Cost and Management Accounting

Cost and Management Accounting

M.E. Thukaram Rao
Head, Department of Commerce
Sri Sathya Sai University
Brindavan Campus
Bangalore, Karnataka

PUBLISHING FOR ONE WORLD

NEW AGE INTERNATIONAL (P) LIMITED, PUBLISHERS

New Delhi • Bangalore • Chennai • Cochin • Guwahati • Hyderabad
Jalandhar • Kolkata • Lucknow • Mumbai • Ranchi
Visit us at www.newagepublishers.com

Published by New Age International (P) Ltd., Publishers
First Edition: 2004
Reprint: 2011

Branches:

- No. 37/10, 8th Cross (Near Hanuman Temple), Azad Nagar, Chamrajpet, **Bangalore** - 560 018.Tel.: (080) 26756823, Telefax: 26756820
  E-mail: bangalore@newagepublishers.com
- 26, Damodaran Street, T. Nagar, **Chennai** - 600 017. Tel.: (044) 24353401, Telefax: 24351463, E-mail: chennai@newagepublishers.com
- CC-39/1016, Carrier Station Road, Ernakulam South, **Cochin** - 682 016. Tel.: (0484) 2377004, Telefax: 4051303, E-mail: cochin@newagepublishers.com
- Hemsen Complex, Mohd. Shah Road, Paltan Bazar, Near Starline Hotel, **Guwahati** - 781 008, Tel.: (0361) 2513881, Telefax: 2543669
  E-mail: guwahati@newagepublishers.com
- No. 105, 1st Floor, Madhiray Kaveri Tower, 3-2-19, Azam Jahi Road, Nimboliadda, **Hyderabad** - 500 027. Tel.: (040) 24652456, Telefax: 24652457
  E-mail:hyderabad@newagepublishers.com
- RDB Chambers (Formerly Lotus Cinema)106A, 1st Floor, S.N. Banerjee Road, **Kolkata** - 700 014, Tel.: (033) 22273773, Telefax: 22275247
  E-mail:kolkata@newagepublishers.com
- 16-A, Jopling Road, **Lucknow** - 226 001. Tel.: (0522) 2209578, 4045297, Telefax: 2204098, E-mail: lucknow@newagepublishers.com
- 142C, Victor House, Ground Floor, N.M. Joshi Marg, Lower Parel, **Mumbai** - 400 013, Tel.: (022) 24927869, Telefax: 24915415
  E-mail: mumbai@newagepublishers.com
- 22, Golden House, Daryaganj, **New Delhi** - 110 002. Tel.: (011) 23262370, 23262368, Telefax: 43551305, E-mail: sales@newagepublishers.com

ISBN : 978-81-224-1513-1

₹ 440.00

C-11-07-5758

Printed in India at Mohanlal Printers, Delhi.
Typeset at Vikas Computers, Delhi.

PUBLISHING FOR ONE WORLD
NEW AGE INTERNATIONAL (P) LIMITED, PUBLISHERS
4835/24, Ansari Road, Daryaganj, New Delhi-110002
Visit us at **www.newagepublishers.com**

PREFACE

I have immense pleasure in placing into the hands of my esteemed readers this book on COST AND MANAGEMENT ACCOUNTING. Although several books are available on the subject, the need for a comprehensive book covering all the important aspects of Cost and Management Accounting has been felt for a long time. My long experience in teaching and the knowledge I have acquired over these years have made it possible for me to satisfy this need.

This book has been divided into two parts. PART I deals with COST ACCOUNTING and PART II deals with MANAGEMENT ACCOUNTING. The book is written in a simple and lucid style. At the end of each chapter, a large number of standard questions of different varieties are given to test the understanding ability of students. A large number of exercises with answers are also given.

In the course of writing this book, I have referred too many standard works of various authors. Some useful definitions and contributions have been incorporated in the text by retaining their originality. I am always thankful to all of them.

The book serves the needs of students preparing for the examinations of B.Com. (Pass & Hons), BBM, BBA, BA (Corporate Secretaryship) M.Com. MBA, CA, CS, ICWA and other diploma courses of management. It will also be of immense use to the practising managers in the private and public industries.

I am thankful to Shri V.R. Damodaran for bringing up this book. I shall appreciate comments and suggestions from readers for the improvement of the book.

M.E. THUKARAM RAO

CONTENTS

PART I

Section A
COST ACCOUNTING

Section B
ELEMENTS OF COST

SECTION C

METHODS OF COSTING

SECTION D

SYSTEMS OF MAINTAINING COST ACCOUNTS

SECTION E

COST CONTROL TECHNIQUES

SECTION F

MISCELLANEOUS TOPICS

PART II

MANAGEMENT ACCOUNTING

PART I

SECTION A

INTRODUCTION

1

NATURE AND SCOPE OF COST ACCOUNTING

INTRODUCTION

In the modern business world, the nature and functioning of business organisations have become very complicated. They have to serve the needs of variety of parties who are interested in the functioning of the business. These parties constitute the owners, creditors, employees, government agencies, tax authorities, prospective investors, and last but not the least the management of the business. The business has to serve the needs of these different category of people by way of supplying various information from time to time. In order to satisfy the needs of all these group of people a sound organisation of accounting system is very essential. In the ancient days the information required by those who were interested with a business organisation was met by practising a system of accounting known as financial accounting system. Financial accounting is mainly concerned with preparation of two important statements, *viz.*, income statement (or profit & loss account) and positional statement (or Balance Sheet). This information served the needs of all those who are not directly associated with management of business. Thus financial accounts are concerned with external reporting as it provides information to external authorities. But management of every business organisation is interested to know much more than the usual information supplied to outsiders. In order to carry out its functions of planning, decision-making and control, it requires additional cost data. The financial accounts to some extent fails to provide required cost data to management and hence a new system of accounting which could provide internal report to management was conceived of.

NEED FOR COST ACCOUNTING

The need for cost accounting arises owing to the following :

To Overcome the Limitations of Financial Accounts

Financial accounting records in an overall manner the results of the operations of a business, using conventional double entry book-keeping techniques. It suffers from the following limitations :

(*i*) *It provides only past data :* Financial accounts provide out of date information to management. But management is interested in current data but not past data as it does not serve any purpose to it. Therefore it has been rightly pointed out that financial accounts provide only a post-mortem analysis of past activities.

(*ii*) *It reveals only over all result of the business :* Financial accounts does not provide data for each and every product, process, department or operation separately. Instead it provides the financial information in a summary form for the entire organisation as a whole.

(*iii*) *It is static in nature :* Modern business is dynamic but not static. Financial accounts does not incorporate the changes that take place within the business.

(*iv*) *It fails to take into account the impact of price level change :* In the modern inflationary conditions the price level has significant impact over financial statement. Under financial accounts, assets are shown at the actual or historical cost. Consequently depreciation is also charged on actual or historical cost. This under charging of depreciation will distort the profit figure.

(*v*) *Possibility of manipulation of financial accounts* : Very often financial accounts are manipulated at the whims and fancies of management so as to project better image in the minds of prospective investors. The chief forms of manipulating the financial accounts assume the form of over or undervaluation of inventory, excessive or inadequate provision for depreciation, creation of secret reserves, etc.

(*vi*) *It fails to exercise control over resources* : Financial accounts fail to exercise control over materials, labour and other expenses incurred in a business enterprise. As a results, avoidable wastages and losses go unchecked under this system of accounts.

(*vii*) *It fails to provide adequate data for price fixation* : Financial accounts fail to provide adequate cost data on the basis of which selling price is fixed. In the absence of fixation of prices in advance, it is not possible to supply quotations to the prospective customers. To that extent the income from such sales diminish.

(*viii*) *It fails to provide adequate data for management in carrying out its functions* : Management of every organisation relies heavily on adequate cost data for formulating policies and in decision-making process. But financial accounts fails to provide such useful cost data to management.

(*ix*) *It does not provide a basis for cost comparison* : Financial accounts does not help in cost comparison over a period of time or between two jobs or two operations. Thus a basis for judging the efficiency of an year with past year or worthfulness of two different jobs or operations cannot be appraised.

(*x*) *It does not make use of control techniques* : Financial accounts fail to make use of certain important cost control techniques such as budgetary control and standard costing. Thus financial accounts do not facilitate measuring the efficiency of the business with the help of control techniques.

(*xi*) *It fails to ascertain break-even point* : Financial accounting does not help in ascertaining the break-even point, *i.e.*, the sale or output where the revenue equals the cost. Hence, the point of no-profit-no-loss cannot be made out under financial accounts.

To Ensure Optimum Utilisation of Resources

In todays business world, the resources available are very scarce. Hence every business unit must strive hard to obtain maximum output with the available input. In order to ensure the optimum utilisation of scarce resources, the value of input is measured against the value of output. This implies matching cost per unit of production against the value of output or selling price. But financial accounts does not provide the information relating to cost per unit of production. Hence the need for cost accounting was felt necessary.

To Achieve Overall Efficiency of Business

Every businessman will make constant effort to improve his business. In order to formulate suitable policy and sound decision, he has to know answers to certain questions such as (*a*) What is the maximum profit which a business can make? (*b*) Is the profit earned by it is more or less compared to the earlier years? (*c*) Which product line is making more profit? (*d*) Has too much capital is blocked in raw materials? (*e*) Whether the cost of production has gone up compared to earlier years? (*f*) Should the selling price requires revision? Cost accounting serves as an useful tool in the hands of management in this direction. By analysing the cost of production of every unit, it helps management to know the answers to the above questions.

GROWTH AND DEVELOPMENT OF COST ACCOUNTING

The history of cost accounting can be traced back to the fourteenth century. In the course of its evolution it passed through following stages.

(1) In the first stage of its development, cost accounting was concerned only with the three prime cost elements, *viz.*, direct material cost, direct labour cost and direct expenses. For recording the transactions relating to materials the important documents used were (*a*) stores ledger, (*b*) a material requisition note, and (*c*) materials received note. To account for labour cost, employee time card and labour cost card were devised by Mr. Metcalfe. Later on a distinction between manufacturing and non-manufacturing cost was made by Mr. Norton. Thus material cost, labour cost and manufacturing cost constituted prime cost.

(2) Secondly, around the turn of the nineteenth century, the importance of non-manufacturing cost (overheads) was recognised as one of the distinct element of cost. The method of charging non-manufacturing cost to the production cost was devised under this stage.

(3) Thirdly, the techniques of estimation and standards are devised. Instead of using actual cost, standard costs are used and by comparing with the actual cost the differences are noted, analysed and disposed off accordingly. This helps in knowing the efficiency of the business undertaking.

(4) Fourthly, cost accounting methods were applied to all types of business undertakings. The costing principles and techniques were also extended to important functions of a business.

(5) In modern times the development of electronic data processing has occupied significant stage in the growth of cost accounting system.

Cost Accounting in Indian Context

The application of cost accounting methods in Indian industries was felt from the beginning of the twentieth century. The following factors have accelerated the system of cost accounting in our country.

(*a*) Increased awareness of cost consciousness by Indian industrialists with a view to ascertain costs more accurately for each product or job.

(*b*) Growing competition among manufacturers led to fixation of prices at a lower level so as to attract more customers.

(*c*) Economic policy of government which laid emphasis on planned economy with a view to achieve the targets led to cost reduction programmes by Indian industrialists.

(*d*) Increased government control over pricing led the Indian manufacturers to give utmost importance to the installation of cost accounts.

(*e*) The establishment of National Productivity Council in 1958 and the Statutory

Recognition of Institute of Cost and Works Accountants of India in 1959 gave further encouragement to install cost accounting system in Indian industries.

DEFINITION AND SCOPE OR COST ACCOUNTANCY

The terminology of cost accountancy published by the Institute of Cost and Management Accountants, London defines cost accountancy as "the application of costing and cost accounting principles, methods and techniques to the science, art and practice of cost control and the ascertainment of profitability. It includes the presentation of information derived therefrom for the managerial decision-making."

On analysis of the above definition, the following features of cost accountancy become evident :

(*a*) "Cost accountancy" is used in the broadest sense when compared to "cost accounting" and "costing". This is so because cost accountancy is concerned with the formulation of principles, methods and techniques to be applied for ascertaining cost and profit.

(*b*) Having ascertained 'cost' and 'profit', cost accountancy is concerned with presentation of information to management. To enable management to carry out its functions, reports must be promptly made available at the right time, to the right person and in a proper form.

(*c*) The information so provided is to serve the purpose of managerial decision-making such as introducing a new line of product, replacement of manual labour by machines, make or buy, decisions, etc.

SCOPE OF COST ACCOUNTANCY

The scope of any subject refers to the various areas of study included in that subject. As regards the scope of cost accountancy is concerned, it has vast scope. The following topics fall under the purview of cost accountancy : (1) Costing, (2) Cost Accounting, (3) Cost Control Techniques, (4) Budgeting and (5) Cost Audit.

1. Costing

The terminology of ICMA, London, defines costing as "the technique and process of ascertaining the cost."

The above definition is very significant in as much as it carries the main theme of cost accountancy. This definition emphasises two important aspects, *viz.*

(*a*) ***The technique and process of costing :*** The technique of costing involves two distinct steps, namely, (*i*) collection and classification of costs according to various elements and (*ii*) allocation and apportionment of the expenses which cannot be directly charged to production. As a process, costing is concerned with the routine ascertainment of cost with a formal procedure.

(*b*) ***Ascertainment of cost :*** It involves three steps, *viz.*, (*i*) collection and analysis of expenses, (*ii*) measurement of production at different stages and (*iii*) linking up of production with the expenses. To achieve the first step, costing has developed different systems such as Historical, Estimated and Standard Cost. For achieving the second step, costing has developed different methods such as single or output costing. Job costing, contract costing, etc. Finally, for achieving the last step costing has developed important techniques such as *Absorption Costing, Marginal Costing* and *Standard Costing.*

The three terms indicated as 'systems', 'methods', 'techniques' are independent factors but co-exist together. Ascertainment of cost of production is based on all these three terms. For example, continuous type of industries may use process costing as a method, using actual cost as a system, under Standard Costing Technique.

2. Cost Accounting

Kohler in his dictionary for Accountants defines cost accounting as "that branch of accounting dealing with the classification, recording, allocation, summarisation and reporting of current and prospective costs."

Mr. Wheldon defines cost accounting as "the classifying, recording and appropriate allocation of expenditure for the determination of the costs of products or services, the relation of these costs to sales values, and the ascertainment of profitability."

The above definitions reveal the following aspects of cost accounting :

(*a*) *Cost classification :* This refers to grouping of like items of cost into a common group.

(*b*) *Cost recording :* This refers to posting of cost transactions into the various ledger maintained under cost accounting system.

(*c*) *Cost allocation :* This refers to allotment of costs to various products or departments.

(*d*) *Cost determination or cost finding :* This refers to the determination of the cost of goods or services by informal procedure, *i.e.*, procedures that do not carry on the regular process of cost accounting on a continuous basis.

(*e*) *Cost reporting :* This refers to furnishing of cost data on a regular basis so as to meet the requirements of management.

Differences between Cost Accountancy, Costing and Cost Accounting

Points of Differences	*Cost Accountancy*	*Costing*	*Cost Accounting*
(1) Scope	Cost accountancy is broadest in its scope.	It is broader in its scope.	It is narrow in its scope.
(2) Function	It is concerned with formulation of costing principles, methods, techniques to be adopted by a business.	It is concerned with ascertainment of cost.	It is concerned with recording of cost.
(3) Periodicity of functioning	It is a starting Point.	It begins where cost accountancy ends.	It begins where costing ends.
(4) Persons involved	The persons involved are experts in the field of cost accountancy such as management accountant.	The person involved is cost accountant.	The persons involved are cost clerks.

3. Cost Control

According to Kohler, cost control represents the employment of management devices in the performance of any necessary operation so that pre-established objectives of quality, quantity and time may be attained at the lowest possible outlay for goods and services. The terminology published by ICMA, London, defines cost control as "The guidance and regulation by executive action of the cost of operating an undertaking." Acccording to this definition, cost control aims at guiding the actuals towards the lines of target and regulates the actuals if they deviate from the targets. This guidance and regulation is done by the executive who is responsible for causing the deviation. This process will become clear by enumerating the steps involved in any cost control technique.

(*a*) Fixation of targets in terms of cost and production performance.
(*b*) Ascertaining the actual cost and production performance.
(*c*) Comparison of actuals with the targets.
(*d*) Analysing the variance by causes and the person responsible for it.
(*e*) Taking remedial steps to set right unfavourable variations.

Cost control is exercised through a variety of techniques such as inventory control, quality control, budgetary control, standard costing, etc. The advantages of cost control are as follows :

(*a*) It helps in utilising the resources to the full extent.
(*b*) It helps in reduction of prices which are benefited by customers.
(*c*) It helps in competing successfully in the market.
(*d*) It increases the profit earning capacity of the business.
(*e*) It increases the goodwill of the business.

4. Budgeting

Mr. Heiser in his book *Budgeting–Principles and Practice*, defines budget as "an overall blue print of a comprehensive plan of operations and actions expressed in financial terms. According to him budgeting process involves the preparation of a budget and its fullest use not only as a devise for planning and co-ordinating but also for control. A detailed study on budgetary control follows in chapter 25.

5. Cost Audit

The terminology of ICMA, London, defines cost audit, as "the verification of the correctness of cost accounts and of the adherence to the cost accounting plan. Cost audit is discussed in chapter 29."

NATURE OF COST ACCOUNTING

The nature of cost accounting can be brought out under the following headings :

1. Cost accounting is a branch of knowledge : Though considered as a branch of financial accounts, cost accounting is one of the important branch of knowledge, *i.e.*, a discipline by itself. It is an organised body of knowledge consisting of its own principles, concepts and conventions. These principles and rules of course vary from industry to industry.

2. Cost accounting is a science : Cost accounting is a science as it is a body of systematic knowledge relating to not only cost accounting but relating to a wide variety of subjects such as law, office practice and procedure, data processing, production and material control, etc. It is necessary for a cost accountant to have intimate knowledge of all these field of study in order to carry on his day-to-day activities. But it is to be admitted that it is not a perfect science as in the case of natural science.

3. Cost accounting is an art : Cost accounting is an art in the sense it requires the ability and skill on the part of cost accountant in applying the principles, methods and techniques of cost accountancy to various management problems. These problems include the ascertainment of cost, control of costs, ascertainment of profitability, etc.

4. Cost accounting is a profession : In recent years cost accounting has become one of the important professions which has become more challenging. This view is evident from two facts. First, the setting up of various professional bodies such as National Association of Accountants (NAA) in USA. The Institute of Cost and Management Accountants in UK, the Institute of Cost and Works Accountants in India and such other professional bodies both in developed and developing countries have increased the growing awareness of costing profession among the people. Secondly, a large number of students have enrolled in these institutes to obtain costing degrees and memberships for earning their livelihood.

RELATIONSHIP BETWEEN FINANCIAL ACCOUNTING AND COST ACCOUNTING

Cost accounting is very closely-related to financial accounting. Some authorities on the subject consider cost accounting to be the branch of financial accounting. But it may be said that cost accounts is complementary to financial accounts, *i.e.*, a subject which is necessary to make financial accounts whole or complete. Financial accounts and cost accounts are both similar in certain respects. But in some other respects they differ from one another. These points of similarities and dissimilarities are enumerated below :

Points of Similarities

(*a*) The fundamental principles of double entry is applicable in both the systems of accounts.

(*b*) The invoices and vouchers constitute the common basis for recording transactions under both the systems of accounts.

(*c*) The results of business are revealed by both the systems of accounts.

(*d*) The causes for losses and wastages of a business are provided by both these systems of accounts.

(*e*) The determination of future business policy is guided by both these systems of accounts.

(*f*) A basis for comparison of expenses is being provided by both the accounting systems.

(*g*) Accuracy of accounts is maintained under both the systems by means of exercising check over errors and commissions which might creep in either of accounts.

Points of Dissimilarities

Points of differences	*Financial Accounts*	*Cost Accounts*
1. Purpose	The purpose of financial accounts is external reporting mainly to owners, creditors, tax authorities, government, and prospective investors.	The purpose of cost accounting is internal reporting, *i.e.*, to the management of every business.
2. Obligation to maintain accounts	This is to be maintained compulsorily by higher forms of business organisations. The preparation of accounts must be in accordance with the statutory provisions.	Cost accounts are maintained voluntarily. In some cases government has directed some companies to maintain cost accounts to improve efficiency.

(Contd.)

Points of differences	*Financial Accounts*	*Cost Accounts*
3. Recording	(*a*) Financial accounts records transactions in a subjective manner, *i.e.*, according to the nature of expenditure. (*b*) In financial accounts expenses are recorded in totals. (*c*) Financial accounts records all transactions which takes place in the business. (*d*) Financial accounts records only historical costs.	(*a*) Cost accounts records transactions in an objective manner, *i.e.*, according to purpose for which costs are incurred. (*b*) In cost accounts costs are expressed by proper analysis and classification in order to find out cost per unit. (*c*) Cost accounts records only those costs which affect production and sales. (*d*) Cost accounts records both historical and estimated costs.
4. Analysis of profit	Financial accounts disclose profit for the entire business as a whole.	Cost accounts show the profitability or otherwise of each product, process or operation so as to reveal the areas of profitability.
5. Control	(*a*) It does not make use of any control techniques. (*b*) It does not control materials by using any technique. (*c*) Control over labour is not exercised.	(*a*) It makes use of some important control techniques such a Marginal Costing, Budgetary Control, Standard Costing, etc. in order to control cost. (*b*) It exercises control over materials using some techniques such as ABC analysis, level setting, economic order quantity, etc. (*c*) Control over labour is exercised and efforts are taken to minimise idle time, over time etc.
6. Duration of reporting	Generally, financial accounts provides financial information once a year.	Cost accounting furnishes cost data at frequent intervals. Some reports are daily. Some are weekly and some monthly.
7. Evaluation of efficiency	The information provided by financial accounts is not sufficient to evaluate the efficiency of the business.	The cost data helps in evaluating the efficiency of the businesses.
8. Pricing	It fails to guide the formulation of pricing policy.	It provides adequate data for formulating pricing policy.
9. Valuation of stock	Stock is valued at cost or market price whichever is less.	Stock is always valued of cost price.

DIFFERENCES BETWEEN COST AND MANAGEMENT ACCOUNTING

The American Accounting Association 1958, committee on management accounting defines management accounting as "the application of appropriate techniques and concepts in processing the historical and projected economic data of an entity to assist management in establishing a plan for reasonable economic objectives and in the making of rational decisions with a view towards achieving these objectives." It includes the methods and concepts necessary for effective planning for choosing among alternative business actions, and for control through the evaluation and interpretation of performance. Its study involves consideration of ways in which accounting information may be accumulated, synthesised, analysed and presented in relation to specific problems, decisions and day-to-day tasks of business management.

The terminology published by ICMA, London, defines management accounting as "the application of professional knowledge and skill in the preparation and presentation of accounting information in such a way as to assist management in the formulation of policies and in the planning and control of the operation of the undertaking."

If we examine the above two definitions of management accounting it appears that both the systems of accounts serve the same purpose. However, they differ from one another in respect of the following :

Points of differences	*Cost Accounting*	*Management Accounting*
1. Growth of Accounting	The history of cost accounting dates back to fourteenth century.	This system of accounting evolved in the middle of 20th century. Hence it is of recent origin where compared to cost accounting.
2. Object	The main objects of cost accounts is to ascertain and control cost.	The main objective of management accounting is to provide useful information to management for decision-making.
3. Basis of recording	It is based on both present and future transactions for cost ascertainment.	It is concerned purely with the transactions relating to future.
4. Scope	Cost accounts has narrow scope as it covers matters relating to ascertainment and control of cost.	It has a wide scope in as much as it covers the areas of financial accounts, cost accounts, taxation, etc.
5. Utility	Cost accounts serves the needs of both internal management and external parties.	Management accounting serves the needs of only internal management.
6. Types of transactions dealt with	It deals only with monetary transactions. *i.e.*, it covers only quantitative aspect.	It deals with both monetary and non-monetary transactions, *i.e.*, both quantitative and qualitative aspects.
7. Observation of principles and format	Cost accounts follow a definite principle for ascertaining cost and a format for recording.	It does not follow a definite principle and format. Instead, the data to be presented depends up on the need of the management.

RELATIONSHIP BETWEEN COST, ESTIMATE AND PRICE

The terms 'estimates', 'costs' and 'prices' are closely related to each other in costing. An estimate is a forecast of the probable cost of a product, job, or process for a future date. Estimation is purely based on past experience. Cost accounts provide reliable data on the basis of which future cost is estimated. However, an estimate is only an opinion because there is every chance of commiting mistake while estimating. Estimation is also based on the future conditions and much depends on guesswork. But such guesswork must be as far as possible closer to the facts.

Cost represents actual total cost incurred in manufacturing a product or in completing a job. The total cost of manufacturing a product broadly consists of material, labour and other expenses. The true cost is ascertained either at the various stages of completing the production or at the end of completion of the job. The current cost serves as the basis for future estimates. Thus cost is considered as a fact as it represents the actual or true cost of manufacturing a product or completing the job.

Price in costing refers to selling price of a product. Selling price is arrived at after adding a certain margin of profit to the actual cost. Of course, certain other factors also determine the price fixation policy such as demand for the product, tastes and preferences of customers, price of competitive products, future trends of prices and so on. So price fixing is regarded as a matter of policy. Hence it has been popularly said that an "estimate is an opinion, cost is a fact and price is a policy."

PURPOSES OR OBJECTS OF COST ACCOUNTS

Costing serves number of purposes among which the following are considered to be most important.

1. Ascertainment of cost : This was considered to be the primary objective of cost accounting in the initial stages of its development. However, in modern times this has assumed the secondary objective of cost accounting. Cost ascertainment involves the collection and classification of expenses at the first instance. Those items of expenses which are capable of charging directly to the products manufactured are allocated. Then the other expenses which are not capable of direct allocation are apportioned on some suitable basis. Thus the cost of production of goods manufactured is ascertained. In this process, cost accounts involves maintenance of different books to record various elements of cost. Cost of production is ascertained by using any of the costing technique such as historical costing, marginal costing, etc.

2. Cost control : At one time cost control was considered as secondary objective of cost accounts. But in modern times it constitutes the primary purpose because of its utmost importance in all business undertakings. Cost control is exercised at different stages in a factory, *viz.*, acquisition of materials, recruiting and deployment of labour force, during the production process and so on. As such we have material cost control, labour cost control, production control, quality control and so on. However, control over cost is exercised through the techniques of budgetary control and standard costing. The control techniques enable the management in knowing the operating efficiency of a business.

3. Determination of selling price : Every business organisation aims at maximising profit. Total cost of production constitutes the basis on which selling price is fixed by adding a margin of profit. Cost accounting furnishes both the total cost of production as well as cost incurred at each and every stage of production. No doubt other factors are taken into consideration before fixing price such as market conditions the area of distribution, volume of sales, etc. But cost plays the dominating role in price fixation.

4. Frequent preparation of accounts and other reports : The management of every business constantly rely upon the reports on cost data in order to know the level of efficiency relating to purchase, production, sales and operating results. Financial accounts provide information only at the end of the year because closing stock value is available only at the end of the year. But cost accounts provide the value of closing stock at frequent intervals by adopting a "continuous stock verification" system. Using the value of closing stock it is possible to prepare final accounts and know the operating results of the business.

5. To provide a basis for operating policy : Cost data to a great extent helps in formulating the policies of a business and in decision-making. As every alternative decisions involve investment of capital outlay, costs play an important role in decision-making. Therefore availability of cost data is a must for all levels of management. Some of the decisions which are based on cost are (*a*) make or buy decision, (*b*) manufacturing by mechanisation or automation, (*c*) whether to close or continue operations in spite of losses.

FUNCTIONS OF COST ACCOUNTANT

The functions of cost accountant may be enumerated under the following :

Traditional Functions

The traditional functions comprise of the routine functions of cost accountant. Such functions are as follows :

(*a*) To establish various cost centres in the organisation.

(*b*) To ascertain the cost of every product, job or process both in terms of total and per unit of product.

(*c*) To design suitable system for defining responsibilities and controlling cost.

(*d*) To provide necessary data to enable management in fixing the price.

(*e*) To prepare reports on wastages of material, loss of labour time, idle capacity of machines so as to improve profitability of business.

(*f*) To implement cost control techniques such as budgetary control and standard costing.

(*g*) To prepare cost schedules to assist management in making decisions anc in formulating policies.

(*h*) To design suitable forms for organising an effective system of reporting which ensures provision of adequate cost data to all levels of management.

(*i*) To assist management in the valuation of closing stock of raw materials and work-in-progress so that too much of capital is not locked up in unnecessary inventories.

(*j*) To prepare periodical cost statements and profit and loss account.

Modern Functions

In recent times the functions of a cost accountant are not only confined to ascertain and control cost but extend far beyond these functions. This is on account of the additional responsibilities arising from the various branches of accounting, works organisation, office management and administration, methods of statistical analysis, systems analysis, O and M studies, modern principles of management, use of computers, etc. These modern functions are as follows :

(*i*) Supervising the functions of mechanised accounting.

(*ii*) Organisation of internal audit in the field of accounting.

(*iii*) To work in close co-ordination with various departmental managers so as to implement cost reduction programmes and methods of improvement.

(*iv*) To undertake cost audit programmes as per the directives issued by the government and the provisions of the Indian Companies Act of 1956.

As regards the role of cost accountant in an industry, it has been beautifully summarised by Mr. Wilmot in his article on "the cost accountant's place in management". According to him, the role of cost accountant is "that of a historian, news agent, and prophet". As historian he must be meticulously accurate, *i.e.*, while supplying cost information to management he has to furnish in greater detail with carefulness and exactness. As news agent, he must be up-do-date, selective and provide full cost information to the needy person. As a prophet he must combine knowledge and experience with foresight and courage.

INSTALLATION OF COST ACCOUNTS

At the outset it is to be understood that a common cost accounting system cannot be installed for all types of business undertakings. The cost accounting system depends upon the nature of business and the product manufactured. Before a suitable system of cost accounting is installed it is necessary to undertake a preliminary investigation so as to know the feasibility of installing cost accounting system to such business. While introducing a system of cost accounts it should be borne in mind that cost accounting system must suit the business. There should not be any attempt to make the business suit the system. One more consideration that is of practical importance is that the benefits derived from cost accounting system must be more than the investment made on it. This means the system must be simple and it must lead to savings through the control of materials, labour and overheads when compared to expenses incurred in maintaining it. For the successful functioning of the costing system, the following conditions are essential :

(*a*) There must be an efficient system of material control.
(*b*) A sound and well designed method of wage payment must be set up.
(*c*) The existence of sound basis for collection of all indirect expenses and a basis for its apportionment to various production departments.
(*d*) The integration of cost and financial accounts to facilitate reconciliation of profit as shown by these two systems of accounts.
(*e*) The use of printed forms so as to facilitate quick compilation of cost reports.
(*f*) The duties and responsibilities of cost accountant must be made clear.

Factors to be Considered before Installing a Cost Accounting System

The following factors are to be considered before installing a cost accounting system :

1. History of business unit : The history of a business unit implies the duration of its existence, position in the industry, the rate of growth, policy and philosophy of management and the like. The history of business unit serves as the basis for designing the cost accounts in respect of necessity, simplicity, and investment involved in installing cost accounts.

2. Nature of the industry : The nature of business such as manufacturing, mining, trading, etc. determines the costing techniques to be applied. Similarly, the type of product manufactured also determine the method of costing that is to be employed. In other words, there is no all purpose technique and method of costing that can be applied universally.

3. Product range : The range of products manufactured and sold also determine the method of costing to be selected. Accordingly range of products must be analysed in terms of size, models, fashions, area of market, competitors and whether the products are made to customers specification or for stocking and selling.

4. Technical considerations : Technical considerations that influence the installation of cost accounts are as follows : .

(*a*) Size and layout of the factory
(*b*) The existence of production and service departments
(*c*) Flow of production
(*d*) Capacity of machines and degree of mechanisation
(*e*) Existence of laboratories
(*f*) Internal transport and material handling equipments
(*g*) Production control techniques
(*h*) Inspection and testing of materials and finished goods.

5. Organisational factors : The problem of installing cost accounting is somewhat difficult in case of an existing business when compared to new business. However, the existing set up of the organisation should be least disturbed should the need arise. In order to fix up responsibility to the executives it may be necessary to group the departments. The organisational factors to be considered are : (*a*) size and the type of organisation such as line, line and staff, functional and committee organisation, (*b*) the levels of management, *viz*., top level, middle level and bottom level management, (*c*) extent of delegation and responsibility, (*d*) extent of centralisation and decentralisation, (*e*) extent of departmentation, (*f*) availability of modern office equipments, and (*g*) number of managerial and supervisory staff.

6. Selling and distribution method : The chief factors to be considered with regard to distribution process are the warehousing facilities, external transport, market research and other promotional measures, terms of sale and procurement of orders from customers.

7. Accounting aspects : The factors to be considered in respect of accounting are : (*a*) number of financial records, (*b*) existing forms, (*c*) registers used, and (*d*) number of copies required.

8. Area of control to be exercised : The areas where cost control is to be exercised is to be identified so that each manager may take action relevant to his activities. If material control occupies significant area of control, it must be given topmost priority for exercising control over materials.

9. Reporting : The cost accounting system to be installed must ensure frequency and promptitude in reporting cost data to all levels of management. It must also to be pointed out that duplication of reporting is to be avoided. Further, only those information which are relevant for the management in a particular context alone should be reported.

10. Uniformity : The practice of adopting uniform costing facilitates inter-firm comparison among various firms belonging to the same industry. Further it also has the benefit of adopting common costing practice if a holding company has number of subsidiaries.

11. Use of electronic data processing : In modern days it has become a common practice to use electronic data processing equipments and computers. In this situation it is essential to ensure that the equipment meets the needs of the system but not the other way round.

12. Practical considerations : The cost accounting system to be installed must be flexible in operation and must be capable of adaptation to changing conditions. The system must be periodically scrutinised so as to make necessary changes owing to development in business.

Practical Difficulties in Installing Cost Accounting

In addition to the above problems, a cost accountant will encounter the following practical difficulties at the time of installation of cost accounting system :

1. Lack of support from management : Wherever costing system is installed. It is essential to seek the support of various departmental managers. Very often the managers show hostile attitude towards the costing system. They feel that this system will interfere in their routine work and probably as a means of checking their efficiency. Under such circumstances it is better to convince them about the utility of costing system for the business as a whole.

2. Resistance by existing accounting staff : Very often the existing accounting staff resist the installation of the cost accounting system on two grounds. Firstly, they feel that the new system of accounting might lead to excess work. Secondly, they are afraid of their job security. But this difficulty may be overcome by encouraging them about the usefulness of cost accounting as a supplement to financial accounts and the generation of more employment opportunities from the installation of cost accounting system.

3. Non-cooperation from middle and bottom level management : At times the middle and bottom level managers such as foremen, supervisors and inspectors also fail to extend their wholehearted cooperation fearing additional work which may be entrusted to them. This problem may be overcome by suggesting them about the simplicity of the system and the existence of a separate cost accounting department to look after costing matters. However, they may be required to provide necessary reports concerning their area of activity so as to enable functioning of cost accounting department efficiently.

4. Lack of trained staff : This was no doubt a problem in olden days. Today this problem is overcome, thanks to the establishment of The Institute of Cost and Works Accountant of India in our country which offers professional course in costing and also offers training facilities through various companies to the candidates undergoing the course. In spite of this facility, it is somewhat difficult to get the competent and experienced staff at the time of installation. This problem can be overcome by paying attractive salaries to the cost accountants.

5. Heavy expenses in installing and maintaining the system : The setting up of a separate costing department with staff often poses a problem. In addition to installation, the operating expenses in the form of printing and stationery, heating and lighting, depreciation and insurance, rent and rates are to be incurred. However, as was mentioned earlier, the system of cost accounting must be a useful investment, *i.e.*, benefits derived from it must be more than the investment made on it. If this is not possible, for the time being the system must be discarded.

REQUISITES OR ESSENTIALS OF COST ACCOUNTING SYSTEM

The following are the essentials of an ideal cost accounting system :

1. Accuracy : The system of cost accounting must provide for accuracy in terms of both cost ascertainment and presentation. Otherwise it will prove to be misleading.

2. Simplicity : Cost accounting system involves detailed analysis of cost. To avoid complications in the procedure of cost ascertainment an elaborate system of costing should be avoided and every care must be taken to keep it as simple as possible.

3. Elasticity : The cost accounting system should be capable of adopting itself to the changing situations of business. It must be capable of expansion or contraction depending upon the needs of the business.

4. Economy : The costs of operating costing system must be less. It must result in increased benefit when compared to the expenditure incurred in installing it.

5. Comparability : The records to be maintained must facilitate comparison over a period of time. The past records must serve as a basis to guide the future.

6. Promptness : An ideal costing system is one which provides cost data in an analytical form to the management. So all the departments of a factory must analyse and record the relevant items of cost promptly in order to furnish cost information on a regular basis to various levels of management. This helps in checking up the progress of the business on a regular basis.

7. Periodical preparation of accounts : With a view to facilitate the comparison of results frequently, it is desirable to prepare accounts periodically. Constant comparison of actual result with standard result enables to spot out areas of inefficiency. This can be set right by taking remedial measures.

8. Reconciliation with financial accounts : The system of cost accounts must be capable of reconciling with financial accounts so as to check accuracy of both the system of accounts.

9. Uniformity : The various forms and documents used under costing system must be uniform in size and quality of paper. Printed forms must be used to avoid delay in the preparation of reports. This also reduces the burden of clerical staff. Forms of different colours can be used to distinguish different documents.

10. Equity : The basis of apportioning indirect expenses to products, departments or jobs must be fair and equitable.

ORGANISATION OF COST ACCOUNTING DEPARTMENT

The organisation of cost accounting department depends upon the size of the concern. Whatever may be the structure of cost accounting department in a factory, it is established to serve the following purposes : (*i*) To compile cost data in order to meet the statutory requirement wherever applicable, (*ii*) To provide necessary cost data to management to carry out its functions efficiently, and (*iii*) To ensure efficiency and economy in the functioning of cost accounting department. To achieve the above purposes cost accounting department usually performs the following functions :

(1) Designing and installation of appropriate method of costing.
(2) Accumulation of cost data by process, department and product.
(3) Analysis of such cost by elements of cost.
(4) Estimation of cost of production.
(5) Reporting of cost information to all levels of management.
(6) Advising management in relation to investment based on cost information.

In a small and medium-sized concern, the cost accounting department may be set up as a section of financial accounting system. The cost accountant who is incharge of cost accounting department may be authorised to report to the chief accountant. In large-sized concern, a separate cost accounting department is established under the supervision of a full-fledged cost accountant. The cost accounting department is equipped with sufficient staff each to look after different facets of cost accounting function. While important functions such as budgeting, cost analysis, etc. are performed by cost accountant, cost recording, cost reporting and such other functions are performed by cost clerks.

The cost accounting department may be organised either on the principle of centralisation or decentralisation. Under centralised system, the functions of cost accounting departments relating to all firms belonging to same industry is performed at a common central place. The extent of centralisation of cost accounting department depends upon the following factors :

(*a*) The philosophy of management regarding divisional responsibility.
(*b*) The ready availability of cost data from each firm.
(*c*) Size of the firm.
(*d*) The area of operations of every firm.
(*e*) The economy involved in centralisation process.

Advantages of Centralised Cost Accounting Department

1. It facilitates full utilisation of services of costing staff.
2. It permits mechanisation of accounting which is not possible under decentralisation system.

3. It reduces paper work and economise stationery costs.
4. It facilitates prompt reporting.

Under decentraiisation system a separate cost accounting department is set up for each and every firm under the supervision of a competent cost accountant. This system has certain advantages.

(*a*) It tends to increase the initiative of the cost accountants of every firm as the responsibility to control lies in their hands.

(*b*) It eliminates duplication of recording and reporting.

(*c*) It increases the speed of functioning of cost accounting department.

Relationship of Cost Department to Other Departments

1. Cost accounting department and production department : It can well be said that production department and cost department are interwoven together as the former cannot function efficiently without the existence of the latter. The production process is concerned with the utilisation of materials, money and human resources. The cost department helps in estimating the material cost, labour cost and other expenses for manufacturing a product. It also helps in controlling these costs so as to minimise the cost of production. In fact, the main objective of cost accounting system is to reduce the cost of production of goods or services manufactured and rendered by business units. The other areas where cost accounting department is helpful in manufacturing process are : (*a*) Engineering department which is concerned with designing a product, (*b*) Research and development department which is concerned with development of a new product, (*c*) Production planning and control department which ensures completion of production within the time schedule, and (*d*) Quality control section, which ensures quality of products. All these departments heavily rely on cost accounting department because costs to be incurred in these departments have a direct impact over the functioning of these departments.

2. Cost accounting department and personnel department : The personnel department which is concerned with proper recruitment, selection, training, time-keeping, fixation of wage rate and preparation of payroll, will work with close co-ordination of cost department. Each and every function performed by personnel department is again influenced by additional cost to be incurred on such function as for example promotion of employees leads to incurrence of additional wages.

3. Cost accounting department and finance department : The finance department is concerned with receiving and disbursement of cash. The allocation of investments on fixed and working capital entirely depends upon the cost reports submitted to it by the cost department. Judicious utilisation of available capital is possible only when priority is given for more important areas of investment. This is facilitated by furnishing prompt report by cost department.

4. Cost accounting department and purchase department : In majority of firms purchase of raw materials at right quantity, of right quality, from right supplier, at a right time not only ensures ready supply but also at a reasonably low price. Any purchase of substandard quality of materials will lead to dissatisfaction among customers and consequently it leads to loss of orders. Further, purchase of materials at high rate will increase the cost of production tremendously. Delay in getting supplies of materials lead to delay in executing customers orders. In these respects cost accounting department can assist purchase department to ensure efficient purchasing. Cost department also help in reducing (*a*) waste of materials, (*b*) the risk from theft, and (*c*) excessive investment in inventories.

5. Cost accounting department and marketing department : Marketing department relies on cost information in order to (*a*) estimate future product cost for fixing the selling price, (*b*) in knowing the expenses incurred in marketing the products so that if the amount exceeds the target, control measures can be taken to reduce such expenses, (*c*) to consider alternative selling methods and promotional measures, and (*d*) to make further investment in warehousing and distribution process. Cost department provides all such information as is required by the marketing department for its efficient functioning.

6. Cost accounting department and financial accounting department : The existence of cost accounting department makes the financial accounting department a complete organisation by furnishing additional cost data to the chief accountant. Cost department enable financial accounts department in carrying out the latter's function furnishing necessary data in respect of the following :

(*a*) Supply of material cost, labour cost and expenses to facilitate preparation of manufacturing account.
(*b*) Provision of the value of closing stock frequently to facilitate the preparation of interim final accounts.
(*c*) Assist financial accounting department in matters relating to taxation, insurance and in solving legal matters.
(*d*) Enables financial accounting department to settle the bills by duly approving them.
(*e*) Helps financial accounting department in budgeting.

ADVANTAGES OF COST ACCOUNTING

A good costing system serves the needs of a large sections of people. The advantages of cost accounting are discussed below.

Advantages of Cost Accounting to Management

1. Fixation of responsibility : Whenever a cost centre is established, it implies establishing a kind of relationship between superior and subordinates. Thus responsibilities are fixed on every individual who is concerned with incurrence of cost.

2. Measures economic performance : By applying cost control techniques such as budgetary control and standard costing it helps in assisting the performance of business.

3. Fixation of price : By providing cost data it helps management to fix the selling price in advance. Hence, quotations can be supplied to prospective customers to secure orders.

4. Aids in decision-making : It helps management in making suitable decisions such as make or buy, replace manual labour by machines, shut down or continue operations based on cost reports.

5. Helps in the preparation of interim final accounts : By the process of continuous stock taking it enables to know the value of closing stock of materials at any time. This facilitates preparation of final accounts wherever desired.

6. Helps in minimising wastages and losses : Cost accounting system enables to locate the losses relating to materials, idle time and under utilisation of plant and machinery.

7. Facilitates comparison : It facilitates cost comparison in respect of jobs, process, departments and also between two periods. This reveals the efficiency or otherwise of each job process or department.

8. Assists in increasing profitability : Costing reports provide information about profitable or unprofitable areas of operation. The management can discontinue that product line or that department which are responsible for incurring losses. Thereby only profitable line of activities alone are retained.

9. Reconciliation with financial accounts : A well maintained cost accounting system facilitates reconciliation with financial accounts to check the arithmetical accuracy of both the systems.

10. It guides future production policy : Cost data help management in determining future production policy. Any expansion or contraction of production for the future is based on past cost data.

Advantages to Employees

1. Cost accounting system enables employees to earn better wages through overtime wages and incentive systems of wage payment.
2. By providing better facilities it ensures job security to employees.
3. Employees benefit by merit rating techniques which is conducted by scientific process.

Advantages to Creditors

1. It increases the confidence of creditors in the capital employed in the business.
2. The frequent preparation of reports and statements help in knowing solvency position of the business.

Advantages to the Government

1. It helps government in formulating policies regarding export, import, taxation, price control measures, wage fixation, etc.
2. It helps in assessing excise duty, sales tax and income tax of the business.
3. Costing information helps in preparing national plans.

Advantages to Society

1. Cost reduction and cost control programmes go to minimise cost of production of goods and services. A portion of the reduced cost of production is shared by customers by paying less price for goods and services.
2. It offers employment opportunities in the cost accounting department in the capacity of cost accountants and cost clerks.

LIMITATIONS OF COST ACCOUNTING

1. It is expensive : The system of cost accounting involves additional expenditure to be incurred in installing and maintaining it. However, before installing it, care must be taken to ensure that the benefits derived is more than the investment made on this system of accounting.

2. The system is more complex : As the cost accounting system involve number of steps in ascertaining cost such as collection and classification of expenses, allocation and apportionment of expenses, it is considered to be complicated system of accounts. Moreover the system makes use of several documents and forms in preparing the reports. This will tend to delay in the preparation of accounts.

3. Inapplicability of same costing method and technique : All business enterprises cannot make use of a single method and technique of costing. It all depends upon the nature of business and type of product manufactured by it. If a wrong technique and method is used, it misleads the results of business.

4. Not suitable for small scale units : A cost accounting system is applicable only to a large-sized business but not to a small-sized one. Hence, there is limitation to its application to all types of business.

5. Lack of accuracy : The accuracy of cost accounts get distorted owing to the use of notional cost such as standard cost, estimated cost, etc.

6. It lacks social accounting : Cost accounting fails to take into account the social obligation of the business. In other words, social accounting is outside the purview of cost accounts.

CRITICISMS OR OBJECTIONS LEVELLED AGAINST COST ACCOUNTS

Despite several benefits offered by cost accounts, critics have levelled the following criticisms against it :

1. Cost accounting is merely a system of estimates and probabilities : Though the main purpose of cost accounting is to ascertain the cost of production with a reasonable degree of accuracy, yet absolute accuracy is not possible owing to the two reasons. (*a*) Indirect expenditures are absorbed on the basis of predetermined rates instead of actual rates, and (*b*) The material cost and labour cost is inflated so as to cover the normal loss and wastage of materials and normal idle time of workers.

2. Cost accounting is unnecessary in such business enterprises which make large profit : It is argued that industries which earn large amount of profit need not have a system of cost accounting. This statement is absolutely wrong. Earning of more profit by industry does not necessarily mean that its cost of production is lowest and there is no scope for further reduction in the cost. Profit represents the difference between the selling price and the cost of a product. Profit earned by a business may be high because of increased price prevailing in the market. Two or more than two products manufactured by business may earn profit for one line of product and loss by other. The profit earned by one product may outweigh the loss suffered by other product thus resulting in overall profit. So it is wrong to judge the efficiency of the business on the basis of overall profitability of the business. If necessary steps are taken to reduce or eliminate losses suffered by a second line product, the industry would earn more amount of profit. It is in this context that a system of costing is felt.

3. It is unnecessary : This criticism is levelled owing to lack of understanding of the objectives and advantages of costing. In the present-day competitive world, every manufacturer must know the cost of production for each article so that he can fix selling price on a reliable and reasonable basis. Further he can also compare his selling price thus fixed with the price prevailing in the market. Cost ascertainment involves application of certain principles and techniques. Having ascertained the cost, control techniques are used to keep the costs under check and thereby increase the profit. Thus it can be said that cost accounting is necessary in most of the concerns.

4. It is expensive : This criticism is true as long as the benefits derived from this system is not commensurate with the investment made on it. But by carefully designing the system so as to suit the business, the criticism can be nullified.

5. Competition governs price and hence there is no need for costing system : Some critics contend that in these days of competition prices are determined by the forces of demand and supply as against fixation of selling price by adding a desired margin of profit on the cost price. This argument is incorrect. Even in this situation cost accounts disclose the margin of profit that is earned by comparing the market price and cost of production. It impresses upon management the need to reduce cost by increasing the volume of production or by elimination of losses and wastages if any. If the cost price tend to be higher than the market price, it is desirable to abandon such product line and pay attention to profitable line of products.

6. There is no need for costing where production efficiency is high : The statement is misleading as without a yardstick to measure the efficiency it is not possible to appraise the efficiency of a business. Cost accounting system offers number of techniques such as standard costing, budgetary control, inter-firm comparison and so on. The cost of production can also be compared between two periods of time to know whether business is currently running efficiently when compared to previous year. In case of inefficient operation remedial measures can be taken to improve the business.

7. Other objections : Some other objections that are raised against the installation of cost accounting system are follows :

(*a*) *It is a mere matter of forms and rulings :* Often it is argued that the cost accounting system degenerates into a matter of mere forms and rulings. This is not the defect of cost accounting system but the way in which the system is maintained. No doubt different forms are necessary under costing system but they must be simplified and altered to meet the changing condition.

(*b*) *Failure in many cases :* The system of cost accounting is often condemned as defective inasmuch as it has failed to produce the desired result. The defect does not lie in the costing system but for some other reasons such as indifferent attitude of the management, lack of adequate facilities, non-cooperations or opposition from employees. These defects can be overcome by reversing the above trend.

(*c*) *For want of necessity :* It is contended by some that costing is of recent origin and that its application was not felt in the past. Though it was not used earlier, still many industries prospered. So it is felt by some critics that the installation of costing involves unnecessary expenditure. However it is to be remembered that todays business functions in a competitive conditions and every manufacturer must know the actual cost of production in order to reduce the selling price. Many industrial failures in the past may be attributed to the lack of knowledge on the part of management relating to the actual cost of production thereby selling product below cost.

QUESTIONS

I. A. Indicate whether the following statements are True or False

1. Cost accounting is not needed for a non-profit organisation such as a club. *T/F*
2. If management is not interested in costing information, there should be no costing department. *T/F*
3. The cost accounting system is designed in such a way the flow of costs parallel the physical movement of products. *T/F*
4. Effective control of cost can be secured only if the responsibility for cost incurrence is clearly defined. *T/F*
5. Installation of a suitable system of cost accounting is restricted to manufacturing concerns only. *T/F*
6. Cost Audit is a part of cost accounting. *T/F*
7. Both financial accounts and cost accounts are written up with the same basic documents. *T/F*
8. Since pricing is a matter of management policy cost information is useless for price fixation. *T/F*

9. A concern that has been quite prosperous needs no costing system. T/F
10. Cost accounting is a branch of financial accounts. T/F

[*Answers* : *True*–2, 3, 4, 6, 7
False–1, 5, 8, 9, 10]

B. Choose the correct answer from the following

1. Which one of the following is most important tool in cost planning
   (*a*) cost unit (*b*) direct cost
   (*c*) cost statement (*d*) budgeting
2. Cost accounting concepts include all the following except
   (*a*) planning (*b*) profit sharing
   (*c*) controlling (*d*) product costing
3. The principal factor to be considered in designing a cost system include
   (*a*) company organisation structure (*b*) nature of business
   (*c*) manufacturing process (*d*) all of the above
4. The chief objective of cost accounting is to
   (*a*) earn more profit (*b*) increase production
   (*c*) provide information for management for planning and control (*d*) fix the prices
5. Cost accounting is
   (*a*) nothing more than a detailed analysis of expenditure
   (*b*) an instrument of management control
   (*c*) useful only in such organisation as have profit as the aim
   (*d*) not needed if prices are beyond the control of the firm
6. The need for cost accounting arises as it helps in
   (*a*) ascertaining and control of cost (*b*) increasing the sales
   (*c*) increasing the production (*d*) solving labour problem
7. The primary objective of cost accounting in modern time is
   (*a*) cost ascertainment (*b*) cost control
   (*c*) ascertainment of profit (*d*) preparation of reports
8. The purpose of financial accounting is to provide information for
   (*a*) fixing prices
   (*b*) recording expenses
   (*c*) locating factors leading to wastage and losses
   (*d*) assessing the profitability and financial position of the firm
9. Which one of the following is not a factor to be considered in designing a cost system
   (*a*) price factor (*b*) organisational factor
   (*c*) economy factor (*d*) reporting factor
10. Cost accounting differs from financial accounting in respect of
   (*a*) recording cost (*b*) ascertaining cost
   (*c*) control of cost (*d*) reporting of cost

[*Answers* : 1(*d*), 2(*b*), 3(*d*), 4(*c*), 5(*b*), 6(*a*), 7(*b*), 8(*d*), 9(*a*), 10(*c*)]

C. Match the following :

List A	*List B*
1. Financial accounting provides	(*a*) management needs
2. One of the objections against costing	(*b*) ascertainment of profit of business
3. Cost accounting was evolved	(*c*) is expensive
4. Financial accounting is concerned with	(*d*) find the actual cost of product
5. Cost accounting is concerned with	(*e*) factual financial information

[*Answers* : 1-*e*, 2-*c*, 3-*d*, 4-*b*, 5-*a*]

SECTION-A – SIMPLE QUESTIONS

1. Define Cost Accounting. (*Bangalore University, B. Com., April 2000*)
2. Distinguish between costing and cost accounting. (*Bangalore University, M. Com., 1998*)

3. Mention any two uses of cost accounting system to management. *(Bangalore University, B. Com., November 1999)*
4. Mention two limitations of costing. *(Bangalore University, B. Com., November 1997)*
5. Distinguish between cost, estimate and price. *(Sri Krishnadevaraya University, B. Com., March 1997)*
6. State any four items which are not included in cost accounts. *(Bangalore University, B. Com., April 1995)*
7. Mention steps that you should take to instal cost accounting. *(Bharathidasan University, B. Com., November 1995)*
8. Mention two objects of cost accounting. *(M G. University, B. Com., April 1994)*
9. What are the limitations of financial accounting? *(Osmania University, B. Com., October 1996)*

SECTION-B

SHORT ANSWER QUESTIONS

1. "Cost accounting is becoming more and more relevant in the emerging economic scenario in India." comment. *(C.S. Intermediate, June 2000)*
2. "Cost accounting system that simply records costs for the purpose of fixing sale price has accomplished only a small part of its mission"–Explain. *(C.S. Intermediate, June 1999)*
3. "Selling price is always based on total cost"—comment. *(C.S. Intermediate, June 1999)*
4. "Cost accounts are key to aconomy in manufacture and one indispensable to the intelligent and economical management of a factory"—Discuss. *(C.S. Intermediate, June 1998)*
5. State the steps involved in the installation of a costing system in a large manufacturing company. *(C.S. Intermediate, June 1997) (S. V. University, B. Com., Sept. 94)*
6. Cost accounting is a system of foresight and not a postmortem examination, it turns losses into profits, speeds up activities and eliminates wastes. comment. *(C.S. Inter. December 1997)*
7. State in differences between financial accounts and cost accounts. *(Bharathidasan University, B. Com., April 1998)*
8. What are the main characteristics of an ideal cost accounting system? *(M.G. University, B. Com., September 1994)*
9. What is costing? What are its objectives? *(Calcutta University, B. Com., October 1997)*
10. Describe the pre-requisites for the installation of cost accounting system. *(Karnataka University, M. Com., April 1997)*
11. Write a note on cost control. *(Mangalore University, B. Com., April 1997)*
12. What is cost accounting? What are its objectives? In what respects does cost accounting differ from financial accounting? *(Mangalore University, B. Com., October 1996)*
13. Distinguish between cost ertimation and cost ascertainment. *(University of Kerala, B. Com., April 1996)*
14. State the advantages of cost accounting. *(Bangalore University, B. Com., November 1992)*

SECTION-C

LONG ANSWER QUESTIONS

1. State the objectives of cost accounting briefly explain the advantages of cost accounting. *(University of Mysore, B. Com., April 1998)*
2. Define "Costing", "Cost" and "Cost Accountancy". Distinguish between cost accounting and financial accounting. *(University of Mysore, B. Com., April 2000)*
3. "A Good system of costing must place the same emphasise on cost control as on cost ascertainment". Comment on this statement. *(University of Mysore, B. Com., October 1999)*
4. "Cost accounting is better understood as a cost control and cost reduction exercise and not a more cost ascertainment process". Discuss. *(University of Mysore, B. Com., April 1997)*
5. "Cost accounting is a system of foresight like pre-natal care, but financial accounting is just a post-mortem examination". Critically examine this statement. *(University of Mysore, B. Com., October 1996)*
6. What one the limitations of financial accounting? How do you overcome item in cost accounting? *(University of Mysore, B. Com., November 1995)*
7. Define costing. How does it differ from financial accounting? Explain its importance under present circumstances. *(University of Mysore, B. Com., November 1998)*

8. State the advantages of costing. How it aids the management and what objections are raised against cost accounts? *(University of Mysore, B. Com., November 91)*
9. Define costing. Discuss briefly the objectives and advantages of costing. *(S. V. University, B. Com., April 1998)*
10. Define cost accounting and bring out the differences between cost accounts and Financial accounts. *(Madurai Kamaraj University, B. Com., April 1998)*
11. Define costing critically evaluate the arguments for the installation of costing system in an industry. *(Mangalore University, B. Com., April 1998)*
12. What one the objectives of cost accounting? What are its advantages and limitations? *(Nagarjuna University, B. Com., March 1998)*
13. Cost accounting has become an essential tool of management. Mention the steps to be taken while installing cost accounting system in a manufacturing concern. *(Sri Krishnadevaraya University, M. Com., April 1998)*
14. What are the objectives of cost accounting and what is the relation with Management accounting department? *(S. V. University, B. Com., September 1995)*
15. "Cost accounting has become an essential tool of modern management". comment. *(Mangalore University, B. Com., April 1994)*
16. Explain briefly the objects advantages and limitations of costing. *(Sri Krishnadevaraya University, B. Com., April 1994)*
17. Define cost accounting. How does a good system of cost accounting serve the management. *(Bharathidasan University, B. Com., April 1994)*
18. Discuss the limitations of financial accounting and explain the importance of cost accounting. *(M.G. University, B. Com., April 1996)*
19. "An efficient system of costing is essential factor for industrial control under modern conditions of business and as such may be regarded as an important part in the efforts of any management to secure business stability"–Elaborate. *(Mangalore University, B. Com., September 1997)*
20. What is meant by cost accounting? Discuss in detail the advantages of the cost accounting. *(Madurai Kamaraj University, B. Com., April 1997)*
21. What do you mean by installation of costing system? Explain the practical difficulties involved in installing such a system in a manufacturing concern. *(Osmania University, B. Com., October 1996)*
22. Explain the advantages of cost accounting. What are the differences between cost accounting and Financial accounting *(Sri Krishnadevaraya University, B. Com., October 1996)*
23. "A good costing system is an involvable aid to management." Discuss. *(Osmania University, B. Com., March 1996)*
24. How cost accounting is superior over financial accounting? Explain the techniques of costing and their application and suitability. *(Karnataka University, M. Com., May 1996)*
25. What is cost accounting? What are its objectives? Discuss. *(Mangalore University, B. Com., October 1995)*
26. "Cost accounting has become an essential tool of management". Comment and state the steps to be taken while installing a costing system in a manufacturing concern. *(Bangalore University, M. Com., May 1995)*
27. Explain the advantages of cost accounting. *(University of Kerala, M. Com., May 1995)*
28. Explain the significance of cost accounting in a manufacturing company. *(Sri Krishnadevaraya University, M. Com., April 1995)*

2

COST ANALYSIS AND CLASSIFICATION

DEFINITION OF COST

The term 'cost' connotes different meanings to different people. But in cost accounting it is used in a special sense. The terminology published by ICMA, defines cost as "the amount of expenditure (actual or notional) incurred on or attributable to a specified thing or activity"

According to Crowningshield cost represents, "an expenditure made to secure an economic benefit, generally resources that promise to produce revenue. The resources may have tangible substance (material or machinery) or they may take the form of services (wages, rent, power)."

In the words of Shillinglaw (Cost Accounting, Analysis and Control) cost represents the resources that must be sacrificed to attain a particular objective.

The AICPA Committee on terminology defines cost as "the amount measured in money, of cash expended or other property transferred, capital stock issued, services performed or a liability incurred in consideration of goods or services received or to be received."

The committee on cost concepts and standards of the American Accounting Association defines cost as "cost is a foregoing, measured in monetary terms incurred or potentially to be incurred to achieve a specific objective."

The term cost is denoted by "expenses" when the cost is incurred after deriving the benefit. The AICPA Committee on terminology defined expenses as "all expired cost which are deductible from revenue". In a narrow sense, expense refers to such items as operating, selling or administrative expenses. Examples of 'expired cost' or 'expense' are rent paid for using the building, wages and salaries paid for deriving the services.

When the cost is incurred before deriving the benefit it is termed as "deferred cost" Examples of deferred costs are insurance premium paid, advertisement expenses incurred and cost of research and development.

When no benefit is derived by the incurrence of cost, it is termed as "loss". Examples of loss are materials destroyed by fire, salary paid for a period of strike, materials spoiled through bad workmanship, high prices paid for materials because of faulty purchases, wages paid to workers for idle time arising from breakdown of machines.

ROLE OF COST IN COST ACCOUNTING

1. It helps in choosing from among various alternative courses of action.
2. It helps in pricing decisions.
3. It helps in determining the optimum level of operation depending upon the behaviour of cost in relation to scale of operation.
4. It helps to make or buy decisions in respect of a component.
5. It helps in matters relating to replacement of capital equipments by a new one.
6. It helps in deciding whether to sell a product at a particular stage of production or to further process and sell at the stage of its completion.

7. It is useful in deciding the acquisition of fixed assets.
8. It helps in deciding to shut down or continue the operation of a certain department owing to losses and wastages arising from such department.
9. It helps in deciding whether an asset is to be bought or hired.
10. It helps in evaluating the incurrence of different elements of cost on different projects.

COST UNIT AND COST CENTRE

Cost Unit

Cost unit is defined by the terminology of ICMA as "a quantitative unit of product or service in relation to which costs are ascertained". A cost unit is a device used for the purpose of splitting total cost into smaller sub-divisions attributable to products or service. A cost unit simply stated is a unit of finished product, service or time or combination of these in relation to which cost is ascertained and expressed. The following are some of the examples of cost units selected by different industries.

Name of the Industry	*Product*	*Cost Unit*
1. Brick kilns	Bricks	1,000 bricks
2. Cement Industry	Cement	Ton
3. Pharmaceutical Industry	Tablets	1,000 Tablets
4. Cosmetics Industry	Talcum powder	1 Tin
5. Furniture Industry	Table	1 Table
6. Hardware Industry	Bolts and nuts	100 pieces
7. Cotton Textile	Yarn	1 Kg
8. Breweries	Beer	1 Barrel
9. Quarry	Granite stone	Ton
10. Construction Company	House	Contract
11. Transport Companies	Service	Passenger-mile
12. Hospital	Service	Bed-day

Cost Centre

A cost centre refers to a section of a factory for which costs are accumulated separately. In order to facilitate charging of costs to cost units, it is necessary to divide the factory into various sections which can be used to accumulate costs for subsequent distribution. Each such section of a factory is known as cost centre. This also facilitates fixation of responsibility for every officer-in-charge of that section. Hence cost centre is also known as responsibility centre.

Cost centre has been defined by ICMA terminology as "a location, person or item of equipment (or group of these) in respect of which costs may be ascertained and related to cost units."

Types of Cost Centre

1. Personal and impersonal cost centre : Personal cost centre consists of a person or group of persons. Personal cost centre follows the organisational structure of a factory. Under this type of cost centre, costs are analysed and accumulated according to, say, works manager, sales manager, store keeper, etc.

Impersonal cost centre consists of a location or item of equipment. A cost centre relating to location may represent a region of sales, a warehouse or storeroom. Cost centre relating to an item of equipment could be a machine or group of machines.

2. Operation and process cost centre : Operation cost centre consist of those machines which carry out the same operation.

A process cost centre is a cost centre in which a specific process or a continuous sequence of operation is carried out.

3. Production and service cost centre : A production cost centre is one where actual production process is carried out. The manufacturing and non-manufacturing costs are charged to production cost centre.

A service cost centre is one which provides services to other cost centre. Only non-manufacturing costs are charged to service cost centre.

Whatever may be the type of cost centre, it is determined by taking into consideration the following factors :

(*a*) The volume of work to be performed.

(*b*) The extent of cost control that can be exercised.

(*c*) Responsibilities to be identified.

(*d*) The uses of cost centres to the cost accounting department.

COSTING TECHNIQUES

Some of the important techniques of costing are as follows :

(*a*) ***Absorption costing :*** Under this technique both fixed and variable costs are charged to costs of production.

(*b*) ***Marginal costing :*** Under this technique a distinction is made between variable cost and fixed cost. Only variable costs are charged to cost of production. Fixed costs are written off to the costing profit and loss account.

(*c*) ***Historical costing :*** Under this technique the actual cost incurred is taken into the cost of production.

(*d*) ***Standard costing :*** Under this technique, standard costs are established for each item of expense based on past experience. The actual cost is compared with standard cost to know the variance. This reflects the efficiency or otherwise of the performance of the organisation.

(*e*) ***Differential costing :*** A technique used in the preparation of *ad hoc* information in which only cost and income difference between alternative courses of action are taken into consideration.

(*f*) ***Uniform costing :*** The use by several undertakings of the same costing systems, *i.e.*, the costing principles and method.

COSTING SYSTEMS

Neuner in his *Accounting System* has defined an accounting system as "an organisation of forms, records and reports, closely co-ordinated to facilitate business management through determining certain basic and required information. A cost system is an aspect of the accounting system designed specifically to provide information concerning costs and efficiency. The following are some of the costing systems."

1. Historical cost system : A historical system is one which accumulates actual costs after the operations have taken place. So under this system cost of a product is ascertained after they have been actually incurred. This system is not so popular because it suffers from the following limitation :

(*i*) As historical costs are recorded after the event takes place it is not possible to rectify the defect until the inefficiency is discovered.

(*ii*) It does not provide any basis against which efficiency can be measured.

(*iii*) It does not facilitate preparation of tender statements and quotations.

(*iv*) It is expensive system as a large number of records and forms are to be maintained under this system.

2. Estimated cost system : It is a system under which the various elements of costs are estimated or predetermined for recording the costs in the books of accounts. Estimated cost system helps in comparing such cost with actual cost to know variations between estimated and actual costs. Estimated cost serve as a basis for fixation of selling price. A serious limitation of estimated cost system is that estimated costs are seldom accurate.

3. Standard cost system : It is a system of cost accounting which makes use of predetermined standards relating to various elements of cost. Having fixed the standard costs, they are compared with actual costs to develop variances to know the efficiency of business. Standard cost system is applicable where the production process is standardised.

Although estimated costs and standard costs are predetermined cost they differ from each other in respect of the following :

(*i*) Estimated costs are established on an average basis taking into account the past performance. While standard costs are established on a scientific basis.

(*ii*) Estimated costs only constitute a statistical information and are not recorded in the books. Standard costs are recorded in the accounting books.

(*iii*) Estimated cost does not serve the purpose of cost control. They are useful in fixing the prices. Whereas standard cost serves the purpose of cost control.

COSTING METHODS

Costing methods help in finding out cost per unit of a product or service. Cost finding is defined as the determination of the cost of goods or services by informal procedure, *i.e.*, procedure that do not carry on regular process of cost accounting on a continuous basis. There are number of methods of cost finding which are used in practice depending upon the nature of the business and the type of its products. The most popular methods of cost finding is shown in the following chart.

Methods of Cost Finding

- Specific order costing
  - Job costing
  - Batch costing
  - Contract costing
  - Cost plus contract
- Operation costing
  - Single or output costing
  - Process costing
  - Service or operating costing
  - Departmental costing
  - Composite costing

Specific Order Costing

The terminology of ICMA defines specific order costing as "the category of basic costing methods applicable where the work consists of separate contracts, jobs or batches each of which is authorised by a special order or contract. This method is adopted in made-to-order type of products which depends entirely on the specification of customers. As such there is no standardisation in the production process for want of uniformity. This method may take any of the following :

1. Job costing : The terminology of ICMA defines job costing as "that form of specific order costing which applies where work is undertaken to customers' special requirements." The work is usually carried out within a factory or workshop where each job moves, through the processes or operations as a continuously identifiable unit although the term may also be applied to such work as building repairs carried out in the customer's premises.

A job costing is also known as 'terminal costing' as the recording of costs ends after the completion of job. Under this method of costing each job is dissimilar in nature and is therefore identified separately by a job order number. Costs are ascertained job wise and profit or loss is known for each job separately.

This method is used in repair workshops, printing press, foundries, film studios, interior decoration, etc.

2. Contract costing : The terminology of ICMA defines contract costing as "that form of specific order costing which applies where work is undertaken to customers' special requirements and each order is of long duration. The work is usually of a constructional nature. In general, the method is similar to job costing although it has certain distinctive features. These features of contract costing are as follow :

(*a*) Most of the contracts take several months (even years) for completion.

(*b*) The work is performed in all cases without exception in the premises of contractee.

(*c*) Most of the expenses chargeable to contracts are direct in nature.

This method is adopted in constructional companies engaged in building houses, road repairs, construction of dams and bridges.

3. Cost plus contract : This is a variation of contract costing which was very popular during the First World War. At present it is used in USA and India to a large extent by constructional contractors. Under this method, the contract price is fixed by adding a percentage of profit to the prime cost, *i.e.*, aggregate of direct material cost, direct labour cost, and direct expenses. This method is followed only when there is need for quick execution of contracts without waiting for the fixing of definite contract price. This method is disapproved because of the following limitations :

(*a*) The contractor may unduly fix a higher margin of profit on a high notional cost.

(*b*) There may be fraudulent agreement between contractor and sub-contractor in arriving at a high total cost, on which profit margin is to be fixed.

(*c*) It may lead to inefficiency and thus, resulting in overtime work to complete the work within the time schedule.

4. Batch costing : The terminology of ICMA defines batch costing as "that form of specific order costing which applies where similar articles are manufactured in batches either for sale or for use within the undertaking." In most cases the costing is similar to job costing. Under this method a convenient batch of production is treated as a job. Cost is ascertained for each batch separately. This method is used in biscuit factories, bakeries, ready-made garments, hardwares like bolts, nuts, screws, drugs and pharmaceuitcals.

Operation Costing

The terminology of ICMA defines operation costing as "the category of basic costing methods applicable where standardised goods or services result from a sequence of repetitive and more or less continuous operations or process to which costs are charged before being averaged over the units produced during the period." The following are the distinctive methods of costing which fall under this category.

1. Single or output or unit costing : It is a method of costing by the unit of production, where manufacturing is continuous and the units are identical. In some cases the units may differ in terms of size, shape, quality, etc. This method is called single costing as only single type of product alone is manufactured. Examples of industries which make use of this method of costing are collieries, quarries, flour-mills, paper mills, textile mills, brick-making.

2. Process or continuous or average costing : The terminology of ICMA defines process costing as "that form of operation costing which applies where standardised goods are produced." It is a method of costing where cost is ascertained at the stage of every process and also after completing the finished production. The industries which make use of this method of costing have the following distinct features :

(*a*) The output of one process is passed on as input of subsequent process until production is complete.

(*b*) The cost of every process is transferred to subsequent process as is done in the above feature.

(*c*) The process industries incur normal and abnormal losses usually.

(*d*) In majority of process costing industries by-products are obtained in addition to main product.

(*e*) The cost of semi-finished goods are expressed in terms of fully finished goods and this process is known as equivalent production.

The examples of industries which make use of process costing are breweries, chemicals, paints, soap, sugar, etc.

3. Service or operating costing : The terminology of ICMA defines service costing as "that form of operation costing which applies where standardised services are provided either by an undertaking or by a service cost centre within an undertaking." This method of costing is used by those undertakings which render service as against manufacturing and supply of tangible products. The important features of industries where this method of costing is applied are as follows :

(*a*) They render uniform service for those who apply for it or who depend on it.

(*b*) It involves heavy capital expenditure in manufacturing and in the supply of services.

(*c*) The cost of production is classified into fixed and variable as economy of operation affects unit cost of service rendered.

(*d*) They make use of composite unit to express the cost per unit.

Examples of industries which make use of this method of costing are (*i*) Transport undertakings which may take the form of Roadways, Railways and Airways, (*ii*) Supply services which may take the form of supply of gas, electricity, water, (*iii*) Welfare services such as Canteen, Hospital and Library.

4. Departmental costing : Under this method of costing the cost incurred in maintaining a particular department is ascertained. There are two reasons for using this method of costing, *viz.*, (*a*) to control the cost of a department as for example the cost of running a research department or a dispensary belonging to the factory, (*b*) To charge the costs of a department to the finished product, as for example, charging the costs of maintenance department to production department.

5. Multiple or hybrid or composite costing : This method of costing is used in those industries which assemble the various component parts. Such industries make use of more than one method of costing. For example, in bicycle manufacturing industries batch costing may be used to ascertain the costs of various component parts. Upon assemblage of these parts output costing may be used in ascertaining the cost of a single bicycle. Other examples of industries which make use of this method of costing are radio manufacturing concerns, refrigeration industries, aeroplanes, TV industries, automobiles and so on.

COST CLASSIFICATION

According to Robert I. Dickey, classification is the process of grouping like facts under a common designation on the basis of similarities of nature, attributes or relations. The committee on National Association of Accountants define classification as "the identification of each item and the systematic placement of like items together according to their common features. Items grouped together under common heads are further defined according to their fundamental differences."

Need for Cost Classification

The need for classification arises owing to use of cost data for a variety of purposes. The same cost data cannot serve all purposes equally well. For different purposes, different kinds of cost information are required. Hence costs must be arranged and classified in such a way that they can be combined in different ways to serve different purposes. The cost classification is directed towards the attainment of the following purposes :

(*a*) ascertainment of profits periodically
(*b*) in budgeting and planning process
(*c*) controlling cost
(*d*) pricing policy and
(*e*) current application of plans and policies.

Methods of Cost Classification

Costs are classified on the basis of large number of methods. This is shown in the following chart. (see next page)

On the Basis of Element of Cost

Under this basis costs can be classified into the following :

(*a*) **Material cost :** The terminology of ICMA defines material cost as "the cost of commodities, other than fixed assets, introduced into products or consumed in the operation of an organisation." Materials cost may be either direct material cost or indirect material cost. The terminology defines direct material cost as "the cost of materials entering into and becoming constituent element of a product or saleable service." Examples of direct materials are cotton in Cotton Textiles, timber in furniture making industries. Indirect material cost has been defined by the terminology as "materials cost other than direct material cost." Examples of indirect materials are consumable stores such as oil, cotton waste, etc.

(*b*) **Labour cost :** Labour cost may relate to direct labour cost or indirect labour cost. The terminology defines direct labour cost as "the cost of remuneration for employees' efforts and skills applied directly to a product or saleable service". Indirect wages cost has been defined by the terminology as "wage cost other than direct, wages cost".

(*c*) **Expenses :** Expenses may relate to direct or indirect expense. The terminology defines direct expenses as "costs other than materials or wages which are incurred for a

CHART SHOWING CLASSIFICATION OF COST

1. On the basis of Elements of Cost
   - (a) Material cost
   - (b) Labour cost
   - (c) Direct expenses
   - (d) Overheads
2. On the Basis of Function
   - (a) Production cost
   - (b) Administration cost
   - (c) Selling cost
   - (d) Distribution cost
   - (e) Finance cost
   - (f) Research & Development cost
3. On the Basis of Variability
   - (a) Variable cost
   - (b) Fixed cost
   - (c) Semi-variable cost
4. On the Basis of Controllability
   - (a) Controllable cost
   - (c) Uncontrollable cost
5. On the Basis of Normally
   - Normal cost
   - Abnormal cost
6. On the Basis of Identifyability
   - Direct cost
   - Indirect cost
7. On the Basis of Investment
   - Capital cost
   - Revenue cost
8. On the Basis of Time
   - Historical cost
   - Predetermined cost
9. On the Basis of Association with the product
   - Product cost
   - Period cost
10. On the Basis of Decision-making
    - Slink cost
    - Out of Pocket cost
    - Opportunity cost
    - Imputed cost
    - Marginal cost
    - Replacement cost
    - Avoidable & unavoidable cost
    - Differential cost
    - Relevant & Irrelevant cost
    - Conversion cost

specific product or saleable service" Indirect expense has been defined by the terminology as "expenses other than direct expense".

(*d*) **Overheads :** The terminology defines overheads as "the total cost of indirect materials, wages and expenses."

Basis of Function

According to this basis costs are classified into:

(*a*) **Production cost :** Production costs refer to those costs incurred in fabricating and assembling units of products. Examples of production costs are material cost, labour cost, and overheads.

(*b*) **Administration cost :** It has been defined by the terminology as the sum of those costs of general management and of secretarial, accounting and administrative services which cannot be directly related to the production, marketing, research or development functions of the enterprise.

(*c*) **Selling cost :** This has been defined as the cost of securing orders.

(*d*) **Distribution cost :** Distribution cost refers to those cost incurred to promote the sale and to facilitate the movement of goods into the hands of purchasers.

(*e*) **Finance cost :** Finance costs are those costs associated with using external sources of funds to finance the firm.

(*f*) **Research and development cost :** The terminology defines research cost as "the cost of seeking new or improved products, applications of materials or methods." Development cost has been defined as the cost of the process which begins with the implementation of the decision to produce a new or improved method and ends with the commencement of formal production of that product or by that method.

Basis of Variability

On the basis of variability, costs are classified into three types, *viz.*, fixed cost, variable cost and semi-variable cost.

(*a*) **Fixed cost :** The terminology of ICMA defines fixed cost as "a cost which accrues in relation to the passage of time and which within certain output or turnover limits, tends to be unaffected by fluctuations in volume of output or turnover. The following are the characteristics of fixed cost :

(*i*) The amount of fixed cost remain constant for varying level of output.
(*ii*) Fixed cost per unit will decrease with increased output.
(*iii*) The control of fixed cost lies in the hands of the top management rather than departmental heads.

Examples of fixed costs are rent and rates, insurance, salaries and such their items.

(*b*) **Variable cost :** The terminology of ICMA defines variable cost as "a cost which in aggregate tends to vary in direct proportion to changes in the volume of output or turnover. The characteristics of variable costs are as follows :

(*i*) They vary in direct proportion to volume of output or sales.
(*ii*) The variable cost per unit of product remains constant.
(*iii*) It is easy to assign variable cost to products or departments.
(*iv*) Control over variable cost lies in the hands of departmental heads.

Examples of variable costs are direct material cost, and direct labour cost.

(*c*) **Semi-variable cost :** The terminology defines semi-variable cost as "a cost containing both fixed and variable elements, which is, therefore, partly affected by fluctuations in the volume of output or turnover. Examples of semi-variable costs are telephone charges (as telephone bill for local calls are fixed and for outstation calls it varies depending upon number of calls made) depreciation (for efflux of time is fixed, for wear and tear it is variable).

Basis of Controllability

On this basis cost is classified into two types *viz.*, (*i*) controllable cost, and (*ii*) non-controllable cost.

(*a*) **Controllable cost :** The ICMA terminology defines controllable cost as "cost chargeable to a cost centre, which can be influenced by the actions of the person in whom control of the centre is vested". Practically all variable costs are controllable cost.

(*b*) **Non-controllable cost :** The ICMA terminology defines non-controllable cost as a "cost chargeable to a cost centre which cannot be influenced by the actions of the person in whom control of the centre is vested". Practically all fixed costs are non-controllable cost.

Basis of Normality

According to this basis costs are classified into two types, *viz.*, (*a*) normal cost, and (*b*) abnormal cost.

(*a*) **Normal cost :** Normal cost is defined as a "cost which is normally incurred at a given level of output in the condition in which that level of output is normally attained.

(*b*) **Abnormal cost :** It is defined as a "cost which is not normally incurred at a given level of output in the conditions in which that level of output is normally attained.

Basis of Identifiability

On this basis costs are classified into two types, *viz.*, (*i*) direct cost, and (*ii*) indirect cost.

(*i*) **Direct cost :** All costs which can be conveniently allocated to cost unit or cost centre is known as direct cost.

(*ii*) **Indirect cost :** Those costs which cannot be allocated to, but which can be apportioned to cost unit or cost centre are known as indirect cost.

This classification is important because of the following :

(*i*) It facilitates accurate ascertainment of cost by means of identifying direct cost to cost unit and by appropriate apportionment and absorption of indirect cost by cost unit.

(*ii*) It facilitates controlling of costs because most of the direct costs are controllable whereas indirect costs are not amenable for control.

(*iii*) It enabies in fixing the responsibility to the executives.

Basis of Investment

On this basis costs are classified into (*a*) capital cost, and (*b*) revenue cost.

(*a*) **Capital cost :** A Capital cost is intended to benefit future periods.

(*b*) **Revenue cost :** A cost which is incurred to benefit the current period is treated as revenue cost.

Capital cost is treated as an asset while revenue cost is treated as an expense.

Basis of Time

On this basis costs are classified into two types : (*a*) Historical cost, and (*b*) predetermined cost.

(*a*) **Historical cost :** This refers to costs which are incurred after the event takes place.

(*b*) **Predetermined cost :** This refers to a cost which is computed in advance of production on the basis of a specification of all the factors affecting cost. Predetermined costs are costs which are set up from analysis and forecast made before the event and represent not what has happened but what is expected to happen. Predetermined costs take a number of forms such as budgeted cost, estimated cost, standard cost and so on.

Basis of Association with the Production

On this basis costs are classified into two types *viz*. (*a*) product cost, and (*b*) period cost.

(*a*) ***Product cost :*** These are the costs which are directly associated with the product. These costs provide no benefit until the product is sold. When the products are sold, the total product costs are recovered as an expense. This expense is called the cost of goods sold. Examples of product costs are direct material, direct labour and factory overheads.

(*b*) ***Period cost :*** Period costs are those costs that can be associated with a particular accounting period rather than with the products delivered to the customers.

Basis of Decision-making

The following costs are classified on the basis of managerial decision-making :

(*a*) **Sunk cost :** The National Association of Accountants defines a sunk cost as "an expenditure for equipment or productive resources which has no economic relevance to the present decision-making process." Sunk cost as its name implies is an historical cost that are irrevocable in a given situation. It is a cost which has been created by a decision that was made in the past which cannot be changed by any decision that will be made in the future. For example, an equipment which is to be discarded at its book value having no scrap value is not effected by a decision to continue or shut down the operation of a department where such equipment is used.

(*b*) **Out-of-pocket cost :** It signifies the cash outlay required for undertaking a project. Here the management is interested in knowing whether the income from a particular project will at least cover the expenditure incurred on that project.

(*c*) **Opportunity cost :** The terminology of ICMA defines opportunity cost as "the value of benefit sacrificed in favour of an alternative course of action". Edwards Hermanson and Salmonson define it as "the benefit lost by rejecting the best competing alternatives to the one chosen". The benefit lost is usually the net earnings or profit that might have earned from the rejected alternative. Opportunity costs are not recorded in the books. It is important in decision-making and in comparing various alternatives to decide the best alternative. An example of opportunity cost would be investment on plant and machinery, cannot be invested on shares of a company. The loss of divident that would have been earned had the investment is made on shares is the opportunity cost.

(*d*) **Imputed cost or notional cost :** The terminology of ICMA defines notional cost as "a hypothetical cost taken into account to represent a benefit enjoyed by the undertaking in respect of which no actual expense is incurred. Examples of imputed costs are rent of owned land, salary of owner and interest on owned capital.

(*e*) **Marginal cost :** The terminology of ICMA defines marginal cost as "the variable cost of one unit of product or a service, *i.e.*, a cost which would be avoided if the unit was not produced or provided.

(*f*) **Replacement cost :** It refers to the cost of replacing an asset at current market value. For example, when the cost of replacing a machniery is considered, it means the cost of purchasing the machinery at the current market price and not at which it was purchased.

(*g*) **Avoidable cost and unavoidable cost :** Avoidable cost can be eliminated in case of product or department is discontinued.

Unavoidable costs are the indirect costs which cannot be eliminated with the discontinuation of a product or department. Such costs are merely allocated if the product or department is discontinued. Example of unavoidable cost is rent of factory and salary of factory manager which cannot be eliminated if a particular product line or a department is discontinued.

(*h*) **Differential cost :** Differential cost has been defined as the increase or decrease in total cost resulting out of (*i*) producing and distributing a few more or few less of products, (*ii*) a change in the method of production or distribution (*iii*) an addition or deletion of product or a territory, and (*iv*) the selection of an additional sales channels.

(*i*) **Relevant and irrelevant cost :** Relevant costs are those costs that would be changed by the decision. Irrelevant costs are those costs that would not be affected by the decision. For example, when a manufacturer decided to close a warehouse, the wages associated with the maintenance of such warehouse is relevant cost as wage payment cease if the warehouse is closed. But rent which was already paid under lease agreement which cannot be recovered is irrelevant cost.

(*j*) **Conversion cost :** This is the aggregate of direct labour cost and overheads. Such costs assume more importance where material value is negligible as in the case of brick manufacturing industries.

COST CONVENTIONS

The cost accounting conventions may be summarised as under :

1. Classification of expenses according to nature of cost : In order to facilitate control over costs the total cost incurred in manufacturing a product is divided into (*a*) direct material cost, (*b*) direct labour cost, (*c*) direct expenses, and (*d*) overheads.

2. Classification of cost into fixed and variable : In order to know the behaviour of costs, total cost is classified into fixed and variable.

3. Classification of costs into normal and abnormal : To facilitate comparison of cost of one period with other period, costs are classified into normal cost and abnormal cost. Normal cost is charged to cost of production and abnormal cost is taken into costing profit and loss account.

4. Principle of exception : Principle of exception which is a technique of management science is used in reporting cost data to management. Under this convention, only such report which are useful in management decision-making is reported and all irrelevant matters are not disclosed to management.

5. Establishment of standards : The standards to be set for each and every task should be practical one which is attainable under a given condition and for attaining a given level of output. In other words standards to be set must be a realistic approach.

6. Classification of cost as controllable and uncontrollable : In order to fix the responsibility on the executives it is necessary to classify the costs into controllable and uncontrollable cost.

7. Consistency : Whenever any method or system or technique is used for ascertaining cost, it should be continued for a reasonably long period of time unless the situation demand for its change. For example, the method of wage payment should not be changed very often. Frequent changes in the methods and techniques will vitiates comparison of cost data. In other words consistency must be maintained for a relatively longer period of time.

8. Cost control to be exercised through close contact with those who incur the costs : The control of cost should not only be the job of cost accountant alone. Everyone such as foreman, supervisors, and departmental managers should be consulted and involved in cost control process.

9. Cost should represent sacrifice involved when a business is operating at an efficient level of operation : Certain items of expenses will not affect cost of production and as such they are not recorded. For example interest on capital is not recorded in cost accounts being a matter of pure finance.

10. The system of cost accounting should be designed so as to meet the specific requirements of a business.

COMPONENTS OF TOTAL COST

The various components of total cost are as follows :

(*a*) Prime cost
(*b*) Factory cost or works cost
(*c*) Office cost or cost of production
(*d*) Cost of sales or total cost.

These components of total cost is explained below :

1. Prime cost : Prime cost is also called by other names such as first cost, basic cost, and foundation cost as it is incurred first in the sequence when compared to other components of total cost. Prime cost consists of three important elements of costs, namely, direct material cost, direct labour cost and direct expenses. Prime cost is important for three reasons. *Firstly*, this is the most important component of total cost because in terms of elements of cost they constitute highest percentage of total cost. It is the foundation upon which stands the whole structure of total cost. *Secondly*, some of the overheads are absorbed on the basis of prime cost elements. *Thirdly*, by analyzing and comparing every element of prime cost of one period with the corresponding element of the previous year, management can know to what extent the prime cost element has varied and take appropriate steps to control such element of prime cost. Expressed in the form of an equation –

Prime cost = Direct material cost + Direct labour cost + Direct expenses

2. Factory cost or works cost : It comprises of prime cost and factory overheads which includes indirect material cost, indirect labour cost and indirect expenses. Works cost denotes the actual expenses that are incurred in converting raw materials into finished products. Works cost is important for two reasons. Firstly, by comparing works cost of current year with the previous year, it shows the variation of the work cost. Management can take suitable steps to control if the variation is adverse. Secondly, works cost constitute the basis for absorption of office overheads in certain cases. Expressed in the form of an equation–

Factory cost or work cost = Prime cost + Factory or works overhead

3. Office cost or cost of production : Office cost is the aggregate of works cost and office and administration overheads. Office cost is important as it serves the purposes of (*a*) knowing the cost of production, (*b*) knowing the percentage of office overheads to office cost. This is turn reflects the relative importance of office department and its efficient functioning, (*c*) selling price is fixed on the basis of cost of production in case of made-to-order type of industries. Expressed in the form of an equation–

Office cost or cost of production = Works costs or factory cost + Office and administration overhead

4. Total cost or cost of sales : When selling and distribution expenses are added to office cost or cost of production, it is known as total cost or cost of sales. Total cost serves the purposes of (*a*) fixing the selling price by adding a margin of profit to the total cost, (*b*) knowing the relation between selling and distribution expenses with office overheads on the one hand and works overheads on the other hand, (*c*) by comparing the total cost of present year with past year it is possible to know increase or decrease in the total cost and thereby to control the total cost if it has gone up. Expressed in the form of an equation–

Total cost or cost of sales = Office cost or cost of production + Selling and distribution overhead

The Fig. 2.1 summarises the various components of total cost.

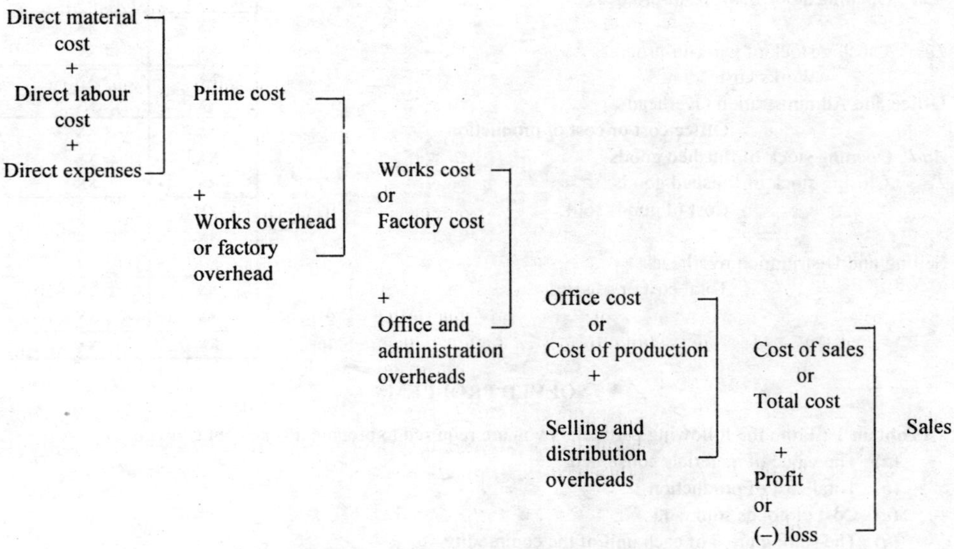

Fig. 2.1 : Chart showing components of total cost.

COST SHEET

A cost sheet is a statement which shows the details regarding the total cost of the job or a product. A cost sheet may include as many columns as is desired to show in detail (*a*) Cost per unit of the product, (*b*) Total cost for all the units produced, (*c*) Particulars of cost relating to the previous year, (*d*) Estimated cost for the succeeding year, and (*e*) A column showing the variation of each and every element of cost. A cost sheet not only shows the total cost but also the various components of total cost. It serves the following purposes :

(1) It discloses the cost per unit as well as total cost of output.

(2) It discloses the various elements of cost which go to make up total cost.

(3) By fixing selling price in advance it facilitates preparation of tender price.

(4) It facilitates comparison of total cost with previous year's cost and standard cost and thereby help management in locating inefficiency in production.

The following is the proforma of a cost sheet :

PROFORMA COST SHEET (*For the period ending......*)

		Total	*Cost per Unit*
Direct material cost :			
Opening stock of raw during the year	xx		
Add : Purchase of raw materials during the year	xx		
Add : Carriage Inwards	xx		
Less : Closing stock of raw materials	xx		
Cost of raw materials consumed	xx	xx	xx
Direct labour cost		xx	xx
Direct expenses		xx	xx
Prime cost		xx	xx
Factory overhead		xx	xx
		xx	xx
		xx	xx
Add : Opening stock of work-in-progress		xx	xx
		xx	xx
Less : Closing stock of work-in-progress		xx	xx
Works cost		xx	xx
Office and Administration Overheads		xx	xx
Office cost or cost of production		xx	xx
Add : Opening stock of finished goods		xx	xx
Less : Closing stock of finished goods		xx	xx
Cost of goods sold		xx	xx
		xx	xx
Selling and Distribution overheads		xx	xx
Total cost or of sales		xx	xx
	Profit	xx	xx
	Sales	xx	xx

SOLVED PROBLEMS

Problem 1 : From the following particulars you are required to prepare a statement showing :

(*a*) The value of materials consumed

(*b*) Total cost of production

(*c*) Cost of goods sold, and

(*d*) The selling price of each unit of the commodity

	Rs.
Opening stock of raw materials	25,000
Opening stock of finished goods (400 Units)	20,000
Wages paid to labourers	1,00,000
Raw materials bought	2,50,000
Closing stock : raw materials	20,000
: Finished goods (800 Units)	25,000
Chargeable expenses	10,000
Rent Rates, and taxes (factory)	25,000
Motive power	10,000
Factory heating & lighting	10,000

Factory Insurance	5,000
Income tax paid	6,000
Experimental expenses	2,500
Waste materials	1,000
Office Salaries	20,000
Printing and stationery	1,000
Salesmen's salary	10,000
Commission to travelling agents	5,000
Cost of free Samples	500
Donations to charitable fund	1,000
Work-in-progress : on 1st January	900
: on 31st December	3,000

Other selling expenses were calculated to be 20 paise per Unit. Total production during the year was 6,400 Units. If a profit of 25% on sales is to be realised what would be the total sales?

(Sri Sathya Sai University, B. Com., August 2000)

Solution :

Cost Sheet

		Total Cost	*Cost Per Unit*
Opening stock of raw materials	25,000		
Add : Purchases of raw materials	2,50,000		
	2,75,000		
Less : Closing stock of raw materials	20,000		
Cost of materials consumed		2,55,000	
Direct Wages		1,00,000	
Chargeable expenses		10,000	
Prime cost		3,65,000	57.03
Factory on cost :–			
Rent	25,000		
Motive Power	10,000		
Heating	10,000		
Insurance	5,000		
Experimental expenses	2,500		
Waste Materials	1,000		
	53,500		
Add : Opening stock of work-in-progress	900		
	54,400		
Less : Closing stock of work-in-progress	3,000		
		51,400	8.03
Works cost		4,16,400	65.06
Office on cost :			
Salaries	20,000		
Printing	1,000		
		21,000	3.28
Cost of production		4,37,400	68.34
Add : Opening stock of finished goods		20,000	—
		4,57,400	68.34
Less : Closing stock of finished goods		25,000	—
Cost of goods sold		4,32,400	72.066

Selling & Distribution overheads			
Salary	10,000		
Commission	5,000		
Free Samples	500		
other selling expenses	1,200		
		16,700	2.784
Cost of sales		4,49,100	74.85
Profit 1/3 on cost		1,49,700	24.95
Sales		5,98,800	99.80

Working notes

(1) Calculation of other Selling expenses on Units Sold

Units produced	6,400 Units
Add : Opening stock of finished goods	400 Units
	6,800 Units
Less : Closing stock of finished goods	800 Units
Units sold	6,000 Units

For 6000 Units @ Rs. 0.20 P = Rs. 1200

(2) Calculation of profit on cost price

Selling price = Cost price + Profit

100 = 75 + 25

$= \frac{25}{75} \times 4,49,100 = 1,49,700$

(3) Donations to charitable fund, and Income tax paid are items of pure finance. Hence they are not taken in calculating cost of production.

Problem-2 : Tirupathi Electronics Ltd., produces a standard product and provides you the following information for the year ending 31st March 1998.

Raw Materials :–	
Opening stock	10,000
Purchases	85,000
Closing stock	4,000
Direct Wages	20,000
Other direct expenses	10,000
Factory overheads	100% of direct wages
Office overheads	10% of Works-cost
Selling expenses	Rs. 2 per unit sold
Finished goods :–	
Opening stock 1,000 Units	(Rs. 16000)
Produced during the year	10,000 Units
Closing stock	2,000 Units

Prepare cost sheet for the year ending 31st March 1998. Also ascertain the selling price per unit so as to yield a profit of 20% on the selling price *(University of Delhi, B. Com. (Pass), April 1999)*

Solution :

Cost sheet of Tirupathi Electronics Ltd. for the period ending 31st March 1998

		Total	*Cost per unit*
Opening stock of raw materials	10,000		
Add : Purchases	85,000		
	95,000		
Less : Closing stock of raw materials	4,000		

Cost of materials consumed		91,000	9.10
Direct wages		20,000	2.00
Other direct expenses		10,000	1.00
Prime cost		1,21,000	12.10
Factory overheads (100% of Direct Wages)		20,000	2.00
Factory cost		1,41,000	14.10
Office & Administration overheads 10/100 × 1,41,000		14100	1.41
Office cost		1,55,100	15.51
Add : Opening stock of finished goods		16,000	
		1,71,100	
Less : Closing stock of finished goods (2,000 units @ Rs. 15.51)		31,020	
Cost of goods Sold		1,40,080	
Selling and Distribution overheads 9,000 units @ Rs. 2 per unit		18,000	
Cost of sales		1,58,080	
Profit		39,520	
Sales		1,97,600	

Selling price per unit : $\frac{1,97,600}{9,000}$ = Rs. 21.96

Working Note :

(1) Calculation of units Sold

Opening stock of Finished goods	1,000
Add : Units produced during the year	10,000
	11,000
Less : Closing stock of finished goods	2,000
Units sold	9,000

(2) Calculation of Profit

Selling price = Cost price + Profit

100 = 80 + 20

$$1,58,080 \times \frac{20}{80} = 39.520$$

Problem-3 : The following data relates to the manufacture of a product during January 1999, prepare a cost sheet showing cost per unit and profit for period

Materials consumed	Rs. 20,000
Direct wages	Rs. 18,000
Machine Hours worked	3,000 hours
Machine hour rate	Rs. 2
Office oncost on works cost	10%
Selling oncost per unit	Rs. 2
Units produced	5,000 units
Units sold	4,600
Selling price per unit	Rs. 30

(Sri Venkateshwara University, B. Com., April 1999)

Solution :

Cost Sheet

		Total Cost	Cost per unit
Direct materials consumed		20,000	4.00
Direct wages		18,000	3.60
	Prime cost	38,000	7.60
Works on cost			
3,000 Hours @ Rs. 2		6,000	1.20
	Works cost	44,000	8.80
Office on cost $44,000 \times \frac{10}{100}$		4,400	0.88
	Office cost	48,400	9.68
Less : Closing stock of finished goods			
Units produced	5,000		
Less units sold	4,600		
400 × 9.68	400	3,872	–
Cost of goods sold		44,528	9.68
Selling oncost			
4,600 @ Rs. 2		9,200	2.00
	Cost of sales	53,728	11.68
Net profit		84,272	18.32
Sales (4,600 × 30)		1,38,000	30.00

Problem-4 : The cost of Sale of product A is made up as follows :

Materials used in manufacturing	55,000
Materials used in primary packing	10,000
Materials used in selling the product	1,500
Materials used in factory	750
Materials used in office	1,250
Labour required in production	10,000
Labour required for factory supervision	2,000
Direct expenses	5,000
Indirect expenses (factory)	1,000
Administration expenses	1,250
Depreciation of office building	750
Depreciation of factory building	1,750
Selling expenses	3,500
Freight on materials purchased	5,000
Advertising	1,250

Assuming that all the products manufactured are sold, what should be the selling price to obtain a profit of 25% on selling price?

(Bangalore University, B.B.M. November 1998)

Solution :

Cost Sheet

Materials used in manufacturing	55,000	
Add : Freight	5,000	
Primary packing materials	10,000	
		70,000
Direct labour cost		10,000

Direct expenses			5,000
	Prime cost		85,000
Factory overheads			
Materials used in Factory		750	
Supervision of factory		2,000	
Indirect expenses		1,000	
Depreciation of factory		1,750	
			5,500
	Works cost		90,500
Office & Administration overheads :			
Materials used in the office		1,250	
Office expenses		1,250	
Depreciation of office building		750	
			3,250
	office cost		93,750
Selling & Distribution overheads :			
Materials used in selling		1,500	
Selling expenses		3,500	
Advertisement		1,250	6,250
	Cost of sales		1,00,000
	Profit $\frac{1}{3}$ on cost		33,333
	Sales		1,33,333

Note :
It has been assumed that the freight has been paid on raw materials purchased.

Problem-5 : The following details have been obtained from the cost records of Comet Paints Ltd.

	Rs.
Stock of raw materials on 1-9-98	75,000
Stock of raw materials on 30-9-98	91,500
Direct wages	52,500
Indirect wages	2,750
Work in progress on 1-9-98	28,000
Work in progress on 30-9-98	35,000
Purchase of raw materials	66,000
Factory rent, rates and power	15,000
Depreciation on plant & Machinery	3,500
Carriage on purchases	1,500
Office rent and taxes	2,500
Stock of finished goods on 1-9-98	54,000
Stock of finished goods on 30-9-98	31,000

It is estimated that selling and distribution overhead is 10% of sales and profit is 10% on Sales. Prepare a cost sheet giving the maximum possible break-up of costs and profit.

(*Sri Sathya Sai University, B. Com., March 1999*)

Solution :

Cost sheet of Comet Paints Ltd. for the year ending 30-9-1998

Opening stock of raw materials	75,000
Add : Purchases of raw materials	66,000
Add : Carriage inwards	1,500

	1,42,500	
Less : Closing stock of raw materials	91,500	
Cost of materials consumed		51,000
Direct wages		52,500
Prime cost		1,03,500
Factory overheads :		
Indirect wages	2,750	
Factory rent, rates & power	15,000	
Depreciation on plant	3,500	
		21,250
		1,24,750
Add : Opening stock of work-in-Progress		28,000
		1,52,750
Less : Closing stock of work-in-progress		35,000
Works cost		1,17,750
Office and administration overhead-office rent		2,500
office cost		1,20,250
Add : Opening stock of finished goods		54,000
		1,74,250
Less : Closing stock of finished goods		
		31,000
Cost of goods sold		1,43,250
Selling and Distribution overheads		17,906
Cost of sales		1,61,156
Profit		17,906
Sales		1,79,062

Working Note :

Let selling price		100
Less : Profit 10%		10
Cost of Sales		90
Less : Selling & Distribution overheads	10% on Sales	10
Cost price		80

Calculation of selling & Distribution overhead

Cost price + profit = cost of sales

$$80 + 10 = 90$$

$$\frac{10}{80} \times 1{,}43{,}250 = 17{,}906$$

Calculation of profit

Selling price = cost price + profit

$$100 = 90 + 10$$

$$= \frac{10}{90} \times 1{,}61{,}156 \text{ (i.e., cost of Sales)}$$

Problem-6 : From the following information prepare cost sheet and find the amount of profit :

	Rs.
Raw materials purchased	24,000
Works overhead	20,000
Stock on 1st Jan. 1997 :–	
Raw material	4,000
Finished goods (800 Quintals)	3,200
Work in progress :	
1st January 1997	960
31st January 1997	3,200
Office and administrative overheads	1,600
Sales (Finished goods)	60,000

Advertising, discount allowed and selling cost is Re. 0.40 per Quintal. During the month 12,800 quintals of the commodity were produced. *(University of Delhi, B. Com. (Pass), April 1998)*

Solution :

Cost Sheet

Opening stock of raw materials	4,000	
Add : Purchases of Raw materials	24,000	
Value of materials consumed or Prime Cost		28,000
Works overhead		20,000
		48,000
Add : Opening stock of work in progress		960
		48,960
Less : Closing stock of work in progress		32,00
Works cost		45,760
Office & Administration overheads		1600
office cost		47,360
Add : Opening stock of finished goods		3,200
Cost of goods sold		50,560
Selling & Distribution overheads :– Advertising, Discount allowed & Selling cost (13,600 × 0.40)		5,440
Cost of Sales		56,000
Profit (Balancing figure)		4,000
Sales		60,000

Working Note :

Calculation of units Sold :

Opening stock of finished goods	800
Add : Units produced during the month	12,800
Units Sold	13,600

Problem-7

From the following information prepare cost sheet for the year ending 31-12-1998.

	1-1-1998		31-12-1998
Raw materials	60,000		40,000
Finished goods	40,000		50,000
Work in progress	30,000		20,000
Chargeable expenses		20,000	

Wages of Labourers	1,00,000
Oil, Grease and Waste	2,000
Factory power	13,000
Depreciation :–	
Office building	5,000
Plant and Machinery	2,000
Repairs :–	
Plant & machinery	15,000
Furniture	2,000
Lighting :–	
Factory	5,000
Office	2,000
Rent :–	
Office	10,000
Show room	5,000
Factory	15,000
Director's remuneration	25,000
Printing and stationery	2,500
Salesmen's salaries	7,000
Postage and telegrams	1,000
Advertisement	7,000
Purchases of raw materials	4,00,000
Carriage inwards	2,000
Carriage outwards	1,500
Wages of foreman	1,000
Wages of store keeper	500
Manager's salary (3/4 Factory 1/4office)	2,000
Income tax	30,000
Donation	5,000
Debenture interest	7,500
Warehousing charges	1,000
Sale of finished goods	7,20,000
Sales commission	1,000

(*University of Mysore, B. Com., April 1999*)

Solution :

Cost sheet for the year ending 31-12-1998

Opening stock of raw materials	60,000	
Add : Purchases of raw materials	4,00,000	
	4,60,000	
Add : Carriage Inwards	2,000	
	4,62,000	
Less : Closing stock of raw materials	40,000	
Cost of materials consumed		4,22,000
Direct wages		1,00,000
Chargeable expenses		20,000
Prime cost		5,42,000
Works overheads :–		
Oil, Grease & Waste	2,000	
Factory power	13,000	
Depreciation on plant	2,000	
Repairs on plant	15,000	

Factory lighting	5,000	
Factory rent	15,000	
Wages of foreman	1,000	
Wages of storekeeper	500	
Manager's Salary $\frac{3}{4} \times 2000$	1,500	
		55,000
		5,97,000
Add : Opening stock of work in progress		30,000
		6,27,000
Less : Closing stock of work-in-progress		20,000
Works cost		6,07,000
Office overheads :–		
Depreciation on office building	5,000	
Repairs on furniture	2,000	
Office lighting	2,000	
Office rent	10,000	
Director's remuneration	25,000	
Printing & stationery	2,500	
Postage & telegrams	1,000	
Manager's Salary $\frac{1}{4} \times 2{,}000$	500	
		48,000
office cost		6,55,000
Add : Opening stock of finished goods		40,000
		6,95,000
Less : Closing stock of finished goods		50,000
Cost of goods Sold		6,45,000
Selling & Distribution overheads :		
Rent of showroom	5,000	
Salesmen's salary	7,000	
Advertisement	7,000	
Carriage outwards	1500	
Warehouse charges	1,000	
Sales commission	1,000	
		22,500
Cost of Sales		6,67,500
Profit		52,500
Sales		7,20,000

Problem-8 : (Cost sheet when missing Information is to be calculated).

The following inventory data relate to X Y Z Ltd.

	Inventories	
	Beginning	*Ending*
Finished goods	Rs. 1,10,000	95,000
Work-in-progress	Rs. 70,000	80,000
Raw materials	Rs. 90,000	95,000

Additional Information :–

	Rs.
Cost of goods available for sale	6,84,000

Total goods processed during the period	6,54,000
Factory overheads	1,67,000
Direct materials used	1,93,000

Requirements :–

(*i*) Determine raw materials purchases

(*ii*) Determine the direct labour cost incurred

(*iii*) Determine the cost of goods sold.

(*University of Delhi, B. Com. (Hons.), April 1999*)

Solution :

Raw Material purchases :–

Raw materials used = Opening stock + Purchases – Closing stock

1,93,000 = 90,000 + Purchases – 95,000

Purchases = 1,93,000 – 90,000 + 95,000

= Rs. 1,98,000

(*ii*) **Direct labour cost** :–

Cost of goods processed	6,54,000
Add : Closing stock of WIP	80,000
	7,34,000
Less : Opening stock of WIP	70,000
	6,64,000
Less : Factory expenses	1,67,000
	4,97,000
Less : Raw materials	1,93,000
Direct labour cost	3,04,000

(*iii*) **Cost of goods sold** :–

Cost of Sales	6,84,000
Add: Closing stock of finished goods	95,000
	7,79,000
Less : Opeing stock of finished goods	1,10,000
Cost of goods sold	6,69,000

Problem-9 : On June 30, 1996, a flash flood damaged the warehouse and factory of ABC corporation completely destroying the work-in-progress inventory. There was no damage to either the raw materials or finished goods inventories. A physical verification taken after the flood revealed the following valuations :

Raw materials	Rs. 62,000
Work-in-progress	0
Finished goods	Rs. 1,19,000

The inventory on Jan. 1, 1996 consisted of the following

Raw materials	Rs. 30,000
Work-in-progress	Rs. 1,00,000
Finished goods	Rs. 1,40,000
	Rs. 2,70,000

A review of the books and records disclosed that the gross profit margin historically approximated 25% of sales. The sales for the first six months of 1996 were Rs. 3,40,000. Raw materials purchases were Rs. 1,15,000. Direct labour cost for this period were Rs. 80,000 and manufacturing overhead has historically been 50% of direct labour.

Compute the cost of work-in-progress inventory lost at June 30, 1996 by preparing a statement of cost and profit.

(*University of Delhi, B. Com. (Hons.), April 1998*)

Solution

Cost sheet of ABC corporation

Opening stock of raw material	30,000	
Add : Purchases	1,15,000	
	1,45,000	
Less : Closing stock of raw materials	62,000	
Cost of materials consumed		83,000
Direct labour		80,000
Prime cost		1,63,000
Factory overhead $\frac{50}{100} \times 80000$		40,000
		203,000
Add : Opening work-in-progress		1,00,000
		3,03,000
Less : Closing work-in-progress (See note below)		69,000
Factory cost		2,34,000
Add : Opening finished stock		1,40,000
		3,74,000
Less : Closing finished stock		1,19,000
Cost of goods sold		2,55,000
Profit		85,000
Sales		3,40,000

Working Notes :

(1) Calculation of profit

$$\frac{25}{100} \times 3{,}40{,}000 = 85{,}000$$

(2) Calculation of closing work-in-progress

Sales	3,40,000
Less : Profit	85,000
	2,55,000
Add : Closing finished stock	1,19,000
	3,74,000
Less : Opening finished stock	1,40,000
Factory cost	2,34,000
Less : Cost before closing work-in-progress	3,03,000
Closing work-in-progress	69,000

Problem-10 : For each of the following cases, find the unknowns designated by letters :

	Case I	*Case II*
	Rs.	*Rs.*
Direct materials used	8,000	6,000
Direct labour	13,000	11,000
Purchase of Direct Materials	9,000	7,000
Factory overhead	7,000	D
Finished goods Inventory on 1-1-88	5,000	4,000
Finished goods Inventory on 31-12-88	B	5,300
Sales	42,000	31,800

Cost of goods sold	A	22,000
Profit	11,300	C
Work-in-progress on 1-1-88	Nil	800
Work-in-progress on 31-12-88	Nil	3,000

(*Sri Sathya Sai University, B. Com., Oct. 1989*)

Solution :

Cost Sheet

		Case I	*Case II*
Raw materials		8,000	6,000
Direct Materials purchased		9,000	7,000
Direct labour		13,000	11,000
Prime cost		30,000	24,000
Factory overheads		7,000	(D) 1,500
		37,000	25,500
Add : Opening stock of work-in-progress		Nil	800
		37,000	26,300
Less : Closing stock of work-in-progress		Nil	3,000
Factory cost		37,000	23,300
Add : Opening stock of Finished goods		5,000	4,000
		42,000	27,300
Less : Closing stock of Finished goods	(B)	11,300	5,300
Cost of goods sold	(A)	30,700	22,000
	Profit	11,300	(C) 9,800
	Sales	42,000	31,800

Problem-11 : The following figures are extracted from the books of factory after close of the year :

		Rs.
Raw materials	– Opening stock	14,000
	– Purchases during the year	1,00,000
	– Closing stock	10,000
Direct wages		20,000

Works overhead – 50% on direct wages

Stores overhead on materials – 10% on the cost of materials

10% of the casting were rejected being not upto specification and a sum of Rs. 800 was realised on sale of scrap. 10% of the finished castings were found to be defective in manufacture and were rectified by expenditure of a additional works overhead charged to the extent of 20% on the proportionate direct wages.

The total gross output of costing during the year-2000 tons. Find out the manufacturing cost of the saleable casting per ton. (*Gulbarga University, B. Com., April 1993*)

Solution :

Cost Sheet

		Quantity	*Amount (Rs.)*
Opening stock of Raw materials	14,000		
Add: Purchases during the year	1,00,000		
	1,14,000		
Less : Closing stock of raw materials	10,000		
Cost of Materials consumed			1,04,000
Direct wages			20,000

Prime cost		1,24,000
Works overhead – 50% of Direct Wages		10,000
Stores overhead – 10% of Direct Materials		10,400
Total cost of gross output	2,000	1,44,400
Less : Sale of rejected costing	200	800
Cost of finished costing	1,800	1,43,600
Additional cost of rectifying	–	360
Manufacturing cost	1,800	1,43,960

Working Note :

Calculation of cost of rectification

$\frac{20}{100}$ of proportionate wages is the additional cost, *i.e.*,

$$\frac{20}{100} \times 20{,}000 = 4{,}000$$

For 2,000 tons the cost is Rs. 4,000

For 180 Tons.........?

$$\frac{180 \times 2{,}000}{100} = 360$$

Problem-12 : Prepare a cost sheet showing cost and profit for 1,000 bricks

Fuel (coal)	2,500 kgs @ Rs. 15 per kg
Wages	10 labourers for 150 days @ Rs. 50 per day
Royalties	0.75 per 1,000 bricks
Depreciation on equipment	@ 10% on Rs. 1,50,000
Handling charges	0.50 per 1,000 bricks
Works expenses	10% of wages and coal
Administrative expenses	5% of wages and coal

Production Data :–

Bricks made	52,00,000
Stock on 1-1-2000	: 1,00,000 @ Rs. 40 per 1,000
Stock on 30-6-2000	: 11,00,000
Actual Breakage	: 2,00,000
Bricks Sold	: 40,00,000 @ Rs. 50 per 1,000

Solution :

Cost Sheet

	Cost per 1,000 bricks	*Total cost for 50,00,000*
Coal : 2,500 kgs @ Rs. 15 per kg	7.50	37,500
Wages : 10 × 150 × 50	15.00	75,000
Royalty	0.75	3,750
Prime cost	23.25	1,16,250
Works expenses – 10% of wages and coal	2.25	11,250
Handling charges	0.50	2,500
Depreciation – 10% on Rs. 1,50,000	3.00	15,000
Works cost	29.00	1,45,000
Administration expenses – 5% of wages & coal	1.125	5,625
cost of production	30.125	1,50,625
Add : Opening stock		4,000

	1,54,625
Less : Closing stock	33,138
Cost of bricks sold	1,21,487
Profit	78,513
Sales	2,00,000

QUESTIONS

I. A. Indicate whether the following element of cost is (1) Direct material (2) Direct labour or (3) Factory overheads :

(*i*) Machine repairs (*ii*) Bottles for packing medicines
(*iii*) Salary of supervisor (*iv*) Wages of carpenter
(*v*) Plant depreciation (*vi*) Carriage on materials purchased
(*vii*) Wages of shoes-maker (*viii*) Thread used in stitching
(*ix*) Salary of works manager (*x*) Bags used in cement mill

[*Answer* : Direct material – (*ii*), (*vi*), (*x*)
Direct labour–(*iv*), (*vii*)
Factory overheads–(*i*), (*iii*), (*v*), (*viii*), (*ix*)]

B. State the method of costing to be used in the following industries :

(*a*) Petroleum refiner (*b*) Meat packing (*c*) Automobile repair shop (*d*) Chocolate manufacturer (*e*) T. V. Sets (*f*) Soft drink (*g*) Furniture making (*h*) Coal (*i*) Textile (*j*) Interior decoration (*k*) Hospital (*l*) Scooter (*m*) Toyes-making (*n*) Nuts and Bolts (*o*) Drugs.

[*Answer* : Single or output costing – (*h*)
Job costing – (*c*), (*g*), (*j*)
Process costing – (*a*), (*b*), (*f*), (*i*)
Batch costing – (*d*), (*m*), (*n*), (*o*)
Multiple costing – (*e*), (*l*)]

C. State whether the following costs are (1) Fixed (2) Variable (3) Semi-variable :

(*a*) Sundry supplies used in a factory (*b*) Supervisor's salary , (*c*) Cost of electric power for the factory, (*d*) Life insurance premium of employee, (*e*) Rent payable on leased land, (*f*) Maintenance on the physical facilities, (*g*) Telephone expenses, (*h*) Cost accountants salary, (*i*) Rent of factory godown , (*j*) Raw materials cost, (*k*) Depreciation, (*l*) Heating, lighting and power, (*m*) Repairs.

[*Answer* : Fixed cost – (*b*), (*d*), (*e*), (*h*), (*i*)
Variable cost – (*a*), (*c*), (*j*), (*l*)
Semi-variable cost – (*f*), (*g*), (*k*), (*m*)]

D. Classify the following industries with respect to the method of costing :

(*a*) Steel, (*b*) Paper box, (*c*) Cooking utensils, (*d*) Pianos, (*e*) Nylon, (*f*) Baby food, (*g*) Office machines, (*h*) Paint, (*i*) Tyres & tubes.

[*Answer* : Single or output – (*a*), (*b*), (*c*), (*d*)
Process costing – (*e*), (*h*)
Batch costing – (*h*), (*i*)
Multiple costing – (*g*)]

E. Classify each of the following costs using the following classes :

(*a*) Direct materials, (*b*) Direct labour, (*c*) Manufacturing overheads, (*d*) Non-manufacturing overheads, (*i*) Managing director's salary, (*ii*) Oil for machine, (*iii*) Wages of machine operator, (*iv*) Salary of supervisor of assembly department for product *A*, *B* and *C*, (*v*) Depreciation on the factory building, (*vi*) Depreciation in the administrative office building, (*vii*) Rent on the sales office, (*viii*) Insurance on the truck used for delivery of finished goods sold.

[*Answer* : Direct labour cost – (*iii*)
Manufacturing overhead – (*ii*), (*iv*), (*v*)
Non-manufacturing overhead – (*i*), (*vi*), (*vii*), (*viii*)]

F. Classify the following manufacturing costs as direct or indirect product cost :

(*a*) Rent on the factory building, (*b*) Salary of the supervisor of costing department, (*c*) Fire Insurance on the factory equipment, (*d*) Labour cost for material handling, (*e*) Power cost for operating machinery, (*f*) Storage for raw materials, (*i*) Wages for tool and die-maker. [***Answer*** : Direct cost – (*b*), (*c*), (*g*), (*i*) Indirect cost – (*a*), (*d*), (*e*), (*f*), (*h*)]

II. Indicate whether the following statements are True or False :

1. All costs are fixed in long run. *T/F*
2. Fixed cost per unit vary with changes in volume. *T/F*
3. Total variable costs remain constant with changes in volume. *T/F*
4. Fixed cost per unit increases with increases in production volume. *T/F*
5. Notional costs and imputed costs mean the same. *T/F*
6. Conversion cost and overheads are interchangeable terms. *T/F*
7. Abnormal cost is uncontrollable. *T/F*
8. The term 'Cost' means price. *T/F*
9. The post of converting raw materials to finished product is known as conversion cost. *T/F*
10. An item of cost that is direct for one business may be indirect for another. *T/F*
11. The salary paid to salesman is an example of a period cost. *T/F*
12. Product costs are inventoriable; period costs are not. *T/F*
13. The job order costing is most suitable for a large steel mill. *T/F*
14. Factory overhead cost applied to job is usually based on a predetermined rate. *T/F*
15. Cost unit in a college may be a student. *T/F*

[***Answer*** : (1) *T*, (2) *F*, (3) *F*, (4) *F*, (5) *T*, (6) *F*, (7) *T*, (8) *F*, (9) *F*, (10) *T*, (11) *T*, (12) *T*, (13) *F*, (14) *T*, (15) *T*]

III. Select the correct answer from the following :

1. Which one of the following constitute conversion cost
   (*a*) Material cost and direct wages
   (*b*) Material cost and factory overheads
   (*c*) Direct wages and factory overheads
   (*d*) Direct expenses and factory overhead
2. Which one of the following is a best example of a variable cost
   (*a*) Interest on capital
   (*b*) Depreciation on machinery
   (*c*) Cost of materials
   (*d*) Rent and taxes
3. Which one of the following constitute the cost of production
   (*a*) Prime cost + factory overhead
   (*b*) Works cost + office and administration overhead
   (*c*) Works cost + prime cost
   (*d*) Works cost + selling and distribution overhead
4. Fixed cost per unit increases when
   (*a*) Variable cost per unit increases
   (*b*) Variable cost per unit decreases
   (*c*) Production value increases
   (*d*) Production volume decreases
5. Increases in total variable cost is due to
   (*a*) Increase in fixed cost
   (*b*) Increase in sales
   (*c*) Increase in production
   (*d*) Increase in semi-variable cost
6. Which one of the following industry adopts batch costing in determining the total cost
   (*a*) Biscuit making
   (*b*) Oil refinery
   (*c*) Cycle manufacturing
   (*d*) Cement industry
7. Multiple costing is followed in
   (*a*) Garment making
   (*b*) Steel industry
   (*c*) Brick making
   (*d*) Cycle manufacturing
8. Which one of the following method of costing is adopted by quarries
   (*a*) Single costing
   (*b*) Multiple costing
   (*c*) Contract costing
   (*d*) Batch costing

9. If the total of production cost is Rs. 40,000 and 20% of sale price is the profit to be added to cost what is the profit?
   (*a*) Rs. 6,000 (*c*) Rs. 10,000
   (*b*) Rs. 8,000 (*d*) Rs. 12,000
10. The total cost of a product is Rs. 32,000 and if 20% of the sale price is the profit to be added what is the sale price?
    (*a*) Rs. 34,000 (*c*) Rs. 38,400
    (*b*) Rs. 36,000 (*d*) Rs. 40,000
11. Welfare expenses will be shown in the cost sheet under
    (*a*) Selling overhead (*c*) Office overhead
    (*b*) Administrative overhead (*d*) Works overhead
12. When a change is made in the level of production the resulting change in the total cost is known as
    (*a*) Imputed cost (*c*) Out of pocket cost
    (*b*) Opportunity cost (*d*) Differential cost
13. An example of a variable cost is
    (*a*) Insurance on machinery (*c*) Labour cost
    (*b*) Manager's salary (*d*) Depreciation
14. An example of fixed cost is
    (*a*) Direct material cost (*c*) Taxes
    (*b*) Direct labour cost (*d*) Lubricants

[***Answer*** : 1. (*c*), 2. (*b*), 3. (*b*), 4. (*d*), 5. (*c*), 6. (*c*), 7. (*d*), 8. (*a*), 9. (*c*), 10. (*d*), 11. (*d*), 12. (*d*), 13. (*c*), 14. (*c*)]

IV. Fill in the blanks :

1. In cement industries cost unit is..............
2. ....costing is based on the classification of costs into fixed and variable.
3. ....costing is used in cinemas.
4. In..............costing the cost of group of products is ascertained.
5. ....is a location, person, or item of equipment in relation to which cost is ascertained.
6. The use by several undertaking of the same technique of costing is known as.............
7. ....is desirable as a common denominator for comparing costs from period to period.
8. ....costs are those chargeable as expense in the current period, which.............costs are those carried forward to future periods.
9. ....costs remain constant with changes in volume, while............costs fluctuate with volume.
10. ....costs are those which follow the item into inventory, and..........costs are those chargeable against current income.
11. ....departments work directly with the product, while...........department render a benefit for other departments.
12. ....costs benefit the current period only, while............cost benefit more than one period.
13. ....costs are determined in advance of production, while..........costs are accumulated as they occur.

[***Answer*** : 1. tonne 2. Marginal 3. Operating
4. batch 5. Cost centre 6. uniform
7. Cost unit 8. Expired and unexpired 9. Fixed and variable
10. Product and period 11. Production and service 12. Revenue and capital
13. Standard and actual]

V. Match the following :

Industry	*Methods of costing*
1. Nursing Home	(*a*) Process
2. Coal	(*b*) Job
3. Bicycle	(*c*) Multiple
4. Bridge construction	(*d*) Single

5. Interior decoration	(*e*) Operating
6. Sugar industry	(*f*) Contract
	(*g*) Batch

[***Answer*** : 1. (*e*), 2. (*d*), 3. (*c*), 4. (*f*), 5. (*b*), 6. (*a*)]

A	*B*
1. Sunk cost	(*a*) Increases in proportion to output
2. Opportunity cost	(*b*) Remains constant
3. Incremental cost	(*c*) Not suitable for decision
4. Fixed cost	(*d*) Added cost of a new product
5. Variable cost	(*e*) Cost of displaced alternative

[***Answer*** : 1. (*c*), 2. (*e*), 3. (*d*), 4. (*b*), 5. (*a*)]

A	*B*
(*a*) Pencil	1. One gross
(*b*) Bricks	2. One litre
(*c*) Cement	3. One bottle
(*d*) Chemical	4. Cubic metre
(*e*) Medicines	5. One thousand
	6. One bag
	7. One batch

[***Answer*** : (*a*) -6, (*b*) -5, (*c*) -7, (*d*) -2, (*e*) -1]

A	*B*
1. Batch costing	(*a*) Railways
2. Multiple costing	(*b*) Buildings
3. Contract costing	(*c*) Garments
4. Unit costing	(*d*) Cycle manufacturing
5. Operating costing	(*e*) Mines
	(*f*) Toys
	(*g*) Painters

[***Answer*** : 1 (*c*), 2. (*d*), 3. (*b*), 4. (*e*), 5. (*a*)]

A	*B*
(*a*) Process costing	1. Ship building
(*b*) Contract costing	2. Hospital
(*c*) Operation costing	3. Chemicals
(*d*) Unit costing	4. Printing press
(*e*) Batch costing	5. Breweries
	6. Pharmaceuticals

VI. Simple Questions

1. What do you mean by cost sheet? (*Bangalore University, B. Com., April 2000*)
2. What is a cost centre? (*Bangalore University, B. Com., April 2000*)
3. What is a cost unit? (*Bangalore University, B. Com., April 1997*)
4. Distinguish between Fixed and Variable cost. (*Sri Krishnadevaraya University, B. Com., March 1998*)
5. State the difference between cost of goods sold and cost of sales. (*Bangalore University, B. Com., April 1999*)
6. What are the techniques of costing? (*Bangalore University, B. Com., April 1999*)
7. What are the different methods of costing? (*Bangalore University, B. Com., Nov. 1997*)
8. What is prime cost? (*Bangalore University, B. Com., Nov. 1997*)
9. Define cost. (*Bangalore University, B. Com., April 1994*)
10. Define the following:
    (*a*) cost unit (*b*) cost centre (*c*) conversion cost (*d*) controllable cost. (*Osmania University, B. Com., April 1994*)
11. What is meant by Semi-variable expenses? (*Bharathidasan University, B. Com., April 94*)

12. Name any four industries in which unit costing would be suitable. *(Bangalore University, B. Com., April 1995)*
13. Mention two purposes served by a cost sheet. *(M.G. University, B. Com., April 1997)*
14. Define service costing. *(M.G. University, B. Com., April 1997)*
15. What is batch costing? *(M.G. University, B. Com., April 1996)*
16. Mention four essentials of Job costing. *(M.G. University, B. Com., April 1995)*
17. What is indirect labour? *(M.G. University, B. Com., September 1994)*
18. What is Sunk cost? *(M.G. University, B. Com., September 1994)*
19. What is direct labour? *(M.G. University, B. Com., April 1994)*
20. What is total cost? *(M.G. University, B. Com., April 1994)*
21. What are indirect materials? *(M.G. University, B. Com., April 1994)*
22. Explain the term Direct expense. *(M.G. University, B. Com., October 1993)*
23. Explain the term indirect expense. Give two examples. *(Bangalore University, M. Com., May 1996)*
24. What is variable cost? *(Karnataka University, B. Com., April 1997)*
25. What is prime cost? *(Karnataka University, B. Com., April 1997)*
26. State the elements of cost. *(Sri Krishnadevaraya University, B. Com., Oct. 1997)*
27. Distinguish between
    (*a*) Cost centre and cost unit
    (*b*) Fixed cost and variable cost. *(Calcutta University, B. Com., October 1997)*
28. Write short notes on
    (*a*) concept of cost (*b*) on cost (*c*) Semi-variable cost. *(Karnataka University, M. Com., 1997)*
29. What is historical costing? *(Bangalore University, B. Com., April 1996)*
30. What is uniform costing? *(Bangalore University, B. Com., April 1996)*
31. Give examples of industries which adopt Batch costing. *(Bangalore University, B. Com., April 1996)*
32. What is cost classification? *(Bangalore University, B. Com., April 1996)*
33. What do you mean by imputed cost? *(University of Kerala, B. Com., April 1996)*
34. How and why do you distinguish between fixed and variable cost? *(University of Kerala, B. Com., April 1996)*
35. What is opportunity cost? *(University of Kerala, M. Com., April 1996)*
36. Classify the following into fixed, variable and Semi-variable cost
    (*a*) Office rent (*b*) Direct materials (*c*) Telephone expenses (*d*) Insurance of factory building *(Kuvempu University, B. Com., October 1995)*
37. State the methods of costing suitable to the following establishments
    (*a*) Printing press (*b*) Transport company (*c*) Mining company (*d*) Construction company (*e*) Breweries *(University of Mysore, B. Com., Nov. 1999)*
38. Distinguish between Direct and Indirect cost. *(University of Mysore, B. Com., April 1996)*

Short and Long answer Questions

1. Explain the terms "product cost" and "period cost" with atleast 2 examples of each. *(C.S. Inter., December 1998)*
2. "While variable costs are controllable fixed costs are not"? Comment. *(C.S. Inter., December 1997)*
3. "The term "Cost" must be qualified according to its context". Comment *(C.S. Inter., June 1996)*
4. Draw a proforma cost sheet. *(C.S. Inter., December 1994)*
5. Describe briefly the different methods of costing together with industries to which they can be applied *(University of Mysore, B. Com., May 1999)*
6. Distinguish between
   (*a*) Cost centre and profit centre
   (*b*) Direct and indirect cost *(Madurai Kamaraj University, B. Com., April 1998)*
7. What are period cost and product cost? Give a few examples of such cost. Explain the significance of such classification. *(Sri Venkateshwara University, B. Com., April 1993)*
8. Define costing and explain the different classification of costing. *(University of Madras, B. Com., March 1994)*
9. What are the components of total cost *(Bharathidasan University, B. Com., April 1994)*

10. State the important ways of classification of cost and discuss each of item in detail
(Bharathidasan University, B. Com., April 1994)

11. Fundamentally, it is said that there are only two methods of costing. Explain them
(M.G. University, B. Com., April 1993)

12. What is the proper method and unit of cost for the following:
    (*a*) Shipping company
    (*b*) Cold storage plant
    (*c*) Advertising company
    (*d*) Pottery
    (*e*) Oil refinery
    (*f*) Architect
    (*g*) Aircraft factory
    (*h*) Hospital
    (*i*) Toy company
    (*j*) Vegitable ghee co.
(M.G. University, B. Com., April 1993)

13. What are the elements of cost? Explain the terms with appropriate examples.
(Sri Krishnadevaraya University, B. Com., April 1996)

EXERCISES

Exercise-1

Find out the cost of raw materials purchased from the data given below :

	Rs.
Prime cost	2,00,000
Closing stock of raw materials	20,000
Direct labour cost	1,00,000
Expenses on purchases	10,000

(University of Delhi, B. Com. (Pass), April 1995)

(Raw materials purchased Rs. 1,10,000)

Exercise-2

Prepare cost sheet :-	Rs.
Opening Materials	30,850
Opening work-in-progress	60,850
Purchase of materials	1,43,250
Direct wages	1,78,500
Works overhead	1,42,800
Office overhead	1,12,700
Closing Materials	37,700
Closing work-in-progress	67,750
Sales for the year	8,60,625

(Sri Venkateshwara University, B. Com., October 1998, Profit Rs. 2,97,125)

Exercise-3

From the following data, prepare cost sheet showing cost per unit and profit for the year 1997 :

Materials consumed	30,000
Direct wages	19,600
Machine hours	2,000
Machine hour rate	0.50
Administration overhead	10% on works cost
Selling overhead	0.50 paise per unit sold
Units produced	20,000
Units sold at Rs. 5 per unit	18,000

(Sri Venkateshwara University, B. Com., April 1998, Net Profit Rs. 30,900)

Exercise-4

From the following information prepare a cost sheet for the month of April 1996 :

	Rs.
Stock (1-4-1996) :–	
Raw materials	2,50,000
Finished goods	1,73,000
Stock (30-4-1996) :–	
Raw materials	2,62,000
Finished goods	1,57,000
Purchase of Raw materials	2,19,000
Carriage on purchases	11,000
Work-in-progress :–	
on 1-4-1996	82,000
on 30-4-1996	91,000
Sale of finished goods	7,23,000
Direct wages	1,72,000
Non-productive wages	8,000
Direct expenses	12,000
Factory overheads	83,000
Administration overheads	32,000
Selling and Distribution overheads	42,000

(*University of Madras correspondence course, B. Com., May 1997,* Profit Rs. 1,49,000)

Exercise-5

From the following particulars, prepare a cost sheet showing the components of total cost and profit for the year ended 31-12-1994 :

	Rs.
Stock on 1-1-1994 :–	
Raw materials	2,500
Work in progress	822
Finished goods	1,736
Stock on 31-12-1994 :–	
Raw materials	2,625
Work-in-progress	910
Finished goods	1,575
Purchase of raw materials	2,190
Direct wages	1,715
Non-productive wages	83
Office expenses	316
Works expenses	834
Selling and Distribution expenses	421
Sale of finished goods	7,331

(*Bangalore University, B. Com., November 1995,* Profit Rs. 1,824)

Exercise-6

The following extract of costing information relates to a commodity for the half year ended 30th June, 1990 :

	Rs.
Stock on 1-1-1990 :–	
Raw materials	22,000
Finished products (1,600 units)	17,600
Purchase of raw materials	1,32,000
Direct wages	1,10,000
Rent, Rates, Insurance and works on cost	44,000
Carriage Inwards	1,584
Stock on 30-6-1990 :–	
Raw materials	24464
Finished products (3,200 units)	35,200

Work-in-progress (1-1-1990)	5,280
Cost of factory supervision	8,800
Sale finished goods	3,30,000

Advertising, discount allowed and selling cost 0.75 paise per unit sold. 25,600 units of commodity was produced during the period.

Yor are required to ascertain :–

(*a*) Value of Materials used
(*b*) Cost of output for the period
(*c*) Cost of turnover for the period
(*d*) Net profit for the period
(*e*) Net profit per unit of commodity

(*Sri Krishnadevaraya University, B. Com., September 1993*)

(*a*) Cost of Materials used	Rs. 1,30,440
(*b*) Cost of output for the period	Rs. 2,99,200
(*c*) Cost of turnover for the period	Rs. 2,81,600
(*d*) Net profit for the period	Rs. 30,400
(*e*) Net profit per unit	Rs. 1.26

Exercise-7

The following extracts of costing information relate to commodity x for the year ending 31-12-1992 :

	Rs.
Purchase of raw materials	6,000
Direct wages	5,000
Rent, Rates and Insurance	2000
Carriage Inwards	100
Stock (1-1-1992) :–	
Raw materials	1,000
Finished products-200 tons	800
Stock (31-12-1992) :–	
Raw materials	1,100
Finished products-400 tons	
Cost of factory supervision	400
Sale of finished products	15,000

Advertising and selling cost is 0.40 paise per ton sold. 3,000 tons of the commodity were sold during the year. Prepare a cost sheet.

(*University of Delhi, B. Com. (Pass), April 1993,* Profit Rs. 1,275)

Exercise-8

Following information are obtained from costing records for the month of March 1999 :

	Rs.
Raw materials purchased during the month	4,50,000
Cost of materials in stock on 1st March, 1999	30,000
Wages paid	2,00,000
Wages outstanding	30,000
Factory overheads	92,000
Work-in-progress on 1st March 99	12,000
Raw materials in stock on 31st March 1999	25,000
Work-in-progress on 31st March 1999	15,000
Opening stock of finished goods	60,000
Closing stock of finished goods	55,000
Selling and distribution overheads	20,000
Sales	9,00,000
Administrative overheads	30,000

Prepare a statement of cost showing cost of goods manufactured and cost of goods sold.

(*University of Mysore, B. Com., April 2000*)

Cost of goods manufactured Rs. 8,04,000 cost of goods sold 8,09,000, profit Rs. 71,000)

Exercise-9

For each of the following cases find out the unknown balances for a given year :

	Case A	*Case B*
Stock of raw materials (1-1-2000)	(a)	3,500
Stock of raw materials (31-12-2000)	3,600	2,900
Work-in-progress (1-1-2000)	2,700	6,720
Work-in-progress (31-12-2000)	3,800	3,100
Finished stock of goods (1-1-2000)	1,900	(d)
Finished stock of goods (31-12-2000)	300	4,400
Purchase of raw materials	16,100	12,000
Cost of production	(b)	27,220
Cost of goods sold	56,050	27,200
Gross profit	(c)	16,400
Direct labour	26,450	3,800
Direct materials	15,300	(e)
Factory overhead	13,800	7,200
Sales	1,03,300	(f)

Exercise-10

From the following information prepare a monthly cost sheet of the Seshagiri Bricks works showing cost per 1,000 bricks. Also find out the profit per 1,000 bricks. Materials used :–

Lime	895 kgs @ Rs. 30 per kg
Coal	829 kgs @ Rs. 25 per kg
Sand	Rs. 10 per 1000 bricks made
Other	Rs. 700
Labour :–	
Sand digging	Rs. 1,800
Brick making	Rs. 8,000
Factory overhead	25% of Direct charges
Office overhead	10% of Factory overhead
Bricks sold	35,00,000 @ Rs. 20 per 1,000 bricks
Stock of bricks at the beginning of the month	1,00,000
Stock of bricks at the end of the month	6,00,000

SECTION B

ELEMENTS OF COST

3

MATERIALS COST – PURCHASE CONTROL

INTRODUCTION

Purchase control is concerned with controlling the kind, amount, location, movement and timing of the various commodities used and produced by industrial enterprise. Materials cost constitute a substantial portion of the capital invested in factories and thus demand a continuing and considerable attention from its management. Many factory failures are the direct outgrowth of excessive inventories. Too much materials cause idle funds, storage and obsolescence problems and marketing difficulties. On the other hand, if the materials are not adequate to meet the needs of the operating and distribution segments of the enterprise, efficiency suffers, costs skyrocket, manufacturing delays are frequent and broken delivery promises will be inevitable.

The term "materials" denote the commodities or substances supplied to factories for the sake of converting them into finished goods. The term "stores" is often interchangeably used to denote the materials. However it is used in a broader sense to include sundry supplies, maintenance, stores, tools and jigs in addition to raw materials used in the production process. Sometimes materials are also denoted by the term "inventory" which is used in the broadest sense. Inventory includes raw materials, semi-finished goods and finished goods. The Institute of Chartered Accountants of India define inventory as "tangible property held (*i*) for sale in the ordinary course of business or (*ii*) in the process of production for sale or (*iii*) for consumption in the production of goods or service for sale, including maintenance supplies and consumables other than machinery spares."

TYPES OF MATERIALS

The following are some of the important types of materials used in a factory :

1. Raw materials : These are the basic materials which undergo change during the manufacturing process so as to become finished goods. Examples of raw materials are coal, steel, lead, copper, rubber, cotton, wool, timber, limestone, etc.

2. Component parts : These are the piece parts manufactured from raw materials so as to assemble them to get a finished product. Usually component parts are the finished products of one industry which become the raw materials of another industry. Some examples of component parts are collar in dress-making, tyres and tubes in cycle industries, battery cells in transistors.

3. Equipments and spares : This type of stock is usually more important in extractive industries, public utility undertakings and such other organisations. They include machines installations, vehicles and other spare parts associated with such equipments.

4. Tools : These may relate to hand tools such as hammers, screwdrivers, etc. used on machines or machine tools such as drills, milling cutters, portable electric and pneumatic tools.

5. Gauges : Gauges are the materials which are used to measure the dimensions of shapes of materials or components. Examples of gauges used are calliper, screw gauge, common balance, etc.

6. Jigs and fixtures : These are the equipments used for handling the materials when they are in the process of manufacturing, fitting, assembly or other processes. They are used mainly in mass-production factories.

7. Work-in-progress : Work-in-progress refers to partly finished goods and which require further processing so as to convert them into finished products.

8. Primary packing materials : Primary packing materials which are used for easy handling of finished goods such as bottles, tins, polythene bags, etc. constitute one of the important types of materials in some factories.

9. Scraps and residues : These are the waste, used or surplus materials arising out of the manufacturing processes which are reused for further manufacturing processes. Examples of materials falling under this category are iron filing and other scrap metals, rejected components, saw dust, etc.

10. Sundry materials or supplies : All other materials which do not fall under any of the above category are classified as sundry materials. Examples of sundry materials are cleaning materials such as cotton waste, jute waste, sand paper, oil, grease, etc.

DIRECT AND INDIRECT MATERIALS

From the cost accounting point of view materials used in a manufacturing organisation may be classified into two types : (*i*) Direct Materials (*ii*) Indirect materials. Materials are called as direct materials when they satisfy the following characteristics :

(*a*) They are capable of being identified with the finished product.

(*b*) They vary directly with the volume of output.

(*c*) They become part and parcel of finished goods.

(*d*) They are measurable in terms of related production units.

(*e*) They are significant in amount and determination of the cost of the same is of practical use for control.

The following are some of the specific examples of direct materials :

- Jute in manufacturing gunny bags
- Steel in manufacturing cars
- Fruits in manufacturing jams
- Timber in manufacturing furniture
- Turpentine oil in manufacturing paint
- Polythene grannules in manufacturing plastic products.

Materials are said to be indirect when a direct relationship cannot be established between materials used with the specific production units. Indirect materials are ancillary to production although some such materials are also used in repairs department, canteen department office and administration department and selling and distribution department as no specific production unit consumes them. Whereas direct material cost forms part of prime cost, indirect material cost is treated as part of overheads. Some of the examples of indirect materials are sewing thread used in dress-making, nails used in furniture making, glue used in book binding, polishing compound used in vessels manufacturing and so on.

DEFINITION AND IMPORTANCE OF PURCHASING

Alford and Beatty in their book *Industrial Organisation and Management* define purchasing as "the procuring of materials, supplies, machine tools and services required for the equipment, maintenance and operation of a manufacturing plant. Dr. Walters defines scientific purchasing as the procurement by purchase of the proper materials, machinery, equipment and supplies of stores used in the manufacture of a product adapted to marketing in the proper quantity and quality at the proper time and the lowest price consistent with the quality desired." The objective of scientific purchasing is to procure materials at :

(*a*) Right price
(*b*) Right quality
(*c*) Right contractual terms
(*d*) Right time
(*e*) Right source
(*f*) Right materials
(*g*) Right place
(*h*) Right mode of transportation
(*i*) Right quantity
(*j*) Right attitude.

The importance of purchasing may be summarised under the following :

(*i*) Purchasing is a primary function and as such it directly influence the total cost of production. The increased or decreased amount of profit earned in a factory is determined by the efficient purchasing.

(*ii*) The purchase department ensures receipt of proper materials, in sufficient quantities, when needed to maintain production process on a continuous basis. It checks unnecessary or excessive investment of capital on purchase of materials.

(*iii*) It is possible to discover new materials which may be used as a substitute for existing material. This is ensured by the purchase department by coming into close contact with other factories.

(*iv*) By discovering new substitute of materials, it enables to introduce new lines of products.

(*v*) It helps in framing plans and policies relating to scheduling of production and marketing.

ORGANISATION OF PURCHASE DEPARTMENT

The organisation of purchase department depends upon the size, the relative importance of procurement, the availability of personnel and the management policy. The purchase function is common for all factories irrespective of the size. But in a large-sized factory, it is under the control of a chief purchase manager who is assisted by assistant purchase officers. In small factories all the purchase functions are performed by a single individual. The organisation of purchase department may be based on any of the following three systems :

1. Centralisation of Purchases

Centralisation of purchases refers to purchase of materials under one purchase department headed by a competent purchase manager. If the firm has one plant, then it has to invariably follow centralisation of purchases. When a firm has many plants certain factors are to be considered before centralising the purchases. These factors are geographical location of plants, similarity of products manufactured, type of materials, the quantity of materials, the location of suppliers and other conditions peculiar to industry. According to National Association of purchasing Management a firm having several plants in the same country manufacturing similar products requiring the same general types of materials should have centralised purchasing.

Advantages of Centralised Purchasing

(*a*) The purchase manager can be solely held responsible for inefficient purchasing.

(*b*) It helps in maintaining a consistent buying policies such as terms of payment, (payment on delivery, cash with order, cash before delivery) packing, marking, etc.

(*c*) It results in economy of purchase records.

(*d*) It tends to reduce the inventories that must be carried and thus helps in low capital investment on materials.

(*e*) Bulk purchasing results in reduced price of materials on account of trade discount, cash discount facilities.

(*f*) Free home delivery facility is available under centralised system owing to bulk purchases.

(*g*) It relieves the departmental heads the responsibility of procuring variety of materials.

(*h*) Specialised and expert knowledge on the purchasing problems connected with specific items of materials can be made available to all the units.

Disadvantages of Centralised Purchases

(*a*) The benefits arising out of local purchase cannot be availed of.

(*b*) This system of purchases leads to communication difficulties between centralised purchasing office and the plants.

(*c*) Emergency purchases cannot be made under this system.

(*d*) Delay in receiving, checking and approving the invoices as central purchasing office has to receive all the reports and invoices from all the plants.

2. Decentralised Purchases

Under decentralised purchasing system a separate purchase department is established to make purchases independently. Decentralised purchasing is applicable to those manufacturing concerns which operates several plants in different localities manufacturing different products and each plant requiring different types of materials. Each purchase department will have a purchase authority who enjoys the freedom of making purchases of materials required for his department. The purchasing authority in each department reports to the chief purchase officer who establishes the general purchase policies and co-ordinates the purchasing functions in all plants.

Advantages of Decentralised Purchases

(*a*) *Greater flexibility :* If a centralised buyer is purchasing for a number of plants he will find it difficult to react rapidly to changes in the requirements of individual plant. But under Decentralisation system, the buyer can buy the required quantity and quality and at the time when materials are required.

(*b*) *Close liaison :* A local buyer will be in close contact with his own manufacturing unit. Therefore he is in a position to make scientific purchase of all kinds of materials.

(*c*) *Quick procurement of materials* : The delay involved in centralised purchasing system where in pooling all the purchase requisition and placing the order and then supply of materials to each and every plant is avoided under this system.

3. Centralised-Decentralised System

Firms which have more than one plant located in and around, adopt this system of purchasing. Though such plants produce different products there are some materials which are common to all plants. Under such circumstance it is desirable to partially centralise and partially decentralise the purchase function. Under this system, it is necessary to make clear that which type of materials are to be bought by the centralised buying officer and which type of materials by departmental buying officer. For the successful operation of this system of buying, the following requirements are essential :

(*a*) The centralised purchase manager has to establish policies, procedures, record keeping methods and exercise central control and restrict the authority and range of buying by each decentralised purchase officer.

(*b*) All decentralised purchases must be reported immediately to the central office.

(*c*) The decentralised buying officer must buy materials for his plant only within the budgeted amount.

(*d*) Approval of the central office must be obtained by the decentralised buying officer for special and excess quantity purchases.

(*e*) The plan should be kept flexible so that specific buying authorities can be reassigned as conditions change.

QUALIFICATIONS OF PURCHASE MANAGER

- He must have considerable experience in buying and must be conversant with the purchasing techniques.
- He must possess technical ability to decide upon the most suitable source and the required quality of material.
- He must know as to how to negotiate with the suppliers.
- He must acquaint himself closely with current quotations and sources of supply.
- He must have practical knowledge of the finance and business methods.
- He must have knowledge of the materials which is required to purchase and their specification, quality and quantity.
- He must be honest and reliable.
- He must be aware of the policy of management and financial resource of the factory and its impact on purchases.
- He must have an up-to-date knowledge of government policies regarding import and export restrictions and various duties and taxes on materials.
- He must be well conversant with economic principles of demand and supply, price, etc.
- He must have a working knowledge of laws relating to contracts, Sale of Goods Act, Negotiable Instruments Act, etc. which have a bearing on purchase of materials.
- He must be aware of the market conditions, and should have a complete knowledge of the market, source of supply, price and purchase formalities.
- He must be able to maintain records and documents like catalogues, price lists, trade magazines, journals, etc. to assist him in locating the best market.

DUTIES AND RESPONSIBILITIES OF PURCHASE MANAGER

The duties of purchase manager can be summarised as under :

1. To establish purchase policies for his department to execute.
2. To locate and select the best source of supply for materials and services required.
3. To receive purchase requisitions from all the departments and know the exact quantity of material requirements of the factory.
4. To purchase the required quantity of materials at the lowest price and at the best possible terms.
5. To place purchase orders with the supplier.
6. To follow-up suppliers so that delivery of materials can be obtained at the proper time.
7. To make sure that materials received from suppliers conform to the orders placed.
8. To verify and check the invoices and approve them for payment.
9. To secure adjustment on claims for materials received which are not in accordance with quality or quantity or which have been damaged.
10. To maintain proper records for efficient operation of the purchase department.
11. To keep constant touch with market conditions and try to secure new goods which are improvement over existing materials.
12. To analyse the effects of changes in general business trends upon purchase plants.
13. To advise on prices for materials to be used in new or modified designs.
14. To prepare and present all reports regarding the purchase of materials to the General Manager.
15. To take part in departmental conferences for planning, formulation of policies or other purposes.

The responsibilities of the Purchase Manager can be summarised as under :

(*a*) He is responsible for organising and directing the purchase department

(*b*) He is responsible for timely purchase of materials so that production process is not interrupted.

(*c*) He is responsible for judicious utilisation of funds while purchasing various types of materials.

(*d*) He is responsible for maintaining the factory's regulation for integrity and fair dealings.

(*e*) He is responsible for preparing purchase budget.

(*f*) He is responsible for conducting research on materials, tools, etc.

(*g*) He is responsible for final check on all goods requisitioned, questioning the need, quantity, quality and specification of materials.

PURCHASE PROCEDURE

The main steps involved in the purchase procedure are as follows :

1. Receiving purchase requisitions.
2. Decision regarding what, when and how much to buy.
3. Determining the source of supply.
4. Selecting the supplier by issuing tenders.
5. Preparing and placing purchase orders.

6. Follow-up of purchase orders.
7. Receiving of materials.
8. Inspection of materials.
9. Checking the invoices and settling the accounts.

The above steps are discussed below.

1. Receiving Purchase Requisitions

The purchase requisition is a formal request made to the purchase manager to arrange for the purchase of materials described in the purchase requisition. It is a statement which contains a list of materials and a request to purchase them. It serves as a basis for purchasing the materials when it is signed and approved by authorised person. The requisition should give clearly and completely all the information that is required for initiation of the purchase procedure. This particulars ensure that the purchases can be made with speed and accuracy. It must contain the following essential information :

(*a*) Name and exact description of materials wanted.
(*b*) Quantity required.
(*c*) Date on which material are needed.
(*d*) Statement of need or record of the use that justifies requisition.
(*e*) The place of delivery within the factory after passing through receiving and inspection or directly in case of machinery which should be unloaded as close to the point of use as possible.
(*f*) Vendor's name, in certain special cases as in repair parts for equipment.
(*g*) Signature of the authority initiating the purchase requisition.
(*h*) A space for use of the purchase department to add supplier's name, price, terms.

The above particulars are presented to depict a typical purchase requisition hereunder :

WELLMAN (INDIA) PRIVATE LIMITED

Purchase Requisition

Department............
Requisition No. ....

To,
The Purchase Manager

Date of Initiating
Purchase Requisition
Required on ....

Dear Sir,
Please purchase the following items in accordance with the following specifications :

Sl. No.	*Quantity*	*Description*	*Material in hand*	*Average Consumption*	*Remark*

Required by ....
Special Instructions ....
Approved by ....

Fig. 3.1. Purchase requisition form.

The purchase requisition form may originate from (*a*) Storekeeper for the purchase of raw materials which have reached reorder level. (*b*) Production control department for special type of materials. (*c*) Head of the concerned department for buying equipment such as almirah, filing cabinet, etc. (*d*) Plant engineer for the purchase of plant and machinery and other tools and equipments. (*e*) Office manager for purchase of office stationery.

Whenever a purchase requisition is received it is reviewed to see whether the items are available in the storeroom or whether the request for some materials could be replaced by a standard item which is readily obtained at lesser price.

The purchase requisition is generally prepared in triplicate so that the original is sent to the purchase department, the duplicate is sent to the production control department and triplicate is retained in the department which initiates the purchase requisition.

2. Decision Regarding What, When and How Much to Buy

The purchase manager before proceeding further in purchasing the materials has to decide the quality, quantity, price and time at which materials are to be purchased.

(*a*) ***Buying the proper quality by purchase specification :*** A specification is an accurate description of material to be purchased. Buying proper quality of materials depends upon (*i*) the accurate specification of materials required; (*ii*) placing the order with a reliable supplier; and (*iii*) checking materials against specification. Definiteness in the specification of materials always tend to minimise cost of materials. The form of specification may be indicated by (*a*) trade name or brand name, (*b*) blue print, (*c*) physical characteristics or chemical analysis, (*d*) detail of materials, (*e*) description of purpose or use, (*f*) suppliers sample, (*g*) buyer's sample.

(*b*) ***Buying the proper quantity :*** As a rule, the quantity of a material to be purchased is specified in the purchase requisition. The quantity is often changed to take advantage of market or speculative purchasing. Quantity of materials required are determined by taking the following factors into consideration : (*i*) sales forecast, (*ii*) customer's orders, (*iii*) production authorisation, (*iv*) transfers from other departments, and (*v*) time taken to supply the materials by the suppliers.

(*c*) ***Buying at proper price :*** In order to purchase materials at reasonable price, the purchase manager must obtain and record the price. Material prices may be classified into : (*i*) prices obtained from market reports and newspapers, (*ii*) prices listed in catalogues, (*iii*) price quoted by the suppliers when tenders are issued.

3. Determining the Source of Supply

After determining the quality and quantity of materials to be bought, the sources of supply are to be tapped. The following are the important sources of supply of materials :

(*i*) Trade directories
(*ii*) Telephone directories
(*iii*) Purchasing periodicals
(*iv*) Newspapers and commerce magazines
(*v*) Catalogues
(*vi*) Supplier's index files
(*vii*) Exhibitions and trade shows
(*viii*) Market survey
(*ix*) Quotations
(*x*) Experience of purchase manager.

While considering suitable source of supply, the following factors should be given due consideration.

(*A*) Whether to purchase from a single supplier or a multiple of them.

Advantages of a Single Source

(*a*) The purchase manager will place an order for all items of materials with a single supplier and thereby get largest possible discount.

(*b*) There is less administration work in the purchase department.

(*c*) A good relation will prevail between buyers and suppliers, wherein the supplier offers all facilities to the buyer such as credit facilities, after sale services, exchange facilities, free transport facility, etc.

Advantages of Multiple Source

Many factories avoid relying on a single source for all items. They try to have at least two suppliers for each item of materials. The main advantages of multiple source are :

(*a*) With several sources, there is less risk of interruption of supply. If one supplier fails the other supplier can take up the supply of materials.

(*b*) With two or more suppliers for one item a healthy competitive spirit can develop in which each vies to improve methods and reduce costs in order to get greater share of the business.

(*B*) Whether to purchase from the local sources or from some distant place.

(*C*) Whether to purchase directly from the manufacturer or through wholesaler.

4. Selecting the Supplier by Issue of Tenders

When there are more than one supplier dealing with materials, the purchase manager has to select the best supplier with whom the purchase manager has confidence as to quality of materials, ability to deliver the materials promptly, at the cheapest price and with better terms of sale. The selection of such a supplier is decided by issuing tenders. A tender is a written letter or an advertisement given in newspaper inviting the prospective suppliers to quote their lowest price and other terms and conditions of sale. The request for quotation should give the following information :

(*i*) Quantity to be ordered.

(*ii*) Name and full specification of materials.

(*iii*) Place where materials are to be delivered.

(*iv*) Other terms and conditions of sale which the supplier wishes to make.

Types of Tender

(*i*) ***Single tender :*** Such a tender is issued where an item is of a proprietary nature or where the material is dealt with by a single supplier.

(*ii*) ***Limited tender :*** When the value of the tender is moderate, limited tenders are issued. Here tenders are invited only from those suppliers who are on the approved list of suppliers. The merits of this method are : (*a*) Being regular suppliers they submit realistic quotations, (*b*) They are fully conversant with the materials, (*c*) The chances of selecting the supplier is better.

(*iii*) ***Open tender :*** This type of tender is issued when the sources are many and the value is large. Anybody who deals with such material and who is willing to supply the materials can quote his prices in response to this tender.

(*iv*) ***Global tender :*** This type of tenders are issued for the suppliers even beyond the boundarise of the country. This tender is mostly used when the factory is under the collaboration of foreign government.

Earnest Money

Earnest money is demanded from the supplier to discourage unreliable suppliers. This is also insisted upon so that the prospective supplier subsequently does not back out from the rate he has quoted for supplying the materials. A specimen of tender form is given below :

ABC CO. LTD.

Request for Quotation

Data..........

Quotation No..........

To,

..............(Name of Supplier)

..............Address

....

Dear Sir,

Please submit your quotation for the materials listed below so as to reach the office of the undersigned on or before.........at..........Please send full details, specifications and other literature if any along with the quotation. Please note the terms and conditions mentioned below :

(*a*) Please mention on the top of the envelop enquiry number..........date on which due.

(*b*) Submit quotations in duplicate.

(*c*) Preferably quote in the same order as in the enquiry letter.

(*d*) Price each item separately and the prices quoted should be for destination.........

(*e*) If you are unable to furnish materials as per our descriptions and wish to offer a substitute, please give details.

(*f*) Quotations should be valid for at least one month from the data of opening.

(*g*) Quotations should be sent in sealed covers.

(*h*) Taxes should be mentioned for each item.

(*i*) The right is reserved to accept or reject quotations on each item separately or as a whole.

The quotations will be opened on........at........in the office of the undersigned.

Sl. No.	*Description*	*Quantity*	*Unit*	*Price*	*Discount*	*Total price*

Your's Faithfully

Sd/-

Fig. 3.2. Tender Form.

The sealed quotations are opened on the last date on which it is to be submitted by all competitive suppliers. The purchase manager will then prepare a comparative tender statement to know the lowest quotation price and best terms and conditions of sale offered. Thus the supplier is choosen with whom the purchase order is to be placed. A specimen form of comparative tender statement is given below :

Comparative Tender Statement

Section..........
Tender Number.........
Data of Opening Quotations.........
Comparative Tender Statement Prepared by...........
Checked by...........

Sl. No.	*Description of materials*	*Quantity*	*Rates*		
			Supplier 1	*Supplier 2*	*Supplier 3*
			Terms and Conditions		
	Delivery data Place of Delivery Terms of Payment Taxes Packing and Forward Charges				

Fig. 3.3 Comparative tender statement.

Problem 1 : The stock position and requirements of a certain material used in a factory are as follows :

Present stock	7000 units
Average weekly requirement	2000 units
Maximum level	16000 units
Minimum level	6000 units

The manager invited tenders for the supply of materials and received the undernoted quotations :

(*a*) Any quantity up to 20,000 units @ Rs. 2.40 per unit; immediate delivery.

(*b*) Any quantity @ Rs. 2.20 per unit plus Rs. 1,000 fixed charges irrespective of quantity ordered; immediate delivery.

Give your decision as regards the choice of tender and quantity to be ordered.

Solution :

Comparative statement

Quantity ordered (units)	*Quotation price as per tender (a) @ Rs. 2.40 per unit*	*Quotation price as per tender (b)*		
		Variable cost @ Rs. 2.20 per unit	*Fixed cost*	*Total*
	Rs.	Rs.	Rs.	Rs.
2,000	4,800	4,400	1,000	5,400
3,000	7,200	6,600	1,000	7,600
4,000	9,600	8,800	1,000	9,800
5,000	12,000	11,000	1,000	12,000
6,000	14,400	13,200	1,000	14,200
7,000	16,800	15,400	1,000	16,400
8,000	19,200	17,600	1,000	18,600
9,000	21,600	19,800	1,000	20,800
10,000	24,000	22,000	1,000	23,000
20,000	48,000	44,000	1,000	45,000

From the above comperative tender statement it is clear that at, 5,000 units the amount quoted by both tenderer is same, *viz*, Rs. 12,000. The present stock is 7,000 units. Whereas the maximum level is 16,000 units. So the purchase manager can purchase 9,000 units. (16,000 – 7,000). As the quotation price for the purchase of 9,000 units are quoted by tenderer (*b*) is less, *i.e.*, Rs. 20,800, he is to be preferred over tender (*a*).

Problem 2 : After inviting tenders, two quotations are received as under :

Supplier *A* – Rs. 2.20 per unit

Supplier *B* – Rs. 2.10 per unit plus Rs. 2,000 fixed charges irrespective of units ordered

(*i*) Calculate the order quantity for which the purchase price per unit will be the same.

(*ii*) Select the supplier if the purchase officer wants to place an order for 15,000 units.

(*C.S., Dec. 1990; Sri Sathya Sai University, B. Com., Oct., 1991*)

Solution : (*i*) Calculation of order quantity for which the purchase price per unit will be the same :

Difference in tender price :

Quotation per unit by supplier 'A'	=	Rs. 2.20
Quotation per unit by supplier 'B'	=	Rs. 2.10
Difference per unit		0.10

In order to cover the fixed charges of Rs. 2,000 of supplier *B*, the order quantity should be 20,000 units *i.e.*, Rs. 2,000 ÷ Re. 0.10. At the quantity of 20,000 units the purchase price will be the same in both cases as shown below :

Supplier *A* 20,000 × Rs. 2.20 = Rs. 44,000

$$\text{Per unit} = \frac{44{,}000}{20{,}000} = \text{Rs. } 2.20$$

Supplier *B* 20,000 × Rs. 2.10 + 2,000 fixed cost
= 42,000 + 2,000 = Rs. 44,000

$$\text{Per unit} = \frac{44{,}000}{20{,}000} = \text{Rs. } 2.20$$

(*ii*) Selection of the best supplier for the purchase of 15,000 units :

Quotation price of supplier *A* = 15,000 × Rs. 2.20 = Rs. 33,000

Quotation price of supplier *B* = 15,000 × Rs. 2.10 + Rs. 2,000
= 31,500 + 2,000 = Rs. 33,500

As the quotation price of supplier *A* is less compared to supplier *B*, it is suggested to select supplier *A* by the purchase officer.

Problem 3 : When two tenders were invited for a stores, two quotations were received as under :

Supplier (*A*) (*a*) Rate Rs. 2 each, (*b*) Trade discount 10% (*c*) Cash discount 5%, if bills are paid within a fortnight after receipt, (*d*) Transport charge Re. 1 per 100 units.

Supplier (*B*) (*a*) Rate Rs. 1.80 each (up to 1,000 units)
Rs. 1.60 each (for order above 1,000 units)

(*b*) 6% interest per annum will be added if bills are not paid within a fortnight after receipt of the material.

(*c*) Transport charges Rs. 3 per 100 units.

Assuming that above 5,000 units are required every month and that quality and other conditions of supply are the same offer your comments as to on whom purchase orders can be issued. The factory pays 50% of its monthly bills every fortnight.

Solution :

	Supplier A	*Supplier B*	
		up to 1,000 units	*above 1,000 units*
Basic rate	2.00	1.80	1.60
Less : Trade discount	0.20		
Net price per unit	1.80	1.80	1.60
Add : Total transport charges	0.01	0.03	0.03
Purchase price per unit	1.81	1.83	1.63

(*Contd.*)

Purchase bill	5,000 × Rs. 1.81 = 9,050.00	5,000 × Rs.1.83 = 9,150.00	5,000 × 1.63 = 8,150.00
Less : Cash discount – 5% on Rs. 9050 for fortnight	= 226.25		
	8,823.75	9,150.00	8,150.00
Add : Interest at 6% on Rs. 9150 and Rs. 8150 for fortnight	–	11.28	10.04
Final Cost	8,823.75	9,161.28	8,160.04

Comments : As the price quoted by supplier *B* is less when more than 1,000 units are bought he must be selected for placing order of 5,000 units.

Working Note :

(1) Calculation of cash Discount

$$9{,}050 \times \frac{1}{2} \times \frac{5}{100} = 226.25$$

(2) Calculation of Interest

$$9{,}150 \times \frac{6}{100} \times \frac{15}{365} \times \frac{1}{2} = 11.28$$

$$8{,}150 \times \frac{6}{100} \times \frac{15}{365} \times \frac{1}{2} = 10.04$$

(3) In the above calculations $\frac{1}{2}$ is equal to 50% of bill paid

5. Preparing and Placing Purchase Order

A purchase order is a contractual document which authorises the supplier to supply the materials. Once the purchase order is issued to a supplier, it is obligatory on the part of purchase manager to take delivery of materials and arrange for the payment of invoice. The purchase order must be carefully drafted by precisely including all essential elements of purchases to be made. It must be prepared in such a manner so as to avoid future misunderstanding and minimise the necessity of correspondence. The purchase order should include the following particulars :

(*a*) ***Purchase order number :*** Purchase order number helps in identifying the transaction in future correspondence. It also helps the supplier in preparing the invoice and in despatching the materials.

(*b*) ***Quantity ordered :*** The quantity ordered is expressed in different units depending upon the type of materials.

(*c*) ***Description :*** The full description of materials enable the supplier to supply the right quantity of materials. It also helps the receiver to inspect the materials on its receipt.

(*d*) ***Delivery instructions :*** This relate to the data on which the materials are to be delivered. It also include the place of delivery, packing, marking, insurance and mode of transportation.

(*e*) ***Terms of payment :***The terms of payment, *i.e.*, cash basis, credit basis, FOB, FOR, CWO, CBO, COD can be made clear under this point.

(*f*) ***Price :*** The unit rate and the total amount of materials purchased are to be included.

(*g*) Name and address of the purchasing company.

(*h*) Name and address of supplier.

(*i*) Data of placing purchase order.
(*j*) Signature of purchase manager.

A specimen form of purchase order is given below :

WELLMAN (INDIA) PRIVATE LIMITED
Regd. Office : Neville House, Currimnbhoy Road, Bombay.
Factory & Adm. Office : Kolshet Road, Thana, Maharashtra
Purchase Order

Phone...................... Purchase Order No............
Cable...................... Data.................................
Telex...................... CST Reg. No. ....

To,
....
....
....

Your reference............dated..........

[Please deliver the undermentioned materials subject to conditions printed on the reverse, quoting the order number on all delivery challans.]

S. No.	*Quantity*	*Description*	*Unit rate*		*Price*	
			Rs.	*P.*	*Rs.*	*P.*

Delivery : Deliveries at our stores should be made before 4.00 p.m. on working days.
Insurance : On despatch of the consignment please TELEGRAPH following information to the attention of purchase department.
(*a*) Our order reference, (*b*) Invoice value, (*c*) Freight charges payable.

For Wellman (India) Pvt. Ltd.

Purchase Manager

Fig. 3.4. Purchase order.

Conditions

(*a*) **Acceptance :** The acceptance of this order will constitute the contract. The buyer reserves the right to cancel or amend this order or any part thereof without assigning any reason.

(*b*) **Quality :** All materials must conform to samples, specification, description and drawings and will be subject to our inspection and approval at any time within a reasonable time from the date of delivery. If not up to specification they will be held for deposition or returned at your risk and expenses. If required, free replacement for rejected materials/equipment should be made.

(*c*) **Quantity :** The buyer assumes no obligation in relation to any goods delivered in excess of those specifically ordered. In any case the quantity of the material must not exceed without permission in writing being first obtained.

(*d*) **Delivery :** Delivery is to be effected within the stipulation of the order and the buyer reserves the right to rescind or cancel the order without prior notice or intimation if the delivery is not effected within the time stated on this purchase order.

(*e*) **Partial delivery :** The buyer may accept partial delivery on condition that the balance will be delivered within a stipulated time from thereon.

(*f*) All the materials must be forwarded by the particular route named. Otherwise difference in freight and extra cost of cartage, etc., will be charged to the account.

(*g*) **Payment :** Ninety days after receipt and inspection of goods at our factory at Thana, unless otherwise specified.

(*h*) **Advice notes :** Advice notes are to be sent to the purchase department at the time goods are despatched.

(*i*) **Bills or invoices :** All bills or invoices must be sent to us in TRIPLICATE mentioning our order number and our Sales Tax Registration number thereon. The RR number or LR number and data under which the materials are despatched must appear on Bills/Invoices.

Itemised bills or invoices should be sent to the purchase department immediately along with a copy of delivery note and a copy of rail/lorry receipt.

A copy of the invoice should be sent along with consignment despatched by lorry or motor to avoid seizure at sales tax check posts.

(*j*) **Cartage and freight :** No charges will be allowed for cartage, freight and/or packing, etc., unless accepted by previous agreement.

(*k*) The statement of account must be sent at stated intervals mutually agreed upon.

The purchase order is prepared in five copies : (*i*) two copies are sent to supplier and the supplier will return back the duplicate as acknowledgement, (*ii*) third copy is sent to production department or department which initiated purchase requisition, (*iii*) fourth copy is sent to costing department, and (*iv*) fifth copy is retained by purchase manager.

6. Follow-up of Purchase Order

The continuation of production process to a large extent depends upon the regular and ready delivery of materials. While placing purchase order the date on which materials are to be delivered must be clearly mentioned. It is the duty of follow-up section to see that this date is kept. Where it is not possible to get delivery of material on the promised date, the follow-up section can take necessary steps to prevent crippling the production process due to lack of materials. To avoid late delivery of materials the following points must be remembered :

(*a*) Use clear and complete specifications.

(*b*) Keep demands for "rush" delivery to minimum.

(*c*) Keep records of the delivery performance of suppliers.

(*d*) Try to find goods alternative suppliers to those whose delivery performances are consistently bad.

(*e*) Keep abreast of suppliers current range of delivery times.

(*f*) Know supplier's policy regarding stock of raw materials.

(*g*) Visit suppliers regularly.

(*h*) Pay suppliers promptly.

7. Receiving of Materials

Before materials are taken delivery of, it is very essential to receive and inspect materials so as to ensure that the supplier has supplied the exact quantity and quality of materials. In large factories a separate receiving and inspection department is set up and receiving clerks are incharge of receiving the materials. To facilitate the receiving clerk to receive and inspect the materials, a copy of purchase order without filling up the quantity of materials can be supplied. This serves as the basis for recording the entries by the receiving clerks. The duties of receiving department are as follows :

(*a*) To check the incoming materials to know whether all items of materials in terms of quantities conform to the purchase order.

(*b*) To record the receipt of the materials.

(*c*) To inform the storekeeper about the receipt of materials.

(*d*) To inform the purchase manager the fact which require an adjustment to be made with supplier in respect of shortage or defective materials.

(*e*) To deliver the materials either to the department where it is required or to the storeroom.

Having received and checked the materials, the receiving clerk will prepare a material received report. A material received report is useful for checking the supplier's invoice. It contains the following particulars :

(*a*) Date of receipt.
(*b*) Supplier's name and address.
(*c*) Types of materials received.
(*d*) Quantity of materials received.
(*e*) Condition in which materials are received.
(*f*) Type of container.
(*g*) Mode of transportation.

A specimen of materials received note is given below :

USHA MARTIN BLACK LTD.
58, Main Road, Whitefield, Bangalore - 560 066
Material Received Note

MRN No.......................
Name of the Supplier.......... Date...............................
RR No...................... Order No. & Date.........

Sl. No.	*Particulars*	*Unit*	*Qty as per order no.*	*Short*	*Excess*	*Rejected*	*Accepted*

Signature of receiving clerk...........

Fig. 3.5. Materials received note.

8. Inspection of Materials

The next step involved in the purchase procedure is inspection of materials received Inspection refers to comparison or checking of quality, size and quantity of materials. The quality of material is ensured if the properties such as shape, colour, dimension, weight, composition, strength, etc. of the required standard are present in the materials. Sometimes materials such as chemicals are taken to laboratory and tested to know their quality.

Importance of Inspection of Materials

Inspection of materials is necessary to ensure that :

(*a*) Materials received are in strict specification of purchase order. In other words only those materials that were ordered have been received.
(*b*) The quantity of materials conform to the quantity of materials ordered.
(*c*) The quality of materials are those specified in purchase order.
(*d*) No damage is caused to materials during transit.

Inspection of materials in a large factory is usually undertaken by Inspection Officer. In small factories inspection function is performed by the receiving clerk or by the storekeeper himself. The duties and responsibilities of Inspection Officer are as follows :

(*a*) To sort out defective raw materials received.
(*b*) To report the management about the quality of materials received.

(*c*) To suggest action regarding rejected materials, *i.e.*, whether they are to be returned to the supplier or deducted from the supplier's invoice.

(*d*) To prepare and sign the material inspection certificate.

(*e*) To maintain and use various inspection devices such as steel rules, callipers, micrometer, electric instruments, etc. for the purpose of inspection.

9. Checking the Invoice and Settling the Account

This is the last step in the purchase procedure. The invoice is checked with the purchase order and the materials received report. The rates and the terms of invoice is compared with those of purchase order. Similarly, the quantity received must tally with the quantity ordered. If there are any discrepancy or defective materials are received, the same is brought to the notice of supplier and accordingly a debit note or credit note is prepared. Finally, if everything is in order, the invoice is approved by purchase manager and forwarded to the costing section for payment.

ASCERTAINING PURCHASE COST OR VALUATION OF MATERIALS RECEIVED

As a matter of rule, the invoice price quoted by the supplier is used for accounting purposes. However, the following items are to be considered while valuing the materials :

(*a*) **Invoice price or supplier's prices :** Invoice quoted by suppliers are of different types such as net price or list price subject to discounts, inclusive or exclusive of freight, customs, insurance or packages. However, for costing purposes we must arrive at a figure which will represent the cost actually incurred up to the point of delivery of the goods. For this reason 'purchase price' is calculated by taking the invoice price as the basis, deducting any trade or quantity discounts and adding other expenses not already included.

(*b*) **Trade discount :** It is a discount allowed by manufacturers to distributors. This is to enable the distributors to cover the cost of storage, repacking goods if any, and such other expenses.

(*c*) **Quantity discount :** It is a discount allowed by the manufacturers to customers who buy goods on large scale basis. This discount take the form of special rebates with a view to encourage them to purchase in bulk quantities.

(*d*) **Cash Discount :** This is a deduction allowed by manufacturer if payment is made promptly with in a specified period. But the treatment of this item depends upon the decision taken by the purchaser to pay the bill promptly to avail the benefit. In some cases, this item is kept outside the purview of costing considering this as an item of pure financial matter.

(*e*) **Transport charges :** Sometimes the manufacturer undertakes to supply the materials meeting the transport charges. But when the supplier fails to meet the transport cost, it is the purchaser who has to bear the transport cost and hence included in the cost of materials.

(*f*) **Storage cost :** The expenses incurred by the purchaser to store the purchased materials is to be taken into account while determining the purchase price.

(*g*) **Insurance :** Any insurance taken to cover the materials in transit is again added to materials cost to calculate its purchase price.

(*h*) **Customs duties :** When raw materials are imported from other countries, it involves payment of custom duties. This is to be added while calculating purchase price of materials.

(*i*) **Excise duty, sales tax, octroi :** These items of expenses are to be paid when materials are bought from a local manufacturer or goods manufactured indegenously are bought. This is added to the cost of materials while calculating purchase price of materials.

(*j*) **Cost of containers :** Some time the manufacturer will not charge any amount to the containers or packing materials. In such circumstances, the cost of containers are not included in the materials cost. Where the manufacturer charges for the containers it will be treated as follows :

(*i*) *Non-returnable containers :* In this situation, the cost of container will be added to the purchase price of materials.

(*ii*) *Crediting returnable containers at its full value :* Where the purchaser returns all the containers safely, it will not be included in the purchase price.

(*iii*) *Crediting returnable containers at reduced value :* Under this situation, the difference between the cost of container and the amount credited by the supplier will be added to purchase price of materials.

(*k*) **Apportionment of joint purchase cost :** Where materials are purchased in different grades in one lot, by incurring common cost, it becomes necessary to apportion the common cost or joint cost to all the grades of materials on an average basis. This may result in undercharging or overcharging of cost to all the grades of materials. To eliminate such differences the existing rates of material can be taken into consideration and the receipt of materials priced accordingly. If any difference is still found, it can be distributed proportionately to the various grades on the basis of market price.

(*l*) **Extra quantity or free supply of excess spare parts :** Sometimes the manufacturer may supply extra quantities of certain types of spare parts at a free of cost. This will reduce the unit price of the consignment.

Problem 4 : Ramprakash & Co. purchases certain quantities of mixed grades of materials for Rs. 9,00,000. On sorting out into the following grades they revealed the following market rates :

Grades	*Units*	*Selling rate per unit*
Grade *X*	50,000	Rs. 12.00
Grade *Y*	30,000	Rs. 10.00
Grade *Z*	20,000	Rs. 5.00

Find out the purchase rate per unit of each grade of materials assuming all grades yield the same rate of profit.

Solution : This problem is worked out based on equation

Selling Price = Cost price or purchase price + Profit

Statement showing profit

Grade *X*	50,000 units @ Rs. 12 each	Rs. 6,00,000
Grade *Y*	30,000 units @ Rs. 10 each	Rs. 3,00,000
Grade *Z*	20,000 units @ Rs. 5 each	Rs. 1,00,000
	Total sale price	10,00,000
Less : Purchase price		9,00,000
	Profit	1,00,000

Calculation of percentage of profit on sale price
For Rs. 10,00,000 Sales, Profit is Rs. 1,00,000
For 100 – ?

$$\frac{1,00,000 \times 100}{10,00,00} = 10\%$$

Ascertainment of purchase rate

Grades	*Selling price per unit (A)*	*Profit 10% per unit of sales (B)*	*Purchase Rate per unit (A) – (B)*
X	Rs. 12	Rs. 1.20	Rs. 10.80
Y	Rs. 10	Re. 1.00	Rs. 9.00
Z	Rs. 5	Re. 0.50	Rs. 4.50

Verification

Purchase price of grade *X* materials	50,000 × Rs. 10.80	= Rs. 5,40,000
Purchase price of grade *Y* materials	30,000 × Rs. 9.00	= Rs. 2,70,000
Purchase price of grade *Z* materials	20,000 × Rs. 4.50	= Rs. 90,000
	Total purchase price	Rs. 9,00,000

Problem 5 : A factory received a consignment of four grades of a material for Rs. 1,20,000. These were sorted in stores and recorded as below :

Grade-I	4,000 units,	Grade-III	10,000 units
Grade-II	8,000 units,	Grade-IV	12,000 units

Grade-I total sales was Rs. 16,000 at a profit of $33\frac{1}{3}$% on cost.

Grade-II was totally sold at a price one and a half time that of Grade-I fetching $33\frac{1}{3}$% profit on sales.

Grade-III, sales of Rs. 50,000 brought at a profit of 20% on sales.

Find out the purchase price of each grade of materials from the above information.

(*Madurai University, B. Com., April 1986*)

Solution : This problem is worked out based on the formula

Selling price = Cost price + Profit

Calculation of profit on Grade-I material

Percentage of profit is given on selling price but not on cost price.

Let cost price be = Rs. 100

Add : Percentage of profit on cost Price = $33\frac{1}{3}$

∴ Selling price = $133\frac{1}{3}$

$$\text{Profit on sales} = \frac{33\frac{1}{3}\%}{133\frac{1}{3}\%} \times 16,000$$

$$= \frac{100}{3} \times \frac{3}{400} \times 16,000 = 4,000$$

Purchase price of Grade-I material = Sales – Profit
= 16,000 – 4,000 = Rs. 12,000

Calculation of profit on Grade-II materials

Selling price of Grade-II materials is $1\frac{1}{2}$ times that of Grade-I materials

i.e., $= \frac{3}{2} \times$ Rs. 4 = Rs. 6

Total sales of Grade-II materials = 8,000 units × Rs. 6 = Rs. 48,000

Percentage profit on sales is $33\frac{1}{3}\%$

i.e., $= \dfrac{33\frac{1}{3}}{100} \times 48,000$

or $\dfrac{100}{3} \times \dfrac{1}{100} \times 48,000 = \text{Rs. } 16,000$

Purchase price of Grade-II materials = Sales – Profit
= 48,000 – 16,000 = Rs. 32,000

Calculation of profit on Grade-III materials

Percentage of profit on sales is 20%

i.e., $\dfrac{20}{100} \times 50,000 = \text{Rs. } 10,000$

Purchase price of Grade III materials = Sales – Profit
= 50,000 – 10,000 = Rs. 40,000

Calculation of purchase price of Grade-IV materials

Total purchase price – (Purchase price of Grade I, II, III materials)
Rs. 1,20,000 – (12,000 + 32,000 + 40,000)
Rs. 1,20,000 – 84,000 = Rs. 36,000

Problem 6 : The following details are available in respect of a consignment of 1,250 kgs of material *X*.

(*a*) Invoice price – Rs. 20 per kg
(*b*) Excise duty – 25% on invoice price
(*c*) Sales tax – 8% on invoice price including excise duty
(*d*) Trade discount – 10% on the invoice price
(*e*) Insurance – 1% on aggregate net price
(*f*) Delivery charges – Rs. 250
(*g*) Cost of containers @ Rs. 60 per container for 50 kgs of materials, Rebate is allowed @ Rs. 40 per container if returned within six weeks, which is a normal feature.
(*h*) One container load of materials was rejected on inspection and not accepted.
(*i*) Cost of unloading and handling @ 0.25% of the cost of materials ultimately accepted. On the basis of above you are required to find out the landed cost of per kg of material *X*

(*ICWA Inter., Dec. 1991*)

Solution : **Statement showing cost per kg of material 'X'**

		Amount (Rs.)	*Cost per kg* *(1,200 kgs)*
Invoice price :			
Total Qty. ordered	1,250 kgs		
Less : Qty. rejected	50 kgs		
Qty. accepted	1,200		
1,200 kgs. @ Rs. 20		24,000	20.00
Less : Trade discount – 10% on invoice price		2,400	2.00
		21,600	18.00
Excise duty – 25% on invoice price $\left(\dfrac{25}{100} \times 24,000\right)$		6,000	5.00
		27,600	23.00
Sales tax – 8% on invoice price and excise duty			
$\dfrac{8}{100} \times 30,000$ (24,000 + 6,000)		2,400	2.00
Delivery charges		250	0.21

Cost of containers :

No. of containers	$\frac{1,250}{50} = 25$		
Less : Return of 1 container full of materials	$\frac{1}{24}$		
24 containers @ Rs. 60	= 1,440		
Less : Credited at Rs. 40 when returned (24 × 40)	= 960		
		480	0.40
Net purchase price		30,730.00	25.61
Insurance 1% on 30,730		307.30	0.25
Cost of materials ultimately accepted		31037.30	25.86
Cost of unloading and handling @ Rs. 0.25% of the cost of materials accepted		77.60	0.06
Landed cost of materials		31,114.90	25.92

Problem 7 : The following quotation is received from Mr. Kumar in respect of a material :

Lot price	*Rate per kg.*
	Rs.
500 kg –	10.00
2,000 kg –	8.50
4,000 kg –	7.75

Trade discount 20% and cash discount 5% if payment is made within one month. One container is required for every 250 kg of the material and containers are charged at Rs. 25 each but credited with Rs. 20, if returned within one month.

Transportation charges for any order Rs. 250

Storage charges Rs. 150

Concern decides to purchase 2,000 kgs

Assuming the payment is made within one month and the containers are also returned, calculate the materials cost per kg. (*Bangalore University, B. Com., Nov. 1990*)

Solution : **Calculation of purchase price for 2,000 kgs**

	Cost per kg.	*Amount (2,000)*
Supplier's price for 2,000 kgs @ Rs. 8.50	8.500	17,000.00
Less : Trade discount $\left(\frac{20}{100} \times 17,000\right)$	1.700	3,400.00
	6.800	13,600.00
Le s : Cash discount $\frac{5}{100} \times 13,600$	0.340	680.00
	5,460	12,920.00

Add : Cost of container :

For 250 kgs : 1 container is needed

For 2000 kgs – ?

$$\frac{2,000 \times 1}{250} \times 1 = 8 \text{ containers}$$

Each container is charged at Rs. 25 *i.e.* 8 × 25 = Rs. 200

Less : Cost of containers returned	8 × 20 = Rs. 160	0.02	40.00
		5.480	12,960.00
Add : Transport charges	250		
Storage charges	150	0.200	400.00
Purchase price		5.680	13,360.00

Problem 8 : A consignment was received from a supplier containing four types of materials. The invoice reveal the following :

		Rs.
Material *P*	1000 kgs @ Rs. 2 per kg	2,000
Material *Q*	500 kgs @ Rs. 2 per kg	1,000
Material *R*	750 kgs @ Rs. 4 per kg	3,000
Material *S*	500 kgs @ Rs. 4 per kg	2,000
Insurance		150
Freight paid by the buyer		500
Other expenses incurred by the buyer		100

Loss due to breakage was as follows :

Material *P* – 10 kgs   Material *Q* – 5 kgs

Material *R* – 10 kgs   Material *S* – 5 kgs

You are to keep a further provision of 10% on the purchase rate so arrived towards normal loss. Calculate the rate at which they should be priced when issued to various departments.

(Sri Sathya Sai University, B. Com., Oct. 1990)

Solution :

Calculation of total purchase price

	P (Rs.)	*Q* (Rs.)	*R* (Rs.)	*S* (Rs.)
Invoice price	2,000	1,000	3,000	2,000
Insurance (on the basis of invoice price)	37.50	18.75	56.25	37.50
Freight (on the basis of quantity)	181.00	91.00	137.00	91.00
Other expenses (on the basis of Invoice)	25.00	12.50	37.50	25.00
Total purchase price	2,243.50	1,122.25	3230.75	2,153.50

Calculation of net quantity of materials

	P	*Q*	*R*	*S*
Quantities bought	1,000	500	750	500
Less : Loss due to breakage	10	5	10	5
Net quantity	990	495	740	495
Purchase rate	Rs. $\frac{2,243.50}{990}$ = 2.26	$\frac{1122.25}{495}$ = 2.27	$\frac{3230.75}{740}$ = 4.36	$\frac{2,153.50}{495}$ = 4.35

Calculation of issue rate

	P	*Q*	*R*	*S*
Purchase rate	Rs. 2.26	2.27	4.36	4.35
Add : 10% provision	Re. 0.22	0.22	0.43	0.43
Issue rate	2.46	2.49	4.79	4.78

Problem 9 : A manufacturing organisation has imported four types of materials. The invoice reveals the following data :

	Quantity *kg.*	Rate *US $ per kg*
Material *A*	1,000	1.50
B	2,000	1.25
C	1,500	2.00
D	3,000	1.00

Import duty – 23% of invoice value
Insurance – 2% of invoice value
Freight & clearing – Rs. 30,000
Exchange rate US $ 1 = Rs. 16.00

50% of the materials imported are issued to production centres. While determining the value of closing stock 5% allowance is provided to cover up storage loss. Determine the value of closing stock of each type of materials. *(ICWA, Inter., Dec., 1989)*

Solution : **Statement of materials cost**

Materials	*A*	*B*	*C*	*D*	*Total*
Value of materials :					
Material *A* – 1,000 @ $ 1.50	1,500	2,500	3,000	3,000	10,000
Material *B* – 2,000 @ $ 1.25					
Material *C* – 1,500 @ $ 2.00					
Material *D* – 3,000 @ $ 1.00					
Import duty – 23% of invoice price	345	575	690	690	2,300
Insurance – 2% of invoice price	30	50	60	60	200
Total cost in US $	1,875	3,125	3,750	3,750	12,500
Converted to Rs.	30,000	50,000	60,000	60,000	2,00,00
Freight & clearing – on the basis of quantity	4,000	8,000	6,000	12,000	30,000
Total cost in Rs.	34,000	58,000	66,000	72,000	2,30,000
Less : 50% of materials issued	17,000	29,000	33,000	36,000	1,15,000
Balance in stock	17,000	29,000	33,000	36,000	1,15,000
Less : 5% allowance of storage loss	850	1,450	1,650	1,800	5,750
Value of closing stock	16,150	27,550	31,350	34,200	1.09,250

Problem 10 : A timber merchant purchased 1,000 cu.ft. of timber logs on 1st April 1991 @ Rs. 100 per cu.ft. and stored them in his timber yard for 6 months for seasoning. In the timber yard the following items of expenses were incurred during the period of seasoning :

(*i*) Rent – Rs. 1,250 p.m.
(*ii*) Salaries of 4 guards @ Rs. 250 p.m.
(*iii*) Incidental expenditure for maintenance, power, lighting, etc. – Rs. 750 p.m.
(*iv*) Annual share of administration overheads Rs. – Rs. 10,000.

50% of the floor area of the godown and other connected operations were incurred for stocking the seasoned timber. Loss in volume of the logs due to seasoning should be taken at 10%.

Calculate the selling price of the seasoned timber per cu.ft., on 1st October, 1991, assuming that the profit margin on cost was 15%. *(ICWA, Inter., June 1992)*

Solution : **Statement showing selling price**

	Qty. (Cu.ft.)	Amount (Rs.)
Cost of timber	1,000	1,00,000
Rent 1,250 × 6 × ½		3,750
Salary of guards 250 × 4 × 6 × ½		3,000
Incidental expenses 750 × 6 × ½		2,250
Overhead 10,000 × ½ × ½		2,500
		1,11,500
Less : Loss in qty. due to seasoning 10%	100	
Total	900	1,11,500
Profit @ 15% on cost	–	16,725
Selling price	900	1,25,225

Selling price per cu.ft. = $\frac{1,28,225}{900}$ = Rs. 142.47

TREATMENT OF MATERIALS RECEIVING AND HANDLING CHARGES

All the expenses such as transport cost, purchase department cost, receiving department cost, inspection department cost, stores department cost and other expenses such as stores accounting cost constitute materials receiving and handling cost.

Materials receiving and handling costs may be treated under any of the following three methods :

(*a*) By adding to the invoice price as part of the purchase cost of the materials.

(*b*) They may be treated as materials overhead and are charged as additional costs of materials at the time of issuing them. A material overhead absorption rate is calculated in the beginning of the year as a percentage of estimated value of materials issued throughout the year. The estimated value of materials issued consists of invoice value of purchased materials minus cash discount. Expressed in the form of a formula :

$$\frac{\text{Estimated receiving and handling cost}}{\text{Estimated value of materials issued}} \times 100$$

This percentage is added to the issue value of materials to absorb materials receiving and handling charges.

(*c*) Treating them as manufacturing overhead by charging to production as a departmental overhead absorption rate.

Problem 11 : You are supplied with the following information extracted from the budget estimates of a company :

	Rs.
Net purchases	2,00,000
Freight and insurance	10,000
Buying expenses	5,000
Receiving expenses	4,000
Inspection expenses	2,000
Storage expenses	3,000

The company made the following purchases during the budget period :

		Rs.
Consignment No.	1	30,000
	2	50,000
	3	70,000

Actual costs during the period were :

	Rs.
Freight and insurance	6,000
Buying expenses	4,000
Receiving expenses	3,000
Inspection expenses	1,500
Storage expenses	1,000

Compute the applied material and receiving handling rate for the period and determine the amount of receiving and handling cost chargeable to purchases. Also ascertain the variance between the actual and the applied costs for the period. (*ICWA, Inter., Dec. 1983*)

Solution : Calculation of applied material receiving and handling rate

Estimated expenses :

	Rs.
Freight and insurance	10,000
Buying expenses	5,000
Receiving expenses	4,000
Inspection expenses	2,000
Storage expenses	3,000
Total Rs.	24,000

For an estimated purchase of Rs. 2,00,000 the estimated expenses are 24,000

For 100 →? $\frac{24,000 \times 100}{2,00,000} = 12\%$

Statement showing amount of receiving and handling cost chargeable to purchases

Consignment No. 1, $\frac{12}{100} \times 30,000$ = 3,600

Consignment No. 2, $\frac{12}{100} \times 50,000$ = 6,000

Consignment No. 3, $\frac{12}{100} \times 70,000$ = 8,400

18,000

Actual Cost :

	Rs.
Freight and insurance	6,000
Buying expenses	4,000
Receiving expenses	3,000
Inspection expenses	1,500
Storage expenses	1,000
Total Rs.	15,000

Variance = Actual cost – Applied cost

Rs. 15,500 × Rs. 18,000 = 2,500 (favourable)

QUESTIONS

I. Mark True or False

1. Purchase requisition note is prepared by the purchase department. *T/F*
2. The purchase manager is himself the controller of materials. *T/F*
3. Routing the purchase requisition through the purchase department entails an unnecessary delay in receiving the required materials. *T/F*

4. The direct materials as a type of materials usually includes materials that are in their raw or natural state. *T/F*
5. Some materials used in the manufacture of a product may not be classified as direct materials. *T/F*
6. The primary criterion for classifying a material as direct is whether it can be clearly traced to and associated with a product. *T/F*
7. The duties and responsibilities of the purchase department differ from factory to factory. *T/F*
8. Centralised purchasing should not be used for any concern operating a single plant. *T/F*
9. Specification of materials means the material standards which are established by the factory to define its major materials requirement. *T/F*
10. Tenders are invited when time permits and money involved is in large amount. *T/F*
11. Once a tender has been received, no alteration or modification is allowed. *T/F*

[***Answer*** : (1) *F*, (2) *F*, (3) *F*, (4) *F*, (5) *T*, (6) *T*, (7) *T*, (8) *F*, (9) *T*, (10) *T*, (11) *T*]

II. Indicate whether each of the following items represent direct or indirect material

(*a*) Clay in bricks (*b*) Lubricants (*c*) Jars for cosmetics (*d*) Nails in wooden furniture (*e*) Sand paper used in polishing (*f*) Ink used in printing (*g*) Shop pattern (*h*) Thread used in stitching shirts (*i*) Fruits in carrying industry (*j*) Pig iron in foundry.

[***Answer*** : Direct Materials : (*a*), (*c*), (*f*), (*e*), (*i*), (*j*), rest are Indirect Materials]

III. Choose the correct answer from the following

(*a*) Which one of the following would not be treated as direct material in the manufacture of furniture :
- (1) Lumber for frames
- (2) Foam rubber padding
- (3) Adhesive past
- (4) Steel wire spring

(*b*) Purchase requisition is generally prepared in :
- (1) Single
- (2) Duplicate
- (3) Triplicate
- (4) Quadruplicate

(*c*) Which of the following items of cost should not be treated as direct material :
- (1) Electricity representing 90% of the total cost
- (2) Sand paper used in production
- (3) Thread used in stitching garments
- (4) All of the above

(*d*) A Purchase requisition is prepared by :
- (1) Purchase manager
- (2) Foreman
- (3) Supplier
- (4) Storekeeper

[**Answer** : (*a*) - 3, (*b*) - 4, (*c*) - 4, (*d*) - 4]

IV. Match the following

A	*B*
1. Raw materials	(*a*) Materials that are used in production but do not become part of the product.
2. In-process materials	(*b*) Materials used directly in the product but have not undergone a major change.
3. Finished products	(*c*) Products ready to be packaged and sold.
4. Supplies	(*d*) Machine parts that are used in manufacturing.
5. Equipment Items	(*e*) Materials used in the product whose form has changed as a result of the production process.

[***Answer*** : 1 - *e*, 2 - *b*, 3 - *c*, 4 - *a*, 5 - *d*]

V. Simple Questions

1. State two advantages of centralised purchasing. (*M.G. University, B. Com., April 96*)
2. Mention two disadvantages of centralised purchasing. (*M.G. University, B. Com., April 95*)
3. What are direct materials? (*M.G. University, B. Com., September 1994*)
4. What is materials received note? (*Bangalore University, B. Com., April 1995*)
5. What are the stages in materials purchase cycle? (*Bangalore University, M. Com., May 1995*)

6. Classify the following into direct materials and indirect materials :-
   (*a*) Oil & grease used in machine
   (*b*) Leather used in shoe
   (*c*) Cotton in textile industry
   (*d*) Nails used in Furniture

   (*Kuvempu University, B. Com., April 1995*)

7. What is meant by Direct materials cost? (*Bangalore University, B. Com., Nov. 97*) (*Karnataka University, B. Com., April 94*)
8. What is meant by centralised buying? (*Bangalore University, B. Com., November 99*)

SHORT ANSWER QUESTIONS

1. Explain the different stages involved in purchase procedure. (*University of Mysore, B. Com., Nov. 1997*)
2. Explain in brief the functions of :–
   (*a*) Purchasing Department
   (*b*) Receiving Department
   (*c*) Inspection Department
   (*d*) Stores Department

   (*University of Mysore, B. Com., April 1997*)

3. Describe the procedure to be followed for purchase of stores till the payment of the bill. (*Sri Krishnadevaraya University, B. Com., March 1998*)
4. What is buying process followed in an industrial organisation? (*Nagarjuna University, B. Com., March 1998*)
5. Describe the procedure for purchasing materials from outside. (*................University, B. Com., April 1994*)
6. What do you understand by Doublebin system? (*Sri Krishnadevaraya University, B. Com., March 1997*)
7. Describe the material purchase procedure. (*Osmania University, B. Com., October, 1996*)
8. Explain the functions of the Purchase Department. (*Kuvempu University, B. Com., October 1995*)

EXERCISES

Exercise on tender

Exercise 1 : After inviting tenders, two quotations are received as follows :

(*a*) Rs. 1.20 per unit

(*b*) Rs. 1.10 per unit plus Rs. 3,000 fixed charges to be added irrespective of units ordered.

Advise with your arguments on whom orders should be placed and what quantity to be ordered. The following additional information may be of interest :

	Units
Present Stock	35,000
Average monthly requirements	10,000
Maximum level	80,000
Minimum level	30,000

Sales tax may be ignored.

[*Answer :* Tender I is desirable if materials to be bought is below 30,000 units. Tender II is desirable if materials to be bought is above 10,000 units. Materials can be bought up to 45,000 units considering the maximum level of 80,000 units and the present stock of 35,000 units.]

Exercises on ascertaining purchase price

Exercise 2 : A small factory purchases different types of materials for Rs. 80,000. After sorting them out the selling price is recorded against each as shown below :

Category *A* 6,000 kgs selling price per unit is Rs. 8.

Category *B* 4,000 kgs selling price per unit is Rs. 6.

Category *C* 7,000 kgs selling price per unit is Rs. 4.

Find out the purchase rate per unit of each category of the materials presuming that all categories yield the same rate of profit.

[*Answer :* Purchase Rates of A = Rs. 6.40, B = Rs. 4.80, C = Rs. 3.20]

Exercise 3 : The following quotation is received from a supplier in respect of Material *A* :

			Rate per kg. Rs.
Lot Price	–	100 units	5.00
	–	500 units	4.50
	–	1,000 units	4.00

Trade discount 20% and cash discount 5% if payment is made with in 15 days. One container is required for every 100 units of the materials and containers are charged at Rs. 10 each but credited Rs. 9 if returned within 3 months.

Transport charges for order	Rs. 50
Storage charges	Rs. 15

Calculate the material cost for 500 units and per unit cost of materials when the purchaser decides to buy 500 units of the materials.

[*Answer* : Assuming that containers are returned within 3 months and cash discount not availed the purchase price amounts to Rs. 1,870 for 500 units and Rs. 3.74 per unit of material.]

Exercise 4 : A consingnment was received by a small business containing four types of materials. The invoice reveals the following :

			Rs.
Material *A*	–	2,000 litres @ Rs. 2 per litre	4,000.00
Material *B*	–	1,000 litres @ Rs. 3 per litre	3,000.00
Material *C*	–	1,500 litres @ Rs. 4 per litre	6,000.00
Material *D*	–	500 litres @ Rs. 4.50 per litre	2,250.00
Insurance			152.50
Freight paid by buyer			1,000
Expenses incurred by the buyer			1,600
Tax paid by the supplier			610

Loss due to breakage was recorded as follows :

Material *A*	–	120 litres,	Material *B*	–	20 litres
Material *C*	–	45 litres,	Material *D*	–	10 litres

It has been a policy of the materials management to keep a further provision of 10% for evaporation. Calculate the rate at which these should be prices when issued to various department.

[*Answer :* Apportioning insurance and taxes on the basis of value of materials and freight and 'other expenses' on the basis of number of units, the issue prices are A–3.05, B–4.11, C–5.36, D–5.88]

Exercise 5 : A timber dealer, who also makes furniture, purchased 20,000 cu.ft of timber logs @ Rs. 20.25 per cu.ft. He stored them in his timber for six months for seasoning. His expenses during the period were. .

Rent of the yard Rs. 300 month, maintenance and lighting, etc. Rs. 200 p.m. Salaries to 3 watchmen @ Rs. 250 p.m., each. Administration expenses amounted to Rs. 12,000 per annum. One-third of the floor area of the yard has been set apart for making furniture and the remaining space used for seasoning timber.

10% of loss in weight due to seasoning is regarded as normal. Calculate the cost of seasoned logs per cu.ft.

(*Bharathidasan University, M. Com., April 1987*)

[*Answer :* Cost per cu.ft of seasoned logs is Rs. 23]

Exercise on material receiving and handling charges

Exercise 6 : The estimated receiving and handling charges in the budget for the Gemini Enterprises were Rs. 3,000. The estimated net cost of materials for the budget period was Rs. 30,000. The actual receiving and handling costs amounted to Rs. 2,500. The actual materials purchases totalled Rs. 24,000 in the year 1982.

(*a*) What is the amount of variance between the acutal and applied material receiving and handling cost.

(*b*) What disposition would you recommend for the variance.

[*Answer :* The variance is Rs. 100 (adverse). This is to be charged to costing P & L a/c]

4

MATERIALS COST-STOREKEEPING

OBJECTIVS OF STOREKEEPING

Storekeeping is that aspect of materials management which is concerned with the physical storage of materials. Storekeeping is essentially a service function and as such it should aim at providing this service efficiently and effectively at a minimum cost. The main objectives of storekeeping are as follows :

1. Easy Identification of Materials

Identification of materials become very difficult especially when varieties of materials are bought in bulk quantities. Unless they are sorted out and stored properly identifying the materials will pose a problem. Production will be delayed to the extent of identification and its issue.

2. To Prepare Purchase Requisitions

By seeing the quantity of materials reaching the reorder level, it is possible to replenish the exhausting materials by requesting the purchase manager to arrange for the purchase of materials. So the danger in the stoppage of production can be overcome by timely purchase of materials.

3. Safe Keeping of Materials

To ensure the safety of all types of materials it is essential to store the materials. Proper storage of materials also facilitates quick issue of materials to various production departments.

4. To Maintain Store Records

The object of maintaining store records is to know the quantity of materials on hand, slow moving and fast moving, dormant and obsolete materials so that prompt action can be taken in respect of each of this materials.

5. Co-ordination with other Department

Co-ordination of storage department with other departments is necessary to know the exact requirements of materials and their specifications, so that only required quantity and quality of materials can be procured.

6. Store Verification

To exercise control over materials stock verification is necessary.

IMPORTANCE OF STOREKEEPING

(*a*) Proper maintenance of stores will help the storekeeper to know the actual quantity of materials available in storeroom. On the other hand, if the materials are not properly stored it does not help in assessing the exact requirements of materials. Whereas those materials which are already available are initiated for purchasing again and again the one which must be bought may go unnoticed by the storekeeper.

(*b*) Systematic arrangement of stores help in easy location of materials. Delay in the process of issue of materials can be avoided once materials are easily located. In fact, a store item 'misplaced' is a store item 'lost' for all practical purposes.

(*c*) By submitting frequent reports regarding the stock position of materials it facilitates the top level management to formulate purchase policies.

(*d*) Losses arising from theft, can be avoided by proper storage of materials.

ESSENTIALS OF GOOD STOREKEEPING

Storekeeping is both an art and a science. It is an art as it involves the day-to-day receipt, storage and issue of materials. It is a science, as it involves recording the stores transactions as per the prescribed principles and rules. Good storekeeping results from experienced and enthusiastic storekeeper and his assistants. The essentials of good storekeeping are outlined below :

(*a*) Allot a proper place for every item of store.
(*b*) Keep every item of store in the alloted place.
(*c*) Maintain proper records of stores and keep them up-to-date.
(*d*) To issue the materials promptly to various departments.
(*e*) Storing the materials in an orderly fashion.
(*f*) Protecting materials against damage and pilferage.
(*g*) Issue oldest materials first.
(*h*) Classify and codify the materials for easy identification.
(*i*) Adequate space must be provided in between tracks and almirah for easy movement of store's assistants.
(*j*) Undertake continuous verification of materials.

LOCATION AND LAYOUT OF STORES DEPARTMENT

The selection of appropriate site for establishing a storeroom is known as location of stores. The ideal location of storeroom must be such that the movement of the materials from the receiving department to the storeroom and from the storeroom to the production departments is minimum. Further the ideal location of store is that where the most efficient transportation and material handling equipment could be utilised. The following storage location factors should be taken into account in order to select the best locality.

(*a*) **Materials Classification :** Materials of the same classification may be stored at a place irrespective of differences in size, weight and place of consumption. For example, one area may be designated for raw materials, Sundry supplies and component parts: another area may be designated for semi-finished products and another for finished stock.

(*b*) **Similarity of materials :** Items of similar size, shape and weight may be stored together although they may be classified differently or required at different production departments. For example, all small items may be kept in one place and bulk items in another place.

(*c*) **Materials handling consideration :** Materials requiring similar handling equipment may be grouped together. For example, those materials which are to be moved by trucks alone may be stored separately. Similarly liquids which are to be specially measured and moved by trolleys may be placed together.

(*d*) **Character of materials to be stored :** The character of the materials to be stored affects the location of storage areas. Materials that are not damaged by weather can be stored in a shed. Materials subject to corrosion must be stored in dry place. Materials whose character is altered by high temperature must be stored in cold storage room. Finished goods which are damaged by dust must be stored in dust proof bins.

(*e*) **The quantity, weight and bulk of materials :** The quantity of each of the materials to be stored must be carefully considered in determining the location of storeroom. When the quantities of materials are known, the weight and bulk of materials can be determined and required space can be alloted.

(*f*) **Miscellaneous factors**

(*i*) Security aspect to prevent theft and explosion of certain types of materials.
(*ii*) The storeroom may be located near the main road, railway stations or wharf to facilitate easy handling of materials.
(*iii*) Heavy and bulky items should be stored near the departments using them.
(*iv*) Location of doors, size of platforms, etc. should suit the storeroom.
(*v*) Fast moving items should be stored near the point of issue.

Layout of Stores

Stores layout refers to physical arrangement of storage space facilities so as to provide for most efficient receipt, storage and issue of materials. The arrangement of storeroom includes arrangement of space for storing materials, records and files and materials handling equipments. The basic principles of good stores layout are :

1. The layout of stores must reduce (*a*) the distance of moving the stores item, (*b*) storage equipment, (*c*) storage space and (*d*) handling cost.
2. The stores layout must be flexible enough to allow for changed condition and future expansion.
3. Free flow of materials into and outside the storeroom, *i.e.*, the principle of minimum distance is to be followed.
4. Provision of different storage facility for different types of materials.
5. Facilitate better supervision of stores.

A well planned layout offers the following advantages :

(*a*) Full utilisation of storage space.
(*b*) Easy accessibility to all the materials.
(*c*) More security of all materials and stores records.
(*d*) Lesser time to receive, issue and store the materials.
(*e*) Minimum spoilage, damage and other kinds of losses.

ORGANISATION OF STORES DEPARTMENT

The organisation of storekeeping department depends upon (*a*) design and layout of the factory, (*b*) the degree of centralisation required, (*c*) need for departmental storeroom and (*d*) frequency of issues of materials. Generally speaking storekeeping department can be organised under (1) Centralised System, (2) Decentralised System and (3) Imprest System.

1. Centralised System

In centralised system all the materials are received and issued from one stores department. The advantages of this system according to *Wheldon* is outlined below :

(*a*) Economy in staff and concentration of experts in one department.

(*b*) Reduced clerical costs and economy in records and stationary.
(*c*) Better supervision is possible.
(*d*) Staff become acquainted with different types of stores, which is very useful if any one is absent from work.
(*e*) Better layout of stores.
(*f*) Inventory check facilitated.
(*g*) Stocks are kept to a minimum, thus reducing storage space.
(*h*) Fewer obsolete articles.
(*i*) The amount of capital invested in stock is minimised.
(*j*) Better security arrangements can be made.

The disadvantages of this system are as follows :

(*a*) When centralised storeroom is located far away from other departments it involves high transportation cost.
(*b*) The supply of materials to distant production department may cause delay and inconvenience.
(*c*) Breakdown of transport or hold-ups in storeroom will hamper production.
(*d*) The chance of risk of loss on account of natural calamities such as occurrence of fire, food, etc. are high.

2. Decentralised System

Under this system, a separate storeroom is located adjacent to the production department from where materials can be drawn. This system is particularly suitable where the plants are dispersed over wider geographical areas. The disadvantages of centralised store system can be overcome by adopting this method.

3. Imprest System

This system is followed in order to minimise materials handling expenses. Under this system a sub-store is located near production department. The exact requirements of stores for each production department is decided in advance and so much of materials are kept on hand in the beginning. At the end of the month, the sub-storekeeper will obtain the quantity of materials required so as to replenish the exhausted stock of materials. The advantages of this system are as follows :

(a) It facilitates personal supervision of materials by the sub-storekeeper.
(*b*) It reduces transport cost involved during frequent issue of materials.
(*c*) It facilitates prompt issue of materials.
(*d*) Space in the main storeroom can be saved.
(*e*) Risk due to fire is spread over a numer of departments.

The disadvantages of this system are :

(*a*) It lacks centralised control over materials.
(*b*) The cost of storage is more with the involvement of more sub-storekeepers and other storekeeping expenses.
(*c*) Additional space is to be provided for every sub-store.

DUTIES AND RESPONSIBILITIES OF STOREKEEPER

The stores department is headed by a competent authority known as storekeeper. He takes care of the stores and keeps a watchful eye on the movement of both men and materials with a view to keep the whole organisation moving. The extent of functions to be performed by him varies depending upon the nature, size and composition of the stores department. However, a good storekeeper must possess the following requisites :

(*a*) He must be hard working.
(*b*) He must be honest.
(*c*) He must have knowledge of accounts.
(*d*) He must possess leadership abilities so as to command his subordinates to carry out storekeeping functions efficiently.
(*e*) He must possess an academic qualification which depend upon the type of industry. For example, the storekeeper of an engineering storeroom should be a science graduate.

Duties of Storekeeper

(*a*) To prepare and issue purchase requisition note for such types of materials which have reached reorder level.
(*b*) To receive the purchased materials from receiving department.
(*c*) To enter the particulars of materials in the bin card.
(*d*) To store materials in their appropriate place for easy identification.
(*e*) To issue the materials to production departments on the basis of, "materials requisition note".
(*f*) To take back the surplus materials returned by production departments.
(*g*) To undertake stock verification of materials.
(*h*) To report on scrap, waste, surplus, obsolete materials to management for taking necessary action.
(*i*) To equip the storeroom with material handling equipments for easy and economical handling.
(*j*) To prevent unauthorised persons from entering into the storeroom.

Responsibilities of Storekeeper

(*a*) The storekeeper is responsible for the materials which he receives. Therefore at the time of receiving the materials into the storeroom he must verify the quantity, quality and the specification of materials.
(*b*) He is responsible for the timely issue of material. So the storekeeper has to classify and codify the materials and store them at appropriate place.
(*c*) He is responsible for shortage of materials on account of theft, damage and spoilage.
(*d*) It is the responsibility of the storekeeper to work in close co-ordination with purchase, production and accounts departments for the smooth functioning of the factory.
(*e*) He is responsible for the negligence of his as well as his subordinates duties.

STOREKEEPING RECORDS

The need for keeping stock records are as follows :

(*a*) To know the amount of materials without depending on physical stock taking.
(*b*) To know the reasons for the discrepancies in the balance of materials as shown by different stock records and the actual balance of materials.
(*c*) To know the quantity and time at which such material are to be bought.
(*d*) To facilitate valuation of materials.

The following documents are used in recording the stores items :

(*a*) **Material receipt book :** This book records the receipt of materials by the storekeeper in a chronological order. This book forms the basis of stores accounting. Before the materials are stored in bins, they are verified in respect of quantity and quality. If there is any shortage or damage of materials, the storekeeper prepares accordingly a shortage or damage report.

(*b*) **Bin card :** A bin card is made out of a thick paper and is meant for recording the receipt, issue and balance of materials in stores. The bin card is attached to the bin or rack in which materials are stocked. It enables to know the quantity of materials on hand, whenever materials are issued or when received from suppliers or returned by the departments as surplus stock. A bin card helps storekeeper to prepare purchase requisition to replenish the exhausted materials. It also helps in locating the discrepancy when physical stock verification is undertaken and the balance compared with bin card. It contains particulars such as bin number, description of materials, code number of materials, maximum, minimum, reorder and danger levels and the columns for the quantity of materials received, issued and in balance. The specimen of a Bin Card is given below :

KMA—BANGALORE

Bin Card

Description.........   Bin card No. ....
Group ....   Units ....   Materials Code ....
Location ....
Max. Level ....
Min. Level ....
Order Level ....

Date	*Ref. No.*	*Receipts (qty.)*	*Issues (qty.)*	*Balance (qty.)*	*Remarks*

Fig. 4.1. Bin card.

Problem 1 : The Kamani Metal and Alloys Co. furnishes the following information to you. Draw are up the Bin Card (Number 32).

1992 Jan.	1,	Opening balance	200 Tons
	2,	Issued on requisition No. 10	57 Tons
	4,	Issued on requisition No. 11	83 Tons
	5,	Received from supplier by Challan No. 74	120 Tons
	8,	Issued on requisition No. 12	92 Tons
	12,	Issued on requisition No. 13	30 Tons
	17,	Received from supplier by Challan No. 76	100 Tons
	24,	Issued on requisition No. 14	69 Tons
	28,	Issued on requisition No. 15	29 Tons
	30,	Received from supplier by Challan No. 80	125 Tons
	31,	Issued on requisition No. 16	85 Tons

Examination by stock verifier on Jan. 27, 1992 revealed a shortage of 5 tons. The maximum quantity of stock permissible at any time is 200 tons and the minimum 50 tons. The ordering level is 100 tons.

Solution : **Bin Card**

Name of Material:	Steel	Bin Card No.	:	32
Unit :	Tons	Max. Qty.	:	200 Tons
		Min. Qty.	:	50 Tons
		Ordering Level	:	100 Tons

Date	*Receipts*		*Issues*		*Balance*	*Remarks*
	Ch. No.	*Qty.*	*Requisition No.*	*Qty.*		
1992 Jan.1	-	-	-	-	200	
2	-	-	10	57	143	
4	-	-	11	83	60	
5	74	120	-	-	180	
8	-	-	12	92	88	
12	-	-	13	30	58	
17	76	100	-	-	158	
24	-	-	14	69	89	
27	-	-	-	5	84	Shortage
28	-	-	15	29	55	
30	80	125	-	-	180	
31	-	-	16	85	105	

(*c*) **Stores ledger card :** A stores ledger card is a record of materials showing receipts, issues and balance of materials both in quantities and values. It is maintained in stores accounting section and is outside the control of storekeeper. A specimen of stores ledger card is given below :

STORES LEDGER CARD

Name of the Materials	Maximum Level ....
Code No. of Material	Minimum Level ....
	Reorder Level ....
	Danger Level ....

Date	*Receipts*				*Issues*				*Balance*		
	PRN	*Qty.*	*Rate*	*Amount*	*MRN*	*Qty.*	*Rate*	*Amount*	*Qty.*	*Rate*	*Amount*

Fig. 4.2. Stores ledger card

A stores ledger card differs from a bin card in the following respects :

Bin Card	*Stores ledger card*
1. It is maintained in the storeroom.	1. It is maintained in the cost accounting department.
2. It contains particulars of materials only in terms of quantities.	2. It contains particulars of materials both in terms of quantity and value.
3. Entries in the bin card is made by storekeeper or his assistants.	3. Entries in the stores ledger card is made by the stores clerks or stores accountant.
4. Entries are made on the basis of actual quantity received or issued.	4. Entries are supported by materials recei. ved note, materials requisition note, etc.
5. Inter-departmental transactions do not appear in a bin card.	5. Inter-departmental transfer of materials are recorded in the stores ledger card.
6. Entries are posted before the trans- actions takes place.	6. Entries are posted after the transactions takes place.
7. Entries are posted individually.	7. Entries are posted periodically.

(*d*) **Stock verification sheet :** This record is prepared at the time of stock taking in the storeroom. After physical verification is over, they may be valued to incorporate the value of materials to record in the balance sheet.

Two-Bin System

Under this system a certain quantity of materials termed as reserve stock is set apart which is not used for daily use. Under this system two bins are used. The first bin is termed as "running bin" which serves the purpose of day-to-day issues. The second bin which is termed as "reserve bin" is set aside with a certain quantity of materials. The reserve stock is set apart by taking into account the time taken by the supplier to deliver the materials. When the materials in the running bin exhaust, the materials of reserve bin is used for issuing them. This serves as a caution for the storekeeper to make immediate arrangement to prepare and place a purchase requisition for procuring the required materials. However, the reserve bin should be kept rotated, *i.e.,* old materials must be issued and reserve should be created out of fresh stock.

MATERIALS HANDLING

Material handling refers to the study of the movement of materials from one place to another place within the factory. The importance of materials handling cannot be underestimated is spite of the fact that mechanical equipments are largely being used. It has been estimated that one out of ten in labour force is involved in handling materials and in a typical factory, fifty tons of product must be handled to produce one ton of finished product. In some factories at least one-quarter of the cost is attributable to the handling of the materials.

Objectives of Material Handling

(*a*) **Reduce the cost for each part handled :** The main objective of material handling is to reduce the overall costs of materials handling by reducing the number of handling involved. But the overall material handling costs can be reduced only if the unit cost, *i.e.*, cost for each part handled are reduced. This approach requires that costs of handling be allocated to its component parts that are moved.

(*b*) **Reduce the manufacturing-cycle time :** Effective handling of materials from the stage of receipt to the stage of completion involves reduction in production time. By means of speedling up or handling over short distance it results in the reduction of inventory cost.

(*c*) **Contribute towards a better control of the flow of goods :** In continuous manufacturing factories, where all the process of production are predetermined and where production of one process depends upon another process, material handling plan can effect considerable amount of savings in flow of materials. Thus the production control can be exercised more efficiently.

(*d*) **Provide for improved working conditions and greater safety :** The Factories Act requires adherence to safe handling practices. Safe handling of materials also reduces industrial accidents. This reduces the tangible saving in the form reduced insurance rates and an intangible saving in the form of improves employee movable.

(*e*) **Lesser rejection of goods :** Handling of material carefully to a large extent reduces breakages and damages of the finished products. This is more so in case of fragile goods such as glass and ceramics. Excess damages and breakages add to the increased cost of production and so a carfeul material handling plan is necessary.

(*f*) **Increases storage capacity :** A well designed material handling plan saves to a considerable extent storage space in factories.

(*g*) **Increased productivity at lower manufacturing cost :** A material handling system improves productivity by moving materials in the fastest, most efficient and economical way possible.

Factors Affecting the Selection of Material Handling Equipment

The following factors are to be considered when choosing material handling equipment:

(*a*) **Types of material to be handled :** This include size, weight and strength of the material to be handled.

(*b*) **Type of production :** For the sake of material handling purpose the type of production can be considered as continuous production or batch production. If continuous production is envisaged, conveyor belts and overhead conveyor might be suitable. In case of batch production, powered trucks and portable conveyors are useful.

(*c*) **Factory building :** The determining factors are number of floors, provision of lifts, heights of ceilings, etc.

(d) **Handling costs :** It is difficult to assess material handling costs. However a full study of cost should be made not only of labour but also of handling equipment and containers.

(*e*) **Adaptability :** The carrying capacity of the equipment should fit the material handling problem. Whenever possible the equipment should have flexibility to handle more than one material.

(*f*) **Speed :** Repidity of movement of material within the limits of production process should be considered.

(*g*) **Space requirements :** The space required to install or operate materials handling equipment is an important factor in selecting the material handling equipment.

(*h*) **Supervision required :** This refers to the degree of automaticity designed into the equipment.

(*i*) **Ease of maintenance :** Equipment selected should be easily maintained at reasonable cost.

(*j*) **Environment :** Equipment selected must conform to any environmental regulation.

Advantages of Mechanised Handling

1. The manufacturing-cycle time can be reduced by the elimination of non-productive time in the manufacturing process. Research has indicated that at least 30 per cent of the total time required in manufacturing is consumed by material handling.
2. Human fatigue in lifting and handling mannually can be reduced and in some cases eliminated.
3. Idle time can be brought to a minimum. Most of the waiting for work that occurs where intermittent and non-mechanical delivery of material is involved can be eliminated by equipment that ensures a steady constant flow of materials.
4. The productivity of employees working on the product is increased by a reduction of time they would otherwise spend in handling materials.
5. Increased safety of handling results where materials are not 'man-handled'.
6. Storage space is conserved, particularly where mechanical equipment is used to stock materials vertically.
7. Non-productive indirect labour can be released for more productive, direct-labour activities.
8. Certain types of mechanised handling equipment tied in with automatic machine controls open up vast vistas in the field of automation.

Material Handling Cost

The cost of materials handling arises from two sources *viz.* (1) the cost of acquiring and maintaining equipment and (2) the cost of operating the system. The material handling cost can be classified on the basis of variability and character of costs. This is shown under the following chart :

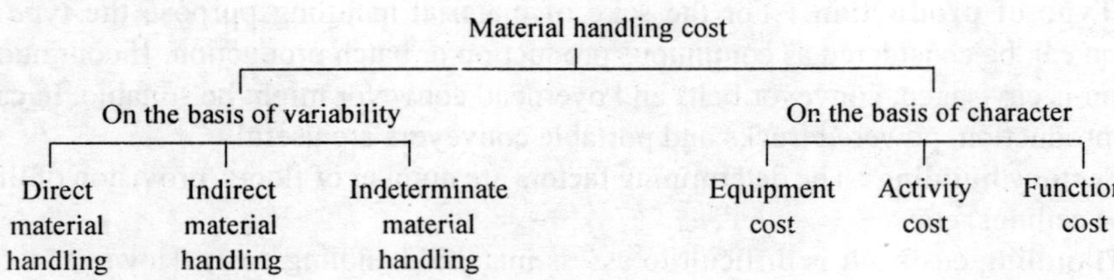

Fig. 4.3. Chart showing material handling cost.

On the basis of variability material handling cost can be classified into the following types:

(*a*) **Direct material handling cost :** Direct costs are those commonly associated with the operation of material handling equipment. Both equipment and manpower costs are included in this category. Some examples of direct material handling costs are depreciation. Interest on investment, wages of operating personnel, fuel and power, etc.

(*b*) **Indirect material handling cost :** Indirect material handling costs are those associated with the investment. Sometimes this cost also include operation cost of an equipment but not in direct proportion. Examples of indirect materials handling costs are rent for space occupied, repair parts, etc.

(*c*) **Indeterminate material handling cost :** Indeterminate material handling costs are those which cannot be precisely determined or which are not known in advance or which do not lend themselves to the determination of a definite cost figure. This category might include some of the following costs; safety, clerical costs, plans for expansion.

On the basis of character of costs, material handling cost can be classified into the following types of costs :

(*a*) **Equipment cost :** Equipment costs are those related to the actual capital investment.

(*b*) **Activity cost :** Activity costs are those expenditures required by a specified handling activity.

(*c*) **Functional cost :** Functional costs are concerned with such organisational units as receiving, warehousing and the like.

Suggestions to Reduce Material Handling Costs

In order to reduce the material handling cost the following suggestions are made :

(a) Keep all handling at a minimum.
(b) Handle as many pieces in one unit as is practical.
(c) Provide large, heavy or bulky objects with handling aids such as hooks.
(d) Always consider handling problems in analysing and designing the overall production system.
(e) Modify existing building facilities to permit full use of available capacity.
(f) Wherever possible manufacturing processing should take place while the product is being moved.
(g) Move the greatest weight or bulk material to the least possible distance.

INVENTORY CONTROL OR MATERIAL CONTROL OR STORES CONTROL

Material control can be defined as the systematic control concerned with procuring, storing and using of materials so as to minimise wastage and losses and at the same time avoiding excess investment in materials.

Objectives of Material Control

1. **To ensure continuity in production :** The success of an undertaking depends upon the continuity in production. Stoppage of production has adverse impact not only in terms of restarting of production as in the case of furnaces but also in the cancellation of orders by the customers. Therefore care must be taken to ensure that production is not stopped for want of raw materials and other sundry supplies.

2. **To purchase requisite quality of materials :** The quality of finished goods depend upon the quality of raw materials used. Any purchase of inferior quality of materials lead to sub-standard production of goods which are likely to be rejected by customers. At the same time a very superior quality of materials should also be avoided as it may entail payment of high prices. This may lead to increased cost of production and consequently increased selling price, which is also likely to be rejected by the customers.

3. **To eliminate losses and wastages :** Materials are subjected to rust, dust, dirt, moisture. Sometimes they are also lost due to theft and careless handling of materials. Hence it must be the endeavour of material management to investigate the causes for the losses and wastages of materials and take prompt action to eliminate such losses.

4. **To avoid overstoking of materials :** Overstocking of materials leads to incurring of the following expenses :

(*a*) *Capital cost :* Any excess purchase of materials results in the sinking of capital in the purchase of materials which could otherwise yield a higher rate of return if invested in profitable investment.

(*b*) *Storage cost :* Storage of excess quantity of materials require incurrence of additional amount of rent, heating, lighting, etc.

(*c*) *Equipment cost :* Additional equipments such as bins, racks, etc. are required to store overstocked materials.

(*d*) *Personal cost :* Personal costs such as salaries and wages are to be paid for additional staff recruited for storing, stock verification, security, etc.

(*e*) *Obsolescence :* The higher the stock of materials, higher is the chances of obsolescence because they are kept in storeroom for longer duration.

(f) Loss on account of deterioration and evaporation in case of certain types of liquid materials.

5. **To avoid understocking of materials :** The understocking of materials results in the following consequences :

(a) There is a danger in the stoppage of production for want of materials.

(b) Stoppage in production results in delayed deliveries thereby leading to cancellation of orders.

(c) While there may not be any revenue earned during the period of stoppage in production, it involves incurring of fixed expenses such as wages, rent, etc.

6. **Purchase at reasonable price :** Purchase of materials must be always at a reasonably low price. Otherwise a large amount of money is lost in purchasing the materials. However, quality should not be sacrificed at the cost of lower price.

7. **Knowledge about the sources of materials :** A good system of material control must facilitate ready availability of information about various sources of suppliers, so that the best terms of purchase can be resorted to.

ESSENTIALS OF MATERIAL CONTROL

Buyers and Holmes in their book *Principles of Cost Accountancy* have summarised the essential requirements of material control as listed below :

(*a*) Co-ordination between the departments involved in the buying, receiving, inspection and storage of materials and in accounting for them.

(*b*) Centralisation of purchasing under the authority of a competitive buyer.

(*c*) The planning and programming of material requirements.

(*d*) Standardisation and simplification of materials.

(*e*) The proper classification and codification of materials.

(*f*) The use of standard forms for orders, requisitition, etc. upon which written and signed instructions are given.

(*g*) Control by budget of material and equipment purchases.

(*h*) The operation of internal check to ensure that all transactions involving materials and equipment are checked by reliable and independent officials.

(*i*) The storage of all materials is well planned and properly designated subject to adequate safeguards and supervision.

(*j*) The operations of efficient stock control procedures and records.

(*k*) Adequate records to control materials during production and the quantities manufactured for stock.

(*l*) Regular reports to management upon purchases of materials, issues, stocks and in paritcular obsolete stocks, returns to suppliers, spoilage and waste, etc.

TECHNIQUES OF MATERIAL CONTROL

The important teachniques used to exercise control over materials are as follows :

1. ABC analysis.
2. Level setting.
3. Economic order quantity.
4. Inventory turnover.
5. Stock checking and stocktaking—Perpetual inventory system.
6. Input-output ratio analysis.
7. Classification and codification of materials.
8. Miscellaneous techniques.
9. New techniques of material control.

1. ABC Analysis or Selective Inventory Control

The concept of ABC analysis was coined by Pareto, an Italian philosopher in the nineteenth century who illustrated graphically the fact that most of the wealth in Italy was owned by a small proportion of the population. This analysis is based on the principle "Vital few—Trivial many". On an analysis of materials consumption in all factories it is revealed that about 80 per cent of total value of issues accounts for 20 per cent of the items. So this technique is sometimes expressed 80 : 20 rule. When this technique is used as a tool of material control, the materials are classified into three categories, designated as '*A*' category materials, '*B*' category material and '*C*' category materials. The features of such materials can be stated as under :

Category '*A*' items—Small in number, high in usage value—the 'vital few' from a financial point of view.

Category '*B*' items—Medium number, medium usage value—'normal items'.

Category '*C*' items—High number, low usage value—the 'trivial many'

This is illustrated in the following graph :

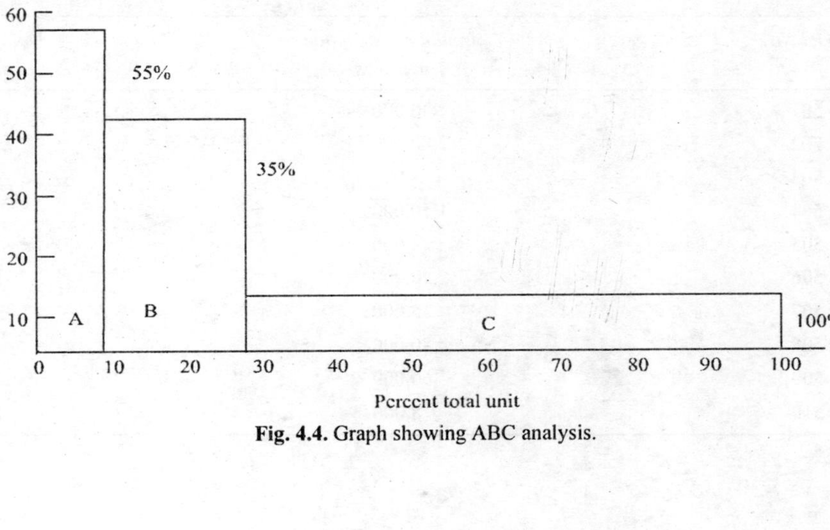

Fig. 4.4. Graph showing ABC analysis.

According to this technique, a strict control is exercised over '*A*' category material, perhaps under the supervision of an experienced person, a moderate control is exercised over '*B*' category materials and relatively lesser degree of control over '*C*' category materials. The object of carrying out ABC analysis is to develop policy guidelines for selective controls. Normally once ABC analysis has been done, the following broad policy guidelines can be established in respect of each category :

From the point of view of	*'A' Items*	*'B' Items*	*'C' Items*
1. Degree of control	Very strict control	Moderate control	Low control
2. Safety stock	No safety stock	Low-safety stock	High safety stock
3. Ordering	Frequent ordering	Once in 3 weeks	Bulk ordering once in 6 months
4. Periodicity of control	Weekly control statements	Monthly control reports	Quarterly control reports
5. Value analysis	Rigorous value analysis	Moderate value analysis	Minimum value analysis
6. Forecasting	Accurate forecasting and planning	Estimate based on past data and present plans	Rough estimates
7. Lead time	Maximum efforts to reduce lead time	Moderate efforts	Minimum efforts

Advantages of ABC Analysis

(*a*) A strict control is exercised on costlier items of materials while exercising moderate control over less costlier materials.

(*b*) Investment on materials are judiciously utilised.

(*c*) Storage cost also will be less as only the required quantity of materials alone are bought.

(*d*) Quick purchase of materials can be ensured by concentrating on fewer items that are required at one time.

(*e*) It is based on the principle of control by exception which gives best results especially when resources and staff are less.

Problem 2 : The following information is known about a group of items. Classify the materials, as *A*, *B* and *C* classification :

Model No.	*Annual consumption in prices*	*Unit price in paise*
501	30,000	10
502	2,80,000	15
503	3,000	10
504	1,10,000	5
505	4,000	5
506	2,20,000	10
507	15,000	5
508	80,000	5
509	60,000	10
510	8,000	10

Solution : **Statement showing value of materials consumed and its relative ranks**

Model No.	*Annual consumption*	*Unit price*	*Value of annual consumption*	*Ranks based on value*
501	30,000	0.10	3,000	6
502	2,80,000	0.15	42,000	1
503	3,000	0.10	300	9
504	1,10,000	0.05	5,500	4
505	4,000	0.05	200	10
506	2,20,000	0.10	22,000	2
507	15,000	0.05	750	8
508	80,000	0.05	4,000	5
509	60,000	0.15	9,000	3
510	8,000	0.10	800	7
Total	8,10,000		87,550	

Statement of ABC classification

Category	*Model No.*	*Percentage items*	*Annual consumption value*	*Percentage to total value*	*Rank*
A	502	10%	42,000	48%	1
	506	10%	22,000	25%	2
	Total	20%	64,000	73%	
B	509	10%	9,000	10%	3
	504	10%	5,500	6%	4
	508	10%	4,000	5%	5
	Total	30%	18,500	21%	
C	501	10%	3,000	3.4%	6
	510	10%	800	1.0%	7
	507	10%	750	1.0%	8
	503	10%	300	1.4%	9
	505	10%	200	0.2%	10
	Total	50%	5,050	6.0%	
	Grand Total	100%	87,550	100%	

Problem 3 : A factory uses 4,000 varieties of inventory. In terms of inventory holding and invesntory usage, the following information is compiled

No. of varieties of Inventory	*%*	*% value of Inventory holding (average)*	*% of Inventory usage (in end product)*
3875	96.875	20	5
110	2.750	30	10
15	0.375	50	85
4000	1,00.000	100	100

Classify the items of inventory as per ABC analysis with reasons (*C A. Inter November 1998*)

Solution : Classification of the items of inventory as per ABC analysis.

(1) 15 number of varieties of inventory items should be classified as '*A*' category items because of the following reasons :

(*a*) They constitute 0.375% of total number of varieties of inventory items handled by stores of the factory, which is minimum as per given classification in the table.

(*b*) 50% of total use value of inventory holding (average) which is maximum according to the given table.

(*c*) Highest consumption of about 85% of inventory usage (in end-product)

(2) 110 number of varieties of inventory items, should be classified as '*B*' category item because of the following reasons :

(*a*) They constitute 2.75% of total number of varieties of inventory items handled by stores of factory.

(*b*) They require moderate investment of about 30% of total use value of inventory holding (average).

(*c*) Moderate consumption of about 10% of inventory usage (in end-production).

(3) 3,875 number of varieties of inventory items, should be classified as '*C*' category items because of the following reasons :

(*a*) They constitute 96.875% of total varieties of inventory items handled by stores of the factory.

(*b*) They require investment of 20% of total use value of inventory holding.

(*c*) Minimum consumption, i.e., about 5% of inventory usage (in end-product).

2. Level Setting

This technique of material control is helpful in avoiding overstocking and understocking of materials in storeroom. The stock levels are fixed by the management and it is the duty of storekeeper to observe them. The various stock levels commonly fixed are as follows :

(*a*) ***Maximum level :*** It is the level beyond which storage of raw materials are not allowed to go. The main purpose of this level is to avoid blocking up of capital unnecessarily on materials. The following factors guide in fixing up this level :

(*i*) Rate of consumption of materials.

(*ii*) Time necessary to obtain new supplies.

(*iii*) Finance—if stocks are unnecessarily high, capital is locked up which could probably be otherwise employed.

(*iv*) Storage cost.

(*v*) Possibility of loss by evaporation, deterioration, etc.

(*vi*) Extent to which price fluctuates.

(*vii*) Risk of changing specification and obsolescence.

(*viii*) Seasonal considerations as to both price and availability of supplies.

(*ix*) Economic order quantity.

(*x*) Rules framed by the government for importing raw materials.

(*b*) ***Minimum level :*** It is the level below which materials should not be allowed to fall. This level serves as safety stock and is not generally used for issue purposes. As soon as this level is reached it indicates the possibility of stoppage in production unless quick arrangement is made for further purchases of materials. Hence the storekeeper and purchase manager have to give topmost priority for the acquisition of new supplies. The following factors are to be considered while fixing up this level :

(*i*) Rate of consumption of the materials.

(*ii*) Time necessary to obtain delivery of materials.

(*iii*) Nature of materials, for example for purchase of special materials against customer's specific order, no minimum level is necessary.

(*c*) ***Danger level :*** This level is fixed in between minimum level and nil stock or zero stock. This level is fixed for such types of materials which are used against more than one order or product. As and when this level is reached the storekeeper normally does not issue materials unless authorised by the production control department as to which job or product is to get the priority for the use of these items. This level is particularly fixed to control materials during the period of emergencey so that urgent and priority orders are not held up.

(*d*) ***Reorder level :*** This is the level on reaching of which a fresh order is prepared and placed with a supplier. This level is fixed in between maximum level and minimum level. This level is fixed after considering the following factors :

(*i*) Maximum usage
(*ii*) Delivery Time
(*iii*) Rate of consumption
(*iv*) Economic order quantity.

Lead Time and Delivery Time

In connection with fixation of various levels for materials, the term 'lead time' refers to the time required for the whole procurement procedure and delivery time refers to the period which is required for execution of orders by the suppliers, i.e., from the time the order reaches the supplier till the commodities are despatched to the purchaser.

Problem 4 : Compute various stock levels from the following data :

Normal consumption	300 Units per day
Maximum consumption	420 Units per day
Minimum consumption	240 Units per day
Reorder quantity	3,600 Units
Reorder period	10 to 15 days
Normal reorder period	12 days

(*Nagarjuna University, M.Com., March 1992*)

Solution :

Reorder level = Maximum usage × Maximum reorder period
= 420 × 15 = 6,300 units

Minimum level = Reorder level – (Normal usage × Normal reorder period)
= 6,300 – (300 × 12)
= 6,300 – 3,600 = 2,700 units

Maximum level = (Reorder level + Reorder quantity) – (Minimum usage × Minimum reorder period)
= (6,300 + 3,600) – (240 × 10)
= 9,900 – 2,400 = 7,500 units

$$\text{Average stock level} = \frac{\text{Minimum level} + \text{Maximum level}}{2}$$

$$= \frac{2,700 + 7,500}{2}$$

$$= \frac{10,200}{2} = 5,100 \text{ units}$$

Problem 5 : Calculate Reorder level, minimum stock level, maximum stock level and average stock level from the following information :

Normal usage	—	300 Units per week
Maximum usage	—	450 Units per week
Minimum usage	—	150 Units per week
Reorder period	—	4 to 6 weeks
Reorder quantity	—	2,400 Units

(*University of Madras, B.Com., March 1997*)

Solution :

(1) Reorder level = Maximum usage × Maximum Reorder period
= 450 × 6 = 2,700 Units per week

(2) Minimum stock level = Reorder level – (Normal usage × Normal Reorder period)
= 2,700 – (300 × 5)
= 2,700 – 1500 = 1,200 Units per week

(3) Maximum Stock level = (Reorder level + Reorder quantity) – (Minimum usage × minimum reorder period)
= (2,700 + 2,400) – (150 × 4)
= 5,100 – 600 = 4,500 Units per week

(4) Average stock level = Minimum level + $\frac{1}{2}$ (Reorder Quantity)
= 1,200 + $\frac{1}{2}$ × 2,400
= 1,200 + 1,200 = 2,400 Units per week

Problem 6 : Two components A and B are used as follows :

(*a*) Reorder quantity :
A : 3,000 units
B : 4,000 units

(*b*) Reorder period
A : 4 to 6 weeks
B : 2 to 4 weeks

(*c*) Normal usage : 3,000 units per week each

(*d*) Minimum usage : 1,500 units per week each

(*e*) Maximum usage : 4,500 units per week each

You are required to calculate for each of the component (1) Reorder level, (2) Minimum level, (3) Maximum level, (4) Average stock level.

(*Sri Venkateshwara University, B.Com., April 1998*)

Solution :

(1) Reorder level = Maximum usage × Maximum reorder period
A = 4,500 × 6 = 27,000 Units per week
B = 4,500 × 4 = 18,000 Units per week

(2) Minimum level = Reorder level – (Normal usage × Average reorder period)
A = 27,000 – (3,000 × 5)
= 27,000 – 15,000 = 12,000 Units per week
B = (18,000 – (3,000 × 3) = 9000 units

(3) Maximum level = (Reorder level + Reorder quantity) – (Minimum usage × Manimum reorder period)
A = (27,000 + 3,000) – (1,500 × 4)
= 30,000 – 6,000 = 24,000 Units per week
B = (18,000 + 3,000) – (1,500 × 2)
= 21,000 – 3,000 + 18,000 Units per week

(4) Average stock level = $\frac{\text{Minimum level + Maximum level}}{2}$

A = $\frac{12,000+24,000}{2} = \frac{36,000}{2}$ = 18,000 units per week

B = $\frac{9,000+18,000}{2} = \frac{27,000}{2}$ = 13,500 Units per week

Problem 7 : Kerala Producers furnish the following information regarding the requirements of material x, y and z in their production activity.

Raw materials	*Usage per unit of production (kgs)*	*Reorder quantity (kgs)*	*Price per kg (Rs.)*	*Delivery period (Weeks)*	*Order level (kg)*	*Minimum level (kg)*
X	20	20,000	1.00	1 to 3	1,6000	-
Y	8	10,000	3.00	3 to 5	9,500	-
Z	12	20,000	1.50	2 to 4	-	4,000

Weekly production various from 350 to 450 units averaging to 400 units. What would you expect the quantities of the following to be :

(*a*) Minimum stock level of x
(*b*) Maximum stock level of y
(*c*) Reorder stock level of z
(*d*) Average stock level of x

(*Calicut University, M.Com., April 1992*)

Solution :

(*a*) Minimum level of *x* = Reorder level – (Average usage × Average delivery period)
= 16,000 – (400 × 20 × 2)
= 16,000 – 16,000 = 0

(*b*) Maximum level of y = (Reorder level + Reorder quantity) – (Minimum usage × Minimum reorder period)
= (9,500 + 10,000) – (350 × 8 × 3)
= 19,500 – 8,400 = 11,100 units

(*c*) Reorder level of z = Maximum usage × Maximum reorder period
= 450 × 12 × 4 = 21,600 units

(*d*) Average stock level of *x* = Minimum level + $\frac{1}{2}$ Reorder quantity
= $0 + \frac{1}{2} \times 20{,}000 = 10{,}000$ units

Problem 8 : The following particulars are furnished by Kiran Stamping Ltd :

Month	*Budget consumption (in units)*	*Month*	*Budget consumption (in units)*
2000 Jan.	300	July	1,000
2000 Feb.	300	Aug.	1,000
2000 Mar.	500	Sept.	1,000
2000 Apr.	600	Oct.	900
2000 May	800	Nov.	600
2000 June	1,000	Dec.	400

Delivery period : 2 to 4 months
Reorder quantity : 1,000 units
Calculate : (1) Maximum level, (2) Minimum level, (3) Reorder level, (4) Average stock level using reorder quantity.

Solution :

(1) Reorder levei = Maximum consumption × Maximum delivery period
= 1,000 × 4 = 4,000 units

(2) Minimum level = Reorder level – (Normal usage × Average reorder period)
= 4,000 – (700 × 3)
= 4,000 – 2,100 = 1,900 units

(3) Maximum level = (Reorder level + Reorder quantity) – (Minimum usage × Minimum reorder period)
= (4,000 + 1,000) – (300 × 2)
= 5,000 – 600 = 4,400 units

(4) Average stock level = Minimum level + $\frac{1}{2}$ reorder quantity
= 1,900 + $\frac{1}{2}$ × 1,000
= 1,900 + 500 = 2,400 units

Working note : Normal usage is calculated by the following formula :

$$\frac{\text{Total consumption per year}}{\text{Number of months in the year}} = \frac{8,400}{12} = 700 \text{ units.}$$

Problem 9 : From the following information calculte the four important levels of stocks :

(*a*)	Average Delivery time	=	20 days
(*b*)	Maximum delivery time	=	30 days
(*c*)	Minimum delivery period	=	15 days
(*d*)	Maximum delivery period for emergency purchase	=	5 days
(*e*)	Average rate of consumption per day	=	25 units
(*f*)	Maximum rate of consumption	=	35 units per day
(*g*)	Minimum rate of consumption	=	14 units per day
(*h*)	Standard ordering quantity	=	600 units

Solution :

(1) Reorder level = Maximum usage × Maximum reorder period
= 35 × 30 = 1,050 units

(2) Minimum level = Reorder level – (Normal usage × Average reorder period)
= 1,050 – (25 × 20)
= 1,050 – 500 = 550 units

(3) Maximum level = (Reorder level + reorder quantity) – (Minimum usage × Minimum reorder period)
= (1,050 + 600) – (14 × 15)
= 1,650 – 210 = 1,440 units

(4) Danger level = Average usage × Maximum reorder period for emergency purchase
= 25 × 5 = 125 units

Problem 10 : It the minimum stock level and average stock level of raw-material A are 4,000 and 9,000 units respectively, find out its 'Reorder quantity'.

Solution :

Minimum stock level of Material A = 4,000 units
Average stock level of material A = 9,000 units

Average stock level = Minimum level + $\frac{1}{2}$ reorder quantity

or $\frac{1}{2}$ Reorder quantity = 9,000 – 4,000 units

or Reorder quantity = 5,000 × 2
= 10,000 units

3. Economic Order Quantity (EOQ)

This technique of material control helps in deciding the purchase of most favourable quantity of materials when fresh supplies are required. One of the problems encountered by the purchase manager at the time of preparing a purchase order is deciding about the quantity of materials to be ordered. The quantity of materials to be ordered at a time is affected by two conflicting cost, termed as "Ordering cost" and "Cost of carrying the inventory". The important components of these are outlined below :

Ordering cost : Ordering cost can be again classified into (*i*) Fixed ordering cost and (*ii*) Variable ordering cost. Examples of fixed ordering costs are salaries of staff, establishment cost, rent and unalterable services in running the department. However fixed ordering cost does not affect the quantity of materials to be ordered. It is the variable ordering cost that affect the quantity of materials that is to be ordered. The examples of variable ordering costs are : cost of documents, postage and stationery, cost of follow-up, telephone and telegram expenses, etc. The fact to be underlined at this stage is that smaller the quantities ordered more frequently, larger is the ordering cost and *vice versa*. Again if a small order is placed at a time, the benefits arising out of large scale purchases such as trade discount, cash discount, free home delivery services, exchange facilities, credit facilities, after sales services cannot be derived.

Cost of carrying the inventory: The important components of carrying cost can be enumerated as under :

(*a*) *Investment cost* : This include the cost of foregone liquidity, interest on borrowed capital and the opportunity cost of investment.

(*b*) *Storage cost* : This include rent, salary of watch and ward staff, electricity charges, maintenance expenses of store room and handling and equipment costs.

(*c*) *Wastage cost* : This include deterioration and damages, obsolescence and handling losses.

(*d*) *Miscellaneous cost* : This include insurance, pilferage, etc.

In addition to the above costs, the following costs also affect the determination of EOQ.

(a) Stock-out cost or outage cost. Such costs are incurred to make product continue without interruptions. Whenever the usual type of materials are not readily available, often a suitable material which may be quite expensive or an inferior quality of materials are bought. Stock-out cost includes the additional cost of an expensive substitute, delayed production cost and customer's dissatisfaction owing to the use of inferior item. If customers reject such goods the cost of waste product is also treated as stock-out cost.

(b) Systemic cost : This type of cost arises from stock-out cost. They include additional cost of emergency purchases such as higher rates, increased transportation costs, cost of job rescheduling, set-up cost, etc.

The cost of carrying inventory will be less when the quantity of materials bought is also less and *vice versa*. Therefore EOQ is a problem of balancing the two conflicting kinds of cost, *i.e.* the cost of ordering and cost of carrying the inventory. The EOQ is taken at that level where the total cost of purchases must be lowest which is possible when the cost of ordering is equal to cost of carrying the inventory. The following formula is used to calculate economic order quantity :

$$EOQ = \sqrt{\frac{2AB}{CS}}$$

where,

A = Annual usage

B = Buying cost per order or ordering cost per order

C = Cost per unit

S = Storage cost or the cost of carrying the inventory.

Problem 11 : The annual demand for a product is 6,400 units. The unit cost is Rs. 6 and inventory carrying cost per unit per annum is 25% of the average inventory cost. If the cost of procurement is Rs. 75. Determine :

(*i*) economic order quantity (E O Q)
(*ii*) number of orders per annum and
(*iii*) time between two consecutive orders

(*C.S. Inter, December 1998*)

Solution :

(*i*) E. O. Q. $= \sqrt{\dfrac{2AB}{CS}}$

$$= \sqrt{\dfrac{2 \times 6,400 \times 75}{6 \times \dfrac{25}{100}}}$$

$$= \sqrt{\dfrac{2 \times 6,400 \times 75 \times 100}{6 \times 25}}$$

$=$ **800 units**

(*ii*) Number of orders per annum :

$$= \frac{\text{Annual usage}}{\text{EOQ}} = \frac{6,400}{800} = 8 \text{ orders}$$

(*iii*) Time between two orders

$$= \frac{\text{Number of months in a year}}{\text{Number of orders}}$$

$$= \frac{12 \text{ months}}{8 \text{ orders}} = 1.5 \text{ months}$$

Problem 12 : ABC company buy in lots of 125 boxes which is a three months supply. The cost per box is Rs. 125 and the ordering cost is Rs. 250 per order. The inventory carrying cost is estimated at 20% of unit value per annum. You are required to as certain.

(*i*) What is the total annual cost of the existing inventory policy?
(*ii*) How much money would be saved by employing the economic order quantity (E O Q)?

(*C.S. Inter, Dec. 1999*)

Solution :

E O Q $= \sqrt{\dfrac{2AB}{CS}}$

$$= \sqrt{\dfrac{2 \times (125 \times 4) \times 250}{125 \times \dfrac{20}{100}}}$$

$$= \sqrt{\dfrac{2 \times 500 \times 250 \times 100}{125 \times 20}}$$

$$= \sqrt{1,00,000}$$

$=$ 100 units

Statement showing annual cost of existing policy :

Cost of purchase		
125 × 4 × 125	=	62,500
ordering cost 4 orders		
each costing Rs. 250	=	1,000

Average Inventory cost = 1562.50

$125 \times 125 \times \frac{20}{100} \times \frac{1}{2}$

= 65062.50

Statement showing annual cost with E O Q

Cost of purchase	=	62,500
ordering cost 5 orders each costing Rs. 250	=	1,250
Average Inventory cost $100 \times 125 \times \frac{20}{100} \times \frac{1}{2}$	=	1,250
	=	65,000

Hence Savings = 65,062.50 – 65,000 = Rs. 62.50

Problem 13 : The complete gardner is deciding on the economic order quantity for two brands of lawn fertilizer : Super Grow and Native's own. The following information is collected :

	Fertilizer	
	Super Grow	Native's own
Annual Demand	2,000 bags	1,280 bags
Relevart ordering cost per purchase order	Rs. 1,200	Rs. 1400
Annual relevant carrying cost per bag	Rs. 480	Rs. 560

Required :

(*i*) Compute E O Q for super grow and native's own.

(*ii*) For the E O Q, what is the sum of the total annual relevant ordering costs and total annual relevant carrying costs for super grow and native's own?

(*iii*) For the E O Q compute the number of deliveries per year for super grow and native's own.

(*C.A., Inter, November 1999*)

Solution :

(i) E O Q $= \sqrt{\frac{2AB}{CS}}$

Super Grow Fertilizer $= \sqrt{\frac{2 \times 2{,}000 \times 1{,}200}{480}}$

$= \sqrt{10{,}000}$

= 100 bags

Native's own fertilizer $= \sqrt{\frac{2 \times 1{,}280 \times 1{,}400}{560}}$

= 80 bags

(ii) **Total annual relevant costs for super grow fertilizer :**

= Total annual ordering cost + Total annual carrying cost

$= \frac{\text{Annual Demand}}{\text{EOQ}} \times \text{ordering cost} + \frac{1}{2}\text{ E O Q} \times \text{Cost of carrying}$

$= \frac{2{,}000}{100} \times 1{,}200 + \frac{1}{2} \times 100 \times 480$

= 24,000 + 24,000

= Rs. 48,000

Total annual relevant costs for native's own fertilizer :

$$= \frac{1,280}{80} \times 1,400 + \frac{1}{2} \times 80 \times 560$$

$$= 22,400 + 22,400$$

$$= \text{Rs. } 44,800$$

(iii) Number of deliveries (i.e. orders)

$$= \frac{\text{Annual Usage}}{\text{EOQ}}$$

Super grow $= \frac{2000}{100} = 20$ orders

Native's own $= \frac{1280}{80} = 16$ orders

Problem 14 : G Ltd, produces a product which has a monthly demand of 4,000 units. The product requires a component x which is purchased at Rs. 20. For every finished product, one unit of component is required. The ordering cost is Rs. 120 per order and the holding cost is 10% per annum.

You are required to calculate :

(i) Economic order quantity.

(ii) If the minimum lot size to be supplied is 4,000 units. What is the extra cost, the company has to incur?

(iii) What is the minimum carrying cost the company has to incur? *(C.A. Inter, May 1999)*

Solution :

(a) E O Q $= \frac{\sqrt{2AB}}{CS}$

$$= \sqrt{\frac{2 \times 48,000 \times 100}{20 \times \frac{10}{100}}}$$

= 2,400 units

(b) **Extra cost incurred by the company :**

Total cost (where order size is 4,000 units) = Total ordering cost + Total Carrying cost

$$\frac{\text{Annual Demand}}{\text{Order size}} \times \text{Ordering cost} + \frac{1}{2}\text{order size} \times \text{cost of carrying}$$

$$= \frac{48,000}{4,000} \times 120 + \frac{1}{2} \times 4,000 \times 20 \times \frac{10}{100}$$

$$= 1,440 + 4,000$$

$$= \text{Rs. } 5,440 \quad \text{(a)}$$

Total cost (when order size is 2400) $= \frac{48,000}{2,400} \times 120 + \frac{1}{2} \times 2,400 \times 20 \times \frac{10}{100}$

$= 2,400 + 2,400$

$= \text{Rs. } 4,800$ (b)

Extra cost $= (a - b)$

$= 5,440 - 4,800 = \text{Rs. } 640$

(iii) Minimum Carrying Cost :

Carrying Cost depends upon the size of the order. It will be minimum on the least order size. In this problem the two orders are 2,400 units and 4,000 units. Here 2,400 units is the least of the two order sizes. At this order size, carrying cost will be minimum.

The minimum carrying cost in this case can be computed as under :

$$= \frac{1}{2} \times 2,400 \times 20 \times \frac{10}{100} = \text{Rs. } 2,400$$

Problem 15 : A publishing house purchase 2,000 units of a particular item per year at unit cost of Rs. 20, the ordering cost per order is Rs. 50 and the inventory ordering cost is 25%. Find the optiomal order quantity and the minimum total cost including purchase cost.

If a 3% discount is offered by the supplier for purchase in lots of 1,000 or more, should the publishing house accept the order? *(C.S. Inter, December 1996)*

Solution : E O Q without discount :

$$\text{E O Q} = \sqrt{\frac{2AB}{CS}}$$

$$= \sqrt{\frac{2 \times 2{,}000 \times 50}{20 \times \frac{25}{100}}}$$

$$= \sqrt{\frac{2 \times 2{,}000 \times 50 \times 100}{20 \times 25}}$$

$$= 200 \text{ units}$$

$$\text{Number of orders to be placed} = \frac{\text{Annual purchase}}{\text{EOQ}}$$

$$= \frac{2{,}000}{200} = 10 \text{ orders}$$

Total cost of purchase without discount

Purchase cost – 2000 units @ Rs. 20	40,000
ordering cost – 10 orders @ Rs. 50	500
carrying cost of average inventory	
Average Inventory $= \frac{200}{2} = 100$ units	
Cost of Carrying per unit	
$\frac{25}{100} \times 20 = \text{Rs. } 5$	
for 100 units @ Rs. 5 per unit	500
	Rs. 41,000

Total cost of purchase with discount

Purchase cost – 2000 units @ Rs. 19.40 (20 – 3% of 20)	= 38,800
Ordering cost – Number of order is 2 $\left(i.e., \frac{2{,}000}{1{,}000}\right)$ @ Rs. 50	= 100
carrying cost of average Inventory	
Average Inventory = 500 units $\left(i.e., \frac{1{,}000}{2}\right)$	
carrying cost $\frac{25}{100} \times 19.40 = 4.85$	
for 500 units @ Rs. 4.85	= 2,425
	41,325

Problem 16 : From the following particulars find out

(a) how much should be ordered each time

(b) when should the order be placed and

(c) what should be the inventory level immediately before the material order is received?

Annual Consumption = 12,000 units (360 days)

Cost per unit	=	Re. 1
ordering cost	=	12 per order
Inventory carrying charge	=	24 %
Normal lead time	=	15 days
Safety stock	=	30 days consumption

(Bangalore University, M.Com., May 1989)

Solution :

(i) E O Q $= \sqrt{\dfrac{2AB}{CS}}$

$$= \sqrt{\dfrac{2 \times 12{,}000 \times 12}{1 \times \dfrac{24}{100}}}$$

$$= \sqrt{\dfrac{2 \times 12{,}000 \times 12 \times 100}{1 \times 24}}$$

$$= \sqrt{12{,}00{,}000} \quad = 1{,}095 \text{ units}$$

(ii) Time of placing the order :

For 12,000 units the period is 12 months (360 days)

For 1,095 units ? $\dfrac{1{,}095}{12{,}000} \times 12$

= 1.095 months

or 33 days

(iii) Inventory level before the order is received :

(Delivery period × normal usage) + safety stock

$$\left(15 \text{ days} \times \frac{12{,}000}{360}\right) + 1{,}000 \text{ (see note)}$$

= 15 × 33.34 + 1,000

= 500 + 1,000 = 1,500

Working note :

For 360 days safety stock is 12,000

For 30 days → $= \dfrac{12{,}000 \times 30}{360} \quad = \quad 1{,}000$ units

Problem 17 : Following information relating to a type of raw material is available

Annual demand	2,400 units
Unit price	Rs. 2.40
Ordering cost per order	Rs. 4.00
Storage cost	2% per annum
Interest rate	10% per annum
Lead time	half month

Calculate E O Q and total annual inventory cost in respect of the particular material.

(Sri Sathya Sai University, B.Com (Hons) August 2000)

Solution :

(*i*) E O Q $= \sqrt{\dfrac{2AB}{CS}}$

$$= \sqrt{\dfrac{2 \times 2{,}400 \times 4}{2.40 \times \dfrac{(10+2)}{100}}}$$

$$= \sqrt{\dfrac{2 \times 2{,}400 \times 4}{2.40 \times \dfrac{(12)}{100}}}$$

$$= \sqrt{\frac{19,200}{0.288}} = 258 \text{ units}$$

Calculation of total Annual Inventory cost :

Cost of 2,400 units @ Rs. 2.40	5,760.00
ordering cost = $\frac{2,400}{258}$ = 9.3 orders	
or say 10 orders @ Rs. 4	40.00
carrying cost of average inventory	
$\frac{285}{258} \times 2.40 \times \frac{1}{2} \times \frac{12}{100}$	37.15
	5,837.15

Problem 18 : Exe Ltd. has received an offer of quantity discount in its order of materials as under :

Price per ton (Rs.)	*Tones*
1,200	less then 500
1,180	500 and less then 1,000
1,160	1,000 and less then 2,000
1,140	2,000 and less then 3,000
1,120	3,000 and above

The annual requirements for materials is 5,000 tonnes. The ordering cost per order is Rs. 1,200 and the stock holding cost is estimated at 20% of materials cost per annuam. You are required to compute the most economical purchase level.

What will be your answer to the above question if there are no discounts offered and the price per tonne is Rs. 1,500 ? *(CA. Inter, November 1990)*

Solution :

E O Q with discount

Ordering Qty. (tonnes) Q	*Price per ton (Rs.) P*	*Cost of purchasing 5,000 tonnes (Rs.)*	*Cost of ordering (Rs)*	*Cost of carrying average inventory*	*Total cost (Rs.)*
		5,000 × P	$\frac{5,000}{Q} \times 1,200$	$\frac{Q}{2} \times P \times 20\%$	
400	1,200	60,00,000	15,000	48,000	60,63,000
500	1,180	59,00,000	12,000	59,000	59,71,000
1,000	1,160	58,00,000	6,000	1,16,000	59,22,000
2,000	1,140	57,00,000	3,000	2,28,000	59,31,000
3,000	1,120	56,00,000	2,000	3,36,000	59,38,000

From the above table it is clear that the most economical purchase level is at 1000 ordering quantity in tonnes. Because it is at this level that total cost. i.e., cost of ordering and cost of carrying inventory is minimum.

E O Q without discount and when the price is Rs. 1,500 per tonne :

$$EOQ = \sqrt{\frac{2AB}{CS}}$$

$$= \sqrt{\frac{2 \times 5,000 \times 1,200}{1,500 \times \frac{20}{100}}}$$

$$= \sqrt{\frac{2 \times 5,000 \times 1,200 \times 100}{1,500 \times 20}}$$

$$= \sqrt{40,000}$$

$$= 200 \text{ units}$$

Problem 19 : Anil company buys its annual requirement of 36,000 units in 6 instalments. Each unit cost Re. 1 and the ordering cost is Rs. 25. The inventory carrying cost is estimated of 20% of unit value. Find the total annual cost of the existing inventory policy. How much money can be saved by economic order quantity? *(C.A. Final, May 1986)*

$$\text{E O Q} = \sqrt{\frac{2AB}{CS}}$$

$$= \sqrt{\frac{2 \times 36,000 \times 25}{1 \times \frac{20}{100}}}$$

$$= \sqrt{\frac{2 \times 36,000 \times 25 \times 100}{1 \times 20}}$$

$$= \sqrt{90,00,000} = 3000 \text{ units}$$

Statement showing annual cost of the existing policy :

Cost of purchase	=	36,000
ordering cost – $\frac{36,000}{6,000}$ = 6 orders @ Rs. 25 per order	=	150
carrying cost – 6,000 × 1 × $\frac{1}{2}$ × $\frac{20}{100}$	=	600
Total cost		36,750

Statement showing annual cost with E O Q

Cost of Purchase	=	36,000
Ordering cost – $\frac{36,000}{3,000}$ = 12 ordrs @ Rs. 25	=	300
carrying cost – 3,000 × 1 × $\frac{1}{2}$ × $\frac{20}{100}$	=	300
Total cost		36,600

Problem 20 : (Problem on Level Setting and EOQ)

The following data pertain to material x :

Supply period	4 to 8 months
Consumption rate :	
Maximum	600 units per month
Minimum	100 units per month
Normal	300 units per month
Yearly	3,600 units

Storage costs are 50% of stock value. Ordering costs are Rs. 400 per order. Price per unit of material Rs. 64. Compute :

(*i*) Reorder level

(*ii*) Minimum stock level

(*iii*) Maximum stock level
(*iv*) Average stock level

(*University of Delhi, B.Com. (Pass), April 1999*)

Solution :

(1) Reorder level = Maximum usage × Maximum reorder period
= 600 × 8 = 4,800 units

(2) Minimum stock level = Reorder level – (Normal usage × Normal reorder period)
= 4,800 – (300 × 6)
= 4,800 – 1,800 = 3,000 units

Note : Normal reorder period is the average reorder period i.e., $\frac{4+8}{2} = 6$ months

(3) Maximum stock level = (Reorder level + Reorder quantity) –
(Minimum consumption × Minimum reorder period)
= 4,800 + 300) – (100 × 4)
= 5,100 – 400 = 4700 units

Note : Reorder quantity or E O Q $= \sqrt{\frac{2AB}{CS}}$

$$= \sqrt{\frac{2 \times 3,600 \times 400}{64 \times \frac{50}{100}}}$$

$$= \sqrt{\frac{2 \times 3,600 \times 400}{32}}$$

= 300 units

(4) Average stock level $= \frac{\text{Minimum stock level} + \text{Maximum stock level}}{2}$

$$= \frac{3,000 + 4,700}{2}$$

$$= \frac{7,700}{2} = \quad 3,850 \text{ units}$$

Problem 21 : Ace Ltd. manufactures a product and the following particulars are collected for the year ended March 2000.

Monthly demand (units)	1,000
Cost of placing on order (Rs.)	100
Annual carrying cost (Rs. per unit)	15
Normal usage (units per week)	50
Minimum usage (units per week)	25
Maximum usage (units per week)	75
Reorder period (weeks)	4–6

you are required to calculate :

(1) Reorder quantity
(2) Reorder level
(3) Minimum level
(4) Maximum level
(5) Average stock level

(*C.S., Inter, June, 2000*)

Solution :

(*i*) Reorder quantity $= \sqrt{\frac{2AB}{S}}$

$$= \sqrt{\frac{2 \times 2,600 \times 100}{15}}$$

= 186 units

Note : Since normal usage is 50 units per week the annual consumption for the year is— 52 weeks × 50 = 2,600 units

(*ii*) Reorder level = Maximum usage × Maximum delivery period
= 75 × 6 = 450 units per week

(*iii*) Minimum level = Reorder level – (Normal usage × Average delivery period)
= 450 – (50×5)
= 450 – 250 = 200 units per week

(*iv*) Maximum level = (Reorder level + Reorder Qty.) – (Minimum usage × Minimum delivery period)
= (450 + 186) – (25 × 4) = 536 units per week

(*v*) Average stock $= \frac{\text{Minimum level} + \text{Maximum level}}{2}$

$= \frac{200+536}{2}$ = 368 units per week

Note : Alternatively, since the monthly demand given in the problem is 1000 units it can be presumed that the annual consumption would be 12000 units. Then the answers would be changed accordingly as regards (*i*) Reorder quantity, (*ii*) Maximum level and (*iii*) Average stock level.

Problem 22 : Shagoon India Ltd. provides the following information in respect of material 'x'

Supply period	:	5 to 15 days
Rate of consumption	:	
Average	:	15 units per day
Maximum	:	20 units per day
Yearly	:	5,000 units

ordering costs are Rs. 20 per order. Purchase price per unit is Rs. 50. Storage costs are 10% of unit value compute :

(*i*) Reorder quantity
(*ii*) Reorder level
(*iii*) Miminum level
(*iv*) Maximum level

(*University of Delhi, B.Com. (Hons), April 1998*)

Solution :

(*i*) Reorder quantity $= \sqrt{\frac{2AB}{CS}}$

$$= \sqrt{\frac{2 \times 5,000 \times 20}{50 \times \frac{10}{100}}}$$

$$= \sqrt{\frac{2 \times 5,000 \times 20 \times 100}{50 \times 10}}$$

= 200 units

(*ii*) Reorder level = Maximum consumption × Maximum delivery period
= 20 × 15 = 300 units

(*iii*) Minimum level = Reorder level – (Normal consumption × Normal delivery period)
= 300 – (15 × 10)
= 300 – 150 = 150 units

(*iv*) Maximum level = (Reorder level + Reorder Qty.) – (Minimum consumption × Minimum delivery period)
= (300 + 200) – 10 × 5)
= 500 – 50 = 450 units

Problem 23 : M/s Tubes Ltd. are the manufactures of picture tubes for T.V. The following are the details of their operation during 1997 :

Average monthly market demand	2000 tubes
Ordering cost	Rs. 100 per order
Inventory carrying cost	20% per annum
Cost of tubes	Rs. 500 per tube
Normal usage	100 tubes per week
Minimum usage	50 tubes per week
Maximum usage	200 tubes per week
Lead time to supply	6-8 weeks

Compute from the above

(1) Economic order quantity. If the supplier is willing to supply quarterly 1,500 units at a discount of 5% is it worth accepting.

(2) Maximum level of stock

(3) Minimum level of stock

(4) Reorder level

(*C.A. Inter, May 1998*)

Solution :

(*i*) E O Q $= \sqrt{\dfrac{2AB}{CS}}$

$= \sqrt{\dfrac{2 \times 5{,}200 \times 100}{500 \times \dfrac{20}{100}}}$

$=$ 102 tubes

If the supplier is willing to supply 1,500 units at a discount of 5% is it worth accepting

Total cost (When order size is 1,500 units) = cost of 5,200 units + ordering cost + carrying cost

$= 5{,}200 \times 475 + \dfrac{5{,}200}{1{,}500} \times 100 + 1{,}500 \times \dfrac{1}{2} \times 475 \times \dfrac{20}{100}$

$= 24{,}70{,}000 + 346.67 + 71.250$

$= 25{,}41{,}596.67$

Total cost (when order size is 102 units) $= 5200 \times 500 + \dfrac{5{,}200}{102} \times 100 + 102 \times \dfrac{1}{2} \times 500 \times \dfrac{20}{100}$

$= 26{,}00{,}000 + 5{,}098.03 + 5{,}100$

$= 26{,}10{,}198.03$

Since, the total cost under quarterly supply of 1,500 units with 5% discount is lower than that when order size is 102 units, therefore the offer should be accepted. While accepting this offer consideration of capital blocked on order size of 1,500 units per quarter has been ignored

(2) Maximum level of stock = (Reorder level + Reorder quantity) – (Minimum usage × Minimum reorder period)
= (1,600 + 102) – (50 × 6)
= 1,402 units

(3) Minimum level = Reorder level – (Normal usage × Average reorder period)
= 1,600 – (100 × 7)
= 900 units

(4) Reorder level = Maximum usage × Maximum reorder period
= 200 × 8
= 1,600 units

4. Inventory Turnover Ratio or Material Turnover Ratio

Inventory turnover ratio as a technique of material control is useful to avoid unnecessary investment on those materials whose consumption is much less. In addition to this, it also helps to avoid obsolescence of stock and incurring of unnecessary storage costs. It may be defined as the ratio of cost of materials consumed to the average stock held during the period. Expressed in the form of formula,

$$\text{Inventory turnover ratio} = \frac{\text{Cost of materials consumed during the period}}{\text{Average stock of materials during the period}}$$

Inventory turnover may be denoted in terms of number of days in which the average inventory is consumed. This is obtained by using the following formula :

$$\text{Inventory turnover ratio in terms of days} = \frac{\text{365 days}}{\text{Inventory turnover ratio}}$$

In this case, if the duration of the inventory turnover period is short (than the anticipated period), material is said to be fast moving.

Whenever the consumption of different types of materials are analysed, it will be observed that not all materials are consumed in the same quantities. Some materials move fast while others are slow in their movement for consumption purposes. On the basis of rate of consumption of materials, the following categories of materials become evident.

(*a*) ***Slow-moving materials :*** Such materials have a low turnover ratio and hence they must not be stocked in excess quantites.

(*b*) ***Dormant materials :*** Materials which are currently not in demand for consumption purpose are regarded as dormant materials. Such materials should not be bought until the entire stock is made use of.

(*c*) ***Obsolete materials :*** Obsolete materials represent a kind of materials for which there is no longer a demand. This may be on account of the fact that the production of goods using this kind of materials must have been discontinued or a better substitute must have been found. The obsolete stock may be treated as scrap.

Problem 24 : The following information is available from the books of a company for the year ended 31st December 1990 :

	Material A (Rs.)	*Material B* (Rs.)
Opening stock	14,000	20,000
Purchases	2,30,000	36,000
Closing stock	10,000	24,000

Calculate the material turnover ratio of the above type of materials and determine which of the two materials is more fast moving.

(*University of Kerala, M.Com., May 1992*)

Solution :

Calculation of materials consumed

	Material A	*Material B*
Opening stock	14,000	20,000
Add : Purchases	2,30,000	36,000
	2,44,000	56,000
Less : Closing stock	10,000	24,000
Cost of material consumed	2,34,000	32,000

Calculation of average inventory

$$\frac{\text{Opening stock} + \text{Closing stock}}{2}$$

Material *A* $\quad \dfrac{14,000+10,000}{2} = 12,000$

Material *B* $\quad \dfrac{20,000+24,000}{2} = 22,000$

Calculation of inventory turnover ratio

$$\text{Inventory turnover ratio} = \frac{\text{Cost of materials consumed}}{\text{Average inventory}}$$

$$\text{Material } A = \frac{2,34,000}{12,000} = 19.5$$

$$\text{Material } B = \frac{32,000}{22,000} = 1.4$$

Material *A* is fast moving

Problem 25 : From the following data for the year ended 31st December 1986. Calculate the inventory ratio of the two items and put forward your comments on them.

	Material A (*Rs.*)	*Material B* (*Rs.*)
Opening stock on 1.1.1986	10,000	9,000
Purchase during the year	52,000	27,000
Closing stock on 31.12.1986	6,000	11,000

(*ICWA, Inter, Dec. 1987*)

Solution : **Calculation of materials consumed**

	Material A (*Rs.*)	*Material B* (*Rs.*)
Opening stock	10,000	9,000
Add : Purchases	52,000	27,000
	62,000	36,000
Less : Closing stock	6,000	11,000
Cost of materials consumed	56,000	25,000

Calculation of average inventory

$$\frac{\text{Opening stock} + \text{Closing stock}}{2}$$

$$\text{Material } A = \frac{10,000+6,000}{2} = \text{Rs. } 8,000$$

$$\text{Material } B = \frac{9,000+11,000}{2} = \text{Rs. } 10,000$$

$$\text{Inventory turnover ratio} = \frac{\text{Cost of materials consumed}}{\text{Average inventory}}$$

$$\text{Material A} = \frac{56,000}{8,000} = 7 \text{ times}$$

$$\text{Material B} = \frac{25,000}{10,000} = 2.5 \text{ times}$$

$$\text{Inventory turnover ratio in terms of number of days} = \frac{\text{Number of days in a year}}{\text{Inventory turnover ratio}}$$

$$\text{Material A} = \frac{365}{7} = 52 \text{ days}$$

$$\text{Material B} = \frac{365}{2.5} = 146 \text{ days}$$

Problem 26 : (Calculation of inventory turnover ratio when stock levels are given) : From the following particular calculate the inventory turnover ratio :

Minimum stock level	Rs. 1,000

Maxminum stock level	Rs. 3,000
Issues during the period	Rs. 10,000

Solution :

$$\text{Inventory turnover ratio} = \frac{\text{Cost of materials consumed during period}}{\frac{1}{2}(\text{Maximum level} + \text{Maximum stock level})}$$

$$= \frac{10,000}{\frac{1}{2}(3,000+1,000)} = 5 \text{ times}$$

Problem 27 : (Calculation of inventory turnover ratio when reorder quantity is given) : From the following particulars, calculate the inventory turnover ratio :

Maximum stock level	1,500 units
Minimum stock level	600 units
Reorder quantity	800 units
Issues during the year	4,000 units

Solution :

$$\text{Inventory turnover ratio} = \frac{\text{Cost of materials consumed during period}}{\text{Minimum level} + \frac{1}{2}\text{Recorder quantity}}$$

$$= \frac{4,000}{600+\frac{1}{2}\times 800} = 4 \text{ times}$$

Problem 28 : (*a*) From the following information available from the Bin Cards of a concern for the period of one year, calculate inventory ratios of materials *A*, *B* and *C*.

(*b*) If the prices of *A*, *B* and *C* be respectively Rs. 10 per unit, Rs. 8 per kg. and Rs. 5 per litre, then what is the total turnover of materials *A*, *B* and *C*?

(*c*) Find the period for which the average inventory in respect of each of *A*, *B* and *C* is held?

	Material A	*Material B*	*Material C*
Opening stock	7,000 units	2,000 kgs.	10,000 litres
Purchases	1,15,000 units	1,10,000 kgs.	12,000 litres
Closing stock	2,000 units	12,000 kgs.	18,000 litres

Solution :

(*a*) Inventory turnover ratio $= \frac{\text{Annual consumption of materials}}{\text{Average inventory}}$

Material *A* $= \frac{1,20,000}{4,500} = 26.67$

Material *B* $= \frac{1,00,000}{7,000} = 14.29$

Material *C* $= \frac{4,000}{14,000} = 0.29$

Note 1 : Annual consumption of material = Opening stock + Purchases – Closing stock.

Material *A*	= 7,000 + 1,15,000 – 2,000	=	1,20,000 units
Material *B*	= 2,000 + 1,10,000 – 12,000	=	1,00,000 kgs.
Material *C*	= 10,000 + 12,000 – 18,000	=	4,000 litres

Note 2 : Average inventory $= \frac{\text{Opening stock} + \text{Closing stock}}{2}$

$$\text{Material } A \quad = \frac{7,000+2,000}{2} \quad = 4,500 \text{ units}$$

$$\text{Material } B \quad = \frac{2,000+12,000}{2} \quad = 7,000 \text{ kgs.}$$

$$\text{Material } C \quad = \frac{10,000+18,000}{2} \quad = 14,000 \text{ litres}$$

$$(b) \text{ Total turnover of materials } A, B \,\&\, C = \frac{\text{Value of materials consumed during the year}}{\text{Value of average inventory}}$$

$$= \frac{20,20,000}{1,71,000} = 11.81$$

Note 3 **:** Value of materials consumed :

Material *A*	1,20,000 units @ Rs. 10	=	12,00,000
Material *B*	1,00,000 kgs. @ Rs. 8	=	8,00,000
Material *C*	4,000 litres @ Rs. 5	=	20,000
			20,20,000

Note 4 **:** Value of average inventory :

Material *A*	4,500 units @ Rs. 10	=	45,000
Material *B*	7,000 kgs @ Rs. 8	=	56,000
Material *C*	14,000 litres @ Rs. 5	=	70,000
			1,71,000

$$(c) \text{ Inventory turnover expressed in days} = \frac{\text{No. of days in the year}}{\text{Inventory turnover ratio}}$$

$$\text{Material } A \quad = \frac{365}{26.67} \quad = 14 \text{ days}$$

$$\text{Material } B \quad = \frac{365}{14.29} \quad = 26 \text{ days}$$

$$\text{Material } C \quad = \frac{365}{0.29} \quad = 1,259 \text{ days}$$

Problem 29 : The following data are available in respect of material 'x' for the year ended 31st March, 1997 :

	(Rs.)
Opening stock	90,000
Purchases during the year	2,70,000
Closing stock	1,10,000

Calculate (*i*) Inventory turnover ratio and, (*ii*) Number of days for which the average inventory is held.

(*C.A. Inter, November 1997*)

Solution :

Cost of materials consumed

	Opening stock of raw materials	90,000
Add :	Material purchased during the year	2,70,000
		3,60,000
Less :	Closing stock of raw materials	1,10,000
	Cost of raw materials consumed	2,50,000

Average stock of raw materials

$$= \frac{\text{Opening stock of raw materials} + \text{Closing stock of raw materials}}{2}$$

$$= \frac{90,000+1,10,000}{2}$$

$$= 1,00,000$$

(*i*) Inventory turnover ratio $= \dfrac{\text{Cost of raw materials consumed}}{\text{Average stock of raw materials}}$

$= \dfrac{2,50,000}{1,00,000} = 2.5$

(*ii*) Average number of days for which the average inventory is held $= \dfrac{365}{\text{Inventory Turnover Ratio}}$

$= \dfrac{365}{2.5} = 146 \text{ days}$

5. Stock Checking the Stock Taking

The term stock taking refers to the process of the verifying the quantity balances of the entire range of materials held in the storeroom. The term stock checking is used to denote verification of materials in terms of quantities which may be undertaken either regularly or intermittently. It is process of counting, weighing or measuring all items of materials and recording the results. Stock checking serves the following purposes :

(*a*) To verify the accuracy of stores records.

(*b*) To furnish value of closing stock to prepare final accounts of the enterprise.

(*c*) To disclose frauds, thefts and losses of materials.

(*d*) To reveal any weakness in the system of storage and control over materials.

Methods of stock taking : There are two method of stock taking, *viz.*, periodic or annual and continuous or perpetual.

1. ***Periodic or annual stock taking :*** Under this method the entire stock of materials are covered at the same time at the end of given period, which is ususally the end of the financial year. However in a large factory it may be impossible to do all the verification work in one day and hence it is extended over several days. Annual stock taking involves a great deal of preparation. Firstly a programme should be drawn up and it is agreed upon by all concerned. Secondly, stock verification sheets are to be prepared in advance. Thirdly, all personnel concerned must be instructed as to their duties. The following points are to be considered while conducting annual stock verification :

(*a*) Appoint one person to control the whole operation.

(*b*) While stock taking is in progress, do not open storeroom for issues and receipts.

(*c*) Consider for verification all normal stock of materials such as packages, scraps, residues and materials under inspection.

(*d*) The stock taking sheets must be under the control of one individiaul, consecutively numbered as issued to staff on duty as required.

(*e*) All damaged, deteriorated or used items must be recorded separately.

(*f*) Make each person taking stock responsible for a particular section or clearly defined area of the storeroom and record everything that is found in that area, Stock takers should proceed in an orderly manner and mark each bin or rack as it is dealt with to avoid the chance of checking any items twice and to ensure that nothing is missed.

(*g*) List separately materials received but still under inspection.

(*h*) Show the method of check, *i.e.*, count, weight, measurement on the stock sheet for each item.

(*i*) The method of pricing should be known and if possible, it is desirable to enter all prices in terms of units of issue on the stock sheets in advance.

(*j*) In case of decentralised store systems, the materials in transit at the date of stock taking must be taken into account.

Having verified the stock of materials, a stock verification report is to be prepared. A specimen form of such a report is given below :

ABC CO. LTD.

Stock Verification Report

Store Room No. .... Section .... Date of verification ....
Date of completion ....

Number of Items checked .... Number of items found incorrect ....

Code	*Description of materials*	*Physical balance*	*Book balance*	*Physical balance over or under book balance*	*Unit code*	*Remarks*

Physical count by .... Unit cost entered by ....
Checked by ....

Fig. 4.5. Stock verification report.

Disadvantages of Annual Stock Taking System :

(*a*) Under this system the factory has to be closed during the period of stock verification which results in the loss of production time.

(*b*) Some times a complete check on materials may not be exercised. Often those materials which are not used go unnoticed.

(*c*) It takes more time to verify the stock.

2. ***Continuous or perpetual inventory control :*** In its broad sense, it means a method of recording stores balance after every receipt and issue, to facilitate regular checking and to obviate closing down of factory for stock taking. Under this method the balance of materials as shown by the bin card and stores ledger card for the same item of materials is compared along with the actual quantity of materials in stock. The book balance and the physically verified balance must agree with each other. The discrepancy if any go to indicate the deficit in the materials for which prompt action is taken to avoid such defects.

Under this system, to verify the materials on a regular basis, a team may be constitituted which verifies the stock continuously throughout the year in accordance with a predetermined programme so that each item is physical verified at least once in the course of year or more frequently. The programme is so designed that a certain number of materials are taken on every working day and compared with the bin cards and the store ledger. Having verified the materials, a stores audit note is prepared. A specimen form of it is given below :

XYZ CO. LTD.

Store Audit Note

Note No. .... Bin No. ....

Items .... Location code ....

Code No. .... Date ....

Date of verification	*Actual stock*	*Bin card stock*	*Shortage*	*Surplus*	*Reasons*	*Adjustment*	*Remarks*

Stock .... Storekeeper .... Stores Accountant ....

Fig. 4.6. Stores audit note.

When the stock is incorrect, and enquiry is made and the discrepancies are adjusted in the records to make them correspond with the physical balance. A surplus or deficiency should be prevented. Deficiency in materials may arise out of malpractice in stores whereas a surplus may tend to introduce and encourage malpractice.

Causes for the discrepancies in the materials : The causes for the discrepancies in the materials may be analysed as shown in the following chart :

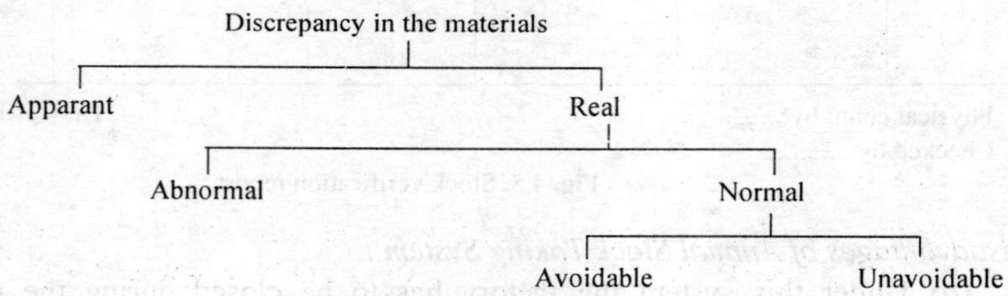

Fig. 4.7. Chart showing causes for discrepancies.

Apparant cause of discrepancy is owing to wrong entry in the bin card or because of wrong verification of materials. These discrepancies can be set right by correcting the bin card entries or by re-verifying the stock.

If the discrepancy is not because of the above reasons it is termed as 'real' discrepancy which requires further investigation.

The causes for abnormal discrepancies are due to occurence of fire, riot, burglary, etc. They are not within the reach of management. Hence they are written off as losses. Normal discrepancies are within the control of management and hence effective steps are to be taken to prevent them.

Avoidable discrepancies arise on account of (*i*) incorrect measurement of issues, (*ii*) carelessness in material handling, (*iii*) improper storage of materials and (*iv*) Pilferage. It is the duty of storekeeper to be vigilant on all these causes and is personally responsible for all surpluses and deficiencies arising out of avoidable causes.

Unavoidable deficiencies are caused by (*i*) handling losses arising out of issuing in small units, (*ii*) loss or gain arising out of atmospheric conditions. For example, evaporation in case of liquids and gain in weight on exposure to air in case of certain chemicals like caustic soda, (*iii*) gains arising out of seasoning of materials. Thought it is unavoidable, the control lies in foreseeing the nature of unavoidable causes, the extent of the differences that could arise out of these and to decide a proper method of treating them.

Advantages of Perpetual Inventory Control

The advantages of perpetual inventory system are as follows :

(*a*) The long and costly work of stock taking is avoided. The stock of materials as shown by the stores ledger can be obtained quickly for the preparation of final accounts at interim periods.

(*b*) A detailed and reliable check on the stores is obtained.

(*c*) It is not necessary to stop production during the period of stock verification.

(*d*) Discrepancies are readily located and appropriate measures can be taken to avoid their recurrence.

(*e*) It boosts the moral effect on the storekeeper and the practice of dishonesty can be curbed.

(*f*) It helps in avoiding the understocking and overstocking of materials and the dangers associated with them.

(*g*) It helps storekeeper in replenishment of stocks on item as he is always in touch with reorder level because of continuous stock taking.

(*h*) The investment in stock can be kept to the minimum in view of the operational requirements.

(*i*) It reveals the existence of surplus, dormant, obsolete and slow moving materials and hence remedial action can be taken.

Limitations

(*a*) The system is expensive and a small concern cannot afford to implement this system.

(*b*) The information about actual stock of a particular item on a particular day may not be available only book figures alone are available.

Differences between Periodic Stock Taking and Perpetual Inventory System

Periodic stock taking	*Perpetual inventory system*
1. Stock verification is done once in the year.	1. Stock verification is spread all over the year.
2. It is undertaken by technical staff.	2. It is undertaken by staff of accounts or the audit department.
3. Discrepancies are adjusted in one consolidated. figure.	3. Discrepancies are adjusted all over the year.
4. There is no secrecy about the items of materials to be verified.	4. Secrecy can be maintained as to the items and dates on which they are verified.
5. It involes closure of the factory during the period of stock verification.	5. It is carried out without affecting the stores and production departments.
6. Discrepancies are brought to the notice of management at the end of the year and hence it becomes too late to take corrective measures.	6. Discrepancies are brought to the notice of management as and when it is detected and hence immediate action can be taken.
7. It is suitable only for small sized concerns as it will be very expensive to have a con tinuous stock taking system.	7. It is suitable for large sized concern which can easily afford to incur expenses on this system.

Accounting of Surpluses and Shortages

1. Apparent discrepancies need no adjustment. The only thing to be done is to correct the bin card or to reverify the stock depending upon the circumstance.
2. Abnormal discrepancies are to be written off to costing profit and loss account.
3. Avoidable discrepancies should be valued and adjusted through the stores consumption account. The difference in the amount is recovered as an item of stores overhead.
4. Unavoidable discrepancies should be estimated in terms of percentages when materials are issued, the issue qnantities should be adjusted by this percentage.

Reconciliation between the Bin Card Balance, Stores Ledger Balance and the Physical Balance

Reconciliation is a three-tier process. They are :

(*a*) ***Reconciliation between physical balance of stores and bin card balances :*** If the physical balance of stores is less than the bin card balance, the shortage is to be entered in the issue column and the excess, should be entered in the receipt column in red ink.

(*b*) ***Reconciliation between bin card and stores ledger with respect to quantities :*** The differences can be avoided by writing the serial number of documents used in connection with recording the material transactions. Another method is by indicating the balance of stock in each and every material document after posting in the bin card. This facilitates automatic reconciliation at the time of posting in stores ledger card.

(*c*) ***Reconciliation between stores ledger and cost ledger in regard to value :*** Various transactions relating to materials such as receipts, issues, returns, shortages, excesses are valued, posted and journalised. The entries are posted in the cost ledger. The value of closing stock of all the stores ledger card should be equal to the value of closing stock in the cost ledger. Any differences should be corrected at regulat intervals.

Problem 30 : After the annual stock taking you come to know of some significant discrepancies between book stock and physical stock. You gather the following information :

Item	*Stock card (units)*	*Stores ledger (units)*	*Physical (units)*	*Cost per unit*
A	600	600	560	60
B	380	380	385	40
C	750	780	720	10

(*a*) What action should be taken to record the information shown above?

(*b*) Suggest reasons for the shortage and discrepancies above and recommend a possible course of action by management to prevent losses. (*C.A., Inter, May 1991*)

Solution :

(*a*) *The following action is to be taken to record the information given in the question :*

(*i*) Check the stock card and stores ledger and to record the correct physical quantities.

(*ii*) Investigate the causes for the losses or gains in the stock.

(*iii*) Once the causes are known, the following treatment is to be given :

(*a*) Factory overhead a/c *Dr.*
To stores ledger control a/c
(When the shortage is normal)

(*b*) Costing profit and loss a/c *Dr.*
To stores ledger control a/c
(When the shortage is abnormal)

(*c*) Work-in-progress a/c *Dr.*
To stores ledger control a/c
(When the shortage is due to non-recording or short-recording)

(*iv*) If there are any clerical errors rectification entries are to be passed.

(*v*) If there is any gain the following entries are required to be passed.

(*a*) Stores ledger a/c *Dr.*
To factory overhead a/c
(When the excess of stock is due to normal course)

(*b*) Stores ledger control a/c *Dr.*
To costing P & L a/c
(When the excess of stock is due to abnormal circumstances)

(*c*) Stores ledger control a/c *Dr.*
To work-in-progress
(When the excess of stock is due to wrong recording)

(*vi*) In the given problem, the losses are with reference to items *A* (Rs. 60 × 40 units = 2,400) and *C* (Rs. 10 × 60 = 600). As the reasons for these loses are not given, they may be debited to profit and loss a/c and stores ledger control a/c is credited accordingly.

(*vii*) The gains are in respect of stock item *B* (Rs. 40 × 5 = 200). This gain is debited to stores ledger control account and profit and loss account is credited.

(*b*) *Reasons for shortage and discrepancies :*

(i) Wastage of materials due to spoilage, evaporation, etc. which may be normal or abnormal.
(ii) Units issued for production without entering in stock card and stores ledger.
(iii) Theft.
(iv) Clerical errors.

Recommendations for preventing Future Losses :

(i) Only authorised persons should make entries.
(ii) Materials should be issed only against material requisition notes.
(iii) A system of internal check should be undertaken for all types of materials.
(iv) Materials are to be issued in the order of their receipts to avoid deterioration or obsolescence.
(v) Entries must be carefully made in both stores ledger card and stock card.

Problem 31 : In the course of physical verification of stores as on 31st March 1991, following differences are revealed in case of *AB* Ltd. :

Material	*Unit*	*Rate per unit (Rs.)*	*Balance Physical*	*Balance Ledger*	*Remarks*
A	Nos.	7,00	600	680	Wrong entry
B	Litres	12,00	1,100	1,155	Normal evaporation loss
C	Nos.	6,00	350	400	Material losses not accounted for
D	Kgs.	22.00	900	930	Shortage due to pilferage and theft
E	Nos.	15.00	1,475	1,325	150 Nos. received but not entered in ledger
F	Meters	10.00	291	291	Obsolete materials realised sale value Rs. 1,650 awaiting despatch.

Prepare journal entries in the cost ledger to give effects to the above adjustments as called for.

(*ICWA, Inter, June 1991*)

Solution :

Material A : No journal entry is required. The stock verification record should be altered to 680 numbers to match with the book balance which is the correct balance.

Material B :

Stores adjustment a/c	*Dr.*	660	
To stores ledger control a/c			660

(Being the adjustment of normal evaporation loss of material *B*, charged off to production overheads.)

Material C :

Work-in-progress control a/c	*Dr.*	300	
To stores ledger control a/c			300
(Being adjustment of issue of materials)			

Material D :

Costing profit & loss a/c	*Dr.*	660	
To stores ledger control a/c			660
(Being the abnormal loss of materials caused by theft charged P & L a/c)			

Material E :

Stores ledger control a/c	*Dr.*	2,250	
To general ledger control a/c			2,250
(Being entry for materials received not taken into stock)			

Material F :

General ledger adjustment a/c	*Dr.*	1,650	
Stores adjustment a/c	*Dr.*	1,260	
To stores ledger control a/c			2,910
(Being obsolete materials written off sale value transferred to general ledger)			

6. Input-output Ratio Analysis

This technique of material control is helpful in knowing the utility or usage of materials in manufacturing a finished product. It refers to the ratio of quantity of a material put in the manufacturing process to the quantity of the material in the finished product. Expressed in the form of a formula :

$$\text{Input-output ratio} = \frac{\text{Input quantity of materials}}{\text{Quantity of materials in the output}}$$

Very often this ratio is expressed in percentages. To know whether the input-output ratio is favourable or adverse a standard input-output ratio is determined. The acutal ratio is compared with the standard ratio. If the actual ratio is higher than the standard ratio, it denotes an inferior quality of materials or inefficiency in the manufacturing process. Accordingly the reasons may be traced and appropriated action is taken. This ratio helps in exercising control over scrap and wastages in the production.

Advantages

(*a*) It helps in knowing whether the usage of material is favourable or adverse.

(*b*) It helps in evaluating the efficiency of production department.

(*c*) It helps in knowing the cost of raw material in the finished product. This is calculated by multiplying cost per unit of the raw material by the input-output ratio.

Problem 32 : The pure chemical industry is using chemical *A* as its raw materials. This chemical costs Rs. 10 per kg. and its input-output ratio is 125 per cent. On account of scarcity of this material, the industry is forced to use one of the following alternative keeping in view, of course the quality of materials :

Material	*Rater per kg.*	*Input-output ratio*
Chemical *B*	Rs. 12	110%
Chemical *C*	Rs. 9	150%

Recommend which material is to be used.

Solution : In order to select the right type of substitute, it is necessary to calculate the cost of raw material in the finished product. The following formula is to be adopted.

$$\frac{\text{Input}}{\text{Output}} \times \text{rate per unit}$$

Chemical B $= \frac{110}{100} \times 12$ = Rs. 13.20 per kg.

Chemical C $= \frac{150}{100} \times 9$ = Rs. 13.50 per kg.

As the cost per kg. of chemical B is less it has to be preferred to chemical 'C'.

7. Classification and Codification of Materials

This technique of material control helps in easy identification of materials and in issuing them quickly to various production departments. Large factories involve purchase of varieties of materials in bulk quantities and they tend to mix up with other materials. Classification of materials prevents from mixing up of materials and in issuing them easily to various departments.

Classification of materials may be defined as a standardised arrangement of materials under a common designation according to its similarities, attributes or relations. Classification of materials are made on the basis of its nature or usage. The following principles of classification helps in quick identification of materials :

(*a*) Every item of material and all related components thereof, should be grouped into logical divisions or classes.

(*b*) Divisions should be specific enough to exclude all duplicate listing of items or ambiguity.

(*c*) Arrangement should be broad enough so that divisions will not become numerous as to be cumbersome.

Having classified the materials the next step is to codify the materials. A code may be defined as a mark, character or group of characters which may consist of figures, letters or signs chosen to typify or represent material. The following principles are to be followed while coding the materials :

(*a*) A code should be exclusive and should completely differentiate the item it represents from every other item in the system.

(*b*) A code should indicate, by its form, the class and principal sub-classes in which the item represented by it belongs.

Methods of Codifying the Materials

(*a*) ***Alphabetic method :*** Under this method, each item of material is indicated by a letter or combination of letters. This method is conveniently used when the materials used are few in number.

(*b*) ***Numerical method :*** Under this method, each item of material is indicated by a number or combination of numbers.

(*c*) ***Mnemonic method :*** When the codes chosen for classification is meant for memory assisting, it is known as mnemonic codification. This includes the use of both alphabetic letters and numbers. The first letter or number of the code denotes the general class to which the materials belong and successive letters or numbers indicate sub-class for which the materials belong.

Advantages of Codification of Materials

(*a*) It helps in easy identification of materials which facilitates quick and prompt issue of materials. Codification is more useful where the same material is known by more than one name.

(*b*) It dispenses with writing full names and other particulars of materials. This also economises space in forms.

(*c*) Codification is a must for mechanised accounting.

(*d*) Codification ensures secrecy as code numbers are not known to all.

8. Miscellaneous Techniques

The following are some of the techniques used to exercise control over materials :

(*a*) ***Automatic order system :*** Under this techniqe purchase orders are automatically placed as soon as the materials reach the reorder level. This technique is used where materials accounting is mechanised. The punched cards are used to record the receipts and issues of materials. When the reorder level is reached, computer automatically sorts the material card. It is then processed by a clerk who places an order for the necessary quantity. This technique enables the purchase department to review material items,forecast the requirements and the lead time, establishes safety stock and in determining economic order quantity.

(*b*) ***Order cycling :*** Under this technique a review of materials in storeroom is made on a regular basis. For example, a review can be made once in a month. Those materials which are more essential can be reviewed more frequently compared to other materials. On review, an order is placed to bring the materials to a desired level, say fortnightly supply. One of the review that is made frequently covering small items of materials (indirect materials) is termed as 90 ÷ 60 – 30 day method. When the materials fall to a 60-day supply, an order is placed for 30-day supply. Similarly adjustments can be made for procuring the materials at the time desired.

(*c*) ***Minimum-maximum method :*** This is based on the technique of level setting. Under this technique, the minimum level represents reordering level. It means as and when the minimum level is reached an order is placed with a view to increase the materials to the maximum level.

9. New Techniques of Materials Control

The following are some of new techniques of material control :

(*a*) ***FSN analysis (Fast-slow and Non-moving materials) :*** Fast moving materials are consumed very frequently in the production process and hence they are to be replenished at very frequent intervals. Slow moving materials on the other hand are consumed less frequently. Non-moving materials may be termed as dormant stock. These are the materials whose demand for the current production requirements are not felt but are needed in the near future. A careful watch is to be kept on all these three category of materials so as to keep further stock of slow moving and dormant stock to a minimum while increasing the stock of fast moving materials.

(*b*) ***HML analysis (High, Medium and Low valued items) :*** As compared to ABC analysis which takes into account the consumption value of materials under this technique the unit value of stores item is considered. Those materials with a high unit value will be given utmost importance and a tight control is exercised. The medium items of materials with a moderate unit value will be given lesser degree of control whereas low valued items will receive least degree of control.

(*c*) ***VED analysis (Vital, Essential, Desirable Materials) :*** The technique of material control is applicable to spare parts. Spares are classified into vital, essential and desirable. Whereas vital category of spares are to be stocked adequately, essential and desirable categories can be stocked as and when required if the lead time of such materials is low.

A modified form of this technique is termed as VEIN (Vital, Essential, Important and Normal) which is used to control plant and machineries. When this technique is used in conjunctions with VED analysis it becomes one of the effective technique of material control. Under this technique, vital spares are arranged for all types of plants, *viz.*, vital, essential, important and normal. Similarly, essential spares are arranged for all the four categories of machines.

(*d*) ***SDE analysis :*** This technique is used to exercise control over materials depending upon their ready availability. Accordingly, materials are classified into scarce, difficult and easy to obtain the materials. Any item of materials which is scarce in supply is to be stocked in excess quantities irrespective of its value, volume and frequency of its movement in order to avoid stoppage in the production process. So also constant efforts are to be made to procure difficult-to-obtain type of materials. However, no extra efforts are required/to be taken in case of 'easy-to-obtain' type of materials.

(*e*) ***SOS analysis :*** Under this technique of material control, materials are classified into two types, *viz.*, seasonal and off-seasonal materials. It is seasonal materials which are given more importance in terms of its procurements.

(*f*) ***GOLF analysis :*** Under this technique of material control, materials are classified on the basis of nature of supply. Accordingly materials are classified into (*i*) government supplies *i.e.*, through government departments like STC, MMTC, etc., (*ii*) open supplies, (*iii*) local supplies and (*iv*) foreign supplies. No problem is posed in case of open and local supplies. Whereas certain formalities are to be observed in case of government and foreign supplies.

(*g*) ***Just-in-time approach (JIT) :*** Just-in-time technique ensures the flow of raw material to the production point just in adequate quantities continuously, thus ensuring the production flow process without any obstruction. Ensuring such an arrangement therefore results in to building up of inventories. When a company practices minimal or zero level inventory the cost of production drastically come down.

QUESTIONS

I. Mark *T* or *F* in the Space Provided

(*a*) Storeroom does not store finished products manufactured in the factory. T/F

(*b*) "Providing a place for everything and everything in its place" is the key to success in a stores organisation. T/F

(*c*) Centralised stores system is more suitable for a large-sized factory. T/F

(*d*) A good layout of stores need not give a good appearance. T/F

(*e*) A bin card is not filled by the storekeeper. T/F

(*f*) A stores ledger card contains the quantity and value of materials received, issued and in-balance. T/F

(*g*) The returned material is received by the stores accountant. T/F

(*h*) Under a decentralised 'storekeeping' system several employees working out of one storeroom are responsible for the issue and control of all items. T/F

(*i*) Stores ledger is maintained in the stores room. T/F

(*j*) A high inventory turnover rate indicates that material in question is a fast moving one. T/F

(*k*) Bin cards are not a part of accounting records. T/F

(*l*) An efficient and experienced storekeeper need not bother himself about classification and codification of materials. T/F

(*m*) The two extremes of overstocking and understocking of materials may be avoided by the fixation of inventory level. T/F

(*n*) The stores ledger is written by the storekeeper. T/F

(*o*) Maintenance of the stores ledger involves additional clerical labour since it contains the same particulars as those in bin card. T/F

[***Answers :*** *(a) F, (b), T, (c) T, (d) F, (e) F, (f) T, (g) F, (h) F, (i) F, (j) T, (k) T, (l) F, (m) T, (n) F, (o) F*]

II. Fill in the blanks :

(*a*) The process of physical verification of stores throughout the year is known as ....

(*b*) .... level is that level of materials at which a new order for material is placed.

(*c*) Allotting symbols to the different items of stores is known as ....

(*d*) The quantity of materials that is to be ordered with a supplier is known as ....

(*e*) Bin card is maintained by ....

[***Answers :*** (*a*) perpetual inventory system, (*b*) reorder, (*c*) codification, (*d*) economic order quantity, (*e*) storekeeper]

III. Selects the correct answer from the following :

(*a*) Which of the following method of stock control aims at concentrating efforts on selected items of materials

(1) Perpetual inventory system
(2) Material turnover
(3) Level setting
(4) ABC analysis

(*b*) The formula to be used to calculate minimum level is

(1) Reorder level × Minimum reorder period
(2) Reorder level + Reorder quantity × Minimum reorder period
(3) Reorder level + Reorder quantity × Minimum usage × Minimum reordeer period
(4) Reorder level – Normal usage × Average reorder period

(*c*) The storekeeper should initiate a purchase requisition when stock reaches

(1) Minimum level
(2) Maximum level
(3) Reorder level
(4) Average level

(*d*) Lead time refers to

(1) The time interval between the date production and the date of sale
(2) The time interval between the date of purchase and the date of sale
(3) The time required to order and receive the materials
(4) The time required to process the order

(*e*) Economic order quantity is computed so that

(1) The ordering and carrying costs are least
(2) The ordering and stock out costs are least
(3) The ordering and back ordering costs are least
(4) The cost of materials are least

[***Answers :*** (*a*)–4, (*b*)–4, (*c*)–3, (*d*)–3, (*e*)–1]

IV. Simple questions

1. Give 2 advantages of codification of materials. (*Bangalore University, B.Com., April 2000*)
2. What is perpetual inventory system? (*Bangalore University, B.Com., April 2000*)
3. State 2 differences between Bin card and stores ledger card. (*Bangalore University, B.Com., April 2000*)
4. What do you mean by ABC analysis? (*Bangalore University, B.Com., April 2000*) (*Bharathidasan University, B.Com., April 1998*)
5. What is Bill of materials? (Bangalore University, B.Com., November 1999)
6. What do you mean by stores discrepancies? State its causes. (*Bangalore University, B.Com., April 1997*)
7. Mention the methods of codification. (*Bangalore University, B.Com., Nov. 1997*)
8. What is E O Q. Give its utility? (*Bherethidasam University, B.Com., April 1994*)
9. What is Bin card? (*Bangalore University, B.Com., Nov. 1997*)
10. What do you mean by maximum level? (*Bangalore University, B.Com., April 1994*)
11. What is danger level of materials? (*Bangalore University, B.Com., April 1994*)
12. Write a specimen of Bin card. (*Bangalore University, B.Com., April 1994*)
13. Give the formula to calculate reorder level. (*Karnataka University, B.Com., April 1994*)
14. What do you mean by material control? (*Bangalore University, B.Com., April 1995*)
15. On what basis is the reorder quantity determined? (*Bharathidasan University, B.Com., November 1995*)

16. What is minimum level? *(M.G. University, B.Com., April 1994)*
17. What is meterial turnover ratio? *(Karnataka University, B.Com., April 1997)*
18. What is stores ledger card? *(Karnataka University, B.Com., April 1997)*
19. What is danger level? *(Bangalore University, B.Com., April 1996)*
20. What is economic order quantity? *(University of Kerala, M.Com., May 1995)*

Short answer questions

1. What is 'economic order quantity'? How is it determined? Is it different from reorder quantity? *(C.S., Inter, June 2000)*
2. Differentiate between 'bin card' and stores ledger card. *(C.S., Inter, December 1999; C.A., Inter, May 1999)*
3. State briefly the various techniques used for inventory control. *(C.S., Inter, June 1999)*
4. Explain perpetual inventory system. *(C.S., Inter, June 1998)*
5. Outline a system of stores control. *(C.S., Inter, June 1997)*
6. "Perpetual inventory system is on integral part of material control". Explain. *(C.S., Inter, December 1997)*
7. Explain ABC analysis of inventory control. *(C.S., Inter, December 1996)*
8. How do you determine economic order quantity? *(C.S., Inter, December 1996)*
9. What is material handling cost? How will you deal it in cost accounts? *(C.S., Inter, May 1999)*
10. At the time of physical stock taking it was found that actual stock level was different from the clerical or compute records? What can be possible reasons for such differences? How will you deal with such differences? *(C.S., Inter, May 1996)*
11. What is perpetual inventory system? Explain its merits over periodic system. *(University of Mysore, B.Com., April 1998)*
12. Explain the meaning and importance of material control and the main requisites of an adequate system of material control. *(University of Mysore, B.Com., October 1999)*
13. Describe the factors which influence different stock levels of a manufacturing unit. *(University of Mysore, B.Com., April 1995)*
14. Explain the tools and techniques of material control. (S.V. *University, B.Com., April 1995)*
15. What do you mean by ABC analysis? What are its advantages? (S.V. *University, B.Com., Sept. 1994)*
16. What is codification of materials? Describe the methods of codification of materials. *(University of Mysore, B.Com., April 1994)*
17. What is meant by 'maximum level', 'minimum level' and 'reorder level' with regard to maintenance of stocks? What are the factors that govern the fixing of levels? *(Bharathidasan University, B.Com., April 1994)*
18. What is a bin card? Give a specimen form of it and discuss its utitity. *(Bharathidasan University, B.Com., April 1994)*
19. What are the duties of a storekeeper? *(M.G. University, B.Com., Sept. 1994)*
20. What is two-bin system? What are the advantages? *(M.G. University, B.Com., Sept. 1994)*
21. What is meant by inventory turnover? Explain it with the help of an example. *(M.G. University, B.Com., Sept. 1994)*
22. Explain the objectives of inventory control. *(M.G. University, B.Com., October 1993)* *(Mangalore University, B.Com., April 1997)*
23. Give the advantages resulting from classification and codification of materials. *(Mangalore University, B.Com., April 1996)*

EXERCISES

Exercise on bin card

Exercise 1 : Sirdhar and Co. furnish the following information regarding receipts and issues of materials :

			kg.
1992, April	1,	Opening stock	25,000
	2,	Issued against requisition no. 1	13,000
	3,	Issued against requisition no. 2	2,000
	4,	Received from a supplier by challan no. 13	30,000

10,	Issed on requisition no. 3	10,000
15,	Issued on requisition no. 4	5,000
25,	Received from supplier by challan no. 14	10,000
30,	Issued on requisition no. 5 examination by the stock verifier on 26th morning revealed a shortage of 500 kg.	50,000

Maximum limit	50,000
Minimum limit	50,000
Ordering level	8,000
You are required to prepare bin card no. 15	25,000

[*Answer* : Balance 30,000 kg.]

Exercise on ABC analysis

Exercise 2 : Analyse the following items into *A*, *B* and *C* categories on the basis of information given below show the percentage of materials in quantity and value under *A*, *B* and *C* categories.

Category *A*—Rs. 4,000 and above (total value)

Category *B*—Rs. 1,000 to Rs. 3,999 of (total value)

Category *C*—Below Rs. 1,000 (total value)

S.No.	*Code No.*	*Quantity*	*Unit rate*
1	*A*	147	3.00
2	*B*	986	2.00
3	*C*	353	4.00
4	*D*	8,931	0.10
5	*E*	1,239	0.15
6	*F*	100	0.25
7	*G*	18	513.00
8	*H*	3,770	2.50
9	*I*	683	2.00
10	*J*	134	0.70
11	*K*	190	0.40
12	*L*	1	43.00
13	*M*	52	0.70
14	*N*	426	0.10
15	*O*	4,725	0.06
16	*P*	10	30.27
17	*Q*	20	1.40
18	*R*	6,542	0.02
19	*S*	329	0.40
20	*T*	10	134.00

[*Answer : Category*	*Quantity in percentage*	*Value in percentage*	*Value of materials*
A	10%	68%	Rs. 18,659
B	20%	22%	Rs. 6,090
C	70%	10%	Rs. 2,715]

Exercises on level setting

Exercise 3 : Two types of materials *X* and *Y* are used as follows :

(1) Normal usage	—	100	units per month
(2) Minimum usage	—	50	units per month
(3) Maximum usage	—	200	units per month
Reorder quantity	— *X* —	800	units
	Y —	1500	units
Reorder period	— *X* —	4 to 8	months
	Y —	2 to 4	months

Calculate for each type of materials : (*a*) Reorder level, (*b*) Minimum level, (*c*) Maximum level.

(*Bangalore University, B.Com., Nov. 1990*)

[*Answer :* Reorder level of *A* = 16,000 units
Reorder level of *B* = 800 units
Minimum level of *A* = 1000 units
Minimum level of *B* = 500 units
Maximum level of *A* = 2,200 units
Maximum level of *B* = 22,000 units]

Exercise 4 : In a manufacturing unit a material is used as follows :

Maximum consumption		450 units per week each
Minimum consumption	—	150 units per week each
Normal consumption	—	300 units per week each
Reorder quantity	— A — 2,400	units
	B — 3,600	units
Time required for deliver	— A — 4 to 6	weeks
	B 2 to 4	weeks

Calculate (*a*) Reorder level, (*b*) Minimum level, (*c*) Maximum level, (d) Average store level.

(*Bangalore University, B.Com., Apr. 1989*)

[*Answer :* Reorder level of *A* 2,700 units
Reorder level of *B* — 1,800 units
Minimum level of *A* — 1,200 units
Minimum level of *B* — 900 units
Maximum level of *A* — 4,500 units
Maximum level of *B* — 5,200 units
Average stock level of *A* — 2,850 units
Average stock level of *B* — 3,050 units]

Exercise 5 : Components *A* and *B* and used as follows :

Normal usage	—	50 units per week each
Minimum usage	—	25 units per week each
Maximum usage	—	75 units per week each
Reorder quantity of *A*	—	300 units
Reorder quantity of *B*	—	500 units
Reorder period of *A*	—	4 to 6 weeks
Reorder period of *B*	—	2 to 4 weeks

Calculate for each component :

(*a*) Reorder level
(*b*) Minimum level
(*c*) Maximum level
(*d*) Average stock level

(*Madras University, B.Com., April 1991; Sri Sathya Sai University, B.Com., Oct. 1987*)

[*Answer :* Reorder level of *A* = 450 units
Reorder level of *B* = 300 units
Minimum level of *A* = 200 units
Minimum level of *B* = 150 units
Maximum level of *A* = 650 units
Maximum level of *B* = 750 units
Average stock level of *A* = 425
Average stock level of *B* = 450 units]

Exercise 6 : In a company weekly minimum and maximum consumption of material *A* are 25 and 75 units respectively. The reorder quantity as fixed by the company is 300 units. The material is received within 4 to 6 weeks from issue of supply order. Calculate minimum level and maximum level of material *A*.

(*C.A., Inter, May 1995*)

[*Answer :* Reorder level — 450 units
Minimum level — 200 units
Maximum level — 650 units]

Exercise 7 : Determine maximum stock and buffer stock to keep stock at a reasonable level while providing a good service where :

		Maximum	Average	Minimum
Daily consumption		75 units	50 units	25 units
Delivery period		5 days	2 days	1 day
I deal order size	=	125 units		
Reorder level	=	375 units		

(*University of Delhi, B.Com. (Hons), April, 1995*)

[***Answer :*** Maximum level = 475 units
Buffer stock or minimum level = 275 units]

Exercise on EOQ

Exercise 8 : From the following particulars find out the economic order quantity :

(*i*) Annual demand	—	12000 units
(*ii*) Ordering cost	—	Rs. 90 per order
(*iii*) Inventory carrying cost	—	Rs. 15 per annum

(*ICWA, Inter, Dec. 1990*)

[***Answer :*** 379 Units App]

Exercise 9 : From the following data prepare economic ordering quantity for the item :

Total annual consumption	—	1,70,000	units
Purchase price (per unit)	—	Rs. 1.50	units
Ordering cost	—	Rs. 80	per order
Cost of carrying inventory	—	20%	per annum

(*C.S., Inter, Dec. 1988*)

[***Answer :*** 8,000 units]

Exercise 10 : From the following particulars with respect to a particular item of materials of a manufacturing company calculate the best quantity to order :

Ordering quantity (tonnes)	*Price per tonne* *Rs.*
Less then 250	6.00
250 but less than 800	5.90
800 but less than 2000	5.80
2000 but less than 4000	5.70
4000 and above	5.60

The annual demand for the material is 4,000 tonnes stock holding costs are 20 per cent of material cost p.a. the delivery cost per order is Rs. 6.00.

[***Answer :*** At 800 order size the total cost of Rs. 23,694 is minimum.
Therefore, the best quantity to be ordered is 800 tonnes]

Exercise 11 : The daily demand for an electronic machine is approximately 25 times every time on order is placed., a fixed cost of Rs. 25 is increased. The daily holding cost per item inventory is Rs. 0.40. If the lead time is 16 days determine the economic lot size and the reorder point. (*ICWA, Final (Rs.) Dec. 1985*)

[***Answer :*** EOQ = 56, Reorder point is 400 items]

Exercise 12 : A company, for one of the 'A' class items placed 6 orders each of size of 200 in a year. Given ordering cost = Rs. 600, holding cost = 40%, cost per unit = Rs. 40. Find out the loss to the company along with your recommendation for the future. (*C.A., Final, November 1995*)

[***Answer :***
EOQ = 300 units
Annual cost of existing policy = Rs. 53,200
Annual cost with EOQ = Rs. 52,800
Loss to the company = 53,200 – 52,800
= Rs. 400

Recommendation : A savings of Rs. 400 can be obtained by placing an economic order quantity of 300 units.]

Exercises on level setting and EOQ

Exercise 13 : ABC Ltd. manufacturers a special product 'Ruby'. The following particulars were collected for the year 1988 :

(*a*) Cost of placing an order Rs. 100

(*b*) Annual carrying cost per unit Rs. 15

(*c*) Usage rate of input 25 units to 75 units per week
(*d*) Reorder period 4 to 6 weeks
(*e*) Normal usage 50 units per week.

Compute for the input for Ruby :

(*i*) Minimum level (*ii*) Reorder level
(*iii*) Reorder quantity (*iv*) Maximum level

(*SSSIHÇ, B.Com., Oct. 1989*)

[*Answer* : (i) Minimum level — 200 units
(ii) Reorder level — 450 units
(iii) Reorder quantity — 186 units
(iv) Maximum level — 536 units]

(**Note :** Annual consumption for determining reorder quantity is find out by multiplying 52 weeks in a year by 50 units which is the normal usage per week)

Exercise 14 : A manufacturer uses 200 units of a component every month and he bags them entirely from an outside supplier. The order placing and receiving cost is Rs.100 and annual carrying cost is Rs. 12. From this set of data calculate the EOQ. (*ICWA, Inter, June 1984*)

[*Answer :* 200 units]

Exercise on inventory turnover ratio

Exercise 15 : The following information is available from the bin cards No. 17 and 18 of Sunshine Co. Ltd. for the year 1992. Calculate inventory turnover ratio and also days the average stock of each material held.

	Material X (*Rs.*)	*Materials Y* (*Rs.*)
Opening stock	30,000	70,000
Purchases	1,20,000	2,05,000
Closing stock	15,000	45,000

[*Answer :* Inventory turnover ratio of material *A* is 6 times and materials *B* is 4 times. Inventory turnover in days for materials *A* is 61 days and material *B* is 91 days]

Exercise 16 : Calculate the material turnover ratio for the year 1979 from the following details :

	Material X (*Rs.*)	*Materials Y* (*Rs.*)
Opening stcok	25,000	87,500
Closing stock	15,000	62,500
Purchase	1,90,000	1,25,000

Determine the fast moving materials.

(*Madurai University, B.Com., Apr. 1981*)

[*Answer :* The material turnover ratio of material *X* is 10 and that of material *Y* is 2 '*X*' is fast moving material]

Exercise on adjustment of discrepancies of material

Exercise 17 : The following differences are noticed in the physical verification of stores. State how you would adjust in the stores ledger and prepare the necessary journal entries for the cost ledger.

Material	*Physical balance* (*units*)	*Ledger balance* (*units*)	*Issue rate per cent* (*Rs.*)	*Reasons*
A	500	550	1.00	Shortage is due to theft. A receipt of 100 units was not recorded in the stores ledger.
B	550	400	0.50	A receipt of 100 units was not recorded in the stores ledger. The balance of 50 units of the excess is due to errors in issuing from stores.
C	540	550	2.00	Discrepancy is shown erroneously due to careless stock taking. Deficiency is considered normal and within units.

Exercise 18 : A manufacturer uses 200 units of a component every month and he buys item entirely from an outside suppliers. The order placing and receiving cost is Rs. 100 and annual carrying cost per unit is Rs. 12. From the given set of data. Calculate the economic order quantity.

P. Ltd. uses three types of materials *A*, *B* and *C* for production of *X*, the final product. The relevant monthly data for the components are as given below :

	A	*B*	*C*
Normal usage (units)	200	150	180
Minimum usage (units)	100	100	90
Maximum usage (units)	300	250	270
Reorder quantity (units)	750	900	720
Reorder period (months)	2 to 3	3 to 4	2 to 3

Calculate for each component :

(1) Reorder level
(2) Maximum level
(3) Minimum level
(4) Average stock level

(*C.S., Inter, June 1998*)

[*Answer :*
(1) EOQ = 200 units
(2) Reorder level = *A* — 900 units; *B* — 1,000 units; *C* — 810 units
(3) Maximum level = *A* — 1,450 units; *B* — 1,600 units; *C* — 1,350 units
(4) Minimum level = *A* — 400 units; *B* — 475 units; *C* — 360 units
(5) Average stock level = *A* — 925 units; *B* — 1,038 units; *C* — 855 units

Exercise 19 : About 50 items are required every day for a machine. A fixed cost of Rs. 50 per order is incurred for placing an order. The inventory carrying cost per item amounts to Rs. 0.02 per day. The lead period is 32 days compute :

(*i*) Economic order quantity
(*ii*) Reorder level

(*C.A., Inter, November 1996*)

[*Answer* : (*i*) EOQ = 500 items
(*ii*) Reorder level = 1,600 items

Exercise 20 : From the details given below, calculate :

(*i*) Reorder level
(*ii*) Maximum level
(*iii*) Minimum level
(*iv*) Danger level

Reordering quantity is to be calculated on the basis of following information; cost of placing a purchase order is Rs. 20 number of units to be purchased during the year is 5,000.

Purchase price per unit inclusive of transportation cost is Rs. 50.

Annual cost of storage per unit is Rs. 5

Details of lead time : Average 10 days
Maximum 15days
Minimum 6 days
For emergency purchases 4 days

Rate of consumption : Average — 15 units per day
Maximum — 20 units per day

(*C.A., Inter, May 1996*)

[**Answer :** (1) Reorder level — 3,000 units
(2) Maximum level — 440 units
(3) Minimum level — 150 units
(4) Danger level — 60 units
(5) EOQ — 200 units

Hint : (6) Average rate of consumption =

$$\frac{\text{Minimum Rate of consumption} + \text{Maximum rate of consumption}}{2}$$

$$15 = \frac{x+20}{2} \text{ or } X = 10 \text{ units per day}$$

Exercise on input-output ratio analysis

Exercise 21 : The Mysore Pharmaceutical Co. uses chemical *X* as its raw materials. The chemical costs Rs. 10 per kg and its input-output ratio being 125 per cent. Due to its scarcity, the company is contemplating to buy one of the following substitues :

Material	*Rater per litre*	*Input-output ratio*
Chemical *Y*	Rs. 15	110%
Chemical *Z*	Rs. 12	140%

Recommend which of the above two material is to be preferred.

[*Answer :* Chemical Y is to be preferred as its cost per litre is Rs. 16.50 when compared to chemical Z whose cost per litre is Rs. 16.80]

5

MATERIALS COST-ISSUE CONTROL

INTRODUCTION

Issue control is that phase of material control which is exercised in the course of usage of materials. Materials for consumption and issue purposes can be classified into three types. *viz.* (*i*) raw materials which are to be issued to production department, (*ii*) spare parts and components, which are to be issued to maintenance department and (*iii*) indirect materials and sundry supplies which are to be issued to both production and service departments. It is desirable to estimate in advance the requirement of materials for every product, job or process both item-wise and quantity-wise so that the exact requirements can be issued to ensure continuity in production. When standard costing is in operation, a standard material schedule is prepared for each job or product. Otherwise for bulk issue of materials, a document known as bill of materials is used.

OBJECTS OF MATERIALS ISSUE CONTROL

The following are the objects of material issue control :

1. Every Issue must be Authentically Authorised

A person is said to be authentically authorised if he derives the power to draw the required quantity of materials from a specified lot. Usually the foreman or a supervisor is authorised to draw materials from the storeroom. The storekeeper keeps a specimen signature of the authority to draw the materials. The document which is used to draw materials is termed as a material requisition note or a stores requisition note. This document is prepared in triplicate. The original and duplicate copies are sent to storekeeper which serves as the basis for issuing the materials. The storekeeper sends the original copy to the stores accountant to facilitate him for pricing the issues. The triplicate copy is retained by the department which initiated the material requisition note. The contents of material requisition note are as follows :

(*a*) Number and date of requisition. The materials requisition note is centrally numbered in the storeroom by a serial number to ensure that all the notes are accounted for.

(*b*) Name of the department needing the materials.

(*c*) Particulars and code number of materials to facilitate the correct issue of materials.

(*d*) The quantity of materials demanded and its unit of measurement.

(*e*) The rate at which the issue is to be priced. This is obtained from stores ledger which is worked out under FIFO, LIFO or other methods of issuing prices.

(*f*) The total value of materials which is obtained by multiplying the unit cost with the quantity issued on the requisition.

(*g*) The signature of the person initiating the materials requisition note.

A specimen form of material requisition note is given below :

W.S. INSULATORS OF INDIA LIMITED

Factory, Porur, Madras

Material requisition note

Please issue the following materials :

No. ....

Date ....

S.No.	*Description of materials*	*Material code*	*Quantity required*	*Quantity issued*	*Unit*	*Rate*	*Value*

Cost centre [ ]

Authorised by .... *Issued by* .... *Received by* ....

Fig. 5.1. Material requisition note.

When all the types of materials required to execute a job is to be drawn at a time, a document known as a 'Bill of materials' is made use of. It is a list of all materials required for a specific job, process or work order. Usually this document is prepared by the production planning department and presented to the storekeeper in lieu of one or more material requisition slips. It serves the following purposes :

(*a*) It serves as an advance intimation to all the persons concerned about the execution of the job.

(*b*) It facilitates the storekeeper to prepare a purchase requisition note and thus ensures ready availability of materials for issue purpose.

(*c*) It facilitates quick accounting of materials consumed as entries can be posted in totals to the concerned jobs.

(*d*) It serves as a substitute to material requisition note especially when all the materials for executing a job is to be drawn.

A specimen form of bill of materials is given below :

ABC CO. LTD.
Bill of materials

Department authorised ....

Job or work order No. ....

Number ....

Date of issue ....

Item No.	*Code No.*	*Description of materials*	*Quantity*	*For department use*		
				MRN No.	*Date*	*Qty.*

Fig. 5.2. Bill of materials.

The authority to draw materials from storeroom must be extended to return the surplus materials from the production departments to storeroom. Otherwise it may involve misappropriation of materials and may go unaccounted. The document used to accompany the return of surplus materials is known as materials return note. This note is used to record not only the return of excess materials but also the rejected materials, scraps, etc. arising out of the materials received in the department. On the basis of this document the returned materials are priced. A specimen form of materials return note is given below :

W.S. INSULATORS OF INDIA LIMITED
Porur, Madras - 602 104
MATERIALS RETURN NOTE

No. ....
Date ....

S. No.	*Description of materials*	*Material code*	*Quantity*	*Rate*	*Amount*	*Remarks*

Returned by ....   *Cost centre* ....   *Received by* ....

Fig. 5.3. Materials return note.

Sometimes the excess quantity of materials of one department may be needed by other departments. In such situations it may not be prudent to return back the surplus materials to the storeroom. Instead it can be directly transferred to the department where it is needed. Though inter-departmental transfer of materials is not generally allowed, under the following two circumstances it is to be encouraged (*a*) where the excess materials are very heavy in weight involving more material handling expenses, (*b*) where the production is not to be delayed for want of materials. A specimen form of material transfer note is given below :

ABC CO. LTD.

From ....(cost centre)   No. ....
To ....(cost centre)   Date ....

Material Transfer Note

Transfer from job No. ....   To job No. ....

S. No.	*Description of materials*	*Material code*	*Quantity*	*Rate*	*Amount*	*Remarks*

Sent by ....   *Received by* ....   *Stores clerk* ....

Fig. 5.4. Material transfer note.

2. Proper Accounting of Every Authorised Issue

The materials issued to various departments from storeroom must be properly accounted both in storeroom as well as in stores accounting section. This ensures proper usage of materials and helps in knowing the correct requirements of materials for every department.

3. Proper Pricing of Materials

Pricing of material issues to a large extent influences the cost of product and the value of closing stock. The method to be followed depends upon number of factors. However, the following basic factors must be satisfied by a good method of pricing material issues :

(*a*) The issue price must cover the cost of purchases of materials.

(*b*) It must reflect current market price.

(*c*) It should not destabilise costs from time to time.

(*d*) It should not lead to adjustment of stock at the end of accounting year.

4. Proper Charging of Material Cost to Product, Process or Job

This objective enables the proper charge of materials cost to various jobs executed. The basis of charging material cost is material requisition notes, which are analysed first on the basis of cost centres and then by job number. Charging of materials cost to every job as and when materials are issued leads to cumbersome process. Sometimes this may also lead to omission of entries thereby under estimating materials cost. So, to facilitate charging of materials cost for all the jobs without omission, a document known as materials abstract or material analysis sheet is prepared. This document contains the analysis of materials by jobs and cost centres. This document is prepared once in a week or fortnight on the basis of various materials requisition notes used during that week or fortnight. From this document entries are posted into stores ledger card at one time and the cost of materials issued to every job or work order ascertained. This document is prepared both for direct and indirect materials. But the cost of indirect materials are charged to factory overheads.

A specimen form of materials abstract or material analysis sheet is given below :

ABC CO. LTD.
Materials analysis sheet

Period...............

Job no.	*Material requisition no.*	*Stores ledger folio no.*	*Quantity*	*Rate*	*Amount*	*Progressive total for each order no.*

Fig. 5.5. Material analysis sheet.

PRINCIPLES REGARDING MATERIALS ISSUE

While issuing the materials to various departments, the following principles should be followed :

(*a*) The exact requirement of materials is to be planned. This ensures the correct issue of materials (neither less nor more) to all the departments.

(*b*) All the materials (direct and indirect) must be issued only on the basis of written requisition forms signed by competent authority.

(*c*) There should be a system of material audit of issues of materials. This helps in checking over-issue of materials.

(*d*) A proper control must be exercised on wastages, scraps and defective materials so that they can be kept to a minimum.

METHODS OF PRICING MATERIALS ISSUE

Before issues of materials are recorded in the stores ledger, the cost accounting department must decide upon the method of pricing the materials issue. However, materials issues could have been recorded at its actual cost, if prices of materials remain uniform. But this phenomenon is rarely observed in practice. The adoption of particular method of pricing material issues serves two purposes, *viz.* (*a*) To charge cost of materials to the jobs on a consistent basis and (*b*) To value the closing stock properly for the preparation of final accounts. Different methods of pricing materials have been devised and the choice of a method is left to the discretion of the enterprise. These methods of pricing materials issues is shown in the following chart :

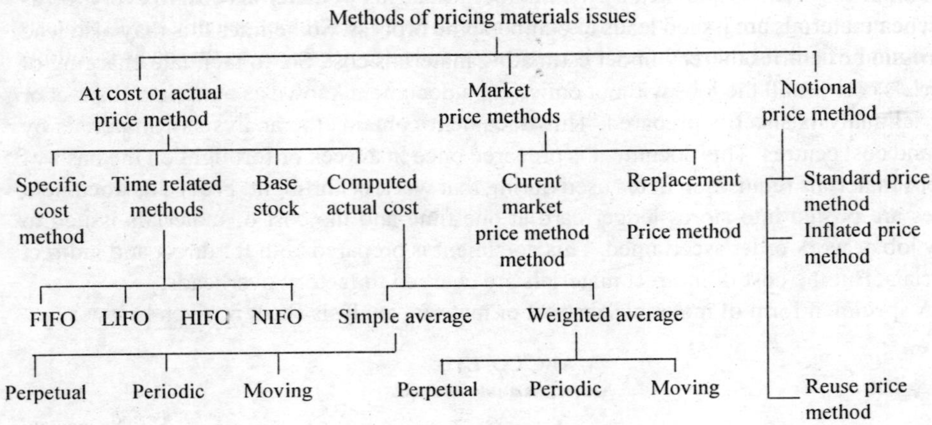

Fig. 5.6. Chart showing various methods of pricing materials.

I. At Cost or Actual Price Method

This method takes into account the price of materials at which they are bought for the purpose of valuing them at the time of issues. The following methods fall under this classification :

1. **Specific cost method :** This method of pricing material issues is adopted where special types of materials are bought for the execution of a job or a contract. The materials to be issued to jobs are identified with the invoices prices and if any handling and inspection costs are incurred such expenses are also included to constitute issue prices. The materials which are thus priced is commonly known as special materials as they are specifically purchased at the instance of customers. Thus under this method, the production is charged with the actual cost of materials. The inventory is also similarly valued at the actual cost.

Advantages : (*a*) No calculations are involved for calculating issue prices and the cost of material when compared to other methods.

(*b*) The production is charged with the acutal cost. Therefore, production is neither undercharged nor overcharged.

(*c*) The closing stock of materials are also valued at actual cost and therefore we do not come across any unrealised profit or loss.

Limitations : (*a*) This method is not suitable in case of continuous manufacturing industries involving repetitive and frequent purchase of materials.

(*b*) As each job differs from other jobs a separate register is to be maintained for the issue of materials which involves more of clerical work.

(*c*) If materials purchased are too frequent it becomes difficult to maintain their identity. Similarly if issues are too frequent it becomes difficult to relate the materials to each and every job.

(*d*) As this method depends on invoices non-receipt of an invoice will obstruct the issue procedure.

2. **First-in-first out (FIFO) method :** Under this method, the issues of materials are priced according to the chronological order of purchased rates of materials. The underlying principle is that purchase price of the earlier consignment is used first for issue purposes and once this consignment exhausts the price of next consignment is taken up. This process is repeated throughout. However it is to be remembered that the physical issue of materials need not be in the above order as it is neither possible nor necessary as this basis is followed only for accounting purposes.

Impact of FIFO method on cost of production : (*a*) As purchase rates of the earliest and subsequent lots of purchases are adopted for issue purposes the cost of production does not reflect the current market price of materials.

(*b*) The cost of production is not accurate but only arbitrary especially when materials price fluctuate widely. This is because cost of production consists of issue prices of different lots of purchases.

(*c*) The cost of production is overstated and understated depending upon the fluctuation in the prices of materials in the market.

Impact of FIFO method on inventory valuation : (*a*) When the materials price increase, the value of stock is understated and when the material price decreases, the value of closing stock is overstated.

(*b*) The total value of stock fluctuates with the rise and fall in the cost of materials. This distorts the valuation of the stock accurately.

(*c*) The value of closing stock reflects current market price.

Impact of FIFO method on The profit : (*a*) The total profit is unaffected by the overstatement in cost as this is compensated by a corresponding understatement in closing stock value and *vice versa*. However as production cost of a particular product or job is distorted by a rise or fall in the material cost, consequently profit on such product or job will also fall or rise.

Advantages : (*a*) As materials are issued at actual cost but not on estimates and approximation, unrealised profit or loss will not arise.

(*b*) where FIFO principle is adopted even for the physical issue of materials, this method gives correct cost of materials consumed. Further oldest materials are exhausted first to avoid deterioration and obsolescence.

(*c*) The value of closing stock will reflect current market price.

(*d*) If purchases are few and if the prices of materials remain stable the method will be simple to operate.

Disadvantages : (*a*) Issue prices do not reflect current market price and so does cost of production.

(*b*) Two similar jobs cannot be compared as different rates of materials are used to execute the jobs.

(*c*) During the period of falling prices cost of production tend to be high. This may lead to cancellation of prospective sales because of high quotations.

Pricing of materials returned to stores room under FIFO : Materials returned to storeroom is recorded at the price at which they were issued originally. These units are to be isued at the old price on the next material requisition received.

Pricing of materials returned to vendor : Materials returned to the vendor is recorded at the price of the oldest materials in stock on the date on which the materials are returned.

Problems on FIFO Method

Problem 1 :-From the following information prepare a stores ledger account under FIFO method :

1.1.96	Opening Stock	1,000 units at Rs. 5 each
5.1.96	Purchased	900 units at Rs. 6 each
10.1.96	Issued	1,200 units
12.1.96	Purchased	800 units at Rs. 6.20 each
15.1.96	Purchased	300 units at Rs. 6.40 each
19.1.96	Issued	400 units
22.1.96	Issued	600 units
27.1.96	Purchased	200 units at Rs. 6.50 each
31.1.96	Issued	600 units

(*University of Madras, B.Com., September 1997*)

Solution : Stores ledger card-FIFO Method

Date	*Receipts*			*Issues*			*Balance*		
	Qty.	*Rate*	*Amount*	*Qty.*	*Rate*	*Amount*	*Qty.*	*Rate*	*Amount*
1.1.96	–	–	–	–	–	–	1,000	5	5,000
5.1.96	900	6	5400	–	–	–	1,000	5	5,000
							900	6	5,400
10.1.96	–	–	–	1000	5	5000			
				200	6	1200	700	6	4,200
12.1.96	800	6.20	4960				700	6	4,200
							800	6.20	4,960
15.1.96	300	6.40	1920	–	–	–	700	6	4,200
							800	6.20	4,960
							300	6.40	1,920
19.1.96	–	–	–	400	6	2400	300	6	1,800
							800	6.20	4,960
							300	6.40	1,920
22.1.96	–	–	–	300	6	1,800	500	6.20	3,100
				300	6.20	1,860	300	6.40	1,920
27.1.96	200	6.50	1300	–	–	–	500	6.20	3,100
							300	6.40	1,920
							200	6.50	1,300
31.1.96	–	–	–	500	6.20	3100	200	6.40	1,280
				100	6.40	640	200	6.50	1,300

Problem 2 : From the following information prepare stores ledger account as per FIFO method :

1st Jan.	Opening stock	200 pieces @ Rs. 2 each
5th Jan.	Purchases	100 pieces @ Rs. 2.20 each
10th Jan.	Purchases	150 pieces @ Rs. 2.40 each
20th Jan.	Purchases	180 pieces @ Rs. 2.50 each
2nd Jan.	Issues	150 pieces

7th Jan.	Issues	100 pieces
12th Jan.	Issues	100 pieces
28th Jan.	Issues	200 pieces

(University of Delhi, B.Com. (Pass), April 1996)

Solution : **Stores ledger card - FIFO method**

Date	*Receipts*			*Issues*			*Balance*		
	Qty.	*Rate*	*Amount*	*Qty.*	*Rate*	*Amount*	*Qty.*	*Rate*	*Amount*
1 Jan.	–			–	–	–	200	2	400
2 Jan.				150	2	300	50	2	100
5 Jan.	100	2.20	220	–	–	–	50	2	100
							100	2.20	220
7 Jan.	–	–	–	50	2	110			
				50	2.20	110	50	2.20	110
10 Jan.	150	2.40	360	–	–	–	50	2.20	110
							150	2.40	360
12 Jan.	–	–	–	50	2.20	110	100	2.40	240
				50	2.40	120			
20 Jan.	180	2.50	450	–	–	–	100	2.40	240
							180	2.50	450
28 Jan.	–	–	–	100	2.40	240			
				100	2.50	250	80	2.50	200

Problem 3 : The following information is extrated from the stores ledger :

Jan. 1, Opening balances	500 units @ Rs. 4
Jan. 5, Purchases	200 units @ Rs. 4.25
Jan. 12, Purchases	150 units @ Rs. 4.10
Jan. 20, Purchases	300 units @ Rs. 4.50
Jan. 25, Purchases	400 units @ Rs. 4

Issues of materials were as follows :

Jan. 4	200 units
Jan. 10,	400 units
Jan. 15,	100 units
Jan. 19,	100 units
Jan. 26,	200 units
Jan. 30,	250 units

Issues are to be priced on the principle of 'First in First out'. Write out the stores ledger account.

Solution : **Stores ledger card - FIFO method**

Date	*Receipts*			*Issues*			*Balance*		
	Qty.	*Rate*	*Amount*	*Qty.*	*Rate*	*Amount*	*Qty.*	*Rate*	*Amount*
1 Jan.	–	–	–	–	–	–	500	4	2,000
2 Jan.	–	–	–	200	4	800	300	4	1,200
5 Jan.	200	4.25	850	–	–	–	300	4	1,200
							200	4.25	850
10 Jan.	–	–	–	300	4	1200			
				100	4.25	425	100	4.25	425
12 Jan.	150	4.10	615	–	–	–	100	4.25	425
							150	4.10	615
15 Jan.	–	–	–	100	4.25	425	150	4.10	615
19 Jan.	–	–	–	100	4.10	410	50	4.10	205
20 Jan.	300	4.50	1,350	–	–	–	50	4.10	205
							300	4.50	1,350

25 Jan.	400	4	1,600	–	–	–	50 300 400	4.10 4.50 4	205 1,350 1,600
26 Jan.	–	–	–	50 150	4.10 4.50	205 675	150 400	4.50 4	675 1,600
30 Jan.	–	–	–	150 100	4.5 4	675 400	300	4	1,200

Problem 4 : From the following transactions extracted from the books of accounts of a manufacturing concern as on 31st December 1994. Work out (*a*) consumption value of raw-materials in the month and (*b*) value of closing stock as on 31st December 1994 under the FIFO method of pricing issues.

		Quantity in units	*Rate per unit (Rs.)*
1994 Dec. 1,	Opening stock	300	9.70
1994 Dec. 3,	Purchases	250	9.80
1994 Dec. 11,	Issues	400	
1994 Dec. 15,	Purchases	300	10.50
1994 Dec. 20,	Issues	210	
1994 Dec. 25,	Purchases	150	10.30
1994 Dec. 29,	Issues	100	

(*University of Madras, B.Com., March 1995*)

Solution : **Stores ledger card - FIFO method**

Date	*Receipts*			*Issues*			*Balance*		
	Qty.	*Rate*	*Amount*	*Qty.*	*Rate*	*Amount*	*Qty.*	*Rate*	*Amount*
1 Dec.	–	–	–	–	--	–	300	9.70	2,910
3 Dec.	250	9.80	2,450	–	–	–	300 250	9.70 9.80	2,910 2,450
11 Dec.	–	–	–	300 100	9.70 9.80	2,910 980	150	9.80	1,470
15 Dec.	300	10.05	3,015	–	-	-	150 300	9.80 10.05	1,470 3,015
20 Dec.	–	–	–	150 60	9.80 10.05	1,470 603	240	10.05	2,412
25 Dec.	150	10.30	1,545				240 150	10.05 10.30	2,412 1,545
29 Dec.	–	–	–	100	10.05	1005	140 150	10.05 10.30	1,407 1,545

Computation of value of raw-materials

11 Dec.	—	400 units	3,890	(2,910 + 980)
20 Dec.	—	210 units	2,073	(1,470 + 603)
29 Dec.	—	100 units	1,005	
Consumption value			6968	

Closing stock

140 units × 10.05	=	1,407
150 units × 10.30	=	1,545
	=	2,452

3. Last-in-first-out (LIFO) Method : This method is exactly the opposite of FIFO method. For pricing the materials issues the price of the latest batch or lot of materials is adopted. If this lot exhausts then the price of earlier lot is made use of. However, before the current lot of materials are used fully, if any further purchases are made, any issue of materials are priced at the rate of recently purchased lot of materials. This process is continued throughout.

Impact of LIFO method on cost of production : (*a*) As the prices of the latest purchased materials are used for issue purpose, the issue price conforms to the current market prices. Consequently, the cost of production also reflects to the current market price.

(*b*) In a rising market, cost of production is overstated and in a falling market the cost of production is understated.

Impact of LIFO method on inventory valuation : (*a*) The value of closing stock does not reflect the current market price as all the rates of latest purchased materials are used for issue purposes. Thus closing stock is valued at old rates but not at the current rates of materials.

Impact of LIFO method on profit : (*a*) The total profit will not get affected under this method because a rise in price may be compensated by a fall in prices over a period of time. However, profits of every product or job differs because of charging of different rates of materials to different products or jobs.

(*b*) In period of rising prices, the higher rates of materials are charged to production, thereby inflating the cost of production. This results in a reduced margin of profit resulting in tax deduction.

Advantages : (*a*) As all issues are priced at the actual cost no unrealised profit or loss is derived.

(*b*) Issue prices reflect current market rates and hence cost of production also conforms to the current market rates which is more realistic.

(*c*) Becasue of the above reason, it will be possible to fix the selling price easily.

(*d*) The method is easy to operate where purchases are made less frequently.

(*e*) As mentioned earlier, because of inflation in the cost of production, the reduced profit margin results in savings in tax.

Disadvantages : (*a*) Two similar jobs cannot be compared because of charging of different rates of materials to different jobs.

(*b*) The closing stock does not reflect current market price. This may not be accepted by income tax authorities.

(*c*) This method cannot be operated when the invoice price does not reach before issues are to be priced.

(*d*) Calculations will be more if transactions are many with frequent price fluctuations.

Pricing of materials returned to storeroom under LIFO method : Materials returned should be recorded at the price at which they were originally issued, and these units should be issued at the old price on the next requisition received.

Pricing of materials returned to vendor under LIFO method : The materials returned to the vendor should be valued at the price of the latest units received and still in stock.

PROBLEMS ON LIFO METHOD

Problem 5 : From the following receipts and issues of material during the month of January 1997 prepare store ledger account according to LIFO method :

1997 Jan. 1, Received	500 units @ Rs. 10 per unit
1997 Jan. 5, Received	250 units @ Rs. 11 per unit
1997 Jan. 8, Issued	300 units

1997 Jan. 10, Received	400	units @ Rs. 12 per unit
1997 Jan. 13, Issued	250	units
1997 Jan. 20, Received	100	units @ Rs. 11 per unit
1997 Jan. 28, Issued	400	units

On 1st January 1997, stock on hand was 200 units valued at Rs. 9 per unit.

(*University of Delhi, B.Com. (Pass), April 1998*)

Solution : Stores ledger card - LIFO method

Date	*Receipts*			*Issues*			*Balance*		
	Qty.	*Rate*	*Amount*	*Qty.*	*Rate*	*Amount*	*Qty.*	*Rate*	*Amount*
1997									
Jan. 1,	–	–	–	–	–	–	200	9	1,800
1,	500	10	5,000	–	–	–	200	9	1,800
							500	10	5,000
5,	250	11	2,750	–	–	–	200	9	1,800
							500	10	5,000
							250	11	2,750
8,	–	–	–	250	11	2,750	200	9	1,800
				50	10	500	450	10	4,500
10,	400	12	4,800	–	–	–	200	9	1,800
							450	10	4,500
							400	12	4,800
13,	–	–	–	250	12	300	200	9	1,800
							450	10	4,500
							150	12	1,800
20,	100	11	1,100	–	–	–	200	9	1,800
							450	10	4,500
							150	12	1,800
							100	11	1,100
28,	–	–	–	100	11	1,100			
				150	12	1,800			
				150	10	1,500	200	9	1,800
							300	10	3,000

Problem 6 : From the following information, prepare the stores ledger account under LIFO method.

1.2.95	Opening balance	100 units at Rs. 10 each
2.2.95	Received	200 units at Rs. 10.50 each
5.2.95	Received	300 units at Rs. 10.60 each
7.2.95	Issued	400 units
10.2.95	Issued	120 units
15.2.95	Received	400 units at Rs. 11 each
19.2.95	Issued	200 units
24.2.95	Received	300 units at Rs. 11.40 each
27.2.95	Issued	200 units
28.2.95	Issued	200 units

(*University of Madras, B.Com. (Correspondence Course), May 1997*)

Solution : Stores ledger card - LIFO method

Date	*Receipts*			*Issues*			*Balance*		
	Qty.	*Rate*	*Amount*	*Qty.*	*Rate*	*Amount*	*Qty.*	*Rate*	*Amount*
1.2.95	-	-	-	-	-	-	100	10	1,000

2.2.95	200	10.50	2,100	–	–	–	100 200	10 10.50	1,000 2,100
5.2.95	300	10.60	3180	–	–	–	100 200 300	10 10.50 10.60	1,000 2,100 3,180
7.2.95	-	-	-	300 100	10.60 10.50	3,180 1,050	100 100	10 10.50	1,000 1,050
10.2.95				100 20	10.50 10	1,050 200	80	10	800
15.2.95	400	11	4,400	–	–	–	80 400	10 11	800 4,400
19.2.95	–	–	–	200	11	2,200	80 200	10 11	800 2,200
24.2.95	300	11.40	3420	–	–	–	80 200 300	10 11 11.40	800 2200 3,420
27.2.95	–	–	–	200	11.40	2,280	80 200 100	10 11 11.40	800 2,280 1,140
28.2.95	–	–	–	100 100	11.40 11	1,140 1,100	80 100	10 11	800 1,100

Problems on FIFO and LIFO methods

Problem 7 : In pricing the diesel sold, service station *A* follows FIFO method, while station *B* follows LIFO method. On 1 January 1992 both had 6,000 litres each@ Rs. 2.60 per litre. During the month, each station received additional supply of 6,000 litres at Rs. 2.75 per litre. Sales for each of these two stations during the month were 8,000 litres @ Rs. 2.90 per litre. Calculate for each station the profit earned during the month and value of diesel in stock at the close of the period.

Solution :

Stores ledger card (FIFO method)

Particulars	*Receipts*			*Issues*			*Balance*		
	Qty.	*Rate*	*Amount*	*Qty.*	*Rate*	*Amount*	*Qty.*	*Rate*	*Amount*
Opening stock	-	-	-	-	-	-	6,000	2.60	15,600
Receipts	6,000	2.75	16,500	-	-	-	6,000 6,000	2.60 2.75	15,600 16,500
Issues	-	-	-	6,000 2,000	2.60 2.75	15,600 5,500	4,000	2.75	11,000

Profit = Sale price – Issue price

= 8,000@ Rs. 2.90 – 21,100 (15,600 + 5,500)

= 23,200 – 21,100 = Rs. 2.100

Stores ledger card (LIFO method)

Particulars	*Receipts*			*Issues*			*Balance*		
	Qty.	*Rate*	*Amount*	*Qty.*	*Rate*	*Amount*	*Qty.*	*Rate*	*Amount*
Opening stock	-	-	-	-	-	-	6,000	2.60	15,600
Receipts	6,000	2.75	16,500	-	-	-	6,000 6,000	2.60 2.75	15,600 16,500
Issues				6,000 2,000	2.75 2.60	16,500 5,200	4,000	2.60	10,400

Profit = Sale price – Issue price
= 23,200 – 21,700 (16,500 + 5,200)
= Rs. 1,500

Problem 8 : Mr. Reddy, a textile dealer in Warangal commenced business on 1 January, 1989. Textile materials used include two types *M* and *N*.

During six months ended on 30 June, 1989, purchase were as follows :

4.1.89	500	meters of type *M* @ Rs. 20 per meter
6.1.89	800	meters of type *N* @ Rs. 30 per meter
18.3.89	1,150	meters of type *M* @ Rs. 24 per meter
16.4.89	1,500	meters of type *N* @ Rs. 32 per meter
26.5.89	400	meters of type *M* @ Rs. 19 per meter

Issues were as follows :

7.1.89	350	meters of *M*
12.1.89	600	meters of *N*
28.3.89	710	meters of *M*
22.4.89	1,430	meters of *N*
1.6.89	790	meters of *M*

Write out the complete stores ledger card in respect of above transactions using (*i*) FIFO and (*ii*) LIFO methods. (*Kakatiya University, B.Com., May 1992*)

Solution : **Stores ledger card (FIFO method)**

Date	Receipts			Issues			Balance		
	Qty.	*Rate*	*Amount*	*Qty.*	*Rate*	*Amount*	*Qty.*	*Rate*	*Amount*
4.1.89	500(*M*)	20	10,000				500	20	10,000
6.1.89	800(*N*)	30	24,000				500	20	10,000
							800	30	24,000
7.1.89				350(*M*)	20	7,000	150(*M*)	20	3,000
							800(*N*)	30	24,000
12.1.89				600(*N*)	30	18,000	150(*M*)	20	3,000
							200(*N*)	30	6,000
18.3.89	1,150(*M*)	24	27,600				150(*M*)	20	3,000
							200(*N*)	30	6,000
							1,150(*M*)	24	27,600
28.3.89				150(*M*)	20	3,000	200(*N*)	30	6,000
				560(*M*)	24	23,440	590(*M*)	24	14,160
16.4.89	1,500(*M*)	32	48,000				200(*N*)	30	6,000
							590(*M*)	24	14,160
							1,500(*N*)	32	48,000
22.4.89				200(*N*)	30	6,000	590(*M*)	24	14,160
				1,230(*N*)	32	39,360	270(*N*)	32	8,640
26.5.89	400(*N*)	19	7,600				590(*M*)	24	14,160
							270(*N*)	32	8,640
							400(*M*)	19	7,600
1.6.89				590(*N*)	24	14,160	270(*N*)	32	8,640
				200(*M*)	19	3800	200(*M*)	19	3,800

Stores ledger card (LIFO method)

Date	Receipts			Issues			Balance		
	Qty.	*Rate*	*Amount*	*Qty.*	*Rate*	*Amount*	*Qty.*	*Rate*	*Amount*
4.1.89	500(*M*)	20	10,000				500(*M*)	20	10,000
6.1.89	800(*N*)	30	24,000				800(*N*)	30	24,000
7.1.89				350(*M*)	20	7,000	150(*M*)	20	3,000
12.1.89				600(*N*)	30	18,000	200(*N*)	30	6,000
18.3.89	1,150(*N*)	24	27,600				150(*M*)	20	3,000
							200(*N*)	30	6,000
							1,150(*M*)	24	27,600
28.3.89				710(*M*)	24	17,040	150(*M*)	20	3,000
							200(*N*)	30	6,000
							440(*M*)	24	10,560
16.4.89	1,500(*N*)	32	48,000				150(*M*)	20	3,000
							440(*N*)	24	10,560
							200(*M*)	30	6,000
							1,500(*N*)	32	48,000
22.4.89				1,430(*N*)	32	47,760	150(*M*)	20	3,000
							440(*M*)	24	10,560
							200(*N*)	30	6,000
							70(*N*)	32	2,240
26.5.89	400(*M*)	19	7,600				150(*N*)	20	3,000
							440(*M*)	24	10,560
							400(*M*)	19	7,600
							200(*N*)	30	6,000
							70(*N*)	32	2,240
1.6.89				400(*M*)	19	7,600	150(*M*)	20	3,000
				390(*M*)	24	9,360	50(N)	24	1,200
							200(*N*)	30	6,000
							70(*N*)	32	2,240

Problem 9 : The following transactions occur in the purchase and issue of a material during the first quarter of 1999.

Jan. 2,	Purchased	4,000 units @ Rs. 4.00 per unit
Jan. 20,	Purchased	500 units @ Rs. 5.00 per unit
Feb. 5,	Issued	2,000 units
Feb. 10,	Purchased	6,000 units @ Rs. 6.00 per unit
Feb. 12,	Issued	4,000 units
Mar. 2,	Issued	1,000 units
Mar. 5,	Issued	2,000 units
Mar. 15,	Purchased	4,500 units @ Rs. 5.50 per unit
Mar. 20,	Issued	3,000 units

From the above, prepare the stores ledger card by using (*a*) FIFO method, (*b*) LIFO method of issuing materials. What would be the value of stock on hand at the end of the period according to each of the two methods. *(Sri Sathya Sai University, B.Com. (Hons), March 1999)*

Solution :

Stores ledger card - FIFO method

Particulars	Receipts			Issues			Balance		
	Qty.	*Rate*	*Amount*	*Qty.*	*Rate*	*Amount*	*Qty.*	*Rate*	*Amount*
Jan. 2	4,000	4	16,000	-	-	-	4,000	4	16,000

Date	Receipts Qty.	Rate	Amount	Issues Qty.	Rate	Amount	Balance Qty.	Rate	Amount
Jan 20,	500	5	2500	–	–	–	4,000	4	16,000
							500	5	2,500
Feb. 5,	–	–	–	2,000	4	8,000	2,000	4	8,000
							500	5	2,500
10,	6,000	6	36,000	–	–	–	200	4	8,000
							500	5	2,500
							6,000	6	36,000
12,	–	–	–	200	4	8,000			
				500	5	2,500			
				1,500	6	9,000	4,500	6	27,000
Mar. 2,				1,000	6	6,000	3,500	6	21,000
3,				2,000	6	12,000	1,500	6	9,000
15,	4,500	5.50	24,750	–	–	–	1,500	6	9,000
							4,500	5.50	24,750
20,	–	–	–	1,500	6	9,000			
				1,500	5.50	8,250	3,000	5.50	16,500

Closing Stock 3,000 units @ Rs. 5.50 = Rs. 16,500

Stores ledger card - LIFO method

Date	*Receipts*			*Issues*			*Balance*		
	Qty.	*Rate*	*Amount*	*Qty.*	*Rate*	*Amount*	*Qty.*	*Rate*	*Amount*
Jan. 2,	4,000	4	16,000	–	–	–	4,000	4	16,000
Jan. 20,	500	5	2,500	–	–	–	4,000	4	16,000
							500	5	2,500
Feb. 5,	–	–	–	500	5	2,500			
				1,500	4	6,000	2,500	4	10,000
Feb. 10,	6,000	6	36,000	–	–	–	2,500	4	10,000
							6,000	6	36,000
Feb. 12,	–	–	–	4,000	6	2,400	2,500	4	10,000
							2,000	6	12,000
Mar. 2,	–	–	–	1,000	6	6,000	2,500	4	10,000
							1,000	6	6,000
Mar. 5,	–	–	–	1,000	6	6,000			
				1,000	4	4,000	1,500	4	6,000
Mar. 15,	4,500	5.50	24,750	–	–	–	1,500	4	6,000
							4,500	5.50	24,750
Mar. 20,	–	–	–	3,000	5.50	16,500	1,500	4	6,000
							1,500	5.50	8,250

Closing stock	=	1,500 units @ Rs. 4	=	6,000
		1,500 units @ Rs. 5.50	=	8,250
			Rs.	14,250

4. **Highest-in-first-out (HIFO) method :** This is a variation of LIFO method and gives similar result as in case of LIFO during the period of continuous rising prices. Under this method issues are priced at the highest rates of materials in stock irrespective of the dates of purchases. The purpose of this method is to charge with the highest rate of materials to the current cost of production.

The impact of this method over cost of production is that cost is overstated. On profit, its impact is understatement of profit. On valuation of closing stock its impact is understatement of the value of stock and a hidden reserve is created in the valuation of stock.

Problem on HIFO method

Problem 10 : The South India Chemical Works had a opening stock of materials of 500 units at Re. 1 per unit on 1.4.03. The following purchases and issues were made thereafter :

Purchases			*Issues*	
Date	*Units*	*Rate*	*Date*	*Units*
6.4.03	100	1.10	9.4.03	500
20.4.03	700	1.20	22.4.03	500
27.4.03	400	1.30	30.4.03	500
13.5.03	1,000	1.40	15.5.03	500
20.5.03	500	1.50	22.5.03	500
17.6.03	400	1.60	18.6.03	500
28.6.03	600	1.70	29.6.03	500

Prepare a store ledger card and determine the value of closing stock as on 30.6.03 under HIFO method.

Solution : **Stores ledger card (HIFO method)**

Material ————	Bin No. ————	Max. level ————
Description ————	Location code No. ————	Min. level ————
Code No. ————	Unit of quantity ————	Reorder level ————
		Danger level ————

Date	*Receipts*			*Issues*			*Balance*		
	Qty.	*Rate*	*Amount*	*Qty.*	*Rate*	*Amount*	*Qty.*	*Rate*	*Amount*
1.4.03							500	1	500
6.4.03	100	1.10	110				500	1	500
							100	1.10	110
9.4.03				100	1.10	110			
				400	1	400	100	1	100
20.4.03	700	1.20	840				100	1	100
							700	1.20	840
22.4.03				500	1.20	600	100	1	100
							200	1.20	240
27.4.03	400	1.30	520				100	1	100
							200	1.20	240
							400	1.30	520
30.4.03				400	1.30	520			
				100	1.20	120	100	1	100
							100	1.20	120
13.5.03	1,000	1.40	1,400				100	1	100
							100	1.20	120
							1,000	1.40	1,400
15.5.03				500	1.40	700	100	1	100
							100	1.20	120
							500	1.40	700
20.5.03	500	1.50	750				100	1	100
							100	1.20	120
							500	1.40	700
							500	1.50	750

22.5.03				500	1.50	750	100	1.00	100
							100	1.20	120
							500	1.40	700
17.6.03	400	1.60	640				100	1.00	100
							100	1.20	120
							500	1.40	700
							400	1.60	640
18.6.03				400	1.60	640	100	1.00	100
				100	1.40	140	100	1.20	120
							400	1.40	560
28.6.03	600	1.70	1,020				100	1.00	100
							100	1.20	120
							400	1.40	560
							600	1.70	1,020
29.6.03				500	1.70	850	100	1.00	100
							100	1.20	120
							400	1.40	560
							100	1.70	170

5. **Next-in-first-out (NIFO) method :** Under this method, the issues are priced at the purchased rates of materials which are yet to arrive, in simple words, the material rates which have been agreed upon by the supplier is used for issue purpose, though materials are not physically received. In this method, materials are issued at the price at which a new order has been placed and this price will hold good for all future issues until a next order is placed. As this method is somewhat complicated it is not normally adopted.

6. **Base stock method :** Strictly speaking this is not a distinct method of pricing materials issue. However, this method is used by some concerns as a safety device to ensure continuity in production. This method works out under the assumption that a certain minimum quantity of materials are to set aside which is to be used during the period of emergencey. This minimum stock is treated as a fixed asset and is known as 'Base Stock'. Materials which are in excess of base stock are issued by adopting either FIFO or LIFO principle. The base stock is deemed to have been created out of the first consignment and therefore valued at this price. The advantages and disadvantages of this method depends upon FIFO or LIFO principle used.

PROBLEM ON BASE STOCK METHOD

Problem 10 : From the following particulars, write up the priced stores ledger card .

2003 Jan. 1, Purchased 500 kgs@ Rs. 2 per kg.
10, Purchased 300 kgs @ Rs. 2.10 per kg.
15, Issued 600 kgs.
20, Purchased 400 kgs@ Rs. 2.20 per kg.
25, Issued 300 kgs.
27, Purchased 500 kgs @ Rs. 2.10 per kg.
31, Issued 200 kgs.

Adopt base stock method of issues using LIFO principle and ascertain the value of closing stock. Base stock being 200 kgs.

Solution : **Stores ledger card (base stock method—LIFO)**

Material ________ Bin No. ________ Max. Level ________
Description ________ Location code No. ________ Min. level ________
Code No. ________ Unit of quantity ________ Reorder level ________
Danger level ________

Date	*Receipts*			*Issues*			*Balance*		
	Qty.	*Rate*	*Amount*	*Qty.*	*Rate*	*Amount*	*Qty.*	*Rate*	*Amount*
1.1.03	500	2	100				500	2	1,000
10.1.03	300	2.10	630				500	2	1,000
15.1.03				300	2.10	630	300	2.10	630
				300	2	600	200	2	400
20-1-03	400	2.20	880				200	2	400
							400	2.20	880
25-1-03				300	2.20	660	200	2	400
							100	2.20	220
27-1-03	500	2.10	1,050				200	2	400
							100	2.20	220
							500	2.10	1,050
31-1-03				200	2.10	420	200	2	400
							100	2.20	220
							300	2.10	630

Computed Actual Cost

This method is based on the assumption that when materials are frequently bought and put in storeroom, they loose their identity. This is more common in industries like chemicals, paints, varnishes, oil refineries, etc. As materials cannot be identified for issue purpose, its actual cost cannot be used for pricing the materials issue. Therefore instead of using actual cost computed actual costs are used. The following are the various methods which fall under this category of pricing material issues.

A. Simple Average Price Methods

1. *Perpetual simple average price :* Under this method issue price is calculated by dividing the total of unit purchase price of different lots of materials from which the materials to be priced could be drawn by the number of prices constituting the total. Expressed in the form of a formula :

$$\text{Simple average price} = \frac{\text{Total unit prices of materials in stock}}{\text{Number of purchases}}$$

The new simple average price is to be calculated when a fresh purchase is made. Similarly the issue rates also changes when the materials from a consignment the price of which was taken into consideration for calculating issue prices is exhausted.

Advantages :

(*a*) The method smoothens out the variations in the material price.

(*b*) Issue rate remains same until a fresh purchase is made or the consignment which gets exhausted before the current issue is made. This reduces clerical work.

Disadvantages

(*a*) The issue prices do not confirm the current market price. So we come across an element of unrealised profit or loss in every job.

(*b*) Closing stock value also does not conform to current market price. This distorts the balance sheet of the concern.

(*c*) It takes into account only the purchase prices but not the quantities.

Pricing of materials returned to storeroom under average price method : Materials returned to storeroom is recorded at the price originally issued but a new average cost is to be computed at the time of such issue as if the goods returned is a new purchase.

Pricing of materials returned to vendor : Materials returned to vendor is valued at the latest average price.

PROBLEMS ON SIMPLE AVERAGE METHOD

Problem 11 : Reccrd the following transactions in a stores ledger card by adopting the simple average price method :

Date	*Purchases*		*Issues*
	Qty.	*Rate*	
1-1-03	500	2.00	
10-1-03	300	2.10	
15-1-03			600
20-1-03	400	2.20	
25-1-03			300
27-1-03	500	2.10	
31-1-03			200

Solution : **Stores ledger card (Simple average price method)**

Material ————	Bin No. ————	Max. level ————
Description ————	Location code No. ————	Min. level ————
Code No. ————	Unit of quantity ————	Reorder level ————
		Danger level .....

Date	*Receipts*				*Issues*				*Balance*	
	Qty.	*Cumu-lative qty.*	*Rate*	*Amt.*	*Qty.*	*Cumu-lative qty.*	*Rate*	*Amt.*	*Qty.*	*Amt.*
1-1-92	500	500	2	1,000					500	1,000
10-1-92	300	800	2.10	630					800	1,630
15-1-92					600	600	2.05	1,230	200	400
20-1-92	400	1,210	2.10	880					600	1,280
25-1-92					300	900	2.15	645	300	635
27-1-92	500	1,700	2.10	1,050					800	1,685
31-1-92					200	1,100	2.15	430	600	1,255

Calculation of Ist issue rate :

Cumulative receipt before issue is 800 : Cumulative issue before actual issue is *Nil.* So the price is

$$\frac{2+2.10}{2} = 2.05$$

Calculation of IInd issue rate :

Cumulative receipt 1,200 : Cumulative issue before actual issue is 600. So issue price is

$$\frac{2.10+2.20}{2} = 2.15$$

Calculation of IIIrd issue rate :

Cumulative receipt is 1,700 : Cumulative issue before actual issue is 900. So the issue price is

$$\frac{2.20+2.10}{2} = 2.15$$

Problem 12 : Record the following transactions in a stores ledger card under simple average price method :

Date	*Receipts*		*Issues*
	Qty.	*Rate*	
1-1-03	1,000	1.00	
10-1-03	260	1.05	
20-1-03			700
4-2-03	400	1.15	
21-2-03	300	1.25	
16-3-03			620
12-4-03			240
10-5-03	500	1.10	
25-5-03			380

Solution : **Stores ledger card (Simple average price method)**

Material	Bin No.	Max. Level ....
Description	Location code No.	Min. level ....
Code No.	Unit of quantity	Reorder level ....
		Danger level ....

Date	*Receipts*				*Issues*				*Balance*	
	Qty.	*Cumu-lative qty.*	*Rate*	*Amt.*	*Qty.*	*Cumu-lative qty.*	*Rate*	*Amt.*	*Qty.*	*Rate.*
1-1-03	1,000	1,000	1	1,000					1,000	1,000
10-1-03	260	1,260	1.05	273					1,260	1,273
20-1-03					700	700	1.025	718	560	555
4-2-03	400	1,660	1.15	460					960	1,015
21-2-03	300	1,960	1.25	375					1,260	1,390
16-3-03					620	1,320	1.11	682	640	708
12-4-03					240	1,560	1.20	288	400	420
10-5-03	500	2,460	1.10	550					900	970
25-5-03					380	1,940 .	1,165	443	520	527

Calculation of Ist issue price :

Cumulative receipts 1,260 : Cumulative issue *Nil*. So the price is

$$\frac{1.00+1.05}{2}=1.025$$

Calculation of IInd issue price :

Cumulative receipt 1,960 : Cumulative issue 700. So issue price is

$$\frac{1.00+1.05+1.15+1.25}{4}=1.11$$

Calculation of IIIrd issue price :

Cumulative receipt is 1,960 : Cumulative issues 1,320 which exceeds the cumulative receipts to January 10 (1,260). So the price is

$$\frac{1.15+1.25}{2}=1.20$$

Calculation of IVth issue price :

Cumulative receipts 2,460 : Cumulative issues 1,560 which exceeds the cumulative receipts to January 10 (1,260) but is still less than cumulative receipts to February 4 (1,660). So price is

$$\frac{1.15+1.25+1.10}{3} = 1.165$$

2. *Periodic simple average price method :* Unlike simple average price method, where issue prices are calculated depending upon purchases and issues of materials, under this method issue prices are calculated for a particular period. Hence the name periodic simple average price method. The issue rate is computed by dividing the total of purchase rates of all materials for a period by the number of rates used in that period. However, rate of opening stock is not included, as it is included in the previous year's calculation. The issue rate thus obtained is used for pricing the material issues.

PROBLEM ON PERIODIC SIMPLE AVERAGE METHOD

Problem 13 : For the problem number 12 prepare a stores ledger card using periodic simple average price method.

Solution : **Stores ledger card (Periodic simple average price method)**

Material .... Bin No. .... Max. level ....

Description .... Location code No. .... Min. level ....

Code No. .... Unit of quantity .... Reorder level ....

Danger level ....

Date	*Receipts*			*Issues*			*Balance*	
	Qty.	*Rate*	*Amount*	*Qty.*	*Rate*	*Amount*	*Rate*	*Amount*
1-1-03	1,000	1	1,000				1,000	1,000
10-1-03	260	1,05	273				1,260	1,273
20-1-03				700			560	
9-2-03	400	1.15	460				960	
21-2-03	300	1.25	375				1,260	
16-3-03				620			640	
12-4-03				240			400	
10-5-03	500	1.10	550				900	
25-5-03				380			520	505
	2,460	5.55	2,658	1,940	1.11	2,153		

Note : The issue rate is calculated at the end of the given period. The issue rate of Rs. 1.11 is calculated as under :

$$\text{Periodic simple average price} = \frac{\text{Total rates of materials}}{\text{Number of rates}}$$

$$= \frac{5.55}{5} = 1.11$$

Value of closing stock = Value of receipts – Value of issues

= 2,658 – 2,153 (1,940 × 1.11)

= Rs. 505

3. *Moving simple average price method :* This method is particularly used when, there is drastic changes in the price level and where it is desired to spread total cost over all the jobs executed. The issue rate is calculated by dividing the total of periodic simple average prices relating to a given period by the number of period. This method therefore involves the fixation of period which can be a month, two months and so on. For example, if three monthly period is fixed, the simple moving average rate is to be calculated for the month of April. The number of prices of purchases for the month of January to March is added and then it is divided by three. Similarly, for calculating issue rate of April, the purchase rate of January is ignored and that of April month is included. The total rates of February to April is then divided by 3 to get the issue rate for April.

PROBLEM ON SIMPLE MOVING AVERAGE PRICE METHOD

Problem 14 : Voltas Ltd. follows simple moving average price method of pricing materials issue. The periodic averge prices are given in order to calculate 3 monthly simple moving average price for use for the period May to September 1992.

Month :	Jan.	Feb.	Mar.	April	May	June	July	Aug.	Sept.
Periodic simple Average price	2.00	2.10	2.20	2.30	2.40	2.50	2.60	2.70	2.80

Solution : **Calculation of 3 monthly simple moving average price**

Month	*Periodic average price*	*3 Monthly moving total*	*Simple moving average price*
Jan.	2.00		
Feb.	2.10	6.30	2.10
Mar.	2.20	6.60	2.20
Apr.	2.30	6.90	2.30
May	2.40	7.20	2.40
June	2.50	7.50	2.50
Jul.	2.60	7.80	2.60
Aug.	2.70	8.10	2.70
Sept.	2.80		

B. Weighted Average Price Methods

1. Perpetual weighted average price method : Under this method the weighted average price is calculated by taking into account both the quantity and amount of materials. Issue rates are calculated by dividing the amount of materials in balance column of stores ledger by the quantity of materials in stock. Issue rates are to be calculated only when a fresh purchase is made, till then all isues are priced at the same issue rate. In other words, the issue rate remains same until a fresh purchase is made. However, the issue rate is calculated up to four decimal places to get more accurate results.

Advantages :

(*a*) The method smoothens out a drastic fluctuation in the prices of materials.

(*b*) Issue rates need be caculated only when materials are purchased. Hence clerical work is reduced.

(*c*) This method gives satisfactory result compared to simple average price method because it takes into account both the quantity and value of materials.

Disadvantages :

(*a*) Calculations will be more when transactions are many.

(*b*) Issue rate does not correspond to current market price Hence we come across an element of unrealised profit or loss.

(*c*) Closing stock value also does not correspond to current market price. Hence balance sheet does not reflect the true position of the business.

(*d*) Issue rates are to be calculated up to four decimal places to ensure more accuracy.

Problem 15 : The stores ledger account of a manufacturing company reveals the following entries of a particular material :

Date	*Receipts*			*Issues*		
	Qty.	*Rate*	*Amount*	*Qty.*	*Rate*	*Amount*
2-1-03	4,000	1.80	7,200			
5-1-03	2,000	1.75	3,500			
18-1-03				10,000		19.500
3-2-03				5,000		9.750
14-2-03	3,000	1.85	5,550			
18-2-03	3,000	1.90	5,700			
20-2-03				10,000		19,200

Opening stock as on 1-1-03 was 20,000 units valued at Rs. 40,000. Closing stock as per physical verification on 28-2-03 was 6,950 units.

Work out the method of pricing the issue which you consider to have been adopted for the issue of the material and show the working of the issue rates (correct to 2 places of decimal). Complete the account of the material and work out the value of the closing stock as on 28-2-03 on the basis of valuation adopted.

Solution : **Stores ledger card (Weighted average price method)**

Material *X*———	Bin No. ———	Max. Level ———
Description ———	Location code No. ———	Min. level ———
Code No. ———	Unit of quantity ———	Reorder level ———
		Danger level ———

Date	*Receipts*			*Issues*			*Balance*	
	Qty.	*Rate*	*Amount*	*Qty.*	*Rate*	*Amount*	*Qty.*	*Amount*
1-1-03							20,000	40,000
2-1-03	4,000	1.80	7,200				24,000	47,200
5-1-03	2,000	1.75	3,500				26,000	50,700
18-1-03				10,000	1.95	19,500	16,000	31,200
3-2-03				5,000	1.95	9,750	11,000	21,450
14-2-03	3,000	1.85	5,550				14,000	27,000
18-2-03	3,000	1.90	5,700				17,000	32,700
20-2-03				10,000	1.92	19,200	700	13,500
28-2-03				50 (Loss being difference of balance of stock)	1.92	96	6,950	13,404

Working note : In the above problem, weighted average method of pricing issues has been followed as is evident from the working of issue price as given below :

(1) On 18-1-03, the issue price per unit is

$$\frac{19,500}{10,000} = \text{Rs. } 1.95$$

This corresponds to weighted average rate which is calculated from the following receipts prior to 18-1-03 :

		Qty. *(Units)*	*Value* *(Rs.)*
Opening stock	1-1-03	20,000	40,000
Purchases on	2-1-03	4,000	7,200
Purchases on	5-1-03	2,000	3,500
		26,000	50,700

$\therefore$ Weighted average rate per unit = $\frac{50,700}{26,000}$ = Rs. 1.95

(2) On 3 February 03, the issue price per unit is

$$= \frac{9,750}{5,000} = \text{Rs. } 1.95$$

(3) On 20 February, the issue price is

$$= \frac{19,200}{10,000} = \text{Rs. } 1.92$$

This corresponds to weighted average rate which is calculated from the following receipts in the stores prior to 20-2-03

	Qty. *(Units)*	*Value* *(Rs.)*
Balance of materials in stores on 3-2-03, *i.e.*, balance left after issue on 3.2.03	11,000	21,450
Purchases on 14-2-03	3,000	5,550
Purchases on 18-2-03	3,000	5,700
	17,000	32,700

$\therefore$ Weighted average rate = $\frac{32,700}{17,000}$ = Rs. 1.92

PROBLEM ON FIFO, LIFO AND WEIGHTED AVERAGE METHOD

Problem 16 : Oil India is a bulk Distributor of high otanc petrol. A periodic inventory of petrol on hand is taken when the books are closed at the end of each month. The following summary of information is a available for the month of June 1985 :

	Rs.
Sales	9,45,000
General administrative cost	25,000
Opening stock : 1,00,000 litres @ Rs. 3 per litre	3,00,000

Purchases :

June 1, 2,00,000 litres @ Rs. 2.85 per litre

June 30, 1,00,000 litres @ Rs. 3.03 per litre

Closing stock June 30—1,30,000 litres

Compute the following data by the first-in-first-out weighted average and last-in-first-out method of inventory costing :

(*a*) Value of inventory on June 30

(*b*) Amount of the cost of goods sold for June

(*c*) Profit or loss for June. (*Sri Sathya Sai University, B.Com., Oct. 1988*)

Solution : **Stores ledger card (FIFO method)**

Material X ————	Bin No. ————	Max. Level ————
Description ————	Location code No. ————	Min. level ————
Code No. ————	Unit of quantity ————	Reorder level ————
		Danger level ————

Date	Receipts			Issues			Balance		
	Qty.	*Rate*	*Amount*	*Qty.*	*Rate*	*Amount*	*Qty.*	*Rate*	*Amount*
June 1							1,00,000	3	3,00,000
June 1	2,00,000	2.85	5,70,000				1,00,000	3	3,00,000
							2,00,000	2.85	5,70,000
June 1 to June 30				1,00,000	3	3,00,000			
				1,70,000	2.85	4,84,500			
June 30	1,00,000	3.03	3,03,000				30,000	2.85	85.500
							1,00,000	3.03	3,03.000

Stores ledger card (Weighted average method)

Date	Receipts			Issues			Balance	
	Qty.	*Rate*	*Amount*	*Qty.*	*Rate*	*Amount*	*Qty.*	*Amount*
June 1							1,00,0000	3,00,000
June 1	2,00,000	2.85	5,70,000				3,00,0000	8,70,000
June 1 to June 30				2,70,000	2.90	7,83,000	30,000	87,000
June 30	1,00,000	3,03	3,03,000				1,30,000	3,90,000

Stores ledger card (LIFO method)

Date	Receipts			Issues			Balance		
	Qty.	*Rate*	*Amount*	*Qty.*	*Rate*	*Amount*	*Qty.*	*Rate*	*Amount*
June 1							1,00,000	3	3,00,000
June 1	2,00,000	2.85	5,70,000				1,00,000	3	3,00,000
							2,00,000	2.85	5,70,000
June 1 to June 30				2,00,000	2.85	5,70,000			
				70,000	3	2,10,000	30,000	3	90,000
June 30	1,00,000	3.03	3,03,000				30,000	3	90.000
							1,00,000	3.03	3,03.000

(*b*) Statement showing cost of goods sold for June

	FIFO	*Weighted average*	*LIFO*
Opening stock of materials	3,00,000	3,00,000	3,00,000
Add : Purchases :			
June 1, 2,00,000 litres @ Rs. 2.85 per litre	5,70,000	5,70,000	5,70,000
June30, 1,00,000 litres @ Rs. 3.03 per liter	3,03,000	3,03,000	3,03,000
	11,73,000	11,73,000	11,73,000
Less : Closing stock of materials	3,88,500	3,90,000	3,93,000
Cost of goods sold	7,84,500	7,83,500	7,80,000

(c) Statement showing profit :

		FIFO	Weighted average	LIFO
Sales		9,45,000	9,45,000	9,45,000
Less :	Cost of goods sold	7,84,500	7,83,000	7,80,000
	Gross Profit	1,60,500	1,62,000	1,65,000
Less :	General adm. cost	25,000	25,000	25,000
	Profit	1,35,500	1,37,000	1,40,000

2. Periodic Weighted Average Price Method

This method is also known as month-end weighted average method. Under this method the issue rate is calculated by dividing the total cost of materials purchased for a month (or quarter) by the total quantity of materials purchased during the period. The opening stock of materials (both quantity and value) is not considered while calculating the issue rate as this is included in calculating the previous year's issue rate. The issue of materials and closing stock is valued at the rate so obtained.

Advantages :

(*a*) Issue rate is calculated once in a month. Hence it reduces clerical work.

(*b*) This method is more accurate when compared to periodic simple average method since it takes into account both the quantity and cost.

(*c*) This method is particularly useful in coutinuous manufacturing industries where accounting entries are made periodically.

(*d*) It even's out wide fluctuation in the prices of materials in a given period.

Disadvantages :

(*a*) This method is not based on actual cost. Hence it gives rise to unrealised profit or loss.

(*b*) The value of closing stock neither reflects current market price nor actual cost.

Problem 17 : Prepare stores ledger card for problem No. 12 adopting periodic weighted average method considering 5 month duration.

Solution : **Stores ledger card (Periodic weighted average method)**

Material ————	Bin No. ————	Max. Level ————
Description ————	Location code No. ————	Min. level ————
Code No. ————	Unit of quantity ————	Reorder level ————
		Danger level ————

Date	Receipts			Issues			Balance	
	Qty.	Rate	Amount	Qty.	Rate	Amount	Qty.	Amount
1-1-03	1,000	1	1,000				1,000	1,000
10-1-03	260	1.05	273				1,260	1,273
20-1-03				700				
4-2-03	400	1.15	460					
21-2-03	300	5.25	375					
16-3-03				620			640	
12-4-03				240			400	
10-5-03	500	1.10	550				900	
25-5-03				380			520	563
	2,460		2,658	1,940	1.08	2,095		

Note : Calculation of issue rate $= \frac{\text{Total cost of purchases of materials}}{\text{Total quantity of materials purchased}}$

$= \frac{\text{Rs.}2{,}658}{2{,}460} = \text{Rs. } 1.08$

Closing stock = Receipts-Issues

= 2,658-2,095 = Rs. 563

or closing stcok = 520 units @ Rs. 1.08 = 563 (App.)

3. Moving Weighted Average Price Method : Under this method the issue price is calculated by dividing the total of the weighted price of the current period and weighted average prices of a given number of preceding periods by the total number of current and preceding periods. The issues of current month or period are valued at this rate.

PROBLEM ON MOVING WEIGHTED AND PERIODIC WEIGHTED AVERAGE PRICE METHOD

Problem 18 : From the following transactions extracted from the books of accounts of a manufacturing concern as on 31-12-2002, work out.

(*a*) The consumption value of raw materials in the month and (*b*) value of closing stock as on 31-12-2002, under the following methods of pricing issues :

(i) Moving weighted average price method

(*ii*) Periodic weighted average price method

Show the results in a tabuler form.

			Quantity in units	*Rate per unit*
2002 Dec.	1	Opening stock	300	9.70
	3	Purchases	250	9.80
	11	Issues	400	
	15	Purchases	300	10.05
	20	Issues	210	
	25	Purchases	150	10.30
	29	Issues	100	

(*I C W A, Inter 1981*)

Solution : **Stores ledger card (Moving weighted average price)**

Material ———— Bin No. ———— Max. Level ————

Description ———— Location code No. ———— Min. level ————

Code No. ———— Unit of quantity ———— Reorder level ————

Danger level ————

Date	*Receipts*			*Issues*			*Balance*	
	Qty.	*Rate*	*Amount*	*Qty.*	*Rate*	*Amount*	*Qty.*	*Amount*
1-1-02							300	2,910
3-12-02	250	9.80	2,450				250	2,450
							550	5,360
11-12-02				400	9.75	3,900	150	1,460
15-12-02	300	10.05	3,015				300	1,015
							450	4,475
20-12-02				210	9.94	2087.40	240	2,387.60
25-12-02	150	10.30	1,545				150	1,545.00
							390	3,932.60
29-12-02				100	10.08	1008	290	2,924.60

Note : Calculation of 1st issue rate $= \frac{5,360}{550} = 9.75$

Calculation of 2nd issue rate $= \frac{4,475}{450} = 9.94$

Calculation of 3rd issue rate $= \frac{3,932.60}{390} = 10.08$

Value of consumption of 710 units is as follows

(*i*) 400 units @ 9.75 per unit	3,900.00
(*ii*) 210 units @ 9.94 per unit	2,087.40
(*iii*) 100 units @ Rs. 10.08 unit	1,008.00
	6,995.40

Stores ledger card (Periodic weighted average price method)

Material	Bin No.	Max. Level
Description	Location code No.	Min. level
Code No.	Unit of quantity	Reorder level
		Danger level

Date	*Receipts*			*Issues*			*Balance*		
	Qty.	*Rate*	*Amount*	*Qty.*	*Rate*	*Amount*	*Qty.*	*Rate*	*Amount*
1-1-02	300	9.70	2,910				300	9.70	2,910
3-12-02	250	9.80	2,450				250	9.50	2,450
15-12-02	300	10.05	3,015				300	10.05	3,015
25-12-02	150	10.30	1,545				150	10.30	1,545
							1,000		9,920
11-12-02				400	9.92	3,968.00			
20-12-02				210	9.92	2,083.20			
29-12-02				100	9.92	992.00	290		2,876.80
	1,000		9,920	710	992	7,043.30			

Note : Calculation of issue rate $= \frac{9,920}{1,000} = 9.92$

Value of consumption = Rs. 7,043.20

Value of closing stock = Rs. 2,876.80

II. Market Price Method

This method is based on market price as against actual cost of materials under the earlier discussed methods. The following two methods fall under this classification of pricing materials issue.

1. Current market price method : As the name itself suggests, under this method, the materials are issued at the current prices prevailing in the market. This method is based on the principle that the cost of production must reflect the current market price. Thus this method is an reimprovement over the earlier methods discussed as all these methods are historical in nature and hence the cost of production does not reflect the current market price. This limitation is overcome by market price method. As the cost of production is charged with the current market price, the value of closing stock will reflect the historical cost.

Advantage : Cost of production reflects current market price.

Disadvantages : (*a*) Issues are not based on actual cost of materails at which they were bought. This results in notional profits.

(*b*) It is diffcult to ascertain market price.

(*c*) The cost of production varies depending upon fluctuation in market prices.

(*d*) The closing stock value does not conform to current market price.

2. Replacement price method : This method is based on the principle that at every issue of material, it is possible to determine the replacement cost of materials. However, determination of replacement price is not so easy and hence involves more work. Under this method, the issues are valued at the replacement price prevailing in the market on the date of issue.

Advantages : (*a*) No calculations are involved for pricing the material issues. The determined rates of issues are used instead.

(*b*) The cost of production reflects current market price.

Disadvantages : (*a*) It is difficult to determine replacement prices of materials.

(*b*) Issues are not made at the actual cost at which they were bought. Hence we come across notional profit or loss.

(c) Closing stock value does not conform to current market price.

PROBLEM ON REPLACEMENT PRICE METHOD

Problem 19 : Prepare stores ledger card showing pricing of material issues in replacement price basis from the following particulars :

10-3-03	Opening balance 400 units @ Rs. 4 each
10-3-03	Received 100 units @ Rs. 4.10 each
15-3-03	Issued 300 units to job *X* vide MRN 1
17-3-03	Received 200 units @ Rs. 4.30 each
20-3-03	Issued 250 units to job *Y* vide MRN 2
25-3-03	Received 400 units @ Rs. 4.50 each
26-3-03	Issued 200 units to job *Z* vide MRN 3
27-3-03	Received 100 units @ Rs. 4.60 each
30-3-03	Issued 300 units to job *A* vide MRN 4
	Replacement price on various dates :
	15-3-03—Rs. 4.20, 20-3-03—Rs. 4.40, 26-3-03—Rs. 4-60 and 30-3-03—Rs. 4-80.

Solution : **Stores ledger card (Replacement price method)**

Material—————	Bin No. —————	Max. Level —————
Description —————	Location code No. —————	Min. level —————
Code No. —————	Unit of quantity —————	Reorder level —————
		Danger level —————

Date	*Receipts*			*Issues*			*Balance*	
	Qty.	*Rate*	*Amount*	*Qty.*	*Rate*	*Amount*	*Qty.*	*Amount*
1-3-03							400	1,600
10-3-03	100	4.10	410				500	2,010
15-3-03				300	4.20	1,260	200	750
17-3-03	200	4.30	860				400	1,610
20-3-03				250	4.40	1,100	150	510
25-3-03	400	4.50	1,800				550	2,310
26-3-03				200	4.60	920	350	1,390
27-3-03	100	4.60	460					
30-3-03				300	4.80	1,440	150	410

III. Notional Price Method of Pricing Material Issues

1. ***Standard price method :*** The terminology of ICMA London defines standard price as "a predetermined price fixed on the basis of a specification of all the factors affecting price." These factors are as follows.

(*a*) The quantity of materials to be purchased which will affect quantity discount.

(*b*) The possibility of a rise in price due to expected wage increase.

(*c*) The liklihood of a rise or fall in prices due to market condition.

(*d*) The charging of fieight and warehousing expenses to the material.

(*e*) The charging of containers to the materials.

Although this method works out in those industries which make use of standard costing technique, yet it can be adopted in other industries as well. This method is used both as a control technique for ensuring efficient purchases as well as to price the materials issues. The actual price of materials purchased is compared with the standard price. If the actual price paid exceeds standard it results in loss. On the other hand if the actual price is less than standard price, it results in profit.

Under this method receipts of materials are recorded in the stores ledger card the actual prices and all issues at the standard price. The difference between actual and standard price is disposed off through price variance account.

Advantages :

(*a*) This method enables to know the efficiency of purchases made. As was mentioned earlier if actual price paid is more than standard price it amounts to inefficient purchase.

(*b*) Comparing of two similar jobs is possible as all materials are priced at the same standard price.

(*c*) The method is simple to operate as all materials are issued at the same standard price.

(*d*) It facilitates fixation of selling price in advance.

Disadvantages :

(*a*) The issue prices do not correspond to the current market price. So an unrealised profit or loss will arise.

(*b*) The closing stock value also does not correspond to the current market price. Hence balance sheet will not show the realistic position.

(*c*) It is difficult to fix up standard price in practice.

(*d*) It involves adjustment of profit or loss arising under this method.

PROBLEMS ON STANDARD PRICE METHOD

Problem 20 : The purchases and issues of materials in the month of December 2002 of Shriram & Co. are as follows :

1-12-02	Purchases 400 units @ Rs. 20.00 per unit
5-12-02	Purchases 350 units @ Rs. 18.00 per unit
10-12-02	Issues 300 units
15-12-02	Issues 400 units
20-12-02	Purchases 400 units @ Rs. 20.00 per unit
25-12-02	Purchases 250 units @ Rs. 25.00 per unit
30-12-02	Issues 500 units

The standard price per unit of material is fixed at Rs. 20 for the year. Prepare the store ledger and determine the price variance for the month of December 2002.

Solution : **Stores ledger card (Standard price method)**

Material ————	Bin No. ————	Max. Level ————
Description ————	Location code No. ————	Min. level ————
Code No. ————	Unit of quantity ————	Reorder level ————
		Danger level ————

Date	*Receipts*			*Issues*			*Balance*	
	Qty.	*Rate*	*Amount*	*Qty.*	*Rate*	*Amount*	*Qty.*	*Amount*
1-12-02	400	20	8,000				400	8,000
5-12-02	350	18	6,300				750	14,300
10-12-02				300	20	6,000	420	8,300
15-12-02				400	20	8,000	50	300
20-12-02	400	20	8,000				450	8,300
25-12-02	250	25	6,250				700	14,550
30-12-02				500	20	10,000	200	4,550
	1,400		28,550	1,200		24,000		

Standard cost of purchases 1,400 units @ Rs. 20	=	28,000
Actual cost of purchases	=	28,550
Adverse material price variance		550

Alternatively value of closing stock of 200 units @ Rs. 20 is 4,000. But the actual value shown in the stores ledger is 4,550. Hence is 550 is transferred to material price varince. The following entry is passed to dispose off the variance :

Material control a/c	*Dr.* 24,000	
Material price variance a/c	*Dr.* 550	
To cost ledger control a/c		24,550

(Being the adverse variance transferred to cost ledger control, etc.,)

Problem 21 : Stocks are issued at standard price and the following transactions have occurred with respect to high speed steel, a basic raw materials of a small tool factory :

Opening stock on 1-1-03 1,000 kgs @ Rs. 9.00 per kg
Purchased on 5-1-03 5,000 kgs @ Rs. 8.50 per kg
Issued on 10-1-03 600 kgs
Issued on 15-1-03 3,750 kgs
Issued on 20-1-03 650 kgs
Purchased on 25-1-03 2,500 kgs @ Rs. 8.00 per kg
The credit balance of price variance account before transfer to costing profit & loss a/c was Rs. 500.
Find out the standard rate at which the above issues should be made and determine the closing stock.

Solution : **Stores ledger card (Standard price method)**

Material ————	Bin No. ————	Max. Level ————
Description ————	Location code No. ————	Min. level ————
Code No. ————	Unit of quantity ————	Reorder level ————
		Danger level ————

Date	*Receipts*			*Issues*			*Balance*	
	Qty.	*Rate*	*Amount*	*Qty.*	*Rate*	*Amount*	*Qty.*	*Amount*
1-1-03							1,000	9,000
5-1-03	5,000	8.50	42,500				6,000	51,500

10-1-03				600	8.50	5,100	5,400	46,400
15-1-03				3,750	8.50	31,875	1,650	14,525
20-1-03				650	8.50	5,525	1,000	9,000
25-1-03	2,500	8	20,000				3,500	29,000
	7,500		62,500	5,000		42,500		

Note : Calculation of issue price standard price : In the previous year the standard price was Rs. 9 per kg. Therefore the total value was 9,000 (1,000×9). As there is a credit balance in the material price variance a/c, the standard rate for current year should be less than Rs. 9.00 (*i.e.*, to be debited). Hence the issue rate is calculated as follows :

Op. balance	Rs. 9,000
Less : Credit variance	500
	8,500

$$\frac{8,500}{1,000} = 8.50$$

Calculation of material price variance

Material price variance = Std. value of closing stock-Actual value of closing stock

= 3,500 × 8.50 - 29,000

29,750 - 29,000 = 750 (*F*)

Cost ledger control a/c	Dr. 43,250	
To material control a/c		42,500
To material price variance a/c		750

(Being material price variance transferred to cost ledger a/c.)

2. ***Inflated price method :*** This is not a distinct method of pricing material issues. Instead it is a method of accounting of materials taking into account the losses, wastages deterioration, evaporation of materials. It was discussed earlier in the previous chapter that all costs related to losses and wastages, material receiving and handling expenses, etc. are absorbed by the cost of production through a overhead recovery rate. But where it is desired that the actual cost of materials are to be known in the cost of production of a job, this method treats all such losses and wastages as also receiving, storage and handling cost as a charge to materials consumed. In other words the cost of good materials is inflated to the extent of loss, scrap and waste materials together with other expenses incurred in procuring storing and issuing them.

Problem 22 : A manufacturer of Surat purchased three chemicals *A, B* and *C* from Bombay. The invoice gave the following information :

		Rs.
Chemical *A*	3,000 kg @ Rs. 4.20 per kg	12,600
Chemical *B*	5,000 kg @ Rs. 3.80 per kg	19,000
Chemical *C*	2,000 kg @ Rs. 4.75 per kg	9,500
Sales Tax		2,055
Railway freight		1,000
	Total cost	44,155

A shortage of 200 kg in chemical *A*, of 280 kg in chemical *B* and 100 kg in chemical *C* was noticed due to breakages. At Surat, manfacturer paid octroi, duty @ Re, 0.10 per kg. He also paid cartage. Rs.22 for chemical *A*, Rs. 63.12 for chemical *B*, Rs. 31.80 for chemical C. Calculate the stock rate that you would suggest for pricing issue of chemicals assuming a provision of 5 per cent towards further deterioration.

(*CA Inter, Nov. 1991*)

Solution : **Statement showing the total price**

	Chemicals		
	A (Rs.)	B (Rs.)	C (Rs.)
Purchase price	12,600	19,000	9,500
Add : Sales tax @ 5% of purchase price (*See Note 1*)	630	950	475
Add : Railway freight in the ratio of 3:5:2 (*See Note 2*)	300	500	200
Add : Octroi @ Re. 0.10 per kg on the quantity of material received	280	472	190
Add : Cartage	22	63.12	31.80
Total price	13,832	20,985.12	10,396.80

Statement showing the net quantity of chemical available for issue

	A (kg)	B (kg)	C (kg)
Quantity purchased	3,000	5,000	2,000
Less : Shortage (assumed to be normal)	200	280	100
Qty. received at the stores	2,800	4,720	1,900
Less : Provision for further deterioration 5%	140	236	95
Quantity available for issue	2,660	4,484	1,805
Rate of issue per kg	$\frac{13,832}{2,660}$	$\frac{20,985.12}{4,484}$	$\frac{10,396.80}{1,805}$
	= 5.20	4.68	5.76

Working Notes :

(1) Rate of sales tax = $\frac{\text{Sales tax}}{\text{Total purchase price of chemical}} \times 100 = \frac{2,055}{41,100} \times 100 = 5\%$

(2) Railway freight : The quantity purchased is taken as the basis, *i.e.* 3,000 : 5,000 : 2,000

Problem 23 : From the following particulars, work out the issue rate per 1,000 of first class and second class bricks.

(*a*) Paid for supply at the kiln site for 30 lakh first class bricks at Rs. 300 per 1,000 bricks.
(*b*) Paid for supply at the kiln site for 60 lakh second class bricks at Rs. 250 per 1,000 bricks.
(*c*) Paid for carrying all bricks from kiln to store yard at Rs. 50 per 1,000 bricks.
(*d*) Paid unloading charges Rs. 600 (lump sum).
(*e*) Paid for stocking in the store yard Rs.1,200 (lump sum).
(*f*) Breakage in handling : 2 per cent for first class bricks and 3 per cent for second class bricks.

(*Bangalore University B. Com., Nov 1991*)

Solution : **Statement showing total cost**

	I Class bricks	II Class bricks
Invoice price of bricks	9,00,000	15,00,000
Carriage inwards	1,80,000	2,70,000

$$\frac{5}{1,000} \times 90,00,000 = 4,50,000$$

$$\frac{2}{5} \times 4,50,000 = 1,80,000$$

$$\frac{3}{5} \times 4,50,000 = 2,70,000$$

Unloading charges in the ratio of 2:3	240	360
Storage cost in the ratio of 2:3	480	720
Total cost	10,80,720	17,71,080
Net number of bricks		
	Ist Class	*II Class*
Cross number of bricks	30,00,000	60,00,000
Less : Breakage in handling	60,000	1,80,000
Net number of bricks	29,40,000	58,20,000
Issue rate	10,80,720 / 29,40,000 = 0.3675 per 1,000 bricks	17,71,080 / 58,20,000 = 0.3043 per 1,000 bricks

3. Re-use price method : Sometimes materials issued to production departments are returned back to stores being considered unfit or in excess. Such retained materials are again re-issued to other department not at its original price but at a different price. The price at which they are valued is known as the re-use price.

COMPARISION OF DIFFERENT METHODS OF PRICING

Points of Differenes	*FIFO*	*LIFO*	*Average Cost*	*Market price*	*Standard price*
1. Recovery of cost	It recovers cost	It recovers cost	It recovers cost	It does not recover the cost	It does not recovers the cost
2. Reflection of market price	Does not reflects market price	It reflects market price	It does not reflects market price. But if the rise and fall in prices is uniform then it reflects market price	It reflects market price	It does not reflects market price
3. Elimination of variation	It does not eliminate price variation	It does not eliminate price variation	It eliminates price variation	It does not eliminate price variation	It eliminates price variation
4. Stock adjustment	Avoids Stock adjustment	It does not avoid stock adjustment	It avoids stock adjust-ment	It does not avoid stock adjustment	It avoids stock adjustment

FACTORS INFLUENCING PRICING OF MATERIAL ISSUES

From the foregoing discussion of various methods of pricing the material issues it is possible to decide which particular method is best suited for adoption. There are no rigid rule which can be applied for selecting a particular method of pricing the material issues. The choice depends upon the following factors :

(*a*) The nature of materials used : If materials are kept for ripening as in the case of fruits or seasoning as in the case of timber, then inflated price is useful.

(*b*) The policy of management wherein if the cost of production is to reflect market price, then market price method is used.

(*c*) The ability to meet clerical expenses in calculating the issue price. Small sized concerns will not have more amount to invest. So they choose a method which does not involve much clerical labour.

(*d*) The frequency of purchases made, receipts obtained and issues to be made.

(*e*) Fluctuations in the price of material in which case weighted average cost method can be used.

(*f*) The application of standard costing technique in which case standard price method is applicable.

(*g*) The nature of business : if it is job order industries it requires use of special type of materials in which case specific price method is to be adopted.

(*h*) The accuracy desired in which case weighted average price method is to be selected.

(*i*) The length of material turnover period. If the material turnover ratio is less FIFO method is to be used.

(*j*) The method of stock valuation.

(*k*) The effect of pricing method on tax payable.

(*l*) Identification of materials in the purchase lot. Where materials loose their identity average price method is to be adopted.

ACCOUNTING OF MATERIALS SUPPLIED BY CUSTOMERS

Sometimes the materials required for processing the goods might be supplied by customers themselves. The examples are supply of dress materials in case of readymade garment factory, gold and silver in case of jewellery, leather in case of footwear industry and other controlled commodities. In accounting of such materials, the following problems arise :

Valuing the Stock of Materials on Hand Supplied by Customers

The quantity of materials supplied by customers must be recorded in the stores ledgers pricing them either at nil value or at a notional value. The clerical work related to receipts and issues will be reduced if materials are valued at nil value. However, this method will not help in claiming the insurance as the value of stock is under-insured. So a prudent manufacturer will always value the materials supplied by the customer at a notional price. The following entries are passed for the receipt and issue of such materials :

(1) For receiving the stock of materials from customer store

Stock a/c *Dr.*

    To stores suspense a/c

(2) For issuing the materials to production

Work-in-progress a/c *Dr.*

    To stores stock a/c

(3) For writing back at the year end the notional value of customers' materials taken into Stock a/c

Stores suspense a/c *Dr.*

    To stores stock a/c

    To work-in-progress a/c

Charging of Handling Charges to Materials Supplied by Customers

Whenever the manufacturer arranges to obtain the materials from the premises of customers, the cost of receiving handling and storage of such materials is to be charged to customer's account. A separate rate is calculated for such materials on a percentage basis and on this basis it is levied.

Treatement of Wastage of Materials Supplied by Customers

An agreement is entered into between manufacturer and customer in respect of a percentage of wastage of material which is common in production process. The output to be delivered must be in accordance with the given quantity of input subject to the provision for waste percentage. Any excess of wastage than the agreed percentage is to be borne by the manufacturer. Thus an excess waste constitutes a loss to manufacturer.

QUESTIONS

I. Mark true or false in the space provided

1. Stores ledger is maintained in the stores room. *T/F*
2. Bill of materials is a cash bill sent by the suplier along with the materials. *T/F*
3. The standard pricing method is a tool of material cost control. *T/F*
4. A bill of material is a special form of material requisition. *T/F*
5. The adoption of FIFO method results in a profit inflation during period of rising prices. *T/F*

[*Answers :* 1-*F*, 2-*F*, 3-*T*, 4-*T*, 5-*T*]

II. Fill in the blanks

1. In..............method of pricing the materials evens out the fluctuations in purchase prices.
2. Under the..............method of pricing the material issues, a new issue price is determined after each purchase.
3. Under..............method of pricing the material issues, materials are issued to production at a predetermined price.
4. The stores ledger card contains information relating to.............. as well as ....
5. The document used to draw materials from store room for production departments is known as ....
6. When excess materials are returned to stores..............note is prepared in the department where the materials are in excess.

[*Answers :* (1) average cost method, (2) weighted average price, (3) standard price, (4) quantity and value, (5) material requisition note (6) materials returned note or stores debit note]

III. Choose the correct answer

1. Materials from the storeroom are issued to production departments on presentment of :
   (*a*) Purchase requisition note (*c*) Stores credit note
   (*b*) Stores requisition note (*d*) Materials received note
2. Pricing of material issues closely resembles the current market value under.
   (*a*) Last-in-first-out (*c*) Simple Average
   (*b*) First-in-first-out (*d*) Weighted average [ ]
3. In base stock method of pricing the material issues, the term base stock represents :
   (a) Quantity of stock being issued (*c*) Minimum stock
   (*b*) Stock in balance (*d*) Maximum stock [ ]
4. In Which of the following methods of pricing costs lag behind the current economic value :
   (*a*) LIFO (*c*) Simple average
   (*b*) FIFO (*d*) Weighted Average [ ]
5. Under which method issue of materials priced at the latest purchase price.
   (*a*) FIFO (*c*) NIFO
   (*b*) LIFO (*d*) HIFO [ ]
6. Material requisition note is prepared by
   (*a*) Purchase department (*c*) Production department
   (*b*) Accounts department (*d*) Production control department [ ]

7. Materials analysis sheet is also known as
   (*a*) Material requisition note
   (*b*) Purchase requisition note
   (*c*) Materials abstract
   (*d*) Bill of materials [ ]
8. When prices fluctuate widely the method of pricing that smooths out the effect of fluctuation is
   (*a*) Simple average
   (*b*) Weighted average
   (*c*) FIFO
   (*d*) LIFO [ ]
9. A material tranfer note is prepared to
   (*a*) Transfer materials from one job to another
   (*b*) Transfer materials from main store to sub-store
   (*c*) Return materials to stores from production department
   (*d*) Return defective materials to suppliers [ ]
10. FIFO method of pricing the issues is suitable
    (*a*) During period of rising prices
    (*b*) During a period of falling prices
    (*c*) During a period of constant prices
    (*d*) During a period when prices move erratically
11. The value of closing stock approximates to the market value under :
    (*a*) LIFO
    (*b*) FIFO
    (*c*) Base stock method
    (*d*) Standard price method [ ]
12. Given : Opening stock on 1-1-92, 200 kgs @ Rs. 4 per kg
    Purchased on 4-1-92, 300 kgs @ Rs. 5 per kg
    Issued on 8-1-92, 350 kgs
    Market price on 8-1-92 was Rs. 5 per kg
    (*a*) The value of materials issued on 8th under FIFO is
    (*i*) Rs. 1,100
    (*ii*) Rs. 1,450
    (*iii*) Rs. 1,700
    (*iv*) Rs. 1,750 [ ]
    (*b*) The amount at which issues are charged under LIFO method is
    (*i*) Rs. 1,550
    (*ii*) Rs. 1,575
    (*iii*) Rs. 1,700
    (*iv*) Rs. 1,750 [ ]
    (*c*) Under simple average method it will be
    (*i*) Rs. 1,550
    (*ii*) Rs. 1,575
    (*iii*) Rs. 1,610
    (*iv*) Rs. 1,700 [ ]
    (*d*) Under weighted average the amount at which issues are charged will be
    (*i*) Rs. 1,575
    (*ii*) Rs. 1,610
    (*iii*) Rs. 1,625
    (*iv*) Rs. 1,700 [ ]

[***Answers :*** 1. (*b*), 2. (*a*), 3. (*c*), 4. (*a*), 5. (*b*), 6. (*c*), 7. (*c*), 8. (*b*), 9. (*a*), 10. (*b*), 11. (*a*), 12. (*a*) (*ii*), (*b*) (*iv*), (*c*) (*ii*), (*d*) (*ii*), (*e*) (*ii*)]

IV. Match the following

A	B
(1) Purchase requisition note	(*a*) Person nominated by the management
(2) Purchased order	(*b*) Stores attendant
(3) Materiasl received note	(*c*) Head of the department
(4) Bill of materials	(*d*) Laboratory technician
(5) Material requisiton note	(*e*) Cost clerk
(6) Stores ledger card	(*f*) Foreman
(7) Material stock verification note	(*g*) Purchase manager
(8) Material transfer note	(*h*) Production control department
(9) Material inspection note	(*i*) Storekeeper
(10) Bin card	(*j*) Material inspection clerk
	(*k*) Cost accountant
	(*l*) General manager

[***Answers :*** (1)-(*i*), (2)-(*g*), (3)-(*j*), (4)-(*h*), (5)-(*f*), (6)-(*e*), (7)-(*a*), (8)-(*c*), (9)-(*d*), (10)-(*b*)]

V. Simple Questions

1. What do you mean by material requisition note? Give its specimen form.
2. What do you mean by a bill of material? Give its specimen from.
3. Distinguish between a material requsition note and a bill of materials.
4. What do you mean by material abstract? Give its specimen form.
5. What do you mean by materials returned note? Give its specimen form.
6. What do you mean by material transfer note? Give its specimen form.
7. What do you mean by FIFO method of pricing material issues?
8. What do you mean by LIFO method of pricing material issues?
9. What do you mean by base stock of pricing material issues?
10. State any two merits and two demerits of FIFO method.
11. State any two merits and two demerits of LIFO method.
12. What do you mean by HIFO method ?
13. What do you mean by NIFO method?
14. What do you mean by simple average price method.
15. What do you mean by weighted average price method.
16. State the advantages and disadvantages of simple average price method.
17. State the advantages and disadvantages of weighted average.
18. Distinguish between simple average and weighted average price method of pricing the material issues.
19. What do you mean by periodic average price?
20. What do you mean by periodic weighted average price?
21. What do you mean by inflation price method?
22. What do you mean by replacement price method?
23. What do you mean by standard price method?
24. State the advantages of standard price method.
25. State the disadvantages of standard price method.

VI. Short and Long Answer Questions

1. Explain the standard method of pricing the material issues. (*Bangalore University, B. Com., April 1987*)
2. Explain the FIFO and LIFO methods of valuation of materials issues. State under what circumstances these methods are used. (*Sri Sathya Sai University, B. Com., Feb. 1991*)
3. Make a comparative study of the following methods pricing materials issues and state in what situations each method would be appropriate (*a*) LIFO, (b) FIFO, (*c*) Weighted average and (*d*) Standard price method. (*Sri Sathya Sai University, B. Com., Oct. 1989*)
4. Explain how LIFO and FIFO methods affect (*i*) Valuation of inventories and (*ii*) Profit during a period of rising prices and falling prices. (*Sri Sathya Sai University, B. Com., Oct. 1987*)
5. Discuss the methods of pricing the issues of materials. (*Bangalore University, M. Com., May. 1991*)
6. What are the circumstances under which "direct transfer of surplus materials from one job to another is justified?" Mention the procedure to be followed for regularising such transfers and draw a specimen form, if any, used for recording such transfer. (*ICWA, Inter, Dec. 1986*)
7. Draw a proforma of bill of materials. List down the advantages of using the same. (*C.A. Inter, May. 1987*)
8. State various methods of pricing the issue of materials. (*Andhra University, B. Com., May. 1992*)
9. How simple average method of pricing the issue differ from the weighted average method. (*Osmania University, B. Com., March. 1992*)

EXERCISES

Exercise-1 (FIFO method)

The following transactions occur in the purchase and issue of a material

Jan. 2nd Purchased 4000 units @ Rs. 4 per unit

Jan. 20th Purchased 500 units @ Rs. 5 per unit

Feb. 5th	Issued 2000 units
Feb. 10th	Purchased 6000 units @ Rs. 6 per unit
Feb. 12th	Issued 4000 units
Mar. 2nd	Issued 1000 units
Mar. 5th	Issued 2000 units
March 15th	Purchased 4500 units @ Rs. 5.50 per unit
Mar. 20th	Issued 3000 units

On March 31st there was a shortage of 100 units. From the above information, prepare a stores ledger by adopting Fifo method of pricing the issue (*Bangalore University, B.B.M., Nov. 1999*)

[Answer : Closing stock 2900 units amounting to Rs. 15950]

Exercise-2

From the following particulars, prepare a stores ledger account, pricing issues to production on the Fifo method.

Purchases :

1996 March 3, 400 kgs at Rs. 2.50 per kg
7, 800 kgs at Rs. 3.00 per kg
17, 500 kgs at Rs. 3.50 per kg

Issues

March 5, 600 kgs
9, 500 kgs
25, 600 kgs

The stock on March 1, was 500 kgs priced at Rs. 2 per kg. There was a return to stores on March 12, of 200 kgs from a job and this has been charged at Rs. 2.25 earlier. The stock verification on March 27, revealed a loss of 10 kgs. (*Mangalore University, B.Com., October 1997*)

[Answer : Closing stock 690 units amounting to Rs. 2177.50]

Exercise-3

The following is the extract of the record of receipts and issues of sulphur in a chemical factory during February 1994

Feb 1, Opening Balance, 500 tonnes at Rs. 200
7, Issued 250 tonnes
13, Received from supplier 200 tonnes at Rs. 190
14, Returned from department, 15 tonnes
16, Issued 180 tonnes
20, Received from supplier 240 tonnes at Rs. 200
24, Issued 300 tonnes
25, Rceived from supplier 320 tonnes at Rs. 190
26, Issued 115 tonnes
27, Returned from department 35 tonnes
28, Received from supplier 100 tonnes at Rs. 190

Issues are to be priced on the principle Fifo. The stock verifier had found shortage of 10 tonnes on 22nd and left a note accordingly. Draw up a priced ledger, showing the above transactions.

(*Calicut University B.Com., October 1995*)

[Answer: Closing stock value Rs. 1,06,000]

Exercise-4 (Lifo)

From the following particulars prepare the stores ledger account for the month of March 1998 adopting the "Last in First out" method

1998 March	1,	Opening stock	500 kgs @ Rs. 5 per kg
	4,	Issued	200 kgs
	9,	Issued	150 kgs
	12,	Purchased	400 kgs @ Rs. 6 per kg
	18,	Issued	300 kgs

21, Purchased 500 kgs @ Rs. 7 per kg
28, Returned from job 50 kgs
30, Issued 300 kgs

There was a stock shortage of 10 kgs on 22nd March 1998

(*Calcutta University B.Com.(pass), 1998*)

[**Answer :** Closing stock 100 units amounting to Rs. 600 and 190 units amounting to Rs. 1330]

Exercise-5

From the following information select the most suitable method of pricing material issues and write up a Stores Ledger card based on that method.

1996 Jan. 1, Opening Balance 24000 kg @ Rs. 7.50 per tonne
Jan. 1, Purchased 44,000 kg @ Rs. 7.60 per tonne
3, Issued 10,000 kg
5, Issued 16,000 kg
12, Purchased 10,000 kg @ Rs. 7.80 per tonne
13, Issued 24,000 kg
18, Issued 25,000 kg
22, Purchased 50,000 kg @ Rs. 8.00 per tonne
28, Issued 20,000 kg
31, Issued 22,000 kg

on 24th January, 1996 a shortage of 200 kg was noticed in stock taking

(*Calcutta University B.Com(Hons.) 1996*)

[**Answer :** Closing Stock 3000 kgs @ Rs. 7.50 Rs. 22,500, 7800 kgs @ Rs. 8.00 Rs. 62,400]

Exercise-6 (Fifo & Lifo)

On 1st March 1994 there are 1500 units of materials at Rs. 12 per unit in stock. The following transactions were made during the month

March 2, Issued 200 units
4, Purchased 1000 units at Rs. 15 per unit
5, Issued 1200 units
6, Purchased 600 units at Rs. 20 per unit
7, Issued 650 units
7, Returned to stores from issues of 2 March, 100 units
9, Purchased 300 units at Rs. 25 per unit
13, Issued 250 units
17, Issued 300 units

Prepare Stores Ledger account by Fifo and Lifo methods (*Kakatiya University, B.Com April 1997*)

[**Answer :** Closing stock under Fifo 900 units amounting to Rs. 18,700]
Closing stock under Lifo 900 units amounting to Rs. 10800

Exercise-7

The owner of Lucky Pumping Station always assumed that he was pumping off the bottom of his tank using Fifo. The owner of Exide Pumping Station assumed that he was pumping off the top of his tank using Lifo. On 31st January 2002, both had the same stock of petrol at the tank totalling 4000 litres which cost Rs. 10 per litre. In February, each owner obtained an additional supply of 4500 litres at Rs. 15 per litre. Sales during February for each pumping station totalled 7800 litres at Rs. 20 per litre. You are required to compute for each pumping station the net profit for the month of February and the value of closing stock.

[**Answer :** Closing stocks under Fifo Rs. 15,000
Profit under Fifo Rs. 59,000
Closing stock under Lifo Rs. 10,000
Profit under Lifo Rs. 54,000]

Exercise-8 (Base Stock Method)

The stock of material A as on 1st June 1994 is 500 units, at Rs. 1 per unit. Following purchases and issues of this item were made subsequently.

	Receipts Qty (units)	Rate per unit	Issue Quantity (units)
June 6	–	–	200
10	400	1.10	–
15	300	1.20	–
20	–	–	500
21	–	–	200
24	500	1.30	–
25	–	–	300
28	–	–	200

Prepare a stores ledger account showing how the value of the above issues should be arrived under Base Stock Method when it operates in conjunction with Lifo. Base stock is 200 units.

(*Annamalai University B.Com., May 1996*)

[Answer : Closing stock 300 units amounting to Rs. 300]

Exercise-9 (Simple Average)

The following transactions took place in respect of a raw material during the month of January 1993

Date	Particulars	kg	Rate per kg (Rs.)
Jan. 1,	Balance	1000	9
2,	Purchased	1500	10
5,	Issued	390	–
8,	Shortage	10	–
15,	Surplus returned by a Production Department	200	12
20,	Issued	1000	–
25,	Received from Vendor	300	14
28,	Issued	1200	–
31,	Issued	100	–

You are required to write up a stores ledger account applying the Simple Average method of pricing issues.

(*Calcutta University, B.Com.(Hons.), 1993*)

[Answer : Closing stock 300 units amounting to Rs. 770]

Exercise-10 (Weighted Average)

From the following record of receipts and issues, draw a stores ledger under weighted average method of pricing.

1995 Aug.	1,	Opening balance 50 units at Rs. 3 per unit
	3,	Issued out to production 60 units
	5,	Purchased 48 units at Rs. 4 per unit
	6,	Issued to production 15 units
	7,	Purchased 40 units at Rs. 5 per unit
	8,	Issued out 20 units
	9,	Purchased 75 units at Rs. 3 per unit
	11,	Received back to stores 10 units out of 20 units issued on 8th
	15,	Issued to production 5 units

(*Kakatiya University, B.Com, Nov. 1996*)

[Answer : Closing stock 177 units amounting to Rs. 637]

Exercise-11 (Replacement price method)

The stock on hand of material as on 1st Sept. 2002 was 500 units at Rs. 1 per unit. The following purchases and issues were subsequently made. Prepare a Stores Ledger card showing the value of materials issue and inventory on hand using replacement cost method. The replacement cost of materials on Sept. 9, 12, and 30, October 15, and 22 and November 18 were Rs. 1.15, Rs. 1.25, Rs. 1.35, Rs. 1.45, Rs. 1.25, and Rs. 1.65 respectively.

Purchased		Issued	
Sept 6	100 units at Rs. 1.10	Sept 9	500 units
Sept 20	700 units at Rs. 1.20	Sept 22	500 units
Sept 27	400 units at Rs. 1.30	Sept 30	500 units
Oct 13	1000 units at Rs. 1.40	Oct 15	500 units
Oct 20	500 units at Rs. 1.50	Oct 22	500 units
Oct 27	400 units at Rs. 1.60	Nov 18	500 units

[**Answer :** Closing stock 620 units amounting to Rs. 560]

Exercise-12 (Standard Price Method)

Stocks are issued at Standard Price and the following transactions occured in a specific material :

2002, Jan 1,	Opening balance	10 tons @ Rs. 240 per ton
4,	Purchased	5 tons @ Rs. 260 per ton
5,	Issued	3 tons
12,	Issued	4 tons
13,	Purchased	3 tons @ Rs. 250 per ton
19,	Issued	4 tons
26,	Issued	3 tons
30,	Purchased	4 tons @ Rs. 280 per ton
31,	Issued	3 tons

The debit balance of price variation on 1st Jan 2002 was Rs. 20. Show the Stores Ledger card for the material for the month of January indicating how would you deal with difference in material price variance.

[**Answer :** Closing stock 5 tons amounting to Rs. 1456. Issue price is Rs. 242]

Exercise-13

A consignment consisted of 2 chemicals A and B. The invoice gave the following data :

	Rs.
Chemical 'A' – 4 tonnes at Rs. 5.00 per kg	20,000
Chemical 'B' – 2 tonnes at Rs. 2.00 per kg	4,000
Sales Tax	1,200
Freight	900
Total	26,100

A shortage of 2 quintals in A and 1 quintal in B was noticed and it was considered normal. What rate per kg would you adopt for pricing issues assuming provision of 20% towards further deterioration?

[**Answer :** Rate per kg A = Rs. 7.10, B Rs. 2.96]

6

ACCOUNTING OF MATERIAL LOSSES

INTRODUCTION

It is a normal tendency in most of the industries to loose a part of materials at all the three stages of dealing with materials, *viz.*, receiving, storing and issuing. Materials like cement, sand, coal and such other materials are lost at least in part at the time of its receipt. During the stage of storage some materials are lost owing to evaporation, shrinkage, breaking the bulk and so on. Similarly during the stage of issue and usage of materials, the quantity of output will be less compared to the quantity of input, which represents the loss of materials. Such losses assume the form of waste, scrap, spoilage and defectives. These losses often pose special problem in dealing with them in cost accounts. Unless the causes and, circumstances which give rise to such losses are carefully analysed, it becomes difficult not only in accounting but also in exercising control over them.

CLASSIFICATION OF MATERIAL LOSSES

For proper accounting and control of material losses, material losses can be classified into the following types. This is shown in the following chart :

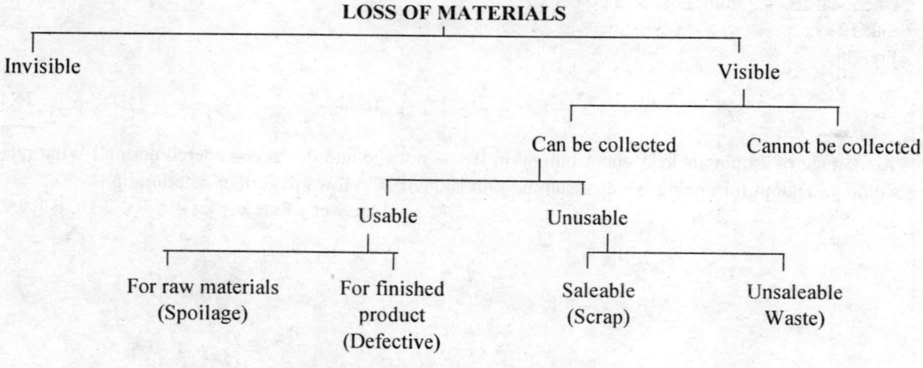

Fig. 6.1. Chart showing types of materials losses.

Invisible Loss

This represents loss in weight on account of shrinkage, evaporation, absorption by moisture, flow of materials in the form of dust, etc.

Visible Loss

Visible loss can be visualised and its presence can be identified.

Collectable and non-collectable loss : The portion of visible loss which is usefully collected and measured is known as collectable loss. The remaining portion of visible loss which is not worthwhile to collect is known as waste.

Usable and Unusable Loss : Usable loss is that portion of collected loss which can be used internally for further processing. This is used either as raw material or rectified to constitute a finished product. In the former case it is termed as a spoilage and in the latter case it is termed as a defective material. Whereas unusable material cannot be used for further processing, they can at best be sold as a scrap or thrown away as a waste.

ACCOUNTING TREATMENT OF WASTE

The residue which is left behind by a production process in known as a waste. Wastage is inevitable and is inherent in the technological process. It has comparatively insignificant value. It cannot be reused nor reworked so as to convert it into good units. Waste comprises of (*a*) invisible loss as for example, shrinkage, in a tanning industry, evaporation in an oil refinery, loss in energy transmission, etc., (*b*) visible loss that cannot be collected as for example, sand in construction industry and (*c*) unsaleable portion of collected loss, as for example, saw dust in furniture making industry, churnings in a machining operation, cuttings in a garment industry, ash in coke industry and so on. In certain cases waste involves further costs of disposing it, as for example, cost incurred for the disposal of effluent, obnoxions gases, etc.

Whenever a waste occurs it is necessary to prepare a report to facilitate accounting and controlling such waste. A specimen form of report on waste materials is given below :

REPORT ON WASTE

Dept .... Period ....

Production order No.	*Units of product*	*Waste qty.*	*Percentage of waste to production*
Total			

Fig. 6.2. Specimen showing report on waste.

Accounting Treatment of Wastage

For the sake of treatment of wastages in cost accounting, it is classified into two types, *viz.*, (*a*) Normal wastage and (*b*) Abnormal wastage.

Normal wastage is unavoidable and uncontrollable and is treated as part of the product cost. The wastage cost is borne by the good units.

Abnormal wastage is unanticipated and is valued as if the output is good. This cost is transferred to the costing profit and loss account.

Sometimes a demand may arise for the wastage, as for example, it may be used as a substitue raw material. In such a case, the selling price has to be suitably fixed on the basis of the market value of the raw material substituted.

ACCOUNTING OF SCRAP

A scrap refers to the incidental residue derived from certain types of manufacture recoverable without further processing. The main feature of scrap is it has some disposable value and it arises from normal production process. Scrap arises from faulty operation, bad supervision, wrong tool setting, defective process and use of defective raw material.

Types of Scrap

(*a*) *Normal scrap* : This is considered to be inevitable in the manufacturing process and hence it is predetermined or anticipated much in advance of production and provided for in the books of accounts.

(*b*) *Administrative scrap* : This arises owing to the decision taken by management such as use of a different method of production or a different design of product.

(*c*) *Defective scrap* : This arises mainly due to the use of sub-standard quality of materials and/or for bad workmanship.

Differences between a Waste and a Scrap

(*i*) The degree of inherence of waste is more when compared to the inherence or the element of inevitability in scrap.

(*ii*) The chance of re-using scrap in the same production process is high when compared to waste.

(*iii*) Scrap has a higher saleable value when compared to waste.

Examples of scraps in engineering industry takes the form of turnings, borings, filings. etc. from the metal. In leather industry it takes the form of pieces of leather. In timber industry it takes the form of saw dust.

To facilitate accounting of scrap a daily or weekly scrap report is to be prepared. This reveals the unexpected items and abnormal variations in scraps. A specimen form of such a report is given below :

SCRAP REPORT

Name of the production Dept. ....

Scrap report for the week ending ....

No.	*Description*	*Units issued*	*Units scrapped*	*Percentage of scrap*	*Cost*	*Reasons*
Total for the week						

Fig. 6.3. Specimen showing scrap report.

Accounting Treatment of Scrap

Depending upon the quantity of scrap and its sale value, it is treated according to the following methods :

(*a*) If the scrap has negligible value, the income earned by such sale is treated as other income.

(*b*) The sale value can be used to mitigate or to reduce the cost of materials by deducting it from materials cost.

(*c*) It can be credited to the cost of production, so as to minimise cost of production and there by minimising selling price.

(*d*) If the scrap, arising from one job is transferred to another job to be used as raw material, the latter job is debited and the formar job is credited with the cost of scrap.

ACCOUNTING OF SPOILAGES

Spoilage is man-made scrap. It results when materials are so damaged in manufacturing operations that they are taken out of process and disposed of in some manner without further processing. They cannot be repaired or reconditioned into a product of acceptable quality. It is either sold as second hand product or reused for further manufacturing as a basic raw material. Spoilages occur due to faults in operation, bad workmanship, use of defective raw materials, defective machines and faulty tool setting.

Spoilage differs from scrap in the following two respects :

(*a*) Spoilage occurs more towards the finishing stage with higher loss of added value whereas scraps occur in the beginning and intermediary stage of production with less added value.

(*b*) Spoilage arises because of some defects in production process or materials which may or may not be inherent in the production process. Whereas scrap arises as a result of inherent production process. Thus it can be said that scrap is inevitable whereas spoilage is not so in all cases.

To facilitate accounting and control of spoilages a spoilage report is to be prepared. A specimen form of spoilage report is given below :

SPOILAGE REPORT

Dept. No. .... Date ....

Production order No. ....

Units produced	*Units spoilt*	*Normal spoilage*	*Abnormal spoilage*	*Cost of abnormal spoilage*	*Reason*	*Action taken*

Fig. 6.4. Specimen showing spoilage report.

Accounting Treatment of Spoilages

(*a*) Loss arising due to normal spoilage can be debited to the job, product or process in which it occurs.

(*b*) Abnormal loss arising out of spoilage which is unexpected and uncontrollable is transferred to costing profit & loss a/c.

(*c*) Where it becomes difficult to identify the normal loss arising out of spoilage to any of the product or job or process, it is charged to factory overhead so that the loss is borne by all products.

ACCOUNTING OF DEFECTIVES

Defectives refer to imperfect products which are transformed into the standard specifications by the application of additional material, labour or both, Defectives differe from spoilage in one important respect, *viz.*, defectives can be reworked and restored to original condition but spoilages cannot be rectified. Defectives occur on account of the following reasons : (*i*) sub-standard raw materials, (*ii*) bad maintenance of machines, (*iii*) wrong setting-up of tools, (*iv*) bad workmanship, (*v*) machines used for unscheduled operations, (*vi*) lack of control such as temperature, humidity, etc., (*vii*) bad design of the product, (viii) bad working conditions.

Defective goods should be separated from spoilages to facilitate reconditioning of work. However, reconditioning work is justifiable only when the revenue earned by the sale of rectified defective goods is more than the cost incurred in rectification of defectives. The rework to be done on defectives should be authorised by a senior official. For this a defective work report is to be prepared and attached to production order representing the defective work. A specimen form of defective work report is given below :

DEFECTIVE WORK REPORT

Production order No. .... No. ....
No. of units .... , Date ....
Dept. responsible ....
Nature of defective ....

Job No.	*Description of additional work required*	*Rework cost*			*Total cost*
		Material cost	*Labour cost*	*Overhead*	

Fig. 6.5. Specimen showing defective work report.

Accounting Treatment of Defectives

1. The estimated quantity or number of defectives are considered to be normal and are treated in the following manner :

(*a*) Charging of loss to good units manufactured.

(*b*) The additional cost of rectifying defectives is charged to factory overhead and apportioned to various units as part of the factory overhead.

(*c*) If a particular department is responsible for the additional cost of rectification, it can be charged to that department.

2. Where the defective units are traceable to a specific job or work-order, the additional costs can be charged to that job or work-order.

3. Where the defectives are considered abnormal and beyond control, the cost of such defectives is to be charged to costing P & L a/c.

CONTROL OF WASTE, SCRAP, SPOILAGE AND DEFECTIVES

The first step in designing a control system is to classify the losses into controllable and uncontrollable losses. Secondly, standards must be set in respect of all types of losses and actual losses are to be compared with standard losses to know whether they are normal or abnormal. Standard levels should be frequently reviewed because some losses may be uncontrollable in the short run but controllable in the long run. A good control system should calculate and report data relating to losses, wastages, defectives and spoilage to management. This facilitates management to evaluate performance and take remedial action. Control over material losses is exercised at the stage of (*a*) occurrence, (*b*) recovery, handling and storage and (*c*) disposal.

Control Over Occurrence

Before control is exercised it is necessary to identify the causes for the occurrence of losses of materials. Material losses occur on account of several reasons. The main causes can be summarised under the following :

(*i*) **Causes related to production method :** The various causes which fall under this category are use of defective equipment, bad design, overloading, excessive utilisation of resources, problems associated with new products.

(*ii*) **Material related causes :** These causes are mainly due to use of sub-standard quality of materials, obsolete materials and deteriorated quality of materials. Other causes which fall under this category are shrinkage, evaporation, breaking the bulk etc.

(*iii*) **Labour related causes :** The causes which fall under this category are inadequate training to the operator, inadequate supervision, lack of skill, damage caused by mishandling, fatigue, etc.

At each and every stage of occurrence of losses, it is necessary to keep a strict vigilance so that they can be minimised, if not eliminated.

Control over Handling and Storage

As soon as materials are received they must be properly stored. The corks of containers should be tightly closed. Material handling equipments must be used to handle heavy and bulk quantity of materials. Proper care must be taken to avoid theft and misappropriation of materials.

Control over Disposal

To increase the revenue of waste, spoilages and defectives it is necessary to consider the following points : (*i*) to make available such scrapped, spoilt or defective material ready for sale, (*ii*) to select the best buyer. Quotations can be obtained and the revenue receivable should be compared with market price, (*iii*) control the quantity of losses. Physical control is to be exercised over such materials before they leave the factory and there must be frequent review of the quantities produced, repaired and sold.

Problem 1 : The normal handling waste is 10 per cent of material *A*. The average price is Rs. 18 per kg. Total material drawn from stores were 170 kg. Job wise analysis of consumption of this material was as follows :

Job		
Job	1	30 kg.
	2	40 kg.
	3	24 kg.
	4	50 kg.

Find out (1) the effective rate of material per kg. to be charged to jobs so that cost of normal wastage is covered, (2) Quantity and value of abnormal loss.

Solution : **Calculation of effective rate of materials**

Normal handling waste is	10%
∴ Good units must be	90%

Average price of materials is Rs. 18

For 90% of units, materials cost is Rs. 18

For 100% – ?	$\frac{18 \times 100}{90}$	= Rs. 20
Total materials drawn form stores		= 170 kgs
Less : Normal of 10%		= 17 kgs
Net units used		= 153 kgs

Total units of materials used on Jobs

Job 1	30
Job 2	40
Job 3	24
Job 4	50
Total	144 kgs

Calculation of abnormal wastage

Units of materials used subject to normal loss	=	153 kgs
Less : Actual units used on various job	=	144 kgs
Abnormal wastage	=	9 kgs
Value of abnormal loss : 9 kgs @ Rs. 20	=	Rs. 180

Problem 2 : 2,000 kgs of Art board valued at Rs. 8,000 were issued for the manufacture of medium-sized cartons. The following details were collected.

(*a*) 2,400 Nos. medium-sized cartons weighted 0.50 kg. each were manufactured.

(*b*) 480 kgs of off cuts were used for the manufacture of small-sized cartons. This would have amounted to Rs. 1,000.

(*c*) 320 Medium-sized cartons were damaged and rectification costs came up to Rs. 160.

(*d*) 120 kgs of offcuts were sold as scrap for Rs. 20.

You are required to calculate the cost of one medium sized carton assuming that there are no opening and closing stock.

Solution : **Calculation of cost of one medium-sized carton**

	Qty. (kg.)	*Value (Rs.)*
Input	2,000	8,000
Less : Offcuts Transferred to small-sized cartons	480	1,000
	1,520	7,000
Less : Value of scrap sold	120	20
	1,400	6,980
Add : Cost of rectification	–	160
	1,400	7,140
Less : Waste in process (Balancing figure)	40	
Output	1,360	7,140

Cost per carton = $\frac{7,140}{2,720}$ = Rs. 2.62

Note 1 : Calculation of quantity of output.

2,400 + 320 = 2,720 cartons and expressed
(Cartons) (Cartons)

in terms of kg. it is $\frac{2,720}{2}$ = 1,360 kg. $\left(\text{each carton weighing } \frac{1}{2}\right)$.

Note 2 : Calculation of number of cartons.

Total output is 1,360 kgs and expressing in terms of cartons it will be 2,700 cartons.

Problem 3 : *XYZ* Co. draws up the standard cost of a product as follows :

		Rs.	Rs.
Direct Material			12
Direct Wages :			
Dept. A–3 hrs.		15	
Dept. B–2 hrs.		12	
Dept. C—5 hrs.		20	47
Factory overheads			
Dept. A		18	
Dept. B		18	
Dept. C		40	76
	Factory cost		135
Administration cost			12
Selling cost			15
Distribution cost			18
	Total cost		180
	Net profit		20
	Selling price		200

Factory overhead is absorbed by means of departmental hour rates. Analysis of these overhead reveal that in each department a rate of Rs. 2 per hour is required to absorb the variable portion, the balance being of a fixed nature. As a general rule, all production is of first class quality.

After a batch of 1,000 units has been processed through all three departments, inspection reveals that half are faulty. The faulty products can be rectified by completely reprocessing through departments *B* and *C*. Alternatively, they can be sold for Rs. 120 each.

Present figures which indicate to management the most economic method of dealing with the faulty product.

Solution : **Calculation of time taken for original processing and rectification**

Dept.	A—1,000 units @ Hrs.	=	3,000 Hrs.
	B—1,000 units @ 2 Hrs plus 500 units @ 2 Hrs.	=	3,000 Hrs.
	C—1,000 units @ 5 Hrs. plus 500 units @ 5 hrs.	=	7,500 Hrs.

Calculation of fixed cost per unit

Dept. A—Rs. 18 – (Rs. 2 × 3 Hrs.) = Rs. 12 per unit
B—Rs. 18 – (Rs. 2 × 2 Hrs.) = Rs. 14 per unit
C— Rs. 40 – (Rs. 2 × 5 Hrs.) = Rs. 30 unit

Alternative 1

Statement showing cost of production (including reprocessing cost)

Direct Materials—1,000 units @ Rs. 12				12,000
Wages :	Dept. A	3,000 × Rs. 7 (5 + 2)		21,000
	B	3,000 × Rs. 8 (6 + 2)		24,000
	C	7,500 × Rs. 6 (4 + 2)		45,000
		Prime cost		1,02,000
Overheads :	Dept. A	1,000 × 12		12,000
	B	1,500 × 14		25,000
	C	1,500 × 30		45,000
		Factory cost		1,80,000
Administration, selling and distribution overhead for 1,000 units @ Rs. 45 per unit			45,000	
Loss no non-recovery of 500 units reprocessed			22,500	67,500

Total cost	2,47,500
Cost	(–) 47,500
Sales	2,00,000

Alternative 2

Cost of production of 1,000 units of which 500 units are disposed off

Sales 500 × 200 + 500 × 120	=	1,60,000
Less : Total cost 1,000 × 180	=	1,80,000
Loss	=	(–) 20,000

The second alternative is better as the loss involved is less.

QUESTIONS

I. Fill in the blanks :

(*a*) Abnormal loss of materials are charged to .... a/c.

(*b*) Normal loss is charged to .... a/c.

[***Answers :*** (*a*) costing profit & loss all, (*b*) cost of production]

II. Mark 'T' or 'F' in the space provided

(*a*) The cost of abnormal wastage is added to the cost of product. *T/F*

(*b*) Defectives can be sold as finished goods without being processed. *T/F*

[***Answers :*** (*a*) *F*, (*b*) *F*]

III. Choose the correct answer

1. Which one of the following is considered to be the normal loss of materials.
   (*a*) Loss due to accident
   (*b*) Pilferage
   (*c*) Loss due to breaking the bulk.
   (*d*) Loss due to careless handling of materials.
2. Defectives are those items
   (*a*) Which are rectifiable, made into good units.
   (*b*) Which are useless and beyond rectification
   (*c*) Which has scrap value and thus be sold
   (*d*) Which is waste having no recoverable value

[***Answers :*** 1. (*c*), 2. (*a*)]

IV. Simple questions

1. What do you mean by 'invisible loss'?
2. What do you mean by 'visible loss'?
3. Distinguish between usable and unusable loss.
4. What do you mean by 'waste'?
5. What do you mean by 'scrap'?
6. Distinguish between a 'waste' and 'scrap'.
7. What do you mean by spoilage?
8. Distinguish between a 'scrap' and 'spoilage'.
9. What do you mean by defective?

V. Short and long answer questions

1. Distinguish between scrap, spoilage and defectives in an engineering industry with specific reference to accounting treatment and control for each. (*Madras University, B.Com., March 1991*)
2. Explain how would you differentiate between normal and abnormal wastage of materials and their treatment in cost accounts. (*ICWA, Inter, Dec. 1990*)
3. Distinguish amongst waste, spoilage, salvage, rectification scrap. How are they treated in cost accounts. (*C.A., Inter, May 1986*)
4. Distinguish between waste, scrap, spoilage and defective and indicate the accounting treatment of each. (*Kerala University, B.Com., April 1989*)

5. Explain the terms waste, scrap, spoilage and defectives. Enumerate the steps for control and the principles of accounting of such losses to be followed in a manufacturing concern.
(ICWA, Inter, Dec. 1991)
6. What is scrap? How is treated in cost accounts? *(Madurai Kamaraj University, B.Com., April 1992)*
7. What do you understand by normal and abnormal waste of materials during the process of manufacture? State briefly how each should be treated in cost accounts? *(Madras University, B.Com., April 1992)*
8. Exaplain the accounting treatment and control of the following in cost accounts.
(*a*) Waste, (*b*) Scrap, (*c*) Defectives and (*d*) Spoilages *(Madras University, B.Com., April 1992)*
9. State brefly the problems connected with waste, scrap, spoilage and defectives and indicate the principle to be followed in control and accounting of such losses. *(Kakatiya University. M.Com., August 1991)*
10. Illustrate normal wastage and abnormal wastage in cost accounts. Also explain how does it affect the cost of the production and the necessity to minimise the same.
(Sri Krishnadevaraya University. B.Com., April 1992)

7

TOOLS, PATTERNS, DESIGNS, BLUE PRINTS AND PACKING MATERIALS

TOOLS

These are small equipments which are used in machine operations. Though they cost relatively less when compared to plant and machines yet they play an important role and has significant financial implications. Where tools constitute an important means of production, a separate tool room is established and it will be under the supervision of a tool room keeper. His duties among other things include maintenance of tools, its issue to various departments, receive them back after their use and undertake verification of tools from time to time.

Types of tools

The following are the different types of tools used in manufacturing concerns :

(*a*) **Tool :** A tool is a device used for working or cutting a material into a desired shape, for holding workpieces or for measuring parts after work has been completed.

(*b*) **Fixture :** A fixture is a device that holds one or more pieces while work is being done.

(*c*) **Jig :** A Jig is a device that keeps the work in position while cutting operations are being performed.

In addition to above tools many other tools such as locating devices, centralisers, clamping devices, dies, gages, etc. are used depending upon the nature of work invoived.

Treatment of Tools Cost in Cost Accounting

For the sake of treating tools in cost accounting it is classified into following types :

(*a*) **Loose tools, jigs, etc. :** The value of these tools are charged to departmental overheads by means of revaluing them.

(*b*) **Tools, jigs of standard types :** The depreciated value of such tools are charged to departmental overhead.

(*c*) **Special tools :** The cost of such tools are directly charged to the order on which special tools are used. The cost to be charged is not only the cost but also the cost of up-keep during the processing of the product.

(*d*) **Maintenance of old tools :** Such costs are charged to various departments in proportion to number of tools used.

Controlling Tool Cost

The tools required for production purpose may be manufactured or purchased. When it is to be manufactured, it involves the following steps :

(*a*) Prepare an estimate of tools required.

(*b*) Determine the unit cost and total cost of production.

(*c*) Add to the above cost of tools.

Instructions are then issued to manufacture such tools. Standard cost is established and used as yardstick for control of actual cost of tool manufactured.

When they are procured they are stored in the tool room. They are subject to perpetual inventory control.

For costly tool a separate tool ticket is maintained. This shows the number of times the tools are used, the extent of wastage and extent of recovery of tool cost.

Whenever any tools are to be drawn, it is to be authorised by a competent authority and the tools are issued only against presentment of a tool ticket. Alternatively metal tokens can be used for drawing the tools. Such tokens are kept in the relevant vacant bin and handed back when tools are returned at the end of day's work. This eliminates the paper work connected with issue of tools. Tools are examined when they are returned.

Damaged tools are sent for repairs. Every employee is made responsible for careful handling, using and return of tools.

The following steps should be taken while controlling the tool cost :

(*a*) The design of tool must be according to the design of the product for which the tools are required. In other words while manufacturing or procuring the tools care must be taken to see that they suit the design of the product to be manufactured.

(*b*) Tools are to be classified according to its requirements for various jobs.

(*c*) Conducting periodic inventory of tools.

(*d*) Recording of receipts, issues and wastages in stock ledger of tools.

(e) Inspection of tools when they are returned back after use in various departments.

(f) The life span of every tool must be indicated on the tools. If they wear out before its life span, the causes for the same is to be investigated.

PATTERNS

A pattern is a model according to which the finished product is to be developed or manufactured. Patterns are mostly used by readymade garment industry, plastic industry, iron and steel industry, etc.

Patterns can be obtained in two different ways, *viz.*, (*i*) they can be manufactured and (*ii*) they may be supplied by customers themselves.

Treatment of Pattern cost in Cost Accounts

(*i*) Where the patterns are manufactured by the manufacture, its cost is charged to the job. Thus the cost of production of job will be higher to the extent of the pattern cost.

(*ii*) Where the pattern is supplied by customers, the cost of pattern is charged to the job.

A separate register is maintained for various types of patterns used so as to enable return of patterns to customers. Records are also necessary for revaluing the patterns and for its depreciation. In big industries a pattern shop and pattern stores is set up as in the case of a tool room.

DESIGNS

The dictionary meaning of design is ""a drawing or sketch, a plan in out-line". However, the term design is much more than a drawing as it gives the three-dimensional view of the various parts and the whole assembly of a product. It is sketch which preceeds the drawing and takes into consideration the shape, constructional materials, method of manufacture, handling and the ultimate function of the various parts and the complete product. Though a design represents a paper sketch, it is supported by notes as to the kind of materials to be used, method of manufacture and so on. Design should be developed by the co-ordinated efforts of designors and cost accountant. This is because the cost of design exerts a powerful influence over the total cost of production. The design so developed must meet the functional efficiency, widest in its use, good in appearance and cheap in its development.

Treatment of Cost of Designs in Cost Accounts

(*a*) When the design is drawn for a specific job, the cost of design should be charged to that job wholly.

(*b*) When the design is meant for production of goods on a repetitive basis, an estimated design cost per unit is predetermined and charged to products manufactured in course of time as research and development cost.

DRAWINGS AND BLUEPRINTS

The term 'drawings' refers to the representation of the products by lines drawn, shades, etc. They are prepared according to a choosen scale. The term 'blueprint' refers to the original or altered (diminished or enlarged) copies of the drawings.

Drawings are prepared as per the list of specification for various parts and the final assembly of the parts into a finished product illustrating the dimensions of raw materials, parts made from such raw materials and finished dimension of the assembled product.

A separate department known as drawing office is established to prepare drawings and blueprints. This is essential in order to prepare the selling price in advance of production for quoting to prospective customers. The draughtsmen will maintain a record of drawings made by him.

Treatment of Cost of Drawings and Blueprints

The cost of drawings and blueprints are charged directly to the customer's orders. Where drawings and blueprints are prepared for manufacturing standard products, its cost are charged over the period of life of drawings.

PACKING MATERIALS

Packing materials are those materials which are used to pack the finished products before they are distributed to customers. Examples of packing materials are wrapping papers, bags, cartons, boxes, bottles, tins, etc. For the sake of accounting of packing materials, it can be classified into two types, *viz.*, (*a*) primary packing materials, (b) secondary packing materials. Primary packing materials are required to pack finished goods before they are ready for sale. Whereas secondary packing materials are those which are requied for safe and convenient distribution of the finished product.

Treatment of Primary Packing Materials in Cost Accounts

(*a*) The cost of primary packing materials are charged as part of the direct materials cost to the finished product. In other words, it forms part of prime cost.

(*b*) The cost of secondary packing materials is treated as distribution overhead.

Control over Packing Materials

(*a*) Select the best packing materials among various available ones. This can be done by a comparative study of the relative merits and demerits of various packing materials in retation to damage, deterioration and pilferage.

(*b*) Select the most durable and economical type of packing materials.

(*c*) By studying the turnover of packing material the slow moving type is to be eliminated.

(*d*) When packing materials such as drums, etc. are used the empty containers returned by customers can be revised for further packing of goods.

(*e*) The cost of packing materials can be reduced by bulk buying or manufacturing on mass scale basis.

(*f*) Mannual method of packing is to be replaced by mechanical method.

QUESTIONS

Short and long answer questions

1. How would you treat the following in cost accounts :
   (*a*) Tools
   (*b*) Designs
   (*c*) Drawings and blueprints
   (*d*) Packing materials.
2. Suggest what control measures would your recommend for (*a*) Tools and (*b*) Packing materials.

8

LABOUR COST CONTROL

INTRODUCTION

Labour cost constitutes the second important element of cost next only to material cost. Research has shown that in majoritiy of the cases labour cost constitutes about 40 per cent to 50 per cent of total cost of production. Though in modern days machines are used on a large scale basis, the importance of manual labour cannot be under estimated. This is so because efficient utilisation of labour reduces the labour cost, increases the productivity and quality and reduces the wastage and spoilage of goods. For the successful utilisation of labour force, it is necessary to account and control the labour. However payment of low labour cost need not result in decreased cost of production as it may result in delayed production, involving more wages and increased overhead. Similarly payment of higher wages need not result in higher cost of production because it may boost the morale of employee, thereby increasing their efficiency, speedier production and reduced overhead cost.

DIRECT AND INDIRECT LABOUR

Labour engaged in a factory may be classified into two types, *viz.*, (1) Direct labour and (2) Indirect labour.

Direct Labour

It refers to labour engaged in altering the construction, composition, conformation or condition of the product. In other words, it is the labour which can be conveniently identified with a particular cost centre or cost unit. The remuneration payable to direct labour is known as direct wages. As such labour cost can be allocated to the cost unit or cost centre. It is the wages which is paid for those employees who actually convert raw materials into finished goods. The examples of direct labour are wages payable to furniture-maker, shoe-maker, baker,tailor, masons, drivers, etc. The following are the important features of direct labour :

(*a*) Direct labour is a part of prime cost.
(*b*) It can be attributed to finished goods.
(*c*) Its cost can be identified with total cost of production.
(*d*) It varies with change in output.
(*e*) It can be controlled.

The ICMA terminology defines direct labour cost as "the cost of remuneration for employees, efforts and skills applied directly to a product or saleable service".

Indirect Labour

Labour that does not alter the construction, conformation, composition or condition of the product, but which contributes to the completion of the product is known as indirect labour. It is the labour which serves as ancillary to the direct labour used in completing the production. The remuneration paid to indirect labour is termed as indirect wages. It is defined by the ICMA terminology as "wage cost other than direct wage cost". Examples of indirect labour are services of watch and ward, supervisor, inspector, foreman, cleaners, time keeping officiers, storekeeper, general manager, etc. The following are the important features of indirect labour :

(1) It is secondary in importance as compared to direct labour.
(2) Its cost cannot be allocated but can only be apportioned.
(3) It does not vary with the change in production.
(4) It cannot be controlled.
(5) Its cost is treated as overheads.
(6) It can not be identified with the finished product.

The nature of work performed need not be necessarily taken as a basis for classifiying labour into direct and indirect. It is instead based on practicability and expediency. A worker who is engaged on a particular job is treated as direct if the above two conditions are satisfied. Thus wages or salary payable to an inspector or supervisor who can devote all his time for a single job is a direct labour. Whereas if he devotes his time on different jobs, his wages or salary is treated as indirect labour. Nevertheless the following are the important points of differences between direct and indirect labour :

Direct labour	*Indirect labour*
(1) It can be identified with finished product.	(1) It cannot be identified with finished product.
(2) The direct labour cost can be allocated to cost centre or cost unit.	(2) The indirect labour cost cannot be allocated but can only be apportioned.
(3) It is a part of prime cost.	(3) It is a part of overheads.
(4) It is primary in the production process.	(4) It is secondary or subsidiary to the production.
(5) Direct labour cost can be easily ascertained.	(5) It is somewhat difficult to ascertain indirect labour cost.
(6) It varies according to change in output.	(6) It remains fixed.
(7) It can be controlled.	(7) It cannot be easily controlled.

Need for Classifying Labour into Direct and Indirect

1. To ascertain the cost accurately in order to provide a basis for control.
2. To maintain efficiency.
3. To allocate overheads.
4. To introduce incentives.
5. To facilitate inter-firm comparision
6. To estimate the total labour cost.

LABOUR CONTROL

It may be defined as a control exercised over labour cost by proper employment and thereafterwards efficient utilisation of labour force. The important aspects over which labour control is exercised are as follows :

(*a*) Recruitment and selection of employees.
(*b*) Provision of good working conditions.
(*c*) Calculation and payment of correct amount of wages.
(*d*) Proper recording of attendance time.
(*e*) Accounting of wages.

By far the most important aspect over which control is exercised is labour cost. For better control, labour cost is classified into the following types.

Monetary Reward

The following are some of the examples of monetary reward.

(*i*) Basic wages.
(*ii*) Dearness allowance.
(*iii*) Production bonus.

Deferred Monetary Reward

These include the following :

(*i*) Employer's contribution to provident fund.
(*ii*) Employer's contribution to state insurance.
(*iii*) Gratuity.
(*iv*) Pension fund.
(*v*) Bonus based on profit.

Fringe Benefits or Non-Monetary Benefits.

These include the following :

(*i*) Canteen.
(*ii*) Housing.
(*iii*) Dispensary.
(*iv*) Education.

Labour-Related Costs

These include the following :

(*i*) Holiday pay.
(*ii*) Leave pay.
(*iii*) Premium pay.
(*iv*) Idle time pay.
(*v*) Overtime pay.

In big industries five separate departments are established to control labour cost. They are as follows :

1. **Personnel department :** This department is concerned with recruitment and selection of employees. Having selected, the employees are inducted and trained on the jobs. On appointment of an employee, this department intimates to the time-keeping and payroll department. This department maintains two important documents, *viz.*, (*a*) labour placement requisition and (*b*) employee history card.

A labour placement requisition is prepared by various departments which are in need of employees. The personnel manager verifies from his records in order to know whether the required number of employees are available within the factory. Otherwise he will arrange for the recruitment of said number of employees by advertising in newspaper or by consulting the employment exchange. The necessary action is then taken to receive applications to conduct interviews, tests, etc.

An employee history card is maintained to keep the record of every employee. It contains the details such as name, address, department where he works, name of the former employers, date of appointment, rate of pay, etc. Whenever any employee leaves the factory on his own or when his services are terminated the cause for such leaving or termination is recorded. This helps to control excessive labour turnover.

2. **Time recording department :** Time recording serves two purposes, *viz.*, (*i*) Time

keeping and time booking. Time keeping refers to recording of incoming and outgoing time of employees in a factory. Time booking refers to recording the time of employees spent on various jobs.

3. **Payroll department :** This department is concerned with calculation and disbursement of wages to employees. It performs the folloing functions :

(*a*) Maintenance of job classification record and wage rate of employees.

(*b*) To collect the hours of time spent in factory as well as on jobs by various employees.

(*c*) To calculate the wages of employees.

(*d*) To prepare payroll for every department separately.

(*e*) To calculate various deductions to be made from gross wages.

(*f*) To pay the net wages to the employees.

(*g*) To maintain pay roll record of every employee.

4. **Engineering department :** This department carries out the following functions :

(*a*) To determine and provide for good working conditions.

(*b*) To determine production method for each job.

(*c*) To prepare designs for each job.

(*d*) To conduct time and motion study.

(*e*) To determine the rate of pay.

5. **Cost accounting department :** Cost accounting department is concerned with proper recording and control of labour cost. It will classify the labour cost into direct and indirect labout cost. The former is recorded under prime cost and the latter under overheads. Proper reports are prepared by cost accountant and submitted to management for controlling excess idle time, overtime, labour turn over, etc. It will also compare actual labour cost with estimated labour cost to know variance between the two.

TIME KEEPING AND TIME BOOKING

Time Keeping

Time keeping refers to the process of recording the arrival and departure time of employees in a factory. In other words it records the incoming and outgoing time of employees in a factory. Every factory will establish a separate time keeping department which is situated near the entrance of factory gate. The time keeping officer will be incharge of the department. His duty is to arrange for accurate time recording of all employees of the factory. Usually time recording is done twice in a day, *i.e.*, at the starting time and at the closing time of the factory. However where employees are allowed to go out of the factory during lunch interval it will be recorded on four occasions. Time keeping serves the following objects :

(*a*) To calculate the wages payable to the employees.

(*b*) To calculate the normal working hours and overtime working hours of the employees.

(*c*) To meet statutory requirements.

(*d*) To calculate labour cost of an operation or job.

(*e*) To apportion overheads if they are based on number of workers or wages.

(*f*) To provide a basis for preparing statistical record which help in controlling labour cost.

(*g*) To introduce incentive system of wage payment.

(*h*) To ensure discipline among workers, *i.e.*, regularity and punctuality. This information is also useful for the management in deciding matters relating to promotion, sanction of increments, termination etc.

Methods of Time Keeping

Broadly speaking there are two methods for time keeping. These are (*i*) Manual method and (*ii*) Mechanical method.

1. **Manual method :** Under this method the attendance time of employees are recorded either by the time keeping officer or by employees themselves. The manual method of time keeping are as follows :

(*a*) ***Muster roll method or attendance register method :*** Under this method, an attendance register is maintained for recording the attendance time. This method is followed in small-sized concerns. This method is more suitable for recording the attendance time of clerical staff and other staff officers. Two separate columns are maintained corresponding the names of every employee. One column is to record the arrival time and second column for recording departure time. The attendance time can be marked by the time keeping officer by calling out the name of every employee or alternatively the attendance register may be signed by every employee.

Merits :

(1) It is simple to maintain attendance register.
(2) It is economical when compared to other methods.

Demerits :

(1) The method is not suitable for medium and large sized business.
(2) Where the attendance is marked by calling out the names of employees, there will be hold-ups near the factory gate.
(3) Dishonest employees may mark the attendance of their absentee employee.
(4) Time keeping officer may show step-motherly treatment to his friends and this will defeat the purpose of time keeping.
(5) It involves additional work for posting the entries into the individual working record.

(*b*) ***Token or disc method :*** A disc or token is a small metallic plate which bears the identification number of an employee. The disc of all employees may be arranged in a spike file or in a box. Whenever a worker enters into the factory gate, he is supposed to pick up his token and place it on another file or box meant for this purpose. The box can be replaced at frequent intervals to know the extent of late arrival of employees. Alternatively, instead of replacing the box, the employees may be asked to report to time keeping officer who inturn will record the late attendance time of employees. The time keeping officier will then prepare an attendance record with the help of disc and the absentees are denoted by the missing discs.

Merits :

(1) It is simple to operate.
(2) It does not involve heavy investment.
(3) It suits to a factory which employs more number of employees.

Demerits :

(1) This dishonest practice of inserting a disc of an absentee worker by another employee may take place..

(2) It involves more clerical work to prepare an attendance record with the help of disc. Where any mistake is committed in recording attendance time on the basis of disc and in case of any disputes between an employee and time keeping officer, disc cannot offer any proof.

2. **Machanical method :** In modern days mechanical methods of time keeping is used to save time and ensure greater accuracy. The machines record the exact time of the arrival and departure of employees. Thus they avoid possible disputes and difference of opinions between employees and time keeping officers. Mechanical methods are used in medium and large sized industries as small sized concerns cannot afford to invest more capital on such equipments. The following are the important mechanical methods of time recording.

(*a*) ***Dial time recorder :*** The features and functioning of this equipment can be summarised as under :

(*i*) It consists of a large dial on which there are about 150 holes corresponding to the number of workers.

(*ii*) A clock is fitted within the circles of the dial together with a dial arm which operates from the centre of the circle.

(*iii*) The worker while entering into the gate turns the dial arm. He then presses the button corresponding to his clock number. The time of his arrival is recorded on a sheet of paper kept inside the machine.

(*iv*) The same procedure is following before the employee leaves the factory gate.

Merits :

(*i*) Time is recorded strictly according to payroll order.

(*ii*) Provision can also be made out not only to record time but also to calculate wages.

Demerits :

(*i*) A worker can record the time of an absentee worker.

(*ii*) Time of arrival and departure are separated out in two different sheets of paper which require additional clerical work.

(*iii*) A worker cannot see the time he has booked and disputes may arise afterwards.

(*b*) ***Card time recorder :*** This is a machine which is fitted with a clock on each side of which there is an 'in' and 'out' rack which contains the cards of the employees. The worker who enters the gate takes his card from the 'in' rack, inserts it in the machine. On pressing a lever the time of arrival is recorded on the card. Then the card is placed in the 'out' rack. At the time of departure from the factory the worker removes his card, inserts it in the machine to record the time of departure and finally places it in the 'in' rack.

Merits :

(*i*) For each and every worker time is recorded individually.

(*ii*) The absence of worker can be checked by a mere look at the 'out' rack.

(*iii*) This can be taken as a basis for wage calculation.

Demerits :

(*i*) An employee can record the time of absenctee worker.

(*ii*) Controlling and checking cards becomes difficult.

(*c*) ***Autograph or signature type time recorder :*** This type of machine is most commonly used in small sized business enterprise where supervision for time recording does not arise. Its features can be summarised as follows :

(*i*) It is a machine which is fitted with a clock and is connected to a printing mechanism on a roll of paper.

(*ii*) To operate the machine, the employee opens the shutter by pressing a lever which is at the side of the machine. This enables to uncover a small signature window.

(*iii*) The employee signs in this signature window and as he signs, the day and time is automatically recorded.

(*iv*) When the lever is released, the paper roll inside the machine (which now bears worker's signature, day and time) is advanced, the shutter slides back over the signature window, and the machine is ready for the signature of the next worker.

Merits :

(*i*) Recording of time is automatic and accurate.

(*ii*) Employees cannot see the recorded time.

Demerits :

(*a*) The worker's name does not appear as per the payroll order.

(*b*) The signature may not be legible.

(*c*) Breakdown in the machine leads to stoppage in the recording of attendance time.

Time booking

Time booking refers to the process of recording the time spent by workers on various jobs in a factory. In other words it is the recording of the starting time and finishing time of employees on a job. Time booking comes next in the sequence after the time keeping in respect of recording time.

Distinction Between Time Keeping and Time Booking

Time keeping	*Time booking*
(1) It records attendance time of employees.	(1) It records the total time worked by employees on jobs.
(2) It is the first step involved in time recording.	(2) It is the second step involved in time recording.
(3) It records the time spent by the employees in the factory.	(3) It records the time spent by the employees on various jobs.
(4) Time keeping is done at the time keeping office.	(4) It is done at various production departments.
(5) It is recorded by time keeping officer.	(5) It is recorded by a foreman or by employees.
(6) Its purpose is to enable preparation of payroll.	(6) Its aim is to ascertain the labour cost of job.

Methods of Time Booking

Time booking can be entrusted to the foreman or to time booking clerks. Some time it is done even by employees. It can be recorded either manually or mechanically. The following are the various methods of time booking.

1. Daily time sheet system : Under this method the time spent by workers on different jobs for a certain day is recorded. For each worker a sheet of paper is issued wherein his time spent on various jobs are recorded. This method is suitable under two situations, *viz.*, (*a*) size of the factory is small, (*b*) where the worker has to attend to more jobs instead of few jobs on the same day. The daily time sheet consists of the following particulars :

(*a*) Worker's name
(*b*) Worker's identification number
(*c*) Name of the department
(*d*) Date of work
(*e*) Job number
(*f*) Nature of work done
(*g*) Starting time on the job
(*h*) Finishing time on the job
(*i*) Actual or normal hours and overtime hours of work done
(*j*) Signature of time booking authority.

A proforma of daily time sheet is shown below :

DAILY TIME SHEET

Name of the worker ____________ Department____________
No. ____________
Machine No. ____________

Worker order no.	*Work done*	*Time*		*Total hrs.*	*Rate*	*Total wages*
		Start	*Finish*			

Signature of time booking authority.........

Fig. 8.1. Specimen showing daily time sheet.

Merits :

(*a*) It is simple to operate.
(*b*) It enables the foreman to know how much of work is done by employee each day.
(*c*) The record shows accurate information as it is checked by the foreman everyday.
(*d*) This method is particularly useful where more number of jobs are to be performed on the same day.

Demerits :

(*a*) It involves more of clerical work by way of consolidation of all the daily time sheets for one full month.
(*b*) It is not suitable for large business concerns.

2. **Weekly time sheet :** This method resembles to daily time sheet of time booking. But instead of booking the time daily, it is recorded for the week. It provides the data relating to the time spent on various jobs for a period of one week. The proforma of such document is shown below :

WEEKLY TIME SHEET

Name of the employee .... Week ending ....
No. ....

Name of the job	*No. of the job*	*Nature of work*	*M*	*T*	*W*	*T*	*F*	*S*	*Total*	
									Ordinery	*OT*

Signature of supervisor/Foreman

Fig. 8.2. Weekly time sheet.

3. **Job cards or job tickets :** Under this method a card is made use of for recording the time spent by workers on various jobs instead of sheets of paper. Each employee will be given a card which contains the particulars of work to be performed by him. This card is to be filled in by employees by noting down the starting time and finishing time of the job which he attends to. When a worker completes a job he will be given a separate job card to book the time on such job. A specimen form of job card is given below :

JOB CARD

Department ____________ Job no. ____________
Work order no. ____________ Date ____________
Machine no. ____________ Starting time ____________
Finishing time ____________

Description of job	*Hours*	*Rate*	*Amount*

Signature of foreman..........

Fig. 8.3. Speciman showing job card.

Merits :

(*a*) It provides information relating to the job to be performed by workers. Thus it serves as an authority to start the work, besides recording the total time spent by workers on jobs.

(*b*) It provides correct and clear information for costing department.

Demerits :

(*a*) It involves more paper work when workers performs several jobs everyday.

(*b*) Reconciliation of attendance time and time booked on job becomes difficult when idle time is not properly recorded.

4. **Combined time and job card :** This document contains two parts. The first part is to be filled in as attendance time and the second part, the total time spent on jobs. This faciliates reconciliation of gate time with the work time and the extent of idle time can be easily detected. This method fullfills the objectives of both time keeping and time booking. A proforma of this document is shown below :

COMBINED TIME AND JOB CARD

Name of the worker ____________ Week ending ____________
No. ____________________
Department ______________

Days in the week	*Job no.*	*Attendance time*		*Job time*		*Total hrs.*		*Rate*	*Amount*
		Arrival	*Departure*	*From*	*To*	*Ordinary*	*OT*		
Monday Tuesday Wednesday Thursday Friday Saturday									

Idle hours

Signature of time keeping officer Signature of time booking officer

Fig. 8.4. Speciman showing combined time and job card.

Merits :

(1) It combines the mertis of both attendance time and time booking.

(2) Compared to maintaining time keeping and time booking separately, it is more economical.

(3) The idle time is properly accounted for.

Demerit : It is no suitable for large sized undertakings.

5. **Labour cost card :** A labour cost card is used to record the time spent by all the workers on various operations of the job. In other words, the time spent by a group of workers attending on a job is recorded in labour cost card. This card is meant for a job instead of workers. As and when a worker records time spent on the job, it shall be pased on to other workers. This record thus shows the total time spent on a job and the wages to be charged to that job. As this card shows the total labour cost of a particular job it is termed as labour cost card.

6. **Piece work card :** This card shows the number of units produced by the worker and the time spent in manufacturing the units. This method is adopted where piece rate system of wage payment is adopted. A separate card is prepared and used by every worker to record the number of units produced and the total time spent by him. A proforma of piece work card is shown below :

PIECE WORK CARD

Name of the worker ___________

No. ___________

Department ___________

Job no.	*Description of the job*	*Units*		*Hours*		*Piece rate*	*Amount*
		Produced	*Rejected*	*Starting*	*Finishing*		

Signature of worker/foreman   Signature of inspector

Fig. 8.5. Specimen of piece work card.

MOTION STUDY, TIME STUDY AND WORK STUDY

In order to fix wage rates it is necessary to classify the jobs in relation to their importance, the skill and time required to complete the jobs and such other factors. Motion study, time study and work study assume more importance in fixing wage rates.

Motion Study

Motion study has been defined by F.B. Gilberth as "the science of eliminating, wastefulness resulting from using unnecessary, ill directed and inefficient motions". Motion study consists of dividing work into the most fundamental elements possible, studying these elements separately and in relation to one another and from these elements, the unnecessary movement of workers' organ's are eliminated.

A micro-motion study is the sub-divison of an operation into motions and their analysis for the improvement of the work cycle. Detailed bodily movements, especially highty skilled motions are recorded and the time is measured by taking motion pictures at a constant speed with a micrometer from the background.

Advantages of Motion Study

(*a*) By simplifying the movements and reducing the sequence, it enables the worker to produce more units per hour and earn more wages. The employer is also benefitted by the increased production.

(*b*) It helps in carefully planning material handling equipments which not only increases speed of production but also reduces material handling cost.

(*c*) It helps the foreman to know the causes for the slow progress of work and enables him to train the workers the best method of performing the task.

(*d*) It helps the personnel department to induct the right type of workers into the jobs for which they are best suited.

(*e*) It leads to better safety measures.

Time Study

The concept of time study was introduced by F.W. Talyor. It refers to the analysis and determination of the time necessary to perform a given task. It replaces the old practice of using past performance, judgement or trial as a method of establishing the time allowed for the performance of a task. Time study has been defined by Alford and Beathy (in their *Industrial Management*) as a scientific analysis of methods and equipments used or planned in doing a piece of work, development is practical detail the best way of doing it and determination of the time required."

Time Study Procedure

The following steps are involved in a time study procedure :

1. The objective of the study is to be clearly defined. This includes a definition of the use of the results, the precision required and the desired confidence in the estimation of the time parameter.
2. The purpose of the study and necessary preparations are reviewed by the supervisor of the operating department.
3. A preliminary analysis of the operation is made to determine whether standard methods and conditions prevail and whether the operator is properly trained.
4. When there is more than one operator, the operator to be choosen is studied.
5. A detailed record is made for the standard methods and conditions, either in writing or by a motion picture.
6. The operation is divided into time study elements.
7. A number of time study observations are taken.
8. The actual measurement is made with the requisite number of observations over a specified time period.
9. The operator is rated during the study by a comparison of his performance level with that of the normal operator.
10. Allowances for various job interruptions and delays are determined by policy.
11. The standard time is derived from the observed time, the rating factor and allowance.

Utility of Time Study

The management makes use of time study for the following purposes :

(*a*) To determine the standard time for the performance of an operation and use the data for establishing a fair incentive system of wage payment.

(*b*) To estimate the time and cost involved in new production orders.

(*c*) To achieve a uniform flow of work in developing or improving the layout of a plant.

(*d*) To aid the analysis of work methods conducted during motion studies.

Work Study

Keith Lockyer (in his *Production Management*) has defined work study as "a management service based on those techniques, particularly method study and work measurement, which are used in the examination of human work in all its contexts and which lead to systematic investigation of all the resources and factors which affect the efficiency and economy of the situation being reviewed, in order to effect improvement." Work study is one of the important tools of management which indicates the areas requiring investigation, so as to set right the defects in manufacturing. Work study includes two closely related techniques, *viz.*, (1) method study and (2) work measurement.

1. **Method study :** Method study is the systematic recording and critical examination of the existing and proposed ways of doing work, as a means of developing and applying

easier and more effective methods and reducing costs. The following are some of the reasons for which method study is conducted.

(*a*) Bottlenecks generating high work-in-progress, long delivery times or unbalanced work-flow.

(*b*) Idle plants giving rise to underutilisation of reasources.

(*c*) Poor morale on account of trivial complaints, high absenteeism.

(*d*) Inconsistent earnings.

(*e*) Poor quality, which may arise from poor working methods or conditions.

2. **Work measurement :** The procedure involved in measuring or forecasting the rate of output of an existing or newly designed operation, as well as in determining how much time is consumed for various productive and non-productive activities of a process, operation or job is known as 'work measurement'. The management of a factory makes use of work measurement as a technique for evaluation of work methods and in determining the standard time for each job.

JOB EVALUATION

Kimball and Kimball (in their *Industrial Organisation*) have defined job evaluation as "an effort to determine the relative value of every job in a plant and to determine what the fair basic wage for such a job should be."

Objectives of Job Evaluation

The main objectives of job evaluation are as follows :

(*a*) To eliminate wage inequalities.

(*b*) To establish sound wage differentials among the jobs.

(*c*) To provide a sound wage for incentive and bonus plan.

(*d*) To establish a sound wage structure.

(*e*) To faciliate maintenance of a consistent wage policy.

Advantages of Job Evaluation

(*a*) Wage rates can be fixed accurately in an organisation by deciding the proper worth of the different jobs.

(*b*) Job evaluation technique is useful for proper selection, training, promotion, transfers of employees within the organisation. These activities can be performed objectively and impartially through job evaluation.

(*c*) It facilitates objective control on the entire organisation and eliminates nepotism and wastage.

(*d*) It eliminates or at least minimises the grievances of the workers about the absolute and relative wage rates. It avoids confusion in the minds of employees as regards the wage rates fixed by the management.

(*e*) Job evaluation technique raises the morale of the employees and also efficiency of labour force in factories.

Methods of Job Evaluation

There are four methods of job evaluation. They are as follows :

1. **Ranking method :** This method is also known as the grading method as it involes assigning grades to various jobs in the order of their relative importance. Under this method, three steps are involved, *viz.*, (*a*) making a thorough job analysis, (*b*) expressing the findings

of this analysis in job description and (*c*) ranking each job by arranging them in an ascending order, starting with the job of minimum requirements of various characteristics and ending with maximum requirements of various characteristics of the job. Ranking can be based on : (*i*) difficulty of work, (*ii*) volume of work, (*iii*) responsibility involved, (*iv*) supervision required, (*v*) knowledge, (*vi*) conditions under which work is done.

After ranking is completed, the jobs are generally grouped into ten or twelve groups, according to their position. The jobs are then evaluated by determining the wage rates prevailing in similar factories. Accordingly, wage rates are increased either by a fixed percentage or by a fixed amount.

2. **Job classification method :** Under this method, standard grade descriptions are used in classifying the various jobs. As and when each job is reviewed, it is placed in the category having the most appropriate description. This is opposite of what happens in the job ranking system, since in that system, jobs are first ranked and then divided into grades.

3. **Points methods :** This method is by far the most widely used method in factories. It consists of a "yardstick containing various factors such as skill, education, responsibility and so on that are inherent in the jobs. The degree of importance of each factor is determined by an arbitrary decision, and a suitable point value is specified for each factor. The total points for all the factors then determine the relative position of that job among other jobs.

4. **Factor comparison method :** This method consists of analysing jobs on the basis of five factors, *viz.*, mental requirements, skill requirements, physical requirements, responsibility involved and working conditions. The jobs are ranked according to each one of these factors, one factor being taken at a time and each job is compared with the other with respect of its worth on this factor alone. The relative weightage of this factor on each job is done by applying money value (*i.e.*, rupees) to the ranking. After all the jobs are rated on each factor, a wage rate for each job is determined by the sum of money weightages determined for each of the five job factors. These wage rates become the basis for determining the wage scale.

MERIT RATING

Merit rating of an employee is the process of evaluating the employee's performance on the job in terms of the requirements of the job for the purposes of placement of workers on appropriate jobs, selection for promotion, providing financial reward and so on. In the words of Alford and Beatty, merit rating is the evaluation or appraisal of the relative worth of man's services on this job.

Objectives of Merit Rating

Merit rating serves the following purposes :

(*a*) It furnishes a periodic record of the relative value of each employee, as judged by his superior.

(*b*) It determines and justifies wage differentials existing for the same job.

(*c*) It provides more accurate information on which promotions, transfers and lay-offs may be based.

(*d*) It provides a means of evaluating the selection and training techniques used.

(*e*) It provides imformation for counselling employees, so that the means of overcoming weakness can be pointed out and programmes for self-improvement developed.

(*f*) It provides a more effective tool for rating the personnel.

(*g*) It establishes better employer-employees relations through mutual confidence, which comes as a result of frank discussions between the leader and the follower regarding merit rating.

(*h*) It ensures better supervision as the supervisors must observe the employees closely if they are to rate them accurately.

Method of Merit Rating

The method used for merit rating are as follows :

(1) **Rank-order method :** Under this method, the rater is expected to keep a list of all the employees under this supervision. The various characteristics which are to be possessed by the employees are then determined. Ranks are assigned to these characteristics, depending upon the fulfilment of traits by the employees.

(2) **Graphic rating scale :** Graphic rating scale provides a series of traits and their definition. The rater places a mark opposite to these traits on a line representing the full distance from the 'highest' to the 'lowest' rating. This approach is one of the most commonly used rating forms in industries today.

(3) **Forced choice :** Under this method, the rater selects from a number of groupings of unrelated 'personal characteristics' statements, one that is most similar and another that is least similar to the rates. Numerical values are assigned on a statistical basis and thus scores are obtained.

(4) **Critical incident :** The rater keeps a running record of activity incidents which are 'critical' for successful and unsuccessful performance. When this method is used over a period of time, it identifies those types of activity which are characteristic of successful and unsuccessful employees in specific types of jobs. Thus, it furnishes the basis for continuing appraisals of subordinates and for day-to-day discussions with them for corrective and development purposes.

LABOUR PRODUCTIVITY

Labour productivity is an indicator of efficiency of eimployees in a factory. It refers to the quantity of output obtained for a given quantity of input. The quantity may be expressed in terms of quantity of output, sales value or cost and input in terms of weight of materials used, hours worked etc.

Measurement of Labour Productivity

The following are the important measurements of labour productivity :

1. **Output per man-hour :** Under this method the total output is divided by the total man-hours worked. This method can be applied where the output obtained is uniform in respect of quality, design, etc. The following formula is used :

$$\text{Labour productivity} = \frac{\text{Total output}}{\text{Total manhours}}$$

2. **Labour hours per unit of production :** Under this method the total labour hours are divided by the total output to get number of labour hour required for manufacturing certain units of products. This method can be used where different products are produced and where an overall productivity is to be measured covering all the production. The following formula is used :

$$\text{Labour productivity} = \frac{\text{Total labour hours}}{\text{Total output}}$$

It can be seen from the above formula that this method is reciprocal to the output per man-hour.

3. **Comparing actual time with standard time :** This method is adopted where production process is standardised and where standard costing is in operation. The following formula is used :

$$\text{Labour productivity} = \text{Std. hours for actual output} - \text{Actual hours for actual output}$$

4. **Extent of lost time :** Under this method the man-hours lost is divided by total man-hours and the quotient is expressed as a percentage. The following formula is used :

$$\text{Percentage of lost time} = \frac{\text{Manhours lost}}{\text{Total manhours}} \times 100$$

5. **Labour productivity based on money value :** The following are some of the measures used to know the labour productivity :

(*a*) ***Based on sales :*** Under this method the sales value is divided by the number of workers. The following formula is used :

$$\text{Labour productivity} = \frac{\text{Sales value}}{\text{No. of workers}}$$

(*b*) ***Based on value added :*** Under this method added value of the product is divided by total wages paid. Here added value represents the difference between sales value and material cost. The following formula is used :

$$\text{Labour productivity} = \frac{\text{Added value of the product}}{\text{Total wages}}$$

where Added value of product = Sales value – Material cost of product.

(*c*) ***Based on direct wages :*** Under this method the direct wages is divided by number of units produced. The following formula is used :

$$\text{Labour productivity} = \frac{\text{Direct wages}}{\text{Number of units}}$$

Measures to be taken for Increasing Labour Productivty

Labour productivity can be improved by the joint efforts of the Government, employers and employees. The following steps may be taken to increase labour productivity :

(*a*) Recruitment and selection of right type and required number of employees.
(*b*) Training the employees.
(*c*) Provision of good working conditions to employees.
(*d*) Adopting production planning and control techniques.
(*e*) Standardisation and simplification of work.
(*f*) Fixation of reasonable rate of wages and incentives.
(*g*) Conducting time motion and work studies.
(*h*) Adopting job evaluation and merit rating techniques.

LABOUR TURNOVER

Whenever employees in a factory gets better terms and conditions of employement elsewhere, they leave the existing factory and join the new factory. This change in labour force is known as labour turnover. Thus labour turnover refers to mobility of empoyees from factory to factory for getting better cpportunities in terms of earnings and position of authority. In concrete terms, labour turnover may be defined as the number of employees who leave the factory during a period in relation to the average number of workers employed during the year.

Although a minimum labour turnover is quite normal and can be allowed in factories, excessive rate of labour turnover is not desirable. This is because efficient and experienced workers leave the factory and new employees come and occupy their places. Naturally, the ability of such new workers is less as compared to that of the experienced workers. The desirable percentage of labour turnover is placed between 3 per cent and 5 per cent.

Causes of Labour Turnover

The causes of labour turnover may be listed under the following headings :

(1) ***Causes arising from the point of view of employees***

(*a*) Incompetence to perform a job satisfactorily.
(*b*) Insubordination to superiors.
(*c*) Accidents.
(*d*) Prolonged illness.
(*e*) Death.
(*f*) Marriage in case of women employees.
(*g*) Housing problem.
(*h*) Discharge on disciplinary ground.
(*i*) Retirement.
(*j*) Personal betterment.

(2) ***Causes arising from the point of view of employer***

(*a*) Payment of low wages.
(b) Bad working conditions.
(*c*) Failure to protect workers against accidents.
(*d*) Hostile attitude on the part of superior towards subordinates.
(*e*) Unfair promotion policies.
(*f*) Inefficient management.
(*g*) Lack of welfare facilities.
(*h*) Lack of job security, social security and training facilities.

Effects of Labour Turnover on Cost of Production

(1) Increased wages due to less speed in production.
(2) Additional expenses incurred on training the newly recruited employees.
(3) Increased cost of labour arising out of rectifying the spoilt and defective products.
(4) Increased idle time wages as new workers are always less efficient.
(5) Overhead expenses will increase cost per unit owing to lower volume of production.
(6) Cost of repairs and maintenance will increase.
(7) Payment of higher compensation to employees involved in industrial accidents.

Remedial Measures to Prevent High Labour Turnover

The following measures are to be taken to control and reduce the high percentage of labour turnover :

(1) Scientific recruitment, selection and training of workers.
(2) Provision of better wages, allowances and other monetary benefits.
(3) Provision of better working conditions.
(4) Introduction of fair promotion policy.
(5) Provision of social security measures such as pension, provident fund, gratuity and so on.
(6) Better motivation and provision of welfare facilities to employees.
(7) Cordial labour management relations.
(8) Reducing fluctuations in the volume of work.
(9) Ensuring job satisfaction and job security.
(10) Measures should be taken to reduce labour disputes to the minimum.

Measurement of Labour Turnover

Labour turnover can be measured by any one of the following three methods. In this connection it is to remembered that once a particular method is adopted, it should not be changed frequently as comparision of labour turnover becomes difficult.

1. **Separation method :** This is the most commonly used method of measuring labour turnover. Under this method, the total number of separations during a period is divided by the average number of workers on roll during that period and multiplying the quotient by 100 to determine the percentage of turnover. The average number of workers during a period is obtained by adding the number of workers in the beginning and at the end of the year and dividing the sum by 2. Expressed in the form of formula :

$$\text{Separation method} = \frac{\text{No. of separation during the period}}{\text{Average no. of employees during the period}} \times 100$$

2. **Replacement method :** Thie method takes into consideration only the actual replacement of labour, *i.e.*, the number required to be replaced during the period, irrespective of total leavings. This is obtained by dividing the number of replacement during the period by the average number of employees during that period and then multiplying it by 100 to determine the percentage. Expressed in the form of a formula :

$$\text{Replacement method} = \frac{\text{No. of replacements during the period}}{\text{Average no. of employees during that period}} \times 100$$

3. **Flux rate method :** This method takes into account both the leavings and the new entrants. This is obtained by adding the leavings and replacements, dividing the total by the average number of employees during the period and multiplying the quotient by 100. Expressed in the form of a formula :

$$\text{Flux rate method} = \frac{\text{No. of Separations + No. of replacements}}{\text{Average no. of employees during the period}} \times 100$$

Problem 1 : From the following data given by the personnel department calculate the labour turnover rate by applying (*a*) separation method, (*b*) replacement method, (*c*) flux method.

Number of workers on the payroll :

At the beginning of the month	900
At the end of the month	1,100

During the month 10 workers left, 40 persons were discharged and 150 workers were recruited of these 25 workers are recruited in the vacancies of those leaving, while the rest were engaged for an expansion.

(*ICWA, Inter, Dec. 1988*)

Solution :

Calculation of average No. of workers during the month

$$= \frac{\text{No. of workers at the beginning of the month + No. of workers at the end}}{2}$$

$$\frac{900 + 1{,}100}{2} = 1{,}000$$

(*a*) Separation method $= \dfrac{\text{No. of separations during the month}}{\text{Average no. of workers during the month}} \times 100$

$$= \frac{10 + 40}{1{,}000} \times 100 = 5\%$$

(*b*) Replacement method $= \dfrac{\text{No. of workers replaced during the month}}{\text{Average no. of workers during the month}} \times 100$

$$= \frac{25}{1{,}000} \times 100 = 2.5\%$$

(*c*) Flux method $= \dfrac{\text{No. of separations + No. of replacement}}{\text{Average no. of workers during the month}} \times 100$

$$= \frac{50 + 25}{1{,}000} \times 100 = 7.5\%$$

Treatment of Labour Turnover Cost

Labour turnover cost can be classified into (*i*) preventive cost and (*ii*) replacement cost. Preventive cost includes all expenses incurred in preventing excess labour turnover. Such costs relate to providing welfare facilitites. Replacement cost include cost spent on new workers in place of workers who leave the factory, such as recruitment cost, training cost, cost of defectives and so on. Labour turnover cost is not treated as direct cost. Hence they are accumulated over a period of time under the above two classification and are charged to various departments as overheads on the basis of number of workers in each department.

Problem 2 : The cost accountant of Y Ltd has computed labour turnover rates for the quarter ended 31st March, 1997 as 10%, 5% and 3% respectively under 'Flux method', 'Replacement method' and 'Separation method'. If the number of workers replaced during the quarter is 30, find out the number of (1) Workers recruited and joined and (2) workers left and discharged. (*CA, Inter, May 1997*)

Solution :

Labour Turnover rate (under replacement method) $= \dfrac{\text{No. of replacements}}{\text{Average number of workers on roll}} \times 100$

$$\frac{5}{100} = \frac{30}{\text{Average no. of workers on roll}}$$

or Average No. of workers on roll $= \dfrac{30 \times 100}{5} = 600$

Labour turnover rate (separation method) $= \dfrac{\text{No. of separations}}{\text{Average no. of workers}} \times 100$

$$\frac{3}{100} = \frac{\text{No. of separations}}{600}$$

$$\text{No. of separations} = \frac{600 \times 3}{100} = 18$$

∴ No. of separations or No. left and discharged is 18

$$\text{Labour turnover rate (flux method)} = \frac{\text{No. of separations + No. of replacements}}{\text{Average no. of workers}}$$

$$= \frac{10}{100} = \frac{18 + \text{No. of replacements}}{600}$$

or $600 \times 10 = 100\,(18 + \text{No. of replacement})$

or $6{,}000 = 1{,}800 + 100 \text{ No. of replacement}$

or $6{,}000 - 1{,}800 = 100 \text{ No. of replacement}$

or $\text{No. of replacement} = \frac{4{,}200}{100} = 42$

∴ No. of replacement or No. recruited and joined is 42

Problem 3 : The cost Accountant of Adarsh Ltd, has computed labour turnover rates for the quarter ended 31st March, 2000 as 20%, 10% and 6% respectively under 'flux method', 'replacement method' and 'separation method'. If the number of workers replaced during the quarter is 80, find out the number of (*i*) Workers left and discharged and (*ii*) Workers recruited and joined including replacements. (*C.S., Inter, December 2000*)

Solution :

$$\text{Labour turnover (under replacement method)} = \frac{\text{No. of replacements}}{\text{Average no. of workers on roll}}$$

$$\frac{10}{100} = \frac{80}{\text{Average No. of workers on roll}}$$

or $10 \text{ Average No. of workers} = 100 \times 80$

or $\text{Average No. of Workers} = \frac{8{,}000}{10} = 800$

(1) $$\text{Labour turnover rate (separation method)} = \frac{\text{No. of separations}}{\text{Average No. of workers on roll}}$$

$$\frac{6}{100} = \frac{S}{800}$$

or $100\,S = 6 \times 800$

$$S = \frac{4{,}800}{100} = 48$$

No. of separations or No. of workers left and discharged = 48

(2) $$\text{Labour turnover (flux method) rate} = \frac{\text{No. of separations + No. of replacements}}{\text{Average No. of workers on roll}}$$

$$\frac{20}{100} = \frac{48 + R}{800}$$

or $20 \times 800 = 100\,(48 + R)$

or $16{,}000 = 4{,}800 + 100\,R$

or $16{,}000 - 4{,}800 = 100\,R$

$11{,}200 = 100\,R$

$$R = \frac{11{,}200}{100} = 112$$

∴ No. of workers recruited and joined including replacement is 112

CASUAL AND OUT WORKERS

A casual worker is a worker who is appointed on a termporary basis on a daily wage basis in order to meet the increased production schedule. Casual workers can also be appointed to replace workers who would have met with industrial accidents. As and when casual workers are appointed a separate accounting is to be maintained for such workers. They should be under the care of supervisor and their output must be certified by the supervisor.

The wages payable to the casual workers are to be treated as direct wages and as such it is charged directly to the job on which casual workers have been worked.

Out workers are engaged to work outside the premises of factory. Out workers may be classified under two categories viz., (*i*) those who work with their own tools in their own houses, (*ii*) those who are sent to the premises of customers by the employers. No record need be maintained in respect of first category of employees. However control is to be exercised over them with regard to issue of materials, prompt production of goods and quality of finished goods. For the second category of workers, it is necessary to maintain records for the purpose of recording attendance time and time spent on the jobs.

QUESTIONS

I. (A) Mark 'T' or 'F' in the space provided

1. The distinction between direct and indirect labour is not influenced by the use of a payroll summary account. *T/F*
2. The dial time recorder economises in clerical work involved in the preparation of the payroll. *T/F*
3. Muster roll is necessary for the preparation of payroll. *T/F*
4. Wages of a crane operator in a factory are direct wages. *T/F*
5. Metal disc method of time keeping can be profitably used in very large undertaking. *T/F*
6. Time keeping and time booking are one and the same thing. *T/F*
7. There is no need to record attendance of piece rate workers since attendance is not relevant for ascertaining the amount of wages to be paid. *T/F*
8. Time booking gives an analysis of the time spent by workers on various jobs. *T/F*
9. Time keeping record gives us the standard time of workers. *T/F*

[***Answers :*** True : 1, 3, 8, 9, False : Rest of the items]

(B) Fill in the blanks :

1. Wages sheet is prepared by .... department.
2. Recording of job time is known as ....
3. Wages which can be identified with and allocated to cost centre or cost unit is known as ....
4. .... department is concerned with proper selection and training employees.
5. An example of labour cost which is direct to a department and indirect to a product is ....

[***Answers :*** (1) payroll, (2) time booking, (3) direct wages, (4) Personnel, (5) foremen's salary]

(C) Choose the correct answers :

1. Time and motion study is conducted by
   (*a*) Time keeping department.
   (*b*) Personnel department.
   (*c*) Payroll department.
   (*d*) Engineering department.
2. Time and motion study is essential for
   (*a*) Rational promotion policy.
   (*b*) Completing a job on time.
   (*c*) Determining the standard time and the correct method of competing a task.
   (*d*) Determining prices of products.
3. The input-output ratio in case of labour means the ratio of
   (*a*) The value of output to the wages paid.
   (*b*) Standard time of the production to the actual time paid for.

(c) Abnormal idle time to normal idle time.
(d) Number of workers employed to the sanctioned strength.

4. Job specification is
   (a) A list of operations to be performed for completing the job concerned.
   (b) The requirement in terms of goods to be produced or work to be done.
   (c) The list of qualities and qualifications which the employee concerned should have to do the job work.
   (d) The name of the employee which will be assigned to a job.
5. Job evaluation aims at
   (a) Comparing a job with others so as to ascertain the proper scale of remuneration for the job.
   (b) Assessing the requirements in terms of personnel required.
   (c) Assessing the profitability of the job.
   (d) Establishing the hierarchial position of the holders of the job.
6. Direct labour means.
   (a) Labour which completes the work mannually.
   (b) Labour which is recruited directly and not through contractors.
   (c) Permanent labour in the production department.
   (d) Labour which can be conveniently associated with particular cost unit.

[*Answers :* 1(d), 2(c), 3(b), 4(c), 5(a), 6(d)]

(D) Classify the following into direct and indirect labour

(1) Repairman, (2) Shoemaker, (3) Baker, (4) Cabinet marker, (5) Time office clerk, (6) Foreman, (7) Bus driver in a transport company, (8) Carpenter, (9) Sweeper, (10) Watchman, (11) Lathe machine operator, (12) Factory clerical worker, (13) Workshop cleaner, (14) internal transport men, (15) General Manager.

[*Answers* : Direct labour (2), (3), (4), (7), (8), (11), Rest of the items is indirect labour]

II. Simple questions

1. Define direct labour.
2. State any four features of direct labour.
3. Define indirect labour.
4. Define any four features of indirect labour.
5. Define direct labour cost.
6. Define indirect labour cost.
7. Distinguish between direct labour and indirect labour.
8. Mention the need for classifying the labour into direct and indirect labour.
9. Mention the five departments established to control labour.
10. What do you mean by time keeping?
11. Mention two manual and two mechanical methods of time keeping.
12. What do you mean by time booking?
13. Mention any four methods of time booking.
14. Distinguish between time keeping and time booking.
15. What do you mean by work study?
16. What do you mean by method study?
17. What do you mean by time study?
18. What do you mean by motion study?
19. What do you mean by merit rating?
20. Distinguish between job evaluation and merit rating.
21. What do you mean by labour productivity?
22. Define labour turnover.
23. What do you mean by separation method of labour turnover?
24. What do you mean by replacement method of labour turnover?
25. What do you mean by flux method of labour turnover?
26. What do you mean by a casual worker?
27. What do you mean by a outworker?

III. Short and long answer questions

1. Explain the difference between direct labour and indirect labour highlighting the importance of such a distinction. *(ICWA, Inter, June 1992)*
2. Write a note on job evaluation. *(ICWA, Inter, June 1992)*
3. Explain the difference between work measurement and motion study. *(ICWA, Inter, Dec. 1991)*
4. Write a note on labour turnover. *(ICWA, Inter, June 1991)*
5. Define productivity. Higher productivity does not always result in lower costs or increased efficiency. Give your comments on this statement. *(ICWA, Inter, June 1990)*
6. Define job evaluation and distinguish it from merit rating. Explain the methods and objectives of job evaluation. *(ICWA, Inter, Dec. 1989)*
7. What is meant by the term 'labour turnover'? What is the effect of labour turnover on cost of production? *(ICWA, Inter, Dec. 1988)*
8. What is labour productivity? How can it be improved? Discuss the steps to be taken to increase labour efficiency and labour productivity. *(ICWA, Inter, June 1989)*
9. What is labour turnover? Explain the important methods of measuring it. *(Nagarjuna University, B.Com., April 1992)*
10. Define 'Labour turnover'. What are the major causes for the same. *(Calicut University, M.Com., April 1992)*
11. Discuss the mertis and demerits of disc method and dial time recorder. *(Mangalore University, B.Com., April 1991)*
12. Give the specimen rulings of the following documents and assess their importance, (*i*) Pay roll. *(Mangalore University, B.Com., Oct. 1987)*
13. What is the meaning of 'labour turnover'? How is it measured? Write the avoidable causes (any three) and unavoidable causes (any three) of labour turnover. *(University of Madras, B.Com., March 1991)*
14. What is labour turnover? Describe the effects of high labour turnover. *(University of Delhi, B.Com. (Hons), 1990)*
15. Why is a job card 'maintained'? How is it different from piece work card? *(University of Delhi, B.Com. (Hons), 1988)*
16. What is labour turnover? What are its causes? How is labour turnover measured. *(Sri Sathya Sai University, B.Com., March 1992)*
17. Distinguish between time keeping and time booking methods. Briefly explain the different method of time keeping. *(Sri Sathya Sai University, B.Com., Oct. 1990)*

Exercise 1 : From the following information, calculate the labour turnover rate and labour flux rate :

Number of workers at the beginning of the year : 3,800.

Number of workers at the end of the year : 4,200.

During the year, 40 workers leave while 160 workers are discharged. 600 workers are recruited during the year of these, 150 workers are recruited because of leavers and the rest are engaged in accordance with an expansion scheme.

(Bharathidarsan University, B.Com., April 1988)

[***Answer :*** Labour turnover rate under replacement method is 3.75 per cent and flux rate method is 20 per cent]

9

LABOUR COST ACCOUNTING

INTRODUCTION

The remuneration payable to labour factor of production is known as wages. One of the major issues confronting the management of every factory is the determination of a satisfactory wage structure. This issue has been further complicated by the fact that many direct components of a wage structure have social and psychological implications. From the point of view of the employer, the selection of a particular system of wage payment determines the future earning capacity of the factory. From the point of view of employees, choosing the appropriate wage plan will play a prominent role in determining employees satisfaction, productivity, morale and turnover. Therefore, the management of every factory must determine how much of wages and salaries are to be paid to employees. The determination of wages payable to employees is based upon a thorough analysis of all factors affecting such remuneration.

CHARACTERISTICS OF A SOUND WAGE SYSTEM

The following are the essential characteristics of a sound system of wage payment :

(1) The system must be agreed upon both by the employer and employees.

(2) The wage system must be such that it must minimise labour turnover.

(3) Wage system should include incentives for efficient and exceptional types of workers.

(4) It should reduce absenteeism and late attendance.

(5) The cost of operation of the system must be low.

(6) The system of wage payment must take into account the working conditions of the employees.

(7) It should guarantee a minimum amount of wages.

(8) Wage system must be flexible and capable of being adjusted in case of need.

(9) Wage system must be commensurate with the earnings of the factory.

(10) It should be consistent with government policy.

METHODS OF WAGE PAYMENT

Originally two systems of wage payment were in practice. *viz.*, time rate and piece rate system of wage payment. In modern days a number of systems of wage payment have been devised based on the time and piece rate system. The following chart shows the various methods of wage payment :

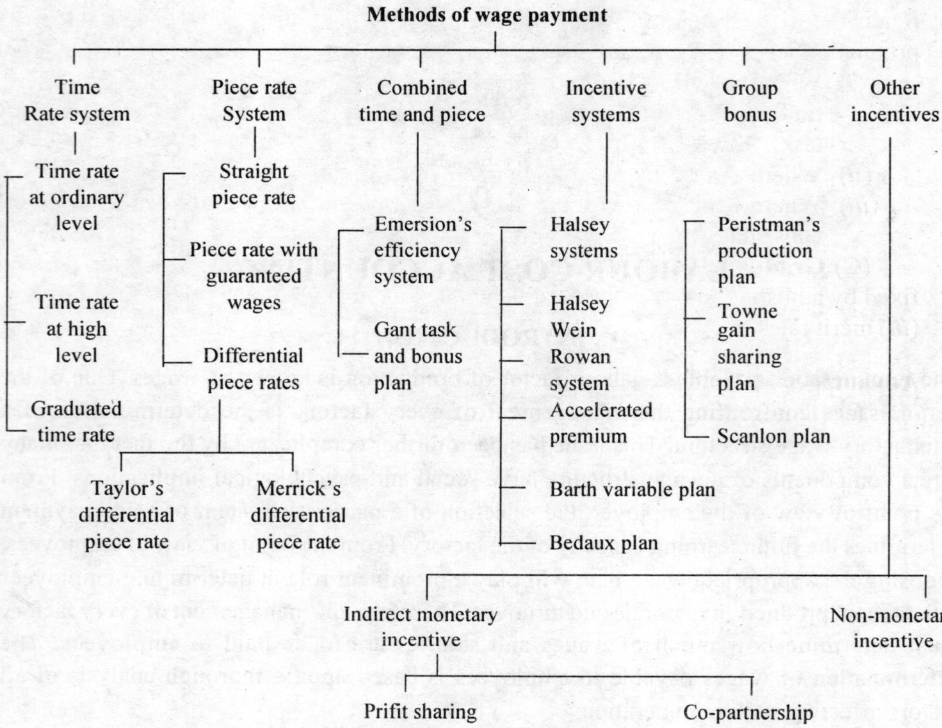

Fig. 9.1. Chart showing various methods of wage payment.

I. Time Rate System

Under this system wages are paid on the basis of time worked by the employees. Time rate system can take any of the following forms :

(A) Time rate at ordinary level : Under this system, the time rate is fixed beforehand and employees are remunerated at this rate. The time rate can be fixed in respect of hour, day or month. The following formula is used to calculate earnings under this method :

$$\text{Earnings} = \text{Time taken} \times \text{Time rate}$$

Suppose the time taken by an employee in a factory is 8 hours and the time rate fixed is Rs. 4 per hour, the employee will earn Rs. 32 under this method.

Time rate at ordinary level is suitable under the following circumstances:

(*i*) Where services rendered by employees cannot be tangibly measured, e.g., watchman, office staff and other indirect workers such as repairer, inspector, etc.

(*ii*) Where quality is more important than quantity of output.

(*iii*) Where the speed of operation is governed entirely by the process time and the operator has little or no control over the rate of production.

(*iv*) Where a worker is learning a job.

(*v*) Where increase in production is not commensurate with the incentive paid, e.g., wages payable to a night watchman.

(B) Time rate at high wage level : Time rate at a high wage level is used to attract and retain the highest quality labour for the purpose of obtaining and maintaining a high production level. The circumstances which favour this system are :

(*i*) Where the effort is strictly measurable in terms of units produced. In effect, the time rate is really a piece rate and high wage is an incentive to achieve a high task.

(*ii*) Where a uniform rate of high quality production is desirable, and

(*iii*) Where work can be graded according to skill and where a worker can be kept consistently at a job operation or machine demanding the same degree of skill.

(C) Graduated time rate : This is a form of time rate under which the time rate is fixed by adjusting to (*i*) the cost of living index numbers, (*ii*) sale price of the product and (*iii*) merit rates.

Advantages of Time Rate System

(*i*) This method is very simple to understand and easy to operate. It does not involve any additional calculations excepting in the case of overtime work. The chances of committing mistakes under this method are very rare.

(*ii*) This method does not give scope for jealousy and hatred amongst the workers as all of them earn the same wages. So rival groups are not formed under this method.

(*iii*) Workers do not do the work in a hurry. So there is little loss due to breakage of tools and accessories.

Disadvantages of Time Rate System

(*i*) This method discourages efficient workers as no distinction is made between efficient and inefficient workers. All are paid the same rate of wage.

(*ii*) The workers tend to work slowly as they are certain about their wages. So in order to ensure that there is no waste of time, a supervisor is appointed which increases the total cost of labour.

II. Piece Rate System

Under this system wages are paid on the basis of the number of articles produced by the workers. This method offers a direct financial incentive to the workers who can earn more wages by producing more number of articles. Piece rate system can be of the following types :

(A) Straight piece rate : Under this mathod, each unit produced is taken as a piece. A piece rate is fixed for a unit of product produced. The number of pieces produced multiplied by piece rate will give piece wages under this method. The following formula is used :

$$\text{Earnings} = \text{No. of pieces produced} \times \text{Piece rate}$$

This system of wage payment is suitable under the following circumstances :

(*i*) Where there is an urgent necessity to increase production.

(*ii*) Where individual output can be easily and quickly determined and priced.

Advantages :

(*i*) This system offers an incentive to the employees inasmuch as they can earn more wages by producing more numer of units.

(*ii*) As the workers tend to work on their own initiative, the need for supervision does not arise.

(*iii*) Cost ascertainment is easy under this method.

Disadvantages :

(*i*) Fixation of piece rate is not an easy task. A low piece rate may lead to discontentment among the employees.

(*ii*) The workers may sacrifice quality for the sake of quantity with a desire to earn more wages.

(*iii*) Excessive speeding up of work may lead to more spoilage and defective work. The cost of rectification may result in increased cost of production.

(*iv*) It is difficult to exercise control over the arrival and departure time of the employees.

(B) Piece rate with guaranteed wages : Piece rate with guaranteed wages is applicable for the new and inefficient employees. Those workers whose capacity is much below the required capacity will earn very meagre salary and hence instead of paying at the normal piece rate, they are given a minimum guaranteed wages. This encourages the workers to improve their efficiency gradually and there afterwards reach the standard of other workers.

(C) Differential piece rate system : Under the differential piece rate system, the wages of workers vary at different stages, within a certain range of output. This variation is sometimes more, sometimes less and sometimes in proportion to output. Workers often feel that beyond a certain stage, any further effort is not worth while. It is at this stage that an additional incentive is given to increase output. Differential piece rate system is useful under the following circumstances :

(*i*) Where production is undertaken on a continuous basis in order to maximise output.

(*ii*) Where learners are to be encouraged.

(*iii*) Where the time required to complete a job can be conveniently fixed.

(*iv*) Where the output can be identified with the individual workers.

(*v*) Where the production process is standardised.

The two systems which work under this principle are : (1) Taylor's differential piece rate system and (2) Merrick's differential piece rate system.

(1) ***Taylor's differential piece rate system :*** This system was designed by F.W. Taylor in 1880. The features of this system of wage payment are as follows :

(*a*) Day wages are not guaranteed.

(*b*) A standard is established for each and every task by means of time and motion studies.

(*c*) Two differential piece rates are applicable for payment of wages to employees. The first rate is called 'low piece rate' and the second is known as 'high piece rate'. Low piece rate is used to remunerate those employees whose efficiency is below standard and high piece rate for those who are above the standard.

(*d*) Taylor's original system of wage payment includes a low rate which is 83 per cent of the normal piece rate. The high piece rate is 125 per cent of the normal piece rate plus 50 per cent incentive in the form of bouns (or 175 per cent of normal piece rate) of the given piece rate.

The main objects of Talyor's differential piece rate system are : (1) To discourage less than average workers denying guaranteed wages and fixing a low piece rate for low production and (2) For rewarding the efficient workers by offering a high piece rate for higher level of production.

Advantages :

(*a*) This system attracts only the efficient workers.
(*b*) With an efficient labour force, the output will increase considerably.
(*c*) The incidence of overhead will be less with an increase in production.

Disadvantages :

(*a*) This leads to discontent among employees, particularly among learners and substandard employees by setting a low piece rate.
(b) This method is also not suitable for those employees whose efficiency level is just below the border line, *i.e.*, by a small margin.
(*c*) It does not guarantee even the minimum day wages, which frustrates the employees.
(*d*) Workers develop hatred and jealoursy towards each other because of the differential wage rates.

PROBLEMS ON TAYLOR'S SYSTEM OF WAGE PAYMENT

Problem 1 : From the following particulars calculate wages earned by workers *A* and *B* respectively under Talyor's system :

Standard time allowed : 10 units per hour
Normal wage rate : Rs. 1 per hour
Differential rates to be applied :
90% of piece rate when below standard efficiency
125% of piece rate when at or above standard. Production on a day of 8 hours : *A* – 75 units
B – 85 units

(*Shri Sathya Sai University, B.Com., March 1992*)

Solution :

	A	*B*
Standard output 10 units × 8 hrs.	80	80
Actual output	75	85

Worker *A*'s efficiency is below standard and therefore low piece rate is applicable. Low piece rate in this case is 90% of Re. 0.1 = 0.09

Worker *B*'s efficiency is above standard and therefore high piece rate is applicable. High piece rate is 125% of Rs. 1 = 0.125

Earnings = Number of pieces × Rate per piece
A = 75 × 0.09 = Rs. 6.75
B = 85 × 0.125 = Rs. 10.63

Working note

$$\text{Calculation of piece rate} = \frac{\text{Rate per hour}}{\text{Pieces per hour}}$$

$$= \frac{1}{10} = 0.1$$

Problem 2 : The workwise production in a department is as follows :
Amar — 600 units, Akbar — 1,000 units, Anthony — 400 units
Calculate their earnings as per :

(*a*) Straight piece rate system at 10 paise per unit
(*b*) Differential piece rate system under which first 400 units are paid at 2 paise per unit, the rate increasing by 2 paise per unit for each subsequent 200 units produced.

(*Osmania University, B.Com., April 1991*)

Solution :

Straight piece rate system		= No. of pieces produced × Rate per piece	
Amar		= 600 × 0.10 = Rs. 60.00	
Akbar		= 1,000 × 0.10 = Rs. 100.00	
Anthony		= 400 × 0.10 = Rs. 40.00	
Differential piece rate system		= No. of pieces produced × Rate per piece	
Amar :	For Ist 400 units	= 400 × 0.12 =	48.00
	For next 200 units	= 200 × 0.14 =	28.00
			Rs. 76.00
Akbar :	For Ist 400 units	= 400 × 0.12 =	48.00
	For next 200 units	= 200 × 0.14 =	28.00
	For next 200 units	= 200 × 0.16 =	32.00
	For next 200 units	= 200 × 0.18 =	36.00
			144.00
Anthony :		= 400 × 0.12 =	48.00

(2) ***Merrick's differential piece rate system :*** This method is also otherwise known as multiple pieces rate system. Under this method, three graded piece rates are used instead of two as in the case of Taylor's differential system. The features of this system are as follows :

(*a*) Minimum day wages are not guaranteed and thus remuneration paid is solely on the basis of output.

(*b*) The three rates of remuneration are as follows :

Up to 83 per cent standard output		ordinary piece rate
83 per cent to 100 per cent standard output	—	110 per cent of ordinary piece rate
Above 100 per cent standard output	—	120 per cent of ordinary piece rate

Advantages :

(*a*) When compared to Talyor's method, this system offers better terms for earning increased wages. Under Taylor's method, to earn a high piece rate wage, an employee has to improve his efficiency to 100 per cent, whereas to earn an incentive under Merrick's system, an employee has to reach only 83 per cent. Thus psychologically, the employee feels that Merrick's system is a better system of wage payment than Taylor's system, as it is felt that it is within their reach to attain 83 per cent efficiency.

(*b*) Having thus reached 83 per cent efficiency, employees strive to achieve even 100 per cent efficiency to earn better wages.

Disadvantage : This system is mostly suitable at the intermediate range of efficiency, *i.e.*, it makes a good upgrading plan.

PROBLEMS ON MERRICK'S SYSTEM OF WAGE PAYMENT

Problem 3 : Given the following data calculate wages payable under Merrick's differential price rate system.

Standard production		—	120 units
Actual production of workers	*A*	—	90 units
	B	—	100 units
	C	—	130 units

Rate per piece 0.10 per unit.

Solution : Calculation of efficiency of each worker

$A = \frac{90}{120} \times 100 = 75\%$

$B = \frac{100}{120} \times 100 = 83.33\%$

$C = \frac{130}{120} \times 100 = 108.33\%$

Earnings = No. of pieces × Rate per piece

$A = 90 \times 0.10 = $ Rs. 9

$B = 100 \times 0.11 = $ Rs. 11

$C = 130 \times 0.12 = $ Rs. 15.60

Problem 4 : Calculated the earnings of workers A, B and C under straight piece rate system and Merrick's multiple piece rate system from the following particulars :

Normal rate per hour : Rs. 5.40

Standard time per unit : 1 Minute

output per day is as follows :

Worker *A* — 390 units

Worker *B* — 450 units

Worker *C* — 600 units

Working hours per day are 8 (*C.A., Inter, May 1998*)

Solution :

Calculation of standard output per hour

For standard time of 1 minute the output is 1 unit

For standard time of 60 minutes or 1 hrs = 60 min × 1 unit

= 60 units

Calculation of normal wage per unit

$$\frac{\text{Normal rate per hour}}{\text{pieces per hour}}$$

$$= \frac{\text{Rs. } 5.40}{60 \text{ units}} = 0.09 \text{ p}$$

Calculation of standard output per day

60 units × 8 hours = 480 units

Calculation of efficiency of employees

$$\frac{\text{Actual output}}{\text{Standard output}} \times 100$$

$A = \frac{390}{480} \times 100 = 81.25\%$

$B = \frac{450}{480} \times 100 = 93.75\%$

$C = \frac{600}{480} \times 100 = 125\%$

Earnings of workers under straight piece rate

Earnings = No. of units × rate per unit

$A = 390 \times 0.09 = $ Rs. 35.10

$B = 450 \times 0.09 = $ Rs. 40.50

$C = 600 \times 0.09 = $ Rs. 54.00

Earnings of workers under Merrick's multiple piece rate system

A = 390 × 0.09 = Rs. 35.10
B = 450 × 0.099 = Rs. 44.55
C = 600 × 0.108 = Rs. 64.80

Problem 5 : The following piect rate system is followed in a small concern manufacturing a single product :

(*a*) Basis piece rate up to 85 per cent efficiency
(*b*) 110 per cent of the piece rate between 85 per cent and 100 per cent efficiency.
(*c*) 120 per cent of the basis piece rate above 100 per cent efficiency. Guaranteed day rate is equal to 70% efficiency. Assuming that 100 per cent efficiency is 100 pieces per day of 8 hours and the piece rate is 50 paise per piece. Calculate labour cost per piece at 5 per cent intervals between 60 per cent and 120 per cent efficiency.

(*University of Kerala, M.Com., May 1992*)

Solution : **Statement showing calculation of wages**

Output per hour	*Effi ciency*	*Piece wages*	*Guaranteed time wages*	*10% Add-itional piece wages*	*20% Add-itional piece wages*	*Total wages*	*Wages per piece*
60	60	30.00	35	-	-	35	0.583
65	65	32.50	35	-	-	35	0.538
70	70	35.00	35	-	-	35	0.500
75	75	37.50	-	-	-	37.50	0.500
80	80	40.00	-	-	-	40.00	0.500
85	85	42.50	-	4.25	-	46.75	0.500
90	90	45.00	-	4.50	-	49.50	0.550
95	95	47.50	-	4.75	-	52.25	0.550
100	100	50.00	-	5.00	-	55.00	0.550
105	105	52.50	-	-	10.50	63.00	0.600
110	110	55.00	-	-	11.00	66.00	0.600
115	115	57.50	-	-	11.50	69.00	0.600
120	120	60.00	-	-	12.50	72.00	0.600

III. Combined Time and Piece Rate System

This system of wage payment is based on the time rate and piece rate system of wages. The following method of wage payment fall under this classification.

1. Emerson's Efficiency System

This method of wage payment was introduced by Harrington Emerson who worked together with F.W. Taylor under scientific management movement. While Talyor introduced differential piece rate system of wages, Emerson devised an empirical system of wage payment which came to be called as Emerson's efficiency system. This system is suitable to (*a*) encourage slow workers to better their performance and (*b*) to faciliate an easy transfer from time wages to payment by result. The features of this system of wage payment can be enumerated as follows :

(*a*) Day wages are guaranteed
(*b*) A standard is fixed in respect of output.
(*c*) Below $66\frac{2}{3}$ per cent efficiency, workers are paid at the normal time rate.
(*d*) Between $66\frac{2}{3}$ per cent and 100 per cent efficiency, payments are made on step

bonus rates. Emerson himself has prepared a table which contains the efficiency level ranging from $66\frac{2}{3}$ to 100 per cent and the corresponding percentage of bonus on time wages earned by the worker. For 67 per cent efficiency, the bonus applicable is 0.01 per cent, for 68 per cent efficiency, it is 0.04 and for 100 per cent efficiency it is 20 per cent.

(*e*) Above 100 per cent efficiency, an additional bonus of 1 per cent of the time rate is paid for each 1 per cent increase in efficiency.

The following formula is used to calculate total earnings under this system :

Earnings = Time taken × Time rate + Emerson's bonus percentage × Time taken × Time rate

PROBLEM ON EMERSON'S EFFICIENCY SYSTEM

Problem 6 : In a manufacturing concern the daily wages guaranteed for workers is Rs. 2. The standard output for the month is 1,000 units representing 100% efficiency. The rate of wages is paid without bonus to those workers who show up to $66\frac{2}{3}$ per cent efficiency. Beyond this, bonus is payable in a graded scale.

Efficiency	*Bonus*
90%	10%
100%	20%

Further increase of 1% of bonus for every 1% further rise in efficiency. Calculate the total earnings of Ramesh, Suresh, Umesh and Mahesh who worked for 26 days in a month and their output being 500, 900, 1,000 and 1,200 respectively.

Solution : Calculation of efficiency of all four workers

$$\text{Ramesh} = \frac{500 \times 100}{1,000} = 50\%$$

$$\text{Suresh} = \frac{900 \times 100}{1,000} = 90\%$$

$$\text{Umesh} = \frac{1,000 \times 100}{1,000} = 100\%$$

$$\text{Mahesh} = \frac{1,200 \times 100}{1,000} = 120\%$$

Earnings = Time taken × Time rate + Emerson's bonus percentage × Time taken × Time rate

Ramesh = 26 × 2 + Nil = Rs. 52.00

$$\text{Suresh} = 26 \times 2 + \frac{10}{100} \times 26 \times 2$$

52 + 5.20 = Rs. 57.20

$$\text{Umesh} = 26 \times 2 + \frac{20}{100} \times 26 \times 2$$

52 + 10.40 = Rs. 62.40

$$\text{Mahesh} = 26 \times 2 + \frac{40}{100} \times 26 \times 2$$

= 52 + 20.80 = Rs. 72.80

Problem 7 : An employee working under a bonus scheme sarves 10 hours in a job for which the standard time is 60 hours. Calculate the rate per hour worked and wages payable to him if incentive bonus of 10% on the hourly rate is payable when standard time (namely, 100% efficiency) is achieved and a further incentive bonus of 1% on hourly rate for each 1% in excess of that 100% efficiency is payable. Assume that the normal rate of payment is Rs. 5 per hour. (*University of Madras, B.Com., September 1995*)

Solution : Hours worked = Standard time – Sarved timed
= 60 hrs. – 10 hrs.
= 50 hrs.

(*a*)	Wages	50 hrs. @ Rs. 5 per hr	=	250
(*b*)	Bonus	10% of Rs. 250	=	25
(*c*)	Incentive	1% of excess of 100 efficiency	= $\frac{60}{50} \times 100 = 120\%$	
	Incentive is 20% of 250		=	50
		Total wages		325
	Effiective rate per hour		$= \frac{325}{50} =$	Rs. 6.50

2. Gantt Task and Bonus Plan

This system was introduced by Henry L. Gantt. It is a combination of time rate system with a step bonus and differential piece rate system of wage payment. The purpose of this method is to reward those who reach a high level of production. The method also guarantees the minimum day wages and at the same time, encourages less skilled employees to improve their performance. Remuneration under this system is computed as under :

Output below standard	—	Time rate wages
Output at standard	—	Bonus of 20 per cent on time rate
Output above standard	—	High piece rate on whole output

Advantages :

(*a*) It provides security to less efficient workers.

(*b*) It is beneficial to more efficient workers by offering a high incentive.

(*c*) The increased output because of increased efficieny reduces the fixed cost per unit.

Disadvantage :

The trade union may not agree to the piece rate fixed. Instead, it may seek a high guaranteed time rate.

PROBLEM ON GANTT'S TASK BONUS PLAN

Problem 8 : From the following particulars calculate the earnings of workers *X*, *Y* and *Z* under Gantt task bonus plan :

Time rate	—	Rs. 2 per hour
Standard output	—	10 units per hour
Number of hours	—	8 hours in a day
High piece rate	—	0.40 per unit
Output of *X*	—	70 units
Output of *Y*	—	80 units
Output of *Z*	—	90 Units

Solution : Calculation of efficiency of all the workers :

X's efficiency is below standard, *i.e.*, his output is lesser than the standard output.

Y's efficiency is at standard.

Z's efficiency is above standard.

Earnings of *X* = Time taken × Time rate
= 8 hrs × Rs. 2 = 16

Earnings of *Y* = 8 Hrs. × Rs. 2.40 = 19.20

Earnings of Z = No. of units produced × High piece rate
= 90 × 0.40 = 36

PROBLEM ON WAGES UNDER TAYLOR'S, MERRICK'S AND GANTT TASK BONUS PLAN

Problem 9 : From the following particulars calculate wages under (1) Taylor's differential piece rate system, (2) Merrick's differential piece rate system and (3) Gantt task and bonus plan.

Number of hours worked in a day	—	8 hours
Standard output per day	—	30 units
Low piece rate	—	Rs. 1 per unit
High piece rate	—	Rs. 1.50 per unit
Time rate	—	Rs. 2 per hour
Output of X	—	25 units
Output of Y	—	30 units
Output of Z	—	40 units

Solution : Taylor's differential piece rate system = No. of units × Rate per unit

X = 25 × Re. 1 = Rs. 25

Y = 30 × Rs. 1.50 = Rs. 45

Z = 40 × Rs. 1.50 = Rs. 60

Merrick's differential piece rate system—

Efficiency of X $= \frac{25}{30} \times 100 = 83.34\%$

Efficiency of Y $= \frac{30}{30} \times 100 = 100\%$

Efficiency of Z $= \frac{40}{30} \times 100 = 133.34\%$

Earnings = No. of units produced × Rate per unit

X = 25 × Rs. 1.10 (Re 1 + 10% of Re 1) = Rs. 27.50

Y = 30 × Rs. 1.10 (Re 1 + 10% of Re 1) = Rs. 33.00

Z = 40 × Rs. 1.20 (Re 1 + 20% of Re 1) = Rs. 48.00

Gantt task and bonus plan

Earnings of X at time rate	=	8 Hrs. × Rs. 2	= Rs. 16
Earnings of Y at time + 20% Bonus	=	8 Hrs. × Rs. 2.40	= Rs. 19.20
Earnings of Z at high piece rate	=	40 units × 1.50 per unit	= Rs. 60.00

IV. Incentive System of Wage Payment

The term, 'inventive' has been defined as "the stimulation of effort and effectiveness by offering monetary inducement or enhanced facilities". It is clear from this definition that an incentive could be a monetary incentive, *i.e.*, cash bonus system or non-monetary incentive, like fringe benefits. Incentives can also be paid to an individual worker or collectively to a group of workers. In the former case, the worker directly gets his share of premium for his increased efficiency, while in the latter case, the incentive is shared by all the workers in an agreed proportion for their collective effort.

The incentive system is in fact, a compromise between the time rate system and the piece rate system. Under the time rate system, the workers will not gain anything even if they complete production in less than the allowed time. On the other hand, under the piece rate system, employers get nothing if the time is saved. So under the incentive system, both the employer and employees benefit from the time saved.

The incentive systems have the following characteristics :

(*a*) In all incentive systems of wage payment, minimum wages are guaranteed.

(*b*) For every job, a standard time is fixed on the basis of time and motion studies.

(c) If a worker completes the job within the time allowed, he will be paid an incentive bonus on the time saved.

Essentials of a Good Incentive System of Wage Payment

David W. Belcher, in his "*Wage and Salary Administration*" enumerates the following essential requirements of a good incentive system of wage payment :

1. An incentive wage plan should be explained and discussed with all employees and supervisors before it is implemented. Employees' cooperation and participation is much more likely if they have a part in its inception.
2. The plan should allow for earnings to be in direct proportion to an employee's output above the work standard.
3. An incentive plan should be easily understood and easy to calculate by the employees. A complicated plan leads to doubts and distrust in the worker's mind.
4. The incentive should be paid in the same month during which the fforts are put. It should not be postponed to a future date.
5. The spread between the guaranteed and incentive pay rates should be large enough to encourage extra effort on the part of employees.
6. All incentive systems should guarantee a minimum day's wages. This infuses an element of security among employees.
7. The standard once set should not be changed unless (*i*) there is an error or (*ii*) a change in the working conditions has been effected.
8. The standard should be scientifically set and it must be within the reach of employees to attain it.
9. The entire production process should be standardised, such as standard control processes, etc.
10. Equitable adjustments should be provided for an employee who fails to meet the standard for reasons beyond his control.
11. Standards of output must be based on established and recognised quality requirements. Employees should not be paid for substandard work. In fact, some provision may be necessary to control waste if it is excessive.
12. Good working conditions are to be created to enable the workers to attain the established standard.
13. An incentive system should be extended so as to include even indirect workers.
14. No upper limit to be fixed for workers' earnings.
15. The incentive system should be conducive to setting up a standard cost and budgetary control.

The following are the most important types of incentive system of wage payment.

1. Halsey System

This system was introduced by F.A. Halsey, an enginerr of America in 1891. The features of this incentive system are as follows :

(a) A standard time is allowed for each job. A worker who takes standard time or more than standard time to complete a piece of work receives his time rate.

(b) If the piece of work is completed in less than the standard time, the employee is paid an incentive of 50 per cent of the time saved. The remaining 50 per cent of the incentive is shared by the employer. The following formula is used to compute wages under this method :

Earnings = Time taken × Time rate + 50% of time saved × Time rate

Advantages :

(*a*) Time wages are guaranteed and thus it offers security to the employees.

(*b*) As the incentive is also shared by the employer, he is interested in improving the working conditions in factories.

(*c*) This method of wage payment is comparatively easy to operate and understand.

Disadvantages :

(*a*) The workers are dissatisfied because employer share half of the incentive earned by employees.

(*b*) It is difficult to fix a standard time in actual practice.

PROBLEMS ON HALSEY SYSTEM OF WAGE PAYMENT

Problem 10 : Calculate wages under Halsey system from the following particulars :

Time allowed	—	16 hours
Time taken	—	10 hours
Time rate	—	Rs. 1 per hour

Solution : Halsey system = Time taken × Time rate + $\frac{50}{100}$ × Time saved × Time rate

$$10 \times 1 + \frac{50}{100} \times 6 \times 1$$

$$= 10 + 3 = \text{Rs. } 13.00$$

Note : Time saved = Time allowed – Time taken

= 16 hours – 10 hours = 6 hours

Problem 11 : A worker completes a job in a certain number of hours. The standard time allowed for the job is 10 hours and the hourly rate of wage is Re. 1. The workers earn at 50% rate bonus of Rs. 2 under Halsey plan. Calculate his wages under Halsey system.

Solution : Here the time taken is not given. It is calculated as shown below :

Time allowed	=	10 hrs
Time saved	=	4 hrs
Time taken	=	6 hrs

Time saved is calculated as shown below :

Bonus at 50% of time saved is Rs. 2

Bonus at 100% or total bonus = Rs. 4

Rate per hour is Rs. 1 Hence time saved is 4 hours.

$$\text{Earnings} = \text{Time taken} \times \text{Time rate} + \frac{50}{100} \times \text{Time saved} \times \text{Time rate}$$

$$= 6 \times 1 + \frac{50}{100} \times 4 \times 1$$

$$= 6 + 2 = \text{Rs. } 8.$$

2. Halsey-Weir System

This system of wage payment was introduced by G.J. Weir in England. This is in fact modified form of Halsey system. All the features of Halsey system also apply to this system, excepting that the percentage of incentive payable too employees is $33\frac{1}{3}$ per cent of the time saved. The remaining $66\frac{2}{3}$ per cent is shared by the employer. The formula as was given under Halsey system holds good for this method also.

PROBLEM ON HALSEY-WEIR SYSTEM

Problem 12 : Calculate the amount of wages and bonus earned by this worker :

Name	:	Surinder
Job commenced	:	Monday, 23rd Sept. 1982, 8 a.m.
Job finished	:	Saturday, 28th Sept. 1982, 1 p.m.
Quantity of pieces of work given out	:	638
Quantity of pieces of work passed	:	600
Worker's rate	:	50 paise per hour
Time allowed	:	10 pieces per hour
Bonus	:	40% of time saved

Assume that the employee worked for 9 hours a day and no overtime.

(Bharathidasan University, B.Com., October 1988)

Solution : Calculation of standard time allowed $= \dfrac{600 \text{ piece}}{10 \text{ piece per hr.}} = 60$ hrs.

Time taken : for 5 days @ 9 hrs. per day (Monday to friday) = 45 hrs.

Saturday = 5 hrs. = 50 hrs.

Time saved 10 hrs.

$$\text{Halsey-Weir system} = \text{Time taken} \times \text{Time rate} + \frac{40}{100} \times \text{Time saved} \times \text{Time rate}$$

$$= 50 \times 0.50 + \frac{40}{100} \times 10 \times 0.50 = 27 \text{ Rs.}$$

3. Rowan System

This incentive system was introduced by James Rowan of Scotland. Under this system also, the incentive is paid on the time saved as in the above-mentioned two methods. But a different method is used to calculate the bonus under this system, bonus hours are calculated as a proportion of the time taken which the time saved bears to the time alloed and they are paid on the basis of the time rate system. The following formula is applicable to compute wages under this system :

$$\text{Earnings} = \text{Time taken} \times \text{Time rate} + \frac{\text{Time saved}}{\text{Time allowed}} \times \text{Time taken} \times \text{Time rate}$$

Advantages :

(*a*) This system is more suitable to beginners and slow workers.

(*b*) The employer benefits more from this system. So he provides good working conditions in the factories.

Disadvantages :

(*a*) This system of wage payment is not easily understood by employees.

(*b*) This system is not beneficial to workers at high level efficiency.

PROBLEMS ON ROWAN SYSTEM

Problem 13 : Mr. Avinash takes 9 hours to complete a job on daily wages and 6 hours on a scheme of payment by results. His day rate is Rs. 3 per hour. The material cost of the job is Rs. 20. Overheads are recovered at 150 per cent of the direct wages. Calculate the factory cost of the product under (*a*) Piece work plan and (*b*) Rowan plan. (*Mangalore University, B.Com., April 1992*)

Solution : **Calculation of time saved**

Time allowed	90 hours
Time taken	6 hours
Time saved	3 hours

(*a*) Earnings under piece work plan

Piece work wages are calculated on the time allowed at the rate of Rs. 3 for 9 hours it amounts to Rs. 27.

(*b*) Rowan system

$$\text{Earnings} = \text{Time taken} \times \text{Time rate} + \frac{\text{Time saved}}{\text{Time allowed}} \times \text{Time taken} \times \text{Time rate}$$

$$6 \times 3 + \frac{3}{9} \times 6 \times 3$$

$$18 + 6 = \text{Rs. } 24$$

Statement of works cost

	Piece rate system	*Rowan system*
Materials	20.00	20.00
Wages	27.00	24.00
Prime cost	47.00	44.00
Works overhead	40.50	36.00
$\frac{150}{100} \times 27$		
$\frac{150}{100} \times 24$		
Works cost	87.50	80.00

Problem 14 : A worker under the Halsey plan is paid Rs. 12 per week of 48 hours a week plus cost of living index bonus of 10 paise per hour. The time required to do a job is 8 hours which he completes in 6 hours. He is given bonus of 30% of time saved. Calculate the hourly rate of wage. Would it make any differece if he was paid under Rowan method. (*Gulbarga University, B.Com., November 1991*)

Solution : Calculation of time saved

Time allowed	8 hours
Time taken	6 hours
Time saved	2 hours

$$\text{Calculation of hourly rate} = \frac{\text{Weekly wages}}{\text{No. of hrs. in a week}}$$

$$= \frac{12}{48} = 0.25$$

$$\text{Halsey-Weir system} = \text{Time taken} \times \text{Time rate} + \frac{30}{100} \times \text{Time saved} \times \text{Time rate}$$

$$= 6 \times 0.25 + \frac{30}{100} \times 2 \times 0.25$$

$$1.50 + 0.15 = 1.65$$

Cost of living bonus 0.10 for 6 hours = 0.60

Total wages = Rs. 2.25

Calculation of wages under Rowan System

$$\text{Time taken} \times \text{Time rate} + \frac{\text{Time saved}}{\text{Time allowed}} \times \text{Time taken} \times \text{Time rate}$$

$$1.50 + \frac{2}{8} \times 1.5$$

= 1.50 + 0.375	=	1.875
Cost of living bonus		0.600
		2.475

Difference in wages

2.250 – 2.475 = 0.225

PROBLEMS ON COMBINATION OF DIFFERENT SYSTEMS OF INCENTIVES

Problem 15 : During the first week of April 1990, a workman Mr. Syam manufactured 300 units. He receives wage for a 48 hours week at the rate of Rs. 4 per hour which is guaranteed. The estimated time to produce one article is 10 minutes, and under incentive scheme the time allowed is increased by 20%. Calculate his gross wages according to (*a*) piece work with a guaranteed weekly wages, (*b*) Halsey premium bonus, (*c*) Rowan system. (*University of Kerala, B.Com., April 1991; Andhra University, M.Com., April 1991*)

Solution : (*a*) Piece work with a guaranteed weekly wages

Under this system Syam is paid for 60 hrs. at the rate of Rs. 4 per hour, *i.e.*, Rs. 240. This is in the absence of the availability of piece rate.

(*b*) Halsey system

Time allowed - Std. Time for 1 article	=	10 mins		
Add : 20% incentive under incentive system	=	2 mins		
For 1 Article	=	12 mins		
For 300 Articles 300 × 12 mins	=	3,600 mins		
or in hours	=	$\frac{3,600 \text{ mins}}{60}$	=	60 hrs.
Time taken			=	48 hrs.
Time saved			=	12 hrs.

$$\text{Earnings} = \text{Time taken} \times \text{Time rate} + \frac{50}{100} \times \text{Time saved} \times \text{Time rate}$$

$$48 \times 4 + \frac{50}{100} \times 12 \times 4$$

$$192 + 24 = \text{Rs. } 216$$

(c) Rowan system $= \text{Time taken} \times \text{Time rate} + \frac{\text{Time saved}}{\text{Time allowed}} \times \text{Time taken} \times \text{Time rate}$

$$= 48 \times 4 + \frac{12}{60} \times 48 \times 4$$

$$= 192 + 38.40 = \text{Rs. } 230.40$$

Problem 16 : Out of the Halsey and Rowan plans of wage payment, which method will be more beneficial to a worker who saves less than 50% of the standard time. Illustrate your answer.

(*C.S., Inter, June 2000*)

Solution : To a worker who saves less than 50% of the standard time, Rowan premium plan of wage payment is always beneficial as illustrated below :

Suppose the standard time to do a Job is 10 hours

Actual time taken is only 6 hours

Wage rage is Re. 1 per hour

$$\text{Earnings under Halsey system} = \text{Time taken} \times \text{Time rate} + \frac{50}{100} \times \text{Time saved} \times \text{Time rate}$$

$$= 6 \times 1 + \frac{50}{100} \times 4 \times 1$$

$$= 6 + 2$$

$$= \text{Rs. } 8$$

$$\text{Rowan system} = \text{Time taken} \times \text{Time rate} + \frac{\text{Time saved}}{\text{Time allowed}} \times \text{Time taken} \times \text{Time rate}$$

$$= 6 \times 1 + \frac{4}{10} \times 6 \times 1$$

$$= 6 + 2.40$$

$$= 8.40$$

Problem 17 : What is the difference between Halsey plan and Rowan plan of remunerating workers? Which one is more beneficial to the workers? *(C.S., Inter, June 1998)*

Under Halsey plan, time rate is guaranteed standard time and work are predetermined the bonus is 50% of the wages for standard time saved.

$$\text{Total wages} = \text{Time taken} \times \text{Hourly rate} + \frac{50}{100} \times \text{Time saved} \times \text{Hourly rate}$$

under the Rowan plan also, the time rate is guaranteed. But here the percentage of bonus to the wages earned is that which the time saved bears to the standard time

$$\text{Total wages} = \text{Time taken} \times \text{Hourly rate} + \frac{\text{Time saved}}{\text{Time allowed}} \times \text{Time taken} \times \text{Time rate}$$

Comparision : If the worker finishes the work in helf the time fixed for it, the wages earned under Halsey and Rowam plans will be the same. If the time saved is less than 50% of the standard time, the Rowan plan is better. If the time saved is more than 50% of the standard time, the Halsey plan is better.

Problem 18 : A worker is allowed 10 hours to complete a job on daily wages. He takes 6 hours to complete the job under a scheme of payment by results. His day rate is Rs. 6 per hour and piece rate is Rs. 36. The material cost of the product is Rs. 40 and the overheads are charged at 150% of the total direct wages. Calculate the factory cost of the product under.

(*i*) Piece work plan
(*ii*) Rowan plan
(*iii*) Halsey plan

(C.S., Inter, Dec. 1998)

Solution :

(1) Piece Rate System

Number of pieces are not given in this problem. Instead time allowed is given as 10 hrs. to complete a job. Presuming that the worker completes one job and is paid Rs. 36 for that job, his piece wage for a day is Rs. 36.

(2) Rowan System

$$\text{Time taken} \times \text{Time rate} + \frac{\text{Time saved}}{\text{Time allowed}} \times \text{Time taken} \times \text{Time rate}$$

$$= 6 \times 6 + \frac{4}{10} \times 6 \times 6$$

$$= 36 + 14.40$$

$$= 50.40$$

(3) Halsey System $= \text{Time taken} \times \text{Time rate} + \frac{50}{100} \times \text{Time saved} \times \text{Time rate}$

$$= 6 \times 6 + \frac{50}{100} \times 4 \times 6$$

$$= 36 + 12$$

$$= 48$$

Factory cost under three plans

	Piece rate	*Rowan plan*	*Halsey plan*
Materials	40	40	40
Wages	36	50.40	48
Factory overhead (150% of direct wages)	54	75.60	72
	130	166	160

Problem 19 : A firm employs five workers at an hourly rate of Rs. 2.00. During the week, they worked for four days for a total period of 40 hours each and completed a job for which the standard time was 48 hours for each worker. Calculate the labour cost under the Halsey method and Rowan method of incentive plan payments. (*C.S., Inter, June 1996*)

Solution : **Calculation of Time saved**

Standard time allowed	48 hrs. × 5 workers	=	240 hrs.
Actual time taken	40 hrs. × 5 workers	=	200 hrs.
	time saved		40 hrs.

(1) Halsey system $= \text{Time taken} \times \text{Time rate} + \frac{50}{100} \times \text{Time saved} \times \text{Time rate}$

$= 200 \times 2 + \frac{50}{100} \times 40 \times 2$

$= 400 + 40 = \text{Rs. } 440$

(2) Rowan system $= \text{Time taken} \times \text{Time rate} + \frac{\text{Time saved}}{\text{Time allowed}} \times \text{Time taken} \times \text{Time rate}$

$= 200 \times 2 + \frac{40}{240} \times 200 \times 2$

$= 400 + 67 = \text{Rs. } 467$

Problem 20 : A skilled worker in XYZ Ltd. is paid a guaranteed wage rate of Rs. 30 per hour. The standard time per unit for a particular product is 4 hours. P, a machineman, has been paid wages under the Rowan incentive plan and he had earned an effective hourly rate of Rs. 37.50 on the manufacture of that particular product.

What could have been his total earnings and effective hourly rate, had he been put on Halsey incentive scheme (50%)? (*C.A., Inter, November 1999*)

Solution :

Let 'T' hours be the total time worked in hours by machineman 'P'

Rate per hour = Rs. 30

Standard time = 4 hours per unit

effective hourly earnings rate = Rs. 37.50

$$\text{Earnings} = \text{Time taken} \times \text{Time rate} + \frac{\text{Time saved}}{\text{Time allowed}} \times \text{Time taken} \times \text{Time rate}$$

$$37.5\text{ T} = \text{T} \times 30 + \frac{(4-\text{T})}{4} \times \text{T} \times 30$$

$$37.5 = 30 + (4 - \text{T}) \times 7.5$$

(T is common)

$$37.5 = 30 + 30 - 7.5\text{ T}$$

$$37.5 = 60 - 7.5\text{ T}$$

$$37.5 - 60 = -7.5\text{T}$$

$$-22.5 = -7.5\text{ T}$$

$$\text{T} = \frac{22.5}{7.5} = 3 \text{ hours}$$

$$\text{Halsey system} = \text{Time taken} \times \text{Time rate} + \frac{50}{100} \times \text{Time saved} \times \text{Time rate}$$

$$= 3 \times 30 + \frac{50}{100} \times 1 \times 30$$

$$= 90 + 15 = \text{Rs. } 105$$

Problem 21 : A job can be executed either through workman A or B. A takes 32 hours to complete the job while B finishes it in 30 hours. The standard time to finish the job is 40 hours.

The hourly wage rate is same for both the workers. In addition the workman A is entitled to receive bonus according to Halsey plan (50% sharing) while B is paid bonus as per Rowan plan. The works overhead are absorbed on the job at Rs. 7.50 per labour hour worked. The factory cost of the job comes to Rs. 2,600 irrespective of the workman engaged.

Find out the hourly wage rate and cost of raw materials input. Also show cost against each element of cost included in factory cost. *(C.A., Inter November 1997)*

Solution :

Calculation of Time saved

	A	*B*
Standard Time allowed	40	40
Actual time taken	32	30
Time saved	8	10

$$\text{Halsey system} = \text{Time taken} \times \text{Time rate} + \frac{50}{100} \times \text{Time saved} \times \text{Time rate}$$

$$= 32 \times x + \frac{50}{100} \times 8 \times x$$

$$= 32x + 4x$$

$$= 36x$$

$$\text{Rowan system} = \text{Time taken} \times \text{Time rate} + \frac{\text{Time saved}}{\text{Time allowed}} \times \text{Time taken} \times \text{Time rate}$$

$$= 30 \times x + \frac{10}{40} \times 30 \times x$$

$$= 30x + 7.5x = 37.5\,x$$

Statement of factory cost of the job

	A	*B*
Material cost (allowed to be)	*Y*	*Y*
Wages	$36x$	$37.5x$
Works overhead	240	225
Factory cost	2,600	2,600

The above particulars can be written as follows :

$$3.6x + Y + 240 = 2{,}600 \quad \text{...(1)}$$

$$37.5x + Y + 225 = 2{,}600 \quad \text{...(2)}$$

Substracting (1) from (2), we have

$$1.5x - 15 = 0$$

or $$1.5x = 15$$

or $$x = \frac{15}{1.5} = \text{Rs. 10 per hour}$$

On Substituting the value of x in (1)

$$36x + y + 240 = 2{,}600$$

$$36 \times 10 + y + 240 = 2{,}600$$

$$360 + y + 240 = 2{,}600$$

$$y = 2{,}600 - 600$$

$$y = 2{,}000$$

Hence the wage rate per hour is Rs. 10 and the cost of raw material input is Rs. 2000 on the job.

Problem 22 : Calculate the earnings of a worker under (*i*) Halsey plan and (*ii*) Rowan plan from the following particulars.

(*i*) Hourly rate of wages guaranteed 0.50 paise per hour

(*ii*) Standard time for producing one dozen articles – 3 hours

(*iii*) Actual time taken by the worker to produce, 20 dozen articles – 48 hours

(*C.A., Inter, November 1998*)

Solution : **Calculation of Time save**

Time allowed for producing one dozen articules	=	3 hrs.
∴ Time allowed for producing 20 dozen articles	=	60 hrs.
Time taken for producing 20 dozen articles	=	48 hrs.
Time saved		12 hrs.

$$\text{Halsey system} = \text{Time taken} \times \text{Time rate} + \frac{50}{100} \times \text{Time saved} \times \text{Time rate}$$

$$= 48 \times 0.50 + \frac{50}{100} \times 12 \times 0.50$$

$$= 24 + 3 = \text{Rs. } 27$$

$$\text{Rowan system} = \text{Time taken} \times \text{Time rate} + \frac{\text{Time saved}}{\text{Time allowed}} \times \text{Time taken} \times \text{Time rate}$$

$$= 48 \times 0.50 + \frac{12}{60} \times 48 \times 0.50$$

$$= 24 + 4.80 = \text{Rs. } 28.80$$

Problem 23 : A worker produced 200 units in a week's time the guaranteed weekly wage payment for 45 hours is Rs. 81. The expected time to produce one unit is 15 minutes which is raised further by 20% under incentive scheme. What will be the earnings per hour of that worker under Halsey (50% sharing) and Rowan bonus schemes?

(*C.A., Inter May 1995*)

Solution : **Calculation of Time saved**

Time allowed under piece rate system		=	15 mins
Add : 20% increase under incentive system		=	3 mins
			18 mins
For 1 unit	— 18 mins		
For 200 units	— 18 × 200	=	3,600 mins
Expressed in Hours $\frac{3,600}{60}$		=	60 hrs.
Time taken		=	45 hrs.
Time saved			15 hrs.

$$\text{Halsey system} = \text{Time taken} \times \text{Time rate} + \frac{50}{100} \times \text{Time saved} \times \text{Time rate}$$

$$= 45 \times 1.80 + \frac{50}{100} \times 15 \times 1.80$$

$$= 81 + 13.50 = \text{Rs. } 94.50$$

$$\text{Earnings per hour} = \text{Rs. } \frac{94.50}{45} = \text{Rs. } 2.10 \text{ per hour}$$

$$\text{Rowan system} = \text{Time taken} \times \text{Time rate} + \frac{\text{Time saved}}{\text{Time allowed}} \times \text{Time taken} \times \text{Time rate}$$

$$= 45 \times 1.80 + \frac{15}{60} \times 45 \times 1.80$$

$$= 81 + 20.25 = \text{Rs. } 101.25$$

$$\text{Earnings per hour} = \text{Rs. } \frac{101.25}{45} = \text{Rs. } 2.25 \text{ per hour}$$

Working note :

$$\text{Calculation of time rate} = \text{Rs. } \frac{81}{45 \text{ hrs}} = \text{Rs. } 1.80$$

4. Accelerated Premium System or Sliding Scale Bonus System

Under this system as in the case of earlier methods a standard output or hour is specified. The actual performance or hours of time taken is compared with standard output or time. Bonus is paid at different rates for different level of efficiency. Under this method a direct relationship exists between the efficiency of workers and the wages earned by them.

Problem 24 : What will be the earning of a worker at Re. 0.55 per hour when he takes 140 hours to do a volume of work for which the standard time allowed is 200 hours? The plan of payment of hours is on a sliding scale as under :

Within the first 10%saving in standard time, bonus is 40% of time saved.
Within the second 10% saving in time, bonus is 50% of time saved.
Within the third 10% saving in standard time, bonus is 60% of time saved.
Within the fourth 10% saving in standard time, bonus is 70% of time saved.
For the rest, bonus is 75% of time saved.

(*University of Madras, B.Com., March 1992; Karnataka University, B.Com., April 1992*)

Solution : Satandard time allowed 200 hours
Actual taken 140 hours

Time saved 60 hours

Calculation of percentage of time saved to standard time

$$\frac{60}{200} \times 100 = 30\%$$

Calculation of the number of hours for which bonus will be allowed.

(*a*) For the first 10% of time saved, *i.e.*, bonus is allowed for 40% of time saved

$$200 \times \frac{10}{100} \times \frac{40}{100} = 8 \text{ hours}$$

(*b*) For the next 10% of time saved bonus will be allowed for 50% of time saved i.e.,

$$200 \times \frac{10}{100} \times \frac{50}{100} = 10 \text{ hours}$$

(*c*) For the next 10% of time, saved, bonus will be allowed for 60% of time saved, i.e.,

$$200 \times \frac{10}{100} \times \frac{60}{100} = 12 \text{ hours}$$

30 hours

Statement showing earnings of worker

Time wages — 140 hrs. @ Re. 0.55 per hour	77.00
Bonus for 30 hours (30 × 0.55)	16.50
Total Rs.	93.50

5. Barth Variable Plan

This incentive system is meant for new entrants, i.e., beginners and for unskilled workers. The purpose is to encourage workers to learn the job and to improve their performance. The following formula is used to calculate earnings under this method.

$$\text{Earnings} = \text{Rate per hour} \times \sqrt{\text{Standard time} \times \text{Actual time}}$$

Problem 25 : Calculate the earnings under Barth variable plan from the following data :

Time allowed	—	15 hours
Time taken	X —	12 hours, Y – 10; Z – 8 hrs.
Time rate	—	Rs. 4 per hour

Solution : Earnings = Rate per hour × $\sqrt{\text{Standard time} \times \text{Actual time}}$

$$X = 4 \times \sqrt{15 \times 12}$$
$$= 4 \times \sqrt{180}$$
$$= 4 \times 13.4 = 53.60$$

$$Y = 4 \times \sqrt{15 \times 10}$$
$$= 4 \times \sqrt{150}\,\sqrt{150}$$
$$= 4 \times 12.2 = 48.80$$

$$Z = 4 \times \sqrt{15 \times 8}$$
$$= 4 \times \sqrt{120}\,\sqrt{120}$$
$$= 4 \times 10.1 = \text{Rs. } 40.40$$

6. Bedaux Plan

This system was introduced by C.E. Bedaux. The following are the important features of this system :

(*a*) Day wages are guaranteed.

(*b*) Bonus is paid if the worker attains 100 per cent efficiency level. Under this method standard time and standard work is measured in terms of Bedaux' points. These points are also known as B's, B refers to a standard work performed in a standard minute.

(*c*) Bonus of 75 per cent of B's saved is paid at the hourly rate.

The following formula is used to calculate earnings under this method—

$$\text{Earnings} = \text{Time taken} \times \text{Time rate} + \frac{75}{100} \times \frac{\text{Hourly rate}}{60} \times \text{B's saved}$$

Problem 26 : From the following data calculate the earnings under Bedaux system :

B's got by the workman	90
Hourly rate	2.40
Time allowed in minutes	60

Solution : B's saved = 90 – 60 = 30 B's

$$\text{Earnings} = \text{Time taken} \times \text{Time rate} + \frac{75}{100} \times \frac{\text{Hourly rate}}{60} \times \text{B's saved}$$

$$1 \times 2.40 + \frac{75}{100} \times \frac{2.40}{60} \times 30$$

$$2.40 + 0.90 = 3.30$$

V. Group Bonus System

When bonus is paid collectively to a group of employees, it is known as group bonus system. In assembly-type of work such as radio, TV, typewriter, refrigerators, automobiles, etc. production depends upon the collective efforts of a group of workers as a whole. In such cases, the output of an individual worker cannot be measured and group effort is inevitable. The work of each worker is dependetn upon the work done by one or more co-workers. So the workers constituting the group is considered for receiving incentives. This system is applicable under the following circumstances :

(*a*) Where individual output cannot be measured.
(*b*) Where output depends upon the combined efforts of group.
(*c*) Where management wants to encourage team spirit.
(*d*) Where workers constituting a group are almost of equal skill.
(*e*) Where indirect workers are also to be included under incentive system.

Advantages :

(*a*) This method of wage payment infuses cooperation and team spirit.
(*b*) Absenteeism is reduced, as an absentee employee weakens the team which he does not like.
(*c*) Accounting system is simplofied as recording relates to the output of the group but not to individuals.
(*d*) Supervision is reduced because efficient workers compensate for less efficient workers.
(*e*) Indirect workers can also be included in the team by taking them into the team.

Disadvantages :

(*a*) This system is unfair to efficient and hard working workers as efficient workers are penalised for their efficiency by the other members of the team.
(*b*) Workers do not easily accept this plan.
(*c*) It is difficult to fix group incentive and distribute it to employees.

The following are some of the important types of group bonus system.

1. Priestman's Production Bonus

Under this system, all employees are paid a guaranteed basic wage. In this system, a production standard is fixed every month. When the actual production exceeds the standard, worker's receive during the following month additional pay equal to the percentage on output over the standard.

2. Towne Gain Sharing Plan

Under this method, standard wages for a group of workers for a particular period is predetermined which is based on the output they are expected to produce. The actual wages of the group is ascertained and then compared with standard wages. When the actual wages is less than the standard wages, half of the gain resulting thereform is paid to the workers as bonus apart from time wages.

3. Scanlon Plan

This plan was introduced by Scanlon in the USA prior to the Second World War. Under this system also day eages are guaranteed. The bonus payable is calculated from the effective reduction in labour cost which is expressed as a ratio of labour cost to total sales value. If the labour cost is reduced or sales value is increased. it results in increased pay for all the employees. This method enables more workers to participate and raise their productivity in factories.

Problem 27 : In a factory group bonus system is in use which is calculated on the basis of earnings under time rate. The following pariticulars are available for a group of 4 workers P, Q, R and S :

(*i*) Output of the group	1,600 units
(*ii*) Piece rate per 100 units	Rs. 2.50
(*iii*) Number of hours worked by	$P-90$, $Q-72$, $R-80$, $S-100$
(*iv*) Time rate per hour for	P = Re. 0.80, Q = Re. 1.00, R = Re. 1.20, S = Re. 0.80

Calculate the total of bonus and wages earned by each worker. (*ICWA, Inter, June 1992*)

Solution : Time wages of the worker = Time taken × Time rate

$P = 90 \times 0.80 = \text{Rs. } 72$

$Q = 72 \times 1.00 = \text{Rs. } 72$

$R = 80 \times 1.20 = \text{Rs. } 96$

$S = 100 \times 0.80 = \text{Rs. } 80$

Total Rs. 320

$$\text{Total piece earning of the group} = \frac{1{,}600}{100} \times 2.50 = 400$$

Total of bonus and wages earned by

$$P = \frac{400}{320} \times 72 = 90$$

$$Q = \frac{400}{320} \times 72 = 90$$

$$R = \frac{400}{320} \times 96 = 120$$

$$S = \frac{400}{320} \times 80 = 100$$

Total Rs. = 400

Problem 28 : In a manufacturing concern 20 workmen work in a group. The concern follows a group incentive bonus system whereby each workman belonging to the group is paid a bonus on the excess output over the hourly production standard of 250 pieces, in addition to his normal wages at hourly rate. The excess of production over the standard is expressed as a percentage and two-thirds of this percentage is considered to be the share of the workmen and is applied on the notional hourly rate of Rs. 6 (considered only for the purpose of computation of bonus). The output data for a week are stated below :

Days	*Man-hours worked*	*Output (in pieces)*
Monday	160	48,000
Tuesday	172	53,000
Wednesday	164	40,000
Thursday	168	52,000
Friday	160	46,000
Saturday	160	42,000
	984	2,81,000

You are required to :

(*i*) Work out the amount of bonus for the week and the average rate at which each workman is to be paid the same.

(*ii*) Compute the total wages including bonus payable to Ram Jadav who worked for 48 hours at an hourly rate of Rs. 2.50 and to Francis Williams who worked for 52 hours at an hourly rate of Rs. 3.

(*ICWA, Inter, December, 1990*)

Solution :

Day	*Man hrs. worked*	*Std. output*	*Actual output*	*Excess output*	*% of excess output (see note2)*	*% of bonus*	*Amount of incentive*
Monday	160	40,000	48,000	8,000	20%	13.40	128.64
Tuesday	172	43,000	53,000	10,000	23.26%	15.58	160.79
Wednesday	164	41,000	40,000	–			
Thursday	168	42,000	52,000	10,000	23.81%	15.95	160.78
Friday	160	40,000	46,000	6,000	15%	10.05	96.48
Saturday	160	40,000	42,000	2,000	5%	3.35	32.16
	984					Total hrs.	578.85

Share of each individual workman

$$\frac{578.85}{984} = 0.59 \text{ per hour worked}$$

Working Notes :

(1) Standard output for Monday 160 × 250 = 40,000 and so on for other days.

(2) Excess output for Monday = $\frac{8,000}{40,000} \times 100 = 20\%$ and so on for other days.

(3) Bonus for Monday = $\frac{160 \times 13.40}{100} \times 6 = 128.64$ and so on.

Computation of wages to Individual workers

	Ram Jadav	Francis William
Time wages		
48 × 2.50	120	
52 × 3		156
Share of Incentive		
48 × 0.59	28.32	
52 × 0.59		30.68
Total wages	148.32	186.68

VI. Other Incentive System

In addition to the above methods of incentive systems, some other incentive systems adopted by some industries can be classified under the following :

1. Indirect Monetary Incentives

Indirect monetary incentives are allowed on the understanding that employees contribute to profit earning capacity of the factory. This can take two forms.

(*A*) ***Profit sharing scheme :*** Under this system, the employer agrees to pay a certain predetermined amount of profit in addition to the ususal salary payable to employees. Profit-sharing scheme, differs from factory to factory in terms of coverage and method of distributing profit. In some factories, it is restricted only to executives, while in others, it is applicable to all employees. Again in some factories, it is paid for the year during which profit is earned while in others, the payment of profit is deferred. This is to enable the employees to get a sizeable fund at the time of retirement, disability or separation. The method of distributing profit also differs from factory to factory. In some factories, the length of service is taken as the basis for determining the percentage of profit. In others, a fixed percentage of the total wages or merit rating of the employees constitutes the basis.

Advantages :

(*a*) It reduces excess labóur turnover.

(*b*) It increases production on account of increased efforts of workers with a view to earn profit.

(*c*) It eliminates conflicts between the employer and employees.

(*d*) It leads to better cooperation, team spirit and increased efficiency of workers.

(*e*) It boosts up labour morale which is responsible for industrial peace.

(f) Workers get a chance to participate in management. This creates a sense of belonging to the factory. Materials and machineries will be handled with care, thus minimising losses and wastages.

Disadvantages :

(*a*) Usually, the worker has no control over profit and it is not directly related to his effort.

(*b*) Unless merit-rating is considered as the basis, both efficient and inefficient workers get profit at the same rate.

(*c*) Payment of profit is at long intervals, usually once a year and the share received by employees is negligible.

(*d*) Employees share only the profit but not the losses.

(*e*) When workers are habituated to the payment of profit on a regular basis, non-payment of profit in any particular year will discourage the employees.

(*B*) ***Co-partnership scheme :*** Co-partnership or co-ownership confers upon employees the opportunity to share in the capital of the factory and to receive a part of the profit that accrue to their share of ownership.

Co-partnership differs from profit sharing in two respects : (1) In co-partnership, employees invest capital in the factory, whereas in a profit sharing scheme, the employees do not contribute to capital. (2) In a co-partnership, the employees share profit and loss if there is any, whereas in profit-sharing scheme, the workers receive only a share in the profit but they are not called upon to bear the losses.

Incentives for indirect workers : In addition to paying incentives to direct employees, it is also paid to indirect workers for the following reasons :

(*a*) To reduce the cost of operating various departments by means of increasing their efficiency.

(*b*) To avoid discrimination between direct and indirect workers by extending incentives to both the categories.

(*c*) To infuse team spirit and co-operative attitude.

(*d*) To eliminate labour unrest and dissatisfaction among employees.

(*e*) To encourage efficient indirect workers by rewarding them.

(*f*) To enable them to improve their skill so that losses and wastages arising out of materials can be avoided.

(*g*) To provide better service by indirect employees to direct employees.

2. Non-Monetary Incentives

Non-monetary incentives are offered with a view to attract better employees, to encourage loyalty, reduce labour turnover, promote better health and reduced absenteeism so as to build up a happy and contended staff. Non-monetary incentives are sometimes provided free of cost, while in some other cases, it may be subsidised. This usually takes the following forms :

(*a*) Canteens.
(*b*) Educational facilities for training the employees or to educate children of employees.
(*c*) Financial assistance in respect of housing.
(*d*) Medical facilities.
(*e*) Transport facilities.
(*f*) Recreational facilities.
(*g*) Co-operative societies.
(*h*) Leave travel concession.
(*i*) Pension contribution to PF, gratuity.
(*j*) Free uniforms.

PROBLEM ON PROFIT-SHARING SCHEME

Problem 29 : A Ltd. Co., has an issued share capital, fully paid up, consistaing of

1,000, 9% preference shares of Rs. 10 each
3,000, equity shares of Rs. 10 each

It is agreed that 25% of the remaining taxed profits be paid to the employees after payment of :

(*a*) the dividend due on the preference shares
(*b*) a dividend of 15% on the equity shares

The profit for the year 1992 after payment of tax amounted to Rs. 20,000.

Calculate the amount of profit that is to be used for profit sharing scheme.

Solution : Amount available for payment of dividend :

Preference shares 9%	900
Equity shares 15%	4,500
Total dividend	5,400

Profit available after paying the total dividends is Rs. 14,600 (20,000 – 5,400)

Profit available for profit sharing scheme is

$$\frac{25}{100} \times 14{,}600 = \text{Rs. } 3{,}650$$

PREPARATION OF PAYROLL

The calculation of wages due to employees is entrusted to the payroll department of the factory. Wage sheets and wage slips are the two important documents used by the payroll department to calculate wages of employees. A payroll or wage sheet is a document which shows the details of gross wages earned by each employee for a particular period, the deductions made and the net wages payable. It is prepared generally once in a month, on the basis of department or shifts of work involved.

The preparations of payroll involve three steps, *viz.*, (*a*) collection of basic data, (*b*) calculation of wages payable and (*c*) preparation of actual payroll.

Preparation of Payroll Under Time Rate System

When time rate system of wage payment is adopted, the clock cards are used to ascertain the attendance time of workers. The cost accounting department then ascertains the normal working hours and overtime working hours. The normal working hours are paid at the normal time rate whereas, the overtime hours are paid at double the normal time. Having thus calculated the gross wages, the following deductions are made wherever applicable :

(*a*) Fines.
(*b*) Employees state insurance contribution.
(*c*) Income tax.
(*d*) Toward house rent.
(*e*) For recovering advances.
(*f*) For life insurance premium.
(*g*) Welfare facilities provided.

Preparation of Payroll Under Piece Wage System

When piece rate system of wage payment is adopted the number of pieces produced is obtained from piece work card or job cards. If there are any defectives, wages can be proportionately deducted out of the gross wages.

The cost accounting department checks the wages payable to the employees. Later on the payroll is prepared for each department separately. It is always better to prepare payroll departmentwise as it serves three purposes, *viz.*, (*a*) the extent of work which is yet to be done can be distributed to various departments, (*b*) a departmental labour rate can be calculated for each department, and (c) control over departmental wages can be exercised by comparing actual wages with budgeted wages.

A payroll consists of the following particulars :

(*a*) Name of the department
(*b*) Duration for which wages are paid
(*c*) Workers name
(*d*) Normal hours worked and time rate
(*e*) Overtime hours worked
(*f*) No. of units produced and piece rate-
(*g*) Total gross wages
(*h*) Dearness allowance
(*i*) Bonus payable
(*j*) Deductions
(*k*) Net wages payable.

A specimen of wages analysis sheet of payroll is given below :

Payroll of ________ Department ________

Sl. No.	*Name of the worker*	*Hours worked*	*Rate*	*Basic wages*	*OT hours*	*OT wages*	*Leave pay etc.*	*Gross wages*	*Deductions*			*Net wages*
									Tax	*PF*	*ESI*	

Fig. 9.2. Specimen showing wage analysis sheet.

Having prepared a payroll for the entire department, the payroll department also prepares yet another document known as a pay slip. It contains all the particulars of a wage sheet. It is prepared for each individual worked and given to them before the wages are distributed. This enables the workers to verify the amount of wages due to them.

Finally the exact amount of wages are drawn from the bank. The wages of each employee is put in an envelop and paid to all employess in the presence of departmental managers.

Measures to Prevent Fradulent Payment of Wages

Buyers and Holmes in their *Cost Accountancy* have summarised the following measures to prevent frauds while paying wages :

(*a*) The system of recording time of arrival and departure should be carefully controlled. Time clocks should be installed and the recording of time adequately supervised.

(*b*) Where piece work and bonus system are in operation, the quantities produced should be certified by a competent Inspector and records should be signed by the foreman responsible. Extra allowances and payments for lost time should be recorded on forms provided for the purpose, which should be signed by a responsible official.

(*c*) Piece work rates should be clearly laid down and the terms of bonus schems defined in writing so that no doubt can exist as to the method of payment.

(*d*) All overtime should be properly authorised and the form of authority should be pased to the wages department for verification of overtime bookings.

(*e*) Standard wage rates schedules should be prepared. All alterations in wage rates should be made out on proper forms and be approved by a responsible official.

(*f*) The clerks who prepare wage sheets should not take part in the make-up of the wages envelopes. Where this is unavoidable no clerk should know in advance which section of the payroll he will be required to makeup.

(*g*) All wages and bonus calculations should be worked out by one clerk and be checked by another and the totalling and cross-checking of the sheets should be done by accounting machine wherever possible.

(*h*) The wage sheets should occasionally be scrutinised by the personnel officer or works manager to guard against the inclusion of 'dummy' workers on the payroll.

(*i*) There should be a satisfactory system for ensuring that all workers are identified before they are handed their wage packets.

(*j*) Wages should not be handed to any person other than the worker concerned except on production of a signed request made out on an authorised form and this should only be permitted in exceptional cases, e.g. disablement or sickness.

Problem 30 : Calculate the earnings of *A* and *B* from the following particulars for a month and allocate the labour cost to each job X, Y and Z :

		A	*B*
(*i*)	Basic wages	Rs. 100	160
(*ii*)	DA	50%	50%
(*iii*)	Contribution to PF. (on basic wages)	8%	8%
(*iv*)	Contribution to ESI (on basic wages)	2%	2%
(*v*)	OT	Hours 10	

The normal working hours for the month are 200. OT is paid at double the total of normal wages and DA Employers's contribution to state insurance and PF are at equal rates with employees' contribution. The two workers were employed on jobs *X*, *Y* and *Z* in the following proportions :

	Jobs		
	X	*Y*	*Z*
Worker *A*	40%	30%	30%
Worker *B*	50%	20%	30%

Overtime was done on Job Y (*C.A., Inter, May 1992*)

Solution : **Statement showing earnings of workers A and B**

	A	*B*
Basic wages	100	160
DA (50% of basic wages)	50	80
OT (*Refer working note 1*)	15	-
Gross wages	165	240
Less : PF 8% of basis wages ESI 2% of basic wages	10	16
Net wages paid	155	224

Statement of labour cost

Gross wages (excluding OT)	150	240
Employer's contribution to PF & ESI	10	16
Ordinary wages	160	256
Labour rate per hour	$\frac{160}{200}$ = 0.80	$\frac{256}{200}$ = 1.24

Statement showing allocation of wages to jobs

	X	*Y*	*Z*	*Total*
Worker *A* :				
Ordinary wages (4:3:3)	64	48	48	160
Overtime	–	15	–	15
Worker *B* :				
Ordinary wages (5:2:3)	128	51.20	76.80	256
	192	114.20	124.80	431

Working Note

$$\text{Over time} = 2 \times \frac{(\text{Basic wages + DA})}{200} \times 10 \text{ hrs.}$$

$$= 2\left(\frac{150}{100}\right) \times 10 = \text{Rs. } 15$$

Problem 31 : Calculate labour cost per man day of 8 hours from the following particulars :

(*i*)	Basic Salary	—	Rs. 20 per day
(*ii*)	Dearness allowance	—	50 paise per every point over 100 cost of living index for working class. Current cost of living index 500 points
(*iii*)	Leave salary	—	10% of (*i*) and (*ii*)
(*iv*)	Employer's contribution to provident fund	—	8% of (*i*), (*ii*) and (*iii*)

(*v*)	Employer's contribution to ESI	—	2.5% of (*i*), (*ii*) and (*iii*)
(*vi*)	Expenditure on amenities to labour	—	Rs. 20 per head per mensem
(*vii*)	Number of working days in a month	—	25 days of 8 hours each.

(*University of Kerala, B.Com., October 1989*)

Solution : **Statement of labour cost per man-day of 8 hours**

(*a*)	Basic salary — Rs. 20 for 25 days	500
(*b*)	Dearness allowance — 400 points @ 0.50	200
(*c*)	Leave salary — 10% of 700	70
(*d*)	Employer's contribution to PF — 8% of 770	62
(*e*)	Employer's contribution to ESI — 2.5% of 770	19
(*f*)	Amenities to labour	20
	Total for 25 days	871

$$\text{Per man-day} = \text{Rs. } \frac{871}{25} = \text{Rs. } 34.84$$

Problem 32 : Calculate the labour hour rate of a worker *P* form the following data :

Basic pay	Rs. 200 PM
DA	Rs. 150 PM
Fringe	Rs. 100 PM

Number of working days in a year 300 days full pay and 20 days half pay leave in a year is availed and allowed. Assume 8 hours days.

What would be the effect on hourly rate if only 30 days full pay leave is allowed. (*C.S., Inter, June 1990*)

Solution : **Calculation of effective working hours**

Working days in a year	300
Less : Leave days (30 + 20)	50
Effiective working days	250
Working hours in a day	8 hours

Total effective working hours = 250 × 8 = 2,000 hrs.

Statement showing total wages paid in a year

Basic wages	200 × 12	2,400
DA	150 × 12	1,800
Fringe benefits	100 × 12	1,200
	Total wages	5,400
Less : 20 days half pay	$\frac{5400}{300} = 18$	
For 1 day — 18		
For 20 days — 360 and ½ pay is		180
	Net amount paid	5,220

$$\text{Hourly Rate} \quad \frac{5,220}{2,000} = 2.61$$

If 30 days full pay leave is allowed

Effective working days	270 days
Effective working hours 270 × 8	2,160 hours
Total wages payable	Rs. 5,400

$$\text{Hourly Rate} \quad = \frac{5,400}{2,160} = 2.50$$

Effect on hourly rate = Rs. 2.61 – 2.50 = Rs. 0.11.

TREATMENT OF CERTAIN ITEMS IN COST ACCOUNTS

1. Idle Time

Idle time arises when time rate system of wage payment is implemented. It refers to the time during which workers will not attend to job although wages are paid for such time. In other words idle time is the time during which employees remain idle without producing any articles. In spite of this fact they are paid for such idle time. The existence of idle time can be known by referring to the attendance time and time booking. The difference between attendance time and time booking indicates the extent of idle time :

Idle time arises on account of the following causes.

(*a*) **Productive causes :** The productive causes closely related to production funtion of the factory. Such causes ae as follows :

(*i*) Time involved in reaching the production department from factory gate.
(*ii*) Setting up time involved in adjusting machines.
(*iii*) Time taken for attending to different jobs by the employees.
(*iv*) For want of instructions regarding the machine to be attended.
(*v*) Waiting for materials.
(*vi*) Waiting for tools and equipments.
(*vii*) Power failure.
(*viii*) Breakdown of machines.

(*b*) **Administrative causes :** Administrative causes arises owing to decisions taken by management. Some such decisions relates to operating the plant at a lower capacity, deliberate reduction in the production during depression, etc.

(*c*) **Economic causes :** Economic causes arise owing to general economic conditions prevailing in the country. Such causes are as follows :

(*i*) Seasonality of products.
(*ii*) Non-availability of materials.
(*iii*) Lack of demand
(*iv*) Period of depression.

In addition to above causes, idle time may also arise for other causes like strikes, lockouts, natural calamities such as, occurrence of fire, floods, etc.

From the point of view of treatment of idle time, it is classified under two types, viz., (*a*) normal and (*b*) abnormal idle time. Normal idle time is regular in nature whereas abnormal idle time arise only under certain circumstances.

From the point of view of control idle time can be classified into, (*a*) controllable and (*b*) uncontrollable idle time. It is very essential to control idle time as it has close relationship with cost of production and efficiency of workers. Controllable idle time it within the purview of management and it is possible to control it by an executive action. Whereas uncontrollable idle time is not within the purview of management to control it. Most of the productives causes resulting in idle time is controllable, whereas idle time arising out of economic and administrative causes are uncontrollable. An idle time card is used to book the idle time hours. This card helps in controlling the idle time. A specimen of it is shown below :

IDLE TIME CARD

Name of the worker .... Date ....
Clock no. ....
Department ....

Causes of idle time	*Time lost*		*Total hours lost*	*Rate*	*Amount*
	From	*To*			
Normal idle time					
(*a*)					
(*b*)					
(*c*)					
Abnormal idle time					
(*a*)					
(*b*)					

Sd. of worker *Sd. of foreman*

Fig. 9.3. Specimen showing idle time card.

Treatment of Idle Time in Cost Accounts

Treatment of normal and controllable idle time: Normal and controllable idle time is treated as overheads and charged to the department where such idle time is spent.

Treatment of abnormal and uncontrollable idle time: Abnormal idle time is charged to costing profit and loss account.

Problem 33 : (Problem on Idle Time) The capacity usage ratio and the capacity utilisation ratio in respect of a machine for a particular month is 80% and 90% respectively. The available working-hours in a month is 200 hours.

The break-up of idle time is as follows :

Waiting for job	5 hours
Break down	4 hours
Waiting for tools	3 hours

Calculate the idle time cost and present the same in a tabular form when the hourly fixed cost of running the machine is Rs. 8. (*ICWA, Inter, June 1993*)

Solution :

Total avoidable working hours	=	200 hrs.
Capacity usage rate	=	80%
Standard capacity expected $\frac{80}{100} \times 200$ hours	=	160 hrs.
Therefore unavoidable idle time (200 – 160)	=	40 hrs.
Capacity utilisation ratio	=	90%
Actual hours worked $\frac{90}{100} \times 16C$ hrs.	=	144 hrs.
Therefore unutilised capacity on idle facilities (160 – 144)	=	16 hrs.
Idle time records reveal the following :		
Waiting for jobs	=	5 hours
Breakdown	=	4 hours
Waiting for tools	=	3 hours
		12 hours

Avoidable idle time = (16 – 12 hrs.) = 4 hrs.

Idle Time Report

	Time	*Amount* @ Rs. 8 *per hrs.*
Unavoidable idle time facilities	40	320
Avoidable idle time facilitites :		
Waiting for job	5	40
Breakdown	4	32

Waiting for tools	3	24
Idle facilities	4	32
	16	128
Total idle time	56 hrs.	Rs. 448

2. Overtime

Overtime work arises whenever normal production work is hampered by power failure, breakdown in machinery, non-availability of material, increase in demand for the products, rush orders from customers, etc. In all such situations overtime work is engaged and workers are paid at a higher rate than the normal rate. According to the Indian Factories Act 1948, any worker who works for more than 9 hours a day or 48 hours a week is said to have worked under overtime and is to be remunerated at double the normal rate. The treatment of overime wages depends upon the circumstance under which it arises. As overtime wages results in excess payment of wages and thereby increases cost of production, it is necessary to control excess overtime work. The following steps are to be taken to control excess overtime work:

(*a*) It is to be resorted to only when it becomes inevitable.
(*b*) It should be authorised by competent authority.
(*c*) The efficiency of workers during overtime work should not be allowed to go down.
(*d*) Separate records must be maintained for overtime work and overtime wages.
(*e*) Overtime work must be properly supervised.
(*f*) More labourers are to be recruited if overtime work becomes a permanent feature.
(*g*) Arrangement for the prompt supply of materials and regular maintenance of machineries is to be ensured if materials and machine breakdown are responsible for overtime.

Treatment of Overtime Wages in Cost Accounts

(*i*) When overtime work is done at the specific instruction given by customer to complete production within a specific date:

Under this circumstance the overtime wages is charged directly to that job and treated as direct labour cost.

(*ii*) When overtime work is done owing to power failure or breakdown in machinery :

Under this circumstance, overtime wages are charged to the number of jobs executed during the period as overheads.

(*iii*) When overtime work is done as a matter of policy due to shortage of labourers :

Under this circumstance, overtime wages is treated as direct labour cost and sperad over the various jobs completed.

PROBLEMS ON OVERTIME WAGES

Problem 34 : Calculate the normal and overtime wages payable to a workman from the following data.

Days	*Hours worked*
Monday	8 hours
Tuesday	10 hours
Wednesday	9 hours
Thursday	11 hours

Friday	9 hours
Saturday	4 hours
	51 hours

Normal working hours	:	8 hours per day
Normal rate	:	0.50 per hour
Overtime rate	:	up to 9 hours in a day at single rate and over 9 hours in a day at double rate.

(*University of Madras, B. Com., March 1991*)

Solution : **Statement showing normal and overtime working hours**

Days	*Total hours worked*	*Normal working hrs.*	*Overtime hours At single rate*	*Overtime hours At double rate*
Monday	8	8		
Tuesday	10	8	1	1
Wednesday	9	8	1	–
Thursday	11	8	1	2
Friday	9	8	1	–
Saturday	4	4		–
	51	44	4	3

Normal wages for 44 hrs. @ 0.50	=	22.00
OT wages— At single rate 4×0.50	=	2.00
At double rate 3×1	=	3.00
Total	Rs.	27.00

Problem 35 : A firm's basic rate is Rs. 3 per hour and overtime rates are time and a half for earnings and double time for week ends. The following details have been recorded on three jobs :

	Job X Clock hrs.	*Job Y Clock hrs.*	*Job Z Clock hrs.*
Normal time	480	220	150
Evening time	120	60	80
Week end	10	30	16

Calculate the labour cost chargeable to each of the jobs in the following situations :

(*i*) When the overtime is worked at the coustomer's request to advance the delivery time.

(*ii*) When overtime is worked occasionally under general pressure of work.

(*Sri Sathya Sai University, B. Com., October 1989*)

Solution : (*a*) Under the first situation the jobs are charged with the following amount of labour cost :

Job X	480 × Rs. 3	=	1,440
	102 × Rs. 4.50	=	459
	10 × Rs. 6	=	60
			1,959
Job Y	220 × Rs. 3	=	660
	60 × Rs. 4.50	=	270
	30 × Rs. 6	=	180
			1,110
Job Z	150 × 3	=	450
	80 × 4.50	=	360
	16 × 6	=	96
			906

(*b*) Under the second situation each job will be charged with labour cost for the number of hours worked at

Job X	480 + 102 + 10	=	592 @ Rs. 3	=	1,776
Job Y	220 + 60 + 30	=	310 @ Rs. 3	=	930
Job Z	150 + 80 + 16	=	246 × Rs. 3	=	738

The overtime wages chargeable to factory overheads will be

102 + 60 + 80	=	242 × 1.50[1] =	363
10 + 30 × 16	=	56× 3[2] =	168
			531

Note 1 : Rs. 1.50 is the difference between the evening overtime rate of Rs. 4.50 and basic wage rate of Rs. 3.

Note 2 : Rs. 3 is the difference between the double overtime rate of Rs. 6 and basic wage rate of Rs.3.

3. Holiday with Pay

Important festivals and days of national importance such as Independence Day, Republic Day, etc. are declared as holidys. On these days workers do not attend the factories and they are paid for these unproductive days. However, the wages payable for these holidays are charged to cost of production. There are two ways of treating holiday with pay in cost accounts, *viz.,* (*a*) to treat it as factory overheads for the entire year and apportioned to the number of jobs executed during the year and (*b*) to charge as direct wages by inflating the wage rate chargeable to different jobs.

4. Leave with Pay

Workers are entitled to different types of leave in a factory such as casual leave, sick leave, special leave, etc., Leave days with pay again constitute unproductive working days. The wages payable for those days are again treated as factory overheads and apportioned to various jobs executed in that year.

5. Work on Holidays

Workers may be requested to work on holidays and other weekly off days owing to unavoidable circumstances. The rate of wage payment of those days are at higher rate than the normal rate. Such extra wages paid are treated as overheads and charged to jobs as indirect wages. However the normal wages paid is treated as direct wages and charged directly to the jobs concerned.

6. Night Shift Allowance

The night shift allowance is treated as departmental overheads and charged to jobs executed as indirect wages.

7. Wages Payable to Defective Work

Defective units can be reworked in order to convert them into good units. The wages payable for converting defecive units into good units may be treated in two ways, *viz,* (*a*) If the amount of wages is negligible it is treated as direct wages and charged to the work order, and (*b*) If the the amount of wages is more it is treated as overheads and charged to the department concerned.

8. Wages Paid to Apprentices

A worker who learns a job cannot work efficiently when compared to other workers. He needs to be trained and the cost of training is treated as overheads. However, where a worker works on a job but takes moer time, then his wages are partly charged to the job as direct wages and partly as overheads.

9. Fringe Benefits

Fringe benefits include all welfare facilities offered to workers by the factory such as medical, housing, recreational, educational and also other contributions such as PF, ESI, gratuity, pension, etc. The expenses incurred towards factory workers are treated as departmental overheads, whereas fringe benefit relating to office staff and selling department of the factory are treated as office and administration overheads and selling and distribution overheads respectively.

QUESTIONS

I. (A) Fill in the Blanks

1. Cost of normal idle time is changed to..........
2. Time not spent on production is known as..........
3. In Taylor's differential piece rate system..........number of piece rates are set for each job.
4. Idle time arises only when workers are paid on..........basis of wage payment.
5. In Halsey-Weir system, a worker gets a bonus equal to..........percentage of time saved.

[*Answers :* (1) overhead, (2) idle time (3) two, (4) time rate, (5) 4%]

(B) Mark 'T' or 'F' in the space provided

1. When wages are paid on piece basis, the quality of work deteriorates. *T/F*
2. In Merrick's differential piece rate system, time wages are guaranteed to each worker. *T/F*
3. Holiday pay and leave pay are labour based cost. *T/F*
4. Rowan incentive system distributes the benefit of time saved equally between employee and employer. *T/F*
5. Cost of idle time due to labour strike should be treated as factory overhead. *T/F*

[*Answer :* True (1); Rest are all false]

(C) Choose the Correct Answer

1. Incentive system of wage payment
   (*a*) Pay bonus for the time saved besides guaranteeing wages for the time taken.
   (*b*) Is a fraud on the employee compensation plan.
   (*c*) Is intended to speed up work for the benefit of the employer.
   (*d*) Pay incersed bonus at an increasing rate as the efficiency increases.
2. Under Emerson's efficiency plan, the worker gets normal wages at
   (*a*) $66\frac{2}{3}$% efficiency (*b*) $33\frac{1}{3}$% efficiency
   (*c*) 80% efficiency (*d*) 100% efficiency
3. Under Bedaux system the point obtained as 'B' represents
   (*a*) No. of units produced. (*c*) No. of hours taken for a job.
   (*d*) No. of workers required for a job. (*b*) No. of minutes taken for a job.
4. Which one of the following is the basis on which bonus is calculated under Rowan system
   (*a*) $\frac{\text{Std. Time}}{\text{Time saved}} \times \text{Std. time} \times \text{Std. rate}$ (*b*) $\frac{\text{Std. Time}}{\text{Time taken}} \times \text{Time saved} \times \text{Time rate}$
   (*c*) $\frac{\text{Std. Time}}{\text{Time rate}} \times \text{Time taken} \times \text{Time saved}$ (*d*) $\frac{\text{Time saved}}{\text{Std. Time}} \times \text{Time taken} \times \text{Time rest}$
5. Which one of the following is a system which combines both time and price rate system.
   (*a*) Bedaux system. (*b*) Merrick's differential system.
   (*c*) Halsey system. (*d*) Emerson's system.

6. Under Gantt task and bonus plan no bonus is available to a worker if his efficiency is below

   (*a*) 50% (*b*) $66\frac{2}{3}\%$

   (*c*) 75% (*d*) 100%

7. Under which of the following bonus system production budget of the department is taken as standard and the actual production, if exceeds the standard bonus is paid to all the workers

   (*a*) Rucker plan (*b*) Scanlon plan

   (*c*) Bush plan (*d*) Prestman's plan

8. The formula to calculate wages under Barth system is

   (*a*) $\sqrt{\text{Std. time} \times \text{Actual time} \times \text{Time wage}}$ (*b*) $\sqrt{\text{Std. time} \times \text{Actual time} \times \text{Time wage}}$

   (*c*) $\sqrt{\text{Std. time} \times \text{Actual time} \times \text{Time wage}}$ (*d*) Std. time × Time wage × Actual wage

9. Which one of the following factor is the most important for reducing the labour cost per unit

   (*a*) Low wage rates (*b*) Higher input-output rates

   (*c*) Strict control and supervision (*d*) Longer hours of work

10. The benefit of time saved by a worker against the standard should

    (*a*) go wholly to the employee.

    (*b*) be shared by the employer and the employee if the work is standardised.

    (*c*) be shared by the two if it is not standardised.

    (*d*) go wholly to the employer.

[***Answers*** : 1 (*a*), 2 (*b*), 3(*b*), 4(*d*), 5(*d*), 6(*d*), 7(*d*), 8(*b*), 9(*b*), 10(*c*)]

(D) Match the Following

A	*B*
(1) Halsey system	(*a*) Indirect monetary incentive
(2) Taylor system	(*b*) Group bonus system
(3) Emerson's system	(*c*) Combination of time and piece rate
(4) Co-partnership	(*d*) Premium bonus plan
(5) Production plan	(*e*) Piece rate system
(6) Barth system	(*f*) Time rate system
	(*g*) Non-monetary incentive
	(*h*) 50% of time saved as bonus

[Answer : 1(*h*), 2(*e*) 3(*c*) 4(*a*) 5(*b*) 6(*d*)]

II. Simple Questions

1. State any two merits and two demerits of time rate system of wage payment.
2. State any two merits and two demerits of piece rate system.
3. State the feature of Taylor's differential piece rate system of wage payment.
4. State the features of Merrick's differential piece rate system.
5. State the features of Gantt task and bonus plan.
6. State the features of Emerson's efficiency system.
7. State the features of Halsey system of wage payment.
8. State the features of Rowan system of wage payment.
9. What do you mean by group bonus system?
10. What do you mean by profit sharing plan?
11. What do you mean by co-partnership?
12. Distinguish between profit sharing and co-partnership.
13. What do you mean by wage abstract?
14. What is idle time?
15. Distinguish between overtime and idle time.
16. What is a fringe benefit?

17. How do you treat holiday with pay in cost accounts?
18. How do you treat leave with pay in cost accounts?
19. Mention any four types of group incentive system?
20. What do you mean by accelerated premium bonus?

III. Short and Long Answer Question

1. Emunerate the causes of idle time indicating the treatment thereof in cost account. *(ICWA, Inter, June 1992)*
2. Write a note on plant register. *(ICWA, Inter, June 1992)*
3. Discuss the advantages and disadvantages of having piece rate system of payment of wages. *(ICWA, Inter, June 1990)*
4. Explain the differences between time rate wages and piece rate wages. *(ICWA, Inter, Dec. 1988)*
5. What are the various incentive plans of wage? Explain. *(Andhra University, B. Com., May 1992)*
6. Give a comparative study of Halsey and Rowan plan with imaginary data about actual time, standard time and rates of wages, etc., *(Kakatiya University, B.Com., November 1991)*
7. Compare and contrast Halsey and Rowan premium plan. *(Kakatiya University, B.Com., October 1989)*
8. Explain the different system of wage payment. *(Kakatiya University, B.Com., April 1990)*
9. What is idle time? From control point of view, how do you categorise different kinds of idle time. *(Nagarjuna University, B.Com., March 1992)*
10. What is idle time? How is cost of idle time treated? *(Osmania University, B.Com., April 1990)*
11. Discuss the importance of the following (*a*) time booking, (*b*) time keeping, and (*c*) group incentive. *(Osmania University, B.Com., March 1992)*
12. Explain briefly the methods of treating overtime wages in cost accounts. *(Bangalore University, M.Com., May 1992)*
13. Outline the general principles to be broke in mind in distinguish a wage incentive scheme. *(University of Madras, B.Com., March 1992)*
14. What is idle time? Who is it treated in cost account ? *(Kakatiya University, M.Com., August 1991)*
15. List the various causes for idle time of workers and machines and give the remedial measures you recommend. *(Mangalore University, B.Com., April 1988)*
16. Explain the following methods of wage payment : (1) Taylor's differential piece rate system, (2) Emerson's efficiency plan, (3) Gantt task and bonus plan, (4) Rowan scheme. *(Mangalore University, B.Com., Oct. 1987)*
17. What are the methods of group incentive payment? What are its limitations? *(University, of Kerala, B.Com., May 1989)*
18. How would you deal with the following expenses :
    (*a*) Overtime wages, (*b*) Expenses for welfare activities, (*c*) Wages paid for re-operation of defectives, (*d*) Research and development cost. *(University of Delhi, B.Com., (Hons.) 1991)*
19. What are the factors to be considered for the introduction of a wage incentive scheme? Explain. *(University of Delhi, B.Com., (Hons.) 1991)*
20. What are the objectives of "Incentive plans of wage payment"? Explain briefly the conditions necessary for their success. *(University of Delhi, B.Com., (Hons.) 1990)*
21. How will you deal with 'Idle time' in cost accounts? How can you control such costs? *(University of Delhi, B.Com., (Hons.) 1989)*
22. How will you deal with "overtime premium cost in cost account"? *(University of Delhi, B.Com., (Hons.) 1988)*
23. What are the objectives of introducing an incentive scheme in a factory? What factors would you take into consideration for the same? *(Calcutta University B.Com., 1991)*
24. What do you understand by "Group bonus scheme"? Briefly narrate its advantages and disadvantages. *(Calcutta University B.Com., 1990)*
25. State the essentials of a good incentive wage plan. In the light of your answer discuss any two incentive wage plans you know of. *(Sri Sathya Sai University B.Com., Oct., 1991)*
26. Draw a payroll sheet filling in imaginary details pertaining to the office staff of a small manufacturing concern. *(Sri Sathya Sai University B.Com., Oct., 1989)*

EXERCISES

Exercise-1 (Tarylor's Differential Piece rate)

With the help of the following information, ascertain the wages paid to workers Somu and Balu under Tarylor's Differential Piece rate system.

Standard time allowed 40 units per hour
Simple time rate wage Rs. 4 per hour
Differential piece rates to be applied :
75% of piece rate when below standard
125% of piece rate when at and above standard
The workers have produced in a day of 8 hours as follows :
Somu 240 units : Balu 400 units

(*Bharathidason University, B.Com., April 1998*)
[**Answer :** Somu's wages Rs. 18, Balu's wages Rs. 50]

Exercise-2

Calculate the earnings of worker Arun under Straight Piece rate system and Tarylor's differential piece rate system from the following :

Normal rate per hour : Rs. 2.40
Standard time per unit : 30 Seconds
Differential to be applied :
80% of piece rate below standard and
120% of piece rate above standard
Worker Arun produces 800 units per day of 8 hours

(*Bharathidason University, B.Com., November 1997*)
[**Answer :** Wages under straight piece rate Rs. 16 and under Tarylor's Differential piece rate Rs. 12.80]

Exercise-3 (Straight Piece rate and Merrick's Multiple rate)

Calculate the earnings of workers A, B and C under straight piece rate system and Merricks multiple piece rate system from the following particulars :

Normal rate per hour = Rs. 1.80
Standard time per unit = 1 minute
Output per day is as follows :
Worker A = 384 units
Worker B = 450 units
Worker C = 552 units
Working hours per day are 8

(*Calicut University, B.Com., Oct. 1995*)
[**Answer :** Straight piece rate A Rs. 11.52, B Rs. 14.85 and C Rs. 19.87
Merrick's system A Rs. 11.52, B Rs. 14.85 C Rs. 19.87]

Exercise-4 (Gautt Tark and Bonns Plan)

The standard output in a day of 8 hours is 30 units. Time rate is Rs. 2 per hour. Low piece rate is Rs. 0.50 per unit and high piece rate is Rs. 0.75 per unit. In a day of 8 hrs, A produces 25 units, B 30 units and C 40 units. Calculate the earnings of A, B and C under Gautt Tark and Bonns plan.

(*Bharathidason University BBA, April 1996*)
[**Answer :** A's wages Rs. 16, B's wages 19.20 and C's wages Rs. 30]

Exercise-5 (Holley System)

Standard time – 10 hours
Time taken – 8 hours
Time rate – Rs. 2.50 per hour

Calculate the total earnings under Halsey plan. (*Bharathidason University B.Com, November 1994*)
[**Answer :** Total Earnings Rs. 22.50]

Exercise-6 (Halsey Weir)

A worker under Halsey method of remuneration has a day rate of Rs. 12 per week of 48 hours plus a cost of living index of 10 paise per hour worked. He is given 8 hours task to perform which he completes in 6 hours. He is allowed 30% of the time saved as premium bonus. What would be his total earnings and hourly rate of earnings. *(Kakatiya University, B.Com., April 1997)*

[**Answer :** Total Earnings Rs. 27.00]

Exercise-7 (Rowom System)

A worker's wage for a guaranteed 44 hour week is Rs. 10 per hour. The estimated time to produce one article is 30 minutes and under the incentive scheme, time allowed is increased by 20%. During the week, he manufactured 100 articles. Calculate the total wages under the Rowom Bonns plan.

(Bangalore University, B.Com., Nov. 1995)

[**Answer :** Total Earnings Rs. 557.33]

Exercise-8 (Holsey and Rowom System)

During the first week of January, 1995, M produced 400 articles. He receives wages for a guaranteed 48 hours a week at Rs. 5 per hour. The estimated time to produce one article is 12 minutes. Calculate his wages according to (a) Holsey Premium plan and (b) Rowom Premium plan.

(Bangalore University, B.Com., April 1997)

[**Answer :** Holsey System Rs. 320, Rowom System Rs. 336]

Exercise-9

It takes 9 hours to complete a job under time rate system. But the same job requires only 6 hours for its completion under piece rate system. Assume daily wages are Re. 1 per hour, cost of material Rs. 4 and other general overheads 150% of wages. Calculate the cost of production under (a) Piece rate system (b) Rowom plan (c) Holsey plan. *(Madras University, B.Com., March 1995)*

[**Answer :** Factory cost under Piece rate Rs. 19, Rowom Rs. 24 and Holsey Rs. 22.75]

Exercise-10 (Group Bonns System)

From the following particulars, calculate the group bonns payable and the amount that will be paid to each member of the group. Standard production in a week 120 units. It is agreed that for every 10% increase in production, bonus of 5% of the total wages payable for the week will be paid and the same will be shared by the group consisting of 4 members in proportion to their total wages of the group.

Total production for the week is 145 units. Wages earned by the four members of the group A, B, C and D are respectively Rs. 80, Rs. 78, Rs. 72, and Rs. 68. *(Kerala University, B.Com., Oct. 1990)*

[**Answer :** Bonus payable – A Rs. 8, B Rs. 7.80, C Rs. 7.20, D Rs. 6.80]

Exercise-11 (Payroll Preparation)

From the following data prepare a statement of labour cost, showing cost per day :

(i) Monthly salary — Rs. 255

(ii) Leave salary — 5% of (i)

(iii) Employer's contribution to provident fund : $8\frac{1}{3}\%$ of (i) and (ii)

(iv) Employer's contribution to ESI : 3% of (i) and (ii)

(v) Pro-rata expenditure on amenities to labour : Rs. 28 per head per month

(vi) No. of working hours in a month of 25 days : 8 hours per day

(Bharathidason University, B.Com., April 1998)

[**Answer :** Rs. 291 per month of 25 days and Rs. 11.64 per day of 8 hours]

Exercise-12

From the following data, prepare a statement showing the cost per man-day of 8 hrs.

(i) Basic salary and D.A Rs. 300 per month.

(ii) Leave salary to workman 6% of the basic and D.A.

(iii) Employers contribution to P.F 6% of (i) plus (ii)

(iv) Employee's contribution to P.F 6% of (i) plus (ii)

(v) Pro-rata expenditure on amenities to labour at Rs. 25 per head per month.

(vi) Number of working hours in a month 200 *(Bharathidason University, B.Com., April 1997)*

[**Answer :** Rs. 14.44]

10

DIRECT EXPENSES

INTRODUCTION

Direct expenses, otherwise known as chargeable expenses, as the name itself indicates, are those expenses, other than direct material cost and direct labour cost, which are directly incurred on a specific cost unit. They form part of prime cost because they are incurred directly on a specific cost unit. The ICMA terminology defines diect expenses as "expenses which can be identified with and allocated to cost centre or cost units". However, in some cases, the direct expenses cannot be very easily identified with the cost unit but it can be identified with cos centre. In such cases these expenses are direct cost of the cost centre and it becomes indirect cost of all jobs manufactured in that department. A factory with large number of departments will have a greater proportion of direct expenses.

FEATURES OF DIRECT EXPENSES

1. Direct expenses are solely incurred on a particular cost unit or cost centre. The benetit of incurring direct expenses is available only for a particular cost unit or cost centre but not for others.
2. Direct expenses may sometimes include material, labour or indirect expense, *e.g.*, cost of a special mould.
3. Direct expenses vary in direct proportion with production volume.
4. The proportion of direct expenses to total cost of production is very less.
5. They can be controlled easily when compared to indirect expenses.
6. The direct expense can be identified with the total cost of production.

The following are some of the examples of direct expenses:

1. Carriage inward and import duty paid on materials purchased.
2. Excise duty and octroi paid on materials specifically purchased for specific job.
3. Primary packing materials.
4. Cost of patents and royalty paid.
5. Travelling expenses incurred in securing an order to supervise a work being carried out at the premises of customer.
6. Architect's or surveyor's fee.
7. Sub-contract cost.
8. Cost of spare parts.
9. Cost of special drawing, design, pattern or mould.
10. Cost of special tools or equipments hired.
11. Maintenance charges of such tools or equipments.

DIRECT EXPENSES vs. DIRECT MATERIALS

Though direct material cost and direct expenses form part of prime cost, yet there is a difference between the two. Direct materials can be conveniently identified with the finished product. Whereas direct expenses are incurred for providing services for the production and cannot be identified with the finished product. For example, when power is used substantially to produce goods, say to the extent of 75 per cent of the total cost of production it is to be treated as direct cost, because power is inevitable to production process.

DIRECT EXPENSES VS. INDIRECT EXPENSES

Direct expenses differ from indirect expenses in following respects :

(*a*) Direct expenses is part of prime cost whereas indirect expenses is part of overheads.

(*b*) Direct expenses vary in direct proportion of output, whereas indirect expenses do not.

(*c*) The benefit of incurring direct expenses with the completion of a job, whereas the benefit of incurring indirect expenses extends to other jobs also.

(*d*) The direct expenses can be identified with the total cost of production, whereas it is not possible in case of indirect expenses.

(*e*) Direct expenses can be allocated whereas indirect expenses are to be apportioned.

(*f*) Direct expenses can be easily controlled when compared to indirect expenses.

ACCOUNTING OF DIRECT EXPENSES IN COST ACCOUNTS

The following entry is passed when direct expenses are incurred.

Direct expenses a/c *Dr.*

To cost ledger control a/c

When charged to respective jobs, the following entry is passed

Individual job a/c *Dr.*

(In the work-in-progress ledger)

To direct expenses a/c

CONTROL OF DIRECT EXPENSES

Though direct expenses constitute only a small proportion to the total cost of production it should not be allowed to go unchecked. Care must be taken to see that these expenses do not exceed the predetermined amount. Standard cost can be fixed for direct expenses and the actuals can be compared with standard cost to know varinaces. In case of adverse variance, it should be analysed and reported for taking remedial measures.

QUESTIONS

Simple Questions

1. Define direct expense.
2. State any four features of direct expenses.
3. Give four examples of direct expenses.
4. Distinguish between direct material and direct expense.
5. Distinguish between direct expense and indirect expense.
6. How is direct expense accounted in cost account?
7. How is direct expenses controlled?

11

FACTORY OVERHEADS

INTRODUCTION

Overheads constitute one of the important elements of the cost of production. The production of goods or services of every kind involves incurring of additional costs apart from the three prime cost elements. Such expenses which are incurred over and above the prime cost elements are known as overheads. Unlike prime cost elements the overheads cannot be easily identified with finished product. As such overheads cannot be allocated but can be apportioned to finished goods only on an equitable basis. Overheads are incurred both inside and outside the production department. The amount of overheads incurred depends upon the nature of industry and as such it cannot be precisely estimated as a percentage to total cost. However, it is inevitable to incur overheads in all factories.

The ICMA terminology defines overheads as the "aggregate of indirect material cost, indirect labour cost and indirect expenses."

There are two tests which can be applied to determine whether an item of cost is overhead or not. Firstly, identification of the item of cost with cost unit or cost centre. If it is not possible to identify the item of cost to a cost unit or cost centre then such item of cost is a overhead cost. For example, rent and rates, heating and lighting, power, etc. cannot be identified with finished products. Hence they are overheads. Secondly, the convenience with which an item of cost can be identified with finished product serves as a second test. Where it is not convenient to identify an item of cost with finished product, again it is a case of overheads. For example, nails used in furniture making and buttons used in readymade garments are overheads though they can be identifed with finished goods.

The following are some of the distinctive features of overheads as an element of cost :

1. The proportion of overheads in the total cost of production is less.
2. Overheads are incurred both inside and outside the production departments.
3. They cannot be allocated but can be apportioned.
4. They cannot be controlled in the strict sense of the term.
5. Most of the overheads are charged on the predetermined basis.
6. Their benefit cannot be measured.
7. Most of them are period cost and not product cost.

Very often the term indirect expenses in interchangeably used to mean overheads. However, these two terms from accounting point of view differs. The term "indirect expense" is used to record the actual indirect expense incurred. Whereas the term "overheads" is used to tecord indirect expenses which are likely to be incurred.

STEPS IN OVERHEAD ACCOUNTING

Unlike prime cost elements overheads cannot be charged directly to the cost of production.

The following steps are involved in overhead accounting procedure.

I. Classification of Overheads

Overheads can be classified in the basis of number of characteristics. The following are the important basis of overhead classification

1. Elementwise Classification

The method of caissification is done on the basis of definition of overhead. Accordingly there are three elements of overheads. They are as follows :

(A) Indirect materials cost : The ICMA Terminology difines indirect material cost as "materials cost other than direct material cost." It cannot be allocated but it can be apportiones to cost centres or cost units. The example of indirect material cost are : oil, grease, cotton waste, sand paper, nails, nuts, bolts, screws, carbon papers, etc.

(B) Indirect labour cost : The ICMA Terminology defines indirect labour cost as "wage cost other than direct wages cost." Indirect laboure cost cannot be allocated but apportioned to cost centres or cost units." The examples of indirect labour cost are wages payable to the staff of peronnel department, purchase department, service and maintenance department. Idle time wages, overtime wages, leave with pay, holiday with pay, fringe benefits and so on.

(C) Indirect expenses : The ICMA terminology defines indirect expenses as "expenses, other than direct expenses." Indirect expenses cannot be allocted but apportioned to cost centres or cost units. The examples of indirect expenses are rent, rates, insurance, heating, lighting, power, depreciation, repairs and maintenance, etc.

2. Functionwise Classification

Under this method of classification, the various functions performed by the factory constitutes the basis. Accordingly overheads are classified as follows :

(A) Factory overheads : All overheads that are incurred in various production and service departments which are ancillary to production process is known as factory overheads. Factory overheads include indirect material cost, indirect labour cost and indirect expenses incurred in the various production and service departments. Some examples of indirect material cost used in the manufacturing process are consumable stores, tiny part of materials such as thread and button in readymade garment industry, nails and polish in furniture making industry and so on. Examples of indirect labour cost incurred in production process are wages and salaries of repair and maintenance staff, salary of foreman, supervisor, inspector, watchman's salary, works manager salary, etc. Example of indirect expenses incurred in production process are depreciation, repairs and maintenance, rent, rates, taxes of factory building, drawing office expenses and so on.

(B) Administration overheads : It is defined by the ICMA terminology as "the cost of formulating the policy, directing the organisation and controlling the operations of an undertaking, which is not related directly to production, selling, and distribution function of an undertaking." Administration overheads include indirect material cost, indirect labour cost and indirect expenses. Some examples of indirect material cost are office stationery such as paper, pen, ink, carbon papers, stapler, etc. Some examples of indirect labour cost incurred in the administration department of a factory are salaries of managing director, accountant, secretary, clerks and attendars. Some examples of indirect expenses incurred in office are lighting and heating, rent and rates, repairs and maintenance, bank charges, leagal charges, telephone charges.

(C) Selling overheads : The overheads which are incurred in promoting sales and retaining customers is known as selling overheads. Selling overheads include indirect material cost, indirect labour cost and indirect expenses. Some examples of indirect material cost are catalogues, price lists, free gifts and samples, etc. Some examples of indirect labour cost incurred in the sales department are salaries of sales manager, salaries and commission of salesmen. Some examples of indirect expenses incurred in the sales department are expenses incurred in training salesman, advertisement, market research expenses, rent, insurance, heating and lighting of sales show room.

(D) Distribution overheads: These are expenses which are incurred from the time finished products are packed until they reach their destination. Distribution overheads include indirect material cost, indirect labour cost and indirect expenses. Some examples of indirect material cost incurred in the distribution department of a factory are packing materials, such as cardboard boxes, hammers, nails, etc. Some examples of indirect labour cost incurred in the distribution department are salaries of warehouse staff, salaries of drivers of delivary vans, etc. Some examples of indirect expenses are rent, heating, lighting, repairs of warehouse, freight, maintenance of delivery vahicles, etc.

3. Behaviourwise Classification

According to this basis overheads are classifed by establishing a relationship with the output. There are certain overheads, which vary in sympathy with production while others remain static. With reference to such behaviour overheads are classifed into the following :

(A) Variable overheads : The ICMA terminology defined variable overheads as "overhead cost related to production which, in the aggregate, tends to vary in direct proportion to changes in the volume of output. In other words variable overheads vary in direct proportion to output produced. Most of the indirect material costs are example of variable overheads.

(B) Fixed overheads : Fixed overheads tend to remain constant whatever may be the output obtained within the installed capacity of plant. All the indirect labour cost and indirect expenses are examples of fixed overheads.

(C) Semi-variable overheads : These overheads vary with production level but not in direct proportion, Indirect expenses such as depreciation of plant, repairs and maintenance, telephone charges, etc. are examples of semi-variable overheads.

4. On the Basis of Normality

According to this basis overheads are classified into the following two types :

(A) Normal overheads : Overheads which are not expected to be incurred in attaining a given output are known as normal overheads. Normal overheads forms part of production cost.

(B) Abnormal overheads : Overheads which are not expected to be incurred in attaining a given level output are known as abnormal overheads. Cost of abnormal idle time is an example of abnormal overheads. It is taken into costing profit and loss account.

Advantages of Behaviourwise Classification of Overheads

***(a)* Cost control :** Fixed overheads are not controllable at all points and levels of management. At the most fixed overheads can be controlled only by the top level management, whereas, variable costs are capable of controlling at all levels of management. Thus a proper classification of overheads into fixed and variable helps in controlling overheads.

(*b*) **Flexible budgets :** A flexible budget is prepared for various levels of production capacity. In its preparation classification of overheads into fixed and variable is very important. Fixed overheads remain constant for all levels of activity, whereas variable overheads vary with every change in the level of activity.

(*c*) **Marginal costing :** Under marginal costing technique only variable overheads are taken into cost of production, whereas fixed overheads are charged to costing profit and loss account. So, for the application of marginal costing technique it becomes inevitable to classify overheads into fixed and variable overheads.

(*d*) **Break-even analysis :** For preparation of preak-even chart it is also very essential to classify overheads into fixed and variable. Only then it is possible to know the point of no-profit-no-loss in a business.

(*e*) **Managerial decision-making :** Management is very often confronted with number of problems and alternate proposals. To take decisions among various proposals it is necessary to classify overheads into fixed and variable. This is so because some decisions such as make or buy, fixation of price, etc. are affected by variable overheads but not by fixed overhead.

(*f*) **Cost analysis :** Analysis of overheads into fixed and variable is important because though fixed overheads remain fixed in respect of its amount, it decreases per unit when the volume of output is increased. Similarly, though variable overheads per unit remains same it increases when production volume is increased. When it is necessary to know the cost per unit, it is necessary to classify overheads into fixed and variable components.

(*g*) **Overhead absorption :** In order to charge overheads to various products or jobs it is essential to calculate two separate overheas rates, *viz.,* fixed overhead rate and variable overhead rates. In order to calculate these rates overheads are to be classified into fixed and variable.

II. Codification of Overheads

Codification of overheads are useful in accumulating and control of overheads. After classification of overheads, the next step involved in overhead accounting is to codify them. This is so because there are number of overheads which are incurred in factories and unless proper attention is given, the chances of accounting of all overheads may not be possible. Thus all overheads falling under the category of depreciation relating to plant and machinery, factory building, factory furniture may be given a separate number. So that depreciation relating to all the assets can be properly accounted for. Codification of overheads refers to assignment of a number or symbol for each item of overheads with a view to accumulate them easily. To facilitate easy identification of different types of overheads different code numbers are given. The code numbers given for factory overheads is known as standing order number and that to administration, selling and distribution overheads is known as cost accounting number. These numbers are listed in a schedule for ready reference.

Objects of Codification of Overheads

(*a*) To accumulate overheads systematically.
(*b*) To facilitate control over them.
(*c*) To distinguish between different types of overheads.
(*d*) To account for all types of overheads.
(*e*) To facilitate convenience of identifying the overheads.

Methods of Codification of Overheads

The following are the important methods of codifying the overheads :

(a) Numerical method : Under this method numerical numbers are used to codify the overheads. In big factories, first of all the various expenses are first identified and a separate number (or main number) is given to each expense. Subsequently a sub-number is given for various overheads incurred under each category of expense. For example, depreciation is given a code number as 1. Then depreciation relating to factory building will be given a code number of 1.1 depreciation relating to plant and machinery 1.2 and that relating to furniture 1.3 and so on. Similarly repairs may be given a code number as 2. Then repairs relating to factory building is given a code number as 2.1 repairs relating to plant and machinery as 2.2 and repairs relating to furniture as 2.3 and so on.

(b) Alphabetic method or mnemonic method : Under this method alphabets are used to codify the overheads. Each item of overhead is given a code letter which happens to be the first letter of the overhead expenditure. However items of overheads beginning with same letter will pose a problem. To avoid confusion the next letter of the overhead can be used along with the first letter.

(c) Decimal method : Under this method the various departments are first identified and a separate number is given to them. Then each and every overhead incurred in the respective departments are given a sub-number. For example, salary of clerk belonging to office department is given a code number as 1.1, The salary of clerk belonging to selling department is given a code number as 2.1 and so on.

(d) Alpha-numerical method : This method combines both the alphabetic and numerical methods. The alphabetic letter denotes the main expenditure while the numerical number denotes its sub-division. For example, depreciation of plant is coded as D_1, depreciation of plant and machinery as D_2, and depreciation of assets as D_3.

III. Collection of Overheads

The process of ascertaining the amount of overheads incurred for a period is called collection of overhead. The classified and coded overheads are collected and recorded under standing order number and cost accounting number. To facilitate recording of overhead a separate ledger known as "overhead ledger" is maintained. Separate accounts are opened for standing order number and cost accounting number in this ledger. Generally, overheads are collected at the end of every month and after totalling them, they are recorded in the overhead ledger.

Sources from Which Various Overheads are Collected

(a) Material requsition slips : Indirect materials such as oil, grease, cotton waste, tiny parts such as bolts, nuts, etc. are drawn by various departments on the basis of material requisition slips. At the time of issue the particulars of issue of indirect materials and the departments to which they are issued are recorded in the materials requisition slip. At the end of the month, the various material requisition slips are summarised in a sheet known as "materials abstract." From the material abstract the total of indirect material cost is posted to the debit of factory overhead control account and credited to stores ledger control acount.

(b) Invoices : Those indirect materials which are directly requisitioned by departmental heads, such as stationery by the office superintendent does not pass through a material requisition note. Such type of indirect materials are collected from invoices. The various invoices supporting the purchase of indirect materials by various departmental heads are entered in purchase journal meant for the purpose of collection of overheads. At the end of the month, the totals from the purchase journal is posted to the debit of factory overhead account and credited to cost control account.

(c) Wages abstract : The indirect wages paid to various employees are recorded in the wage abstract on the basis of time cards or job cards. From wages abstract, the total indirect labour cost is posted to the debit of factory overhead account and credited to wages control account.

(d) Cash book : Sundry items of expenses or indirect expenses are recorded in an analytical petty cash book. The total of Indirect expenses are collected from the petty cash book on the basis of standing order number and cost accounting number. They are then posted to the debit of factory overhead control account and credited to cost control ledger account.

(e) Subsidiary records : Certain items of overheads are recorded separately in some special or subsidiary records. For example, depreciation on machinery is recorded in a plant register. Similarly scraps can be recorded in a "Scrap report" and postal expenses in a postage book. So overheads of these nature are collected from a subsidiary register or records meant for this purpose.

(f) Journal : All notional expenses and transactions requiring adjustments, such as accrued expense, prepaid expenses are posted into the journal. The total of these expenses are posted to the debit of factory overhead control account and credited to cost control ledger account.

IV. Departmentalisation of Overheads

In a large sized factories there exists number of departments. Some departments are concerned with production process, while other departments render useful services to production departments. The former typer of department is known as production department and latter is known as service department. Whenever overheads are incurred in a factory, they have to be charged to these two types of departments. The precess of allocation and apportionment of overheads to various departments is known as departmentalisation of overheads. Proper allocation and apportionment of overheads serve the following purposes:

(a) It helps in accurate ascertainment of cost.
(b) It helps in controlling of overheads by comparing actuals with budgeted overheads.
(c) An effective control can be exercised over service departments.
(d) Responsibility can be fixed over various executives for efficient functioning of the different departments of the factory.
(e) It facilitates correct ascertainment of work-in-progress.
(f) It helps in accurate forecasting and estimating.

Allocation of Overheads

The term "allocation of overheads" refers to identifying an item of overhead and the allotment of the whole amount to one department or cost centre. In other words it means charging the entire amount of overhead to a department or cost centre. Some examples of allocation are salary of a foreman, wages of a machine operator, power expenses if separate meter is installed for each production department.

Apportion of Overheads

Those overheads which connot be allocated to a specific department or cost centre need to be apportioned to various departments or cost centres. The process of charging proportionate amount of overheads to various departments is known as apportionment of overheads. As overheads are to be charged proportionatle to various departments it has to be done on some equitable basis. For example, salary of general manager is to be apportioned to various departments on the basis of time devoted by him on several departments.

Difference between Allocation and Apportionment of Overheads

Under allocation of overheads the entire amount is charged to a department. Under apportionment of overthead only a proportionate amount is charged to a department. Allocation is the first step in the departmentalisation of overheads, whereas apportionment comes next. Allocation is a simple process, whereas apportionment is a cumbersome process. In case of allocation, overheads can be conveniently identified with a department, whereas it is not possible to identify overheads to a department under apportionment process.

Basis of Apportionment of Overheads

Items of overhead expenses which are ineurred as a common expense is to be apportioned among all the departments. Though different basis are available for apportionment, it is essential to satisfy that the overhead is closely related to the basis selected. In other words the overheads should involve a direct impact on the basis selected. The basis should also ensure accuracy under the prevailing situations. Some of the basis used for apportionment are as follows.

(*a*) **Direct wages :** The following overheads are apportioned on this basis :

(*i*) Workmen's compensation.
(*ii*) Contribution to provident fund.
(*iii*) Contribution to ESI.

(*b*) **Number of labour hours :** The following overheads are apportioned on this basis :

(*i*) Salaries of inspector.
(*ii*) Salaries of supervisors.
(*iii*) Other administrative expenses.

(*c*) **Number of employees :** The following overheads are apportioned on this basis :

(*i*) Canteen expenses :
(*ii*) Welfare expenses.
(*iii*) Salaries of time keeping staff.
(*iv*) Medical expenses.
(*v*) Fringe benefits.

(*d*) **Floor Area :** The following overheads are apportioned on this basis :

(*i*) Rent and rates.
(*ii*) Taxes.
(*iii*) Heating and lighting.
(*iv*) Repairs and maintenance of building.
(*v*) Accident prevention cost.

(*e*) **Capital value of the asset :** The following overheads are apportioned on this basis:

(*i*) Depreciation.
(*ii*) Repairs and maintenance
(*iii*) Insurance.

(f) **Machine hours :** The following overheads are apportioned on this basis :

(*i*) Consumable stores.

(*ii*) Supervision charges.

(*iii*) Repairs and maintenance.

(g) **Number of watts, kilowatt, hours or light points :** The following overhead expenses are apportioned on this basis :

(*i*) Electricity charges for lighting, heating, air-conditioning.

(*ii*) Electricity charges for productive purposes.

(h) **Technical estimate:** The following overheads are apportioned on this basis :

(*i*) Sundry overheads which cannot be apportioned on any of the above-mentioned basis.

(*ii*) Internal transport cost.

(*iii*) Director's salaries.

Principles on which Apportionment of Overhead is Based

Overheads which are incurred for various departments are to be apportioned by using a suitable criterion. The choice of a criterion for appropriate apportionment is referred to as principle on which overheads are to be apportioned. The following are the important principles adopted while selecting a basis for the apportionment of overheads.

1. Service or use criterion : This principle is based on the assumption that the service rendered to various departments are capable of easy measurement. Accordingly overheads are apportioned on the basis of service rendered to various departments. In other words that department which derives of maximum service or benefit should share more amount of overheads, when compared to other departments.

2. Analysis or survey criterion : This criterion is adopted where it is not possible to measure the services rendered directly because of its variation from time to time. In such a situation a survey or analysis is made to know the impact of overheads on different departments and accordingly a fair share of overheads are apportioned to all the departments. The best examples are apportionment of salary of general manager to various departments based on the assessment of his time spent on different department. Similarly, the salary of sales manager can be apportioned to different products based upon the time spent on promoting the sales of all products.

3. Ability to pay criterion : This principle is applied where overheads are to be apportioned to different departments or products of which one of them happens to be a new line. In such a situation it will not be proper to overburden a new department or new product by charging a higher share of overheads. According to this principle the overheads are charged on what is termed as "what the traffic can bear or ability to pay." This means those departments or products which earn more profit should bear a higher share of overheads as compared to a new department or product.

4. Efficiency or incentive principle : Under this principle production target is fixed for each department and overheads are apportioned according to the targets set. In order to encourage the departmental managers to attain the targets they are also given incentives. When the targets are attained. The unit cost of production decreases, which reveals the efficiency of the department. On the other hand, if the targets are not attained the unit cost of production will be high and thereby proves inefficiency of the department.

PROBLEMS ON APPORTIONMENT OF OVERHEADS

Problem 1: The Modern Co., is having four departments *A, B* and *C* are the producing departments and *D* is a servicing department. The actual cost for a period are as follows :

	Rs.
Rent	2,000
Repair	1,200
Depreciation	900
Lighting	200
Supervision	3,000
Insurance—Stock	1,000
Employees' insurance—Employer's liability	300
Power	1,800

The following data are also available in respect of four departments :

	Dept. A	*Dept. B*	*Dept. C*	*Dept. D*
Area sq ft.	150	110	90	50
Number of workers	24	16	12	8
	Rs.	Rs.	Rs.	Rs.
Total wages	8,000	6,000	4,000	2,000
Value of plant	24,000	18,000	12,000	6,000
Value of stock	15,000	9,000	6,000	—

Apportion the cost to the various departments on the most equitable method.

(University of Madras, B.Com., March 1991)

Solution : **Statement showing apportionment of overheads**

Expenses	*Basis of apportionment*	*Total*	*A*	*B*	*C*	*D*
Direct wages	Allocated	2,000	–	–	–	2,000
Rent	Areas of sq ft	2,000	750	550	450	250
Repair	Value of plant	1,200	480	360	240	120
Depreciation	Value of plant	900	360	270	180	90
Lighting	Area in sq ft	200	75	55	45	25
Supervision	No. of workers	3,000	1,200	800	600	400
Insurance	Value of stock	1,000	500	300	200	–
Employee's Insurance	Total wages	300	120	90	60	30
Power	Value of plant	18,00	720	540	360	180
	Total	10,400	4,205	2,965	2,135	3,095

Problem 2 : Bharat Engineering Works has three production departments *A, B,* and *C* and one service department *S*. From undermentioned particulars calculate labour hour rate for each of production departments :

Expenses for the period of 12 months

	Rs.
Rent	36,000
Power	8,250
Indirect wages	5,200
Depreciation on machinery	22,000
Electricity	5,600
Canteen expenses	6,500

Additional inormation :

	A	*B*	*C*	*S*
Light point (Nos.)	7	7	9	5
Floor space (sq. mts)	300	250	450	200
Horse power of machines (Hp)	65	30	30	40
No. of workers (Nos.)	2	3	6	2
Direct wages (Rs.)	12,000	14,000	18,000	8,000
Cost of machine (Rs.)	50,000	60,000	80,000	10,000

Working days : 200 days of 8 hours each. Service rendered by service department *S* to production departments *A*, *B* and *C* is 30%, 20% and 50% respectively. *(Calcutta University, B.Com., (Hons.) 1990)*

Solution : **Statement showing overhead apportionment**

Expenses	*Basis of apportionment*	*Total*	*A*	*B*	*C*	*S*
Direct wages	Allocated	8,000	-	-	-	8,000
Rent	Floor space	36,000	9,000	7,500	13,500	6,000
Power	H.P. of machine	8,250	3,250	1,500	1,500	2,000
Indirect wages	Direct wages	5,200	1,200	1,400	1,800	800
Depreciation of machinery	Cost of machine	22,000	5,500	6,600	8,800	1,100
Electricity	Light points	5,600	1,400	1,400	1,800	1,000
Canteen expenses	No. of workers	6,500	1,000	1,500	3,000	1,000
		83,550	21,350	19,900	30,400	19,900
Expenses of service dept. apportioned	30%, 20%, 50%		5,970	3,980	9,950	(-) 19,900
	Total overheads		27,320	23,880	40,350	
Labour hour rate			$\frac{27,320}{1,600}$	$\frac{23,880}{1,600}$	$\frac{40,350}{1,600}$	
			= 17.07	14.92	25.21	

V. Reapportionment of Overheads

It refers to the process of apportioning service department's overheads to production departments. Reapportionment of overheads is necessary because service departments are established to render service to production departments and whatever expenses that are incurred in service departments must naturally be borne by production departments. The following guidelines are to be considered while reapportioning the services department overhead to production departments :

(*a*) The nature of service rendered by each service department.

(*b*) The extent of service rendered to production.

(*c*) Determining or identifying the production departments which derived services from service departments.

(*d*) Selecting the basis of apportionment.

PROBLEM ON REAPPORTIONMENT OF OVERHEADS

Problem 3: In an engineering factory, the following particulars have been extracted for the quarter ended 31st Dec. 1981 compute the departmental overhead rate for each for each of the production departments, assuming that overheads are recovered as a percentage of direct wages.

	Production Department			*Service Dept.*	
	A (Rs.)	*B (Rs.)*	*C (Rs.)*	*X (Rs.)*	*Y (Rs.)*
Direct wages	30,000	45,000	60,000	15,000	30,000
Direct material	15,000	30,000	30,000	22,000	22,500
Staff number	1,500	2,250	2,250	750	750
Electricity (kwh)	6,000	4,500	3,000	1,500	1,500
Asset value	60,000	40,000	30,000	10,000	10,000
Light points	10	16	4	6	4
Area sqmts	150	250	50	50	50

The expenses for the period were :

Power	Rs. 1,100
Lighting	200
Stores	800
Welfare to staff	3,000
Deperciation	30,000
Repairs	6,000
General overheads	12,000
Rent and taxes	550

Apportion the expenses of service department *Y* according to direct wages and those of service department *X* in the ratio of 5 : 3 : 2 to the production departments.

Solution : **Statement showing overhead apportionment**

Expenses	*Basis of apportionment*	*Production Dept.* A	B	C	*Service Dept.* X	Y
Power	Kilo watt hrs.	400	300	200	100	100
Lighting	Light points	50	80	20	30	20
Stores overhead	Direct materials	100	201	201	147	151
Welfare to Staff	No. of staff	600	900	900	300	300
Depreciation	Value of asset	12,000	8,000	6,000	2,000	2,000
Repairs	Value of asset	2,400	1,600	1,200	400	400
General overheads	Direct wages	2,000	3,000	4,000	1,000	2,000
Rent & Rates	Area	150	250	50	50	50
Direct materials	Allocated	–	–	–	22,000	22,500
Direct Wages	Allocated	–	–	–	15,000	30,000
		17,700	14,331	12,571	41,027	57,521
Service Dept. *Y*'s overheads apportioned	Wages	12,782	19,174	25,565		(-5,754)

Sevice Dept. X's overheads apportioned	5 : 3: 2	20,513	12,308	8,206	(- 41,027)
		50,995	45,813	46,343	
Overhead rate as percentage of direct wages		169.98%	101.80%	77.23%	

Inter-service Departmental Overheads

Under the reapportionment of service department's overheads to production departments, as discussed above, it was presumed that service departments render service only to production departments. However in most of the industries, the service departments not only render service to production departments but also to other service departments. For example, canteen department provides service to both production and other. Service department, say, repairs department. The repairs deartment undertakes to serve not only the production department but also the canteen department. Thus the overheads incurred in the canteen department is to be apportioned not only to production departments but also to the repairs department. Similarly, the overheads incurred in repairs department must be apportioned to canteen department apart from other production departments. This process of reapportioning the service departments, overheads to other service departments is known as interservice departmental overheads or secondary distribution of overheads.

There are two methods which are used for secondary distribution of overhead. They are as follows :

1. Repeated distribution method or step ladder method : Under this method the overheads are apportioned by adopting a repeated number of steps. As this method involves number of steps in apportioning overheads it is also known as step ladder method.

The following steps are involved under this method :

(*a*) By applying the given percentages, the primary distribution overheads of the first service department is reapportioned to all production and service departments. In this process the first service department's account is closed.

(*b*) The second service department now consists of primary distribution overhead and a share of overhead from the first service department. The total of overheads of the second service department is now reapportioned according to the given percentages. This step closes the account of the second service department.

(*c*) The first service department now has only a share of overheads reapportioned from the second service department. Applying the given percentages this amount of overheads is again reapportioned to all the other departments.

(*d*) the above process in repeated until the amount of overheads become negligible for further reapportionment.

2. Simultaneous equation method : This method involves the following two steps:

(a) The amount of overhead for the two service departments is to be obtained by solving two simultaneous equations.

(b) By applying the given percentages the service departments overheads are reapoortioned to production departments. This process involves only one step as compared to first method which involves number of repeated steps.

PROBLEMS ON REPEATED DISTRIBUTION METHOD

Problem 4: Strongman Ltd. has three production departments *A, B* and *C* and two service departments *X* and *Y*. The following particulars are available for the month of March 1991 concerning the organisation :

	Rs.
Rent	15,000
Muncipal taxes	5,000
Electricity	2,400
Indirect wages	6,000
Power	6,000
Depreciation on machinery	40,000
Canteen expenses	30,000
Other labour related costs	10,000

Following further details are also available :

	Total	*A*	*B*	*C*	*X*	*Y*
Floor space (sq mts)	5,000	1,000	1,250	1,500	1,000	250
Light points (Nos.)	240	40	60	80	40	20
Direct wages (Rs.)	40,000	12,000	8,000	12,000	6,000	2,000
Horse power fo machines (Nos.)	150	60	30	50	10	–
Cost of machine (Rs.)	2,00,000	48,000	64,000	80,000	4,000	4,000
Working hours		2,335	1,510	1,525		

The expenses of service departments are to be allocated in the following manner :

	A	*B*	*C*	*X*	*Y*
X	20%	30%	40%	–	10%
Y	40%	20%	30%	10%	–

You are required to calculate the overhead absorption rate per hour in respect of the three production departments. *(ICWA, (Inter), June 1991)*

Solution : **Statement showing apportionment of overheads**

Expenses	*Basis of apportionment*	*Total*	*Production depts.* *A*	*B*	*C*	*Service Depts.* *X*	*Y*
Rent	Floor area	15,000	3,000	3,720	4,500	3,000	750
Municipal taxes	Floor area	5,000	1,000	1,250	1,500	1,000	250
Electricity	Light point	2,400	400	600	800	400	200
Indirect wages	Direct wages	6,000	1,800	1,200	1,800	900	300
Power	HP of machine	6,000	2,400	1,200	2,000	400	–
Depreciation	Value of machine	40,000	9,600	12,800	16,000	800	800
Canteen expenses	Direct wages	30,000	9,000	6,000	9,000	4,500	1,500
Other costs	Direct wages	10,000	3,000	2,000	3,000	1,500	500
Direct wages	Allocated	–	–	–	–	6,000	2,000
Total primary distribution		11,4400	30,200	28,800	38,600	18,500	6,300
Service dept. *X*			3,700	5,550	7,400	(–18,500)	1,850
Service dept. *Y*			3,260	1,630	2,445	815	(–81,50)
Service Dept. *X*			164	244	326	–815	81
Service Dept. *Y*			33	15	25	8	(–81)
Service Dept. *X*			3	1	4	(–8)	
	Total overhead		37,360	36,240	48,800		

Rate per hour	$\frac{37,360}{2,335}$ = 16	$\frac{36,240}{1,510}$ = 24	$\frac{48,800}{1,525}$ = 32

Problem 5: *XYZ* Ltd. have three production departments P_1, P_2 and P_3 and two service departments S_1 and S_2, the details pertaining to which are as under :

	P_1	P_2	P_3	S_1	S_2
Direct wages (Rs.)	3,000	2,000	3,000	1,500	195
Working hours	3,070	4,475	2,419	–	–
Value of machines (Rs.)	60,000	80,000	1,00,000	5,000	5,000
HP of machines	60	30	50	10	–
Light points	10	15	20	10	5
Floor space (sq ft)	2,000	2,500	3,000	2,000	500

The following figures extracted from the accounting records are releveant

	Rs.
Rent and rates	5,000
General lighting	600
Indirect wages	1,939
Power	1,500
Depreciation on machine	10,000
Sundries	9,695

The expenses of the service departments are distributed as under :

	P_1	P_2	P_3	S_1	S_2
S_1	20%	30%	40%	–	10%
S_2	40%	20%	30%	10%	

Find out the total cost of product LEO which is processed for manufacture in Dept. P_1, P_2, P_3 for 4, 5, and 3 hours respectively given that its direct material cost is Rs. 50 and direct labour cost is Rs. 30.

(Sri Sathya Sai University, B. Com., March 1999)

Solution : **Statement showing apportionment of overheads**

Expenses	*Basis of apportionment*	*Production Dept.* P_1	P_2	P_3	*Service Depts.* S_1	S_2
Direct wages	Allocated				1,500	195
Rent & rates	Floor space	1,000	1,250	1,500	1,000	250
Lighting	Light point	100	150	200	100	50
Indirect wages	Direct wages	600	400	600	300	39
Power	HP of machine	600	300	500	100	–
Depreciation of machines	Value of machines	2,400	3,200	4,000	200	200
Sundries	Direct wages	3,000	2,000	3,000	1,500	195
Total departmental overhead		7,700	7,300	9,800	4,700	929
Dept. S_1		940	1,410	1,280	(-4,700)	470
Dept. S_2		560	280	420	140	1,399
Dept. S_1		28	42	56	(-140)	14
Dept. S_2		6	2	4	2	
		9,234	9,034	11,560		
Hourly rate		$\frac{9,234}{3,070}$ = 3	$\frac{9,034}{4,475}$ = 2.101	$\frac{11,560}{2,419}$ = 4.77		

Statement showing total cost of product LEO

Materials cost				50
Labour cost				30
	Prime cost			80
Overheads				
Dept. P_1	—	4 × 3 =	12	
Dept. P_2	—	5 × 2.01 =	10.05	
Dept. P_3	—	3 × 5.02 =	15.06	37.11
			Total cost	117.11

Problem 6 : In a factory there are two service departments *P* and *Q* and three production departments *A, B* and *C*. In April 1990 the departmental expenses were :

A — Rs. 6,50,000
B — Rs. 6,00,000
C — Rs. 5,00,000
P — Rs. 1,20,000
Q — Rs. 1,00,000

The service departments expenses are allotted on a percentage basis as follows :

	Production dept.			*Service dept.*	
	A	*B*	*C*	*P*	*Q*
P	30%	40%	15%	–	15%
Q	40%	30%	25%	5%	–

Prepare a statements showing the distribution of the service departments costs to the production departments under the repeated distribution method.

(*University, of Madras, March 1996 Sri Sathya Sai University, B.Com., March 1993*)

Solution : **Statement showing secondary distribution of overheads**

	Production dept.			*Service dept.*	
	A	*B*	*C*	*P*	*Q*
As per primary Distribution of overheads	6,50,000	6,00,000	5,00,000	1,20,000	1,00,000
Service dept. *P*	36,000	48,000	18,000	(–1,20,000)	18,000
Service dept. *Q*	47,200	35,400	29,500	5,900	(–118,000)
Service dept. *P*	1,770	2,360	880	(–5,900)	890
Service dept. *Q*	350	270	220	50	(–890)
Service dept. *P*	15	20	7	–50	8
Total overheads	7,35,335	6,86,050	5,48,607		

PROBLEMS ON SIMULTANEOUS EQUATION METHOD

Problem 7 : A company has three production departments and two service departments. Distribution summary of overhead is as follows :

Production Departments

A Rs. 13,600
B Rs. 14,700
C Rs. 12,800

Service Departments

X Rs. 9,000

Y Rs. 3,000

The expenses of service departments are charged on a percentage basis which is as follows :

	A	*B*	*C*	*X*	*Y*
X Dept.	40%	30%	20%	–	10%
Y Dept.	30%	30%	20%	20%	–

Apportion the cost of service departments by using the Repeated Distribution method

(*CA, Inter., November 1998*)

Solution : Statement showing reapportionment of service dept. overheads to production departments

	Production Departments			*Service Departments*	
	A	B	C	*P*	*Q*
Total overheads as per Distribution summary	13,600	14,700	12,800	9,000	3,000
Dept. X overhead re-apportioned	3,600	2,700	1,800	–9,000	900
Dept. Y overhead re-apportioned	1,170	1,170	780	780	–3,900
Dept. X overhead re-apportioned	312	234	156	–780	78
Dept. Y overhead re-apportioned	23	23	16	16	–17
Dept. X overhead reapportioned	6	5	3	–16	2
Dept. Y overhead reapportioned	1	1	–	–	–2
	18,712	18,833	15,555		

Problem 8 : (Simultaneous equation method)

A factory is having three production departments A, B and C and two service departments, Boiler-hourse and pump-hourse. The boiler house has to depend upon the pump-room for supply of water and pump room in its turn is dependent on the boiler house for supply of steam power for driving the pump. The expenses incurred by the production departments during the period are A–Rs. 8,00,000, B–Rs. 7,00,000 and C–Rs. 5,00,000. The expenses for boiler-house is Rs. 2,34,000 and the pump-house Rs. 3,00,000.

The expenses of boiler-house and pump-room are apportioned to the production departments on the following basis :

	A	*B*	*C*	*B.H*	*P.R*
Expenses of boiler-house	20%	40%	30%	–	10%
Expenses of pump-room	40%	20%	20%	20%	–

Show dearly as to how the expenses of boiler-house and pump-room would be apportioned to A, B and C department use algesraisal equation

(*University of Madras, B. Com., September 1995*)

Solution : Let x = Total expenses of B.H (Boiler-House)

Let y = Total expenses of P.R (Pump-Room)

$$x = 2{,}34{,}000 + \frac{20}{100}y \quad ....(1)$$

$$y = 3{,}00{,}000 + \frac{10}{100}x \quad ....(2)$$

$$x - 0.2y = 2{,}34{,}000$$

$$-0.1x + y = 3{,}00{,}000 \times 10$$

$$x - 0.2y = 2{,}34{,}000$$

$$-x + 10y = 30{,}00{,}000$$

$$9.8y = 32{,}34{,}000$$

$$y = 3{,}30{,}000$$

Substituting the value of y in 1st equation

$$x - 0.2y = 2{,}34{,}000$$

$$= x - 0.2 \times 3{,}30{,}000 = 2{,}34{,}000$$

$$= x = 3{,}00{,}000$$

Apportionment of Service Dept. Expenses

	A	B	C
Primary overheads	8,00,000	7,00,000	5,00,000
Service Dept. B.H (3,00,000 in the ratio of 20 : 40 : 30)	60,000	1,20,000	90,000
Service Dept. P.R (3,30,000 in the ratio of 40 : 20 : 20)	1,32,000	66,000	66,000
	9,92,000	8,86,000	6,56,000

Problems 9 : You are supplied with the following information and required to work out the production hour rate of absorption of overheads in departments *A, B* and *C* under simultaneous equation method of distributing service departments costs to production department :

Particulars	*Total*	*Production dept*			*Service dept.*	
		A	*B*	*C*	*P*	*Q*
Total overheads	46,000	11,310	13,050	8,040	7,500	6,100
No. of hrs. worked		5,000	4,000	3,000		
Percentage of service rendered by dept. *P*		30%	40%	20%	–	10%
Percentage of service rendered by dept. *Q*		15%	25%	40%	20%	–

(*Sri Sathya Sai University, B. Com., March 1992*)

Solution :

Let *x* be the service dept. *P*

y be the service dept. *Q*

$$x = 7{,}500 + \frac{20}{100}y$$

$$y = 6{,}100 + \frac{10}{100}x$$

or

$$x - 0.2y = 7{,}500 \quad ...(1)$$

$$-0.1x - 1y = 6{,}100 \quad ...(2)$$

or

$$5x - 1y = 37{,}500 \text{ on multiply (1) by 5}$$

$$-0.1x + 1y = 6{,}100$$

$$4.9x = 43{,}600$$

$$x = \frac{43{,}600}{4.9} = 8{,}898$$

Substituting the value of *x* in 1st equation

$$5x - 1y = 37{,}500$$

$$5 \times 8{,}898 - 1y = 37{,}500$$

$$44{,}490 - 1y = 37{,}500$$

$$-1y = -44{,}490 + 37{,}500$$

$$y = 6{,}990$$

Summary of overhead distribution :

	A	*B*	*C*	*P*	*Q*
Primary distribution	11,310	13,050	8,040	7,500	6,100
Service dept. *P*	2,670	3,557	1,780	–8,898	890
Service dept. *Q*	1,049	1,748	2,796	1,397	–6,990
	15,029	18,355	12,616		

Production hour rate = $\frac{15,029}{5,000}$ = 3 ; $\frac{18,355}{4,000}$ = 4.58 ; $\frac{12,616}{3,000}$ = 4.20

Problem 10 : Chandra Bhanu & Co. has 3 production and 2 service departments. Distribution of overheads is done as follows :

Production departments		*Service departments*	
A	Rs. 3000	*X*	Rs. 234
B	Rs. 2000	*Y*	Rs. 300
C	Rs. 1000		

Expenses of service departments are to be allocated on percentage basis as follows :

	A	*B*	*C*	*X*	*Y*
X	20%	40%	30%	–	10%
Y	40%	20%	20%	20%	–

Find out the amount to be distributed among production departments under simultaneous equation.

(*Andhra University, B. Com., May 1992*)

Solution :

$$x = 234 + \frac{20}{100}y$$

$$y = 300 + \frac{10}{100}x$$

$$x = 234 + 0.2y$$

$$y = 300 + 0.1x$$

or $x - 0.2y = 234$ ...(1)

$-0.1x + 1y = 300$ ...(2)

or $5x \times 1y = 1,170$ on multiply equation (1)

$-0.1x + 1y = 300$

$4.9x = 1,470$

$$x = \frac{1,470}{4.9} = 300$$

Substituting the value of x in the first equation

$x - 0.2y = 234$

$-0.2y = x + 234$

$-0.2y = -300 + 234$

$$-y = \frac{66}{0.2} = 330$$

Statement showing secondary distribution of overheads

	A	*B*	*C*	*X*	*Y*
Primary distribution	3,000	2,000	1,000	234	300
Service dept. *X*	60	120	90	–300	30
Service dept. *Y*	132	66	66	66	–330
	3,192	2,186	1,156		

VI. Absorption of Overheads

This is the last step in the accounting procedure of overheads. After all the overheads are reapportioned from the service departments to production departments, it involves charging of production department overheads to the number of units produced in those departments. The process of charging the overheads from cost centre to cost units is known as absorption of overheads. In other words the recovery of overheads by the finished goods from various production departments is known as absorption of overheads. The finished products absorb the factory overhead through overhead absorption rates. The overhead absorption rates are obtained by dividing the overheads to be absorbed by a basis to be decided by the management.

Actual vs. Predetermined Overhead Rates

The absorption of overheads can be based either on actual basis or predetermined basis. Accordingly overhead rates are of two types (1) Actual rate and (2) Predetermined rate.

(1) **Actual rate :** An actual rate is obtained by dividing the actual overheads to be absorbed by the actual base selected. Actual overhead rate can be calculated only historically, *i.e.*, after the overheads are incurred and measured. This rate can be calculated either periodically or annually. Actual overhead rates are not popularly used because they suffer from the following limitations :

(*a*) The cost ascertainment will be delayed as actual overheads are available only at the end of accounting period.

(*b*) It is not possible to prepare tender statement for quotation. Thus prospective orders are lost if actual overhead rates are used.

(*c*) Control cannot be exercised over actual overhead rates.

(*d*) Cost comparison is not facilitated when actual overhead rates are used. This is so because certain overheads like overtime wages, leave and holiday pay, repairs and maintenance are not uniformly spread over the entire accounting year. So overheads rate fluctuates making difficult cost comparison.

(2) **Predetermined overhead rates :** Because of the above limitations suffered by the actual overhead rate, in majority of the cases predetermined overhead rate is used. This rate is calculated in advance of incurrence of overheads. It is calculated by dividing predetermined overheads by a predetermined base. Budgeted overheads and budgeted base could be used to calculate this overhead rate.

Single or Blanket Rate vs. Multiple Rate

When a single overhead rate of absorption is set up for the entire factory it is known as blanket rate. This is calculated by adding up the overheads of all the production departments and dividing by the base which is the total of the quantity or amount. The use of a blanket rate may not give accurate result when the amount of overheads differ from department to department.

When a separate overhead rate is set up for each department for absorption of overheads it is known as multiple rates. This is calculated by dividing departmental overheads by the departmental base. Multiple absorption rates are popularly used because they give accurate results.

Methods of Absorption of Factory Overheads

The following are the various methods of absorption of overheads :

(1) **Percentage on direct material cost :** Under this method the overhead to be absorbed is divided by direct material cost and the quotient is expressed as a percentage. Expressed as a formula,

$$\text{Factory overhead rate} = \frac{\text{Amount of factory overhead}}{\text{Direct material cost}} \times 100$$

This method is suitable under the following situations :

(*a*) Where only one variety of product is manufactured

(*b*) Where the materials used are common for different jobs or process or products

(*c*) Where raw material prices remain stable

(*d*) Where material cost constitutes highest proportion to total cost.

Merits :

(*a*) The method is simple and easy to operate.

(*b*) The method gives satisfactory results where material prices are uniform, quantity and quality of materials used is uniform.

Demerits :

(*a*) Most of the factory overheads are not directly related to direct materials cost. So the method is not logically correct and hence gives misleading result.

(*b*) The method is again based on an illogical relationship, *viz.*, a job requiring costlier material requires more of overheads. This is wrong and instead the reverse is true because a job requiring cheap materials may require more of overheads.

(*c*) This method does not take time factor into account. Most of the overheads are related to time element. A job which requires a longer period to complete may need more of overheads than a job which is completed in a shorter period of time.

(*d*) This method also fails to take into account the jobs performed by skilled and unskilled worker. A job which is done to a large extent by unskilled workers requires more amount of overheads. Similarly this method also fails to distinguish the jobs done by manual labour and machines.

(2) **Percentage on direct labour cost :** Under this method the overheads to be absorbed is divided by direct labour cost and the quotient is expressed in the form of percentage. This is the oldest method of overhead absorption and still it is more popularly used. Expressed in the form of a formula :

$$\text{Overhead absorption rate} = \frac{\text{Overhead to be absorbed}}{\text{Direct wages}} \times 100$$

This method is suitable under the following situations :

(*a*) Where labour cost forms a high proportion to total cost of production.

(*b*) Where the skill of labour, *i.e.*, grade and sex composition does not differ widely.

(*c*) Where the wage rate does not fluctuate widely.

Merits :

(*a*) The method is simple to understand and easy to operate. All the details are available and there is no need to keep separate account for collecting particulars.

(*b*) Wages are directly related to time factor and so does overheads. Hence the method gives satisfactory results.

(*c*) Labour cost fluctuates less frequently compared to materials cost. Thus this method gives stable results.

Demerits :

(*a*) The method is not suitable where a large part of the work is done by machines.

(b) Where piece rate system of wage payment is adopted the method is again unsuitable as it ignores time factor.

(c) Where the work is done by both skilled and unskilled workers the method is again not suitable. As a matter of fact the overheads incurred will be more where work is done by unskilled workers. This fact is ignored by this method.

(3) **Percentage on prime cost :** Under this method the factory overheads to be absorbed is divided by the prime cost and the quotient is expressed in terms of percentage. Expressed as a formula :

$$\text{Overhead absorption rate} = \frac{\text{Overhead to be absorbed}}{\text{Prime cost}} \times 100$$

This method is suitable where both direct material cost and direct labour cost are equally important and overheads are related to both.

Merits :

(a) This method is simple to operate.

(b) Particulars about materials and wages are readily available and there is no need to keep separate account for them.

(c) The method takes into account both direct material cost and direct labour cost and hence gives satisfactory results.

Demerits :

(a) Equal importance is given for both materials and labour, though most of the overheads are closely related to labour cost.

(b) Where material cost is predominant element of cost, the method ignores time factor.

(4) **Labour hour rate method :** Under this method overheads are absorbed on the basis of direct labour hours worked. The overhead rate is obtained by dividing the overheads to be absorbed by the number of direct labour hours. Expressed as a formula :

$$\text{Overhead absorption rate} = \frac{\text{Overhead to be absorbed}}{\text{Direct labour hours}}$$

This method is most suitable where manual labour is engaged in factories.

Merits :

(a) This method recognises the time factor which is also closely related to overheads. Hence the method gives satisfactory result.

(b) This method is not affected by the method of wage payment.

Demerits :

(a) This method involves additional clerical work and separate records are necessary for recording direct labour hours.

(b) This method is not suitable where machines are used predominantly for production purposes.

(5) **Machine hour rate :** It refers to the overheads incurred for running a machine for one hour. By far this is the most scientific method of overhead absorption when compared to all other methods. The ICMA terminology defines machine hour rate as "an actual or predetermined rate of cost of apportionment or overhead absorption, which is calculated by dividing the cost to be apportioned or absorbed by the number of hours for which a machine

or machines are operated or expected to be operated". In simple words, machine hour rate is obtained by dividing the amount of overhead related to a machine by the number of machine hours. Expressed in the form of a formula :

$$\text{Machine hour rate} = \frac{\text{Overheads to be absorbed}}{\text{Machine hours}}$$

This method is most suited where machines are used predominantly for production purpose.

Types of machine hour rates : There are two types of machine hour rate, *viz.*, (*a*) simple or ordinary machine hour rate and (*b*) Composite or comprehensive machine hour rate. A simple or ordinary machine hour rate takes into account only the fixed expenses incurred in operating a machine. The variable cost, mostly the direct wages is not included under operating expenses of the machine for calculating the machine hour rate. A comprehensive machine hour rate includes both fixed and variable cost per hour incurred for operating the machine.

Merits :

(*a*) This is most scientific, accurate and logical method of overhead absorption.
(*b*) It is an ideal method for estimating the quotation price of a job.
(*c*) It helps in knowing the existence and extent of idle time of machines.
(*d*) This method takes into account time factor and hence gives accurate resutls.
(*e*) It helps in comparing the efficiency and cost of operating different machines.
(*f*) It helps management in choosing between manual labour and machines.

Demerits :

(*a*) This method is not suitable where most of the production work is done by manual labour.
(*b*) it involves maintenance of additional records for noting down the number of machine hours operated.

Computation of machine hour rate : The following steps are involved in calculating a machine hour rate :

(*a*) To allocate and apportion the factory overheads to all the production departments.
(*b*) To charge the departmental overheads to machine or a group of machines.
(*c*) Those overheads which can be allocated directly to the machine, such as depreciation, power, repairs and maintenance are to charged, specifically to the machine.
(*d*) Where comprehensive machine hour rate is desired include direct wages along with other expenses incurred for operating the machine.
(*e*) Along with the above, include cost of standby equipment to calculate machine hour rate.
(*f*) Classify the overheads into fixed and variable overheads if possible.
(*g*) Make necessary adjustments for calculating the effective machine hours by deducting cleaning or warming up time.
(*h*) Divide the expenses incurred for operating the machine for a given period by the number of hours for which machines were operated for that period.

(6) **Rate per unit of output :** Under this method the overheads are absorbed on the basis of number of units produced. The overhead absorption rate is obtained by dividing the

overheads to be absorbed by the number of units produced. Expressed as a formula :

$$\text{Overhead absorption rate} = \frac{\text{Overheads to be absorbed}}{\text{No. of units produced}} \times 100$$

This method is suitable where the finished goods are identical in nature.

Merits :

It is the simplest of all the methods.

Demerits :

(*a*) This method is not suitable where different varieties of finished products are manufactured.

(*b*) If historical overhead rate of recovery is adopted it involves considerable delay in computing the overhead rate as one has to wait for the completion of production for the given period.

(7) **Standard rate :** This method is adopted by those industries which adopt standard costing technique. The standard overheads and a standard base is set on the basis of past experience and necessary adjustments are made based on the factors which affect it. The standard overhead divided by a standard base gives a standard rate of overhead absorption. The following formula is applicable.

$$\text{Overhead rate} = \frac{\text{Standard overhead for a period}}{\text{Standard base for the period}}$$

Problem 11 : A manufacturing company has supplied the following particulars relating to the activity of its production department for the month of March 1988 :

Materials used	Rs. 36,000
Direct labour cost	Rs. 30,000
Direct labour hours worked	24,000
Hours of machine operations	20,000
Factory overhead chargeable to the department	Rs. 25,000

On one production order wholly carried out within the department during this period, the relevant data were :

Materials used	Rs. 2,000
Direct labour	Rs. 1,650
Direct labour hours	1,650
Machine hours	1,200

Prepare a comparative statement of cost of this order by using the following three methods of recovery of overheads :

(1) Direct labour hour rate method.

(2) Direct labour cost rate method.

(3) Machine hour rate method *(University of Delhi, B. Com.,(Hons.) 1990)*

Solution :

(1) Direct labour hour rate $= \dfrac{\text{Factory overheads}}{\text{Direct labour hours}}$

$= \dfrac{25,000}{24,000} = \text{Rs. } 1.042 \text{ per hour}$

(2) Direct labour cost rate $= \dfrac{\text{Factory overheads}}{\text{Direct labour cost}} \times 100$

$= \dfrac{25{,}000}{30{,}000} \times 100$ = 83% of direct labour cost

(3) Machine hour rate $= \dfrac{\text{Factory overheads}}{\text{Machine hour}}$

$= \dfrac{25{,}000}{20{,}000}$ = Rs. 1.25 per hr.

Statement showing cost of the order

	(1) *LHR*	(2) *LCR*	(3) *MHR*
Materials	2,000	2,000	2,000
Direct labour	1,650	1,650	1,650
Overheads (*See note* below)	1,719	1,375	1,500
	5,369	5,025	5,150

Note : Overheads under each method is calculated as shown below :

(1) 1,650 × Rs. 1.042 = 1,719

(2) $\frac{5}{6} \times 1{,}650$ = 1,375

(3) 1,260 × 1.25 = 1,500

Problem 12 : Atlas Engineering Ltd. accepts a variety of Jobs which require both manual and machine operations. The budgeted profit and loss account for the period 1996-97 is as follows :

		(in lakh of Rupees)
Sales		75
Cost :		
Direct materials	10	
Direct labour	5	
Prime cost	15	
Production overhead	30	
Production cost	45	
Administrative, selling and distribution overhead	15	
		60
Profit		15

Other budgeted data :

Labour hours for the period	2,500
Machine hours for the period	1,500
No. of Jobs for the period	300

An enquiry has been received recently from a customer and the production department has prepared the following estimate of the prime cost required for the Job

Direct materials	Rs. 2,500
Direct labour	2,000
	4,500

Labour hours required = 80

Machine hours required = 50

You are required to :

(*a*) Calculate by different methods, six overhead absorption rates for absorption of production overhead and comment on the suitability of each.

(*b*) Calculate the production overhead cost of the order based on each of the above rates.

(*c*) Give your recommendation to the company. (*ICWA Inter., December 1997*)

Solution :

(1) Direct labour hour rate $= \dfrac{\text{Overheads to be absorbed}}{\text{Direct labour hours}}$

$$= \frac{3,00,000}{2500} = 120$$

(2) Machine hour rate $= \dfrac{\text{Overheads to be absorbed}}{\text{Machine hours}}$

$$= \frac{3,00,000}{1500} = 200$$

(3) Percentage on direct material cost $= \dfrac{\text{Overheads to be absorbed}}{\text{Direct Materials cost}} \times 100$

$$= \frac{3,00,000}{1,00,000} \times 100 = 300\%$$

(4) Percentage on direct wages cost $= \dfrac{\text{Overheads to be absorbed}}{\text{Direct wages}} \times 100$

$$= \frac{3,00,000}{50,000} \times 100 = 600\%$$

(5) Percentage on prime cost $= \dfrac{\text{Overheads to be absorbed}}{\text{Prime cost}} \times 100$

$$= \frac{3,00,000}{1,50,000} \times 100 = 200\%$$

(6) Production unit $= \dfrac{\text{Overheads to be absorbed}}{\text{No. of jobs for the period}}$

$$= \frac{3,00,000}{300} = \text{Rs. } 10,000$$

Statement showing overheads under different methods

Methods		*Production overhead for the Job*
(1) Direct labour hour rate	80 hrs. × 120	9,600
(2) Machine hour rate	50 hrs. × 200	10,000
(3) Percentage of direct material cost	$\frac{300}{100} \times 2,500$	7,500
(4) Percentage of direct labour cost	$\frac{600}{100} \times 2,000$	12,000
(5) Percentage of prime cost	$\frac{200}{100} \times 4,500$	9,000
(6) Production Unit/Job	1 × 10,000 = 10,000	

Comments :

(1) For labour hour rate and machine hour rate the rates are based on time and hence generally considered equitable as most overheads vary with time.

(2) In case of percentage of Direct Material cost it may be suitable only if all the jobs use the same materials.

(3) If wage rates vary, percentage of direct wages may cause distortion.

(4) Percentage of prime cost is simple but has the disadvantages of percentage of Direct Material cost and percentage of Direct Labour cost.

(5) In case of production unit (Job) method, it is very simple and acceptable if all the jobs are same. If they are different, this method is not appropriate for charging overhead.

Recommendations :

Separate overhead rates based on labour hours and machine hours for absorption of labour related overhead and machine related overhead respectively, is the ideal solution. However, if the degree of mechanisation is very high in the factory, the Management wants a single rate, the machine hour rate may be used for absorption of production overhead.

PROBLEMS ON LABOUR HOUR RATE

Problem 13 : Calculate labour hour rate from the following information for a department.

(*i*) Annual rent of a factory having an area of 10,000 sq. feet Rs. 27,500, this department has 4,000 sq. feet.

(*ii*) Annual rates of the factory Rs. 24,000.

(*iii*) Annual lighting of the factory having 80 light points Rs. 10,000 this department has 60 light points.

(*iv*) Meeting charges of the department Rs. 7,500 per year.

(*v*) Sundry materials issued to the department for one year Rs. 10,400.

(*vi*) One foreman looks after the department who is paid a salary of Rs. 700 per month.

The department has 28 workers. On an average 3 workers will be on leave. It is estimated that the department will run for 2,000 hours per year. (*Bangalore University, B.Com, April 1990*)

Solution : **Statement showing labour hour rate**

		PA (Rs.)
Rent $\frac{4}{10} \times 27,500$		11,000
Rates $\frac{4}{10} \times 24,000$		9,600
Lighting $\frac{6}{8} \times 10,000$		7,500
Meeting charges		7,500
Sundry materials		10,400
Salary of foreman 700 × 12		8,400
	Total overheads	54,400
Labour hour rate		$\frac{54,000}{50,000}$
		Rs. = 1.88

Working Note : Calculation of labour hours

Number of workers in the department	28
Less : No. of workers on leave	3
	25

Departmental working hours = 2,000 × 25 = 50,000 hrs.

PROBLEMS ON MACHINE HOUR RATE

Problem 14 : A machine was purchased on Ist January 1998 for Rs. 5 lakhs. The total cost of all machinery inclusive of the new machine was Rs. 75 lakhs. The following further particulars are available :

Expected life of the machine 10 years

Scrap value at the end of 10 years Rs. 5,000

Repairs and maintenance for the machine during the year Rs. 2,000

Expected number of working hours of the machine per year 4,000 hours

Insurance premium annually for all machines Rs. 4,500

Power consumption for the machine per hour @ 75 paise per unit — 25 units

Area occupied by the machine 100 sq ft.

Rent per month of the department Rs. 800

Lighting charges for 20 points for the whole department out of which three points are for the new machine — Rs. 120 per month

Compute the machine hour rate for the new machine. (*University of Delhi, B Com. (Hons), April 1999*)

Solution : **Computation of machine hour rate**

(1) ***Standing expenses :***		
Insurance	300	
Rent	600	
Lighting	216	
Annual standing expenses	1,116	
Standing expenses per hour	$\frac{\text{Rs. } 1{,}116}{4{,}000 \text{ hrs}}$	0.279
(2) ***Running expenses :***		
Depreciation $\left(\frac{5{,}00{,}000 - 5{,}000}{10 \text{ yrs} \times 4{,}000 \text{ hrs.}}\right)$		12.375
Repairs & Maintenance $\frac{\text{Rs. } 2{,}000}{4{,}000 \text{ hrs.}}$		0.500
Power 25 units @ 0.75		18.750
Machine hour rate		31.904

Working Note :

Insurance premium is calculated as under

$$= \frac{\text{Rs.} 5{,}00{,}000}{75{,}00{,}000} \times 4{,}500 = \text{Rs. } 300$$

$$\text{Rent} = \frac{\text{Rs. } 9{,}600 \times 100 \text{ sq. ft.}}{1{,}600 \text{ sq. ft.}} = \text{Rs. } 600$$

Problem 15 : From the following information, compute machine hour rate for a machine for the month of April 1999 :

	Per annum (*Rs.)*
Rent and Rates	12,000
$\left(\frac{1}{4}\text{th space is occupied by the machine}\right)$	
Machine operator's wages	3,000
(10 operators are engaged in the department out of them four are working on this machine)	
Supervisor's salary	6,000
$\left(\frac{1}{3}\text{rd time is devoted for this machine}\right)$	

Insurance	600
Lubricants and cotton waste	60

The cost of the machine is Rs. 16000 and its scrap value is estimated at Rs. 1,000. From the past experience it has been ascertained that :

(*a*) The working life of the machine is 20,000 hours.
(*b*) The machine will work for 2,000 hours annually
(*c*) The estimated cost of repairs and maintenance is Rs. 1,000 over the life of the machine
(*d*) The machine consumes 4 units per hour, rate of power is 5 paise per unit.

(*Sri Sathya Sai University, B.Com. (Hons), August 2000*)

Solution : **Computation of machine hour rate**

	Per Annum	*Rate per hour*
Standing charges :		
Rent	3,000	1.50
Machine operator's wages	1,200	0.60
Supervisor's salary	2,000	1.00
Insurance	600	0.30
Lubricants & waste	60	0.03
Total standing charges	6,860	3.43
Variable charges :		
Depreciation	—	0.75
Repairs	—	0.05
Power	—	0.20
Machine hour rate		4.43

Problem 16 : (a) Calculate the machine hour rate of a machine with information given below :

Operating data :

Total number of weeks per quarter	=	13
Total number of hours per week	=	48
Stoppage due to maintenance	=	8 hrs. p.m.
Time taken for set-up	=	2 hrs. per week

Cost details :

Cost of machine	=	Rs. 2,00,000
Repairs and Maintenance	=	Rs. 24,000 p.a
Consumable stores	=	Rs. 30,000 p.a
Rent, Rates & taxes	=	Rs. 80,00 per quarter
Operator's wages	=	Rs. 3,000 p.m.
Supervisor's salary	=	Rs. 5,000 p.m.
Cost of power	=	15 units per hour at Rs. 3 per unit

Notes :

(*i*) Life of the machine is 10 years. Depreciation is provided on straight line basis and is treated as variable cost.
(*ii*) Repairs and maintenance and consumable stores are variable costs.
(*iii*) Power is consumed for production runs only and for set-up maintenance. But cost of power is to be borne by the total time excluding maintenance stoppages.
(*iv*) The supervisor is supervising work on 5 identical machines including the one now considered.
(*v*) The company hires out excess capacity in the machine shop for outside jobs. Assuming that hire charges are fixed at variable cost plans 20%, what rate should be quoted by the company?

(*ICWA, Inter, June 1999*)

Solution : **Calculation of machine hours for the quarter**

Total hours in a quarter	13 × 48	=	624
Less : Maintenance stoppage for 3 months	8 × 3	=	24
			600

Less : Set-up hours in a quarter	13 × 2	=	26
Machine hours per quarter			574

Computation of machine hour rate

			Amount per quarter
Variable :			
Repair and Maintenance $\frac{24,000}{4}$			6,000
Consumable stores $\frac{30,000}{4}$			7,500
Depreciation $\frac{2,00,000}{10 \text{ years}} = \frac{20,000}{4}$			5,000
Power 15 units @ Rs. 3 for 574 hours of a quarter			25,830
Total variable cost			44,330
Fixed cost :			
Rent, rates & taxes			8000
Operator's wages @ Rs. 3,000 p.m.			9,000
Supervisor's salary			
$\frac{1}{5}$ × 5,000 = 1,000 p.m. and per quarter			3,000
Total cost per quarter			64,330
Machine hour rate	$\frac{64,330}{600}$	=	107.22
(*b*) Rates to be quoted			
Variable cost per hour	$\frac{44,330}{600}$	=	73.88
Add : 20% profit		=	14.78
			Rs. 88.66

Problem 17 : From the following information, compute machine hour rate :

Cost of the machine	Rs. 44,000
Scrap value	Rs. 4,000
Rent for the workshop	Rs. 25,000 per annum
General lighting for the workshop	Rs. 160 per month
Power consumption 20 units per hour @ Rs. 20 for every 100 units	
Administrative expenses allocated to the machine	Rs. 4,000 per annum
Repairs and maintenance 75% of depreciation	
workshop supervisor's salary	Rs. 3,000 per month
Estimated working time per year	
55 weeks of 40 hours each	
Setting up time which is regarded as productive time 200 hours per year	
Effective life of the machine 10 years	

The machine occupies $\frac{1}{4}$th area of the workshop. The supervisor is expected to devote $\frac{1}{3}$rd of his time in supervising the machine. *(University of Delhi, B.Com. (Pass), April 1998)*

Solution : **Calculation of machine hours**

50 weeks of 40 hours = 2000 hrs

Computation of machine hour rate

	per annum	per hour
Standing charges		
(1) Rent $\frac{25,000}{4}$	6,250	
(2) General lighting $\frac{160 \times 12}{4}$	480	
(3) Administrative expenses	4,000	
(4) Supervisor's salary $\frac{3,000 \times 12}{3}$	12,000	
Total	22,730	
Standing charges per hour		11.37
Machine expenses :		
(1) Depreciation $\frac{44,000 - 4,000}{10 \times 2,000}$		2.00
(2) Repairs & maintenance 75% of depreciation		1.50
(3) Power* $\left(\frac{20 \times 20 \times 1,800}{100 \times 2,000}\right)$		3.60
Machine hour rate		18.47

Note : It is pressumed that the machine does not take the current during setting up time.

Problem 18 : X Ltd. having 15 different types of automatic machines furnishes information as under for 1996-97 :

(1) Overhhead expenses :

Factory rent Rs. 96,000 (Floor area 80,000 sq. ft.). Heat and gas Rs. 45,000 and supervision Rs. 1,20,000.

(2) Wages of the operator are Rs. 48 per day of 8 hours. He attends to one machine when it is under set-up and two machines while they are under operation.

In respect of machine B (one of the above machines). The following particulars are furnished :

(*i*) Cost of the machine Rs. 45,000. Life of machine – 10 years and scrap value at the end of its life Rs. 5,000.

(*ii*) Annual expenses on special equipment attached to the machine are estimated at Rs. 3,000.

(*iii*) Estimated operation time of the machine is 3,600 hours while set-up time is 400 hours per annum.

(*iv*) The machine occupies 5,000 sq. ft. of floor area.

(*v*) Power cost Rs. 2 per hour while machine is in operation.

Find out the comprehensive machine hour rate of machine B. Also find out machine costs to be absorbed in respect of use of machine B on the following two work-orders :

	Work-order 31	*Work-order 32*
Machine set-up time (hrs.)	10	20
Machine operation time (hrs.)	90	180

(*C.A., Inter, May 1997*)

Solution : **Computation of machine hour rate of machine B**

Fixed cost :

Factory rent $\frac{\text{Rs. } 96000}{80000 \text{ sq. ft.}} \times 5{,}000$ sq. ft.	6,000
Heat and gas $\frac{45{,}000}{15 \text{ machines}}$	3,000
supervision $\frac{1{,}20{,}000}{15 \text{ machines}}$	8,000
Depreciation $\frac{45{,}000 - 5{,}000}{10 \text{ years}}$	4,000
Annual expenses on special equipment	3,000
	24,000
Fixed cost per hour	$\frac{24{,}000}{4{,}000 \text{ hrs.}} = 6$

	Set-up rate per hour	*Operation rate per hour*
Fixed cost	6	6
Power	-	2
Wages	6	3
Comprehensive machine hour rate	12	11

Statement of 'B' machine costs to be absorbed on the two work orders

	Work order 31			*Work order 32*		
	Hrs.	*Rate*	*Amount*	*Hrs.*	*Rate*	*Amt.*
Set-up time cost	10	12	120	20	12	240
Operation time cost	90	11	990	180	11	1,980
			1,110			2,220

Problem 19 : A machine costs Rs. 90,000 and is deemed to have a scrap value of 5% at the end of its effective life (19 years). Ordinarily the machine is expected to run for 2,400 hours per annum but it is estimated that 150 hours will be lost for normal repairs and maintenance and further 750 hours will be lost due to staggering. The other details in respect of the machine shop are :

(*a*)	Wages of each of two operators (each operator is in charge of two machines)	Rs. 6,000 P.A
(*b*)	Rent & rates of the shop	Rs. 3000 P.A
(*c*)	General lighting of the shop	Rs. 250 P.M
(d)	Insurance premium for the machine	Rs. 200 P.Q
(*e*)	Cost of repairs & maintenance per machine	Rs. 250 P.M.
(*f*)	Shop supervisor's salary	Rs. 500 P.M
(g)	Power consumption of the machine per hour — 20 units, rate of power per 100 units @ Rs. 10	
(*h*)	Other factory overhead attributed to the shop	Rs. 4,000 P.A

There are four identical machines in the shop. The supervisor is expected to devote $\frac{1}{5}$th of his time for supervising the machine. Compute a comprehensive machine hour rate from the above details.

(Sri Sathya Sai university, B.Com. (Hons) March 1999)

Solution :

Computation of machine hour rate

Fixed charges		*(yearly)*
Rent & rates $\frac{3,000}{4}$		750
General lighting 250×12 = $\frac{3,000}{4}$		750
Insurance premium per machine		800
Shop supervisor's salary $\frac{6,000}{5}$		1,200
Allocation of overheads $\frac{4,000}{4}$		1,000
Total fixed charges		4,500
Fixed oh per hour $\frac{4,500}{1,500}$	=	3.00
Variable charges :		
Wages per operator per hour $\frac{3,000}{1,500}$	=	2.00
Power	=	2.00
Repairs & Maintenance $\frac{250 \times 12}{1,500}$	=	2.00
Depreciation	=	3.00
Machine hour rate		12.00

Working notes :

(1) **Calculation of machine hours**

Annual working hours		2,400
Less : Maintenance & repair hours	150	
Less : Hours lost due to staggering	750	
		900
Annual working hours		1,500

(2) **Calculation of Depreciation**

Cost of Machine	=	90,000
Less Scrap (5%)	=	4,500
		85,000
Life time 19 years		
Yearly depreciation $\frac{85,500}{19}$	=	4,500
Hourly depreciation $\frac{4,500}{1,500}$	=	Rs. 3

Problem 20 : The following particulars relate to a new machine

	Rs.
Purchase price	4,00,000
Installation expenses	1,00,000
Rent per quarter	3,750

General lighting for the total area	1,000 PM
Foreman's salary	30,000 PM
Insurance premium for the machine	3,000 PA
Estimated repairs for the machine	5,000 PA
Consumable stores	4,000 PA
Power-2 units per hour at Rs. 50 per 100 units	

The estimated life of the machine is 10 years and scrap value at the end of 10th year is Rs. 1,00,000. The machine is expected to run 20,000 hours in its life time. The machine occupies 25% of total area. The foreman devotes $\frac{1}{6}$th his time for the machine. Calculated the machine hour rate for the machine.

(University of Delhi, B.Com. (Pass), April 1996)

Solution : **Computation of machine hour rate**

Fixed cost

Rent $3,750 \times 4 \times \frac{1}{4}$	=	3,750
Lighting $1,000 \times 12 \times \frac{1}{4}$	=	3,000
Foreman's salary $30,000 \times \frac{1}{6}$	=	5,000
Insurance	=	3,000
Repairs	=	5,000
Consumable stores	=	4,000
		23,750
Fixed cost per hour $\frac{23,750}{2,000}$	=	11.875
Variable cost :		
Depreciation $\frac{4,00,000+1,00,000-10,000}{20,000}$	=	20.00
Power 2 units @ 50 paise per unit	=	1.00
Machine hour rate		32.875

Problem 21 : Calculate the machine hour rate from the following :

	Rs.
Cost of the machine	8,000
Cost of installation	2,000
Scrap value after 10 years	2,000
Rent for a quarter	300
General lighting per month	20
Salary of supervisor per quarter	100
Insurance premium for a machine P.A	60
Repair charges per year	100
Power 2 units per hour at 5 paise per unit	
Estimated working hours per year	2,000 hours

(University of Madras, B.Com., March 1997)

Solution : **Computation of machine hour rate**

Fixed Costs :

Rent per year 300×4	=	1,200
General lighting 20×12	=	240
Supervisor's salary 100×4	=	400

Insurance premium	=	60
		1,900
Fixed cost per hour = $\frac{1,900}{2,000}$	=	0.95
Variable cost :		
Depreciation	=	0.40
Estimated repairs	=	0.05
Power		
Per hour — 2 units		
For 2,000 hours — 4,000 units @ 0.05 = $\frac{200}{2,000}$	=	0.10
Machine hour rate		1.50

Working note :

$$\text{Depreciation} = \frac{\text{Cost} - \text{Soap}}{\text{Life of Machine}}$$

$$= \frac{8,000 + 2,000 - 2,000}{10 \text{ years}} = \frac{800}{2,000} = 0.40$$

Problem 22 : Calculate machine hour rate from the following :

Life of the machine	10 years
Cost of the machine	Rs. 80,000
Cost of freight and installation	Rs. 20,000
Scrap value after 10 years of its life	Rs. 10,000
Rent, Rates and taxes for the shop (per quarter)	Rs. 3,000
Shop supervisor's salary (per quarter)	Rs. 6,000
Insurance premium for the machine (per annum)	Rs. 600
Estimated repairs and maintenance charges during the life time	Rs. 10,000
Factory lighting per month	Rs. 2,400
Power 5 units per hour at 0.20 per unit	
Estimated working hours per annum 2,000 hours	

The machine occupies $\frac{1}{4}$th of the total area of the factory shop and lighting should be apportioned on this basis. The supervisor is expected to devote $\frac{1}{6}$th of his time for supervising the machine.

(Sri Sathya Sai university, B.Com. (Hons), March 1997)

Solution :

Computation of machine hour rate

(1)	Depreciation :		
	Cost of the machine	80,000	
	Add : Freight and installation cost	20,000	
		1,00,000	
	Less : Scrap value	10,000	
		90,000	
	Per hour $\frac{90,000}{10 \text{ yrs}} \times \frac{1}{2,000}$		= 4.50
(2)	Rent and rates per year 3000 × 4	= $\frac{12,000}{2,000}$ = 6	
	Per hour	$\frac{6}{4}$	= 1.50

(3) Shop supervisor's salary per year

$6,000 \times 4 = \frac{24,000}{2,000}$

Per hour $= \frac{12}{6} = 2.00$

(4) Insurance premium $\frac{600}{2,000} = 0.30$

(5) Repairs and maintènance $\frac{10,000}{10 \times 2,000} = 0.50$

(6) Factory lighting per year $2,400 \times 12 = \frac{28,800}{2,000}$

Per hour $= \frac{14.4}{4} = 3.60$

(7) Power : 5 units @ 0.20 per unit = 1.00

Machine hour rate 13.40

Problem 23 : Calculate the machine hour rate for machine no. 101 from the particulars given below. The department had five machines of similar type and value :

(*a*) Rent of the department – Rs. 4,805 per annum
(*b*) Depreciation on each machine – Rs. 500 per annum
(*c*) Repairs and maintenance of the department – Rs. 1,000 per annum
(*d*) Light charges of the department – Rs. 540 per annum
(*e*) Attendants – two attendant in the department and each paid Rs. 60 per month
(*f*) Supervision – one supervisor in the department who is paid at Rs. 250 per month
(*g*) Cotton waste and lubricants for the departments – Rs. 495 per annum
(*h*) Hire purchase instalment payable for machines – Rs. 1,200 per annum (including Rs. 300 as interest)
(*i*) Each machine consumes 10 units of power per hour at Re. 1 for 15 units.
(*j*) Each machine will work 1,200 hours per annum (*Karnataka University, B. Com., April 1992*)

Solution : **Computation of machine hour rate**

Rent and rates of the dept.	=	4,805 per annum
Repairs and maintenance of the dept.	=	1,000 per annum
Light charges of the dept.	=	540 per annum
Attendants salary 60 × 12 = 720		
For 2 attendants 720 × 2	=	1,440 per annum
Supervisor's salary 250 × 12	=	3,000 per annum
Cotton waste for the department	=	495 per annum
		11,280 per annum

For 1 machine $= \frac{11,280}{5} = 2,256$

For 1 hour $\frac{2,256}{1,200} = \frac{2,256}{1,200} = 1.88$

Depreciation $\frac{500}{1,200} = \frac{500}{1,200} = 0.41$

Power $\frac{1}{15} \times 10$	=	0.66
		2.95

Note : Interest on hire purchase instalment is purely a financial matter and has not been included in calculating machine hour rate.

Problem 24 : From the following data of a textile factory machine room, compute an hourly machine rate, assuming that the machine room will work on 90% capacity throughout the year and that breakdown of 10% is reasonable. There are 3 day's, holiday at Deepawali. 2 days at Holi, and 2 days at Christmas exclusive of Sundays. The factory works 8 hours a day and 4 hours on Saturday. Number of machines (each of the same type) – 40.

Expenses per annum		Rs.
Power		3,120
Light		640
Salaries to foremen		1,200
Lubricating oil		66
Repairs of machine		1,446
Depreciation		785.60
	Total	7,257.60

(University of Kerala, M. Com., May 1992)

Solution : **Computation of machine hour rate**

Lighting	$640 \times \frac{1}{40}$	= 16.00		
Salary of foremen	$1,200 \times \frac{1}{40}$	= 30.00		
Lubricating oil	$66 \times \frac{1}{40}$	= 1.65		
		47.65		
Per hour	$\frac{47.65}{1,814}$		=	0.03
Depreciation	$785 \times \frac{1}{40}$	= 19.64		
Per hour	$\frac{19.64}{1,814}$		=	0.01
Repairs to machine	$1,446 \times \frac{1}{40}$	= 36.15		
Per hour	$\frac{36.15}{1,814}$		=	0.02
Power	$3,120 \times \frac{1}{40}$	= 78		
Per hour	$\frac{78}{1,814}$		=	0.04
		Machine hour rate		0.10

Working Note : Calculation of machine hours

Total number of days in a year		365
Less : Number of holidays exclusive of Sundays		
Deepawali	3 days	
Holi	2 days	
Christmas	2 days	7
		358
Less : Number of Sundays in a year		52
		306
Less : Number of Saturdays which are half working days		52
Number of full working days		254
Half working days		
Number of half working days, *i.e.*, Saturdays		52
Effective working hours of the machine		
Number of working hours during 254 days (254 × 8)		2,032
Add : Number of working hours during 52 Saturdays (52 × 4 hrs.)		208
		2,240
For 90% capacity $\frac{90}{100} \times 2,240$		= 2,016
Less : 10% for breakdown allowance $\frac{10}{100} \times 2,016$		= 202
Effective working hrs. of machine		1,814

Problem 25 : From the following particulars compute a comprehensive machine hour rate :

(*i*) Cost of the machine Rs. 1,00,000. Essimated life 15 years. Residual value : Rs. 10,000

(*ii*) Machine running hours 2,040 hours per machine per annum including idle time of 40 hours due to routine repairs and maintenance and 20 hours due to breakdown of machine.

(*iii*) Power consumption of the machine per hour : 20 units : rate of power per 100 units Rs. 80.

(*iv*) There are two operators in the shop and wages, workmen's compensation, insurance, etc. of an operator who is in charge of two machine is Rs. 12,000 per annum.

(*v*) Rent and taxes of the shop per month : Rs. 4,800 per annum.

(*vi*) Insurance premium for the machine : Rs. 400 per quarter.

(*vii*) General lighting of the shop per month : Rs. 600.

(*viii*) Repairs and maintenance expenses per month : Rs. 400 per machine.

(*ix*) Shop supervisor's salary per month : Rs. 1,500.

(*x*) Other factory overhead allocated to the shop : Rs. 6,000 per annum.

There are four identical machines in the machine shop. The supervisor devotes one-fifth of his time for supervising the machine. (*Calcutta University, B. Com., Hons. 1991*)

Solution : **Computation of machine hour rate**

Depreciation :		
Cost of the machine	1,00,000	
Less : Residual value	10,000	
	90,000	
Estimated life 15 years		
Depreciation	$\frac{90,000}{15} \times \frac{1}{1,980}$ =	3.03

Power	$\frac{80}{100} \times 20$	=	16.00
Operator's wages etc.			
For 2 machines	Rs. 12,000 per annum		
For 1 machine	Rs. 6,000 per annum		
Per hour	$\frac{6,000}{1,980}$	=	3.03
Rent	$4,800 \times \frac{1}{4} \times \frac{1}{1,980}$	=	0.60
Insurance	$400 \times 4 = 1,600 \times \frac{1}{1,980}$	=	0.808
General lighting	$600 \times 12 = \frac{7,200}{4} \times \frac{1}{1,980}$	=	0.919
Repairs & maintenance	$400 \times 12 = \frac{4,800}{1,980}$	=	2.42
Shop supervisor's salary	$\frac{1,500 \times 12 \times 1}{4 \times 1,980} \times \frac{1}{5}$	=	0.45
Other factory overhead	$\frac{6,000}{4} \times \frac{1}{1,980}$	=	0.75
	Machine hour rate		27.98

UNDER-ABSORPTION AND OVER-ABSORPTION OF FACTORY OVERHEADS

As was mentioned earlier the absorption of factory overheads could be based either on the actual rate or predetermined rate. When the actual rates are used the overheads are fully absorbed and no difference will arise between the overheads actually incurred and that absorbed. However when predetermined rates are used, the overheads absorbed may not be equal to overheads incurred. This gives rise to under or over absorption of overheads.

When the overheads absorbed by the finished products are less than the actual overhead incurred, it is known as under absorption of overheads. For example, when overheads absorbed are Rs. 4,500 as against the actual overhead of Rs. 5,000, it is a case of under absorption of overheads. When the overheads absorbed by the finished products are more than the actual overheads it is known as over absorption of overheads. For example, if the overheads absorbed by the finished goods are Rs. 5,500 as against the actual overheads of Rs. 5,000 it is a case of over absorption of overheads.

The following are some of the causes which are responsible for the occurrence of over or under absorption of overheads :

(*a*) Wrong estimation of factory overheads.
(*b*) Change in the method of production which affects actual overheads.
(*c*) Change in the production capacity unexpectedly.
(*d*) Seasonal change in overheads.
(*e*) Change in production volume.

Treatment of Over-absorption and Under-absorption of Factory Overheads in Cost Accounts

The following methods are followed to treat the over and under absorption of overheads :

(*a*) **Use of supplimentary overhead rates :** This method is used when the over or under absorption of overheads are of considerable amount. The over or under absorbed overheads are adjusted to the cost of goods produced. Otherwise this will give rise to misleading picture. The cost of production is revised by making use of supplementary rates of overheads. The supplementary rates is obtained by dividing the amount of over absorption or under absorption of overheads by the actual base selected. There are two supplementary rates *viz.*, positive and negative supplementary rates. In case of under absorption the overhead is adjusted by adding it back through a positive supplementary rate. In case of over-absorption, the over absorbed overhead is deducted through a negative supplementary rate. The effect of this treatment is overheads are absorbed at the actual rate.

(*b*) **Write off to costing profit and loss account :** This method is used when the over or under absorption of overheads are of small amount. According to this method the difference of under or over absorption of overheads is transferred to costing profit and loss at the end of accounting period. In case of under-absorption it is debited, and in case of over-absorption it is credited to costing profit and loss account.

(*c*) **Carry over to next year's overhead account :** Under this method the under absorption or over absorption of overheads of one year is carried forward to the next year in order to determine the overhead absorption rate of the next year. This method is criticised on the ground that the overheads of one year should be absorbed in the same year but not to carry over to the next year as it distorts the cost of production of next year.

Problem 26 : Separate departmental overhead application rates based on direct labour hours are being used by a manufacturing company. At the end of the year, the following information is supplied to you :

	Dept. I	*Dept. II*	*Dept. III*
Overhead absorption rates used	Rs. 4	3	7
Actual overhead incurred	81,900	1,20,960	79,360
Overheads absorbed	72,800	1,00,800	86,800
Direct labour hours – recorded againt :			
Work-in-progress	2,800	4,930	820
Finished goods stock	5,400	3,700	1,210

(*a*) Calculate the revised overhead application rate in rupees per direct labour hour in the light of actual figures for the year supplied to you.

(*b*) Calculate also the total amounts by which the work-in-progress and finished goods stock in each department will have to be increased or decreased in the light of the revision of the overhead application rate :

	Dept. I	*Dept. II*	*Dept. III*
(*a*) Actual overhead	Rs. 81,900	1,20,960	79,360
(*b*) Overhead absorbed	72,800	1,00,800	86,800
(*c*) Over (–) or under (+) absorption (a – b)	+ 9,100	+ 20,160	– 7,440
(*d*) Direct labour hours = $\frac{\text{Overhead absorbed}}{\text{Overhead rate}}$	18,200	33,600	12,400

(*e*) Supplementary rate $c \div d$	+ 0.50	+ 0.60	– 0.60
(*f*) Revised overhead rate	4.50	3.60	6.40
(*g*) Adjustment to work-in-progress :			
Labour hours × supplementary rate	+ 1,400	+ 2,958	– 492
(*h*) Adjustment to finished goods stock :			
Labour hours × supplementary rate	+ 2,800	+ 2,220	+ 726

Problem 27 : The cost accountant of NOVO Chemicals Ltd. determined the overhead recovery rate for the year 1989 (based on direct labour hours) with the following estimates :

Indirect labour	Rs. 1,15,000
Inspection	70,000
Factory supervision	50,000
Depreciation and maintenance	1,25,000
Total factory overhead	3,60,000
Direct labour hours	75,000
Hourly wage rate	Rs. 15

The actual results for the year are as follows :

Indirect labour	Rs. 99,000
Inspection	73,000
Factory supervision	51,000
Depreciation and maintenance	1,15,000
	3,38,000
Direct labour hours	67,600
Hourly wage rate	Rs. 16

Calculate the predetermined overhead recovery rate and find out the amount of over/under absorption if any. (*University of Delhi, B. Com.,(Hons.) 1991*)

Solution :

$$\text{Direct labour hour rate} = \frac{\text{Estimated total factory overheads}}{\text{Direct labour hour}} = \frac{3,60,000}{75,000} = \text{Rs. 4.80 per hour}$$

Overhead recovered = 67,600 × 4.80 = Rs. 3,24,480

Under absorption = Actual total overhead – overheads recovered

= 3,38,000 – 3,24,480

= Rs. 13,520

Problem 28 : The actual total expenditure of a hight engineering factory was Rs. 6,75,912 overheads were recorded at the rate of Rs. 2 per-hour at normal capacity of the factory. Out of 10,000 units produced, only 8,000 units were sold. 500 units were in work-in-progress. Actual hours worked were 2,84,756. Sixty per cent of the difference between the actual and applied overheads was due to fluctuations in material prices and labour rates. There was a fire in the factory during this accounting period and the company lost Rs. 50,000 of which the building accounted for Rs. 30,000 and the balance represented loss of materials stored in the godown. A sum of Rs. 10,000 was paid as wages to workmen during the strike period. The balance amount represented the difference between the actual and applied overheads due to operational efficiency or inefficiency.

Calculate the under/over absorption of production overheads for the period and state the appropriate treatment in cost accounts (Journal entries not required) (*University of Delhi, B. Com.,(Hons.), April 1999*)

Solution :

Actual overhead	6,75,912
Less : Overhead recovered (2,84,756 × Rs. 2)	5,69,512
Under recovered overhead	1,06,400

Division according to reasons :–

Due to price fluctuations	63,840
$1{,}06{,}400 \times \frac{60}{100}$	
Due to labour strike	10,000
Due to loss of materials	20,000
Due to inefficiency (balance)	12,500
Total	10,6,400

Under-absorption due to price fluctuations will be apportioned to total units produced at the supplementary rate calculated as follows :

Supplementary rate = Rs. $\frac{63{,}840}{10{,}000 \text{ units}}$ = Rs. 6.384

Charge to cost of sales = 80,00 units × 6.384 = Rs. 51,072
Charge to finished stock = 1,500 units × 6.384 = Rs. 9,576
Charge to work-in-progress = 500 units × 6.384 = Rs. 3,192
Balance of under-absorbed overhead will be transfered to costing P & C a/c

Problem 29 : ABC Ltd. manufactures a single product and absorbs the production overheads at a predetermined rate of Rs. 10 per machine hour.

At the end of financial year 1998-99, it has been found that actual production overheads incurred were Rs. 6,00,000. It included Rs. 45,000 on account of "written off" obsolete stores and Rs. 30,000 being the wages paid for the strike period under an award.

The production and sales data for the year 1998-99 is as under production :–

Finished goods	20,000 units
Work-in-progress (50% complete in all respects)	8,000 units

Sales :–

Finished goods	18,000 units

The actual Machine Hours Worked during the period were 48,000. It has been found that $\frac{1}{3}$ of the under absorption of production overheads was due to lack of production planning and the rest was attributable to normal increase in costs.

You are required to :

(1) Calculate the amount of under-absorption of production overhead during the year 1998-99

(2) Show the accounting treatment of under-absorption of production overheads

(CA, Inter., November 1999)

Solution : Calculation of under-absorption of production overhead during the year 1998-99

		Rs.
Total production overhead actually incurred during the year 98-99		6,00,000
Less : "Written off" obsolete stores	45,000	
Wages paid for strike period	30,000	
		75,000
Net production overhead actually incurred (A)		5,25,000
Production overhead absorbed by 48,000 machine hours @ Rs. 10 per hour (B)		4,80,000
Amount of under-absorption of production overhead (A – B)		45,000

(*ii*) Accounting Treatment of under absorption of production overheads

It is given in the statement of the question that 20,000 units were completely finished and 8,000 units were 50% complete, one third of the under-absorbed overheads were due to lack of production planning and the rest were attributable to normal increase in costs

(*a*) $33\frac{1}{3}$% of 45,000 = 15,000 of under-absorbed overheads were due to lack of production planning. This being abnormal, should be delited to the profit & loss a/c — 15,000

(*b*) Balance ($66\frac{2}{3}$% of Rs. 45,000) *i.e.*, 30,000 of under absorbed overheads should be distributed over work-in-progress, finished goods and cost of sales by using supplementary rate — 30,000

Total under absorbed overheads — 45,000

Calculation of supplementary absorption rate

$$\text{Rs. } \frac{30,000}{24,000 \text{ units}} = \text{Rs. } 1.25 \text{ per unit}$$

Apportionment of unabsorbed overheads of Rs. 30,000 over, work-in-progress, finished goods and cost of sales

Work-in-Progress (equivalent completed)			
Units $\frac{50}{100} \times 8,000$	= 4,000 × Rs. 1.25	=	5,000
Finished goods (20,000 – 18,000 = 2,000)	= 2,000 × Rs. 1.45	=	2500
Cost of Sales (18,000 units)	= 18,000 × Rs. 1.25	=	22,500
	24,000		30,000

Accounting Treatment :

Work in progress control a/c	Dr.	5,000	
Finished goods control a/c	Dr.	2,500	
Cost of sales a/c	Dr.	22,500	
Profit & Loss a/c	Dr.	15,000	
To overhead control a/c			45,000

Problem 30 : Sweet Dreams Ltd. uses a historical cost system and absorb overheads on the basis of predetermined rate. The following data are available for the year ended 31st March, 1997

Manufacturing overheads :–	
Amount actually spent	1,70,000
Amount absorbed	1,50,000
Cost of goods sold	3,36,000
Stock of finished goods	96,000
Work in progress	48,000

Using two methods of disposal of under-absorbed overheads show the implication on the profits of the company under each method. (*CA, Inter., November 1997*)

Solution :

According to first method, the total unabsorbed overhead amount of Rs. 20,000 will be written off to costing profit & loss a/c. The use of this method will reduce the profits of the concern by Rs. 20,000 for the period.

According to second method, a supplementary rate may be used to adjust the overhead cost of each unit. The under absorbed amount in total money, at the end of accounting period, be apportioned on proportionate basis over cost of goods sold, stock of finished goods and work in progress. This is shown below :

Apportionment of overhead under absorbed

Cost of goods sold	3,36,000	14,000	3,50,000
Stock of finished goods	96,000	4,000	1,00,000
Work in progress	48,000	2,000	50,000
	4,80,000	20,000	5,00,000

Working Note :

under-absorbed oh to be absorbed by cost of goods sold $= \dfrac{3,36,000}{4,80,000} \times 20,000 = 14,000$

under-absorbed oh to be absorbed by stock of finished goods $= \dfrac{96,000}{4,80,000} \times 20,000 = 4,000$

under-absorbed oh to be absorbed by work in progress $= \dfrac{48,000}{4,80,000} \times 20,000 = 2,000$

Problem 31 : A factory has three production departments the policy of the factory is to recover the production overheads of the entire factory by adopting a single blanket rate based on the percentage of total factory overheads to total factory wages. The relevant data for a month are given below :

Department	*Direct Materials Rs.*	*Direct wages Rs.*	*Factory overheads Rs.*	*Direct Labour Hour*	*Machine Hours*
Budget :–					
Machining	6,50,000	80,000	3,60,000	20,000	80,000
Assembly	1,70,000	3,50,000	1,40,000	1,00,000	10,000
Packing	1,00,000	70,000	1,25,000	50,000	–
Actuals :–					
Machining	7,80,000	96,000	3,90,000	24,000	96,000
Assembly	1,36,000	2,70,000	84,000	90,000	11,000
Packing	1,20,000	90,000	1,35,000	60,000	–

The details of one of the representative jobs produced during the month are as under Job No. CW 7083.

Department	*Direct Materials Rs.*	*Direct wages Rs.*	*Direct Labour Hours*	*Machine Hours*
Machining	1,200	240	60	180
Assembly	600	360	120	30
Packing	300	60	40	–

The factory adds 30% on the factory cost to cover administration and selling overheads and profit required :–

(1) Calculate the overhead absorption rate as per the current policy of the company and determine the selling price of the job No. CW 7,083

(2) Suggest any suitable alternative mathods of absorption of the factory overheads and calculate the overhead recovery rates based on the methods so recommended by you

(3) Determine the selling price of Job CW 7,083 based on the overhead application rates calculated in (2) above :

(4) Calculate the department wise and total under or over recovery of overheads based on the company's current policy and the methods recommended by you. *(CA, Inter., November 1994)*

Solution : **Calculation of overhead absorption rate (as per the current policy of the company)**

Department	*Budgeted Factory overheads Rs.*	*Budgeted Direct wages Rs.*
Machinery	3,60,000	80,000
Assembly	1,40,000	3,50,000
Packing	1,25,000	70,000
	6,25,000	5,00,000

$$\text{Overhead Absorption Rate} = \frac{\text{Budgeted factory oh}}{\text{Budgeted Direct Wages}} \times 100$$

$$= \frac{6,25,000}{5,00,000} \times 100 = 125\% \text{ of Direct Wages}$$

Selling price of Job No. CW – 7083

Direct Materials (1,200 + 600 + 300)	2,100
Direct Wages (240 + 360 + 60)	660
Overheads $\frac{125}{100} \times 660$	825
Factory cost	3,585
Profit $\frac{30}{100} \times 3{,}585$	1,075.50
Selling price	4,660.50

***(ii)* Methods available for absorbing factory overheads and their overhead recovery rates in different departments :–**

(1) Machining Department :–

$$\text{Machine Hour Rate} = \frac{\text{Budgeted Factory overheads}}{\text{Budgeted Machine Hours}}$$

$$= \frac{\text{Rs. } 3,60,000}{80,000 \text{ hrs.}} = \text{Rs. } 4.50 \text{ per hr.}$$

(2) Assembly Department :–

$$\text{Direct Labour Hour Rate} = \frac{\text{Budgeted factory overheads}}{\text{Budgeted direct labour hours}}$$

$$= \frac{1,40,000}{1,00,000} = \text{Rs. } 1.40 \text{ per hour}$$

(3) Packing Department :–

$$\text{Direct labour hour rate} = \frac{\text{Budgeted factory overheads}}{\text{Direct labour hours}}$$

$$= \frac{1,25,000}{50,000} = \text{Rs. } 2.50 \text{ per hour}$$

Selling price of Job CW – 7083

(Based on overhead application rates calculated in (*ii*) above)

Direct Materials	2,100
Direct Wages	660
Overheads (See working note)	1078
Factory cost	3,838
Profit $\frac{30}{100} \times 3838$	1,151.40
Selling price	4,989.40

Working Note :

Calculation of overheads

Machining Dept.	180 hrs. × 4.50	=	810
Assembly Dept.	120 hrs. × 1.40	=	168
Packing	40 hrs. × 2.50	=	100
	Total		1,078

(*iii*) Department wise statement of total under or over recovery of overheads

(*a*) Under current policy :–

	Machine Dept. *Rs.*	*Assembly Dept.* *Rs.*	*Packing Dept.* *Rs.*	*Total*
Actual Direct Wages	96,000	2,70,000	90,000	
Overheads recovered e 125% of Direct Wages (A)	1,20,000	3,37,500	1,12,500	5,70,000
Actual overheads (B)	3,90,000	84,000	1,35,000	6,09,000
(under)/over recovery of overheads	(2,70,000)	2,53,500	(22,500)	(39,000)

(*b*) As per method suggested :

	Basis of overhead recovery			
	Machine Hours	*Direct labour Hours*	*Direct labour Hours*	*Total*
Hours Worked	96,000	90,000	60,000	
Rate per hr.	4.50	1.40	2.50	
Overhead recovered (A)	4,32,000	1,26,000	1,50,000	7,08,000
Actual overheads (B)	3,90,000	84,000	1,35,000	6,09,000
(under)/over recovery (A – B)	42,000	42,000	15,000	99,000

CAPACITY COST

The capacity of a factory is its ability to produce with the present resources and facilities which it commands. Plant capacity may be expressed in terms of physical unit of products, direct labour hour, machine hour, or value of production. The capacity of a plant is closely related to overheads. While discussing about the various methods of absorption of overheads, different bases such as direct labour hours, machine hours, number of units produced, etc. were used for the sake of absorption of overheads. Computation of overheads rates based on actual basis, *i.e.*, capacity, is quite easy because the actual capacity is readily available. But a problem would arise while computing the predetermined rate, since the determination of the most suitable level of activity is somewhat difficult. The overhead recovery rates will vary if various levels of activities like maximum capacity, practical capacity, normal capacity, etc. are used as the basis. This has given rise to the study of various types of plant capacities adopted in factories.

Types of Capacities

(1) **Maximum or theoretical capacity :** If the plant or department works without interruption and without any loss of operation it is known as maximum capacity. The maximum capacity cannot be achieved as the capacity is lost owing to normal operating interruptions such as time lost during repairs, breakdowns, set up time, labour absenteeism,

etc. which are inevitable in factories and hence deducted from maximum capacity. Because maximum capacity cannot be utilised in full, it is also known as theorertical capacity.

(2) **Practical or operating capacity :** If the capacity is lost due to operating interruptions like time lost for repairs, supply of materials, etc. is deducted from the maximum capacity, the balance of capacity is known as practical capacity. Practical capacity will become the maximum capacity of the plant to manufacture the goods and services for all practical purposes, as in practice it is impossible to operate maximum capacity of the plant.

(3) **Capacity to make and sell or capacity based on expected sales :** It is the capacity which is installed when there is lack of demand and it is not possible to sell the entire quantity produced in a factory. In other words it represents the capacity to meet the demand or sales.

(4) **Actual capacity :** The capacity that is achieved during a given period of time is known as actual capacity.

(5) **Idle capacity :** The excess of practical capacity over the actual capacity achieved is known as idle capacity. It represents the capacity which remains unutilised on account of lack of demand, scarcity of materials, or labour or other factors of production. The cost arising out of idle capacity is treated as factory overheads.

(6) **Normal capacity :** It is somewhat difficult to define normal capacity, as what is 'normal' at one time may not to be true at other time. Two views are expressed to indicate normal capacity. According to one view, the average of the sales level expectancy for a period should be treated as normal capacity. The period so selected for this purpose should cover business cycle and seasonal fluctuations. According to a second view, the capacity which would be worked if there is no lack of orders should be treated as normal capacity. In other words, it refers to capacity available for utilising during a period.

Problem 32 : A manufacturing unit produces electronic circuits at the rate of 6 pieces an hour. The unit works in a single shift of 8 hours during a six-day week and remains closed for 18 days in a year, on account of holidays. Average idle hours per month is 20 for cleaning and maintenance of equipments. Against an average annual output of 12,000 pieces during last 10 years, the actual output achieved during the year was 10,800 pieces. The fixed overheads for the year amounted to Rs. 5,40,000.

You are required to calculate the idle capacity on the assumption that overhead recovery rates are based on maximum capacity, practical capacity, normal capacity and actual capacity utilisation respectively.

(*ICWA, Inter., December 1993*)

Solution : **Ascertainment of various capacities in terms of hours**

(1) Maximum capacity = Total days during the year on single shift of 8 hours
= 365 × 8 = 2,920 hours

(2) Practical capacity = Maximum capacity – Idle time due to various reasons

Maximum capacity			2920 Hrs.
Less : Idle capacity due to :–			
Sundays 52 × 8	=	416 hours	
Holidays 18 × 8	=	144 hrs.	
Maintenance 20 × 12	=	240 hrs	
			800 hrs.
Practical capacity			2120 hrs.

(3) Normal capacity $= \dfrac{\text{Normal sales expected}}{\text{Rate of production}}$

$= \dfrac{12{,}000 \text{ pieces}}{6 \text{ pieces per hr.}} = 2{,}000 \text{ Hrs.}$

(4) Actual capacity $= \dfrac{\text{Actual output}}{\text{Rate of production}}$

$= \dfrac{10{,}800 \text{ pieces}}{8 \text{ pieces per hr.}} = 1{,}800 \text{ hrs.}$

Statement showing idle capacity and machine hour rate

Basis	*Base capacity (hrs.)*	*Capacity utilised (hrs.)*	*Idle capacity*	*Machine hour rate* $= \dfrac{\text{Overheads}}{\text{Base capacity (hrs)}}$
Maximum capacity	2,920	1,800	1,120	184.93
Practical capacity	2,120	1,800	320	254.72
Normal capacity	2,000	1,800	200	270.00
Actual capacity	1,800	1,800	–	300.00

Statement showing Idle capacity cost

Base capacity	*Overhead absorption rate*	*Applied oh.*		*Idle capacity cost*	
		Hrs.	*Amt. (Rs.)*	*Hrs.*	*Amt. (Rs.)*
Maximum	184.93	1,800	3,32,874	1,120	2,07,126
Practical	254.72	1,800	4,58,496	320	81,504
Normal	270.00	1,800	4,86,000	200	54,000
Actual	300.00	1,800	5,40,000	–	–

QUESTIONS

I. Classify the Following Costs into Prime Cost and Overheads. In Case of Overheads Classify by Function.

1. Salary of the Accountant.
2. Temporary labour employed to increase production in order to meet unusual demand of product 'C'.
3. Uniforms of sanitary workers.
4. Gatekeeper's salary.
5. Dividends received on investments.
6. Freight on purchase of raw materials.
7. Remuneration for legal advise.
8. Consultation fee of advertisement designs.
9. Rent of godown for storing finshed goods.
10. Rent of godown for storing raw materials.
11. Salary paid to the wife of the managing director. She is designated as whole time director but does not come to the factory at all.
12. Loss due to accidental falling of the roof of a section of the factory.
13. Primary packing material.

14. Secondary packing with the name of the company.
15. Packing of boxes of finished product in wooden cases for transportation.
16. Income for sale of bags in which raw materials were procured.
17. Depreciation of patterns and dyes.
18. Bad debts.
19. Cost of stolen materials.
20. Commission paid to salesman as a percentage of sales price.
21. Expenses incurred for repairs and maintenance of water supply lines, sewage pipes, etc.
22. Royalties paid on the basis of sales.
23. Amount paid to lawyer for appearing before a labour tribunal.
24. Allowance made to custoumers for late deliveries of goods.
25. Carriage inwards.

[***Answer :*** Prime cost—2, 6, 13, 16, 25; Factory overheads—3, 4, 10, 17, 21; Administrative overheads—1, 7, 23; Selling overheads—8, 16, 18, 20, 22; Distribution Overheads—9, 15; Costing P & L a/c—5, 11, 12, 19, 24]

II. Classify the Following costs into Fixed, Semi-Variable and Variable

(*a*) Salary of H.D., (*b*) Salary of foreman, (*c*) Raw materials, (*d*) Wages of permanent workers, (*e*) Commission to salesman as a percentage of sales. (*f*) Depreciation on plant (*g*) Rent of factory, (*h*) Power consumption in the production process, (*i*) Canteen expenses, (*f*) Salary of storekeeper.

[***Answer :*** (*a*), (*b*), (*d*), (*g*), (*i*), (*f*); Semi-variable—(*e*), (*f*), (*h*); Variable—(*c*)]

III. Mark *T* of *F* in the Space Provided

1. The actual overhead incurred in a month is the amount of overhead that is usually assigned to work-in-process and the production of the month. *T/F*
2. Manufacturing overhead consists of a rather homogeneous group of services that aid in the manufacture of a product. *T/F*
3. Factory overhead is said to to be overabsorbed when actual costs are greater than the amount assigned to production. *T/F*
4. The amount of manufacturing overhead assigned to the production of a given month may be more or less than the amount to overhead costs incurred in that same month. *T/F*
5. Initially, overhead costs should be classified according to the function fulfilled by their incurrence. *T/F*
6. A cost accounting system may contain many sub-groups of accounts for overhead each of which contains an account with the same title. *T/F*
7. Generally, all indirect manufacturing overheads will the allocated to the production departments after being first accumulated in service departments. *T/F*
8. Any basis of allocating overhead costs to producing departments in arbitrary irrespective of its apparent logic. *T/F*
9. A factory may operate at a level greater then practical capacity. *T/F*
10. An idle capacity loss cannot be isolated if an overhead rate is set using expected activity. *T/F*
11. The overhead rate can be based on practical capacity even through the company fully expects to operate at a lower level. *T/F*
12. The machine hour rate is appropriate where direct labour costs are relatively low and machine costs are relatively high. *T/F*
13. The historical (actual) overhead rate is generally preferred over the predetermined overhead rate because it is precise and the predetermind overhead rate is only an estimate. *T/F*
14. If activity fluctuates widely during a year due to seasonal variations, the actual overhead rate will provide more constant unit costs from month to month than will a predetermined rate. *T/F*
15. Allocation of overhead costs to producing department is necessary to identify operating inefficiencies in service department. *T/F*
16. The actual overhead incurred in a month is the amount of overhead that is usually assigned to work-in-process and the production of the month. *T/F*
17. It is commonly accepted theory that a part of the overhead costs incurred in a period should be attached to every unit of product manufactured during that period. *T/F*

18. Factory overhead is said to be overabsorbed when actual costs are greater than the amount assinged or applied to production T/F

[*Answer* : 4, 6, 8, 9, 11, 12, 17; False Rest of the statements are false]

IV. Choose the Correct Answer from the Following :

1. The allotment of whole items of cost to centre or cost unit is called
   (*a*) Cost apportionment (c) Cost allocation
   (b) Cost reapportionment (d) Cost absorption
2. Predetermined overhead is calculated as follows :
   (*a*) $\frac{\text{Budgeted overhead}}{\text{Budgeted base}}$ (*b*) $\frac{\text{Acual overhead}}{\text{Budgeted base}}$
   (*c*) $\frac{\text{Acual overhead}}{\text{Standard base}}$ (*d*) $\frac{\text{Standard overhead}}{\text{Standard base}}$
3. Information regarding depreciation is obtained from
   (*a*) Stores requisition (*c*) Invoice
   (*b*) Cash book (*d*) Plant register
4. Normal capacity of a plant is
   (*a*) The maximum productive capability
   (*b*) Maximum capacity less inevitable interruption
   (*c*) Actual volume of production overhead
   (*d*) Long term average capacity based on sales expectancy
5. Idle capacity of plant refers to the service between
   (*a*) Maximum capacity and practical capacity
   (*b*) Practical capacity and normal capacity
   (*c*) Practical capacity and capacity based on sales expectancy
   (*d*) Maximum capacity and actual capacity
6. Maximum possible productive capacity of a plant when no operating time is lost is its
   (*a*) Practical capacity (*c*) Theoretical eapacity
   (*b*) Normal capacity (*d*) Capacity based on salse expectancy
7. Factory overheads include all of the following except
   (*a*) Taxes on factory building (*c*) Deperciation on delivery equipment
   (*b*) Small tool expenses (*d*) Salary of plant manager
8. The level of capacity or activity which when used in setting overhead reates would yield the lowest average unit product costs is most likely to be
   (*a*) Practical capacity (*c*) Expected capacity
   (*b*) Normal capacity (*d*) Actual capacity
9. Departmental overhead rates are used to
   (*a*) Allocate service department costs to production departments
   (*b*) Make sure that more overhead is applied to production
   (c) Assign overhead to production whenever a factory overhead applied account is used
   (*d*) Secure an assignment of overhead to production that reflects the benefits a product receives from a department better than does a single plant wide overhead rate
10. When fixed and variable overhead rates are used
    (*a*) Both rates should be based on actual activity
    (*b*) Both rates should be based upon expected activity
    (*c*) The variable rate should be based upon expected activity, while several alternative bases may be used of the fixed rate
    (*d*) Overhead will probably be rather fully absorbed when both rates are based upon practical capacity

[*Answer* : 1-(*c*), 2-(*a*), 3-(*d*), 4-(*d*), 5-(*c*), 6-(*c*), 7-(*c*), 8-(*a*), 9-(*d*), 10-(*c*)]

V. Match the Following :

A	*B*
1. Canteen expenses	(*a*) Sales
2. Depreciation of plants	(*b*) Hours used

3. Electric power
4. Rent
5. Electric light

(c) Light points
(d) Weight
(e) Asset value
(f) Horse power
(g) Floor area
(h) Number of employees

[***Answer :*** 1-(b), 2-(e), 3-(f), 4-(g), 5-(c)]

VI. Simple Questions

1. Define overheads.
2. Distinguish between indirect expenses and overheads.
3. Give two tests for identifying an item of expenditure as overheads.
4. Distinguish between standing order number and cost accounting number.
5. What do you mean by codification of overheads?
6. What do you mean by collection of overheads?
7. What do you mean by classification of overheads?
8. Mention any four bases of classification of overheads.
9. Define allocation of overheads.
10. Define apportionment of overheads.
11. Distinguish between allocation and apportionment of overheads.
12. List out the important steps involved in the accounting procedure of overheads.
13. What do you mean by departmentalisation of overheads?
14. What do you mean by reapportionment of overheads?
15. Distinguish between primary and secondary distribution of overheads.
16. Define absorption of overheads.
17. Mention the different methods of overhead absorption.
18. What do you mean by percentage on direct material cost method of overhead absorption?
19. What do you mean by percentage on direct labour cost method of overheads absorption?
20. What do you mean by percentage on prime cost method of overheads absorption?
21. What do you mean by direct labour hour rate method of overheads absorption?
22. What do you mean by machine hour rate?
23. Distinguish between direct labour hour rate and machine hour rate.
24. Distinguish between actual and predetermined rate of overhead recovery.
25. What do you mean by over absorption of overheads?
26. What do you mean by under absorption of overheads?
27. Distinguish between over and under absorption of overheads.
28. What do you mean by normal capacity?
29. What do you mean by practical capacity?
30. What do you mean by maximum capacity?

VII. Short and Long Answer Questions

1. State the need for pre-determined overhead rate in fa factory. *(Calcutta University, B.Com., (Hons.) 1991)*
2. What is meant by absorption of overhead ? Explain briefly the different methods of absorption of overheads. *(University of Delhi, B.Com., 1989)*
3. Explain how you will deal with under or over absorption of overheads in cost accounts. *(University, of Delhi B.Com., (Hons.) 1989)*
4. Explain the different mathods of apportionment of service departments costs over production department. *(University, of Delhi B.Com., (Hons.) 1989)*
5. Briefly explain diefferent methods of absorption of overheads. *(Andhra University, B.Com., May 1992)*
6. Enumerate the different methods of absorption of overhead. *(Kakatiya University, B.Com., November 1991)*
7. What is meant by machine hour rate? Explain as to how it is ascertained using imaginary figures. *(Kakatiya University, B.Com., October 1990)*

8. Explain different methods of re-apportionment of service department costs.
(*Nagarjuna University, B.Com., April 1992*)
9. How do you treat the follwing in cost accounts (*i*) Bad debts, (*ii*) Expenses of costing department, (*iii*) Royalties, (*iv*) Packing materials, (*v*) Income tax. (*Osmania University, B.Com., April 1990*)
10. How do you treat under absorption and overabsorption of overhead in costing.
(*Osmania University, B.Com., April 1990*)
11. State the different methods of absorption of factory overhead.(*Osmania University, B.Com., April 1990*)
12. Distinguish between "Allocation" and "Absorption." (*Calicut University, M.Com., April 1992*)
13. Define overheads and state the problems connected with overhead accounting. Mention different methods of classification of overheads. (*Kakatiya University, M.Com., August 1991*)

EXERCISES

Exercise 1

Mention the basis of apportioning the following overheads :

(1) Fire insurance, (2) Delivery expenses, (3) Purchasing department expenses, (4) General administration expenses, (5) Advertising, (6) Sales assistants' salaries, (7) Personnel department expenses, (8) Sales commission, (9) Time office expenses, (10) Interval transport.

[*Answer :* (1) Asset value, (2) Weight of goods, (3) Value of materials, (4) Cost of sales, (5) Actual, (6) Actual, (7) Number of employees in each department, (8) Actual, (9) Number of employees, (10) Value of material handled]

Exercise 2 (Reapportionment):

The following particulars have been collected for the three months ending 31st December 1993. You are required to prepare an overhead distribution summary.

	Production Dept.			*Service Dept.*	
	A	B	C	D	E
Direct Wages (Rs.)	2,000	3,000	4,000	1000	2000
Direct Materials (Rs.)	1,000	2,000	2,000	1500	1500
Staff (Nos)	100	150	150	50	50
Electricity (kwh)	4,000	3,000	2,000	1000	1000
Light Points (Nos)	10	16	4	6	4
Asset Value (Rs.)	60,000	40,000	30,000	10,000	10,000
Area Occupied (SqFt)	150	250	50	50	50

The expenses for the period were :

Motive power	550
Lighting	100
Stores overhead	400
Amenities to staff	1,500
Depreciation	15,000
Repairs	3,000
General overhead	6,000
Rent	275

Apportion the cost of service department E on the basis of direct wages and that of department D in the ratio of 5:3:2 to production departments (*Manonmaniom Sudranar University, B.Com., November 1994*)

[**Answer :** Dept. A Rs. 12,442, Dept. B 10523, Dept. C Rs. 9860]

Exercise 3 (Apportionment of overhead)

A company has four departments out of which X, Y and Z are production departments and S is a service department. The following are the costs for a period of 3 months relating to these departments.

	Rs.
Rent	1000
Repairs	600
Depreciation	450
Light	100

Supervision	1500
Insurance	500
Employee's Insurance paid by Employer	150
Power	900

The following data are also available for the four departments.

	Dept. X	*Dept. Y*	*Dept. Z*	*Dept. S*
Area SqFt	75	55	45	25
No. of Workers	12	8	6	4
Total Wages	Rs. 4000	Rs. 3000	Rs. 2000	Rs. 1000
Value of plant	Rs. 12000	9000	6000	3000
Value of stock	Rs. 7500	4500	3000	–

Make the apportionment of the costs to the various departments on the most equitable method.

(*Mahatma Gandhi University, B.Com., April 1997*)

[**Answer :** Apportioned overhead Dept. X, Rs. 2102, Dept. Y, Rs. 1482, Dept. Z, Rs. 1067 and Dept. S, 547]

Exercise-4 (Repeated Distribution Method)

A factory has three production departments A, B and C and two service departments X and Y. The budgeted expenditure for the month of March 1999 are given below :

	Rs.
Stores overhead	2500
Indirect Wages	20,000
Insurance	7000
Rent	10500
Power	14000
Lighting	5000
Depreciation	1,05,000
Other indirect expenses	40,000
	204000

The other details are :

	Total	A	B	C	X	Y
Direct Wages (Rs.)	2,00,000	75,000	40,000	60,000	10,000	15,000
Floor Area (Sq Mts)	2100	400	500	600	300	300
Value of Machines (Rs.)	7,00,000	2,00,000	2,50,000	2,00,000	30,000	20,000
Horse Power	140	40	50	40	5	5
Direct Materials (Rs.)	50,000	10,000	20,000	10,000	5,000	5,000
No of light points	25	8	7	5	3	2

Service department overheads are apportioned on the following basis.

	A	B	C	X	Y
Service Dept. X	50	30	10	–	10
Service Dept. Y	30	40	20	10	–

Assuming that overheads are recovered as a percentage on direct wages. Calculate the overhead recovery rates

(*Bangalore University, B.Com., November 1999*)

[**Answer :** Dept. A – 95.64%, B – 75.42%, and C – 103.50%]

Exercise-5

A company has three production departments A, B and C and two service departments X and Y. The following data are extracted from the records of the company for a particular given period.

(i)	Rent and rates	25,000
(ii)	General lighting	3,000
(iii)	Indirect Wages	7,500
(iv)	Power	7,500
(v)	Depreciation on machinery	50,000
(vi)	Sundries	50,000

Additional data departmentwise

	Total	A	B	C	X	Y
Direct Wages (Rs.)	50,000	15,000	10,000	15,000	7,500	2,500
Horse Power of machines used	150	60	30	50	10	–
Cost of Machinery	12,50,000	3,00,000	4,00,000	5,00,000	25,000	25,000
Production Hrs Worked	–	6,226	4,028	4,066	–	–
Floor space used (SqFt)	10,000	2,000	2,500	3,000	2,000	500
Lighting points	60	10	15	20	10	5

Service departments expenses allocation :

	A	B	C	X	Y
X	20%	30%	40%	–	10%
Y	40%	20%	30%	10%	–

You are required to :

(a) Compute the overhead rate of production departments using the repeated distribution method; and

(b) Hence determine the total cost of a product whose direct material cost and direct labour cost are respectively Rs. 250 and Rs. 150 and which would consume 4 hours, 5 hours, and 3 hours in departments A, B and C respectively.

(*ICWA Inter, June 1997*)

[Answer : Production cost Rs. 531.25]

Exercise-6 (Simultaneous Equation Method)

A company has three production departments and two service departments and for a period, the departmental distribution summary has the following totals:

A – Rs. 1,600; B – Rs. 1,400; C – Rs. 1,000 4000

P – Rs. 702; Q – Rs. 900 1602

5602

The expenses of service departments is charged as a percentage as follows :

	A	B	C	P	Q
Service Dept. P	20%	40%	30%	–	10%
Service Dept. Q	40%	20%	20%	20%	–

Prepare a statement showing the apportionment of two service department expenses to production departments by simultaneous equation method. (*Bharathidason University, B.Com., April 1997*)

[Answer : Dept. A – Rs. 2176
Dept. B – Rs. 1958
Dept. C – Rs. 1468]

Exercise-7 (Repeated and Simultaneous Equation Methods)

The following particulars relate to a manufacturing company which has three production departments A, B and C and two service departments X and Y.

	A Rs.	B Rs.	C Rs.	X Rs.	Y Rs.
Total departmental overheads as per primary distribution	6300	7400	2800	4500	2000

The company decided to charge the service department cost on the basis of the following percentages.

	Production Depts.			*Service Depts.*	
	A	B	C	X	Y
X	40%	30%	20%	–	10%
Y	30%	30%	20%	20%	–

Find out the total overheads of production departments charging service department cost to production departments on :

(i) Repeated distribution method

(ii) Simultaneous equation method.

(*Bangalore University, B.Com., April 1998*)

[Answer : Dept. A – Rs. 9050; Dept. B – Rs. 9650; Dept. C – 4300]

Exercise-8 (Labour Hour Rate)

Calculate direct labour hour rate from the following :

Total number of workers	100
Working days in a year	300
Number of hours per day worked	8
Idle time	5%
Factory overhead	Rs. 11,400
Gift to workers	Rs. 1,000

(*Osmania University, B.Com., March 1996*)

[Answer : Rs. 0.05]

Exercise-9 (Different Methods of Absorption of Overheads)

From the budgeted figures of a company :

(i) Prepare normal overhead application rate using

(a) Direct labour hour method

(b) Direct labour cost method

(c) Machine hour rate method

Budgeted figures :

Factory overhead for the year	Rs. 58,000
Direct labour hours	1,34,600
Direct labour cost	97,500
Machine Hours	50,500

(ii) Prepare a statement of cost showing the result of application of each of the above rates to job No. 101 from the data given below :

Cost of materials consumed	Rs. 420
Direct Wages	450
Direct labour hours	300
Machine Hours	200

(*Bharathidason University, M.Com., Nov. 1996*)

[Answer : Direct labour hour rate Re. 0.43

Direct labour cost rate 59%

Machine hour rate Re. 1.15]

Factory cost (a) Rs. 1100 (b) Rs. 1138 (c) Rs. 999.

Exercise-10 (Machine Hour Rate)

The following particulars relate to a processing machine :

(a) Cost of machine Rs. 10,000

(b) Estimated life 10 years

(c) Scrap value Rs. 1000

(d) Yearly working time 50 weeks of 44 hours each

(e) Machine maintenance 200 hours p.a

(f) Setting up time estimated at 5% of total productive time and is regarded as productive time.

(g) Electricity is 16 units per hour at 10 paise per unit.

(h) Chemical required Rs. 20 per week.

(i) Maintenance cost per year Rs. 1200

(j) Two attendants control the operations of machine together with 6 others. Their combined weekly wages are Rs. 140.

(k) Departmental overhead allocated to this machine per annum Rs. 2000.

Calculate Machine Hour Rate

(*Bangalore University, B.Com., November 1997*)

[Answer : Rs. 4.810]

Exercise-11

The following expenses were incurred in respect of a shop having 5 identical machines.

	Per month Rs.
(1) Rent and Rates	21,600
(2) Repairs and maintenance	10,000
(3) Power (at 54 paise per unit)	32,400
(4) Lighting	9,700
(5) Supervisor's Salary (He devotes his time equally on all the 5 machines)	3,120
(6) Oil, grease and cotton waste	560
(7) Hire purchase instalment including interest (Rs. 6600)	46,600
(8) Each machine consumes 8 units of power per hour	
(9) The purchase price of each machine is	92,000

The life of each machine is estimated as 10 years at the end of which, it would have a residual value of Rs. 12,000

Calculate the machine Hour rate. *(Mangalore University, B.Com., April 1997)*

[**Answer** : Machine Hours are 1500]

[Machine Hour Rate 10.76]

Exercise-12

A machine was purchased on January 1990 for Rs. 5 lakhs. The total cost of all machinery inclusive of the new machinery was Rs. 75 lakhs. The following further particulars are available.

Expected life of the machine 10 years,

Scrap value at the end of 10 years Rs. 5000

Repairs and maintenance for the machine during the year Rs. 2000

Expected number of working hours of the machine per year 4000 hours

Insurance premium annually for all the machines Rs. 4500

Electricity consumption for the machine per hour (@ 75 paise per unit) 25 units

Area occupied by the machine 100 SqFt.

Area occupied by other machines 1500 SqFt.

Rent per month of the department Rs. 800;

Lighting charges for 20 points for the whole department out of which 3 points are for the machine Rs. 120 per month.

Compute the machine hour rate for the new machine on the basis of the data given above

(Madurai Kamaraj University, M.Com., April 1998)

[**Answer : Machine Hour Rate Rs. 31.90]**

Exercise-13

Prepare a machine hour rate to cover overhead expenses indicated below :

	Per Hour Rs.	Per year Rs.
(1) Electric power	0.85	
(2) Steam	0.35	
(3) Water	0.15	
(4) Repairs		160
(5) Rent		320
(6) Running hours : 2000 Hrs.		

Original cost price of machine Rs. 4000

Book value of machine Rs. 400

Replacement value of machine Rs. 3200

Depreciation at 7% p.a on original costs.

(Calicut University, B.Com., October 1995)

[**Answer :** Machine Hour rate Rs. 1.74]

Exercise-14

A production department in a factory purchased four new machines costing Rs. 20,000; Rs. 25,000; Rs. 30,000 and Rs. 40,000 respectively. All the machines occupy equal space. Other particulars relating to the machines are as follows :

	Rs.
Rent	10,000
Rate and Water	4,250
Heat and light	3,150
Power :	
Machine 1	5,100
Machine 2	5,000
Machine 3	12,000
Machine 4	14,500
Administration	9,500

Running expenses, repairs, sundries amount to Rs. 20,000

Calculate machine hour rate for each machine assuming 45 hours week, 50 weeks per annum, 80% utilisation and 10 years life for machine with 200 scrap value.

(*Osmania University, B.Com., April 1997*)

[*Answer* : Machine 1 Rs. 9.612
Machine 2 Rs. 10.31
Machine 3 Rs. 14.96
Machine 4 Rs. 17.87]

Exercise 15 : Compute machine hour rate from the following data :

		Rs.
(*i*)	Cost of machine	1,00,000
(*ii*)	Installation charges	10,000
(*iii*)	Scrap value after the expiry of its life of 15 years	5,000
(*iv*)	Rent, rates, for the shop per month	200
(*v*)	General lighting for the shop per month	300
(*vi*)	Insurance charges for the machine per month	960
(*vii*)	Repairs and maintenance of the machine throuht its life time	1,500
(*viii*)	Shop supervisor's salary per month	600

(*ix*) The machine consumes 10 units of electricity per hour at the rate of Rs. 0.25 paise per unit.

Additional information :

(*a*) Estimated working hours per annum—2,200 hours
(*b*) Setting up per annum estimated @ 200 hours
(*c*) The machine occupies 1/4 area of the shop
(*d*) The supervisor is expected to devote 20% of his time on this machine.

(*Karnataka University, B.Com., May 1990*)

[***Answer :*** Machine hour rate is 8.00]

Exercise 16 (Under and over absorption of overheads): The budgeted working conditions for a cost centre are as follows :

Normal working per week		42	hrs.
No. of machineries		14	
Normal weekly loss of hours on maintenance		5	hrs. per machine
No. of weeks worked per year		48	
Estimated annual overhead	Rs.	1,24,320	
Estimated direct wage rate	Rs.	4	per hour
Actual result in respect of a 4 week period are wages incurred	Rs.	9,000	
Overheads incurred	Rs.	10,200	
Machine hours produced		2,00	

You are required to calculate. :

(*a*) the overhead rate per machine hour and

(*b*) The amount of under or overabsorption of wages and overheads. (*ICWA Inter, Dec. 1988*)

[***Answer :*** Machine hour rate is 5 overhead under-absorbed Rs. 200, wages overabsorbed Rs. 408]

Exercise 17 : The total overhead expenses a factory are Rs. 4,50,608. Taking into account the normal working of the factory, overhead was recovered in production at Rs. 1.25 per hour. The actual hours worked are 2,93,104. How would you proceed to close the work of account assuming that besides 7,800 units produced of which, 7,000 were sold, there were 200 equivalent units in work-in-progress? On investigation it was found that 50% of the unabsorbed overhead was in account of increase in the cost of indirect material and indirect labour and the other 50% was due to factory inefficiency.

[***Answer :*** Under absorption of Rs. 42,114 is apportioned to cost of sales Rs. 36,849.75, finished goods Rs. 4,211.40 and work-in-progress Rs. 1,052.85].

12

OFFICE, ADMINISTRATION, SELLING AND DISTRIBUTION OVERHEADS

DEFINITION AND FEATURES OF OFFICE AND ADMININSTRATION OVERHEADS

Office overheads are those overheads which are incurred in carrying out the day-to-day routine of office. Examples of office overheads are offfice rent, office insurance, printing and stationery, salaries payable to office clerks and office supervisors. Administration overheads are defined by the ICMA terminology as "the sum of those costs of general management and of secretarial, accounting and administrative services, which cannot be directly related to the production, marketing, research or development functions of the enterprise." In other words, the cost of formulating the policy, directing the organisation and controlling the operations of an undertaking may be termed as administration overheads.

Features of Office and Administration Overheads

(*a*) The amount of office and administration overhead constitutes lowest proportion to the total cost when compared to other types of overheads.

(*b*) Most of the office and administration overheads are fixed in nature.

(*c*) They are not amenable for control. This is so because the nature of these overheads are such that, it is not possible to set norms or standards against which actual overheads could be compared.

(*d*) These overheads cannot be charged accurately to cost of production. Hence cost ascertainment cannot be accurate.

CLASSIFICATION AND COLLECTION OF ADMINISTRATION OVERHEADS

Administration overheads are classified according to their type, nature, purpose or department. Each type of overhead is to be denoted by a specific cost accounting number. For the sake of exercising control it would be appropriate to classify admininstration overheads on the basis of various administration departments such as accounting department, secretarial department, general office and so on. The administration overheads are collected for each department by means of preparing a summary statement of administration overhead. A specimen of such a statement is shown below :

SUMMARY OF DEPARTMENTAL ADMINISTRATION OVERHEADS

Name of the Dept. .... General office......................
Month .... Year ....

Cost Account No.	*Expense*	*Actual*	*Budgeted*	*Variances*
A_1	Postage			
A_2	Telephone			

A_3	Printing & stationery
A_4	Office lighting
A_5	Office rent
A_6	Salary of office staff
Total	

Fig. 12.1 Specimen of summary of departmental administration overheads.

Where a common item of expense is incurred for all the administrative departments, it is to be apportioned to all the departments on some equitable basis. The following are some of the common expenses incurred in the administration department and the basis for their apportionment.

Items of expenses	*Basis of apportionment*
Filing expenses	No. of documents handled
Correspondence expenses	No. of documents handled
Typing expenses	No. of documents handled
Invoicing expenses	No. of documents handled
Personnel department expenses	Number of employees
Depreciation of office building	Floor area
Rent of office	Space occupied
Telephone expenses	Number of extensions

ACCOUNTING OF ADMINISTRATION OVERHEADS IN COST ACCOUNTS

There are three methods of accounting of office and administration overheads. They are as follows.

1. Apportionment to Production and Selling and Distribution Departments of the Factory

This method recognises the fact that a factory has two important functions to perform, *viz.*, production and distribution. As such office and administration overheads must be apportioned to these two departments. The effect of this treatment is administration overheads lose their identity and are absorbed by production and selling & distribution departments. The reasons advocated for adopting this method are as follows :

(*a*) Administration is only an auxiliary service which is rendered to the two important departments *viz.*, production and selling & distribution departments of the factory. So administration overhead should not have any separate entity and all such overheads should be borne by only these two departments.

(*b*) As administration overheads cannot be controlled easily, the merger of such overheads with factory and selling & distribution overheads facilitates easy control.

(*c*) Production and distribution costs can be correctly calculated only when administration overheads are charged to these two departments.

This method is subjected to the following criticisms :

(*a*) A suitable basis of apportionment may not to be available for apportioning administration overheads to production and selling and distribution departments. So the method will give absurd figure.

(*b*) Administration is also one of the important function performed in all factories. Administration department and the overheads incurred in this department is as important as overheads incurred in production and selling and distribution departments. Merger of such cost with other departments distorts the relationship between the three functions.

(*c*) When administration overheads are not possible to control, its merger with other controllable overheads connot make the former controllable.

The following entries are passed to record the office and administration overheads in the cost ledger :

(*a*) For recording administration overheads incurred :

Administration overhead control a/c *Dr.*
To general ledger adjustment a/c

(*b*) When the overheads are apportioned between the production and selling and distribution overheads :

Works overhead control a/c *Dr.*
Selling and distribution overhead control a/c *Dr.*
To administration overhead control a/c

The amount of administration overheads thus apportioned to production and selling and distribution departments are ultimately recovered in the total cost of sales.

2. Charging to Costing Profit and Loss Account

Under this method administration overheads are treated as period or fixed cost and hence written off to costing profit and loss account of the period in which it is incurred. This method is advocated on the following grounds :

(*a*) Administration overheads are related to cost of formulating the policies and are not directly related to production or selling function.

(*b*) The administration overheads are very small when compared to other overheads. So they must be charged to costing profit & loss account instead of apportioning to production and selling departments.

(*c*) These overheads have no direct bearing with production and sales. Hence it should not be taken into cost of production.

This method of accounting is criticised on the following grounds;

(*a*) It is as important as production and selling function and as such it should form an important component of total cost.

(*b*) If it is taken into profit and loss account, the cost of production of a job is understated.

(*c*) The static nature cannot be taken as a reason for excluding it from cost of production.

The following entries are passed under this method :

(*a*) When administration overheads are incurred

Administrative overhead control a/c *Dr.*
To general ledger adjustment a/c

(*b*) When the overheads are charged to costing profit and loss account

Closing profit & loss a/c *Dr.*
To administration overhead control a/c

3. As a Separate Item of Cost

The method is based on the assumption that administration function is one of the distinct and important function in any organisation and as such its expenses should be borne by the finished products sold. So under this method, administration overheads are added as a separate item of cost to the number of units sold. According to this method, the stock of finished goods and work-in-progress should not bear the burden of administration cost.

For the sake of adding as a separate item of cost, the office and administration overheads are classified and collected under suitable cost accounting number. The various departments of the office such as cash, filing, secretarial accounting, etc. are identified as separate cost centres. Wherever it is possible to allocate the overheads to these cost centres, they are allocated. Other overheads are apportioned to these cost centres on some suitable basis. For the sake of calculating the rate the following basis can be used.

(*a*) Factory cost
(*b*) Factory overheads
(*c*) Sales value
(*d*) Units sold
(*e*) Units produced.

CONTROL OF ADMINISTRATION OVERHEADS

It was already mentioned that administration overheads are fixed in nature and therefore not succeptible for exercising control over it. However, the top management can devise the following control techniques for the sake of controlling administration overheads.

1. Control Through Classification and Analysis

The overheads incurred for various departments may be classified and compared with the budgeted figures. Similarly overheads incurred for the previous year can be compared with current year to know whether more overheads are incurred. Alternatively, the absorption rates for different periods can also be calculated to know the increase or decrease in the overheads incurred.

2. Control Through Budgets

Under this techique overheads are budgeted for different sections of the office. The actuals are compared with the budgeted overheads and variations are calculated and analysed. The person incharge of the concurred department has to report the variance to the top level management for taking remedial measures.

3. Control Through Standards

Under this technique standard costs are set for each item of administration overhead. The actual overheads incurred in each section is compared with standards to know the efficiency or otherwise of the sections.

DEFINITION AND CLASSIFICATION OF SELLING AND DISTRIBUTION OVERHEADS

The main aim of all business undertakings is to earn maximum amount of profit. This aim can be achieved by maximising the production and sales. Incereased production results in decreased cost of production. But necessary efforts must also be taken to boost up sales of increased production. This is possible by incurring selling and distribution overheads for the sake of creating demand and promoting sales. Though technological development and automation to a large extent are responsible for lowering the cost of production still the total cost has not been able to be reduced owing to increased selling and distribution overheads. It is estimated that in most of the factories, selling and distribution overheads accounts for about 15 to 20 per cent and therefore requires proper accounting and control.

Definition of Marketing Cost

The ICMA terminology has used marketing cost as a broader concept to include three componets *viz.,* selling, publicity and distribution cost. Marketing cost has been defined by the terminology as the cost incurred in publicising and presenting to customers the products of the undertaking in suitably attractive forms of all relevant research work, securing of orders, and usually, delivery of the goods to customers. In certain cases, after sales service and/or order processing may also be included.

Definition of Selling Cost

It is defined by the ICMA terminology as that portion of marketing cost which is incurred in securing orders.

Publicity Cost

It is defined by the ICMA terminology as that portion of marketing cost which is incurred in advertising and promotion as aids to the eventual sales of goods or services.

Distribution Cost

It is defined by the ICMA terminology as that portion of marketing cost which is incurred in wardhousing saleable products and in delivering products to customers.

Classification of Selling Overheads

Selling overheads may be classified into the following types :

1. Direct selling expense : The overheads which are directly related to securing orders, market research, retaining the customers, etc. fall under this category. The common examples are salaries payable to sales manager, salesmen, showroom expenses, sales depot expenses, etc. expenses incurred in preparation and quotation of selling price, cost incurred in meeting enquiries and after sales service costs, such as repairs and maintenance.

2. Sales promotion cost : These are the overheads which are incurred in creating the demand for the products of the company. Examples of costs which fall under this category are advertisement expenses, distribution of free gifts, cost of exhibition, expenses incurred for marker analysis in order to expand the market and so on.

3. Financial cost : These overheads include actual or notional interest payable or working capital which is required to finance cost of stock of goods and for dealing on credit basis, credit collection expenses such as legal expenses, incurred for realising debts, and bad debts.

Classification of Distribution Overheads

Distribution overheads can be classified into the following types ;

1 Transportation cost : These include expenses incurred for delivering goods sold and the cost incurred to receive back the goods when they are sold on sale or return basis. Examples are wages payable to the drivers of delivery van, depreciation of delivery van, insurance premium payable for goods in transit, etc.

2. Warehousing cost : All expenses incurred in storing the finished goods is known as warehousing cost. Examples are rent of godown, heating and lighting expenses, insurance of godown, wages of godown kepeers, etc.

3. Packing and cost of containers : This include the cost of packing and employing the reconditioned containers for re-use. Examples are cost fo secondary packing materials, cost of tools used in packing such as hammers, etc.

Though the term selling and distribution overheads are used together, they differ in the following respects :

(*a*) Selling overheads are incurred for promoting sales, whereas distribution overheads are incurred in moving the finished goods from the godown of the fatory to customer's place.

(*b*) The object of selling overhead is to create demand and ratain the customers, whereas the object of distribution overhead is to deliver the goods safely to the required place.

ACCOUNTING OF SELLING AND DISTRIBUTION OVERHEAD

The accounting of selling and distribution overhead is necessary for the following purposes :

(*a*) To contorl selling and distribution overheads,

(*b*) To fix selling price,

(*c*) To determine optimum sales volume,

(*d*) To determine cost of sales of each product in order to know the profit.

The accounting of selling and distribution overheads involves the following steps.

1. Analysis of Overheads

Selling and distribution of overheads may be analysed under any of the following basis :

(*a*) According to nature and object : Under this basis the overheads are classified according to the purpose for which they are incurred. The examples of overheads which may be analysed on this basis are freight, warehousing expenses, packing material and so on. Some time these overheads can also be classified on the basis of variability, such as variable, semi-variable and fixed. Best example is salary payable to salesman is fixed, travelling allowance is semi-variable and commission is variable.

(*b*) According to function : Overheads can be analysed based on the functional division of the factory. Examples are advertising and sales promotion, credit collection, storage, transportation, etc. The functional basis of analysis can also be made according to area covered by sales. The area may represent a territory, or sales office.

(*c*) Analysis by products : Overheads can also be analysed on the basis of products so that, those overheads which can be attributed to the products can be directly allocated.

2. Apportionment of Overheads

After collection and analysis, the second step involved is to apportion the overheads on suitable basis. The following are some of the basis used for apportionment. :

Expenses	*Basis of apportionment*
Advertisement	Sales value
Warehousing	Sales value
Credit collection	Number of orders
Transport cost	Weight

3. Absorption of Overheads

Selling and distribution overheads may be absorbed under the following two methods :

(a) A percentage of sales value : Under this method selling and distribution overheads and sales value is predetermind. A percentage of this overhead is calculated over sales value. It is at this percentage that selling and distribution overheads are absorbed by the unmber of finished goods sold.

(b) An estimated rate per unit : Under this method the selling and distribution overheads and the number of units to be sold are predetermined. The predetermined selling and distribution overhead divided by the predetermined units to be sold gives a rate and it is at this rate the overheads are absorbed. This method can be conveniently used where only one variety of goods are produced and sold.

The following entries are passed in the cost books to record selling and distribution overheads :

(a) For recording the actual expenses incurred for selling and distributing the goods
Selling and distribution overhead ledger control a/c *Dr.*
To cost ledger control a/c

(b) For issue of materials from store room for the purpose of selling and distribution function
Selling and distribution overhead ledger control a/c *Dr.*
To stores ledger control a/c

(c) When wages or salaries are incurred towards this function selling and distribution overhead ledger control a/c *Dr.*
To wages ledger control a/c

(d) Whe selling and distribution overheads are recovered on goods sold.
Cost of sales ledger control a/c *Dr.*
To selling and distribution overhead ledger control a/c

CONTROL OF SELLING AND DISTRIBUTION OVERHEADS

There are three methods of controlling selling and distribution overheads. They are as follows :

1. By Analysis of expenses and Comparison with Past Performance

This method is suitable only for a small organisation. Under this method selling and distribution overheads are analyesed on the basis of nature, product, territory, etc. Each item of overheads is compared with the corresponding item of the previous year. Alternatively, the overheads can also be expressed as a percentage of sales and compared with similar percentages of previous year.

2. Budgetary Control

Under this method first of all a sales forecast is made and on this basis a sales budget is prepared. Then selling and distribution overheads are budget based on sales budget. The selling and distribution overheads are classified into fixed and variable overheads. These overheads are then compared with the budgeted overheads to know whether more expenses are incurred than the budgeted overheads. If so remedial measures are taken to minimise such overheads. Flexible budgets are used to control overheads in most of the cases.

3. Standard Costs

Fixation of standard cost for selling overheads in comparatively difficult than distribution overheads. Still, standard cost are set carefully for these overheads and actuals are compared with standards to know the variances. In case of adverse variances, the causes for the same are analysed and reported to the top level management for taking remedial measures to control such variance.

Problem 1 : A company is making a study of the relative profitability of the two products – A and B. In addition to direct costs, indirect selling and distribution costs to be allocated between the two products are as under :

	Rs.
Insurance charges for inventory (finished)	78,000
Storage costs	1,40,000
Packing and forwarding charges	7,20,000
Salesmen salaries	8,50,000
Invoicing costs	4,50,000

Other details are :–

		Product A	*Product B*
Selling price	(Rs.)	500	1,000
Cost per unit (exclusive of indirect selling & distribution costs)	(Rs.)	300	600
Annual sales in units		10,000	8,000
Average Inventory	(units)	1,000	800
Number of Invoices		2,500	2,000

One unit of product A requires a storage space twice as much as product B. The cost to pack and forward one unit is the same for both the products. Salesmen are paid salary plans commission @ 5% on sales and equal amount of efforts are put forth on the sales of each of the products

Required :

(*i*) Set up a schedule showing the apportionment of the indirect selling and distribution costs between the two products.

(*ii*) Prepare a statement showing the relative profitability of the two products. (*CA, Inter., May 1996*)

Solution : **Statement Showing Apportionment of the Indirect Selling and distribution costs between the two products**

Items	*Basis of Apportionment*	*Total*	*A*	*B*
Insurance charges	Average Inventory Value (1,000 × 500 : 800 × 100)	78,000	30,000	48,000
Storage cost	Average Inventory storage space (1000 × 2 : 800 × 1)	1,40,000	1,00,000	40,000
Packing & forwarding charges	Annual sales in units (10000 : 8000)	7,20,000	4,00,000	3,20,000
Salesmen salaries	Efforts of salesman (1; 1)	8,50,000	4,25000	4,25,000
Salesmen commission	Annual sales value (5 : 8)	6,50,000	2,50,000	4,00,000
Invoicing costs	No of Invoices (2,500 : 2,000)	4,50,000	2,50,000	2,00,000
		28,88,000	14,55,000	14,33,000

Statement Showing Relative profitability of Two products

	A	B
Annual sales :	50,00,000	80,00,000
A 10,000 units × 500		
B 8,000 units × 1,000		
Less : Cost of sales	30,00,000	48,00,000
A 10,000 × 300		
B 8,000 × 600		
Gross profit	20,00,000	32,00,000
Less : Indirect selling & Distribution cost	14,55,000	14,33,000
Profit	5,45,000	17,67,000
Profit percentage on sales	$\frac{5,45,000}{50,00,000} \times 100$ = 10.9%	$\frac{17,67,000}{80,00,000} \times 100$ = 22.08%

Problem 2 : Cosmos Ltd. produces three types of products A, B & C. The sales territory of the company is divided in three areas as North, South and Central. The estimated sales for the year are as under

Product	*Territories*		
	North (*Rs.*)	*South* (*Rs.*)	*Central* (*Rs.*)
A	1,00,000	40000	–
B	60,000	–	1,60,000
C	–	1,40,000	80000

Budgeted advertising cost is as under :–

	Rs.
North	6,400
South	9,000
Central	7,800
Common	11,600

You are required to work out the advertising cost per cent on sales for each product and each territory and prepare a suitable statement for presentation to the management. (*ICWA, Inter., June 1995*)

Solution : Apportionment of common Advertising cost on the basis of sales value :

		Sales value		*Common Adrt. cost*	
Territory North –	A	1,00,000		2,000	
	B	60,000		1,200	
			160,000		3,200
Territory South –	A	40,000		800	
	C	1,40,000		2,800	
			1,80,000		3,600
Territory Central –	B	1,60,000		3,200	
	C	80,000		1,600	
			2,40,000		4,800
	Total		5,80,000		11,600

Apportionment of Local Costs on the basis of sales value

			Sales value		*Common Advt. cost*	
Territory North	–	A	1,00,000		4,000	
	–	B	60,000		2,400	
				1,60,000		6,400
Territory South	–	A	40,000		2,000	
	–	C	1,40,000		7,000	
				1,80,000		9,000
Territory Central	–	B	1,60,000		5,200	
	–	C	80,000		2,600	
				2,40,000		7,800
		Total		5,80,000		23,200

Statement of Advertisement cost

Product	*Territories* North	South	Central	Total	*% on Sales*
A	6000	2800	–	8800	6.29
B	3600	–	8400	12000	5.45
C	–	9800	4200	14000	6.36
Total	9600	12600	12600	34800	
Percentage on Sales	6%	7%	5.25%		

Problem 3 : Progressive Company Ltd. manufacture three products *A, B* and *C* and sells them direct through own sales force in three zones *X, Y* and *Z*. The overall control of distribution and sales is taken care of at the headquarters, responsible also for sales promotion.

You are presented with the following data for the year end 31st March 1992.

			Sales (Rs.)	*Direct selling and distribution expenses* (Rs.)
Zone *X*	Product	*A*	1,50,000	10,200
		B	1,00,000	10,500
		C	50,000	5,300
			3,00,000	26,000
Zone *Y*	Product	*A*	2,00,000	14,200
		B	2,00,000	18,800
		C	1,00,000	10,500
			5,00,000	43,500
Zone *Z*	Product	*A*	50,000	4,200
		B	40,000	3,400
		C	1,10,000	14,400
			2,00,000	22,000

Selling and sales promotion expenses at the headquatrer are as follows :

Selling expenses	Rs. 18,000
Advertisement expenses	Rs. 20,000
Other expenses	Rs. 24,000

While advertisement expenses are allocated to zones and products on the basis of sales, the other two types of expenses are allocated equally to zones and products.

Cost of sales should be taken as following percentage of sales

Product *A*	80%
B	75%
C	70%

You are required to tabulater the above information to present comparative profit and loss statements for each zone and for each product. *(ICWA Inter, June 1992)*

Solution : **Comparative zonewise profit or loss statement**

		Zone X	ZoneY	ZoneZ	Total
(1)	Sales	3,00,000	5,00,000	2,00,000	10,00,000
(2)	Cost of sales :				
	Product *A*	1,20,000	1,60,000	40,000	3,20,000
	B	75,000	1,50,000	30,000	2,55,000
	C	35,000	70,000	77,000	1,82,000
	Total	2,30,000	3,80,000	1,47,000	7,57,000
(3)	Margin	70,000	1,20,000	53,000	2,43,000
(4)	Direct selling expenses	26,000	43,500	22,000	91,500
(5)	Selling cost :				
	Selling expenses	6,000	6,000	6,000	18,000
	Advertisement expenses	6,000	10,000	4,000	20,000
	Other expenses	8,000	8,000	8,000	24,000
	Total selling cost	46,000	67,500	40,000	1,53,500
	Profit	Rs. 24,000	52,500	13,000	89,500

Comparative productwise profit/loss statement

		Product A (Rs.)	Product B (Rs.)	Product C (Rs.)	Total (Rs.)
(1) Sales :	Zone *X*	1,50,000	1,00,000	50,000	3,00,000
	Zone *Y*	2,00,000	2,00,000	1,00,000	5,00,000
	Zone *X*	50,000	40,000	1,10,000	2,00,000
		4,00,000	3,40,000	2,60,000	10,00,000
(2) Cost of sales		3,20,000	2,55,000	1,82,000	7,57,000
(3) Margin		80,000	85,000	78,000	2,43,000
(4) Direct selling expenses		6,000	6,000	6,000	18,000
Advertisement expenses		8,000	6,800	5,200	20,000
Other expenses		8,000	8,000	8,000	24,000
Indirect selling expenses (at headquarter)		28,600	32,700	30,200	91,500
Total selling expenses		50,600	53,500	49,400	1,53,500
Profit		29,400	31,500	38,600	89,500

Problem 4 : A company is producing three types of products *A, B, C*. The sales territory of the company is divided into three areas *X, Y*, and *Z*.

The estimated sales and the advertising cost for the next year are as under :

Sales	*Territories*		
	X (Rs.)	*Y (Rs.)*	*Z (Rs.)*
Product *A*	25,000	10,000	–
B	15,000	–	40,000
C	–	35,000	20,000

Advertising cost

	Territories			Total
	X (Rs.)	Y (Rs.)	Z (Rs.)	(Rs.)
Local direct cost	3,200	4,500	4,200	11,900
Common cost	–	–	–	5,800
				17,700

You are required to prepare a statement showing territorywise advertising cost expressesd as a percentage of sales. The allocation of advertising cost should be based on. Sales as given above.

(ICWA Inter, June 1992)

Solution :

Territories	*Products*	*Sales*		*Local direct cost*		*Common cost*	
		Rs.	*Rs.*	*Rs.*	*Rs.*	*Rs.*	*Rs.*
X	*A*	25,000		2,000		1,000	
	B	1,500	40,000	1,200	3,200	600	1,600
Y	*A*	1,000		1,000		400	
	C	35,000	45,000	3,500	4,500	1,400	1,800
Z	*B*	40,000		2,800		1,600	
	C	20,000	60,000	1,4000	4,200	800	2,400
			1,45,000		11,900		5,800

The local direct costs have been apportioned on the basis of percentages of territorywise sales and the common cost has been apportioned on the basis of total sales.

Statement showing advertisement cost

Products	*Territories*			*Total*
	X	*Y*	*Z*	
A	3,000	1,400	–	1,400
B	1,800'	–	4,400	6,200
C	–	4,900	2,200	7,100
Total cost	4,800	6,300	6,600	17,700
Sales	40,000	45,000	60,000	1,45,000
% of cost to sales	12%	14%	11%	12.21

TREATMENT OF CERTAIN ITEMS IN COST ACCOUNTS

While treating certain items on cost accounts, the following guidelines are to be considered :

(*a*) To identify the item of expenditure with the units of production.

(*b*) Where it is not possible to identify the expenditure with the unit of production, or where the process of identifying is difficult or if the cost of identifying exceeds the cost of materials, then such an item of expenditure is to be treated as overheads.

(*c*) When an expenditure incurred results the benefits over a period of time, it is to be treated as deferred revenue expenditure and to be spread over the number of years during which benefit accrues. Only a part of the expenditure is charged to the production cost for that year.

(*d*) If the expenditure is of abnormal nature, it is to be included in the costing profit and loss account so that the cost of production is not distorted.

The following are some of the expenses which deserve special treatement in cost accounts.

1. Repairs and Maintenance Expenses of Machines

The repairs and maintenance department is a service department which is established in most of the factories. For the sake of treating this item of expenditure, repairs and maintenance can be classified into two types, *viz.,* (*a*) minor reparirs and normal maintenance and (*b*) heavy repairs and major overhauls. The expenses of minor repairs and normal maintenance is to be treated as factory overheads. Heavy repairs and major overhauls can be underaken for two purposes, *viz.,* (*a*) to increase the earning capacity of the machinery and (*b*) to keep the machine in good running condition. In the former case the expense is treated as capital expenditure. In the latter case, it is treated as a deferred revenue expense and spread over to number of years' cost of production.

2. Audit Fees, Bank Charges, Legal Expenses and Postage and Stationery

These expenses are incurred in the day-to-day working of the office. Hence all these expenses are treated as office and administration overheads.

3. Advertising

This is one of the most commonly incurred expenses in most of the business enterprises. Advertising may relate to (*a*) common or general one to cover all the products to be sold and (*b*) specifically spent on one existing line of product or for a new line of product. If the advertising expenses incurred is a general one to cover all products, it is treated as selling and distribution overheads and is recovered from the cost of goods sold on a suitable basis. If it is spent specifically to a particular line of existing product, it is treated as selling overhead and allocated directly to those products sold. If the advertising expenses are incurred specifically on a new line of product, then it is treated as deferred revenue expenditure to be recovered over a period of time.

4. Cost Accounting Department Expenses

This expenditure include salary of staff of cost accounting department and other expenses incurred to maintain it. Where the cost accounting department is established in small concern, then such expenses are treated as administration overhead. In big organisation, where the expenditure is large, it is charged to works, administration, selling and distribution overheads.

5. Bad Debts

When selling departments bills the credit sales then bad debts is treated as selling overhead. If collection of bad debts is the responsibility of accounting or administration department, then it is treated as administration overheads.

6. Transport Cost

The carriage inwards is treated as part of material cost. The cost of internal transport, *i.e.*, cost of carrying materials from stores department to production departments and *vice versa* is treated as factory overheads. Carriage outwards is treated as distribution overheads.

7. Insurance of Building and Plant

The Insurance policy in a factory may relate to fire insurance, burgalary insurance and so on. The premium paid on such policies is treated as overheads. Where a policy is taken in respect of a single department, the premium is allocated to that department. If the policy is taken for the entire factory, the premium is apportioned to all the departments on a suitable basis. Where a policy is taken to cover risk of administration and selling and distribution departments, the premium is apportioned to these departments.

8. Sales Commission

Commission on sales is paid to sales manager, salesmen or agents on a fixed basis for all products or as a percentage for each product sold. Where it is paid as a fixed rate it is charged to the cost of product sold. Where it is paid as a percentage for different products, then it is treated as selling overheads.

9. Discounts Received

Discounts on purchase of materials may be trade discount or cash discount. Such discounts are deducted from the invoice price of the materials bought.

10. Research and Development Cost

The ICMA terminology has defined research cost as "the cost of searching for new or improved products, new applications of materials, or new improved methods." Whereas development cost as "the cost of the process which begins with the implementation of the decision to produce a new or improved product or to employ a new or improved method and ends with the commencement of formal production of that product or by that method."

The distinction between research and development costs thus lies in the fact that while research costs are incurred in the hope of getting a new or improved product or a new or improved method of production, etc., development costs are incurred on successful research projects only. The examples of research costs are salaries of research supervisor and of research assistants, *viz.*, chemists, technicians, etc., costs of materials used, cost of equipments etc.

Treatment of research cost : Research may normally be of two types, *viz.*, (*a*) fundamental research and (*b*) applied research. The aim of fundamental research is to increase the general fund of knowledge and no specific tangible results are aimed at. Neverthless, they facilitate applied research work. If such research work is carried out on a continuous basis, the cost should be charged to the manufacturing overhead of the period in which the research work is carried out. However, if such research work is carried out at the intervals of certain periods, then the cost should be treated as deferred revenue expenditure to be spread over the manufacturing overhead of such periods.

Cost of applied research is treated in the following manner :

(i) For improvement of existing products or methods **:** Usually a lump-sum amount is earmarked every year for conducting research work on all existing products and methods. In such cases, the actual costs should be charged to manufacturing overhead of the period. If, any separate sums are allotted for any particular product, the actual expenses should also be collected accordingly and charged directly.

(ii) For new products and methods **:** Separate project number is allotted for each individual research project costs collected accordingly. Costs of incompleted projects are carried over. Costs of projects ending in failure are charged off to costing profit & loss account. Cost successful research projects should be merged with development cost of the relevant project.

Treatment of development cost : For successful research projects, development costs should be merged with research cost and the total research and development cost for each such project temporarily capitalised and treated as deferred revenue expenditure to be spread over a number of future periods depending upon the size of the expenditure and period likely to be benefited. If the project is related to a product, the cost is charged directly and if it is related to method it is treated as factory overhead of the future periods.

11. Royalties, Patent Fees

The treatment of royalty depends upon the method of payment. If royalty is paid as a fixed amount or on the basis of a fixed percentage of output, it is treated as direct expenses. If it is paid on the units sold it is treated as selling expense.

The expenditure incurred in registering and renewal of patent is treated as administration overhead.

12. Rent of Building

Depending upon the use of building for production, administration and selling, it is treated as overheads.

13. Heating, Lighting and Air-conditioning

Depending upon the location of installation, *i.e,* production, administration, and selling, lighting charges are treated as overheads. However, where meters are installed lighting expenses are allocated directly to the departments. Where meters are not installed, it is apportioned on the basis of number of light points. Heating and air-conditioning expenses is, apportioned on the basis of cubic capacity of the department.

14. Head Office Expenses

Where a firm has number of plants, the expenses incurred in running the head office is apportioned to various plants on the basis of service rendered by the head office to each plant. In each plant such expense is treated as its administration overheads.

15. Warranty Claims

A warranty clause is inserted in sales clause for replacing a defective part of a product. This clause will be in force for a specific period of time. Any expenses relating to replacement of defective parts within a stipulated period are treated as selling expenses.

16. Depreciation

Depreciation is the gradual and permanent decrease in the value of an asset from any cause. It has been defined as the dimunition in intrinsic value of an asset due to its use or lapse of time. The main causes for depreciation in an asset may be classified into physical and functional causes. The physical causes include wear and tear with constant use and the action of other elements. The functional causes include obsolescence and supersession.

The depreciation of various assets are booked under various standing order number and the amount of depreciation is charged to the concerned departments as overheads. The following reasons are attributed for charging depreciation as overheads to cost of production :

(*a*) It will not be possible to calculate the correct cost of manufacturing goods without taking depreciation into account.

(*b*) It will not be possible to show the correct value of an asset in the balance sheet if depreciation is not provided for. In fact, the balance sheet will be overstated if depreciation is not provided for.

(*c*) It will become difficult to replace an asset if depreciation is not provided for.

(*d*) The profit and loss account also will not show the correct profit if depreciation is not taken into consideration.

(*e*) If depreciation is not proveided for, it will show a higher profit. But the consequences of increased profit are (*i*) It leads to the entry of competitors, (*ii*) There will be no incentive to minimise the expenses, (*iii*) It involves payment of more tax, and (*iv*) Payment of more commission, if it is based on profit.

Methods of Calculating Depreciation

(*a*) Fixed instalment method : Under this method, the assets are depreciated at a fixed amount throughout its life span. The amount of depreciation is calculated by dividing the value of an asset by the number of years of the estimated life of the machine. At the end of its life, the value of the asset will become zero. This method of depreciation is followed where the services rendered by the asset is uniform as in the case of furniture. But the chief limitation of this method is that the amount of depreciation remains the same, although the value of the asset diminishes every year.

(*b*) Diminishing balance method or written down value method : Under this method, the depreciation is calculated every year on the diminishing value of the asset. For example, suppose, the original value of asset, is say Rs. 10,000 and the rate of depreciation is say, 10 per cent. Then according to this method, the asset will be depreciated by Rs. 1,000 in the first year. The diminished value of the asset in the second year will become Rs. 9,000. Then the depreciation for the third year will be charged on 9,000 which works out to Rs. 900 and this practice is continued till the end.

(*c*) Annuity method : Under this method, depreciation is calculated not only on the cost of the asset but also on the interest forgone would have been earned had the amount been invested in some other form. The depreciation to be charged is obtained by referring to the annuity table.

(*d*) Depreciation fund method : Under this method, to facilitate ready replacement of asset without facing a financial problem, the depreciation amount is set aside from the divisible profit every year and a fund known as depreciation fund is created. The fund is invested in good securities. At the time of replacing the asset, the securities are sold out and the sale proceeds are utilised for the purchase of the new asset.

(*e*) Insurance policy method : This method resembles the above method but with a difference, *viz.*, the amount so set apart is invested in an insurance company in the form of premium. When the asset gets complete by worn out, the policy money is realised from the insurance company and thus the asset is replaced.

(*f*) Annual valuation method : According to this method, the asset is valued at the end of the year and if this valuation is less than the book value, the difference is treated as depreciation and charged to profit and loss account. However, if the valuation amount is higher, the excess amount is ignored as it is in the nature of a temporary charge and no depreciation is charged on this excess amount.

(*g*) Kilometer method : This method of depreciation is used to depreciate motar vans, cars, and other delivery vahicles such as truks. Under this method, depreciation is calculated by dividing the original cost of the asset by the estimated life of vehicle in kilometers.

***(h)* Machine hour rate method :** Under this method, depreciation of machinery is calculated on the basis of hours for which it is used but not on a yearly basis.

***(i)* Replacement cost method :** Under this method, the replacement cost of the asset is estimated and depreciation is calculated on the replacement cost but not on the original cost.

17. Training Cost

It is compulsory under the Apprentices Act of 1961 to train apprentices by every factory. There are different schemes of training employees. Firstly, learners may be appointed and trained them before they are appointed as employees. Secondly, existing employees may be trained while they work in factory in order to make them more familiar with the work. Thirdly, before promotions, workers may be trained so that they can discharge their newly assigend jobs more satisfactorily.

The training cost comprises of cost of material and equipment used for training, pay and allowance of training staff, and the allowance payable to the trainees. There are two methods of treating training cost in cost accounting. Firstly, training expenses including the spoiled work is treated as factory overheads. Secondly, where the trainees are given some jobs to perform, part of the training cost is treated as factory overhead and the balance is charged to the job concerned as direct labour cost.

18. Erection and Installation Cost of New Plant and Machinery

The cost of installing the new plant and machinery is capitalised along with the acquisition value of the asset.

19. Re-erection Cost

The dismantling of an asset and its reinstallation may be on account of error or because of a policy decision of management. Where the cost of dismantling an asset and its refixation is due to an error it is treated as factory overhead. Where it is on account of management policy and the amount involved is more it is written off as a loss.

20. Interest on Capital

The inclusion of interest paid on capital in the total cost of production is a controversial issue. The following arguments are put foward for the inclusion of interest on capital in cost accounts :

(*a*) Just as wages are remuneration paid to labour factor, interest is the remuneration paid on capital. As wages forms part of production cost, interest must also form part of production cost.

(*b*) As interest paid on borrowed capital is included in cost accounts, under the same principle, the notional interest on capital should also be included in cost accounts.

(*c*) Cost comparison and profit evaluation is possible when interest is included in cost of production

(*d*) The inclusion of interest in cost accounts also facilitates make or buy decision and to own or hire a machine.

(*e*) It enables in determining the cost of holding the inventory.

(*f*) If interst is not included in cost of production, the cost of goods sold is understated and profit is overstated.

The following arguments are put forward against the inclusion of interest on capital in cost accounts :

(*a*) The remuneration payable on capital is profit and as such interest should not be included in cost accounts.

(*b*) Actual interest paid can be included in cost accounts but not the notional interest.

(*c*) Interest is a matter of pure finance and hence it should be taken into costing profit and loss account but not to cost of production account.

(*d*) Interest need not be included in determining the comparative cost of installation of a new asset at it is governed by depreciation, repairs and maintenance cost, etc.

(*e*) It involves additional clerical work and creates unnecessary complications in cost accounts.

(*f*) Estimating the actual capital to be utilised and interest thereof is somewhat difficult. So interest is to be excluded in cost accounts.

(*g*) It increases the cost of closing stock-in-hand when there is not of much sales in an year. It results in increased value of closing stock which is not justified.

(*h*) Finally, it does not affect the profit figure. It increases cost of production on the one hand and simultaneously increases the profit on the other.

Where it is decided to include interest on capital in cost accounts, the interest amount for each department is to be recorded under standing order number. The following entries are passed in the cost ledger :

(*a*) For recording the notional interest
Factory overhead control a/c *Dr.*
To costing P & L a/c

(*b*) When interest is charged to cost of production :
Work-in-progeress ledger control a/c *Dr.*
To factory overhead control a/c

21. Rent

Rent paid on building is treated as overheads. It is apportioned on the basis of area occupied by production, administration, selling and distribution departments of the factory.

QUESTIONS

I. Choose the Correct Answer

1. Which one of the following is a cost of seeking to create and stimulate demand and of securing orders
(*a*) Research cost (*c*) Selling cost
(*b*) Administrative cost (*d*) Distribution cost [ ]

2. Administration overheads are generally recovered as a percentage of
(*a*) Direct materials (*c*) Prime cost
(*b*) Direct wages (*d*) Factory cost [ ]

3. Warehouse expenses in an example of :
(*a*) Factory overhead (*c*) Administration overhead
(*b*) Selling overhead (*d*) Distribution overhead [ ]

4. Bad debts is shown under the head
(*a*) Factory overhead (*c*) Selling overhead
(*b*) Administration overhead (*d*) Distribution overhead [ ]

[***Answer :*** 1—(*c*), 2—(*d*), 3—(*d*), 4—(*c*)]

II. Simple Questions

1. Define office overheads.
2. Mention the different methods of treating office and administration overheads in cost accounts.
3. Give four examples of indirect materials used as office overheads.
4. Define selling overheads.
5. Define distribution overheads.
6. Distinguish between selling and distribution overheads.
7. How is selling and distribution overheads accounted for in costs accounts?
8. How are office and administration overheads and selling and distribution overheads controlled?
9. How are the following expenses treated in cost, accounts :
   (*a*) Royalty, (*b*) Research and development cost, (*c*) Inspection cost, (*d*) Drawing office expenses, (*e*) Transport cost, (*f*) Bad debts, (*g*) Advertising, (*h*) Tabulation expenses, (*i*) Repairs and maintenance cost, (*j*) Insurance on plant and building, (*k*) Office cost, (*l*) Erection of a new palnt, (*m*) Dismantling and re-erection of old plant, (*n*) Subscriptions and donations, (*o*) Packing expenses.

Short Answer Questions

1. Explain the arguments for and against inclusion of interest in cost accounts.
2. Explain the arguments for and against inclusion of depreciation on cost accounts.
3. Explain the different methods of calculating depreciation on assets.

EXERCISES

Exercise 1 : A firm is producing three types of products A_1,A_2,A_3. The sales territory of the company is divided into three areas X_1,X_2,X_3

The estimated sales for 1992 are as follows :

Product		Territory X_1	X_2	X_3
A_1	Rs.	40,000	16,000	–
A_2	Rs.	24,000	–	64,000
A_3		–	56,000	32,000

The estimated cost for advertisement is as under :

Territory	X_1	X_2	X_3	*Tatal*
Local cost	2,560	3,600	3,360	9,520
General expenses	–	–	–	4,640

Calculate the advertisement cost per cent on sales for each product and territory showing how you will present the statement to the management.

[*Answer :* Percentage of advertisement cost to sales are 6%, 7%, and 5.5%]

Exercise 2 : The Pure Chemical Manufacturing Company has three salesmen *A*, *B*, and *C*. *A* is paid a salary of Rs. 3,000 per annum plus a commission of 5% on sales. *B* receives a salary of Rs. 2,000 and a commission of 5% on his sales and *C* is employed on a straight commission basis of 10%. Apart from the sales by salesmen, the company has the direct sales :

For the year 1992 the following information are obtained.

	Rs.
Net sales by *A*	1,00,000
Net sales by *B*	60,000
Net sales by *C*	40,000
Direct house sales	2,10,000
Advertising costs	42,000
General selling costs	72,000

Cost of goods sold averages 50% of net sales travelling costs incured by *A* is Rs, 4,000, *B* is Rs. 2,000, *C* is Rs. 1,000.

Prepare comparative profit and loss statement for each salesman and house sales and total net profit the company. Assume one-half of the advertising and general selling costs are incurred for the house sales.

[*Answer :* Net profit of *A* is Rs. 9,500, *B* is Rs. 5,900, *C* is 3,600 house sales is Rs. 48,000]

Exercise 3 : The multiproducts manufacturers electric fans, bicycles, and electric heaters, which are distributed in three main territories—Calcutta, Bombay, and Madras. The sales in Delhi region is controlled by the Calcutta head office. The analysis of sales for the month of March is as follows :

	Territories			
Line of products	*Calcutta*	*Bombay*	*Madras*	*Total*
Bicycles	1,20,000	2,00,000	50,000	3,70,000
Fans	60,000	40,000	20,000	1,20,000
Heaters	20,000	10,000	5,000	35,000
	2,00,000	2,50,000	75,000	5,25,000

The gross profit based on an analysis of pricing is estimated to be 15% of sales for bicycles 40% of sales for fans and 30% of sales for heaters.

Tho costs during the month were tabulated as under :

Selling costs directly chargeable	*Territory 1*			*Territory 2*			*Territory 3*		
	Bicycles (Rs.)	*Fans (Rs.)*	*Heaters (Rs.)*	*Bicycles (Rs.)*	*Fans (Rs.)*	*Heaters (Rs.)*	*Bicycles (Rs.)*	*Fans (Rs.)*	*Heaters (Rs.)*
Advertising through newspapers	5,000	1,000	2,000	10,000	4,000	2,000	5,000	1,000	1,000
Advertising through cinema	1,000	500	500	2,000	1,000	1,000	500	200	200
Sales commission	6,000	3,000	1,000	10,000	2,000	500	2,500	1,000	250
Telephone	300	100	100	500	100	100	100	100	150
Entertainment	4,000	1,000	2,000	5000	1,500	1,500	1,000	500	500
	16,300	5,600	5,600	27,500	8,100	5,100	9,000	2,800	2,100

Indirect selling costs are :	*Rs.*
Executive office	12,000
Service dept. cost	15,000
Other sales promotion expenses	25,000

Prepare comparative profit and loss statement for each territory and for each line of product. Distribute executive office and service department costs equally among territories and lines of products. Other sales promotion expenses are to be distributed on the basis of actual sales.

[*Answer :* Profit of Territory 1, Rs. 2,000; Loss of Territory 2, Rs. 12,620 and Loss of Territory 3, Rs. 9,580; Loss of by cycles Rs. 24,030; Profit on fans Rs. 16,790; loss on heaters Rs. 12,960]

SECTION C

METHODS OF COSTING

13

SINGLE OR OUTPUT OR UNIT COSTING

INTRODUCTION

As was discussed in chapter 2, the methods of costing can be broadly classified into two types, *viz.*, specific order costing and operation costing. Single or output or unit costing is a method of costing that belongs to the group of operation costing method. It is defined by the ICMA terminology as "the basic costing method applicable where goods or services result from a series of continuous or repetitive operations or processes to which costs are charged before being averaged over the units produced during the period". This method is known as "single" method of costing as industries adopting this method manufactures, in most cases a single variety of product. It is termed as unit costing because cost units are identical. Though under this method of costing a single variety of product is manufactured, it may vary in respect of size, grade, colour etc. The examples of industries which make use of this method of costing are : quarries, brick, sugar, cloth, coal, cement, fisheries, food canning, plantation industry, etc.

FEATURES AND OBJECTS OF OUTPUT COSTING

The features of industries which adopt single or output method of costing are as follows :

(*a*) The production of goods are undertaken on a continuous basis in anticipation of demand both in the short run and long run.

(*b*) The goods are produced on a large scale basis.

(*c*) Excepting in newly started industry in all other cases there always exists opening and closing work-in-progress.

(*d*) Cost of production is ascertained at the end of accounting year which may be a financial year or calender year.

(*e*) The cost is ascertained both per unit of finished product and for all the units manufactured.

(*f*) The end products are always homogeneous or uniform in all respects.

(*g*) Equality of costs is one of the basic feature of unit costing. In other words, identical cost unit will have identical cost.

The specific objects of this method of costing are (*a*) To ascertain total cost and unit cost of production, (*b*) Comparing cost of one period with another period to know efficiency or otherwise of it, and (*c*) To ascertain profit or loss from production.

COST COLLECTION

The various elements of cost is accumulated for the entire accounting period. As under this method, the variety of goods manufactured is restricted to one or to a few varieties, the method does not demand maintaining of elaborate records. The accounting procedure can be summarised under the following stages :

(*a*) The accumulation and tabulating various elements of costs for a given period say, a month, quarter, or year.

(*b*) Measurement of output either in terms of number or quantity.

(*c*) Calculating the cost per unit by dividing the total cost by number or quntity produced.

Collection of Materials Cost

The materials cost is accumulated from materials abstract. Alternatively, cost of raw materials consumed is ascertained by adding purchased raw materials during the period to the opening stock and deducting closing stock of materials therefrom. Any normal loss of materials is adjusted by inflating the rate of good units of raw materials.

Collection of Labour and Overhead

The labour cost is obtained from the pay rolls prepared separately for different sections or departments of the factory.

In majority of the cases overheads are charged at a predetermined rate where quotation prices are to be prepared. Otherwise overheads are collected under the heads of factory, office and administration and selling and distribution for the period for which they relate. When more than one variety of product is manufactured the overheads are apportioned on some suitable basis.

TREATMENT OF WORK-IN-PROGRESS AND SCRAP

The incomplete units of production is termed as work-in-progress. It is valued on the basis of material cost, labour cost and factory overheads. The opening stock of work-in-progress is added to the current cost of production (factory cost) and the closing stock of work-in-progress is deducted from the above total. After this treatment is given, the office and administration overheads are added to arrive at office cost.

Alternatively if the work-in-progress is analysed in terms of materials cost, labour cost and overheads, then the amount of materials, wages and overheads included in the work-in-progress in the beginning will be added and that included in work-in-progress at the end, deducted to ascertain the cost of materials labour and factory overheads respectively. There afterwards no other treatment need be given to the work-in-progress

The value of "scrap" realised is to be deducted from works cost or works overhead. This is so because all the elements of costs are incurred on scrapped units also.

Any extra expenses incurred on rectifying "defectives" is added to works cost. However, if the cost of rectifying is high due to abnormal reasons it should be transferred to a separate "Defective account".

COST PRESENTATION–PREPARATION OF COST SHEET

The information derived from various records is presented in the form a statement of cost or a cost sheet. According to Walter W. Biggs, "the expenditure which has been incurred upon production for a period, is extracted from the financial books and the stores' records and set out in a memorandum or statement. If this statement is confined to the disclosure of the cost of the units produced during the period, it is termed as a cost sheet". The purposes which a cost sheet serves and its proforma is already presented in second chapter.

Problem 1 : A factory can produce 60,000 units per annum at its 100% capacity. The estimated cost of production are as under :

Direct materials	Rs. 3 per unit
Direct labour	Rs. 2 per unit
Fixed overheads	Rs. 1,50,000 per annum
Variable overheads	Rs. 5 per unit

Semi-variable Rs. 50,000 per annum up to 50% capacity and an extra expenses of Rs. 10,000 per annum for every 25% increase in capacity or part thereof.

The factory produces only against orders. If the production programme of the factory is as indicated below and the management desires to ensure a profit of Rs. 1,00,000 for the year. Work out the average selling price at which unit should be quoted.

First 3 months of the year 50% of capacity, remaining 9 months of the year 80% of capacity.

(Bangalore University, B. Com., Nov. 1991)

Solution :

Cost sheet

Direct materials	43,500 units @ Rs. 3 per unit		1,30,500
Direct labour	43,500 units @ Rs. 2 per unit		87,000
	Prime cost		2,17,500
Indirect expenses :			
Fixed		1,50,000	
Variable–43,500 units @ Rs. 5		2,17,500	
Semi-variable :			
For first 3 months at 50% capacity $50,000 \times \frac{3}{12}$		12,500	
For 9 months at 80% capacity $70,000 \times \frac{9}{12}$		52,500	4,32,500
	Cost of production		6,50,000
Estimated profit			1,00,000
	Estimated sales		7,50,000

$$\text{Selling price per unit} = \frac{\text{Estimated sales}}{\text{Total units}}$$

$$= \frac{7,50,000}{43,500} = \text{Rs. } 17.24$$

Working Note : Calculation of units produced

output for first 3 months at 50% capacity

$$60,000 \times \frac{50}{100} \times \frac{3}{12} = 7,500 \text{ units}$$

For next 9 months 80% capacity

$$60,000 \times \frac{80}{100} \times \frac{9}{12} = 36,000 \text{ units}$$

Total units produced 43,500 units

Problem 2 : A manufacturing company has an installed capacity of 1,20,000 units per annum. The cost structure of the product manufactured is as under

	Rs.
(*i*) Variable cost per unit :–	
Materials	8
Labour (subject to a minimum of Rs. 56,010 per month)	8
Overheads	3

(*ii*) Fixed overhead – Rs. 1,68,750 per annum.

(*iii*) Semi-variable overheads Rs. 48,000 per annum at 60% capacity. Which increase by Rs. 6,000 per annum for increase of every 10% of the capacity utilisation or any part thereof, for the year as a whole.

The capacity utilisation for the next year is estimated at 60% for two months; 75% for six months and 80% for the remaining part of the year. If the company is planning to have a profit of 25% on the selling price, calculate the selling price per unit. Assume that there are no opening and closing stocks.

(*CA Inter., November 1997*)

Solution : **Calculation of capacity utilisation for the next year**

$$\frac{60}{100} \times \frac{2}{12} \times 1{,}20{,}000 = 12{,}000 \text{ units}$$

$$\frac{75}{100} \times \frac{6}{12} \times 1{,}20{,}000 = 45{,}000 \text{ units}$$

$$\frac{80}{100} \times \frac{4}{12} \times 1{,}20{,}000 = 32{,}000 \text{ units}$$

89,000 units

Calculation of labour cost (subject to a minimum of Rs. 56,000 PM)

For 2 months	=	12,000 × Rs. 8	=	1,12,000
For 6 months	=	45,000 × Rs. 8	=	3,60,000
For 8 months	=	32,000 × Rs. 8	=	2,56,000
				7,28,000

Calculation of semi-variable oh

At 60% capacity	=	48,000
For 80% capacity at Rs. 6,000		
For every 10% capacity utilisation	=	12,000
		60,000

Cost sheet

Materials – 89,000 units e Rs. 8 per unit		7,12,000
Labour cost		7,28,000
	Prime cost	14,40,000
Variable overhead – 89,000 units @ Rs. 3 per unit		2,67,000
Semi variable overhead		60,000
Fixed overhead		1,68,750
	Factory cost	19,35,750
	Profit $\frac{1}{3}$ on cost price	6,45,250
	Sales	25,81,000

Selling price per unit $= \frac{25{,}81{,}000}{89{,}000}$ = Rs. 29.00

Problem 3 : Enterprising Engineering works manufacture product "useful" having a very good demand in the market. The annual accounts of the concern for the year ending March 31, 1995 reveal the following details

	Rs.
Purchase of Raw materials	7,75,800
Wages paid to workmen	
Direct	3,12,400
Indirect	34,000
Salaries :	
Works	1,30,900
Administrative	1,20,000
Sales staff	2,40,000
Travelling expenses (for sales staff)	35,000
Income-tax paid	2,00,000
Interest on Bank borrowing	15,000
Advertisements	2,20,000
Power	62,000
Fuel	47,500
Maintenance :	
Plant	51,500
Building	50,000
Freight (outwards)	2,05,000
Rent	40,000
Depreciation :	
Plant	38,500
Building	25,000
Rates & Taxes	12,000
Sundry office expenses	56,000
Bad debts	30,000
Opening stock :	
Raw materials	55,000
Work-in-progress	1,56,200
Finished goods (4,000 Pcs)	40,000

During the year the concern produced a total output of 1,42,000 pieces out of which 6,000 pieces remained unsold. The stock of raw materials and work-in-progress as on 31st March 1995 were Rs. 1,35,000 and Rs. 56,800 respectively. Other data available are as under :

(*i*) Expenses relating to building are apportioned between works and administration in the ratio of 80 : 20.

(*ii*) Rent is shared between plant and administration in the ratio of 75 : 25.

(*iii*) Entire rates and taxes are identified as administrative expenses.

(*iv*) The Sales Manager is to receive a commission calculated at the rate of 6% of the net profit.

(*v*) Total sales turnover for the year was Rs. 30 lakhs and bad debts to the tune of 1.5% thereof are considered normal.

Prepare a statement of cost showing (a) cost of production in aggregate and per unit (b) cost of goods sold and (c) cost of sales and profit earned. (*ICWA, Inter., June 1995*)

Solution : **Cost sheet of Enterprising Engineering works for the year ending 31st Mar. 1995**

		Total	*Per unit*
Opening stock of Raw materials	55,000		
Add : Purchases	7,75,800		
	8,30,800		
Less : Closing stock of raw materials	1,35,000		
Cost of materials consumed		6,95,800	4.90

Direct wages		3,12,400	2.20
Prime cost		10,08,200	7.10
Works overheads :–			
Indirect wages	34,000		
Power	62,000		
Fuel	47,500		
Maintenance – plant	51,500		
– Building (80%)	40,000		
Rent (75%)	30,000		
Depreciation – plant	38,500		
– Building	20,000		
Salaries	1,30,900		
		4,54,400	3.20
		14,62,600	10.30
Add : Opening stock of work-in-progress		1,56,200	1.10
		16,18,800	11.40
Less : Closing stock of work-in-progress		56,800	0.40
Works cost		15,62,000	11.00
Administration overheads :–			
Rates & Taxes	12,000		
Repairs – Building (20%)	10,000		
Rent (25%)	10,000		
Depreciation – Building (20%)	5,000		
Salaries	1,20,000		
Sundry expenses	56,000		
		2,13,000	1.50
Cost of production		17,75,000	12.50

Statement of cost of sales and profit

		Rs.	*Units*
Opening stock of finished goods		40,000	4,000
Add : Cost of production		17,75,000	1,42,000
		18,15,000	1,46,000
Less : Closing stock of finished goods @ Rs. 12.50 per unit		75,000	6,000
Cost of goods sold		17,40,000	1,40,000
Selling and Distribution overheads :			
Freight	2,05,000		
Travelling expenses	35,000		
Advertisement	2,20,000		
Salaries	2,40,000		
Sales Manager's Commission @ 6% on Net profit	30,000		
Bad debts	30,000	7,60,000	
Cost of sales		25,00,000	
Profit		5,00,000	
Sales		30,00,000	

Working note

Calculation of Sales Manager's commission

Let profit = x

Sales manager's commission 6% of x or $\frac{6x}{100}$

Total profit before charging commission

$$x + \frac{6x}{100}$$

$$\text{or} \quad x + \frac{6x}{100} = \text{sales} - \text{cost of sales excluding sales manager's commission}$$

$$x + \frac{6x}{100} = 30{,}00{,}000 - 24{,}70{,}000$$

$$x + \frac{6x}{100} = 5{,}30{,}000$$

$$100\,x + 6x = 5{,}30{,}000 \times 100$$

$$106x = 5{,}30{,}00{,}000$$

$$x = \frac{5{,}30{,}00{,}000}{106} = 5{,}00{,}000$$

$$\text{Sales Managers Commission} = \frac{6}{100} \times 5{,}00{,}000$$

$$= \text{Rs. } 30{,}000$$

Problem 4 : Delta Engineering Ltd. produces a uniform type of product and has a manufacturing capacity of 3,000 units per week of 48 hrs. From the cost records of the company, the following data are available relating to output and cost for three consecutive weeks :

Week no.	*Units manufactured*	*Direct materials Rs.*	*Direct labour Rs.*	*Factory overhead (variable and fixed) Rs.*
1	1,200	9,000	3,600	31,000
2	1,600	12,000	4,800	33,000
3	1,800	13,500	5,400	34,000

Assuming that the company charges a profit of 20% on selling price find out the selling price per unit when the weekly output is 2,000 units. (*ICWA, Inter, June 1990*)

Solution :

Cost sheet

	Per unit	*Total for 2,000 units*
Materials (In the last three weeks material per unit has been Rs. 7.50)	7.50	1,500
Labour (In the last three weeks labour cost per unit is Rs. 3)	3.00	6,000
Prime cost	10.50	21,000
Overhead :		
Variable overhead 5 per unit (*see note 1*)	5.00	10,000
Fixed overhead (see note 2)	12.50	25,000
Total cost	28.00	56,000
Profit 25% on cost	7.00	14,000
Selling price	35.00	70,000

Working note 1 : Calculation of variable overhead :

Week		*Units manufactured*	*Factory overhead*
1		1,200	Rs. 31,000
2		1,600	Rs. 33,000
	Difference	400	Rs. 2,000

For 400 units : Rs. 2,000

For 2,000 units – ? $\frac{2,000 \times 2,000}{400}$ = Rs. 10,000

Verification of the above figure of Rs. 10,000 considering figures of third week.

Week		*Units manufactured*	*Factory overhead*
2		1,600	33,000
3		1,800	34,000
	Difference	200	1,000

For 200 : 1,000 : 2,000 : x

i.e., $\frac{1,000 \times 2,000}{200}$ = Rs. 10,000

Working note 2 : Calculation of fixed cost

Total factory overheads for 1,200 units	= 31,000
Less : Total variable overhead for 1,200 units	
For 400 : 2,000	
For 1,200 :– ? $\frac{2,000 \times 1,200}{400}$ (output of Ist week)	– 6,000
Fixed overhead	25,000

Fixed overhead by definition remains fixed throughout.

PROBLEMS ON CALCULATION OF MISSING INFORMATION

Problem 5 (Where selling price and cost of sales is missing) : A firm purchased a plant to manufacture a new product, the cost data for which is given below :

Estimated annual sales	24,000 units
Estimated costs :	
Materials	Rs. 4 per unit
Direct labour	Re. 0.60 per unit
Overheads	Rs. 24,000 per year
Administrative expenses	Rs. 28,800 per year
Selling expenses	15% on sales

Calculate the selling price if profit per unit is Rs. 1.02. (*ICWA Inter., Dec. 1990*)

Solution : **Cost sheet**

		Cost per unit	*Amount*
Materials		4.00	96,000
Direct labour		0.60	14,400
	Prime cost	4.60	1,10,400
Overheads		1.00	24,000
	Factory cost	5.60	1,34,400
Administrative expenses		1.20	28,800
	Office cost	6.80	1,63,200
Selling & distribution overheads		1.38	33,120

Cost of sales	8.18	1,96,320
Profit	1.0200	24,480
Sales	9.20	2,20,800

Working note : Calculation of selling price

Let the selling price be $= x$ Rs.

∴ Sales value $= 24{,}000 \times x$ Rs.

Office cost + Selling expense + Profit = Sales

$$1{,}63{,}200 + \left(\frac{15}{100} \times 24{,}000\,x\right) + 24{,}480 = 24{,}000\,x$$

$$1{,}63{,}200 + 3{,}600\,x + 24{,}480 = 24{,}000\,x$$

$$1{,}63{,}200 + 24{,}480 = -\,3{,}600\,x + 24{,}000\,x$$

$$1{,}87{,}680 = 20{,}400\,x$$

$$x = \frac{1{,}87{,}680}{20{,}400} = 9.2$$

$$\text{Sales} = 24{,}000 \times 9.2 = 2{,}20{,}800$$

$$\text{Selling \& distribution overhead} = \frac{15}{100} \times 2{,}20{,}800 = 33{,}120$$

Problem 6 (When the quantity of scrap, value of closing stock of raw materials and value of finished goods are missing) : The following particulars relating to the year 1986 have been taken from the books of a chemical works manufacturing and selling a chemical mixture :

	Kg.	*Rs.*
Stock on 1-1-86 :		
Raw materials	2,000	2,000
Finished mixture	500	1,750
Factory stores		7,250
Purchases :		
Raw materials	1,60,000	1,80,000
Factory stores		24,250
Sales :		
Finished mixture	1,53,050	9,18,000
Factory scrap	?	8,170
Factory wages		1,78,650
Power		30,400
Depreciation of machinery		18,000
Salaries :		
Factory		72,220
Office		37,220
Selling		41,500
Expenses :		
Direct		18,500
Office		18,200
Selling		18,000
Stock on 31-12-86 :		
Raw materials	1,200	?
Finished mixture	450	?
Factory stores		5,550

The stock of finished mixture at the end of 1986 is to be valued at the factory cost of the mixture for that year. The purchase price of raw materials remained unchanged throughout 1986.

Prepare a statement giving the maximum possible information about cost and its break up for the year 1986.

Solution : **Cost sheet for the year ending 31.12.86**

	Quantity (Kg.)	Amount (Rs.)
Opening stock of raw materials	2,000	2,000
Add : Purchases	1,60,000	1,80,000
	1,62,000	1,82,000
Less : Closing stock of raw materials (*see note 1*)	1,200	1,350
Cost of materials consumed	1,60,800	1,80,650
Factory wages		1,78,650
Direct expenses		18,500
Prime cost		3,77,800
Factory overhead :		
Factory stores consumed (*see note 2*)		25,950
Power		30,400
Depreciation of machinery		18,000
Factory salaries		72,220
		5,24,370
Less : Factory scrap sold (*see note 3*)	7,800	8,170
Works cost	1,53,000	5,16,200
Office salaries		37,220
Office expenses		18,200
Office cost	1,53,000	5,71,620
Add : Opening stock of finished mixture	500	1,750
	1,53,500	5,73,370
Less : Closing stock of finished mixture (*see note 4*)	450	1,518
Cost of finished mixture sold	1,53,050	5,71,852
Selling & distribution overhead :- salaries of selling dept.		41,500
Selling expenses		18,000
Cost of sales		6,31,352
Profit		2,86,648
Sales	1,53,050	9,18,000

Working note 1 : Calculation of value of closing stock of raw materials

For 1,60,000 kgs. of purchases, the value is 1,80,000

For 1,200 kgs. – ? (Purchases price of raw materials remains same throughout 1986)

$$\frac{1,80,000 \times 1,200}{1,60,000} = \text{Rs. } 1,350$$

Working note 2 : Calculation of value of factory stores consumed

Opening stock of factory stores	Rs.	7,250
Add : Purchases of factory stores	Rs.	24,250
		31,500
Less : Closing stock of factory stores		5,550
	Rs.	25,950

Working note 3 : Calculation of quantity of scrap sold using reverse method

	Kg.
Quantity of finished mixture sold	1,53,050
Add : Closing stock of finished mixture	450
	1,53,500

Less : Opening stock of finished mixture	500
	1,53,000
Quantity of scrap sold (balancing figure)	7,800
Quantity of materials consumed	1,60,800

Working note 4 : Calculation of value of closing stock of finished mixture : (at works cost)

For 1,53,000 kgs. the works cost is Rs. 5,61,000

For 450 kgs.— ? $= \dfrac{5,16,000 \times 450}{1,53,000}$ = Rs. 1,518

Problem 7 (When purchases is missing) : The books of Adarsh Manufacturing Company present the following data for the month of April 1992 :

Direct labour cost Rs. 17,500 being 175% of works overhead

Cost of goods sold excluding administrative expenses Rs. 56,000

Inventory accounts showed the following opening and closing balances :

	April 1 (Rs.)	*April 30 (Rs.)*
Raw materials	8,000	10,600
Work-in-progress	10,500	14,500
Finished goods	17,600	19,000

Other data are :

Selling expenses	3,500
General & Administration expenses	2,500
Sales for the month	75,000

You are required to

(1) Compute the value of materials purchased.

(2) Prepare a cost statement showing the various elements of cost and also the profit earned.

(CA (Inter), May, 1992)

Solution :

Statement showing value of materials purchased

Cost of goods sold		56,000
Add : Clossing stock of finished goods		19,000
		75,000
Less : Opening stock of finished goods		17,600
	Cost of goods manufactured	57,400
Add : Closing stock of work-in-progress		14,500
		71,900
Less : Opening stock of work-in-progress		10,500
	Work cost	61,400
Less : Factory overhead $\frac{100}{175}$ of direct labour cost		10,000
	Prime cost	51,400
Less : Direct labour		17,500
	Raw materials consumed	33,900
Add : Closing stock of raw materials		10,600
		44,500
Less : Opening stock of raw materials		8,000
Value of materials purchased		36,500

Cost sheet

Cost of raw materials consumed		33,900
Direct labour cost		17,500
	Prime cost	51,400
Add : Factory overhead		10,000
		61,400
Add : Opening stock of work-in-progress		10,500
		71,900
Less : Closing stock of work-in-progress		14,500
	Net works cost	57,400
Add : Opening stock of finished goods		17,600
		75,000
Less : Closing stock of finished goods		19,000
	Cost of goods sold	56,000
Add : General & administration expenses		2,500
Add : Selling expenses		3,500
	Cost of sales	62,000
	Profit	13,000
	Sales	75,000

Problem 8 (When prime cost is missing) : From the following information prepare a cost statement showing maximum possible breakup of cost and total profit :

	Rs.
Sales for January 1990	30,00,000
Cost of goods sold	24,80,000
Administration expenses	1,80,000
Selling expenses	40,000

	1.1.1990 *(Rs.)*	*31.1.1990* *(Rs.)*
Raw materials stock	3,20,000	4,00,000
Work-in-progress	3,20,000	4,80,000
Finished goods	4,20,000	3,40,000

Direct wages were 30% of prime cost
Raw materials consumed were 50% of prime cost
Direct expenses were 20% of prime cost
Factory overheads were 20% of prime cost

(*University of Bombay, B.Com., May 1990*)

Solution :

Cost sheet for the period ending 31.1.1990

Opening stock of raw materials	3,20,000		
Add : Purchases of raw materials	10,71,667		
	13,91,667		
Less : Closing stock of raw materials	4,00,000		
Cost of raw materials consumed			9,91,667
Wages			5,95,000
Direct expenses			3,96,667
		Prime cost	19,83,334
Factory overheads			3,96,666
		Works cost	23,80,000

Add : Opening stock of work-in-progress		3,20,000
		27,00,000
Less : Closing stock of work-in-progress		4,80,000
		22,20,000
Office & administration expenses		1,80,000
	Office cost	24,00,000
Add : Opening stock of finished goods		4,20,000
		28,20,000
Less : Closing stock of finished goods		3,40,000
	Cost of goods sold	24,80,000
Selling expenses		40,000
	Cost of sales	25,20,000
	Profit	4,80,000
	Sales	30,00,000

Note : In this problem prime cost is the basis for calculating various elements of cost. Prime cost in this problem is calculated as under :

	Rs.
Let prime cost be	100
Add : Factory overhead	20
Works cost	120

Calculation of factory overheads on work cost

$$\frac{20}{120} \times 23{,}80{,}000 = 3{,}96{,}666$$

Prime cost = Works cost – Factory overheads

= 23,80,000 – 3,96,666

= Rs. 19,83,334

PROBLEMS ON OUTPUT COSTING AS APPLIED TO VARIOUS INDUSTRIES

Problem 9 (Output costing as applied to plastic industry) : From the following particulars supplied by Pure Plastic Ltd. You are required to prepare a monthly cost sheet showing profit for 1,000 plastic spoons. The opening stock was valued at the same price per 1,000 spoons of the production of the month concerned :

Materials	— Plastic granules	1,400 kgs @ Rs. 5 per kg.
	— Stores	Rs. 5,000
Labour	— Direct	Rs. 16,000
	— Indirect	Rs. 3,000
Overheads	— Works	25% of direct labour
	— Office	10% of works cost

Production for the month of October 1992 was 10,00,000 spoons.

Sales for the month : 90,00,000 spoons @ Rs. 50 per 1,000 spoons.

Stock at the end of the month : 3,00,000 spoons.

Solution : **Cost sheet of Pure Plastic Ltd.**

		Cost per 1,000 spoons	*Total for 10,00,000 spoons*
Raw materials (*see note 1*)		7,00	7,000
Labour (*see note 2*)		16.00	16,000
	Prime cost	23.00	23,000

Stores (*see note 3*)		5.00	5,000
Indirect labour (*see note 4*)		3.00	3,000
Works overhead (*see note 5*)		4.00	4,000
	Works cost	35.00	35,000
Office overhead		3.50	3,500
	Office cost	38.50	38,500
Add : Opening stock of spoons (*see note 6*)		7.70	7,700
		46.20	46,200
Less : Closing stock of spoons (*see note 7*)		11.55	11,550
	Cost of goods sold	34.65	34,650
	Profit	10.35	10,350
	Sales (*see note 8*)	45.00	45,000

Working note 1 : Calculation of material cost per 1,000 spoons

for 10,00,000 spoons : Rs. 7,000

for 1,000 spoons → ? $= \frac{7,000 \times 1,000}{10,00,000}$ = Rs. 7.00

Working note 2 : Calculation of labour cost per 1,000 spoons

for 10,00,000 spoons : Rs. 16,000

for 1,000 spoons → ? $= \frac{16,000 \times 1,00}{10,00,000}$ = Rs. 16.00

Working note 3 : Calculation of stores cost per 1,000 spoons

for 10,00,000 spoons Rs. 5,000

for, 1,000 spoons → ? $= \frac{5,000 \times 1,000}{10,00,000}$ = Rs. 5.00

Working note 4 : Calculation of indirect labour per 3,000 spoons

for 10,00,000 spoons Rs. 3,000

for 1,000 spoons → ? $= \frac{3,000 \times 1,000}{10,00,000}$ = Rs. 3.00

Working note 5 : Calculation of works overheads per 1,000 spoons

for 10,00,000 spoons Rs. 4,000

for 1,000 spoons → ? $= \frac{4,000 \times 1,000}{10,00,000}$ = Rs. 4.00

Working note 6 : Calculation of value of opening stock of spoons

for, 1,000 spoons cost of production is Rs. 38.50

for 2,00,000 spoons → ?$= \frac{2,00,000 \times 38.50}{1,000}$ = Rs. 7,700

Opening stock = Closing stock + Sales – production

= 3,00,000 + 9,00,000 – 10,00,000 = 2,00,000

Working note 7 : Calculation of value of closing stock of spoons

for 1,000 spoons the cost of production is 38.50

for 3,00,000 spoons → ?$= \frac{3,00,000 \times 38.50}{1,000}$ = Rs. 11,550

Working note 8 : $\frac{50}{100} \times 9,00,000 = 45,000$

Problem 10 (Output costing as applied to brick manufacturing industries) : From the following information prepare a monthly cost sheet of the Hard Brickworks showing cost per 1,000 bricks. Also find out the profit per 1,000 bricks.

Materials used :	
Lime	895 tonnes @ Rs. 30 per tonne
Coal	820 tonnes @ Rs. 25 per tonne
Sand	Rs. 10 per 1,000 bricks made
Others	Rs. 700
Labour :	
Sand digging	Rs. 1,800
Brick making	Rs. 8,000
Factory overhead	25% of direct charges
Office overhead	10% of factory cost
Bricks sold	35,00,000 @ Rs. 20 per 1,000 bricks
Stock of bricks at the beginning of the month	1,00,000
Stock of bricks at the end of the month	6,00,000

Solution :

Cost sheet of Hard Brickworks

		Cost per 1,000 bricks	*Amount for 40,00,000 bricks*
Materials used :			
Lime		6.712	26,850
Coal		5.125	20,500
Sand		10.000	40,000
Others		0.175	700
	Total materials cost	22.012	88,050
Labour Sand digging		0.450	1,800
Brick making		2.000	8,000
	Prime cost	24.426	97,850
Factory overheads			
25% direct charges, *i.e.* prime cost		6.115	24,462
	Factory cost	30.577	1,22,312
Office overheads			
10% of factory cost		3.058	12,231
Office cost or cost of production		33.635	1,34,543

Statement showing profit for 1,000 bricks

	No. of bricks	*Per 1,000 bricks*	*Total*
Opening stock	1,00,000	33.635	3363.50
Add : Cost of production	40,00,000	–	1,34,540.00
	41,00,000	33.635	1,37,903.50
Less : Closing stock	6,00,000	–	20,181.00
Cost of goods sold	35,00,000	33.635	1,17,722.50
Loss			47,222.50
Sales			70,000.00

Working note 1 : Calculation of materials cost, lime per 1,000 bricks
for 40,00,000 bricks, materials cost is 26,850

for 1,000 bricks → ? $= \frac{26,850 \times 1,000}{40,00,000}$ = Rs. 6.712

Working note 2 : Calculation of coal consumed per 1,000 bricks

for 40,00,000 bricks : coal cost is Rs. 20,500

for 1,000 bricks → ? $= \dfrac{20,500 \times 1,000}{40,00,000}$ = Rs. 5.125

Working note 3 : Calculation of sand cost per 1,000 bricks

for 40,00,000 bricks : sand cost is 40,000

for 1,000 bricks → ? $= \dfrac{40,000 \times 1,000}{40,00,000}$ = Rs. 10

Working note 4 : Calculation of other cost per 1,000 bricks

for 40,00,000 bricks, other costs is Rs. 700

for 1,000 bricks → ? $= \dfrac{700 \times 1,000}{40,00,000}$ = Rs. 0.175

Working note 5 : Calculation of labour cost per 1,000 bricks

for 40,00,000 bricks, labour cost is Rs. 1,800

for 1,000 bricks → ? $= \dfrac{1,800 \times 1,000}{40,00,000}$ = Rs. 0.450

Working note 6 : Calculation of factory overheads per 1,000 bricks

for 40,00,000 bricks, factory overhead is Rs. 24,462

for 1,000 bricks → ? $= \dfrac{24,462 \times 1,000}{40,00,000}$ = Rs. 6.115

Working note 7 : Calculation of office overheads per 1,000 bricks

for 40,00,000 bricks, office overheads is Rs. 12,231

for 1,000 bricks → ? $= \dfrac{12,231 \times 1,000}{40,00,000}$ = Rs. 3.058

Working note 8 : Calculation of value of opeing stock

for 1,000 bricks : cost of production is Rs. 33.635

for 1,00,000 bricks → ? $= \dfrac{33,635 \times 1,00,000}{1,000}$ = Rs. 3,363.50

Working note 9 : Calculation of value of closing stock

for 1,000 bricks cost of production is Rs. 33.635

for 6,00,000 bricks → ? $= \dfrac{33,635 \times 6,00,000}{1,000}$ = Rs. 20,181

Working note 10 : Calculation of sales

for 1,000 bricks sale price is Rs. 20

for 35,00,000 bricks → ? $= \dfrac{20 \times 35,000}{1,000}$ = Rs. 70,000

Working note 11 : Number of bricks manufactured

Number of bricks sold	35,00,000
Add : Closing stock	6,00,000
	41,00,000
Less : Opening stock	1,00,000
Bricks manufactured	40,00,000

Problem 11 (Output costing as applied to quarries) : The following particulars relate to a manufacturing company :

Slates quarried : 10,000 tons on which a royalty @ Rs. 2 per ton paid

	Rs.
Wages	40,000
Coal	10,000

Internal transport	20,000
Works overhead — 20% on direct charges	
Office overheads — 10% on works cost	
Cost of removal of overburden @ 0,01 paise per slate manufactured	
Opening stock	10,000 slates
Manufactured slates purchased	20,000 @ Re. 1 per slate
Slates sold	1,00,000 @ Rs. 2 per slate
Closing stock	30,000 slates
Selling expenses	0.10 paise per slate sold

Prepare a cost sheet showing the cost per unit of each and every element

Solution :

Cost sheet

	Cost per unit	*Total for 1,00,000 slates*
Royalty on slates quarried — 10,000 tons @ Rs. 2 per ton	0.20	20,000
Wages	0.40	40,000
Coal	0.10	10,000
Internal transport	0.20	20,000
Direct cost or charge	0.90	90,000
Works overhead — 20% on direct charges $\frac{20}{100} \times 90,000$	0.18	18,000
Cost of removal of overburden @ 0.01 paise on 1,00,000 slates	0.01	1,000
Works cost	1.09	1,09,000
Office overhead — 10% of works cost	0.10	10,900
Cost of production	1.19	1,19,900

Statement showing profit

	Number of slates quarried	*Amount*
Opening stock	10,000	11,990
Add : Quarried quantity	1,00,000	1,19,900
Add : Purchases of manufactured slates	20,000	20,000
	1,30,000	1,51,890
Less : Closing stock of slates	30,000	35,700
Cost of goods sold	1,00,000	1,16,190
Selling expenses — 1,00,000 slates @ 0.10 paise		10,000
Cost of sales		1,26,190
Profit		73,810
Sales		2,00,000

Note : Calculation of number of slates quarried

Sale of slates		1,00,000
Add : Closing stock		30,000
		1,30,000
Less : Opening stock	10,000	
Less : Slates purchased	20,000	30,000
Number of slates quarried		1,00,000

Problem 12 (Cost sheet when certain rate of return is expected on share capital) : The Government of India has instituted a dual pricing system in the industry in which your organisation operates. You are the head of the costing division of Rajan Taxtiies Co. Ltd. Your company produces a standard type of cloth 50% of which is procured by the Government at a price of Rs. 4 per metre. You are required by the managing director of your company to suggest a suitable price for the cloth to be sold in the open market. Production during 1990-91 has been 20,00,000 meteres of cloth. Relevant information is given below :

	Rs.
Cotton consumed	10,00,000
Direct labour in factory	10,00,000
Carriage inwards	50,000
Indirect labour in factory	4,00,000
Salary of works manager	2,50,000
Water, power and local taxes (factory)	5,00,000
Dyeing, bleaching, etc.	10,00,000
Excise and other taxes	30,00,000
Depreciation of factory	2,00,000
Depreciation of office	1,00,000
Miscellaneous expenses of factory	1,00,000
Miscellaneous expenses of office	1,00,000
Purchase of computer (office)	20,00,000
Purchase of furniture & machines (office)	5,00,000
Expenditure on sales department	4,00,000
Dividends paid	1,22,00,000
Office salaries	10,00,000
Director's fee	2,00,000
Advertisement & publicity	10,00,000
Salary to M.D.	1,00,000
Commission paid on sales	10,00,000
Commission paid to foreign buyers	1,00,000
Packing and forwarding (sales)	2,00,000

The following further information is made available :

(*i*) The company expects a fair return of 20% on its paid up capital

(*ii*) The paid up capital of the company is Rs. 1,00,00,000.

(*iii*) Marketing expenses outstanding are Rs. 1,00,000.

Suggest the open market price after preparing a cost sheet.

(*Sri Sathya Sai University, B.Com., March 1993*)

Solution :

Cost sheet of Rajan Textiles Co. Ltd.

Cotton consumed		10,00,000
Direct labour cost		10,00,000
Carriage inwards		50,000
Prime cost		20,50,000
Excise & other duties	30,00,000	
Indirect labour	4,00,000	
Salary of works manager	2,50,000	
Water, power, etc.	5,00,000	
Dyeing & bleaching	10,00,000	
Depreciation of factory	2,00,000	
Miscellaneous factory expenses	1,00,000	54,50,000
Factory cost		75,00,000
Depreciation of office	1,00,000	
Miscellaneous office expenses	1,00,000	
Salary to M.D.	1,00,000	

Office salaries	10,00,000	
Director's fee	2,00,000	
		15,00,000
Office cost		90,00,000
Expenditure on sales dept.	4,00,000	
Advertisement	10,00,000	
Commission paid	10,00,000	
Commission to foreigners	1,00,000	
Packing	2,00,000	
Marketing expenses o/s	1,00,000	28,00,000
Cost of sales		1,18,00,000
Expected rate of return		20,00,000
Sales		1,38,00,000

Working note

Cost of production and sale of cloth per meter $= \dfrac{1,18,00,000}{20,00,000}$ = 5.9

Less : Government procurement price = 4.0

Loss per meter 1.9

Total loss on 10,00,000 mts. @ Rs. 1.9 per meter	19,00,000
Fair return on capital (20% on 1 crore)	20,00,000
	39,00,000

Amount to be recovered per meter

$$\frac{39,00,000}{10,00,000} = 3.90$$

Thus the price of remaning 10,00,000 mts. should be fixed up as follows :

Cost of sale per meter	5,90
Amount to be recovered per meter	3.90
	9.80

Note 2 : Purchase of computers, furnitures and equipment are assets. They will not come in cost sheet. Dividend paid is a matter of pure finance. It will not affect cost of production and hence excluded from cost sheet.

PREPARATION OF COMPARATIVE COST SHEET

A comparative cost sheet can be prepared for any of the following purposes :

(*a*) To know the comparative profitability of two or more than two lines of existing products.

(*b*) To know the cost of production, profit and sales of two or more than two products over two different period of time.

(*c*) To compare the actual cost of production with predetermined cost to know the efficiency or otherwise.

(*d*) To compare the profit of one line of product with the existing product and thereby to decide whether a new line of product could be introduced.

(*e*) To evaluate the performance of different types of machineries.

Problem 13 (On comparative cost sheet) : M/s Vidya Pen Company manufactures two types of pens 'Sharada' and 'Viveka'. The particulars for the year ended 31st March, 1999 were as follows :

	Rs.
Direct materials	5,00,000
Direct wages	2,25,000
Direct expenses	75,000
Total sales	10,00,000

There was no work-in-progress at the beginning or at the end of the year. On the study it is as certained that :

(1) Direct material per unit in 'Sharada pen' consists twice as much as that in type 'Viveka pen'

(2) The direct wages per unit for 'Viveka pen' were 40% of those for 'Sharada pen'

(3) Direct expenses were same per unit for viveka as well as 'Sharada pen'.

(4) Factory overhead were 20% of the prime cost.

(5) Administrative overhead were 50% of direct wages

(6) 2,500 units of Sharada pen were produced of which 2,000 were sold and 5,000 units of Viveka pen were produced of which 4,000 were sold, during the year.

(7) Selling overheads were Rs. 8 per unit for Sharada pen and Rs. 9 per unit for Viveka pen.

(8) Selling price per unit for Sharada pen was 250 and Viveka pen was Rs. 125 respectively.

You are required to prepare a statement showing cost and profit in total as well as per unit for Sharada pen and Viveka pen. *(University of Bombay, B.Com., October 1999)*

Solution : **Cost sheet of Vidya Pen Co. for the year ended 31st March**

	Sharada Pen		*Viveka Pen*	
	Amount	*Cost per pen*	*Amount*	*Cost per pen*
Direct materials	2,50,000	100	2,50,000	50
Direct wages	1,25,000	50	1,00,000	20
Direct expenses	25,000	10	50,000	10
Prime cost	4,00,000	160	4,00,000	80
Factory overheads 20% of Prime cost	80,000	32	80,000	16
Works cost	4,80,000	192	4,80,000	96
Administrative overhead 50% of direct wages	62,500	25	50,000	10
Cost of production	5,42,500	217	5,30,000	106
Less : Closing stock of finished goods	1,08,500	–	1,06,000	–
Cost of goods sold	4,34,000	217	4,24,000	106
Selling overheads	16,000	8	36,000	9
Cost of sales	4,50,000	225	4,60,000	115
Profit	50,000	25	40,000	10
Sales	5,00,000	250	5,00,000	125

Working notes :

(1) Calculation of direct materials :

Let material used per unit in Viveka be Rs. x

Material used per unit in 'Sharada' = $2x$

$$2x\,(2{,}500) + x\,(5{,}000) = 5{,}00{,}000$$

$$10{,}000x = 5{,}00{,}000$$

$$x = 50$$

∴ per unit in Viveka = Rs. 50

per unit in Sharada = Rs. 100

(2) Calculation of direct wages :

Let direct wages per unit in 'Sharda' be Rs. x

$\therefore$ Direct wages per unit in 'Viveka' = $\frac{40}{100}x$ or $0.4x$

$$x\,(2{,}500) + 0.4x\,(5{,}000) = 2{,}25{,}000$$
$$2{,}500x + 2{,}000x = 2{,}25{,}000$$
$$4{,}500x = 2{,}25{,}000$$
$$x = \text{Rs. } 50$$
$$\text{Wages per unit in Sharada} = \text{Rs. } 50$$
$$\text{Wages per unit in Viveka} = \frac{40}{100} \times 50 = \text{Rs. } 20$$

(3) Calculation of direct expenses

Per unit : $\frac{75{,}000}{7{,}500}$ = Rs. 10

(4) Valuation of closing stock of finished goods

	Sharada	*Viveka*
Quantity produced	2,500	5,000
Less : Quantity sold	2,000	4,000
Qty. in closing stock	500	1,000
Value of closing stock		
Sharada 500 × 217	1,08,500	
Viveka 1,000 × 106		1,06,000

Problem 14 : A & Co. manufactures two types of products, *viz.*, A and B. The following information is available for the year ended 31st March, 1998.

	Rs.
Direct material	6,75,000
Direct wages	9,90,000
Works overheads	1,95,000

(1) Direct material used per unit in product A were 3 times that of product B.

(2) Direct wages per unit in product B were $\frac{2}{3}$ that of product A.

(3) Works overhead per unit were the same for both the products.

(4) Administration overheads were 100% of the prime cost in each of the products.

(5) Selling and distribution cost per unit was Rs. 6 for both A and B.

(6) 35,000 units of product A were produced, out of which 32,000 units were sold @ Rs. 100 per unit.

(7) 30,000 units of product B were produced, out of which 25,000 units were sold @ Rs. 65 per unit.

Prepare cost sheet showing total cost and cost per unit for both the products.

(University of Bombay, B.Com., October 1998)

Solution :

Cost sheet for the year ended 31st March, 1998

	Product A		*Product B*	
	Per unit	*Total*	*Per unit*	*Total*
Direct materials	15	5,25,000	5	1,50,000
Direct wages	18	6,30,000	12	3,60,000
Prime cost	33	11,55,000	17	5,10,000
Factory overhead	3	1,05,000	3	90,000
Works cost	36	12,60,000	20	6,00,000

Administration overhead	33	11,55,000	17	5,10,000
Cost of production	69	24,15,000	37	11,10,000
Less : Closing stock	—	2,07,000	—	1,85,000
Cost of goods sold	69	22,08,000	37	9,25,000
Selling & Distribution overheads	6	1,92,000	6	1,50,000
Cost of sales	75	24,00,000	43	10,75,000
Profit	25	8,00,000	22	5,50,000
Sales	100	32,00,000	65	16,25,000

Working notes :

(1) *Calculation of direct materials :*

Let materials cost per unit of product B = x

$\therefore$ Materials cost per unit of product A = $3x$

$\therefore$ $3x \times 35{,}000 + x \times 30{,}000 = 6{,}75{,}000$

$1{,}05{,}000x + 30{,}000x = 6{,}75{,}000$

$1{,}35{,}000x = 6{,}75{,}000$

$$x = \frac{6,75,000}{1,35,000} = 5$$

Product A $3x = 15$

$\therefore$ Materials for A = 35,000 × 15 = 5,25,000

Materials for B = 30,000 × 5 = 1,50,000

(2) *Calculation of direct wages :*

Let wages per unit of product A = x

$\therefore$ wages per unit of product B = $\frac{2}{3}x$

$= x \times 35{,}000 + \frac{2}{3}x \times 30{,}000 = 9{,}90{,}000$

$= 35{,}000x + 20{,}000x = 9{,}90{,}000$

$= 55{,}000\,x = 9{,}90{,}000$

$$x = \frac{9,90,000}{55,000} = 18$$

$\therefore$ $\frac{2}{3}x = 12$

$\therefore$ Wages for product A = 35,000 × 18 = 6,30,000

Wages for product B = 30,000 × 12 = 3,60,000

9,90,000

(3) *Calculation of closing stock valuation :*

	Product A	*Product B*
Units produced	35,000	30,000
Units sold	32,000	25,000
Units in stock	3,000	5,000
Value of closing stock		
A — 3,000 units @ Rs. 69	2,07,000	
B — 5,000 units @ Rs. 37		1,85,000

Problem 15 : M/s Vishal manufacturing company manufactures two types of products *viz.*, A and B. The information for the year ended on 31st March, 1998 is as under :

Particulars	*Products*	
	A	*B*
	Rs.	*Rs.*
Direct material per unit	100	120
Direct labour per unit	60	50
Direct expenses per unit	40	80

Additional Information :

(1) Factory expenses are charged at 20% of prime cost.

(2) Office expenses are charged at 25% of works cost.

(3) 2,000 units of product A were produced of which 1500 units were sold and 5,000 units of product B were produced of which 4,500 units were sold

(4) Selling expenses are Rs. 15 per unit for product A and Rs. 20 per unit for product B.

(5) Company charges a profit at 20% on sales for both the products.

Prepare a cost sheet showing the cost and profit in total as well as in per unit.

(University of Bombay, B.Com., April 1998)

Solution : **Comparative cost sheet of M/s Vishal Manufacturing Company**

	Product A		*Product B*	
	Total	*Per unit*	*Total*	*per unit*
Direct materials	2,00,000	100	6,00,000	120
Direct labour	1,20,000	60	2,50,000	50
Direct expenses	80,000	40	4,00,000	80
Prime cost	4,00,000	200	12,50,000	250
Factory overheads 20% of prime cost	80,000	40	2,50,000	50
Works cost	4,80,000	240	15,00,000	300
Office overheads 25% of works cost	1,20,000	60	3,75,000	75
Cost of production	6,00,000	300	18,75,000	375
Less : Closing stock	1,50,000	–	1,87,500	-
Cost of goods sold	4,50,000	300	16,87,500	375
Selling & Distribution overhead	22,500	15	90,000	20
Cost of sales	4,72,500	315	17,77,375	395
Profit @ 20% on sales or 25% on cost	1,18,125	78.75	4,44,375	98.75
Sales	590625	393.75	22,21875	493.75

Working notes :

(1) **Calculation of materials :**

A = 100 × 2,000 units = 2,00,000

B = 120 × 5,000 units = 6,00,000

(2) **Calculation of wages :**

A = 60 × 2,000 units = 1,20,000

B = 50 × 5,000 units = 2,50,000

(3) **Calculation of selling overheads**

A = 15 × 1,500 units = 22,500

B = 20 × 4,500 units = 90,000

PREPARATION OF TENDER STATEMENT

Very often the purchase of goods and component parts by the buyers are based on the tender price or quotation price quoted by the supplier, *i.e.*, manufacturer. This is to take advantage of the lowest price quoted by the manufacturer. So it is implied that to increase the sales and to attract more customers towards business it is very essential to prepare the quotation price very carefully. At the some time once the tender price is issued it cannot be reversed. Any increased, quotation price leads to rejection of the tender and consequently loss of orders. Any low quotation price results in a loss to the business. Therefore care must be taken to prepare tenders based on actual facts and in precise terms.

The cost accountant plays a significant role in preparing the tender price. First of all, he has to collect all the information relating to cost of materials, wages and other expenses. The exact requirements of the various inputs can be obtained from production planning department. If necessary, advise can also be obtained from industrial engineer. The estimated price of raw materials can be known from market survey. The labour cost for manufacturing so many units can be known from previous years records and providing for additional charges in case of revision of wage rates. Similarly direct expenses and overheads are worked out based on past experience and considering new factors. Wherever it is necessary overheads may be classified into fixed and variable to know the impact of variable overhead. Fixed overheads should be critically examined to ascertain the possible increase for the new work load. The office and administration overheads can be charged on a predetermined basis. Once the estimated cost is prepared the last step is to add a margin of profit to ascertain the quotation price or tender price.

Problem 16 : The following figures ralate to the manufacture of electric fans for three months ending 31st Dec., 2000 :

	Rs.
Completed stock on 1st Oct. 2000	NIL
Completed stock on 31st Dec. 2000	20,250
Stock of raw materials on 1st Oct. 2000	5,000
Stock of raw materials on 31st Dec. 2000	3,500
Factory wages	75,000
Indirect charges	12,500
Materials purchased	32,500
Sales	1,12,500

The number of fans manufactured during these three months was 3,000.

Prepare a statement showing the cost per fan and the price to be quoted for 750 fans to realise the same percentage of profits as was realised during the said period, assuming the same condition.

(*Sri Sathya Sai University, B.Com., Feb. 2001*)

Solution : **Statement of cost for the three months ending**

		31.12.1982	
		Cost for 3,000 fans	*Cost for fan*
Opening stock of raw materials	5,000		
Add : Purchases	32,500		
	37,500		
Less : Closing stock	3,500		
		34,000	11.33
Factory wages		75,000	25.00

	Prime cost	1,09,000	36.33
Indirect charges		12,500	4.17
	Cost of production	1,21,500	40.50
Less : Closing stock of fans		20,250	
	Cost of goods sold	1,01,250	
	Profit	11,250	
	Sales	1,12,500	

Quotation for 750 fans

		Total	*Per fan*
Materials Rs. $\frac{34,000}{3,000} \times 750$		8,500	11.33
Wages Rs. $\frac{75,000}{3,000} \times 750$		18,750	25.00
	Prime cost	27,250	36.33
Indirect wages Rs. $\frac{12,500}{3,000} \times 750$		3,125	4.17
	Cost of production	30,375	40.50
Add : Profit $\frac{1}{9} \times 30,375$		3,375	4.50
	Quotation price	33,750	45.00

Problem 17 : The trading profit & loss a/c of Vijaya manufacturing company for the year ending 31.12.1998 was as follows :

To Raw materials Purchased	80,000	By sales (2,500 units)	2,50,000
To Direct wages	30,000	By closing stock of raw materials	5,000
To Direct expenses	25,000		
To Factory expenses	40,000		
To Gross profit c/d	80,000		
	2,55,000		2,55,000
To Office salaries	25,000	By gross profit b/d	80,000
To Office rent	12,000	By dividend received	10,000
To Selling expenses	12,500	By discount received	7,500
To preliminary expenses written-off	2,500		
To Goodwill written off	5,500		
To Net profit c/d	40,000		
	97,500		97,500

For the year 1999, it is estimated that :

(1) Units produced and sold will rise by 20%

(2) Prices of raw materials per unit will rise by 10%

(3) Direct wages per unit will increase by 25%.

(4) Direct expenses will increase by Rs. 5,000 in Total.

(5) Factory expenses per unit will increase by 25%

(6) The office premises which was on rental basis in 1998 would be purchased by the company, on which depreciation would be Rs. 6,000 on 1999.

(7) Selling expenses per unit will remain same

You are required to prepare a statement showing estimated cost and profit for the year ended 31.12.1999 considering that company shall charge a profit at 20% on sales. (*University of Bombay B.Com., April 1999*)

Solution : **Cost sheet and tender statement**

	1998 (for 2,500 units)		1999 (for 3,000 units)	
	Total	*Per unit*	*Total*	*per unit*
Raw materials	75,000	30	99,000	33
Direct wages	30,000	12	45,000	15
Direct expenses	25,000	10	30,000	10
Prime cost	1,30,000	52	1,74,000	58
Factory expenses	40,000	16	60,000	20
Works cost	1,70,000	68	2,34,000	78
Office & administration overheads	37,000	148		
Office salaries 25,000				
Depreciation 6,000			31,000	10.33
	207,000	82.8	2,65,000	88.33
Selling expenses	12,500	5	15,000	5
Cost of sales	2,19,500	87.8	2,80,000	93.33
Profit	30,500	12.2	70,000	23.33
Sales	2,50,000	100	3,50,000	116.66

Working notes :

(1) *Calculation of units produced in 1999*

No. of units produced in 1998	=	2,500
Add increase of 20% in 1999		500
		3,000

(2) *Calculation of raw materials in 1999*

$$\text{Raw materials per unit} = \frac{75,000}{2,500} = \text{Rs. } 30$$

	In 1998 per unit cost	=	Rs. 30
Add :	Increase of 10% in 1999	=	3
			33

(3) *Calculation of direct wages :*

	In 1998 wages per unit cost	=	Rs. 12
Add :	Increase of 25% in 1999	=	3
			15

(4) *Calculation of factory expenses :*

Factory expenses in 1998 = 40,000

$$\text{Per unit in 1998} = \frac{40,000}{2,500} = \text{Rs. } 16$$

Add :	Increase by 25%	=	4
			20

Factory expenses in 1999 = 20 × 3,000 = 60,000

(5) It is assumed that salaries will remain same

(6) Rent will not appear in 1999, instead of the rent, depreciation will be Rs. 6,000.

So total expenses = 25,000 + 6,000 = 31,000

(7) Selling expenses for 1999 per unit Rs. 5 as in 1998 will remain same

(8) Profit = 20% on sales or 25% on cost

$$= 2{,}80{,}000 \times \frac{25}{100} = 70{,}000$$

(9) Preliminary expenses written off and goodwill written off are purely financial expenses and dividend received and discount received are purely financial incomes, hence excluded from cost sheet.

Problem 18 : Swadeshi Electronics Ltd., furnishes to you the following information for the year ended 31 March, 1996 :

Production and sales	15,000 units
Sales	Rs. 12,75,000
Direct wages	Rs. 2,70,000
Direct materials	Rs. 3,30,000
Factory overheads	Rs. 2,25,000
Administrative overheads	Rs. 1,05,000
Sales overheads	Rs. 90,000

On account of intense competition following changes are estimated in the subsequent year.

(1) Production and sales activity will be increased by one-third.

(2) Material rate will be lower by 25%. However there will be increase in consumption by 20% due to quality differences

(3) Direct wages cost would be reduced by 20% due to automation

(4) Out of the above factory overhead, Rs. 45,000 are of fixed nature. The remaining factory expenses are variable in proportion to the number of units produced

(5) Total administrative overheads will be lower by 40%

(6) Sales overhead per unit would remain the same

(7) Sale price per unit would be lower by 20%

Prepare a statement of cost for both the years ending 31st March, 1996 and 31st March, 1997, showing maximum possible details. *(University of Bombay, B.Com., April 1996)*

Solution : **Cost sheet for the years 1996 and 1997**

	1996		*1997*	
	Total	*Per unit*	*Total*	*Per unit*
Materials	3,30,000	22	3,96,000	19.80
Wages	2,70,000	18	2,88,000	14.40
Prime cost	6,00,000	40	6,84,000	34.20
Factory overhead	2,25,000	15	2,85,000	14.25
Works cost	8,25,000	55	9,69,000	48.45
Administration overhead	1,05,000	7	63,000	3.15
Cost of production	9,30,000	62	10,32,000	51.60
Selling overheads	90,000	6	1,20,000	6.00
Cost of sales	10,20,000	68	11,52,000	57.60
Profit	2,55,000	17	2,08,000	10.40
Sales	12,75,000	85	13,60,000	68

Working notes :

(1) *Calculation of production & sales :*

$$15{,}000 + \frac{1}{3} \times 15{,}000 = 20{,}000 \text{ units}$$

(2) *Calculation of material rate :*

$1996 = \dfrac{3,30,000}{15,000}$	=	22.00
Less Reduction in price by 25%		5.50
		16.50
Add Rise in consumption by 20%		3.30
Rate of materials		19.80

(3) *Calculation of wages*

Wage rate	18.00
Less : 20% reduction	3.60
Rate of wages	14.40

(4) *Calculation of factory overheads*

	1996	*1997*
Fixed	45,000	45,000
Variable	1,80,000	2,40,000
	2,25,000	2,85,000

(5)	Administration cost in 1996	1,05,000
	Less decrease in expenditure 40%	42,000
	Cost in 1997	63,000
(6)	Sales overheads per unit is Rs. 6	
	So for 20,000 units it would be 1,20,000	
(7)	Selling price in 96	85
	Less 20% reduction	17
	Selling price in 97	68

Problem 19 : The following information for the years ending 31st Dec. 1989 is taken from the books of a company manufacturing TV valves :

Materials consumed	6,00,000
Direct wages	4,00,000
Direct expenses	2,00,000
Indirect wages	30,000
Stereo and spares consumed	55,000
Workman's welfare expenses	40,000
Cost of rectifying defective work	15,000
Depreciation on machinery	25,000
Other factory expenses	1,50,000
Sale of factory scrap	15,000
Administrative staff salaries	1,55,000
Other administrative expenses	1,10,000
Professional charges, audit fee, director's fee	35,000
Commission paid to selling agents	1,20,000
Neon sign expenses	25,000
Show room expenses	35,000
Sales	26,40,000

10,000 units has been manufactured and sold for the year ending 31st Dec. 1989

For the year ending 31st Dec. 1990 the following estimates have been made :

(*i*) Production and sales will be 12,000 units

(*ii*) Materials cost per unit will rise by 50%

(*iii*) Wage rates per unit will rise by 25%

(*iv*) Direct expenses per unit will be in the same proportion to wages as before

(*v*) Factory expenses will be in the same proportion to prime cost. Administration overheads in the same proportion to factory cost and selling overheads in the same proportion to cost of production as before

(*vi*) Profit desired per unit is 25% on selling price.

Prepare a cost statement showing total cost, cost per tin, total profit and profit per unit for 1989 and 1990.

(*University of Bombay, B.Com., Oct. 1990*)

Solution :

Cost sheet for 1989 (output 10,000 units)

			Cost per unit	*Amount*
Materials			60.00	6,00,000
Wages			40.00	4,00,000
Direct expenses			20.00	2,00,000
		Prime cost	120.00	12,00,000
Works overheads :				
Indirect wages	30,000			
Stereo and spare parts	55,000			
Workmen's welfare expenses	40,000			
Cost of rectifying defectives	15,000			
Depreciation on machinery	25,000			
Other factory expenses	1,50,000			
	3,15,000			
Less : Sale of factory scrap	15,000		30	3,00,000
		Factory cost	150.00	15,00,000
Administration overheads :				
Administrative staff salaries	1,55,000			
Other administrative expenses	1,10,000			
Profession charges, etc.	35,000		30.000	3,00,000
		Office cost	180.00	18,00,000
Selling & distribution overheads :				
Commission paid	1,20,000			
Neon sign expenses	25,000			
Show room expenses	35,000		18.00	1,80,000
		Cost of sales	198.00	19,80,000
		Profit	66.00	6,60,000
		Sales	264.00	26,40,000

Quotation price for 1990 (output 12,000 units)

			Cost per unit	*Amount*
Materials	60		90.00	10,80,000
Add : 50% Increase	30			
Labour	40		50.00	6,00,000
Add : 25% Increase	10			
Direct expenses (*see note 1*)			25.00	3,00,000
		Prime cost	165.00	19,80,000
Works overhead (*see note 2*)			41.25	4,95,000
		Factory cost	206.25	24,75,000
Administrative expenses (*see note 3*)			41.25	4,95,000

Office cost	247.50	29,70,000
Selling and distribution expenses (*see note 4*)	24.75	2,97,000
Cost of sales	272.25	32,67,000
Profit	90.75	10,89,000
Sales	363.00	43,56,000

Working note 1 : Calculation of direct expenses

In 1989, for Rs. 40 wages : the direct expenses 20

In 1990 for Rs. 50 wages → ? $\frac{50 \times 20}{40}$ = Rs. 25 per unit

Working note 2 : Calculation of factory overheads

For 12,00,000 prime cost, factory expenses was, 3,00,000

For 100 → ? $\frac{3,00,000 \times 100}{12,00,000} = 25\%$

Working note 3 : Calculation of administration overhead

For 15,00,000 of factory cost, the adm. overhead is Rs. 3,00,000

For 100 → ? $\frac{3,00,000 \times 100}{15,00,000} = 20\%$

Working note 4 : Calculation of selling overheads

For 18,00,000 of cost of production the selling overhead is Rs. 1,80,000

For 100 → ? $\frac{1,80,000 \times 100}{18,00,000} = 10\%$

Problem 20 : A company produces a plant that sells for Rs. 1,800. An increase of 7½% in cost of materials and 6¼% in cost of labour is anticipated. What must be the selling price to produce the same percentage of gross profit as before. Only data available are :

Material cost have been 50% of cost of sale

Wages cost have been 20% of cost of sale

Overhead cost have been 30% of cost of sale

The anticipated increased costs in relation to the present sales price would cause a 25% decrease in the amount of present gross profit.

Prepare a statement of profit or loss per unit, showing the new selling price desired and new cost per unit.

Solution :

Let x be the present cost of sales

Let y be the present gross profit

Then for the present condition $x + y = 1,800$ ....(1)

Rs. x is made up of :

Materials	50% or =	$0.5\,x$
Labour	20% or =	$0.2\,x$
Overheads	30% or =	$0.3\,x$

This would increase :

Materials by	7½% = $0.5x + 0.0375x$ =	$0.5375x$
Labour by	6¼% = $0.2x + 0.0125x$ =	$0.2125x$
Overhead as before		$0.3000x$
		$1.0500x$

This increase in cost would result in a decrease of gross profit by 25% at the same selling price. So the gross profit would be $0.75\,y$

i.e., $1.05\,x + 0.75\,y = 1,800$ ....(2)

$x + y = 1,800$ $- \times 1.5$

$1.05\,x + 0.75\,y = 1,800$

$$1.05\,x + 1.05\,y = 1{,}890$$
$$1.05\,x + 0.75\,y = 1{,}800$$

Subtracting 0.30 y = 90

$$y = \frac{90}{0.30} = 300$$

Substituting the value of y in the 1st equation

$$x + y = 1{,}800$$
$$x + 300 = 1{,}800$$
$$x = 1{,}800 - 300$$
$$= 1{,}500$$

Cost sheet showing present and revised cost

	Present cost		Revised cost
Materials 50%	750.00	Add 7½%	806
Labour 20%	300.00	Add 6¼%	318
Overhead 30%	450.00		450
Cost of sales	1,500		1,575
Profit	300		315
Selling price	1,800		1,890

Problem 24 (When fixed and variable overheads are given) : The following information is available from the books of a company manufacturing luxury ceiling fans. Production and sales during the year ending 31.3.1988 was 1,000 units.

	Rs.
Direct materials	2,00,000
Direct wages	1,50,000
Factory expesnes	1,37,500
Administration expenses	60,000
Selling expenses	45,000
Sales	7,30,000

The following estimates have been made for 1988-89 :

(*i*) Production and sales will be 1,500 units

(*ii*) Materials price per unit will increase by 25% but due to economy in consumption the cost per unit will reduce by 12%

(*iii*) The wages rates per unit will increase by 20%

(*iv*) Factory expenses Rs. 50,000 are fixed. The remaining factory expenses will be in the same proportion to materials consumed and wages as in the previous year

(*v*) The total administration expenses will increase by $66\frac{2}{3}\%$

(*vi*) Selling expenses will be Rs. 90,000

(*vii*) The profit desired is 20% on sales

Prepare a cost statement showing maximum possible break-up of cost per unit and total cost for 1987-88 and 1988-89 profit per unit and total profit for 1987-88 and 1988-89.

(*University of Bombay, B.Com., Oct. 1988*)

Solution : **Cost sheet for 1987-88 (output 1,000 fans)**

			Cost per fan	Amount
Direct materials			200	2,00,000
Direct wages			150.00	1,50,000
		Prime cost	350.00	3,50,000
Factory overheads	— Fixed		50.00	50,000
	— Variable		87.50	87,500

	Factory cost	487.50	4,87,500
Administration expenses		60.00	60,000
	Office cost	547.50	5,47,500
Selling expenses		45.00	45,000
	Cost of sales	592.50	5,92,500
	Profit	137.50	1,37,500
	Sales	730.00	7,30,000

Quotation for 1,500 fans

			Cost per fan	*Amount*
Materials	200		226	3,39,000
Add : 13% increase	26			
Wages	150			
Add : 20% increase	30		180	2,70,000
		Prime cost	406	6,09,000
Factory overhead — Fixed			33.33	50,000
— Variable (*see note*)		101.50	1,52,250	
		Factory cost	540.83	8,11,250
Administration expenses			66.67	1,00,000
		Office cost	607.50	9,11,250
Selling expenses			60.00	90,000
		Cost of sales	667.50	10,01,250
		Profit	166.875	2,50,312.50
		Sales	834.375	12,51,562.50

Note : For prime cost of 350 variable overhead is 87.50
For prime cost of 406 variable overhead is 101.50.

PRODUCTION ACCOUNT

A production account is another form of cost sheet which is prepared to ascertain cost of production, profit and sales. Strictly speaking a cost sheet is prepared to ascertain the cost of production of goods and services. But when the cost sheet is extended further so as to reveal profit and sales, it is termed as production a/c. However, production account is prepared in the form ledger accounts so as to give the exact cost of production, loss in output, sale of scrap, etc.

Problem 22 (Problem on Iron production) : The Sandur Iron and Manganese production for the quarter ending 31st March, 2003 amounted to 32,000 tons. The standard cost of production of one ton of pig iron is Rs. 21.00.

From the particulars given below, prepare pig iron production account showing profit on production and cost per ton of each expenditure.

	Stock on 1-1-03 (Rs.)	*Purchases (Rs.)*	*Stock on 31-1-03 (Rs.)*
Lime stone	3,100	42,300	5,400
Coal and coke	17,400	2,93,500	14,900
Iron ore	14,600	1,77,200	27,800
	Stock on 1-1-03	*Sales during the quarter*	*Stock on 31-3-03*
Pig iron	(Rs.) 2,97,000	10,33,000	2,99,000

Other production expenses during the quarter were—Furnace wages Rs. 92,000, carriage inwards Rs. 22,000, furnace repairs Rs. 26,000.

Solution :

Production A/c

	Cost per ton	*Tatal*		*Cost per ton*	*Total*
To materials used :			By trading a/c		
Lime stone	1.25	40,000	(32,000 tons @ Rs. 21)	21	6,72,000
Coal and coke	9.25	2,96,000			
Iron ore	5.12	1,64,000			
To carriage inwards	0.69	22,000			
To furnace wages	2.88	92,000			
To furnace repairs	0.81	26,000			
To profit on production	1.00	32,000			
	21.00	6,72,000		21	6,72,000

Trading a/c for the quarter ended 31.3.91

To opening stock	2,97,000	By sales	10,33,000
To production a/c	6,72,000	By closing stock	2,99,000
To gross profit	3,63,000		
	13,32,000		13,32,000

Working note : Calculation of cost of materials consumed

	Lime stone	*Coal & coke*	*Iron ore*
Opening stock	3,100	17,400	14,600
Add : Purchases	42,300	2,93,500	1,77,200
	45,400	3,10,900	1,91,800
Less : Closing stock	5,400	14,900	27,800
Materials consumed	40,000	2,96,000	1,64,000

Problem 23 (Problem on coal production) : The following are the balances of the impersonal ledger of a colliery relating to revenue at the end of the year :

	Rs.
Wages paid for coal production	5,80,000
Coal for colliery consumption	45,000
Timber used in coal production	64,000
Ropes used in coal production	12,000
Stores used in coal production	76,000
Royalties paid for coal production	42,000
General charges for coal production	70,000
Salaries for coal production	36,000
Coal sold (including colliery consumption 1,12,000 tons)	8,84,000
Wages paid for coke making	50,000
Stores used	37,000
Salaries paid ·	8,000
Coke sold 43, 500 tons	5,40,000

The stock of coal at the beginning of the year amounted to 7,000 tons valued at Rs. 5 per ton and at the end of the year 15,000 tons at a similar rate. The stock of coke at the beginning of the year amounted to 2,000 tons valued at Rs. 10 pet ton and at the end of the year 500 tons valued at a similar rate.

The total production of the colliery was 1,85,000 tons of coal and 42,000 tons of coke, 65,000 tons of coal being used for coke making.

Prepare separate production accounts for coal and coke showing the cost of each item of expenses per ton of coal and coke separately, taking coal used for coke making at cost price.

(Sri Sathya Sai University, B.Com., March 1992)

Solution :

Coal production a/c

	Per ton	Amount		Per ton	Amount
To wages	3.14	5,80,000	By cost of production a/c	5.00	9,25,000
To coal	0.24	45,000			
To timber	0.34	64,000			
To ropes	0.06	12,000			
To stores	0.42	76,000			
To royalties	0.23	42,000			
To general charges	0.38	70,000			
To salaries	0.19	36,000			
	5.00	9,25,000		5.00	9,25,000
To opening stock		35,000	By sales		8,84,000
To cost of production		9,25,000	By coke production		
To gross profit c/d		3,24,000	65,000 @ Rs. 5		3,25,000
			By closing stock		75,000
		12,84,000			12,84,000

Coke production a/c

To wages	1.19	50,000	By cost of production a/c	10	4,20,000
To stores	0.88	37,000			
To salaries	0.19	8,000			
To coal used	7.74	3,25,000			
	10.00	4,20,000		10	4,20,000
To opening stock		20,000	By sales		5,40,000
To cost of production		4,20,000	By closing stock (500×10)		5,000
To profit & loss a/c		1,05,000			
		5,45,000			5,45,000

Problem 24 (Problem on yarn and cloth production a/c) : Given below is the cloth and yarn manufacturing a/c of Utter Pradesh Cotten Mills for the year ended 31.12.99 :

To opening stock		By sale of 2,24,000 kgs	
Yarn 44,800 kgs	33,600	of waste being that portion	
Cloth 88,200 kgs	88,200	of 11,53,600 kgs of cotton	28,000
To cotton consumed			
11,53,600 kgs	9,01,250	By sales :	
To spinning wages	57,050	Yarn — 1,68,000 kgs	1,89,000
To weaving wages	91,700	Cloth — 7,56,000 kgs	8,97,750
To stores consumed in spinning which increased yarn 5,600 kgs in weight	41,300	By cloing stock :	
		Yarn — 1,40,000 kgs	1,48,750
To stores and sizing materials consumed in weaving which increased cloth by 1,86,200 kgs	1,48,400	Cloth — 1,90,400 kgs	2,14,200
To spinning fuel	36,050		
To weaving fuel	22,400		
To gross profit	57,750		
	14,77,700		14,77,700

For the satisfaction of income tax authorities, who contend that gross profit is suppressed by the company, you are required to prepare (1) yarn production and (2) cloth production account separately showing the following details :

(1) Gross profit of the department.
(2) Total quantity produced (including the opening balance).
(3) The cost production including the value of opening stock which was at cost.

Solution :

Yarn production a/c

	Qty.	Amt.		Qty.	Amt.
To opening stock	44,800	33,600	By sales of waste	2,24,000	28,000
To cotton consumed	11,53,600	9,01,250	By cost of production		
To stores consumed	5,600	41,300	including opening stock		
To spinnig wages		57,050	@ Rs. 1.0625	9,80,000	10,41,250
To spinning fuel		36,050			
	12,04,000	10,69,250		12,04,000	10,69,250
To cost of production	9,80,000	10,41,250	By sale of yarn	1,68,000	1,89,000
To gross profit		10,500	By cloth production	6,72,000	7,14,000
			a/c @ 1.0625		
			By closing stock	1,40,000	1,48,750
	9,80,000	10,51,750		9,80,000	10,51,750

Cloth production a/c

	Qty.	Amt.		Qty.	Amt.
To opening stock	88,200	88,200	By cost of production	9,46,400	10,64,700
To yarn	6,72,000	7,14,000			
To stores consumed	1,86,200	1,48,400			
To weaving wages		91,700			
To weaving fuel		22,400			
	9,46,400	10,64,700		9,46,400	10,64,700
To cost of production	9,46,400	10,64,700	By sale	7,56,300	8,97,750
To gross profit		47,250	By closing stock	1,90,400	2,14,200
	9,46,400	11,11,950		9,46,400	11,11,950

Problem 25 : From the following particulars of Swadeshi Cotton Mills for the half year ended 30.6.92, prepare two separate production accounts, *viz.*, yarn production a/c and cloth production a/c :

	Rs.
Opening stock of yarn at cost (60,000 kgs)	30,000
Opening stock of cloth at cost (1,20,000 kgs)	90,000
Cotton purchased (10,40,000 kgs)	2,60,000
Weaving wages	60,000
Stores weaving	40,000
Wages of spinning	30,000
Stores	20,000
Fuel	10,000
Yern sales (2,00,000 kgs)	40,000
Stock at the end at cost :	
Yarn (2,00,000 kgs)	41,000
Cloth (2,05,000 kgs)	1,50,000
Fuel—Weaving	10,000
Sales : Waste (2,11,000 kgs)	29,000
Cloth (4,20,000 kgs)	3,00,000

Stores consumed increased the weight of production by 4,000 kgs for spinning stores and 1,20,000 kgs for weaving stores.

Solution :

Yarn production a/c

	Weight	*Amount*		*Weight*	*Amount*
To cotton	10,40,000	2,60,000	By sales of waste	2,11,000	29,000
To stores	4,000	20,000	By cost of production	8,33,000	2,91,000
To wages		30,000			
To fuel		10,000			
	10,44,000	3,20,000		10,44,000	3,20,000
To opening stock	60,000	30,000	By sales	2,00,000	40,000
To cost of production	8,33,000	2,91,000	By cloth production a/c (*see note 1*)	4,93,000	1,77,215
			By closing stock	2,00,000	41,000
			By P & L a/c		62,785
	8,93,000	3,21,000		8,93,000	3,21,000

Cloth production a/c

To yarn production	4,93,000	1,77,215	By loss in weight (*see note 2*)	1,08,000	
To stores	1,20,000	40,000	By cost of production a/c	5,05,000	2,87,215
To wages		60,000			
To fuel		10,000			
	6,13,000	2,87,215		6,13,000	2,87,215
To opening stock	1,20,000	90,000	By sale	4,20,000	30,00,000
To cost of production	5,05,000	2,87,215	By closing stock	2,05,000	1,50,000
To P & L a/c		72,785			
	6,25,000	4,50,000		6,25,000	4,50,000

Working note 1 : Calculation of the value of yarn transferred to cloth production a/c :
For processing a total weight of yarn of 8,93,000 kgs the cost of production is 3,21,000.
For 4,93,000 kgs of yarn output the value is

$$\frac{3,21,000 \times 4,93,000}{8,93,000} = \text{Rs. } 1,77,215$$

Working note 2 : Calculation of weight lost

Total production = Sales + Closing stock – Opening stock
4,20,000 + 2,05,000 – 1,20,000 = 5,05,000

Total weight put in	6,13,000
Actual weight of production	5,05,000
Loss in weight	1,08,000

Problem 26 (Mica and talcum production account) : The following particulars are extracted from the books of M/s Rao Insulating Company as on 31.12.90.

Wages paid	6,04,000
Timber used	58,000
Sundry stores	97,000
Rent and taxes ($\frac{1}{3}$ applicable to talcum powder)	72,000
Wages paid for manufacturing talcum powder	71,000
Royalties paid on mica produced	72,000
Ropes used	12,000
Salaries paid ($\frac{1}{4}$ applicable to talcum powder)	28,000
Mica sold, 1,94,000 tons	7,02,000

Talcum powder sold 72,000 tons 4,50,000

The total production of the company was 3,04,000 tons of Mica and 72,000 tons of talcum powder, 1,10,000 tons of mica were used for making talcum powder.

You are required to prepare mica production and talcum powder production account showing the profit resulting from the sale of Mica and talcum powder, showing the cost per ton of mica and the cost per ton of talcum powder taking mica used for talcum powder at cost price.

Solution :

Mica production a/c (output 3,04,000)

To wages paid		6,04,000	By cost of production @ Rs. 3		9,12,000
To timber used		58,000			
To sundry stores		97,000			
To rent & taxes $\frac{2}{3}\times 72{,}000$		48,000			
To royalties		72,000			
To ropes used		12,000			
To salaries $\frac{3}{4}\times 28{,}000$		21,000			
		9,12,000			9,12,000
To cost of production	3,04,000	9,12,000	By sales	1,94,000	7,02,000
To P & L a/c	–	1,20,000	By talcum powder a/c	1,10,000	3,30,000
	3,04,000	10,32,000		3,04,000	10,32,000

Talcum powder production a/c

To Mica production a/c		3,30,000	By cost of production @ Rs 6 per ton		4,32,000
To rent & taxes $\frac{1}{3}\times 72{,}000$		24,000			
To salaries $\frac{1}{4}\times 28{,}000$		7,000			
To wages		71,000			
		4,32,000			4,32,000
To cost of production	1,10,000	4,32,000	By normal waste	38,000	
To profit	–	18,000	By sales	72,000	4,50,000
	1,10,000	4,50,000		1,10,000	4,50,000

QUESTIONS

Short and Long Answer Questions

1. Define "unit costing" what are its characteristics? What are the types of industries to which it is applicable? *(Calicut University, B.Com., Apr. 1988)*
2. Describe the objects of cost sheets. Give an examle of a cost sheet, indicating clearly the headings and important items supplying imaginary figures. *(Kerala University, B.Com., April. 1990)*
3. Define unit costing. Mention the names of industries that can adopt such a costing. *(Calicut University, B.Com., Oct. 88)*
4. Define unit costing. How does it differ from job costing. *(S.V University, B.Com., April. 1985)*
5. Describe the role of a cost accountant in determining the quotation price as against a tender. *(ICWA, Inter, Dec. 1989)*
6. Write short notes on unit cost and job cost. *(Andhra University, B.Com., May. 1992)*
7. What is a cost sheet? What are its purposes? *(University, of Kerala, M.Com., May 1992)*
8. What is a cost sheet? Give a specimen cost sheet for the manufacture of an acid measured in terms of kiloliters and explain the different items included in that cost sheet. *(Osmania University, B.Com., March. 1992)*

EXERCISES

Exercise-1

From the following particulars prepare a cost-sheet and ascertain the sales by adding a profit of 25% on sales.

	1-1-1998 *(Rs.)*	*31-1-1998* *(Rs.)*
Raw materials	30,500	48,500
Work in progress	8,000	9,000
Finished goods	20,400	10,000
Purchase of Raw materials	Rs. 25,000	
Direct wages	20,400	
Factory expenses	10,500	
Office expenses	5,400	
Selling and distribution expenses	7,300	

(*Bangalore University, B.B.M, April 1999*)

[Answer : Sales Rs. 80,000**]**

Exercise-2

Following data are extracted from Pavan Kishore industries for the year 1995 :

Opening stock of raw materials	25,000
Closing stock of raw materials	40,000
Purchases of raw materials	85,000
Carriage inwards	5,000
Wages (direct)	75,000
Wages (indirect)	10,000
Other direct charges	15,000
Rent and rates - factory	5,000
Rent and rates - office	500
Indirect Materials	500
Depreciation - plant	1,500
Depreciation - office furniture	100
Salary - office	2,500
Salary - salesman	2,000
Other office expenses	900
Other factory expenses	5,700
Managing Director's remuneration	12,000
Other selling expenses	1,000
Travelling expenses	1,100
Carriage outwards	1,000
Sales	2,50,000
Advance income tax paid	15,000
Advertisement	2,000

Managing Director's remuneration is to be allocated as Rs. 4000 to the factory, Rs. 2000 to the office and Rs. 6000 to the selling departments. From the above information prepare a cost-sheet showing (a) Prime cost (b) Works cost (c) Cost of production (d) Cost of sales (e) Net profit.

(*Andhra University, B.Com., Sept. 1996*)

[Answer : (a) Rs. 1,65,000 (b) 1,91,700 (c) Rs. 1,97,000 (d) Rs. 2,10,100 (e) 39,900**]**

Exercise-3 (Comparative Cost Sheet)

In a factory two types of articles, *viz.* o and p are manufactured. From the following particulars prepare a statement of cost showing the total cost of each variety and ascertain the total profit. There is no opening stock or closing stock.

	Article 'o'	Article 'p'
	Rs.	Rs.
Materials	30,000	50,000
Labour	60,000	70,000

Works on cost is charged at 40% of works cost and office oncost is taken at 20% on total cost.

'o' articles sold during the period are 360 at Rs. 600 each and 'p' articles sold are 400 at Rs. 750 each.

(Bharathidason University, B.Com., November 1998)

[**Answer** : Profit of article 'o' Rs. 28,500
Profit of article 'p' Rs. 50,000]

Exercise-4 (Tender Statement)

AP Scooters Ltd., finds that in 1996, the total cost of producing 100 scooters was Rs. 20,00,000 which were sold at Rs. 22,000 each. The cost consisted of :

Materials Rs. 8,00,000, Direct Wages Rs. 9,00,000, Factory overhead Rs. 1,80,000, office overhead Rs. 94,000 and distribution overhead Rs. 260 per scooter.

For 1997, the cost estimate is :

(a) That each scooter will require material of Rs. 9000 and labour Rs. 9000.
(b) That factory overhead will bear the same relation to wages as in the previous period.
(c) That the percentage of office overhead on factory cost will be the same as in the past and
(d) That there will be an increase of Rs. 60 per scooter in selling and distribution overhead.

Prepare a statement showing the profit that the company would make per scooter if it increases the price of scooter by Rs. 2000. *(Karnataka University, B.Com., April 1997)*

[**Answer :** Profit Rs. 2,00,000, per scooter 2000]

Exercise-5

Following are the particulars for the production of 2000 sewing machines of Nath Engineering Company Ltd. for the year 1994. Cost of materials Rs. 1,60,000, wages Rs. 2,40,000, manufacturing expenses Rs, 1,00,000, salaries Rs. 1,20,000, rent rates and Insurance Rs. 20,000, selling expenses Rs. 60,000, general expenses Rs. 40,000 and sales Rs. 8,00,000.

The company plans to manufacture 3000 sewing machines during 1995. You are required to submit a statement showing the price at which machines would be sold so as to show a profit of 10% on selling price. The following additional information is supplied to you.

(i) Price of material is expected to rise by 20%,
(ii) Wage rates are expected to show an increase of 5%,
(iii) Manufacturing expenses will rise in proportion to the combined cost of materials and wages,
(iv) Selling expenses per unit will remain the same,
(v) The other expenses will remain unaffected by the rise in output.

(Bharathiar University, B.Com., November 1997)

[**Answer :** 12,25,000]

Exercises on production accounts

Exercise 6 (On coal production account) : Prepare a pig iron production account showing total cost and cost per tonne for each element of cost :

Particulars	*Coal*	*Coke*	*Limestone*	*Iron ore*	*Sundries*
	(Rs.)	*(Rs.)*	*(Rs.)*	*(Rs.)*	*(Rs.)*
Stock on 1.1.91	4,720	3,580	1,450	3,930	2,700
Purchases during the year	21,880	29,740	5,080	18,690	7,810
Stock on 31.12.91	3,600	2,050	1,530	3,620	3,010

The total production of pig iron was 32,000 tons. Sale of slag amounted to Rs. 10,500. General works charges and wages were Rs. 4,500 and Rs. 17,000 respectively. [*Answer :* Cost of production Rs. 96,500]

Exercise 7 (On yarn and cloth production account) : From the following particulars of Ramkumar Cotton Mills Ltd. for the half year ended 30th June 1991, prepare two separate production accounts relating to yarn and cloth :

	(Rs. '000)
Opening stock of yarn at cost (60 kgs)	30
Opening stock of cloth at cost (120 kgs)	90
Cotton purchased (1,040 kgs)	260
Weaving wages	60
Stores weaving	40
Wages of spining	30
Stores	20
Fuel	10
Yarn sales (200 kgs)	40
Stock at the end at cost :	
Yarn (200 kgs)	41
Cloth (205 kgs)	150
Fuel; weaving	10
Sales : waste (211 kgs)	20
Cloth sales (420 kgs)	303

Stores consumed increased the weight of production by 4 kgs for spinning stores and 120 kgs for weaving stores. [***Answer :*** Loss of Rs. 6.2785 in yarn production a/c and profit of Rs. 7.2785 in cloth production a/c].

14

JOB AND BATCH COSTING

INTRODUCTION

Job costing as a distinctive method of costing is a form of specific order costing which is adopted to execute the work strictly according to customers specification. The production process depends upon the number of orders received from customers. As such production is not standardised and intermittent in nature. The goods manufactured is not for stocking but for immediate delivery once it is complete in all respects. The cost is ascertained separately for each job as every work order differs from customer to customer. The purpose of job costing is to ascertain the profit or loss made on each job. Further cost of job is compared with the estimated cost to indicate whether estimation was defective or the actual cost incurred is excessive. Such an analysis helps in taking remedial action to improve efficiency and also facilitate revision of estimates.

DEFINITION AND FEATURES OF JOB COSTING

Kohler in his 'Dictionary for Accountants' defines job costing as "a method of cost accounting whereby cost is compiled for a specific quantity of product, equipment, repair or other service that moves through the production process as a continuously identifiable unit, applicable material, direct labour, direct expense and usually a calculated portion of the overhead being charged to a job order".

Industries which employ job costing have the following characteristic features :

(*a*) Each job is dissimilar in nature requiring special treatment. Hence the operations, processes and the sequence may differ from job to job.

(*b*) Production is intermittent and not continuous.

(*c*) Production is undertaken against customer's orders and not for stock.

(*d*) The industries need not incur selling and distribution expenses as the customers themselves come place orders and collect the goods after production.

(*e*) Each job is treated as a cost unit under this method of costing.

(*f*) Each job is distinctively identified by a production order throughout the production stage.

(*g*) The cost of production of every job is ascertained after the completion of the job.

Examples of industries which employ job costing are; foundries, printers, machine tool making industries, engineering workshops, toy making concerns, furniture making concerns, management consulting concerns, interior decorations, musical instruments, advertising concerns and so on.

Though job costing is applied in manufacturing concerns where production process is not standardised it can still be used in conjuction with standard costing. For example, a company which manufactures machine tools against customers specification, can do so by the use of standard parts and sub-assemblies that can be pre-costed. Subsequently job costing can be applied for accounting non-standard component parts and for final assembly of all parts.

PROCEDURE OF JOB COSTING

The procedure that is commonly applicable to a normal sale transaction equally applies in case of job costing. This is explained under the following steps :

1. Receiving an Enquiry

Before placing an order with the manufacturer, usually the customer will enquire about the price, quality to be maintained, the duration within which the order is to be executed and other specification of the job.

2. Estimation of the Price of the Job

The cost accountant estimates the cost of job after considering the various elements of cost and keeping in mind the specification of customer. This is based on the cost of execution of similar job in the previous year and considering the possible changes in the various elements of cost. The estimated cost of the job is then informed to the prospective customer.

3. Receiving of Order

The customer will then place the order if he is satisfied with the quotation price and other terms of executing the job. The production control department receives the order and it will give a number for every order thus received which is known as job order number. The job is known by this number until it is completed.

4. Preparation of Production Order

A production order is prepared by the production control department and is sent to the concerned persons such as the employees to enable them to carry out the job, to the storekeeper to facilitate him to stock all the required materials, to cost accountant to enable him to prepare job cost sheet in order to ascertain the profit on every job completed. The production order consists of the following particulars :

(*a*) Date on which the order is prepared.
(*b*) Job order number.
(*c*) Description of the article's to be produced
(*d*) Number of articles to be produced.
(*e*) Date of starting the work.
(*f*) Date of completing the work.
(*g*) Listing of materials to be used.
(*h*) Sequence of production process.
(*i*) Signature of production manager.

5. Preparation of Design

When the job to be executed requires special treatment, a design to meet the customers specification is prepared by the production planning department. This is done by the engineering department in consultation with the production planning department.

6. Execution of Job and its Inspection

The job will be started as per the schedule of production. Necessary materials, employees, tools are used to complete the production. The production process is supervised by the production manager or supervisor from time to time to ensure that the job executed is in accordance with customer's specification and that it is completed as per the production schedule.

7. Despatch of Goods

The finished products are then packed and delivered to the customer as per the delivery schedule. Payment is settled as per the agreed mode of payment.

ACCOUNTING SYSTEM UNDER JOB COSTING

As in any other method of costing, the four important elements of cost enter into the cost of production. They are :

1. Materials Cost

Materials are classified into direct and indirect on the basis of traceability of materials to the job. Those materials which are traceable to the job are treated as prime cost element and those not traceable to the job are treated as manufacturing overhead.

The following procedure is followed for recording materials :

(*a*) *When materials are purchased from supplier :* The following entry is passed :

Materials a/c *Dr.*
 To cash a/c

Stock of materials is an asset account and appears in the balance sheet. The cost of any unused materials will be included in the stock of materials account at the end of the accounting period.

(*b*) *When materials are issued to job :* A material requisition note or a bill of materials is prepared to draw materials from stores to start the work on the job. The following entry is passed to record the issue of materials to the job :

Job order no. *Dr.*
 To materials

The production manager identifies the nature, quantity and quality of materials required and places the materials requisition note with the storekeeper. Once the materials are issued a copy of the requisition is sent to the cost accounting department to show that such materials have been used and to that extent the stock of mateials has been reduced.

However, in large-sized concern, after the issue and pricing of materials are made, the cost of materials so issed are recorded in a material abstract. This facilitates the analysis and collection of cost of direct materials according to job or work orders. The cost of direct materials are then posted to individual job cost sheet. The transactions are posted weekly or fortnightly. However overheads from materials abstract is posted to jobs periodically.

(*c*) Any surplus materials unused on the job is returned back to storeroom supported by a material transfer note. The following entry passed :

Materials a/c *Dr.*
 To job order no.

2. Direct Labour Cost

The direct labour cost is debited to the job on which work is directly performed. Clock card is used to record the hours worked by each employee. At the end of each week, the payroll department uses the information on the clock card to calculate each employee's pay. The clock card only records the total time worked by each employee. It is used by the employee to indicate how much time he worked in a period and by the employer to determine how much to pay the employee for that work. A clock card does not record the time spent by each employee on the jobs. This information is recorded by the employees on a time ticket. A time ticket shows the date on which the work was completed, the employees name, name of the department, the time of starting and finishing the work. If the work is performed directly on a job, the employee would record the job number, indicating the labour as direct labour.

The cost accounting department collects all the labour time tickets, records the pay rate of the employee on the ticket and calculate the labour cost of the operation.

Treatment of overtime wages in job costing : When overtime work is done on a job to speed up production with a view to expedite the delivery, the overtime wages is to be debited to that job on which overtime work is performed. Where overtime work is performed as a routine work it forms part of factory overhead.

3. Direct Expenses

The direct expenses under job order industries usually include cost of designs, moulds, hiring of special tools and equipments and maintenance cost of such tools.

4. Factory Overheads

In most cases predetermined overhead rates are used for the absorption of factory overheads. The predetermined overhead rate is calculated at the beginning of the year by estimating the total overhead cost for the year and then dividing either by direct labour cost or direct labour hours. Throughout the year the overhead rate is applied to calculate the overheads and thus charged to job.

Preparation of Job Cost Sheet

A separate job cost sheet is prepared for every job undertaken. This is to facilitate the calculation of cost of the job separately, with a view to know the amount of profit earned on every job. All the elements of cost discussed above are recorded in the job cost sheet. Its contents are as follows :

(*a*) Identity or name of the customer.
(*b*) Date of starting the job.
(*c*) Date on which the job is to be completed.
(*d*) Date on which the job is actually completed.
(*e*) The job number.
(*f*) The name of the product—its description in brief.

The job cost sheet constitutes the heart of job order industries. In the words of Blocker and Weltmer (*Cost Accounting*) "the heart of job order system is the job cost sheet which is used as a daily record of material, direct labour and estimated factory overhead cost for each department or operation for the entire course of production". A specimen form of job cost sheet is given below :

JOB COST SHEET

Name of the customer	Job no. ....
Quantity on order	Date promised ....
Name of the product	Date started ....
	Date completed ....

Materials cost			Labour cost			Overheads		
Date	*Requisition number*	*Amount*	*Date*	*Hours*	*Amount*	*Hours*	*Rate*	*Amount*

Cost summary	
Materials cost	....
Labour cost	....
Direct expenses	....
Prime cost	....
Overheads	....
Total profit	....
Selling price	....

Fig. 17.1. Job cost sheet.

Advantages of Job Costing

1. It records costs more accurately.
2. Comparison of two jobs enables to know profit or loss on jobs. Only profitable jobs alone can be taken up by the enterprise.
3. It facilitates estimation of cost of similar jobs.
4. It facilitates cost control by comparing actuals with estimates.
5. As cost of materials, labour and overhead for every job is available daily, the trend of costs can be known by management.
6. The use of predetermined overhead rates involve application of budgetary control technique.
7. It facilitates identification and control of spoilages and defectives.
8. It is useful in quoting cost plus contract.

Disadvantages

1. It is expensive as cost is accumulated and ascertained for each job separately.
2. The scope of commiting mistakes are high as the costs of one job may wrongly be posted to the cost of other job.
3. When drastic economic changes take place cost comparison becomes difficult.

TREATMENT OF SPOILAGES, DEFECTIVES, UNDER JOB COSTING

Spoiled Goods

Spoilages are goods that do not meet production standards and are either sold for their salvage value or discarded. When spoiled goods are discovered, they are taken out of production and no further work is performed on them.

Spoilages can be of two types, *viz.*, (1) Normal spoilage and (2) Abnormal spoilage. Normal spoilage arises from efficient production and are considered as an unavoidable cost of producing good units. It is treated either as factory overheads or the sale proceeds of spoilages are deducted from the cost of production.

Any spoilage of goods which are in excess of normal spoilage is treated as abnormal spoilage. It is arises on account of inefficient operations. The cost of abnormal spoilages are kept outside the purview of cost of production. Instead they are charged to costing profit and loss account.

Defective Goods

The goods which do not meet production standards and requires further processing in order to sell them as good units are known as defective goods.

Defectives are again classified into normal and abnormal defectives. The cost of reworking normal defective goods are treated as factory overheads. The total cost of reworking abnormal defective units are to be charged to costing profit and loss account because it is the result of inefficient operation and it should not become part of the production cost.

REPORTS IN JOB COSTING

The following are the important reports prepared under job costing :

1. Monthly Gross Profit Report on the Jobs Completed

This report shows an analysis of gross profit earned on various jobs completed during the month. A proforma of such a report is given below :

ABC CO. LTD.

Gross profit analysis on completed jobs
For the month of ....

Job no.	*Production cost*	*Selling price*	*Gross profit*
101	–	–	–
102	–	–	–
103	–	–	–
104	–	–	–
105	–	–	–
Total			

Fig. 17.2. Monthly gross profit report.

2. Completed Job Reports

Such reports are prepared and submitted to the concerned authority to investigate the differences between actual cost and estimated cost. A proforma of such a report is given below :

ABC CO. LTD.
Completed job report

Job no. ....
Started on ....
Completed on ....

Elements of cost	*Actual cost*	*Estimated cost*	*Defference*
Materials cost	–	–	–
Labour	–	–	–
Overheads	–	–	–
Total			
Gross profit			
Sales			

Fig. 17.3. Completed job report.

3. Defective Work Reports

This type of report enables management to know the extent of defective units obtained and cautions management to take remedial steps to minimise the defectives.

4. Other Reports

Some of the reports which are prepared in addition to those mentioned above are, (*a*) Purchasing report, (*b*) Inventory report, (*c*) Idle time report, (*d*) Overhead analysis report.

Problem 1 : The following direct costs, were incurred on Job no. 678 of standard T.V. company.

Materials Rs. 4,020

Wages : Dept. *A* — 60 hours @ Rs. 3 per hour
Dept. *B* — 40 hours @ Rs. 2 per hour
Dept. *C* — 20 hours @ Rs. 5 per hour

Overhead expenses were estimated as follows :

Variable overheads :

Dept. *A* Rs. 5,000 for 5,000 labour hours
Dept. *B* Rs. 3,000 for 1,500 labour hours
Dept. *C* Rs. 2,000 for 500 labour hours

Fixed overhead

Estimation at Rs. 20,000 for 10,000 normal working hours

You are required to calculate the cost of job no. 678 and calculate the price to give profit of 25% on selling price. (*S.V. University, B.Com., Oct. 1999*)

Solution : **Job cost sheet for Job no. 678**

Direct materials		4,020
Direct wages :		
Dept. *A* — 60 × 3	= 180	
Dept. *B* — 40 × 2	= 80	
Dept. *C* — 20 × 5	= 100	
		360
	prime cost	4,380

Overheads :

Variable :

Dept. *A* $\frac{5,000}{5,000} \times 60 = 60$

Dept. *B* $\frac{3,000}{1,500} \times 40 = 80$

Dept. *C* $\frac{2,000}{500} \times 20 = 80$

	220
Fixed $\frac{20,000}{10,000} \times 120$	240
Total cost	4,840
Profit 25% on SP or $\frac{1}{3}$ on cost price	1,613
Selling price	6,453

Problem 2 : A factory has three production departments. The policy of the factory is to recover the production overheads of the entire factory by adopting a single blanket rate based on the percentage of total factory overheads to total factory wages. The relevant data for a month are given below :

Department	*Direct materials Rs.*	*Direct wages Rs.*	*Factory overheads Rs.*	*Direct labour hours*	*Machine hours*
Budget :					
Machining	6,50,000	80,000	3,60,000	20,000	80,000
Assembly	1,70,000	3,50,000	1,40,000	1,00,000	10,000
Paking	1,00,000	70,000	1,25,000	50,000	–
Actuals :					
Machining	7,80,000	96,000	3,90,000	24,000	96,000
Assembly	1,36,000	2,70,000	84,000	90,000	11,000
Packing	1,20,000	90,000	1,35,000	60,000	–

The details of one of the representative jobs produced during the month are as under :

Job no. CW 7,083

Department	*Direct materials Rs.*	*Direct wages Rs.*	*Direct labour*	*Machine hours*
Machining	1,200	240	60	180
Assembly	600	360	120	30
Packing	300	60	40	–

The factory adds 30% on the factory cost to cover administration and selling overheads and profit.

Calculate the overhead absorption rate as per the current policy of the company and determine the selling price of the job no. CW 7083. (*C.A., Inter, Nov. 1999*)

Solution : **Calculation of oh absorption rate**

Department	*Budgeted factory oh*	*Budgeted direct wages*
Machining	3,60,000	80,000
Assembly	1,40,000	3,50,000
Packing	1,25,000	70,000
	6,25,000	5,00,000

$$\text{Overhead absorption rate} = \frac{\text{Budgeted factory oh}}{\text{Budgeted direct wages}} \times 100$$

$$= \frac{6,25,000}{5,00,000} \times 100$$

= 125% of direct wages

Job cost sheet of job no. CW 7083

Direct mateials (1200 + 600 + 300)		2100
Direct wages (240 + 360 + 60)		660
	Prime cost	2760
Overheads	125% of 660	825
	Factory cost	3585
	Profit 30% of 3585	1075.50
	Selling price	4660.50

Problem 3 : New product company is contemplating to launch a new product in the market. The estimated cost details me as follows :

(*i*) Material cost per unit — Rs. 40

(*ii*) Labour cost per unit — Rs. 36

(*iii*) Production overheads are to be calculated from the following data :

Production departments	*Hourly overhead rate (Rs.)*	*Normal monthly hours for oh rates*	*Fixed oh included in oh (Rs.)*	*Time to be taken by new product (Hour)*
A	3.60	30,000	36,000	5
B	4.80	20,000	12,000	2.5
C	6.00	40,000	60,000	4

(*iv*) Annual administration and selling expenses — Rs. 2,50,000 (applicable to the new product)

(*v*) Estimated sales quantity —50,000 per annum.

Based on the above information prepare a cost-sheet and find out the unit selling price with a profit margin of 40% on total cost. (*ICWA, Inter, Dec. 1992*)

Solution :

Calculation of variable and fixed overhead rates

	A	*B*	*C*
Total monthly overhead (normal hours × oh rate)	108,000	96,000	2,40,000
Less fixed overhead	36,000	12,000	60,000
variable overhead	72,000	84,000	1,80,000
Variable oh rate per hr.	2.40	4.20	4.50
Fixed oh rate per hr.	1.20	0.60	1.50

Job Cost Sheet

Direct materials			40.00
Direct labour			36.00
		Prime cost	76.00
Variable oh :			
Dept. *A* — Rs. 2.40 × 5 hrs.	=	12.00	
Dept. *B* — Rs. 4.20 × 2.5 hrs.	=	10.50	
Dept. *C* — Rs. 4.50 × 4	=	18.00	
		40.50	
Fixed oh :			
Dept. *A* — Rs. 1.20 × 5 hrs.	=	6.00	
Dept. *B* — Rs. 0.60 × 2.5 hrs.	=	1.50	
Dept. *C* — Rs. 1.50 × 4	=	6.00	
			54.00

Factory cost	130.00
Administration & selling expense $\frac{\text{Rs. } 2,50,000}{50,000 \text{ pieces}}$	5.00
Cost of sales	135.00
Profit 40% on cost of sales	54.00
Selling price	189.00

Problem 4 : The Hind Manufacturing Co. used to absorb overheads by means of a blanket rate based on the direct labour hours employed. From Ist July, 1992, It decides to adopt separate rates for the three main production activities, *viz.*, (*a*) Store keeping and material handling, (*b*) Machining and (*c*) Assembly. The estimates of costs and output upon which overhead absorption rates are predetermined remain unchanged as are the rates of absorption for selling and distribution costs.

Overhead absorption rates are :

Prior to Ist July, 1992 :

0.50 paise per direct labour hour

Selling and distribution overhead — 20% of production cost

After Ist July 1992 :

Production overhead :

Storekeeping and material handling — 5% of direct material cost

Machining — 0.75 paise per machine hour

Assembly — 0.30 paise per direct labour hour

Selling and distribution overhead — 20% of production cost

Direct costs of Job 120 have been :

Direct materials cost	400
Direct wages :	
Machining — 200 hrs. at 0.60 P	120
Assembly — 100 hrs. at 0.40 P	40
	560

The quotation price of the job is Rs. 896 and it required 184 machine hours to complete.

Show the job cost sheet for job 120 :

(*a*) As it would appear if the job had been completed entirely in the month of June, and

(*b*) As it would appear if the job were completed entirely in the month of July.

Solution : **Job cost sheet for the month of June**

Customer : Job no. 120

Particulars :

Started on .... June Finished .... June

Direct materials cost		400
Direct wages :		
Machining — 200 hrs. @ 0.60 P		120
Assembly — 100 hrs. @ 0.40 P		40
	Prime cost	560
Production overhead — 300 hrs. @ 0.50 P		150
	Factory cost	710
Selling & distribution overheads 20% on factory cost		142
	Cost of sales	852
	Profit	44
	Selling price	896

Job cost sheet for the month of July

Customer			Job no. 120
Particulars			
Commenced no : 1st July 92			Finished 31st July 92

Direct materials		400	
Storekeeping & material handling		20	420
Machining :			
Direct wages : 200 hrs. @ 0.60 P			120
Overhead : 184 hrs. @ 0.75 P (*see note*)			138
Assembly :			
Direct wages : 100 hrs. @ 0.40 P			40
Overhead : 100 hrs. @ 0.30 P			30
		Factory cost	748
Selling and distribution overhead : 20% on 784			150
		Cost of sales	898
		Loss	2
		Selling price	896

Note : Overhead is absorbed on 184 machine hours.

Problem 5 : A factory produces goods against customer's order. Its manufacturing section consists of three department *P*, *Q* and *R*. It is the practice of the company to prepare quarterly budgets for the purposes of control and the absorption of overheads. The following information is extracted from the first quarter budget of the company :

	Departments			
	P (*Rs.*)	*Q* (*Rs.*)	*R* (*Rs.*)	*Total* (*Rs.*)
Direct materials	10,000	20,000	30,000	60,000
Direct labour cost	7,000	8,000	8,500	23,500
Variable factory overheads	5,000	4,000	6,000	15,000
Fixed factory overhead	–	–	–	15,000
Administrative overhead	–	–	–	10,000
Machine hours	6,000	4,000	10,000	20,000

The factory overheads are absorbed on the basis of machine hours and the administration overhead is absorbed as a percentage of factory cost.

The factory has received an order from its regular customer for the supply of a specific veriety of products that pass through two departments only, i.e., *P* and *Q*. In respect of the order, the following particulars are available :

	P	*Q*
Material cost (Rs.)	1,500	2,500
Direct labour cost (Rs.)	700	800
Machine hours	600	400

Prepare a job order cost sheet and ascertain the price of the order if the margin of 25% on sales is added to the total cost of production :

Solution : **Job order cost sheet**

Materials Cost		
Dept. *P*	1,500	
Dept. *Q*	2,500	4,000

Direct wages			
Dept. P		700	
Dept. Q		800	1,500
	Prime cost		5,500
Factory overheads (on the basis of machine hours)			
Variable : Dept. $P - \frac{5,000}{6,000} \times 600 = 500$			
Dept. $Q - \frac{4,000}{4,000} \times 400 = 400$			900
Fixed overhead $\frac{15,000}{20,000} \times 1,000$			750
	Factory cost		7,150
Administration overhead — 8.81% of factory cost			629.91
	Cost of production		7,779.91
	Profit $\frac{1}{3}$ of cost		2,593.30
	Selling price		10,373.21

Problem 6 : A jobber used to quote to his customer on the basis of cost plus a certain percentage to cover overheads and profit. He now follows departmental rate of recovery of overheads based on direct labour hours. The following information is available from his books for the period ending 31.3.92 :

Expenses	*Total (Rs.)*	*Suggested base for apportionment to departments*
Consumables stores	500	Direct labour hours
Rent & rates	3,000	Floor area
Depreciation	2,500	Plant value
Indirect labour	4,000	Direct labour hours
Repairs & renewals	1,000	3 : 3 : 4
Labour amenities	1,500	No. of employees
E.S. Insurance	400	- Do -
Works manager's salary	3,600	Equally
General administration	6,000	5 : 4 : 3
Sundry expenses	400	12 : 7 : 1

Departments	X	Y	Z
Direct labour hours	5,000	3,000	2,000
Wage rate per hour (Re.)	0.60	0.50	0.40
Number of employees	20	20	10
Floor area (in sq. ft.)	3,000	2,000	1,000
Value of plant (Rs.)	15,000	9,000	6,000

You are required to (*a*) Calculate the hourly overhead rates to be charged for work in each department, (*b*) Prepare a quotation for a job to which the following data relates :

Material		Rs. 300
Direct labour :	X	20 hrs.
	Y	15 hrs.
	Z	10 hrs.

Profit = 20% of selling price

Solution :

Statement showing overhead apportionment

Expenses	*Ratio*	*Dept. X*	*Dept. Y*	*Dept. Z*
Consumable stores	5 : 3 : 2	250	150	100
Depreciation	5 : 3 : 2	1,250	750	500
Indirect labour	5 : 3 : 2	2,000	1,200	800
Rent & rates	3 : 2 : 1	1,500	1,000	500
Repairs & renewals	3 : 3 : 4	300	300	400
Labour amenities	2 : 2 : 1	600	600	300
E.S. Insurance	2 : 2 : 1	160	160	80
Works manager's salary	1 : 1 : 1	1,200	1,200	1,200
Gen. administration	5 : 4 : 3	2,500	2,000	1,500
Sundry expenses	12 : 7 : 1	240	140	20
		10,000	7,500	5,400
Labour (hrs.)		5,000	3,000	2,000
Labour hour rate		$\frac{10,000}{5,000}$ = Rs. 2	$\frac{7,500}{3,000}$ = Rs. 2.50	$\frac{5,400}{2,000}$ = Rs. 2.70

Estimate for job

Materials			300
Direct labour cost :			
Dept. *X*	20 hrs. @ Rs. 0.60	= 12.00	
Dept. *Y*	15 hrs. @ Rs. 0.50	= 7.50	
Dept. *Z*	10 hrs. @ Rs. 0.40	= 4.00	23.50
	Prime cost		323.50
Overheads :			
Dept. X	20 hrs. @ Rs. 2.00	= 40.00	
Dept. Y	15 hrs. @ Rs. 2.50	= 37.50	
Dept. Z	10 hrs. @ Rs. 2.70	= 27.00	104.50
	Factory cost		428.00
	Profit 20% on S.P.		107.00
	Selling price		535.00

Problem 7 : A job manufacturing company has received an equiry for the supply of 2,00,000 number of a special type of machine screw. Capacity exists for manufacture of the screws in the company's department number 2 but a fixed investment of Rs. 60,000 and working capital to the extent of 25% of the sale value will be required if the job is undertaken. The cost are estimated as follows :

Raw materials — 20,000 kgs. at Rs. 2.30 per kg.

Labour hours — direct 18,000 of which 2,000 — would be overtime hours payable at double the labour rate.

Labour rate — Re. 1 per hour

Factory overhead — Rs. 1 per direct labour hour

Selling and distribution on cost — Rs. 23,000

Material recovered as scrap at the end of the operations is estimated at Rs. 2,000

The company expects a net return of 25% on the capital employed.

Prepare a job cost sheet indicating the price which should be quoted to the customer.

Solution :

Job cost sheet

Raw materials : 20,000 kgs. @ Rs. 2.30		46,000
Direct labour :		
Normal wages 16,000 hrs. @ Re. 1	16,000	
Overtime wages 2000 hrs. @ Rs. 2	4,000	20,000

	Prime cost	66,000
Factory overhead : Re. 1 for 18,000 hrs.		18,000
		84,000
Less : Sale of scrap		2,000
	Factory cost	82,000
Selling & distribution cost		23,000
	Cost of sales	1,05,000
	Profit	23,000
	Selling price	1,28,000

Note **:** Calculation of selling price

Let Sales $= x$

Then $S.P. = C.P. + \text{Profit}$

$$x = 1,05,000 + \frac{25}{100}\text{ (Fixed capital + Working capital)}$$

$$x = 1,05,000 + \frac{25}{100}\text{ (Fixed capital + 25\% of Sales)}$$

$$x = 1,05,000 + \frac{1}{4}\left(60,000 + \frac{x}{4}\right)$$

$$x = 1,05,000 + 15,000 + \frac{x}{16}$$

$$x = 16,80,000 + 2,40,000 + 16x$$

$$19,20,000 = -x + 16x$$

$$19,20,000 = 15x$$

$$x = \frac{19,20,000}{15} = 1,28,000$$

Problem 8 : The process plant division of a group of companies has built a food packaging machine to a customer's requirement. A price of Rs. 49,000 had been quoted with the intention of achieving a profit of 25% on the selling price.

Customer :	Bond Food Ltd.
Customer's order no.	72, dated 3.2.03
Job order no.	141
Date of commencement	5.3.03
Date of completion	29.4.03
Date of delivery	2.5.03

	March	*April*
Material used :		
Machine dept.	Rs. 2,900	700
Assembly dept.	Rs. 1,900	1,400
Direct wage rate per hour :		
Machine dept.	Rs. 4	4.40
Assembly dept.	Rs. 5	5.25
Direct labour hours :		
Machine dept.	Hrs. 200	100
Assembly dept.	Hrs. 50	500
Machine hours in machinery dept. :	Hrs 350	180
Technical drawing (direct cost)	Rs. 2,115	

Production overhead is absorbed at the predetermined rate of Rs. 10 per direct labour hour in the assembly department and Rs. 15 per machine hour in the machining department.

Commissioning cost, *i.e.*, installation and initial running of the machine were Rs. 750 and these are to be treated as a direct production cost.

Selling and general administration cost are charged to jobs at the rate of $33\frac{1}{3}$% of production cost.

You are required to prepare a job order cost sheet.

Solution : **Job order cost sheet**

Customer : Bond Food Ltd.
Customer order : 72
Date commenced : 5.3.92
Date completed : 29.4.92

Job order no. : 141
Date of delivery : 2.5.92

Materials :					
March	—	Machinery		2,900	
	—	Assembly		1,900	4,800
April	—	Machine		700	
		Assembly		1,400	2,100
Direct wages :					
March	—	Machine	200 × 4	800	
		Assembly	50 × 5	250	1,050
April	—	Machine	100 × 4.40	440	
		Assembly	500 × 5.25	2,625	3,065
Direct cost :					
Technical drawing				2,115	
Commission cost				750	2,865
			Prime cost		13,800
Production overhead :					
March	—	Machinery	350 × 15		5,250
		Assembly	50 × 10		500
April	—	Machinery	180 × 15		2,700
		Assembly	500 × 10		5,000
			Factory cost		27,330
Selling and administration cost					9,110
			Cost of sales		36,440
			Profit		12,560
			Sales		49,000

Note : Profit is the difference between sales value given in the problem and cost of sales.

Problem 9 (Calculation of missing items) : A fire occurred in a factory and records containing information about the allocation of overhead charges were destroyed. It is however known that works overhead is absorbed at 100% of wages and office overhead is a fixed percentage of factory cost.

The following further information regarding two previous jobs is also available :

Job no.	*Materials*	*Wages*	*Direct expenses*	*Profit (% on total cost)*	*Selling price*
101	20,000	16,000	4,000	10%	80,080
102	32,000	24,000	2,000	15%	1,22,590

Find out the percentage and actual office overhead and hence total cost.

Solution : **Job cost sheet for job nos. 101 and 102**

	Job 101	*Job 102*
Materials	20,000	32,000
Wages	16,000	24,000
Direct expenses	4,000	2,000
Prime cost	40,000	58,000

Works overhead — 100% on wages		16,000	24,000
	Factory cost	56,000	82,000
Office overhead (balancing figure)		16,800	24,600
	Total cost	72,800	1,06,600
	Profit	7,280	15,990
	Sales	80,080	1,22,590

Working notes :

Calculation of office overheads for job 101 :

$$\text{Profit on sales} = \frac{10}{110} \times 80{,}080 = \text{Rs. } 7{,}280$$

$$\text{Sales} - \text{Profit} = \text{Actual cost}$$

$$80{,}080 - 7{,}280 = 72{,}800$$

$$\text{Total cost} - \text{Prime cost} = \text{All overheads}$$

$$72{,}800 - 40{,}000 = 32{,}800$$

$$\text{Total overhead} - \text{factory overhead} = \text{Office overhead}$$

$$32{,}800 - 16{,}000 = 16{,}800$$

For 56,000 factory cost the office overhead is 16,800

$$\text{For } 100 \rightarrow ? \qquad \frac{16{,}800 \times 100}{56{,}000} = 30\%$$

Calculation of office overhead for job 102

$$\text{Profit on sales } \frac{15}{115} \times 1{,}22{,}590 = 15{,}990$$

$$\text{Sales} - \text{profit} = \text{Total cost}$$

$$1{,}22{,}590 - 15{,}990 = 1{,}06{,}600$$

$$\text{Total cost} - \text{Prime cost} = \text{Total overhead}$$

$$1{,}06{,}600 - 58{,}000 = 48{,}600$$

$$\text{Total overhead} - \text{Factory overhead} = \text{Office overhead}$$

$$48{,}600 - 24{,}000 = 24{,}600$$

For 82,000 factory cost the office overhead is Rs. 24,600

$$\text{For } 100 \rightarrow ? \qquad \frac{24{,}600}{82{,}000} \times 100 = 30\%$$

Problem 10 : The elements comprising the cost of a factory output for the three years 1987, 1988, 1989 were as follows :

		Years		
		1987	*1988*	*1989*
Materials	Rs.	1,50,000	1,12,500	1,87,500
Labour	Rs.	67,000	65,000	69,000
Works on cost	Rs.	30,000	22,500	37,500
Administration oncost	Rs.	18,000	18,000	18,000
Selling and distribution cost	Rs.	9,000	7,000	5,000
Output	Tons	10,000	7,500	12,500

Following an examination of the figures, you are required to state on what basis would you allocate on cost in quoting for a job to supply 17,500 tons of the commodity representing the whole of the anticipated output for the year 1990. What price would you quote assuming there was no change in the organisation and that a profit of 15% on works cost is considered adequate.

Solution : **Quotation for a job to supply 17,500 tons**

Raw materials	— It is Rs. 15 for all the 3 years so 17,500 × 15		2,62,500
Labour	— It has been increasing @ Rs. 2,000 for every 2,500 tons		
Labour cost for 12,500 tons		= 69,000	

Labour cost for 5,000 tones	=	4,000	73,000
		Prime cost	3,35,500
Works on cost — It bears 20% relationship with materials			
∴ 20% of 2,62,500			52,500
		Works cost	3,88,000
Administration cn cost : It is same for all the years. This year also it remains same			18,000
		Office cost	4,06,000
Selling and distribution cost —It shows a reduction by Rs. 2,000 for every year			
So this year also it goes down by 2,000 (*i.e.*, 5,000 – 2,000)			3,000
		Cost of sales	4,09,000
		Profit	58,200
		Selling price	4,67,200

Problem 11 : A company has two manufacturing shops. The shop floor supervisor presented the following cost for job *A* to determine the selling price :

	Rs. per unit
Material	70
Direct wages : 14 hrs. @ Rs. 2.50 per hr. (Dept. *X* – 8 hrs. and Dept. *Y* – 6 hrs.)	35
Chargeable expenses (stores)	5
	110
Add : $33\frac{1}{3}$% for expenses (oh)	37
	147

Analysis of the P & L account shows the following :

Materials	1,50,000	Sales less returns	2,50,000
Direct wages :			
Dept. *X*	10,000		
Dept. *Y*	12,000		
Stores expenses	4,000		
Overheads :			
Dept. *X*	5,000		
Dept. *Y*	9,000		
Gross profit	60,000		
	2,50,000		2,50,000

It is noted that average hourly rates for the two department *X* and *Y* are similar. You are required to :

(*i*) Draw up a job cost sheet.

(*ii*) Calculate the revised cost using overhead figures as shown in the P & L a/c as the basis for charging overhead to Dept. X and Y.

(*iii*) Add 20% of total cost to determine the selling price. (*C.S., Inter, June 1991*)

Solution :

Job cost sheet

Job : A — Date started ....

Description................ — Date completed ....

Materials		70.00
Direct wages :	Dept. *X* — 8 × 2.50	20.00
	Dept. Y — 6 × 2.50	15.00
Chargeable expenses		5.00

		Prime cost	110.00
Overheads :	Dept. *X* (50% of direct wages) *i.e.*, 8 × 1.25		10.00
	Dept. *Y* (75% of direct wages) *i.e.*, 6 × 1.875		11.25
		Total cost	131.25
		Profit (20% on cost)	26.25
		Selling price	157.50

Working note :

Direct wages as per P & L a/c	Rs. 10,000.00	12,000.00
Hourly rate	2.50	2.50
Number of hours	$\frac{10,000.00}{2.50}$	$\frac{12,000}{2.5}$
	= 4,000 hrs.	= 4,800 hrs.
Calculation of overhead rate	$\frac{5,000}{4,000}$	$\frac{9,000}{4,800}$
	= 1.25 hrs.	= 1.875 hrs.

At the above rates for 8 and 6 hrs. for X and Y it comes to 21.25 Rs. (10 + 11.25)

On the basis of percentage on direct wages :

$$\frac{\text{oh}}{\text{wages}} \times 100$$

$$\frac{5,000}{10,000} \times 100 \qquad \frac{9,000}{12,000} \times 100$$

$$= 50\% \qquad = 75\%$$

Problem 12 : In an Engineering company the factory overheads are recovered on a fixed percentage basis on direct wages and the administrative overheads are absorbed on a fixed percentage basis on factory cost. The company has furnished, the following data relating to two jobs undertaken by it in a period.

	Job 101	*Job 102*
	Rs.	Rs.
Direct materials	54,000	37,500
Direct wages	42,000	30,000
Selling price	1,66,650	1,28,250
Profit percentage on total cost	10%	20%

Required :

(1) Computation of percentage recovery rates of factory overheads and administrative overheads

(2) Calculation of the amount of factory overheads, administration overheads and profit for each of the two jobs.

(3) Using the above recovery rates fix the selling price of job 103. The additional data being.

Direct materials	Rs. 24,000
Direct wages	Rs. 20,000
Profit percentage on selling price	$12\frac{1}{2}\%$

(*C.A., Inter, May 1995*)

Solution :

Let factory overhead recovery rate as percentage of direct wages be F and administration overhead recovery rate as percentage of factory cost be A

Total cost of production :

Job 101	=	(96,000 +	42,000 F)	+	A (96,000 +	42,000 F)	=	1,51,500
Job 102	=	(67,500 +	30,000 F)	+	A (67,500 +	30,000 F)	=	10,6875
or	=	96,000 +	42,000 F	+	96,000 A +	42,000 AF	=	1,51,500
	=	67,500 +	30,000 F	+	67,500 A +	30,000 AF	=	10,6875

or = 42,000 F + 96,000 A + 42,000 AF = 55,500 × 5

30,000 F + 67,500 A + 30,000 AF = 39,375 × 7

or 2,10,000 F + 4,80,000 A + 2,10,000 AF = 2,77,500

or (–) 2,10,000 F + 4,72,500 A + 2,10,000 AF = 2,75,625

(–) (–) (–) (–)

On Subtracting

7,500A = 1,875

$$A = \frac{1,875}{7,500} = 0.25$$

Substituting the value of A in first equation

= 96,000 + 42,000 F + 96,000 A + 42,000 AF = 1,51,500

or = 96,000 + 42,000 F + 96,000 × 0.25 + 42,000 × 0.25 × F = 1,51,500

= 96,000 + 42,000 F + 24,000 + 10,500 F = 1,51,500

= 52,500 F = 1,51,500 – 96,000 – 24,000

= 52,500 F = 1,51,500 – 1,20,000

52,500 F = 31,500

$$F = \frac{31,500}{52,500} = 0.60$$

Job cost sheet of job 101 and 102

	Job 101	*Job 102*
Direct materials	54,000	37,500
Direct wages	42,000	30,000
Prime cost	96,000	67,500
Factory overheads 60% of direct wages	25,200	18,000
Factory cost	1,21,200	85,500
Administration overheads 25% of factory cost	30,300	21,375
Total cost	1,51,500	1,06,875
Profit	15,150	21,375
Sales	1,66,650	1,28,250

Job cost sheet of job 103

Direct materials		24,000
Direct wages		20,000
	Prime cost	44,000
Factory oh — 60% of direct wages		12,000
	Factory cost	56,000
Administration oh — 25% of factory cost		14,000
	Total cost	70,000
	Profit $\frac{12.5}{87.5} \times 70,000$	10,000
	Selling price	80,000

BATCH COSTING

As the name itself suggest, under this method the cost is ascertained in respect of a batch of goods or components manufactured. There are certain products whose cost of production cannot be ascertained in isolation, *i.e.*, for each and every unit of article produced. Examples of such products are hardware (such as bolts, nuts, screws, pins, etc.) Bakery products such as breads, biscuits, cakes, etc. So industries which manufacture products of this nature make use of batch costing. Other examples of industries which adopt batch costing are readymade garments, drugs and pharmaceuticals, spare parts and component parts as in the case of automobiles, radios, TV's, refrigerators, machineries, etc.

Batch costing does not differ from job costing in respect of accounting procedure. However, there are two points of differences between job costing and batch costing. Firstly, under job costing, each job is treated as a cost unit, whereas in case of batch costing, a batch of articles produced constitute a cost unit. Secondly, a job is undertaken for execution only on receiving an order, whereas, production under batch costing is taken up in anticipation of demand for such products as well as on receiving specific orders.

In order to know the cost of production of a batch of articles, a batch cost sheet is prepared. The production planning department determines the batch of articles to be produced depending upon the orders received or the potential demand for such articles. The other factors considered in determining a batch of articles to be manufactured are the capacity of machines, flow of work, treatment of work-in-progress and such other operation factors. The cost per article is obtained by dividing the total cost of batch by the number of articles manufactured in the batch. The units manufactured in a batch are identical in nature.

Advantages of Batch Costing

When compared to job costing, batch costing has the following advantages :

1. The accounting work is considerably reduced as a group of homogeneous jobs constitute a batch.
2. The variations in the costs arising under job costing is smoothened by means of averaging such costs and spreading over the batch of articles. This gives a consistent cost of production of every article in the batch.
3. It takes the benefit of reduced cost of production arising out of economic batch quantity.
4. Supervision becomes easy and more effective by means of spreading over the supervisor's time over all the units constituting the batch. Thus, the idle time of supervisor's as well as workers are eliminated.
5. The loss of time under job costing arising out of inter-job transfer of materials, labourers and tools is minimised under batch costing.

Disadvantages

1. Determination of a batch from various jobs often pose problem. It is difficult to come across absolute homogeneity of jobs.
2. When quantity of goods to be manufactured differs from customer to customer, again it becomes difficult to determine the batch.
3. If the production of a batch is wrongly undertaken, say, owing to sub-standard materials or defective operations, the whole batch of articles are to be discarded which will become a great loss to the manufacturer. Drugs and pharmaceutical products offer best example to this point of disadvantage.

Determination of Economic Batch Quantity

The concept of economic batch quantity is quite similar to economic order quantity discussed earlier under chapter 3. In batch costing, the determination of economic lot size or economic batch quantity assumes more importance. In fact, determining the size of the batch is a problem by itself under batch costing. This is so because, if the batches are many, the (*i.e.*, quantity of production is less in every job) economies arising out of large scale production is not taken advantage of. On the other hand, if a batch is very large, it involves more of inventory and it has its own disadvantages. Therefore, it is always necessary to determine the optimum size of the batch or economic batch quantity before the production is started. The economic batch quantity also helps in eliminating the setting up time involved whenever a batch of articles are produced.

Thus it can be said that the concept of 'Economic batch quantity' is an example of the law of increasing returns and takes advantage of economies of large scale production. By producing the goods in an optimum batch, it reduces the cost of production, thereby maximising the profit. In determining the economic batch quantity, two conflicting forces operate. They are : (1) Production cost which include set up cost and other factors such as loss of time due to change of work, loss of speed of work when work is frequently changed on different jobs, wastage in materials, increased supervision cost, all these forces are responsible for increased cost of production, (2) Production in a very large batch quantity will lead to certain disadvantages such as, increased wear and tear of machines, breakdown of machines, problem of inspection, excessive defectives of goods, large inventory, locked up capital and so on. Thus economic batch quantity strickes a balance between these two factors in order to take maximum benefit from production process.

Different formulae are developed to determine the economic batch quantity. One such formula is given below :

$$EBQ = \sqrt{\frac{2US}{C}}$$

where EBQ = Economic Batch Quantity
U = Units to be produced in a year
S = Set up cost per batch
C = Carrying cost per unit of production.

Where rate of interest and cost of production per unit is given, the following formula is applicable

$$EBQ = \sqrt{\frac{2US}{i \times C}}$$

where EBQ = Economic Batch Quantity
U = Units to be produced
S = Set up cost per batch
i = Interest rate per year
C = Cost of manufacture per unit.

Problem 13 (Determination of economic batch quantity) : M/s. Kobo Bearings Ltd., is committed to supply 24,000 bearing per annum to M/s Deluxe Fans on a steady daily basis. It is eatimated that it costs 10 paise as inventory holding cost per bearing per month and that the set up per run of bearing manufacture is Rs. 324.

1. What should be the optimum run size for bearing manufacture?
2. What would be due interval between two consecutive optimum runs?
3. Find out the minimum inventory holding cost. (*ICWA, Final, Dec. 1979*)

Solution : **1. Determination of economic batch quantity**

$$EBQ = \sqrt{\frac{2US}{C}}$$

$$= \sqrt{\frac{2 \times 24,000 \times 324}{12 \times 0.10}}$$

$$= 3,600 \text{ units}$$

2. Interval between two consecutive optimum runs expressed in terms of days

$$\frac{24,000}{12} = 2,000 \text{ bearings per month of 25 working days}$$

$$\frac{EBQ}{\text{Monthly production}} \times \text{No. of days in the month}$$

$$\frac{3,600}{2,000} \times 25 = 45 \text{ days interval}$$

3. Average inventory

$$= \frac{3,600}{2} = 1,800 \text{ bearings}$$

Minimum inventory holding cost per month is :

$$1,800 \times 0.10 = \text{Rs. } 180$$

Per annum it is $1,800 \times 0.10 \times 12 = \text{Rs. } 2,160$

Problem 14 : A contractor has to supply 10,000 paper cones per day to a Textile unit. He finds that, when he starts a production run he can produce 25,000 paper cones per day. The cost of building a paper cone is stock for one year is 2 paise and the set up cost of a production run is Rs. 18. How frequently should production run be made. (*ICWA, Final, Dec. 1983*)

Solution :

For 365 days at the rate of 10,000 paper cones it works out to 36,50,000 cones

$$EBQ = \sqrt{\frac{2US}{C}}$$

$$= \sqrt{\frac{2 \times 36,50,000 \times 18}{0.02}}$$

$$= 81,100 \text{ cones}$$

= Producion run in terms of days

$$= \frac{EBQ}{\text{Daily production}}$$

$$= \frac{81,100}{10,000} = 8 \text{ calendar days App.}$$

Problem 15 (Problem involving setting up cost and production cost) : Component 'Pee' is made entirely in cost centre 100. Material cost is 6 paise per component and each component takes 10 minutes to produce. The machine operator is paid 0.72 paise per hour, and the machine hour rate is Rs. 1.50. The setting up of the machine to produce component pee takes 2 hrs. 20 minutes.

On the basis of this information prepare cost sheets showing the production and setting-up costs, both in total and per component, assuming that a batch of (*a*) 10 components, (*b*) 100 components and (*c*) 1,000 components and produced. (*C.A., Inter, Nov. 1992*)

Solution :

Cost sheet for a batch of 10 components

	Cost of the batch	*Cost per unit*
Setting up cost		
Wages : 2 hrs, 20 mins at 0.72 paise per hr.	1.68	
Overheads : 2 hrs. 20 mins at 1.50 per hr.	3.50	
	5.18	0.518
Production cost		
Materials cost — 10 @ 0.06 P	0.60	0.060
Wages — 1 hr. 40 mins @ 72 paise per hr.	1.20	0.120
Overheads — 1 hr. 40 mins @ 1.50 per hr.	2.50	0.250
Total production & setting up cost	9.48	0.948

Cost Sheet for a batch of 100 components

Setting up cost		
Wages : 2 hrs. 20 mins @ 72 P per hr.	1.68	
Overhead : 2 hrs. 20 mins @ 1.50 per hr.	3.50	
	5.18	0.05
Production cost		
Material cost — 100 @ 0.60 P	6.00	0.06
Wages — 16 hrs. 40 mins @ 72 P per hr.	12.00	0.12
Overhead — 16 hrs. 40 mins @ 1.50 per hr.	25.00	0.25
	48.18	0.48

Cost sheet for a batch of 1,000 components

Setting up cost		
Wages — 2 hrs. 20 mins @ 72 P per hr.	1.68	
Overheads — 2 hrs. 20 mins @ 1.50 per hr.	3.50	
	5.18	0.005
Production cost		
Materials cost — 1,000 @ 0.06 P	60.00	0.060
Wages — 166 hrs. 40 mins @ 72 P per hr.	120.00	0.120
Overhead — 166 hrs. 40 mins @ 1.50 per hr.	250.00	0.250
Total of setting up & production cost	435.18	0.435

Problem 16 : A printing press is proposing to offer a leaflet advertising service to local trader. The following costs have been estimated for a batch of 10,000 leaflets

Setting up cost		
Setting up machine	:	6 hrs. @ Rs. 10 per hr.
Art work	:	Rs. 20 per batch
Production cost		
Paper	:	Rs. 1.80 per 100 sheets
Other printing materials	:	Rs. 15
Direct labour cost	:	4 hrs. @ Rs. 6 per hr.

Fixed overheads allocated to this side of business are Rs. 1,000 per annum and recovered on the basis of orders received, which are expected to be 2 per week for 50 week in the year :

The management requires 25% profit on selling price.

You are required to

(*a*) Prepare a price to be quoted for the leaflets for batches of 2,000, 5,000, 10,000 ad 20,000 leaflets

(*b*) Show the price per 1,000 leaflets on the basis of price ascertained above.

Solution : **Batch cost sheet**

	Batch sizes			
	2,000	*5,000*	*10,000*	*20,000*
Setting up cost				
Cost of setting up machine	60	60	60	60
Art work	20	20	20	20
Production cost				
Paper	36	90	180	360
Other printing materials	3	7.50	15	30
Labour cost	4.80	12	24	48
Fixed overhead 1,000 ÷ 100	10	10	10	10
Total cost	133.80	199.50	309	528
Profit	44.60	66.50	103	176
Selling price	178.40	266	412	704
Selling price per 1,000 leaflets	89.20	53.20	41.20	35.70

Working note : Calculation per 1,000 leaflets

For 2,000 leaflets the selling price is 178.40

For 1,000 → ? $\frac{178.40 \times 1,000}{2,000} = 89.20$

For 5,000 leaflets the selling price is 266

for 1,000 → ? $\frac{266 \times 1,000}{5,000} = 53.20$

For 10,000 leaflets the selling price is 412.20

For 1,000 × ? $\frac{412 \times 1,000}{10,000} = 41.20$

For 20,000 leaflets the selling price is 704

For 1,000 → ? $\frac{704 \times 10,00}{20,000} = 35.70$

Problem 17 : K. Ltd., designs and manufactures deluxe containers for various industries. The company has been requested to submit quotations for supplying a specially designed container to which the following data relate :

Estimated design & development costs

Engineer's time	—	50 hrs. @ Rs. 6 per hour
Draughtsman's time	—	30 hrs. @ Rs. 3 per hour
Materials	—	Rs. 30
Engineering machine shop time	—	20 hrs. @ 5 per hour
Project supervision	—	Rs. 200
General overhead allocation	—	Rs. 350

Manufacturing cost including setting up costs

The production machine to be used require 20 hours of an engineer's time @ Rs. 3 per hour and has an output of 50 containers per hour.

Operatives are paid an hourly rate of Rs. 1.50 and production overhead is absorbed at Rs. 2.50 per direct labour hour worked. The direct material cost per containers is Rs. 1.25. It is companies practice to provide for a profit of 10% on design and development costs and 30% on production cost.

Calculate the price to be quoted for the supply of (*a*) 5,000 containers, (*b*) 20,000 containers and (*c*) 50,000 containers.

Solution : **Batch cost sheet**

	Batch size		
	5,000	*20,000*	*50,000*
Estimated design & development cost :			
Engineer's time — 50 hrs. @ 6 per hr.	300	300	300
Draughtsman's time — 30 hrs. @ Rs. 3 per hr.	90	90	90
Materials	30	30	30
Engineer's machine shop time — 20 hrs. @ Rs. 50 per hr.	100	100	100
Project supervision	200	200	200
General overhead allocation	350	350	350
(*A*) Total estimated & design and development cost	1,070	1,070	1,070
Manufacturing cost including setting up cost :			
Materials cost :	6,250	25,000	62,500
Wages :			
(*a*) Engineer's 20 hrs. @ Rs. 3	60	60	60
(*b*) Operatives (*see working note 1*)	150	600	1,500
Overheads (*see working note 2*)	250	1,000	2,500
(*B*) Total manufacturing & setting up cost	6,710	26,660	66,560
Profit — 10% on design & development cost	107	107	107
— 30% on manufacturing cost	2,013	7,998	19,968
(*C*) Total profit	2,120	8,105	20,075
Statement showing selling price :			
(*A*) Total estimated design & development cost	1,070	1,070	1,070
(*B*) Total maunfacturing cost	6,710	26,660	66,560
(C) Total profit	2,120	8,105	20,075
Selling price	10,575	35,835	87,705

Working note 1 : Calculation of wages of operatives

$$\text{Calculation of direct labour hours} = \frac{\text{Total containers}}{\text{No. of containers per hour}} = \frac{5{,}000}{50} = 100 \text{ hrs.}$$

$$= \frac{20{,}000}{50} = 400 \text{ hrs.}$$

$$= \frac{50{,}000}{50} = 1{,}000 \text{ hrs.}$$

Wages 100 hrs. @ 1.50 = Rs. 150
400 hrs. @ 1.50 = Rs. 600
1,000 hrs. @ 1.50 = Rs. 1,500

Working note 2 : Calculation of overheads

100 hrs. @ 2.50 = 250
400 hrs. @ 2.50 = 1,000
1,000 hrs. @ 2.50 = 2,500

Problem 18 : A Jobbing factory has undertaken to supply 200 pieces of a component per month for the ensuing 6 months. Every month a batch order is opened against which materials and labour hours are booked at actuals. Overheads are levied at a rate per labour hour. The selling price contracted for is Rs. 8 per piece. From the following data present the cost and profit per piece of each batch order and overall position of the order for 1,200 picees :

Month	*Batch output*	*Material*	*Direct wages*	*Direct labour hrs.*
Jan.	210	650	120	240
Feb.	200	640	140	280
Mar.	220	680	150	280
Apr.	180	630	140	270
May	200	700	150	300
June	220	720	160	320

The other details are :

Month	*Chargeable expense*	*Direct labour hrs.*
Jan.	12,000	4,800
Feb.	10,560	4,400
Mar.	12,000	5,000
Apr.	10,580	4,600
May	13,000	5,000
June	12,000	4,800

Solution :

Batch cost sheet

	Jan.	*Feb.*	*Mar.*	*Apr.*	*May*	*June*	*Total*
Materials	650	640	680	630	700	720	4,020
Wages	120	140	150	140	150	160	1,860
Chargeable expenses (*see working note 1*)	600	672	672	621	780	800	4,145
Total	1,370	1,452	1,502	1,391	1,630	1,680	9,025
Profit	310	148	258	49	–30	80	815
Sales	1,680	1,600	1,760	1,440	1,600	1,760	9,840
Total cost per unit	$\frac{1,370}{210}$	$\frac{1,452}{200}$	$\frac{1,502}{220}$	$\frac{1,391}{180}$	$\frac{1,600}{200}$	$\frac{1,680}{220}$	$\frac{9,025}{1,230}$
	= 6.52	= 7.26	= 6.83	= 7.73	= 8.15	= 7.64	= 7.33

Overall position of the order for 1,200 units

Sales value of 1,200 units @ Rs. 8 per unit	9,600
Total cost for 1,200 units @ Rs. 7.33	8,796
Profit	804

Working note :

Jan. : For 4,800 labour hrs. : The chargeable expenses expended were 12,000

For 240 → ? $\frac{12,000 \times 240}{4,800} = 600$

Problem 19 : The output for April 1987 for ABC Ltd. includes one batch of the Ranji model consisting of 500 units. The following data are taken from the works records :

(1) Standard batch data for Ranji :

Materials :

Body and lid	Rs. 136
Fittings	Rs. 27

Department			
I	:	Labour time	20 hrs.
II	:	Machine time	10 hrs.
III	:	Machine time	8 hrs.
IV	:	Labour time	20 hrs.

(2) Department cost for April 1987 :

Dept.	*Machine hours*	*Labour hours*	*Wages*	*Variable overheads*	*Fixed expenses*
I	–	6,000	1,800	3,600	0.50 P per labour hour
II	4,000	8,000	3,600	4,000	0.60 P per machine hour
III	6,000	12,000	7,200	9,000	0.80 P per machine hour
IV	–	10,000	3,000	4,500	0.40 P per labour hour

(3) Administrative overheads are absorbed at the rate of $12\frac{1}{2}$% of works conversion cost. Selling and distribution costs are charged to the products at 10% of the selling value.

Required : Prepare the batch cost sheet of the Ranji model and suggest the minimum unit selling price which will yield a profit of 10% on the selling price. *(Sri Sathya Sai University, B.Com., Mar., 1989)*

Solution :

Batch cost sheet

Materials :			
Body and lid		136	
Fittings		27	
Labour cost (*see working note 1*)			
Dept. I		6.00	
Dept. II		9.00	
Dept. III		9.60	
Dept. IV		6.00	30.60
	Prime cost		193.60
Overhead			
Variable (*see working note 2*)			
Dept. I		12.00	
Dept. II		10.00	
Dept. III		12.00	
Dept. IV		9.00	43.00
Fixed			
Dept. I 20 × 0.50		10.00	
Dept. II 10 × 0.60		6.00	
Dept. III 8 × 0.80		6.40	
Dept. IV 20 × 0.40		8.00	30.40
	Work cost		267.00
Administration overhead : 12½% of conversion cost (i.e., wages + ohs)			
Wages 30.63			
Oh — Fixed 43.00			
Variable 30.00			
Conversion cost 104.00			13.00
	Cost of production		280.00
Selling & distribution overhead (*see working note 3*)			35.00
	Cost of sales		315.00

Profit $\frac{1}{9}$ on cost	35.00
Sales	350.00

Working note 1 : Calculation of labour cost

Dept. I $\quad \frac{\text{Rs. } 1,800}{6,000} = 0.30$

20 hrs. @ 0.30 = Rs. 6

Dept. II $\quad \frac{\text{Rs. } 3,600}{4,000} = 0.90$

10 hrs. @ 0.90 = Rs. 9

Dept. III $\quad \frac{\text{Rs. } 7,200}{6,000} = 1.20$

8 hrs. @ 1.20 = Rs. 9.60

Dept. IV $\quad \frac{\text{Rs. } 3,000}{10,000} = 0.30$

20 hrs. @ 0.30 = Rs. 6.00

Working note 2 : Calculation of variable overheads

Dept. I $\quad \frac{\text{Rs. } 3,600}{6,000} = 0.60$

20 hrs. @ 0.60 = 12.00

Dept. II $\quad \frac{\text{Rs. } 4,000}{4,000} = 1.00$

10 hrs. @ 1.00 = 10.00

Dept. III $\quad \frac{\text{Rs. } 9,000}{6,000} = 1.50$

8 hrs. @ 1.50 = 12.00

Dept. IV $\quad \frac{\text{Rs. } 4,500}{10,000} = 0.45$

20 hrs. @ 0.45 = 9.00

Working note 3 : Calculation of selling and distribution overheads
Selling and distribution ohs is 10% of sales. But sales itself is not given. So

Let selling price	100
Less : Profit 10%	10
Cost of sales	90

Cost of sales = Cost of production + Selling and distribution overhead

90 = 80 + 10

$$\frac{10}{80} \times 280 = \text{Rs. } 35$$

On verification of this amount of selling and distribution overhead, *i.e.*, 35, with sales, i.e. 10% on 350 we get the same amount of Rs. 35.

Problem 20 : Following information for the month of April is extracted from the cost records of Hilton Ltd., which specialises in the manufacture of automobile spares. The parts are manufactured in Dept. *A* and assemble in Dept. *B*.

	Total	Dept. A	Dept. B
Direct labour hrs. worked	80,000	30,000	50,000
Machine hours worked	30,000	25,000	5,000
Machine horsepower (H.P.)	400	353	47
Book value of machines (Rs.)	50,000	40,000	10,000
Floor space (sq. ft.)	20,000	10,000	10,000
Direct materials (Rs.)	65,000	50,000	15,000
Direct labour (Rs.)	90,000	40,000	50,000
Factory rent (Rs.)	15,000	–	–
Supervision (Rs.)	6,000	2,500	3,500
Depreciation on machines (Rs.)	5,000	–	–
Power (Rs.)	4,000	–	–
Repairs to machines (Rs.)	2,000	1,600	400
Indirect labour (Rs.)	4,000	2,000	2,000
The prime cost of batch B-401 have been booked as under :			
Materials (Rs.)	3,200	2,700	500
Labour (Rs.)	7,500	3,000	4,500

Direct labour hours worked on batch B-401 were 2,500 in Dept. *A* and 5,000 in Dept. *B*. Machine hours worked on this batch were 1,250 in Dept. *A* and 600 in Dept. *B*. Allocate overhead expenditure and calculate the cost of each unit in batch B-401 which consists of 1,000 units. *(C.S. Inter, June 1993)*

Solution : **Departmentalisation of overhead costs**

Items of expenses	*Basis*	*Total*	*Dept. A*	*Dept. B*
Depreciation	Plant value (4.1)	5,000	4,000	1,000
Power	H.P. (353; 47)	4,000	3,530	470
Repairs to machines	Actual	2,000	1,600	400
Total machine cost		11,000	9,130	1,870
Other overhead costs				
Factory rent	Floor space	15,000	7,500	7,500
Supervision	Actual	6,000	2,500	3,500
Indirect labour	Actual	4,000	2,000	2,000
Total other overheads		25,000	12,000	13,000
Machine hour rate			$\frac{9,130}{25,000}$ = 0.3652	$\frac{1,870}{5,000}$ = 0.374
Labour hour rate			$\frac{12,000}{30,000}$ = 0.40	$\frac{13,000}{50,000}$ = 0.26

Cost sheet of batch B-401

	Total	Dept. A	Dept B
Materials	3,200	2,700	500
Labour	7,500	3,000	4,500
Overhead (*see note*)	2,981	1,457	1,524
	13,681	7,157	6,524

Cost of each unit $\frac{13,681}{1,000} = 13.68$

Working note :

Dept. A	= 2,500 hrs. × 0.40	=	1,000	
	= 1,250 hrs. × 0.3652	=	475	
				1,457
Dept. B	= 5,000 hrs. × 0.26	=	1,300	
	= 600 hrs. × 0.374	=	224	1,524

Note : **It seems both men and machines are playing equally important roles in production, hence it will be appropriate to charge overheads according to dual rate method. Consequently machine cost have been absorbed on the basis of machine hour rate and other overhead costs on the basis of direct labour hours.**

QUESTIONS

I. Chosse the correct answer :

1. Which of the following methods of costing can be used in a factory where the products differ in type of materials and work performed
   (*a*) Single or output costing (*b*) Job costing
   (*c*) Process costing (*d*) Contract costing [ ]
2. Tyre and tubes manufacturing company adopts
   (*a*) Output costing (*b*) Job costing
   (*c*) Contract costing (*d*) Batch costing [ ]
3. Given cost of production of a job Rs. 7,50,000 and profit percentage 20% on sales, the profit would be
   (*a*) Rs. 1,87,500 (*b*) Rs. 1,78,500
   (*c*) Rs. 1,57,800 (*d*) Rs. 1,85,700 [ ]
4. Job costing is used in
   (*a*) Repairs shops (*b*) Brick making
   (*c*) Road repairs (*d*) Cycle manufacturing [ ]
5. Job order means
   (*a*) An order received from a customer for the production of a specific item
   (*b*) Instructions to the shops to proceed with the production of the product
   (*c*) An order to the storekeeper to issue necessary materials for production
   (*d*) All of the above [ ]
6. Which one of the following industries is properly matched with its method of costing
   (*a*) Boiler — job costing (*b*) Hotel — operating costing
   (*c*) Readymade garments — contract costing (*d*) Oil refinery — process costing [ ]
7. Which one of the following method of costing is best suited for interior decoration
   (*a*) Job costing (*c*) Process costing
   (*b*) Contract costing (*d*) Operating costing [ ]
8. Which one of the following method of costing is best suited for garment manufacturing
   (*a*) Unit costing (*c*) Batch costing
   (*b*) Job costing (*d*) Process costing [ ]
9. In shoe manufacturing industries the most suitable method of costing is
   (*a*) Output costing (*c*) Job costing
   (*b*) Batch costing (*d*) Process costing [ ]
10. If the total cost of a product is Rs. 40,000 and 20% of the sale price is the profit to be added to cost, then the profit is
   (*a*) Rs. 6,000 (*b*) Rs. 10,000
   (*c*) Rs. 8,000 (*d*) Rs. 12,000 [ ]
11. Pharmaceutical industries adopt
   (*a*) Output costing (*c*) Job costing
   (*b*) Batch costing (*d*) Process costing [ ]
12. At the level of production of the economical lot size
   (*a*) Set-up cost is minimum (*b*) Carrying cost is minimum
   (*c*) Total cost of production is minimum (*d*) Set-up cost is greater than carrying cost [ ]

13. Job costing is used in

(*a*) Paper maills (*c*) Paints & varnishing

(*b*) Printing press (*d*) Pharmaceutical products [ ]

[***Answers :*** 1 (*b*), 2 (*d*), 3 (*a*), 4 (*a*), 5 (*b*), 6 (*a*), 7 (*a*), 8 (*c*), 9 (*c*), 10 (*c*), 11 (*b*), 12 (*c*), 13 (*b*)]

II. Fill in the blanks :

1. The formula for determining economic batch quantity is ....
2. Under job costing each job is known by its ....
3. In industries where batch costing is employed an important point is the determination of ....
4. An item of cost which is common to prime cost and conversion cost is .... cost.
5. The backbone of job costing is ....
6. In .... method of costing, the cost of a group of products is ascertained.
7. Under job costing each .... is a cost unit to which all elements of costs are assigned.

[***Answer :*** 1. $\sqrt{\frac{2US}{C}}$ 2. job number, 3. economic batch qty, 4. labour, 5, job cost sheet, 6. batch, 7. job]

III. Mark true or false in the space provided

1. In job costing each job should be continuously identifiable from the raw materials stage to the stage or completion. *T/F*
2. In Asian Paints Co. job costing method should be applied. *T/F*
3. A job cost sheet is used to collect, classify and summarise costs. *T/F*
4. In job costing method a cost sheet is prepared for each job. *T/F*
5. Job costing cannot be used in industries using standard costing. *T/F*
6. Job costing can be more conveniently used in concerns producing uniformly any specific product. *T/F*
7. Batch costing is a variant of job costing. *T/F*
8. A production order is an order received from a customer for a particular job. *T/F*
9. Compared to process, cost control under job costing is more completed. *T/F*
10. The concept of economic batch quantity is similar to that of economic order quantity. *T/F*

[*Answer* : 1. *F*, 2. *F*, 3. *T*, 4. *T*, 5. *T*, 6. *F*, 7. *T*, 8. *F*, 9. *T*, 10. *T*]

IV. Match the following :

A	*B*
1. Road transport	(*a*) Multiple costing
2. Cement	(*b*) Operating costing
3. Engineering industry	(*c*) Output costing
4. Bicycle industry	(*d*) Process costing
5. Pharmaceuticals	(*e*) Job costing
	(*f*) Batch costing
	(*g*) Contract costing

[***Answer :*** 1. (*b*), 2. (*c*), 3. (*e*), 4. (*a*), 5. (*f*)]

V. Short answer question

1. What are the salient features of batch costing? (*Calicut University, B.Com., Oct. 1989; Kerala University, B.Com., April 1990*)
2. What are the salient features of job costing? Indicate the industries to which it is suitable. (*Calicut University, B.Com., Oct. 1989*)
3. What is the importance of estimation in job costing? (*Calicut University, B.Com., April 1988*)
4. What do you understand by Batch costing? In what industries is it applied? (*C.A., Inter, May 1987*)

EXERCISES

Exercise 1 : *A* Co. Ltd., had absorbed overhead by means of a blanket rate based on direct labour hours. As from 1.1.90, it decides to adopt separate rates for the three main activities—storekeeping and material

handling, maching and assembly. The estimates of costs and absorption rates for selling and distribution cost remain unchanged overhead absorption rates are :

Prior to 1st January 1990 :

Production overhead — 0.50 paise per direct labour hour. Selling and distribution overhead — 25% of factory cost.

From 1.1.1990 :

Storekeeping & material handling — 10% of direct material cost

Machining — 0.75 paise per machine hour

Assembly — 0.30 paise per labour hour

Selling and distribution overhead — 25% of factory cost

The direct cost of job no. 501 have been :	
Direct material cost	90
Direct wages :	
Machining 200 hrs. @ 0.60	120
Assembly 100 hrs. @ 0.40	40
	250

The estimated price of the job is Rs. 525 and it requires 180 machine hours to complete.

Show the job cost sheet for job 501

(*a*) As it would appear if the job had been completed prior to 1st Jan. 1990.

(*b*) As it would appear if the job were completed on 1.1.1990.

[***Answer :*** Profit prior to 1.1.90 is Rs. 25, Loss on 1.1.90 is Rs. 5]

Exercise 2 : M/s Diamond Tools Co. Ltd. has undertaken a job no. 5. As per cost ledger, the following expenses have been debited to this job. You are reqquired to prepare a job cost sheet and calculate the total amount to be charged to the customer in order to secure 20% profit on sale.

Additional information based on normal capacity if furnished below :

Capacity	*Department* A	*Department* B	*Total for the factory as a whole*
Budgeted production in items of direct labour hours	6,000	9,000	20,000
Budgeted variable overheads (Rs.)	9,000	10,800	
Budgeted fixed overhead (Rs.)			20,000

Job cost details :

Direct materials :

Cast Iron — 10 kgs. @ Rs. 1 per kg.

Gun metal — 5 kgs. @ Rs. 10 per kg.

Direct labour :

Dept. A — 20 hrs. @ Re. 0.50 per hr.

Dept. B — 15 hrs. @ Re. 0.40 per hr.

Direct expenses

Special tool — Rs. 21

[***Answer :*** Selling price Rs. 225]

Exercise 3 : The information given below has been taken from the records of an engineering works in respect of job no. 303.

Materials Rs. 4,010

Wages : Dept. *A* — 60 hrs. at Rs. 3 per hr.

Dept. *B* — 40 hrs. at Rs. 2 per hr.

Dept. *C* — 20 hrs. at Rs. 5 per hr.

The works overheads are as follows :

Variable : Dept. *A* — Rs. 5,000 for 5,000 labour hours

Dept. *B* — Rs. 3,000 for 1,500 labour hours

Dept. *C* — Rs. 2,000 for 500 labour hours

Fixed expenses : Rs. 20,000 for 10,000 working hours

Calculate the cost of job 303 and price for the job to earn a profit of 25% on the selling price.

(Bangalore University, B.Com., Nov. 1988)

[***Answer :*** Selling price Rs. 6,440]

Exercise 4 : The following information is extracted from the books of Kohinor Mossac Tiles factory :

	1990 (*Rs.*)	*1991* (*Rs.*)	*1992* (*Rs.*)
Materials	75,000	50,000	1,00,000
Labour	50,000	40,000	60,000
Works overheads	35,000	30,000	40,000
Administrative overheads	20,000	20,000	20,000
Selling overheads	10,000	9,000	8,000
Number of tiles	15,000	10,000	20,000

On the basis of the data given above prepare an estimate for the supply of 40,000 tiles under job number 55, to fetch a profit of 25% on works cost.

[***Answer :*** Selling price for 40,000 tiles is Rs. 4,77,000]

Exercise 5 (Batch costing) : Leo Ltd., undertaken to supply 1,000 units of a component per month for the months of January, February and March 1987. Every month a batch order is opened against which materials and labour costs are booked at actuals, overheads are levied at a rate per labour hour. The selling price is contracted at Rs. 15 per unit.

From the following data present the cost and profit per unit of each batch order and the overall position of the order for the 3,000 units.

Manths	*Batch output*	*Materials cost* (Rs.)	*Labour cost* (Rs.)
Jan. 87	1,250	6,250	2,500
Feb. 87	1,500	9,000	3,000
Mar. 87	1,000	5,000	2,000

Labour is paid at the rate of Rs. 2 per hour. The other details are :

Month	*Overheads (Rs.)*	*Total labour hours*
Jan. 87	12,000	4,000
Feb. 87	9,000	4,500
Mar. 87	15,000	5,000

(C.A., Inter, May 1987)

[***Answer :*** Cost per unit Rs. 10 each when batch output is 1,250, 1,500, and 1,000 profit per unit Rs. 5 each when batch output is 1,250, 1,500 and 1,000]

15

CONTRACT COSTING

FEATURES OF CONTRACT COSTING

Contract costing is a variation of job costing applied in those undertakings which are engaged in constructional and repair works. There lies a thin line of difference between these two methods of costing—the difference lies in the size of order received. In fact a big order is termed as a contract and a small contract as a job. Contract costing is also known as terminal costing as the preparation of contract account is terminated or closed after the completion of contract. Examples of undertakings which adopt contract costing are builders, civil engineering contractors, road repairing concerns, dams and bridge constructional concerns. The following are the distinctive characteristic features of industries which adopt contract costing :

1. The work is executed in the premises of contractee.
2. Most of the contracts involve longer duration for completion.
3. Expenses chargeable to contracts are direct in nature.
4. The work to be executed depends upon customer's specification. Hence very rarely two contracts resemble one another.
5. Each contract is treated as a cost unit, *i.e.*, the cost of construction is ascertained in respect of each and every contract separately.
6. The payment is received depending on the stage of completion of work.

SIMILARITIES AND DISSIMILARITIES BETWEEN JOB AND CONTRACT COSTING

Points of Similarities

In both the methods of costing :

1. Production starts on received orders from customers.
2. Quotation price is asked before giving orders.
3. Every job and contract is dissimilar in nature.
4. No need to create demand, customers come on their own.
5. Profit is determined in respect of each job and contract separately.
6. Work is to be executed according to the specification of customers.
7. A job and contract is identified by a separate number and is known by that number until it is completed.
8. They belong to the category of specific order costing.

Points of Dissimilarities

1. A job is small in size, contract is big in size.
2. Work under job costing is performed in the premises of manufacturer. Whereas in contract costing, a contract is executed in the premises of customer.
3. A job usually takes less time to complete. Whereas a contract takes more time to complete.

4. The selling price of a job is paid after completing the job in full. Under contract costing, the price is paid in various instalments depending upon the progress of work.
5. Job costing involves heavy investment on assets initially. This is not so under contract costing.
6. Expenses under job costing takes the form of both direct and indirect, whereas under contract costing most of the expenses are direct in nature.
7. Profit earned on a job is entirely taken to P & L a/c. In case of incomplete contract only proportionate profit is taken to P& L a/c.

PROCEDURE OF CONTRACT COSTING

The preparation of contract account is the essense of contract costing. The contract account is prepared by the contractor in his books. In addition to this account the contractor also prepares contractee's account. A separate account is opened for each contract and a serial number is given to it in order to distinguish it from other contracts. The purpose of preparing a contract account is to know the profit or loss on every contract executed. The preparation of contract account involves recording of the following items :

1. Materials

Materials required for the execution of contract in most of the cases are ordered specifically and then used on the contract. The following entries are passed to record the materials cost :

(*a*) When materials are specifically purchased for the contract
Materials a/c *Dr.*
To cash or supplier's a/c
Note : usually the materials bought are sent to the storeroom of the contractor.

(*b*) When materials are sent to site by the contractor
Contract a/c *Dr.*
To materials a/c

(*c*) When materials are transferred from one contract to another
Transferee contract a/c *Dr.*
To transferor contract a/c

(*d*) When materials are supplied by the contractee, the value of such materials should not be charged to the contract account. Instead, a separate record for such materials should be kept because the unused materials will have to be returned back to the contractee.

(*e*) When any materials are sold at work site
Cash a/c *Dr.*
To contract a/c

(*f*) For recording accidental loss of materials
Insurance company a/c *Dr.* (with the admitted claim)
Profit & loss a/c *Dr.* (with the residue)
To contract a/c

(*g*) For recording materials remaining at site at the end of the year
(*i*) At the end of the current year :
Materials at site a/c *Dr.*
To contract a/c

(*ii*) At the beginning of the next year

Contract a/c *Dr.*

To materials on site a/c

(*h*) When materials are sent to stores

Stores control a/c *Dr.*

To contract

2. Labour Cost

All labour engaged at the contract site is regarded as direct irrespective of the nature of the job performed by the employee. Even salary of supervisors are charged as direct labour cost when they spend all their time on a particular contract. However salaries payable to the staff of head office and central stores are treated as indirect wages.

3. Direct Expenses

Some of the direct expenses which are charged to contract account are; Architects' and consultant fees, the hire of plant from outside firms, electricity charges, insurance, telephone, postages and other general expenses.

4. Plant and Machinery

Some of the assets that are to be depreciated while on use on a contract are : Bulldozers, mobile crane, cement mixer, tiles-polishing machines, tractors and lorries. There are two ways of dealing with the plant and machineries used on a contract.

(*a*) Where a plant is specially purchased for a particular contract to be used for longer duration, the contract account is debited with the value of plant. At the end of the accounting period the depreciated value of the plant is credited to the contract account.

(*b*) When the plant is used relatively for a shorter duration on a contract, the contract account is charged with the depreciation of the plant.

5. Indirect Expenses

When a contractor undertakes more than one contract simultaneously, he will set up a common office and engages common supervisory staff. The administration expenses incurred and the supervisor's salary is apportioned among the contracts on some suitable basis.

6. Sub-contract

The contractor may entrust certain types of specialised work such as electrical, plumbing, painting, carpentry, special flooring, etc. to a sub-contractor. The sub-contractor is responsible to the main contractor in terms of performing the work and he will get the payment from the main contractor. The cost of such sub-contract is debited to contract account.

7. Retention Money

Usually the contractee stipulates in the contract deed that he would withhold a part of the contract price to be paid at a later stage after completion of the contract. This is to make sure that the contractor has performed all work relating to contract on the most satisfactory manner and that no repair work arises within a prescribed time limit. The amount so withheld by the contractee is known as retention money. It safeguards the interest of the contractee against the contractor, who may at time perform sub-standard work and gain therefrom.

8. Progress Payment

In a large contract, which takes longer duration to complete, the contractee pays to the contractor a certain amount from time to time depending upon the stage of satisfactory completion of work. The progress of work from time to time will be certified by the architect or engineer of the contractee. Thus every instalment of money paid by the contractee to the contractor depending upon the progress of work is known as progress payment.

9. Escalation Clause

Sometimes, owing to fluctuation in the prices of materials and labour costs the contract price is altered so that neither party suffers the loss arising out of the change in price level. To protect his interest against the rise in prices, the contractor inserts a clause known as the 'escalation clause', under which, the contractee will be obliged to pay the enhanced price of the contract because of increase in the rates of materials, labour and other expenses. Similarly, to protect the interest of the contractee against the fall in the rates of materials, labour and overheads, a 'descalation clause' is inserted. However, it is to be noted that the terms and condition under which the contract price is to be altered is to be specifically mentioned. The reasons which gives rise to change in price level is to be stipulated. There should be no ambiguity in the wordings of this clause. The essentials of the escalation clause are as follows :

(*a*) The elements of costs on the basis of which quotation price is submitted must be specified.
(*b*) The elements in relation to which escalation clause applies should be specified.
(*c*) The escalation clause should apply to only those factors which are beyond the control of contractor.
(*d*) The escalation clause should mention the date from which the rise in price of the contract comes into effect.
(*e*) The records of the contractor is to be made available to the contractee for inspection.
(*f*) The provision for alteration of contract price must relate only to change in design, or any major alteration of the work but not on account of defective work.

10. Cost-plus Contract

It is a modified method of contract costing. This method of costing is resorted to when it is not possible to determine the cost of the contract in advance with a reasonable degree of accuracy. Under such circumstance, the contractee agrees to pay to the contractor, the actual cost incurred together with an agreed amount of profit which the contractor earns in the usual course of business. This type of contract is mostly followed during the period of urgency when certain types of products are to be manufactured and suppled as in the case of defence products, component parts and so on.

Advantages of Cost-plus Contract to the Contractor

(*a*) The contractor will not suffer any risk of loss as he will receive the contract price as is assured by the contractee.
(*b*) There is bargain in the contract price in future under this type of contract.
(*c*) The contractor is releived from the botheration of preparing quotation price for the sake of submitting it to the contractee.

Advantages to the Contractee

(*a*) Since the contract price is governed by the contract, the contractee will also not suffere from risk of loss.

(*b*) The contractee also stands to benefit in a period of uncertain market condition as he is expected to pay only a reasonable price after satisfying the ruling prices.

11. Work Certified and Work Uncertified

Work certified represents that portion of the contract that has been duly approved by the architect of the contractee. This is denoted in terms of money value in contract account and appears on the credit side of the contract account. Work uncertified refers to that portion of work completed by the contractor but disapproved by the architect on the ground that it has not reached a stipulated stage. The value of work uncertified also appears on the credit side of the contract account.

12. Work-in-Progress

The work-in-progress represents the value of work which is in progess on a contract and requires further completion. The value of work-in-progress appears on the asset side of the balance sheet and is ascertained as under :

Amount of work certified		xxx
Amount of work uncertified		xxx
		xxx
Less : Profit transferred to WIP	xxx	
Less : Cash received	xxx	xxx
Work-in-progress		xxx

13. Profit on Uncompleted Contract

As regards profit on a completed contract, it may be safely taken to profit and loss account. This is so because it is the actual profit earned on a contract which is taken for granted to be the profit earned on a completed contract. But in case of incomplete contract the profit made on it cannot be taken to be the actual profit. Since the completion of contract in the subsequent years may be subjected to risk of loss, a prudent contractor will not consider the profit on incomplete contract to be the actual profit. Instead, it is treated as notional profit and necessary provision is made in anticipation of probable losses. The question is what percentage of notional profit is to be transferred to profit and loss account on an incomplete contract in an accounting year. There are no hard and fast rules laid down to calculate a proportionate amount of profit to be taken into profit and loss account. However, the following rules are followed in practice as laid down by contractors of yester years.

(*a*) **When the work completed is less than 25 per cent of the contract :** Under this situation no profit is transferred to profit and loss account. The entire amount of profit is carried forward in the form of reserve.

(*b*) **When the work completed is more than 25 per cent but less than 50 per cent :** In this case $\frac{1}{3}$ of the notional profit is transferred to profit and loss account and the balance is carried forward in the form of reserve. The following formla is used :

$$\frac{1}{3} \times \text{Notional profit} \times \frac{\text{Cash received}}{\text{Work certified}}$$

(*c*) **When the amount of work completed is more than 50 per cent but not nearing a stage of completion :** Under such situation $\frac{2}{3}$ of notional profit is transferred to profit and loss account and the balance to work-in-progress account.

(*d*) **When the contract is nearing the stage of completion :** In this case the cost of completing the contract is estimated. Then the estimated profit is calculated by deducting the total estimated cost from the contract price. For calculating the profit to be taken to profit and loss account, the following formula is adopted :

$$\text{Estimated profit} \times \frac{\text{Work certified}}{\text{Contract price}}$$

14. Contractee's Account

The contractee's account is prepared by the contractor in his books. When the various instalments of contract price is received from the contractee, the following entry is passed :

Cash a/c *Dr.*
To contractee's a/c

When the contract is fully completed the following entry is passed :

Contractee's a/c *Dr.*
To contract a/c

Thus it is clear that the contractee's account will show a debit balance indicating the amount due from him to the contractor till it is paid fully.

15. Loss on Uncompleted Contract

The loss on incomplete contract is taken into the debit side of profit and loss account.

16. Balance Sheet

At the time of preparation of balance sheet, the contractee's account deserves a special mention. The contractee's a/c is not to be shown as a debtor for the full contract price unless the work has been completed. Likwise the sum received from the contractee under various instalments should not be shown as a liability on the balance sheet. On completion of contract, if the contractee still owes the amount to the contractor, his account is shown as a debtor for the amount due from him. When the contractee pays full amount, his account is closed and his account will not appear in the balance sheet.

17. Target Costing

This is a variation of cost-plus contract. Under this method, the contractee agrees to pay the profit as per the agreement on the total contract price. In addition to the profit, sometimes, it is agreed upon by the contractor to complete the contract within a target price. In case, if he completes the contract within the target price, he is entitled to receive a bonus which is in proportion to the savings made, saving being difference between original contract price and target price.

Problem 1 (Treatment of materials and plant) : Gangaram Construction Limited undertook a number of contracts during 1987. Following particulars are available as regards the constractions of a conteen building :

Materials at site on 1.1.87	2,000
Materials purchased	50,000
Materials supplied from stores	10,000
Materials returned to stores	1,000
Materials costing Rs. 2,000 were stolen	

Materials worth Rs. 200 destroyed by fire	
Materials costing Rs. 1,000 were sold for 800	
Materials in hand at the end of the year	10,000
Materials received from hospital contract which was completed	20,000
Materials transferred to cinema contract	500
Plant issued to contract on 1.1.87	50,000
Plant returned to stores	1,000
Plant costing Rs. 2,000 sold for Rs. 2,500	
Plant worth Rs. 500 was stolen	
Plant worth Rs. 300 was destroyed by an accident	
Plant in hand at the site at the end of the year was Rs. 10,000	

Show how these transactions will appear in a contract account. (*Mangalor University, B.Com., April 1988*)

Solution :

Contract a/c

To materials at site	2,000	By materials returned to stores	1,000
To materials purchased	50,000	By profit & loss a/c — materials stolen	2,000
To materials supplied from stores	10,000	— materials destroyed by fire	200
To materials received from hospital contract	20,000	By loss on sale of materials (1,000 – 800)	200
		By materials sold	800
		By materials in hand	10,000
		By materials transferred to cinema contract	500
To plant	50,000	By plant returned to stores	1,000
To profit & loss a/c :		By profit & loss a/c :	
Profit on sale of plant (2,500 – 2,000)	500	Plant stolen	500
		Plant lost by fire	300
		By plant sold	2,500
		By plant in hand	10,000

Note : Since the rate of depreciation is not given the net value of plant is not shown on the credit side of the contract.

Problem 2 (Treatment of plant in contract a/c) : Mr. Amar undertook a contract on 1.1.1990. The books are closed on 30th June every year, A second-hand plant of Rs. 1,50,000 was purchased on Ist March 1990 and Rs. 10,000 were spent on reconditioning it. On 30th June a portion of the plant costing Rs. 20,000 was sold for Rs. 14,000 on the same date a component of the plant costing Rs. 5,000 was returned to stores. Plant costing Rs. 6,000 was stolen. Depreciate plant by 15% per annum. Show contract account.

Solution :

Contract a/c

To plant	1,50,000		By plant returned to stores	5,000	
Add : Expenses	10,000	1,60,000	*Less* : Depreciation @ 15% for 4 months	250	4,750
			By plant sold		14,000
			By P & L a/c – cost	20,000	
			Less : Depreciation for 4 months @ 15%	1,000	
				19,000	
			Less : Sale	14,000	
				5,000	5,000
			Plant stolen		6,000
			By plant in hand		1,22,550

Working note : Plant in hand

Cost of plant installed		1,60,000
Less : Cost of plant sold	20,000	

Less : cost of plant returned	5,000	
Less : Cost of plant stolen	6,000	31,000
		1,29,000
Less : Depreciation @ 15% p.a. for 4 months		6,450
Plant in hand		1,22,550

Problem 3 (Contract completed in the same year) : The following particulars are in respect of contract no. 20 which commenced on 1.1.1990 :

	Rs.
Materials issued	58,000
Direct wages	75,000
Cost of special plant	30,000
Direct expenses	12,000
Establishment charges	8,000

The contract was completed by 31st December, 1990. The contract price was Rs. 1,75,000. The value of materials returned to stores was Rs. 5,000. The special plant was returned to stores subject to depreciation at 20% per annum contract price was received in full on 31st December, 1990. Prepare contract account.

(Bangalor University, B.Com., Nov. 1991)

Solution :

Contract a/c

To materials issued	58,000	By materials returned		5,000
To direct wages	75,000	By plant returned	30,000	
To plant	30,000	*Less* : Depreciation	6,000	24,000
To direct expenses	12,000	By contractee's a/c		1,75,000
To establishment charges	8,000			
To P & L a/c	21,000			
	2,04,000			2,04,000

Contractee's a/c

To contract a/c	1,75,000	By bank	1,75,000

Problem 4 (Incomplete contract) : Mr. Sai undertook a contract for the construction of a building on 1st January 1998. The contract price is Rs. 7,50,000. The following particulars are available prepare contract account and show the account that should be transferred to profit and loss a/c and prepare contract a/c

	Rs.
Materials purchased	1,20,000
Materials issued from stores	1,50,000
Labour employed on site	45,000
Plant installed on site	60,000
Direct expenses	30,000
Proportionate establishment charges	7,500
Cash received (80% of work certified)	3,00,000
Work uncertified	75,000
Materials returned to stores	7,500
Materials in hand at the end	3,000
Plant on hand at the end	45,000
Wages outstanding	9,000
Direct expenses accrued	12,000

(S.V. University, B.Com., April 1999)

Solution :

Contract a/c for the year ended 31.12.1998

To materials purchased	1,20,000	By materials returned	7,500
To materials issued	1,50,000	By materials on hand	3,000
To labour employed	45,000		
To plant installed	60,000	By work-in-progress :	
To direct expenses	30,000	work certified	3,75,000
To establishment charges	7,500	Work uncertified	75,000
To wages o/s	9,000		
To direct expenses accrued	12,000		
To balance c/d	72,000		
	5,05,500		5,05,500
To profit & loss a/c $72,000 \times \frac{2}{3} \times \frac{3,00,000}{3,75,000}$	38,400	By balance b/d	72,000
To work-in-progress a/c-reserve	33,600		
	72,000		72,000

Working note :

Calculation of work certified

Let work certified $= x$

Cash received is $\frac{80}{100}x = 3,00,000$

$80x = 3,00,000 \times 100$

$80x = 3,00,00,000$

$x = \frac{3,00,00,000}{80}$

$x = 3,75,000$

Problem 5 (When work uncertified is not given) : X Ltd., closes its accounts on 31st December each year. The company commenced work on a contract on 1st January 1998. The following information relates to the contract as on 31st December 1998

	Rs.
Materials issued	1,25,500
Wages	2,82,800
Salary to foreman	40,650

A machine costing Rs. 1,30,000 had been on the site for 146 days. Its working life is estimated at 7 years and its final scrap value at Rs. 7,500. A supervisior, who is paid Rs. 4,000 per month has devoted half of his time to this contract. Other expenses and administration charges amounted to Rs. 68,250. Materials at site at the end of the year cost Rs. 17,700. The contract price is Rs. 10 lakhs. On 31st December 1998, two-thirds of the contract was completed. The architect had issued certificate of approval convering 50% of the contract price and the contractor had been paid Rs. 3,75,000 on account.

Prepare the contract account and work-in-progress account. Also show how the work-in-progress will appear in the balance sheet of the contractor as on 31st December 1998. (*C.S., Inter, June 1999*)

Solution :

Contract a/c for the year ended 31st Dece. 1998

To materials	1,25,500	By materials at site	17,700
To wages	2,82,800		

To salary to foreman	40,650	By work-in-progress a/c	
To depreciation on machinery	7,000	Work certified	5,00,000
		Work uncertified	1,32,625
To other expenses & adm. charges	68,250		
To supervisor's salary	24,000		
To balance c/d	1,02,125		
	6,50,325		6,50,325
To profit & loss a/c	51062.50	By balance b/d	1,02,125
To WIP a/c —(reserve)	51062.50		
	1,02,125		1,02,125

Work-in-progress a/c

To contract a/c :		By contract a/c	51,062.50
Work certified	5,00,000	(reserve)	
Work uncertified	1,32,625	By balance c/d	5,81,562.50
	6,32,625		6,32,625

Balance sheet as on 31st Dec. 1998

Work-in-progress	
Work certified	5,00,000
Work uncertified	1,32,625
	6,32,625
Less : Reserve	51,062.50
	5,81,562.50
Less : Cash received	3,75,000
	2,06,562.50

Working note :

(1) *Calculation of profit taken into P & L a/c*

$$1,02,125 \times \frac{2}{3} \times \frac{3,75,000}{5,00,000} = 51062.50$$

(2) *Calculation of work uncertified*

$$\text{Work completed} = \frac{2}{3} \text{ and work certified} = \frac{1}{2}$$

$$\text{Hence} \quad \text{work uncertified} = \frac{2}{3} - \frac{1}{2}$$

$$\frac{4-3}{6} = \frac{1}{6}$$

Cost of $\frac{2}{3}$ work completed :

Materials	1,25,500
Wages	2,82,800
Salary to foreman	40,650
Depreciation on machinery	7,000
Other expenses	68,250
Supervisor's salary	24,000
	5,48,200
Less : Materials at site	17,700
	5,30,500

Cost of $\frac{1}{6}$ work completed =

For $\frac{2}{3}$rd completion the cost is 5,30,500

$$\text{For } \frac{1}{6} \rightarrow ? \quad = \frac{5,30,500 \times \frac{1}{6}}{\frac{2}{3}}$$

$$5,30,500 \times \frac{3}{2} \times \frac{1}{6} = 1,32,625$$

Alternatively, cost of work uncertified can also be found out by the following calculation :

The cost of $\frac{2}{3}$ or 66.67% is 5,30,500

$$\text{For } 100\% \rightarrow \frac{5,30,000 \times 100}{66.67}$$

$$= 7,95,710$$

The cost of 50% of the contract which has been certified by the architect is

$$7,95,710 \times \frac{50}{100} = 3,97,855$$

∴ Cost of work uncertified is

$$5,30,500 - 3,97,855 = 1,32,645$$

Problem 6 : A company undertook a contract for construction of a large building complex. The construction work commerced on 1st April 1993 and the following data are available for the year ended 31st March 1994.

	Rs. '000
Contract price	35,000
Work certified	20,000
Progress payment received	15,000
Materials issued to site	7,500
Planning & estimating costs	1,000
Direct wages paid	4,000
Materials returned from site	250
Plant hire charges	1,750
Wage related costs	500
Site office costs	678
Head office expenses apportioned	375
Direct expenses incurred	902
Work not certified	149

The contractor owns a plant which originally cost Rs. 20 lakhs has been continuously in use in this contract throughout the year. The residual value of the plant after 5 years of life is expected to be Rs. 5 lakhs. Streight line method of depreciation is in use.

As on 31st March, 1994. The direct wages due and payable amounted to Rs. 2,70,000 and the materials at site were estimated at Rs. 2,00,000.

Required :

(*i*) Prepare the contract a/c for the year ended 31st March, 1994.

(*ii*) Show the calculation of profit to be taken to the profit & loss account of the year.

(*iii*) Show the relevant balance sheet enteries. (*C.A., Inter, November 1994*)

Solution : Contract a/c for the year ended 31st March 1994 (Rs. '000)

To materials issued	7,500	By materials returned	250
To direct wages paid	4,000		
To direct wages accrued	270	By materials at site	200
To wage related costs	500	By work-in-progress	
To direct expenses	902	Work certified	20,000
To plant hire charges	1,750	Work uncertified	149
To planning & estimating cost	1,000		
To site office cost	678		
To head office expenses apportioned	375		
To plant depreciation	300		
To balance c/d	3,324		
	20,599		20,599
To P & L a/c	1,662	By balance b/d	3,324
$\frac{2}{3} \times 3{,}324 \times \frac{15{,}000}{20{,}000}$			
To WIP-Reserve	1,662		
	3,324		3,324

Balance sheet

P & L a/c	1,662	Plant at site		1,700
Wages accrued	270	(2,000 – 300)		
		Materials at site		200
		Work-in-progress		
		Work certified	2,000	
		Work uncertified	149	
			20,149	
		Less reserve	1,662	
			18,487	
		Less cash received	15,000	
				3,487

Working note :

Calculation of Depreciation : ('000)

Original cost of plant	2,000
Less : Residual value	500
	1,500
Life of plant 5 year	
Annual depreciation	$\frac{1{,}500}{5} = 300$

Problem 7 : The Maharashtra Construction Company undertook the construction of a building at a contract price of Rs. 12,00,000. The date of commencement of contract was 1st April 1998.

The following cost information is given for the year ended 31st March 1999

	Rs.
Materials sent to the site	3,00,000

Wages	4,40,000
Architect fees	55,500
Office & administration overhead	1,51,000
Uncertified work	55,000
Materials at the site at the end of the year	10,000
Cash received from the contractee	9,45,000
(Being 90% of the work certified)	
Materials destroyed by fire	5,000
Plant and Machinery at cost	2,00,000

(Date of purchase — 1st July 1998. The estimated working life of the plant 10 years and its estimated scrap value at the end Rs. 20,000)

Supervisor's salary	60,000

You are required to prepare a contract a/c for the year ended 31st March 1999.

(University of Bombay, B.Com., April 1999)

Solution :

Contract a/c for the year ended 31.3.1999

To materials sent to site	3,00,000	By P & L a/c : Mateirals lost	5,000
To wages	4,40,000	By WIP :	
To architect's fees	55,500	Work certified	10,50,000
To office & adm. oh	1,51,000	Work uncertified	55,000
To depreciation	13,500	Materials at site	10,000
To Supervisor's salary	60,000		
To balance c/d	1,00,000		
	11,20,000		11,20,000
To P & L a/c	60,000	By balance b/d	1,00,000
$\frac{2}{3} \times 1{,}00{,}000 \times \frac{9{,}45{,}000}{10{,}50{,}000}$			
To WIP reserve	40,000		
	1,00,000		1,00,000

Working notes :

(1) *Calculation of depreciation*

$$\text{Depreication for 1 year} = \frac{\text{Cost} - \text{Scrap value}}{\text{Working life}}$$

$$= \frac{2{,}00{,}000 - 20{,}000}{10}$$

$$= \frac{1{,}80{,}000}{10} = 18{,}000$$

$$\text{For nine months } 18{,}000 \times \frac{9}{12} = 13{,}500$$

(2) *Calculation of work certified*

$$\text{Let work certified} = x$$

$$\text{Cash received is } \frac{90}{100}x = 9{,}45{,}000$$

$$90x = 9,45,000 \times 100$$
$$90x = 9,45,00,000$$
$$x = \frac{9,45,00,000}{90} = 10,50,000$$

Problem 8 (Comparative contract a/c) : Mr. Behram contractor has undertaken two contracts one at Mumbai and another at Thane. The details of the contracts are given below for the year ended 31st March 1998 :

Particulars	*Contract at Mumbai*	*Contract at Thane*
Date of commencement	1st July 97	1st Oct. 97
	Rs.	*Rs.*
Contract price	10,00,000	15,00,000
Direct labour	2,55,000	1,82,000
Materials issued from stores	2,20,000	2,00,000
Materials returned to stores	10,000	15,000
Plant installed at site	2,00,000	3,50,,000
Direct expenses	40,000	30,000
Office overheads	15,000	10,000
Materials sold (cost Rs. 8,000)	10,000	–
Materials at site	18,000	16,000
Cash received from contractee (representing 80% of work certified)	4,80,000	2,40,000
Work uncertified	13,000	9,000
Architects fees	7,000	3,000

(*i*) Provide depreciation on plant at 20% p.a.

(*ii*) During the year materials costing Rs. 10,000 were transferred from Thane contract to Mumbai contract.

You are required to prepare contract a/c of Mumbai and Thane contracts.

(*University of Bombay, B.Com., Oct. 98*)

Solution : **Mumbai contract a/c for the year ended 31st March 1998**

	Rs.		Rs.
To materials issued	2,20,000	By work certified	6,00,000
To direct labour	2,55,000		
To plant installed	2,00,000	By materials returned	10,000
To direct expenses	40,000	By materials sold	8,000
To office overheads	15,000	By materials at site	18,000
To Thane contract	10,000	By work uncertified	13,000
To Architect fees	7,000	By plant at site	1,70,000
To balance c/d	72,000		
	8,19,000		8,19,000
To P & L a/c $\left(\frac{2}{3} \times 72,000 \times \frac{4,80,000}{6,00,000}\right)$	38,400	By balance b/d	72,000
To work-in-progress (reserve)	33,600		
	72,000		72,000

Working note :

Calculation of work certified :

Let work certified = x

Cash received is $\frac{80}{100}x = 4,80,000$

or $80x = 4,80,000 \times 100$

$80x = 4,80,00,000$

$$x = \frac{4,80,00,000}{80} = 6,00,000$$

Thane contract a/c for the year ended 31st March 1998

To materials issued	2,00,000	By work certified	3,00,000
To direct labour	1,82,000	By materials returned	15,000
To plant installed	3,50,000	By Mumbai contract	10,000
To direct expenses	30,000	By materials at site	16,000
To office overheads	10,000	By work uncertified	9,000
To Architect fees	3,000	By plant at site	3,15,000
		By P & L a/c	1,10,000
	7,75,000		7,75,000

Working note :

Calculation of work certified

Let work certified = x

Cash received is $\frac{80}{100}x = 2,40,000$

or $80x = 2,40,00,000$

$$x = \frac{2,40,00,000}{80} = 3,00,000$$

Problem 9 : Navnirman Ltd. has undertaken three contracts. It furnishes the following information for the year ended 31st March 1996.

(Figures in 00's)

	Goa Contract *Rs.*	*Roha Contract* *Rs.*	*Surat Contract* *Rs.*
1. Balances on 1.4.95 :			
Materials at site	100	2,000	–
Uncertified work	2,500	4,000	–
Plant at site	2,200	3,100	–
Work certified	19,500	1,400	–
Provision for contingencies	1,000	600	–
2. Transactions during the year :			
Materials issued	–	6,200	8,000
Sub-contract charges	600	11,800	9,000
3. Balances on 31.3.96 :			
Materials at site	–	1,000	800
Uncertified work	–	1,000	3,850
Plant at site	–	2,000	950
Work certified	25,000	30,000	12,000
4. Contract price	25,000	40,000	50,000
5. Amount received	25,000	27,000	10,800

6. Value of plant tranferred from Goa contract to Surat contract Rs. 1,550.

The company consistently adopts the policy of taking credit for the contract profit considering the proportion of amounts received to the contract price

You are required to :

(*a*) Prepare the respective contract accounts for the year ended 31st March 1996.

(*b*) Find the net profit as per profit and loss account. (*University of Bombay, B.Com., April 1996*)

Solution :

Goa contract a/c **(*Fig. in 00's*)**

To opening balance :		By provision for contingencies	1,000
Materials	100	By contractee's a/c	25,000
Uncertified work	2,500		
Certified work	19,500		
To sub contract charges	600		
To depreciation (*see note*)	650		
To net profit	2,650		
	26,000		26,000

Roha contract a/c

To opening balance :			
Materials	2,000	By provision for contingencies	600
Uncertified work	4,000	By work-in-progress :	
Certified work	1,400	Work certified	30,000
To materials issued	6,200	Work uncertified	1,000
To sub contract charges	11,800	Materials at site	1,000
To depreciation on plant (*see note*)	1,100		
To balance c/d	6,100		
	32,600		32,600
To P & L a/c	3,660	By balance b/d	6,100
$6{,}100 \times \frac{2}{3} \times \frac{27{,}000}{30{,}000}$			
To Work-in-progress	2,440		
	6,100		6,100

Surat contract

To materials issued	8,000	By work-in-progress :	
To sub-contract charges	9,000	Work certified	12,000
To depreciation on plant (*see note*)	600	Work uncertified	3,850
		Materials at site	800
		By P & L a/c	950
	17,600		17,600

Profit & Loss a/c

To Surat contract	950	By Goa contract	2,650
To net profit	5,360	By Roha contract	3,660
	6,310		6,310

Working note :

Calculation of depreciation

(1) Goa contract a/c

Opening balance	2,200
Less : Value of plant transferred to Surat contract	1,550
Depreciation	650

(2) Roha contract

	Opening balance	3,100
Less :	Closing balance	2,000
	Depreciation	1,100

(3) Surat contract

	Value of plant transfered from Goa contract	1,550
Less :	Closing balance	950
	Depreciation	600

Problem 10 : From the following information, prepare contract a/c in tabuler from and show how these figures appear in the balance sheet as on 31st Dec. 1995.

Particulars	*Contract* A	B	C
Commencement	1.1.95	1.7.95	1.10.95
	Rs.	*Rs.*	*Rs.*
Contract price	80,000	54,000	60,000
Raw materials	14,400	11,600	4,000
Wages	22,000	22,400	2,800
General charges	800	560	200
Plant installed	4,000	3,200	2,400
Materials on hand	800	800	400
Wages accrued	800	800	360
Work certified	40,000	32,000	7,200
Work uncertified	1,200	1,600	420
Cash received in respect of work certified	30,000	24,000	5,400

Depreciation is to be charged on the plant @ 10% which was installed on the opening date of the contract in each case. (*C.S., Inter, June 1997*)

Solution :

Contract Accounts

	A	B	C		A	B	C
To raw materials	14,400	11,600	4,000	By materials in land	800	800	400
To wages paid	22,000	22,400	2,800	By plant in hand	3,600	3,040	2,340
To general charges	800	560	200	By work-in-progress :			
To plant	4,000	3,200	2,400	Work certified	40,000	32,000	7,200
To wages accrued	800	800	360	Work uncertified	1,200	1,600	420
To balance c/d	3,600	–	600	By profit & loss a/c	–	1,120	–
	45,600	38,560	10,360		45,600	38,560	10,360
To P & L a/c	1,800	–	–	By balance b/d	3,600	–	600
To WIP Reserve	1,800	–	600				
	3,600	–	600		3,600	–	600

Working note :

(1) Depreciation on plant is provided at 10% per annum. So depreciation is deducted in order to arrive at the closing value of plant in hand.

(2) Profit transferred to P & C a/c of contract 'A'

$$3,600 \times \frac{2}{3} \times \frac{3}{4} = 1,800$$

Balance sheet as on 31.12.95

P & C a/c :		**Materials on hand :**	
Profit of contract A	1,800	Contract A	800
Less : loss of contract B	1,120	B	800
	680	C	400

Wages o/s		Plant in hand	
Contract A	800	Contract A	3,600
Contract B	800	B	3,040
Contract C	360	C	2,340
		WIP	
		Contract A	9,400
		B	9,600
		C	1,620
			20,620

Work-in-progress

	A	*B*	*C*
Work certified	40,000	32,000	7,200
Work uncertified	1,200	1,600	420
	41,200	33,600	7,620
Less cash received	30,000	24,000	5,400
	11,200	9,600	2,220
Less reserve	1,800	–	600
	9,400	9,600	1,620

Problem 11 (Contract a/c with balance sheet) : On 1.1.1999, Archana & Co., undertook one contract for a price of Rs. 25,00,000. Of the plant and materials sent to the contract; plant which cost Rs. 25,000 and materials worth Rs. 20,000 were lost in transit. On 31st December 1999, plant which originally cost Rs. 25,000 was returned to stores. The cost of work done but uncertified was Rs. 10,000 and materials costing Rs. 20,000 were at site. Charge depreciation at 10% pa on plant. Prepare contract account and balance sheet, from the following trial balance as on 31.12.99.

	Dr.	*Cr.*
Share capital		6,00,000
Creditors		50,000
Contractee's a/c		10,00,000
(80% of work certified)		
Land & Buildings	2,15,000	–
Bank	1,25,000	–
Contract a/c :		
Materials	4,50,000	
Plant at cost	1,25,000	
Wages	7,00,000	
Expenses	35,000	
	16,50,000	16,50,000

(*Sri Sathya Sai University, B.Com., February 2001*)

Solution :

Contract a/c

To materials	4,50,000	By P & L		
To plant	1,25,000	Materials lost		20,000
To wages	7,00,000	Plant lost		25,000
To expenses	35,000	By plant returned to stores	2,500	
To balance c/d	1,05,000	Less Dep.	2,500	
				22,500
		By materials at site		20,000
		By work-in-progress		
		Work certified	12,50,000	
		Work uncertified	10,000	

				12,60,000
		By plant at site	1,25,000	
		Less lost	25,000	
			1,00.000	
		Less returns	25,000	
			75,000	
		Less depreciation	7,500	
				67,500
	14,15,000			14,15,000
To P & L a/c	56,000	By balance b/d		1,05,000
To work-in-progress – reserve	49,000			
	1,05,000			1,05,000

Balance sheet

Share capital		6,00,000	Land & Buildings		2,15,000
Crditors		50,000	Bank		1,25,000
P & L a/c			Plant returned		22,500
Profit on contract	56,000		Materials at site		20,000
Less Plant lost	25,000		**Work-in-progress :**		
	31,000		Work certified	12,50,000	
			Work uncertified	10,000	
Less loss of materials	20,000	11,000		12,60,000	
			Less cash received	10,00,000	
				2,60,000	
			Less reserve	49,000	
					2,11,000
			Plant at site		67,500
		6,61,000			6,61,000

Problem 12 : The following trial balance was extracted on 30th April 1998 from the books of General contractors Ltd.

	Debit	*Credit*
Share capital		70,360
Profit & losss a/c (last year)		5,000
Provision for depreiciation on plant		12,600
Cash received on contract no. 15		2,56,000
Creditors		16,240
Land & Buildings at cost	14,800	
Plant at cost	10,400	
Cash at bank	9,000	
Contract no. 15		
Materials issued	1,20,000	
Direct labour	1,66,000	
Expenses	8,000	
Plant at cost	32,000	
	3,60,200	3,60,200

Contract no. 15 was begun on May 1, 1997. The contract price is Rs. 4,80,000 and the customer has so far paid Rs. 2,56,000 being 80% of the work certified. The cost of work done since certification is estimated at Rs. 3,200 on April 30, 1998. After the above trial balance was extracted, plant costing Rs. 6,400 was returned to stores and materials then on site were valued at Rs. 5,400. Provision is to be made for labour accured Rs. 1,200 and depreciation on plant at 12½%.

You are required to (a) write up contract a/c (b) prepare balance sheet as on that date.

(*Sri Sathya Sai University, B.Com., October 1998*)

Solution :

Contract a/c

To materials used	1,20,000	By materials at site	5,400
To direct labour	1,66,000	**By work-in-progress**	
To expenses	8,000	Work certifed	3,20,000
To depreciation on plant	4,000	$2{,}56{,}000 \times \frac{100}{80}$	
$\frac{12.5}{100} \times 32{,}000$		Work uncertified	3,200
To provision for labour accrued	1,200		
To balance c/d	29,400		
	3,28,600		3,28,600
To P & L a/c	15,680	By balance b/d	29,400
$\frac{2}{3} \times 29{,}400 \times \frac{2{,}56{,}000}{3{,}20{,}000}$			
To WIP reserve	13,720		
	29,400		29,400

Balance sheet

Share capital	70,360	Plant	42,400	
P & L a/c (*see note*)	19,380	(32,000 + 10,400)		
Creditors	16,240	Less provision for dep.	17,900	
Provison for labour accrued	1,200	(*see note*)		24,500
		Land & Building		14,800
		Work-in-progress		58,880
		(*see note*)		
		Cast at bank		9,000
	1,07,180			1,07,180

Working note :

(1) *Calculation of profit transferred to B/S*

P & L a/c

To depreciation on plant	1,300	By balance b/d	5,000
(other then issued to contract)		By profit from contract no. 15	15,680
To profit transferred to B/s	19,380		
	20,680		20,680

(2) *Calculation of depreciation :*

Provision for depreciation on plant	12,600
Add : depreciation on plant issued to contract	4,000
Add : Depreciation on general plant	1,300
	17,900

(3) *Calculation of WIP*

Work certified	3,20,000
Work uncertified	3,200
	3,23,200
Less : Cash received	2,56,000
	67,200
Less : Reserve	13,720
	53,480
Add : Materials at site	5,400
	58,880

Problem 13 : Modern Construction company with a paid up share capital of Rs. 50 lakhs undertook a contract to construct LIC houses. The contract was commercial on 1.1.1994 and the contract price was Rs. 50 lakhs. Cash received on account of contract on 31.12.94 was Rs. 18 lakhs (90% of the work certified) work completed but not certified was estimated at Rs. 1,00,000. As on 31.12.94, materials at site was estimated at Rs. 30,000 and machinery at site costing Rs. 2,00,000 was returned to stores. Plant and machinery at site is to be depreciated at 5%. Wages outstanding on 31.12.94 was Rs. 5,000.

The following trial balance was extracted as on 31.12.94.

	Debit	*Credit*
Paid up share capital		50,00,000
Cash received (90% of work certified)		18,00,000
Land and Buildings	15,00,000	
Machinery at cost (60% at site)	25,00,000	
Lorries and vehicles	8,00,000	
Furniture	50,000	
Office equipment	10,000	
Materials sent to site	14,00,000	
Site expenses	5,000	
Postage etc.	4,000	
Office expenses	8,000	
Retes & taxes	15,000	
Fuel & power	1,25,000	
Cash at bank	1,33,000	
Wages	2,50,000	
	68,00,000	68,00,000

Prepare the contract a/c to as certain the profit from the contract and show the work-in-progress in the balance sheet. (*ICWA, Inter, December 1995*)

Solution :

Contract a/c

To materials		14,00,000	By materials at site	30,000
To wages	2,50,000		**By work-in-progress**	
Wages o/s	5,000	255,000	Work certified	20,00,000
To site expenses		5,000	Work uncertified	1,00,000
To postage		4,000		
To power & fuel		1,25,000		
To office expenses		8,000		
To rates & taxes		15,000		
To depreciation		75,000		

$\frac{5}{100} \times \frac{60}{100} \times 25,00,000$			
To balance c/d	2,43,000		
	21,30,000		21,30,000
To P & L a/c	72,900	By balance b/d	2,43,000
$\frac{1}{3} \times \frac{90}{100} \times 2,43,000$			
To WIP Reserve	1,70,100		
	2,43,000		2,43,000

Working note :

(1) *Calculation of work-in-progress*

Work certified $18,00,000 \times \frac{100}{90}$	= 20,00,000
Work uncertified	1,00,000
	21,00,000
Less : Cash received	18,00,000
	3,00,000
Less : Reserve	1,70,100
Work-in-progress	1,29,900

(2) *Value of plant returned to stores :*

Plant returned to stores	2,00,000
Less : Depreciation $\frac{5}{100} \times 2,00,000$	10,000
	1,90,000

Balance sheet

Paid up capital	50,00,000	Land & Building		15,00,000
Wages o/s	5,000	Lorries & vehicles		8,00,000
P & L a/c	72,900	Furniture		50,000
		Office equipment		10,000
		Machinery at site	15,00,000	
		Less : Machinery returned	1,90,000	
			13,10,000	
		Less : Dep.	75,000	
				12,35,000
		Machinery in stores	10,00,000	
		Add : Machinery returned	1,90,000	
				11,90,000
		Materials at site		30,000
		Work-in-progress		1,29,900
		Cash at bank		1,33,000
	50,77,900			50,77,900

Problem 14 (Contract a/c with trial balance when two contracts are in progress) : The following trial balance was extracted from the books of Gemini Contractor as on 31.12.89 :

	Dr.	Cr.
Contractees a/c		3,30,000
Buildings	1,00,000	
Creditors		62,000
Bank	35,000	
Capital a/c		3,00,000
Materials	1,00,000	
Wages	70,000	
Expenses	37,000	
Plant	2,50,000	
Work-in-progress (contract no. 83)	1,00,000	
Contract 83 a/c (1.1.89) unadjusted profit		30,000
	6,92,000	6,92,000

Contract no. 83 which was in progress on 1.1.89 was completed on 31.3.89. Contract no. 84 commenced on 1.1.89. Rs. 20,000 materials and Rs. 10,000 wages were paid for contract no. 83. Rs. 60,000 materials were sent to contract no. 84 but Rs. 3,000 worth was lost there by accident Rs. 60,000 wages were paid for contract no. 84. Rs. 50,000 plant was used in contract no. 84 all through but plant costing Rs. 2,00,000 was used on contract no. 84 from 1st April 1989; prior to that, above machinery was used on contract no. 83. Rs. 4,000 materials were at site on contract no. 84 at the end of the year. Provide 10% depreciation of the plant and 2% on buildings.

Contract no. 83 was for Rs. 1,50,000 and certifed work up to last year was Rs. 1,00,000. The work has been certified up to the full extent but payment has been received up to 80% of the certified amount. The balance has not been paid yet nor any entry has been passed on completion of the contract.

Expenses are charged to contracts on the basis of 50% of direct wages. The new contract is for Rs., 4,00,000 and 90% is paid on certification. The uncertified work of contract as on 13st Dec. 1989 is estimated at Rs. 15,000.

You are required ot prepare : (*a*) Contract 83 a/c, (*b*) Contract no. 84 a/c, (*c*) P & L a/c for 1989, (*d*) Contract no. 83 contractee's a/c, (*e*) Contract no. 84 contractee's a/c, (*f*) Balance sheet as on 31. 12. 89.

(*Sri Sathya Sai University, B. Com., Mar. 1993*)

Solution :

Contract no. 83

To work-in-progress a/c (1.1.89)	1,00,000		By contractee's a/c	1,50,000
Less : Unadjusted profit on 1.1.89	30,000	70,000		
To materials		20,000		
To wages		10,000		
To expenses (50% of direct wages)		5,000		
To depreciation on plant		5,000		
To profit & loss a/c		40,000		
		1,50,000		1,50,000

Contract no. 84

To materials	60,000	By P & L a/c—Abnormal loss	3,000
To wages	60,000	By materials at site	4,000
To expenses 50% of wages	30,000	By work certified	2,00,000
To depreciation on plant		$\frac{100}{90} \times 1,80,000$	
(5,000 + 15,000)	20,000		
To P & L a/c	31,200	By work uncertified	15,000
To work-in-progress a/c—Reserve	20,800		
	2,20,000		2,20,000

Contractee's a/c on contract 1983

1988 To Balance c/d	80,000	1988 By Bank	80,000
1989 To Balance c/d	1,20,000	1989 By Balance b/d	80,000
		By cash	
		$\frac{80}{100} \times 1,50,000 = 1,20,000$	
		Less : Cash already received 80,000	40,000
	1,20,00		1,20,000
1990 To Contract a/c	1,50,000	1990 By Balance b/d	1,20,000
		By Balance c/d	30,000
	1,50,000		1,50,000

Profit & loss a/c

To expenses not charged to contract	2,000	By contract no. 83	40,000
To contract no. 83 :		By contract no. 84	31,200
Abnormal loss	3,000		
To depreciation on building	2,000		
To balance c/d	64,200		
	71,200		71,200

Balance sheet

Creditors	62,000	Bank		35,000
P & L a/c	64,200	Amount due from contractee of no. 83		30,000
Capital	3,00,000	Materials at stores	20,000	
		A contract no. 84 site	4,000	24,000
		Work-in-progress a/c :		
		Work certified	2,00,000	
		Work uncertified	15,000	
			2,15,000	
		Less : Reserve	20,800	
			1,94,200	
		Less : Cash received	1,80,000	
				14,200
		Plant	2,50,000	
		Less : Dep.	25,000	
				2,25,000
		Building	1,00,000	
		Less : Dep.	2,000	
				98,000
	4,26,200			4,26,200

Working note :

(1) *Calculation of work certified*

It is calculated on the basis of percentage of cash received to work certified

Let work certified = x

Cash received to work certified ratio

$$\frac{90x}{100} \times 1,80,000 = 2,00,000$$

(2) *Calculation of cash received on contract 84*

Contractee's a/c - cash received as per trial balance	3,30,000
Less : cash due (see contractee's a/c)	30,000
Total cash received from contractee	3,00,000
Less : Cash received on contract no. 83 upto 1989	1,20,000
∴ Cash received on contract no. 84 (balancing figure)	1,80,000

(3) *Calculation of profit taken to P & L a/c*

Profit made to date 52,000

Since half of the contract is complete

Profit taken to the P & L a/c has been calculated as under

$$52{,}000 \times \frac{2}{7} \times \frac{90}{100} = 31{,}200$$

(4) *Profit & loss a/c*

Profit from contract 83	40,000
Profit from contract 84	31,200
	71,200
Less : unabsorbed expenses (37,000 – 35,000)	2,000
	69,200
Less : materials lost	3,000
	66,200
Less : depreciation in building	2,000
	64,200

Problem 15 (Long term contract) : Rajesh contractor obtained a contract to build a house at a contract price of Rs. 15,00,000. The contractee agrees to pay 90% of the value of the work done as certified by the architect immediately on receipt of the certificate and to pay the balance after completion of the contract.

The contractor commenced the work on 1st May 1999. A plant costing Rs. 20,000 was specially bought for the contract. The value of the plant at the end of 1996, 1997 and 1998 was Rs. 16,000, Rs., 10,000 and Rs. 4,000 respectively. The work done and certified by the architect as at the end of 1996 and 1997 was Rs. 3,50,000 and Rs. 11,50,000 respectively. Work costing Rs. 20,000 done as at the end of 1997 was not certified as on that date.

Other details of the contract were as under :

	1996 *Rs.*	*1997* *Rs.*	*1998* *Rs.*
Materials sent to site	1,80,000	2,20,000	1,26,000
Wages paid	1,70,000	2,30,000	1,70,000
Direct expenses	7,000	25,000	9,000
Indirect expenses	3,000	4,000	–

You are required to prepare contract a/c for the year ended 31st Dec. 1996, 1997 and 1998, considering that contract is fully completed in 1998. (*University of Bombay, B.Com., October 1999*)

Solution :

Contract a/c for the year ended 31st Dec. 1996

To materials	1,80,000	By work-in-progress	3,50,000
To wages paid	1,70,000	By P & L	14,000
To direct expenses	7,000		
To indirect expenses	3,000		
To depreciation on plant (20,000 - 16,000)	4,000		
	3,64,000		3,64,000

Contract a/c for the year ended 31st Dec. 1997

	Rs.		Rs.
To work-in-progress : work certified	3,50,000	By work-in-progress : Work certified	11,50,000
To materials	2,20,000	Work uncertified	20,000
To wages	2,30,000		
To direct expenses	25,000		
To indirect expenses	4,000		
To depreciation on plant (16,000 - 10,000)	6,000		
To balance c/d	3,35,000		
	11,70,000		11,70,000
To P & L a/c $\frac{2}{3} \times 3,35,000 \times \frac{90}{100}$	2,01,000	By balance b/d	3,35,000
To WIP reserve	1,34,000		
	3,35,000		3,35,000

Contract a/c for the year ended 31st Dec. 1998

		Rs.		Rs.
To work-in-progress a/c			By work-in-progress :	
Work certified	11,50,000		Provision for contingencies	1,34,000
Work uncertified	20,000		By contractee's a/c	15,00,000
		11,70,000		
To materials		1,26,000		
To wages		1,70,000		
To direct expenses		9,000		
To depreciation on plant (10,000 - 4,000)		6,000		
To P & L		1,53,000		
		16,34,000		16,34,000

Problem 16 : Bal Ram contractors undertook a contract for Rs. 15,00,000 on 1st July 1996. The contract was complete on 31st March 1998. The contractor prepares his accounts on 31st March. The details of the contract are

Particulars	Period: From 1.7.96 to 31.3.97	From 1.4.97 to 31.3.98
	Rs.	Rs.
Materials issued	1,52,000	3,30,000
Direct wages	1,25,000	4,65,000
Direct expenses	30,000	45,000
Materials returned to stores	22,000	15,000
Materials at site	20,000	8,000
Uncertified work	48,000	-
Office overheads	23,000	66,000
Materials lost by fire	–	5,000
Work certified	3,00,000	15,00,000
Plant issued	3,00,000	1,50,000

Provide depreciation @ 20% p.a. on plant. Prepare contract accounts for the years ended 31.3.1997 and 31.3.1998.

(University of Bombay, B.Com., April 1998)

Solution : **Contract a/c for the period 1.7.96 to 31.3.97**

To materials issued	1,52,000	By materials returned to stores		22,000
To direct wages	1,25,000	By work-in-progress :		
To direct expenses	30,000	Work certified	3,00,000	
To office overheads	23,000	Work uncertified	48,000	
To depreciation on plant	45,000	Materials at site	20,000	
$3,00,000 \times \frac{9}{12} \times \frac{20}{100}$				
To profit reserve for contingency	15,000			3,68,000
	3,90,000			3,90,000

Contract a/c for the period 1.4.97 to 31.3.1998

To work-in-progress :				
Work certified	3,00,000		By reserve for contingency	15,000
Work uncertified	48,000		By materials returned to stores	15,000
Materials at site	20,000		By materials at site	8,000
		3,68,000	By materials lost by fire	5,000
To materials issued		3,30,000	By contractee's a/c	15,00,000
To direct wages		4,65,000		
To direct expenses		45,000		
To office overheads		66,000		
To depreciation on plant		90,000		
4,50,00 (3,00,000 + 150,000) @ 20%				
To net profit		1,79,000		
		15,43,000		15,43,000

Problem 17 : Yuti space contractors and Builder have obtanined a contract for constructing alternate accomodation to the slum dwellers. The contract work commenced on 1st July 1994 and was completed on 31st January 1997. The year ending of the company is 31st March. The contract price was Rs. 800 lakhs the contractee agree to pay 90% of the value of the work done as certified by the architect immediately. The entire contract price was received before 31st March 1997.

A machine costing Rs. 60,00,000 was specially bought and used for the contract. The residual value of the machine as on 31.1.1997 was Rs. 29,00,000 depreciation to be effected on straight line basis.

As a cost consultant, you are provided with the following relevant information :

	Accounting years		
	1994-95	*1995-96*	*1996-97*
	Rs.	*Rs.*	*Rs.*
Materials purchased	27,50,000	86,25,000	19,75,000
Direct labour	77,52,500	89,36,500	1,02,00,000
Supervision charges	1,22,000	1,85,000	2,76,000
Architect fees	2,50,000	4,50,000	5,00,000
Construction overheads	49,50,000	32,16,500	80,15,000
Administration overheads	19,25,500	10,50,000	7,96,000
Uncertified work at the end of the year	2,00,000	4,00,000	
Material on site at the end of the year	50,000	1,25,000	75,000
Money received from the contractee during the year	1,80,00,000	3,60,00,000	2,60,00,000

As per the policy of the company no profit is to be considered unless the certified work completed exceeds 20% of the total contract price. Thereafter profit is to be taken credit for in the same proportion as the amount received bears to the contract price.

Prepare contract accounts for all the three years and show the relevent extracts in the balance sheet as on 31st March of every year. *(University of Bombay, B.Com., October 1997)*

Solution :

Contract a/c for the year ended 31st March 1995

To materials purchased	27,50,000	By work-in-progress : work certified	2,00,00,000
To direct labour	77,52,500	Work uncertified	2,00,000
To supervisor's charges	1,22,000	Materials at site	50,000
To architects fee	2,50,000		
To construction overheads	49,50,000		
To administrative overheads	19,25,500		
To depreciation	9,00,000		
To balance c/d	16,00,000		
	2,02,50,000		2,02,50,000
To P & L a/c	3,60,000	By balance b/d	16,00,000
$16,00,000 \times \frac{1,80,00,000 \text{ (C.R.)}}{8,00,00,000 \text{ (C.P.)}}$			
To WIP reserve	12,40,000		
	16,00,000		16,00,000

Extract of balance sheet for the year 1995

P & L a/c	3,60,000	Plant	60,00,000	
		Less : dep.	9,00,000	
				51,00,000
		Work-in-progress :		
		Work certified	2,00,00,000	
		Work uncertified	2,00,000	
		Materials at site	50,000	
			2,02,50,000	
		Less : cash received	1,80,00,000	
			22,50,000	
		Less : reserve	12,40,000	
				10,10,000

Contract a/c for the year ended 31.12.96

To work-in-progress b/d			By reserve for contingency b/d		12,40,000
Work certified	2,00,00,000		**By work-in-progress**		
Work uncertified	2,00,000		Work certified	6,00,00,000	
Materials at site	50,000				
		2,02,50,000			
To materials purchased		86,25,000	Work uncertified	4,00,000	
To direct labour		89,36,500			
To supervision charges		1,85,000	Materials at site	1,25,000	
					6,05,25,000
To architect fees		4,50,000			
To construction overhead		32,16,500			
To administration overhead		10,50,000			
To depreciation		12,00,000			
To balance c/d		1,78,52,000			
		6,17,65,000			6,17,65,000

To P & L a/c $1,78,52,000 \times \frac{5,40,00,000}{8,00,00,000}$	1,20,50,100	By balance b/d	1,78,52,000
To WIP reserve	58,01,900		
	1,78,52,000		1,78,52,000

Extracts of the B/s for the year 31.3.1996

P & L	1,24,10,100	Plant (WDV)	51,00,000	
		Less : dep.	12,00,000	
				39,00,000
		Work-in-progress		
		Work certified	6,00,00,000	
		Work uncertified	4,00,000	
		Materials at site	1,25,000	
			6,05,25,000	
		Less : Cash received	5,40,00,000	
			65,25,000	
		Less : reserve	58,01,900	
				7,23,100

Contract a/c for the year ended 31.3.97

To work-in-progress b/d			By reserve for contingency	58,01,900
Work certified	6,00,00,000		By materials at site	75,000
Work uncertified	4,00,000		By contractee's a/c	8,00,00,000
Materials at site	1,25,000			
		6,05,25,000		
To materials purchased		19,75,000		
To direct labour		1,02,00,000		
To supervision charges		2,76,000		
To architects fees		5,00,000		
To construction overheads		80,15,000		
To administrative overheads		7,96,000		
To depreciation		10,00,000		
To P & L		25,89,900		
		8,58,76,900		8,58,76,900

Extract of balance sheet for the year 31.3.1997

P & L a/c	25,89,900	Plant (WDV)	39,00,000
		Less : dep. charged to contract	10,00,000
			29,00,000
		Less : dep. charged for 31.1.97 to 31.3.97	2,00,000
		(non-contract period)	27,00,000
		Materials at site	75,000

Working note :

Calculation of depreciation

Purchased on 1.7.94	60,00,000
Written down value (WDV) on 31.1.1997	29,00,000
	31,00,000

Depreciation for period 1.7.94 to 31.1.97 *i.e.*, 31 months

$$\text{Depreciation per month} = \frac{31,00,000}{31} = 1,00,000 \text{ P.M.}$$

Problem 18 (Contract nearing the stage of completion) : A contractor commenced a building contract on October 1, 1997. The contract price is Rs. 4,40,000. The following data pertaining to the contract for the year 1998-99 has been compiled from his books and is as under :

		Rs.
Apr. 1st 1998,	Work-in-progress not certified	55,000
	Materials at site	2,000
1998-99	Expenses incurred :	
	Materials issued	1,12,000
	Wages paid	1,08,000
	Hire of plant	20,000
	Other expenses	34,000
March 31, 1999	Materials at site	4,000
	Work-in-progress : not certified	8,000
	Certified	4,05,000

The cash received represents 80% of work certified. It has been estimated that further costs to complete the contract will be Rs.. 23,000 including the materials at site as on March 31, 1999.

Required :

Determine the profit on the contract for the year 1998-99 on prudent basis, which has to be credited to P & L a/c. *(C.A., Inter, November 1999)*

Solution :

Contract a/c for the year 1998-99

1.4.98			
To work-in-progress (Not certified)	55,000	By materials at site	4,000
To materials at site	2,000	By cost of contract c/d	3,27,000
1998-99			
To materials issued	1,12,000		
To wages paid	1,08,000		
To hire of plant	20,000		
To other expenses	34,000		
	3,31,000		3,31,000
31.3.99			
To cost of contract b/d	3,27,000	By work certified	4,05,000
To P & L a/c	66,273	By work not certified	8,000
To reserve WIP	19,727		
	4,13,000		4,13,000

Profit for the year 1998-99
4,13,000 – 3,27,000 = Rs. 86,000

Estimated profit (on the completion of the contract)

Cost of the contract	3,27,000
Add : Further cost of completing the contract	23,000
Total cost	3,50,000

Estimated profit = contract price – total estimated cost
= 4,40,000 – 3,50,000
= 90,000

Profit to be taken to P & L a/c

$$\text{Estimated profit} \times \frac{\text{cash received}}{\text{contrast price}}$$

$$90{,}000 \times \frac{3{,}24{,}000}{4{,}40{,}000} = 66{,}273$$

Problem 19 : Compute a conservative estimate of profit on a contract (which has been 80% complete) from the following particulars. Illustrate four methods of computing the profit.

	Rs.
Total expenditure to date	1,70,000
Estimated further expenditure to complete the contract (including the contingencies)	34,000
Contract price	3,06,000
Work certified	2,00,000
Work not certified	17,000
Cash received	1,63,200

(*CA, Inter, May 1998*)

Solution :

Calculation of estimated profit

	Total cost to date	1,70,000
Add :	Estimated further cost to complete the contract (including contingencies)	34,000
	Total estimated cost	2,04,000

Estimated profit = contract price – total estimated profit
= 3,06,000 – 2,04,000
= 1,02,000

Calculation of notional profit

Contract a/c

To total cost	1,70,000	By work certified	2,00,000
To notional profit	47,000	By work uncertified	17,000
	2,17,000		2,17,000

Four methods of computing conservative estimates of profit.

(1) $$\text{Estimated profit} \times \frac{\text{work certified}}{\text{contract price}}$$

$$1{,}02{,}000 \times \frac{2{,}00{,}000}{3{,}06{,}000} = 66{,}666.67$$

(2) $$\text{Estimated profit} \times \frac{\text{cash received}}{\text{contract price}}$$

$$1{,}02{,}000 \times \frac{1{,}63{,}200}{3{,}06{,}000} = 54{,}400$$

(3) $$\text{Notional profit} \times \frac{\text{work certified}}{\text{contract price}}$$

$$47{,}000 \times \frac{2{,}00{,}000}{3{,}06{,}000} = 30718.95$$

(4) $$\frac{2}{3} \times \text{notinal profit} \times \frac{\text{cash received}}{\text{work certified}}$$

$$\frac{2}{3} \times 47{,}000 \times \frac{1{,}63{,}200}{2{,}00{,}000} = 25{,}568$$

Problem 20 : M/s New Century Builders have entered into a contract to build an office building complex for Rs. 480 lakhs. The work started in April 1997 and it is estimated that the contract will take 15 months to be completed. Work has progressed as per schedule and the actual costs charged till March 1998 are as follows :

	Rs. (in lakhs)
Materials	112.20
Labour	162.00
Hire charges for equipments and other charges	36.00
Establishment charges	32.40
	342.60

The following information are available :

	Rs. (in lakhs)
Materials in hand (March 31, 1998)	6,60
Work certified (of which Rs. 324 lakhs have been paid) at March 31,1998	400
Work not yet certified at March 31, 1998 at cost	7.50

As per management estimates, the following further expenditure will be incurred to complete the work.

	Rs. (in lakhs)
Materials	10.50
Labour	16.00
Sub-contractors	20.00
Equipments hire and other charges	3.00
Establishment charges	6.90

You are required to prepare contract a/c after considering a reasonable margin of profit. Make a provision for contingencies amounting to 5% of total costs. (*ICWA, Inter, December 1998*)

Solution :

Contract a/c

To materials	1,12,20,000	By mateials in hand	6,60,000
To labour	1,62,00,000	By cost of contract c/d	3,36,00,000
To hire charges	36,00,000		
To establishment charges	32,40,000		
	3,42,60,000		3,42,60,000
To cost of contract b/d	3,36,00,000	By work certified	4,00,00,000
To profit c/d	71,50,000	By work uncertified	7,50,000
	4,07,50,000		4,07 50,000
To P & L a/c	50,00,000	By profit b/d	71,50,000
To WIP reserve	21,50,000		
	71,50,000		71,50,000

Contractee's a/c

To contract a/c	4,00,00,000	By cash	3,24,00,000
		By balance c/d	76,00,000
	4,00,00,000		4,00,00,000

Calculation of estimated profit

Expenditure upto 31.3.1998 (3,42,60,000 – 6,60,000)		3,36,00,000
Add : Estimated expenditure to complete		
Materials	10,50,000	
Less : Materials in hand	6,60,000	
	17,10,000	

Labour	16,00,000	
Sub-contractors	20,00,000	
Hire charges	3,00,000	
Establishment charges	6,90,000	
		63,00,000
		3,99,00,000
Add : Provision for contingencies $\frac{5}{95} \times 3{,}99{,}00{,}000$		21,00,000
Estimated cost		4,20,00,000

Estimated profit = contract price – toatal estimated cost
= 4,80,00,000 – 4,20,00,000
= 60,00,000

Proportionate profit taken to P & L a/c

$$\frac{\text{work certified}}{\text{contract price}} \times \text{estimated profit}$$

$$\frac{4{,}00{,}00{,}000}{4{,}80{,}00{,}000} \times 60{,}00{,}000$$

= 50,00,000

Problem 21 : M/s Everfine constructions commenced a contract for the construction of a Bunglow on 1st July 1994. Originally the contract price was Rs. 50,00,000 but finally the same was fixed at Rs. 45,00,000.

Their actual expenditure during the year 1994 and estimated expenditure during 1995, till the completion of the contract is as under :

Particulars	*Actual expenditure upto 31.12.94* *Rs.*	*Estimated expenditure during 1995* *Rs.*
Building materials	8,00,000	13,00,000
Labour charges	6,00,000	6,00,000
Plant installed at site (at cost)	4,00,000	-
Materials at site on 31.12.94	50,000	-
General expenses	2,50,000	3,55,000
Plant returned to stores at cost at the end of the year	1,00,000	-
Work certified	20,00,000	contract completed
Work uncertified	75,000	-
Cash received	90% of the work certified	45,00,000

The contract is expected to be completed by 30th September 1995. The plant is subject to depreciation at 20% p.a. on the original cost.

In order to calculate the correct account of profit made on the contract for the year 1994, it was decided to take certain proportion of the estimated profit on completion of the contract to the credit of profit and loss a/c; such proportion being cash received to the total contract price.

Prepare the contract a/c for the year ending 31st December 1994 and work out the estimated profit on the completion of the contract by 30th Sept. 1995 (*University of Bombay, B.Com., October 1995*)

Solution : **Contract a/c for the year ended 31.12.1994**

To building materials	8,00,000	By WIP a/c :-	
To labour charges	6,00,000	Work certified	20,00,000
To depreciation $4{,}00{,}000 \times \frac{6}{12} \times \frac{20}{100}$	40,000	Work uncertified	75,000

To general expenses	2,50,000	Materials at site	50,000
To balance c/d	4,35,000		
	21,25,000		21,25,000
To P & L a/c	2,04,000	By balance b/d	4,35,000
To WIP reserve	2,31,000		
	4,35,000		4,35,000

Statement of total contract

	Actual	*Estimated*	*Total*
Materials	8,00,000	13,00,000	21,00,000
Labour	6,00,000	6,00,000	12,00,000
Depreciation plant	40,000	45,000	85,000
General expenses	2,50,000	3,55,000	6,05,000
Total estimated cost			39,90,000

Estimated profit = contract price – total estimated cost
= 45,00,000 – 39,90,000
= 5,10,000

Profit transferred to P & L a/c

$$\text{Estimated profit} \times \frac{\text{Cash Received}}{\text{Contract price}}$$

$$5,10,000 \times \frac{18,00,000}{45,00,000} = 2,04,000$$

Working note :

Calculation of depreciation on plant for estimated period of 9 months

	Book value issued	4,00,000
Less :	Plant returned to stores at cost at the end of the year	1,00,000
		3,00,000

$$3,00,000 \times \frac{20}{100} \times \frac{9}{12} = 45,000$$

Problem 22 : Prabhu Builders commenced work on 1st April 1993 on a contract of which the agreed price was Rs. 5 lakhs. The following expenditure was incurred during the year upto 31st March 1994.

	Rs.
Wages	1,40,000
Plant	35,000
Materials	1,05,000
Head office expenses	12,500

Materials costing Rs. 10,000 proved unsuitable and were sold for Rs. 11,500 and a part of the plant was scrapped and sold for Rs. 1,700.

Of the contract price Rs. 2,40,000 representing 80% of the work certified had been received by 31st March, 1994 and on that date the value of the plant on the job was Rs. 8,000 and the value of materials was Rs. 3,000. The cost of work done but not certified Rs. 25,000.

It was decided to (a) estimate what further expenditure would be incurred in completing the contract (b) compute from the estimate and the expenditure already incurred, the total profit that would be made on the contract and (c) ascertain the amount of profit to be taken to the credit of P & L a/c for the year ending 31st March 1994. While taking profit to the credit of P & L a/c that portion of the total profit should be taken which the value of work certified bears to the contract price. Details of the estimates were as follows :

(1) That the contract would be completed by 30th September 1994.

(2) The wages to complete would amount to Rs. 84,750.

(3) That materials in addition to those in stock on 31st March 1994 would cost Rs. 50,000.

(4) That further Rs. 15,000 would have to be spent on plant and the residual value of the plant on 30th September 1994 would br Rs. 6,000.

(5) The head office expenses to the contract would be the same annual rate as in 1993-94.

(6) That claims, temporary maintenance and contingencies would require Rs. 9,000.

Prepare contract a/c for the year ended 31st March, 1994 and show your calculations of the sum to be credited to P & L a/c for the year. *(C.S., Inter June 1995)*

Solution :

Contract a/c

To wages	1,40,000	By cash—Materials sold	11,500
To materials	1,05,000	By cash—plant sold	1,700
To plant	35,000	By materials	3,000
To H.O. expenses	12,500	By plant	8,000
To P & L a/c profit on materials sold	1,500	**By work-in-progress :**	
To balance c/d	55,200	Work certified	3,00,000
		Work uncertified	25,000
	3,49,200		3,49,200
To P & L a/c	36,120	By balance b/d	55,200
To work-in-progress reserve	19,080		
	55,200		55,200

Calculation of estimated profit

Total net expenditure upto 31.3.1994 :			
Wages			1,40,000
Plant		35,000	
Less : Scraped & sold	1,700		
Plant in hand	8,000		
		9,700	
			25,300
Materials		1,05,000	
Less : Cost of materials sold	10,000		
Cost of materials in hand	3,000		
		13,000	
			92,000
H.O. expenses			12,500
			2,69,800
Add : Further estimated expenses :			
Wages		84,750	
Materials	50,000		
Add : Materials on hand	3,000	53,000	
Plant	15,000		
Add : plant on hand	8,000		
	23,000		
Less : Residual value	6,000		
		17,000	

H.O. expenses (6 months @ last year $\frac{12,500}{2}$)	6,250	
Contingencies	9,000	
		1,70,000
Total estimated cost		4,39,800

Estimate profit = contract price – estimated cost
= 5,00,000 – 4,39,800
= 60,200

Profit to be credited to P & L a/c

$$\text{Estimated profit} \times \frac{\text{work certified}}{\text{contract price}}$$

$$60{,}200 \times \frac{3,00,000}{5,00,000} = 36{,}120$$

Problem 23 : Excellent engineers undertook a contract which involves the fabrication of pre-stressed concrete blocks and the erection of the same at the consumer's site. The following information is supplied regarding the contract which is incomplete on 31st December :

Cost incurred	*Rs.*
Fabrication cost to date :	
Direct materials	8,30,000
Direct labour	2,85,000
Overheads	1,65,000
	12,80,000
Erection costs	1,20,000
	14,00,000
Contract price	25,00,000

Cash received being 80% of work certified 12,80,000

Technical estimates of work completed to-date :

Fabrication : Direct materials 80%

: Direct labour and overheads 75%

: Erection 25%

Prepare a statement showing :

(*a*) Estimated profit on completion of contract

(*b*) Estimated profit to-date the contract

(*Sri Sathya Sai University, B. Com., April 1986*)

Solution :

Statement showing estimated profit

	Cost to date		*Further cost*		*Total*
	Percentage of completion	*Amount*	*Percentage of completion*	*Amount*	
Fabrication cost :					
Direct material	80%	8,30,000	20%	2,07,500	10,37,500
Direct labour	75%	2,85,000	25%	95,000	3,80,000
Overhead	75%	1,65,000	25%	55,000	2,20,000
Erection cost	25%	1,20,000	75%	3,60,000	4,80,000
Total		14,00,000		7,17,500	21,17,500

Estimated profit = Contract price – Total estimated cost
= 25,00,000 – 21,17,500 = 3,82,500

$$\text{Profit to be taken} = \text{Estimated profit} \times \frac{\text{Cash received}}{\text{Contract price}}$$

$$3{,}82{,}500 \times \frac{12{,}80{,}000}{25{,}00{,}000} = \text{Rs. } 1{,}95{,}840$$

Working notes : Calculation of further cost of materials

For 80% the cost incurred is 8,30,000

$$\text{For 20\%} \quad ? \rightarrow \quad \frac{8{,}30{,}000 \times 20}{80} = \text{Rs. } 20{,}75{,}000$$

Labour cost to be incurred subsequently

For 75% the labour cost incurred is Rs. 2.85,000

$$\text{For 25\%} \quad ? \rightarrow \quad \frac{2{,}85{,}000 \times 25}{75} = \text{Rs. } 95{,}000$$

Overheads to be incurred subsequently

For 75% the overhead incurred is 1,65,000

$$\text{For 25\%} \quad ? \rightarrow \quad \frac{1{,}65{,}000 \times 25}{75} = \text{Rs. } 55{,}000$$

Erection cost to be incurred subsequently

For 25% the erection cost incurred is Rs. 1,20,000

$$\text{For 75\%} \quad ? \rightarrow ? \rightarrow \quad \frac{1{,}20{,}000 \times 75}{25} = \text{Rs. } 3{,}60{,}000$$

Problem 24 (Escalation clause in contract) : The escalation clause of a long term contract stipulates the following quantites and rates of materials of *A*, *B* and *C* and the following number of labour hours of *X*, *Y* and *Z* and their rates of pay. The actuals are shown below :

			Actual	
Materials	*Qty. (Tons)*	*Rate* (Rs.)	*Qty. (Tons)*	*Rate* (Rs.)
A	500	50	500	45
B	1,000	30	1,000	35
C	20	1,000	20	1,010
Labour	*Hours*	*Hourly rate*	*Hours*	*Hourly rate*
X	4,800	2.00	4,800	2.25
Y	2,400	1.00	2,400	1.50
Z	9,600	1.50	9,600	1.50

Compute the amount of final claim so far as the rate is concerned.

Solution : **Statement showing material escalation**

Material	*As per contract*		*Actual*	*variation*	*material*
	qty.	*rate*	*rate*	*in rate*	*escalation claim*
(1)	(2)	(3)	(4)	(5)	(6) = (2) × (5)
A	500 tons	Rs. 50	45	- Rs. 5	- 2,500
B	1,000 tons	Rs. 30	35	+ Rs. 5	+ 5,000
C	20 tons	Rs. 1,000	1,010	+ Rs. 10	+ 200
			Materials escalation		2,700

Statement showing labour escalation

Labour	As per contract		Actual variation wages		
	hrs	rate	rate	in rate	escalation claim
(1)	(2)	(3)	(4)	(5)	(6) = (2) × (5)
X	4,800	2.00	2.25	+ 0.25	+ 1,200
Y	2,400	1.00	1.50	+ 0.25	+ 1,200
Z	9,600	1.50	1.50	–	–
				Wages escalation	2,400

Final escalation claim							
Materials escalation							2,700
Labour eacalation							2,400
Add : Claim as per contract :							
Material	*A*	—	500 tons @	Rs. 50	=	25,000	
	B	—	1,000 tons @	Rs. 30	=	30,000	
	C	—	20 tons @	Rs. 1,000	=	20,000	75,000
Labour :	*X*	—	4,800 hrs. @	Rs. 2	=	9,600	
	Y	—	2,400 hrs @	Rs. 1	=	2,400	
	Z	—	9,600 hrs @	Rs. 1.50	=	14,400	1,01,400
						Total claim	1,60,500

Problem 25 : A contract for reinforced cement concrete building is governed by an escalation clause in respect of prices of steel, cement, and stone aggregate. The prices ruling on the date of the tender for the building and the actual prices paid by the contractor were as under :

Particulars	*Price on the date of tender (Rs.)*	*Actual Price (Rs.)*
Steel (per ton)	610	675
Cement (per ton)	100	105
Stone aggregate (per ton 100 cft.)	40	38

3,00,000 c.ft. reinforced concrete was laid in the building. If 100 eb steel, 2,400 lb cement and 90 c.ft. stone aggregate are the net quantities to cost 100 c.ft. of reinforced cement concrete and the wastage was 5,3, and 10 per cent respectively, calculate the difference in selling price according to the escalation clause.

Solution :

Net quantities required for 3,00,000 c.ft. reinforced cement conrete :

Steel : 100 lb × 3,000	=	3,00,000	lbs
Cement : 2,400 lbs × 3,000	=	72,00,000	lbs
Stone aggregate : 90 cft. × 3,000	=	2,70,000	c.ft.

Gross quantities required for 3,00,000 c.ft. of reinforced cement concrete

Steel : 3,00,000 lbs + 5%	=	3,15,000	lbs or
		140.65	tons
Cement : 72,00,000 lbs + 3%	=	74,16,000	lbs or
		3,310.71	tons
Stone aggregate : 2,70,000 cft. + 10%	=	2,97,000	cft

Statement showing increase in selling price as per escalation clause

	Rs.
Steel @ Rs. 65 per ton on 140.63 tons	9,140.95
Cement @ Rs. 5 per ton on 3,310.71 tons	16,553.55
	25,694.50
Less— Decrease for stone aggregate @ 2 per 100 c.ft. on 2,97,000 c.ft.	5,940.00
Increase in selling price	19,754.50

Note : It is assumed that the percentage of wastage are based on the net quantities of materials.

AS 7 : ACCOUNTING FOR CONSTRUCTION CONTRACTS*

The following is the text of the Accounting Standard 7 (AS-7) issued by the Institute of Chartered Accountants of India on "Accounting for Construction Contracts". The Standard deals with accounting for construction contracts in the financial statements of contractors.

In the initial years, this Accounting Standard will be recommendatory in character. During this period, this standard is recommended for use by companies listed on a recognised stock exchange and other large commercial, industrial and business enterprises in the public and private sectors.

Introduction

1. This Statement deals with accounting for construction contracts in the financial statements of enterprises undertaking such contracts (hereafter referred to as 'contractors'). The Statement also applies to enterprises undertaking construction activities of the type dealt with in this Statement not as contractors but on their own account as a venture of a commercial nature where the enterprise has entered into agreements for sale.
2. The feature which characterises a construction contract dealt with in this Statement is the fact that the date at which the contract is secured and the date when the contract activity is completed fall into different accounting periods. The specific duration of the contract performance is not used as a distinguishing feature of a construction contract. Accounting for such contracts is essentially a process of measuring the results of relatively long-term events and allocating those results to relatively short-term accounting periods.
3. For the purposes of this Statement a construction contract is a contract for the construction of an asset or of a combination of assets which together constitute a single project. Examples of activity covered by such contracts include the construction of bridges, dams, ships, buildings and complex pieces of equipment.
4. Contracts for the provision of services come within the scope of this Statement to the extent that they are directly related to a contract for the construction of an asset. Examples of such service contracts are contracts for the services of project managers and architects and for technical engineering services related to the construction of an asset.

Explanation

5. The principle problem relating to accounting for construction contracts is the allocation of revenues and related costs to accounting periods over the duration of the contract.
6. Types of Construction Contracts

   Construction contracts are formulated in a variety of ways but generally fall into two basic types :

   (i) fixed price contracts - the contractor agrees to a fixed contract price or rate, in some cases subject to cost escalation clauses;

   (ii) Cost plus contracts - the contractor is reimbursed for allowable or otherwise defined costs, and is also allowed a percentage of these costs or a fixed fee.

Both types of contracts are within the scope of this Statement.

---

* Issued in December, 1983.

7. Accounting Treatment of Construction Contract Costs and Revenues

7.1 Two methods of accounting for contracts commonly followed by contractors are the percentage of completion method and the completed contract method.

7.2 Under the percentage of completion method, revenue is recognised as the contract activity progresses based on the stage of completion reached. The costs incurred in reaching the stage of completion are matched with this revenue, resulting in the reporting of results which can be attributed to the proportion of work completed. Although (as pwer the principle of 'prudence') revenue is recognised only when realised, under this method, the revenue is recognised as the activity progresses wven though in certain circumstances it may not be realised.

7.3 Under the completed contract method, revenue is recognised only when the contract is completed or substantially completed; that is, when only minor work is expected other than warranty obligation. Costs and progress payments received are accumulated during the course of the contract but revenue is not recognised until the contract activity is substantially completed.

7.4 Under both methods, provision is made for losses for the stage of completion reached on the contract. In addition, provision is usually made for losses on the remainder of the contract.

7.5 It may be necessary for accounting purposes to combine contracts made with a single customer or to combine contracts made with several customers if the contracts are negotiated as a package or if the contracts are for a single project. Conversely, if a contract covers a number of projects and if the costs and revenues of such individual projects canbe identified within the terms of the overall contract, each such project may be treated as equivalent to a separate contract.

8. Costs to be Accumulated for Construction Contracts

8.1 Costs attributable to a contract are identified with reference to the period that commences with the securing of the contract and closes when the contract is completed.

8.2 Costs not specially attributable to any contract incurred by the contractor before a contract is secured are usually treated as expenses of the period in which they are incurred. However, if costs attributable to securing the contract can be separately identified and either the contract has been secured or there is a clear indication that the contract will be obtained the costs are sometimes treated as applicable to the contract and are deferred. As a practical measure, costs directly identifiable with a contract are sometimes deferred until it is clear whether the contract has been secured or not.

8.3 Costs attributable to a contract include expected warranty costs. Warranty costs are provided for when such costs can be reasonably estimated.

8.4 Costs incurred by a contractor can be divided into :

(i) Costs that relate directly to a specific contract;

(ii) Costs that can be attributed to the contract activity in general and can be allocated to specific contracts;

(iii) Costs that relate to the activities of the contractor generally, or that relate to contract activity but cannot be related to specific contracts.

8.5 Examples of costs that related directly to a specific contract include :

(*i*) site labour costs, including supervision;
(*ii*) materials used for project construction;
(*iii*) depreciation of plant and equipment required for a contract;
(*iv*) cost of moving plant and equipment to and from a site.

8.6 Examples of costs that can be attributed to the contract activity in general and can be allocated to specific contracts include :

(*i*) insurance;
(*ii*) design and technical assistance;
(*iii*) construction overheads.

8.7 Examples of costs that relate to the activities of the contractor generally or that relate to contract activity but cannot be related to specific contracts, include :

(*i*) general administration and selling costs;
(*ii*) finance costs;
(*iii*) research and development costs;
(*iv*) depreciation of plant and equipment that cannot be allocated to a particular contract.

8.8 Costs referred to in paragraph 8.7 are usually excluded from the accumulated contract costs because they do not relate to reaching the present stage of completion of a specific contract. However, in some circumstances general administrative expenses, development costs and finance costs are specifically attributable to a particular contract and are sometimes included as part of accumulated contract costs.

Basis for Recognising Revenue on Construction Contracts

9. Percentage of completion method

9.1 Under the percentage of completion method, the amount of revenue recognised is determined by reference to the stage of completion of the contract activity at the end of each accounting period. The advantage of this method of accounting for contract revenue is that it reflects revenue in the accounting period during which activity is undertaken to earn such revenue.

9.2 The stage of completion used to determine revenue to be recognised in the financial statements is measured in an appropriate manner. For this purpose no special weightage should be given to a single factor; instead, all relevant factors should be taken into consideration; for example, the proportion that costs incurred to date bear to the estimated total costs of the contract, by the surveys which measure work performed and completion of a physical proportion of the contract work.

9.3 Progress payments and advances received from customers may not necessarily reflect the stage of completion and therefore, cannot usually be treated as equivalent to revenue earned.

9.4 If the percentage of completion method is applied by calculating the proportion that costs to date bear to the latest estimated total costs of the contract, adjustments are made to include only those costs that reflect work performed. Examples of items which may need adjustment include :

(*i*) the costs of material that have been purchased for the contract but have not been installed or used furing contract performance; and

(*ii*) payments to subcontractors to the extent they do not reflect the amount of work; performed under the subcontract.

9.5 The application of the percentage of completion method is subject to a risk of error in making estimates. For this reason, profit is not recognised in the financial statements unless the outcome of the contract can be reliably estimated. If the outcome cannot be reliably estimated, the percentage of completion method is not used.

9.6 While recognising the profit under this method, an appropriate allowance for future unforeseeable factors which may affect the ultimate quantum of profit is generally made on either a specific or a percentage basis.

9.7 In the case of fixed price contracts, the conditions which will usually provide this degree of reliability are :

(*i*) total contract revenues to be received can be reliably estimated,

(*ii*) both the costs to complete the contract and the stage of contract performance completed at the reporting date can be reasonably estimated, and

(*iii*) the costs attributable to the contract can be clearly identified so that actual experience can be compared with prior estimates.

9.8 Normally, the profit is not recognised in fixed price contracts unless the work on a contract has progressed to a reasonable extent. Ordinarily this is not considered as having been satisfied unless 20 to 25% of the work is completed.

9.9 In the case of cost *plus* contracts, the conditions which usually provide this degree of reliability are :

(*i*) costs attributable to the contract can be clearly identified, and

(*ii*) costs other than those that are specifically reimbursable under the contract can be reliably estimated.

10. Completed contract method

10.1 The principal advantage of the completed contract method is that it is based on results as determined when the contract is completed or substantially completed rather than on estimates which may require subsequent adjustment as a result of unforeseen costs and possible losses.

The risk of recognising profits that may not have been earned is therefore, minimised.

10.2 The principal disadvantage of the completed contract method is that periodic reported income does not reflect the level of activity on contracts during the period. For example, when a few large contracts are completed in one accounting period but no contracts have been completed in the previous period or are to be completed in the subsequent period, the level of reported income can be erratic although the level of activity on contracts may have been relatively constant throughout. Even when numerous contracts are regularly completed in each accounting period, and reported income may appear to reflect the level of activity on contracts, there is a continuous lag between the time when work is performed and the related revenue is recognised.

11. Selection of Method

11.1 The selection of a method of accounting for a construction contract depends on considerations discussed earlier. The contractor may use both methods simultaneously for different contracts depending upon circumstances.

11.2 When a contract uses a particular method of accounting for a contract, then in respect of all other contracts that meet similar criteria, the same method is used.

11.3 The methods of accounting used by the contractor and the criteria adopted in selecting the method/s represent an accounting policy.*

12. Change in Accounting Policy

When there is a change in the accounting policy used for construction contracts, there is disclosure of the effect of the change and its amount. If the contractor changes from the percentage of completion method to the completed contract method, it is sometimes not possible to quantify the full effect of the change in the current accounting period. In such cases, there is disclosure of at least the amount of attributable profits reported in prior years, in respect of contracts in progress at the beginning of the accounting period.**

13. Provision for Foreseeable Losses

13.1 When current estimates of total contract costs and revenues indicate a loss, provision is made for the entire loss onthe contract irrespective of the amount of work done and the method of accounting followed. In some circumstances, the foreseeable losses may exceed the costs of work done to date. Provision is nevertheless made for the entire loss on the contract.

13.2 When a contract is of such magnitude that it can be expected to absorb a considerable part of the capacity of the enterprise for a substantial period, indirect costs to be incurred during the period of the completion of the contract are sometimes considered to be directly attributable to the contract and included in the calculation of the provision for loss on the contract.

13.3 If a provision for loss is required, the amount of such provision is usually determined irrespective of :

(i) whether or not work has commenced on the contract; and

(ii) the stage of completion of contract activity; and

(iii) the amount of profits expected to arise on other unrelated contracts.

13.4 The determination of a future loss on a contract may be subject to high degree of uncertainty. In some of these cases, it is possible to provide for the future loss and in other cases only the existence of a contingent loss is disclosed.***

14. Claims and Variations Arising Under Construction Contracts

14.1 Amounts due in respect of claims made by the contractor and of variations in contract work approved by the customer are recognised as revenue in the financial statements only in circumstances when, and only to the extent that, the contractor has evidence of the final acceptability of the amount of the claim or variation.****

---

* Refer to AS-1 on "Disclosure of Accounting Policies."

** Refers to AS-5 on "Prior Period and Extraordinary Items and Changes in Accounting Policies."

*** Refer to AS-4 on "Contingencies and Events Occurring After the Balance Sheet Date."

**** Refer to AS-1 on "Disclosure of Accounting Policies."

14.2 Claims or penalties payable by the contractor arising out of delays in completion or from other causes are provided for in full in the financial statements as costs attributable to the contract. Claims in the nature of contingency are treated as indicated in Accounting Standard 4 on "contingencies and Events Occurring After the Balance Sheet Date."

15. Progress Payments, Advances and Retentions

15.1 Progress payments and advances received from customers in respect of construction contracts in relation to the work performed thereon are disclosed in financial statements either as a liability or shown as a deduction from the amount of contract-work-in-progress.

15.2 In case progress payments and advances received from customers in respect of construction contracts are not in relation to the work performed thereon, these are shown as a liability.

15.3 Amounts retained by customers until the satisfaction of conditions specified in the contract for release of such amounts are either recognised in financial statements as receivables or alternatively indicated by way of a note.

Accounting Standard

(The Accounting Standard comprises paragraphs 16-21 of this statement. The Standard should be read in the context of paragraphs 1-15 of this Statement and of the 'Preface to the Statements of Accounting Standards'.)

16. In accounting for construction contracts in financial statements, either the percentage of completion method or the completed contract method may be used. When a contractor uses a particular method of accounting for a contract, then the same method should be adopted for all other contracts which meet similar criteria.

17. The percentage of completion method can be used if the outcome of the contract can be reliably estimated.

17.1 In the case of fixed price contracts, this degree of reliability would be provided if the following conditions are satisfied :

(i) total contract revenues to be received can be reliably estimated.

(ii) both the costs to complete the contract and the stage of contract performance completed at the reporting date can be reasonably estimated; and

(iii) the costs attributable to the contract can be clearly identified so that actual experience can be compared with prior estimates.

17.2 Profit in the case of fixed price contracts, normally should not be recognised unless the work on a contract has progressed to a reasonable extent.

17.3 In the case of cost plus contracts, this degree of reliability would be provided only if both the following conditions are satisfied :

(i) costs attributable to the contract can be clearly identified; and

(ii) costs other than those that are specifically reimbursable under the contract can be reliably estimated.

17.4 While recognising the profit under percentage of completion method, an appropriate allowance for future unforeseeable factors should be made on either a specific or a percentage basis.

18. The costs included in the amount at which construction contract work is stated should comprise those costs that relate directly to a specific contract and those that are attributable to the contract activity in general and can be allocated to specific contracts.

19. A foreseeable loss on the entire contract should be provided for in the financial statements irrespective of the amount of work done and the method of accounting followed.

Disclosure

20. There should be disclosure in the financial statements of :
   (i) the amount of construction work-in-progress;
   (ii) progress payments received and advances and retentions on account of contracts included in construction work-in-progress; and
   (iii) the amount receivable in respect of income accrued under cost plus contracts not included in construction work-in-progress.

If both the percentage of completion method and the completed contract method are simultaneously used by the contractor, the amount of contract work described in (i) above should be analysed to disclose separately the amounts attributable to contracts accounted for under each method.

21. Disclosure of changes in an accounting policy used for construction contracts should be made in the financial statements giving the effect of the change and its amount. However, if a contractor changes from the percentage of completion method to the completed contract method for contracts in progress at the beginning of the year, it may not be possible to quantify the effect of the change. In such cases, disclosure should be made of the amount of attributable profits reported in prior years in respect of contracts in progress at the beginning of the accounting period.

Problem-26 (Problem on AS-7): A limited undertakes civil contracts. For the year ending 31st March 2002, it has undertaken two contracts. From the information given below relating to the two contracts, determine the amount of profit (or loss) to be recognised in respect of each contract for the year ended 31st March 2002 in accordance with AS-7.

	Contract 1 (Rs. 000)	*Contract 2* (Rs. 000)
Total Contract Price	600	100
Cost incurred to date	400	100
Estimated future costs to complete the contract	400	800
Progress payment received and receivable	500	80

(*Sn Sathya Sai University B.Com. Hons., October 2002*)

Solution :

Contract-I

	(Rs. 000)
Contract Price	600
Less : Total cost of construction (400 + 400)	800
Total foreseeable loss	200

Stage of completion $\frac{400}{800} \times 100 = 50\%$

Turnover to be recognised $600 \times \frac{50}{100} = 300$

∴ The loss to be recognised is Rs. 3,00,000 – Rs. 4,00,000 = Rs. 1,00,000

Since the foreseeable loss is 2,00,000 an additional provision of Rs. 1,00,000 is to be provided in accordance with para 19 of AS-7

Contract-2

		(Rs. 000)
Contract Price		1000
Total cost of construction (100 + 800)		900
Total foreseeable profit		100
Stage of completion $\frac{100}{900} \times 100 = 11.1\%$		
Turnover to be recognised 1000 × 11.11 =	111 Thousands	111
Less : Cost incurred till date =		100
∴ profit to be recognised		11

As the work completed is less than 25%, the profit of Rs. 11000 must be carried as provision for contingencies.

Problem-27: Ram has undertaken two contracts to constract two primary health centres during the calender year 2000. From the information given below, compute for him, the profit to be considered or loss to be provided for in accordance with AS-7

	Contract I (Rs. 000)	*Contract II* (Rs. 000)
Total contract price (fixed)	1500	1000
Cost incurred to date	160	500
Estimated costs for completion	1440	300
Progress payments received and receivable	100	600

Ram receives 90% of the work certified in cash (Sn Sathya Sai University, B.Com. Hons., October 2001)

Solution :

Contract-1 Statement Showing Estimated Foreseeable loss

		(Rs. 000)
Total cost of construction (160 + 1440) =		1600
Stage of completion $\frac{160}{1600} \times 100 =$		10%
Revenue to be recognised 10% of 1500 =		150
Total foreseeable loss :		
Total cost of construction		1600
Total contract price		1500
Foreseeable loss on the contract		100
Loss to be recognised on the accounting date :		
Revenue recognised on percentage of completion basis		150
Cost incurred on accounting date		160
Loss for the accounting period		10
Further loss to be provided as per para 19 of AS-7		90
Net loss including provision		100

Note : As the contract has progressed very little, revenue may not be recognised during the period and loss for the period need not be computed. However, the foreseeable loss of 1,00,000 must be provided for in accordance with para 19 of AS-7

Contract-2 Estimated profit or loss on the contract

	(Rs. 000)
Total contract price	1000
Total estimated costs on the contract (500 + 300)	800
Estimated profit	200
Stage of completion $\frac{500}{800} \times 100$	62.5%
Revenue to be recognised 62.5% of Rs. 1000	625
Profit to be recognised on the balance sheet :	
Revenue recognised on the accounting date	625
Less : Cost incurred to date	500
	125

Note :

Since the contract has progressed only to the extent of 62.5% it is prudent to set apart $\frac{1}{3}$ of the profit towards contingencies. As 90% of the work certified is received in cash, a sum of Rs. 75000 is to be considered as the profit for the year and carry forwards Rs. 50000 towards contingencies. The working is shown below :

$$1,25,000 \times \frac{2}{3} \times \frac{90}{100} = \text{Rs. } 75000$$

QUESTIONS

I. Select the Correct Answer from the Following

1. Most of the expenses are direct in :
   (*a*) Output costing (*c*) Contract costing
   (*b*) Job costing (*d*) Process costing [ ]
2. When a contract is not complete at the end of the year, loss on incomplete contract is
   (*a*) Transferred to P & L a/c (*c*) Transferred partly to P & L a/c and partly to work-in-progress
   (*b*) Transferred to work-in-progress (*d*) Debited to contract account [ ]
3. Contract price in not fixed in case of
   (*a*) Cost plus contracts (*c*) De-escalation clause
   (*b*) Escalation clause (*d*) All of the above [ ]
4. Work-in-progress in contract accounts comprises
   (*a*) Work certified and work uncertified (*c*) Work certified and profits carried forward
   (*b*) Work uncertified (*d*) Work certified, work uncertified and profits carried forward [ ]
5. When the job is big and spread over long periods of time, the method of costing used is
   (*a*) Job costing (*c*) Contract costing
   (*b*) Process costing (*d*) Multiple costing [ ]
6. Terminal costing is also known as
   (a) Contract costing (*c*) Unit costing
   (*b*) Job costing (*d*) Operating costing [ ]
7. Profit on an incomplete contract is called notional profit because
   (*a*) It is an imaginary profit (*c*) The profit is only an approximation
   (*b*) Real profit will be known at the end of the contract (*d*) Of no special reason [ ]

8. Which one of the following holds good as regards transfer of profit to P & L a/c, when the work completed is less than ¼ of the total work of the contract
   (*a*) ¼ of notional profit
   (*b*) ⅓ of notional profit
   (*c*) ½ of notional profit
   (*d*) No profit

[***Answers :*** 1. (*c*), 2. (*a*), 3. (*d*), 4. (*d*), 5. (*c*), 6. (*a*), 7. (*b*), 8. (*d*)]

II. Fill in the Blanks

1. In a contract, provision for changes in cost of material is made in............clause.
2. In contract costing, the cost unit is..........
3. When 60% of contract price is certified, the formula to be used for calculating the profit to be taken to P & L a/c is............
4. A contract which guarantees a certaing percentage of profit is called............contract.

[***Answers :*** 1. escalation 2. contract, 3. $\frac{2}{3} \times$ Notional profit $\times \frac{\text{Cash received}}{\text{Work certified}}$, 4. cost-plus]

III. Mark True or False in the Space Provided

1. In cost-plus contract, the contractor runs a risk of incurring a loss *T/F*
2. When a contract is spread over more than one accounting year, profit is calculated only after the completion of the contract. *T/F*
3. Profit made on the sale of assets brought for the contract should not be treated as profits for the contract. *T/F*
4. Plant returned to central stores becomes the opening stock of plant for the subsequent period of the same contract. *T/F*
5. When the contract is completed the contract price is credited to the contractee's a/c. *T/F*
6. Amount received from the sale of surplus materials is credited to the contract a/c. *T/F*
7. In contract costing, profit on each contract is computed when the contract is completed. *T/F*
8. Only a reasonable proportion of the estimated profit on uncompleted contract is taken to account. *T/F*

[***Answers :*** 1. *F*, 2. *F*, 3. *F*, 4. *T*, 5. *F*, 6. *T*, 7.*F*, 8. *T*]

IV. Short Answer Questions

1. State the features of contract costing.
2. State the points of similarities and dissimilarities between job costing and contract costing.
3. Explain the following terms :
   (*a*) Cost-plus contract
   (*b*) Sub-contract
   (*c*) Retention clause
   (*d*) Escalation clause.
4. State with formula the principles relating to transfer of profit in case of incomplete contract.
5. What is a cost plus contract? State its merits and demerits.

EXERCISES

Exercise-1 (Contract Completed in the Same Year)

The following is the condensed record of the transactions on 31st Dec. 1994 relating to a special contract completed during the year.

Materials bought from the market	1500
Materials issued from the stores	500
Wages	2440
Direct expenses	294
Works on cost 25% of direct wages	
Office on cost 10% of prime cost	
contract price	6000

You are required to prepare a contract account keeping in view that material returned amounted to Rs. 240. (*Calicut University, B.Com., April 1995*)

[**Answer :** Profit on completion of contract Rs. 476]

Exercise-2 (When Contract is 50% Complete)

Mr. A has undertaken several contract works. He maintains a separate record for each contract. From the records for the year ending 31-12-98 prepare contract a/c for contract No. 45 and find the amount transferred to profit & loss a/c.

Direct purchase of materials	1,80,000
Materials issued from stores	50,000
Wages	2,44,000
Direct expenses	24,000
Machinery purchased	1,60,000
Establishment charges	54,000

The contract price was Rs. 15,00,000. Cash received upto 31-12-1998 was Rs. 6,00,000 which is 80% of work certified. Materials at site Rs. 16,000. Depreciation for machine Rs. 16,000.

(*Bharathidason University, B.Com., April 1999*)

[**Answer :** Profit transferred to P & L a/c 1,05,600
Reserve transferred to WIP 92,400]

Exercise-3

Noble Contractors Ltd. undertook a contract on 1-4-1998. From the following particulars, prepare a contract account for the year ending 31-3-1999.

	Rs.
Contract price	6,00,000
Materials issued	1,60,000
Materials returned	4,000
Materials on site (on 31-3-99)	22,000
Labour	1,50,000
Establishment expenses	25,000
Direct expenses	66,000
Plant installed	80,000
Plant value (on 31-3-99)	65,000
Work certified	4,20,000
Uncertified work	23,000
Engineer's fees	2,000
Cash received from contractee	3,78,000

(*Bangalore University, B.Com., April 1999*)

[**Answer :** Profit transferred to P & L a/c Rs. 27,200
Reserve transferred to WIP 23,800]

Exercise-4

The following information relates to contract No. 58. Prepare contract a/c.

	Rs.
Direct materials	45,600
Direct wages	24,400
Special plant	18,400
Stores issued	6,040
Loose tools	3,560
Expenses of tractor :	
Running materials	3,500
Wages of drivers	4,540
Other direct charges	2,560

The contract was completed in 26 weeks at the end of which plant was returned subject to depreciation at 15% p.a. on original cost. The value of loose tools and stores returned were Rs. 2260 and Rs. 640 respectively. The value of tractor was Rs. 40,000 and depreciation was to be charged to this contract at 20% p.a. Administration expenses at 10% on total works cost. The contract price was Rs. 1,25,000.

(*Bangalore University, B.Com., April 1997*)

[**Answer :** Profit on contract Rs. 21,754]

Exercise-5

A firm of building contractors began the work on 1-1-95. The following was the expenditure incurred on a contract. The contract price was Rs. 6,00,000.

Materials issued from stores	1,50,000
Materials purchased for the contract	40,000
Plant installed at cost	70,000
Wages paid	2,40,000
Direct expenses paid	22,000
Establishment expenses	10,000
Direct expenses due	3,000
Wages accured	4,000

of the plant and materials charged to the contract, plant which cost Rs. 5000 and materials costing Rs. 4000 were lost. On 31-12-95, plant which cost Rs. 2000 was returned to stores and plant which cost Rs. 3000 was transferred to some other contract. The work certified was Rs. 4,80,000 and 80% of the same was received in cash. The cost of work done but uncertified was Rs. 3000. Charge depreciation at 10% on plant. Prepare contract a/c.

(*Nagarjuna University, B.Com., November 96*)

[**Answer :** Profit transferred to P & L a/c 6133
Reserve transferred to WIP 5367]

Exercise-6 (Calculation of Work Uncertified)

The following information relates to a contract for the year 1997.

Work on the contract started on 1-1-1997 and the total contract cost is Rs. 40,00,000.

	Rs.
Materials sent to contract	12,00,000
Direct purchase of materials	1,60,000
Wages	4,40,000
Supervisor's salary	90,000
Miscellaneous expenses	2,40,000
Plant and machinery issued	6,60,000
Materials on site on 31-12-97	60,000

Supervisor's salary is Rs. 7500 PM and he has spent $\frac{2}{3}$ of his time on this contract. Scrap value of the plant and machinery is Rs. 60,000 and its working life is estimated at 4 years. It was used in the contract for 146 days. The architect has certified 60% of the contract value on which the contractor has received payment of 75% of the value of work certified. The contractor claims to have completed 75% of the work. Prepare contract account showing the calculation of profit, if any, to be taken credit for.

(*Calicut University, B.Com., April 1998*)

[**Answer :** Profit transferred to P & L a/c 3,60,000
Reserve transferred to WIP 3,60,000]

Exercise-7 (Long term Contract)

The following information relates to a building contract the price of which was agreed at Rs. 10,00,000 and 80% of work certified was to be paid by the contractee.

	I year *Rs.*	*II year* *Rs.*	*III year* *Rs.*
Materials issued	1,20,000	1,45,000	84,000
Direct Wages	1,10,000	1,55,000	1,10,000
Chargeable expenses	5,000	17,000	6,000
Indirect charges	2000	2600	500
Work certified	2,35,000	7,50,000	10,00,000
Work done but not certified	3000	8000	–
Plant issued	14,000	–	–
Materials at site at the end	2000	5000	8000

The value of plant at the end of I, II and III year was Rs. 11,200, Rs. 7000 and Rs. 3000 respectively.

Prepare contract account for three years taking into account such profit as you think proper on incomplete contract.

(*Mangalore University, B.Com., April 1997*)

[**Answer :** Profit for the III year Rs. 1,33,553.]

Exercise-8 (Contract with Balance-sheet)

A company of contractors began to trade on 1-1-96. During 1996, the company was engaged on only one contract of which the contract price was Rs. 5,00,000.

Of the plant and materials charged to contract, plant costing Rs. 5000 and materials costing Rs. 4000 were distroyed in an accident.

On 31st December 1996, plant costing Rs. 5000 was returned to stores. Cost of work uncertified but finished Rs. 2000. Materials costing Rs. 4000 were on hand on site charge 10% depreciation on plant and make a reserve of $\frac{1}{3}$ of the profit to meet future events.

Prepare the contract account and Balance sheet as on 31-12-1996 from the following :

	Dr	*Cr*
Share capital		1,20,000
Creditors		10,000
Cash received (80%) of the work certified		2,00,000
Land & Buildings	43,000	
Bank balance	25,000	
Charged to contract :		
Material	90,000	
Wages	1,40,000	
Plant	25,000	
Expenses	7,000	
	3,30,000	3,30,000

(*Bharathidason University, B.Com., April 1998*)

[**Answer :** Profit transferred to P & L a/c 11,200
Total of Balance sheet Rs. 1,42,000]

Exercise-9

The following is the trial balance of a construction co. as on 31-12-97.

	Dr	*Cr*
Contractor's a/c		6,00,000
Building	3,20,000	
Creditors	–	1,44,000
Bank Balance	70,000	
Capital	–	10,00,000
Materials	4,00,000	
Wages (only for contract)	3,60,000	
Expenses	94,000	
Plant & Machinery	5,00,000	
	17,44,000	17,44,000

Only one contract was taken up during 1997 and the work on the same was commenced on 1-1-1997. Materials of the value of Rs. 3,40,000 were sent to the contract but materials of the value of Rs. 12,000 were destroyed in an accident at the site.

Plant and machinery costing Rs. 1,00,000 was used throughout the year and remaining plant and machinery costing Rs. 4,00,000 was used from 1-1-97 to 30-9-97 and thereafter returned to stores. Materials at site on 31-12-97 were valued at Rs. 8000.

The contract was for Rs. 12,00,000 and the contractee was required to pay 75% of the work certified. The work certified was 80% of the total contract value and uncertified work was Rs. 30,000 on 31-12-97.

Expenses are to be charged to the contract at 25% of wages and plant and machinery is to be depreciated at 10% p.a.

Prepare contract account, and Balance sheet as at 31-12-97

(*Bangalore University, B.B.M., April 1998*)

[**Answer :** Profit transferred to P & L a/c Rs. 90,000
Total of Balance sheet Rs. 13,08,000]

Exercise-10 (Contract nearing Completion)

The following information is extracted from the books of a contractor :

	Rs.
Contract Price	5,00,000
Materials sent to site	1,26,000
Direct labour paid	88,000
Overhead expenses allocated	46,000
Plant sent to site	60,000
Depreciation on plant on straight-line method	20%
Materials at close at site	6,000
Work certified	4,00,000

It is estimated that the contract will be completed in 6 months. The additional cost required for completion of contract are as follows :

	Rs.
Materials (in addition to those in stock)	40,000
Labour	24000
Overheads	10,000

Contingency reserve is to be created at 5% on cost before creating reserve. Prepare contract account showing calculation of estimated cost; profit and profit transferred to profit & loss a/c.

(*Kakatiya University, B.Com., October 1996*)

[**Answer :** Estimated profit:
Profit transferred to P & L a/c Rs. 1,09,360
Reserve transferred to WIP Rs. 24,640]

16

PROCESS COSTING

INTRODUCTION

Process costing refers to a method of accumulating cost of production by process. It represents a method of cost procedure applicable to continuous or mass production industries. Output in such industries consists of like units and every unit of product undergoes similar operation in the process. So it is implied that the same cost of material, labour and overhead is charged to each unit of product processed. Process costing is also known as continuous costing because industries which adopt this method of costing undertake manufacturing of goods on a continuous basis. This method is also known as average costing because the total cost of production is charged to all the units produced irrespective of the fact that on any day the expense incurred is more or less. Under this method, costing an individual unit is impossible. The period of time is adopted as the basis for determining the average cost per unit of production.

There are three types of process costing method. They are : (1) Sequential process cost method, under which all products pass through a series of process in sequence. Under this type, output and cost of production is transferred from process to process until finished products are obtained. This type is used by industries which manufacture a single uniform product or products that are uniformly processed; (2) Parallel process cost method, under which two or more products pass through two or more separate sets of processes. The different sets of processes may be carried on simultaneously or one set may be run for a while and then another started; (3) Selective process cost method, under which cost is accumulated from various processes for various products. They are used where the products pass through only some of the processes but not all the processes of the industry. Thus the process cost vary for different products. Meat packing industry is an example of this type of process costing.

DEFINITION AND FEATURES OF PROCESS COSTING

According to Koheler (Dictionary for Accountants) "process costing is a method of cost accounting whereby costs are charged to processes or operations and averaged over units produced".

According to ICMA terminology "process costing is that form of operation costing which applies where standardised goods are produced".

The distinctive features of process costing can be enumerated under the following points :

1. The factory is divided into various processes or departments which perform a certain limited operation. Each process or department is known as cost centre.
2. The finished products are uniform in all respects such as shape, size, weight, quality, colour, chemical content, etc.
3. The output of one process goes to constitute input of subsequent process/processes until finished product emerges out.

4. It is not possible to distinguish finished products while they are in the stage of processing.
5. The cost of production of one process is transferred to subsequent process/ processes just as output of one process is transferred as input of other process.
6. It is quite common to incur normal loss and wastages. Sometimes, owing to abnormal conditions even abnormal loss is also observed.
7. The production of main product is often accompanied by secondary products which are termed as joint and by-products.
8. The semi-finished products are expressed in terms of complete products. This is technically termed as equivalent production.
9. Cost of production is ascertained at each process and finally after completion of production.
10. Production is accumulated and reported by process.
11. Production process is predetermined and a definite sequence of production is followed. The raw materials and work-in-progress flow from process to process according to the sequence of production.
12. The unit of cost is the "process" under this method of costing.
13. Production is undertaken on a continuous and large scale basis in anticipation of demand.

APPLICATION OF PROCESS COSTING

Gillespie in his book *Cost Accounting and Control* states that a process cost system is used where it is not possible or not desirable to identify the successive jobs or lots of production for cost accumulation purposes. Under the following circumstances process costing method is most suitable :

1. Where the product of one process becomes the materials of another process.
2. Where production undertaken is simultaneous.
3. Where it is not possible to distinguish the products when they are under manufacturing process.
4. Where identical units are produced through an ongoing series of uniform production process.
5. Where production is continuous and undertaken on large scale basis.
6. Where production is standardised.

In addition to the above, Blocker and Weltmer in their book *Cost Accounting* list the following conditions which are favourable for the use of process costing :

1. Production of single product in a plant.
2. Division of a plant into processes or departments, each responsible for the manufacture of a single product.
3. Processing of a single product for a scheduled time, followed by successive runs of other products, each run being separated as to production and costs.
4. Production of several products of standard design in the same plant, process or department under conditions which permit computation of weighted averages to denote relative importance of each product as to quantities and costs.
5. Division of a factory into separate operation or production centres, each performing standard operations.

Examples of industries to which process costing can be applied are : oil refinery, chemical, electronics, baby food, soaps, breweries, dairy, paints and varnish, ink, rubber, textiles, perfumery, fertilizers, beer, ice-cream and many such other industries.

DIFFERENCES BETWEEN JOB AND PROCESS COSTING

Points of difference	*Job costing*	*Process costing*
1. Commencement of work.	On receiving order.	In anticipation of demand.
2. Continuity of work.	Intermitten.	Continuous.
3. Standardisation of product.	To suit the specific requirement of customers. Products are not identical.	Production is standardised. Finished products are identical.
4. Charging of cost	Specifically to the job.	Charged to process concerned.
5. Preparation of accounts.	On completion of job.	As and when required generally once in year.
6. Diversification.	Possible.	Not possible unless altogether a new set of machineries are installed.
7. Reporting.	In respect of a job after completion of job.	Reporting is processwise and in respect of time.
8. Investment of capital.	Less.	More.
9. Work-in-progress.	It may or may not exist.	It always exists.
10. Creation of demand.	No need to creat demand.	Demand creation is necessary for the products.
11. Identification.	Each job can be identified in respect of other jobs.	Products cannot be identified when they are under processing.
12. Transfer.	Generally no transfer of materials or labour is made unless it is necessary.	Output of one process is transferred to other process.
13. Supervision.	More because of differences in jobs.	Less because of standardisation of production.
14. Control of losses and wastages.	Losses and wastages can be controlled.	Only normal losses can be controlled but not abnormal losses and wastages.

RECORDING OF ELEMENTS OF COSTS IN PROCESS COSTING

1. Direct Materials cost

Materials used in process costing industries can be classified into two types, *viz.*, (1) Basic materials or raw materials as in the case of milk in ice-cream industry, fruit in fruit canning industries. (2) Process materials, which are incurred to convert raw materials into finished product as for example, chemicals added to preserve fruit juice content in the finished product. Materials are usually drawn in bulk quantities by various departmental heads from the storeroom through the issue of bill of materials. When solid materials are issued, they are weighted, counted or measured and then recorded in the stores ledger or material consumed report. When liquids or gases are issued, the flow of materials can be recorded by installing meters, readings of which are taken for costing purpose at appropriate intervals. In most of the cases raw materials are fed in the first process and occassionally materials are added in other processes. The cost of raw materials consumed can be ascertained in any of the following ways :

(*a*) By recording the issue prices in stores ledger card,

(*b*) The cost of raw materials purchased is added to the opening stock of raw materials and subtracting the closing stock of raw materials therefrom.

(*c*) Materials of identical nature when issued on a continuous basis can be obtained from material consumed report.

2. Direct Labour Cost

Labour cost constitutes least element of production cost. This is because, production is continuous and standardised, for which reason machines are used on large scale and mannual labour employed is less. This results in reduced labour cost per unit with increased overhead cost per unit.

Usually employees are engaged on one particular process. Labour cost of such employees are debited to the process account concerned. Where employees attend to more than one process, the time spent on more than one process is recorded and the wages are allocated to all the processes.

3. Direct Expenses

Hire of special plant, maintenance cost of such plant and other direct expenses are debited to process account.

4. Overheads

One problem encountered in accounting the overhead, under process costing is when more than one product is manufactured in the factory or in the same process. A suitable basis is to be decided for apportioning overheads to all products so manufactured. Overheads can be charged under any of the two methods : (*i*) Based on predetermined rate which is expressed mostly as a percentage on direct labour. This method is suitable when production capacity or overheads fluctuate from month to month. The pre-determined rate so used eliminates distortion in the monthly unit cost caused by such fluctuations, (*ii*) Actual overhead incurred is charged to process account concerned. This method is used where volume of production and factory overhead remain constant over a period of time. Common items of overhead such as head office cost, salary of executives, maintenance cost, indirect materials, indirect expenses such as heating, lighting, taxes, rent, etc. are apportioned to all the processes. Other expenses such as power, process steam, compressed air etc. are apportioned to the process concerned.

ADVANTAGES AND DISADVANTAGES OF PROCESS COSTING

The following are the advantages of process costing :

1. When standard costing is in operation, it is possible to find out cost of production periodically by using predetermined rates of material, labour cost, and overheads.
2. The accounting system is simpler and is less expensive compared to job costing.
3. Control can be exercised through standard costing technique and it is possible to evaluate the performance of every process.
4. It is easy to quote tender price because of standardised process.
5. Because cost of production is ascertained periodically, management is in a position to receive various reports periodically and review the progress and efficiency of the production process.

The following are the disadvantages of process costing :

1. When costs are recorded at the end of the period, it is not possible to exercise control over costs.
2. It is difficult to value work-in-progress.
3. It is difficult to value losses, wastes and scraps.
4. It is difficult to apportion total cost among joint products and by-products.
5. Cost of production obtained under process costing is only average cost. Hence cost of production is inaccurate. This makes measurement of efficiency difficult.
6. It involves difficulty in ascertaining closing stock value when output of one process is transferred to another process at transfer price or market price.

COSTING PROCEDURE INVOLVED IN PROCESS COSTING

Costing procedure aims at :

1. Accumulation and apportionment of service department expenses.
2. Computation of cost of production of each process at the end of a given period.
3. Transfer of costs from process to process.
4. Valuation of closing stock of work-in-progress.

The following procedure is involved in a process costing method :

1. Each process is separately identified and named and numbered and a separate account is opened for each process.
2. The various elements of cost are recorded in respect of each and every process.
3. Output of every process is recorded in convenient units such as kilogram, tonne, litre etc. on a periodical basis such as daily, weekly, monthly depending upon processing time.
4. The cost per unit in every process is calculated by dividing the net cost by goods units manufactured.
5. Incomplete units at the end of every period in every process is converted in terms of completed units. The degree of completion serves as the basis for such conversion.

The various situations and problems encountered and the method of calculating cost in relation to each of the situation are outlined below :

1. Production involving two or more processes, in which case output of one process is transferred in full to the subsequent process.
2. Output of a process partly transferred to the next process and partly retained in stock.
3. Process consisting of fully completed opening and closing stock.
4. Process costing involving normal loss, abnormal loss, and abnormal gain.
5. Process consisting of partially completed closing stock (equivalent production) and may involve the following :
   (*a*) Normal loss, abnormal loss, and abnormal gain,
   (*b*) Partially completed opening stock,
   (*c*) Normal loss, abnormal loss, partially completed opening and closing stock.
6. Process costing involving joint products and byproducts. This is discussed separately in the next chapter.

Regarding the costing technique to be employed in process costing, standard costing can be conveniently applied because of production of uniform units. The standard cost can be set in respect of each process and compared with actual cost. This technique gives management an excellent measure of efficiency of production. Application of standard costing technique is widely practised by modern process industries.

Problem 1 (When the output of a process is fully transferred to subsequent process) : The manufacture of product *P. J* requires three distinct processes, numbered 1, 2 and 3. On completion, the product is passed from process 3 to finished stock. During May 1992, the following information was obtained in respect of the product :

	Process 1 (*Rs.*)	*Process 2* (*Rs.*)	*Process 3* (*Rs.*)
Direct materials	5,600	1,250	750
Direct labour	620	860	1,880
Direct expenses	800	200	

Production overhead incurred was Rs. 5,040 which is to be absorbed by processes on the basis of 150% of direct wages. Production during the period was 100 units. There was no stock of raw material or work-in-progress either at the beginning or end of the period. The output was sold for Rs. 20,000.

Prepare process cost accounts.

Solution :

Process 1 A/c

	Amount	*Cost per unit*		*Amount*	*Cost per unit*
To direct materials	5,600	56.00	By process 2 a/c	7,950	79.50
To direct labour	620	6.20			
To direct expenses	800	8.00			
To production overhead	930	9.30			
	7,950	79.50		7,950	79.50

Process 2 A/c

To process 1 A/c	7,950	79.50	By process 3 a/c	11,550	115.00
To direct materials	1,250	12.50			
To direct labour	860	8.60			
To direct expenses	200	2.00			
To production overhead	1,290	12.90			
	11,550	115.50		11,550	115.50

Process 3 A/c

To process 2 A/c	11,550	115.50	By Finished stock a/c	17,000	170.00
To direct materials	750	7.50			
To direct labour	1,880	18.80			
To production overhead	2,820	28.20			
	17,000	170.00		17,000	170.00

Finished stock A/c

By process 3 a/c	17,000	170	By sales	20,000	200
By P & L a/c–profit	3,000	30			
	20,000	200		20,000	200

Problem 2 (When output of one process is partially transferred to subsequent process and balance retained) : The Andhra Products Ltd., manufacture and sell their chemical produced by consecutive processes.

The product of the three processes are dealt with as under :

	Process I	*Process II*	*Process III*
Transferred to next process	$66\frac{2}{3}\%$	60%	
Transferred to warehouse for sales	$33\frac{1}{3}\%$	40%	100%

In each process, 4% of the total weight put in is lost and 6% is scrap, which from process *I* realise Rs. 6 per ton, from process *II* Rs. 10 per ton and from process *III* Rs. 12 per ton.

The following particulars relate to October 1989 :

Raw materials used :

Process *I*	2,800 tons at Rs. 40 per ton
Process *II*	320 tons at Rs. 64 per ton
Process *III*	2,520 tons at Rs. 28 per ton

Manufacturing wages and expenses

Process *I*	Rs. 20,608
Process *II*	Rs. 12,560
Process *III*	Rs. 11,580

Prepare process accounts.

(*Kakatiya University, B. Com., May 1992*)

Solution :

Process I A/c

	Qty.	*Amt.*		*Qty.*	*Amt.*
To raw materials	2,800	1,12,000	By loss in wt.	112	–
To wages & expenses		20,608	By sale of scrap	168	1,008
			By process *II* a/c	1,680	87,733
			By warehouse a/c	840	43,867
	2,800	1,32,608		2,800	1,32,608

Process II A/c

To process *I* a/c	1,680	87,733	By loss in wt.	80	
To materials	320	20,480	By sale of scrap	120	1,200
To wages & expenses		12,560	By process *III* a/c	1,080	71,743
			By warehouse a/c	720	47,830
	2,000	1,20,773		2,000	1,20,773

Process III A/c

To process *II* a/c	1,080	71,743	By loss in wt.	144	–
To raw materials	2,520	70,560	By sale of scrap	216	2,592
To wages & expenses		11,580	By finished stock a/c	3,240	1,51,291
	3,600	1,53,883		3,600	1,53,883

Problem 3 (When the output is mutually transferred between two processes) : In a chemical factory two process *A* and *B* are dependent on each other. The process *A* supplies 30% to *B* and the balance elsewhere. The process *B* supplies 25% to *A* and the balance elsewhere. Both transfers are of good materials and not of scraps. The expenditure incurred in two departments as recorded in accounts are *A* Rs. 1,22,000 and *B* Rs. 55,900.

Show how inputs in departments *A* and *B* are to be evaluated.

Solution :

Let x be the expenditure of process *A*

y be the expenditure of process *B*

Now, $x = 1{,}22{,}000 + 0.25\,y$

$y = 55{,}900 + 0.30\,x$

or $y = 5{,}900 + 0.30\,(1{,}22{,}000 + 0.25\,y)$

$$
\begin{aligned}
\text{or} \quad y &= 55{,}900 + 36{,}600 + 0.075\,y \\
\text{or} \quad y &- 0.075\,y = 55{,}900 + 36{,}600 \\
\text{or} \quad & 0.925\,y = 92{,}500 \\
y &= 1{,}00{,}000 \\
x &= 1{,}22{,}000 + \frac{1}{4} \text{ of } 1{,}00{,}000 \\
\text{or} \quad x &= 1{,}22{,}000 + 25{,}000 = 1{,}47{,}000
\end{aligned}
$$

Problem 4 (When part of output is transferred to next process and part of output is sold) : JAVA manufacturing co. supplies you the following information for the year ended 31st March, 1999

Particulars	*Process* A	B	C
Raw material introduced in the process (units)	12,000	2,440	2,600
Cost of Raw materials per unit (Rs.)	5	5	5
Direct wages (Rs.)	34,000	24,000	15,000
Production overheads (Rs.)	16,160	16,200	9,600
Normal loss (% on Number of units entering into the process having no realisable value)	4%	5%	3%
Wastage (% on number of units entering to the process having scrap value)	6%	5%	4%
Scrap value per unit of wastage (Rs.)	3	4	5
Output transferred to subsequent process	70%	60%	–
Output sold at the end of the process	30%	40%	100%
Selling price per unit of the output sold at the end of the process (Rs.)	12	16	17

You are required to prepare the process A, B and C accounts showing the profit earned at each process

(*University of Bombay. B. Com., October 1999*)

Solution :

Process 'A' A/c

	Qty.	*Amount*		*Qty.*	*Amount*
To Raw materials introduced	12,000	60,000	By normal loss $\frac{4}{100} \times 12{,}000$	480	–
To Direct wages		34,000			
To production overhead		16,160	By wastage $\frac{6}{100} \times 12{,}000$	720	2,160
			By output c/d @ Rs. 10 per unit	10,800	1,08,000
	12,000	1,10,160		12,000	1,10,160
To output b/d	10,800	1,08,000	By sales	3,240	38,880
To P & L a/c		6,480	By output transferred to process B	7,560	75,600
	10,800	1,14,480		10,800	1,14,480

$$\text{Cost per unit} = \frac{\text{Total Amount of Debit side} - \text{Scrap value}}{\text{Input Qty.} - \text{Normal loss} - \text{Wastage}}$$

$$= \frac{1,10,160 - 2,160}{12,000 - 480 - 720}$$

$$= \frac{1,08,000}{10,800} = \text{Rs. } 10$$

Process 'B' A/c

	Qty.	Amount		Qty.	Amount
To output from process 'A' a/c	7,560	75,600	By normal loss $\frac{5}{100} \times 10,000$	500	–
To materials introduced	2,440	12,200	By wastage $\frac{5}{100} \times 10,000$	500	2,000
To direct wages		24,000	By output c/d e Rs. 14 per unit	9,000	1,26,000
To production overhead		16,200			
	10,000	1,28,000		10,000	1,28,000
To output b/d	9,000	1,26,000	By sales	3600	57,600
To P & L a/c		7,200	By output transferred to process 'C' a/c	5400	75600
	9,000	1,33,200		9,000	1,33,200

$$\text{Cost per unit} = \frac{\text{Total cost of Debit side} - \text{Scrap Value}}{\text{Input Qty.} - \text{Normal loss} - \text{Wastage}}$$

$$= \frac{1,28,000 - 2,000}{10,000 - 500 - 500} = \frac{1,26,000}{9000} = \text{Rs. } 14$$

Process 'C' A/c

	Qty.	Amount		Qty.	Amount
To output from process 'B' A/c	5,400	75,600	By normal loss $\frac{3}{100} \times 8,000$	240	–
To materials introduced	2,600	13,000			
To direct wages	–	15,000	By wastage $\frac{4}{100} \times 8,000$	320	1600
To production overhead	–	9,600			
			By output c/d @ Rs. 15 per unit	7,440	1,11,600
	8,000	1,13,200		8,000	1,13,200
To output b/d	7,440	1,11,600	By sales	7,440	1,26,480
To P & L a/c		14,880			
	7,440	1,26,480		7,440	1,26,480

$$\text{Cost per unit} = \frac{\text{Total cost of Debit side} - \text{Scrap Value}}{\text{Input Qty.} - \text{Normal loss} - \text{Wastage}}$$

$$= \frac{1,13,200 - 1,600}{8,000 - 240 - 320}$$

$$= \frac{1,11,600}{7,440} = \text{Rs. } 15$$

Problem 5 : Ajay manufacturing Pvt. Ltd. Provides you the following data for the month of March 1998

Particulars	*Process* X	Y	Z
Basic raw materials introduced in the process (units)	6,000	1,220	1,300
Cost of basic raw material per unit (Rs.)	5	5	5
Labour charges (Rs.)	17,000	12,000	7500
Manufacturing overhead (Rs.)	8,080	8,100	4,800
Normal loss (% on number of units entering to the process, having no realisable value)	4%	5%	3%
Scrap (% on number of units entering to the process having scrap value)	6%	5%	4%
Scrap value per unit (Rs.)	3	4	5
Output sold at the end of the process	30%	40%	100%
Output transferred to next process	70%	60%	–
Selling price per unit of the output sold at the end of the process (Rs.)	12	16	17

You are required to prepare process accounts indicating clearly profit earned in each process.

(*University of Bombay, B. Com., April 1998*)

Solution :

Process 'X' A/c

	Qty.	*Amount*		*Qty.*	*Amount*
To raw materials	6,000	30,000	By normal loss	240	–
To labour charges		17,000	By scrap	360	1,080
To manufacturing overheads	–	8,080	By output c/d @ Rs. 10 per unit	5,400	54,000
	6,000	55,080		6,000	55,080
To output b/d	5,400	54,000	By sales	1,620	19,440
To P & L a/c	–	3,240	By process *y* a/c	3,780	37,800
	5,400	57,240		5,400	57,240

$$\text{Cost per unit} = \frac{\text{Total cost of debit side} - \text{Scrap value of net loss Qty.}}{\text{Total input Qty} - \text{Normal loss Qty.} - \text{Scrap units}}$$

$$= \frac{55,080 - 1,080}{6,000 - 240 - 360}$$

$$= \frac{54,000}{5,400} = 10 \text{ per unit}$$

Process Y A/c

	Qty.	*Amount*		*Qty.*	*Amount*
To process *x* a/c	3,780	37,800	By normal loss	250	–
To raw material	1,220	6,100	By scrap	250	1,000
To labour		12,000	By output c/d @ Rs. 14 per unit	4,500	63,000
To manufacturing overheads		8,100			
	5,000	64,000		5,000	64,000
To output b/d	4,500	63,000	By sales	1,800	28,800
To P & L a/c		3,600	By process Z a/c	2,700	37,800
	4,500	66,600		4,500	66,600

$$\text{Cost per unit} = \frac{\text{Total cost of debit side} - \text{Scrap value of net loss Qty.}}{\text{Total input Qty} - \text{Normal loss Qty.} - \text{Scrap units}}$$

$$= \frac{64,000 - 1,000}{5,000 - 250 - 250}$$

$$= \frac{63,000}{4,500} = \text{Rs. } 14 \text{ per unit}$$

Process Z a/c

	Qty.	Amount		Qty.	Amount
To process y a/c	2,700	37,800	By normal loss	120	–
To raw materials	1,300	6,500	By scrap	160	800
To labour charges	–	7,500	By output c/d @ Rs. 15 per unit	3,720	55,800
To manufacturing overheads	–	4,800			
	4,000	56,600		4,000	56,600
To output b/d	3,720	55,800	By sales	3,720	63,240
To P & L a/c		7,440			
	3,720	63,240		3,720	63,240

$$\text{Cost per unit} = \frac{\text{Total cost of debit side} - \text{Scrap value of net loss Qty.}}{\text{Total input Qty} - \text{Normal loss Qty.} - \text{Scrap units}}$$

$$= \frac{56,600 - 800}{4,000 - 120 - 160} = \frac{55,800}{3,720}$$

Rs. = 15 per unit

TREATMENT OF NORMAL LOSS, REJECTS AND RECTIFICATION, ABNORMAL LOSS AND ABNORMAL GAIN ACCOUNT

1. Normal Loss

The loss which is inherent in the production process and which cannot be controlled is known as normal loss. Because they are inherent in any production process they are capable of estimating in advance of production. The estimation is usually expressed as a certain percentage of input quantity. Normal loss may occur due to evaporation, shrinkage chemical reaction, moisture, withdrawal for test, or for sampling. Normal loss may take the form of (*a*) normal waste and (*b*) normal scrap.

Normal waste, according to Theodore Lang (*The Cost Accountants Hand Book*) refers to "that portion of a basic raw material lost in processing, having no recovery value". Scrap has been defined by Theodore Lang as "the incidental residue from certain types of manufacture usually of small amount and low value, recoverable without further processing". There are two points of differences between a waste and scrap. Firstly, waste, is invisible, whereas scrap is visible. Secondly, waste does not yield any income whereas scrap does.

Treatment of normal loss in process cost accounts : The cost of normal loss units will be charged to the good units manufactured. Thus the cost of good units is inflated to the extent of normal loss quantity. For example, if the total cost of processing 1,000 units is Rs. 5,400 the cost per unit would be Rs. 5.40. Suppose if wastage is 100 units, then the cost per good unit is Rs. 6 (5,400 ÷ 900). The increase in the unit cost due to normal waste is 0.60.

If the normal loss is in the form of scrap material such as metal turning or faulty parts, it may have a saleable value. The process account is to be credited with the saleable value, thereby reducing the cost of production to this extent.

2. Rejects and Rectification

The ICMA terminology defines rejects as "output units which fail to reach the required standard of quality or specification before despatch to customers or subsequent users".

The rejects may be reworked so as to meet the required standards. This is subject to the condition that the cost of such rectification does not exceed the additional value obtained from the sale proceeds of such rejects. Where cost of rectification is considered to be more, rejects can be sold as scrap and treated in the same manner as discussed under normal loss.

Treatment of rejects in process cost accounts : The cost incurred to the point of rejection is credited to the process account and a separate "rejects account is opened to which is debited with the cost incurred on such rejects". The "reject account" will also be debited with the rectification cost and is credited with its sale value.

3. Abnormal Loss Account

Losses which are incurred over and above normal loss is known as abnormal loss. Abnormal loss is incurred in abnormal conditions. So it is not possible to anticipate abnormal units in advance of production. Abnormal loss can be controlled by taking corrective steps. Some of the causes which gives rise to abnormal loss are use of sub-standard materials, carelessness and accidents, bad plant design, bad workmanship and so on.

Treatment of abnormal loss in process cost accounts : The treatment of abnormal loss differs from that of treatment of normal loss. Instead of charging the cost of abnormal loss units to good units manufactured, abnormal units have to bear the respective cost of production. The following formula is used to value abnormal loss units :

$$\frac{\text{Normal cost of normal output}}{\text{Normal output}} \times \text{abnormal loss units}$$

Problem 6 (Treatment of rejected units) : Ten units were rejected at the end of a process and unit cost in the process was calculated as Rs. 5. The management decided that four units should be rectified and sold at the normal price of Rs. 12 each, two items could be sold as "seconds" at Rs. 8 each and the remainder would be scrapped at nil value. Rectification costs amounted to Rs. 16.

Prepare rejects account.

Solution :

Rejects account

	Units	*Amt.*		*Units*	*Amt.*
To process a/c	10	50	By sale	4	48
To rectification cost		16	By sale as seconds	2	16
			By scrap	4	–
			By P & L a/c	–	2
	10	66		10	66

Abnormal loss

Problem 7 : Units of raw materials introduced	– 100 units
Rate per unit	– Rs. 10
Normal loss	– 10% of input
Sale of normal loss units	– Rs. 3 per unit
Output	– 75 unit

Wages incurred Rs. 600. Calculate the abnormal loss units and its value.

Solution :

Process a/c

	Units	*Amt.*		*Units*	*Amt.*
To raw materials	100	1,000	By normal loss	10	30
To wages		600	By abnormal loss	15	262
			By output of the process	75	1,308
	100	1,600		100	1,600

Working Note :

Normal cost of normal output = 1,600 – 30 = Rs. 1,570

Normal output :

Units introduced	100
Less : Normal loss units	10
	90 units

Abnormal loss units :

Normal output	90
Less : Actual output	75
	15 units

$$\text{Value of abnormal loss units} = \frac{\text{Normal cost of normal output}}{\text{Normal output}} \times \text{abnormal loss units}$$

$$= \frac{1,570}{90} \times 15 = \text{Rs. 262 App.}$$

4. Abnormal Gain

It was referred earlier that normal loss units are estimated on the basis of past experience. Sometimes the normal loss actually incurred may be less than anticipated loss. This results in abnormal gain or abnormal effectiveness or abnormal efficiency. Abnormal gain can also be considered as the difference between actual units produced and expected units.

Treatment in process cost accounts : The value of abnormal gain is debited to the process account from which it originated. A separate abnormal gain account is opened and the corresponding credit is given to this account. The sale of abnormal gain is utilised to reduce the cost of normal loss units. This is so because abnormal gain is the difference between actual normal loss and anticipated normal loss. Thus in effect the normal loss is set off against abnormal gain by debiting abnormal gain a/c.

Problem 8 (Calculation of abnormal gain) : From the following data compute abnormal gain and prepare process account :

Input quantity in process *A*	–	1,000 kg
Total cost incurred in process *A*	–	Rs. 10,000
Output expected	–	900 kgs
Actual output	–	920 kgs
Sale of scraps	–	Rs. 2 per kg.

Solution :

Process A a/c

	Qty.	*Amt.*		*Qty.*	*Amt.*
To input	1,000	10,000	By normal loss	100	200
To abnormal gain	20	218	By output	920	10,018
	1,020	10,218		1,020	10,218

Abnormal gain a/c

To scrap not relised 20 units @ Rs. 2	40	By process a/c	218
To P & L a/c	178		
	218		218

Working Note : Calculation of abnormal gain units and its value.

	Units	Rs.
Input	1,000	10,000
Less : Normal loss	100	200
Output expected	900	9,800
Abnormal gain $\frac{9,800}{900} = 10.89$		
20 Units @ Rs. 10.89	20	218
Actual production	920	10,018

Problem 9 : The following information is available in respect of process *B* of Product *X*.

Input	5,000 units at a cost of Rs. 25,000
Process material added	Rs. 12,000
Direct labour	Rs. 8,000
Overheads	Rs. 3,000
Output of process B	4,800 units
Normal wastage	5% of input
Scrap value of wastage	Rs. 2 per unit
Prepare process B account	

(*Delhi University, B.Com. (Pass), April 1991*)

Solution :

Process B A/c

	Qty.	Amt.		Qty.	Amt.
To input	5,000	25,000	By normal wastage	250	500
To process material		12,000	By output of process	4,800	48,000
To direct labour		8,000			
To overheads		3,000			
To abnormal gain	50	500			
	5,050	48,500		5,050	48,500

Working Note : Calculation of abnormal gain

Input	5,000	Rs. 48,000
Less : Normal loss	250	Rs. 500
	4,750	47,500

$$\frac{47,500}{4,750} \times 50 = \text{Rs. } 500$$

Problem 10 (Normal loss, Abnormal loss and Abnormal gain) : A product passes through two processes A and B prepare the process accounts from the following :

	Process A	*Process B*
10,000 units introduced at cost (Rs.)	20,000	–
Materials consumed (Rs.)	24,000	12,000
Direct labour (Rs.)	28,000	16,000
Manufacturing expenses (Rs.)	8,000	8,566
Normal wastage on input	5%	10%

Scrap value of normal wastage (Rs. per 100 units)	40	50
Output (units)	9,400	8,500

Also prepare the Abnormal wastage/effectives account, as the case may be, with each process account

(C.S. Inter., Dec. 1999)

Solution :

Process A A/c

	Qty.	*Amt.*		*Qty.*	*Amt.*
To cost of Input	10,000	20,000	By normal loss a/c	500	200
To materials		24,000	By Abnormal wastage a/c	100	840
To direct labour		28,000	By process B a/c	9,400	78,960
To manufacturing expenses		8,000			
	10,000	80,000		10,000	80,000

$$\text{Cost per unit} = \frac{\text{Total cost of debit side} - \text{Scrap value of normal loss units}}{\text{Total input Qty} - \text{Normal loss units}}$$

$$= \frac{80,000 - 200}{10,000 - 500} = \frac{79,800}{9,500} = 8.40$$

Cost of Abnormal wastage = 100 × 8.4 = 840

Process 'B' a/c

	Qty.	*Amt.*		*Qty.*	*Amt.*
To process 'A' a/c	9,400	78,960	By normal loss	940	470
To materials		12,000	By finished stock a/c	8,500	1,15,600
To direct labour		16,000			
To manufacturing expenses		8,566			
To Abnormal effectives	40	544			
	9,440	1,16,070		9,440	1,16,070

$$\text{Cost per unit (good units)} = \frac{\text{Cost of production} - \text{Sale value of normal loss units}}{\text{Input Qty.} - \text{Normal loss units}}$$

$$= \frac{1,15,526 - 470}{9,400 - 940}$$

$$= \frac{1,15,056}{8,460} = 13.60$$

Cost of Abnormal effectives = 40 × 13.60 = Rs. 544

Normal loss A/c

	Qty.	*Amt.*		*Qty.*	*Amt.*
To process 'A' A/c	500	200	By sale of normal loss :–		
To process 'B' a/c	940	470	Process A	500	200
			Process B	900	450
			By Abnormal effectives	40	20
	1,440	670		1440	670

Abnormal Wastage A/c

To process 'A' a/c	100	840	By sales	100	40
			By P & L a/c	–	800
	100	840		100	840

Abnormal Effectives A/c

	Qty.	Amount		Qty.	Amount
To normal loss a/c	40	20	By process B a/c	40	544
To P & L a/c	–	524			
	40	544		40	544

Problem 11 : Product 'A' is obtained after it is processed through process X, Y and Z. The following cost information is available for the month ended 31st March 1999

Particulars	*Processes* X	Y	Z
Number of units introduced in the process	500	–	–
Rate per unit of units introduced (Rs.)	4	–	–
Cost of materials	2,600	2,000	1,025
Direct wages	2,250	3,680	1,400
Production overheads	2,250	3,680	1,400
Normal loss (% on units introduced in each process i.e., input)	10%	20%	25%
Value of scrap per unit	2	4	5
Output in units	450	340	270

There is no stock in any process. You are required to prepare :–

(1) The Process Accounts

(2) The abnormal loss and Abnormal gain a/c (*University of Bombay, B. Com., April 1999*)

Solution :

Process x A/c

	Qty.	*Amount*		*Qty.*	*Amount*
To input	500	2,000	By normal loss	50	100
To materials		2,600	By process y a/c	450	9,000
To direct wages		2,250			
To production overheads		2,250			
	500	9,100		500	9,100

$$\text{Cost per unit} = \frac{\text{Total cost of debit side} - \text{Scrap value of normal loss Qty.}}{\text{Input Qty} - \text{Normal loss units}} = \frac{9100-100}{500-50} = 20$$

Process 'Y' A/c

	Qty.	*Amount*		*Qty.*	*Amount*
To process 'x' a/c	450	9,000	By normal loss	90	360
To material		2,000	By abnormal loss	20	1,000
To direct wages		3,680	By process z a/c		
To production overhead		3,680	@ Rs. 50 per unit	340	17,000
	450	18,360		450	18,360

$$\text{Cost per unit} = \frac{\text{Total cost of debit side} - \text{Scrap value of normal loss Qty.}}{\text{Input Qty} - \text{Normal loss units}}$$

$$= \frac{18,360-360}{450-90} = \frac{18,000}{360} = \text{Rs. } 50$$

Process 'Z' A/c

	Qty.	Amount		Qty.	Amt.
To process 'y' a/c	340	17,000	By normal Loss	85	425
To materials		1,025	By finished stock	270	21,600
To direct wages		1,400	@ Rs. 80 per unit		
To production overhead		1,400			
To abnormal gain	15	1,200			
	355	22,025		355	22,025

$$\text{Cost per unit} = \frac{20,825-425}{340-85} = \text{Rs. } 80$$

Normal loss A/c

	Qty.	Amt.		Qty.	Amt.
To process A a/c	50	100	By sale of normal loss		
To process B a/c	90	360	units :–		
To process C a/c	85	425	process A	50	100
			process B	90	360
			process C	70	350
			By abnormal Gain a/c	15	75
	225	885		225	885

Abnormal loss A/c

	Qty.	Amt.		Qty.	Amt.
To process 'y' a/c	20	1,000	By sale	20	80
			By P & L a/c		920
	20	1,000		20	1,000

Abnormal Gain a/c

To normal loss a/c	15	75	By process z a/c	15	1,200
To P & L a/c		1,125			
	15	1,200		15	1,200

Problem 12 : A product is manufactured by passing through three processes A, B and C. In process C, a by-product is also produced which is then transferred to process D where it is completed. For the first week in January, the actual data included :

	Process A	B	C	D
Normal loss of input (%)	5	10	5	10
Scrap value (Rs. per unit)	1.50	2	4	2
Estimated sale value of by-product (Rs. per unit)	–	–	8	–
Output (units)	5,760	5,100	4,370	–
Output of by-products (units)	–	–	510	450
Direct Materials (6,000 units) (Rs.)	12,000	–	–	–
Direct materials added in process (Rs.)	5,000	9,000	4,000	220
Direct wages (Rs.)	4,000	6,000	2,000	200
Direct expenses (Rs.)	800	1,680	2,260	151

Budgeted production overhead (based on direct wages) for the week is Rs. 30,500

Budgeted direct wages for the week is Rs. 12,200. You are required to prepare

(1) Accounts for processes A, B, C and D

(2) Abnormal loss and Abnormal gain accounts. (*C.S. Inter., June 2,000*)

Solution :

Process 'A' A/c

	Qty.	*Amount*		*Qty.*	*Amount*
To input	6,000	12,000	By normal loss	300	450
To direct materials		5,000	By process 'B' a/c		
To direct wages		4,000	@ Rs. 5.50 per unit	5,760	31,680
To direct expenses		800			
To production overhead (250% of Direct wages)		10,000			
To Abnormal gain @ Rs. 5.50 per unit	60	330			
	6,060	32,130		6,060	32,130

Working Notes :

(1) Calculation of production overhead

$$\frac{30,500}{12,200} \times 100 \qquad = 250\%$$

(2) Calculation of cost per unit

$$\frac{31,800 - 450}{6000 - 300} = \frac{31,350}{5,700} = \text{Rs. } 5.50$$

Process 'B' A/c

	Qty.	*Amount*		*Qty.*	*Amount*
To process 'A' a/c	5,760	31,680	By normal loss	576	1,152
To direct material cost		9,000	By abnormal loss	84	1,008
To direct wages		6,000	By process 'C' a/c	5,100	61,200
To direct expenses	–	1,680			
To production overhead	–	15,000			
	5,760	63,360		5,760	63,360

$$\text{Cost per unit} = \frac{63,360 - 1,152}{5,760 - 576} = \frac{62,208}{5,184} = \text{Rs. } 12$$

Process 'C' A/c

	Qty.	*Amount*		*Qty.*	*Amount*
To process 'B' a/c	5,100	61,200	By normal loss	255	1,020
To direct material		4,000	By finished goods	4,370	69,920
To direct wages		2,000	@ Rs. 16		
To direct expenses		2,260	By process D a/c	510	4080
To production overhead		5,000			
To Abnormal gain	35	560			
	5,135	75,020		5,135	75,020

$$\text{Cost per unit} = \frac{74,460 - 1,020 - 4,080}{5,100 - 255 - 510}$$

$$= \frac{69,360}{4,335} = \text{Rs. } 16$$

Process 'D' A/c

	Qty.	Amount		Qty.	Amount
To process 'C' A/c	510	4,080	By normal loss	51	102
To direct materials	–	220	By finished goods	450	4,950
To direct wages	–	200	By abnormal loss	9	99
To direct expenses	–	151			
To production oh	–	500			
	510	5,151		510	5,151

$$\text{Cost per unit} = \frac{5{,}151-102}{510-51} = \frac{5{,}049}{459} = \text{Rs. } 11$$

Abnormal loss A/c

	Qty.	Amt.		Qty.	Amt.
To process B a/c	84	1,008	By sales	84	168
To process D a/c	9	99	By sales	9	18
			By P & L a/c	–	921
	93	1,107		93	1,107

Abnormal Gain a/c

	Qty.	Amt.		Qty.	Amt.
To normal loss a/c	60	90	By process A A/c	60	330
To normal loss a/c	35	140	By process C A/c	35	560
To P & L a/c		660			
	95	890		95	890

Problem 13 (Calculation of normal loss units) : The following data are available pertaining to a product after passing through two processes A and B.

Output transferred to process C from process B – 9,120 units for Rs. 49,263.

Expenses incurred in process C :–

Sundry materials	Rs. 1,480
Direct labour	Rs. 6,500
Direct expenses	Rs. 1,605

The wastage of process C is sold at Re. 1.00 per unit. The overhead charges were 168% of direct labour. The final product was sold at Rs. 10 per unit fetching a profit of 20% on sales.

Find the percentage of wastage in process C and prepare process C account

(University of Delhi, B. Com., (Hons.) April 1999)

Solution :

Process 'C' A/c

	Qty.	Amt.		Qty.	Amt.
To process B	9,120	49,263	By normal loss	456	456
To sundry materials		1,480	By finished goods a/c	8,664	69,312
To Direct labour		6,500			
To Direct expenses		1,605			
To overhead		10,920			
	9,120	69,768		9,120	69,768

Working Note :

Calculation of normal loss units

Let normal loss units : x

No. of units of finished product = $9{,}120 - x$

Value of normal loss @ Re. 1 per unit = $1x$

Cost of finished goods per unit = 10 – 20%
Rs. = 8

Cost of finished goods = (9,120 – x) Rs. 8
i.e., cost per unit × No. of units produced = 72,960 – 8x
Total cost of process C = 69,768 – 1x

or = $69{,}768 - 1x = 72{,}960 - 8x$

or $8x - 1x = 72{,}960 - 69{,}768$

$7x = 3{,}192$

$$x = \frac{3{,}192}{7} = 456$$

% of normal loss in process C

$$\frac{456}{9{,}120} \times 100 = 5\%$$

Finished goods units = 9,126 – 456
= 8,664 units

Cost of finished goods = 8,664 × Rs. 8
= 69,312

Problem 14 (Process cost accounts with stock) : The product manufactured by the standard chemicals Ltd. passes through three processes I, II and III. The following costs have been incurred for the month of September 96

Details	*Process 1*	*Process II*	*Process III*
Rs.	*Rs.*	*Rs.*	
(1) Materials consumed	40,000	7,500	5,000
(2) Direct wages	22,500	10,000	10,000
(3) Direct expenses	20,500	2,250	2,505
Total Rs.	83,000	19,750	17,505
	Units	*Units*	*Units*
(4) Output	3,900	3,850	3,200
(5) Finished process stock			
(*i*) 1-9-1996	600	550	800
(*ii*) 30-9-1996	500	800	Nil
(6) Stock valuation on 1-9-96 (Rs. per unit)	24.50	31	37
(7) Percentage of wastage	2	5	10
(8) Net realisable value of wastage per unit (Rs.)	13.50	16.25	21

4,000 units of raw materials were introduced in process. No I at a cost of Rs. 20,000.

Stocks are valued and transferred to subsequent processes at weighted average cost. The percentage of wastage is computed on the number of units entering the process concerned.

Prepare (*i*) Process a/c s (*ii*) Process stocks a/c s (*iii*) Normal wastage a/c (*iv*) Abnormal wastage/Effective a/c.

(*University of Delhi, B. Com.,(Hons.) April 1997*)

Solution :

Process I A/c

	Qty.	*Amount*		*Qty.*	*Amt.*
To units introduced	4,000	20,000	By normal wastage @ Rs. 13.50	80	1,080
To total cost		83,000	By abnormal wastage @ Rs. 26	20	520
			By process I stock a/c @ Rs. 26 per unit	3,900	1,01,400
	4,000	1,03,000		4,000	1,03,000

Process I stock a/c

To opening balance @ Rs. 24.50	600	14,700	By process II A/c @ 25.80	4,000	1,03,200
To process A a/c	3,900	1,01,400	By balance c/d	500	12,900
	4,500	1,16,100		4,500	1,16,100

Cost per unit $\frac{1,03,000-1,080}{4,000-80} = 26$

Weighted Average Rate = $\frac{1,16,100}{4,500} = 25.80$

Process II A/c

	Qty.	Amt.		Qty.	Amt.
To process I stock a/c	4,000	1,03,200	By normal wastage @ 16.25 per unit	200	3,250
To total cost		19,750			
To Abnormal effectives	50	1,575	By process II stock a/c @ 31.50 per unit	3,850	1,21,275
	4,050	1,24,525		4,050	1,24,525

Process II stock a/c

To balance b/d @ Rs. 31 per unit	550	17,050	By process III A/c @ Rs. 31.44 per unit	3,600	1,13,175
To process II A/c	3,850	1,21,275	By Balance c/d	800	25,150
	4,400	1,38,325		4,400	1,38,325

Cost per unit $= \frac{1,22,950-3,250}{4,000-200} = \frac{1,19,700}{3,800} = 31.50$

Weighted average rate $= \frac{1,38,325}{4,400} = 31.44$

Process III A/c

	Qty.	Amount		Qty.	Amount
To process II stock a/c	3,600	1,13,175	By normal wastage @ Rs. 21 per unit	360	7,560
To total cost		17,505	By abnormal wastage @ Rs. 38	40	1,520
			By process III stock a/c	3,200	1,21,600
	3,600	1,30,680		3,600	1,30,680

Process III stock a/c

To balance b/d	800	29,600	To cost of – goods sold	4,000	1,51,200
To process III a/c	3,200	1,21,600			
	4,000	1,51,200		4,000	1,51,200

Cost per unit $= \frac{1,30,680-7,560}{3,600-360} = \frac{1,23,120}{3,240} = 38$

Abnormal Effectives A/c

	Qty.	Amt.		Qty.	Amt.
To normal wastage a/c	50	812.50	By process II A/c	50	1,575
To P & L a/c		762.50			
	50	1,575		50	1,575

Normal wastage A/c

	Qty.	Amt.		Qty.	Amt.
To process I A/c	80	1,080	By process I A/c	80	1080
To process II A/c	200	3,250	By process II A/c	150	2437.50
To process III A/c	360	7,560	By process III A/c	360	7560
			By Abnormal effectives a/c	50	812.50
	640	11,890		640	11,890

Abnormal wastage a/c

	Qty.	Amt.		Qty.	Amt.
To process I A/c	20	520	By sales	60	1,110
To process II A/c	40	1,520	By P & L a/c		930
	60	2,040		60	2,040

Problem 15 : Satyug Times Ltd. submits the following information in respect of its product which passes through three consecutive process, *viz.*, Ingestion process, Digestion process and Assimilation process, for the month ended 31st Jan. 1997

Particulars		*Ingestion process*	*Digestion process*	*Assimilation process*
Quantitative information (kgs)				
Basic Raw Material @ Rs. 40 per kg.		80,000	–	–
Normal yield		80%	60%	50%
Output during the month		62,000	36,000	21,000
Stock of process output				
31-12-1996		8,000	8,000	5,000
31-1-1997		10,000	4,000	4,000
Other additional information :–				
Process material	Rs.	3,45,000	8,26,000	6,17,000
Labour man-days		2,400	1,500	1,000
Labour rate per man-day	Rs.	80	100	150
Machine overheads		60% of wages	50% of process material	Rs. 2,34,000
Other manufacturing overheads	Rs.	2,75,800	1,63,000	1,27,000
Value of opening stock per kg.	Rs.	60	140	300
Scrap value per kg.	Rs.	10	15	20
Sale price per unit of finished stock		–	–	350

(*University of Bombay, B. Com., October 1997*)

Ingestion process A/c

	Qty.	Amt.		Qty.	Amt.
To materials introduced	80,000	32,00,000	By normal loss	16,000	1,60,000
To process materials	–	3,45,000	By abnormal loss	2,000	1,24,000

	Qty.	Amount		Qty.	Amount
To labour	–	1,92,000	By process stock @ Rs. 62 per unit	62,000	38,44,000
To machine overhead	–	1,15,200			
To manufacturing overhead	–	2,75,800			
	80,000	41,28,000		80,000	41,28,000

Process stock a/c

	Qty.	Amt.		Qty.	Amt.
To balance b/d	8,000	4,80,000	By digestion process	60,000	37,04,000
To ingestion process a/c	62,000	38,44,000	By balance c/d	10,000	6,20,000
	70,000	43,24,000		70,000	43,24,000

$$\text{Cost per unit} = \frac{41,28000 - 1,60,000}{80,000 - 16,000} = \text{Rs. } 62$$

Digestion process A/c

	Qty.	Amount		Qty.	Amount
To Ingestion process stock a/c	60,000	37,04,000	By normal loss	24,000	3,60,000
To process materials		8,26,000	By process stock a/c @ 136 per unit	36,000	48,96,000
To labour		1,50,000			
To machine overhead	–	4,13,000			
To manufacturing overhead	–	1,63,000			
	60,000	52,56,000		60,000	52,56,000

Process stock a/c

	Qty.	Amount		Qty.	Amount
To balance b/d	8,000	11,20,000	By assimilation	40,000	54,72,000
To digestion process a/c	36,000	48,96,000	By balance c/d	4,000	5,44,000
	44,000	60,16,000		44,000	60,16,000

$$\text{Cost per unit} = \frac{52,56,000 - 3,60,000}{60,000 - 24,000} = \text{Rs. } 136$$

Assimilation process A/c

	Qty.	Amount		Qty.	Amount
To digestion process stock a/c	40,000	54,72,000	By normal loss	20,000	4,00,000
To process materials	–	6,17,000	By process stock a/c @ Rs. 310 per unit	21,000	65,10,000
To labour	–	1,50,000			
To machine overhead	–	2,34,000			
To other manufacturing overheads	–	1,27,000			
To abnormal gain	1,000	3,10,000			
	41,000	69,10,000		41,000	69,10,000

Process stock a/c

	Qty.	Amount		Qty.	Amount
To balance b/d	5,000	15,00,000	By sales	22,000	77,00,000
To assimilation process a/c	21,000	65,10,000	By Balance c/d	4,000	12,40,000
To P & L a/c	–	9,30,000			
	26,000	89,40,000		26,000	89,40,000

$$\text{Cost per unit} = \frac{66,00,000 - 4,00,000}{40,000 - 20,000} = \text{Rs. } 310$$

Normal loss a/c

	Qty.	Amt.		Qty.	Amt.
To ingestion process a/c	16,000	1,60,000	By sale :–		
			Ingestion process	16,000	1,60,000
To digestion process a/c	24,000	3,60,000	Digestion process	24,000	3,60,000
To assimilation process a/c	20,000	4,00,000	Assimilation process	19,000	3,80,000
			By abnormal gain a/c	1,000	20,000
	60,000	9,20,000		60,000	9,20,000

Abnormal loss A/c

To ingestion process a/c	2,000	1,24,000	By sales	2,000	20,000
			By P & L a/c	–	1,04,000
	2,000	1,24,000		2,000	1,24,000

Abnormal gain a/c

To normal loss a/c	1,000	20,000	By Assimilation process a/c	1,000	3,10,000
To P & L a/c		2,90,000			
	1,000	3,10,000		1,000	3,10,000

P & L a/c

To abnormal loss a/c	1,04,000	By abnormal Gain a/c	2,90,000
To net profit	11,16,000	By assimilation stock a/c	9,30,000
	12,20,000		12,20,000

Working Note :

Calculation of Abnormal loss/Gain

	Ingestion process	*Digestion process*	*Assimilation process*
Materials introduced	80,000	60,000	40,000
Less : Normal loss	16,000	24,000	20,000
	64,000	36,000	20,000
Less : Actual output	62,000	36,000	21,000
Abnormal loss/Gain	(–) 2,000	Nil	(+) 1,000

Problem 16 (Calculation of input quantity) : Find out the number of units initially introduced in process I when normal wastage is 10%, 5% and 8% of the input respectively. There are 3,933 units of finished stock. There was no Abnormal loss or Effectives in any of the process.

(University of Delhi, B. Com,(Pass) April 97)

Solution :

Let output quantity = 100 units

Wastage is the difference between units introduced and units produced wastage is 10%, 5%, and 8% in three processes. So input is calculated as follows :

	Let the units introduced =	100
Less :	Wastage 10% (process I)	10
	Final units in process I	90
Less :	Wastage 5% (process II)	4.5
	Final units in process II	85.50
Less :	Wastage 8% (process III)	6.84
	Final units	78.66

For 78.66 Finished stock : The actual output is 3,933

For 100 → $\frac{3,933 \times 100}{7,866}$ = 5,000 units

So, 5,000 units must have been initially introduced.

Problem 17 (Calculation of initial input when final output is given) : An article passes through three successive operations from the materil to the finished product stage. The following data are available from the production records of a particular month :

Operation No.	*No. of pieces input*	*No. of pieces rejected*	*No. of pieces output*
1	60,000	20,000	40,000
2	66,000	6,000	60,000
3	48,000	8,000	40,000

(*i*) Determine the input required to be introduced in the first operation in number of pieces in order to obtain finished output of 100 pieces after the last operation.

(*ii*) Calculate the cost of raw materials required to produce one piece of finished product, given the following : weight of the finished price is 0.10 kg. and the price of raw materials is Rs. 20 per kg.

(*CA, Inter, May 1982*)

Solution :

(i) Statement of input rejection and output

Operation No.	*Input No.*	*Rejections No.*	*Output No.*	*Rejection as % of output*
1	60,000	20,000	40,000	50%
2	66,000	6,000	6,000	10%
3	48,000	8,000	40,000	20%

The input required to be indtroduced in the first operation for finished output of 100 pieces will be as follows :

Output of operation No. 3	100
Add : Rejection of operation No. 3 on output 20%	20
Output of operation No. 2	120
Add : Rejection on output (10%)	12
Output of operation No. 1	132
Add : Rejcetions on output (50%)	66
Input at the beginning of operation No. 1	198

So, for an output of 100 pieces, an input of 198 pieces are required

(*ii*) Input of raw materials required for one finished piece will be as follows :

$$\frac{0.10 \text{ kg} \times 198}{100} = 0.198 \text{ kg.}$$

∴ Cost of raw materials @ Rs. 20 per kg. for 0.198 kg. = Rs. 3.96 per finished piece.

Problem 18 : In a manufacturing unit, raw materials passes four processes *I, II, III* and *IV* and the output of each process is the input of the subsequent process. The loss in the four process, *I, II, III* and *IV* are respectively 25%, 20%, 20%, $16\frac{2}{3}$% and of the input. If the end product at the end of process *IV* is 40,000 kg., what is the quantity of raw materials required to be fed at the beginning of process *I* and the cost of same at Rs. per kg.

Find out also the effect of increase and decrease in the material cost of the end product for variation of every rupee in the cost of the raw material.

Solution : Let the weight of input in process *I* be 100 units.

Statement showing input loss and output

Process	*Input*	*Loss*	*Output*
I	100	25	75
II	75	15	60
III	60	12	48
IV	48	8	40

For 40 kg. output : the end product actual is 40,000

For 100 kg. → ? $\frac{40,000 \times 100}{40} = 1,00,000$ kg.

Total cost of materials is 1,00,000 × Rs. 5 = Rs. 5,00,000

$$\text{Cost per unit} = \frac{5,00,000}{40,000} = \text{Rs. } 12.50$$

For an increase in the material cost :

In case the raw materials cost increases by Re. one

Now the total cost= 5,00,000 + 100,000 = 6,00,000

$$\text{Cost per kg. of final product } \frac{6,00,000}{40,000} = \text{Rs. } 15$$

In case the raw materials cost decreases by Re. one

5,00,000 – 1,00,000 = 4,00,000

$$\text{Cost per kg. of final product } \frac{4,00,000}{40,000} = \text{Rs. } 10$$

Problem 19 (Process costing as applied to oil manufacturing company) : The following details are extracted from the costing records of Parachut Cocount Oil Mills for the year ended 31st March 1993 :

Purchase of 500 kgs. of copra Rs. 2,00,000

The production of oil was undertaken in the following three process :

	Crushing	*Refining*	*Finishing*
	Rs.	*Rs.*	*Rs.*
Wages	2,500	1,000	1,500
Electric power	600	360	240
Sundry materials	100	2,000	–
Repairs to machinery	280	330	140
Steam	600	450	450
Factory expenses	1,320	660	220

Cost of casks Rs. 7,500.

300 tons of crude oil were produced.

250 tons of oil were produced from the refining process.

248 tons of refined oil were finished for delivery.

Copra sacks sold Rs. 400.

175 tons of copra residue were sold for Rs. 11,000.

Loss in weight in crushing 25 tons.

45 tons of by-products obtained from refining process realised Rs. 6,750. The entire output of finished oil was sold for Rs. 2,50,000.

You are required to show the account in respect of each of the following stages of manufacture for the purpose of arriving at the cost per ton of each process and the total cost per ton of finished oil :

(*a*) Copra crushing process, (*b*) Refining process, (*c*) Finishing process including casking.

Solution :

Copra crushing process

	Qty.	*Amt.*		*Qty.*	*Amt.*
To copra used	500	2,00,000	By sale of sacks	–	400
To labour		2,500	By sales of copra residue	175	11,000

To electric power		600	By loss in weight	25	–
To sundry materials		100	By refining process a/c	300	1,94,000
To repairs to machinery		280			
To steam		600			
To factory expenses		1,320			
	500	2,05,400		500	2,05,400

Refining process

To crushing process a/c	300	1,94,000	By sale of by-product	45	6,750
To labour		1,000	By loss in weight	5	–
To electric power		360	By finished process	250	1,92,050
To sundry materials		2,000			
To repairs to machinery		330			
To steam		450			
To factory expenses		660			
	300	1,98,800		300	1,98,800

Finishing process

To refining process	250	1,92,050	By loss in weight	2	–
To labour		1,500	By finished stock a/c	248	1,94,600
To power		240			
To repair to machinery		140			
To steam		450			
To factory expenses		220			
	250	1,95,600		250	1,94,600

Finishing stock A/c

To finishing process a/c	248	1,94,600	By sales	248	2,50,000
To cost of casks		7,500			
To profit & loss a/c		47,900			
	248	2,50,000		248	2,50,000

INTER-PROCESS PROFIT

In some process costing industries, the management may decide not to transfer the output of a process to other process at cost price but at market price. The market price may relate to current market price prevailing in the market or determined by fixing a margin of profit. The market price is also known as transfer price. The ICMA terminology defines transfer price as 'a price related to goods or other benefits transferred from one process or department to another or from one member of a group to another. The extent to which costs and profit are recovered by the price is a matter of policy. The difference between the transfer price and the cost price is known as inter-process profit.

The output of one process is transferred to a subsequent process at transfer price with two objects. Firstly, to know efficiency of one company's production process with other company's production process. This is possible by comparing the cost of production with the sale price of similar products in the market. Secondly, to enable each process to achieve its own economy and efficiency but not to depend upon the efficiency of preceding process. This is possible by way of transferring the output of transfer process to the transferee process at market price. The input of every process is charged at current market price. Hence, no process will derive any benefit of efficiency or penalised by the variation in the cost. This facilitates timely action to be taken on those processes where true profit is inadequate.

Advantages of Transferring Output at Market Price

1. Comparison of cost of output with market price at each and every process helps in evaluating efficiency or otherwise of the process.
2. It helps in make or buy decision. When the cost of production is higher as compared to market price, it can well be bought rather than to manufacture.
3. The true profit or loss of each process can be ascertained and appropriate action can be taken if profit of any process is inefficient.

Disadvantages

1. It is necessary to adjust closing stock value so as to get cost price of stock. This is because closing stock is valued in the balance sheet at cost price.
2. If the adjustment is not effected in the closing stock, such valuation is not accepted by auditor and tax authorities.
3. The method involves additional clerical work by way of calculationg transfer price and subsequently ascertaining cost price of stock.

Problem 20 : *A* Product passes through three process *A*, *B* and *C*. The output of process *A* and process *B* is charged to next process at a price calculated to give a profit of $16\frac{2}{3}$% on transfer price while the output process *C* is charged to the finished stock accout at a profit of $13\frac{1}{3}$% on the transfer price.

From the following particulars, parepare the process cost accounts and calculate the amount of reserve that should be made in respect of the stock in hand :

	Process A *Rs.*	*Process B* *Rs.*	*Process C* *Rs.*
Material & labour	7,000	2,800	4,800
Closing stock	2,000	2,800	2,000

There was no stock in hand at the beginning of the period and the question of oncost has been ignored. The closing stocks are valued at prime cost in each process. (*Univeresity of Kerala, M.Com., May 1992*)

Solution :

Process A A/c

	Total	*Cost*	*Profit*		*Total*	*Cost*	*Profit*
To materials and labour	7,000	7,000	–	By process B a/c	6,000	5,000	1,000
Less : Closing stock	2,000	2,000	–				
Prime cost	5,000	5,000	–				
To profit @ $16\frac{2}{3}$ on tranfer price	1,000	–	1,000				
	6,000	5,000	1,000		6,000	5,000	1,000

Process B A/c

To process *A* a/c	6,000	5,000	1,000	By process C a/c	7,200	5,318	1,882
To materials & wages	2,800	2,800	–				
	8,800	7,800	1,000				
Less : Closing stock	2,800	2,482	318				
Prime cost	6,000	5,318	682				

To profit @ $16\frac{2}{3}$ on							
Transfer price	1,200	–	1,200				
	7,200	5,318	1,882		7,200	5,318	1,882

Process C A/c

To process *B* a/c	7,200	5,318	1,882	By finished			
To materials & labour	4,800	4,300	–	stock a/c	11,538	8432	3,106
	12,000	10,118	1,882				
Less : Closing stock	2,000	1,686	314				
Prime cost	10,000	8,432	1,568				
Profit @ $13\frac{1}{3}$% on							
transfer price	1,538	–	1,538				
	11,538	8,432	3,106		11,538	8,432	3,106

Working notes : 1. Calculation of profit included in the closing stock

Process *A* = NIL

Process *B* $\frac{\text{Cost}}{\text{Total}}$ × closing stock

$$\frac{7,800}{8,800} \times 2,800 = 2,482$$

Process *C* $\frac{10,118}{12,000} \times 2,000 = 1,686$

2. Calculation of actual realised profit

Process	*Apparent profit*	–	*unrealised profit in closing stock*	=	*Actual profit*
A	1,000	–	Nil	=	1,000
B	1,200	–	318	=	882
C	1,538	–	314	=	1,224

Problem 21 : From the following information given by a manufacturing company which manufactures a product. You are required to prepare process accounts.

	Process I *Rs.*	*Process II* *Rs.*	*Process III* *Rs.*
Direct material	30,000	7,500	7,500
Direct wages	22,500	15,000	15,000
Closing stock	7,500	8,750	21,300

Finished goods sold for Rs. 1,30,000. Value of closing finished stock Rs. 5,612. It is the policy of the company to charge 20% on transfer price or 25% on cost price while transferring the goods from process *I* to process *II* and 20% on cost price from process *II* to process *III* and from process *III* to the finished stock.

(*Madras University, M.Com., April 1992*)

Solution :

Process I A/c

	Total	*Cost*	*Profit*		*Total*	*Cost*	*Profit*
To direct materials	30,000	30,000	–	By process *II* a/c	56,250	45,000	11,250
To direct wages	22,500	22,500	–				
	52,500	52,500	–				
Less : Closing stock	7,500	7,500	–				
	45,000	45,000	–				
Profit 25% on cost price	11,250	–	11,250				
	56,250	45,000	11,250		56,250	45,000	11,250

Process II A/c

To process *I* a/c	56,250	45,000	11,250	By process *III* a/c	84,000	60,000	24,000
To direct material	7,500	7,500	–				
To direct wages	15,000	15,000	–				
	78,750	67,500	11,250				
Less : Closing stock	8,750	7,500	1,250				
Prime cost	70,000	60,000	10,000				
Profit – 20% on cost price	14,000	–	14,000				
	84,000	60,000	24,000		84,000	60,000	24,000

Process III A/c

To process *II* a/c	84,000	60,000	24,000	By finished stock a/c	1,02,240	66,018	26,122
To direct materials	7,500	7,500					
To direct wages	15,000	15,000					
	1,06,500	82,500	24,000				
Less : Closing stock	21,300	16,482	4,818				
Prime cost	85,200	66,018	19,182				
Profit – 20% on cost price	17,040	–	17,040				
	1,02,240	66,018	26,222		1,02,240	66,018	26,222

Finished stock A/c

To process *III* a/c	1,02,240	66,018	36,222	By sales	1,30,000	62,394	67,606
Less : Closing stock	5,612	3,624	1,988				
Cost of goods sold	96,628	62,394	34,234				
Profit	33,372		33,372				
	1,30,000	62,394	67,606		1,30,000	62,394	67,606

Working note :

Proccess *I* $\frac{\text{Cost}}{\text{Total}} \times \text{Closing stock} = \text{NIL}$

Process *II* $\frac{67,500}{78,750} \times 8,750 = 7,500$

Process *III* $\frac{82,500}{1,06,500} \times 21,300 = 16,482$

Finished stock $\frac{66,018}{1,02,240} \times 5,612 = 3,624$

Problem 22 : Product *B* passes through three processes before it is completed and transferred to finished stock. The following data were available for the month of June 1993 :

	Process 1 (*Rs.*)	*Process 2* (*Rs.*)	*Process 3* (*Rs.*)	*Finished stock* (*Rs.*)
Opening stock	5,000	8,000	10,000	20,000
Direct materials	40,000	12,000	15,000	–
Direct labour	35,000	40,000	35,000	–
Production overhead	20,000	24,000	20,000	–
Closing stock	10,000	4,000	15,000	30,000

Output of process 1 is transferred to process 2 at 25% on transfer price, from process 2 to process 3 at 20% on transfer price and from process 3 to finished stock at 10% on the trnasfer price. Stock in process have been valued at prime cost. Finished stock has been valued at the price at which it was received from process 3. Sales amounted to Rs. 4,00,000. Provisions for internal process profits as at June 1, 1993 were :

Included in process 2 Rs. 1,395
Included in process 3 Rs. 2,690
Included in finished stock Rs. 6,534
Prepare process accounts.

Solution :

Process 1 A/c

	Total	Cost	Profit		Total	Cost	Profit
To opening stock	5,000	5,000	–	By process 2 A/c	1,20,000	90,000	30,000
To direct materials	40,000	40,000	–				
To direct labour	35,000	35,000	–				
	80,000	80,000	–				
Less : Closing stock	10,000	10,000	–				
Prime cost	70,000	70,000	–				
To production overhead	20,000	20,000	–				
Process cost	90,000	90,000	–				
Profit 25% on transfer price	30,000	–	30,000				
	1,20,000	90,000	30,000		1,20,000	90,000	30,000

Process 2 A/c

	Total	Cost	Profit		Total	Cost	Profit
To opening stock	8,000	6,605	1,395	By process 3 a/c	2,50,000	1,69,303	80,697
To process 1 a/c	1,20,000	90,000	30,000				
To direct material	12,000	12,000	–				
To direct labour	40,000	40,000	–				
	1,80,000	1,48,605	31,395				
Less : Closing steok	4,000	3,302	698				
Prime cost	1,76,000	1,45,303	30,697				
Production overhead	24,000	24,000	–				
Process cost	2,00,000	1,69,303	30,697				
Profit @ 20% on transfer price	50,000	–	50,000				
	2,50,000	1,69,303	80,697		2,50,000	1,69,303	80,697

Process 3 A/c

	Total	Cost	Profit		Total	Cost	Profit
To opening stock	10,000	7,310	2,690	By finished stock a/c	3,50,000	2,35,648	1,14,352
To process 2 a/c	2,50,000	1,69,303	80,697				
To direct material	15,000	15,000	–				
To direct labour	35,000	35,000	–				
	3,10,000	2,26,613	83,387				
Less : Closing stock	15,000	10,965	4,035				
Prime cost	2,95,000	2,15,648	79,352				
Production overhead	20,000	20,000	–				
Process cost	3,15,000	2,35,648	79,352				
Profit 10% on transfer price	35,000	–	35,000				
	3,50,000	2,35,648	1,14,352		3,50,000	2,35,648	1,14,352

Finished stock A/c

To opening stock	20,000	13,466	6,534	By sales	4,00,000	2,28,916	1,71,084
To process 3 a/c	3,50,000	2,35,648	1,14,352				
	3,70,000	2,49,114	1,20,886				
Less : Closing stock	30,000	20,198	9,802				
Cost of goods sold	3,40,000	2,28,916	1,11,084				
Gross profit	60,000	–	60,000				
	4,00,000	2,28,916	1,71,084		4,00,000	2,28,916	1,71,084

Working note : Computation of actual realised profit

	Apparent profit	+	*Unrealised profit in opening stock*	–	*Unrealised profit in closing stock*	=	*Actual profit*
Process 1	30,000	+	*NIL*	–	*NIL*	=	30,000
Process 2	50,000	+	1,395	–	698	=	50,697
Process 3	35,000	+	2,690	–	4,035	=	33,655
Finished stock	60,000	+	6,534	–	9,802	=	56,732

Problem 23 : *A* Ltd., produces a product which passes through two processess it is completed and transferred to finished stock. The following data relate to Dec. 1992 :

	Process I Rs.	*Process II* Rs.	*Process III* Rs.
Opening stock	7,500	9,000	22,500
Direct material	15,000	15,750	
Direct wages	11,200	11,250	
Factory overhead	10,500	4,500	
Closing stock	3,700	4,500	11,250
Inter process profit included in opening stock	–	1,500	8,250

Output of process *I* is transferred to process *II* at 25% profit on the transfer price and from process *II* to finished stock at 25% on cost price. Stock in process are valued at prime cost. Finished stock is valued at the price at which it is received from process *II*. Sales during the period are Rs. 1.,40,000.

Prepare process account and finished stock account showing the profit element at each stage.

Solution :

Process I A/c

	Total	*Cost*	*Profit*		*Total*	*Cost*	*Profit*
To opening stock	7,500	7,500	–	By process *II* A/c	54,000	40,500	13,500
To materials	15,000	15,000	–				
To labour	11,200	11,200	–				
	33,700	33,700	–				
Less : Closing stock	3,700	3,700	–				
Prime cost	30,000	30,000	–				
Overhead process cost	10,500	10,500	–				
	40,500	40,500	–				
Profit 25% on transfer price	13,500	–	13,500				
	54,000	40,500	13,500		54,000	40,500	13,500

Process II A/c

To opening stock	9,000	7,500	1,500	By finished stock	1,12,500	75,750	36,750
To process *I* a/c	54,000	40,500	13,500				
To material	15,750	15,750	–				

To labour	11,250	11,250	–				
	90,000	75,000	15,000				
Less : Closing stock	4,500	3,750	750				
Prime cost	85,500	73,250	14,250				
Overhead	4,500	4,500	–				
	90,000	75,750	14,250				
Profit 25% on 90,000	22,500	–	22,500				
	1,12,500	75,750	36,750		1,12,500	75,750	36,750

Finished stock A/c

To opening stock	22,500	14,250	8,250	By sales	1,40,000	82,500	57,000
To process *II* a/c	1,12,500	75,750	36,750				
	1,35,000	90,000	45,000				
Less : Closing stock	11,250	7,500	3,750				
	1,23,750	82,500	41,250				
Profit	16,250	–	16,250				
	1,40,000	82,500	57,500		1,40,000	82,500	57,500

Working note : Computation of actual profit

	Apparent profit	+	*Unrealised profit in opening stock*	–	*Unrealised profit in closing stock*	=	*Actual profit*
Process *I*	13,500	+	*NIL*	–	*NIL*	=	13,500
Process *II*	22,500	+	1,500	–	750	=	23,250
Finished stock	16,250	+	8,250	–	3,750	=	20,750
							57,500

EQUIVALENT PRODUCTION

The continuous nature of the production process implies that in many cases there always exists opening and closing work-in-progress. This poses a problem in accounting of work-in-progress. The process costing method is based on the 'homogeneity approach'. In other words each unit completed is supposed to have received the same treatment compared to all other units. This means each completed unit contains the same amount of materials, wages and overheads. All units at the same stage of completion are supposed to contain the same amount of each element of cost. In addition to the above assumption, it is also further assumed that the elements of costs are evenly incurred. These two notions provide key to the treatment of the work-in-progress which invariably exists in process costing.

To illustrate from cost point of view, 100 units of opening work-in-progress which are 10% complete are the exact equivalent of 10 units of opening work-in-progress which are 100% complete. In either case, 100 units, 10% complete or 10 units, 100% complete, the number of 'equivalent units' in opening work-in-progress is 10. Similarly, in the absence of opening work-in-progress, suppose 200 units are started during a period and all 200 units are 60% completed at the end of the period, then the equivalent production for the period is 120 units. That is to say, the expected cost for the period equals the cost that would have been expected to incur if 120 units had been started and completed in the period.

It should be emphasised that a separate equivalent production figure must be calculated for each element of cost which varies in its own way. Cost that are applied in an identical manner in the production process can be grouped and a single equivalent production unit figure can be calculated. For instance, labour cost and factory overheads are often incurred at the same rate and therefore are grouped together. This is not true for materials as they are added at discrete point in the production process. But in some processes they may be added at more than one point. For instance, material *X* may be added at the beginning of the process and material *Y* may be added at the midpoint. Thus, any unit of production that is started will be complete as to material *X* but any unit that is less than 50% complete will not have material *Y* and any unit that is more than 50% complete will be complete as to material *Y*. So, the number of equivalent production units will be different for material *X* and *Y*.

Methods of Computing Equivalent Production

There are two methods of computing equivalent production. They are (1) FIFO method and (2) Average method.

(1) **FIFO method :** Under this method, costs are shown separately for (*a*) Opening work-in-progress carried over and remaining to be completed and (*b*) Units introduced and completed during the current period. Under this method, the units transferred to next process or finished stock are issued on FIFO principle. In other words, the units transferred contains the units from opening inventory as well as the units introduced and completed during the current period. Equivalent units and costs of opening inventory is distinguished from units introduced and completed as if they are different batch of units. Cost per unit under each process is obtained by applying the following formula :

$$\frac{\text{Cost added in each process during the current period}}{\text{Equivalent production units}}$$

The cost added in each process during the current period is then apportioned between opening inventory, units completed and transferred to next process (or finished stock) and the closing inventory. The main object of FIFO method is to value the inventory at current cost.

During inflationary period, cost of production will be less, profit will be more and closing stock value will reflect current market price. Reverse is the trend under deflationary period.

(2) **Average method :** Under this method, no distinction is made between opening work-in-progress and current production units. The cost of opening work-in-progress is added to the cost incurred during current period and the total process cost is divided by the total equivalent units to arrive at an average cost of equivalent units.

Procedure Involved in Calculating Equivalent Units

1. Express the opening stock of work-in-progess in terms of equivalent units. This is done by applying the percentage of work yet to be done. For example, if the opening work-in-progress is 100 units, which is 60% complete, then the equivalent of this will be $100 \times \frac{40}{100} = 40$ units.

2. Find out the number of units started and finished during the year. This is found out by deducting the units in closing work-in-progress from the number of new units put into the process. Add these units to the opening stock of work-in-progress as was claculated in the first step.

3. Add to the above, the equivalent completed units of closing work-in-progress. This

is calculated by applying the percentage of work already done on unfinished units at the end of the period. For example, if 100 units of closing work-in-progress is 60% then the equivalent completed units of closing work-in-progress is $100 \times \frac{60}{100} = 60$ units.

4. Find out the net process cost after considering, additional cost incurred, normal losses, etc. in respect of each and every element of cost.

5. Obtain the cost per unit of equivalent production. This is obtained by dividing cost of each element by the number of equivalent units.

6. Ascertain the value of every form of output, such as abnormal loss/gain, finished product and work-in-progress.

In applying the above steps we will prepare three statements, they are (1) Statement of equivalent production, step number 1 to 3 fall under this statement (2) Statement of cost, step number 4 and 5 fall under this statement (3) Statement of evaluation, step number of 6 fall under this statement.

Problem 24 (Equivalent production without losses) : Shakthi Pvt. Ltd. is a manufacturer of processed goods and the results in process 2 for April 1993 were as follows :

Opening stock	NIL
Materials input from process 1	4,000 units
Cost of input :	
Materials from process 1	6,000
Labour cost	1,080
Overheads	1,720

Output is transferred into the next process, *i.e.*, process 3
Closing work-in-progress amounted to 800 units complete as to :

Process 1material	100%
Labour cost	50%
Overheads	30%

Prepare the account for process 2 and a statement of equivalent unit, a statement of cost and statement of evaluation.

Solution :

Statement of equivalent unit

Input qty.	*Particulars of output*	*Output qty.*	*Equivalent units*					
			Process 1 material		*Labour cost*		*Overhead*	
			%	Units	%	Units	%	Units
4,000	Finished stock	3,200	100%	3,200	100%	3,200	100%	3,200
	Closing work-in-progress	800	100%	800	50%	400	30%	240
4,000		4,000		4,000		3,600		3,440

Statement of cost per equivalent unit

Materials cost	6,000	÷	4,000	=	1.50
Labour cost	1,080	÷	3,600	=	0.30
Overhead	1,720	÷	3,440	=	0.50

Statement of evaluation

Finished stock :

Materials	3,200 × Rs. 1.50	=	Rs. 4,800
Labour cost	3,200 × Rs. 0.30	=	Rs. 960
Overhead	3,200 × Rs. 0.50	=	Rs. 1,600
		=	Rs. 7,360

Closing work-in-progress :

Materials	800 × Rs. 1.50	=	Rs. 1,200
Labour cost	400 × Re. 0.30	=	Rs. 120
Overhead	240 × Re. 0.50	=	Rs. 120
		=	Rs. 1,440

Process A/c

	Qty.	Amt.		Qty.	Amt.
To process 1 material	4,000	6,000	By process 3 a/c		
To labour		1,080	-Finished output	3,200	7,360
To overhead		1,720	By closing stock	800	1,440
	4,000	8,800		4,000	8,800

Problem 25 (Equivalent production with normal loss) : The following particulars are extracted from the books of East-West Co. Ltd. as on 31.3.1993.

	Units	Cost (Rs.)
Materials introduced in the process 1	20,000	1,99,800
Wages		1,37,600
Overheads 100% of wages		
Units completed and transfered to process 2	16,000	
Closing work-in-progress	3,000	

Degree of completion :

60% as to materials

40% as to labour and overhead

Normal loss 5% of materials introduced which realises Rs. 4 per unit

Prepare (1) Statement of equivalent units (2) Statement of cost per unit.

Solution :

Statement of equivalent unit

Input	Particulars of output	Units	Equivalent units: Materials %	Materials Units	Labour and overheads %	Labour and overheads Units
20,000	Normal loss	1,000	–	–	–	–
	Finished goods	16,000	100%	16,000	100%	16,000
	Closing WIP	3,000	60%	1,800	40%	1,200
20,000		20,000		17,800		17,200

Statement of cost per unit

Materials	1,99,800				
Less : Scrap value of normal loss	4,000				
	1,95,800	÷	17,800	=	11.00
Wages	1,37,600	÷	17,200	=	8.00
Overheads	1,37,600	÷	17,200	=	8.00

Statement of evaluation

Finished goods :

Materials	16,000	×	11	=	1,76,000	
Wages	16,000	×	8	=	1,28,000	
Overhead	16,000	×	8	=	1,28,000	
						4,32,000

Closing work-in-progress :

Materials	1,800	×	11.00	=	19,800	
Wages	1,200	×	8	=	9,600	
Overhead	1,200	×	8	=	9,60	39,000
						4,71,000

Process 1 A/c

	Qty.	*Amt.*		*Qty.*	*Amt.*
To materials	20,000	1,99,800	By normal loss	1,000	4,000
To wages		1,37,600	By process 2 a/c	16,000	4,32,000
To overheads		1,37,600	By closing WIP	3,000	39,000
	20,000	4,75,000		20,000	4,75,000

Problem 26 : During January, 1,000 units costing Rs. 6,000 were introduced in process *I*. There was no work-in-progress at the beginning. At the end of January, 600 units were transferred to process *II*; 250 units were incomplete and 150 units had been scrapped. The normal process loss was 10% of input. It was estimated that incompleted units had reached the following stages :

Material 80%, Labour 60%, Overhead 60%, Direct materials introduced Rs. 2,700, Direct wages Rs. 3,200, Production overhead Rs. 1,600.

Value of scrap is Rs. 2 each. The units scrapped had passed through the process and is 100% complete as regards material, labour and overhead.

You are required to

(*a*) Prepare a statement of equivalent production.
(*b*) Statement of cost for each element.
(*c*) Statement of apportionment of process cost.
(*d*) Process *I* account.
(*e*) Abnormal loss account. (*Madras University, B.Com., March 1992*)

Solution : **Statement of equivalent production**

Input	*Particulars of output*	*Output*	*Equivalent units*					
			Materials		*Labour*		*Overhead*	
			%	*Units*	*%*	*Units*	*%*	*Units*
1,000	Normal loss	100	–	–	–	–	–	–
	Abnormal loss	50	100%	50	100%	50	100%	50
	Finished goods	600	100%	600	100%	600	100%	600
	Closing WIP	250	80	200	60%	150	60%	150
1,000		1,000		850		800		800

Statement of cost per unit

Materials	6,000				
Add : Further materials	2,700				
	8,700				
Less : Normal loss	200	8,500 ÷ 850	=	Rs.	10
Labour		3,200 ÷ 800	=	Rs.	4
Overhead		1,600 ÷ 800	=	Rs.	2

Statement of evaluation

Abnormal loss :				
Materials	50 × 10	=	500	
Labour	50 × 4	=	200	
Overhead	50 × 2	=	100	800
Finished goods :				
Materials	600 × 10	=	6,000	
Labour	600 × 4	=	2,400	
Overhead	600 × 2	=	1,200	9,600
Closing work-in-progress :				
Materials	200 × 10	=	2,000	
Labour	150 × 4	=	600	
Overhead	150 × 2	=	300	2,900
				13,200

Process '1' A/c

	Qty.	*Amt.*		*Qty.*	*Amt.*
To units introduced	1,000	6,000	By normal loss	100	200
To materials		2,700	By output transferred		
To labour		3,200	to process '2' a/c	600	9,600
			By abnormal loss	50	800
To overhead		1,600	By closing WIP	250	2,900
	1,000	13,500		1,000	13,500

Abnormal wastage A/c

To process '1' a/c	50	800	By sale of abnormal wastage	50	100
			By P & L a/c		700
	50	800		50	800

Problem 27 (Equivalent production relating to two process) : Attractive and Co., operates a department producing a component which passes through two processes. During November 1990, materials for 40,000 components were put into process. There was no opening process stock 30,000 units were finished and passed to next process. Those not passed forward were calculated to be one-half finished as regards wages and overheads. The costs incurred were as follows :

	Rs.
Direct material	10,000
Factory overhead	12,000
Direct wages	8,000

Of those passed to the second process, 28,000 units were completed and passed to finished stores. 200 units were scrapped, which was not abnormal. 1,800 units remained unfinished in process, one-quarter finished as regards wages and overheads no further process material costs occur after introduction at the first process until the end of the second process, when protective packing is applied to the completed components. The process and packing costs incurred at the end of the second process were :

	Rs.
Direct material (packing)	4,000
Factory overhead	4,500
Direct wages	3,500

Prepare a cost analysis tatement for November 1990 accounting for total costs incurred analysed into elements of costs for process, covering finished and part-finished items and process accounts.

(C.S., Inter, June 1991)

Solution : **Statement of equivalent production (cost analysis)**

Input	*Particulars of output*	*Output*	*Equivalent units*					
			Materials		*Labour*		*Overhead*	
			Units	*%*	*Units*	*%*	*Units*	*%*
40,000	Finished goods	30,000	3,000	100%	30,000	100%	30,000	100%
	Closing WIP	10,000	10,000	100%	5,000	50%	5,000	50%
40,000		40,000	40,000		35,000		35,000	

Statement of cost per unit of equivalent production

Materials	10,000 ÷ 40,000	=	0.25
Labour	8,000 ÷ 35,000	=	0.2286
Overhead	12,000 ÷ 35,000	=	0.3429

Statement of evaluation

Finished goods :						
Materials	30,000	×	0.25	=	7,500	
Labour	30,000	×	0.2286	=	6,857	
Overhead	30,000	×	0.3429	=	10,286	24,643
Closing stock WIP						
Material	10,000	×	0.25	=	2,500	
Labour	5,000	×	0.2286	=	1,143	
Overhead	5,000	×	0.3429	=	1,714	5,357
						30,000

Process I A/c

	Qty.	*Amt.*		*Qty.*	*Amt.*
To direct materials	40,000	10,000	By process *II* A/c	30,000	24,643
To direct wages		8,000	By closing WIP	10,000	5,357
To factory overhead		12,000			
	40,000	30,000		40,000	30,000

Process II A/c

Statement of equivalent production

Input	*Particulars of output*	*Output*	*Equivalent units*					
			Materials		*Labour*		*Overhead*	
			Qty.	*%*	*Qty.*	*%*	*Qty.*	*%*
30,000	Finished goods	28,000	28,000	100%	28,000	100%	28,000	100%
	Normal loss	200	–	–	–	–	–	–
	Closing WIP	1,800	1,800	100%	450	25%	450	25%
30,000		30,000	29,800		28,450		28,450	

Statement of cost per unit of equivalent production

Materials					
Cost of materials	4,000				
From process I	24,643				
	28,643	÷	29,800	=	0.8269
Wages	3,500	÷	28,450	=	0.123
Overhead	4,500	÷	28,450	=	0.158

Statement of evaluation

Finished goods					
Materials	28,000	×	0.8269	=	23,153
Add : Primary packing materials				=	4,000
Labour	28,000	×	0.123	=	3,444
Overhead	28,000	×	0.158	=	4,424
					35,021
Closing WIP					
Material	1,800	×	0.8269	=	1,488
Labour	450	×	0.123	=	54
Overhead	450	×	0.153	=	70
					1,612

Process II A/c

	Qty.	*Amt.*		*Qty.*	*Amt.*
To process I a/c	30,000	24,643	By normal loss	200	–
To direct materials		40,000	By finished goods	28,000	35,021
(primary packing materials)			By closing WIP	1,800	1,612
To direct wages		3,500			
To factory overhead		4,500			
	30,000	36,643		30,000	36,643

Problem 27 (Equivalent production with abnormal gain) : The books of Sunflower Oil Co. Pvt. Ltd. revealed the following :

Units introduced into process *A*	6,000 units
Cost incurred in process *A* was a follows :	
Direct materials	Rs. 55,200
Direct labour cost	Rs. 30,600
Factory overhead	Rs. 14,400
Normal loss in process *A*	10% of the input
Output obtained and transferred to process *B*	4,000 units
Units scrapped in process *A*	500 units
Closing work-in-progress in process *A*	1,500 units
Degree of completion :	
Materials	100%
Direct labour	80%
Factory overhead	60%
Realisable value of scrapped units	Rs. 2 per unit

Compute (*a*) Equivalent production, (*b*) Cost per unit of equivalent production, (*c*) Process a/c, (*d*) Normal loss a/c, (*e*) Abnormal gain a/c. (*Sri Sathya Sai University, B.Com., Feb. 2001*)

Solution : **Statement of equivalent production (cost analysis)**

Input	*Particulars of output*	*Output*	*Equivalent units*					
			Materials		*Labour*		*Overhead*	
			%	*Units*	*%*	*Units*	*%*	*Units*
6,000	Normal loss	600	–	–	–	–	–	–
	Finished goods	4,000	100%	4,000	100%	4,000	100%	4,000
	Closing WIP	1,500	100%	1,500	80%	1,200	60%	900

6,000		6,100		5,500		5,200	4,900
	Less : Abnormal gain	100	100%	100	100%	100	100%	100
6,000		6,000		5,400		5,100	4,800

Statement of cost per unit of equivalent production

Materials	55,200					
Less : Sale of normal loss units	1,200					
	54,000	÷	5,400	=	Rs.	10
Labour	30,600	÷	5,100	=	Rs.	6
Overhead	14,400	÷	4,800	=	Rs.	3

Statement of evaluation

Finished goods :						
Materials	4,000	×	Rs. 10	=	Rs. 40,000	
Labour	4,000	×	Rs. 6	=	Rs. 24,000	
Overhead	4,000	×	Rs. 3	=	Rs. 12,000	76,000
Abnormal gain :						
Materials	100	×	Rs. 10	=	Rs. 1,000	
Labour	100	×	Rs. 6	=	Rs. 600	
Overhead	100	×	Rs. 3	=	Rs. 300	1,900
Closing work-in-progress						
Materials	1,500	×	Rs. 10	=	Rs. 15,000	
Labour	1,200	×	Rs. 6	=	Rs. 7,200	
Overhead	900	×	Rs. 3	=	Rs. 2,700	24,900

Process A A/c

	Qty.	*Amt.*		*Qty.*	*Amt.*
To materials	6,000	55,200	By normal loss	600	1,200
To labour		30,600	By finished goods	4,000	76,000
To overhead		14,400	By closing WIP	1,500	24,900
To abnormal gain	100	1,900			
	6,100	1,02,100		6,100	1,02,100

Normal loss A/c

To process *A* a/c	600	1,200	By sales	500	1,000
			By abnormal gain	100	200
	600	1,200		600	1,200

Abnormal gain A/c

To normal loss a/c	100	200	By process A a/c	100	1,900
To P & L a/c		1,700			
	100	1,900		100	1,900

Problem 28 : AB Ltd., is engaged in the process engineering industry. During the month of April 1999; 2000 units were introduced in process '*x*'. The normal loss is estimated at 5% of input. At the end of the month 1,400 units had been produced and transferred to process Y. 460 were incomplete units and 140 units had to be scrapped at the end of the process. The incomplete units reached the following degree of completion :

Materials	:	75%
Labour	:	50%
Overhead	:	50%

Following are the further details regarding process x

Cost of 2,000 units introduced	Rs. 58,000
Additional materials consumed	Rs. 14,400
Direct labour	Rs. 33,400
Allocated overheads	Rs. 16,700

Note : The scrapped units fetched Rs. 10 each. Required :

(1) Statement of equivalent production

(2) Statement of cost

(3) Statement of evaluation

(4) Process 'x' a/c

(ICWA, Inter, June 1999)

Solution :

Statement of equivalent production

Input	*Output*	*Units*	*Equivalent Production*					
			Materials		*Labour*		*Overhead*	
			% of completion	*Units*	*% of completion*	*Units*	*% of completion*	*Unit*
2,000	Normal loss	1,000	–	–	–	–	--	–
	Abnormal loss	40	100%	40	100%	40	100%	40
	Finished goods	1,400	100%	1,400	100%	1,400	100%	1,400
	Closing WIP	460	75%	345	50%	230	50%	230
2,000		2,000		1,785		1,670		1,670

Statement of cost

Cost of Materials introduced	58,000
Additional materials	14,400
	72,400
Less : Sale of scrapped units	1,000
	71,400

Cost per unit $= \frac{71,400}{1,785} = 40$

Labour cost per unit $= \frac{33,400}{1,670} = 20$

Overhead per unit $= \frac{16,700}{1,670} = 10$

70

Statement of evaluation

Finished goods	1,400 × 70	= 98,000
Abnormal loss	40 × 70	= 2,800
Closing WIP		
Materials	345 × 40	= 13,800
Labour	230 × 20	= 4,600
Oh	230 × 10	= 2,300
		20,700

Process 'X' A/c

	Qty.	Amt		Qty.	Amt.
To units introduced	2,000	58,000	By normal loss	100	1,000
To materials		14,400	By abnormal loss	40	2,800
To labour		33,400	By process Y a/c	1,400	98,000
To overheads		16,700	By closing WIP	460	20,700
	2,000	1,22,500		2,000	1,22,500

Problem 29 (When opening work-in-progress is given) : Khomainee & Co. uses process cost system production and inventory data for February 1991 are given below :

Units put in process : 60,000
Units completed in February : 70,000

February 1, work-in-progress was composed of 40,000 units with 30% materials content and 40% of the conversion cost complete.

February 28, work-in-process was composed of 30,000 units with 60% of the materials content and 70% of the conversion cost complete.

Compute the equivalent units. *(Sri Sathya Sai University, B.Com., March 1991)*

Solution : **Statement of equivalent production**

Input	*Particulars of output*	*Output*	*Equivalent units*					
			Materials		*Labour*		*Overhead*	
			%	*Units*	*%*	*Units*	*%*	*Units*
40,000	Opening WIP	40,000	70%	12,000	60%	24,000	60%	24,000
60,000	Finished goods	30,000	100%	30,000	100%	30,000	100%	30,000
	Closing WIP	30,000	60%	18,000	70%	21,000	70%	21,000
1,00,000		1,00,000		60,000		75,000		75,000

Problem 30 : From the following particulars extracted from the books of Unique Ltd. for the month of March 1998. You are required to (*i*) Prepare the statement of equivalent units of production, (*ii*) Compute the cost per equivalent unit for each cost element, (*iii*) Compute the cost of finished output and closing work-in-progress and (*iv*) Prepare process account. Assume that FIFO method is used by the company

	Units
(*i*) Opening stock as on 1st March 1998 @ Rs. 4 per unit	200
Degree of completion	
- Materials 100% and	
- Labour and overhead 40%	
(*ii*) Introduced during March 1998	1,050
(*iii*) Transferred to next process	1,100
(*iv*) Closing stock as on 31st March 1998	150
Degree of completion	
- Materials 100% and	
- Labour and overhead 70%	

Other relevant information regarding the process account is as under :

	Rs.
Materials cost	3,150
Labour cost	4,500
Production overheads	2,250
Total	9,900

(C.S., Inter, Dec. 1998)

Solution : **Statement of equivalent production**

Input	*Output*	*Units*	*Equivalent units*					
			Materials		*Labour*		*Overhead*	
			%	*Units*	*%*	*Units*	*%*	*Units*
	Opening stock of WIP	200	–	–	60%	120	60%	120
	Finished goods	900	100%	900	100%	900	100%	900
	Closing stock of WIP	150	100%	150	70%	105	70%	105
		1,250		1,050		1,125		1,125

Statement showing cost per unit

Materials cost per unit $= \frac{3,150}{1,050} = 3$

Wages per unit $= \frac{4,500}{1,125} = 4$

Overheads per unit $= \frac{2,250}{1,125} = 2$

Statement of Evaluation

(1) Opening stock of WIP :		
Materials	Nil	Nil
Labour	120 × 4	480
Overheads	120 × 2	240
		720
(2) Finished goods :		
Materials	900 × 3	2,700
Labour	900 × 4	3,600
Overheads	900 × 2	1,800
		8,100
(3) Closing WIP :		
Materials	150 × 3	450
Labour	105 × 4	420
Overheads	105 × 2	210
		1,080

Process A/c

	Qty.	*Amt.*		*Qty.*	*Amt.*
To opening stock of WIP	200	800	By output transferred to next process (800 + 720 + 8100)	1,100	9,620
To materials	1,050	3,150			
To labour		4,500			
To overheads		2,250	By closing WIP	150	1,080
	1,250	10,700		1,250	10,700

Problem 31 : Roy & Johnson (P) Ltd., gives the following particulars relating to process A in its plant for the month of December 1997 :

Work-in-progress (opening balance) on 1.12.97			–	500 units
Cost :	Materials	Rs. 4,800		
	Labour	3,200		
	Overhead	6,400		
		14,400		

Units introduced during the month — 19,500

Processing cost incurred during the month

Materials	Rs.	1,86,200
Labour		72,000
Overheads		1,06,400
		3,64,600

Output :	Units transferred to process *B*	18,200
	Units scrapped (completely processed)	1,400
	Work-in-process (closing balance)	400
	Degree of completion :	
	Materials 100%	
	Labour and overheads 50%	

Normal loss in processing is 5% of total input and normal scrapped units fetch Rs. 1 each.

Prepare the following statements for process A for December 1997 :

(*a*) Statement of equivalent production

(*b*) Statement of cost

(*c*) Statement of evaluation

(*d*) Process '*A*' a/c

(*ICWA, Inter, June 1998*)

Solution : **Statement of equivalent production**

Input	*Output*	*Units*	Equivalent units: *Materials* %	*Materials* Units	*Labour of Overhead* %	*Labour of Overhead* Units
500	Opening WIP					
19,500	Units introduced					
	Finished goods	18,200	100%	18,200	100%	18,200
	Normal loss 5% on 20,000	1,000	–	–	–	–
	Abnormal loss	400	100%	400	100%	400
	Closing WIP	400	100%	400	50%	200
20,000		20,000		19,000		18,800

Statement of cost per unit

Materials :	Opening balance	4,800
	Materials consumed	1,86,200
		1,91,000
Less :	Sale of normal loss units 1,000 units e 1	1,000
		1,90,000

Materials cost per unit $= \dfrac{1,90,000}{19,000} = 10$

Labour :	Opening balance		3,200	
	Labour cost during the year		72,000	
			75,200	
Labour cost per unit			$\frac{75,200}{18,800}$	= 4
Overhead :				
	Opening balance		6,400	
	Cost during the month		1,06,400	
			1,12,800	
Overhead per unit			= $\frac{1,12,800}{18,800}$	= 6
		Total		20

Statement of evaluation

(1)	Abnormal loss units - 400 units @ 20	=	8,000
(2)	Output or finished goods - 18,200 units @ 20	=	3,64,000
(3)	Closing work-in-progress :		
	Materials 400 units @ Rs. 10	=	4,000
	Labour & overheads 200 units @ Rs. 10	=	2,000
			6,000

Process 'A' A/c

	Qty.	*Amt.*		*Qty.*	*Amt.*
To opening WIP	500	14,400	By normal loss	1,000	1,000
			By abnormal loss	400	8,000
To units introduced	19,500	1,86,200	By process *B* a/c	18,200	3,64,000
To labour		72,000	By closing WIP	400	6,000
To overhead		1,06,400			
	20,000	3,79,000		20,000	3,79,000

Problem 32 : The following data relate to process Q

(*i*) Opening work-in-process 4,000 units

Degree of completion :

Materials	100%	Rs. 24,000
Labour	60%	Rs. 14,400
Overheads	60%	Rs. 7,200

(ii) Received during the month of April 1998 from process P

4,000 units Rs. 1,71,000

(*iii*) Expenses incurred in process Q during the month

Materials	Rs. 79,000
Labour	Rs. 1,38,230
Overhead	Rs. 69,120

(*iv*) Closing work-in-process 3,000 units

Degree of completion

Mateials	100%
Labour & overheads	50%

(*v*) Units scrapped 4,000 units
Degree of completion :
Materials 100%
Labour & overheads 80%

(*vi*) Normal loss : 5% of current input.

(*vii*) Spoiled goods realised Rs. 1.50 each on sale.

(*viii*) Completion units are transferred to warehouse.

Required :

(*i*) Equivalent units statement.

(*ii*) Statement of cost per equivalent unit and total costs.

(*iii*) Process Q account.

(*iv*) Any other account necessary.

(*C.A., Inter, May 1998*)

Solution :

Statement of equivalent production

Input	*Output*	*Units*	*Materials* %	*Materials* Units	*Labour* %	*Labour* Units	*Overhead* %	*Overhead* Units
4,000	Opening WIP	4,000	–	–	40%	1,600	40%	1,600
40,000	Normal loss	2,000	–	–	–	–	–	–
	Abnormal loss	2,000	100%	2,000	80%	1,600	80%	1,600
	Finished goods	33,000	100%	33,000	100%	33,000	100%	33,000
	Closing WIP	3,000	100%	3,000	50%	1,500	50%	1,500
44,000		44,000		38,000		37,700		37,700

Statement of cost

Materials from process '*P*'		1,71,000		
Materials cost incurred in process Q	79,000			
Less : Sale of scrapped units	3,000			
		76,000		
		2,47,000		
Materials cost per unit		$\frac{2,47,000}{38,000}$	=	6.50
Labour cost per unit		$\frac{1,38,230}{37,700}$	=	3.66
Oh per unit		$\frac{69,120}{37,700}$	=	1.84
				12.00

Statement of evaluationt

OP WIP :		
Material		NIL
Labour	1,600 × 3.66	5,856
Oh	1,600 × 1.84	2,944
		8,800
Finished goods :		
	33,000 × 12.00	3,96,000

Abnormal loss		
Materials	2,000 × 6.50	13,000
Labour	1,600 × 3.66	5,856
Oh	1,600 × 1.84	2,944
		21,800
Closing WIP		
Materials	3,000 × 6.50	19,500
Labour	1,500 × 3.66	5,490
Oh	1,500 × 1.84	2,760
		27,750

Process Q a/c

	Qty.	*Amt.*		*Qty.*	*Amt.*
To op. WIP	4,000	45,600	By normal loss	2,000	3,000
To input qty.	40,000	1,71,000	By abnormal loss	2,000	21,800
To materials		79,000	By finished stock a/c	37,000	4,50,400
To labour		1,38,230	(45,600 + 8,800 + 3,96,000)		
To oh		69,120	By cl WIP	2,000	27,750
	44,000	5,02,950		44,000	5,02,950

Abnormal loss A/c

To process Q a/c	2,000	21,800	By sales	2,000	3,000
			By P & L a/c	–	18,800
			(Balancing figure)		
	2,000	21,500		2,000	21,800

Problem 33 : A manufacturing company furnishes the following data in respect of process 3 for the month of April 1993 :

Direct material added in process	776
Direct labour	386
Production overhead	768
Transfer from process 2	4,200 units valued at Rs. 1,560
Transfer to process 4	3,650 units
Stock at 1st April 1993	600 units valued at Rs. 390
Degree of completion :	
Material added in process	60%
Labour	50%
Overhead	40%
Stock at 30th April 1993	800 units
Degree of completion :	
Materials added in process	80%
labour	70%
Overhead	60%
Units scrapped	350 units
Degree of completion :	
Mater'als added to process	100%
Labour	80%
Overhead	80%

Normal loss is 10% of output (opening stock + output of the process – closing stock). All units scrapped can be sold for Re. 0.10 per unit you are required to prepare :

(*a*) A statement showing the cost per unit of production and the value of the output.
(*b*) Process '3' account.
(*c*) Abnormal loss or abnormal gain account.

Solution :

Statement of equivalent production

Input	*Particulars of Output*	*Units*	*Material 1* %	*Material 1* Units	*Materials 2* %	*Materials 2* Units	*Labour* %	*Labour* Units	*Overhead* %	*Overhead* Units
600	Op. stock	600	–	–	40%	240	50%	300	60%	360
4,200	Normal loss	400	–	–	–	–	–	–	–	–
	Finished goods	3,050	100%	3,050	100%	3,050	100%	3,050	100%	3,050
	Closing stock	800	100%	800	80%	640	70%	560	60%	480
4,800		4,850		3,850		3,690		3,610		3,530
	Less : Ab. gain	50	100%	50	100%	50	100%	50	100%	50
4,800		4,800		3,800		3,640		3,560		3,480

Statement of cost per equivalent unit

	Process 1 material	*Process 2 material*	*Labour*	*Overhead*
Cost incurred	1,560	776	386	768
Less : Sale proceeds of normal loss	40	–	–	–
Column (1)	1,520	776	386	768
Equivalent units (Column 2)	3,800	3,880	3,860	3,840
Cost per equivalent unit (1 ÷ 2)	0.40	0.20	0.10	0.20

Statement of evaluation

	Process 1 material	*Process 2 material*	*Labour*	*Overhead*
Opening stock	–	48	30	72
Finished goods	1,220	610	305	610
Abnormal gain	(20)	(10)	(5)	(10)
Closing stock	320	128	56	96
	1,520	776	396	768

Process 3 A/c

	Qty.	*Amt.*		*Qty.*	*Amt.*
To opening stock	600	390	By normal loss	400	40
To process '2' a/c	4,200	1,560	By process '4' a/c	3,650	3,285
To direct materials		776	(390 + 150 + 2,745)		
To direct labour		386			
To overhead		768	By closing WIP	800	600
To abnormal gain	50	45			
	4,850	3,925		4,850	3,925

Abnormal gain A/c

To normal loss a/c 50 units @ 10 P	50	5	By process '3' a/c	50	45
To P & L a/c	–	40			
	50	45		50	45

Problem 34 (Equivalent production under weighted average cost method) : *XYZ* Co., produces an item which is manufactured in two consecutive processes. Information relating to process '2' during September 2002 is as follows :

Opening stock		800 units
Degree of completion		
Process '1' materials	100%	Cost Rs. 4,700
Added materials	40%	600
Conversion cost	30%	1,000
		6,300

During September 2002, 3,000 units were transferred from process '1' at a valuation of 18,100. Added materials cost Rs. 9,600 and conversion costs were, 11,800.

Closing stock on 30th September 2002 amounted to 1,000 units which were 100% complete with respect to process '1' materials and 60% completed with respect to added materials and conversion cost work was 40% complete.

XYZ Co. Uses a weighted average cost system for the valuation of output and closing stock. Prepare the process '2' a/c for September 2002.

Solution : Opening stock units count as a full equivalent unit of production when the weighted average cost system is applied. Closing stock equivalent units are assessed in the usualy way.

Statement of equivalent production

Input	*Particulars of Output*	*Outuput*	*Equivalent units*					
			Materials 1		*Material 2*		*Conversion cost*	
			%	*Units*	*%*	*Units*	*%*	*Units*
800	Opening stock	800	100%	800	100%	800	100%	800
3,000	Finished goods	2,000*	100%	2,000	100%	2,000	100%	2,000
	Closing stock	1,000	100%	1,000	60%	600	40%	400
3,800		3,800		3,800		3,400		3,200

* 3,000 units from process '1' minus closing stock of 1,000 units.

Statement of cost per equivalent unit

The cost of opening stock is added to costs incurred in September 1992 and a cost per equivalent unit is then calculated.

	Material 1	*Material 2*	*Conversion cost*
Opening stock	4,700	600	1,000
Added in September 1992	18,100	9,600	11,800
Total cost	22,800	10,200	12,800
Equivalent units	3,800 units	3,400 units	3,200 units
Cost per equivalent unit	Rs. 6	Rs. 3	Rs. 4

Statement of evaluation

	Material 1	*Material 2*	*Conversion*	*Total*
Finished goods (2,800 units)	16,800	8,400	11,200	36,400
Closing stock	6,000	1,800	1,600	9,400
				45,800

Process '2' A/c

	Qty.	Amt.		Qty.	Amt.
To opening stock	800	6,300	By finished goods	2,800	36,400
To process '1' A/c	3,000	18,100	By closing stock	1,000	9,400
To added material		9,600			
To conversion cost		11,800			
	3,800	45,800		3,800	45,800

QUESTIONS

I. Fill in the blanks :

(*a*) The unit cost for a department in process costing is computed by dividing the total cost by ....

(*b*) The counterpart in the process cost system of the job order cost sheet is the ....

(*c*) Production completed and no hand in a process department is considered as ....

(*d*) Spoilage that occurs under efficient operating conditions and is ordinarily uncontrollable is called ....

(*e*) Spoilage that occurs under inefficient operating condition and is ordinarily controllable is called ....

(*f*) Abnormal process losses should be transferred to ....

(*g*) .... represents the productions of process in terms of completed units.

(*h*) .... and .... are the two methods of calculating equivalent production.

(*i*) Of 50 units are 60% complete in a process, it is equivalent to .... number of completed units.

(*j*) Under .... method of costing the costs are accumulated by department, cost centre or operation.

(*k*) Under .... method of computing equivalent production, the cost of opening work-in-progress is not kept separate and is added to the cost incurred during the period.

(*l*) The procedure followed intransferring output of one process to another at market price is known as ....

[*Answers :* (*a*) equivalent unit, (*b*) cost of production a/c, (*c*) work-in-progress, (*d*) normal spoilage, (*e*) abnormal spoilage, (*f*) costing P & L a/c, (*g*) Equivalent production, (*h*) FIFO & average cost, (*i*) 300, (*j*) process, (*k*) average cost, (*l*) inter-process profit]

II. Mark 'T' or 'F' in the space provided

1. The process costing method is suitable for a large paper manufacuturing plant. *T/F*
2. The number of requisition for materials is greater in a process cost system than in a job order cost system. *T/F*
3. Process costing is ordinarily used where all the operations are performed in one department. *T/F*
4. The cost of abnormal process loss is not included in the cost of process. *T/F*
5. In process costing there is a transfer of cost from one process to another as the product moves from one process to another. *T/F*
6. Process costing is employed where production is undertaken against specific orders and where the production is not continuous. *T/F*
7. Normal losses are avoidable losses arising from the nature of the productive process. *T/F*
8. The output of one process may be transferred to the next process at cost or at market price. *T/F*

[*Answers :* 1. *T*, 2. *F*, 3. *F*, 4. *T*, 5. *T*, 6. *F*, 7. *T*, 8. *T*]

III. Choose the correct answer :

1. The type of spoilage that should not affect the cost of inventories is
   (*a*) Abnormal spoilage (*c*) Seasonal spoilage
   (*b*) Normal spoilage (*d*) Indirect spoilage [ ]
2. Materials may not be put into process
   (*a*) At the beginning of an operation (*c*) At the end of the operation
   (*b*) Continuously (*d*) In the shipping department. [ ]

3. Process cost method is especially suitable for
   (*a*) Custom production
   (*b*) Standard costs
   (*c*) FIFO
   (*d*) LIFO. [ ]
4. In process costing, costs follow :
   (*a*) Price rise
   (*b*) Price declines
   (*c*) Product flow
   (*d*) Finished goods. [ ]
5. When average costing is used, the opening inventory costs are
   (*a*) Kept separate from the costs for the new period
   (*b*) Added to the costs for the new period
   (*c*) Substracted from the new costs
   (*d*) Averaged with other costs to arrive at total cost. [ ]
6. A disadvantage of FIFO costing is that
   (*a*) The first units production cannot be distinguished from later production
   (*b*) Several units costs are used at the same time
   (*c*) The units have to be kept separate
   (*d*) The shipping costs are higher. [ ]
7. Which of the following method of costing can be used in a large oil refinery
   (*a*) Process costing
   (*b*) Operating costing
   (*c*) Unit costing
   (*d*) Job costing [ ]
8. Which of the following pair is odd :
   (*a*) Construction-Contract costing
   (*b*) Ship-building-Job costing
   (*c*) Brick manufacturing-Process costing
   (*d*) Transport undertaking-Operating costing. [ ]
9. A product which has practically no sales or utility value is
   (*a*) Waste
   (*b*) Scrap
   (*c*) Spoilage
   (*d*) Defectives. [ ]
10. Trimmings in timber industry should be treated as a :
    (*a*) Waste
    (*b*) Scrap
    (*c*) Spoilage
    (*d*) Defectives. [ ]
11. In certain processes, the quantity of output is less than that of the input because of shrinkage, evaporation etc., such a loss of output is known as :
    (*a*) Waste
    (*b*) Normal spoilage
    (*c*) Scrap
    (*d*) Abnormal spoilage. [ ]
12. Defectives are those items
    (*a*) Which are rectifiable and made into good units
    (*b*) Which are useless and beyond rectification
    (*c*) Which has scrap value and then to be sold
    (*d*) Which is waste having no recoverable value. [ ]
13. The essential difference between a job order and a process cost system is that
    (*a*) The process system does not embrace the use of a predetermined overhead rate
    (*b*) The process cost system accumulates costs for a particular operation or department, while the job order system accumulates costs for a given job
    (*c*) The process system generally requires the use of predetermined rates to allocate service department costs to production departments
    (*d*) The process cost method requires a more accurate and detailed classification of costs than the job order system. [ ]

[***Answers :*** 1. (a), 2. (*d*), 3. (*b*), 4. (*c*), 5. (*a*), 6. (*b*), 7. (*a*), 8. (*c*), 9. (*a*), 10. (*b*), 11. (*a*), 12. (*a*), 13. (*b*)]

IV. Simple questions :

1. State any four features of process costing.
2. Define process costing.
3. What do you mean by normal loss? How is it treated in process cost accounts?
4. What do you mean by abnormal loss? How is it treated in process cost accounts?
5. Distinguish between normal loss and abnormal loss.
6. What do you mean by abnormal effective? How is it treated in process cost accounts?

7. What do you mean by inter process profit? What purpose does it serve?
8. What do you mean be equivalent production?

V. Short answer questions

1. Describe the main features of process costing. *(Madurai Kamaraj University, B.Com., April 1992)*
2. Explain the features of process costing. *(University of Kerala, B.Com., May 1991)*
3. How would you treat abnormal gain? *(University of Kerala, B.Com., 1991)*
4. Distinguish between job costing and process costing. *(C.A., Inter, June 1990)*
5. Define normal loss and abnormal process loss explaining their possible causes. *(Madras University, M.Com., April 1992)*
6. What motivational criteria are applicable to transfer pricing? *(Madras University, M.Com., April 1992)*

EXERCISES

Exercise-1 (Simple Process Accounts)

A product passes through three distinct processes to completion. There processes are numbered respectively 1, 2 and 3. During the month ended 31st January 1997, 500 units are produced. The following information is obtained :

	Process 1	*Process 2*	*Process 3*
	Rs.	*Rs.*	*Rs.*
Direct Material	3000	1500	1000
Direct Labour	2500	2000	2500
Direct expenses	500	100	500

The overhead expenses for the period Rs. 1400 were apportioned to the process on the basis of wages. No work in progress or process stock existed at the beginning or at the end of the week. Prepare process accounts. *(Bharathiar University, B.Com., November 1997)*

[Answer : Process 3 a/c output transferred to finished stock a/c 30 units amounting to Rs. 15,000]

Exercise-2 (Normal and Abnormal Loss)

A product passes through three processes to completion. During the quarter ending 31st March 1998, the cost and production were as under :

	Total	*A*	*B*	*C*
Direct Material	84,820	20,000	30,200	34,620
Direct labour	1,20,000	30,000	40,000	50,000
Direct expenses	7,260	5,000	2,260	–
Production overhead	60,000	–	–	–
Normal loss in input	–	10%	5%	10%
Sale of scrap per unit	–	Rs. 30	Rs. 50	Rs. 60
Production in units	–	920	870	800

1000 units at Rs. 50 per unit were introduced to process A. There was no stock of materials or work in progress in any process at the beginning or end of the period. Production overhead is allocated to each process on the basis of 50% of direct labour cost.

Prepare process accounts.

(Bangalore University, B.Com., April 1998)

[Answer : Output of process c transferred to finished stock a/c 800 units amounting to Rs. 3,20,000]

Exercise-3 (Partial Sale of Output at Profit)

X Ltd., processes a patent material used in building. The material is produced in three consecutive grades—soft, medium and hard.

	Soft	*Medium*	*Hard*
	I	*II*	*III*
Raw material used (tons)	1000	–	–
Cost per ton	Rs. 200	–	–
Manufacturing wages and expenses	87,500	39,500	10,710

Weight lost (% of the input of the process)	5%	10%	20%
Scrap (sale price Rs. 50 per tonne)	50 tons	30 tons	51 tons
Sale price per ton	Rs. 350	Rs. 500	Rs. 800

Management expenses were Rs. 17,500 and selling expenses were Rs. 10,000. Two-thirds of the output of process I and one-half of the output of process No. II are passed on to the next process and the balance is sold. The entire output of process No. III, is sold. Prepare the three process accounts and a statement of profit. (*Mangalore University, B.Com., September 1997*)

[**Answer :** Profit of process I Rs. 10,000, process II 13,515, process III 205 and Net loss Rs. 3780]

Exercise-4 (Inter Process Profit)

A Ltd., produces a product which passes through two processes before it is completed and transferred to finished stock. The following data relate to December 1994.

	Process 1 Rs.	*Process 2* Rs.	*Finished Stock* Rs.
Opening Stock	7,500	9000	22,500
Direct Materials	15,000	15,750	
Direct Wages	11,200	11,250	
Factory overheads	10,500	4,500	
Closing Stock	3,700	4,500	11,250
Inter-process profit included in opening stock	–	1,500	8,250

Output of process 1 is transferred to process 2 at 25% profit on the transfer price. Output of process 2 is transferred to finished stock at 20% profit on the transfer price. Stocks in process are valued at prime cost. Finished stock is valued at the price at which it is received from process 2. Sales during the period are Rs. 1,40,000.

Prepare process accounts and finished stock a/c showing the profit element at each stage.

(*University of Madras, B.Com., April 1995*)

[**Answer :** Profit of process-1 Rs. 13,500, process-2, 22,500, process-3 Rs. 16,250]

Exercise 5 : Product *A* is undertaken in two process. The following are the relevant information in a period :

	Process I	*Process II*
Opening stock	Rs. 5,000	6,000
Direct materials	10,000	10,500
Direct wages	7,500	7,500
Overhead	7,000	3,000
Closing stock	2,500	3,000
Percentage of profit on transfer price	25%	20%
Inter process for opening stock	–	1,000

Stocks in process are valued at materials + Conversion cost

Prepare process accounts and calculate actual profit on each process.

[*Answer :* Profit of process *I* is Rs. 9,000 and process *II* Rs. 15,500]

Exercise 6 (Equivalent production without opening work-in-progress) : R.P. Ltd. furnished you the following information relating to process *B* for the month of October 1986 :

(1)	Opening WIP	NIL
(2)	Units introduced	1,000 units @ Rs. per unit
(3)	Expenses debited to the process :	
	Direct materials	RS. 14,650
	Labour	Rs. 21,148
	Overhead	Rs. 42,000
(4)	Normal loss in process :	one per cent on input
(5)	Closing WIP	350
	Degree of completion	
	Materials	100
	Labour and overhead	50%

(6) Finished output 9,500 units

(7) Degree of completion of abnormal loss

Materials 100%

Labour and overhead 80%

(8) Units scrapped as normal loss were sold at Rs. 1 per unit

(9) All the units of abnormal loss were sold at Rs. 2.50 per unit

Prepare :

(1) Statement of equivalent production

(2) Statement of cost of finished goods, abnormal loss and closing WIP

(3) Process *B* a/c. *(ICWA (Inter), December 1988)*

[*Answer :* Total of process *B* A/c is Rs. 1,07,998]

Exercise 7 : Following particulars are extracted from the books of New India Chemical Co. Ltd. during July 1992. Normal loss estimated in the process *I* 10% cost of direct materials introduced Re. 0.92 per unit.

Number of units introduced to process *I*	5,000 units
Direct wages	Rs. 1,075
Overheads	Re. 2,100
Units scrapped realised	Rs. 0.20 per unit

At the end of July the output was as follows :

Work-in-progress	400 units
Scrap	600 units
Finished goods	4,000 units

Work-in-progress had reached the following stage

Direct material	100%
Direct wages	50%
Production overhead	25%

Prepare (*a*) Statement of equivalent production, (*b*) Statement of cost, (*c*) Statement of evaluation, (*d*) Process *I* a/c.

[*Answer :* Total of process I a/c is Rs, 7,775]

Exercise 8 (Opening & closing work-in-progress with abnormal gain) : The following data pertains to process *I* for March 1987 of Beta Ltd.

Opening work-in-progress : 1,500 units amounting to Rs. 15,000

Degree of completion :

Materials 100%, Labour and overhead $33\frac{1}{3}\%$

Input of materials :	18,500 units amounting to Rs. 52,000
Direct labour	Rs. 14,000
Overheads	Rs. 28,000
Closing work-in-progress	5,000 units

Degree of completion :

Materials 90%, Labour and overhead 30%

Normal process loss is 10% of total input (opening work-in-progress units + units put in)

Scrap value Rs. 2 per unit

Units transferred to the next process 15,000 units

You are required to :

(*a*) Compute equivalent units of production.

(*b*) Compute cost per equivalent unit for each cost element, *i.e.*, materials, labour and overhead.

(*c*) Compute the cost of finished output and closing work-in-progress.

(*d*) Prepare the process and other accounts.

Assume : (*i*) FIFO method is used by the company.

(*ii*) The cost of opening work-in-progresss is fully transferred to next process.

(C.A., Inter, May 1987)

[*Answer :* Total of process cost Rs. 1,21,000 profit transferred from abnormal gain a/c to P & L a/c is Rs. 8,000]

Exercise 9 (Opening and closing work-in-progress with abnormal loss) : Hindustan Ltd. is a manufacturer of processed goods and the following information relates to process '2' during September 1992 :

Work-in-progress :

Opening	–	300 units cost Rs. 2,000
Closing	–	400 units

The degree of completion of both opening and closing stock was as follows :

Process 1 cost	100%
Added materials in process 2	60%
Conversion cost	30%

During the month 2,000 units were transferred from process 1, at a valuation of 10,000. Other costs in process 2 were

Added materials	Rs. 4,650
Labour and overhead	Rs. 3,580

Units are inspected in process '2' when added. Materials are 50% complete and conversion cost 30% complete. Actual loss during September 1992 was 200 units, which were sold as scrap for Rs. 2 each.

The company uses a FIFO method of stock valuation. Prepare process '2' account and abnormal loss account for September 1992.

[*Answer :* Total of process '2' a/c is Rs. 20,230. Profit transferred to P & L a/c from abnormal loss is Rs. 970]

17

JOINT PRODUCTS AND BY-PRODUCTS

DEFINITION AND FEATURE OF JOINT PRODUCTS

Sam R. Goodman and James S. Reece in their book *Controller's Handbook* define joint product as "when a group of individual products is simultaneously produced, with each product having a significant relative sales value, the outputs are usually called joint products." According to Matz-Curry-Frank, joint products are produced simultaneously by a common process or series of processes, with each product possessing more than a nominal value in the form in which it is produced. This definition emphasises the point that the manufacturing process creates the products in a somewhat definite quantitative relationship. An increase in the output of one product will bring about an increase in the quantity of the others or *vice versa*, but not necessarily in the same proportion.

According to Theodore Lang, joint products represent two or more products separated in the course of the same processing operation, usually requiring further processing, each product being in such proportion that no single product can be designated as a major product.

According to this definition when two or more products of equal importance are simultaneously produced from the same basic raw materials from a common process they are known as joint products.

Features of Joint Products

1. Joint products are produced simultaneously with respect to common raw material and common manufacturing process.

2. Each product has a significantly relative sales value.

3. The "Jointness" may be associated with the complete transformation from raw materials into finished goods or it may be characteristic of only part of the complete transformation process.

4. There exist a direct quantitative relationship among various joint products such that an increase in the output of one increases the output of others, although not necessarily in the same ratio.

Some examples of joint products are : In oil refinery, the joint products obtained are, petrol, diesel, gasoline, kerosene, nephtha, lubricant oil and paraffin. In dairy industry, the joint products are, butter, ghee, cheese, etc. In gold mining, the joint products are gold, silver and copper.

Definition of Joint Cost

All costs associated with the manufacture of a joint product up to the point in the production process, where they are clearly differentiable as distinct products are called joint cost. Kohler in his *Dictionary for Accountants* defines joint cost as "the common cost of facilities or of services employed in the output of two or more simultaneously produced or otherwise related operations, commodities or services".

According to NAA Research Series No. 31–Costing Joint Products—States "costs are joint when two or more distinguishably different products are producted together from a single input cost factor. The characteristic condition of a joint cost is that the cost of several different products is incurred as a lump sum for the combination and not separately for the individual products".

Definition of Split-off-point

The exact point in a manufacturing process where two or more products can be distinguished is denoted as the split-off-point. This split-off-point can be either at the stage when the manufacturing process is complete, *i.e.*, when the raw materials have been converted into finished goods or alternatively at some intermediate point in the manufacturing process.

Difference Between Joint Cost and Separable Cost

The expenses incurred up to the point of separation is known as joint cost and after the point of split-off is known as separate cost. Joint costs incurred prior to the point of split-off cannot be traced to the particular products involved.

Definition of Minor Products

All jointly produced products of lesser economic significance are termed as "minor products".

Problems Associated with Joint Products

Joint products are obtained incidentally from the same manufacturing process. Some joint products are controllable while others are not. In most of the cases, the management has no alternative course of action. While some are useful, others are not and sometimes even unwanted. To the extent possible, the products that could be made separately are linked together to secure the economies of large scale operation. Further markets are developed for joint products previously discarded as waste. Joint products have assumed more importance today because increasing competition has compelled many industries to consider products which were formerly regarded as waste. Necessary steps are taken to make joint products more useful either at the point of derivation or after post split-off-point.

Some of the problems associated with joint products can be summarised as follows :

1. Classification of joint products into important and incidental.
2. Deciding the method of allocating the joint cost among joint products.
3. The method of treating the revenue earned by the sale of incidental or minor products.
4. Furnishing of information periodically to management for the purpose of deciding what products should be manufactured in what quantities?
5. Not all joint products are sold at the same time. To that extent it becomes difficult to account joint product.

OBJECTS OF TREATING JOINT COSTS

The man objectives of treating joint cost are as follows :

1. To know unit cost of every joint product.
2. For the purpose of stock valuation.
3. For the determination of profitability of different products.
4. For determining and appraising efficiency of various joint products.

5. For exercising internal control over various joint products obtained.
6. For fixing up the selling price of joint products.
7. For setting up standard output in advance of production.

CO-PRODUCTS

According to the NAA Research Study, "when two or more major products appear in a jointly produced combination, these products are called co-products to indicate that they are products of like importance". Co-products are the products which are manufactured in different varieties by the same industry. They may not arise from the same operation or raw material but are produced in different quantities without any co-relation to the other. Examples of co-products in a furniture-making industries are tables, chairs, benches, desks, almirahs. Similarly in fan manufacturing industry, the various co-products are ceiling fans, table fans, and exhaust fans. In automobile industry, the various co-products are buses, lorries, tractors and so on.

Difference between Joint Product and a Co-product

The important difference between a joint product and co-product is, there exists a linear relationship in terms of quantities among various joint products. Whereas no such relationship exists under co-products. They may be produced in different quantities depending upon the demand for them.

TREATMENT OF JOINT COST OF JOINT PRODUCTS

The purpose of accounting of joint product is to know individual product cost. This is done by means of allocating joint cost to all joint products which are obtained at the point of split-off. The following methods are adopted for allocating the joint expenses to all the joint products.

1. Physical Unit Method

This method of allocating costs uses a physical measure such as weight, volume, length and so on as the criterion for allocating joint costs. The joint products are measured in terms of a measuring rod such as a kg, litre, meter and so on. Process loss if any is borne by joint products in proportion to the volume of output. This method cannot be adopted where it is not possible to measure joint products with a common measuring rod. This situation arises when the joint products obtained are in different forms such as solid, liquid and gases.

Problem 1 : One tonne of raw materials put into a common process yields four joint products *P*, *Q*, *R*, and *S*, their weights being 63 kgs, 117 kgs, 180 kgs and 540 kgs respectively. The balance in weight is considered as normal wastage.

Based on the total processing cost of Rs. 20,000 per tonne of raw material input, you are required to apportion the joint cost to products *P*, *Q*, *R*, and *S*. *(C.S. (Final) Dec. 1986)*

Solution : **Statement showing apportionment of joint cost**

Products	*Yield (kg.)*	*Basis* = $\frac{Yield}{Output}$ × *Joint cost*	*Share of joint cost*
P	63	$\frac{63}{900} \times 20{,}000$	1,400
Q	117	$\frac{117}{900} \times 20{,}000$	2,600

R	180	$\frac{180}{900} \times 20{,}000$	4,000
S	540	$\frac{540}{900} \times 20{,}000$	12,000
Output	900		20,000
Normal loss	100		–
Input	1,000		20,000

Problem 2 : In a process line of *X Y* Company three joint products are produced. For the month of May 1990 the following data were available :

	L	*M*	*N*
Sales price per kg	Rs. 5	Rs. 10	Rs. 20
Post-separation point costs	10,000	5,000	15,000
Output in kg	2,500	1,000	1,500

Pre-separation point costs amounted to Rs. 20,000.

The joint products are manufactured in one common process, after which they are separated and may undergo further individual processing. The pre-separation point costs are apportioned to joint products according to weight. You are required to prepare a statement showing the estimated profit or loss for each product and in total. *(ICWA, Inter., June 1990)*

Solution : **Statement showing apportionment of joint cost**

	L (2,500)		*M (1,000)*		*N (1,500)*	
	Total	*Per unit*	*Total*	*Per unit*	*Total*	*Per unit*
Pre-separation cost (5 : 2 : 3)	10,000	4	4,000	4	6,000	4
Post-separation cost	10,000	4	5,000	5	15,000	10
Total cost	20,000	8	9,000	9	21,000	14
Profit/loss (balancing-figure)	(7,500)	(–3)	1,000	1	9,000	6
Sales price	12,500	5	10,000	10	30,000	20

Problem 3 : The following data have been extracted from the books of Bhaskar Coke Works :

Joint products	*Yield in kgs of recovered products per ton of coal*
Coke	1,420
Coal tar	120
Benzol	22
Ammonium sulphate	26
Gas	412
Total	2,000

The price of coal is Rs. 80 per ton. Direct labour and overhead costs to point of split-off are Rs. 40 and 60 respectively per ton of coal.

Calculate material cost, labour, overhead and total cost of each product on the basis of weight.

Solution : **Statement showing apportionment of joint cost per ton of coal**

Products	*Yield in kg of product per ton of coal*	*% of weight of products to coal*	*Cost of coal*	*Direct labour*	*Overhead*	*Total*
Coke	1,420	71.0%	56.80	28.40	42.60	127.8
Coal tar	120	6.0%	4.80	2.40	3.60	10.8

Benzol	22	1.1%	0.88	0.44	0.66	1.9
Ammonium sulphate	26	1.3%	1.04	0.52	0.8	2.4
Gas	412	20.6%	16.48	8.24	12.38	37.1
	2,000	100	80	40	60	180

2. Sales Value Method

Under this method, the criterion for allocating joint costs is the relative sales value associated with each individual product. Thus joint costs are allocated to the joint products on the basis of their ability to earn revenue. The assumption is that if a higher selling price exists for one product as compared with another product, then the production costs associated with that product must also be higher. The disadvantages of this method are : (*a*) Market prices of various products at the point of separation are not always available, (*b*) The joint product of one year may be sold in the next year. To this extent accounts are distorted. The joint products can be sold at any of the following three stages. So the treatment also differs between these stages of sale.

(*a*) Market value at the point of separation : The market prices of the joint products at the point of separation is ascertained and joint cost is apportioned in the ratio of these prices. This method is followed when further processing involves disproportionate costs.

Problem 4 : From the information below, find the profit made by each product, apportioning joint costs on the sale-value basis :

Joint costs		*Rs.*
Direct materials		1,26,000
Power		25,000
Petrol, oil and lubricants		5,000
Labour		7,500
Other charges		4,100
	Product X (Rs.)	*Product Y (Rs.)*
Selling costs	20,000	80,000
Sales	1,52,000	168,000

(*Andhra University, B. Com., May 1992*)

Solution : **Statement showing apportionment of joint cost**

	X	*Y*	*Total*
Direct materials	59,850	66,150	1,26,000
Power	11,875	13,125	25,000
Petrol, oil, lubricants	2,375	2,625	5,000
Labour	3,563	3,937	7,500
Other charges	1,947	2,153	4,100
Cost of production	79,610	87,990	1,67,600
Selling cost	20,000	80,000	1,00,000
Cost of sales	99,610	1,67,990	2,67,600
Profit	52,390	10	52,400
Sales	1,52,000	1,68,000	3,20,000

(b) Market value at finished stage : Usually it is difficult to obtain the selling price of joint products at the point of separation and it is comparatively easy to know selling price of joint products after further processing. Therefore this method is used more frequently compared to the above method.

Problem 5 : In a manufacturing concern a certain product *A* yield by-products *B* and *C*. The joint expenses of manufacture are, materials Rs. 10,200, labour Rs. 11,400 and on cost Rs. 7,600 while subsequent expenses are :

	A	*B*	*C*
Materials	2,500	1,200	1,400
Labour	1,900	1,600	2,000
Oncost	1,500	900	1,050
	5,900	3,700	4,450

The selling prices are : *A* – 30,000, *B* – 20,000, *C* – 15,000. The estimated profits on turnover are : A – 40%, B – 30%, C – 25%.

Show how would you apportion the joint expenses of manufacture and prepare process accounts

(*Bangalore University, B. Com., May 1992*)

Solution :

Statement showing apportionment of overhead

	A	*B*	*C*	*Total*
Sales	30,000	20,000	15,000	65,000
Less : Profit	12,000	6,000	3,750	21,750
Cost of production	18,000	14,000	11,250	43,250
Less : Subsequent expenses	5,900	3,700	4,450	14,050
Share in the joint cost	12,100	10,300	6,800	29,200

Main product 'A' A/c

To materials			By by-product *B* a/c	10,300
Joint	10,200		By by-product *C* a/c	6,800
Subsequent	2,500	12,700	By sales	30,000
To labour :				
Joint	11,400			
Subsequent	1,900	13,300		
To oncost				
Joint	7,600			
Subsequent	1,500	9,100		
To P & L a/c – profit		12,000		
		47,100		47,100

By-product 'B' A/c

To main product A a/c	10,300	By sales	20,000
To material	1,200		
To labour	1,600		
To on cost	900		
To P & L a/c – profit	6,000		
	20,000		20,000

By-product 'C' A/c

To main product A a/c	6,800	By sales	15,000
To material	1,400		
To labour	2,000		
To oncost	1,050		
To P & L – profit	3,750		
	15,000		15,000

Problem 6 : A concern while producing product A, also produces a by-product *B*. The by-product can be sold after a separate process.

From the under-mentioned information prepare accounts to show the cost per kg. of *A* and *B*

	Joint expense	*Separate expense*	
		A	*B*
Material	Rs. 60,000	22,000	2,500
Labour	Rs. 35,000	24,000	8,000
Overhead	Rs. 10,000	4,000	1,500
Output	–	450 kgs	150 kgs

The selling price of *B* is Rs. 300 per kg. It is estimated that profit is 50% of selling price.

(*Sri Sathya Sai University, B. Com., March 1992*)

Solution : **Statement showing share of B in the joint cost**

Sale value product *B* – 150 × Rs. 300			45,000
Less : Profit – 50% of sales value			22,500
Cost of production			22,500
Less : Separate expenses --	Materials	2,500	
	Labour	8,000	
	Overhead	1,500	12,000
Share of *B* in the joint cost			10,500

Product 'A' A/c

To materials			By by-product *B* a/c	10,500
Joint	60,000		By cost of production	1,44,500
Separate	22,000	82,000	@ Rs. 321.11	
To Labour				
Joint	35,000			
Separate	24,000	59,000		
To overhead				
Joint	10,000			
Separate	4,000	14,000		
		1,55,000		1,55,000

By-product 'B' A/c

To main product A A/c		10,500	By sales	45,000
To separate expense	– Material	2,500		
	– Labour	8,000		
	– Overhead	1,500		
To profit		22,500		
		45,000		45,000

Problem 7 (When profit of main product is not given) : *X*, *Y*, *Z* Ltd. manufactures product *A* which yields two by-products *B* and *C*. In a month, the joint cost was Rs. 20,600. Subsequent expenses were :

	A (Rs.)	*B (Rs.)*	*C (Rs.)*
Material	300	200	150
Direct wages	400	300	200
Overhead	300	270	280
	1,000	770	630

Gross sales value of products *A*, *B* and *C* was Rs. 15,000, Rs. 10,000, and Rs. 5,000 respectively. It was estimated that the net profit as percentage of sales in the case of B and C would be 25% and 20% respectively.

Ascertain the profit earned by *A* and prepare process cost accounts.

(Sri Sathya Sai University, B. Com., March 1989; Kerala University, B. Com., May 1991)

Solution :

Note : First of all calculate the share of joint cost of product *B* and *C* and prepare product *A* a/c. The balancing figure in product *A* will be the profit. Subsequently the share of joint cost of product *A* can be known.

Statement showing share of joint cost

	A	*B*	*C*	*Total*
Sales	15,000	10,000	5,000	30,000
Less : Profit	3,500	2,500	1,000	7,000
Cost of production	11,500	7,500	4,000	23,000
Less : Subsequent expenses	1,000	770	630	2,400
Share in joint cost	10,500	6,730	3,370	20,600

Product 'A' A/c

To share in the joint cost	20,600	By product B a/c	6,730
To materials	300	By product C a/c	3,370
To direct wages	400	By sales	15,000
To overhead	300		
To profit (balancing figure)	3,500		
	25,100		25,100

Product 'B' A/c

To product A A/c	6,730	By sales	10,000
To materials	200		
To labour	300		
To overhead	270		
To profit	2,500		
	10,000		10,000

Product 'C' A/c

To product A A/c	3,370	By sales	5,000
To materials	150		
To labour	200		
To overhead	280		
To profit	1,000		
	5,000		5,000

% of profit of product A on sales

$$\frac{3{,}500 \times 100}{15{,}000} = 23.33\%$$

Problem 8 (Physical unit and sales value method) : Three joint products are produced by passing chemicals through two consecutive processes. Output from process 1 is transferred to process 2 from which three joint products are produced and immediately sold. The data regarding the process for April 1990 is given below :

	Process 1	*Process 2*
Direct materials–2,500 kilo at Rs. 4 per kilo	Rs. 10,000	–
Direct labour	Rs. 6,250	Rs. 6,900

Overheads	Rs. 4,500	Rs. 6,900
Normal loss	10% of input	Nil
Sale value of loss	Rs. 2 per kilo	
Output	2,300 kilo	Joint products *A* – 900 kilo *B* – 800 kilo *C* – 800 kilo

These were no opening or closing stocks in either process and the selling price of the output from process '2' were :

Joint product *A*	–	Rs. 24 per kilo
Joint product *B*	–	Rs. 18 per kilo
Joint product *C*	–	Rs. 12 per kilo

Required :

(a) Prepare an account for process 1 together with any loss or gain a/c you consider necessary to record the month's activities.

(b) Calculate the profit attributable to each of the joint product by approtioning the total costs from process 2

(i) According to weight of output

(ii) By market value of production. (*C.A., Inter., May 1991*)

Solution :

Process '1' A/c

	Qty.	*Amt.*		*Qty.*	*Amt.*
To direct materials	2,500	10,000	By normal loss	250	500
To direct labour		6,250	By process '2' a/c	2,300	20,700
To overhead		4,500			
To abnormal gain	50	450			
	2,550	21,200		2,550	21,200

Normal loss A/c

To process '1' a/c	250	500	By abnormal gain	50	100
			By sales	200	400
	250	500		250	500

Abnormal gain A/c

To normal loss a/c	50	100	By process 1 a/c	50	450
To costing P & L a/c		350			
	50	450		50	450

Joint cost of three products under process 2

From process '1'–cost of production	20,700
Direct labour	6,900
Overheads	6,900
Total	34,500

Statement showing apportionment of joint cost under weight of output

A – For 2,300 kilo joint cost is Rs. 34,500

$$\text{For 900 kilo} = \frac{900 \times 34{,}500}{2{,}300} = \text{Rs. } 13{,}500$$

B – For 2,300 kilo joint cost is Rs. 34,500

$$\text{For 800 kilo} = \frac{800 \times 34{,}500}{2{,}300} = \text{Rs. } 12{,}000$$

C – For 2,300 kilo joint cost is Rs. 34,500

$$\text{For 600 kilo } \frac{600 \times 34{,}500}{2{,}300} = \text{Rs. } 9{,}000$$

Statement of profit under weight of output

Joint product	*Output*	*S.P. per unit*	*Sales value*	*Share of joint cost*	*Profit/loss*
A	900	24	21,600	13,500	8,100
B	800	18	14,400	12,000	2,400
C	600	12	7,200	9,000	1,800

Statement showing share of joint expense

Joint product	*Output*	*S.P. per unit*	*Sales revenue*
A	900	24	21,600
B	800	18	14,400
C	600	12	7,200
			43,200

A – For total sale of 43,200 total joint expense is 34,500

$$\text{For } 21{,}600 = \frac{21{,}600 \times 34{,}500}{43{,}200} = \text{Rs. } 17{,}250$$

B – For total sale of 43,200, total joint expense is 34,500

$$\text{For } 14{,}400 = \frac{14{,}400 \times 34{,}500}{43{,}200} = \text{Rs. } 11{,}500$$

C – For total sale of 43,200 total joint expense is 34,500

$$\text{For } 7{,}200 = \frac{7{,}200 \times 34{,}500}{43{,}200} = \text{Rs. } 5{,}750$$

Statement of profit under sales value method

Joint product	*Output*	*S.P. per unit*	*Sales*	*Share of joint cost*	*Profit*
A	900	24	21,600	17,250	4,350
B	800	18	14,400	11,500	2,900
C	600	12	7,200	5,750	1,450
			43,200	34,500	8,700

(c) Net realisable value : Under this method, in addition to deducting the profit and subsequent expenses from the sales value, the non-manufacturing costs such as selling and distribution overheads are also deducted. This gives rise to net saleable value of the various joint products.

Problem 9 : Calculate the estimated cost of production of by-product *X* and *Y* at the point of separation from the main product.

	By products	
	X	*Y*
Selling price per unit	Rs. 12	Rs. 24
Cost per unit after separation from main product	Rs. 3	Rs. 5
Units produced	500	200

Selling expenses amount to 25% of the total works cost—*i.e.*, including both pre-separation and post-separation works cost.

Selling prices are arrived at by adding 20% to toal cost—*i.e.*, the sum of works cost and selling expense.

(*Sri Sathya Sai University, B.Com., March 1991*)

Solution :

Statement showing share of joint expense

		X	Y
Sales		6,000	4,800
Less : Profit	$\frac{20}{120} \times 6,000$	1,000	
	$\frac{20}{120} \times 4,800$		800
Cost of production		5,000	4,000
Less : Subsequent expense		1,500	1,000
		3,500	3,000
Less : Selling expenses 25% on total cost of production $\left(\frac{25}{100} \times 5,000 \text{ and } \frac{25}{100} \times 4,000\right)$		1,250	1,000
Share in the joint cost		2,250	2,000

Product 'X' a/c

To share in joint cost	2,250	By sales	6,000
To subsequent expense	1,500		
To selling expense	1,250		
To profit	1,000		
	6,000		6,000

Product 'Y' a/c

To share in joint cost	2,000	By sales	4,800
To subsequent expense	1,000		
To selling expense	1,000		
To profit	800		
	4,800		4,800

Problem 10 : In a manufacturing concern production of *A* yields by-products *B* and *C*. The joint expenses of manufacture are :

Materials Rs. 8,500, Labour Rs. 9,000, Overheads Rs. 7,500. Subsequent expenses are as follows :

		Material	*Labour*	*Overhead*
A	Rs.	2,500	1,900	1,500
B	Rs.	1,200	1,600	900
C	Rs.	1,400	2,000	1,050

Selling price : *A* Rs. 30,000, *B* Rs. 20,000, *C* Rs. 15,000

Profit on S.P. : *A* 40%, *B* 30%, *C* 25%

Show how you would apportion the joint expenses and ascertain profit of each product.

(*Osmania University, B. Com., March 1992*)

Solution :

Statement showing approtionment of joint cost

	A	*B*	*C*	*Total*
Sales	30,000	20,000	15,000	65,000
Less : Profit	12,000	6,000	3,750	21,750

Cost of production	18,000	14,000	11,250	43,250
Less : Subsequent expenses	5,900	3,700	4,450	14,050
	12,100	10,300	6,800	29,200
Less : Selling & distribution oh.	1,938	1,291	971	4,200
Share in the joint cost	10,162	9,009	5,829	25,000

Note : The total joint cost given in the problem is Rs. 25,000. Whereas the total as per the above statement is Rs. 29,200. The difference of Rs. 4,200 (29,200 – 25,000) is selling and distribution overheads apportioned on the basis of sales value.

Main product 'A' A/c

To material	8,500		By by-product *B* a/c	9,009
Add : Addition	2,500	11,000	By by-product *C* a/c	5,829
To labour	9,000		By sales	30,000
Add : Addition	1,900	10,900		
To overhead	7,500			
Add : Addition	1,500	9,000		
By selling & distribution oh.		1,630		
To profit		12,000		
		44,838		44,838

By-product 'B' A/c

To main product *A* a/c	9,009	By sales	20,000
To materials	1,200		
To labour	1,600		
To overhead	900		
To selling & distribution oh.	1,291		
To profit	6,000		
	20,000		20,000

By-product 'C' A/c

To main product A a/c	5,829	By sales	15,000
To materials	1,400		
To labour	2,000		
To overhead	1,050		
To selling & distribution oh.	971		
To profit	3,750		
	15,000		15,000

Problem 11 : In a manufacturing company 10,000 kilolitre of *A* is processed to produce 6,000 kilolitre of *B* and 4,000 kilolitre of *C*. The joint cost before separation point came to an amount of Rs. 24,000. From the following particulars, calculate the apportionment of joint cost and the profit of each product under (*a*) physical measurement, (*b*) market value at separation point, and (*c*) market value after further processing.

	B (Rs.)	*C (Rs.)*
Unit selling price at separation point	5.00	3.75
Unit selling price after further processing	7.00	7.50
Further processing cost after separation	5,000	7,500

(*ICWA, Inter., June 1992*)

Solution :

(a) Physical unit method

Ratio of products *B* and *C*	6,000 K.L.	4,000 K.L.
	or 6 : 4	
	or 3 : 2	

Statement showing profit under physical unit method

	B	*C*	*Total*
Joint cost of Rs. 24,000 apportioned	14,400	9,600	24,000
Selling price	30,000	15,000	45,000
Profit	15,600	5,400	21,000

Statement showing profit under market value at separation point

	B	*C*	*Total*
Market value	30,000	15,000	45,000
Less : Joint cost allocated in the ratio of market Value, *i.e.*, 2 :1	16,000	8,000	24,000
Profit	14,000	7,000	21,000

Statement of profit under market value after further processing

	B	*C*	*Total*
Market value	42,000	30,000	72,000
Less : Joint cost allocated in the ratio of 7 : 5	14,000	10,000	24,000
	28,000	20,000	48,000
Less : Further processing cost	5,000	7,500	12,500
	23,000	12,500	35,500

3. Points Value Method or Survey Method or Weighted Average Cost Method

Where it is not possible to apply the physical unit method and sales value method because of their disadvantages, survey method is adopted to apportion the joint cost to joint products. Each joint products is assigned weights or points based upon quantity, size, difficulty of manufacture, time taken to manufacture, types of labour engaged, the cost of material used, etc. The output is multiplied by the weights or points thus assigned to get the product of each joint product. The total weight of all joint products is then obtained by adding them together. The product is divided by the total weight of all the joint products to get a quotient. The quotient multiplied by the joint cost gives the share of joint cost for every joint product. Expressed in the form of formula :

$$\text{Joint cost} = \frac{\text{Total weight assigned to each joint product}}{\text{Total weight of all products}} \times \text{Joint cost}$$

Where :

Total weight assigned to each joint product =

No. of units produced × Weights or points assigned

Problem 12 : From the following particulars calculate the share of every joint product

Units produced :	*X*	–	30,000 units
	Y	–	32,000 units
	Z	–	20,000 units
Joint cost incurred		–	Rs. 1,32,000
Weights assigned to each joint product	*X*	–	3 points
	Y	–	2.5 points
	Z	–	4 points

Solution : **Statement showing share of joint cost**

Joint product	*Units*	*Weight*	*Total weight*
X	30,000	3	90,000
Y	32,000	2.5	80,000
Z	20,000	4	80,000
			2,50,000

$$A = \frac{90,000}{2,50,000} \times 1,32,000 = \text{Rs. } 47,520$$

$$B = \frac{80,000}{2,50,000} \times 1,32,000 = \text{Rs. } 42,240$$

$$C = \frac{80,000}{2,50,000} \times 1,32,000 = \text{Rs. } 42,240$$

Problem 13 : *A* And *B* Chemicals Ltd., manufacture three varieties of mannures by mixing chemical fertilizer in different proportions. The three varieties *X*, *Y*, and *Z* are manufactured in two operations, (*a*) mixing and (*b*) packing and had the following relative cost values on a point-value-basis per cwt of output :

Variety	*Mixing*	*Packing*
X	2	1
Y	3	1.5
Z	5	2.5

The total cost for each process for January is as follows :

Mixing	Rs. 1,45,000
Packing	Rs. 2,900
	1,47,900

Production for the month was

Mixture X	2,500 cwts
Mixture Y	1,500 cwts
Mixture Z	1,000 cwts
	5,000 cwts

Prepare a statement showing the cost per cwt of each variety per operation.

Solution : **Statement showing point value of output**

Mixture	*Cwt*	*Points value (Total)*	
		Mixing	*Packing*
X	2,500	5,000	2,500
Y	1,500	4,500	2,250
Z	1,000	5,000	2,500
	5,000	14,500	7,250

Statement showing apportionment of overhead

Mixture	*Mixing*		*Packing*		*Total*	
	Total	*Per cwt*	*Total*	*Per cwt*	*Amt.*	*Per cwt*
X	50,000	20	1,000	0.40	51,000	20.40
Y	45,000	30	900	0.60	45,900	30.00
Z	50,000	50	1,000	1.00	51,000	51.00
	1,45,000		2,900		1,47,900	

Working Note : The costs are apportioned on the basis of their point values. For *X* it is calculated thus :

$$\frac{5,000}{14,500} \times 1,45,000 = \text{Rs. } 50,000$$

and similarly for products *Y* and *Z*.

Problem 14 : Growmore chemicals Ltd. manufacture three varieties of mannures *X*, *Y* and *Z* by mixing chemical fertilizers in different proportions. Two operations (i) mixing and (ii) packing are involved. There is no costing system. On technical estimation, relative cost values are fixed on points, basis per weight of output. However, the financial accounts data are segregated into two operations mentioned above. The relevant data for a particular month are as follows :

Varieties	*Point-Values per unit weight*		*Production*
	Mixing	*Packing*	*(Tons)*
X	2	5	250
Y	3	3	150
Z	5	2	100
Total cost (Rs.)	1,45,000	19,000	

Compute cost per ton of each variety per operation (*C.S. Inter., June 1997*)

Solution :

Calculation of cost per point

Variety	*Production*	*Mixing*		*Packing*	
	(Tons)	*Points*	*Total*	*Points*	*Total*
(1)	(2)	(3)	4(2 × 3)	5	6(2 × 5)
X	250	2	500	5	1,250
Y	150	3	450	3	450
Z	100	5	500	2	200
			1,450		1,900

Cost per point of mixing $\frac{1,45,000}{1,450} = 100$

Cost per point of packing $\frac{19,000}{1,900} = 10$

Statement showing cost per Ton

Variety	*Mixing*		*Packing*		*Total*
	Points	*Rs.*	*Points*	*Rs.*	
X	2	200	5	50	250
Y	3	300	3	30	330
Z	5	500	2	20	520

4. Average Unit Cost Method

Under this method, the total joint cost of manufacturing is divided by the total number of physical units produced. This results in average cost associated with the production of each unit of product regardless of its physical characteristics. Joint cost is apportioned to all joint products at this average cost.

Problem 15 : From the tollowing particulars calculate the share of joint cost of each joint product under average unit cost method :

Joint cost – Rs. 1,00,000

Joint products *X* – 2,500 units
Y – 3,500 units
Z – 4,000 units

Solution :

$$\text{Average cost per unit} = \frac{\text{Total joint cost}}{\text{Total units of joint product}} = \frac{1,00,000}{10,000} = \text{Rs. } 10$$

Statement showing apportionment of joint cost

Joint products	*Units*	*Cost per unit*	*Amount*
X	2,500	10	25,000
Y	3,500	10	35,000
Z	4,000	10	40,000
			1,00,000

5. Marginal Cost Method

Under this method marginal cost is allocated to joint products on the basis of weight or quantity of each product. Fixed cost is apportioned on the basis of contribution made by each product. This method has the advantage of maximising profit by proper planning and product mix.

Problem 16 : JBS Company operates a chemical process which jointly produces two joint products. The total joint cost is Rs. 2,750. It is the policy of the company to allocate the joint cost to products at different basis as mentioned below :

	Joint cost (Rs.)	*Basis of allocation*
Direct material	1,400	Sales value
Variable conversion	600	Weight
Fixed conversion	750	Contribution
	2,750	

	A	*B*
Sales	kg. 50	100
Selling price per kg	Rs. 30	20

Calculate cost of *A* And *B*

Solution : **Statement showing allocation of joint cost**

	Total	*A*	*B*
Materials 15 : 20	1,400	600	800
Variable conversion 5 : 10	600	200	400
Total variable cost	2,000	800	1,200
Sales	3,500	1,500	2,000
Contribution	1,500	700	800
Fixed cost 7 : 8	750	350	400

Statement of cost of *A* and *B*

	Total	*A*	*B*
Total variable cost	2,000	800	1,200
Fixed cost	750	350	400
Total cost	2,750	1,150	1,600

DEFINITION AND FEATURES OF BY-PRODUCT

According to Sam R. Goodman and James S. Reece by-product is a term which is applied to products produced simultaneously that have a very minor sales value as compared with that of main product. According to Theodore Lang, by-products refer to any saleable or usable value incidentally produced in addition to the main product. In the words of Neuner, by-products are produced from the same process as joint products but that the by-products are essentially the secondary results of the operations. According to him the rule that is suggested for interpreting the meaning of "secondary" is that, if the value of a product is less than 10% of the total value of all products, it could be considered a by-product; not a co-product or joint product. According to Schlatter (cost accounting), by-product split-off from the original material in process and thus do not become part of the main product.

The characteristic features of a by-product may be listed out as follows :

(*a*) By-products are obtained simultaneously along with main product.

(*b*) The quantity of by-product obtained is less than the main product.

(*c*) By-products yield only minor sales value when compared to main product.

(*d*) By-products cannot be used as such and therefore require further processing to make it more acceptable by customer.

(*e*) Only limited control can be exercised over by-products.

Some examples of by-products are as follows :

1. *Meat packing*—Meat is main product, whereas bones, fats, hides hairs are by-products.
2. *Sugar industry*—Sugar is main product—Baggasse and molasses are by-products.
3. *Cotton ginning*—Cotton fibre is main product cotton seeds are by-product.
4. *Coke making*—Coke is main product, ammonia, coal tar, benzol and gas are by-products.
5. *Soap making*—Soap is main product—glycerin is by-product.

DIFFERENCES BETWEEN JOINT PRODUCTS AND BY-PRODUCTS

1. Obtaining the joint products is the main objective of an industry, whereas obtaining by-product is secondary objective.

2. There exists a direct quantitative relationship among joint products. It may not be true in case of by-products.

3. The value of joint product is significance whereas it is negligible in case of by-product.

4. Joint product differs from by-products in respect of accounting treatment.

5. Greater degree of control can be exercised on joint products, whereas it is not possible to exercise utmost control over by-products.

TREATMENT OF BY-PRODUCTS

By-products need not bear any portion of the joint costs incurred prior to the point of separation. This is so because production is undertaken not with the intention of obtaining by-product but with the intention of obtaining/main product. However separate expenses or additional processing costs and selling and distribution expenses are to be charged to by-products obtained.

The only treatment that is to be given to by-products is the proper disposition of the net revenue received from by-product. There are two ways of measuring revenue obtained from by-products. First is in terms of net sales revenue obtained from by-product actually sold. Secondly, in terms of the net sales value of the by-product recovered, whether sold or not. Under the first method there exists no closing stock on hand at the end of the period. Whereas the second method carries a stock of by-products.

The accounting treatment of by-products depend upon two main consideration, i.e., (*i*) the by-product is of little value, (*ii*) the by-product is of considerable value.

1. Where the By-product is of Little Value

This consideration of treating by-product is based on two difficulties, *viz.*, (*a*) It is uneconomical to incur expenses in determining the price of each unit of by-product produced, (*b*) It is also equally difficult to ascertain the cost of producing a by-product up to the point of separation. The amount realised on the sales of by-product is treated as a profit and recorded in the profit and loss account. If the amount realised is too less, the amount so realised may be credited to the main product, thereby reducing the cost of the main product.

2. Where By-product is of Considerable Value

Here, the cost of by-product is ascertained accurately on account of increased costs incurred. A separate account is opened for each by-product to which is debited the estimated cost up to the point of split-off. The main product account is credited with the amount realised on sale of by-product.

Accounting of By-products

Two methods are followed in accounting of by-products. This is shown in the following chart :

Accounting of By-products

Non-cost method or sales value method

(1) Other income method
(2) Sales value of by-product included in the main product sale
(3) Sale value of by-product deducted from total cost
(4) Credit of by-product at sale value less selling and distribution cost
(5) Credit of by-product at sales value less cost incurred after split-off-point
(6) Credit of by-product at sale value less an estimated profit, (or reverse cost method) post split-off-cost, and selling and distribution cost

Cost method

(1) Opportunity or replacement cost method
(2) Standard cost method
(3) Joint cost method

Non-cost or Sales Value Method

1. Other income method : Under this method the sale value of by-product is credited to profit and loss account as "other income". The circumstances under which this method is used are as follows :

(*a*) Where the value of by-product is very less;
(*b*) Where the use of a more detailed method entails too much expense in comparison to benefits obtained;
(*c*) Where the carrying of by-product with the main product does not entail any appreciable difference in the cost of the main product.

The chief limitations of this method are as follows :

(*a*) Sometimes by-product may arise in one accounting period but they may be sold in another accounting year. This time gap distorts profits in different year;

(*b*) No value is given to by-product stock. This results in the overvaluation of main product stock. This again distorts the balance sheet;

(*c*) No attempt is made to control the by-product and it may result in losses due to fraud.

Problem 17 : From the following data, prepare a profit and loss account to show the total profit earned by the sale of main product and by-product :

Total cost of production – 12,000 units @ Rs. 1.50 per unit
Closing stock – 2,000 units @ Rs. 1.50
Administration & selling expenses – Rs. 2,000
Sales of main product – 10,000 units @ Rs. 2
Sales of by-product – Rs. 1,500

Solution :

Statement showing profit earned by main product

Cost of production	12,000 × 1.50	18,000	
Less : Closing stock	2,000 × 1.50	3,000	15,000
Administration and selling expenses			2,000
		Cost of sales	17,000
		Profit	3,000
		Sales	20,000

P & L a/c

By main product a/c	3,000
By by-product a/c	1,500
	4,500

2. Sale of by-product included in the main product sales : This method is resorted to (*a*) when by-product could be sold without altering the condition in which they arise, (*b*) when by-product is not significant in relation to main product. The costs incurred on main product and by-product are ascertained and the total cost is deducted from the combined sales value to know the profit.

Problem 18 : Prepare process account of main product for problem 17 under sale of by-product included in the main product sales.

Solution :

Process a/c of main product

To cost of production	18,000	By sales a/c	
To adm. & selling expenses	2,000	Main product	2,000
To profit & loss a/c	4,500	By product	1,500
		By closing stock	3,000
	24,500		24,500

Note : The total profit credited under this method is Rs. 4,500 whereas in the first method it is inly Rs. 3,000.

3. Sales value of by-product deducted from total cost : Under this method the sales value of by-product is deducted from total cost of by-product and main product. Its disadvantages are :

(*a*) Any inefficiency in the cost of manufacture of main product cannot be ascertained correctly if the credit from by-product is fluctuating.

(*b*) Closing stock for balance sheet purpose is valued at selling price of by-product.

4. Credit of by-product at sales less selling and distribution cost : The selling and distribution costs incurred on by-product are deducted from sale value of by-product and the net income thus obtained is deducted from the total cost of main product and by-product together or credited to the process account. The closing stock is valued at selling price less an estimated cost of selling and distribution cost of by-product.

5. Credit of by-product at sales value less cost incurred after split-off-point and selling and distribution cost : If by-product requires further processing after split-off-point then the post-split-off cost and selling and distribution cost incurred are deducted from the sale value of by-product and the net amount thus obtained is deducted from total cost or credited to process account. The closing stock is valued at selling price less an estimated selling and distribution cost and further processing costs after split-off-point.

6. Credit of by-product at sale value less an estimated profit, post-split-off-cost and selling and distribution overhead : Under this method, the credit is given to process account after deducting an estimated profit, post-split-off-cost and selling and distribution cost from the sale of by-products.

Problem 19 : During November 1992, Splatter Ltd. recorded the following results :

Opening stock of main product	Nil
Opening stock of by-product	Nil
Cost of production	Rs. 1,20,000

Sale of main product amounted to 90% of output during the period and 10% of production was held as closing stock at 30th November 1992. Sales revenue from the main product during November 1992 was 1,50,000.

A by-product X is produced and output had a net sales value of Rs. 1,000. Of this output value of Rs. 700 was sold during the month and Rs. 300 was still in stock at 30th November 1992.

Calculate the profit under :

1. Other income method.
2. By-product income added to sales of main product.
3. Sale income of the by-product deducted from the cost of production in the period.
4. Saleable value of the by-product deducted from the cost of product in the period.

Solution :

1. Other income method

Opening stock of main product	NIL
Add : Cost of production	1,20,000
	1,20,000
Less : Closing stock 10% of cost of production	12,000
Cost of goods sold	1,08,000
Profit	42,000
Sales	1,50,000
Profit from sale of main product	Rs. 42,000
Profit from sale of by-product	Rs. 700
Total profit	42,700

2. By-product income added to sales of main product

Opening stock of main product	NIL
Add : Cost of production	1,20,000
	1,20,000
Less : Closing stock 10% of cost of production	12,000
Cost of goods sold	1,08,000
Profit	42,700
Sale (1,50,000 + 700)	1,50,700

3. Sales income of the by-product deducted from the cost of production in the period

Opening stock		NIL
Add : Cost of production (1,20,000 – 700)		1,19,300
Less : Closing stock 10% of cost of production		11,930
	Cost of goods sold	1,07,370
	Profit	42,630
	Sales	1,50,000

4. Saleable value of the by-product deducted from the cost of product in the period

Opening stock		NIL
Add : Cost of production (1,20,000 – 1,000)		1,19,000
		1,19,000
Less : Closing stock—10% of cost of production		11,900
	Cost of goods sold	1,07,100
	Profit	42,900
	Sales	1,50,000

Problem 20 : From the following particulars calculate the amount of profit under :

1. Other income method.
2. When sales value of by-product is added to sale of main product.
3. When sales value of by-product deducting selling and distribution expenses and expenses incurred after split-off-point is credited to main product sales a/c.

Total production cost	Rs. 31,500
Quantity produced	18,000 units
Sale of main product	15,000 units @ Rs. 2.50 per unit
By-product revenue received	Rs. 2,275
Selling & distribution expenses of main product	Rs. 3,250
Closing stock of main product	3,000 units @ Rs. 1.75
Selling & distribution expenses of by-product	Rs. 500
Additional process cost of packing by-product	Rs. 100

Solution :

1. Other income method—Statement showing profit

Cost of production	18,000 × 1.75 =	31,500	
Less : Closing stock	3,000 × 1.75 =	5,250	26,250
Add : Selling & distribution overhead			3,250
	Cost of sales		29,500
	Profit		8,000
	Sales		37,500

Total income :

Profit from main product		Rs. 8,000
Sale of by-product		Rs. 2,275
	Net income	10,275

2. Statement showing profit when sales value of by-product is added to sale of main product :–

Cost of production	18,000 × 1.75 =	31,500	
Less : Closing stock	=	5,250	26,250
Add : Selling & distribution overhead			3,250
	Cost of sales		29,500
	Profit		10,275
	Sales (37,500 + 2,275)		39,775

3. Statement showing profit by crediting sales value less selling and distribution expenses and expenses incurred after split-off-point.

Cost of production	31,500	
Less : Closing stock	5,250	
Cost of goods sold		26,250
Add : Selling & distribution expenses of main product		3,250
		29,500
Profit		9,675
Sales (main product sales *i.e.*, 37,500 + 2,275 – 500 – 100 = 39,175 from sale of by-product less S & D expenses and additional cost of by-product		39,175

Problem 21 (Reverse cost method) : From the following data obtained from the books of Grace Co. (Pvt.) Ltd. calculate (*a*) unit cost of main product and (*b*) unit cost of by-product :

	By-product Rs.	*Main product* Rs.
Sales	12,000	1,50,000
Process cost before separation	–	75,000
Process cost after separation	2,200	23,000
Selling & distribution expenses	1,500	12,000
Units produced	9,000	20,000

There is no opening and closing stock of inventories. The company allows a 20% gross profit for by-product.

Solution : **Statement showing the cost of production of main product and by-product**

			By-product Rs.	*Main product* Rs.
Process cost before separation				75,000
Sale of by-product		12,000		
Less : Gross profit @ 20%	= 2,400			
Less : S & D expenses	= 1,500	3,900		
		8,100		
Less : Process cost after separation		2,200		
Amount credited to main product			5,900	5,900
Net cost to produce main product at separation			5,900	69,100
Add : Process cost after separation			2,200	23,000
Total cost			8,100	92,100
Unit cost			$\frac{8,100}{9,000}$ = 0.90	$\frac{92,100}{20,000}$ = 4.605

II. Cost Methods

1. Opportunity cost method or replacement cost method : Under this method, the by-products obtained in the production process is utilised either as indirect material or as raw material (direct material). The by-products are valued at the cost of replacing them. Hence the name replacement cost method. The term opportunity cost is used because it represents the cost which would have been incurred had the by-products been bought from external source. Examples of by-products which are treated under this method is, use of cotton waste arising from the processing of fine yarn may be used either as indirect material, *i.e.*, for cleaning the machines or as raw materials used in producing low quality yarn. Similarly, coke oven gas which is a by-product of coke may be used for heating the open hearth furnace. The equivalent heat units produced by its consumption may be ascertained and the coke account will be credited with the value thereof.

Problem 22 (Opportunity cost method) : From problem no. 19 calculate the net income from the sale of main product under opportunity cost method taking the replacement cost of by-product used in production as Rs. 2,275.

Solution : **Statement showing net income of main product under opportunity cost method**

Cost of production	18,000 × 1.75 =	31,500	
Less : Replacement cost of by-product used in production		2,275	
		29,225	
Less : Closing stock—3,000 units @ 1.6236		4,871	
i.e., $\frac{29,225}{18,000} = 1.6236$			24,354
Add : Selling & distribution expenses			3,250
Cost of sales			27,604
Profit			9,896
Sales			37,500

2. Standard cost method : Under this method a standard cost is determined for each type of by-product based upon past exerience. The main product account is credited with this standard cost of by-products. This enables to judge efficiency of main product because the standard cost of by-products is a constant figure.

3. Joint cost method : This method is used when the value of by-products is comparatively of a higher value. So the cost incurred up to the point of split-off (joint cost) is apportioned among the main product and all by-products using any of method discussed under the topic treatment of joint products.

Problem 23 : *A* Ltd. manufactures one main product and two by-products. During January 1993 the following data is available :

	Main product	*By-products*	
		A	*B*
Sales	Rs. 4,00,000	32,000	48,000
Joint cost	Rs. 1,55,200		
Subsequent expenses	Rs. 40,000	6,400	7,200
Percentage of profit to sales		10%	15%
Selling expenses as % of sales value	10%	5%	6%

No. Stock exists. Prepare a statement showing profit under joint cost method.

Solution : **Statement showing apportionment of joint cost**

	A	*B*
Sales	32,000	48,000
Less : Profit	3,200	7,200
	28,800	40,800
Less : Separation cost	6,400	7,200
	22,400	33,600
Less : Selling expenses	1,600	2,800
Shares in the joint cost	20,800	30,800
Joint cost to be borne by main product		1,55,200
Less : Share of by product *A* & *B* (20,800 + 30,800)		51,600
		1,03,600

Statement showing profit

	Main product	*A*	*B*
Share of joint expense	1,03,600	20,800	30,800
Post separation cost	40,000	6,400	7,200
Selling expenses	40,000	1,600	2,800
	1,83,600	28,800	40,800
Profit	2,16,400	3,200	7,200
Sales	4,00,000	32,000	48,000

QUESTIONS

I. Mark 'T' or 'F' in the space provided

1. In theory, joint products can be distinguished from by-products. *T/F*
2. Under the relative sales value method of allocating costs to joint products, each of the joint products will show the same gross margin percentage if sold at the split-off-point. *T/F*
3. A common processing operations may yield several joint products and a number of by-products. *T/F*
4. If Rs. 1,00,000 of common processing costs are incurred to produce two products *A* and *B* with market value at split-off-point of *A*–Rs. 1,16,000 and *B*–Rs. 84,000, Rs. 58,000 of costs should be allocated to product *A*. *T/F*
5. Cost per unit of each product is the same if joint costs are apportioned on the basis of the physical measure of product. *T/F*
6. The sales value method apportions the joint costs on the basis of respective capacities of individual products to bear joint costs. *T/F*
7. The allocation of joint cost to joint and by-products does not affect the total profit or loss. *T/F*
8. Joint costs can be obtained separately and are thus divisible common costs cannot be obtained separately and are thus indivisible. *T/F*
9. Standard cost method of evaluating by-products can be used only in standard costing technique. *T/F*
10. It is possible for a main product of one industry to be the by-product of another. *T/F*

[*Answers :* True 1, 2, 3, 4, 6, 7, 10, False 5, 8, 9]

II. Choose the correct answer

1. Which one of the following statement relative to joint products and by-products is false
   (*a*) The preferred accounting treatment of by-products is to set them up in inventory at their net realisable-value and credit this amount to accounts in which the costs of the main product are recorded.
   (*b*) The common costs incurred in producing joint products may, under certain circumstances, be allocated to the products on a physical unit basis.
   (*c*) For product costing purposes, the common costs incurred in producing joint products should be allocated to the products on a physical units basis.
   (*d*) Costs allocated to joint products are useful to management for a variety of decisions. [ ]
2. Trimmings in timber industry should be treated as a
   (*a*) Waste (*c*) Joint product
   (*b*) Scrap (*d*) By-product [ ]
3. The primary purpose of apportioning joint costs of a processing centre to various products produced is to :
   (*a*) Develop accurate processing cost variance product-wise
   (*b*) Report more correct standard product costs for comparative analysis
   (*c*) Establish inventory cost assigned to unsold units
   (*d*) Record accurate cost of sales by product lines [ ]
4. The method of accounting for joint product costs that will produce the same gross profit rate for all the product is
   (*a*) Sales value method (*c*) Opportunity cost method
   (*b*) Other income method (*d*) Reverse cost method [ ]

5. Individual products, each of a significant value, produced simulataneously from the same raw material is known as :
   (*a*) By-product (*c*) Joint product
   (*b*) Main product (*d*) Co-product [ ]
6. Which one of the following method of accounting of by-product should be applied, when the by-product is to be utilised in the undertaking itself as material for some other process :
   (*a*) Sales value method (*c*) Opportunity cost method
   (*b*) Joint income method (*d*) Standard cost method [ ]
7. A backery producing cakes, biscuits, and breads should be treated as :
   (*a*) Main products (*c*) By-product
   (*b*) Joint product (*d*) Co-product [ ]
8. A method of apportionment of joint costs to various joint products on the basis of their respective capacities to bear joint cost is
   (*a*) Sales value method (*c*) Average cost method
   (*b*) Physical unit method (*d*) Survey method [ ]
9. Credit is given to the process account at a predetermined value of the by-product under :
   (*a*) Standard cost method (*c*) Opportunity cost method
   (*b*) Sales value method (*d*) Points value method [ ]
10. Which one of the following are virtually always subsequent costs :
   (*a*) Direct materials (*c*) Administration overhead
   (*b*) Direct labour (*d*) Selling & distribution overhead [ ]

[***Answers :*** 1. (*d*), 2. (*b*), 3. (*d*), 4. (*a*), 5. (*c*), 6. (*c*), 7. (*b*), 8. (*a*), 9. (*a*), 10. (*d*)]

III. Simple Questions
1. Define joint product.
2. Define by-product.
3. Define a co-product.
4. Distinguish between a joint product and a by-product.
5. Distinguish between a by-product and scrap.
6. What is split-off-point?
7. What is a subsequent expense?
8. List out four methods of apportioning joint expense.
9. List out four methods of accounting of by-product.
10. List out four examples of industries producing joint products.

IV. Short Answer Questions
1. Explain the methods of treating joint cost in cost accounts.
   (*Shri Sathya Sai University, B. Com., March 1992*)
2. Distinguish between joint product and by-product. Explain as to how cost share allocated between main product and by-products in cost account.
3. Enumerate the methods which may be employed in costing joint products.
   (*University of Kerala, B. Com., April 1989*)
4. Explain briefly the methods of accounting for "by-product". (*Calicut University, B. Com., Oct. 89*)
5. What are the three most common methods of allocating joint cost of production to joint product? Write a brief explanatory note on each. (*Delhi University, B. Com.,(Hons) 1990*)
6. How would you deal with by-products in costing
   (*i*) Where they are of small total value?
   (*ii*) Where they are of considerable total value?
   (*iii*) Where they require further processing? (*CA, (Inter.) May 1988*)
7. Distinguish between by-product and joint product. (*Madras University, M. Com., April 1992*)

EXERCISES

Exercise 1 (Physical unit method) : *A* coke manufacturing company produces the following products by putting 5,000 tonnes of coal @ Rs. 25 per ton into a common process :

Coke	3,500 tonnes
Tar	1,200 tonnes

Ammonium sulphate	52 tonnes
Benzol	48 tonnes

Apportion the joint cost amongst the products on the basis of the physical unit method.

[*Answer:* Share of joint expenses are coke Rs 91,150, Tar 31,250, Ammonium sulphate 1,350, Benzol 1,250]

Exercise 2 (Sales value method) : From the following information find out the cost of product *X* and *Y*. Product *Y* is the by-product of *X* and on sale of *Y* a profit of 20% on selling price is obtained usually :

	Joint cost	*Separate expense*	
		X	*Y*
Materials	15,000	3,000	2,000
Wages	8,000	1,200	800
Other expenses	6,000	1,500	700

Total amount realised by sale of *Y* was Rs. 8,000 (*Bangalore University, B. Com., Nov. 1991*)

[*Answer:* Cost of production of product *A* is Rs. 16,100 and total of product *B* a/c is 8,000]

Exercise 3 (When profit of a product is not given) : Product *X* yields by-products *Y* and *Z*. The joint expenses of production and separate expenses are as follows :

	Joint expense	*Separate expenses*		
		X	*Y*	*Z*
Material	Rs. 4,000	800	640	720
Labour	Rs. 3,200	960	560	680
Overheads	Rs. 3,600	1,040	400	600
Selling price	–	16,800	8,000	7,200
Profit on sale	–	–	50%	$33\frac{1}{3}\%$

Show how would you apportion the joint expenses prepare the necessary accounts.

(*Bangalore University, B. Com., November 1990*)

[*Answer:* Profit of product is Rs. 8,400. Total of product *Y* and *Z* a/cs are Rs. 8,000 and Rs. 7,000 respectively]

Exercise 4 : A factory producing article *P* also produces a by-product *Q* which is further processed into finished product. The joint cost of manufacture is given below :

Material	Rs. 5,000
Labour	Rs. 3,000
Overheads	Rs. 2,000
	Rs. 10,000

Subsequent costs are given below :

	P	*Q*
Material	3,000	1,500
Labour	1,400	1,000
Overheads	600	500
Selling prices	16,000	8,000
Estimated profit on selling price	25%	20%

Assume that selling and distribution expenses are in proportion of sales price. Show how you would apportion joint costs of manufacture and prepare process accounts relating to products *P* and *Q*.

(*Sri Sathya Sai University, B. Com., July 1990*)

[*Answer:* Share in the joint costs are *P* – Rs. 6,733, *Q* – 3,267, Total of product *P* a/c is Rs. 19,267 and *Q* a/c is Rs. 8,000]

Exercise 5 : In an oil mill, flour products emerge from a refining process. The total cost of input during the quarter ending March 1983 is Rs. 1,48,000. The output sales and additional processing costs are as under :

Products	*Output in liters*	*Additional processing cost after split-off-point*	*Sales value*
AOXE	8,000	Rs. 43,000	Rs. 1,72,500
BOXE	4,000	Rs. 9,000	Rs. 15,000
COXE	2,000	–	–
DOXE	4,000	Rs. 1,500	Rs. 45,000

In case these products were disposed off at the split-off-point, that is before further processing, the selling price would have been

AOXE	*BOXE*	*COXE*	*DOXE*
Rs. 15	Rs. 6	Rs. 3	Rs. 7.50

Prepare a statement of profitability based on

(*i*) If the products are sold after further processing is carried out in the mill

(*ii*) If they are sold at the split-off-point (*CA, Inter., May 1983*)

[***Answer :*** Profit under case (*i*) – AOXE Rs. 30,833, BOXE – loss Rs. 13,733, COXE – profit Rs. 1,067, DOXE – profit Rs. 18,833. Under case (*ii*) – AOXE Rs. 21,333, BOXE Rs. 4,267, COXE Rs. 1,067, DOXE Rs. 5,333]

Exercise 6 (Points value method) : It is the policy of a company to allocate joint cost on points basis. The data are as follows :

Joint cost incurred – Rs. 1,08,000

Product	*No. of units produced*	*Relative evaluation of points*
P	100	40
Q	150	30
R	200	20
S	100	20

Calculate how joint cost will be allocated.

[***Answer :*** *P's* share Rs. 28,800, *Q's* share – Rs. 32,400, *R's* share Rs. 28,800, *S's* Rs. 68,000]

Exercise 7 (On by-product) : The yield of a certain process is 80% as to the main product, 15% as to the by-product and 5% as to the process loss. The material put in process (5,000 units) cost Rs. 23.75 per unit and all other charges are Rs. 14,250, of which power cost a accounted for $33\frac{1}{2}$%. It is ascertained that power is chargeable as to the main product and by-product in the ratio of 10 : 9.

Draw up a statement showing the cost of the by-product. (*CA, Inter., May 1988*)

[***Answer :*** Cost of by-product is Rs. 22,500]

18

OPERATING OR SERVICE COSTING

DEFINITION, CHARACTERISTICS AND APPLICATIONS OF OPERATING COSTING

The ICMA terminology defines operating cost as "the cost of providing a service" and operating costing as "that form of operation costing which applies where standardised services are provided either by an undertaking or by a service cost-centre within an undertaking. The method may be used where the service is not completely standardised but it is convenient to regard it as such, and to calculate average costs per period in relation to the standardised unit of measurement. From these definitions it is clear that the cost of providing a service is known as operating cost and the method employed to ascertain the cost of such service is known as operating costing.

Characteristic Features of Operating Costing

The characteristic features of operating costing are as follows :

1. The industries which adopt this method of costing do not produce any tangible goods. Instead they are concerned with rendering the services to public at large. They render uniform service to all those who apply for such services.
2. The cost unit used by such undertakings is known as composite unit as compared to the use of simple cost unit by rest of the undertakings. Some of the examples of composite units used by the undertakings are as follows :

   Railways – Passanger – kilometer or ton-kilometer
   Hospitals – Patient-day
   Hotel (Lodging) – Room-day
   Hotel (Boarding) – Plate-meals
   Gas distribution – Cublic-meter
3. Classification of expenses into fixed and variable plays an important role. The cost of rendering additional service is affected by variable cost.
4. In most of the cases, it involves many stages and processes in converting basic materials to the ultimate service.
5 Costs are usually computed period-wise. However, under special circumstances costs are computed order-wise as in the case of utilisation of vehicles, use of road-roller, etc.
6. The demand for the services of industries adopting this method of costing fluctuates. Hence it is difficult to estimate the cost accurately.
7. There is no difficulty faced in respect of valuation of work-in-progress or closing stock when compared to other industries.
8. Only medium and large sized undertakings deal in manufacturing and rendering services. Such industries assume the position of monopolistic undertakings or public utility undertakings.

Applications : Operating costing is applied to those organisations which render service externally (*i.e.*, to public at large) or internally (*i.e.*, to various departments of the same organisation). Some examples of services rendered to outsiders are electricity supply, water supply, gas supply, boarding and lodging and so on. While services such as repairs and maintenance, purchasing and storage, internal transport, etc. constitute services rendered internally. There is a point of difference in respect of accounting of services rendered. Whereas the objective of accounting external service is to know the total cost of manufacturing and profit on provision of such service, the object of internal service is to facilitate apportionment of service departments cost to various other departments.

Operating costing is applied to the following undertakings :

1. Transport undertakings such as Roadways, Railways, Tramways and Airways.
2. Municipal services such as supply of water, street lights, etc.
3. Steam and electricity undertakings.
4. Hotels covering boarding and lodging.
5. Hospitals.
6. Educational institutions.
7. Public libraries.
8. Service departments in big factories.
9. Cinemas.
10. Distribution of gas, air compressor, air-conditioning.
11. Sports and recreational clubs.
12. Services such as supply cranes, road roller, water pumping, fire extinguishers, etc.

COMPONENTS OF TOTAL COST IN OPERATING COSTING

As compared to other methods of costing, where the total cost comprises of prime cost, factory cost, and office cost, the total cost under operating costing is classified under the following headings :

1. Capital expenditure : This includes :
- (*a*) Buildings
- (*b*) Plant
- (*c*) Vehicles
- (*d*) Equipments from the use of which service is provided.

2. Direct or variable cost : This includes :
- (*a*) Expenses on medicines (in hospitals)
- (*b*) Fuel (in railways, buses, trucks, taxies)
- (*c*) Pilots salaries (in hotels)
- (*d*) Provisions (in hotels).

3. Fixed cost : This includes :
- (*a*) Depreciation
- (*b*) Rent and rates
- (*c*) Taxes and insurance
- (*d*) Licence fee.

TRANSPORT COSTING

The main objects of transport costing are (*a*) to ascertain the cost of operating a vehicle and (*b*) to fix up a fair for carrying passangers or goods for a certain distance.

Advantages of Transport Costing

The advantages of operating costing are as follows :

1. To decide whether to own a vehicle or to hire a vehicle.
2. To provide a basis for apportioning service departments expenses to production departments.
3. To enable the owner of a vehicle to charge fair to the clients, including concessional and special rates.
4. To know efficiency by comparing the cost of maintaining and running one vehicle with similar type of other vehicle; e.g., car vs. matador.
5. To choose between two modes of transport, as for example between lorry or railway in order to deliver goods to customers.

Components of Transport Costing

The total cost of operating service by a transport company is as follows :

1. Standing charges or fixed cost : These include :

(*a*) Administrative expenses such as salaries of manager, accountant, machanic, etc.

(*b*) Garage rent

(*c*) Taxes and insurance of vehicles

(*d*) Wages of drivers, conductors, and cleaners

(*e*) Depreciation of vehicles.

2. Running charges or variable cost : These include :

(*a*) Petrol

(*b*) Diesel, oil

(*c*) Lubricant.

3. Maintenance cost :

(*a*) Repairs and maintenance charges

(*b*) Tyres, tubes, batteries, etc.

Recording of Cost Under Transport Costing

Two important documents are used under transport costing. They are as follows :

(1) Daily report sheet or log sheet : This document is used when a owner owns a fleet of vehicles. This report is prepared either by a driver, foreman or a clerk at the garage or depot. The purpose of this document is to enable the accumulation and control of cost. This document contains particulars about each journey made by the vehicle. These particulars enable the owner to utilise the vehicle without allowing for idle running capacity. Besides this, the data in this report also enables to apportion expenses to other vehicles. A proforma of this document is shown below :

DAILY REPORT SHEET OR LOG SHEET

Vehicle No....................................	No. of sheet....................................
Route..	Date..
Driver..	Starting time..................................
Registration No.............................	

Particulars of trip

Trip No.	*From*	*To*	*Passanger/or Goods*		*Distance*	*Time*	
			Out	*Enroute*		*Out*	*In*

Employees name :	*Delays :*	*Supplier :*
Driver..................	Loading..............	Petrol.........................
Cleaner................	Traffic..............	Oil............................
Conductor...........	Accident............	Greese.......................
Machanic.............	Breakdown..........	Tyre..........................

(2) Operating cost sheet or cost summary performance statement : This document helps in calculating cost per carrying passanger or goods for one kilometer. The cost of operating the vehicles help the owner in the following ways :

(*a*) To avoid waste of oil, fuel, etc.

(*b*) To know the efficiency by comparing with other vehicles.

(*c*) Facilitates in quoting hire charges.

(*d*) Cost of idle vehicle and lost running time can be known.

(*e*) Helps in apportioning overheads to other departments.

(*f*) Helps in controlling cost by comparing operating cost of one year with previous year.

The operating cost sheet is prepared on a periodical basis. The information for this purpose is collected from log sheets.

A specimen of this document is shown below :

COST SUMMARY AND PERFORMANCE STATEMENT

Registration No........... Month ended.........

Capacity...........

Monthly charges

A – Operating charges	B – Maintenance charges	C – Fixed charges
(1) Petrol.........	(1) Tyres.........	(1) Insurance.........
(2) Oil.........	(2) Repairs.........	(2) Interest.........
(3) Grease.........	(3) Overhead.........	(3) Depreciation.........
(4) Driver.........	(4) Garage.........	(4) Tax, licence.........
(5) Assistant.........		(5) Others.........
(6) Mechanics.........		
Total		

Monthly cost sheet

1.	Total capital cost	
	Performance record	
2.	Days operated	
3.	Days idle	
4.	Days maintained	
5.	Total hours operated	
6.	Total kilometers covered	
7.	Total trips made	
	Performance averages	
8.	Average kilometers per day maintained	6 ÷ 4
9.	Average kilometers per day operated	6 ÷ 2
10.	Average kilometers per trip	6 ÷ 7
	Costs for the month	
11.	Total expenses for the month (A + B + C)	
12.	Cost per day operated	11 ÷ 2
13.	Cost per day maintained	11 ÷ 4
14.	Cost per kilometer operated	11 ÷ 6
15.	Cost per hour	11 ÷ 5

Units of Costs in Transport Costing

To measure the efficiency of running vehicles different cost units are used. Important among those are :

(1) The tonne-kilometer : These are of two types :

(*a*) *The absolute tonne-kilometer :* It refers to unit cost of carrying one tonne of goods over a distance of 1 kilometer. Expressed in the form of formula :

Absolute tonne km. = Weight carried × Kilometer run for each section of the trip

Problem 1 (Calculation of absolute tonne-kilometer) : A truck carries 4 tonnes of goods. It unloads 1 tonne after 7 km and the balance after travelling 5 km. It runs empty on the return trip. Calculate absolute tonne-kilometer.

Solution : (1 ton × 7) + (3 tons + 12) + (0 ton × 12)

7 + 36 + 0 = 43 Absolute ton-km.

(*b*) *Commercial tonne-kilometer :* This unit is used to overcome the limitation of calculating the unloaded capacity at various distance covered. This method is based on the assumption of an average, wherein it is assumed that the vehicle runs with half load throughout the distance covered (after having unloaded part of the goods at different places). Expressed in the form of formula :

$$\text{Commercial tonne kilometer} = \frac{\text{Tonnage loaded on lorry + Distance travelled}}{2}$$

Problem 2 : A truck starts with a load of 10 tonnes of goods from station P. It unloads 4 tonnes at station Q and rest of the goods at station R. It reaches back directly to station P after getting reloaded with 8 tonnes of goods at station R. The distances between P to Q, Q to R and then from R to P are 40 kms., 60 kms., and 80 kms., respectively.

Compute absolute tonne-kms.

(*University of Delhi, B. Com.,(Hons.) April 98*)

Solution :

From	P to Q	10 tonnes × 40 kms.	=	400
From	Q to R	6 tonnes × 60 kms	=	360
From	R to P	8 tonnes × 80 kms.	=	640
	Total Tonne-kms.			1,400

Problem 3 (Calculation of commercial ton-kilometer) : A vehicle Ka–03-2,758 runs with 6 tonnes on a trip. 2 tonnes were unloaded after travelling a distance of 10 km; 1 ton after a further travels of 8 km; yet another ton after travelling a further distance of 4 kms and the remaining 2 tonnes after a further 5 km travel. It then returns empty, covering a distance of 13 kms.

Calculate (*a*) The absolute ton-km

(*b*) Commercial ton-kilometer.

Solution :

(*a*) **Absolute ton-km**

$(6 \times 10) + (4 \times 8) + (3 \times 4) + (2 \times 5) + (0 \times 13)$

$= 60 + 32 + 12 + 10 + 0$

$= 114$ tonne-kilometer

(*b*) **Commercial ton-km**

$$\frac{6 \times 40}{2} = 120 \text{ ton-kilometer}$$

(2) **The kilometer run :** This unit is used to know the performance of vehicles, where carrying of goods is not involved. The cost of transporting the staff of a company can be related to this unit of cost.

(3) **Cost per hour :** This unit is used when vehicles are hired out to customers at a certain rate per hour. This unit covers all the costs of operating the vehicle along with a profit margin. The hour for this purpose is taken as "hired-out hour".

Steps to ensure optimum utilisation of vehicles : In order to increase the efficiency of operating the services, the following steps are suggested :

1. To select the shortest routes for the journey.
2. To utilise the full loading capacity. As far as possible the return journey is to be so planned that it does not return empty.
3. Delay in transit is to be totally avoided. Repairs are to constantly undertaken even if there is minor defect in the vehicle so as to avoid frequent breakdown of vehicle.
4. To ensure economic consumption of petrol, diesel.
5. The size of the vehicle should suit the specific purpose. The owner has to buy different sizes of vehicles or with different capacities for the right useful of vehicles for the right purpose.

Problem 4 : A lorry starts with a load of 20 tonnes of goods from station *A*. It unloads 8 tonnes at station *B* and rest of goods at station *C*. It reaches back directly to station *A* after getting reloaded with 16 tonnes of goods at station *C*. The distance between *A* to *B*, *B* to *C* and then from *C* to A are 80 kms. 120 kms. and 160 kms. respectively compute "Absolute tonnes-kms" and "Commercial tonnes-kms"

(*CA, Inter., November 1999*)

Solution :

Absolute Ton-kms = 20 tonnes × 80 kms + 12 tonnes × 120 kms + 16 tonnes × 160 kms

= 5,600 tons-kms

Commercial Ton-kms = Average load × Total kms Travelled

$$\left(\frac{20 + 12 + 16}{3}\right) \times 360 \text{ kms}$$

= 5,760 tons-kms

Problem 5 : A truck starts with a load of 10 tonnes of goods from station *P*. It unloads 4 tonnes at a station Q and rest of the goods at station R. It reaches back directly to station *P* after getting reloaded with 8 tonnes of goods at station *R*. The distances between *P* to *Q*, *Q* to *R* and then from *R* to *P* are 40 kms. 60 kms and 80 kms respectively compute "Absolute tonne-kms" and commercial-tonne km. (*CA, Inter., May 1995*)

Solution :

Absolute Ton-km = 10 tons × 40 kms + 6 tons × 60 kms + 8 tons × 80 kms

= 1,400 Ton-kms

Commercial Ton-km = Average load × Total kilometer travelled

$$= \left(\frac{10+6+8}{3}\right) \times 180 \text{ kms}$$

8 × 180 = 1,440 ton-kms

Problem 6 : A 40 seater tourist bus operates in a month as follows :

	Capacity	*From*	*To*	*Distance*
First 10 days	Full	Hyderabad	Khammam	160 km
Next 15 days	75%	Hyderabad	Khazipet	250 kms
Next 5 days	60%	Hyderabad	Koppidi	100 kms

The total expenses are Rs. 3,77,000. Ascertain cost of one passanger km

(*S. V. University, B. Com., April 1999*)

Solution :

No. of passanger kilometers = No. of Days × Capacity × Capacity used × Distance × To & From

$$\text{First 10 days} = 10 \times 40 \times \frac{100}{100} \times 160 \times 2 = 1{,}28{,}000$$

$$\text{Next 15 days} = 15 \times 40 \times \frac{75}{100} \times 250 \times 2 = 2{,}25{,}000$$

$$\text{Next 5 days} = 5 \times 40 \times \frac{60}{100} \times 100 \times 2 = 24{,}000$$

Total passanger-kms 3,77,000

$$\text{Cost per passanger km} = \frac{\text{Total expenses}}{\text{Total passenger kms}}$$

$$= \frac{3,77,000}{3,77,000} = 1. \text{ per P. kms}$$

Problem 7 : Sri Venkate Rao runs a tempo service at Anatapur. He furnishes you, the following data and wants you to compute the operating cost per running kilometer :–

Cost of vehicle	Rs. 1,50,000
Road licence	Rs. 1,500 p.a.
Supervisors salary	Rs. 26,500 p.a.
Driver's wages per hour	Rs. 10
Cost of fuel per litre	Rs. 8
Repairs & Maintenance per km	Rs. 5
Tyre cost per km	Rs. 2
Garage rent p.a.	Rs. 7,200
Insurance	Rs. 2,000 p.a.
Kilometers running per litre	5
Kilometers run during the year	6,000
Estimated life of the vehicle	75,000 kms

Charge interest at 10% p.a. on the cost of vehicle

The vehicle runs 20 kms per hour on an average (*S. V. University, B. Com., October 1999*)

Solution : **Operating cost sheet**

	Per annum	Per running km
Standing charges :–		
Road licence	1,500	
Supervisor salary	26,500	
Garage rent	7,200	
Insurance	2,000	
Interest $\left(1{,}50{,}000 \times \frac{10}{100}\right)$	15,000	
	52,200	
per running km	$= \frac{52{,}200}{6{,}000}$	8.70
Operating charges :–		
Driver's wages $\frac{10}{20} \times 6{,}000$	= 3,000	
Fuel $\frac{8}{5} \times 6{,}000$	= 9600	
Repairs & Maintenance $5 \times 6{,}000$	= 30,000	
Tyre cost $2 \times 6{,}000$	= 12,000	
Depreciation $\frac{1{,}50{,}000}{75000} \times 6{,}000$	= 12,000	
	66,600	
Per Running km = $\frac{66{,}600}{6{,}000}$		11.10
Operating cost per running km		19.80

Problem 8 : A transport service company is running five buses between two towns which are 50 kms apart. Seating capacity of each bus is 50 passangers. The following particulars were obtained from their books for April 1998 :

	Rs.
Wages of drivers, conductors and cleaners	24,000
Salaries of office staff	10,000
Diesel oil and other oil	35,000
Repairs & maintenance	8,000
Taxation, insurance etc	16,000
Depreciation	26,000
Interest and other expenses	20,000
	1,39,000

Actually passangers carried were 75% of seating capacity. All buses ran on all days of the month. Each bus made one round trip per day.

Find out the cost per passanger kilometer. (*CA, Inter., Nov. 1998*)

Solution : **Calculation of passanger kilometer**

No of Buses × Distance × "To" and "Fro" × Seating capacity × Percentage of seating capacity × No of days in a month

$= 5 \times 50 \times 2 \times 50 \times \frac{75}{100} \times 30 = 5{,}62{,}500$ kms

Operating cost sheet

Standing charges :–		
Wages of drivers, conductcrs and cleaners	24,000	
Salaries of office staff	10,000	
Taxation, Insurance	16,000	
Interest & other expenses	20,000	
		70,000
Running & Maintenance cost :–		
Repairs and maintenance	8,000	
Diesel and other oil	35,000	
Depreciation	26,000	
		69,000
		1,39,000

Cost per passanger km = $\frac{1,39,000}{5,62,500} = 0.2471$

Problem 9 : Anami Transport company has been given a route 40 km long to run a bus. The bus costs the company a sum of Rs. 1,00,000. It has been insured at 3% p.a. and the annual tax will amount to Rs. 2,000. Garage rent is Rs. 200 p.m. Annual repairs will be Rs. 2,000 and the bus is likely to last for 5 years.

The driver's salary will be Rs. 300 PM and the conductor's salary will be Rs. 200 PM in addition to 10% of takings as commission (to be shared by the driver and the conductor equally)

Cost of stationery will be Rs. 100 PM. Manager-cum-Accountant's salary is Rs. 700 PM.

Petrol and oil will be Rs. 50 per 100 km. The bus will make 3 up and down trips carrying, on an average, 40 passangers on each trip. Assuming 15% profit on takings, calculate the bus fare to be charged from each passanger. The bus will run on an average 25 days in a month *(ICWA, Inter., December 1998)*

Solution : **Calculation of Effective passanger-km per month**

40 km × 2 (up & down) × 3 trips × 25 days × 40 passangers
= 2,40,000 passanger-kms per month

Calculation of total passangers carried per month

40 passangers × 2 (up & down) × 3 trips × 25 Days
= 6,000 passangers

Operating cost sheet

		P.A. *Rs.*	*P.M.* *Rs.*
Standing charges :–			
Insurance @ 3% on Rs. 1,00,000		= 3,000	
Tax		= 2,000	
Garage rent @ Rs. 200 PM		= 2,400	
Driver's salary e Rs. 300 PM		= 3,600	
Conductor's salary @ Rs. 200 PM		= 2,400	
Stationery @ Rs. 100 PM		= 1,200	
Manager cum Accountant's salary @ Rs. 700 PM		= 8,400	
	Total	23,000	1,916.67
Variable charges :–			
Depreciation	$\frac{1,00,000}{5}$	20,000	1666.67
Repairs		2,000	166.66
Petrol and oil	$\left(\frac{5}{100} \times 40 \text{ km} \times 2 \times 3 \times 25\right)$		3,000.00
	Total cost without commission		6,750.00

Commission (See note 1)		900.00
Profit (See note 2)		1,350.00
	Total takings	9,000.00

Fare per passanger km $\frac{9,000}{2,40,000}$ = 0.0375

Or Fare per passanger $\frac{9,000}{6,000}$ = 1.50

Working Note :

Commission to driver and conductor @ 10% of total takings and profit @ 15% of the same

Let total taking be *x*

Commission @ 10% = $\frac{x}{10}$

Profit @ 15% of takings = $\frac{15x}{100} = \frac{3x}{20}$

Total cost without commission = 6,750

$$\therefore x = \frac{6,750}{1} + \frac{x}{10} + \frac{3x}{10}$$

$$x = \frac{1,35,000 + 2x + 3x}{20}$$

$$\text{or} \quad 20 \times x = 1,35,000 + 2x + 3x$$

$$20x - 2x - 3x = 1,35,000$$

$$15x = 1,35,000$$

$$x = \frac{1,35,000}{15} = 9,000$$

(1) Commission @ 10% on 9,000 = 900

(2) Profit @ 15% on 9,000 = 1,350

Problem 10 : From the following data calculate the cost per running km of a vehicle

	Rs.
Cost of vehicle	75,000
Garage rent p.a.	1,200
Insurance premium p.a.	2,500
Life tax	3,500
Drivers wages P.M.	1,000
Cost of Diesel per litre	15
Tyre depreciation per km	0.20
Estimated life of vehicle	1,50,000 kms
Annual mileage	10,000 kms
Mileage per litre of diesel	15 kms

(*S.V. University, B. Com., October 1998*)

Solution :

Operating cost sheet

	Per annum	*Per running km*
Standing charges :–		
Garage rent	1,200	
Insurance premium	2,500	
Life Tax 3,500 × $\frac{10,000}{1,50,000}$	233	
Driver's wages (1,000 × 12)	12,000	
	15,933	
Per running km $\frac{15,933}{10,000}$		1.59

Operating charges :–

Depreciation of vehicle		
$75{,}000 \times \frac{10{,}000}{1{,}50{,}000}$	5,000	
Depreciation of Tyre		
$0.20 \times 10{,}000$	2,000	
Diesel $\frac{15}{15} \times 10{,}000$	10,000	
	17,000	
Per running km = $\frac{17{,}000}{10{,}000}$		1.70
Operating cost per running km		3.29

Problem 11 : SMS is a public school having five buses each plying in different directions for the transport of its school students. In view of a large number of students availing of the bus service, the buses work two shifts daily in the morning and two in the afternoon one shift is for senior students and the other for Junior students.

The distance travelled by each bus one way is 8 kms. The school works 25 days in a month and remains closed for vacation in May, June and December. Bus fee, however, is payable by the students for all the 12 months in a year. The details of expenses for a year are as under :–

Driver's salary	Rs. 450 per month per driver
Cleaner's salary	Rs. 350 per month
Salary payable for all 12 months :–	
(One cleaner employed for all the five buses)	
Licence fee, taxes etc.	Rs. 860 per bus per annum
Insurance	Rs. 1,000 per bus per annum
Repairs and maintenance	Rs. 3,500 per bus per annum
Purchase price of the bus	Rs. 1,50,000 each
Life	12 years
Scrap value	Rs. 30,000
Diesel cost	Rs. 2.00 per litre

Each bus gives an average mileage of 4 kms per litre of diesel
The seating capacity is fully occupied during the whole year
Seating capacity of each bus – 50 students

Students are picked up and dropped within a range upto 4 kms of distance from the school are charged half fare and fifty percent of the students travelling in each trip are in this category. Ignore interest. Since the charges are to be based on average cost, you are required to :

(*i*) Prepare a statement showing the expenses of operating a single bus

(*ii*) Work out the average cost per student per month in respect of :

(*a*) Students coming from a distance of upto 4 kms from the school

(*b*) Students coming from a distance beyond 4 kms from the school.

(*University of Delhi. B. Com.(Hons.) April 1995*)

olution : **Calculation of Diesel cost per bus per annum**

No of trips of 8 kms per day per bus = 8 Trips

Distance travelled per bus per day =

$8 \times 2 \times 4 \times = 64$ kms

Distance travelled during the month =

$64 \times 25 = 1{,}600$ kms

Distance travelled during the year = $1{,}600 \times 9 = 14{,}400$ kms

(May, June, and December being vacation/cost of Diesel $14{,}400 \times \frac{2}{4}$ = Rs. 7,200 p.a.)

Operating cost sheet

		Per bus Per annum
Driver's salary	450×12	5,400
Cleaner's salary	$\frac{350 \times 12}{5}$	840
Licence fee, taxes etc		860
Insurance		1,000
Repairs and maintenance		3,500
Depreciation of bus	$\left(\frac{1,50,000-30000}{12}\right)$	10,000
Diesel cost		7,200
		28,800

(1) Operating cost per month (For both trips)

$$\frac{28,800}{12} = \text{Rs. } 2,400$$

Operating cost per month per trip

$$\frac{2,400}{2} = 1,200$$

Apportionment of operating cost per bus per month per trip (Rs. 1,200) over half fare and full fare students

Ratio of charging to these two categories of students 1 : 2

∴ cost charged to

(*a*) $\frac{1}{2}$ fair students $\frac{1}{3} \times 1,200 = 400$

(*b*) Full fair student $\frac{2}{3} \times 1,200 = 800$

(*ii*) (*a*) Operating cost per half fair student $= \frac{\text{Rs. } 400}{25} = \text{Rs. } 16$

(*b*) Operating cost per full fair student $= \frac{800}{25} = \text{Rs. } 32$

Problem 12 : Mr X owns a bus which runs according to the following schedule :

(*i*) Delhi to Chandigarh and back on the same day,
Distance covered : 150 kms, one way, number of days run each month 8, seating capacity occupied 90%

(*ii*) Delhi to Agra and back, the same day :
Distance covered : 120 kms, one way, number of days run each month 10, seating capacity occupied 85%

(*iii*) Delhi to Jaipur and back the same day distance covered : 270 kms, one way, Number of days run each month : 6. Seating capacity occupied 100%

(*iv*) Following are the other details :

Cost of the bus	Rs. 6,00,000
Salary of the driver	Rs. 2,800 p.m.
Salary of the conductor	Rs. 2,200 p.m.
Salary of the part time accountant	Rs. 200 p.m.
Insurance of the bus	Rs. 4,800 p.a.
Diesel consumption 4 kms per litre	@ Rs. 6 per litre
Road Tax	Rs. 1,500 p.a.
Lubricant oil	Rs. 10 per 100 kms.
Permit fee	Rs. 315 p.m.
Repairs and maintenance	Rs. 1,000 p.m.

Depreciation of the bus	@ 20% p.a.
Seating capacity of the bus	50 persons

Passanger tax is 20% of the total takings. Calculate the bus fare to be charged from each passenger to earn a profit of 30% on total takings. The fares are to be indicated per passenger for the Journeys :

(*i*) Delhi to Chandigarh
(*ii*) Delhi to Agra
(*iii*) Delhi to Jaipur

(*C.A., Inter, May 1994*)

Solution :

Calculation of total run per month

	Km. per trip	×	Trips per day	×	Days per month	=	kms per month
Delhi to Chandigarh	150	×	2	×	8	=	2,400
Delhi to Agra	120	×	2	×	10	=	2,400
Delhi to Jaipur	270	×	2	×	6	=	3,240
							8,040

Calculation of passanger-kms per month

	Total seats available per month	*Capacity utilised % seats*	*Kms. per trip*		*Passen-ger kms. per month*
Delhi to Chandigarh & back	50 seats × 2 trips × 8 days = 800	90	720 × 150	=	108,000
Delhi to Agra & back	50 Seats × 2 trips × 10 days = 1,000	85	850 × 120	=	102,000
Delhi to Jaipur & back	50 seats × 2 trips × 6 days = 600	100	600 × 270	=	1,62,000
			Total		3,72,000

Operating cost sheet

	P.M.
Fixed cost :	
Salary of driver	2,800
Salary of conductor	2,200
Salary of part-time accountant	200
Depreciation $6,00,000 \times \frac{20}{100} \times \frac{1}{2}$	10,000
Insurance $4,800 \times \frac{1}{12}$	400
Road tax $1,500 \times \frac{1}{12}$	125
Repairs and maintenance	1,000
Permit fee	315
Total fixed cost	17,040
Variable cost :	
Diesel $8,040 \times \frac{6}{4}$	12,060
Lubricant oil $8,040 \times \frac{10}{100}$	804
Total cost per month	29,904
Profit and passenger tax together account for 50% of total takings or 100% of cost	29,904

	Total takings	59,808
Passenger tax	20% of takings	11,961.60
Profit	30% of takings	17,942.60

Rate per passenger kilometer $= \frac{59,808}{3,72,000}$ = 0.16

Fare to be charged

Delhi to Chandigarh, per passenger	= 150 × 0.16	= Rs. 24
Delhi to Agra, per passenger	= 120 × 0.16	= 19.20
Delhi to Jaipur, per passenger	= 270 × 0.16	= 43.20

Problem 13 : Mr. Prakash has been promised a contract to run a tourist car on a 20 km. long route for the chief executive of a multinational firm. He buys a car costing Rs. 1,50,000. The annual cost of insurance and taxes are Rs. 4,500 and Rs.. 900 respectively. He has to pay Rs. 500 per month for a garage where he keeps the car when it is not in use. The annual repair costs are estimated at Rs. 4,000. The car is estimated to have a life of 10 years at the end of which the scrap value is likely to be Rs. 50,000.

He hires a driver who is paid Rs. 300 per month plus 10% of the takings as commission. Other incidental expenses are estimated at Rs. 200 per month.

Petrol and oil will cost Rs. 100 per 100 kms. The car will make 4 round trips each day. Assuming that a profit of 15% on taking is desired and that the car will be on the road for 25 days on an average per month, what should he charge per round trip? *(University of Delhi, B.Com. (Hons.) April 1993)*

Solution : **Calculation of total kilometers run**

20 kms × 2 × 4 round trips × 25 days = 4,000 kms.

Operating cost sheet

Fixed charges :	*P.A.*	*P.M.*
Depreciation	10,000	
Insurance	4,500	
Taxes	900	
Garage Rent (500 × 12)	6,000	
Annual repairs	4,000	
Drivers salary (300 × 12)	3,600	
Incidental expenses (200 × 12)	2,400	
	31,400	2,616.17
Variable expenses :		
Petrol and oil $4,000 \times \frac{100}{100}$		4,000.00
Total cost (without commission)		6,616.17
Drivers commission 10% of 8,822.22		882.22
Profit 15% of 8,822.22		1,323.33
Takings		8,822.22

Working Note :
Calculation of takings

Let x be the total takings for the month drivers commission 10% of x or $\frac{x}{10}$

Profit 15% of x or $\frac{3x}{20}$

Takings = Total cost + drivers commission + profit

or, $x = TC + \frac{x}{10} + \frac{3x}{20}$

$$\text{or,} \quad x - \frac{x}{10} - \frac{3x}{20} = 6{,}616.67$$

$$\text{or,} \quad \frac{20x - 2x - 3x}{20} = 6{,}616.67$$

$$\text{or,} \quad 15x = 6{,}616.67 \times 20$$

$$\text{or,} \quad x = \frac{6{,}616.67 \times 20}{15}$$

$$x = 8{,}822.22$$

Total number of round trips per month 25 × 4 = 100

$$\text{Hence charge per round trip} = \frac{8{,}822.22}{100} = 88.22$$

Problem 14 : The following information is available for estimating the cost for the year 1997. Full operating cost per truck-hour applicable to the trucks operated for a service department of a telephone company. The 1996 actual costs are used to calculate the 1997 rate :

(*a*) Cost of rent, insurance etc. of the garage was Rs. 15,576 of which one-third was allocated to the service department.

(*b*) The foreman of the garage was paid a salary of Rs. 4,800. All his time was devoted to the trucks.

(*c*) The trucks belonging to the service department represent one-quarter of the trucks handled by the garage.

(*d*) The heating, lighting cost of the garage amounted to Rs. 3,540.

(*e*) Other running expenses, which fluctuated with the truck operating homs, amounted to Rs. 4,794 for the six trucks in the service department.

(*f*) The trucks operate 40 hours a week for 52 weeks each year. During the working hours each of the trucks in down for approximately 60 hours per year for repairs and maintenance. As a result of a strike in July. The garage was closed for 2 weeks.

(*g*) Cost of each truck was Rs. 3,500 and its scrap value is estimated at Rs. 400. The life of a truck has been estimated at 12,000 operating hours.

(*h*) The estimated repairs over the life of a truck are expected to amount Rs. 1,400.

(*i*) Driver's wages paid amounted to Rs. 18,720 for the year.

You are required to calculate the applicable rate per hour to be used to reflect the full operating cost for 1997 for trucks operating in the service department of the telephone company.

(*Sri Sathya Sai University, B.Com., March 1998*)

Solution : **Calculation of hours operated**

40 hrs. × 50 weeks	=	2,000	hrs.
Less : Repairs & maintenance	=	60	hrs.
Per truck		1,940	hrs. for the year
For 6 trucks 1,940 × 6 trucks	=	11,640	hrs.

Operating cost sheet of service department of telephone company

Standing charges :

Depreciation :

Cost	3,500 per truck	
Less : Scrap value	400	
	3,100	
$\frac{3{,}100}{12{,}000 \text{ hrs}} \times 1{,}940 \text{ hrs.} \times 6 \text{ trucks}$		3,007
Foreman's salary $4{,}800 \times \frac{1}{4}$		1,200
Rent & Insurance $15{,}576 \times \frac{1}{3}$		5,192

Maintenance charges :

Repairs $\frac{1,400}{12,000 \text{ hrs}} \times 1,940 \times 6$ trucks	1,358
Heating, Lighting of garage 3,540 × $\frac{1}{3}$	1,180
Running charges :	
Running expenses for 6 trucks	4,794
Driver's wages	18,720
	35,451
Cost per hour $\frac{35,451}{11,640}$	3.04

Problem 15 : Mr 'x' runs a tempo service to chennai. He furnishes you the following data and wants you to compute the cost of running the tempo per tonne kilometer.

	Rs.
Cost of vehicle	1,50,000
Road licence fee p.a.	750
Supervisor's salary p.a.	26,500
Driver's wage per hour	40
Repairs and maintenance per k.m.	0.20
Cost of fuel per litre	9.00
Tyre depreciation per k.m.	0.80
Garage rent p.a.	3,600
Insurance p.a.	500
Kilometer running per litre	5
Kilometer run during the year	6,000
Estimated life of the vehicle	75,000 kms.
Tonnes per k.m. (average)	5

Charge interest @ 10% p.a. on cost of vehicle. The vehicle runs 20 kms. per hour an am average.

(*Sri Sathya Sai University, B.Com., March 1999*)

Solution : **Operating cost sheet**

Fixed cost

Road licence	$\frac{750}{30,000}$	= 0.025
Supervisor's salary	$\frac{26,500}{30,000}$	= 0.883
Garage rent	$\frac{3,600}{30,000}$	= 0.120
Interest	$1,50,000 \times \frac{10}{100} \times \frac{1}{30,000}$	= 0.500
Insurance	$\frac{500}{30,000}$	= 0.016

Variable cost :

Driver's wages	$\frac{40}{20}$	= 2.000
Cost of fuel	$\frac{9}{5}$	= 1.800
Repairs & maintenance		= 0.200
Tyres cost		= 0.800

Depreciation	$\frac{1,50,000}{75,000}$	= 2.000
	Cost per ton. km.	8.344

Problem 16 : A transport company supplies the following details in respect of a truck of 5 ton. capacity

Cost of truck	Rs. 1,80,000
Estimated life	10 years
Diesel oil	@ Rs. 100 per trip each way
Repairs	Rs. 500 per month
Drivers wages	Rs. 2,000 per month
Cleaner's wages	Rs. 1,500 per month
Insurance	Rs. 9,600 per year
Taxes	Rs. 2,400 per year
General supervision	Rs. 4,800 per year

The trucks carries goods to and from a city covering a distance of 50 miles each way. While going to the city, freight is available to the extent of full capacity and on return 20% of capacity.

Assuming that the truck runs on an average 25 days a month, work out (*a*) operating cost per ton-mile, (*b*) rate per ton. per trip that the company should charge if a profit of 50% on the freightage is to be earned.

(*Sri Sathya Sai University, B.Com., Oct. 1998*)

Solution :

(*a*) Operating cost sheet

		P.M.
Depreciation	$\frac{1,80,000}{10} = \frac{18,000}{12}$	1,500
Repairs		500
Driver's wages		2,000
Clearner's wages		1,500
Insurance	$\frac{9,600}{12}$	800
Taxes	$\frac{2,400}{12}$	200
General supervision	$\frac{4,800}{12}$	400
		6,900
Per ton-mile	$= \frac{6,900}{7,500}$	0.920
Diesel 100 × 50 =	$\frac{5,000}{7,500}$	0.667
	Operating cost	1.587

(*b*) Freight rate per ton-mile

Operating cost per ton-mile	1.587
Add : Profit of 50% on freightage or 100% on operating cost. (For verification see note below)	1.587
Freight rate per ton.km.	3.174
Onward trip 50 × 5 × 3.174	= 793.5
Return trip $50 \times 5 \times \frac{20}{100} \times 3.174$	= 158.7
Total for one trip both ways	952.2

Note :

Total freight collected in 25 days 952 × 25	= 23,800
Less : Operating cost per month 6,900 + 5,000	= 11,900
Profit at 50% on freightage	11,900

Problem 17 : Comparative operating cost sheet : From the following date relating to two different vehicles *A* and *B*, compute the cost per running kilometer.

	A (Rs.)	*B (Rs.)*
Kilometers run (Annual)	15,000 km.	6,000 km.
Cost of vehicles	25,000	15,000
Road licence (Annual)	750	750
Insurance (Annual)	700	400
Garage rent (Annual)	600	500
Salaries	1,200	
Driver's wages per hour	3	3
Cost of petrol per litre	3	3
Km. run per litre	20 km.	15 km.
Repair charges per km.	1.65	2.00
Tyre cost per km.	0.80	0.60
Estimated life of the vehicle	5%	5%
Vehicle run per hour	20 kms.	20 kms.

(*University of Madras, B.Com., Sept. 1997*)

Solution :

Comparative operating cost sheet

	Vehicle A	*Vehicle B*
Standing charges :		
Road licence	750	750
Insurance	700	400
Garage rent	600	500
Salaries	1,200	1,200
Interest on capital vehicle *A* $\frac{25,000 \times 5}{100}$	1,250	
B $\frac{15,000 \times 5}{100}$		750
Total fixed cost	4,500	3,600
Variable cost :		
Drivers wages	2,250	900
Vehicle *A* $\frac{15,000}{20 \text{ km per hr}} = 750 \text{ hrs} \times 3$		
Vehicle *B* $\frac{6,000}{20 \text{ km per hr}} = 300 \text{ hrs.} \times 3$		
Cost of petrol		
Vehicle *A* $\frac{3}{20} \times 15,000 = 2,250$	2,250	1,200
Vehicle *B* $\frac{3}{15} \times 6,000 = 1,200$		
Repair charges		
Vehicle *A* 15,000 × 1.65	24,750	12,000
Vehicle *B* 6,000 × 2		

Tyre cost		
Vehicle A 15,000 × 0.80	12,000	3,600
Vehicle B 6,000 × 0.60		
Depreciation	3,750	1,200
	49,500	22,500
Cost per running km.	$\frac{49,500}{15,000 \text{ kms}}$	$\frac{22,500}{6,000 \text{ kms}}$
	= 3.30	= 3.75

Problem 18 : Global Transport Ltd. charges Rs. 90 per ton. for its 6 ton truck lorry load from city '*A*' to city '*B*'. The charges for the return journey are Rs. 84 per ton. No concessions or reduction in these rates is made for any delivery of goods at intermediate station '*C*'. In January 1997. The truck made 12 outward Journeys for city *B* with full load out of which 2 tons were unloaded twice in the way at city '*C*'. The truck carried a load of 8 ton in its return journey for 5 times but once caught by police and Rs. 1,200 was paid as fine. For the remaining trips the truck carried full load out of which all the goods on load were unloaded once at city 'C'. The distance from city '*A*'. to City '*C*'. and City '*B*' are 140 and 300 kms. respectively.

Annual fixed costs and maintenance charges are Rs. 60,000 and Rs. 12,000 respectively. Running charges spent during January 1997 are Rs. 2,944.

You are required to find out the cost per absolute ton-kilometer and the profit for January 1997.

(*C.A., Inter, May 1997*)

Solution :

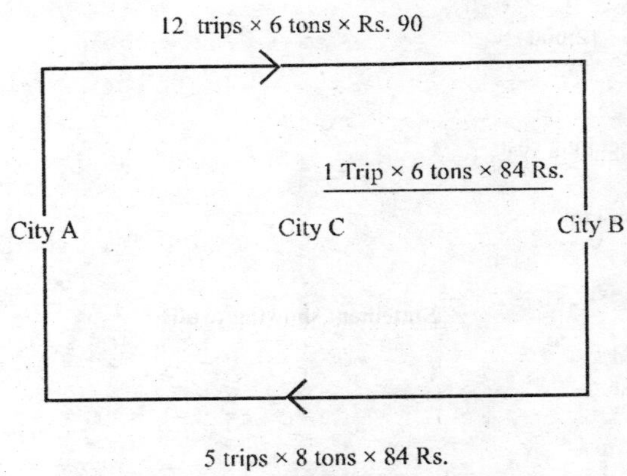

Calculation of net revenue received

Based on the above diagram net revenue received is as follows :

		Rs.
From city A to B		
12 trucks/Journeys × 6 tons × Rs. 90	=	6,480
From city B to city A		
5 trucks/journey × 8 tons × Rs. 84	=	3,360
6* trucks/journeys × 6 tons × Rs. 84	=	3,024
From city B to city C		
1 truck/journey × 6 tons × 84	=	504
Total revenue		13,368
Less : Fine paid		1,200
Net revenue received		12,168

*** 6 Journeys is the difference between 12 outward journey and 6 (5 + 1) inward journeys.**

Calculation of ton-kilometers :

Outward Journeys :		
(*i*) From city *A* to city *B*		
10 (12 – 2) journeys × 300 km. × 6 tons	=	18,000
(*ii*) From city *A* to *C*		
2 journeys × 140 km. × 6 tons	=	1680
(*iii*) From city *C* to City *B*		
2 journeys × 160 kms. × 4 tons	=	1,280
		20,960
Return Journey		
(*i*) *From city B to city A*		
5 journeys × 300 kms. × 8 tons	=	12,000
6 journeys × 300 kms. × 6 tons	=	10,800
(*ii*) *From city B to city C*		
1 journey × 160 kms. × 6 tons	=	960
Total absolute ton-kms.		44,720

Operating cost sheet

Fixed cost $\frac{60,000}{12}$	5,000
Maintenance charges $\frac{12,000}{12}$	1,000
Running charges	2,944
Total operating cost	8,944
Cost per absolute ton-km.	$\frac{8,944}{44,720}$ = 0.20

Statement showing profit

Net revenue received	12,168
Less : Operating cost	8,944
Profit	3,224

Problem 19 (Problem involving decision-making) : A practising chartered accountant now spends Re. 0.90 per km on taxi for his clients work. He is considering two other alternatives, the purchase of a new small car or an old biggar car. The estimated cost figures are :

	New small car (Rs.)	*Old bigger car* (Rs.)
Purchase price	35,000	20,000
Sale price, after 5 years	19,000	12,000
Repairs & servicing per annum	1,000	1,200
Taxes and insurance per annum	1,700	700
Petrol consumption per litre	10 km.	7 km.
Petrol price per litre	3.50	3.50

His estimates that he does 10,000 km annually. Which of the three alternatives will be the cheapest. If his practice expands and he has to do 19,000 kms per annum, what should be his decision? At how many kms per annum, will the cost of the two breakeven and why? Assume petrol only as variable cost. Ignore interest and income tax. *(Delhi University, B. Com.,(Hons) April 88)*

Solution :

Statement of comparative cost

1st alternative		*New small car*	*Old big car*	*Taxi*
(*a*) Fixed cost :				
Depreciation	$\frac{35,000-19,000}{5}$	3,200	1,600	–
	$\frac{20,000-12,000}{5}$			
Repairs & servicing		1,000	1,200	–
Taxes & Insurance		1,700	700	–
	Total fixed cost	5,900	3,500	–
(*b*) Variable cost				
Petrol :				
$\frac{3.50}{10} \times 10,000, \frac{3.50}{7} \times 10,000$		3,500	5,000	–
Hire charges (10,000 × 0.90)		–	–	9,000
	Total cost	9,400	8,500	9,000
2nd alternative				
Petrol for 19,000 kms		6,650	9,500	–
Fixed cost		5,900	3,500	–
Hire charges (19,000 × 0.90)		–	–	17,100
	Total cost	12,550	13,000	17,100

It is clear from the above statement that out of the three alternatives, old bigger car is the cheapest for his present practice. But if his practice expands new small car will be the cheapest.

Break-even point :

$$= \frac{\text{Difference in fixed cost}}{\text{Difference invariable cost per km}}$$

$$= \frac{5,900-3,500}{50p-35p} = \frac{2,400}{15p} = 16,000 \text{ kms}$$

At 16,000 km, the cost of operating new small car and old biggar car will be the same.

POWER HOUSE COSTING OR BOILER HOUSE COSTING

The power house or boiler house is concerned with generation of electricity or steam as a form of power or energy. The purpose of power house costing is to ascertain the cost of electricity or steam produced. The components of total cost in such undertakings include cost of boiler service, depreciation on capital assets, fuel cost, salaries and wages of power house employees, salaries of supervisors and managers, and other overheads. For the sake of exercising control on various elements of cost, the total cost of generating the service is classified into the following types :

(*a*) *Cost of fuel*—This includes cost of coal or fuel oil, handling and storage cost of fuel.

(*b*) *Water*—This includes the cost of purification, softening and supply.

(*c*) *Labour*—This includes coal handlers and ash removers.

(*d*) *Supervision*—This includes salary of foreman, and supervisors.

(*e*) *Maintenance*—This includes repairs and maintenance cost of furnace and boiler house.

(*f*) *Fixed overhead*—This includes rent, rates, depreciation, insurance and interest on capital.

A cost sheet is prepared to record all the above-mentioned costs. A specimen of such cost sheet is given below :

Boiler house cost sheet for the month of......

Items of expenses	*Total cost*		*Percentage*
	Current year	*Previous year*	*Increase or decrease*
Fuel			
Fuel handling			
Ash removal & disposal			
Water purchased			
Water softened			
Sundry indirect materials			
Gas and electric light			
Repairs & maintenance			
Wages of boiler house			
Wages of generating house			
Salaries of supervisors			
Rent and rates			
Depreciation on plant			
Depreciation on building			
Share of Administration charges			
Interest on capital			
Total cost			

Problem 20 (Cost of generating electricity) : From the following data, find out in an appropriate cost sheet form, the cost of generating per unit of electricity in an iron and steel works, during the month of April 1989.

(1) Fuel : Coal at the beginning of the month 500 tonnes
Supply during the month 1,100 tonnes
Balance at the end of the month 400 tonnes
Annual contract for supply of coal F.O.R. Colliery at Rs. 10 per tonne.
Add 10% to cover freight and handling charges.

(2) Oil : 10 tonnes at Rs. 250 per tonne.

(3) Water : 50,000 litres. Pumping charges at 30 paise per 100 litres.

(4) Depreciation of steam boiler : Capital value Rs. 24,000 and the rate of depreciation $12\frac{1}{2}$ per cent per annum.

(5) Salaries and wages of the boiler house :
10 Men at Rs. 100 each per month
40 Coolies at Rs. 20 each for month

(6) Recovery on account of sale of ash :
100 tonnes at Re. 1 per tonne

(7) Salaries and wages of the generating station :
50 Men at Rs. 100 per month each
20 Coolies at Rs. 20 per month each

(8) Repairs and maintenance of the generating equipment Rs. 2,600.

(9) Depreciation of generating equipment : Capital value Rs. 1,20,000 and the rate of depreciation $12\frac{1}{2}$ per cent per annum.

(10) Share of administration charges Rs. 1,750.

(11) Number of units generated; 1,46,000.

(12) Loss in process : 2,000 units generated. (*Sri Sathya Sai University, B. Com., March 1990*)

Solution :

Operating cost sheet

Coal at the beginning	500 tons	
Add : Supply during the month	1,100 tons	
	1,600 tons	
Less : Balance of coal at the end	400 tons	
Coal consumed @ Rs. 10 Per ton	1,200 tons	
		12,000
Freight & handling charges 10% on coal consumed		1,200
Oil : 10 tons at Rs. 250 per ton		2,500
Water : $\frac{0.30}{100} \times 50,000$		150
Depreciation : $24,000 \times \frac{12.5}{100} \times \frac{1}{12}$		250
Salaries & wages of boiler house :		
10 Men @ Rs. 100 each p.m.		1,000
40 Coolies @ Rs. 20 each p.m.		800
Salaries & wages of generating station :		
50 Men @ Rs. 100 each p.m.		5,000
20 Coolies @ Rs. 20 each p.m.		400
Repairs & maintenance of generating equipment		2,600
Depreciation of generating equipment. $1,20,000 \times \frac{12.5}{100} \times \frac{1}{12}$		1,250
		27,150
Less : Recovery on account of sale of ash		100
Works cost		27,050
Share of administration charges		1,750
Total cost		28,800

Net units generated :

Total units generated	1,46,000	units
Less : Loss in process	2,000	units
Net units	1,44,000	

$$\text{Cost per unit of electricity generated} = \frac{24,300}{1,44,000} = 0.16$$

Problem 21 : A manufacturing firm facing shortage of electric power supply from the State Electricity Board has set up its own power generation plant for efficient running of its production units in the factory. The following information has been taken from the records in connection with the generation of power for a month.

(1) Number of units generated was 10,00,000 for the month of which 10% was utilised by the generation department

(2) Consumption data of materials etc. for the month :

(*a*) Coal consumed 300 MTs @ Rs. 3600 per M.T

(*b*) Oil consumed 4.5 MTs @ Rs. 40,000 per M.T

(*c*) Cost of water extraction and treatment for 6 lakhs litres @ Rs. 1.25 per litre.

(3) Steam boiler costs Rs. 20 lakhs with a residual value of Rs. 2 lakhs after a life of 10 years.

(4) Salaries and wages per month

(*a*) For staff of generating plant

(*i*) 100 skilled workers @ Rs. 3,000 PM

(*ii*) 150 helpers @ Rs. 1,500 PM

(*b*) For staff of boiler house :–

(*i*) 60 category A workers @ Rs. 1500 PM

(*ii*) 100 category B workers @ Rs. 1,000 PM

(5) Cost of generating plant : Rs. 36 lakhs with no residual value. Depreciation @ 10% on straight line basis is to be charged.

(6) Repairs and maintenance of generating plant and boiler Rs. 50,000 PM

(7) Share of administrative charges Rs. 40,000 PM

(8) Sales value of ash disposed of Rs. 15,000 PM

Calculate the per unit cost of electricity generated using a cost sheet format. (*ICWA, Inter., June 1996*)

Solution :

Operating cost sheet for the month

		Total Rs. in lakhs	*Cost per unit*
(1) Coal 300 MT @ Rs. 3,600 MT		10.80	1.200
(2) Oil 4.5 MT @ Rs. 4,000 MT		1.80	0.200
(3) Water extraction and treatment charges (6 lakhs litres @ 1.25)		7.50	0.833
(4) Depreciation on steam boiler $\frac{20-2}{10}$ = 1.8 per annum or 0.15 PM		0.15	0.017
		20.25	2.250
(5) *Less :* Sale of ash		0.15	0.017
		20.10	2.233
(6) Salaries and wages :–			
Generating plant	1.90		
Boiler house	5.25		
	7.15 PM	7.15	0.794
(7) Repairs & Maintenance		0.50	0.056
(8) Depreciation on generating plant 10% of 36 lakhs or 3.6 lakhs per annum or 0.30 PM		0.30	0.033
(9) Share of administrative expenses		0.40	0.045
		28.45	3.161
(10) *Add :* Cost of electricity used by generation dept 10% of 10 lakhs units or 1 lakh unit and 10% of cost is		2.84	0.315
Total cost		31.29	3.476

Note :

The cost of generation should bear the cost of electricity used by generation department. As such total cost is calculated on 9 lakh units and not on 10 lakh units.

CANTEEN OR HOTEL COSTING

A canteen is established in most of the factories as a welfare facility. Canteens provide wholesome food and snacks at a subsidised rates. The real problem in canteen costing is use of perishable provisions. This involves careful planning and controlling of various provisions to be bought from time to time. The record problem is determination of menu which again depends upon the canteen manager. Menu is sold against the purchase of coupons and therefore the number of coupons sold in terms of value constitutes the sale value.

For enabling proper accounting three important records are maintained. They are : (1) stock register, which is maintained by canteen store keeper. As and when issues are made they are recorded to ascertain the cost of materials consumed in the canteen. (2) wage analysis sheet is maintained by the personal department to record labour cost and supervision of canteen, (3) overhead analysis sheet, to calculate proportionate overhead charge.

The purpose of canteen costing is to determine a price at which menu is to be sold. For this purpose it involves classifying the expenses according to the following types :

(*a*) *Provisions* : Such as rice, wheat flour, oil, sugar, vegitables, fruits, milk, coffee and tea powder.

(*b*) *Labour* : Cook's wages, salary of supervisor, wages of kitchen assistants, porter's wages.

(*c*) *Service* : Such as water, gas, electricity, steam, light.

(*d*) *Consumable stores* : Such as table cloths, crockery, glassware, cleaning materials, dustbins, brushes, etc.

(*e*) *Overheads* : Such as rent and rates, insurance, depreciation, etc.

(*f*) *Sales* : This includes revenue from meals, tea and coffee, sale of snacks, etc.

A cost sheet is prepared to record all the above items, a specimen of which is given below :

Cost sheet of a canteen for the month.......

	This month	*This month last year*
Provisions :		
Rice		
Wheat flour		
Oil		
Sugar		
Milk		
Coffee		
Tea		
Vegetables & fruits		
Soft drinks		
Wages and salaries :		
Cooks		
Supervisor		
Counter helpers		
Miscellaneous cost		
Crockery & glassware		
Maintenance & repairs		
Table clothes		
Consumable stores		
Rent		
Gas		

Electricity & lighting	
Profit	
Income from sales	

As compared to canteen costing which is concerned with the supply of food and refreshments, big hotels are concerned with the provision of boarding and lodging facilities. The main object of accounting in such hotels is to ascertain rental rates and charges to be fixed for supplying food.

Problem 22 (Hotel costing) : Following are the information given by an owner of a hotel. You are required to advise him that what rent should he charge from his customers per day so that he is able to earn 25% on cost other than interest.

1. Staff salaries : Rs. 80,000 per annum.
2. Room attendants salary Rs. 2 per day. The salary is paid on daily basis and services of room attendant are needed only when the room is occupied. There is one room attendant for one room.
3. Lighting, heating and power :
   The normal lighting expenses for a room if it is occupied for the whole month is Rs. 50. Power is used only in winter and normal charge per month if occupied for a room is Rs. 20.
4. Repairs to building—Rs. 10,000 p.a.
5. Linen etc.—Rs. 4,800 p.a.
6. Sundries—Rs. 6,600 p.a.
7. Interior decoration—Rs. 10,000 p.a.
8. Cost of building—Rs. 4,00,000 rate of depreciation 5%
9. Other equipments—Rs. 1,00,000 rate of depreciation 10%
10. Interest @ 5% is to be charged on its investment of Rs. 5,00,000 on the building and equipment.

There are 100 rooms in the hotel and 80% of the rooms are normally occupied in summer and 30% of the rooms are busy in winter. You may assume that period of the summer and winter is 6 months each. Normal days in a month may be assumed to be 30. *(University of Madras, B. Com., March 1996)*

Solution : **Operating cost sheet** **P.A.**

1. Salaries of staff		80,000
2. Room attendants salary :		
Summer—$2 \times 100 \times \frac{80}{100} \times 30 \times 6$	= 28,000	
Winter—$2 \times 100 \times \frac{30}{100} \times 30 \times 6$	= 10,800	39,600
3. Lighting :		
Summer—$50 \times 6 \times 100 \times \frac{80}{100}$	= 24,000	
Winter—$50 \times 6 \times 100 \times \frac{30}{100}$	= 9,000	33,000
Power—$20 \times 6 \times 100 \times \frac{30}{100}$		3,600
4. Repairs		10,000
5. Linen		4,800
6. Sundries		6,600
7. Interior decoration		10,000
8. Depreciation		
On building $\frac{5}{100} \times 4,00,000$	= 20,000	
Other equipment $\frac{10}{100} \times 1,00,000$	= 10,000	30,000

9. Interest on investment $\frac{5}{100} \times 5,00,000$ — 25,000

— 2,42,600

10. *Add* : Profit 25% on cost other than interest

$(2,42,600 - 25,000)\ 2,17,000 \times \frac{25}{100}$ — 54,400

— 2,97,000

$$\text{Rent per room for one day} = \frac{2,97,000}{19,800} = \text{Rs. } 15$$

Calculation of total room days :

$$\text{Summer} = 100 \times \frac{80}{100} \times 30 \times 6 = 14,400$$

$$\text{Winter} = 100 \times \frac{30}{100} \times 30 \times 6 = 5,400$$

Total room days — 19,800

Problem 23 : Hotel Fidalgo, Goa, provides economy lodging facilities. From the following information ascertain the rent to be charged in a suitable statement form

1. Single rooms 20
   Double rooms 30
2. Annual expenses summary
   (*a*) Salary :
   (*i*) Manager @ Rs. 1,200 P.M.
   (*ii*) Accountant @ Rs. 1,000 P.M.
   (*iii*) 2 Receptionists @ Rs. 800 P.M. each
   (*iv*) 2 Clerks @ Rs. 500 p.m. each
   (*v*) 10 Attenders @ Rs. 300 p.m. each
   (*b*) Lighting & heating—Rs. 30,000
   (*c*) Interior decoration & garden keeping—Rs. 22,500
   (*d*) Licence fee—Rs. 14,070
   (*e*) Repairs & maintenance—Rs. 18,000
   (*f*) Depreciation on building—5% on Rs. 10,00,000
   (*g*) Depreciation on furnishing—10% on Rs. 2,50,000
   (*h*) Miscellaneous expenses—Rs. 20,000
   (*i*) Insurance & water—Rs. 22,000
3. Occupancy ratio
   (*a*) During summer—30 weeks
   Single room—100%
   Double room—90%
   (*b*) During winter—22 weeks
   Single room and double room—50%
4. Profit margin—20% on cost
5. For the purpose of fixing rentals having regard to the space and facilities; the double room shall be regarded $1\frac{1}{2}$ of the single room.

(*Karnataka University, B. Com., April 1990*)

Solution :

Operation cost sheet

Salary —Manager 1,200 ×12	14,400
—Accountant 1,000 × 12	12,000

—Receptionists 2 × 800 × 12	19,200
—Clerks 2 × 500 × 12	12,000
—Attendars 10 × 300 × 12	36,000
Lighting & heating	30,000
Interior decoration	22,500
Licence fee	14,070
Repairs & maintenance	18,000
Depreciation on building $\frac{5}{100} \times 10,00,000$	50,000
Depreciation on furniture $\frac{10}{100} \times 2,50,000$	25,000
Miscellaneous expenses	20,000
Insurance & water	22,000
Total cost	2,95,170
Profit 20% on cost	59,030
	3,54,200

Rent to be charged per day for single room $= \frac{3,54,200}{2,530} = 140$

Rent to be charged per day for double room is $1\frac{1}{2}$ of the single room, *i.e.*, Rs. = 210

Note : Calculation of room days Single room :

$$\text{Summer}: 20 \times 30 \times \frac{100}{100} = 600$$

$$\text{Winter}: 20 \times 22 \times \frac{50}{100} = 220$$

$$820$$

Double room :

$$\text{Summer}: 30 \times 30 \times \frac{90}{100} = 810$$

$$\text{Winter}: 30 \times 22 \times \frac{50}{100} = 330$$

$$= 1,140$$

For fixing rent the space and facilities of double room shall be regarded as

$1\frac{1}{2}$ the single room, *i.e.*, $\frac{3}{2} \times 1,140 = 1,710$

Total room days $= 2,530$

Problem 24 : A lodging home is being run in a small hill station with 50 single rooms. The home offers concessional rates during six off-season months in a year. During this period, half of the full-room rent is charged. The management's profit margin is targeted at 20% of the room rent. The following are the cost estimates and other details for the year ending 31st March 1996 (assume a month to be of 30 days) :

(*a*) Occupancy during the season is 80% while in the off season is 40% only

(*b*) Expenses :

	Rs.
(*i*) Staff salary (excluding room attendants)	2,75,000
(*ii*) Repairs to buildings	1,30,500
(*iii*) Laundry & linen	40,000
(*iv*) Interior and tapestry	87,500
(*v*) Sundry expenses	95,400

(*c*) Annual depreciation is to be provided for buildings at 5% and on furniture and equipments at 15% on straight line basis,

(*d*) Room attendants are paid Rs. 5 per room day on the basis of occupancy of the rooms in a month,

(*e*) Monthly lighting charges are Rs. 120 per room, except in four months of winter when it is Rs. 30 per room and this cost is on the basis of full occupancy for a month; and

(*f*) Total investment in the home is Rs. 100 lakhs of which Rs. 80 lakhs relate to buildings and balance for furniture and equipments.

You are required to work out the room rent chargeable per day both during the season and the off season months on the basis of the foregoing information. (*ICWA, Inter., Dec. 1995*)

Solution : **(1) Calculation of No of Room days in a year**

Season's occupancy for 6 months

$$50 \times \frac{80}{100} \times 6 \times 30 = 7{,}200 \text{ Room Days}$$

Off-season's occupancy for 6 months

$$50 \times \frac{40}{100} \times 6 \times 30 = 3{,}600 \text{ room days}$$

Total room days during the year 10,800

(2) **Full-room days :–**

Season..........	7,200
Off-season (50% rate on 3,600 Days)	1,800
Full-room days	9,000

(3) **Calculation of light bill :–**

Light bill during 8 months @ Rs. 120 PM per room-day $\frac{120}{30}$ = Rs. 4 per room Day

Light bill during 4 months of winter at Rs. 30 PM per room-day $\frac{30}{30}$ = Re 1 per room day

Total light bill

– During season @ Rs. 4 for 7,200 days	28,800
– During 2 months of off-season @ Rs. 4 for 1,200 days (2/6 × 3,600)	4,800
– During 4 months of winter at Re 1 for 2,400 days (4/6 × 3,600)	2,400
	36,000

Operating cost sheet for the year 1996

Salary	2,75,000
Repairs	1,30,500
Laundry and linen	40,000
Interior decoration	87,500
Depreciation :–	
5% on 80 lakhs	7,00,000
15% on 20 lakhs	
Miscellaneous expenses	95,400
Attendants salary for 10,800 room days @ Rs. 5 per day	54,000
Lighting charges	36,000
Total	14,18,400

Cost per room-day	$\frac{14,18,400}{9,000}$	= 157.60
Add : Profit 20% of rent or 25% on cost		= 39.40
Room rent		197.00

During season, room rent of Rs. 197 Rs. to be charged
During off-season, room rent of Rs. 98.50 Rs. to be charged

Problem 25 : A hotel has three types of rooms, *viz.*, *A*, *B* and *C*. You are to suggest what rent should be charged for each type of rooms on the basis of the following information :

(1) The rent of *B* type rooms is to be fixed at $1\frac{1}{2}$ times of the *C* type rooms and that of A type rooms as twice of the *C* type rooms.

(2) There are 20 *A* type rooms, 30 *B* type rooms and 100 *C* type rooms.

(3) Normally 60% of A type rooms, 80% of *B* type rooms and 90% of *C* type rooms are occupied in summer; and in winter 20% of *A* type rooms, 20% of *B* type rooms and 50% of *C* type rooms are occupied.

(4) Actual expenses are as follows :–

(*a*) Staff salary : Rs. 2,20,000 per annum

(*b*) Room attendants salary (when occupied)

Room Type	*Summer*	*Winter*
A	Rs. 4 per day	Rs. 6 per day
B	Rs. 3 per day	Rs. 4.50 per day
C	Rs. 2 per day	Rs. 3.00 per day

(*c*) Lighting per month if occupied for full month for both summer and winter

A	type room Rs. 80
B	type room Rs. 60
C	type room Rs. 40

(*d*) Power per month if occupied for full month for both summer and winter :

A	type room Rs. 40
B	type room Rs. 30
C	type room Rs. 20

(*e*) Repairs and maintenance : Rs. 42,000 p.a.

(*f*) Decoration : Rs. 50,000 per month

(*g*) Sundry expenses : Rs. 76,550 per annum

(*h*) Depreciation on :
– Building @ 5% : cost of building is Rs. 14 lakhs
– Furniture @ 10% : cost of furniture is Rs. 3 lakhs

(5) Summer may be assumed for 7 months and winter for 5 months in a year. Normal days in a month may be taken as 30.

(6) Profit on cost is 25%. (*C.S. Inter., December 2000*)

Solution :

Calculation of Room-days

No of months × No of Days in a month × No of Rooms × occupancy percentage

'A' Type

Summer :–

$$7 \times 30 \times 20 \times \frac{60}{100} = 2,520$$

Winter :–

$$5 \times 30 \times 20 \times \frac{20}{100} = 600$$

3,120

'B' Type

Summer :–

$$7 \times 30 \times 30 \times \frac{80}{100} = 5{,}040$$

Winter :–

$$5 \times 30 \times 30 \times \frac{20}{100} = 900$$

5,940

'C' Type

Summer :–

$$7 \times 30 \times 100 \times \frac{90}{100} = 18{,}900$$

Winter :–

$$5 \times 30 \times 100 \times \frac{50}{100} = 7{,}500$$

26,400

Room Days	*'A' type*		*'B' type*		*'C' type*
	3,120		5,940		26,400
Multiple of 'C' type	2		1 1/2		1
Total Room Days =	6240	+	8910	+	26400
Total of A, B & C =			41,550 Room-days		

Calculation of salary of room attendants

Type A					
Summer	2,520	× 4	=	10,080	
Winter	600	× 6	=	3,600	
					13,680
'B' type					
Summer	5,040	× 3	=	15,120	
Winter	900	× 4.5	=	4,050	
					19,170
'C' type					
Summer	18,900	× 2	=	37,800	
Winter	7,500	× 3	=	22,500	
					60,300
		Total			93,150

Calculating of lighting charges

Type A $\frac{3{,}120 \times 80}{30}$ = 8,320

Type B $\frac{5{,}940 \times 60}{30}$ = 11,880

Type C $\frac{2{,}640 \times 40}{30}$ = 35,200

Total 55,400

Calculation of power charges

Type A	$\frac{3,120 \times 40}{30}$	=	4,160
Type B	$\frac{5,940 \times 30}{30}$	=	5,940
Type C	$\frac{26,400 \times 20}{30}$	=	17,600
	Total		27,700

Operating cost sheet

Staff salaries		2,20,000
Decoration		50,000
Room attendant's salary		93,150
Lighting		55,400
Power		27,700
Repairs and maintenance		42,000
Sundry expenses		76,550
Depreciation		
Building	70,000	
Furniture	30,000	
		1,00,000
	Total cost	6,64,800
	Profit 25% on cost	1,66,200
Total amount to be recovered as Rent		8,31,000
Rent for 'C' type room per day		$= \frac{8,31,000}{41,550}$
		= Rs. 20
Rent for 'A' type room (Twice of C type)		= Rs. 40
Rent for 'B' type room ($1\frac{1}{2}$ times of C type)		= 30

HOSPITAL COSTING

Hospital costing may relate to ascertaining the cost of medical service rendering by a dispensary belonging to a factory or an hospital or a nursing home owned by government or private doctors. The main object of hospital costing is to ascertain the cost of rendering service per patient per day. For this purpose a cost sheet is prepared to record the various expenses incurred in the hospital. Such costs are classified under the following headings :

(1) Medicines
(2) Cost of operation theater
(3) Cost of out-patient department
(4) Cost of in-patient wards
(5) Salary of physicians, surgeons and nurses
(6) Cost of equipments and instruments

(7) Cost of blood bank

(8) Cost of X-ray and pathological services.

Problem 26 (On hospital costing) : A public health centre runs an intensive medical care unit. For this purpose, it has hired a building at a rent of Rs. 5,000 per month with the understanding that it would bear the repairs and maintenance charges also.

The unit consists of 25 beds and 5 more beds can be comfortably accomodated when the occassion demands. The permanent staff attached to the unit are as follows :

2 Supervisors, each at a salary of Rs. 500 p.m.
4 Nurses, each at a salary of Rs. 300 p.m.
2 Wardways, each at a salary of Rs. 150 p.m.

Though the unit is open for patients all the 365 days in a year. Scrutiny of accounts in 1990 reveals that only for 120 days in the year the unit had the full capacity of 25 patients per day and for another 80 days it had on an average 20 beds occupied per day. But there were occassions when the beds were full, extra beds were hired at a charge of Rs. 5 per bed per day and this did not come to more than 5 beds extra above the normal capacity on any one day. The total hire charges for extra beds incurred for the whole year amounted to Rs. 2,000.

The unit engaged doctors from outside to attend on the patients and the fees were paid as basis of the number of patients attended and time spent by them which on an average worked out to Rs. 10,000 p.m. in 1990.

The other expenses for the year were as under :

Repairs & maintenance	3,600
Food supplied to patients	44,000
Janitor services	12,500
Laundry charges for bed linen	28,000
Medicines supplied	35,000
Cost of oxygen, x-ray, etc.	54,000
General administration charges allocated to the unit	49,550

If the unit recovered an overall amount of Rs. 100 per day on an average from each patient. What is the profit per patient day made by the unit in 1990.

Solution :

Operating cost sheet

Variable cost :		
Food	44,000	
Janitor services	12,500	
Laundry	28,000	
Medicines	35,000	
Doctros fee 10,000 × 12	1,20,000	
Hire charges for extra beds	2,000	2,41,500
Fixed cost :		
Salaries (2 × 500 + 4 × 300 + 2 × 150) 12		30,000
Rent 5,000 × 12		60,000
Repairs & maintenance		3,600
General administration		49,550
Cost of oxygen		54,000
	Total cost	4,38,650
	Profit	61,350
	Income received	5,00,000

$$\text{Profit per patient day} = \frac{61,350}{5,000} = 12.27$$

Calculation of patient days :

25 beds × 120 days	3,000
20 beds × 80 days	1,600
Extra bed days (*See note below*)	400
Total patient days	5,000

$$\text{Extra bed days} = \frac{\text{Total hire charges of extra beds}}{\text{Charges}}$$

$$= \frac{2{,}000}{5} = 400 \text{ patient days}$$

CINEMA COSTING

Cinema theaters are one of the service rendering undertakings. The service rendered being a recreational one. The objects of cinema costing is to determine the rate per ticket per show.

Problem 27 (On cinema costing) : The data given relates to Vasanth Talkies, a mini theatre, for the year ending 31st March 1976 :

	Rs.
1 Manager	800 p.m.
10 Gatekeepers	200 p.m. each
2 Operators	400 p.m. each
4 Clerks	250 p.m. each
Electricity and oil	11,655
Carbon	7,235
Miscellaneous expenditure	5,425
Advertisement	34,710
Administration expenses	18,000
Hire of print	1,40,700

The premises are valued at Rs. 6,00,000 and the estimated life is 15 years. Projector and other equipments cost Rs. 3,20,000 on which 10% depreciation is to be charged.

Daily 3 shows are run throughout the year. The total capacity is 625 seats which are divided into three classes as follows :

Janatha circle	250 seats
Sanman circle	250 seats
Lords's circle	125 seats

Ascertain cost per man-show assuming that :

(*a*) 20% of the seats remain vacant

(*b*) Weightage to be given to the three classes in the ratio of 1 : 2 : 3

Determine the rates for each class if the management expects 30% returns on gross proceeds, ignore entertainment taxes. (*Madras University, B. Com., April 1983*)

Solution :

Operating cost sheet

Fixed cost :			
Salaries :	Manager		9,600
	Gate-keepers		24,000
	Operators		9,600
	Clerks		12,000
Administrative expenses			18,000
Depreciation : Premises			40,000
	Projector & other equipments		32,000
Variable cost :			
Electricity and oil			11,655
Carbon			7,235
Miscellaneous expenses			5,425
Advertisement			34,710
Hire of print			1,40,700
		Total cost	3,44,925
		Add : Profit @ 30%	1,47,825
		Gross proceeds	4,92,750

$$\text{Cost per man-show} = \frac{4,92,750}{9,85,500} = 0.50$$

Calculation of man-shows

No. of seats : Janata : 250, Sanman : 250, Lord's : 125.

Weightage :

Janata	250 × 1 = 250
Sanman	250 × 2 = 500
Lord's	125 × 3 = 375
Total	1,125

Total number of shows 3 × 1,125	=	3,375
Less : Vacant 20%		675
Total daily man-shows		2,700

Man-show per annum 2,700 × 365 = 9,85,500

Rate per each class :

Janata :	0.50 × 1 = 0.50
Sanman :	0.50 × 2 = 1.00
Lords :	0.50 × 3 = 1.50

Problem 29 (Problem involving decision-making) : A 20 HP unit is required to drive a pump for watering an agricultural farm. Two plans *A* and *B* for supplying power are under consideration :

	A	*B*
Purchase and installation	10,000	4,000
Life in years	4	4
Salvage value	1,000	–
Interest as capital	10%	10%
Maintenance per year	3,000	0.50
Operating wages per hour	0.20	0.60
Power per hour	1.00	
Fuel and oil per hour		2.00

Assuming that 3 million litres of water is to be pumped in a year and that the pump will pump 1,000 litres in an hour, find out the cost per 1,00 litres of water under both the plans and find out the number of hours for which the operating costs of both the machines will be even.

Solution :

Operating cost sheet

		Plan A	*Plan B*
Depreciation			
$\frac{10,000}{4}$	$\frac{4,000}{4}$	2,250	1,000
Interest as capital—10%		1,000	400
Maintenance 3,000 × 0.50		3,000	1,500
Operating wages			
3,000 × 0.20		600	
3,000 × 0.60			1,800
Power 3,000 × 1		3,000	
Fuel & oil 3,000 × 2		–	6,000
		9,850	10,700
Cost per 1,000 litres		$\frac{9,850}{3,000}$ = 3.28	$\frac{10,700}{3,000}$ = 3.57

$$\text{No. of hrs. in a year} = \frac{30,00,000}{1,000} = 3,000$$

If the number of hours for which the operating costs of both the machine is even, say x then

1.20 x (*i.e.*, 0.20	+	1.00) +	6,250 =	3.10 +	1,400
Operating wages per hour		Power per hour	(Cost under A)	(Cost under B)	

$x = 2{,}553$ hrs.

Thus the cost of operating the machines under both the plans will be even when they have worked for 2,553 hrs.

Problem 30 : Materials are transported from the depots of a factory namely X and Y to nearest Railway station.

X is at a distance of 10 kms from the Railway station

Y is at a distance of 15 kms from the Railway station

A fleet of trucks of 5 tonnes carrying capacity is used for transporting materials from depots to the Railway station.

Average speed of the trucks is 30 kms per hour when running and regularly take 10 minutes to unload the materials at the Railway station.

At depot X the loading time is 30 minutes per load, while at depot Y the loading time is 20 minuted per load.

Drivers wages, depreciation insurance and taxes are found to cost Rs. 9 per hour operated. Fuel oil, tyres, repairs and maintenance cost Rs. 1.20 per km.

Required :

Draw up a statement showing the cost per ton-kilometer of carrying the materials from depots to Railway station. (*Sri Sathya Sai University, B. Com., March 1993*)

Solution :

	Factory X	*Factory Y*
Distance	10	15
Ton-km.	5 × 10 = 50	5 × 15 = 75
Time per trip in minutes :		
Loading time	30	20
Unloading time	10	10
Running time	40	60
	80 mts.	90 mts.

For 30 km : 60 mins

For 10 km → ? $\frac{60 \times 10}{30}$ = 20 mts to and fro = 40 mts

For 30 kms → ? 60 mts

For 15 kms → ? $\frac{60 \times 15}{30}$ = 30

Operating cost sheet

	Factory X	Factory Y
Drivers wages, depreciation, etc.		
For 60 mins → 9		
For 80 mins → ? $\frac{9 \times 80}{60}$	= 12	
For 60 mins → ? 9		
For 90 mins → ? $\frac{9 \times 90}{60}$		= 13.50
Fuel, oil, repair 1.20 × 10 = 12 to & fro 12 × 2	= 24	
1.20 × 15 = 18 to & fro		36.00
	36	49.50
Cost per ton	$\frac{36}{50}$ = 0.72	$\frac{49.50}{75}$ = 0.66

QUESTIONS

I. (A) Choose the correct answer

1. Classification and accumulation of costs by fixed and variable costs is a distinctive feature of
   (*a*) Process costing (*b*) Unit costing
   (*c*) Operating costing (*d*) Batch costing [ ]
2. Composite unit is distinctive feature of
   (*a*) Single or output costing (*b*) Process costing
   (*c*) Job costing (*d*) Operating costing [ ]
3. Electricity generating company should employ
   (*a*) Unit costing (*b*) Process costing
   (*c*) Operating costing (*d*) Multiple costing [ ]
4. Cinema houses must adopt
   (*a*) Operating costing (*b*) Job costing
   (*c*) Batch costing (*d*) Contract costing [ ]
5. For a library the best method of costing suitable is
   (*a*) Output costing (*b*) Operating costing
   (*c*) Process costing (*d*) Multiple costing [ ]
6. For an educational institutes the right method of costing is
   (*a*) Output costing (*b*) Job costing
   (*c*) Operating costing (*d*) Process costing [ ]
7. Hospitals must make use of
   (*a*) Operating costing (*b*) Batch costing
   (*c*) Process costing (*d*) Multiple costing [ ]
8. For hotels the best method of costing is
   (*a*) Single or output (*b*) Contract costing
   (*c*) Process costing (*d*) Operating costing [ ]
9. Air India Co. must make use of
   (*a*) Job costing (*b*) Operating costing
   (*c*) Batch costing (*d*) Process costing [ ]
10. Indian Railways must adopt
    (*a*) Operating costing (*b*) Unit costing
    (*c*) Batch costing (*d*) Multiple costing [ ]
11. Public utility undertakings must invariably adopt
    (*a*) Operating costing (*b*) Output costing
    (*c*) Contract costing (*d*) Multiple costing [ ]
12. Karnataka Electricity Board must make use of
    (*a*) Single or output costing (*b*) Job costing
    (*c*) Process costing (*d*) Operating costing [ ]
13. The Karnataka State Road Transport Corporation must use
    (*a*) Operating costing (*b*) Contract costing
    (*c*) Process costing (*d*) Multiple costing [ ]

[***Answer :*** 1. (*c*), 2. (*d*), 3. (*c*), 4. (*a*), 5. (*b*), 6. (*b*), 7. (*a*), 8. (*d*), 9. (*b*), 10. (*a*), 11. (*d*), 12. (*a*)]

(B) Fill in the blanks

1. The book in which expenses incurred for different trips by a transport company is recorded is known as.................
2. In hospitals, the cost unit is.................
3. The method of costing to be used by a gas distributing company is.................
4. The cost unit in an educational institute is.................
5. The cost unit in an electricity generating concern is.................
6. The cost unit used in a canteen is.................
7. The industries which render services must make use of.................method of costing.
8. Operating costing is a variation of.................category of costing method.

[***Answer :*** (1) log book, (2) bed-day, (3) operating costing, (4) student, (5) kilo-watt, (6) plate-meals, (7) operating, (8) operation]

(C) Simple Questions

1. Define operating cost.
2. Define operating costing.
3. Distinguish between operating cost and operating costing.
4. What do you mean by a composite unit?
5. List out any eight undertakings which makes use of operating costing.
6. Give the composite unit of the following undertakings :
   (*a*) Roadways carrying passanger
   (*b*) Railways carrying goods
   (*c*) Hospital and
   (*d*) College.
7. Mention the basis of classifying the costs under operating costing.
8. Mention the basis of classifying the costs under transport costing.
9. What is a log sheet?
10. What do you mean by cost summary performance statement?
11. What do you mean by absolute tonne-kilometer?
12. What do you mean by a commercial tonne-kilometer?
13. Distinguish between absolute tonne-kilometer and commercial tonne kilometer.
14. What do you mean by "kilometer run"?
15. What do you mean by "cost per hour" under operating costing?

EXERCISES

Exercise-1

From the following data, calculate the cost per running km.

	Rs.
Cost of vehicle	25,000
Road licence per year	750
Salaries per year	4300
Insurance per year	850
Driver's wages per hour	4
Cost of fuel per litre	1.50
Repairs & maintenance per km	1.50
Type cost per km	1.00
Garage rent per year	3,600
Kms run per litre	6
Kms run during the year	15,000
Estimated life of vehicle (kms)	1,00,000
Vehicle run per hour (km)	20

(*Madras University, B.Com., May 1997*)

[Answer : Cost per running km Rs. 3.83]

Exercise-2

Sugama Transport Ltd., owns a bus which runs between Delhi and Chandigarh and back for 10 days in a month. The distance from Delhi to Chandigarh is 240 kms. The bus completes the trip from Delhi to Chandigarh and back on the same day. It goes another 10 days in a month towards Agra and the distance between Delhi and Agra is 190 kms. This trip is also completed on the same day. For the rest of 4 days of its operations in a month, it runs in the local city covering a distance of 70 kms per day calculate the rate per passenger km, when a profit of 33⅓% on takings is maintained. Other information is as follows :

Cost of the bus	4,00,000
Driver's salary per month	2100
Insurance	1080 P.A

Lubricent oil 40 per 100 kms	
permit fee	1000 PM
Diesel consumption 9 kms, per litre at Rs. 9 per litre	
Accountant's salary	960 PM
Repairs and Maintenance	3000 PM
Token Tax	3600 PM
Scrap value of the bus after 10 years of its life	Rs. 40,000
Salary of conductor	2100 PM

Normal capacity of the bus : 50 passengers. The bus is generally occupied 90% of the capacity between Delhi and Chandigarh 80% between Delhi and Agra and it is always full when it runs within the city.

(*Mangalore University, B.Com., April 1997*)

[Answer : Rate per passenger kilometer Re. 0.11 passenger kilometers : 3,82,000]

Exercise-3

Speed Motor Transport Co. furnishes the following details in respect of a Truck of 10 Tonne capacity.

	Rs.
Cost of Truck	6,00,000
Scrap value after its life	30,000
Estimated life : 10 years	
Diesel @ Rs. 10 per litre, mileage per litre	5kms
Repairs and Maintenance	Rs. 1500 PM
Drivers wages	1500 PM
Cleaners wages	750 p.a
Insurance	30,000 p.a
Tax	15000 p.a
Supervision charges	30,000 p.a

The truck carries goods between two towns which are 50 kms apart. On outward journey, it carries weight of full capacity. But, on return journey only 20% of the capacity is assured. Calculate the operating cost per tonne-km, assuming the truck runs on an average for 25 days in a month

(*Bangalore University, B.Com., April 1999*)

[Answer : Operating cost per ton-km = Re. 1.316]

Exercise-4

From the following data, you are required to ascertain the cost of running the lorry per tonne mile :

Total tonnage carried in a week : 30 tonnes and total mileage carried in a week was 600 miles. Details of the above are as follows :

Days	*Miles*	*Tonnes*
Monday	120	6
Tuesday	125	5
Wednesday	110	4
Thursday	100	5.5
Friday	80	4.5
Saturday	65	5
	600	30

Expenses for the week were as follows :

Driver's salary Rs. 200 per month

Cleaner's salary Rs. 100 per month

Repairs and Maintenance Rs. 300 per month

Depreciation Rs. 3800 per annum

Other expenses Rs. 200 per month

(There are four weeks in a month)

(*Mangalore University, B.Com., October 1997*)

[Answer : Cost per Tonne-mile = Re. 0.092]

Exercise 5 : From the fo llowing data relating to vehicle *A* compute the cost per running ton-km.

Kilometer run (annual)	15,000
Tonnes per km (average)	6
	Rs.
Cost of vehicle	2,50,000
Road licence (annual)	800
Insurance (annual)	700
Garage rent (annual)	1,300
Supervision and salaries	2,700
Driver's wages per hour	4
Cost of fuel per litre	6
Kms run per litre	20
Repairs & maintenance per km	2
Tyre allocation per km	1
Estimated life of vehicles	1,00,000 kms

Charge interest at 5% per annum on cost of vehicle. The vehicle runs 20 kms per hour on an average.

(*Madras University, B. Com., March 1991*)

[***Answer :*** Cost per ton-km is Rs. 7.297]

SECTION-D

SYSTEMS OF MAINTAINING COST ACCOUNTS

19

NON-INTEGRAL OR COST LEDGER ACCOUNTING SYSTEM

INTRODUCTION

Just as financial accounting system is maintained with certain objectives in view, cost accounting system is often distinctively maintained with a view to achieve its objectives. All transactions are collected from the same invoices; vouchers or receipts which are also common for financial accounts. Costs are then classified according to functions, departments or products. Though real accounts and nominal accounts are of direct relevance in ascertaining the cost of products, personal accounts and cash or bank account are not directly related to cost ascertainment. When cost accounting system is maintained it involves maintenance of certain books for recording day-to-day transactions. It is not necessary to maintain cost accounts under double entry system of book keeping. However, in order to ensure arithmetical accuracy of data often the principles of double entry system of book keeping is followed. Under double entry system cost accounts are maintained in the main ledger which is termed as cost ledger. In addition to this, many subsidiary ledgers are also maintained. In the cost ledger, control accounts are maintained pertaining to each subsidiary ledger. In addition to control accounts, two other accounts, viz., cost of sales account and costing profit and loss account are also maintained in the cost ledger in order to match costs with revenue. Apart from these accounts, a general ledger adjustment account is opened in cost ledger to accomodate entries relating to transactions adjustable against cash, bank, debtors, creditors etc. Entries in the accounts are made once in each accounting period on the basis of periodical totals of transactions contained in subsidiary ledgers.

INTERLOCKING SYSTEM

There are two systems of maintaining cost records *viz.*, interlocking system and integral accounting system. Under interlocking system cost records are maintained in a separate set of books independent of financial accounts. The ICMA terminology defines interlocking system of accountings as "a system in which the cost accounts are distinct from the financial accounts, the two sets of accounts being kept continuously in agreement or readily recognizable".

The following are some of the advantages of interlocking accounting system :

(*a*) When separate set of costing books are maintained it facilitates ready accomplishment of its objectives.

(*b*) It avoids the complications of recording the entries if it is integrated with financial accounts.

(*c*) It can be maintained according to convenience as it need not be statutorily maintained.

The following are some of the limitations of this accounting system :

(*a*) When cost accounts are independently maintained, it amounts to duplication of expenses along with financial accounts.

(*b*) The profits shown by cost books may vary with that shown by financial accounts. This requires reconciliation which involves time and effort.

The integral accounting system is discussed in a separate chapter.

LEDGERS MAINTAINED UNDER INTERLOCKING SYSTEM

The following are some of the subsidiary books maintained under interlocking system of accounting :

(1) **Stores ledger :** This ledger is used to record both the quantity and amount of receipts, issues and balance of materials and supplies. The basis for recording the transactions are (*a*) Materials received note, (*b*) Material requisition note, (*c*) Material transfer note, and (*d*) Materials returned note.

(2) **Payroll and wage analysis book :** This ledger is used to record the wages. The basis for recording the transactions are : (*a*) clock cards, (*b*) time tickets, and (*c*) piece work tickets.

(3) **Job ledger :** This ledger is used to record the material cost, wages and overheads incurred in respect of a job.

(4) **Finished goods stock ledger :** This ledger is used to record the receipt of finished goods from production department, the sale and stock of finished goods both in terms of quantity and value. The basis for recording the transactions are delivery note issued by the production departments, sales returns note and sales order requisitions.

(5) **Standing order ledger :** This ledger is used to record overheads incurred.

(6) **Cost ledger :** This is the principal ledger of the cost department in which impersonal accounts are recorded. This ledger also contains a control account for each subsidiary ledger.

ACCOUNTS MAINTAINED UNDER COST BOOKS

(1) **Cost Ledger Control Account:** This account is also known as General Ledger Adjustment Account. This account is made to complete double entry. All items of expenditure are credited to this account. Sales are debited to this account and net profit or loss is transferred to this account. The balance in this account represents the net total of all the balances of the impersonal accounts.

(2) **Stores Ledger Control Account:** Total of material purchases are debited to this account. Whereas issues of material are credited. The balance in this account indicates the total balance of all the individual stores accounts. Abnormal losses or gains if any in this account, are transferred to costing profit & loss account.

(3) **Work in Progress Control Account:** This account is debited with the total cost of production, which includes—direct materials, direct labour, direct expenses, production, overhead recovered and is credited with the amount of finished goods completed and transferred. The balance in this account represents total balances of jobs/work-in-progress as shown by several job accounts.

(4) **Finished goods control account:** This account is debited to the tune of "Value of goods" transferred from work-in-progress account and administration costs recovered. This account is credited with the cost of goods sold and cost of sales account is debited. The balance of this account represents the value of goods lying at hand.

(5) **Wage control account:** This account is debited with total wages paid (direct and indirect). Direct wages are further transferred to work-in-progress and indirect wages to production overhead. Wages paid for abnormal idle time are transferred to costing profit & loss account either directly or through abnormal loss account.

(6) **Production or works overhead account:** This account is debited with indirect costs of production such as indirect material, indirect labour, indirect expenses. Overhead recovered is credited to this account. The difference between overhead incurred and overhead recovered is transferred to overhead adjustment account.

(7) **Administrative overhead account:** This account is debited with overhead incurred and credited with overhead recovered. The overhead recovered are debited to finished goods account. The difference between administrative overhead incurred and recovered are transferred to overhead adjustment a/c.

(8) **Selling and Distribution overhead account:** This account is debited with selling and distribution overhead incurred and debited with the recovered overhead. The difference between incurred and recovered overhead is transfered usually to overhead adjustment a/c.

(9) **Cost of Sales account:** This account is debited with the cost of finished goods transfered from finished goods account for sale as well as with the amount of selling and distribution overhead costs recovered. The balance of this account is ultimately transfered to sales account or costing profit & loss a/c.

(10) **Costing profit & loss account:** The net profit or loss in this account is transfereed to cost ledger control account.

(11) **Overhead adjustment account:** This account is to be debited for under recovery of overhead and credited with over recovery of overhead amount. The net balance in this account is transferred to costing profit & loss account.

(6) **Cost ledger :** This is the principal ledger of the cost department in which impersonal accounts are recorded. This ledger also contains a contrast account for each subsidiary ledger.

ENTRIES TO RECORD TRANSACTIONS UNDER INTERLOCKING SYSTEM

1. Materials :

(a) Purchase of materials (cash or credit)
Stores Ledger Control a/c Dr.
To General Ledger Adj. a/c

(b) Returns to suppliers
General ledger Adj. a/c Dr.
To Stores Ledger Control a/c

(c) Materials Purchased specially for a job (ie. direct issue)
Work-in-progress control a/c Dr.
To General ledger adj. a/c

(d) Direct material issued from stores to Jobs
Work-in-progress control a/c Dr.
To Stores Ledger Control a/c

(e) Materials returned from jobs to Stores
Stores Ledger Control a/c Dr.
To work-in-progress a/c

(f) Issue of indirect materials :
Factory overhead control a/c Dr.
To Stores Ledger Control a/c

(g) Transfer of material from one job to another
Receiving job a/c Dr.
To Giving job a/c

(h) Normal Wastage of materials and stores
Factory overhead control a/c Dr.
To stores ledger control a/c

(i) Abnormal Wastage of materials
Costing P & L a/c Dr.
To Stores Ledger Control a/c

2. Labour :

(a) Payment of Direct Wages :
Wages Control a/c Dr.
To General Ledger adj. a/c

(b) Allocation of direct labour :
Work-in-progress a/c Dr.
To Wages Control a/c

(c) Payment of indirect labour cost :
Wage Control a/c Dr.
To General ledger adj. a/c

(d) Allocation of indirect labour cost :
Overhead Control a/c Dr.
To Wage Control a/c

(e) Normal idle time cost :
Factory overhead control a/c Dr.
To Wages Control a/c

(f) Abnormal idle time cost :
Costing P & C a/c Dr.
To Wages Control

3. Direct expenses :

Work in progress control a/c
To General ledger adj.

4. Overheads :

(a) For recording overhead incurred and accrued
Factory oh control a/c Dr.

Adm. oh control a/c Dr.
S & D oh control a/c Dr.
To General ledger Adj. a/c

(b) Allocation of factory overheads
Work in progress control a/c Dr.
To factory oh control a/c

(c) Absorption of administration overheads
Finished Stock Ledger Control a/c Dr.
To Adm. oh control a/c

(d) Absorption of Selling & Distribution overheads :
Cost of Sales a/c Dr.
To Selling & Distribution of control a/c

(e) Of under/over absorbed amounts are carried forward to subsequent year, the balance of each overhead a/c will have to be transferred to respective overhead suspense (or Reserve) accounts as follows :

(i) Production overhead a/c
To production overhead suspense a/c
(For over recovery)

(ii) Administrative overhead suspense a/c
To Administrative oh a/c
(For under recovery)

(iii) Selling & Distribution of suspense a/c
To Selling & Distribution oh a/c
(For under recovery)

(f) In case the under/over absorbed overheads are transferred to costing profit & loss a/c then the relevant entries will be as follows :

(i) For over recovery :
Overhead Control a/c Dr.
To Costing profit & loss a/c

(ii) For under recovery :
Costing profit & loss a/c Dr.
To overhead control a/c

5. Finished goods or completed Jobs :

(a) Transfer of completed jobs to Finished Goods ledger :
Finished Stock Ledger Control a/c Dr.
To work-in-progress

(b) Transfer of cost of goods sold
Cost of sales a/c Dr.
To Finished Stock Ledger Control a/c

(c) Transfer of cost of sales a/c to P & C a/c
Costing P & C a/c Dr.
To cost of sales a/c

(d) To record sales :
General ledger Adj. a/c Dr.
To costing P & C a/c

6. Transfer of profit or loss :

(a) In case of profit :

Costing P & L a/c	Dr.
To General Ledger Adj. a/c	

(b) In case of loss :

General Ledger Adj. a/c	Dr.
To costing P & L a/c	

Problem 1 : The following figures have been ascertained from the costing records. You are required to pass the necessary entries in the cost journal. Assume that a system of maintaining control accounts prevails in the organisation.

		Rs.
(1)	Purchases	3,90,000
(2)	Carriage Inwards	5,850
(3)	Stores issued	3,58,800
(4)	Productive wages	3,46,320
(5)	Unproductive wages	1,21,680
(6)	Works on cost	3,48,400
(7)	Materials used in repairs	3,120
(8)	Cost of completed jobs	12,80,630

Solution :

Cost Journal

(1)	Stores ledger control a/c	*Dr.*	3,90,000	
	To general ledger adj. a/c			3,90,000
	(Being the entry for purchase of Materials)			
(2)	Stores ledger control a/c	*Dr.*	5,850	
	To general ledger adj. a/c			5,850
	(Being carriage inward treated as part of the cost of materials purchased)			
(3)	Work-in-progress ledger control a/c	*Dr.*	3,58,800	
	To stores ledger control a/c			3,58,800
	(Being stores issued to production)			
(4)	Wages control a/c	*Dr.*	3,46,320	
	To gen. ledger adj. a/c			3,46,320
	(Being payment of wages)			
(5)	Factory overhead control a/c	*Dr.*	1,21,680	
	To cost ledger control a/c			1,21,680
	(Being indirect wages incurred)			
(6)	Factory oh. control a/c	*Dr.*	3,48,400	
	To cost ledger control a/c			3,48,400
	(Being works overhead other than indirect wages)			
(7)	Factory overhead control a/c	*Dr.*	3,120	
	To stores ledger control a/c			3,120
	(Being materials used in repairs)			
(8)	Finished stock ledger control a/c	*Dr.*	12,80,630	
	To work-in-progress ledger control a/c			12,80,630
	(Being completed production transferred to finished stock)			

Problem 2 : The following transactions pertaining to materials took place during March 2001 in A B C Co. Ltd. Enter the transactions in the cost books.

(1) Materials purchased

Credit purchases	10,000
Cash purchases	8,000

	Credit purchases for job no. 20	1,000
(2)	Return to suppliers	500
(3)	Direct materials issued to jobs	4,000
(4)	Indirect materials issed to jobs	400
(5)	Materials returned from jobs to stores	200
(6)	Materials transferred from job no. 8 to job no. 12	300

Solution :

Cost Journal

		Dr.	Cr.
1. (*a*)	Stores ledger control a/c Dr.	10,000	
	To gen. ledger adj. a/c		10,000
	(Being the amount of credit purchases)		
(*b*)	Stores ledger control a/c Dr.	8,000	
	To gen. ledger adj. a/c		8,000
	(Being cash purchases)		
(*c*)	Work-in-progress ledger control a/c Dr.	1,000	
	To general ledger adj. a/c		1,000
	(being purchases for a special job no. 20)		
2.	General ledger adj. a/c Dr.	500	
	To stores ledger control a/c		500
	(Being the return to supplier)		
3.	Work-in-progress ledger control a/c Dr.	4,000	
	To stores ledger control a/c		4,000
	(Being the direct materials issued to jobs)		
4.	Factory overhead control a/c Dr.	400	
	To stores overhead control a/c		400
	(Being issue of indirect materials)		
5.	Stores ledger control a/c Dr.	200	
	To work-in-progress control a/c		200
	(Being the materials returned from jobs to stores)		
6.	Job no. 12 a/c Dr.	300	
	To job no. 8 a/c		300
	(Being the transfer of materials from job no. 8 to job no. 12)		

Problem 3 : Pass Journal entries in the cost books (non-integrated system) for the following transactions :

(1) Materials worth Rs. 25,000 returned to stores from job.

(2) Gross total wages paid Rs. 48,000. Employer's contribution to PF and state insurance amount to Rs. 2,000. Wages analysis book detailed Rs. 20,000 direct labour, Rs. 12,000 towards indirect factory labour, Rs. 10,000 towards salaries to office staff and Rs. 8,000 for salaries to selling and distribution staff.

(University of Delhi, B.Com. (Hons), April 1999)

Solution :

Journal Entries

		Dr.	Cr.
(*i*)	Stores ledger control a/c Dr.	25,000	
	To work-in-progress a/c		25,000
	(Being raw materials returned to stores)		
(*ii*)	Wages control a/c Dr.	50,000	
	To gen. ledger control a/c		50,000
	(Being payment of wages)		
	Work-in-progress control a/c Dr.	20,000	
	Factory overhead a/c Dr.	12,000	
	Office overhead a/c Dr.	10,000	
	Selling overhead a/c Dr.	8,000	
	To wages control a/c		50,000
	(Allocation of wages to direct and indirect cost)		

Problem 4 : As at 31st March 2001, the following balances existed in a company's cost ledger

	Dr.	*Cr.*
Stores ledger control a/c	6,02,870	
Work in progress control a/c	2,44,730	
Finished stock ledger control a/c	5,03,890	
Manufacturing oh. control a/c		21,050
Cost ledger control a/c		13,30,440
	13,51,490	13,51,490

During the next three months the following items arose

		Rs.
(1)	Raw materials purchased	2,46,000
(2)	Materials returned to suppliers	5,800
(3)	Materials issued to production	2,54,630
(4)	Factory wages	1,01,060
(5)	Manufacturing oh incurred	1,83,020
(6)	Indirect labour	43,330
(7)	Manufacturing oh charged to production	1,54,400
(8)	Cost of sales	3,71,780
(9)	Sales returns at cost	10,760
(10)	Finished product at cost	4,21,670

Pass the necessary entries, open ledger accounts and prepare trial balance

Solution :

Journal Entries

Stores ledger control a/c	*Dr.*	2,46,000	
To general ledger adj. a/c			2,46,000
(Being materials purchased)			
(2) General ledger adj. a/c	*Dr.*	5,800	
To stores ledger control a/c			5,800
(Entry for materials returned to suppliers)			
(3) Work-in-progress control a/c	*Dr.*	2,54,630	
To stores ledger control a/c			2,54,630
(Entry for issue of materials to production)			
(4) Wages control a/c	*Dr.*	1,01,060	
To general ledger adj. a/c			1,01,060
(Entry for direc wages incurred)			
(5) Work-in-progress control a/c	*Dr.*	1,01,060	
To wages control a/c			1,01,060
(Entry for direct wages charged to production)			
(6) Works overhead control a/c	*Dr.*	1,83,020	
To general ledger adj. a/c			1,83,020
(Entry for works overhead incurred)			
(7) Works overhead control a/c	*Dr.*	43,330	
To general ledger adj. a/c			43,330
(Entry for indirect wages in curred)			
(8) Work-in-progress control a/c	*Dr.*	1,54,400	
To works oh control a/c			1,54,400
(Entry for oh charged to production)			
(9) General ledger adj. a/c	*Dr.*	3,71,780	
To finished stock ledger control a/c			3,71,780
(Entry for cost of sales)			

		Dr.	
(10)	Finished stock ledger control a/c	Dr. 10,760	
	To general ledger adj. a/c		10,760
	(Entry for sales return)		
(11)	Finished stock ledger control a/c	Dr. 4,21,670	
	To work-in-progress control a/c		4,21,670
	(Entry for finished goods transferred)		

General ledger Adj. A/C

To stores ledger control a/c	5,800	By balance b/d	13,30,440
		By stores ledger control a/c	2,46,000
To finished stock ledger control a/c	3,71,780	By wages control a/c	1,01,060
To balance c/d	15,37,030	By works oh control a/c	1,83,020
		By works oh control a/c	43,330
		By finished stock ledger control a/c	10,760
	19,14,610		19,14,610

Stores ledger control a/c

To balance b/d	6,02,870	By general ledger control	5,800
To general ledger adj. a/c	2,46,000	By work-in-progress control a/c	2,54,630
		By balance c/d	5,88,440
	8,48,870		8,48,870

Manufacturing overhead control a/c

To general ledger control a/c	1,80,020	By balance b/d	21,050
		By work-in-progress control a/c	1,54,000
To general ledger control a/c	43,300	By balance c/d	50,900
	2,26,350		2,26,350

Work-in-progress control a/c

To balance b/d	2,44,730	By finished stock ledger control a/c	4,21,670
To stores ledger control a/c	2,54,630	By balance c/d	3,33,150
To wages control a/c	1,01,060		
To Mfg overhead control a/c	1,54,400		
	7,54,820		7,54,820

Finished Stock ledger control a/c

To balance b/d	5,03,890	By cost ledger control a/c	3,71,780
To work-in-progress control a/c	4,21,670	By balance c/d	5,64,540
To gen ledger adj. a/c	10,760		
	9,36,320		9,36,320

Trial Balance

	Dr.	Cr.
Cost ledger control a/c		15,37,030
Stores ledger control a/c	5,88,440	
Mfg. oh control a/c	50,900	
WIP control a/c	3,33,150	
Finished stock ledger control a/c	5,64,540	
	15,37,030	15,37,030

Problem 5 : A fire destroyed some accounting records of a company. You have been able to collect the following from the spoilt papers/records and as a result of consultation with accounting staff in respect of January 1997.

***(i)* Incomplete ledger entries**

Raw Materials A/c

Beginning Inventory	32,000		

Work-in-progress A/c

Beginning Inventory	9,200	Finished stock	1,51,000

Creditors a/c

Closing balance	19,200	Opening balance	16,400

Manufacturing overhead a/c

Amount spent	29,600		

Finished goods a/c

Opening Inventory	2,400		
		Closing Inventory	30,000

***(ii)* Additional information :**

(1) Cash book showed that Rs. 89,200 have been paid to creditors for raw materials.

(2) Ending inventory of work-in-progress included materials Rs. 5,000 on which 300 direct labour hours have been booked against wages and overheads.

(3) The job card showed that workers have worked for 7,000 hours. The wage rate is Rs. 10 per labour hour.

(4) Overhead recovery rate was Rs. 4 per direct labour hour.

You are required to complete the above accounts in the cost ledger of the company.

(C.A., Inter, May 1997)

Solution :

Creditors A/c

To cash & bank (1)	89,200	BY balance b/d	16,400
To balance c/d	19,200	By purchases (Balancing figure)	92,000
	1,08,400		1,08,400

Work-in-progress a/c

To balance b/d	9,200	By finished goods	1,51,000
To raw materials (Balancing figure)	53,000	By balance c/d Materials (2)	5,000
To wages (3) 7,000 hrs. × Rs. 10	70,000	Labour (2) (300 hrs. × 10)	3,000
To overheads (4) 7,000 hrs. × Rs. 4	28,000	Overhead (2) 300 hrs. × Rs. 4	1,200
	1,60,200		1,60,200

Raw materials a/c

To balance b/d	32,000	By work-in-progress a/c	53,000
To purchases	92,000	By balance c/d	71,000
	1,24,000		1,24,000

Finished Goods a/c

To balance b/d	24,000	By cost of sales (Balancing figure)	1,45,000
To work-in-progress a/c	1,51,000	By balance c/d	30,000
	1,75,000		1,75,000

Manufacturing overhead a/c

To sundries (Amount spent)	29,600	By work-in-progress a/c (7,000 × 4)	28,000
		By under-absorbed overhead	1600
	29,600		29,600

Problem 6 : The following balances were extracted from a company's ledger as on 31st December 1997.

	Rs.	Rs
Raw materials control a/c	48,836	
Work-in-progress control a/c	14,745	
Finished stock control a/c	21,980	
Nominal ledger control a/c		85,561
	85,561	85,561

Further transactions took place during the following quarter as follows :

	Rs.
Factory overhead — allocation to WIP	11,786
Goods finished — at cost	36,834
Raw materials purchased	22,422
Direct wages — allocated to WIP	18,370
Cost of goods sold	42,000
Raw materials — issued to production	17,000
Raw materials — credited by suppliers	1,000
Inventory audit — raw materials losses	1,300
WIP rejected (with no scrop value)	1,800
Customer's returns (at cost) of finished goods	3,000

Prepare all the ledger accounts in cost ledger. (*C.A., Inter, November 1998*)

Solution :

Raw materials control a/c

To balance b/d	48,836	By WIP control a/c	17,000
To nominal ledger control a/c	22,422	By nominal ledger control a/c	1,000
		By nominal ledger control a/c	1,300
		By balance c/d	51,958
	71,258		71,258

Work-in-progress control a/c

To balance b/d	14,745	By finished stock control a/c	36,834
To nominal ledger control a/c	11,786	By nominal ledger control a/c	1,800
To raw material control a/c	17,000		
To nominal ledger control a/c	18,370	By balance c/d	23,267
	61,901		61,901

Finished stock control a/c

To balance b/d	21,980	By nominal ledger control a/c	42,000
To WIP control a/c	36,834	By balance c/d	19,814
To nominal ledger control a/c	3,000		
	61,814		61,814

Nominal ledger control a/c

To raw material control a/c	1,000	By balance b/d	85,561
To raw material control a/c	1,300	By raw materials control a/c	22,422
To finished stock control a/c	42,000	By WIP control a/c	11,786
To WIP control a/c	1,800	By WIP control a/c	18,370
To balance c/d	95,039	By finished stock control a/c	3,000
	1,41,139		1,41,139

Problem 7 : From the following balances and transactions extracted from the books of East-West Co. Ltd., journalise and write up the accounts in the cost ledger and prepare a trial balance as at 31st December 1992. Also show the profit or loss for the month :

	Dr.	Cr.
Balances as on 1.12.1992 :		
Work-in-progress a/c	5,200	
Finished goods a/c	2,300	
Factory overhead suspense a/c	50	
Office overhead suspense a/c	30	
Stores ledger control a/c	1,150	
General ledger adjustment a/c		8,730
	8,730	8,730

Transactions for the month were :

	Rs.
Direct wages	7,500
Indirect wages	500
Works overhead absorbed in production	2,200
Office overhead absorbed in production	1,200
Stores issued to production	4,900
Goods finished during the month	18,000
Finished goods sold	21,000
Stores purchased	5,000
Stores issued to factory repair orders	200
Carriage inwards on stores issued for production	80
Factory expenses	1,450
Office expenses	1,170

Solution :

Journal entries

Work-in-progress ledger control a/c	*Dr.*	5,200	
Finished goods ledger control a/c	*Dr.*	2,300	
Factory overhead suspense a/c	*Dr.*	50	
Office overhead suspense a/c	*Dr.*	30	
Stores ledger control a/c	*Dr.*	1,150	
To general ledger adjustment a/c			8,730
(Being the opening entries for the balances)			
Stores ledger control a/c	*Dr.*	5,000	
To general ledger adjustment a/c			5,000
(Being stores purchased)			
Work-in-progress ledger control a/c	*Dr.*	4,980	
To stores ledger control a/c			4,980

Particulars		Dr. (Rs.)	Cr. (Rs.)
(Being the stores issued to production Rs, 4,900 and carriage in ward on stores issued Rs. 80)			
Factory overhead control a/c	Dr.	200	
To stores ledger control a/c			200
(Being stores issued to factory repairs)			
Work-in-progress ledger control a/c	Dr.	7,500	
To wages control a/c			7,500
(Being direct wages charged to production)			
Factory overhead control a/c	Dr.	500	
To wages control a/c			500
(Being indirect wages charged to factory overhead)			
Wages control a/c	Dr.	8,000	
To general ledger adjustment a/c			8,000
(Being the total wages brought into costing book from financial books)			
Factory overhead control a/c	Dr.	50	
To factory overhead suspense a/c			50
(Being the latter transferred to former a/c)			
Factory overhead control a/c	Dr.	1,450	
To general ledger adjustment a/c			1,450
(Being the actual factory expenses brought into costing books)			
Work-in-progress ledger control a/c	Dr.	2,200	
To factory overhead control a/c			2,200
(Being the overheads charged to production)			
Office overhead control a/c	Dr.	30	
To office overhead suspense a/c			30
(Being suspense a/c transferred to former a/c)			
Office overhead control a/c	Dr.	1,170	
To general ledger adjustment a/c			1,170
(Being the actual office overheads brought into costing books)			
Work-in-progress ledger control a/c	Dr.	1,200	
To office overhead control a/c			1,200
(Being the office overheads charged to production)			
Finished goods control a/c	Dr.	18,000	
To work-in-progress ledger control a/c			18,000
(Being the finished goods transferred to former a/c			
Cost of sales a/c	Dr.	20,300	
To finished goods control a/c			20,300
(Being the finished stock transferred to former a/c)			
Costing profit & loss a/c	Dr.	20,300	
To cost of sales a/c			20,300
(Being cost of sales transferred to profit & loss a/c)			
General ledger adjustment a/c	Dr.	21,000	
To costing profit & loss a/c			21,000
(Being the amount of sales brought into costing profit & lose a/c)			
Costing profit & loss a/c	Dr.	700	
To general ledger adjustment a/c			700
(Being the amount of profit)			

COST LEDGER

General ledger adjustment a/c

To costing P & L a/c	21,000	By balance b/d	8,730
To balance c/d	4,050	By stores ledger control a/c	5,000
		By wages control a/c	8,000
		By factory overhead control a/c	1,450
		By office overhead control a/c	1,170
		By costing P & L a/c	700
	25,050		25,050

Stores ledger control a/c

To balance b/d	1,150	By WIP ledger control a/c	4,980
To general ledger adjustment a/c	5,000	By factory overhead control a/c	200
		By balance c/d	970
	6,150		6,150

Wages control a/c

To general ledger adjustment a/c	8,000	By WIP ledger control a/c	7,500
		By factory overhead control a/c	500
	8,000		8,000

Factory overhead control a/c

To stores ledger control a/c	200	By WIP ledger control a/c	2,200
To wages control a/c	500		
To factory overhead suspense a/c	50		
To general ledger adjustment a/c	1,450		
	2,200		2,200

Office overhead control a/c

To office overhead suspense a/c	30	By WIP ledger control a/c	1,200
To general ledger adjustment a/c	1,170		
	1,200		1,200

Work-in-progress ledger control a/c

To balance b/d	5,200	By finished goods control a/c	18,000
To stores ledger control a/c	4,900	By balance c/d	3,080
To wages control a/c	7,500		
To factory overhead control a/c	2,200		
To office overhead control a/c	1,200		
	21,080		21,080

Finished goods control a/c

To balance b/d	2,300	By cost of sales a/c	20,300
To WIP ledger control a/c	18,000		
	20,300		20,300

Cost of sales a/c

To finished goods control a/c	20,300	By costing P & L a/c	20,300

Costing profit & loss a/c

To cost of sales a/c	20,300	By general ledger adjustment	
To general ledger adjustment a/c (profit)	700	a/c (sales)	21,000
	21,000		21,000

Trial balance as on 31.12.1992

	Dr.	*Cr.*
General ledger control a/c		4,050
Stores ledger control a/c	970	
WIP ledger control a/c	3,080	
	4,050	4,050

Problem 8 : On 31.3.1989, the following balances were extracted from the books of the Supreme Manufacuturing Company :

	Dr.	*Cr.*
Stores ledger control a/c	35,000	
WIP control a/c	38,000	
Finished goods control a/c	25,000	
Cost ledgr control a/c		98,000
	98,000	98,000

The following transactions took place in April 1989 :

Raw materials :	
Purchased	Rs. 95,000
Returned to suppliers	3,000
Issued to production	98,000
Returned to stores	3,000
Productive wages	40,000
Indirect labour	25,000
Factory overhead expenses incurred	50,000
Selling and administration expenses	40,000
Cost of finished goods transferred to warehouse	2,13,000
Cost of goods sold	2,10,000
Sales	3,00,000

Factory overheads are applied to production at 150% of direct wages and under or over absorbed overhead being carried forward for adjustment in the subsequent months. All administrative and selling expenses are treated as period cost and charged off to the profit and loss a/c of the month in which they are incurred :

Show the following accounts.

(*a*) Cost ledger control a/c
(*b*) Stores ledger control a/c
(*c*) WIP control a/c
(*d*) Finished goods stock control a/c
(*e*) Factory overhead control a/c
(*f*) Costing P & L a/c
(*g*) Trial balance as at 30.4.1989 (*CA, Inter, May 1989*)

Solution :

Cost ledger control a/c

To costing P & L a/c (sales)	3,00,000	By balance b/d	98,000
To stores ledger control a/c	3,000	By stores ledger control a/c	95,000
To balance c/d	95,000	By wage control a/c (production and indirect)	65,000

		By factory overhead control a/c	50,000
		By selling & adm. overhead	40,000
		By costing P & L a/c	50,000
	3,98,000		3,98,000

Stores ledger control a/c

To balance b/d	35,000	By cost ledger control a/c	3,000
To cost ledger control a/c	95,000	By work-in-progress control a/c	98,000
To WIP control a/c	3,000	By balance c/d	32,000
	1,33,000		1,33,000

Work-in-progress control a/c

To balance b/d	38,000	By stores ledger control a/c	3,000
To stores ledger control a/c	98,000	By finished goods a/c	2,31,000
To wages control a/c	40,000	By balance c/d	20,000
To factory overhead control a/c	60,000		
	2,36,000		2,36,000

Finished goods control a/c

To balance b/d	25,000	By cost of goods sold a/c	2,10,000
To work-in-progress control a/c	2,13,000	By balance c/d	28,000
	2,38,000		2,38,000

Factory overhead control a/c

To wage control a/c (indirect labour)	25,000	By WIP control a/c	60,000
To cost ledger control a/c	50,000	By balance c/d	15,000
	75,000		75,000

Costing P & L a/c

To cost of goods sold a/c	2,10,000	By cost ledger control a/c	3,00,000
To selling & adm. overhead	40,000		
To cost ledger control a/c (costing profit)	50,000		
	3,00,000		3,00,000

Trial balance as on 30.4.1989

	Dr.	*Cr.*
Stores ledger control a/c	32,000	
Work-in-progress control a/c	20,000	
Finished goods control a/c	28,000	
Factory overhead control a/c	15,000	
General ledger control a/c		95,000
	95,000	95,000

Working Notes :

Wages control a/c

To cost ledger control a/c	65,000	By WIP control a/c	40,000
		By factory overhead control a/c	25,000
	65,000		65,000

Cost of goods sold

To finished goods control a/c	2,10,000	By costing P & L a/c	2,10,000
	2,10,000		2,10,000

Selling and distribution overhead

To cost ledger control a/c	40,000	By costing P & L a/c	40,000

Problem 9 : The following balances are extracted from Gujarat Chemical Companay's cost ledger as on 31st March 1993 :

	Figures in 000	
	Rs. (Dr.)	*Rs. (Cr.)*
Control accounts		
Raw materials	500	
Work-in-progress	230	
Finished stock	130	
General ledger adjustment a/c		860
	860	860

Further transactions took place during the following quarter as follows :

	Fig. in 000's
Factory overhead — allocated to WIP	120
Goods finished at cost	400
Raw materials purchased	225
Direct wages allocated to work-in-progress	80
Raw materials issued to production	165
Cost of goods sold	515
Raw materials — returned to suppliers	10
Sales returns (at cost)	50
Inventory audit — raw material shortage	12
Work-in-progress rejected (scrap value—nil)	18

You are required to :

(*a*) Write up the four accounts in the cost ledger

(*b*) Prepare a trial balances as on 31.3.1993

Solution :

Raw materials control a/c (Rs. '000)

To balance b/d	500	By WIP (materials issued)	165
To general ledger adjustment a/c	225	By general ledger adjustment (purchase returns)	10
		By general ledger adjustment (stock shortage)	12
		By balance c/d	538
	725		725

Work-in-progress control a/c

To balance b/d	230	By finished stock control a/c	400
To general ledger adjustment a/c (factory oh)	120	By general ledger adjustment a/c (rejections)	18
To raw materials control a/c (raw materials)	165		
To general ledger adjustment a/c (direct wages)	80	By balance c/d	177
	595		595

Finished stock control a/c

To balance b/d	130	By general ledger adjustment a/c (sales at cost)	515
To WIP (completed production)	400	By balance c/d	45
To general ledger adjustment (sales returns)	30		
	560		560

General ledger adjustment a/c

To Finished stock control a/c (sales of cost)	515	By balance b/d	860
To raw material control a/c (purchase returns)	10	By WIP (factory oh)	120
To raw materials control a/c (stock shortage)	12	By WIP (direct wages)	80
To WIP (rejections)	18	By raw material control a/c	225
To balance c/d	760	By finished stock control a/c (sales returns)	30
	1,315		1,315

Trial balance as on 31.3.1993 (figures in '000)

	Dr.	*Cr.*
Raw materials ledger control a/c	538	
Work-in-progress control a/c	177	
Finished stock control a/c	45	
General ledger adjustment a/c		760
	760	760

Problem 10 : The following balances appear in the books of M.K. Co. Ltd. on 1.1.2002 :

General ledger adjustment a/c		15,200
Stores ledger control a/c	8,750	
WIP ledger control a/c	4,280	
Finished goods ledger control a/c	2,170	
	15,200	15,200

On 31.12.2002, the following information was supplied :

Purchase of stores		60,640
Purchase for special job		1,950
Direct wages	38,627	
Indirect factory wages	9,543	
Administrative salaries	6,731	
Selling & distribution salaries	4,252	59,153
Production expenses		10,432
Administration expenses		9,546
Selling and distribution expenses		6,430
Stores issued to production		56,501
Stores issued to maintenance a/c		2,556
Returns to suppliers		312
Production overhead absorbed by production		23,410
Administration overhead absorbed by finished goods		15,150
Selling overhead recovered on sales		9,515
Products finished during the year		1,18,517
Finished goods sold at cost		1,33,382
Sales		1,55,000

You are required to record the entries in cost ledger for the year 1992 and prepare a trial balance.

Solution :

COST LEDGER

General ledger adjustment a/c

To stores ledger control a/c (returns)	312	By balance b/d	15,200
To P & L a/c (sales)	1,55,000	By stores ledger control a/c — purchases	60,640
To balance c/d	18,697	By WIP control a/c (special purchases)	1,950
		By wages control a/c	59,153
		By production overhead a/c	10,432
		By administration overhead a/c	9,546
		By selling overhead a/c	6,430
		By costing P & L a/c	10,658
	1,74,009		1,74,009

Stores ledger control a/c

To balance b/d	8,750	By work-in-progress control a/c	56,501
To general ledger adjustment a/c	60,640	By prodouction oh. a/c	2,586
		By general ledger adjustment a/c	312
		By balance c/d	9,991
	69,390		69,390

Wages control a/c

To general ledger adjustment a/c	59,513	By WIP control a/c	38,627
		By production oh. a/c	9,543
		By administration oh. a/c	6,731
		By selling & distribution overhead a/c	4,252
	59,513		59,513

Production overhead a/c

To general ledger adjustment a/c	10,432	By WIP control a/c	23,410
To stores ledger control a/c	2,586		
To wages control a/c	9,543		
To overhead adjustment a/c	849		
	23,410		23,410

WIP ledger control a/c

To balance b/d	4,280	By finished goods ledger control a/c	1,18,517
To general ledger adjustment a/c	1,950	By balance c/d	6,251
To stores ledger control a/c	56,501		
To wages control a/c	38,627		
To production oh. a/c	23,410		
	1,24,768		1,24,768

Administration overhead a/c

To general ledger adjustment a/c	9,546	By finished goods ledger control a/c	15,150
To wages control a/c	6,731	To overhead adjustment a/c	1,127
	16,277		16,277

Selling & distribution overhead a/c

To general ledger adjustment a/c	6,430	By cost of sales a/c	9,515
To wages control a/c	4,252	By overhead adjustment a/c	1,167
	10,682		10,682

Finished goods ledger control a/c

To balance b/d	2,170	By cost of sales a/c	1,33,382
To administration oh. a/c	15,150	By balance c/d	2,455
To WIP control a/c	1,18,517		
To wages control a/c	6,731		
	1,35,837		1,35,837

Cost of sales a/c

To selling & distribution overhead a/c	9,515	By P & L a/c	1,42,897
To finished goods ledger control a/c	1,33,382		
	1,42,897		1,42,897

Overhead adjustment a/c

To administration overhead a/c	1,127	By production overhead a/c	849
To selling & distribution oh. a/c	1,167	By costing P & L a/c	1,445
	2,294		2,294

Costng P & L a/c

To cost of sales a/c	1,42,897	By sales	1,55,000
To overhead adjustment a/c	1,445		
To general ledger adjustment a/c — net profit	10,658		
	1,55,000		1,55,000

Trial balance

	Dr.	*Cr.*
Stores ledger control a/c	9,991	
Work-in-progress control a/c	6,251	
Finished goods ledger control a/c	2,455	
General ledger adjustment a/c		18,697
	18,697	18,697

QUESTIONS

Exercise 1 : The following are the balances in the cost ledger of a manufacturing company on Ist January 1981 :

	Dr.	*Cr.*
Stores ledger	4,500	
Work-in-progress ledger	10,200	
Finished goods ledger	6,800	
Financial ledger		21,500

Summary of transactions during the year 1981 :

Materials purchased	20,000
Materials issued to jobs	18,000
Materials issued for repairs in a factory	1,000
Direct wages paid	15,000
Indirect wages paid	5,000

Factory expenses paid	6,000
Administration expenses paid	15,000
Selling expenses paid	7,000
Cost of finished goods produced	56,000
Cost of finished goods sold	70,000
Sales	1,00,000

Prepare control accounts and costing profit & loss account in the cost ledger assuming that the overheads recovered and incurred are the same and that administration overheads we charged to finished goods.

(Madurai University, M.Com., Nov. 1988)

[***Answer :*** Costing profit is Rs. 23,800]

Exercise-2

Hewlet and Plackard Company maintains cost control accounts. The following balances have been extracted from the books :

	Dr *Rs.*	*Cr* *Rs.*
Cost ledger control		60,000
Stores ledger control	20,000	
Work-in-Progress ledger control	10,000	
Finished goods control	30,000	
	60,000	60,000

Following transactions are recorded for the period :	
Materials supplied to stores	1,00,000
Materials supplied directly to production	30,000
Materials returned from stores to supplier	5,000
Materials issued to production	70,000
Indirect materials	10,000
Wages and salaries (Direct Wages Rs. 80,000, Factory Wages 10,000, Administrative salary Rs. 40,000, marketing salary Rs. 20,000)	1,50,000
Production overhead incurred	60,000
Factory overhead recovered at 90% of Direct wages	–
Administrative expenses	40,000
Office overhead absorbed	85,000
Marketing expenses	28,000
Marketing expenses recovered at Re 1 per unit sold	–
Cost of production	2,50,000
Cost of goods sold	3,20,000
Sales at Rs. 10 per unit	4,00,000

Prepare necessary ledger accounts in cost ledger and extract trial balance as on the last date of period.

(Bangalore University, B.B.M. of, April 1999)

[**Answer :** Balances : Cost ledger control Rs. 92,000. Stores ledger control Rs. 35,000. WIP ledger control Rs. 12,000. Finished goods control Rs. 45,000. Net profit Rs. 29,000]

20

RECONCILIATION OF COST AND FINANCIAL ACCOUNTS

INTRODUCTION

While discussing the relationship between cost and financial accounts under chapter 1, it was stated that cost accounts resemble to financial accounts in one important respect, *viz.*, that the basis for recording transactions is common for both the accounting methods. As for example, invoices constitutes the basis for recording transactions relating to materials, payroll for recording wages and salaries and vouchers for recording indirect expenses such as rent, taxes, insurance, etc. From this point of view, the result shown by cost accounts must be the same as shown by financial accounts. But owing to the subjective recording of transactions (*i.e.*, according to the nature of expense) in financial accounts and objective recording (*i.e.*, according to purpose for which costs are incurred) in cost accounts often gives rise to a difference in profit as revealed by these two sets of books. Hence, a need arises to reconcile the profit as shown by these two accounting systems.

NEED FOR AND OBJECTIVES OF RECONCILIATION

The profit reconciliation is necessary to fulfil the following objectives :

(*a*) **To ensure reliability of cost accounts :** The correct ascertainment of cost of production in cost accounts depends upon proper analysis, allocation, apportionment and recording of costs. If these steps are incorrect, naturally the cost of production will be incorrect. Reconciliation with financial accounts help in checking the reliability of cost accounts.

(*b*) **To check the arithmetical accuracy of cost accounts :** Sometimes some transactions in cost accounts are ignored while recording. At other times some items would have been wrongly recorded. This again is responsible for inaccurate results. So to check the arithmetical accuracy of cost accounts, a reconciliation is necessary.

However the need for reconciliation does not arise when cost and financial accounts are integrated.

REASONS FOR DIFFERENCES IN PROFIT

The various reasons or causes for the differences in the profit as shown by cost and financial accounts may be outlined as under :

I. Items Included in the Finanacial Accounts but not in Cost Accounts

(*A*) *Purely Financial Charges*

(*a*) Expenses incurred on share transfer,
(*b*) Interest paid on bank over draft,
(*c*) Damages payable at law,
(*d*) Penalties payable at law,

(*e*) Losses on scrapping machinery,
(*f*) Losses arising out of natural calamities such as fire, flood, etc.,
(*g*) Donations and charities,
(*h*) Loss on sale of investments.

(*B*) *Purely Financial Incomes*

(*a*) Interest on bank deposit received,
(*b*) Dividends on investments received,
(*c*) Rent receivable,
(*d*) Profit made on sale of assets,
(*e*) Amount received on sale of old magazines and newspapers,
(*f*) Transfer fee received.

(*C*) *Appropriation of Profits*

(*a*) Transfer to reserve fund, general reserves, etc.,
(*b*) Transfer to income tax,
(*c*) Dividend paid,
(*d*) Creation of depreciation fund, sinking fund, dividend equalisation fund, workmen's compensation fund, investment fluctuation fund, reserve for bad and doubtful debts,
(*e*) Goodwill, preliminary expenses underwriting commission, etc. written off.

II. Items Included in Cost Accounts Only

The items of transactions recorded only in cost accounts are in the form of notional costs, such as notional rent, notional interest and notional salary,

III. Under or Over-adsorption of Overheads

In financial accounts manufacturing and office expenses are written off as and when they are incurred. However, in cost accounts such expenses are not included until production is completed. Till then, such costs are accumulated in suspense account in the cost ledger. This difference in the treatment gives rise to difference in the amount of profit shown by two sets of books.

One important point that is to be remembered in this connection is, overheads are charged in the cost accounts on the basis of estimates. Manufacturing overheads are recovered as a percentage of wages, office and administration overheads on cost of production and selling and distribution overheads on the basis of sales. The difference between actual and estimated overheads (either over or under absorption) is written off either to overhead adjustment account or to costing profit and loss account. The effect of such transfer is the actual amount shown in the financial accounts will now agree with the amount shown in cost accounts. This means, when reconciling cost and financial accounts no further adjustment is necessary in respect of such overheads.

However it must also be emphasised that when under or over absorbed overheads are not written off to costing profit and loss, but has been carried forward to next year, the amount of overhead (under or overabsorbed) must be considered for reconciliation purpose. This method of treating over or under absorption is not very popular. But when decided by cost accountant, the adjustment of overhead is to be duly considered while preparing reconciliation statement.

IV. Adoption of Different Bases for Stock Valuation

In cost accounts closing stock for balance sheet purpose is valued at cost, while in financial accounts the basis is cost or market price whichever is less. This difference in the basis of valuation of closing stock is reponsible for the disagreement of profit in these sets of books.

V. Adoption of Different Bases for Depreciation

In cost accounts the assets may be depreciated on the straight line method, whereas in financial accounts a different method of depreciation such as reducing balance method or sinking policy method or a different method is followed. The difference in the method of depreciation followed in these systems of accounts results in a difference of profit.

VI. Adoption of Different Bases for Valuing Work-in-progress

Work-in-progress is valued either at the stage of prime cost, works cost or cost of production. In cost accounts, the basis followed may be quite different than that followed in financial accounts. This difference in the method of valuing work-in-progress gives rise to preparation of reconciliation statement.

VII. Expenses of Abnormal Nature are Excluded in Cost Accounts

VIII. Recording of Costs by Approximation in Cost Accounts in Some Cases

PROCEDURE OF RECONCILIATION

The following steps are involved in reconciling the profits as revealed by cost and financial accounts :

1. Find out the reasons responsible for the disagreement in the profits. The various reasons are already discussed in the previous sub-topic. However notional charges are to be ignored in reconciliation, as they do not affect costing profit and loss account. If a notional cost is included in cost accounts the entry made is
   Production overhead control a/c *Dr.*
   To costing P & L a/c
2. Adjust the stock of raw materials, work-in-progress and closing stock depending upon their impact on profit. The impact of stock values are shown below :
   (*a*) More opening stock — Profit is less
   (*b*) Less opening stock — Profit is more
   (*c*) More closing stock — Profit is more
   (*d*) Less closing stock — Profit is less
3. If profit figure is not given prepare a cost sheet to know profit as per cost accounts and a profit and loss account to know the profit as per financial accounts.

The following proforma can be followed to make necessary adjustments while reconciling the profit :

Start with profit as per cost accounts		xx
Add : (1) Items of incomes included in financial accounts but not in cost accounts.	xx	
(2) Items of expenditure included in cost accounts but not in financial accounts	xx	

	(3) Excess income shown in financial accounts over corresponding incomes in cost accounts	xx	
	(4) Excess expenditure shown in cost accounts over corresponding items in financial accounts	xx	
	(5) Over-absorption of overheads in cost accounts	xx	
	(6) Over-valued closing stock in financial accounts	xx	
	(7) Over-valued opening stock in cost accounts	xx	xx
Less :	(1) Items of income included in cost accounts but not in financial accounts	xx	xx
	(2) Items of expenditure included in financial accounts but not in cost accounts	xx	
	(3) Excess income shown in cost accounts over corresponding items in financial accounts	xx	
	(4) Excess expenditure shown in financial accounts over corresponding entries in cost accounts	xx	
	(5) Under-absorption of overheads in cost accounts	xx	
	(6) Under-valuation of closing stock in financial accounts	xx	
	(7) Under-valuation of opening stock in cost accounts	xx	xx
	Profit as per financial accounts		xx

ADVANTAGES OF RECONCILIATION

1. The arithmetical accuracy can be checked in both the sets of books.
2. It enables to set right under or over-absorption of overheads in cost accounts by making use of supplementary rates.
3. Reconciliation facilitates location of areas of inefficiencies. For example, if predetermined overheads are fixed fairly and actual expenditure incurred are more it is a case of inefficiency requiring remedial measure.
4. It helps in detecting frauds as for example, any wrong entry of stock of material in stores ledger owing to theft can be brought to light by comparing with the stock of financial accounts.
5. Separate maintenance of cost accounts has the advantage of exemption from statutory audit as the purpose of cost accounts is to ascertain and control cost rather than ascertainment of profit.

PRESENTATION OF RECONCILIATION STATEMENT

The reconciliation of profit can be presented under two methods, *viz.*, (1) Adjustment method and (2) Memorandum reconciliation account method. Under the first method, the various adjustments are made in a statement form. Under the second method the adjustments are made in a memorandum reconciliation account. Whichever method is followed is immaterial, because reconciliation is only a memorandum account. For balance sheet purpose, the profit shown in financial accounts holds good. Reconciliation facilitates only internal control by highlighting various causes responsible for increase or decrease in profit. Memorandum reconciliation is only an account to show adjustment of transactions and hence does not form part of double entry books.

A proforma memorandum reconciliation account is shown below :

In the cost ledger

Memorandum reconciliation a/c

To Expenses recorded in financial accounts :		By profit as per cost accounts :	
Discount		By Income from financial accounts :	
Fines & penalties			
Bank interest on O.D.		Rent	
Underwriter's commission		Interest	
Donation		Dividends	
Good will written off		Profit on sale of assets	
To under absorption of overheads		By over-absorption of overheads in cost a/cs	
To closing stock under-valued in financial accounts		By closing stock overvalued in financial accounts	
To opening stock undervalued in cost accounts		By opening stock over-valued in cost accounts	
To profit as per cost a/c			

Problem 1 : From the following particulars prepare a statement of reconciliation

Opening stock of meterials	1,44,000
Opening stock of finished goods	2,88,000
Purchase of materials	8,64,000
Closing stock of materials	2,16,000
Closing stock of finished goods	72,000
Wages	3,60,000
Actual works expenses	2,27,150
Actual office expenses	1,85,950
Profit as per costing books	3,56,544

Works expenses are recovered at 20% on prime cost and office expenses at 80% on works oncost in costing books. (*S.V. University, B.Com., April 1999*)

Solution :

Cost Sheet

Opening stock of materials	1,44,000	
Add : Purchases of materials	8,64,000	
	10,08,000	
Less : Closing stock of raw materials	2,16,000	
Cost of materials consumed		7,92,000
Direct wages		3,60,000
Prime cost		11,52,000
Factory on cost $\frac{20}{100} \times 11,52,000$		2,30,400
Factory cost		13,82,400
Office overheads $\frac{80}{100} \times 2,30,400$		1,84,320
Office cost		15,66,720

Reconciliation Statement

Profit as per cost books	3,56,544
Add : over absorption of works oncost (2,30,400 – 2,27,150)	3,250
	3,59,794
Less : under-absorption of office oncost (1,85,950 – 1,84,320)	1,630
Profit as per financial books	3,58,164

Problem 2 : From the following figures, prepare a reconciliation statement and find out profit as per financial accounts :

	Rs.
Net profit as per costing records	17,24,000
Works overhead under-recovered in cost-books	31,200
Administration overhead over recovered in excess	17,000
Depreciation charged in financial a/cs	1,12,000
Depreciation recovered in cost books	1,25,000
Interest received but not included in costing	80,000
Obsolescence loss charged in financial records	57,000
Income tax provided in financial books	4,03,000
Stores adjustment (credited in financial books)	4,750
Bank interest credited in financial books	7,500
Depreciation of stock charged in financial books	67,500

(*S.V. University, B.Com., October 1999*)

Solution :

Reconciliation Statement

Net profit as per costing records		17,24,000
Add : Administrative overhead over recovered	17,000	
Depreciation over charged in cost books	13,000	
Interest received but not recovered in cost books	80,000	
Bank interest credited only in financial books	7,500	
Stores adjustment (credited in financial books only)	4,750	
		1,22,250
		18,46,250
Less: Works overhead under recovered	31,200	
Obsolescence loss charged in financial records only	57,000	
Income-tax provided in financial books only	4,03,000	
Depreciation on stock charged only in financial books	67,500	
		5,58,700
Net profit as per financial records		12,87,550

Problem 3 : From the following data prepare a reconciliation statement

Profit as per cost accounts	1,45,500
Works overhead under-recovered	9,500
Administrative overhead under-recovered	22,750
Selling overhead over-recovered	19,500
Over valuation of opening stock in cost accounts	15,000
Over valuation of closing stock in cost accounts	7,500
Interest earned during the year	3,750
Rent received during the year	27,000
Bad debts written off during the year	9,000
Preliminary expenses written off during the year	18,000

(*ICWA, Inter, June 1998*)

Solution : **Reconciliation Statement**

Profit as per cost books			1,45,500
Add : Over-recovery of selling overheads		19,500	
Over-valuation of opening stock		15,000	
Income excluded from cost accounts :			
Interest earned		3,750	
Rent received		27,000	65,250
			2,10,750
Less : Under-recovery of works overhead		9,500	
Under-recovery of administrative overhed		22,750	
Over-valuation of closing stock		7,500	
Expenses excluded from cost accounts :			
Bad debts	9,000		
Preliminary expenses	18,000	27,000	66,750
Profit as per financial accounts			1,44,000

Problem 4 : From the following figures prepare a reconciliation statement :

	Rs.
Net loss as per costing records	1,72,400
Works overhead under recovered in costing	3,120
Administrative overhead recovered in excess	1,700
Depreciation charged in financial records	11,200
Depreciation recovered in costing	12,500
Interest received not included in costing	8,000
Obsolescence charged (loss) in financial records	5,700
Incom-tax provided in financial records	40,300
Bank interest credited in financial books	750
Stores adjustment (credit) in financial books	475
Value of opening stock in :	
Cost accounts	52,600
Financial accounts	54,000
Value of closing stock in :	
Cost accounts	52,000
Financial accounts	49,600
Interest charged in cost accounts but not in financial accounts	6,000
Preliminary expenses written off in financial accounts	800
Provision for doubtful debts in financial accounts	150

(*C.S., Inter, December 1997*)

Solution : **Reconciliation Statement**

Loss as per cost accounting		1,72,400
Add : Works overhead under recovered in costing	3,120	
Obsolescence loss charged in financial accounts	5,700	
Income-tax provided in financial accounts	40,300	
Opening stock (under-valued) in costing (54,000–52,600)	1,400	
Over valued closing stock in costing (52,000–49,600)	2,400	
Preliminary expenses written off in financial accounts	800	
Provision for doubtful debts in financial accounts	150	
		53,870
		2,26,270

Less : Administrative overhead recovered in excess	1,700	
Depreciation overcharged in cost accounts (12,500–11,200)	1,300	
Interest received not included in costing	8,000	
Bank interest credited in financial books	750	
Stores adjustment credited in financial books	475	
Interest charged in cost accounts but not in financial accounts	6,000	
		18,225
Loss as per financial account		2,08,045

Problem 5 : Enthusiasts Ltd. commenced business on 1st April 1996, cost and financial records are maintained for the year ended 31st March 1997. From the following information prepare statements :

(1) Showing the results as per costing records

(2) Showing result as per financial records

(3) Reconciling these results

Particular	*As per costing Records*	*As per Financial Records*
Materials consumed (20,000 kgs.)	Rs. 28.50 per kg.	Rs. 26 per kg.
Direct wages (3,000 man-days)	Rs. 80 per man-day	Rs. 85 per man-day
Factory overhead	20% of prime cost	Rs. 3,60,000
Administrative overhead	Rs. 30 per kg. of output produced	Rs. 4,00,000
Sales overhead	Rs. 50 per kg. of output sold	Rs. 9,60,000
Stock (of output produced) as on 31-3-97, 2,000 kgs.	At cost of production	Rs. 1,50,000
Work-in-progress as on 31-3-97	Rs. 162,000	Rs. 1,62,000
Sales (16,000 kgs.)	Rs. 130 per kg.	Rs 129.50 per kg.
Rent income	–	Rs. 1,20,000
Preliminary expenses written off	–	Rs. 30,000

(University of Bombay, B.Com., October 1997)

Solution :

Cost Sheet for the year ended 1997

	Total Cost	*Per kg. (18,000 kgs.)*
Materials consumed	5,70,000	31.67
Direct wages	2,40,000	13.33
Prime cost	8,10,000	45.00
Factory overheads	1,62,000	9.00
	9,72,000	54.00
Less : Closing stock of work-in-progress	1,62,000	9.00
Factory cost	8,10,000	45.00
Administration overheads	5,40,000	30.00
	13,50,000	75.00
Less : Closing stock of finished goods	1,50,000	–
Cost of goods sold	12,00,000	75.00
Selling overheads	8,00,000	50.00
Total cost	20,00,000	125.00
Profit	80,000	5.00
Sales (16,000 × 130)	20,80,000	130.00

Quantity produced	=	Sales + cl stock – op stock
	=	16,000 + 2,000 – Nil
	=	18,000 kgs.

Profit & Loss a/c

To materials consumed	5,20,000	By sales	20,72,000
To direct wages	2,55,000	By rent	1,20,000
To factory overheads	3,60,000	By closing stock	
To administration oh	4,00,000	Finished goods	1,50,000
To sales oh	9,60,000	WIP	1,62,000
To preliminary expenses written off	30,000	By net loss	21,000
	25,25,000		25,25,000

Reconciliation Statement

Net profit as per cost books		80,000
Add : Materials consumed over charged in cost books	50,000	
Administrative overheads overabsorbed in cost books	1,40,000	
Rent recorded in finance book only	1,20,000	
		3,10,000
		3,90,000
Less : Wages underrecovered in cost books	15,000	
Factory overhead under recovered in cost books	1,98,000	
Selling overhead under recovered in cost books	1,60,000	
Preliminary expenses written off in finance book only	30,000	
Sales per unit differ @ Rs. 0.5 in cost and finance books	8,000	
(above in cost books)	(–)	(4,11,000)
Net lost as per financial books	(–)	21,000

Problem 6 : A company's profit as per the costing system was Rs. 46,126 whereas the audited financial accounts showed a profit of Rs. 33,248. From the following additional information you are required to prepare a reconciliation statement, showing clearly the reasons for the difference between the two figures :

P & L a/c for the year ended 31-12-93

Opening stock	4,94,358		Sales	6,93,000
Purchases	1,64,308			
	6,58,666			
Closing stock	1,50,242			
		5,08,424		
Direct wages		46,266		
Factory overheads		41,652		
Gross profit c/d		96,658		
		6,93,000		6,93,000
Administrative expenses		19,690	Gross profit sundry	96,658
Selling expenses		44,352	Income	632
Net profit		33,248		
		97,290		97,290

The cost records show :

(1) Closing stock balance of Rs. 1,56,394
(2) Direct wages absorbed during the year Rs. 49,734
(3) Factory overhead absorbed Rs. 39,428
(4) Administration expenses charged @ 3% on sales
(5) Selling expenses charged @ 5% of value of sales
(6) No. mention of sundry income

(*C.S., Inter, June 1995*)

Solution :

Reconciliation Statement

Profit as per cost accounts		46,126
Add : Sundry income shown in financial accounts	632	
Over recovery of direct wages	3,468	
Over absorption of administration expenses in cost accounts	1,100	
		5,200
		51,326
Less : Over-valuation of closing stock in cost accounts	6,152	
Under-absorption of factory expenses in cost accounts	2,224	
Under absorption of selling expenses in cost a/cs	9,702	
		18,078
Profit as per financial accounts		33,248

Problem 7 : From the following information prepare :

(*a*) P & L a/c
(*b*) Cost sheet
(c) Reconciliation statement

	Rs.	*Units*
Sales	2,50,000	20,000
Materials	1,00,000	
Wages	50,000	
Factory overheads	45,000	
Office overheads	26,000	
Selling and distribution overheads	18,000	
Closing stock of finished goods	15,000	1,230
Work-in-progress :		
Materials	3,000	
Wages	2,000	
Factory overheads	2,000	
Good will written off	20,000	
Interest on capital	2,000	

In costing books, factory overheads is charged at 100% on wages, administration overheads at 10% of factory cost and selling distribution overheads at the rate of Rs. 1 per unit sold.

(*University of Delhi, B.Com. (Pass), April 1996*)

Solution :

Profit & Loss a/c

To materials	1,00,000	By sales	2,50,000
To wages	50,000	By closing stock	15,000
To factory overheads	45,000	By work-in-progress	7,000
To office overheads	26,000	(3,000+ 2,000 + 2,000)	
To selling & distribution overhead	18,000		
To good will	20,000		

To interest	2,000	
To profit	11,000	
	2,72,000	2,72,000

Cost Sheet

Materials	1,00.000
Wages	50,000
Prime cost	1,50,000
Factory overhead	50,000
	2,00,000
Less : Work-in-progress (closing) (3,000 + 2,000 + 2,000)	7,000
Factory cost	1,93,000
Administration overhead	19,3000
Cost of production	2,12,300
Less : Closing stock of finished goods $\frac{2,12,300}{21,230} \times 1,230 = 12,300$	12,300
Cost of goods sold	2,00,000
Selling & distribution overhead @ Rs. 1 for 20,000 units	20,000
Cost of sales	2,20,000
Profit	30,000
Sales	2,50,000

Reconciliation Statement

Profit as per cost accounts		30,000
Add : Over charged factory overhead in cost accounts		5,000
Overcharged selling and distribution overhead in cost accounts		2,000
Closing stock under valued in cost accounts		2700
Less : Goodwill written off in financial a/cs	20,000	39,700
Interest on capital cost included in cost accounts	2,000	
Under charged office overhead in cost accounts	6,700	28,700
Profit as per financial accounts		11,000

Problem 8 : The following information is available from the financial books of a company having a normal production capacity of 60,000 units for the year ended 31-3-1995 :

(*i*) Sales Rs. 10,00,000 (50,000 units)
(*ii*) There was no opening and closing stock of finished units
(*iii*) Direct materials and direct wages cost were Rs. 5,00,000 and Rs. 2,50,000 respectively
(*iv*) Actual factory expenses were Rs. 1,50,000 of which 60% are fixed
(*v*) Actual administrative expenses were Rs. 45,000 which are completely fixed
(*vi*) Actual selling and distribution expenses were Rs. 30,000 of which 40% are fixed
(*vii*) Interest and dividends received Rs. 15,000. You are required to :

(*a*) Find out profit as per financial books for the year ended 31st March, 1995
(*b*) Prepare the cost sheet and ascertain the profit as per cost accounts for the year ended 31-3-1995 assuming that the indirect expenses are absorbed on the basis of normal production capacity and
(*c*) Prepare a statement reconciling profits shown by financial and cost books.

(*C.A., Inter, May 1995*)

Solution :

Profit & Loss a/c for the year ended 31-3-1995

To direct material	5,00,000	By sales (50,000 units)	10,00,000
To direct wages	2,50,000	By interest and dividends	15,000
To factory expenses	1,50,000		
To adm. expenses	45,000		
To S & D expenses	30,000		
To profit	40,000		
	10,15,000		10,15,000

Cost Sheet for the year ended 31-3-1995

Direct Materials		5,00,000
Direct wages		2,50,000
Prime cost		7,50,000
Factory expenses :		
Variable	6,000	
Fixed $90,000 \times \frac{5}{6}$	75,000	1,35,000
Works cost		8,85,000
Administrative expenses $45,000 \times \frac{5}{6}$		37,500
Cost of production		9,22,500
Selling & Distribution expenses		
Variable	= 18,000	
Fixed $12,000 \times \frac{5}{6}$	= 10,000	28,000
Cost of sales		9,50,500
Profit		49,500
Sales		10,00,000

Reconciliation Statement

Profit as per cost accounts		49,500
Add : Income from interest & dividends		15,000
		64,500
Less : Factory expenses under charged in cost accounts (1,50,000 – 1,35,000) =	15,000	
Less : Adm. expenses undercharged in cost accounts (45,000–37,500) =	7,500	
Less : S & D expenses under charged in cost accounts (30,000 – 28,000) =	2,000	24,500
Profit as per financial accounts		40,000

Problem 9 : Following the profit & loss account of M/s Anubhav Manufacturing Company for the year ended 31st December, 1994

To Opeing stock of :			By sales		9,20,000
Raw materials	60,000		By closing stock of :		
Work-in-process	35,000		Raw materials		60,000
Finished goods	80,000		Work-in-progress		41,000
		1,75,000	Finished goods		30,000
To Purchases		2,40,000			
To Factory wages		60,000			
To Electricity charges		66,000			
To Factory overheads		90,000			
To Gross profit c/d		4,20,000			
		10,51,000			10,51,000
To Administrative expenses		25,000	By gross profit b/d		4,20,000
To Selling & Distribution expenses		1,15,000	By miscellaneous income		20,000
To Bad debts		30,000			
To Net profit		2,70,000			
		4,40,000			4,40,000

Their cost accounts showed a profit of Rs. 2,81,750. on scruting of their costing profit and profit & loss a/c it was found that

(1) Their opening stock and closing stock were valued as under :

Opening stock of Raw materials	Rs. 80,000
Opening stock of Work-in-progress	Rs. 40,000
Opening stock of Finished goods	Rs. 60,000
Closing stock of Raw materials	Rs. 70,000
Closing stock of Work-in-progress	Rs. 44,000
Closing stock of Finished goods	Rs. 20,000

(2) They charged administrative expenses at Rs. 18,000 and selling & distribution expenses at Rs. 1,27,000

(3) They had charged depreciation @ 25% on written down value method on its plant which was purchased on 1st July 1991 for Rs. 80,000. In financial accounts, however, the depreciation was provided on straight line method and the same was included in the factory overheads of Rs. 90,000. Prepare a statement reconciling, the difference in the profits as disclosed by the two records.

(University of Bombay, B.Com., April 1995)

Solution :

Reconciliation Statement

	Profit as per cost accounts		2,81,750
Add :	Under valuation of opening stock of raw materials in financial accounts	20,000	
	Under valuation of opening stock of WIP in financial a/c	5,000	
	Over absorption of selling and distribution expenses in cost accounts	12,000	
	Over valuation of stock of financial accounts	10,000	
	Miscellaneous income taken in financial accounts only	20,000	
			67,000
			3,48,750
Less :	Over-valuation of closing stock of finished goods in financial a/c	20,000	
	Under absorption of Adm. expenses in cost a/cs	7,000	
	Under valuation of closing stock of raw materials in financial accounts	10,000	
	Under valuation of closing stock of WIP in financial accounts	3,000	
	Bad debts written off in financial accounts	30,000	
	Under provision for depreciation in cost accounts (20,000 – 9,844)	10,156	
			2,68,594
	Add undelected difference		1,406
	Profit as per financial accounts		2,70,000

Working note :

Depreciation as per financial a/c $80,000 \times \frac{25}{100} = 20,000$

Depreciation as per cost a/c

Machine purchased on 1.7.91	80,000
Less : Depreciation upto 31-12-91 @ 25%	10,000
Written down value on 1.1.92	70,000
Less : Depreciation @ 25%	17,500
Written down value on 1.1.93	52,500
Less : Depreciation @ 25%	13,125
Written down value on 1.1.94	39,375
Less : Depreciation @ 25%	9,844
	29,531

Problem 10 : From the following figures prepare a reconciliation statement :

	Cost Books (Rs.)	*Financial Books (Rs.)*
Profit	50,000	?
Marketing overheads	8,000	8,000
Provision for bad debts	–	5,000
Factory overheads	8,500	7,000
Directors fees	–	2,000
Income tax paid	–	15,000
Rent of owned premises	6,000	–
Depreciation	11,250	12,000
Share transfer fee (cr.)	-	1,000
Administrative overheads	5,000	8,000

(*University of Delhi, B.Com., April 1995*)

Solution :

Reconciliation Statement

Profit as per cost accounts		50,000
Add : Over absorption of factory overheads	1,500	
Rent of own building	6,000	
Share transfer fees	1,000	
		8,500
		58,500
Less : Provision for bad debts	5,000	
Directors fees	2,000	
Income tax	15,000	
Depreciation under charged in cost a/c	750	
Administration overhead under absorbed in cost accounts	3,000	
		25,750
Profit as per financial accounts		32,750

Problem 11 : A factory is producing two products, Anusha and Bhanusha. Their particulars are as follows :

	Anusha	*Bhanusha*
Materials (per unit)	Rs. 12.50	7.50
Wages (per unit)	Rs. 10.00	6.00

Factory expenses are to be calculated as 100% of wages and office expenses as 25% of works cost.

Product. Anusha was produced 200 units and Bhanusha 500 units. Price of product Anusha was Rs. 50 per unit and Bhanusha at Rs. 30. Actual factory expenses were Rs. 4,800 and office expenses Rs. 4,200. Reconcile both the profit (*Andhra University, B. Com., May 1992*)

Solution :

Cost sheet

	Anusha		*Bhanusha*		*Total*
	Per unit	*Total*	*Per unit*	*Total*	
Materials	12.50	2,500	7.50	3,750	6,250
Wages	10.00	2,000	6.00	3,000	5,000
Prime cost	22.50	4,500	13.50	6,750	11,250
Factory expenses	10.00	2,000	6.00	3,000	5,000
Factory cost	32.50	6,500	19.50	9,750	16,250
Office expenses	8.125	1,625	4.875	2,438	4,063
Office cost	40.625	8,125	24.375	12,188	20,313
Profit	9.375	1,875	5.625	2,812	4,687
Sales	50.00	10,000	30.000	15,000	25,000

Profit & loss A/c

To Materials :		By sales :	
Anusha	2,500	Anusha	10,000
Bhanusha	3,750	Bhanusha	15,000
To Wages :			
Anusha	2,000		
Bhanusha	3,000		
To factory expenses	4,800		
To office expenses	4,200		
To P & L a/c profit	4,750		
	25,000		25,000

Reconciliation statement

Profit as per cost accounts	4,687
Add : Overabsorption of factory expenses in cost accounts (5,000 – 4,800)	200
	4,887
Less : Under absorption of office expenses in cost accounts (4,200 – 4,063)	137
Profit as per financial accounts	4,750

QUESTIONS

Simple Questions

1. When does the need for reconciling the profit of cost accounts with financial accounts arise?
2. Mention two forms of reconciling the profits of cost and financial accounts. Which do you prefer?
3. State four reasons for profit as per cost books being more than that shown in financial books.
4. State four reasons for profit as per cost books being less than that shown in financial books.
5. List out any four items (transactions) included in cost accounts but not in financial accounts.
6. List out any four transactions included in financial accounts but not in cost accounts.
7. Mention different bases of valuing closing stock in cost and financial accounts.
8. Mention any two methods of depreciation followed in cost and financial accounts.

Short Answer Questions

1. What is the purpose of reconciling cost and financial accounts when two accounts are separately maintained? State the causes which are responsible for the disagreement in the profit.
2. "When separate sets of books are maintained for financial and cost accounts the profits computed in one set many differ from profit computed in the other set". Indicate the possible reasons for such variation.
3. Compile a proforma reconciliation statement (withcut figures) to explain profit variation between cost and financial accounts.
4. "For computing the profits, the methods adopted in financial accounts differ from those used in cost accounts." Elucidate.
5. "The reconciliation between cost and financial accounts help not only explaining profit variations in the past but also enables evolving better estimates, for future guidance". Comment.
6. Why is reconciliation of cost and financial accounts necessary? Give any eight items which appear in the financial accounts but do not appear in the cost accounts.
(*Kakatiya University, B.Com., November 1991 and May 1992*)
7. Explain the procedure of reconciling the profit as shown by cost and financial accounts.
(*Sri Sathya Sai University, B. Com., July 1990*)
8. What do you understand by reconciliation of cost and financial accounts? Indicate the possible reasons (causes) for difference between them. (*Kakatiya University, B. Com., October 1990*)
9. Write a note on profit reconciliation statement. (*Osmania University, B. Com., March 1992*)
10. Explain the causes of difference between profit shown by financial accounts and profit shown by cost accounts. (*Delhi University, B. Com.,(Hons.) April 1989*)

EXERCISES

Exercise-1

In a factory, works overhead is absorbed @ 60% of labour and office expenses @ 20% of works cost. The total expenditure is as follows :

	Rs.
Material	2,00,000
Labour	1,50,000
Factory expenses	98,000
Office expenses	85,000
	5,33,000

10% of the output is in stock and sales Rs. 5,10,000. Prepare a cost-sheet and a reconciliation statement.
(*Bharathiar University, B.Com., April 1998*)

[**Answer :** Profit as per cost A/cs Rs. 26,000 and as per financial accounts Rs. 21,800]

Exercise-2

The following information has been obtained from the records of a machine manufacturer.

(a) Materials per machine Rs. 1750
(b) Wages per machine Rs. 1,000
(c) Number of machines manufactured and sold 80
(d) Works overhead to be charged at 60% of wages.
(e) Office overhead to be charged at 20% of works-cost.
(f) There was no opening or closing stock of machines.
(g) Selling price per machine Rs. 4750.

Prepare a statement showing the profit per machine sold. Also prepare a statement showing the actual profit if the works expenses were Rs. 48,000 and office expenses were Rs. 47,500 as per financial books.

Reconcile the profit as shown by costing and financial records.

(*Bangalore University, B.Com., April 1997*)

[**Answer :** Profit as per cost accounts Rs. 58,400 and as per financial accounts Rs. 64,500]

Exercise-3

From the following particulars, prepare (*a*) statement of cost of manufacture for the year (*b*) a statement of profit as per cost accounts (*c*) profit and loss account in the financial books and (*d*) reconciliation of the difference in the profit as shown by (*b*) and (*c*) above.

	Rs.
Opening stock of raw materials	1,00,000
Closing stock of raw materials	1,50,000
Opening stock of finished product	2,00,000
Closing stock of finished product	50,000
Purchase of raw materials	6,00,000
Wages	2,50,000

Calculate factory overhead at 25% of prime cost, office overhead will be levied at 75% on factory overhead. Actual works expenditure amounted to Rs. 1,93,750 and actual office expenses amounted to Rs. 1,52,500. The selling price was fixed at 25% above cost price

(*Calicut University, M.Com., April 1997*)

[Answer : Profit as per cost Accounts Rs. 3,25,000. As per financial accounts Rs. 3,28,750.]

Exercise-4

Papanna and Company Ltd., maintains separate cost accounting system which revealed a profit of Rs. 57,6C0 for the period ending 31st March 1999. The financial accounting revealed a different profit. On verification, the following information was obtained :

(a) Preliminary expenses written off Rs. 12,200
(b) Factory overhead incurred Rs. 8900 but absorbed Rs. 10,000
(c) Provision for doubtful debts Rs. 800
(d) Discount on issue of shares Rs. 6,200
(e) Transfer fees received Rs. 1,700
(f) Underwriting commission paid Rs. 5,000
(g) Dividend received Rs. 7,300
(h) Depreciation charged Rs. 10,800 but recovered only Rs. 10,000
(i) Closing stock valued in financial accounts Rs. 7,800 but in cost accounts Rs. 9,000
(j) Interest on own capital recorded in cost accounts Rs. 1,300

Prepare a reconciliation statement as on 31-3-1999 and show profit as per financial accounts.

(*Bangalore University, B.B.M., April 1999*)

[Answer : Profit as per financial books Rs. 42,800.]

Exercise-5

From the following data, prepare a reconciliation statement.

	Rs.
Profit as per cost accounts	1,45,500
Works overhead under-recovered	9,500
Administrative overhead under-recovered	22,750
Selling overheads over-recovered	19,500
Over valuation of opening stock in cost accounts	15,000
Over valuation of closing stock in cost accounts	7500
Interest earned during the year	3750
Rent received during the year	27,000
Bad debts written off during the year	9000
Preliminary expenses written off during the year	18,000

[Answer : Profit as per financial accounts Rs. 1,44,000]

21

INTEGRAL ACCOUNTING

INTRODUCTION

Cost and financial accounts are said to be integrated when only one set of account is operated to serve the purpose of both the accounts. Under this method a general ledger is maintained which contains both cost and financial accounts. In general ledger, purchases, wages and expenses undergo functional analysis instead of grouping under various account heads. Entries in general ledger are made in summarised form supported by detailed day-to-day postings in related subsidiary ledgers. The main objective of integrated account is to avoid duplication of work. It also obviates the necessity of reconciliation between cost and financial accounts. It facilitates short term closing of accounts without going through the tedious process of stock-taking and valuation.

DEFINITION AND FEATURES OF INTEGRATED ACCOUNTING

The ICMA terminology defines integrated accounts as "a single set of accounts which provides both financial and management accounting information".

The following are the features of integrated accounting system :

(*a*) Only one set of book is maintained for both financial and cost accounts.

(*b*) The general ledger adjustment account is dispensed with under this system.

(*c*) Transactions which affect cost accounts are recorded in the general ledger just as they are recorded in cost accounts.

(*d*) Transactions which affect financial accounts are recorded in the general ledger just as they are recorded in financial accounts.

(*e*) Instead of a double entry for every transaction in the financial books and further double entry in cost books, this system requires only one debit and one credit.

Advantages and Limitations

The following are the advantages of integral accounting system :

1. The preparation of reconciliation statement does not arise as only one profit and loss account is prepared.
2. It avoids duplication of work which is involved in non-integral accounts.
3. It results in economy in maintaining accounts.
4. It facilitates control of accounting procedure and co-ordination of accounting function in different departments.
5. Because of centralisation principle the accounting procedure is simplified.
6. It facilitates quick reporting as all accounting information is readily available.

Integrated accounting suffers from one limitation. Financial accounts have to be prepared in a proforma prescribed by the Companies Act to satisfy statutory requirements. This would necessitate classification of income and expenses according to their natural headings. Similarly, total purchases figures will have to be shown in the accounts as per law, whereas the integrated accounts do not have a purchase account maintained. A common flexible code of accounts to suit both statutory accounting and integrated accounting would be necessary for the purpose. Purchases, wages and expenses would then undergo natural analysis followed by functional analysis.

Books and Accounts Under Integral Accounting

The following are the subsidiary ledgers and the accounts that are maintained under integral accounting system :

(1) **Sales ledger :** This ledger consists of accounts of customers. The account that is prepared in this ledger is known as sales ledger control account.

(2) **Bought ledger :** This ledger is maintained to record the accounts of suppliers. The account that is maintained in this ledger is known as bought ledger control account.

(3) **Stores ledger :** This ledger is maintained for recording accounts relating to individual items of materials and stores kept in stock. The account maintained in this ledger is known as stores ledger control account.

(4) **Stock ledger :** This ledger is maintained for recording accounts relating to individual items of finished goods in stock. The account maintained in this ledger is known as stock ledger control account.

(5) **Job ledger :** This ledger contains accounts of individual jobs on hand. The account maintained in this ledger is known as work-in-progress account.

(6) **Expenses ledger :** This ledger contains accounts of expenses kept separately for factory, office and selling and distribution expenses. The accounts maintained in this ledger are : (*a*) works overhead account, (*b*) office overhead account, and (*c*) selling and distribution overhead account.

JOURNAL ENTRIES UNDER INTEGRAL ACCOUNTS

1. Materials

(*a*) Materials purchased on credit for stock :–
Stores control a/c Dr.
To creditors a/c

(*b*) Cash purchase of materials for stock :–
Stores control a/c Dr.
To cash

(*c*) Material purchased for special Jobs :–
Work-in-progress a/c Dr.
To creditors/cash

(*d*) Purchase of materials for immediate repair work
Factory overhead control a/c Dr.
To creditors/cash

(*e*) Materials returned to suppliers from stock
Sundry creditors a/c Dr.
To stores control a/c

(*f*) Payment to creditors for purchases made
Creditors a/c Dr.
To cash

(2) Payment of wages

Wages control a/c Dr.
To cash

(3) Payment for expenses

Overhead control a/c	Dr.		
To cash			

(4) Recording of goods completed

Finished goods control a/c	Dr.		
To WIP			

(5) Recording of cost of goods sold

Cost of sales	Dr.		
To P & L a/c			
To Finished goods control a/c			

Problem 1 : Journalise the following transactions assuming that cost and financial transactions are integrated

Raw materials purchased	2,00,000
Direct materials issued to production	1,50,000
Wages paid (30% indirect)	1,20,000
Wages charged to production	84,000
Manufacturing expenses incurred	84,000
Manufacturing overhead charged to production	92,000
Selling and Distribution costs	20,000
Finished products (at cost)	2,00,000
Sales	2,90,000
Receipts from Debtors	69,000
Payments to creditors	1,10,000

Solution :

Journal Entries

Stores ledger control a/c	Dr.	2,00,000	
To cash/creditors a/c			2,00,000
(Being materials purchased)			
Work-in-progress control a/c	Dr.	1,50,000	
To stores ledger control a/c			1,50,000
(Materials issued to production)			
Wages control a/c	Dr.	1,20,000	
To cash			1,20,000
(Being wages paid)			
Work-in-progress control a/c	Dr.	84,000	
To Wages control a/c			84,000
(Direct wages charged to production)			
Factory overhead control a/c	Dr.	36,000	
To wages control a/c			36,000
(30% of wages paid being indirect charged to overhead)			
Factory overhead control a/c	Dr.	84,000	
To Bank a/c			84,000
(Manufactured overhead incurred)			
Work in progress control a/c	Dr.	92,000	
To factory overhead control a/c			92,000
(Being manufactured overhead charged to production)			
Selling & Distribution oh control a/c	Dr.	20,000	
To Bank			20,000
(Being selling & Distribution oh incurred)			
Finished goods ledger control a/c	Dr.	2,00,000	
To WIP control a/c			2,00,000
(Being cost of goods finished)			

Cost of sales a/c	Dr.	2,20,000	
To Finished stock ledger control a/c			2,00,000
To S & D oh control a/c			20,000
(Being cost of goods sold)			
Sundry Debtors a/c	Dr.	2,90,000	
To sales			2,90,000
(Being Finished stock sold)			
Bank a/c	Dr.	69,000	
To sundry Debtors			69,000
(Receipts from Debtors)			
Sundry creditors a/c	Dr.	1,10,000	
To Bank			1,10,000
(Being payment made to creditors)			

Problem 2 : Shivalika Enterprises operates an integrated system of accounting. You are required to pass journal entries for the following transactions that took place for the year ended 31st March 1992 (Naration is not required)

(1)	Raw materials purchased (50% on credit)	Rs.	6,00,000
(2)	materials issued to production	Rs.	4,00,000
(3)	Factory overhead incurred	Rs.	80,000
(4)	Sales (50% credit)	Rs.	7,50,000
(5)	Receipt from Debtors	Rs.	2,00,000
(6)	Payment to creditors	Rs.	2,00,000

(University of Delhi, B. Com.,(Hons.) April 98)

Solution :

Journal Entries

(1)	Stores Ledger control a/c	Dr.	6,00,000	
	To cash a/c			3,00,000
	To credit a/c			3,00,000
(2)	Work-in-progress control a/c	Dr.	4,00,000	
	To stores ledger control a/c			4,00,000
(3)	Factory overhead control a/c	Dr.	80,000	
	To cash			80,000
(4)	Cash a/c	Dr.	3,75,000	
	Debtors a/c	Dr.	3,75,000	
	To sales			7,50,000
(5)	Cash a/c	Dr.	2,00,000	
	To Debtors a/c			2,00,000
(6)	Creditors a/c	Dr.	2,00,000	
	To cash			2,00,000

Problem 3 : Journalise the following transactions under the Integral accounting system

	Rs.
Direct wages paid in cash	60,000
Indirect wages paid in cash	30,000
Purchases made in cash	15,000
Purchases (credit)	2,90,000
Stores issued against production order	2,75,000
Works expenses incurred and paid in cash	55,000
Works expenses allocated to Jobs	80,000
Administration expenses paid in cash	40,000
Administration expenses allocated to Jobs	48,000
Finished goods transferred to warehouse	4,50,000

(ICWA, Inter., June 1995)

Solution :

Journal Entries

	Particulars		Dr. (Rs.)	Cr. (Rs.)
(1)	Wages control a/c	Dr.	90,000	
	To cash			90,000
	(Cash paid towards direct wages Rs. 60,000 + Indirect wages Rs. 30,000)			
(2)	WIP control a/c	Dr.	60,000	
	To wage control a/c			60,000
	(Direct wages transferred to WIP)			
(3)	Works expenses control a/c	Dr.	30,000	
	To wages control a/c			30,000
	(Indirect wages transferred to works expenses control a/c)			
(4)	Stores ledger control a/c	Dr.	3,05,000	
	To creditors			2,90,000
	To cash			15,000
	(To record cash and credit purchases)			
(5)	WIP control a/c	Dr.	2,75,000	
	To stores ledger control a/c			2,75,000
	(To record transfer of stores issued to production)			
(6)	Works expenses control a/c	Dr.	55,000	
	To cash a/c			55,000
	(To record work expenses disbursed in cash)			
(7)	WIP control a/c	Dr.	80,000	
	To works expenses control a/c			80,000
	(Works expenses allocated to jobs)			
(8)	Administration expenses-control a/c	Dr.	40,000	
	To cash			40,000
	(Administration expenses paid in cash)			
(9)	WIP control a/c	Dr.	48,000	
	To Administrative expenses			48,000
	(Administration expenses charged to production)			
(10)	Finished goods control a/c	Dr.	4,50,000	
	To WIP control a/c			4,50,000
	(To record finished goods transferred)			

Problem 4 : Journalise the following transactions assuming that the cost and financial records are integrated and prepare necessary ledger accounts

Raw materials purchased on credit	14,800
Direct Materials issued to production	12,800
Wages paid	16,800
Wages productive	14,800
Wages unproductive	2,000
Factory expenses	6,500
Factory expenses charged to production	8,600
Administration expenses	4,400
Administration expenses charged to production	4,350
Selling expenses charged to sales	4,500
Finished goods at cost	30,000
Cash sales	39,000

No.	Particulars		Dr. (Rs.)	Cr. (Rs.)
(2)	Work-in-progress control a/c	Dr.	12,800	
	To stores control a/c			12,800
	To stores control a/c			
	(Being materials issued to jobs)			
(3)	Wages control a/c	Dr.	16,800	
	To Bank			16,800
	(Being wages paid)			
(4)	Work-in-progress control a/c	Dr.	14,800	
	To wages control a/c			14,800
	(Being the wages charged to production)			
(5)	Factory overhead control a/c	Dr.	2,000	
	To wages control a/c			2,000
	(Being the indirect wages charged to Factory overheads)			
(6)	Factory overhead control a/c	Dr.	6,500	
	To Bank			6,500
	(Being the factory expenses incurred)			
(7)	WIP control a/c	Dr.	8,600	
	To Factory oh control a/c			8,600
	(Being factory oh charged to production)			
(8)	Administration oh control a/c	Dr.	4400	
	To Bank			4,400
	(Being Administration expenses incurred)			
(9)	WIP control a/c	Dr.	4,350	
	To Adm. oh control a/c			4,350
	(Being Adm. oh charged to production)			
(10)	S & D oh control a/c	Dr.	4,500	
	To Bank			4,500
	(Being selling expenses incurred)			
(11)	Finished stock control a/c	Dr.	30,000	
	To WIP control a/c			30,000
	(Being Finished stock transferred at cost)			
(12)	Cost of sales a/c	Dr.	34,500	
	To Finished stock control a/c			30,000
	To S & D oh control a/c			4,500
	(Being the cost of production of goods sold)			
(13)	Bank a/c	Dr.	39,000	
	To sales control a/c			39,000
	(Being cash sales)			

Stores control A/c

To creditors	14,800	By WIP control a/c	12,800
		By Balance c/d	2,000
	14,800		14,800

Wages control a/c

To Bank	16,800	By WIP control a/c	14,800
		By Factory oh control a/c	2,000
	16,800		16,800

Work-in-progress control a/c

To wages control a/c	14,800	By Finished stock Control a/c	30,000
To stores control a/c	12,800	By Balance c/d	10,550
To factory oh control a/c	8,600		
To Adm. oh control a/c	4,350		
	40,550		40,550

Factory oh control A/c

To wages control	2,000	By WIP control a/c	8,600
To Bank	6,500		
To oh suspense a/c (Balancing figure)	100		
	8,600		8,600

Adm. oh control a/c

To Bank	4,400	By WIP control a/c	4,350
		By oh suspense a/c (Balancing figure)	50
	4,400		4,400

S & D oh control a/c

To Bank	4,500	By cost of sales	4,500

Finished stock control a/c

To WIP control a/c	30,000	By cost of sales	30,000

Cost of sales a/c

To finished stock control a/c	30,000	By sales control a/c	39,000
To S & D oh control a/c	4,500		
To P & C a/c (Balancing figure)	4,500		
	39,000		39,000

Bank a/c

To sales control a/c	39,000	By wages control a/c	16,800
		By Factory oh control a/c	6,500
		By Administration oh control a/c	4,400
		By S & D oh control a/c	4,500
		By Balance c/d	6,800
	39,000		39,000

Creditors A/c

To Balance c/d	14,800	By stores control a/c	14,800

Sales control a/c

To cost of sales a/c	39,000	By Bank a/c	39,000

oh suspense a/c

To Adm. oh control a/c	50	By factory oh control a/c	100
To Balance c/d	50		
	100		100

Trial Balance

	Dr.	*Cr.*
Stores control a/c	2,000	
WIP control a/c	10,550	
Bank	6,800	
Creditor's control a/c		14,800
oh suspense a/c		50
P & C a/c		4,500
	19,350	19,350

THIRD ENTRY METHOD

Intergral accounting is sometimes called thired entry accounting. In fact third entry accounting is a modified form of self-balancing system. In a self-balancing ledger, four entries are passed in respect of each transaction affecting accounts maintained in two different ledgers. For example, general ledger and stores ledger are kept under self-balancing system, then in general ledger a total account under the heading 'stores ledger control account' is opened. In stores ledger, in turn, a total account is opened under the heading 'General ledger control account'. When raw materials are purchased for stock the following four transactions are passed.

In general ledger

Stores ledger control a/c Dr.

To sundry creditors a/c

In stores ledger

Stores a/c Dr.

To general ledger control a/c

But in practice, the general ledger control a/c in stores ledger is not maintained, in which case the transaction involves only three entries, *i.e.*, two entries in the general ledger and a third entry in stores ledger card. This process is extended to any or all subsidiary ledgers which are "controlled" by a total account in general ledger.

Problem 5 : Dutta Enterprises operates an integral system of accounting. You are required to pass the journal entries for the following transactions that took place for the year ended 30.6.90. Narration not required.

	Rs.
Raw materials purchased (50% on credit)	6,00,000
Materials issued to production	4,00,000
Wages paid (50% direct)	2,00,000
Wages charged to production	1,00,000
Factory overheads incurred	80,000
Factory overheads charged to production	1,00,000
Selling and distribution overhead incurred	40,000
Finished goods at cost	5,00,000
Sales (50% credit)	7,50,000

Closing stock	NIL
Receipts from debtors	2,00,000
Payments to creditors	2,00,000

(*C.A., Inter., November 1990*)

Solution :

Journal entries

Particulars		Dr. (Rs.)	Cr. (Rs.)
Stores ledger control a/c	*Dr.*	6,00,000	
To sundray creditors a/c			3,00,000
To cash			3,00,000
Work-in-progress control a/c	*Dr.*	4,00,000	
To stores ledger control a/c			4,00,000
Wages control a/c	*Dr.*	1,00,000	
To cash a/c			1,00,000
Factory overhead control a/c	*Dr.*	1,00,000	
To wages control a/c			1,00,000
Factory overhead control a/c	*Dr.*	80,000	
To cash			80,000
Work-in-progress control a/c	*Dr.*	1,00,000	
To factory overhead control a/c			1,00,000
Selling and distribution overhead control a/c	*Dr.*	40,000	
To cash			40,000
Finished stock ledger control a/c	*Dr.*	5,00,000	
To WIP control a/c			5,00,000
Cost of sales a/c	*Dr.*	5,40,000	
To finished stock ledger control a/c			5,00,000
To selling & distribution overhead control a/c			40,000
Sundry debtors	*Dr.*	3,75,000	
Cash a/c	*Dr.*	3,75,000	
To sales a/c			7,50,000
Cash	*Dr.*	2,00,000	
To sundry debtors			2,00,000
To sundry creditors a/c	*Dr.*	2,00,000	
To cash			2,00,000

Problem 6 : In the absence of the chief accountant, you have been asked to prepare a month's cost accounts for a company which operates a batch costing system fully integrated with the financial accounts. The following relevant information is provided to you :

Balances at the beginning of the month :		
Stores ledger control a/c		25,000
Work-in-progress control a/c		20,000
Finished goods control a/c		35,000
Prepared production overhead brought forward from the previous month		3,000
Transactions during the month :		
Materials purchased		75,000
Materials issued		
To production	30,000	
To factory maintenance	4,000	34,000

Materials transferred between batches		5,000
Total wages paid		
To direct workers	25,000	
To indirect workers	5,000	30,000
Direct wages charged to batches		20,000
Recorded non-productive time of direct workers		5,000
Selling and distribution overheads incurred		6,000
Other production overheads incurred		12,000
Sales		1,00,000
Cost of finished goods sold		80,000
Cost of completed and transferred into finished goods during the month		65,000
Physical value of work-in-progress at the end of the month		40,000

The production overhead absorption rate is 150% of direct wages charged to work-in-progress :

Prepare the following accounts for the month :

(*a*) Stores ledger control a/c
(*b*) Work-in-progress control a/c
(*c*) Finished goods control a/c
(*d*) Production overhead control a/c
(*e*) Profit & loss a/c. (*CA, Inter., May 1988*)

Solution :

Stores ledger control a/c

To balance b/d	25,000	By WIP control a/c	30,000
To creditors (or bank)	75,000	By production oh. control a/c	4,000
		By balance c/d	66,000
	1,00,000		1,00,000

WIP control a/c

To balance b/d	20,000	By finished goods control a/c	65,000
To stores ledger control a/c	30,000	By balance c/d (physical value)	40,000
To wages control a/c	20,000		
To production overhead control a/c (150% of direct wages)	30,000		
To P & L a/c (stock gain)	5,000		
	1,05,000		1,05,000

Finished goods control a/c

To balance b/d	35,000	By cost of goods a/c or P & L a/c	80,000
To work-in-progress control a/c	65,000	By balance c/d	20,000
	1,00,000		1,00,000

Production overhead control a/c

To balance b/d (prepaid amount)	3,000	By WIP control a/c (150% of direct wages)	30,000
To stores ledger control a/c	4,000		
To wages control a/c			
Direct workers	5,000		
Indirect workers	5,000		
To bank	12,000		
To P & L a/c (overabsorption–balancing figure)	1,000		
	30,000		30,000

Profit & loss a/c

To finished goods control a/c or cost of goods sold a/c	80,000	By sales a/c	1,00,000
To selling & distribution overhead a/c	6,000	By production overhead control a/c	1,000
To balance c/d	20,000	By work-in-progress control a/c (stock gain)	5,000
	1,06,000		1,06,000

Notes :

(1) Materials transferred between batches will not affect the control accounts.

(2) Non-production time of direct workers is a production overhead and therefore will not be charged to WIP control a/c.

(3) Production overheads absorbed in WIP control a/c will then equal Rs. 30,000 (150% of Rs. 20,000).

(4) In the WIP control a/c the excess physical value of stock is taken resulting in stock gain. Stock gain is transferred to P & L a/c.

COST RECORD RULE

Introduction :

The Government of India is empowered under section 209 of the companies Act 1956 to prescribe that certain classes of companies, engaged in production, processing, manufacturing or mining activities should keep records showing particulars of utilisation of materials or labour or other costs. The central Government is also empowered to frame rules in respect of such industries to maintain cost accounting records. These rules are framed to ascertain the cost of production in the various units of the selected industries. Accordingly, rules have been framed in the case of 28 products/industries which are consumer oriented, earners of high margin of profit etc. viz. cement, cycles, rubber tyres and tubes, canetic soda, room air conditioners, refrigerators, automobiles, batteries, electric lamps, electric fans, electric motors, motor vehicles, tractors, aluminium, bulk drugs, sugar, infant milk food, industrial alcohal jute goods, paper, rayon, dyes, soda alh, polyster, nylon, cotton textiles, dry cell batteries and sulphuric acid. According to these rules, proper accounts should be maintained in respect of the various items of cost. If a company defaults in the maintenance of cost records, the company and every officer of the company who is in default is punishable with fine which may extend to Rs. 500 and if the default is a continuing one, with a further fine upto Rs. 50 for each day of default. It may be mentioned that separate rules have been framed for each industry. However, there are some similar requirements for all the industries in respect of each element of cost. They are briefly stated below:

(1) Raw materials and purchased componenets:

(a) Adequate records should be kept showing the receipts, issues and balances, both in quantities and values of raw materials and components required for the manufacture of the product.

(b) The basis on which the value of purchases and issues have been calculated should be indicated in the records and the basis adopted should be followed consistently throughout the relevant period.

(c) The value should include all direct charges such as freight, insurance etc. and also the wastage, whether in storage, transit or for other reasons.

(d) If the consumption value is determined on any basis other than actual, the method adopted should be explained and a reconciliation with acuals and the treatment of variations should be dealt with in the records.

(2) Manufactured components:

Detailed records showing the cost of manufactured components should be maintained in the form prescribed in the rules. The records should also indicate quantities, values and wastages as in the case of purchased components. Quantities manufactured, rejected and accepted together with the losses on account of rejection should also be mentioned in the records.

(3) Stores and spare parts

(a) Adequate records should be kept showing the receipts, issues and balances, both in quantities and value of various items of stores and spares required for repairs, maintenance or manufacture. The value should include all direct changes upto the works such as freight, insurance etc.

(b) The value of issues and balances may be recorded monthly or at such shorter intervals as may be decided by the company or may be kept in the form of control accounts, the balances being reconciled at least once a year with the values of the quantity shown by the quantity accounts for each items of stores.

(c) The value of stores consumed should be charged to relevant heads like manufacturing, repairs to plant and machinery, repairs to buildings, maintenance of vehicles, capital items etc.

(d) The value of stores charged to manufacture should further be allocated to the different departments or manufacturing units or cost centres and products, if any, manufactured therein

(e) Stores issued for capital works like additions to plant and machinery and other assets should be shown separately under the capital heads

(f) Any wastage, whether in stores or transit or for other causes should be recorded separately and their treatment explained.

(g) Stores should be valued consistently during the relevant period on a reasonable basis and the method adopted should be recorded.

4. Labour

With regard to labour, proper and systematic accounts should be maintained in respect of:

(a) attendance of workers and other staff

(b) all payments made for overtime work

(c) cost of wages and salaries relating to various manufacturing departments or units in the factory being the amount payable and allocated to the different departments or units.

(d) Idle time, giving reasons for such idle time and the method of its treatment in calculating cost of products.

(e) The extent of wages and salaries capitalised as additions to plant and machinery and other assets.

(f) Where piece rate payment system is applicable, the records should be so maintained as to enable ascertainment of wages payable to such workers.

5. Overheads:

(a) The overhead expenses should be classified as works overhead, administration overhead and selling and distribution overhead.

(b) Adequate records should be kept showing the accounts comprising the overhead expenses and the details of opportionment of overhead expenses to the various departments, manufacturing units and cost centres. The details of such expenses should be collected from the financial accounts.

(c) Capital jobs carried out during the year should bear their appropriate share of overhead expenses. The basis of allocation of such expenses should be indicated in relevant records.

(d) The works overhead should include among other items, indirect wages and salaries relating to works, indirect materials consumed, staff and labour welfacre expenses, and expenditure on repairs and maintenance.

(e) The method of opportioning overheads to various departments or manufacturing units or cost centres should be followed consistently and explained in the records.

(f) If overheads are recovered on a basis other than actuals, the method of reconciliation with actuals and treatment of variances should be disclosed in the cost records.

(g) The shares of selling and distribution expenses if any, applicable to products sold should be shown separately in the cost records stating clearly the basis of apportionment.

6. Service

(a) proper records should be maintained so that the cost of services such as power, water, electricity and steam produced and utilised in manufacturing operations can be ascertained.

(b) The power cost should include cost of units consumed, fixed charges and duties.

(c) If power, water or steam is generated by the company, the records maintained should show the different items making up the cost of such power. Water or steam produced and consumed.

(d) The allocation of the consumption of services by different departments or manufacturing units should be shown in the records. If actual allocation is not possible, the basis of allocation should be indicated in the cost records.

7. Depreciation:

(a) Adequate records should be maintained in respect of fixed assets showing (i) the cost of each item of asset (ii) date of acquisition (iii) rate of depreciation and (iv) the amount of depreciation provided.

(b) Depreciation chargeable to the different departments or cost centres should not be less than the amount chargeable under section 205(2) of the companies Act, 1956 and should relate to the plant and machinery and other assets utilised in the department or cost centre. The method of depreciation, once adopted should be applied consistently.

8. Production and Sale:

Adequate records should be maintained in respect of production, showing the receipts, issues and balances of the goods produced by the company. The value should be based on the cost of production of the items concerned. The value of the issues and balances may be recorded monthly or at such shorter intervals as may be decided.

(9) Inventories:

(a) Inventories may be classified as (1) raw materials (ii) stores and spare parts (iii) work-in-progress and (iv) finished goods. The records required for raw materials, stores and spares and finished goods, production have already been dealt with

(b) Proper records should be maintained to show the quantities and value of work-in-progress at the end of period for which the costs are made up. It should represent the cost incurred upto the relevant stage of manufacture.

(c) Stock verification records should be maintained in respect of all raw materials components, stores, and spares including tools etc. The method of dealing with the discrepancies arising out of such verification should be indicated in the records.

QUESTIONS

Exercise 1 : From the following transaction pass journal entries under integral accounting system.

	Rs.	
Purchases	2,00,000	(30% in cash)
Wages	1,00,000	(25% indirect)
Stores issued to production	3,00,000	
Factory overhead paid	60,000	
Factory overhead allocated	80,000	
Administration expenses incurred	15,000	
Outstanding administration expenses	2,000	
Administration expenses allocated	20,000	
Finished goods transferred	4,55,000	

Exercise 2 : From the following information write up the control accounts in the general ledger of Sujatha Enterprises where cost and financial accounts are integrated and prepare a trial balance as on 31st March, 1993 :

Ledger balances as on 1 April 1992 :		
Share capital		1,00,000
Reserves		25,000
Sundry debtors		20,000
Plant and machinery		1,25,000
Sundry creditors		30,000
Bank overdraft		40,000
Raw materials		50,000
Transactions during the year :		
Raw materials purchases		80,000
Raw materials issued to production		1,00,000
Raw materials on hand 31.3.1993		26,000
Direct wages	– Incurred	95,000
	– Charged to production	93,000
Manufacturing expenses	– Incurred	87,500
	– Charged to production	93,000
Selling & distribution expenses		10,000
Finished stock	– Production (at cost)	1,91,000
	– Sales (at selling price)	86,000
	– Closing stock	NIL
Payments to creditors		85,000
Receipts from debtors		3,00,000

[***Answer :*** Total of trial balance Rs. 4,59,000]

SECTION E

COST CONTROL TECHNIQUES

22

MARGINAL COSTING

ABSORPTION COSTING

Absorption costing is a conventional technique of ascertaining the cost of production. It is, therefore, sometimes referred to as 'orthodox costing'. It is a technique of ascertaining cost of goods or services manufactured under which both variable and fixed cost are taken into cosideration. As under this technique all costs—fixed and variable—are taken into account, it is also known as 'full costing' technique. The total or 'full' cost is classified on the functional basis into production cost, administration cost, selling and distribution cost. Under this technique, the total cost per unit remains constant only when the level of output remains same from time to time. But in today's dynamic world the level of activity differs from time to time and so does the cost. The cost of production may be Rs. 18 today and Rs. 20 next week. This change in the cost of production is on account of change in the volume of output and the way in which fixed cost tend to behave. The differences in the cost of production from time to time often poses a problem to the management in decision-making process. Hence, the marginal costing technique is used to enable management in carrying out its day-to-day functions of planning, decision-making and controlling. However, the proponents of absorption costing technique argue that both fixed and variable costs must be charged to the cost of production in order to meet the requirements of generally accepted accounting principles and income tax reporting.

The total cost under this technique is classified into two types, *viz.*, (*i*) production cost and (*ii*) period cost. These costs are further classified into various types of costs. These costs are shown in the following chart :

COST CLASSIFICATION UNDER ABSORPTION COSTING

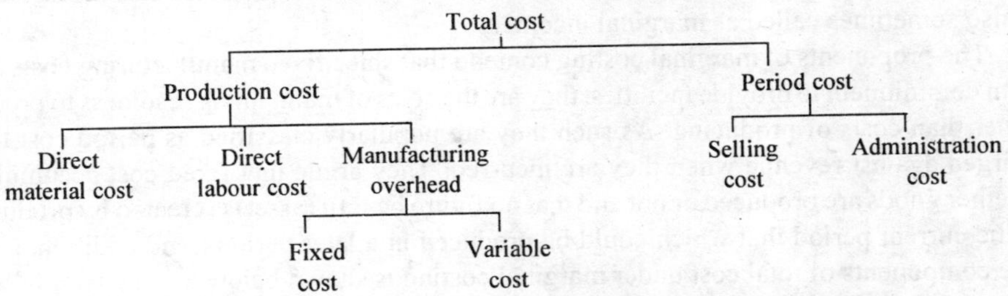

Fig. 22.1 : Chart showing total components of total cost under absorption costing.

MARGINAL COSTING

Before dealing with the marginal costing technique; it would be appropriate at this stage to know the meaning and definition of 'marginal cost'.

Marginal Cost

From the Economist's point of view, the cost incurred in producing an additional unit of product is known as marginal cost. However, from the cost accounting point of view marginal cost applies to the total cost obtained by adding prime cost and variable cost. In other words all costs other than fixed costs are the marginal cost.

The ICMA Terminology defines marginal cost as 'the amount at any given volume of output by which aggregate costs are changed if the volume of output is increased or decreased by one unit. In practice, this is measured by the total variable costs attributable to one unit. In this context a unit may be a single article, a batch of articles, an order, a stage of production capacity, a man hour, a process or a department. It relates to change in output in the particular circumstance under consideration.

Marginal Costing

This is one of the technique of ascertaining cost of production of goods or services manufactured. It is not a method of costing but it could be used in conjunction with any method of costing such as job or process costing. This technique can also be used along with other techniques of costing such as standard costing and budgetary control. This technique is also known by other names such as direct costing, variable costing, attributable costing, out-of-pocket costing and so on. Whereas in USA it is termed as 'direct costing', in UK it is referred to as 'marginal costing'.

Definition of marginal costing : According to NAA Bulletin on Direct Costing Research Series 23, "direct costing should be defined as seggregation of manufacturing cost between those which are fixed and those which vary directly with volume. Only the prime cost plus variable factory overheads are used to value inventory and cost of sales. The remaining factory expenses are charged off currently to profit and loss account".

In simple words, marginal costing may be defined as "the ascertainment of marginal costs and the effect on profit of changes in volume by differentiating between fixed cost and variable cost".

It is a technique whereby marginal costs of cost units are ascertained. Only variable costs are charged to cost units. The fixed costs attributable to a relevant period being written off in full against the contribution for that period.

The term contribution represents excess of sales over total variable costs. Contribution is also sometimes called as marginal income.

The proponents of marginal costing contend that since fixed manufacturing costs arise from commitment to provide facilities, they are the costs of maintaining readiness to produce rather than costs of producing. As such they are popularly classified as period cost to be charged against revenue when they are incurred. They argue that fixed cost accumulates whether goods are produced or not and that no future benefit (asset) is created by producing in the current period that which could be produced in a later period at no additional cost. The components of total cost under marginal costing is shown below :

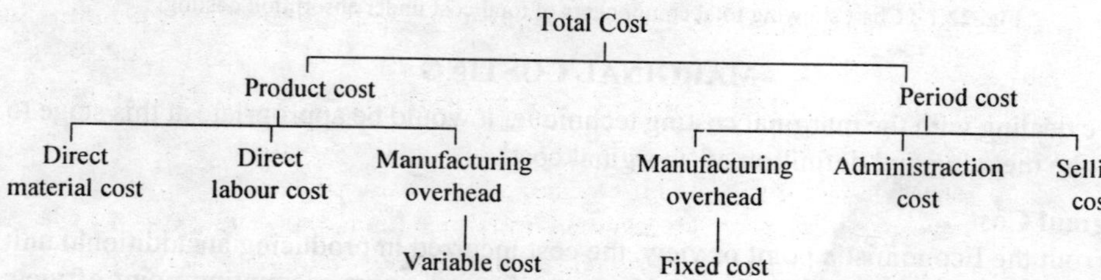

Fig. 22.2 : Chart showing components of total cost under marginal costing.

Theory of marginal costing : The theory of marginal costing is very clearly laid down by the ICMA, London, in the booklet on *A Report on Marginal Costing*. It can be stated thus; in relation to a given volume of output, additional output can normally be obtained at less than proportionate cost because within limits the aggregate of certain items of cost will tend to remain fixed and only the aggregate of the remainder will tend to rise proportionately with the increase in output. Coversely, a decrease in the volume of output will normally be accompanied by a less than proportionate fall in the aggregate cost. In simple words, when the volume of output increases the cost per unit will decrease. Similarly, if the volume of output is reduced, the cost per unit will increase. For example, if a company produces 100 units at a cost of Rs. 200, and by increasing the output by 2 units, the cost goes up to Rs. 204. The marginal cost of the increased output is Rs. 4.

Features of marginal costing : The features of marginal costing may be summarised under the following points :

(*a*) It is a technique of costing used to ascertain the marginal cost and to know impact of variable cost on the volume of output.

(*b*) All costs are classified on the basis of variability into fixed and variable cost. Semi-variable costs are segregated into fixed and variable costs.

(*c*) Variable costs alone are charged to production. Fixed costs are recovered from contribution.

(*d*) Stock of work-in-progress and finished goods are valued on the basis of marginal cost.

(*e*) Selling price is based on marginal cost plus the contribution.

(*f*) Profit is calculated not in the usual manner. When marginal cost is deducted from sales it gives rise to contribution. When fixed cost is deducted from conbtribution it results in profit.

(*g*) Break-even analysis and cost-volume-profit analysis (discussed in the next chapter) are integral part of this technique.

(*h*) The profitability of product or department is based on contribution made availabe by each department or product.

SIMILARITIES AND DISSIMILARITIES BETWEEN ABSORPTION AND MARGINAL COSTING

Similarities

1. Both the techniques agree that fixed and variable administration and selling expenses are period cost.
2. Both agree that the variable manufacturing costs are product cost.
3. Both agree that marginal costing presents the data for internal use.

Dissimilarities

Absorption Costing	*Marginal Costing*
1. All costs are charged to the cost of production.	1. Only variable cost is charged to cost of production. Fixed costs are recovered from contribution.
2. Stock of work-in-progress and finished goods are valued at fuil or	2. Stock of work-in-progress and finished goods are valued at marginal

Absorption Costing	Marginal Costing
total cost. Fixed costs are carried over from one period to another period which distort cost comparison.	cost. This facilitates cost comparison.
3. The differences between sales and total cost constitute profit.	3. The excess of sales revenue over variable cost is known as contribution. When fixed cost is deducted from contribution, it results in profit.
4. The apportionment of fixed costs on an arbitrary basis gives rise to under or over absorption of overheads.	4. As only variable costs are charged to products, it does not give rise to over or under absorption of overheads.
5. Costs are classified according to functional basis such as production cost, administration cost, selling and distribution cost.	5. Costs are classified according to variability.

Cost Presentation under Absorption and Marginal Costing

The difference between absorption and marginal costing in respect of cost ascertainment and cost presentation can be better understood by considering the following problems :

Problem 1 (Without stock balance) : Given the following data :

	Rs.
Direct material cost per unit	5.00
Direct labour cost per unit	9.00
Variable manufacturing overhead per unit	0.60
Total fixed manufacturing overhead per year	92,000
Number of units produced per year	10,000

Calculate the cost of production per unit under (*1*) absorption costing and (*2*) marginal costing.

Solution : Statement of cost under absorption and marginal costing

	Absorption costing	*Marginal costing*
Direct material cost	5.00	5.00
Direct labour cost	9.00	9.00
Variable manufacturing cost	0.60	0.60
Fixed mfg. cost $\frac{92,000}{10,000}$	9.20	—
Cost of production per unit	23.80	14.60

Note : Under marginal costing fixed manufacturing cost of Rs. 92,000 is treated as period cost.

Problem 2 (When closing stock balance is given) : Considering the data given in the above problem and the following additional information. Calculate the profit under (*i*) absorption costing and (*ii*) marginal costing.

Opening stock of finished goods	*NIL*
Units produced	10,000
Units sold	8,000
Sale price per unit	Rs. 35
Variable selling and administration expenses	Rs. 1.20 per unit sold
Fixed administration and selling expenses	Rs. 58,000

Solution :

Statement of profit under absorption and marginal costing

Absorption costing

Sales 8,000 × 35		2,80,000
Opening stock	NIL	
Add : Cost of goods produced 10,000 × 23.80	2,38,000	
(as per the Ist problem)		
	2,38,000	
Less : Closing Stock 2,000 × 23.80	47,600	1,90,400
		89,600
Less : Selling and distribution expenses		
Fixed 58,000		
Variable 9,600 8,000 × 1.20		67,600
Profit		22,000

Marginal costing

Sales 8,000 ×35		2,80,000
Opening Stock	NIL	
Add : Cost of goods produced (10,000 × 14.60)	1,46,000	
	1,46,000	
Less : Closing Stock 2,000 × 14.60	29,2000	1,16,800
		1,63,200
Less : Variable selling and administration expenses		9,600
contribution		1,53,600
Less : Fixed cost :		
Mfg. Overhead 92,000		
Fixed selling & Admn. exp. 58,000		1,50,000
Profit		3,600

The difference in the profit of Rs. 18,400 (22,000 – 3,600) is because of the different accounting treatment of fixed manufacturing costs under marginal costing and absorption costing. Under the marginal costing, the fixed manufacturing costs are accounted for as a period cost and the entire fixed manufacturing cost of Rs. 92,000 is deducted in calculating profit. Under absorption costing, the fixed manufacturing costs are treated as a product cost and charged to 10,000 units produced during the year. This means the closing stock of finished goods of 2,000 units will 'absorb' a part of the fixed manufacturing cost. The valuation of closing stock of finished goods under absorption costing is shown below :

Variable manufacturing cost	2,000 × 14.60	= 29,200
Fixed manufacturing cost	2,000 × 9.20	= 18,400
Total manufacturing cost	2,000 units @ 23.80	= 47,600

The fixed manufacturing cost of Rs. 18,400 assigned to closing finished goods is carried forward in the balance sheet until these, 2,000 units are sold in the next accounting year. In fact the difference in the profit under the two methods shown earlier is this amount of Rs. 18,400. When this 2,000 units are sold, the fixed cost of Rs. 18,400 is deducted in the profit statement. In other words, under absorption costing, the total fixed manufacturing cost of Rs. 92,000 is divided between the unsold finished goods (18,400) and finished goods that are sold (73,600).

Thus, in calculating net profit under absorption costing only Rs. 73,600 of fixed manufacturing costs are included in cost of goods sold, whereas, under marginal costing the entire fixed manufacturing cost of Rs. 92,000 is included as part of the fixed cost in the profit statement.

COST BEHAVIOUR AND ITS IMPACT OVER MARGINAL COSTING

The concept of marginal costing is based on the behaviour of the costs with volume of output. The assumption is that some components of costs change directly in proportion to the change in volume of activity and some remain unchanged with the change in the activity level. The pattern of cost behaviour is the result of an interplay of many forces which cause some costs to fluctuate and others to remain constant. The most important of these forces are the following :

(a) Volume
(b) Inherent nature of the cost
(c) Capacity
(d) Managerial policies
(e) Effective control
(f) Prices of input factors
(g) Strikes and lockouts
(h) Weather and economic conditions

Accordingly, the costs can be classified on the basis of their behaviour into three types. They are as follows :

1. Fixed Cost

A fixed cost is defined as "a cost which accrues in relation to the passage of time and which within certain output and turnover limits tend to be unaffected by fluctuations in the level of activity, *i.e.*, output or turnover.

The key points in this definition are :

(1) Fixed costs are time related.
(2) It remains fixed within the limits of output or turnover.
(3) It is unaffected by changes in the level of activity.
(4) Though it is called fixed cost in the short run, in the long it may vary as for example when the policy of management is to expand after 10 years, fixed cost will increase no matter what volume of output is produced. Therefore, fixed cost is sometimes called as 'policy cost'.

Fixed costs are of two types. They are as follows :

(a) **Committed cost :** These costs are related to the provision of a capacity to do business. The amount of committed costs is fixed by decisions which were made in the past and is not subject to management control in the present on a short run basis. Since there is no direct relationship between committed costs and either the planned or actual utilisation of existing facilities, the amount will remain constant over the whole range of operating activity.

(b) **Programmed or managed cost :** These costs are related to the utilisation of the capacity provided :

Fixed cost can be shown graphically as under :

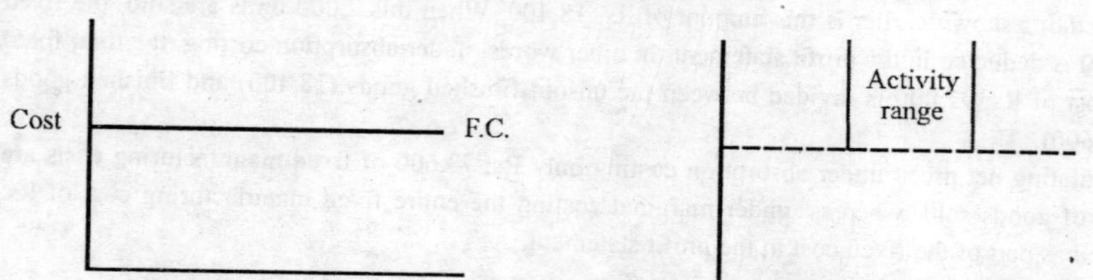

Fig. 22.3 : Graphic presentation of fixed cost.

Fixed cost can be expressed algebraically thus :

Cost = a

where 'a' is contant, 'v' the volume of output does not appear in this equation to indicate the change in activity is deemed not to affect the fixed cost.

2. Variable Cost

It is defined as a cost which, in the aggregate, tends to vary in direct proportion to changes in the volume of output or turnover.

Variable costs are of two types. They are as follows :

(*A*) Linear variable cost or engineered cost : When the relationship between variable cost and output can be shown as a straight line on a graph, they are termed as linear variable cost. This is shown graphically below :

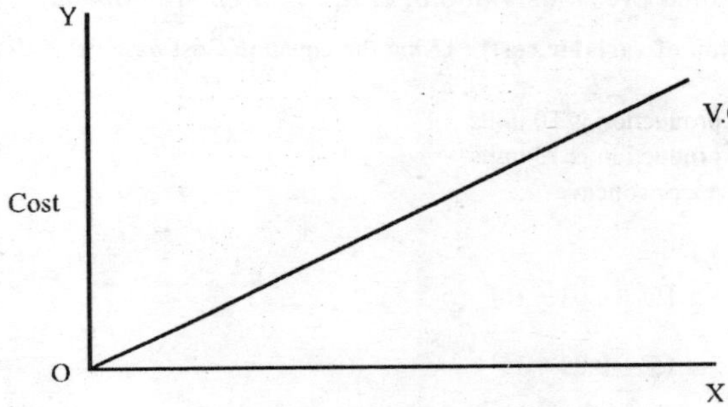

Fig. 22.4 : Graph showing linear variable cost.

A variable cost is called as engineered cost because an optimum relationship can be carefully determined by work measurement technique between input and output. Direct material cost and direct labour cost are good examples of engineered cost.

For calculation and analysis it is more convenient to express the linear relationship algebraically, thus

Cost = bx

where x is the volume of output in units, b is a constant representing the variable cost per unit.

(B) Non-linear or curvilinear variable cost : When the relationship between variable cost and output can be shown as a curved line on a graph, it is said to be curvilinear. This is shown graphically below :

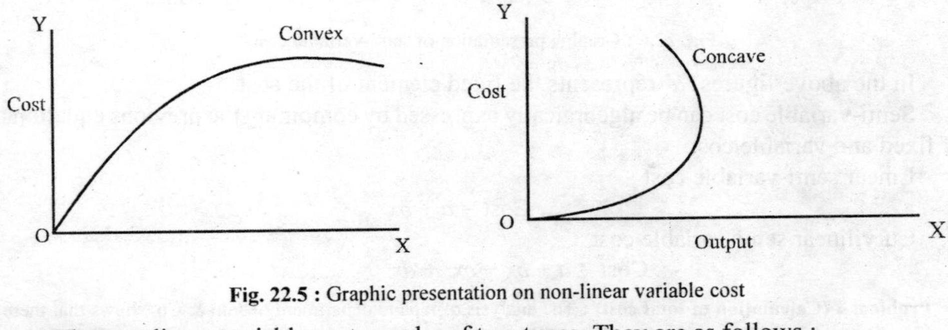

Fig. 22.5 : Graphic presentation on non-linear variable cost

The non-linear variable cost may be of two types. They are as follows :

(*a*) *Convex-linear variable cost :* It is a cost where each extra unit of output causes a less than proportionate increase in cost.

(*b*) *Concave-linear variable cost* : It is a cost where each extra unit of output causes a more than proportionate increase in cost. Differential piece rate system of wage payment is a good example for this type of cost.

Curvilinear variable cost—the parabola : When the slope of the cost function changes uniformly with changes in output, the curve is known as a parabola and is algebraically expressed thus :

Cost : $bx + cx^2 + dx^3$ ....px^4

where x is as defined previously and b, c, d, ... p are constant.

Problem 3 (Calculation of variable cost) : Using the equation Cost $bx + cx^2 + dx^3$, where $b = 8$, $c = 0.5$ and $d = 0.03$, calculate

(*i*) variable cost when production is 10 units.

(*ii*) variable cost when production is 15 units.

Is the function convex or concave?

Solution :

Cost = $bx + cx^2 + dx^3$

$8 \times 10 + 0.5 \times 10^2 + 0.03 + 10^3$

Rs. 160

= $8 \times 15 + 0.5 \times 15^2 + 0.03 \times 15^3$

= Rs. 333.75

From the above it is seen that the increase in activity from 10 to 15 units results in more than a doubling of variable cost. This shows that there is a more than proportionate increase in the unit cost of extra production. Hence the function is concave.

3. Semi-variable Cost

It is defined as a cost containing both fixed and variable elements, which is, therefore partly affected by fluctuation in the volume of output or turnover. It is also sometimes called as a stepped cost or hybrid cost.

Semi-variable cost can be shown graphically thus :

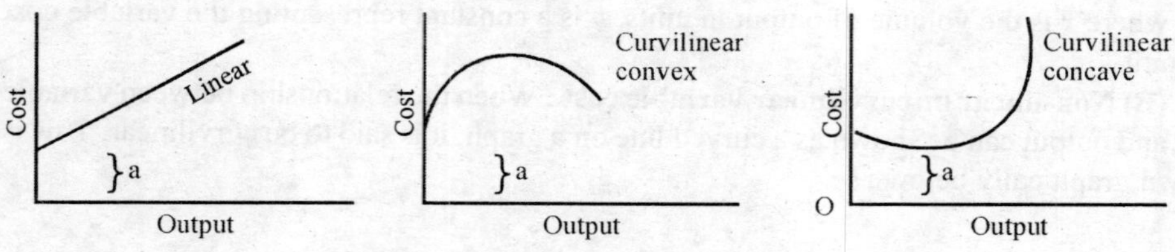

Fig. 22.6 : Graphic presentation of semi-variable cost.

In the above figures '*a*' represents the fixed element of the cost.

Semi-variable cost can be algebraically expressed by combining the previous equations of fixed and variable cost.

Linear semi-variable cost

$$\text{Cost} = a + bx$$

Curvilinear semi-variable cost

$$\text{Cost} = a + bx + cx^2 + dx^3 \text{ .... } px^4$$

Problem 4 (Calculation of total cost) : The analysis of repairs department of Jain & Co. shows that there is a fixed cost of Rs. 500 per month and a variable cost related to machine hours amounting to Rs. 2.25 per machine hour.

What is the expected cost for a month when the budgeted activity level is (*i*) 1,500 machine hours and (*ii*) 1,800 machine hours.

Solution :

Total cost	=	$a + bx$
(*i*)		500 × 2.25 (1,500)
	=	Rs. 3,875
(*ii*)		500 × 2.25 (1,800)
	=	Rs. 4,550

As, under marginal costing technique, only variable cost alone is charged to the product, it becomes necessary to segregate semi-variable cost into fixed and variable cost. Besides this, the segregation of semi-variable cost into fixed and variable has the following uses :

1. It facilitates budgeting the expenses for various levels of production.
2. It helps in exercising control over variable cost once semi-variable cost is segregated into fixed and variable.
3. It helps in fixing prices especially during the period of depression.
4. It helps in making useful decisions.

Methods of Segregating Semi-variable Cost

1. High-low method : This method is based on the analysis of past records of expenses. This method takes into account only the highest and lowest values contained in the data in order to determine the rate of cost change and thereafter variable cost. The variable cost is then deducted from total cost to get fixed cost.

Limitations : (*i*) It is not based on all the items of the given data.

(*ii*) It assumes that the variable portion of semi-variable cost has linear relationship. In other words, the variable portion of cost per unit is constant which is not always true.

Steps involved : 1. Take the difference between high and low costs.

2. Take the difference between level of activity corresponding these costs.
3. Divide the difference in cost by the difference in level of activity. We get variable cost per unit.
4. Find out the variable cost by multiplying the rate so obtained under step 3 by the number of units.
5. Deduct this variable cost from semi-variable cost to get fixed cost.

Problem 5 (Segregation of semi-variable cost under high-low method) : From the following data segregate the semi-variable cost into fixed and variable cost under High-Low method.

Level of activity (Units)	*Cost (Rs.)*	*Level of activity (Units)*	*Cost (Rs.)*
36	800	72	950
48	700	75	1,170
49	970	76	1,020
55	790	82	1,200
57	1,050	86	1,060
59	900	92	1,100
65	880	94	1,310
66	1,020	97	1,250
67	1,180		

Solution :

High point	94 units at a cost of Rs.	1,310
Low point	48 units at a cost of Rs.	700
Difference	46	610

Variable cost per unit = $\frac{610}{46}$ = 13.26 per unit.

Semi-variable cost at 48 units = Rs. 700

Less : Variable cost 48 × 13.26	=	Rs. 636
Fixed cost	=	Rs. 64

In this process for each level of activity, fixed cost and variable cost can be found out.

2. Scatter graph technique : This is a graphic method of segregating semi-variable cost into fixed and variable cost. This method is also known as regression line method. This method is also based on past data, but it takes into account all the data when compared to the high-low method. The following steps are involved under this method :

(1) On the *X*-axis is taken to represent the output sales.
(2) On the *Y*-axis the cost is represented.
(3) Plot the points on the graph.
(4) Draw a line through the points plotted, with the same number of points on each side of the line. In the process of drawing the line ignore any abnormal cost if there is any. The line so drawn is known as the line of best fit.
(5) Extend the line so drawn above the *Y*-axis. The point where the line of best fit intersects the Y-axis is taken to be the amount of fixed cost.

One main limitation of this method is that there will be a change in fixed cost even if there is a slight bias in drawing the straight line.

Problem 6 (Scatter graph method of segregating semi-variable cost into fixed and variable cost) : From the following data extracted from the books of Arun Food Products Ltd. Calculate the fixed cost using scatter graph method :

Output (units)	*Semi-variable cost (Rs.)*	*Output (units)*	*Semi-variable cost (Rs.)*
500	2,500	900	3,700
600	2,800	840	3,520
700	3,100	800	3,400
940	3,820	860	3,580
740	3,220	760	3,280
880	3,640	540	2,620

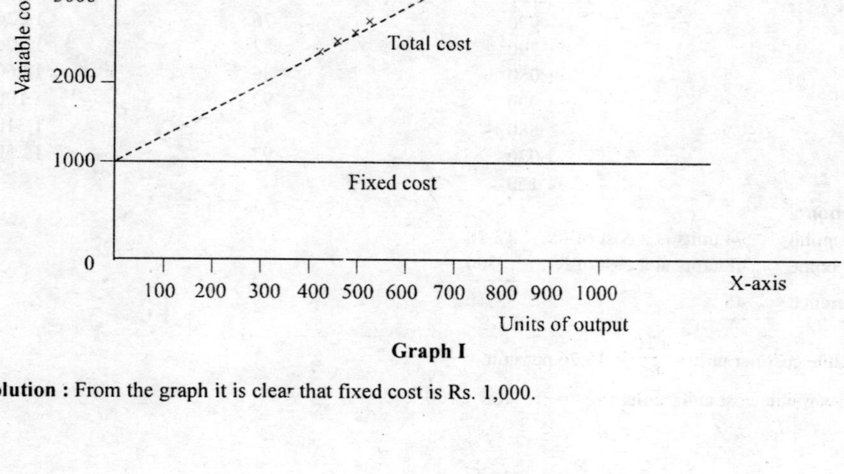

Graph I

Solution : From the graph it is clear that fixed cost is Rs. 1,000.

(3) Method of least squares : This is a statistical method used for establishing a line of best fit to data. The linear cost function can be represented by the following equation :

$$y = a + bx$$

where y = cost. Other symbols are as defined previously.

To find out the values of '*a*' and '*b*' which are constants, we have to solve two simultaneous equations

$$\Sigma y = an + b\,\Sigma x$$

$$\Sigma xy = a\Sigma x + b\Sigma x^2$$

Where n = number of pairs of cost and activity figures.

Problem 7 (Simultaneous equation method of segregating semi-variable cost) : From the following data obtain an equation to indicate the linear cost function under the method of least squares :

Unit x	*Cost y*
4	56
5	62
7	80
7	72
9	88
10	94

Solution :

x	y	xy	x^2
4	56	224	16
5	62	310	25
7	80	560	49
7	72	504	49
9	88	792	81
10	94	940	100
$\Sigma x = 42$	$\Sigma y = 452$	$\Sigma xy = 3,330$	$\Sigma x^2 = 320$

$$\Sigma y = ax + b\Sigma x^2$$

$$\Sigma xy = a\Sigma x + b\Sigma x^2$$

$$452 = 6a + 42b \times 7$$

$$3,330 = 42a + 320b$$

$$3,164 = 42a + 294b$$

$$3,330 = 42a + 320b$$

Subtracting

$$166 = 26b$$

$$b = 6,385$$

Substituting the value of b in equation 1

$$6a + 42b = 452$$

$$6a = -42 \times 6.385 + 452$$

$$6a = -268 + 452$$

$$a = 30.6$$

∴ The linear cost function is $y = 30.6 + 6.385x$

When the given problems has many digits of variables and costs, it becomes difficult to adopt the above method. An alternate method which could be termed as short-cut method or indirect method can be followed in such situations. The steps involved under this method are as follows :

(*a*) Calculate the average of '*x*' series. This is found out by the formula $x = \dfrac{\Sigma x}{N}$.

(*b*) Calculate the average of '*y*' series. This is found out the formula $y = \dfrac{\Sigma y}{N}$

(c) Take the deviations from the average of 'x' series for each and every item of 'x' series.
(d) Take the deviations from the average of 'y' series for each and every item of 'y' series.
(e) Square the deviations of 'x' series to get x^2.
(f) Obtain the products of the deviations of 'x' and 'y' series. This is denoted under the column 'xy'.
(g) Add up the products so obtained under step (f) and denote it with Σxy.
(h) Apply the following formula $b = \frac{\Sigma xy}{\Sigma x^2}$

Problem 8 (Short-cut or indirect method of segregating semi-variable cost) : The following semi-variable costs are taken from Ajanta Metal Works for the period January to June, 1993 :

Month	*Machine hours*	*Semi-variable cost*
Jan.	2,000	300
Feb.	2,200	320
Mar.	1,700	270
Apr.	2,400	340
May	1,800	280
June	1,900	290

Find out the amount of variable and fixed cost.

Solution :

Month	*Machine hours (x)*	*Semi-variable Cost (y)*	*Deviations from x (2,000)*	*Deviations from y (300)*	x^2	xy
Jan.	2,000	300	0	0	0	0
Feb.	2,200	320	+200	+20	40,000	+4,000
Mar.	1,700	270	−300	−30	90,000	+9,000
Apr.	2,400	240	+400	+40	1,60,000	+16,000
May	1,800	280	−200	−20	40,000	+4,000
June	1,900	290	−100	−10	10,000	+1,000
	$\Sigma x = 12{,}000$	$\Sigma xy = 1{,}800$			$\Sigma xy = 3{,}40{,}000$	$\Sigma xy = 34{,}000$

$$x = \frac{\text{Total machine hrs}}{\text{No. of months}} = \frac{12{,}000}{6} = 2{,}000$$

$$y = \frac{\text{Total semi-variable cost}}{\text{No. of months}} = \frac{1{,}800}{6} = 300$$

$$b = \frac{\Sigma xy}{\Sigma x^2} = \frac{34{,}000}{3{,}40{,}000} = 0.10$$

The variable element of the semi-variable cost is 0.10 per unit.

The fixed cost can be calculated thus :

$$\begin{aligned} & y &= a + bx \\ \text{Jan.} \quad & 300 &= a + 2{,}000 \times 0.10 \\ & 300 &= a + 200 \\ & a &= 100 \\ \text{Feb.} \quad & 320 &= a + 2{,}200\ (0.10) \\ & 320 &= a + 220 \\ & a &= 100 \end{aligned}$$

Fixed cost of Rs. 100 is thus same whatever may be the level of activity.

ARGUMENTS IN FAVOUR OF MARGINAL COSTING

The exclusion of fixed costs in the ascertainment of cost of production (marginal costing) is justified on the following grounds :

1. Fixed costs relate to a particular period of time and therefore, it should be charged for that period. Thus, it is treated as a period cost not as a product cost.

2. There is no accurate basis to apportion fixed cost. So it is charged to profit and loss account instead of charging to cost of production.
3. Since fixed cost remain constant irrespective of change in the level of activity, it does not affect production capacity. It is only variable cost that affects various levels of productive activity. Hence fixed cost is excluded from cost of production.
4. To facilitate cost comparison and to maintain accuracy of trading results, fixed costs are excluded from cost of production.
5. Fixed costs under absorption costing is carried over from one period to another as part of inventory value. Such carrying forward is not justified as it does not facilitate matching of cost with revenue.
6. For the current operation of any level of activity only variable cost alone is relevant but not the fixed cost. Hence it is excluded from cost of production.

MARGINAL COST EQUATION

The marginal cost equation is stated below :

Sales – Variable Cost = Contribution

or S – V = C

Contribution = Fixed cost + Profit

or C = F.C. + P

or S – V = F.C. + P

If there is loss

S – V = FC – L

At the point of no-profit-no-loss (break-even point)

S – V = F + Zero

The usefulness of marginal cost equation is, given any of the three pariturculars, we can find out the fourth unknown particular. From the above equation it is clear that contribution is used to meet fixed cost and any balance left out is equal to profit.

Problem 9 : From the following particulars extracted from the books of Sunshine Enterprises for the period ending 31st Dec., 1992. Find out the amount of profit.

Number of units produced	=	500 units
Variable cost for the period	=	Rs. 2 per unit
Fixed cost for the period	=	Rs. 800
Selling price per unit	=	Rs. 4

Solution :

Sales – Variable cost = Fixed cost + Profit

or Sales – Variable cost – Fixed cost = Profit

$500\,(4-2) - 800 = P$

$1{,}000 - 800 = P$

P = Rs. 200

MARGINAL COSTING AND VALUATION OF FINISHED STOCK

Under marginal costing technique closing stock is valued at marginal cost. However, under absorption costing, fixed cost is included in the value of closing stock. Because of this treatment the amount of fixed overhead charged under absorption costing for the current year will differ from the actual fixed overhead pertaining to that year. The reason is the amount of fixed cost carried down from the previous year, will differ from the amount of fixed cost carried forward to the next year. This can better be understood by the following examples :

> *Example :* On 1.1.92, Opening stock of finished goods of 2,000 units is valued at Rs. 4 of which fixed cost is Rs. 1.
>
> On 31.12.1992, closing stock of finished goods of 1,600 units valued at Rs. 5 per unit of which fixed cost is Rs. 1.50.

Value of fixed cost brought in is 2,000 (2,000 × Re. 1). Whereas the value of fixed cost carried forward is Rs. 2.400 (1.600 × 1.50).

If the actual fixed cost for the year 1992 is Rs. 50,000, then the fixed cost charged for the year will be Rs. 49,600 (50,000 + 2,000 – 2,400).

When compared to absorption costing, considering the output, sales and closing stock the following conclusions are arrived at :

1. When production volume is equal to sales volume, net profit is same under both marginal costing and absorption costing.
2. When sales are less than production, profit under marginal costing are less than that of absorption costing.
3. When sales exceed production, profit under marginal costing are more than that of absorption costing.

UTILITY, ADVANTAGES AND LIMITATIONS OF MARGINAL COSTING

Utility of Marginal Costing

1. It is used as one of the techniques of costing, *i.e.*, to ascertain the cost of production.
2. It aids management for making useful decision by providing useful information.
3. It serves as a tool of cost control.

Advantages

1. It avoids the complications of over or under absorption of fixed cost by excluding it from cost of production.
2. The technique provides useful data for managerial decision-making.
3. By not carrying forward fixed cost from period to period, it facilitates cost comparison.
4. The impact of profit on sales fluctuations are clearly shown under marginal costing.
5. The technique is flexible in the sense it can be used along with other techniques such as budgetary control and standard costing.
6. It establishes a clear relationships between cost, sales and volume of output and break-even analysis which shows the effect of increasing and decreasing production acitivity on the profitability of the company.
7. It provides useful data for the management in determination of policies regarding future production and sales.
8. Stock of work-in-progress and finished goods are valued at marginal cost, which is uniform.

Limitations

1. The segregation of semi-variable costs often poses a problem.
2. Closing stock of work-in-progress and finished goods are understated which is not acceptable to tax authorities.

3. With the change of technology and owing to automation of industries, it results in more fixed cost. Marginal costing fails to reflect the exact change because of adoption of new technology.
4. It does not provide any yardstick to exercise control. So an effective means of control cannot be exercised.
5. The technique is not suitable under cost plus contract because the technique ignores fixed cost in calculating total cost.
6. Variable cost per unit remains constant only in the short run but not in the long run.
7. Cost comparison of two jobs will be difficult. Though marginal costing may be same for both the jobs, yet a job which takes more time to complete involves more of overhead.
8. When sales are based on marginal cost or marginal cost with some contribution, it may result in losses or low profit.

PRECAUTIONS TO BE TAKEN WHILE ADOPTING MARGINAL COSTING

1. As fixed cost is not included in the cost of production, care must be taken to see that while fixing the selling price, profit is realised after full recovery of fixed cost.
2. It is necessary to check composition of marginal cost from time to time. There can be a change of variable cost into fixed and *vice versa* when production method is changed.
3. Based on contribution margin, orders are accepted with a view to increase profits. This may lead to uneconomic expansion in the business involving more capital. However, during the period of falling business this proves to be burden.

APPLICATIONS OF MARGINAL COSTING

The technique of marginal costing is largely used in the managerial decision-making process. The application of marginal costing in the day-to-day decision-making process are as follows :

1. Make or Buy Decision

Very often management is confronted with the problem of deciding whether to buy a component or product from an outside source or to manufacture the same if it is economical as compared to the price quoted by a supplier. In deciding this absorption costing (total cost analysis) would mislead. If the decision is to buy from an external source the price quoted by the supplier should be less than marginal cost. If the decision is to make within the organisation, the cost of production should include all additional cost such as depreciation on new plant interest on capital, etc. If this cost of production is less than the quotation price, it should be decided in making the product rather than procure it from an external source.

Problem 10 (Make or buy decision) : Expansion Ltd. manufactures automobiles accessories and parts. The following are the total costs of processing 1,00,000 units :

Direct materials cost	Rs. 5 lakhs
Direct labour cost	Rs. 8 lakhs
Variable factory overhead	Rs. 6 lakhs
Fixed factory overhead	Rs. 5 lakhs

The purchase price of the component is Rs. 22. The fixed overhead would continue to be incurred even when the component is bought from outside, although there would have been reduction to the extent of Rs. 2,00,000.

Required :

(*a*) Should the part be made or bought considering that the present facility when released following a buying decision would remain idle?

(*b*) In case the released capacity can be rented out to another manufacturer for Rs. 1,50,000 having good demand. What should be the decision? (*C.S., Inter, June 1990*)

Solution :

Cost Analysis

Particulars	*(1) Whether to make*	*(2) Whether to buy at Rs. 22 each present facility remaining idle*	*(3) Whether to buy at Rs. 22 each when released capacity is rented out*
1. Variable cost of production	19	–	–
2. Cost of buying from outside	–	22	22
3. Saving in fixed cost when bought	–	(2)	(2)
4. Rent receipt when idle capacity is rented out	–	–	(1.5)
	19	20	18.5

Recommendations :

1. For decision to situation (*a*)—make the component.
2. For decision to situation (*b*)—buy the component.

Problem 11 (Make or buy decision) : Stoner Company uses three different components (materials) in manufacturing its primary product. Stoner manufactures two of the components and purchases one (designated as component 1) from outside suppliers. The company is currently developing the annual profit plan. Sales are highly seasonal. Component 2 cannot be acquired from outsiders. However, component 3 can be purchased. The three components have critical specifications. The annual profit plan provided data for the following computations :

	Components 3 *(Unit cost at 12,000 units)*
Material (direct)	Rs. 1.40
Labour (direct)	Rs. 2.20
Factory overhead (apportioned)	Re. 0.40
Annual machine rental (special machine used only for component 3)	Rs. 0.50
Variable factory overhead	Rs. 1.00
Average storage cost per year (fixed)	Rs. 0.40
Total	Rs. 5.90
Average inventory level	500 units

The purchase manager investigated outside suppliers and found one that would sign a one year contract to deliver "12,000 top quality units as needed during the year at Rs. 5.20 per unit". Serious consideration is being given to this alternative. Should Stoner make or buy component 3? Explain the relevant factors influencing your decision. (*ICWA, Inter, Dec., 1988*)

Solution :

Total cost of component 3 can be bifurcated into fixed and variable portion as follows :

Variable cost :

Material (direct)	Rs. 1.40
Labour (direct)	Rs. 2.20
Annual machine rental (special machine used only for component 3)	Re. 0.50
Variable factory overhead	Re. 1.00
	Rs. 5.10

Fixed cost :

Fixed overhead apportioned	Re. 0.40
Average storage cost per year	Re. 0.40
	Re. 0.80
Total	Rs. 5.90

On comparison of the price offered by outside supplier with the variable cost, if made inhouse, it is observed that variable cost of inhouse production is lower (fixed cost remains same whether made in-house or purchased). This is also on the assumption that labour (direct) is variable if it is possible to get rid of the workers when required. Hence, labour cost is treated as fixed. If labour is treated as fixed, variable cost of inhouse production is Rs. 2.90 (5.10–5.20) per unit which is per unit less than the purchase price per unit (5.20 – 2.90 = 2.30).

Hence it is advisable to make component no. 3.

2. Comparing mannual with machine labour : Whenever a new product is launched management may have to decide whether the new product is to be manufacutured mannually or mechanically. Some of the factors which are to be considered in this regard are the (*i*) savings arising in the labour cost, (*ii*) additional investment on machinery, (*iii*) additional capacity of machine, (*iv*) the possible displacement of employees and (*v*) the danger of obsolescence of the machine. However, cost of production is the significant factor which determines the method of production. Under marginal costing that method which gives the largest contribution, *i.e.*, lowest marginal cost would be preferred. Under absorption costing that method of manufacture which gives lowest cost will be selected.

Problem 12 (Manual vs. machanical production) : The Navabharath Enterprise has a plan to introduce a new product A numbering 10,000 units for the year 1993. The following details are available :

	Machine (Rs.)	*Mannual labour (Rs.)*
Purchase price of machine	20,000	–
Direct material	5,000 PA	5,000 PA
Direct labout	500 PA	3,000 PA
Variable overheads	2,000 PA	1,000 PA
Fixed overheads (not including depreciation)	1,500 PA	1,00 PA

The selling price of the products has been fixed at Rs. 3 each. If the machines is purchased it will have an estimated life of 10 years with little or no residual; value.

You are required to show the decision to be taken regarding the method of production under (*i*) marginal costing and (*ii*) absoption costing including interest @ 5%.

Solution :

Statement of marginal cost

			Machine (Rs.)	*Mannual labour (Rs.)*
Sales			30,000	30,000
Less : *Variable cost* :				
Direct material	5,000	5,000		
Direct labour	500	3,000		
Variable overheads	2,000	1,000	7,500	9,000
Contribution			22,500	2,000

On this basis (the lower marginal cost and large contribution) the machine is preferable.

Statement of total cost

	Machine (Rs.)	Mannual labour (Rs.)
Direct material	5,000	5,000
Direct labour	500	3,000
Overheads : Variable	2,000	1,000
Fixed	1,500	1,000
Depreciation $\frac{1}{10} \times 20,000$	2,000	–
	11,000	10,000
Interest @ 5%	550	500
	11,550	10,500

From the above statement, mannual method of production is cheaper. This problem illustrates a weakness of the marginal costing. Obviously, fixed costs have to be covered as they are incurred on the specific products.

3. Replacing existing machinery with new machinery : Sometimes with a view to derive maximum efficiency an existing plant may have to be replaced by a new one. Again the guiding factors mentioned earlier will help in such decision-making process.

Problem 13 : A factory engaged in the manufacture of electronic goods has a ten-year old equipment depreciated on straight-line basis. The useful life of the equipment was estimated to be 20 years with a residual value of Rs. 3 lakhs (original cost of the equipment being Rs. 23 lakhs). The output of the equipment is 1,200 units per hour.

The management now proposes to install a new equipment worth Rs. 50 lakhs which has an estimated life of 15 years and a residual value of Rs. 5 lakhs. The payment terms for the new equipment include a part exchange provision of Rs. 6 lakhs in respect of the existing equipment. The output of the new equipment is 3,000 units per hour.

Other comparative annual cost data relating to the two equipments are as under :

	Existing equipment (Rs.)	*New equipment (Rs.)*
Wages	1,00,000	1,20,000
Repairs and maintenance	20,000	52,000
Consumables	3,20,000	4,80,000
Power	1,20,000	1,50,000
Allocation of fixed cost	60,000	80,000
Total hours run per year	2,400	2,400

You are required to prepare a comparative schedule showing total conversion cost as well as cost per 1,000 units after considering interest @ 10% on net cash out flow for procuring the new equipment and also for providing for the yearly recovery of the loss suffered in the transaction. *(ICWA, Inter, Dec. 1991)*

Solution :

Comparative statement of cost of equipment

	Existing equipment (Rs.)	*New equipment (Rs.)*
Capital cost of equipment including cost of installation	23,00,000	50,00,000
Less : Residual value	3,00,000	5,00,000
	20,00,000	45,00,000
Less : Depreciation written off	10,00,000	
	10,00,000	45,00,000

Comparative statement of operation cost of equipment

Annual depreciation	—New	–	3,00,000
(See Note 1)	—Old	1,00,000	70,000
Interest on capital (new cash outflow) *(See Note 2)*		–	4,40,000
Wages		1,00,000	1,20,000
Repairs and maintenance		20,000	52,000
Consumables		3,20,000	4,80,000
Power		1,20,000	1,50,000
Allocation of fixed expense		60,000	80,000
		7,20,000	16,92,000
Total hours run per annum		2,400	2,400
Operating cost per hour		Rs. 300	Rs. 705
Output per hour (units)		1,200	3,000
Operating cost per 1,000 unit		Rs. 250	Rs. 235

Therefore, there is a net saving in cost of Rs. 15 per, 1,000 units.

Working Note 1 : Depreciation on new equipment

$$= \frac{\text{Original cost} - \text{Residual value}}{\text{Estimated life}}$$

$$= \frac{45,00,000}{15} = 3,00,000$$

Depreciation (yearly recovery) on loss on sale of existing equipment

$$= \frac{\text{Book value of existing equipment} - \text{Part exchange value}}{\text{Residual life of existing equipment}}$$

$$= \frac{13,00,000 - 6,00,000}{10 \text{ years}} = \text{Rs. } 70,000$$

Working note 2 : Interest is calculated on net cash outflow in procuring the new equipment is Rs. 44,00,000 (Cost of old equipment Rs. 50 lakhs less part exchange value Rs. 6 lakhs).

4. Alternative use of plant or productive facility : To take advantage of alternative use of production facility or alternative use of plant it is necessary to know the contribution margin. That alternative which yields highest contribution margin shall be selected.

Problem 14 : The management of Alpha Co. Ltd. are considering the following two alternative proposals :

(*a*) A semi-automatic lathe costing Rs. 58,000. The annual cost for its operation being estimated at Rs. 42,000 and

(*b*) A fully automatic lathe costing Rs. 95,000 the annual costs for its operation being estimated at Rs. 38,000.

The life of each is estimated as 12 years with zero salvage value. The capacity of the automatic plant is assessed as 30% more than that of semi-automatic plant, but this extra capacity is likely to remain unutilised for two years. Using straight line depreciation with an interest charge of 6% on the capital investment. Make your recommendations as to which alternative is preferable.

Solution :

	Semi-automatic lathe	*Fully automatic lathe*
Purchase cost (Rs.)	58,000	95,000
Expenses on machines :		
Operating expenses	42,000	38,000
Depreciating $\frac{1}{12}$ of cost	4,833	7,917
Interest 6%	3,480	5,700
	50,313	51,617
Percentage increase		2.5%

In the first two years the semi-automatic lathe is more profitable because extra 30% capacity of fully automatic lathe is not utilised. But in the remaining 10 years the fully automatic lathe will be much more profitable because the extra cost incurred by that plant is only about 2.5%, whereas the extra output capacity is 30%. So the fully automatic lathe is preferable. However, it is assumed that (*i*) additional 30% output will have ready market and (*ii*) revenue from the same is more than the additional expenses imparted above.

Problem 15 : Given below are the details of cost of production of two products *X* and *Y* manufactured by Adam's Co. Pvt. Ltd. Both the products use the same raw materials.

	X	*Y*
% of total capacity utilised	60%	40%
Units produced	1,200	2,000
Selling price per unit	Rs. 2,000	Rs. 1,200
Cost per unit :		
Raw materials	Rs. 1,400	700
Direct labour	Rs. 200	150
Variable expense	Rs. 180	230
Contribution per unit	Rs. 220	10
Fixed overhead	Rs. 3,00,000	

Would you recommend increasing the capacity utilised on product *X*.

Solution :

	1		2		3	
	X	Y	X	Y	X	Y
Percentage of capacities	60%	40%	50%	50%	70%	30%
Units produced	1,200	2,000	1,000	2,500	1,400	1,500
Contribution per unit	220	120	220	120	220	120
Contribution	2,64,000	2,40,000	2,20,000	3,00,000	3,08,000	1,80,000
Total contribution	5,04,000		5,20,000		4,88,000	
Fixed overhead	3,00,000		3,00,000		3,00,000	
Net profit	2,04,000		2,20,000		1,88,000	

Thus by increasing capacity usage on product *Y* profit is increased whereas by increasing capacity usage on product *X*, profit is reduced.

This is so because contribution per unit percentage of capacity for product *X* is $\frac{2,64,000}{60\%}$ = Rs. 4,400 and for product *Y* is $\frac{2,400,000}{40\%}$ = Rs. 6,000. Hence it is better to increase 40% of the capacity utilised on product *Y* and not on product *X*.

5. Product-mix, profit planning and profit maximisation : Companies manufacturing varieties of products often have to decide which product-mix is more profitable. That product-mix which gives maximum contribution is to be considered as best product-mix. Similarly, profit planning is often considered so as to earn reasonable profit if not maximum profit. The profit planning is affected by factors such as (*i*) volume of output, (*ii*) product mix, (*iii*) costs to be incurred, (*iv*) prices to be charged and so on. Marginal costing techniques guides the management in this regard.

Problem 16 : The directors of *A* Ltd. are considering the sales budget for the budget period 1993. You are required to present to the board a statement showing the marginal cost of each product and to recommend which of the following product-mix should be adopted :

(*a*) 450 units of *A* and 300 units of *B*
(*b*) 900 unit of *A* only
(*c*) 600 units of *B* only
(*d*) 600 units of *A* and 200 units of *B*

The following additional information is furnished :

	Product A	Product B
Fixed overhead Rs. 10,000 p.a.		
Direct labour @ Re. 1 per hour	10 hrs.	15 hrs.
Variable overheads—100 % of labour		
Direct material	Rs. 20	Rs. 25
Selling price	Rs. 60	Rs. 100

Solution :

Marginal cost statement

	Product A	Product B
Direct materials	20	25
Direct labour	10	15
Variable overhead	10	15
Marginal cost	40	55
Contribution	20	45
Sales	60	100

Product-mix

	A	B		Total
(*i*) 450 units of *A* and 300 units of *B*				
Contribution	9,000	13,500		22,500
Less : Fixed overheads				10,000
			Profit	12,500
(*ii*) 900 units of A				
Contribution	18,000			18,000
Less : Fixed overheads				10,000
			Profit	8,000
(*iii*) 600 units of *B*				
Contribution		17,000		27,000
Less : Fixed overhead				10,000
			Profit	17,000
(*iv*) 600 units of *A* and 200 units of *B*				
Contribution	12,000	9,000		21,000
Less : Fixed overhead				10,000
			Profit	11,000

Thus alternative (*iii*) is the one recommended.

Problem 17 : From the following particulars find the most profitable product-mix and prepare a statement of profitability of that product-mix.

	Product A	Product B	Product C
Units budgeted to be produced and sold	1,800	3,000	1,200
Selling price per unit (Rs.)	60	55	50
Requirement per unit :			
Direct materials	5 kg.	3 kg.	4 kg.
Direct labour	4 hrs.	3 hrs.	2 hrs.
Variable overhead	Rs. 7	Rs. 13	Rs. 8
Fixed overhead	Rs. 10	Rs. 10	Rs. 10
Cost of direct material per kg.	Rs. 4	Rs. 4	Rs. 4
Direct labour hour rate	Rs. 2	Rs. 2	Rs. 2
Maximum possible units of sale	4,000	5,000	1,500

All the three products are produced from the same direct material using the same type of machines and labour, direct labour which is the key factor, is limited to 18,600 hours. (C.A., Inter, May 1990)

Solution :

Statement showing most profitable product-mix

				A	*B*	*C*
Selling price per unit				60	55	50
Less : variable cost :						
Direct material	20	12	16			
Direct labour	8	6	4			
Variable overhead	7	13	8	35	31	28
Contribution				25	24	22
Contribution per hour = $\frac{\text{Contribution per unit}}{\text{Direct labour hour per unit}}$				$\frac{25}{4}$ = 6.25	$\frac{24}{3}$ = 8	$\frac{22}{2}$ = 11
Ranking of most profitable product-mix				III	II	I

Statement of profitability of the most profitable product-mix.

	A	*B*	*C*	*Total*
Total contribution on unit sold	3,750	1,20,000	33,000	1,56,750
Less : Fixed cost	18,000	30,000	12,000	60,000
			Profit	96,750

Note : Here direct labour hour is the key factor and only 18,600 hours are avaiable to produce the three products. The available 18,600 hours are utilised in the order of the ranking assigned, i.e. product *C*, *B* an *A*.

The number of units of each product to be produced will depend upon the maximum possible sale of each product. The details of the products to be produced keeping in view of available hours and their ranking are as below :

		Total hrs. utilised
Product *C*	1,500 × 2 Hrs.	3,000
Product *B*	5,000 × 3 Hrs.	15,000
Product *A*	150 × 4 Hrs.	600
		18,600

Problem 18 : A farmer wants your recommendations for optimal mix of production for the coming year. The current data is given below :

	Items produced			
	A	*B*	*C*	*D*
Area occupied (acres)	25	20	30	25
Yield per acre (tonnes)	10	8	9	12
Sale price per tonne (Rs.)	1,000	1,250	1,500	1,350
Variable cost per acre :				
Material (Rs.)	700	600	950	900
Labour (Rs.)	2,000	2,500	3,000	3,700
Variable overhead (Rs.)	2,000	2,000	2,000	2,000
Fixed overhead	*(Rs.)*			
Cultivation and growing	1,00,000			
Harvesting and transport	2,40,000			
Land revenue	90,000			
Administration	1,10,000			
	5,40,000			

The land which is being used for producing items *A* and *B* can be used for either items but not items *C* and *D*. The land which is being used for producing items *C* and *D* can be used for either items but not for items *A* and *B*.

In order to provide adequate market service, the farmer must produce each year at least 40 tonnes each of *A* and *B* and 36 tons each of *C* and *D*.

You are requried to calculate the following :

(*a*) The profit for the current year and

(*b*) The profit for the production-mix which you would recommend. (*C.S., Inter, Dec., 1989*)

Solution :

Statement showing profit for the current year

	Products			
	A	*B*	*C*	*D*
Sale value (per acre)	10,000	10,000	13,500	16,200
Variable cost (per acre)	4,700	5,100	5,950	6,600
Contribution per acre	5,300	4,900	7,550	9,600
Total acres	25	20	30	25
Total contribution	1,32,500	98,000	2,26,500	2,40,000
Total contribution $(A + B + C + D)$		6,97,000		
Less : Fixed cost		5,40,000		
Profit		1,57,000		

Statement of profit for the profitable product-mix

	A	*B*	*C*	*D*
Minimum required production (tonnes)	40	40	36	36
Yield per acre (tonnes)	10	8	9	12
Acre required for minimum production	4	5	4	3
Surplus area allocated to profitable production (*i.e. A* and *B*)	36	–	–	48
Total acres	40	5	4	51
Contribution per acre	5,300	4,900	7,550	9,600
Total contribution	2,12,000	24,500	30,200	4,89,600
Total contribution $(A + B + C + D)$	= 7,56,300			
Less : Fixed overhead	5,40,000			
Profit	2,16,300			

***Note* :** The distribution of area to different products has been made in the manner given because the area is not interchangeable between all products but only partly interchangebale, *i.e.*, between *A* and *B* and *C* and *D* only. Therefore, the total area denoted to *A* and *B* is 45 acres (25 + 20) so that, on the basis of the per acre contribution, maximum possible land to the production of product *A* and similarly to product *D*.

6. Profitability of the department or products : The preparation of a departmental profit and loss account under marginal costing is useful in determining which department is making profit and which department is incurring a loss. This enables the management to decide whether a particular department must continue operation or it should be eliminated. The decision is taken by referring to the contribution made or loss incurred by the department or product.

Problem19 : A company produces three products. The cost data are as under :

		A	*B*	*C*
Direct materials		Rs. 64	152	117
Direct labour :				
Department	Rate per hour *(Rs.)*	Hrs.	Hrs.	Hrs.
1	5	18	10	20
2	6	5	4	7
3	4	10	5	20
Variable overhead		Rs. 16	9	21

Fixed overheads Rs. 4,00,000 per annum

The budget was prepared at a time, when the market was sluggish. The budgeted quantities and selling prices are as under :

Product	*Budgeted qty.*	*Selling price (Rs.)/unit*
A	9,750	270
B	7,800	280
C	7,800	400

Later the market improved and the sales quantities could be increased by 20 for product '*A*' and 25% for product '*B*' and '*C*'. The sales manager confirmed that the increased quantities could be achieved at the prices originally budgeted. The production manager stated that the output cannot be increased beyond the budgeted level due to limitation of direct labour hours in department *Z*.

Required :

(*i*) Present a statement of budeted profitability.

(*ii*) Statement of optimal product mix and calculate the optimal profits.

(*C.A., Inter, May 1998*)

Solution : **Statement of budgeted profitability**

	A	*B*	*C*	*Total*
Selling price (p.u.)	270	280	400	
Variable cost (p.u.) :				
Direct materials	64	152	117	
Direct labour	160	94	222	
Variable overheads	16	9	21	
Total variable cost	240	255	360	
Contribution per unit	30	25	40	
Budgeted qty. (units)	9,750	7,800	7,800	
Total contribution	2,92,500	1,95,000	3,12,000	7,99,500
Less fixed cost				4,00,000
			Profit	3,99,500

Statement of optimal product mix and profit

	A	*B*	*C*	*Total*
Contribution (*A*)	30	25	40	
Direct labour hors. in dept. 2 (*B*)	5	4	7	
Contribution per hr. $\frac{A}{B}$	6	6.25	5.71	
Ranking	II	I	III	

Optimal product-mix				
Units (*C*) (*See Notes*)	11,700	9,750	5,292	
Total contribution ($A \times C$)	3,51,000	2,43,750	2,11,680	8,06,430
Less : Fixed cost				4,00,000
			Optimal profit	4,06,430

Working note :

Total hours aviable in dept. 2

Products	*Units*	*Hours per unit*	*Total hours*
A	9750	5	48,750
B	7800	4	31,200
C	7800	7	54,600
			1,34,550

Maximum sales quantities of products (under improved market conditions)

Products	*Units*	*Increase in percentae*	*Total number of units*
A	9750	20	11700
B	7800	25	9750
C	7800	25	9750

Problem 20 : A Ltd. Co. has three departments. The following data relates to the period ending 31st Dec., 1992 :

	Department		
	A	*B*	*C*
Sales (Rs.)	80,000	40,000	60,000
Marginal cost :			
Direct material	10,000	5,000	10,000
Direct labour	4,000	5,000	16,000
Variable overhead	10,000	5,000	20,000
Fixed overheads	20,000	10,000	20,000
Total cost	44,000	25,000	66,000

The manager in charge of department is disappointed with the results because of higher marginal cost and there is no hope of being reduced further. You are required to present the information in the most suitable manner indicating whether or not department *C* should be closed down.

Solution :

Marginal profit and loss 'A' Ltd. Co.

Dept.	*Sales Value (Rs.)*	*Marginal Cost (Rs.)*	*Contribution (Rs.)*
A	80,000	24,000	56,000
B	40,000	15,000	25,000
C	60,000	46,000	14,000
	1,80,000	85,000	95,000
Less : Fixed cost			50,000
Net profit			45,000

Department *C* makes a contribution of Rs. 14,000 towards fixed cost. If this department is eliminated altogether, the following would be the position :

Dept.	*Sale value*	*Marginal cost*	*Contribution*
A	80,000	24,000	56,000
B	40,000	15,000	25,000
	1,20,000	39,000	81,000
Less : Fixed cost			50,000
	Net profit		31,000

From the above is clear that the net profit has fallen down to Rs. 31,000 from 45,000, if Department *C* is eliminated.

Problem 21 : *XYZ* Ltd. is selling three brands of its products in the brand names *X*, *Y* and *Z*. The details regarding unit costs and selling prices are as under :

	X (Rs.)	*Y (Rs.)*	*Z (Rs.)*
Direct materials	6	12	16
Direct labour	8	8	20
Variable overheads	6	20	14
Selling price	36	50	96

The monthly fixed expenditure is Rs. 5,40,000.

Sales volume for the months of July and August of 1989 are as follows :

	X	*Y*	*Z*
July	20,000	20,000	20,000
August	40,000	26,000	10,000

Find out the monthly profits and if your computations brings out that higher profit was earned in the month having lower sales volume, kindly justify the finding with reasons. (*ICWA, Inter, Dec. 1989*)

Solution :

Statement of cost per unit

	X (Rs.)	*Y (Rs.)*	*Z (Rs.)*
Direct material	6	12	16
Direct labour	8	8	20
Variable overhead	6	20	14
Marginal cost	20	40	50
Selling price	36	50	96
Contribution	16	10	46

For July	*X*	*Y*	*Z*	*Total*
Sales (units)	20,000	20,000	20,00	60,000
Contribution per unit	16	10	46	
Total contribution	3,20,000	2,00,000	9,20,000	1,44,000
Less : Fixed cost				5,40,000
			Profit	Rs. 9,00,000

For August				
Sales (units)	40,000	26,000	10,000	76,000
Contribution pe. unit	16	10	46	
Total contribution	6,40,000	2,60,000	4,60,000	13,60,000
Less : Fixed cost				5,40,000
			Profit	Rs. 8,20,000

Here it can be seen that although the sale quantity has been more in August at 76,000 than 60,000 in July, both contribution and profit were lower in August. The reason for this apparent mismatch is a drop in sales of product *Z* having the highest contribution of Rs. 46 per unit when compared to figure of Rs. 16 and 10 for products *X* and *Y* respectively. This means one unit of *Z* earns Rs. 20 more compared to one unit of *X* and *Y* taken together. Thus the increase in sales of *X* and *Y* though significant in quantitative measurement could not compensate the loss in contribution due to reduction of sales of Z in the month of August.

7. Selling at or below marginal cost : Some time it may become necessary to sell the goods at a price below the marginal cost. Some such situations are as follows :

(*a*) Where mateials are of perishable nature.

(*b*) Where large quantities of stock is accumulated and whose market prices have fallen. This will save the carrying cost of stocks.

(*c*) In order to popularise a new product.

(*d*) In order to increase sales of those products which have higher margin of profit.

If the selling price is below the total cost but above the marginal cost, the contribution will leave an under-recovering of fixed cost. If the selling price fixed is equal to marginal cost, there will be a loss which is equal to fixed cost. However, where the selling price fixed is lesser than the marginal cost, the loss will be greater then fixed cost.

Problem 22 : Garden Product Limited manufactures the 'Rainpour' garden spray. The accounts of the company for the year 1981 are expected to reveal profit of Rs. 14,00,000 from the manufacturer of 'Rainpour' after charging fixed costs of Rs. 1,00,000. The rainpour is sold for Rs. 50 per unit and has a variable unit cost of Rs. 20.

Market sensitivity tests suggest the following response to price changes L

Alternatives	*Selling price reduced by*	*Quantity sold increased by*
A	5%	10%
B	7%	20%
C	10%	25%

Evaluate these alternatives and state which, on profitability consideration, should be adopted for the forthcoming year,assuming cost structure unchanged from 1981. (*University of Delhi, B.Com. (Hons.) 1988*)

Solution :

	Present	*Proposed*		
		A	B	C
Selling price	50	47.50	46.50	45
Less : Variable cost	20	20	20	20
Contribution	30	27.50	26.50	25
Quantity (units)	80,000	88,000	96,000	1,00,000
Total contribution	24,00,000	24,20,000	25,44,000	25,00,000
Less : Fixed cost	10,00,000	10,00,000	10,00,000	10,00,000
	14,00,000	14,20,000	15,44,000	15,00,000

Contribution and profit of proposal *B* is the largest and should, therefore, be adopted.

Note : Units produced and sold is calculated by employing the formula of $= \frac{\text{Total contribution}}{\text{Contribution per unit}}$

8. Determination of selling price and volume of output : The determination of selling price and volume of output is based on 'differential costing'. The difference in total cost due to difference in sales volume is known as differential costing. The increase in sales value due to increase in sales volume is known as 'incremental revenue'. The analysis of differential cost and incremental revenue helps in determining selling price which will yield the optimum profit. So long as incremental reneue is more than the differential cost it is advantageous to increase the output. But as soon as incremental revenue equals the differential cost further increase in output is not advantageous. Differential cost analysis thus helps to determine the selling price and the level of activity which are expected to yield the highest profit.

9. Determination of sales volume for a desired profit : Sometimes one of the decisions that is to be taken by the management is to determine the volume of sales in order to earn a desired profit. The cost-volume-profit analysis which is again based on marginal costing helps management in taking such decisions.

Problem 23 : Frazer Ltd. manufactures and sells a product the selling price and raw material cost which have remained unchanged during the past two years. The following are the relevant data :

	Year 1	*Year 2*
Quantity sold (kgs.)	100	150
	Rs.	*Rs.*
Sales value	20,000	?
Raw materials	10,000	?
Direct wages	3,000	?
Factory overheads	5,000	5,700
Profit	2,000	2,550

During year 2 direct wages rates increased by 50% but there was a saving of Rs. 300 in fixed factory overhead.

Required : What quantity (in kgs) the company should have produced and sold in year 2 in order to maintain the same amount of net profit per kg. as it earned during the year. (*C.A., Inter, Nov., 1988*)

Solution : **Statement of quantity to be produced and sold during year 2**

		Rs.
Selling price per kg. (*See Working Note 1*)		200
Variable costs per kg :		
Raw material	100	
Direct wages (*See Working Note 2*)	45	
Variable factory overhead (*See Working Note 3*)	20	165
		35
Less : Profit required per Kg. (at 100 kgs. of sales)		20
Balance contribution per kg. for meeting fixed cost		15
Total fixed cost (*See Working Note 4*)		2700

Quantity of kgs. produced sold $\frac{2,700}{15} = 180$ kgs.

Working notes:

(1) Selling price per kg. = $\frac{\text{Rs } 20,000}{100 \text{ kg}}$ = Rs. 200 per kg.

(2) Direct wages = Rs. $\frac{\text{Rs. } 3,000}{100 \text{ kg}}$ = Rs. 150% = Rs. 45

(3) Variable factory overhead per kg. :

	Rs.
Total factory overhead in year 2	5,700
Add : Savings in fixed factory overhead	300
	6,000
Less : Total factory overhead in year 1	5,000
Increase in factory overhead	1,000

Increase in quantity (150 kg. – 100 kg.) = 50 kg.

∴ Variable factory overhead per kg. $\frac{\text{Rs } 1,000}{50 \text{ kg}}$ = Rs. 20

		Year 1	Year 2
(4)	Fixed factory overhead		
	Total factory overhead	5,000	5,700
	Less : Variable factory overhead	2,000	3,000
		3,000	2,700

Problem 24 : X Ltd. manufactures and markets a single product. The following information is available :

	Rs. per unit
Materials	8.00
Conversion costs (variable)	6.00
Dealers margin	2.00
Selling price	20.00

Fixed cost Rs. 2,50,000

Present sales 80,000 units

Capacity utilisation 60 per cent

There is accute competition. Extra efforts are necessary to sell. Suggestions have been made for increasing sales :

(1) By reducing sales price by 5%

(2) By increasing dealers margin by 25% over the existing rate.

Which of the two suggestions you would recommend if the company desires to maintain the profit? Give reasons :

Solution :

Present Marginal cost per unit

Materials	8.00
Conversion costs	6.00
Dealer's margin	2.00
Total	16.00

Contribution per unit = Selling price – Marginal cost

= 20 – 16 = 4

Total contribution= 90,000 × 4 = 3,60,000

Profit = Contribution – Fixed cost

= 3,60,000 – 2,50,000 = 1,10,000

Since in both suggestions, fixed costs remain unchanged, the present profit can be maintained by keeping the total contribution at the present level, *i.e.*, Rs. 3,60,000

(1) **Reducing sales price by 5%**

New sales price = (20 – 1) = 19

New dealers margin = 10% of Rs. 19

= 1.90

∴ Variable cost = 8 + 6 + 1.90 = Rs. 15.90

Contribution per unit = 19 – 15.90 = Rs. 3.10

Sales (units) required to maintain the present level of profit =

$$= \frac{\text{Total contribution}}{\text{Contribution per unit}} = \frac{3.60,000}{3.10}$$

= 1,16,111 units

(2) **Increasing dealers margin by 25%**

New dealer's margin = Rs. 2 + 25% = 2.50

New variable cost = 8 + 6 + 2.50 = 16.50

Contribution = 20 – 16.50 = Rs. 3.50

$$\text{Sales (units)} = \frac{3,60,000}{3.50} = 1.02$$

The second proposal is recommended because the contribution per unit is higher and the sales (in units) are lower. Lower sales efforts and less finance would be required in implementing the proposal (*ii*)

10. Acceptance or rejection of a special order within the country : Sometimes a decision regarding acceptance of a special order is to be made. This, however, depends on the availability of spare capacity. The contribution available from such an order helps in making such decision.

Problem 25 : *Z* Ltd. manufactures and sells a soft drink at 0.20 paise per cup. Current output is 4,00,000 cups per month which represents 80% of capacity. They have the opportunity to utilise their surplus capacity by selling their product at 0.13 paise per cup to a supermarket chain who will sell it as 'own lable' product.

Total costs for the previous month were Rs. 56,000 out of which Rs. 16,000 were fixed costs. This represented a total cost of 14 paise per cup.

Based on the above data should Z accept the super market order. What other factors should be considered.

Solution : **Statement showing the present situation**

Sales 4,00,000 @ 0.20 p	80,000
Less : Marginal cost 0.10 per cup	40,000
Contribution	40,000
Less : Fixed cost	16,000
Net profit	24,000

On the assumption that fixed costs are unchanged, the special order will produce the following contribution :

Sales 1,00,000 × 0.13	13,000
Less : Marginal cost 1,00,000 × 0.10)	10,000
Contribution	3,000

However, there are several other factors which would need to be considered before a final decision is taken :

(*a*) Will the acceptance of one order at a lower price lead other customers to demand lower prices as well?

(*b*) Is this special order the most profitable way of using the spare capacity?

(*c*) Will the special order lock up capacity which could be used for future full price business?

Problem 26 : A mechanical toy factory presents the following information for the year 1990 :

Material cost (Rs.)	1,20,000
Labour cost (Rs.)	2,40,000
Fixed overhead (Rs.)	1,20,000
Variable overhead (Rs.)	60,000
Units produced	12,000
Selling price per unit (Rs.)	50

The available capacity is a production of 20,000 units per year. The firm has an offer for the purchase of 5,000 additional units at a price of Rs. 40 per unit. It is expected that by accepting this offer there will be saving of rupee one per unit in the material cost on all units manufactured, the fixed overhead will increase by Rs. 35,000 and the overall efficiency will drop by 2% on all production.

State whether offer is aceptable or not? (*C.S., Inter, June 1993*)

Solution :

Available capacity — 20,000 units : 100%

Capacity utilised — 12,000 units : 60%

Statement of production and sales of 12,000 units

		Total	*Per unit*
(*A*)	Sales	6,00,000	50.00
	Variable cost of sales :		
	(*a*) Materials	1,20,000	10.00
	(*b*) Labour cost	2,40,000	20.00
	(*c*) Variable overheads	60,000	5.00
(*B*)	Total variable cost of sales	4,20,000	35.00

(*C*)	Contribution (*A* – *B*)	1,80,000	15.00
(*D*)	Fixed overheads	1,20,000	10.00
(*E*)	Profit	60,000	5.00

Profit prospect of the offer for 5,000 units is accepted.

Existing sales revenue	6,00,000	
Additional sales revenue (5,000 × Rs. 40)	2,00,000	
		8,00,000
Less : Variable cost of sales :		
Materials 17,000 units × Rs. 9	= 1,53,000	
Labour 17,000 units ×Rs. 20.40	= 3,46,800	
Variable overhead 17,000 units × Rs. 5	= 85,000	
		5,84,800
Total contribution from sales		2,15,200
Less : Original fixed overhead	1,20,000	
Additional fixed overhead	35,000	1,55,000
	Total profit	60,200
Total profit		60,200
Original profit before acceptance of offer		60,000
Additional profit		200

The offer is not acceptable in view of insignificant incremental profit. However, if the offer is likely to result in a wider market for the future.

Working note :

New marginal cost Rs. 10 – 10% of 10 = Rs. 9
New labour cost Rs. 20 + 2% of 20 = Rs. 22
Note : Efficiency is related to labour cost.

Problem 27 : *PQR* Ltd. manufactures medals for winners of athletic events and other contests. Its manufacturing plant has the capacity to produce 10,000 medals each month. The company has current production and sales level of 7,500 medals per month. The current domestic market price of the medal is Rs. 150.

The cost data for the month of October 1999 is as under :

Variable costs : (That vary with units produced)	
Direct materials	Rs. 2,62,500
Direct labour cost	3,00,000
Variable costs (That vary with number of batches)	
Set ups : Materials handling :	
Quality control	
150 batches × Rs. 500 per batch	75,000
Fixed manufacturing costs	2,75,000
Fixed marketing costs	1,75,000
	10,87,500

PQR Ltd. has received a special one-time-only order for 2,500 medals at Rs. 100 per medal.

PQR Ltd. makes medals for its existing customers in batch sizes of 50 medals (150 batches × 50 medals per batch = 7,500 medals).

The special order for 2,500 medals required *PQR* Ltd. to manufacture the medals in 25 batches of 100 each :

Required :

(*i*) Should *PQR* Ltd. accept the special order? Why? Explain briefly.

(*ii*) Suppose the plant capacity was 9,000 medals instead of 10,000 medals each month. The special order must be taken either in full or rejected totally. Should *PQR* Ltd. accept the special order? Why? (*C.A., Inter, November 1999*)

Solution : Statement of contribution margin on accepting the special order of 2,500 medals

Sales revenue (2,500 medals × Rs. 100 per medal)		2,50,000
Less : Variable costs :		
Direct materials (2,500 × 35)	87,500	
Direct wages (2,500 × 40)	1,00,000	
Setups, materials handling, quality control (25 batches × 500)	12,500	
		2,00,000
	Contribution	50,000

Decision :

PQR Ltd. should accept the special order, because its acceptance would increase the operating profit of the concern by Rs. 50,000.

Statement showing present contribution on 7,500 medals

Sales revenue (7,500 × 150)		11,25,000
Less : Variable costs :		
Direct materials (7,500 × 35)	2,62,500	
Direct wages (7,500 × 40)	3,00,000	
Setups, material handling and quality control (150 × 500)	75,000	6,37,500
	Contribution	4,87,500

Statement showing contribution margin on 6,500 medals

Sales revenue (6,500 × 150)		9,75,000
Less : Variable cost :		
Direct materials (6,500 × 35)	2,27,500	
Direct labour cost (6,500 × 40)	2,06,000	
Setups, material handling and quantity control	65,000	
		5,52,000
	Contribution	4,22,500

Statement showing acceptance of special order when the plant capacity was 9,000 medals

Gain in contribution because of Special order of 2,500 medals	50,000
Contribution on reduction of 1,000 medal sales in the internal market (4,87,500 – 4,22,500)	(–65,000)
Loss of contribution	(–15,000)

Decision :

The special order of 25,000 medals (when the plant capacity was reduced to 9,000 medals) should not be accepted, as its acceptance will result in a loss of margin by Rs. 15,000.

11. Acceptance or rejection of an offer from foreign market : The acceptance or rejection of an offer from a foreign market depends upon the incremental cost and incremental revenue.

Problem 28 : A manufacturer has planned his level of operation at 50% of his plant capacity of 30,000 units. His expenses are estimated as follows, if 50% of the plant capacity is utilised :

(*i*) Direct materials	Rs. 8,280
(*ii*) Direct wages	Rs. 11,160
(*iii*) Variable and other manufacturing expenses	Rs. 3,960
(*iv*) Total expenses irrespective of capacity utilisation	Rs. 6,000

The expected selling price in the domestic market is Rs. 2 per unit. Recently, the manufacturer has received a trade enquiry from an overseas organisation interested in purchasing 6,000 units at a price of Rs. 1.45 per unit.

As a professional management what would be your suggestion regarding acceptance or rejection of the offer? Support your suggestion with suitable quantitative information. (*ICWA, Inter, Dec. 1991*)

Solution :

Statement of costs and profits

Particulars	*15,000 units (Expected output for domestic market)*		*6,000 units (Additional output for the foreign market)*		*Total*
	Amount	*Unit*	*Amount*	*Unit*	
Direct materials	8,280	0.552	3,312	0.552	11,592
Direct wages	11,160	0.744	4,464	0.744	15,624
Variable and other mfg. expenses	3,960	0.264	1,584	0.264	5,544
Variable cost	23,400	1.560	9,360	1.560	32,760
Sales	30,000	2.000	8,700	1.450	38,700
Contribution	6,600	0.440	(660)	0.11	5,940
Less : Fixed cost	6,000				6,000
Profit (Loss)	600		(660)		(60)

The price that can be obtained from the foreign market is Rs. 1.45 per unit of additional product which is less than the estimated variable cost of production, *i.e.*, Rs. 1.56 per unit. This will result in an estimated negative contribution of Re. 0.11 per unit and thereby will generate an expected loss of Rs. 660 on 6,000 additional costs.

Therefore, if the offer from the overseas organisation is accepted, the profit of Rs. 6,000 on 15,000 units (based on the 50% plant capacity utilisation) will be wiped out and expected net loss of Rs. 60 will arise. Therefore, it is suggested not to accept the offer.

Problem 29 : *A* company manufacturing electric motors at a price of Rs. 6,900 each made up as under :

Direct material	Rs. 3,200
Direct labour	400
Variable overheads	1,000
Fixed overheads	200
Depreciation	200
Variable selling overheads	100
Royalty	200
Profit	1,000
	6,300
Central excise duty	600
	6,900

(1) A foreign buyer has offered to by 200 such motors at Rs. 5,000 each. As a cost accountant of the company, would you advise acceptance of the offer?

(2) What should the company quote for a motor to be purchased by a company under the same management if it should be at cost. (*CS, Inter, June 1990*)

Solution : **Statement showing contribution**

	Price offered		5,000
Less :	Variable cost		
(*i*)	Direct material	3,200	
(*ii*)	Direct labour	400	
(*iii*)	Variable overhead	1,000	
(*iv*)	Variable selling overheads	100	
(*v*)	Royalty (presumed to be production based)	200	4,900
	Contribution		100

From the above it appears that is would be worthwhile to accept the offer since the price offered covers marginal cost in full and gives Rs. 100 contribution towards the recovery of fixed cost. Secondly there will not be the incidence of central excise duty because this is an export order. Further there will also be government incentive for export order. This will help the company to recover further the fixed cost and balance if any the depreciation.

Problem 30 : *ABC* Ltd. has been operating at 70% capacity and the following particulars relate to the present level of activity :

Units	3,500
Direct materials	Rs. 10,500
Direct labour	Rs. 5250
Variable overhead (200% of direct labour)	
Fixed overhed	14,000
Sales	47,250

ABC Ltd. receivied an export order for 1,000 units of its product @ Rs. 10 per unit. The export order will entail on extra expenditure in the form of special packing at Re 0.50 per unit.

Is the export order worth trying. (*University of Madras, B.Com., March 95*)

Solution : **Statement showing profit**

	Present 70% capacity		Extra order		Total	
	3,500 units @ Rs. 13.50		*1,000 units @ Rs. 10*			
Sales :						
Less : Variable cost :		47,270		1,000		57,250
Direct materials @ Rs. 3	10,500		3,000		13,500	
Direct labour @ Rs. 1.50	5,250		1,500		6,750	
Variable cost @ Rs. 3	10,500		3,000		13,500	
Packing @ Rs. 0.50	-		500		500	
		26,250		8,000		34,250
Contribution		21,000		2,000		23,000
Less : Fixed overhead		14,000		–		14,000
Profit		7,000		2,000		9,000

Comments :

The extra order is worth and it will earn extra profit of Rs. 2,000 subjected to reduction of selling price for Rs. 13.50 to Rs. 10 in export will not affect the local market. Therefore the export order may be worth trying.

12. Differential pricing in the different markets/pricing in depression or recession : Under normal circumstances, the selling price is fixed by adding a margin of profit to the total cost. However, selling price is not always determined by the total cost of production.

The market conditions play an important factor and hence, selling price is sometimes fixed considering market condition. In the long run they tend to equal the cost of production of marginal firm. Occasionally, a factory may have to sell below the total cost. Such pricing has the following advantages :

(*a*) The services of talented employees can be utilised without discharging them.
(*b*) The idle capacity of plant may be prevented.
(*c*) The factory will be in a position to take the benefit arising out of a favourable condition at a later stage.
(*d*) The business can complete successfully.

Problem 31 : A Company is at present working at 90% of its capacity and producing 13,500 units per annum. It operates a flexible budgetary control system. The following figures (excluding material and labour cost) are obtained from its budget.

		90%	*100%*
(*a*)	Sales	Rs.15,00,000	16,00,000
(*b*)	Fixed expenses	Rs. 3,00,500	3,00,500
(*c*)	Semi-fixed expenses	Rs. 97,500	1,00,500
(*d*)	Variable expenses	Rs. 1,42,000	1,49,500

Material and labour cost per unit are constant under present conditions. Profit margin is 10% at 90% capacity.

(*a*) You are required to determine the cost of producing an additional 1,500 units.
(*b*) What would you recommend for an export price for these 1,500 units taking into account that overseas are much lower than indigenous prices. (*ICWA, Inter, June 1990*)

Solution :

(*i*) Calculation of material and labour cost for 13,500 units :

	Amount (Rs.)	*Per Unit (Rs.)*
Sale of 13,500 units	15,00,000	111.11
Less : 10% profit	1,50,000	11.11
	13,50,000	100.00
Less : Overhead —Fixed, semi-fixed and variable	5,40,000	40.00
Material & labour cost	8,10,000	60.00

Statement of cost of producting 1,500 units

	Total	*Per unit*
Material & Labour cost	90,000	60.00
Semi-fixed expenses (Differential cost 1,00,500 – 97,500)	3,000	2.00
Variable expenses (Differential cost 1,49,500 – 142,000)	7,500	5.00
Marginal cost	1,00,500	67.00

(*ii*) Indegenous price is Rs. 111.11. Though overseas prices are much lower than indigenous prices, an export price of Rs. 67 per unit plus any direct costs incurred for export is recommended in view of the foreign exchange earnings.

Problem 32 : Banu Co. Ltd. produces three products *A*, *B* and *C* through two departments, *viz.*, machining department and finishing department. The production costs are as follows :

	A (Rs.)	*B (Rs.)*	*C (Rs.)*
Material cost per unit	46	70	100
Labour Hours :			
Machine Dept. at Rs. 5 per hr.	3	4	2
Finishing Dept. at Rs. 10 per hr.	2	2	6
Selling price per unit	140	160	275

Overhead rates based on normal production budget are :
Machine Dept. Rs. 15 per hour (40% variable)
Finishing Dept. 8 per hour (50% variable)

Present information to the management to enable relative profitability of the three products to be assessed in :

(*a*) a time of depression
(*b*) normal times
(*c*) when there is a shortage of labour in finishing department.

Solution :

		A	*B*	*C*
Selling price per unit		140	160	274
Less : Material		46	70	100
Added value		94	90	175
Variable cost :				
Machine dept. :	Labour	15	20	10
	Overhead	18	24	12
Finishing dept. :	Labour	20	20	60
	Overhead	8	8	24
	Total variable cost	61	72	106
Contribution		33	18	69
Fixed cost :	Machinery	27	36	18
	Finishing	8	8	24
	Total fixed cost	35	39	42
Profit/Loss		–2	–26	27

(*a*) During depression all the products are to be manufactured.

(*b*) During normal times, *Z* is the only profitable product to be manufactured.

(*c*)

	A	*B*	*C*
Finishing hours per unit	2	2	6
Contribution per hour	Rs. 16.5	Rs. 9	Rs. 11.5
Profitability ranking	*A*	*C*	*B*

13. Decision-making and profit miximisation based on key factor : It is a situation under which a company has a choice between various types of product which it can manufacture but subjected to a limiting factor. A limiting factor or a key factor is a factor involved in the productive activity of a company, which at a point of time will limit the production capacity. It is also, therefore, termed as scarce factor, principal budget factor and so on. The limiting factor is affected by both internal and external environment. The contribution per unit of key factor is ascertained and it can be maximised according to the priority needs. Some of the examples of key factors are scarce raw materials, shortage of labour, plant capacity, inefficient, management, shortage of capital and shortage of demand.

Probleme 33 : You are given the following information in respect of products *X* and *Y* of *AB* Co. Ltd.

	Product *X*	*Product* *Y*
Selling price	Rs. 42	Rs. 33
Direct materials	Rs. 15	Rs. 15
Labour hours	18 hrs.	9 hrs.
(50 paise per hour)		

Variable overheads 50% of direct wages Rs. 6,750

Show which product is more profitable during labour shortage :

Solution :

Statement showing contribution

	Product X	Product Y
Selling price	42	33
Less : Variable cost	28.50	21.75
Contribution	13.50	11.25

$$\text{Profitability} = \frac{\text{Contribution}}{\text{Key Factor}}$$

$$\text{Product X} = \frac{13.5}{18} = 0.75$$

$$\text{Product Y} = \frac{11.25}{9} = 1.25$$

Thus, product *Y* is more profitable then *X* during labour shortage.

14. Dropping out a product : When a company produces several range of products, a decision that is to be often taken is whether all the products are to be produced in spite of the fact that one or two products are responsible for incurring losses. Marginal costing helps in taking decision of such nature by calculating the margin of contribution.

Problem 34 : Synthetic Rubber Co. Ltd. manufactures and sell three varieties of shoes. The income statement for the year ending 31.12.1992 is as follows :

		Varieties of shoes (Rs. in lakh)		
		A	*B*	*C*
Sales		1.00	4.00	2.00
Works cost	Variable	50	1.80	70
	Fixed	30	1.00	40
Selling cost	Variable	12	50	20
	Fixed	10	40	20
Profit/Loss		(2)	30	50

The income statement reveals loss in the product *A*, previous years also. The management is considering a proposal to discontinue product *A* and intensify production of *C*. It is anticipated that an advertisement of Rs. 20,000 annually would yield an increase of 30% in its sales volume and this would exactly fit in the plant facilities released by discontinuance of the product *A*.

The variable overheads both worl.s and selling, etc. are directly proportional to sales. The total fixed overheads will remain the same irrespective of the change in production policy. The present allocations are based on capacity utilisation on works side and sales effort on selling side.

The management desires to know comparative positions whether (*a*) the present production/sales policy should be continued, (*b*) the product *A* to be discontinued without any further change or (*c*) the proposal of increasing the product *C* in lieu of the product *A* should be accepted. Present the information assuming sales and costs will remain the same as in last year.

Solution :

(*a*) Present policy

				Products (Rs. in lakh)			
				A	*B*	*C*	*Total*
Sales				1.00	4.00	2.00	7.00
Variable cost :				0.62	2.30	0.90	3.82
Works	0.50	1.80	0.70				
Selling	0.12	0.50	0.20				
	0.62	2.30	0.90				
Contribution				0.38	1.70	1.10	3.18

Fixed Cost :							
Works	0.30	1.00	0.40				
Selling	0.10	0.40	0.20	0.40	1.40	0.60	2.40
	0.40	1.40	0.60				
		Profit or loss		0.02	0.30	0.50	0.78

(*b*) If 'A' is discontinued

	Products *B*	*C*	*Total*
Sales	4.00	2.00	6.00
Variable cost	2.30	0.90	3.20
Contribution	1.70	1.10	2.80
Less : Fixed cost			2.40
Profit			0.40

(*c*) If C is expanded

	Products *B*	*C*	*Total*
Sales	4.00	2.60	6.60
Variable cost	2.30	1.17	3.47
Contribution	1.70	1.43	3.13
Fixed cost & Advt.			2.60
Profit			0.53

From the above statement it is clear that the profit is highest under the present policy. Hence, the present policy should continue.

QUESTIONS

I. Choose the correct answer

1. Production cost under marginal costing include:
   (*a*) Prime cost only
   (*b*) Prime cost and variable overhead
   (*c*) Prime cost and fixed overhead
   (*d*) Price cost, variable overhead and fixed overhead [ ]
2. One of the primary difference between marginal costing and absorption costing is regarding the treatment of :
   (*a*) Direct material (*c*) Fixed overhead
   (*b*) Variable overhead (*d*) Prime cost [ ]
3. Period costs are :
   (*a*) Variable costs (*c*) Prime cost
   (*b*) Fixed cost (*d*) Overhead costs [ ]
4. Absorption costing offeres from marginal costing in the
   (*a*) fact that standard costs can be used with absorption costing but not with marginal costing
   (*b*) amount of fixed costs that will be incurred
   (*c*) kind of activities for which each can be use
   (*d*) amount of costs assigned to individual units of products [ ]
5. Chosse the true statement from the following :
   (*a*) Variable costing is a method of costing in which only direct materials and direct labour are charged to work-in-process.
   (*b*) Under variable costing, all costs which vary with sales volume are changed to work-in-progress.
   (*c*) Because certain manufacturing costs are treated as period costs, net earnings will always be lower under variable costing than under full costing.

(*d*) Variable costing clearly points out the fact that if additional units of product can be sold for more than the variable costs of producing and selling them, net earnings will increase. [ ]

[*Answers :* 1. (b), 2. (*c*), 3. (*c*), 4. (*d*), 5. (*d*)]

(B) Mark true or false

1. In marginal costing, fixed costs are excluded in the valuation of work-in-progress and finished goods stocks. *T/F*
2. Marginal costing may be used in conjunction with standard costing or budgetary control. *T/F*
3. In marginals costing, fixed costs are apportioned on some arbitrary basis. *T/F*
4. In absorption costing, the valuation of stock in higher than in marginal costing. *T/F*
5. In marginal costing, managerial decisions are guided by contribution margin than by profit. *T/F*
6. Absorption costing is generally accepted approach to product cost determination. *T/F*
7. Under marginal costing, variable overhead is treated as part of the cost of an assets, the goods produced, while fixed overhead is viewed as an expense. *T/F*
8. Marginal costing is sometimes referred to as variable costing. *T/F*
9. Under marginal costing, variable overhead is a period costs. *T/F*
10. Under variable costing only the costs of materials and labour are reviewed as product cost. *T/F*
11. Fixed factory overhead is not treated as a product cost under variable costing while it so treated under full costing. *T/F*
12. Variable selling expenses are deducted from revenue under the variable costing technique in arriving at net earnings. *T/F*
13. In general, if production volume exceeds sales volume, net earnings under full costing will be greated than under marginal costing. *T/F*
14. In the earning statement under marginal costing, marginal earnings are directly related to the volume of units sold. *T/F*
15. An unresolved issue in the variable full costing controversy is whether fixed overhead costs are period cost or product costs. *T/F*
16. The effect upon net earnings of the sale of some additional units of product is readily determinable under full costing. *T/F*

[*Answer : True* : 1, 2, 4, 5, 6, 7, 8, 11, 13, 14, 15, *False* : 3, 9, 10, 12, 16]

II. Short answer questions

(1) What is 'analysis of margin of contribution'? Discuss the need for it.

(*Calicut University, M.Com., April 1992*)

(2) Define marginal costing. What are the features of marginal costing?

(*Bangalore University, B.Com., April, 1992*)

EXERCISES

Exercise 1 (High/Low method of segregating semi-variable cost) : From the following data segregate semi-cariable cost into fixed and variable cost :

Month	*Units*	*Semi-variable cost*
Jan.	15,000	12,000
Feb.	12,000	11,400
Mar.	14,000	11,800
Apr.	16,000	12,200
May	18,000	12,600
June	17,000	12,400
	92,000	72,400

[*Answer :* For the month of Jan. variable cost is Rs. 3,000 and fixed cost is Rs. 9,000. For the month of Feb. the variable cost is Rs. 2,400 and fixed cost is Rs. 9,000 and so on]

Exercise 2 (High/Low method and method of least square) : From the following semi-variable cost calculate the fixed and variable cost under (*i*) High and low method, (*ii*) Method of least squares :

Month	*Units*	*Semi-variable cost*
Jan.	500	2,500
Feb.	600	2,800
Mar.	700	3,100
Apr.	940	3,820
May	740	3,220
June	880	3,640
July	900	3,700
Aug.	840	3,520
Sept.	800	3,400
Oct.	860	3,580
Nov.	760	3,280
Dec.	540	2,620

[***Answer :*** For the month of Dec. the fixed cost under High-low method is Rs. 1,000 and variable cost is Rs. 2,820. Under method of least squares the fixed cost is Rs. 1,000 and variable cost per unit is Rs. 3]

Exercise 3 : The following figures have been extracted from the books of a manufacturing company for the first half year ending 30th June, 1979 :

Month	*Volume (Units)*	*Semi-variable cost overhead cost (Rs.)*
Jan.	150	2,700
Feb.	300	3,900
Mar.	450	5,100
Apr.	750	7,500
May	1,050	9,900
June	1,350	12,300

Find out the fixed and variable cost. (*University of Kerala, B.Com., May 1989*)

[***Answer :*** Adoting indirect method the variable cost per unit is Rs. 8. The fixed cost is Rs. 1,500]

Exercise 4 (Make or buy decision) : *X* Ltd. manufactures component *A*-100 and the costs for the year 1992 when 50,000 units are produced is as follows :

Materials	Rs. 2.50
Labour	Rs. 1.25
Variable overheads	Rs. 1.75
Fixed overhead	Rs. 3.50
Total cost	Rs. 9.00

Component *A*-100 could be bought in for Rs. 7.75 and if so the production capacity at utilised in 1992 would be unused. Assuming that there is no technical cnsideration. Should component *A* be bought in or manufactured.

[***Answer :*** The component should be manufactured and not bought because marginal cost of manufacture is Rs. 5.50 and the buying price is Rs. 7.75. The reason for this is that the fixed cost of Rs. 17,500 (50,000 units × Rs. 3.50) would continue and as the capacity is not used, the fixed overhead would not be absorbed into production. If component *A*-100 is bought, overall profit will fall by Rs. 1,12,500 being the difference between buying price and marginal cost of manufacture *i.e.* (7.75 – 5.50 × 50,000)]

Exercise 5 (Make or buy decision based on cost savings) : A firm is considering whether to manufacture or purchase a particular component. This would be in batches of 10,000 and the buying price is Rs. 6.50. The marginal cost of manufacturing this component is Rs. 4.75 per unit and the component will have to be made on a machine which was currently working at full capacity. If the component is manufactured, it is estimated that the sales of the finished product would be reduced by 1,000 units. The finished product has a marginal cost of Rs. 60 per unit and is sold at Rs. 80 per unit.

Should the firm manufacture or purchase the component.

[***Answer :*** Marginal cost of manufacture is Rs. 47,500.

Add lost contribution of the finished product 100 × Rs. 20 = 20,000/67,500. Buying price is Rs. 65,000 (10,000 × Rs. 6.50). Thus there is a saving of Rs. 1.500 per 10,000 batch by buying rather than manufacture.]

Exercise 6 : A radio manufacture company finds that while it costs Rs. 6.75 each to make component of 376 R, the same is available in the market at Rs. 5.75 each with the assurance of continued supply. The breakdown of cost is as follows :

Materials	Rs. 2.75 each
Labour	Rs. 1.75 each
Other variable	Re. 0.50 each
Fixed cost	Rs. 1.25 each
	Rs. 6.25

(*a*) Should you make or buy.
(*b*) What would be your decision if the supplier offered the component at Rs. 4.55 each.

(Bangalore University, M.Com., May 1990)

[***Answer :*** The marginal cost of production is Rs. 5 whereas market price is Rs. 5.75. Since market price is more, the component is to be manufactured. If the offer is 4.85, the proposal to buy may be examined in relation to other factors, *viz*., more profitable use of available resources, the fixed cost to be borne by other products, the ability to sell at the same rate in the long run by the supplier etc.]

Exercise 7 (Product mix) : Tourus Ltd. produces three products : *A*, *B* and *C* from the same manufacturing facilitites. The cost and other details of the three products are as follows :

	A	*B*	*C*
Selling price per unit (Rs.)	200	160	100
Variable cost per unit (Rs.)	120	120	40
Fixed expenses per unit (Rs.)			2,76,000
Maximum production per month (units)	5,000	8,000	6,000
Total hours available for the month			
Maximum demand per month (unit)	2,000	4,000	2,400

The processing hours cannot be increased beyond 200 hours per month.

You are required to compute the most profitable product mix. *(CA, Inter, May 1988)*

[***Answer :*** Contribution of A = 1,60,000, B = 64,000, C = 1,44,000. Total contribution is 3,68,000 and profit is Rs. 92,000]

Exercise 8 (Product mix) : A company engaged in plantation activities has 200 hectares of virgin land which can be used for growing jointly or individually tea, coffee and cardamom. The yield per hectare of the difference crops and their selling prices per kg. are as under :

	Yield kg.	*Selling price Rs. per kg.*
Tea	2,000	20
Coffee	500	40
Cardamom	100	25

The relevant cost data are given below :

(*a*) Variable cost per kg.

	Tea (Rs.)	*Coffee (Rs.)*	*Cardamom (Rs.)*
Labour charges	8	10	120
Packing materials	2	2	10
Other costs	4	1	20
Total cost	14	13	150

(*b*) Fixed cost per annum

Cultivation and growing cost	10,00,000
Administrative cost	2,00,000
Land revenue	50,000

Repairs and maintenance	2,50,000
Other costs	3,00,000
Total cost	18,00,000

The policy of the company is to produce and sell all the three kinds of products and maximum and minimum area to be cultivated per products is as follows :

	Maximum Area (Hectares)	*Minimum Area (Hectares)*
Tea	160	120
Coffee	50	30
Cardamom	30	10

Calculate the priority of production, the most profitable product mix and the maximum profit which can be achieved. (*CS, Inter, June 1988*)

[***Answer :*** Contribution per heactare for tea is Rs. 12,000, for coffee Rs. 13,500 and for cardamom Rs. 10,000. Profits is Rs. 6,55,000]

Exercise 9 (Acceptance or rejection of an offer) : A factory produces 5,000 articles for home consumption at the following costs :

Materials		Rs. 50,000
Wages		Rs. 30,000
Factory overheads		
Fixed	30,000	
Variable	10,000	40,000
Adm. overheads (fixed)		28,000
Selling and distribution overheads		
Fixed	15,000	
Variable	10,000	25,000
Total		1,73,000

The home market can consume only 5,000 articles at a price of Rs. 40 each and no more. The foreign market for this product can, however, consume 3,000 additional pieces at a price of Rs. 22 each C.I.F. If this export order is extended, the following additional costs will be incurred :

(1) Special packing, forwarding charges etc. Rs. 1.00 per unit.

(2) Freight, insurance etc. Rs. 2.00 per unit.

The following 'export benefits' should also be considered :

(1) Duty drawback on direct materials cost at 10%.

(2) Cash subsidy at 10% on F.O.B. value if foreign market worth trying?

(*Bangalore University, M.Com., May 1990*)

[***Answer :*** The acceptance of foreign market results in an additional profit of Rs. 5,000. Hence the foreign market is worth trying]

23

COST-VOLUME-PROFIT ANALYSIS

INTRODUCTION

Earning of maximum profit is the ultimate objective of all business establishments. The profit in its turn is determined by a number of factors, both internal and external. One such factor is the sales revenue of the business. Increase in the sales revenue will lead to increase in the profits. But the sales itself is based on other factors such as demand for the product, the competition, the selling price fixed, marketing strategies adopted by the management. The other important factor that determines the amount of profit is the cost of production. A reduced cost of production will result in an increased profit, keeping the selling price constant. But cost of production itself is affected by many factors such as volume of production, product mix, capacity utilisation, efficiency in production and so on. Though all these factors affect the profit earning capacity of a business, a speical mention about the volume of output deserves to be mentioned in this regard. This is because volume of output changes more frequently and rapidly, and are not susceptible to management control. More than this the profit is more closely related to volume rather than cost. This is because costs seldom vary in direct proportion to volume. Hence, small change in the volume has a significant effect on profit. Whereas a change in other factors such as an order size or lot size will have insignificant effect on profit. However, it is the duty of management to consider the cost and volume while planning the profit earning capacity of the business. One such technique which is used by the management is known as cost-volume-profit analysis. As the name suggests, cost-volume-profit analysis examines the relationship of costs and profit to the volume of business with a view to maximise profit.

Kohler in his *Dictionary for Accountants* defines cost-volume-profit relationship as "the area of interest within an organisation, of management and accountants in observing and controlling the relations between prospective and actual manufacturing costs—both fixed and variable—rates of production and gross profit.

OBJECTIVES OF COST-VOLUME-PROFIT ANALYSIS

According to *NAA Research Bulletin*, Vol. 31, "the cost-volume-profit analysis appears to be useful principally as a technique for the study of problems encountered in business planning. As such it is a tool used largely by those executives responsible for strategic planning and policy-making". More specifically the objectives of cost-volume-profit analysis are as follows :

(*a*) To forecast the profit accurately.

(*b*) To facilitate in the preparation of flexible budgets.

(*c*) To evaluate the performance of the business. For evaluating the profit earned and cost increased, it is necessary to know the impact of cost on the changed volume of output.

(*d*) To enable management in determining the pricing policies.

(e) To enable the charging of overheads to cost of production at different levels of operation.

ASSUMPTIONS OF COST-VOLUME-PROFIT ANALYSIS

1. The analysis is valid for a limited range of values, *i.e.*, 'the relevant ranges' and for a limited period of time.
2. Costs can be classified as fixed and variable. The latter type of cost changes proportionately with the volume within the relevant volume range. Fixed costs are constant within the relevant volume of range.
3. Revenues change proportionately with volumes.
4. There exists a constant product mix.
5. There is no significant change in the inventories in terms of physical units. In other words, the units produced are assumed to be sold.
6. Changes in volume alone are responsible for changes in costs and revenues.
7. The analysis is deterministic in nature. It ignores uncertainty and probabilistic approach.

LIMITATIONS OF COST-VOLUME-PROFIT ANALYSIS

1. It is presumed that the anticipated capacity of production remains same. But it may be increased depending upon the need.
2. The analysis of cost-volume-profit gives satisfactory result only if elements of costs remain stable. But in actual practice it varies.
3. It is again presumed that plant capacity remains same. However, the cost-volume-profit relationship does not hold good if mannual labour is replaced by machines or high cost of materials are substituted by low cost materials.
4. In a business with many varieties of products, it becomes difficult to forecast the profits more accurately.

PRESENTATION OF COST-VOLUME-PROFIT ANALYSIS OR BREAK-EVEN ANALYSIS

One method of presenting cost-volume-profit analysis is by the method of break-even-analysis. It is a technique which is designed to help management in planning and decision-making functions involving the effect of change in volume on the profitability. This method helps management by establishing relationship between cost, volume and profit at different levels of activity. The management of every business desires to know the impact of changes in sales volume on profit. It is interesting in knowing the level at which the cost of production is equal to the sales value. This point where no-profit or no-loss is incurred is known as break-even point. Below this point any production will result only loss and beyond this point it brings profit to the business. Hence, break-even anlalysis and its study beyond the break-even point only relates to cost-volume-profit analysis.

There are two methods of presenting break-even analysis. They are (*i*) Algebraic method and (*ii*) Graphic method. The method to be used depends upon the choice of management and the data available.

ALGEBRAIC METHOD OF PRESENTING CVP ANALYSIS

This method of analysing cost-volume-profit relationship is based on the fundamental equation of marginal costing, *i.e.*, Sales – Variable cost = Fixed cost + Profit. Given any of the three variables, it is possible to find out the fourth unknown variable. This formula can be modified in different ways according to the need. For example, at the break-even point, the profit is nil. So the equation can be written as $S - V = F + 0$ (zero). Similarly, in order to calculate the sales, at the break-even point, it is possible to arrive at the following formula by multiplying it with sales :

$$S(S - V) = F \times S$$

or S (Sales at break-even point) $= \dfrac{F \times S}{S - V}$

Because sale minus variable cost constitute contribution, the above formula may also be written as follows :

$$S = \frac{F \times S}{C}$$

Alternative, fixed cost and profit must be equal to contribution. So the formula can be written as follows :

$$S = \frac{F \times S}{F + P}$$

In the same way for determining different requirements different formula are available. They are indicated below :

1. To determine the break-even sales in terms of units, the formula is

$$\text{BEP (units of Sales)} = \frac{\text{Fixed cost}}{\text{Contribution per unit}}$$

$$\text{or} \quad = \frac{\text{Fixed cost}}{\text{Unit selling price} - \text{Unit variable cost}}$$

2. To determine break-even Sales in terms of rupees

$$\text{BEP (Sales in Rs.)} = \frac{\text{Fixed cost} \times \text{Selling price}}{\text{Contribution per unit}}$$

$$\text{or BEP (Sales in Rs.)} = \frac{\text{Fixed cost} \times \text{Sales}}{\text{Fixed cost} + \text{Profit}}$$

$$\text{or BEP (Sales in Rs.)} = \frac{\text{Fixed cost}}{1 - \dfrac{\text{Variable cost}}{\text{Sales}}}$$

3. Level of sales in units to earn a desired amount of profit

$$\text{BEP (Sales in units)} = \frac{\text{Fixed cost} + \text{Desired profit}}{\text{Contribution per unit}} \times \text{SP}$$

4. To determine the value of sales to earn a desired profit before tax

$$\text{BEP (Sales in Rs.)} = \frac{\text{Fixed cost} + \text{Desired profit}}{1 - \dfrac{\text{Variable cost}}{\text{Sales}}}$$

5. To determine the level of sales (in units) to result a desired prodit after tax.

$$\text{BEP (Sales in units)} = \frac{\text{Fixed cost} + \dfrac{\text{After tax profit}}{1 - \text{Tax rate}}}{\text{Contribution rate per unit}}$$

6. To determine BEP after additional fixed cost owing to plant expansion.

$$\text{BEP} = \frac{\text{Present fixed cost} + \text{Additional fixed cost}}{1 - \dfrac{\text{Variable cost}}{\text{Sales}}}$$

7. To determine sales volume required to earn existing profit

$$\text{BEP (Sales in units)} = \frac{\text{Present fixed cost + Additional fixed cost + Existing profit}}{1 - \frac{\text{Variable cost}}{\text{Sales}}}$$

8. To determine shut down point

$$= \frac{\text{Fixed cost} - \text{Shut down cost}}{1 - \frac{\text{Variable cost}}{\text{Sales}}}$$

Problem 1 : From the following particulars find out break-even point :

Variable cost per unit	Rs.	10
Selling price per unit	Rs.	15
Fixed expenses	Rs.	40,000

What will be the selling price per unit if break-even point is brought down to 5,000 units.

(SV University, B.Com., October 1999)

Solution :

$$\text{BEP} = \frac{\text{Fixed cost}}{\text{Sales} - \text{Variable cost}}$$

$$= \frac{40,000}{15-10} = \frac{40,000}{5} \quad 8,000 \text{ units}$$

Selling price per unit if BEP is brought down to 5,000 units :

Variable cost 5,000 × 10	= 50,000
Fixed cost	= 40,000
Total cost	90,000
Profit/loss	NIL
Sales value	90,000

$$\text{Selling price per unit} = \frac{90,000}{5,000} = 18$$

Note : There is no profit or loss as is clear from the following :

Sales (8,000 × 15)		1,20,000
Less : Variable cost	8,000 × 10	80,000
	Contribution	40,000
	Less : Fixed cost	40,000
	Profit	–

Problem 2 : You are given the following particulars

Selling price	Rs. 200 per unit
Variable cost	Rs. 100 per unit
Total fixed cost	Rs. 96,000

Calculate :

(1) Break-even units and value

(2) Sales to earn a profit of Rs. 20 per unit. *(University of Delhi, B.Com. (Pass), April 1993)*

Solution:

Contribution = Sales – Variable cost
= 200 – 100 = 100 per unit

$$(i) \quad \text{BEP} = \frac{\text{Fixed cost}}{\text{Contribution per unit}}$$

$$\frac{96,000}{100} = 960 \text{ units}$$

BEP in value = 960 × 200 = Rs. 1,92,000

(*ii*) Sales to earn a profit of Rs. 20 per unit

Let Sales = x units

Then total sales = $200x$

Sales = Fixed cost + Variable cost + Profit

$$200x = 96,000 + 100x + 20x$$

$$200x - 120x = 96,000$$

$$80x = 96,000$$

$$x = \frac{96,000}{80} = 1,200 \text{ units}$$

Problem 3 : From the following data calculate :

(*i*) Break-even point expressed in amount of sales in rupees

(*ii*) How many units must be sold to earn a net profit of 10% of sales?

Selling price	Rs. 20 per unit
Variable cost	Rs. 12 per unit
Fixed cost	Rs. 2,40,000

(*University of Delhi, B.Com. (Pass), April 1991*)

Solution :

$$\text{BEP} = \frac{\text{Fixed cost}}{\text{Contribution per unit}}$$

$$= \frac{2,40,000}{20-12} = \frac{2,40,000}{8}$$

$$= 30,000 \text{ units}$$

(1) BEP in rupees = 30,000 units × 20 = Rs. 6,00,000

Units to be sold to earn a net profit of 10 % on sales

Let Sales units = x

Selling price = Rs. 20

Total sales = $20x$

$$\text{Profit 10\% of sales} = \frac{10}{100} \times 20x = 2x$$

Sales value = Fixed cost + Variable cost + Profit

$$20x = 2,40,000 + 12x + 2x$$

$$20x - 12x - 2x = 2,40,000$$

$$6x = 2,40,000$$

$$x = \frac{2,40,000}{6} = 40,000 \text{ units}$$

Problem 4 : Gifts Land Ltd. is considering hiring a machine at an annual charge of Rs. 12,000 to increase the output of a product from its present level of 6,000 units. It is anticipated that with the introduction of the machine, the variable cost per unit will be reduced by Re. 1 due to saving in labour cost. The new machine will not affect fixed cost in total apart from the hiring charges. The selling price of the product is Rs. 12 per unit. The present cost structure of the products is variable cost Rs. 9 per unit and fixed cost per unit Re. 1 per unit.

(*University of Madras, B.Com., September 1995*)

Solution :

$$\text{Break-even point for new machine} = \frac{\text{Revised total fixed cost}}{\text{Revised contribution per unit}}$$

Calculation of revised contribution per unit :

Selling price per unit		12
Less : Revised variable cost :		
Variable cost	9	
Less : Saveing in labour cost	1	
		8
Revised contribution per unit		4

Calculation of revised total fixed cost :

Present fixed cost 6,000 × 1	=	6,000
Add : Additional Hire charges	=	12,000
Revised total fixed cost		18,000

New BEP $= \dfrac{18{,}000}{4} = 4{,}500$ units

Existing BEP $= \dfrac{\text{Total Fixed cost}}{\text{Contribution per unit}}$

Exiting fixed cost $= 6{,}000 \times 1 = 6{,}000$

Contribution per unit $= S - V$

$= 12 - 9 = 3$

Exiting BEP $= \dfrac{6{,}000}{3} = 2{,}000$ units

∴ Extra units produced in justifying Hiring machine is (4,500 units – 2,000 units) = 2,500 units for break even.

Problem 5 : Indian Plastics make plastic buckets. An analysis of their accounting reveal

Variable cost per bucket	Rs. 20
Fixex cost	Rs. 50,000 for the year
Capacity	2,000 buckets per year
Selling price per bucket	Rs. 70

Required :

(*i*) Find the break-even point.

(*ii*) Find the number of buckets to be sold to get a profit of Rs. 30,000.

(*iii*) If the company can manufacture 600 buckets more per year with an additional fixed cost of Rs. 2,000 what should be the selling price to maintain the profit per bucket as at (*ii*) above?

(*University of Delhi, B.Com. (Hons.), April 1991*)

Solution :

(*i*) BEP $= \dfrac{\text{Fixed cost}}{SP - VC \text{ per unit}}$

$= \dfrac{50{,}000}{70-20} = \dfrac{50{,}000}{50} = 1{,}000$ units

Verification :

Total cost (at 1,000 units) $= FC + VC$

$= 50{,}000 + 20{,}000$

Rs. $= 70{,}000$

Sales = 1,000 buckets @ Rs. 70 = Rs. 70,000

Total cost of Rs. 70,000 is equal to total sales of Rs. 70,000, *i.e.*, no-profit-no-loss or BEP.

(*ii*) Number of buckets to be sold to earn profit of Rs. 30,000

$\dfrac{\text{Fixed cost + Desired profit}}{\text{Contribution}}$

$= \dfrac{50{,}000+30{,}000}{50}$ or $\dfrac{80{,}000}{50} = 1{,}600$ buckets

Varification :

Total cost (at 1,600 buckets) $= FC + VC$

$= 50,000 + 32,000 = 82,000$

Sales = 1,600 buckets @ Rs. 70= Rs. 1,12,000

Profit = Sales – Total cost

= 1,12,000 – 82,000 = Rs. 30,000

(*iii*) Selling price to maintain the profit per bucket as at (*ii*) :

Further profit per bucket under (*ii*) will be

$$\frac{\text{Rs. } 30,000}{1,600 \text{ buckets}} = \text{Rs. } 18.75 \text{ per bucket}$$

And fixed cost will be Rs. 52,00 (50,000 + 2,000)

$$\text{Desired sales (units)} = \frac{FC + \text{Desired profit}}{\text{Contribution}}$$

$$2,600 = \frac{52,000 + (2,600 \times 18.75)}{SP - VC}$$

$$2,600 = \frac{52,000 + 48,750}{SP - 20}$$

$$2,600\,(SP - 20) = 1,00,750$$

$$SP - 20 = \frac{1,00,750}{2,600}$$

$$SP - 20 = 38.75$$

$$SP = 38.75 + 20 = \text{Rs. } 58.75$$

Verification :

At 2,600 buckets, capacity utilisation :

Fixed cost = Rs. 52,000

Variable cost = 20 × 2,600 = 52,000

Total cost = 52,000 + 52,000 = 1,04,000

Sales = 2,600 buckets @ Rs. 58.75 = Rs. 1,52,750

Profit = Sales – Total cost

= 1,52,750 – 1,04,000 = Rs. 48,750

Problem 6 : Quickwell Ltd. manufactures pressure cookers, the selling price of which is Rs. 300 per unit. Currently, the capacity utilisation is 60% with a sales turnover of Rs. 18 lakhs. The company proposes to reduce the selling price by 20% but desires to maintain the same profit position by increasing the output. Assuming that the increased output could be made and sold, determine the level at which the company should operate to achieve the desired objective.

The following further data are available :

(*i*) Variable cost per unit = Rs. 60.

(*ii*) Semi-variable cost (including a variable element of Rs. per unit) = Rs. 1,80,000

(*iii*) Fixed cost Rs. 3,00,000 will remain constant up to 80% level. Beyond this an additional amount of Rs. 60,000 will be incurred. (*ICWA, Inter December 1998*)

Solution : **Statement of present profitability at 60% capacity**

		Amount	*Per Unit*
(*a*)	Sales	18,00,000	300
	Variable cost	3,60,000	60
	Variable portion of semi-variable cost	60,000	10
(*b*)	Total variable cost	4,20,000	70
(*c*)	Contribution (*a* – *b*)	13,80,000	230

		Rs.	Rs.
(*d*)	Fixed cost	3,00,000	50
	Fixed portion of semi-variable cost	1,20,000	20
(*e*)	Total fixed cost	4,20,000	70
	Profit ($c - e$)	9,60,000	160
	Revised selling price per unit Rs. 300 – 20% of Rs. 300		240
	Total variable cost per unit		70
	Revised contribution per unit		170

$$\text{BEP (Sales in units)} = \frac{FC + \text{Profit}}{\text{Contribution per unit}}$$

$$= \frac{4,20,000 + 9,60,000}{170}$$

$$= \frac{13,80,000}{170} = 8,118 \text{ units } i.e., 81.18\% \text{ of capacity.}$$

But if the level of capacity is beyond 80%, an additional amount of Rs. 60,000 will be increased towards fixed cost. Then in such the position will be as follows :

$$\text{Sales in unit} = \frac{(4,20,000 + 60,000) + 9,60,000}{170}$$

$$= \frac{14,40,000}{170} = 8,470.58$$

8,471 units are to be sold to maintain the same profit. Therefore, the company should operate at 84.71% level of capacity.

Problem 7 : You are given the following data :

Sales price	Rs. 350 per unit
Variable cost	Rs. 200 per unit
Fixed expenses	Rs. 16,50,000

Ascertain :

(*a*) Break-even point.

(*b*) Sales per unit, if break-even point is brought up to 15,000 units.

(*c*) Sales per unit if break-even point is brought down to 10,000 units.

(*Bangalore University, B.Com., April 1992*)

Solution :

Contribution = Sales price – Variable cost
= 350 – 200 = Rs. 150

(*a*) $\text{BEP} \ \dfrac{\text{Fixed expenses}}{\text{Contribution}} = \dfrac{16,50,000}{150} = 11,000 \text{ units}$

(*b*) Selling price if BEP is brought up to 15,000 units.

Variable cost 15,000 × 200	30,00,000
Add : Fixed cost	16,50,000
Total cost	46,50,000

$$\text{Selling price} = \frac{46,50,000}{15,000} = \text{Rs. } 310$$

(*c*) Selling price if break-even point is brought down to 10,000 units

Variable cost 10,000 × 200	20,00,000
Add : Fixed cost	16,50,000
Total cost	36,50,000

$$\text{Selling price} = \frac{35,50,000}{10,000} = \text{Rs. } 365$$

Problem 8 : A manufacturer provides you the following data regarding his operations for the year 1991 :

	Rs.
Break-even sales	6,66,667
Direct materials	2,20,000
Gross profit	2,50,000
Contribution margin	3,00,000
Direct labour	3,00,000
Sales	10,00,000
Variable manufacturing overhead	5,000

Calculate the following using the above data :

(*a*) Fixed manufacturing overhead.

(*b*) Variable selling and administrative overhead.

(*c*) Fixed selling and administrative overhead. (*Calicut University, M.Com., April 1992*)

Solution :

$$\begin{aligned}\text{Cost of goods sold} &= \text{Sales} - \text{Gross profit}\\ &= 10,00,000 - 2,50,000 = 7,50,000\end{aligned}$$

(*a*) Fixed factory overhead

Let fixed factory overhead = x

Then cost of goods sold will be equal to

$$\begin{aligned}2,20,000 + 3,00,000 + 5,000 + x &= 750,000\\ 5,25,000 + x &= 7,50,000\\ x &= 2,25,000\end{aligned}$$

(*b*) Calculation of fixed selling and administrative overhead

Sales at BEP	6,66,667
Less : Contribution	3,00,000
Total fixed cost	3,66,667
Less : Fixed factory overhead	2,25,000
Fixed selling and administrative overhead	1,41,667

(*c*) Calculation of variable selling and administrative overhead

$$\begin{aligned}\text{Sales} - \text{Variable cost} &= \text{Contribution}\\ 10,00,000 - (2,20,000 + 3,00,000 + 5,000 + x) &= 3,00,000\\ 10,00,000 - 5,25,000 + x &= 3,00,000\\ 4,75,000 + x &= 3,00,000\\ x &= -4,75,000 + 3,00,000\\ x &= 1,75,000\end{aligned}$$

Problem 9 : Sharada Painters Ltd., manufactures and sells four types of points under the brand names of P, Q, R and S. The sales mix in value comprises of $33\frac{1}{3}\%$, $41\frac{2}{3}\%$, $16\frac{2}{3}\%$ and $8\frac{1}{3}$ respectively.

The total budgeted sales are Rs. 60,000 per month. Operating costs are :

Variable cost of P	60% of selling price
Variable cost of Q	68% of selling price
Variable cost of R	80% of selling price
Variable cost of S	40% of selling price

Fixed cost amount to Rs. 14,700 per month. Calculate BEP for all paints on an overall basis.

(*Bangalore University, M.Com., May 1989*)

Solution :

	Products				Total
	P	*Q*	*R*	*S*	
Sales mix	$33\frac{1}{3}\%$	$41\frac{2}{3}\%$	$16\frac{2}{3}\%$	$8\frac{1}{3}\%$	100%
Sales (Rs.)	20,000	25,000	10,000	5,000	60,000
Variable cost	12,000	17,000	8,000	2,000	39,000
Contribution					21,000
Less : Fixed cost					14,700
				Profit	6,300

$$\text{BEP} = \frac{\text{Fixed cost}}{\text{Contribution}} \times \text{Sales}$$

$$= \frac{14,700}{21,000} \times 60,000 = \text{Rs. } 42,000$$

PROFIT-VOLUME RATIO OR CONTRIBUTION—SALES PERCENTAGE

The profit volume (P/V) ratio establishes the relation between contribution to sales. The ratio is expressed as a percentage and it furnishes the details of profitability of various products, processes or departments. A high P/V ratio shows that even a slight rise in the volume without a corresponding increase in fixed cost would result in high profit. Therefore, it is advisable for management to increase sales by taking suitable measures such as advertising and other sales promotional measures. The P/V ratio can be increased by maximising contribution, which is possible by increasing the selling price, reducing the variable cost and by improving the product mix. The formula to calculate P/V ratio is as follows :

$$\text{P/V Ratio} = \frac{\text{Contribution}}{\text{Sales}} \times 100$$

Uses of P/V Ratio

1. It helps in the determination of BEP. The formula is

$$\text{BEP} = \frac{\text{FC}}{\text{P / V Ratio}}$$

2. It helps in the determination of profit at any volume of sales. The formula is

$$\text{Volume} \times \text{P/V Ratio} = \text{Contribution} - \text{FC} = \text{Profit}$$

3. It helps in the determination of sales to earn a desired amount of profit. The formula is

$$\text{Sales} = \frac{\text{F} + \text{P}}{\text{P / V Ratio}}$$

4. It helps in determining the required selling price per unit. The formula is

$$\text{Selling price} = \frac{\text{Variable cost}}{(100 - \text{P / V Ratio})}$$

5. It helps in ascertaining the variable cost for any volume of sales by reverse method, *i.e.*, by deducting P/V ratio from sales considering it as 100%.

Margin of Safety

The excess of actual sales oveer the break-even sales is known as margin of safety. The formula is as follows :

$$MS = \text{Sales Volume} - \text{Break-even sales volume}$$

The soundness of the business can be known by looking into the margin of safety. If the distance between sales revenue and break-even point on the graph is long, it shows the soundness, of the business. On the other hand a small margin of safety involving a fall in sales revenue results in a loss. The margin of safety can be improved by taking the following measures :

(*a*) Increasing the selling price.
(*b*) Increasing the sales volume by increasing the capacity.
(*c*) By improving the contribution margin through reducing the variable cost.
(*d*) By lowering BEP through reduction of fixed cost.
(*e*) By adopting a better profitable product mix.

Margin of safety can be calculated by using the following formula :

$$\text{MS (in rupees)} = \frac{\text{Profit}}{\text{P / V Ratio}} \text{ or Profit} \times \frac{\text{Contribution}}{\text{Sales}}$$

$$\text{MS (in units)} = \frac{\text{Profit}}{\text{Contribution per unit}}$$

It can also be expressed as a percentage using the following formula :

$$\text{MS Ratio} = \frac{\text{MS}}{\text{Sales}} \times 100$$

$$\text{MS Ratio} = \frac{\text{Actual Sales} - \text{BEP Sales}}{\text{Sales}} \times 100$$

The other formulae used to calculate P/V ratio are as follows :

$$\text{P/V Ratio} = \frac{\text{Contribution}}{\text{Sales}}$$

$$\text{P/V Ratio} = \frac{\text{FC + Profit}}{\text{Sales}}$$

$$\text{P/V Ratio} = \frac{\text{FC + Loss}}{\text{Sales}}$$

$$\text{P/V Ratio} = \frac{\text{Change in contribution}}{\text{Change in sales}}$$

$$\text{P/V Ratio} = \frac{\text{Change in profit (or loss)}}{\text{Change in sales}}$$

Angle of Incidence

The angle at which sales line cuts the total cost line is known as angle of incidence. In other words it represents the angle between sales line and total cost line. The angle of incidence shows the profit earning capacity of the business. Hence, higher the angle of incidence, higher the profit and *vice versa*. A high margin of safety with a broader angle of incidence reveals a highly favourable position of the business.

Problem 10 : Given the following information :

Fixed cost	= Rs. 4,000
Break even sales	= Rs. 20,000
Profit	= Rs. 1,000

Selling price per unit = Rs. 20

You are required to calculate :

(*i*) Sales and marginal cost of sales and

(*ii*) New break-even point if selling price is reduced by 10%

(*University of Delhi, B.Com. (Pass), April 1999*)

Solution :

Contribution at BEP = Fixed cost is 4,000

$$\text{P/V ratio} = \frac{\text{Contribution}}{\text{Sales}} \times 100$$

$$= \frac{4,000}{20,000} \times 100 = 20\%$$

(*i*) Sales of earn a profit of Rs. 1,000

$$= \frac{\text{Fixed cost + Profit}}{\text{P / V Ratio}}$$

$$= \frac{4,000+1,000}{20\%} = \frac{5,000}{20\%} = 25,000$$

Marginal cost at sales of Rs. 25,000 is found as follows :

$$\text{Contribution} = \text{Sales} \times \text{P/V ratio}$$

$$= 25,000 \times \frac{20}{100} = 5,000$$

$$\text{Marginal cost} = \text{Sales} - \text{Contribution}$$

$$= 25,000 - 5,000 = \text{Rs. } 20,000$$

(*ii*) New BEP if selling price is reduced by 10%

$$\text{New sales} = 25,000 - 10\%$$

$$= 22,500$$

$$\text{New contribution} = 22,500 - 20,000 = \text{Rs. } 2,500$$

$$\text{New P/V Ratio} = \frac{\text{New Contribution}}{\text{New Sales}}$$

$$= \frac{2,500}{22,500} = \frac{1}{9}$$

$$\text{New BEP} = \frac{\text{Fixed cost}}{\text{P / V Ratio}}$$

$$= \frac{4,000}{\frac{1}{9}} \text{ or} = 36,000$$

Problem 11 : Ascertain profit when

Sales	= Rs. 2,00,000
Fixed cost	= Rs. 40,000
BEP	= Rs. 1,60,000

(*CA, Inter, May 1999*)

Solution :

$$\text{P/V Ratio} = \frac{\text{Fixed cost}}{\text{BEP}} \times 100$$

$$= \frac{40,000}{1,60,000} \times 100 = 25\%$$

$$\text{Contribution} = \text{Sales} \times \text{P/V Ratio} = \text{FC + Profit}$$

$$= 2,00,000 \times 25\% = \text{FC + Profit}$$

$$50,000 = 40,000 - \text{Profit}$$

$$\text{or Profit} = 10,000$$

Problem 12 : Ascertain sales, when

Fixed cost	= Rs. 20,000
Profit	= Rs. 10,000
BEP	= Rs. 40,000

(CA, Inter, May 1999)

Solution :

Contribution = Fixed cost + Profit
= 20,000 + 10,000
= 30,000

$$\text{P/V Ratio} = \frac{\text{Fixed cost}}{\text{BEP}} \times 100$$

$$= \frac{20{,}000}{40{,}000} \times 100 = 50\%$$

$$\text{Also P/V Ratio} = \frac{\text{Contribution}}{\text{Sales}} \times 100$$

$$\text{or Sales} = \frac{\text{Contribution}}{\text{PV Ratio}} \times 100$$

$$= \frac{30{,}000}{50\%}$$

$$= \frac{30{,}000 \times 100}{50} = 60{,}000$$

Problem 13 : Raj Ltd. manufactures three products *X*, *Y* and *Z*. The unit selling prices of these products are Rs. 100, Rs. 160 and Rs. 75 respectively. The corresponding unit variable costs are Rs. 50, Rs. 80 and Rs. 30. The proportions (quantity wise) in which these products are manufactured and sold are 20%, 30% and 50% respectively. The total fixed costs are Rs. 14,80,000.

Calculate break-even quantity and the productwise break up of such quantity. *(CA, Inter, May 1999)*

Solution :

Overall Break-even Quantity

Products	*X*	*Y*	*Z*
Selling price per unit	100	160	75
Less : Variable cost per unit	50	80	30
Contribution per unit	50	80	45
Contribution at break-even point	$0.20x \times 50$	$0.30x \times 80$	$0.50x \times 45$
(*see working note*)	$10x$	$24x$	$22.5x$

At break-even point, contribution = Fixed cost

Hence $10x + 24x + 22.5x$ = Rs. 14,80,000

$$\text{or} \quad x = \frac{14{,}80{,}000}{56.5} = 26{,}195 \text{ units}$$

Productwise break-up of overall break-even quantity

Product *X* = 26,195 units × 0.20 = 5,239 units

Product *Y* = 26,195 units × 0.30 = 7,858 units

Product *Z* = 26,195 units × 0.50 = 13,098 units

Working note :

Let x be the overall break-even quantity of three products *X*, *Y* and *Z*. At break-even *X* has 20%, 30% and 50% units of *X*, *Y* and *Z*. The productwise production and sale of three given products in terms of overall break-even quantity are $0.20x$, $0.30x$ and $0.50x$ units respectively.

Problem 14 : When volume is 3,000 units, average cost in Rs. 4 per unit. When volume is 4,000 units, average cost is Rs. 3.50. The break-even point is 5,000 units. Find the P/V ratio. *(ICWA, Inter, Dec. 1999)*

Solution :

	Output	*Average Cost*	*Total Cost*
	3,000	4	12,000
	4,000	3.50	14,000
change	1,000		2,000

Variable cost per unit $= \frac{2,000}{1,000} =$ Rs. 2

Total fixed cost = Total cost – Variable cost
= 12,000 – 3,000 units × Rs. 2
= 12,000 – 6,000
= 6,000

or = 14,000 – 4,000 units × Rs. 2
= 14,000 – 8,000
= 6,000

At BEP, BEP sales = Variable cost + Fixed cost
5,000 units = 5,000 × 2 + 6,000
= 10,000 + 6,000
= 16,000

$$\text{BEP} = \frac{\text{Fixed Cost}}{\text{P / V Ratio}}$$

$$\text{or P/V Ratio} = \frac{\text{Fixed cost}}{\text{BEP}}$$

$$= \frac{6,000}{16,000} = \frac{3}{8} \text{ or } 37.5\%$$

Problem 15 : ABC Ltd. fixed costs of Rs. 2,00,000. It has two products, that it can sell; *A* and *B*. The company sells these products at a rate of 2 units of *A* to 1 unit of *B*. The unit contribution is Re. 1 per unit for A and 2 per unit for B. How many units of A and B would be sold at the break-even point.

(ICWA, Inter, Dec. 1999)

Solution :

Products	*A*	*B*	*Total*
Sales unit be (in the ratio of 2 : 1)	2	1	3 units
Contribution per unit	Re. 1	Rs. 2	
Total contribution	Rs. 2	2	Rs. 4

Hence, contribution per unit (composite) $= \frac{4}{3}$

Total fixed cost = Rs. 2,00,000

$$\text{BEP (composite)} = \frac{\text{Fixed cost}}{\text{Contribution per unit}}$$

$$= \frac{2,00,000}{\frac{4}{3}}$$

$$\text{or BEP in units} = \frac{2,00,000 \times 3}{4}$$

= 1,50,000 units

$\frac{2}{3} A$ = 1,00,000 units

$\frac{1}{3} B$ = 50,000 units

Problem 16 : A company had incurred fixed expenses of Rs. 2,25,000 with sales of Rs. 7,50,000 and earned a profit of Rs. 1,50,000 during the first half year. In the second half year, it suffered a loss of Rs. 75,000 calculate :

(*i*) The P/V ratio, break-even point and margin of safety

(*ii*) Expected sales-volume for the second half year assuming that selling price and fixed expenses remained unchanged during second helf year. (*CS, Inter, June 1998*)

Solution : **Calculations for the first half-year**

$$\text{P/V Ratio} = \frac{\text{Fixed cost + Profit}}{\text{Sales}}$$

$$= \frac{2,25,000 + 1,50,000}{7,50,000} = 50\%$$

$$\text{BEP} = \frac{\text{Fixed Cost}}{\text{P / V Ratio}} =$$

$$= \frac{2,25,000}{50\%} = 4,50,000$$

Margin of safety = Actual sales – Sales at BEP

= 7,50,000 – 4,50,000 = Rs. 3,00,000

(*ii*) Expected sales volume for second half year

$$= \frac{\text{Fixed Cost} - \text{Loss}}{\text{P / V Ratio}}$$

$$= \frac{2,25,000 - 75,000}{50\%}$$

$$= \frac{1,50,000}{50} \times 100 \qquad = 3,00,000$$

Problem 17 : The profit volume ratio of X Ltd. is 50% and the margin of safety is 40%. You are required to calculate the net profit if the sales value is Rs. 1,00,000. (*CA, Inter, November 1998*)

$$\text{Margin of safety ratio} = \frac{\text{Margin of safety in absolute terms}}{\text{Actual sales}} \times 100$$

$$40 = \frac{\text{Margin of safety in absolute terms}}{1,00,000} \times 100$$

or $$\text{Margin of safety in absolute terms} = \frac{1,00,000 \times 40}{100}$$

$$= 40,000$$

$$\text{Also Margin of safety in absolute terms} = \frac{\text{Profit}}{\text{P/V Ratio}}$$

or $$40,000 \times \frac{\text{Profit}}{50\%}$$

or $$\text{Profit} = 40,000 \times \frac{50}{100} = \text{Rs. } 20,000$$

Problem 18 : A Single product company sells its products at Rs. 60 per unit. In 1996, the company operated at a margin of safety of 40%. The fixed costs amounted to Rs. 3,60,000 and the variable cost ratio to sales was 80%.

In 1997, it is estimated that the variable costs will go up by 10% and the fixed costs will increase by 5%. Find the selling price required to be fixed in 1997 to earn. The same P/V ratio as in 1996.

Assuming the same selling price of Rs. 60 per unit in 1997, find the number of units required to be produced and sold to earn the same profit as in 1996. (*CA, Inter, May 1998*)

Solution : **Calculation of P/V ratio (in 1996)**

$$\text{P/V ratio} = \frac{\text{Selling price} - \text{Variable Cost per unit}}{\text{Selling price}} \times 100$$

$$= \frac{60-48}{60} \times 100$$

$$= \frac{12}{60} \times 100 = 20\%$$

Calculation of units sold (in 1996)

$$\text{BEP} = \frac{\text{Fixed cost}}{\text{Contribution per unit}}$$

$$= \frac{3,60,000}{12} = 30,000 \text{ units}$$

Since, Margin of safety is 40%, therefore BEP is 60% of units sold

$$\text{or, No. of units sold} = \frac{\text{BEP}}{60\%}$$

$$= \frac{30,000 \text{ units}}{60\%} = 50,000$$

Calculation of profit earned in 1996

Profit = Total contribution – Fixed cost
= 50,000 units × Rs. 12 per unit – 3,60,000
= 6,00,000 – 3,60,000 = 2,40,000

Selling price to be fixed in 1997

Variable cost per unit in 1997 =
Rs. 52.80 (Rs. 48 + 4.80)
Fixed cost in 1997 :
Rs. 3,78,000 (3,60,000 + 18,000)
P/V ratio in 1996 = 20%
Since P/V ratio is 20% variable cost is 80%

$$\text{Hence, the required SP} = \frac{52.80}{80\%}$$

$$\text{or} \quad \frac{52.80}{80} \times 100$$

= Rs. 66

Number of units to be produced and sold in 1997 to earn the same profit as in 1996

Profit in 1996 = Rs. 2,40,000
Fixed cost in 1997 = Rs. 3,78,000
Desired contribution in 1997
(2,40,000 + 3,78,000) = Rs. 6,18,000
Contribution per unit in 1997 = SP – Variable cost per unit
= 60 – 52.80
= 7.20

$$\text{No. of units to be produced and sold in 1997} = \frac{\text{Fixed cost in 1997}}{\text{Contribution per unit in 1997}}$$

$$= \frac{3,78,000}{7.20}$$

= 52,500 units

Problem 19 : A Ltd. maintains, a margin of safety of 37.5% with an overall contribution to sales ratio of 40%. Its fixed costs amount to Rs. 5 lakhs.

Calculate the following :

(*i*) Break-even sales
(*ii*) Total sales
(*iii*) Total variable costs
(*iv*) Current profit
(*v*) New margin of safety if the sales value is increased by $7\frac{1}{2}$%.

(*ICWA, Inter, December 1998*)

Solution :

(1) Break-even sales $= \dfrac{\text{Fixed Cost}}{\text{Contribution / Sales}}$

$= \dfrac{\text{5 lakhs}}{40\%} = 12.50$ lakhs

(2) Total sales = Break-even sales + Margin of safety

$= \text{Break-even sales} + \dfrac{37.5}{100} \times \text{Sales}$ [Given MS = 37.5% of sales]

or, Break-even sales $= \text{Sales} - \dfrac{37.5}{100}$ sales

or, 12.50 lakhs $= \dfrac{62.5}{100}$ sales

or, Sales $= \dfrac{12.50 \text{ lakhs} \times 100}{62.5} = 20$ lakhs

(3) Total variable cost = 60% of Rs. 20 lakhs
= 12 lakhs

Because, Sales – Variable cost = Contribution

(4) Current profit = Sales – (Variable cost + Fixed cost)
= 20 lakhs – (12 lakhs + 5 lakhs)
= 20 lakhs – 17 lakhs
= 3 lakhs

(5) **New margin of safety if sales value is increased by $7\frac{1}{2}$%**

New sales value = Rs. 20 lakhs + $7\frac{1}{2}$%
= 21.50 lakhs

Hence, new margin of safety = New sales – Break-even sales
= 21.50 lakhs – 12.50 lakhs
= Rs. 9 lakhs

Problem 20 :

(*i*) Find out BEP sales if budgeted output is 80,000 units, Fixed cost is Rs. 4,00,000, Selling price per unit is Rs. 20 and variable cost per unit is Rs. 10.
(*ii*) Calculate selling price, if marginal cost as Rs. 2,400 and P/V Ratio is 20%.
(*iii*) Find out margin of safety if profit is Rs. 20,000 and P/V Ratio is 40%.

(*University of Delhi, B.Com. (Pass), April 1997*)

Solution :

(*i*) BEP $= \dfrac{\text{Fixed Cost}}{\text{Contribution}}$

$= \dfrac{4,00,000}{20-10} = \dfrac{4,00,000}{10} = 40,000$ units

BEP Sales = 40,000 units × Rs. 20
= Rs. 8,00,000

(*ii*) When P/V Ratio is 20%, then variable cost is 80% of sales

$$\text{Thus, Selling price} = 2{,}400 \times \frac{100}{80} = \text{Rs. } 3{,}000$$

$$(iii)\ \text{Margin of safety} = \frac{\text{Profit}}{\text{P/V Ratio}}$$

$$= \frac{20{,}000}{40\%} = \text{Rs. } 50{,}000$$

Problem 21 : From the following data, you are required to calculate : (*a*) P/V Ratio, (*b*) Break-even sales, (*c*) Sales required to earn a profit of Rs. 4,50,000.

Fixed expenses	Rs. 90,000
Variable cost per unit :	
Direct material	Rs. 5
Direct labour	Rs. 2
Direct expenses	Rs. 2
Selling price per unit	Rs. 12

(*University of Madras, B.Com., Sept. 1997*)

Solution :

$$(a)\ \text{P/V Ratio} = \frac{\text{Sales} - \text{Variable Cost}}{\text{Sales}} \times 100$$

$$= \frac{12-9}{12} \times 100$$

$$= \frac{3}{12} \times 100 = 25\%$$

$$(b)\ \text{BEP Sales} = \frac{\text{Fixed Cost}}{\text{P/V Ratio}}$$

$$= \frac{90{,}000}{25\%} \text{ or } \frac{90{,}000 \times 100}{25} = 3{,}60{,}000$$

(*c*) Sales required to earn profit of Rs. 4,50,000

$$= \frac{\text{Total Fixed Cost + Profit required}}{\text{P/V Ratio}}$$

$$= \frac{90{,}000 + 4{,}50{,}000}{25\%}$$

$$= \frac{90{,}000 + 4{,}50{,}000}{25} \times 100$$

$$= \text{Rs. } 21{,}60{,}000$$

Problem 22 : The Sales Turnover and Profit during two years were as follows :

Year	*Sales* *Rs.*	*Profit* *Rs.*
1991	1,40,000	15,000
1992	1,60,000	20,000

Calculate :

(*a*) P/V Ratio

(*b*) BEP

(*c*) Sales required to earn a profit of Rs. 40,000

(*d*) Fixed expenses

(*University of Madras, B.Com., March 1997*)

Solution :

Year	*Sales*	*Profit*
1991	1,40,000	15,000
1992	1,60,000	20,000
Difference	20,000	5,000

(*i*) P/V Ratio $= \frac{\text{Difference in profit}}{\text{Difference in Sales}} \times 100$

$= \frac{5,000}{20,000} \times 100 \quad = 25\%$

Total fixed cost :

Contribution $=$ Sales × P/V Ratio

$= 1,40,000 \times \frac{25}{100} \quad = 35,000$

Less : Profit $=15,000$

Total fixed cost $20,000$

(*ii*) BEP $= \frac{\text{Total Fixed Cost}}{\text{P / V Ratio}}$

$\frac{20,000}{25} \times 100 = 80,000$

(*iii*) *Sales to earn a profit of Rs. 40,000*

$\frac{\text{Total Fixed Cost + Profit}}{\text{P / V Ratio}}$

$= \frac{20,000 + 40,000}{25\%} = 2,40,000$

(*iv*) Fixed cost as calculated above is Rs. 20,000.

Problem 23 : Given the following, find the margin of safety :

(1) Profit earned Rs. 24,000

(2) Selling price per unit Rs. 10

(3) Marginal cost per unit Rs. 7 (*CS, Inter, June 1997*)

Solution :

Contribution per unit $= 10 - 7 = \text{Rs. } 3$

Margin of safety sales (units) $= \frac{\text{Profit earned}}{\text{contribution per unit}}$

$= \frac{24,000}{3} = 8,000 \text{ units}$

Margin of safety sales (value) $= 8,000 \times \text{Rs. } 10 = \text{Rs. } 80,000$

Problem 24 : Given the following, calculate P/V ratio and profit when sales are Rs. 20,000, fixed cost Rs. 4,000 and Break-even point Rs. 10,000. (*CS, Inter, June 1997*)

Solution :

Variable cost $=$ Break-even point – Fixed cost

$= 10,000 - 4,000$

$= 6,000$

P/V Ratio $= \frac{\text{Contribution}}{\text{Sales}} \times 100$

$= \frac{10,000 - 6,000}{10,000} \times 100$

$= \frac{4,000}{10,000} \times 100 \quad = 40\%$

Profit when sales are Rs. 20,000

$$S \times P/V = F + P$$

$$20{,}000 \times \frac{40}{100} = 4{,}000 + P$$

$$8{,}000 = 4{,}000 + P$$

$$P = 4{,}000$$

Problem 24 : The ratio of variable cost to sales is 70%. The break-even point occurs at 60% of the capacity sales. Find the capacity sales when fixed costs are Rs. 90,000. Also compute profit at 75% of the capacity sales. (*CA, Inter, November 1997*)

Solution :

Basic Data Given

Since $\frac{\text{Variable Cost}}{\text{Sales}} = 70\%$

Therefore, $\frac{\text{Contribution}}{\text{Sales}} = 30\%$ which is also P/V ratio

Capacity sales

$$BEP = \frac{\text{Fixed Cost}}{P/V\ \text{Ratio}}$$

$$= \frac{90{,}000}{30\%} \text{ or } \frac{90{,}000 \times 100}{30}$$

$$= 3{,}00{,}000$$

BEP (as given) = 60% of capacity sales

Hence capacity sales = $\frac{3{,}00{,}000}{60\%} = 5{,}00{,}000$

Calculation of profit at 75% of the capacity sales

75% of capacity sales (75% of Rs. 5,00,000)	3,75,000
Less : Variable cost	2,62,500
Contribution	1,12,500
Less : Fixed cost	90,000
Profit	22,500

Problem 26 : If margin of safety is Rs. 2,40,000 (40% of sales) and P/V Ratio is 30% of AB Ltd., calculate its (*i*) Break-even sales, (*ii*) Amount of profit on sales of Rs. 9,00,000. (*CA, Inter, May 1997*)

Solution :

Calculation of Margin of Safety

$$MS = \frac{\text{Profit}}{P/V\ \text{Ratio}}$$

$$\text{or Profit} = MS \times P/V\ \text{Ratio}$$

$$= 2{,}40{,}000 \times \frac{30}{100} = \text{Rs. } 72{,}000$$

Calculation of Total sales

$$\frac{\text{Margin of Safety}}{40\%}$$

$$\text{or } \frac{2{,}40{,}000 \times 100}{40} = \text{Rs. } 6{,}00{,}000$$

Calculation of contribution

$$\text{Contribution} = \text{Sales} \times \text{P/V Ratio}$$
$$= 6{,}00{,}000 \times \frac{30}{100} = 1{,}80{,}000$$

Calculation of fixed cost

$$\text{Fixed cost} = \text{Contribution} - \text{profit}$$
$$= 1{,}80{,}000 - 72{,}000$$
$$= \text{Rs. } 1{,}08{,}000$$

(*i*) Break-even sales $= \dfrac{\text{Fixed Cost}}{\text{P / V Ratio}}$

$$= \frac{1{,}08{,}000}{30\%} = \text{Rs. } 3{,}60{,}000$$

(*ii*) *Amount of profit on sales of Rs. 9,00,000*

$$S \times P/V = F + P$$
$$9{,}00{,}000 \times \frac{30}{100} = 1{,}08{,}000 + P$$
$$2{,}70{,}000 = 1{,}08{,}000 + P$$
$$P = 2{,}70{,}000 \times 1{,}08{,}000$$
$$P = \text{Rs. } 1{,}62{,}000$$

Problem 27 : X Ltd. has earned contribution of Rs. 2,00,000 and net profit of Rs. 1,50,000 on sales of Rs. 8,00,000. What is its margin of safety. (*CA, Inter, May 1997*)

Solution :

$$\text{P/V Ratio} = \frac{\text{Contribution}}{\text{Sales}} \times 100$$
$$= \frac{2{,}00{,}000}{8{,}00{,}000} \times 100 = 25\%$$

$$\text{Margin of safety} = \frac{\text{Profit}}{\text{P / V Ratio}}$$
$$= \frac{1{,}50{,}000}{25\%} = \text{Rs. } 6{,}00{,}000$$

Problem 28 : From the following data, calculate :

(1) Break-even point expressed in amount of sales in rupees

(2) Number of units that must be sold to earn a profit of Rs. 1,60,000 per year

Selling price	Rs. 20 per unit
Variable manufacturing cost	Rs. 11 per unit
Variable selling cost	Rs. 3 per unit
Fixed factory overheads	Rs. 5,40,000 P.A
Fixed selling cost	Rs. 2,52,000 P.A.

(*University of Delhi, B.Com. (Pass), April 1996*)

Solution :

Given Data

$$\text{Variable cost per unit} = \text{Rs. } 11 + 3 = \text{Rs. } 14$$
$$\text{Total fixed cost} = 5{,}40{,}000 + 2{,}52{,}000$$
$$= 7{,}92{,}000$$
$$\text{Contribution} = SP - VC$$
$$= 20 - 14 = \text{Rs. } 6$$
$$\text{P/V Ratio} = \frac{\text{contribution}}{\text{sales}} \times 100$$
$$= \frac{6}{20} \times 100 = 30\%$$

(1) BEP $= \frac{\text{Total Fixed Cost}}{\text{P / V Ratio}}$

$= \frac{7,92,000}{30\%} = \text{Rs. } 26,40,000$

(2) *Sales to earn a profit of Rs. 1,60,000*

$= \frac{\text{Fixed Cost + Profit}}{\text{Contribution per unit}}$

$= \frac{7,92,000 + 1,60,000}{6} = 1,58,667 \text{ units}$

Problem 29 : The records of a company show the following :

Period	*Sales*	*Profit*
	Rs.	*Rs.*
I	1,20,000	9,000
II	1,40,000	13,000

Find out : (*a*) P/V ratio, (*b*) Break-even point, (*c*) Fixed cost, (*d*) Profit when sales are Rs. 10,00,000, (*e*) Sales required to earn a profit of Rs. 20,000, (*f*) Margin of safety and, (*g*) Variable cost for period *II*.

(*University of Madras, B.Com., Sept. 1996*)

Solution :

(*a*) P/V Ratio $= \frac{\text{Difference in Profit}}{\text{Difference in Sales}} \times 100$

$= \frac{4,000}{12,000} \times 100 = 20\%$

(*b*) BEP $= \frac{\text{Total Fixed Cost}}{\text{P / V Ratio}}$

$= \frac{15,000}{20\%} = 75,000$

(*c*) Total fixed cost :

Taking sales of period *III*	=	1,20,000
Contribution = $1,20,000 \times \frac{20}{100}$	=	24,000
Less : Profit		9,000
Fixed cost		15,000

(*d*) *Profit when sales is Rs. 1,00,000*

$$S \times P/V = F + P$$

$$1,00,000 \times \frac{20}{100} = 15,000 + P$$

$$20,000 = 15,000 + P$$

$$P = 5,000$$

(*e*) *Sales when profit is Rs. 20,000*

$$S \times P/V = F + P$$

$$S \times \frac{20}{100} = 15,000 + 2,000$$

$$S \times \frac{1}{5} = 35,000$$

$$S = 35,000 \times 5$$

$$S = 1,75,000$$

(*f*) *Margin of safety for period II*

Margin of safety = Actual sales – Break-even sales

= 1,40,000 – 75,000

= 65,000

(*g*) *Variable cost for period II*

Sales for period *II*	1,40,000
Less : Contribution $\left(1{,}40{,}000 \times \frac{20}{100}\right)$	28,000
Variable cost	1,12,000

Problem 30 : R.S. Manufacturing Ltd., budgets production of 3,00,000 units at a variable cost of Rs. 10 each. The fixed cost are Rs. 20,00,000. The selling price is fixed to yield 20% profit on cost.

You are required to calculate :

(*i*) P/V Ratio

(*ii*) Break-even production units

(*University of Delhi, B.Com. (Pass), April 1995*)

Solution :

Variable cost = 3,00,000 × 10	=	30,00,000
Fixed cost	=	20,00,000
Total cost		50,00,000
Profit		10,00,000
Sales		60,00,000

$$\text{P/V Ratio} = \frac{S-V}{S} \times 100$$

$$= \frac{60{,}00{,}000 - 30{,}00{,}000}{60{,}00{,}000} \times 100$$

$$= \frac{30{,}00{,}000}{60{,}00{,}000} \times 100 = 50\%$$

$$\text{Selling price per unit} = \frac{60{,}00{,}000}{3{,}00{,}000} = \text{Rs. } 20$$

Variable cost = Rs. 10 per unit

Contribution = S – V

= 20 – 10 = 10

$$\text{BEP} = \frac{\text{Fixed cost}}{\text{Contribution per unit}}$$

$$= \frac{20{,}00{,}000}{10} = 2{,}00{,}000 \text{ units}$$

Problem 31 : Firm '*X*' manufactures Surgical goods. Its normal production is 2,600 units per month at a total cost of Rs. 32,000. At full capacity it can manufacture 3,400 units per month at a total cost of Rs. 38,000 calculate :

(1) Average cost per instrument under normal operating condition.

(2) Average variable cost per instrument.

(3) Total fixed cost.

(4) Average fixed cost under normal operating condition. (*University of Madras, B.Com., March 95*)

Solution :

Note : Since the selling price is not given in problem, it is assumed as Rs. 15 per unit.

	Sales	*Total cost*	*Profit*
Normal production (2,600 units × 15)	39,000	32,000	7,000
Full capacity (3,400 units × 15)	51,000	38,000	13,000
	12,000		6,000

$$\text{P/V Ratio} = \frac{\text{Difference in profit}}{\text{Difference in Sales}} \times 100$$

$$= \frac{6,000}{12,000} \times 100 = 50\%$$

(*a*) ***Average cost per instrument under normal operating condition :***

$$\frac{\text{Total cost}}{\text{Normal production}} = \frac{32,000}{2,600 \text{ units}} = 12.31$$

(*b*) ***Average variable cost per instrument***

P/V Ratio = 50%

Variable cost = 50% (balance %)

Normal production sales = 39,000

Variable cost $39,000 \times \frac{50}{100}$ = 19,500

Variable cost per unit = $\frac{19,500}{2,600}$ units = Rs. 7.50

(*c*) *Total fixed cost* :

Taking normal production total cost	= 32,000
Less : Variable cost 2,600 × 7.50	19,500
Total fixed cost	12,500

(*d*) Average fixed cost under normal operating

Total fixed cost = 12,500

Normal production = 2,600 units

Average fixed cost $= \frac{12,500}{2,600}$ = Rs. 4.81

Problem 32 :

	Sales Rs.	*Profit* Rs.
Period 1	10,000	2,000
Period 2	15,000	4,000

You are required to calculate :

(*i*) P/V Ratio

(*ii*) Fixed cost

(*iii*) Break-even sales volume

(*iv*) Sales to earn a profit of Rs. 3,000 and

(*v*) Profit when sales are Rs. 8,000

(*CS, Inter, June 1995*)

Solution :

(*a*) $\text{P/V Ratio} = \frac{\text{Change in profit}}{\text{Change in sales}} \times 100$

$$= \frac{2,000}{5,000} \times 100 = 40\%$$

(*b*) $\frac{\text{Fixed Cost}}{S \times P/V = F + P}$

$$= 10{,}000 \times \frac{40}{100} = F + 2{,}000$$

$$= 4{,}000 = F + 2{,}000$$

$$F = \text{Rs. } 2{,}000$$

(*c*) Break-even sales value $= \frac{\text{Fixed Cost}}{P/V \text{ Ratio}}$

$$= \frac{2{,}000}{40\%} = \text{Rs. } 5{,}000$$

(*d*) Sale value to earn a profit of Rs. 3,000

$$= \frac{\text{Fixed Cost + Desired Profit}}{P/V \text{ Ratio}}$$

$$= \frac{2{,}000 + 3{,}000}{40\%} = \frac{5{,}000}{40\%} = \text{Rs. } 12{,}500$$

(*e*) Profit when sales are Rs. 8,000

$$S \times P/V = F + P$$

$$8{,}000 \times \frac{40}{100} = 2{,}000 + P$$

$$3{,}200 = 2{,}000 + P$$

$$P = 1{,}200$$

Problem 33 : A Company had incurred fixed expenses of 4,50,000 with sales of Rs. 15,50,000 and earned a profit of Rs. 3,00,000 during the first half year. In the second half, it suffered a loss of Rs. 1,50,000.

Calculate :

(*i*) The profit valume ratio, Break-even point and margin of safety for the first half year

(*ii*) Expected sales-volume for the second half year assuming that selling price and fixed expenses remained unchaged during the second half year

(*iii*) The break-even point and margin of safety for the whole year.

(*CA, Inter, May 1996*)

Solution :

(*i*) *Calculation of P/V Ratio BEP and M.S*

$$\text{P/V Ratio} = \frac{\text{Contribution}}{\text{Sales}} \times 100$$

$$\text{or,} \quad = \frac{(\text{Fixed expenses + Profit})}{\text{Sales}} \times 100$$

$$= \frac{4{,}50{,}000 + 3{,}00{,}000}{15{,}00{,}000} \times 100$$

$$= \frac{7{,}50{,}000}{15{,}00{,}000} \times 100 = 50\%$$

$$\text{BEP} = \frac{\text{Fixed Cost}}{P/V \text{ Ratio}}$$

$$= \frac{4{,}50{,}000}{50\%} = 9{,}00{,}000$$

Margin of safety = Actual sales – Break-even sales

= 15,00,000 – 9,00,000

= 6,00,000

(*ii*) Expected sales value for the second half year :

$$\text{Expected sales value} = \frac{\text{Fixed cost} - \text{loss}}{\text{P / V Ratio}}$$

$$= \frac{4{,}50{,}000 - 1{,}50{,}000}{50\%}$$

$$= \frac{3{,}00{,}00}{50\%} = 6{,}00{,}000$$

(*iii*) *BEP and MS for the whole year*

$$\text{BEP} = \frac{\text{Fixed cost for the whole year}}{\text{P / V Ratio}}$$

$$= \frac{9{,}00{,}000}{50\%} = \text{Rs. } 18{,}00{,}000$$

$$\text{MS} = \frac{\text{Profit for the year}}{\text{P / V Ratio}}$$

$$= \frac{3{,}00{,}000 - 1{,}50{,}000}{50} = \text{Rs. } 3{,}00{,}000$$

or M S = Sales above BEP
= Actual sales – Break even sales
= (15,00,000 + 6,00,000) – 18,00,000
Rs. 3,00,000

Problem 34 : A company sells its product at Rs. 15 per unit. In a period, if it produces and sells 8,000 units, it incurrs a loss of Rs. 5 per unit. If the volume is raised to 20,000 units, it earns a profit of Rs. 4 per unit. Calculate BEP both in terms of rupees as well as in units. (*CA, Inter, November 1996*)

Solution :

Average Cost at 8,000 units

= Selling price per unit + Less Component per unit
= 15 + 5 = Rs. 20

Average cost at 20,000 units

Selling price per unit – profit component per unit
= 15 – 4 = Rs. 11

Total cost at 8,000 units = 8,000 × 20 = 1,60,000
Total cost at 2,000 units = 20,000 × 11 = 2,20,000

$$\text{Variable cost per unit} = \frac{\text{Change in the total cost}}{\text{Change in the volume of production}}$$

$$= \frac{2{,}20{,}000 - 1{,}60{,}000}{20{,}000 - 8{,}000 \text{ units}}$$

$$= \frac{60{,}000}{12{,}000} = \text{Rs. } 5$$

Fixed cost = Total cost – Variable cost
= 1,60,000 – 40,000
= 1,20,000

$$\text{P/V Ratio} = \frac{S - V}{S} \times 100$$

$$= \frac{15 - 5}{15} \times 100 = 66\frac{2}{3}\%$$

$$\text{BEP (in Rs.)} = \frac{FC}{P/V \text{ Ratio}}$$

$$= \frac{1,20,000}{66\frac{2}{3}\%} = \text{Rs. } 1,80,000$$

$$\text{BEP (in units)} = \frac{FC}{\text{Contribution per unit}}$$

$$= \frac{1,20,000}{15-5}$$

$$= \frac{1,20,000}{10} = 12,000 \text{ units}$$

Problem 35 : Two firms A & Co. and B & Co. sell the same type of product in the same market. Their budgeted profit & loss a/c for the year ending 31.3.1966 are as follows :

	A & Co			*B & Co.*
Sales		5,00,000		6,00,000
Variable cost	4,00,000		4,00,000	
Fixed cost	30,000	4,30,000	70,000	4,70,000
	Net profit	70,000		1,30,000

Required :

(1) Calculate at which sales value both the firms will earn equal profit.

(2) State which firm is likely to earn greater profits in condition of

(*i*) heavy demand for the product

(*ii*) Low demand for the product give reasons. (*CA, Inter, November 1995*)

Solution :

	A & Co.	*B & Co.*
(1) Sales	5,00,000	6,00,000
Less : Variable cost	4,00,000	4,00,000
Contribution	1,00,000	2,00,000
P/V Ratio = $\frac{C}{S} \times 100$	20%	$33\frac{1}{3}\%$

$$\text{Sales volume for both the firm to earn equal profits} = \frac{\text{Difference in FC}}{\text{Difference in P/V Ratio}}$$

$$= \frac{40,000}{13.33\%} = \text{Rs. } 3,00,000$$

(2) The P/V Ratio of B & Co. at $33\frac{1}{3}\%$ is higher than that of A & Co. at 20% and therefore B & Co., will earn higher profit if the sales volume exceeds Rs. 3,00,000 level.

In fact, for each additional unit of products sales above Rs. 3,00,000; the profit of B & Co. will rise by Rs. $33\frac{1}{3}$ which exceeds by Rs. $13\frac{1}{3}\%$. The profit of A & Co. under similar conditions. However, below that level profit for A & Co. will be greater. We can therefore, generally conclude that B & Co. is likely to earn higher profit under conditions of heavy demand for the product above Rs. 3,00,000. On the other hand, A & Co. is likely to earn higher profits under conditions of low demand for the product (below Rs. 3,00,000)

Problem 36 : A company earned a profit of Rs. 30,000 during the year 1994-95. If the marginal cost and the selling price of a product are Rs. 8 and Rs. 10 per unit respectively, find out the amount of margin of

Solution :

$$\text{P/V Ratio} = \frac{\text{Contribution}}{\text{Sales}} \times 100$$

$$= \frac{2}{10} \times 100 = 20\%$$

$$\text{Margin of safety} = \frac{\text{Profit}}{\text{P/V Ratio}}$$

$$= \frac{30,000}{20\%} = \text{Rs. } 1,50,000$$

Problem 37 : From the following data, compute break-even sales and margin of safety :

Sales	10,00,000
Fixed cost	3,00,000
Profit	2,00,000

(*CS, Inter, December 1994*)

Solution :

$$S - V = F + P$$

$$10,00,000 - V = 3,00,000 + 2,00,000$$

$$V = -10,00,000 + 3,00,000 + 2,00,000$$

$$V = \text{Rs. } 5,00,000$$

$$\text{P/V Ratio} = \frac{S - V}{S} \times 100$$

$$= \frac{10,00,000 - 5,00,000}{10,00,000} \times 100$$

$$= \frac{5,00,000}{10,00,000} \times 100 = 50\%$$

$$\text{BEP (Sales)} = \frac{\text{Fixed Cost}}{\text{P / V Ratio}}$$

$$= \frac{300,000}{50\%} = \text{Rs. } 6,00,000$$

$$\text{Margin of safety} = \text{Sales} - \text{Break-even sales}$$

$$= 10,00,000 - 6,00,000$$

$$= \text{Rs. } 4,00,000$$

Problem 38 : From the following data find out (*i*) Sales and (*ii*) New break-even sales, if selling price is reduced by 10%

	Rs.
Fixed cost	4,000
Break-even sales	20,000
Profit	1,000
Selling price per unit	20

(*CS, Inter, December 1994*)

Solution :

$$\text{P/V Ratio} = \frac{\text{Contribution}}{\text{Sales}} \times 100$$

Fixed cost = 4,000 *i.e.*, contribution at BEP sales

$$\text{P/V Ratio} = \frac{4,000}{20,000} \times 100 = 20\%$$

(*i*) Sales $= \dfrac{FC + P}{P/V \text{ Ratio}}$

$= \dfrac{4,000 + 1,000}{20\%} = \text{Rs. } 25,000$

(*ii*) New selling price = 20 – 10% = Rs. 18 per unit
Variable cost = 80% of Rs. 20 = 16 per unit

New contribution Rs. 2 per unit

New P/V Ratio $= \dfrac{2}{18} \times 100 = 11\dfrac{1}{9}\%$

New break-even sales $= \dfrac{\text{Fixed Cost}}{P/V \text{ Ratio}}$

$= \dfrac{4,000}{11\frac{1}{9}\%} = \text{Rs. } 36,000$

Problem 39 : From the following data, calculate BEP

Selling price per unit	20
Variable cost per unit	15
Fixed overheads	20,000

If sales are 20% above BEP, determine the net profit. (*CS, Inter, Dec. 1994*)

Solution :

Contribution per unit = 20 – 15 = Rs. 5

P/V Ratio $= \dfrac{\text{Contribution}}{\text{Sales}} \times 100$

$= \dfrac{5}{20} \times 100 = 25\%$

BEP $= \dfrac{\text{Fixed Cost}}{P/V \text{ Ratio}} = \dfrac{20,000}{25\%} = \text{Rs. } 80,000$

If sales are 20% above BEP :

Sales = 80,000 + 20% = Rs. 96,000

= S × P/V Ratio = F + P

$96,000 \times \dfrac{25}{100} = 20,000 + P$

$24,000 = 20,000 + P$

$P = \text{Rs. } 4,000$

Problem 40 : The following figures are extracted from books of a manufacturing concern for the year 1990-91 :

Direct material	2,05,000
Direct labour	75,000
Fixed overhead	60,000
Variable overhead	1,00,000
Sales	5,00,000

Calculate the break-even point. What will be the effect on BEP on an increase of 10% in (*i*) Fixed expenses and (*ii*) Variable expenses. (*CS, Inter, June 1992*)

Solution :

P/V Ratio $= \dfrac{\text{Contribution}}{\text{Sales}} \times 100$

$= \dfrac{1,20,000}{5,00,000} \times 100 = 24\%$

$$\text{BEP} = \frac{\text{Fixed Cost}}{\text{P / V Ratio}} = \frac{60{,}000}{24\%} = \text{Rs. } 2{,}50{,}000$$

(*i*) If fixed cost increases by 10%.

Revised fixed cost = 60,000 + 10% = Rs. 66,000

$$\text{BEP} = \frac{\text{FC}}{\text{P / V Ratio}} = \frac{66{,}000}{24\%} = \text{Rs. } 2{,}75{,}000$$

(*ii*) If variable cost increases by 10% :

Variable cost :

Direct material	2,05,000
Direct labour	75,000
Variable overhead	1,00,000
	3,80,000
Add : 10 % Increase	38,000
Revised variable cost	4,18,000

$$\text{P/V Ratio} = \frac{\text{Contribution}}{\text{Sales}} \times 100$$

$$= \frac{82{,}000}{5{,}00{,}000} \times 100 = 16.4\%$$

$$\text{BEP} = \frac{60{,}000}{16.4\%} = \text{Rs. } 3{,}65{,}854$$

Problem 41 : The profit ratio of BB & Co. dealing in precision instrument is 50% and the margin of safety is 40%.

You are required to work out the break-even point and the net profit if the sale volume is Rs. 50 lakhs.

(*CS, (Inter), June 1991*)

Solution :

(1) Sales of break-even point

Sales	50,00,000
Less : Margin of safety 40%	20,00,000
Sales at break-even point	30,00,000

(2) Contribution at break even point = Sales at BEP × P/V Ratio

= Rs. 3,00,000 × 50% = Rs. 15,00,000

(3) Calculation of fixed cost

Sales at BEP	3,00,000
Less : Contribution at BEP	15,00,000
Fixed cost	15,00,000

(4) Calculation of net profit for total sales :

Contribution on total sales = Sales × P/V Ratio	
= 50,00,000 × 50% =	25,00,000
Less : Fixed cost	15,00,000
Net profit	10,00,000

Problem 42 : *XY* Ltd. has been offered a choice to buy machine *A* or machine *B*. From the following data, you are required to compute :

(*a*) Break-even point for each of the machines.

(*b*) The level of sales at which both machines earn equal profits.

(*c*) The range of sales at which one is more profitable than the other.

	Machine	
	A	*B*
Annual output (in units)	10,000	10,000
Fixed cost (Rs.)	30,000	16,000
Profit at given level of production (Rs.)	30,000	24,000

The market price of the product is expected to be Rs. 10 per unit. *(CS, Inter, Dec., 1990)*

Solution : **Calculation of break-even point**

	Machine	
	A	*B*
Sales 10,000 @ Rs. 10	1,00,000	1,00,000
Less : Variable cost (balancing figure)	40,000	60,000
Contribution	60,000	40,000
Less : Fixed cost	30,000	16,000
Profit	30,000	24,000

$$\text{P/V Ratio} = \frac{\text{Contribution}}{\text{Sales}} \times 100 = \frac{60,000}{1,00,000} \times 100 = 60\% \qquad \frac{40,000}{1,00,000} \times 100 = 40\%$$

$$(a)\ \text{BEP} = \frac{\text{Fixed Cost}}{\text{P / V Ratio}} \qquad \frac{30,000}{60} \times 100 \qquad \frac{16,000}{40} \times 100$$

$$= \text{Rs. } 50,000 \qquad = \text{Rs. } 40,000$$

$$\text{BEP in units} \qquad = \frac{50,000}{10} \qquad \frac{40,000}{10}$$

$$= 5,000 \text{ units} \qquad = 4,000 \text{ units}$$

(*b*) Since the selling price of the products produced by *A* and *B* are equal the machines will earn equal profit. When the total cost of operation of both the machines are the same.

So, if '*x*' be the output where the total cost of operation on each machine is as below :

For *A* $= 4x + 30,000$

For *B* $= 6x + 16,000$

$$4x + 30,000 = 6x + 16,000$$
$$2x = 14,000$$
$$x = 7,000$$

At a production of level of 7,000 units the profits made by the machine *A* and *B* are equal.

(*c*) The breakdown points *A* is at 5,000 units compared to that of 4,000 units in case of *B* and at a production level of 7,000 units they earn equal profit. Therefore, it is quite ciear that the profit earning for machine *B* is more in the range of 4,000 to 6,999 units.

Problem 43 : A Japanese soft drink company is planning to establish a subsidiary company in India to produce mineral water.

Based on the estimated annual sales of 40,000 bottles of the mineral water cost studies produced the following estimates for the Indian subsidiary :

	Total annual Cost (Rs.)	*Per cent of total annual cost which is variable*
Material	2,10,000	100%
Labour	1,50,000	80%
Factory overhead	92,000	60%
Administration overhead	40,000	35%

The Indian production will be sold by manufacturer's representatives who will receive a commission of 8% of the sale price. No portion of the Japanese office expenses is to be allocated to the Indian subsidiary. Required to :

(*a*) Compute the sale price per bottle to enable the management to realise an estimated 10% profit on sale proceeds in India.

(*b*) Calculate break-even point in Rupee Sales as also in number of bottles for the Indian subsidiary on the assumption that the sale price is Rs. 14 per bottle. (*CS, Inter, June, 1992*)

Solution : **Calculation of sales value**

Commission is 8% of sales revenue

Profit is 10% of sales revenue

Hence cost of sales is 82% of sales value

For a cost of sales of Rs. 82, the sales value is 100

For a cost of sales of Rs. 4,92,000, the sales value is $\frac{4,92,000 \times 100}{82}$ = Rs. 6,00,000

Calculation showing selling price per bottle = $\frac{\text{Sales Value}}{\text{No. of bottles sold}} = \frac{6,00,000}{40,000}$ = Rs. 15

Calculation of variable cost

	Total	*Per unit*
No. of bottles	40,000	1.00
Materials	2,10,000	5.25
Labour (80% of 1,50,000)	1,20,000	3,00
Factory overhead (60% of 92,000)	55,200	1.38
Administration expenses (35% of 40,000)	14,000	0.35
Commission (14 × 40,000 × 8%)	44,800	1.12
	4,44,000	11.10

Calculation of fixed cost

Fixed labour cost + Fixed factory overhead + Fixed Adm. overhead

(1,50,000 × 20% + 92,000 × 40%) + (40,000 × 65%)

= 30,000 + 36,800 + 26,000

= Rs. 92,800

$$\text{P/V Ratio} = \frac{\text{Sales} - \text{Variable Cost}}{\text{Sales}} \times 100$$

$$= \frac{14 - 11.10}{14} \times 100$$

Contribution per bottle = Sales – Variable cost

= 14 – 11.10 = 2.90

$$\text{BEP (in rupee sales)} = \frac{\text{Fixed Cost}}{\text{P / V ratio}}$$

$$= \frac{92,800}{20.7142\%} = 4,48,000$$

$$\text{BEP (in number of bottles)} = \frac{\text{FC}}{\text{Contribution per bottle}}$$

$$= \frac{92,800}{2.90} = 32,000 \text{ bottles}$$

Problem 44 : The cost accountant of *X* Co. Ltd. furnishes you the following informations :

Fixed cost for the year	Rs. 40,000
Net profit for the year	Rs. 50,000
P/V Ratio	30%

What is the amount of sales made during the year?
What will be the selling price per unit when variable cost per unit is Rs. 8.40 and P/V ratio is 40%?

(University of Delhi, B.Com. (Pass), April 1990)

Solution :

$$\text{Sales} = \frac{\text{Fixed cost + Profit}}{\text{P / V ratio}}$$

$$= \frac{40,000 + 50,000}{30\%} = \text{Rs. } 3,00,000$$

Variable cost = Rs. 8.40% per unit
P/V Ratio = 40%
Variable cost ratio = 100 – 40 = 60%
If 60% = 8.40,

$$\text{then } 100\% = 8.40 \times \frac{100}{60} = \text{Rs. } 14.$$

Selling price is Rs. 14.

Problem 45 : The projected output of a plant, when sold, would earn Rs. 70,000 in sales income to Mixers Ltd. The variable costs for this production volume would be Rs. 30,000. The fixed cost are Rs. 20,000. Determine the following :

(*a*) The break-even point of the company.
(*b*) The profit or loss to the company on sales of Rs. 49,000 and Rs. 28,000.
(*c*) The amount of sales that will enable the company to earn a net profit of Rs. 28,000.

(University of Delhi, B.Com., (Hons.), April 1990)

Solution :

At projected capacity of 100%

$$\text{P/V Ratio} = \frac{\text{Contribution}}{\text{Sales}} \times 100$$

$$= \frac{40,000}{70,000} \times 100 = 57.14\%$$

$$(i) \text{ BEP} = \frac{\text{FC}}{\text{P / V ratio}} = \frac{20,000}{57.14\%} = \text{Rs. } 35,000$$

Verification :

Sales at BEP = Rs. 35,000

$$\text{VC at BEP} = \frac{1}{2} \text{ of } 30,000 = 15,000$$

FC = 20,000

Hence no profit and no loss.

(*ii*) **Profit or loss on sale of Rs. 49,000 and Rs. 28,000**

	Rs. 49,000 *i.e.*, 70% capacity	Rs 28,000 40% capacity
Variable cost	21,000	12,000
Fixed cost	20,000	20,000
Total cost	41,000	32,000
Profit or loss	+8,000	– 4,000
Sales	49,000	28,000

(*iii*) **Sales to earn profit of Rs. 28,000**

$$\text{Sales} = \frac{\text{FC + Desired profit}}{\text{P / V ratio}} = \frac{20,000 + 28,000}{57.14\%} = \text{Rs. } 84,000$$

At 100% capacity company is making profit of Rs. 20,000. So company will have to run over and above its capacity. Assuming fixed costs will remain same even at this exceeded capacity, sales to earn profit of Rs. 28,000 should be Rs. 84,000.

Verifications :

For a sale of Rs. 70,000, VC is Rs. 30,000

For a sale of Rs. 84,000, VC is

$VC = \frac{30,000 \times 84,000}{70,000} =$	36,000
Fixed cost	20,000
Total cost	56,000
Profit	28,000
Sales	84,000

Problem 46 : From the following particulars calculate break-even point :

Sales	Rs. 2,00,000
Variable cost	Rs. 1,20,000
Fixed overhead	Rs, 30,000

Also calculate

(*a*) New BEP if selling price is reduced by 10%

(*b*) New BEP, if variable cost increased by 10%

(*c*) New BEP, if fixed cost increases by 10%. (*Madurai Kamaraj University, B.Com., April 1992*)

Solution :

$$\text{P/V ratio} = \frac{\text{Contribution}}{\text{Sales}} \times 100$$

$$= \frac{80,000}{2,00,000} \times 100 = 40\%$$

$$\text{BEP} = \frac{\text{FC}}{\text{P/V ratio}} = \frac{30,000}{40\%} = 75,000$$

(*a*) Now BEP if selling price is reduced by 10%

Original sales	2,00,000
Less : 10%	20,000
Revised sales	1,80,000

$$\text{P/V ratio} = \frac{\text{Contribution}}{\text{Sales}} \times 100$$

$$= \frac{60,000}{1,80,000} = 33\frac{1}{3}\%$$

$$\text{BEP} = \frac{\text{FC}}{\text{P/V ratio}}$$

$$= \frac{30,000}{33\frac{1}{3}} = 90,000$$

(*b*) New BEP, if variable cost increases by 10%

Present variable cost	1,20,000
Add : 10%	12,000
Revised variable cost	1,32,000

$$\text{P/V ratio} = \frac{68,000}{2,00,000} \times 100 = 34\%$$

$$\text{BEP} = \frac{\text{FC}}{\text{P/V}}$$

$$= \frac{30,000}{34\%} = 88,325$$

(*c*) Now BEP if fixed cost increases by 10%

Original fixed cost	30,000
Add : 10%	3,000
Revised fixed cost	33,000

$$\text{BEP} = \frac{\text{Fixed Cost}}{\text{P/V ratio}}$$

$$= \frac{33,000}{40\%} = 82,500$$

Problem 47 : From the following data find out :

(*d*) P/V Ratio

(*b*) Sales required to break-even and

(*c*) Sales required to earn a profit of Rs. 1,60,000

Selling price per unit	Rs.40
Variable costs per unit :	
Direct materials	Rs. 10
Direct labour	Rs. 7
Variable overheads—100% direct labour cost	
Fixed expenses	Rs. 64,000

(*Kakatiya University, M. Com., Aug. 1991*)

Solution :

Selling price		Rs. 40
Less : Variable cost		
Direct materials	10	
Direct labour	7	
Variable overhead	7	Rs. 24
Contribution		16

(*a*) P/V ratio

$$= \frac{\text{Contribution}}{\text{Sales}} \times 100$$

$$= \frac{16}{40} \times 100 = 40\%$$

(*b*) BEP (sales volume)

$$= \frac{\text{Fixed cost}}{\text{Contribution per unit}}$$

$$= \frac{64,000}{16} = 4,000$$

Sales value $= 4,000 \times 40 = 1,60,000$

(*c*) Sales required to earn a profit of Rs. 1,60,000

$$\text{Sales} = \frac{\text{Fixed cost + Desired profit}}{\text{Contribution per unit}}$$

$$= \frac{64,000 + 1,60,000}{16}$$

$$= \frac{2,24,000}{16} = 14,000 \text{ units}$$

Problem 48 : The P/V ratio of a firm dealing with electrical goods is 50% and the margin of safety is 40%. You are required to workout the break-even point and the net profit if the sales volume is Rs. 5,00,000.

(Kakatiya University, M. Com., Aug. 1991)

Solution :

$$\text{M.S. Ratio} = \frac{\text{Margin of safety}}{\text{Sales}} \times 100$$

$$40 = \frac{\text{Margin of safety}}{50,00,000} \times 100$$

$$100 \text{ M.S.} = 20,00,00,000$$

$$\text{M.S.} = 20,00,000$$

$$\text{Margin of safety} = \frac{\text{Profit}}{\text{P/V ratio}}$$

$$20,00,000 = \frac{\text{Profit}}{40\%}$$

$$20,00,000 \times 40 = \text{Profit} \times 100$$

$$100 \text{ profit} = 80,00,00,000$$

$$\text{Profit} = 8,00,000$$

Problem 49 : From the following information pertaining to a company find out (*a*) P/V ratio, (*b*) BEP, (*c*) Profit when sales amounted to Rs. 12,00,000 and (*d*) Sales required to earn a profit of Rs. 2,00,000.

Variable cost	Rs. 6,00,000
Fixed cost	Rs. 3,00,000
Net profit	Rs. 1,00,000
Sales	Rs. 10,00,000

(Gulbarga University, B. Com., November 1991)

Solution :

(*a*) P/V ratio

$$= \frac{\text{Contribution}}{\text{Sales}} \times 100$$

$$= \frac{4,00,000}{10,00,000} \times 100 = 40\%$$

(*b*) BEP

$$= \frac{\text{Fixed cost}}{\text{P / V ratio}}$$

$$= \frac{3,00,000}{40\%} = \text{Rs. } 7,50,000$$

(*c*) Profit when sales amounted to Rs. 12,00,000

$$\text{S (P/V)} = \text{F} + \text{P}$$

$$12,00,000 \times \frac{40}{100} = 3,00,000 + \text{P}$$

$$4,80,000 = 3,00,000 + \text{P}$$

$$\text{P} = 1,80,000$$

(*d*) Sales required to earn a profit of Rs. 2,00,000

$$\text{S (P/V)} = 3,00,000 + 2,00,000$$

$$\text{S} \times \frac{40}{100} = 5,00,000 = 1,25,000$$

Problem 50 : Two businesses *Y* Ltd. and *Z* Ltd. sell, the same type of product in the same type of market. Their budgeted profit and loss accounts for the coming year are as follows :

		Y Ltd.		*Z Ltd.*
Sales		1,50,000		1,50,000
Less : Variable cost	1,20,000		1,00,000	
Fixed cost	15,000	1,35,000	35,000	1,35,000
Budgeted net profit		15,000		15,000

You are required to :

(*a*) Calculate the break-even point of each business.

(*b*) Calculate the sales volume at which each of business will earn Rs. 5,000 profit.

(*c*) State which business is likely to earn greater profit in conditions of (*i*) Heavy demand for the product, (*ii*) Low demand for the product and briefly give your reasons.

(*University of Madras, B. Com., March 1991*)

Solution :

Y Ltd. :

$$\text{BEP} = \frac{\text{Fixed cost}}{1-\dfrac{\text{Variable cost}}{\text{Sales}}}$$

$$= \frac{15,000}{1-\dfrac{1,20,000}{1,50,000}} = \frac{1,50,000}{2} = \text{Rs. } 75,000$$

$$\text{P/V ratio} = \frac{\text{Contribution}}{\text{Sales}} \times 100$$

$$= \frac{30,000}{1,50,000} \times 100 = 20\%$$

Margin of safety = 1,50,000 – 75,000 = Rs. 75,000

M/S ratio = 50%

Z Ltd.

$$\text{BEP} = \frac{\text{Fixed cost}}{1-\dfrac{\text{Variable cost}}{\text{Sales}}}$$

$$= \frac{35,000}{1-\dfrac{1,00,000}{1,50,000}} = \frac{35,000}{0.333} = \text{Rs. } 1,05,000$$

$$\text{P/V ratio} = \frac{\text{Marginal contribution}}{\text{Sales}} \times 100$$

$$= \frac{50,000}{1,50,000} \times 100 = 33\frac{1}{3}\%$$

$$\text{M/S Ratio} = \frac{45,000}{1,50,000} \times 100 = 30\%$$

(*b*) (*i*) From the above calculation it is clear that P/V ratio is higher in case of *Z* Ltd. therefore, in case of heavy demand *Z* Ltd. will earn higher profits.

(*ii*) In case of low demand *Y* will be an advantageous position as fixed costs and break-even point are low and consequently margin of safety is higher. Assuming sales at Rs. 1,00,000. *Y* Ltd. will still earn profit while *Z* Ltd. will incur a loss.

GRAPHIC METHOD OF PRESENTING CVP ANALYSIS

This method is preferred under two conditions *viz.* (*a*) where a simple overview is sufficient and (*b*) to avoid detailed calculations involved under equation method. The following procedure is involved under the graphic method :

(*a*) **Vertical line :** Draw a vertical line on the left side of the graph paper to show cost and sales revenue.

(*b*) **Horizontal line :** Draw a horizontal line to show the number of units in such a way it should intersect the vertical line at the point of zero.

(*c*) **Fixed cost line :** A line parallel to X-axis (horizontal line) is to be drawn to represent the fixed cost considering the units manufactured and fixed cost incurred.

(*d*) **Total sales revenue line :** This line is drawn starting at the zero point on the left hand corner and ending on the right hand side considering the sales revenue.

(*e*) **Total cost line :** This is the total of fixed and variable cost. This line is drawn starting at the Y-axis fixed cost point and moving to the right considering the total cost.

(*f*) **BEP :** This is the point where total cost line intersects the sales line.

A typical graph depicting the BEP is shown in the Fig. 23.1.

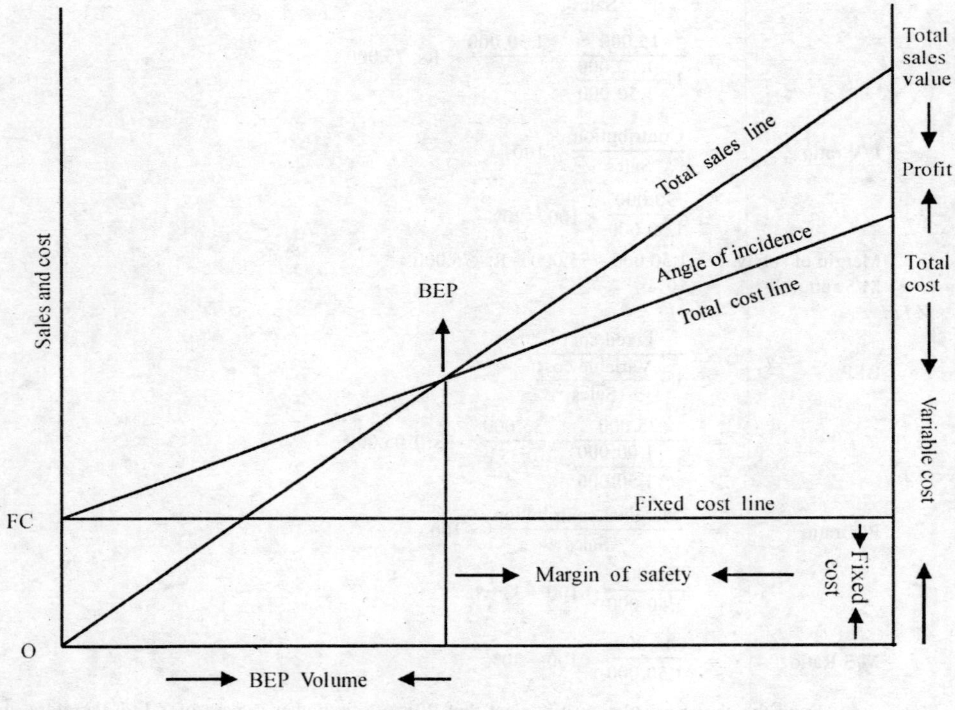

Fig. 23.1 Break-even chart.

Problem 45 : From the following data, draw a single break-even chart :

Selling price per unit	Rs. 10.00
Trade discount	5%
Direct material cost per unit	Rs. 3.00
Direct labour cost per unit	Rs. 2.00
Fixed overhead	Rs. 10.000

Variable overhead 100% of direct labour cost. If sales are 10% and 15% above the break even-volume, determine the net profit. (*Bangalore University, M. Com., April 1992*)

Solution :

Contribution = Selling price – Variable cost

Sales		Rs. 10
Less : 5% trade discount		9.50
Less : Variable costs :		
Direct materials	3.00	
Direct labour	2.00	
Variable overhead : 100% of labour cost	2.00	7.00
Contribution		Rs. 2.50

$$\text{BEP} = \frac{\text{Fixed cost}}{\text{Contribution per unit}} = \frac{10,000}{2.50} = 4,000 \text{ units}$$

Profit if sale is 10% above BEP	
Sales = 4,000 × Rs. 9.50 + 10%	41,800
Less : Variable cost 4,400 × 7	30,800
	11,000
Less : Fixed cost	10,000
Profit	1,000
Profit is sales are above 15%	
4,000 × Rs. 9.50 + 15%	43,700
Less : Variable cost = 4,600 × 7	32,200
	11,500
Less : Fixed cost	10,000
Profit	1,500

For break-even chart see fig. 23.2.

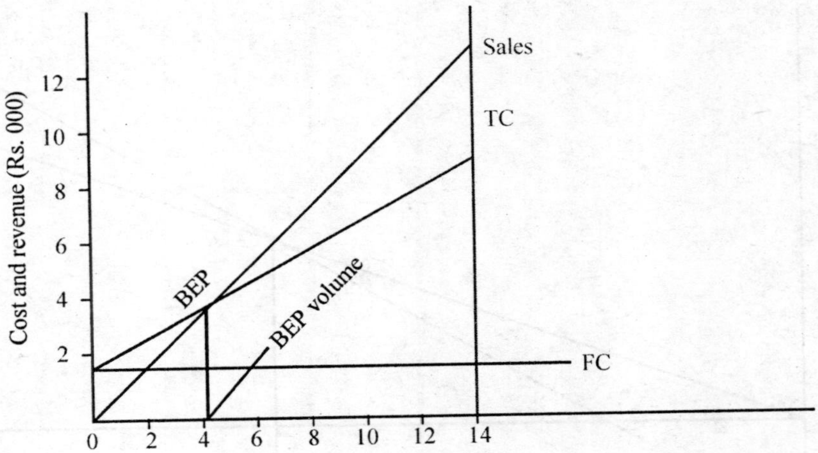

Fig. 23.2

Problem 52 : You are given the following data for a costing year for a factory :

Budgeted output	1,00,000 units
Fixed expenses	Rs. 5,00,000
Variable expense per unit	Rs. 10
Selling price per unit	Rs. 20

Draw a break-even chart showing the break-even point, if the selling price is reduced to Rs. 18 per unit. What will be the new break-even point? (*Bangalore University, M. Com., April 1991*)

Solution : *See* Figs. 23.3 and 23.4.

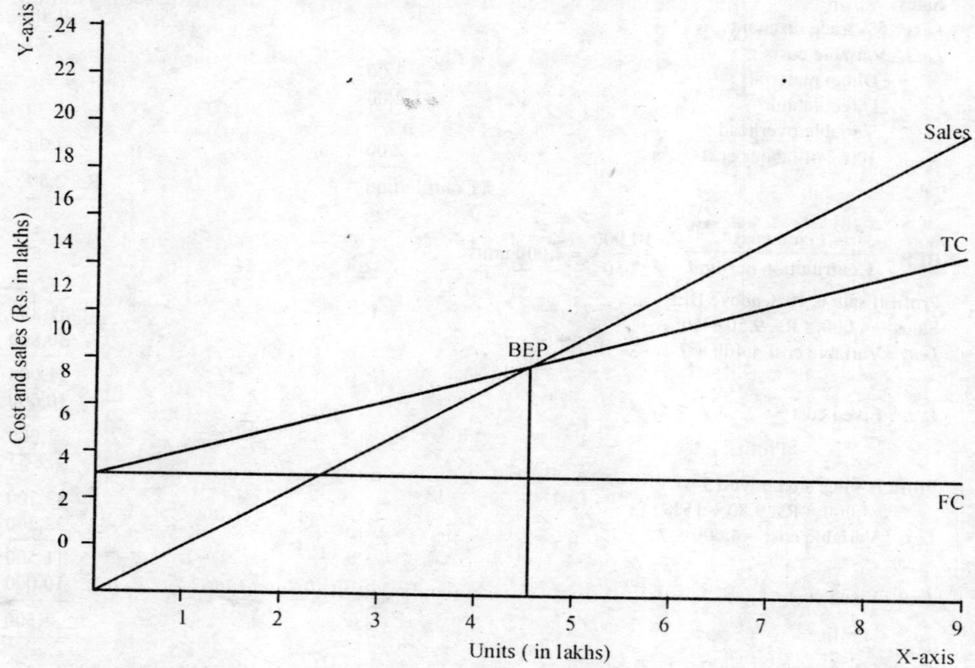

Fig. 23.3 BEP if selling price is Rs. 20.

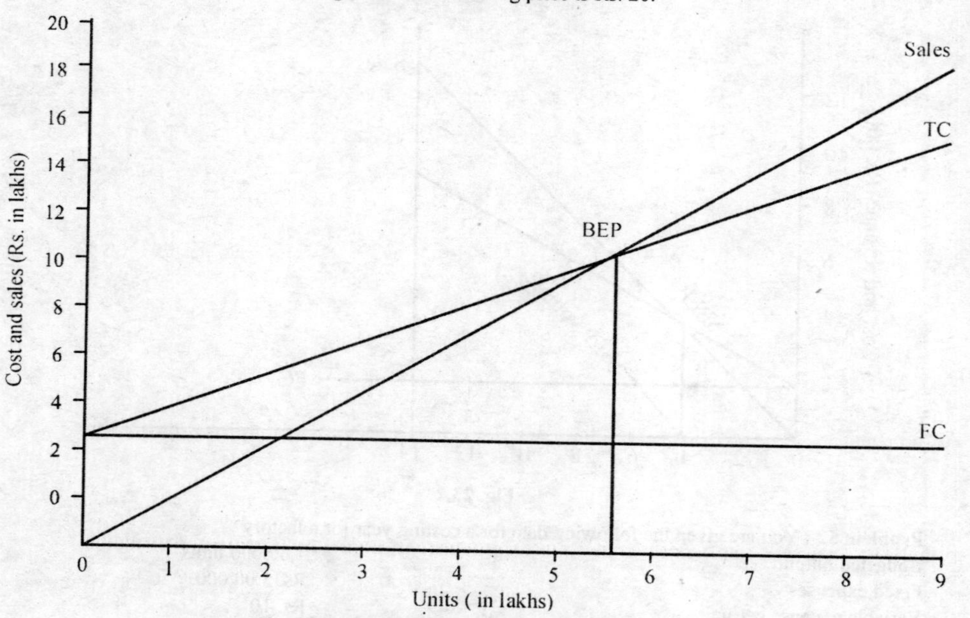

Fig. 23.4 BEP if selling price is reduced to Rs. 18.

TYPES OF BREAK-EVEN CHARTS

1. Break-even chart showing profit appropriation : This is one of the orthodox type of break-even chart which shows additional information as to how the profit is distributed. This is illustrated below :

Problem 53 : From the following information draw up a break-even chart showing the distribution of profit :

Fixed cost	Rs. 20,000
Variable cost	Rs. 2 per unit
Debenture interest not included in the fixed cost	Rs. 10,000
Preference shares dividends	Rs. 10,000
Equity shares dividends	Rs. 20,000
Sales	10,000 units at Rs. 10 each.

Solution : *See* Fig. 23.5.

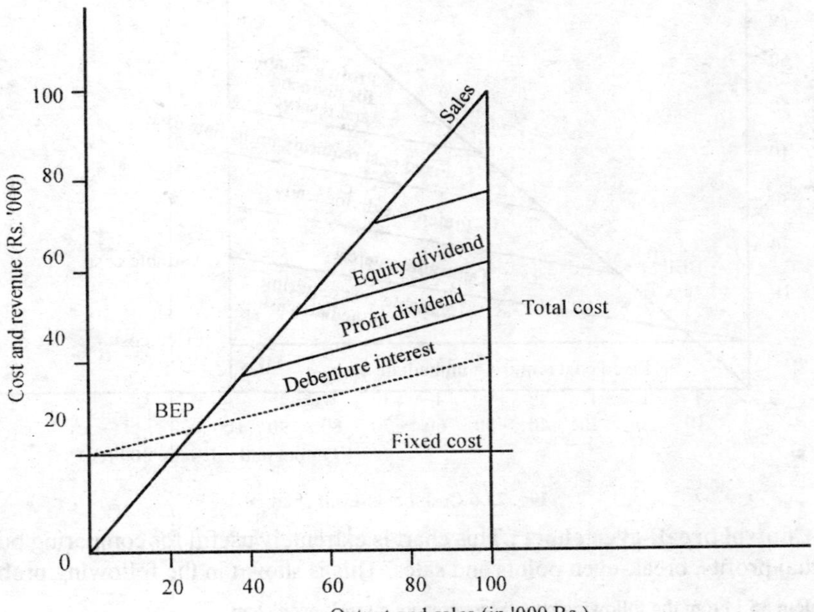

Fig. 23.5 BEP showing profit appropriation.

2. Cash break chart : Under this type the fixed costs are classified into two types *viz.* (*i*) fixed cost requiring immediate cash. Some examples of this type of cost are rent and rates, wages and salaries, insurance, etc. The term "immediate" here refers to the period covered by the chart and (*ii*) fixed cost not requiring immediate cash. Some examples of such costs are depreciation, advertising, research and development cost. The presentation of these two types of fixed cost in the chart deserve special mention. The fixed cost requiring immediate cash is shown at the base line (horizontal line) of the chart. Whereas the fixed cost not requiring immediate cash is shown last. The variable cost is assumed to be payable in cash. Where credit transactions are involved their impact on cash available is measured and cash payments are adjusted. This is shown in the following problem :

Problem 54 : From the following particulars prepare a cash break-even chart :

Fixed cost	Cash Rs. 1,00,000
Already paid	Rs. 10,000
Variable cost	Rs. 2 per unit
Preference dividend and debenture interest	Rs. 10,000 each
Sales	10,000 units of Rs. 10 each

Solution : *See* Fig. 23.6.

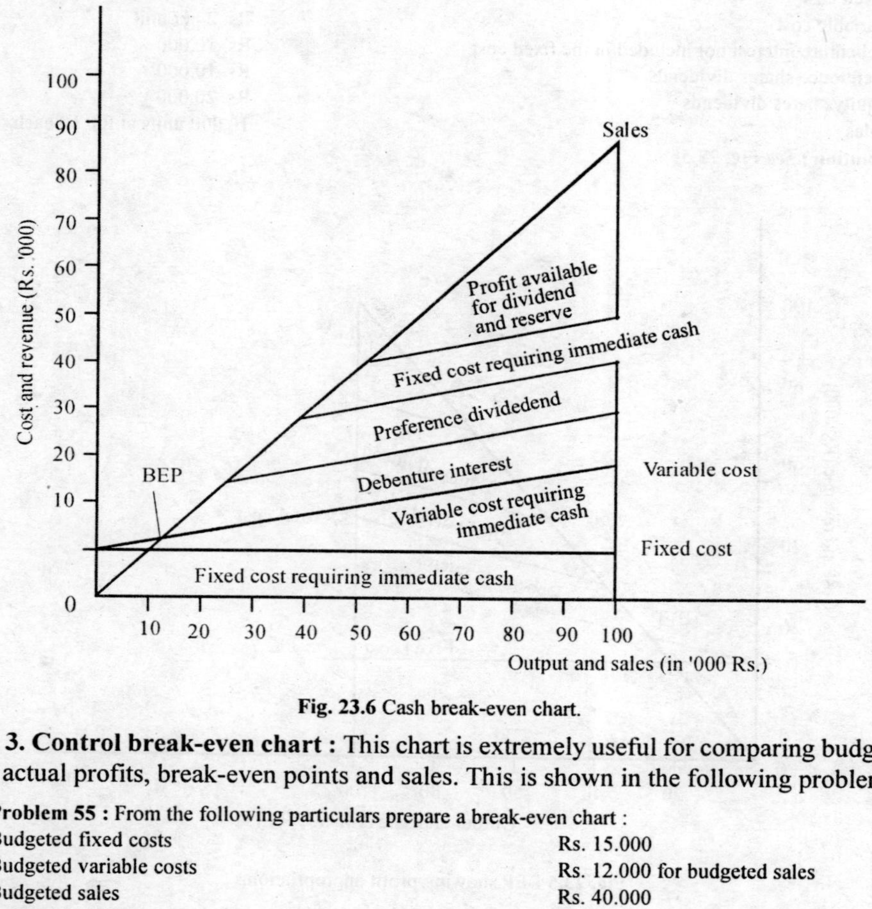

Fig. 23.6 Cash break-even chart.

3. Control break-even chart : This chart is extremely useful for comparing budgeted and actual profits, break-even points and sales. This is shown in the following problem :

Problem 55 : From the following particulars prepare a break-even chart :

Budgeted fixed costs	Rs. 15.000
Budgeted variable costs	Rs. 12.000 for budgeted sales
Budgeted sales	Rs. 40.000
Actual fixed costs	Rs. 15.000
Actual variable costs	Rs. 16.200
Actual sales	Rs. 45.000

Solution : *See* Fig. 23.7 on next page.

Notes :

Profit for budgeted sales	=	Rs. 13,000
Profit for actual sales :		*Rs.*
Budgeted profit—Actual profit		16,500
		13,800
Profit variance		2,700

Note : The budgeted total cost line and actual cost line have been drawn on the variable costs for sales amount of Rs. 50,000. For 40,000 amount of sales, the variable costs are Rs. 12,000. Therefore, for Rs.

50,000, amount of sales, the variable cost should be Rs. 15,000, *i.e.*, at the rate of Rs. 3,000 for every Rs. 10,000 amount of sales. Hence, the total budgeted costs for Rs. 50,000 amount of sales should be Rs. 15,000 variable + Rs. 15,000 fixed costs, *i.e.*, total Rs. 30,000 as shown by budgeted total cost line. For actual sales amount of Rs. 45,000, variable costs are Rs. 16,200 considering Rs. 50,000 amount of sales, the actual respective costs will be Rs. 18,000 and the actual total cost will be Rs. 18,000 + 15,000 (fixed cost), *i.e.*, Rs. 33,000 which is represented by budgeted actual cost.

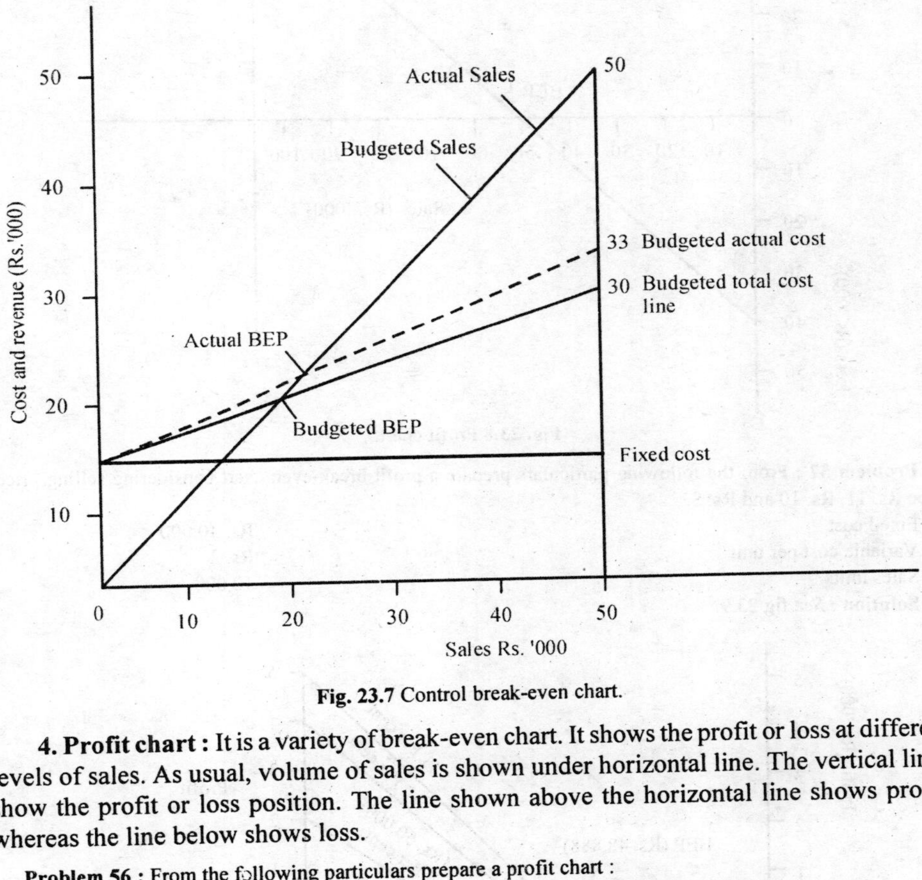

Fig. 23.7 Control break-even chart.

4. Profit chart : It is a variety of break-even chart. It shows the profit or loss at different levels of sales. As usual, volume of sales is shown under horizontal line. The vertical lines show the profit or loss position. The line shown above the horizontal line shows profit, whereas the line below shows loss.

Problem 56 : From the following particulars prepare a profit chart :

Fixed cost	Rs. 40,000
Variable cost	Rs. 2 per unit
Sales	10,000 units @ Rs. 10 per unit

Solution :

$$BEP = \frac{\text{Fixed cost}}{\text{Contribution per unit}}$$

$$= \frac{40,000}{8} = \text{Rs. } 5,000$$

For chart *see* Fig. 23.8 on next page.

5. Profit chart for different prices : This chart shows the effect on profit of charging different prices.

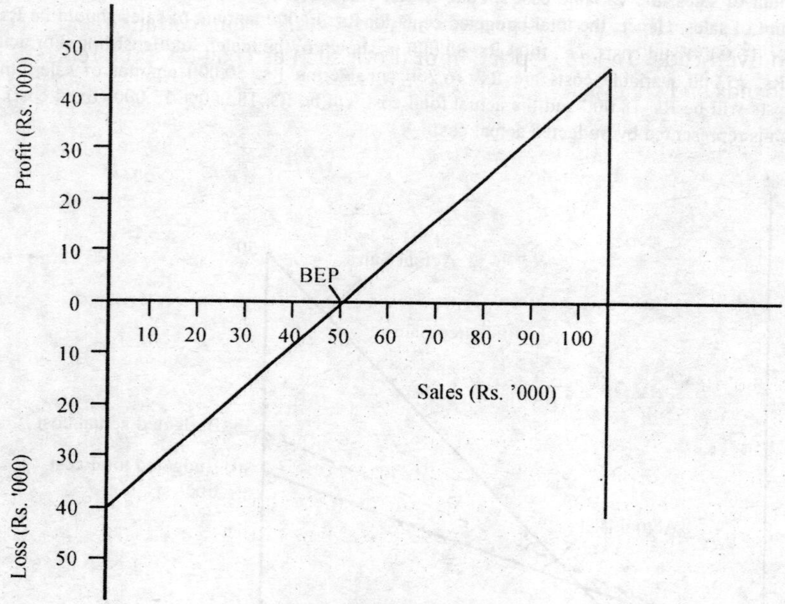

Fig. 23.8 Profit chart.

Problem 57 : From the following particulars prepare a profit break-even chart considering selling prices to be Rs. 11, Rs. 10 and Rs. 8.

Fixed cost	Rs. 40,000
Variable cost per unit	Rs. 2
Sales units	10,000

Solution : *See* fig 23.9..

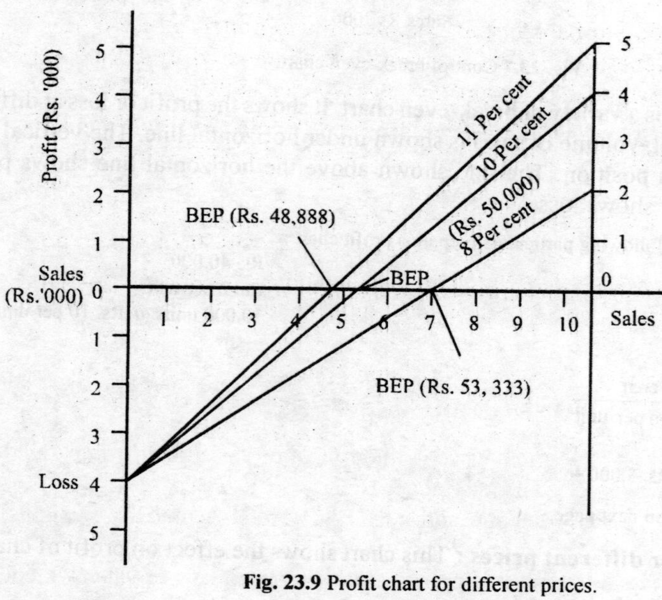

Fig. 23.9 Profit chart for different prices.

6. Analysis break-even chart : This chart portrays the components of variable cost such as direct material, direct labour and variable factory, administrative and selling and distribution overheads. The appropriation of profit such as taxation, preference dividend, equity dividends and creation of various reserves.

Problem 58 : From the following particulars prepare an analysis break-even chart :

Fixed cost	Rs. 10,000
Variable cost Rs. 30,000 divided into	
Direct labour	Rs. 5,000
Direct materials	Rs. 4,000
Factory overheads	Rs. 6,000
Administration overheads	Rs. 5,000
Selling overheads	Rs. 5,000
Distribution overheads	Rs. 5,000
Taxation Rs. 2,000 at maximum output decreasing in direct proportion to reduction in profit	
Preference dividend	Rs. 4,000
Equity dividend	Rs. 5,000

Solution : *See* Fig. 23.10.

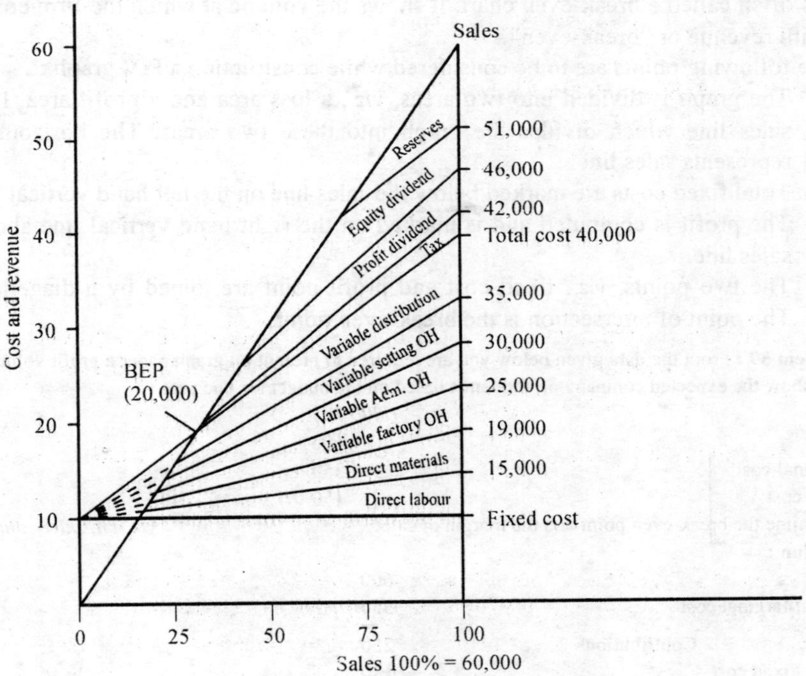

Fig. 23.10 Analysis break-even chart.

LIMITATIONS OF BREAK-EVEN CHARTS

1. The preparation of BEP involves separation of semi-variable cost into fixed and variable, which cannot be carried out accurately.
2. It is presumed that the revenue and cost can be represented by straight lines which may not always be true.
3. It assumes that a selling price is constant at different levels of sales which may

not be true. Selling price either increases or decreases due to decrease or increase in sales units.

4. Apportionment of fixed cost over a variety of products poses a problem.
5. It assumes that the business conditions may not change which is not true.
6. Under a break-even chart only one product is studied. It fails to provide the effects of various product mixes on profit.
7. Capital employed which is one of the important guiding factors determining profitability is ignored by the break-even chart.

PROFIT-VOLUME CHART OR P/V CHART

Vance in his *Theory and Techniques of Cost Accounting* defines a profit graph as a graph showing the amounts of fixed and variable costs and sales revenue at different volumes of operation. The name P/V chart has arised from the fact that the difference between the total of fixed on variable costs and the sales revenue at any volume gives the profit at that volume. Because of the importance of the point at which the total costs and revenue are equal the graph is often called a break-even chart. It shows the volume at which the firm covers all costs with revenue or "break-even".

The following points are to be considered while constructing a P/V graph :

(*a*) The graph is divided into two areas, *viz.*, a loss area and a profit area. It is the sales line which divides the graph into these two areas. The horizontal line represents sales line.

(*b*) Total fixed costs are marked below the sales line on the left hand vertical line.

(*c*) The profit is computed and is marked on the right hand vertical line above the sales line.

(*d*) The two points, *viz.*, fixed cost and profit point are joined by a diagonal line. The point of intersection is the break-even point.

Problem 59 : From the data given below you are required to present on graph paper a profit volume (P/V) graph to show the expected company performance based on the budget for one year :

	('000 Rs.)
Sales	600
Marginal cost	350
Fixed cost	150

Determine the break-even point and the margin of safety. (*ICWA, Inter., June 1990*)

Solution :

Sales	600
Less : Marginal cost	350
Contribution	250
Less : Fixed cost	150
Profit	100

Calculation of BEP (for verification)

$$\text{C/S Ratio} = \frac{\text{Contribution}}{\text{Sales}} = \frac{250}{600} = 41.66\%$$

$$\text{BEP} = \frac{\text{Fixed cost}}{\text{C/S ratio}} = \frac{1{,}50{,}000}{41.66} \times 100$$

$$= 3{,}60{,}000$$

Margin of safety = Sales – BES
6,00,000 – 3,60,000 = Rs. 2,40,000

For P/V graph *see* Fig. 23.11.

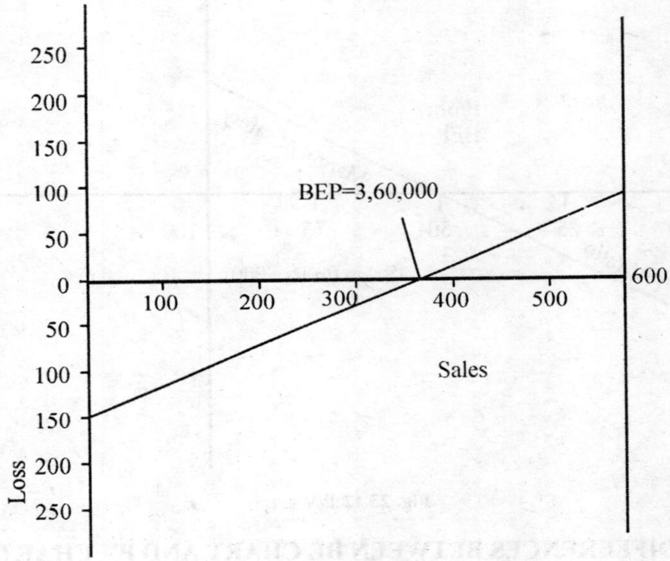

Fig. 23.11 P/V graph.

Problem 60 : From the particulars given below relating to Avinash (Pvt.) Co. Ltd. find out (*a*) P/V ratio, (*b*) BEP, (*c*) Margin of safety and (*d*) Plot P/V graph :

Sales	Rs. 1,00,000
Total cost	80,000
Fixed cost	20,000
Net profit	20,000

Solution :

$$\text{P/V Ratio} = \frac{\text{Sales} - \text{Variable expenses}}{\text{Sales}} \times 100$$

$$= \frac{1,00,000 - 60,000}{1,00,000} \times 100 = 40\%$$

$$\text{BEP} = \frac{\text{Fixed cost}}{\text{P / V ratio}}$$

$$= \frac{20,000}{40\%} = \text{Rs. } 50,000$$

$$\text{Margin of safety} = \frac{\text{Profit}}{\text{P/V ratio}}$$

$$= \frac{20,000}{40\%} = \text{Rs. } 50,000$$

For P/V graph *see* Fig. 23.12.

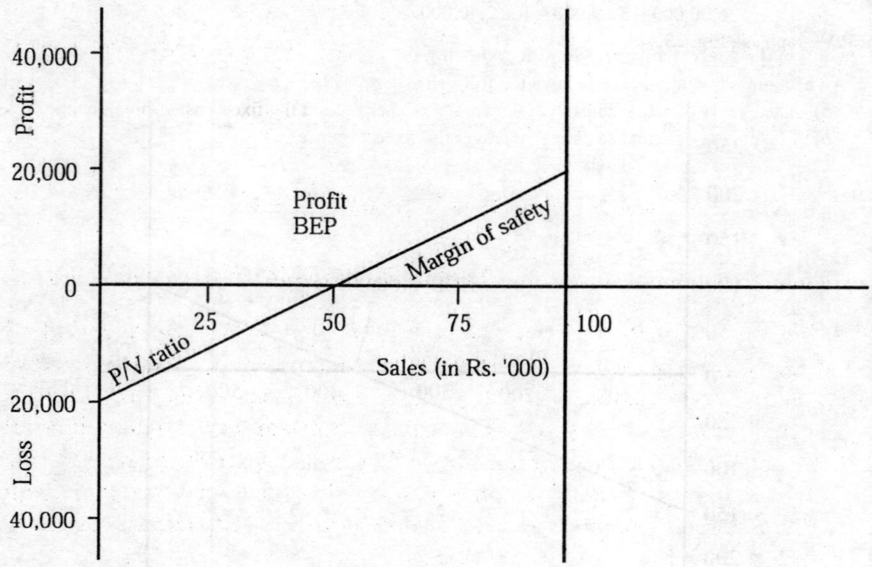

Fig. 23.12 P/V graph.

DIFFERENCES BETWEEN BE CHART AND PV CHART

P/V Chart	*BE Chart*
1. Only one line, *viz.*, profit line is shown.	1. Profit line is not shown instead sales and cost lines are shown.
2. Profit line starts below the horizontal line. Fixed cost incurred at zero point of production indicates loss. This loss is indicated below the horizontal line.	2. All lines are drawn above the horizontal line. The area up to the point of break-even shows loss and the area beyond the point shows profit.
3. The break-even point is found on the horizontal axis.	3. The break-even point is at the intersection of cost and sales lines.
4. Fixed cost is always considered as fixed and the ratio of sales and variable cost is again assumed as constant at different levels of sales.	4. The break-even chart can even measure break-even point when sales line is a curve because of price changes at different volumes of sales.
5. It is possible to measure the impact of individual products in a sales mix.	5. This chart can show the effect of a sales mix only in aggregate. For different items of sales, separate charts are to be prepared.
6. The chart shows profit and loss at different sales.	6. It can be drawn even to show the various elements of cost and profit appropriation.

QUESTIONS

I. Choose the correct answer from the following :

1. An accountant would typically have the following in mind when referring to the "margin of safety" :
   (*a*) The excess of actual sales over the variable expenses and the fixed cost at break-even.
   (*b*) The excess of actual sales revenue over the fixed expense.
   (*c*) The excess of actual sales over budgeted sales.
   (*d*) The excess of sales revenue over the variable cost. [ ]
2. Which of the following alternatives would generally decrease contribution margin per unit the most?
   (*a*) A 15% decrease in selling price.
   (*b*) A 15% increase in variable cost.
   (*c*) A 15% increase in selling price.
   (*d*) A 15% decrease in variable cost. [ ]
3. If fixed cost decrease while variable cost per unit remains constant, the new contribution margin in relation to the old will be
   (*a*) unchanged (*c*) higher
   (*b*) higher (*d*) intermediate [ ]
4. If a firm has a negative contribution margin, to reach break-even :
   (*a*) Sales volume must be increased. (*c*) Fixed cost must be decreased.
   (*b*) Sales volume must be decreased. (*d*) Fixed cost must be increased. [ ]
5. If total contribution margin is decreased by a given amount, operating profit would
   (*a*) Decrease by the same amount.
   (*b*) Decrease by more than the given amount.
   (*c*) Increase by the same amount.
   (*d*) Remain unchanged. [ ]
6. The break-even point would be increased by
   (*a*) a decrease in fixed cost.
   (*b*) an increase in contribution margin ratio.
   (*c*) an increase in variable cost.
   (*d*) a decrease in variable cost. [ ]
7. Given the following formula, which one represents the break-even sales level in units. P = Selling price per unit, F = Fixed cost, V = Variable cost per unit.
   (*a*) $\frac{F}{P-V}$ (*c*) $\frac{F}{V \div P}$
   (*b*) $\frac{P}{F \div V}$ (*d*) $\frac{F}{SP - V}$ [ ]
8. Which one of the following assumptions is not made in break-even analysis?
   (*a*) Volume is the only factor affecting cost.
   (*b*) No change between beginning and closing stock.
   (*c*) The sales mix is maintained as volume changes.
   (*d*) All of the above are assumptions sometimes required in break-even analysis. [ ]
9. The cost-volume-profit analysis underlying the conventional break-even chart does not assume that
   (*a*) prices will remain fixed.
   (*b*) production will equal sales.
   (*c*) some costs vary inversely with volume.
   (*d*) costs are linear and continuous over the relevant range. [ ]
10. The most useful information derived from a break-even chart is the
    (*a*) amount of sales revenue needed to cover enterprise variable cost.
    (*b*) amount of sales revenue needed to cover enterprise fixed costs.
    (*c*) relationship among revenues, variable cost and fixed costs at various levels of activity.
    (*d*) volume or output level at which the enterprise break-even. [ ]

11. The major assumption as to cost and revenue behaviour underlying conventional cost-volume-profit calculation is the
    (*a*) Constancy of fixed cost.
    (*b*) Variability of unit prices and efficiency.
    (*c*) Curvilinearity of relationships.
    (*d*) Linearity of relationships. [ ]
12. Given the following notations, what is the break-even sales level in units? SP = Selling price, FC = Fixed cost, VC = Variable cost per unit :
    (*a*) $\frac{SP}{FC \div VC}$
    (*b*) $\frac{VC}{SP - FC}$
    (*c*) $\frac{FC}{VC \div SP}$
    (*d*) $\frac{FC}{SP - FC}$ [ ]
13. P/V ratio is an indicator of :
    (*a*) the volume of sales.
    (*b*) the volume of profit.
    (*c*) the rate at which goods are sold.
    (*d*) all of the above. [ ]
14. When P/V ratio is 40% and sales value Rs. 10,000, the variable cost will be
    (*a*) Rs. 4,000
    (*b*) Rs. 6,000
    (*c*) Rs. 10,000
    (*d*) Variable cost cannot be calculated from the data given. [ ]
15. Cost-volume-profit analysis is most important for the determination of the
    (*a*) volume of operations necessary to break-even.
    (*b*) variable revenues necessary to equal fixed cost.
    (*c*) relationship between revenues and costs at various levels of operations.
    (*d*) sales revenue necessary to equal fixed cost. [ ]

II. Mark True or False in the space provided

1. At break-even point, contribution is equal to fixed cost. T/F
2. Margin of safety shows the excess of actual sales over budgeted saels. T/F
3. When P/V ratio is 50% and margin of safety is 40%, the net profit is 20% of sales. T/F
4. Margin of safety may come before or after the break-even point. T/F
5. Marginal costing and cost-volume-profit analysis is useful in profit planning. T/F
6. If the selling price per unit is assumed to be constant, total revenue will be proportionate to number of units sold. T/F
7. Decreasing the selling price decreases the break-even point. T/F
8. The contribution margin perunit is proportional to volume. T/F
9. It is impossible to obtein a break-even point with a negative contribution margin. T/F
10. To obtain the break-even point in units, the total fixed costs should be divided by the contribution margin ratio. T/F
11. The margin of safety is found by subtracting fixed cost from sales. T/F
12. If the variable cost per unit increase, the contribution margin ratio will increase. T/F
13. As production volume increases, the contribution margin rate increases. T/F
14. Accountants usually assume that variable costs are linear. T/F

III. Simple Questions

1. Define cost-volume-profit analysis.
2. State any four objectives of cost-volume-profit analysis.
3. State any four assumptions of cost-voiume-profit analysis.
4. State any four limitations of cost-volume-profit analysis.
5. Define break-even analysis.
6. Mention any four assumptions underlying break-even analysis.
7. What do you mean by margin of safety? What purpose does it?
8. What do you mean by angle of incidence?
9. Define profit-volume ratio.
10. State any usefulness of profit-volume ratio.
11. Distinguish between break-even chart and profit-volume chart.

IV. Short Answer Questions

1. What do you mean by break-even point? Discuss in detail. *(ICWA, Inter., Dec. 1990)*
2. What is meant by cost-volume-profit analysis? What are its limitations? Discuss the utility of determining cost-volume-profit relationship? *(Kakatiya University, M. Com., Aug. 1991)*
3. What do you understand by the term break-even analysis? Enumerate its assumptions and uses. *(Calicut University, B. Com., Oct. 1989)*
4. What is break-even point and state its usefulness to management? *(University of Kerala, B. Com., April 1990)*
5. What are the uses of cost-volume-profit analysis? Discuss the various ways of presenting the CVP relationship? *(Bangalore University, M. Com., May 1990)*

EXERCISES

Exercise-1: Following is the statement of cost and sales :

Fixed cost	Rs. 1,80,000
Variable costs	2,80,000
Sales	4,20,000

Determine how much sales should be increased in order to reach the break even point.

(Bangalore University, B.Com., November 1997)

[Answer : Additional sales needed to reach the break even point is Rs. 1,20,000.]

Exercise-2: From the following particulars, calculate the break even point in terms of both quantity and value.

Production in units	10,000
Sale price	Rs. 5 per unit
Variable costs	Rs. 20,000
Fixed cost	Rs. 12,000

(Kakatiya University, B.Com., 1997)

[Answer : BEP in value Rs. 20,000
BEP in units 4000 units]

Exercise-3 : The following information has been extracted from the accounts of Ramesh Equipments Ltd.

	Rs.
Sales	80,00,000
Variable cost	40,00,000
Fixed cost	24,00,000
Selling price per unit	40

Compute the following :

(a) The break even point

(b) If the price increase is 20% is followed by a reduction in volume by 25%, then the effect on net profit.

(Bangalore University, B.Com., October 1998)

[Answer : (a) Rs. 48,00,000
(b) A price increase by 20% followed by reduction in volume by 25% results in reduction in profit by Rs. 4,00,000.]

Exercise-4 : Given :

Fixed cost	Rs. 16,000
Profit earned	Rs. 4,000
Break even sales	Rs. 80,000

Find out actual sales.

(Osmania University, B.Com., March 1996)

[Answer : Actual sales Rs. 1,00,000.]

Exercise-5 : The following information is obtained from A Ltd. in a certain year.

Sales	Rs. 1,00,000
Variable cost	60,000
Fixed cost	30,000

(a) Find the P/V ratio and BEP
(b) Calculate the effect of
(i) 20% increase in selling price
(ii) 10% decrease in selling price

Exercise-6 : The following are obtained from the records of a factory :

	Rs.
Sales (4000 units @ Rs. 25 each)	1,00,000
Variable cost	72,000
Fixed expenses	16,800

Calculate (i) P/V ratio (ii) Break even point in rupees (iii) margin of safety (iv) It is proposed to reduce the selling price by 20% what extra units should be sold to obtain the same amount of profit?

(Bangalore University, B.B.M., November 1999)

[**Answer** : (i) P/V ratio = 28%
(ii) BEP = Rs. 60,000
(iii) M.S = Rs. 40,000
(iv) Extra units to be sold = 10,000 units]

Exercise-7 : S.N. Ltd., a multi-product company furnishes you the following data relating to the year 1996 :

	First half of the year *Rs.*	*Second half of the year* *Rs.*
Sales	45,000	50,000
Total cost	40,000	43,000

Assuming that there is no charge in prices and variable cost, and that the fixed expenses are incurred equally in the two half year period, calculate for the year 1996 : (a) The P/V ratio (b) Fixed expenses (c) Break-even sales and (d) Percentage of margin of safety. *(Calicut University, M.Com., March 1997)*

[**Answer** : (a) P/V Ratio, 40%, (b) Fixed cost Rs. 13,000 (Rs. 26,000 for the whole year) (c) BEP Rs. 65,000, (d) M.S = 31.58%.]

Exercise-8 : The selling price of a product was Rs. 200 per unit as against variable cost of Rs. 100 per unit. The total fixed costs were Rs. 2,00,000. Calculate the effect of a reduction in price by Rs. 40 on P/V ratio, Break-even Point and Margin of Safety. If 4000 units were produced and sold.

(University of Madras, B.Com., March 1995)

[**Answer** : BEP in units = 2000 units
P/V ratio = 50%
Revised P/V ratio = 37.5%
Revised BEP = Rs. 5,33,333
Margin of Safety = Rs. 1,06,667.]

24

DIFFERENTIAL COSTING

INTRODUCTION

Differential costing is a broader and more fundamental concept than marginal costing and hence has a much wider application. It helps in making appropriate decision by examining all the revenues and cost differences between alternatives. While marginal costing analyses the changes in only the variable costs, differential costing examines the differences in both variable and fixed costs. Hence this technique is more useful for those situations where fixed costs also differ and thus more appropriate for both short run and long run decisions.

Differential costs are costs that change in respect of an alternate course of action. The A.A.A. Committee on cost concepts and standards (*Accounting Review*, Vol. 27) defines it as "the increase or decrease in total cost or the change in specific elements of cost that result from any variation in operation". The alternative actions may be owing to change in sales, volume, price, product mix, or methods of production or change in decision. When two levels of activity are under review, differential cost is obtained by deducting the cost at one level from another level.

The technique used for analysing differential costs is known as differential costing. The ICMA terminology defines differential costing as "a technique used in the preparation of *ad hoc* information in which only cost and income differences between alternative courses of action are taken into consideration."

It is the process of determining how costs in particular and profit in general will be affected if one alternative is chosen over another.

The term "incremental cost" is used to denote differential cost when the increase in cost in due to increase in the level of production. Similarly the term "decremental cost" is used when the difference in cost is due to decrease in the level of production.

FEATURES AND IMPLICATIONS OF DIFFERENTIAL COSTING

The features of differential costing can be enumerated under the following points :

(*a*) It is expressed in total but not cost per unit.

(*b*) The data considered for such analysis are (*i*) cost, (*ii*) revenue, (*iii*) investment which are relevant to the problem under consideration.

(*c*) It is not a part of accounting though it is a form of budgeting. It is used only by the management to make decisions.

(*d*) The constant cost at different levels are ignored and only the differentials are considered. Absolute cost is not much importance in this analysis.

(*e*) Differentials are measured from a common position or level of activity.

(*f*) Where the difference between revenue and cost is highest, that course of action is adopted.

The differential costing is based on the implication that only the relevant cost, which will change as a result of the decision is useful for decision-making. Any costs which are not expected to alter, then they are irrelevant for decision-making. The following are the examples of cost that are irrelevant :

(*a*) Sunk cost, *i.e.*, those costs which have already been incurred are irrelevant.
(*b*) Book values of assets.
(*c*) Cost of fully utilised resources, *i.e.*, where a limiting factor exists it will be used to the full extent and will, therefore, cost the same whatever alternative is considered.
(*d*) *Fixed cost* : Any item which remains constant whichever alternative is chosen is not a differential cost and can be ignored in choosing alternatives.

MARGINAL VS. DIFFERENTIAL COSTING

The differential costing is similar to marginal costing under the following respects :

(*a*) Both the techniques are based on cost analysis for presenting the information to management.
(*b*) Costs are analysed on the basis of their behaviour under both the techniques.
(*c*) Both the techniques serve the same purpose of planning and decision-making by the management.
(*d*) Both the techniques will be same if the fixed costs remain same for alternative proposals.
(*e*) Differential cost resembles to economist's concept of marginal cost.

However, differential costing differs from marginal costing in the following respects :

(*a*) The scope of marginal costing is narrow, while that of differential costing is broader and hence it has wider applications.
(*b*) Marginal costing technique is useful in making decisions in the short run, whereas differential costing is useful in taking both short run and long run decisions where fixed costs do alter.
(*c*) Marginal cost is defined as the sum of all variable costs. Such a concrete definition is not possible under differential cost. It can at best be defined as an increase or decrease of total cost owing to rise or fall in production.
(*d*) Marginal costing presents cost information under contribution margin approach. Whereas differential costing can be presented both under absorption costing and marginal costing techniques.
(*e*) Under marginal costing technique the performance is judged by the "contribution" and P/V ratio. Whereas under differential costing, the performance is evaluated by comparing differential cost with incremental revenue.
(*f*) Marginal costing is a part of accounting system whereas differential cost analysis is not a part of accounting system. It may be a part of budgeting.
(*g*) Marginal cost is expressed in terms of cost per unit whereas differential cost is expressed in total.

APPLICATIONS OF DIFFERENTIAL COSTING

Differential costing techniques is used to solve the problems relating to the following :

(*a*) Make or buy decisions.
(*b*) Expanding the marketability of the products.

(*c*) Changing the product mix.
(*d*) Further processing of products.
(*e*) Changing the method of production.
(*f*) Introducing a new product line.
(*g*) Replacing mannual labour with mechanical labour.
(*h*) Fixation of selling price below the competitive price.
(*i*) Accepting or rejecting a new order.
(*j*) Dealing about the most profitable level of production.
(*k*) Shut down or continue operation.

Problem 1 (Determination of level of production) : A company's flexible budget reveals the following market conditions and costs :

Output in units	*Selling price per unit (Rs.)*	*total semi-fixed cost (Rs.)*	*Total variable cost (Rs.)*	*Total fixed cost (Rs.)*
60,000	12	1,50,000	4,18,000	1,42,000
1,20,000	11	1,50,000	8,18,000	1,42,000
1,80,000	10	1,70,000	12,78,000	1,42,000
2,40,000	9	1,70,000	15,78,000	1,42,000
3,00,000	8	2,00,000	17,78,000	1,42,000
3,60,000	7	2,00,000	19,02,000	1,42,000

(*a*) Prepare a schedule.showing the total differential costs and incremental revenue.
(*b*) At what level should the company set its level of production?
(*c*) What selling price should be established in order to obtain the most profitable operations for the year?

Solution :

(*a*) **Statement showing projected cost and revenue**

	Output (Units)					
	60,000	*1,20,000*	*1,80,000*	*2,40,000*	*3,00,000*	*3,60,000*
Fixed cost	1,42,000	1,42,000	1,42,000	1,42,000	1,42,000	1,42,000
Semi-fixed cost	1,50,000	1,50,000	1,70,000	1,70,000	2,00,000	2,00,000
Variable cost	4,18,000	8,18,000	12,78,000	15,78,000	17,78,000	19,02,000
Total cost	7,10,000	11,10,000	15,90,000	18,90,000	21,20,000	22,44,000
Differential cost		40,00,000 (Col 2 – Col 1)	4,80,000 (Col 3 – Col 2)	3,00,000 (Col 4 – Col 3)	2,30,000 (Col 5 – Col 4)	1,24,000 (Col 6 – Col 5)
Sales value	7,20,000	13,20,000	18,00,000	21,60,000	24,00,000	25,20,000
Marginal revenue	–	6,00,000	4,80,000	3,60,000	2,40,000	1,20,000

(*b*) As long as the increment in total revenue exceeds the differential costs, it pays to increase output, but as soon as the incremental revenue equals differential costs, it is no longer profitable to read the volume of production. In the above case the incremental revenue is about equal to differential costs at 3,00,000 output level and beyond that it is decreasing so the production should be fixed at this level (correctly between 3,00,000 and 3,60,000 levels).

(*c*) The sale price at this level is Rs. 8 per unit which should be adopted for the year, which would bring in maximum profit.

Problem 2 (Acceptance or rejection of an offer) : The following particulars are extracted from the books of Adarsh Co. Ltd. for the period ending 31st Dec., 1992 :

Capacity	*Unit cost (Rs.)*	*Unit selling price (Rs.)*
6,000	80	100
7,000	75	97
8,000	74	95
9,000	72	
10,000	71	

The firm is operating at 8,000 units capacity and has received an order for 2,000 units from an export market at a price of Rs. 70 per unit. Advise the company as to whether the export order should be accepted or not?

Solution : **Statement showing incremental cost and revenue**

Capacity	*Unit cost*	*Total cost*	*Incremental cost*	*Unit price*	*Total sales*	*Incremental revenue*
6,000	80	4,80,000		100	6,00,000	
7,000	75	5,25,000	45,000	97	6,79,000	79,000
8,000	74	5,92,000	67,000	95	7,60,000	8,000
9,000	72	6,48,000	56,000			
10,000	71	7,10,000	62,000			

At 8,000 level of output, the total sales revenue is Rs. 7,60,000 and the total cost is Rs. 5,92,000 leaving a profit of Rs. 1,68,000. The fact that this level of output leaves a profit means that the fixed costs have been recovered already. Hence we have to take only the incremental cost for further level of output. For an additional sales of 2,000 units the incremental cost is Rs. 7,10,000 – Rs. 5,92,000 = Rs. 1,18,000. The cost per unit, therefore, is $\frac{1,18,000}{2,000}$ = Rs. 59 for which the price quoted is Rs. 70 per unit. Hence the offer is to be accepted.

Problem 3 (Increasing production capacity) : A company is at present working at 90% of its capacity and producing 13,500 units per annum. It operates at flexible budgetary control system. The following figures are obtained from its budget :

	Capacity 90% (Rs.)	*Utilisation 100% (Rs.)*
Sales	15,00,000	16,00,000
Fixed	3,00,500	3,00,600
Semi-fixed expenses	97,500	1,00,500
Variable expenses	1,45,000	1,49,500
Units manufactured	13,500	15,000

Labour and material costs per unit are constant under the present conditions. Profit marging is 10%.

(*a*) You are required to determine the differential cost of producing 1,500 units by increasing capacity utilisation to 100 per cent.

(*b*) What would you recommend as an export price for these 1,500 units after considering that overseas prices are much lower than in land prices? (*ICWA, Inter., June 1992*)

Solution :

Sales at 90% capacity utilisation	15,00,000
Less : Profit (10%)	1,50,000
Cost of goods sold	13,50,000
Less : Expenses (fixed, semi-fixed and variable)	5,43,000
Cost of materials and labour	8,07,000

∴ Cost of materials and labour at 100% capacity utilisation

$$8,07,000 \times \frac{100}{90} = \text{Rs. } 8,96,667$$

Differential cost analysis will be as follows :

	90% Capacity *utilisation*	100% Capacity *utilisation*
Production (Units)	13,500	15,000
Materials and Labour (Rs.)	8,07,000	8,96,667
Variable expenses (Rs.)	1,45,000	1,49,500
Semi-fixed expenses (Rs.)	97,500	1,00,500
Fixed expenses (Rs.)	3,00,500	3,00,600
	13,50,000	14,47,267

(*a*) Differential cost = 14,47,267 – 13,50,000
= Rs. 97,267

(*b*) Minimum price per export = $\frac{97,267}{1,500}$ = Rs. 64.84 per unit.

At this price, there is no addition to revenue. Any price above Rs. 64.84 per unit may be accepted. A price below this may be considered, if other benefits, i.e. other than mere sales and revenue are likely to accrue. It is assumed that no capital investment is necessary and no export changes have to be incurred and that the export price will have no effect on the home market where the product will continue to be sold at the old price.

Problem 4 (Equipment replacement) : A factory engaged in the manufacture of electronic goods has a ten-year old equipment depreciated on straight-line basis. The useful life of the equipment was estimated to be 20 years with a residual value of Rs. 3 lakhs (original cost of the equipment being Rs. 23 lakhs). The output of the equipment is 1,200 units per hour.

The management now proposes to instal a new equipment worth Rs. 50 lakhs which has an estimated life of 15 years and a residual value of Rs. 5 lakhs. The payment terms for the new equipment include a part exchange provision of Rs. 6 lakhs in respect of the existing equipment. The output of the new equipment is 3,000 units per hour.

Other comparative annual cost data relating to the two equipments are as under :

	Existing equipment (Rs.)	*New equipment (Rs.)*
Wages	1,00,000	1,20,000
Repairs and maintenance	20,000	52,000
Consumables	3,20,000	4,80,000
Power	1,20,000	1,50,000
Allocation of fixed cost	60,000	80,000
Total hours run per year	2,400	2,400

You are required to prepare a comparative schedule showing total conversion cost as well as cost per 1,000 units after considering interest @ 10% on net cash outflow for procuring the new equipment and also for providing for the yearly recovery of the loss suffered in the transaction. (*ICWA, Inter., Dec. 1991*)

Solution : **Comparative statement of cost of equipment**

	Existing equipment	*New equipment*
Capital cost of equipment including cost of installation	23,00,000	50,00,000
Less : Residual value	3,00,000	5,00,000
	20,00,000	45,00,000
Less : Depreciation written off	10,00,000	–
	10,00,000	45,00,000

Comparative statement of operation cost of equipment

Annual depreciation		
New equipment	–	3,00,000
Old equipment	1,00,000	70,000

Interest on capital (net cash outflow)	–	4,40,000
Wages	1,00,000	1,20,000
Repairs and maintenance	20,000	52,000
Consumables	3,20,000	4,80,000
Power	1,20,000	1,50,000
Allocation of fixed expenses	60,000	80,000
	7,20,000	16,92,000
Total hours run per annum	2,400	2,400
Operating cost per hour (Rs.)	300	705
Output per hour (Units)	1,200	3,000
Operating cost per 1,000 unit (Rs.)	250	235

Therefore, there is a net saving in cost of Rs. 15 per 1,000 units.

Working Note 1 : Depreciation on new equipment

$$\text{Depreciation} = \frac{\text{Original cost} - \text{Residual value}}{\text{Estimated life}}$$

$$= \frac{45,00,000}{15} = 3,00,000$$

Working Note 2 : Depreciation (yearly recovery) on loss on sale of existing equipment

$$= \frac{\text{Book value of existing equipment} - \text{Part exchange value}}{\text{Residual life of existing equipment}}$$

$$= \frac{\text{Rs, } 13,00,000 - \text{Rs. } 6,00,000}{10 \text{ years}} = \text{Rs. } 70,000$$

Working Note 3 : Interest is calculated on net cash outflow in procuring the new equipment is Rs. 44,00,000 (cost of old equipment Rs. 50 lakhs less part exchange value of Rs. 6 lakhs).

Problem 5 (Evaluating profitability of different products) : *G* Ltd. is a process industry which manufactures three joint products, *viz., A, B* and *C*. The joint costs of production are Rs. 4,80,000 and sales are :

A = 30,000 units @ Rs. 6 per unit
B = 10,000 units @ Rs. 20 per unit
C = 20,000 units @ Rs. 12 per unit

It is possible to adopt two alternative production programmes after completion of the joint products. First, product *C* can further processed, which will create a new product *D*. This additional processing will cost Rs. 1,60,000 p.a., but the 20,000 units of product *D* can be sold for Rs. 24 per unit. Secondly, processing of product *C* need not be continued further, but the resources which could have been used in converting product *C* to product *D* can be used to produce an additional product *E*. The cost of this programme would be Rs. 60,000 per annum, but sales of *E* would be obtained of 5,000 units at Rs. 16 per unit. Evaluate the two alternative production programmes.

Solution : **Statement showing incremental cost**

Details	*Proposal I*	*Total*	*Proposal II*	*Total*	*Incremental cost*
Sales					
A	1,80,000		1,80,000		
B	2,00,000		2,00,000		
C	–		2,40,000		
D	4,80,000		–		
E	–	8,60,000	80,000	7,00,000	1,60,000
Costs					
A, *B*, C	4,80,000		4,80,000		

D	1,60,000		–		
E	–	6,40,000	60,000	5,40,000	1,00,000
Profit		2,20,000		1,60,000	60,000

Statement of profit for the opportunity foregone

Sales of *D*			4,80,000
Less : Costs of *D*			1,60,000
			3,20,000
Sales foregone if *D* produced	*C* =	2,40,000	
	E =	80,000	
		3,20,000	
Costs foregone if *D* produced	*E* =	60,000	2,60,000
		Profit	60,000

Problem 6 (Dropping or continuing an area for effecting sales) : *X* Co. Ltd. produces and sells three products : *A*, *B* and *C*. These products are sold in a local market and in a regional market. At the end of the first quarter of the year 1993, the following income statement has been prepared :

	Total	*Local*	*Regional*
Sales Revenue	13,00,000	10,00,000	3,00,000
Cost of goods sold	10,10,000	7,75,000	2,35,000
Gross margin	2,90,000	2,25,000	65,000
Marketing cost	1,05,000	60,000	45,000
Administrative cost	52,000	40,000	12,000
Cost production and sales	1,57,000	1,00,000	57,000
Operating profit	1,33,000	1,25,000	8,000

The management has expressed special concern with the regional market because of the extremely poor return on sales. This market was entered a year ago because of excess capacity. It was originally believed that the return on sales would improve with time, but after a year, no noticeable improvement can be seen from the results as reported in the above quarterly statement.

In attempting to decide whether to eliminate the regional market, the following information has been gathered :

	Product A	*Product B*	*Product C*
Sales revenue (Rs.)	5,00,000	4,00,000	4,00,000
Variable cost as a percentage to sales	60%	70%	60%
Variable marketing cost as a percentage to sales	3%	2%	2%

	Sales by market	
	Local	*Regional*
A	Rs. 4,00,000	Rs. 1,00,000
B	Rs. 3,00,000	Rs. 1,00,000
C	Rs. 3,00,000	Rs. 1,00,000

All administrative cost and fixed manufacturing costs are common to the three products and the two markets and are fixed for the period. Remaining marketing costs are fixed for the period and separable by market. All fixed costs are based upon a prorated yearly amount.

Required :

(*a*) Assuming there are no alternative used for the *X* Co. Ltd.'s present capacity, would you recommend dropping the regional market.

(*b*) Prepare the quarterly income statement showing contribution margin by products.

(*c*) It is believed that a new product can be ready for sale next year. The new product can be produced

increase fixed cost by Rs. 10,000 per quarter. What must be the minimum contribution margin per quarter for the new product to make the changeover financially feasible.

Solution :

(*a*) The regional market should not be dropped as this market not only covers all the variable costs and separable fixed costs but also gives net market contribution of Rs. 65,000 towards the common fixed cost

Sales = Rs. 3,00,000

Variable manufacturing cost = (6 × 1,00,000) + (7 × 1,00,000) + (6 × 1,00,000)
= 1,90,000

Marketing costs = Rs. 45,000

(*b*) **Statement showing quarterly income statement**

In thousands

		A	*B*	*C*	*Total*
Sales (Rs.)		500	400	400	1,300
Less :	Variable cost				
	Manufacturing	300	280	240	820
	Marketing	15	8	8	31
	Total variable cost	315	288	248	851
	Contribution margin	185	112	152	449
Less :	Fixed costs :				
	Manufacturing				190
	Marketing				74
	Administrative				52
	Total fixed cost				316
	Operating profit				133

(*c*) The new product must contribute at least Rs. 1,62,000 (Rs. 1,52,000 + Rs. 10,000) per quarter so as not to leave the company worse off when product *C* is replaced.

Problem 7 (Acceptance of rejection of an export order) : *MX* Ltd. having an installed capacity of 1,00,000 units of a product is currently operating at 70% utilisation. At current levels of input prices the FOB unit cost (after credit for applicable export incentives) works out as follows :

Capacity utilisation%	*FOB unit cost (Rs.)*
70	97
80	92
90	87
100	82

The company has received three foreign offers from different sources as under :

Source *A*	5,000 units @ Rs. 54 per unit FOB
Source *B*	10,000 units @ Rs. 52 per unit FOB
Source *C*	10,000 units @ Rs. 51 per unit FOB

Advise the company as to whether any or all the export orders should be accepted or not.

Solution : **Statement showing differential cost**

Capacity	*Production (Units)*	*FOB unit cost (Rs.)*	*Installed total cost*	*Differential cost*	*Per unit differential cost*
70	70,000	97	67,90,000	–	–
80	80,000	92	73,60,000	5,70,000	57
90	90,000	87	78,30,000	4,70,000	47
100	1,00,000	82	82,00,000	3,70,000	37

Statement showing gain or loss on accepting various export orders

Source of export order	*Export order in units*	*Capacity utilisation*	*Differential cost per unit*	*Differential cost Total*	*FOB price per unit*	*Sales revenue from the export*	*Gain or loss*
A	5,000	75	57	2,85,000	55	2,75,000	(10,000)
B	10,000	85	5,000 @ 57 5,000 @ 47	5,20,000	52	5,20,000	NIL
C	10,000	95	5,000 @ 47 5,000 @ 37	4,20,000	51	5,10,000	90,000
	25,000	95%		12,25,000		13,05,000	80,000

From the above analysis it can be said that when all the three export orders are accepted, the company will make a profit of Rs. 80,000. But accepting only source *A* and *B* orders will give a loss of Rs. 10,000.

Problem 8 (Accepting an order at a lower selling price) : The overhead expenses of a factory, producing a single article at different operating levels are as follows :

Operating level capacity	*Works overhead (Rs.)*
80%	36,000
100%	40,000
120%	50,000
60%	33,000

The factory is currently working at 60% operating level and its annual sales amount is Rs. 1,44,000.

Selling prices have been based on 100% capacity and have the following relationship with costs at this level :

Factory cost	66.67% of sales value
Price cost	75% of factory cost
Adm. and selling expenses (of which 75% is variable)	20% of sales value.

The management receives an offer for carrying out some work for another company valued at Rs. 33,000 per annum which will take up 40% of capacity. The price cost for the work is estimated at Rs. 20,000. There will be an addition to administration expenses of Rs. 1,500 per annum.

The sales manager estimates that the sales of the company's own product will increase to 80% capacity by the time new order materialises.

Calculate the profit on current production. Give your views, supported by figure, on the advisability of taking on the new work. (*Sri Venkateshwara University, M. Com., Sept. 1988*)

Solution :

Statement showing profitability

			100%	*60%*
Sales			2,40,000	1,44,000
Less : Cost sales :				
Prime cost	1,20,000	72,000		
Works overhead	40,000	33,000		
Factory cost	1,60,000	1,05,600		
Adm. and selling	48,000	33,600	2,08,000	1,38,600
		Profit	32,000	5,400

At 100% capacity :

Factory cost 66.67% of sales value or $\frac{2}{3}$ of sales

$$\frac{2}{3} \times 2,40,000 = \text{Rs. } 1,60,000$$

Prime cost = –75% of factory cost

$$\frac{75}{100} \times 1,60,000 = \text{Rs. } 1,20,000$$

Factory overhead at 100% level given in the problem is 40,000

Administration and selling overhead

$$\frac{20}{100} \times 2,40,000 = \text{Rs. } 48,000$$

of 48,000, 75% is variable, *i.e.*, Rs. 36,000 and Rs. 12,000 is fixed.

At 60% capacity :

Prime cost is 60% of Rs. 1,20,000 = Rs. 72,000

Works overhead is Rs. 33,000 as is given

Administration and selling overhead

Variable 75% and fixed Rs. 12,000

Statement showing profitability for new work

Capacity	*80%*	*40% Additional*	*Total 100%*
Sales	1,92,000	33,000	2,25,000
Less : Cost of sales			
Prime cost	96,000	20,000	1,16,000
Works overhead	36,000	14,000	50,000
Factory overhead	1,32,000	34,000	1,66,000
Adm. and selling	40,800	6,450	47,250
	1,72,800	40,450	2,13,250
Profit or loss	19,200	7,450	11,750

As profit is reduced by Rs. 7,450 additional order is not profitable.

Problem 9 (Expanding the marketability of the product) :

The following extracts are taken from sales budget of a company for the current year

	(Rs. '000)
Sales : 40,000 units @ Rs. 25 per unit	1,000
Selling costs :	
Advertising	100
Salesmen salaries	80
Travelling expenses	50
Rent of sales office	10
Others	10
	250

The management is considering a proposal to establish a new market in the eastern region in the next year. It is proposed to increase the advertising expenditure by 25% and appoint an additional sales supervisor at a salary of Rs. 30,000 per year to establish a market. This will involve additional travelling, and the travelling expenses shall increase by 10%.

Target annual sales volume at the existing selling price for the new market is 10,000 units. The estimated variable cost of production is Rs. 12 per unit. Should the company try to establish the new market?

(C.S., Inter., Dec. 1997)

Solution :

Statement showing profit

	Current cost and Revenue	*Budget cost and Revenue*	*Incremental cost and Revenue*
Sales (units)	40,000	50,000	10,000
		(Rs. in '000)	

Sales salaries	80		110		30	
Travelling expenses	50		55		5	
Rent	10		10		–	
Others	10		10		–	
	250		310		60	
Variable cost of	480		600		120	
Production		730		910		180
Profit		270		340		70

On the incremental sale, return is 28% of additional sales value and is higher than the current return. Hence the proposal is acceptable.

QUESTIONS

Simple Questions

1. Define "differential cost".
2. Define differential costing.
3. State any four characteristics of differential costing.
4. State any four implications of differential costing.
5. State any four similarities between marginal costing and differential costing.
6. State any four dissimilarities between marginal costing and differential costing.
7. Mention any eight uses of differential costing technique to management of an industry.

EXERCISES

Exercise 1 (Acceptance or rejection of an offer) : A company currently operating at full capacity, manufactures and sells, saucepans at Rs. 2 each current volume is 1,00,000 pans per annum with the following cost structure.

Operating statement for the year 1992

Sales 1,00,000 @ Rs. 2		Rs. 2,00,000
Less : Materials cost	50,000	
Labour cost	80,000	Rs. 1,30,000
	Contribution	70,000
Less : Fixed cost		30,000
	Profit	Rs. 40,000

An opportunity has arisen to supply 30,000 pans per annum at Rs. 1.80.

Acceptance of this order would incur extra materials cost of Rs. 15,000 per annum and fixed cost of Rs. 8,000 per annum for the hire for additional machinery and the payment of an overtime premium of 20% for the extra direct labour required.

Should this order be accepted?

[*Answer :* The incremental revenue generated by accepting order is Rs. 2,200. So the order is to be accepted.]

Exercise 2 (Equipment replacement) : *P* Ltd. is considering the replacement of machine *A* by a new machine *B*. Comparative data are as follows :

	Existing machine A	*Proposed machine B*
Purchase price	Rs. 2,000	6,000
Disposal value now	600	
Disposal value in one year's time	450	
Rate of depreciation	10%	10%
Estimated scrap value (Rs.)		500

Indirect labour and materials	1,000	1,000
Scrap losses	200	100
Direct wages	2,000	1,000

[*Answer :* Saving is Rs. 700 per annum. So new machine is to bought.]

Exercise 3 (Acceptance or rejection of order) : A company has a capacity of producing 1,00,000 units of a certain product in a month. The sales department reports that the following schedule of sale prices is possible :

Volume of production	*Selling price per unit (Re.)*
60%	0.90
70%	0.80
80%	0.75
90%	0.67
100%	0.61

The variable cost of manufacture between these levels is Re. 0.15 per unit and fixed cost Rs. 40,000.

(*a*) Prepare a statement showing incremental revenue and differential cost of each stage. At which volume of production will the profit be maximum?

(*b*) If there is a bulk offer at Re. 0.50 per unit of the balance capacity over the maximum profit volume for export and the price quoted will not affect the internal sale, will you advise this bid?

[*Answer :* As the incremental revenue is higher than differential cost up to the level of 80%, the level of production should be set out 80%.

The bulk offer for export for the balance capacity of 2,000 units (over and above 80%) at 50 paise per unit will add Rs. 7,000 to profit. Hence the offer for export is to be accepted.]

...

25

BUDGETARY CONTROL

INTRODUCTION

A budget is a quantitative expression of a plan of action prepared in advance of the period to which it relates. It may be prepared for the entire organisation or for various departments or for various functions involved in that organisation. Budget is a means of translating the overall objectives of the business into detailed feasible plan of action.

The concept of "budget" is being made use of by every individual who undertake a work involving expenditure. While some express it orally others put it in written form. For example, a person who wants to go on a holiday tour will prepare a budget involving expenditure on fares, boarding, lodging, purchasing, etc. After returning, he will compare the actual expenses incurred with budgeted expenses to know whether he spent more or less as compared to budgets and if so what factors were responsible for it. This enables him to increase or decrease his budget for the next year.

In the same way, every business undertakes to budget its expenditure for utilising the available funds more judiciously. Similarly, to ensure proper utilisation of scarce raw materials and other factors of production, the management of every business will prepare a budget relating to material, labour, production and various expenditure. This enables in proper planning of all activities, there co-ordination and finally controlling such activities. In this process it enables the management to know the performance of business for a given period of time.

BUDGET AND BUDGETARY CONTROL

Definition of a Budget

The ICMA terminology defines a budget as "a plan quantified in monetary items, prepared and approved prior to a defined period of time, usually showing planned income to be generated and/or expenditure to be incurred during that period and the capital to be employed to attain a given objective".

George R. Terry defines budget as "an estimate of future needs arranged according to an orderly basis, covering some or all the activities of an enterprise for a definite period of time".

Definition of Budgetary Control

According to F.H. Rowland and W.H. Barr, budgetary control is a "Tool of management used to plan, carryout and control the operations of the business".

In the words of C.L. Van Sickle, "a budgetary control system is a carefully worked out financial plan, including the procedure involved in its operations for conducting the various divisions of a business for the ultimate purpose of earning a profit".

The ICMA terminology defines budgetary control as "the establishment of budgets relating the responsibilities of executives to the requirements of a policy and the continuous comparison of actual with budgeted result either to secure by individual action the objective of that policy or to provide a basis for its revision".

An analysis of this definition reveal the following important points.

(*a*) **Executive responsibility :** It means that every manager has to do his job directed towards the overall objects of the business, *i.e.*, the policy. In other words, every manager is responsible for attaining the task delegated to him and thereby the ultimate object of the business.

(*b*) **The requirements of a policy :** The budget is a statement of policy relating to the position of business and plans to attain it. The business has to establish certain goals and necessary actions must be taken to achieve those aims. This is essential for proper growth and development of the business and for efficient utilisation of labour force and other assets.

(*c*) **Comparison of actual with budgeted results :** This facilitates control over the planned activities. The actual result is measured and compared with budgets. When there exists any unfavourable difference, management can take remedial steps.

(*d*) **The revision of policy :** The policy may have to be revised in order to make the best use of prevailing situation after considering unfavourable factors.

The budgetary control is exercised by applying the following steps :

1. **Preparation of the budget :** The process of preparing the budget will be explained under the heading "budget organisation".

2. **Publishing the budget :** This implies informing each executive what is expected of him. The publishing of the budget is most important, as no system is able to work unless the people concerned with it understand and are prepared to make it work.

3. **Measuring the results :** This implies the measurement of actual results achieved in order to know whether they are as per plan or otherwise.

4. **Comparing the results with the budget :** The comparison of actual results with the budget enables to know the efficiency or otherwise of the activity.

5. **Reporting the results of the above activity :** This is done by means of budgetary control statements, which enable the budget officer to know whether the objectives set out in the budget are being fulfilled and if not, in which areas attention should be concentrated.

6. **Correcting the unfavourable variances :** Necessary steps are then taken to avoid the occurrence of unfavourable variances. This is the function of the departmental manager or the supervisor. The budgetary control statements will assist as tools to the manager in correcting the unfavourable differences.

OBJECTIVES OF BUDGETARY CONTROL

1. Planning and Co-ordination

Budgeting involves preparation of a detailed operational plans to achieve the objectives of a business. The success of every business depends upon the planning of activities and budgeting forces planning to become more effective. As budgets are prepared covering all the activities and departments of a business, it also serves as a means of co-ordinating the efforts of all concerned in such a way that every department contributes towards the overall plan. The summary of all such plan is known as master plan. The budget forces every departmental manager to establish relationship with other departments and contribute to the achievement of objectives.

2. Clarification of Authority and Responsibility

Budgeting enables the superior to delegate the authority to his subordinates. This also clarifies the responsibility of each manager who can be held accountable if the targets are not reached. Thus budgeting facilitates management by exception.

3. Communication

Since all levels of management are involved in the preparation of budget, it facilitates communication process to become more effective. The objectives of the business, problems involved in achieving them, and finalisation of budgets are all promptly communicated. It also co-ordinates the various functions such as sales, purchases and production more efficiently.

4. Motivation

The preparation of budgets by middle and lower management against which performance can be judged serves as a good motivation for them.

5. Control

The control over various activities is achieved by comparing the achievements with the targets. If there are any deviations, the causes for the same is investigated and remedial action taken.

ESSENTIAL REQUIREMENTS OF BUDGETARY CONTROL

The essential requirements of a budgetary control system as quoted by Robert I Dickey are as follows :

1. Budget must have the complete cooperation of the chief executive.
2. The ultimate realisation of the maximum amount of profit should always be kept uppermost.
3. Responsibility for the preparation of the estimate should rest on those individuals responsible for performance.
4. The budget must be realistic and the goals attainable.
5. A budget committee should be established consisting of the budget director, the chief executive officer, and the executives of the various divisions of the organisation.
6. The budget should cover all phases of operations.
7. Budgeting should be continuous.
8. Periodic reports should be prepared promptly, comparing budget and actual results.
9. The accounting system must be adequate.
10. A good organisation must be developed.

ADVANTAGES AND LIMITATIONS OF BUDGETARY CONTROL

Advantages

The important advantages of budgetary control are as follows :

1. It helps the process of planning by reducing it to concrete numerical goals. Through the budgets, the executives know what they are to produce or sell, how much they can spend, how much income to expect and so on.

2. It provides an effective means by which top management can delegate authority and responsibility without sacrificing its overall control. Limits for each department or division are laid down in the budget.
3. It keeps expenditure under check and constantly reminds employees and management of the targets and goals to be achieved. It helps in the cautious utilisation of resources and promotion of efficiency.
4. As a control devise, it supplies the means of checking results and comparing performance, of revealing weaknesses and making corrections.
5. The budget is not merely an instrument of planning but also a tool of co-ordination. It brings together the activities of various sections, departments and divisions in an overall perspective.
6. It helps in determining the policies of the factory.
7. It gives complete information in advance regarding the amount of capital needed for the budget period.
8. It gives the idea of where executive action is required.
9. It aids in measuring performance of each department of the factory.
10. It promotes cooperation among the different executives for determining future plans.
11. It acts as a control tool for administration.
12. It centralises management control.

Limitations of Budgetary Control

1. The budget is always based on estimates. The success or failure of a budget, to a large extent, depends upon the accuracy of estimates. The estimates cannot be accurately made in this dynamic world, although many statistical techniques are available.
2. To evolve a budgetary control system, normally, it takes several years as it has to be tried, improved, and discarded, depending upon the changing circumstances.
3. The success of budgetary control depends upon the enthusiastic participation of all levels of management. But it is difficult to secure the wholehearted cooperation of all in a factory.
4. Budgeting is only a tool of management but it cannot replace management.
5. It may be difficult to instal a system of budgetary control in small factories owing to expenditure involved.

ORGANISATION FOR BUDGETARY CONTROL

A sound organisation is essential for an effective budgeting programme. It ensures cooperation from all levels of management. The organisation should facilitate control of all elements of cost. The essential ingredients of a sound organisation are as follows :

1. Organisation Chart

An organisation chart depicts the functional responsibilities of every manager. It shows the relative position of every manager and his relationship with others. A typical organisation chart is shown below :

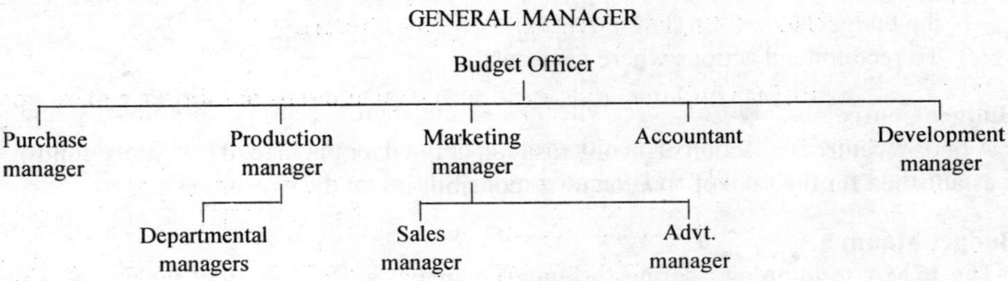

Fig. 25.1. Budgetary control organisation chart.

From the chart it is clear that, the entire responsibility of budgetary control process lies with general manager. He entrusts the authority to implement the budget programme to the budget officer. He shall co-ordinate the budgets prepared by all the departmental managers.

2. Budget Officer

A budget officer is a person who is nominated by the general manager to look after the functions of budgeting. He is responsible to general manager for completing the budgeting process. He acts as co-ordinator and adviser integrating the budgets prepared by the departmental managers so as to get a master budget. His functions are as follows :

(*a*) Issuing instructions to departments regarding requirements, dates of submission of data, etc.
(*b*) Providing historical information to departmental managers to help them in their forecasting.
(*c*) Receiving and checking budget estimates.
(*d*) Suggesting possible revisions.
(*e*) Discussing difficulties with managers.
(*f*) Ensuring that budgets are received in agreed time.
(*g*) Preparing budget summaries.
(*h*) Charting the departmental estimates on a master plan.
(*i*) Submitting budgets to the committee and furnishing explanations on particular points.
(*j*) Informing the departmental managers of any revisions made in their budgets by the committee.
(*k*) Preparing the final master plan approved by the committee.
(*l*) Co-ordinating all budget work.

3. Budget Committee

It serves as a co-ordinating authority of the budgeting process. It is concerned with resolving difficulties or disputes which may arise among functional heads and to take decisions so as to alter production, price, etc. The budget officer will submit the draft master budget to the committee for consideration after which it is finally approved by board of directors. The budget committee will functions in an advisory capacity and it performs the following functions :

(*a*) To receive and review individual budget estimates.
(*b*) To suggest revisions.
(*c*) To decide on general policies affecting more than one primary department.
(*d*) To revise and approve the budgets.

(*e*) To receive and consider budget reports showing actual results compared with the budget.

(*f*) To recommend actions where necessary.

4. Budget Centre

A budget centre is a section of an organisation defined for the sake of budgetary control. It is established for the sake of fixation of responsibilities on the executives.

5. Budget Mannual

The ICMA terminology defines a budget mannual as "a document which sets out standing instructions governing the responsibilities of persons and the procedures, forms and records relating to the preparation and use of budgets". It serves as a basis of guidance and information about budgeting process. It is more like an instructional mannual about the way budget operates. Lucey, in his book *Costing* sets out the contents of a budget mannual as under :

Foreword :

Preferably by managing director

- Objectives/explanation of the budgetary process.
- Explanation of budgetary control.
- Objectives of each stage of the budgetary process.
- Relationship to long term planning.

Organisation structure and responsibilities :

- Structure of the organisation showing titles, responsibilities and relationships.
- Titles and names of current budget holders.

Main budgets and relationship :

- Outline of all main budgets and their accounting relationships.
- Explanation of key budgets (master budget, cash budget)

Budget development :

- Budget committee, membership and terms of reference.
- Sequence of budget preparation.
- Time-table for budget preparation and publication.

Accounting procedure :

- Name and terms of reference of the budget officer.
- Coding lists.
- Sample forms.
- Time-table for accounting procedures, production of reports, closing date.

6. Chart of Accounts

It refers to maintaining a systematic set of accounting books which should be able to record and analyse the information required. A chart of accounts may be maintained separately for every budget centre. In simple words, a chart of accounts denotes accounting structure useful for budgetary control.

7. Budget Period

It is a period relating to which a budget is prepared. A budget period may relate to a short term period or a long term period. Some time these period may relate even to a month for monitoring and control of budgets. It is always desirable to have a short-term budget period excepting those functions which may prolong for a longer period as for example, research and development. The duration of the budget period depends upon type of business, the length of manufacturing cycle, the ease or difficulty of forecasting future market conditions and so on. The budget period may be accordingly short-term budget period or long-term budget period.

The short-term budget period may cover a period of 3 months to 1 year. According to Matz-Curry and Frank (*Cost Accounting*) the following factors should be considered in determining the length of budget period :

(*a*) The budget period should be long enough to complete production of the various products.

(*b*) For a business of a seasonal nature, the budget period should cover at least one entire seasonal cycle.

(*c*) The budget period should be long enough to allow for the financing of production well in advance of actual needs.

(*d*) Major operations and drastic changes in plant layout or manufacturing methods must be planned far in advance to determine financial requirements.

(*e*) The budget period should coincide with the financial accounting period to compare actual results with budget estimates.

A long-term budget may be taken to mean a budget prepared for a period of more than a year. Such a budget is best suited for research and development activities, long-term capital investment, financial and profit planning. It is mostly based on probability of events. It is very much affected by risk factor.

8. Key Factor

The factor which governs the quantity which is manufactured or sold is known as key factor. The ICMA terminology defines a key factor as "a factor which at any time or over a period may limit the activity of an entity often one where there is a shortage or difficulty of supply". This will have an adverse effect over the achievement of budget. Therefore it must be identified and its effect on each of the budget is to be carefully considered during the preparation of budget. Key factor can be changed by the management action. For example, when production process is hampered by plant capacity, the purchase of additional plant will allow increase in production. The following are considered as key factors :

(*a*) *Materials :* (*i*) Availability of supply.
(*ii*) Restrictions imposed by licences, quotas, etc.

(*b*) *Labour :* (*i*) General shortage.
(*ii*) Shortage in certain key processes.

(*c*) *Plant :* (*i*) Insufficient capacity due to lack of capital.
(*ii*) Insufficient or lack of space.
(*iii*) Insufficient or lack of market.
(*iv*) Bottlenecks in certain key processes.

(*d*) *Sales :* (*i*) Low market demand.
(*ii*) Shortage of experienced salesmen.
(*iii*) Inadequate advertisement for want of money.

(*e*) *Management :* (*i*) Lack of "know-how".
(*ii*) Inefficient executives.
(*iii*) Insufficient research into product design and methods.
(*iv*) Lack of capital thereby restricting policy.

ROLLING BUDGET

The concept of rolling budget or continuous budgeting is an attempt to update budgets. The ICMA terminology defines it as "the continuous updating of a short term budget by adding, say, a further month or quarter and deducting the earliest month or quarter, so that the budget can reflect current condition". Rolling budget is used to indicate continuity in the budgeting process. Suppose a budget is prepared for a period of 1 year, then at the end of each month, the results of the previous month's operations together with any new information or changes in business conditions are used to revise the budget for the next 11 months and to prepare a budget for one additional month beyond so that the budget always covers the next 12 months. Each month the budget "rolls" forward one month by adding one month to replace the month just past. The advantage of the rolling budget is that it makes planning a continuous activity.

TYPES OF BUDGET

The various types of budgets are shown in the following chart :

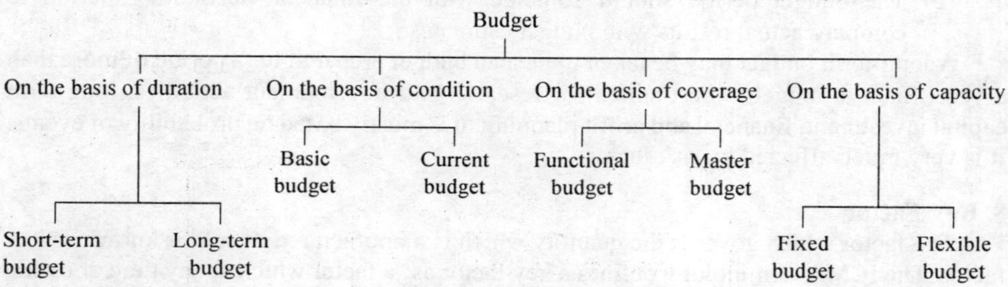

Fig. 25.2. Chart showing types of budgets.

1. On the Basis of Duration

On the basis of duration, budget can be classified into two types, *viz.*, (*a*) short-term budget and (*b*) long-term budget.

(*a*) **Short-term budget :** A short-term budget is prepared to cover a duration of less than 1 year. Sometimes they are prepard for a month also. Cash budget is an example of short-term budget. Short-term budget is followed in many cases as it difficult to forecast events on a long-term basis.

(*b*) **Long-term budget :** A budget which is prepared to cover a period of more than a year is known as long-term budget. The examples of a long-term budget are research and development budget, capital expenditure budget.

2. On the Basis of Condition

On the basis of conditions prevailing, a budget can be classified into two types : (*a*) basic budget and (*b*) current budget.

(*a*) **Basic budget :** The ICMA terminology defines a basic budget as "a budget which is established for use unaltered over a long period of time". The budget does not take into account changes occurring from external environment which are beyond the control of management. This budget is more useful to top level management for formulating policies.

(*b*) **Current budget :** The ICMA terminology defines a current budget as "a budget which is established for use over a short period and is related to the current conditions". The budget under review will be adjusted to the current conditions prevailing in the business. This budget motivates the people preparing the budgets as they are sure of attaining the budget.

3. On the Basis of Coverage

On the basis of coverage of information and activities of a business, budget can be classified into two types, *viz.*, (*a*) Functional budget and (*b*) Master budget.

(*a*) **Functional budget :** As the name suggests functional budgets are prepared in respect of various functions performed in a business. Accordingly we have the following functional budgets.

1. ***Sales budget :*** A sales budget is a statement of planned sales in terms of quantity and value and analysed by products. It is the most important budget as it is most difficult to forecast and attain. It is prepared by the sales manager based on sales forecast. The factors to be considered in forecasting sales are (*a*) Past years sales, (*b*) Forecast of business conditions, (*c*) Market analysis and (*d*) Assessment by the sales department on the basis of (*i*) Products or group of similar products, (*ii*) Areas, (*iii*) Salesmen, (*iv*) Types of customers, (*v*) Period, such as a month or a quarter. While assessing the probable sales, the following are to be considered :

(*i*) The firms own sales and those of its competitors, areawise.
(*ii*) Whether its share of business is increasing or decreasing.
(*iii*) Seasonal fluctuations.
(*iv*) The effect of rise in the level of population.
(*v*) The changes in consumer's tastes and habits.
(*vi*) The effect of introducing new products.
(*vii*) Advertising.
(*viii*) The effect of sales promotion.
(*ix*) The possibility of extending the market.

Problem 1 : Dutta Enterprises sells two products, *A* and *B*. During the year 2003, it plans to sell the following quantities of each product.

Sales budget (in units)

	Total	I Quarter	II Quarter	III Quarter	IV Quarter
A	7,00,000	90,000	2,30,000	3,00,000	80,000
B	3,00,000	85,000	75,000	55,000	85,000

Each of these two products is sold on a seasonal basis. Product *A* tends to sell better in summer months, while product *B* sells better during the winter. Dutta Enterprises plan to sell product *A* throughout the year at a price of Rs. 10 a unit and product *B* at a price of Rs. 20 a unit.

A study of the past experience reveals that Dutta Enterprises has lost about 3% of its invoice each year because of returns (constituting 2% of loss of revenue) allowances and bad debts (1% of loss).

Prepare a sales budget incorporating the above information.

Solution :

Sales budget

	I Quarter	II Quarter	III Quarter	IV Quarter	Total
Product *A*	9,00,000	23,00,000	30,00,000	8,00,000	70,00,000
Product *B*	17,00,000	15,00,000	11,00,000	17,00,000	60,00,000
(*A*) Total sales	26,00,000	38,00,000	41,00,000	25,00,000	1,30,00,000

Loss for returns @ 2% on total sales	52,000	76,000	82,000	50,000	2,60,000
Loss for bad debts and allowance @ 1% of total sales	26,000	38,000	41,000	25,000	1,30,000
(*B*) Total deductions	78,000	1,14,000	1,23,000	75,000	3,90,000
Net sales (*A* – *B*)	25,22,000	36,86,000	39,77,000	24,25,000	1,26,10,000

Problem 2 : Ambitions company Ltd. has three sales divisions at Mumbai, Chennai and Kolkata. It sells two products – product *X* and product *Y*. The budgeted sales for the year ending 31st December 2,000 at each place are given below :

Mumbai :	Product X	1,00,000 units @ Rs. 8 each
	Product Y	70,000 units @ Rs. 5 each
Chennai :	Product Y	1,10,000 units @ Rs. 5 each
Kolkata :	Product X	1,50,000 units @ Rs. 8 each

The actual sales during the same period were as follows :

Mumbai :	Product X	1,25,000 units @ Rs. 8 each
	Product Y	75,000 units @ Rs. 5 each
Chennai :	Product Y	1,25,000 units @ Rs. 5 each
Kolkata :	Product X	1,55,000 units @ Rs. 8 each

From the reports of the sales personal, it was considered that the sales budget for the year ending 31st December 2001 would be higher than 2,000 budget in the following aspects

Mumbai :	Product X	8,000 units
	Product Y	5,000 units
Chennai :	Product Y	13,000 units
Kolkata :	Product X	10,000 units

Intensive sales compaign in Chennai and Kolkata is expected to result in additional sales of 25,000 units in product X in Chennai and 18,000 units of product Y in Kolkata.

You are required to prepare a sales budget for the period ending 31st December 2001.

Solution : **Ascertainment of quantity of Budgeted sales for the year 2001**

Mumbai Division

Product X :–

		Units
	Budgeted sales for the year 2,000	1,00,000
Add :	Expected increase in the sales for the year 2001	8,000
	Budgeted sales for 2001	1,08,000

Product Y

	Budgeted sales for the year 2,000	70,000
Add :	Expected increase in the sales for the year 2001	5,000
	Budgeted sales for 2001	75,000

Chennai Division

Product X :–

		Units
	Budgeted sales for the year 2,000	NIL
Add :	Expected sales for the year 2001	25,000
	Budgeted sales for the year 2001	25,000

Product Y :–

	Budgeted sales for the year 2,000	1,10,000
Add :	Expected increase in the sales for the year 2001	13,000
	Budgeted sales for the year 2001	1,23,000

KolKata Division :–

Product 'X'

	Budgeted sales for the year 2,000	1,50,000
Add :	Expected increase in the sales for the year 2001	10,000
		1,60,000

Product Y

	Budgeted sales for the year 2,000	NIL
Add :	Expected sales for the year 2001	18,000
	Budgeted sales for the year 2001	18,000

Sales Budget

Sales Division	*Pro-duct*	*Budget for the year 2,000* Qty.	Rate	Amt.	*Actuals for the year 2,000* Qty.	Rate	Amt.	*Budget for the year 2001* Qty.	Rate	Amt.
Mumbai	X	1,00,000	8	8,00,000	1,25,000	8	10,00.000	1,08,000	8	864,000
	Y	70,000	5	3,50,000	75,000	5	3,75,000	75,000	5	3,75,000
		1,70,000		11,50,000	200,000		13,75,000	1,83,000		1239000
Chennai	X	–	–	–	–	–	–	25,000	8	2,00,000
	Y	1,10,000	5	5,50,000	1,25,000	5	6,25,000	1,23,000	5	6,15,000
		1,10,000		5,50,000	1,25,000		6,25,000	1,48,000		815,000
Kolkota	X	1,50,000	8	12,00,000	1,55,000	8	12,40,000	1,60,000	8	12,80,000
	Y	–	–	–	–	–	–	18000	5	90,000
		1,50,000		12,00,000	1,55,000		12,40,000	1,78,000		13,70,000

Problem 3 : Adventurous Co. Ltd. manufactures two products *X* and *Y* and sells them through two divisions Bangalore and Cochin. For the purpose of submission of sales budget to the budget committee, the following information has been made available.

Budgeted sales for the current year were :–

Product	*Bangalore*	*Cochin*
X	2,000 units @ Rs. 9	3,000 units @ Rs. 9
Y	1,500 units @ Rs. 21	2,500 units @ Rs. 21

Actual sales for the current year were :–

Product	*Bangalore*	*Cochin*
X	2,500 units @ Rs. 9	3,500 units @ Rs. 9
Y	1,000 units @ Rs. 21	2,000 units @ Rs. 21

Market survey reveal that product 'Y' is popular but under-priced. It is observed that if the price of product '*X*' is increased by Re. 1, it will still find a ready market. On the other hand, product *Y* is over-priced to the customers and the mar'.et could absorb more if the sales price of product *Y* is reduced by Re. 1. The management has agreed to give effect to the above price changes.

From the information relating to these price changes and reports from salesmen, the following estimates have been prepared by divisional managers.

Percentage increase in sales over current budget is

Product	*Bangalore*	*Cochin*
X	+ 10%	+ 5%
Y	+ 20%	+ 10%

With the help of an intensive advertisement campaign, the following additional sales above the estimated sales of divisional managers are possible

Product	*Bangalore*	*Cochin*
X	300 units	350 units
Y	200 units	250 units

You are required to prepare a budget for sales incorporating the above estimates and also show the budgeted and actual sales of the current year.

Solution :

Working notes :

Ascertainment of Quantity of budgeted sales for future period

Bangalore Division :–

Product X		*Units*
	Budgeted sales for the current year	2,000
Add :	Expected increase in sales	
	10/100 × 2,000	200
Add :	Further increase in sales with intensive advertising	300
	Budgeted sales for future period	2,500

Product Y		
	Budgeted sales for the current year	1,500
Add :	Expected increase in sales	
	$\frac{20}{100} \times 1{,}500$	300
Add :	Further increase in sales with intensive advertising	200
	Budgeted sales for future period	2,000

Cochin Division

Product X		
	Budgeted sales for the current year	3,000
Add :	Expected increase in sales–5%	150
Add :	Further expected increase	350
	Budgeted sales for future period	3,500

Product Y		
	Budgeted sales for the current year	2,500
Add :	Expected increase in sales–10%	250
Add :	Further expected sales	250
		3,000

Sales Budget

Sales Division	*Product*	*Budget for the current year*			*Actuals for the current year*			*Budget for the future period*		
		Qty.	*Rate*	*Amt.*	*Qty.*	*Rate*	*Amt.*	*Qty.*	*Rate*	*Amt.*
Bangalore	X	2,000	9	18,000	2,500	9	22,500	2,500	10	25,000
	Y	1,500	21	31,500	1,000	21	21,000	2,000	20	40,000
		3,500		49,500	3,500		43,500	4,500		65,000
Cochin	X	3,000	9	27,000	3,500	9	31,500	3,500	10	35,000
	Y	2,500	21	52,500	2,000	21	42,000	3,000	20	60,000
		5,500		79,500	5,500		73,500	6,500		95,000

2. *Selling and distribution cost budget :* The success of sales depends upon selling and distribution expenses incurred. Selling expenses are incurred to increase the sales volume. While preparing a selling budget, a classification is made according to the variability of cost. This budget is prepared by the sales managers. Common examples of selling expenses included in a selling cost budget are salesmen's salaries, commissions, and travelling expenses. Sometimes a separate distribution cost budget is prepared apart from selling cost budget. The purpose is to know the expenditure involved in making available finished goods safely to customers. Two important costs go to make up distribution cost budget *viz.*, (*a*) storage and warehousing cost and (*b*) transportation cost. As in the case of selling cost budget, distribution costs are also classified into fixed and variable cost. A specimen of selling and distribution cost budget is shown below :

SELLING & DISTRIBUTION COST BUDGET
(For the period ending 31st Dec. 1993)

	Previous year's budget	*Previous year's actual*	*Current budget*
A. Personnel cost :			
Salaries			
Commission			
Travelling			
B. Sale's office cost			
Office supplies			
Salaries			
Postage			
Telephone			
Rent & rates			
C. Publicity :			
Salaries			
Press			
Journals			
Television			
Samples			
D. Warehousing packing & despatch			
Salaries			
Packing wages			
Driver's wages			
Sundries			

Fig. 25.3. Specimen of selling and distribution cost budget.

Problem 4 : Prepare a sales overhead budget for the months of January, February and March from the estimates given below :

	Rs.
Advertisement	2,500
Salaries of sales department	5,000
Expenses of the sales department	1,500
Counter salesman's salaries & D.A.	6,000

Commission to counter salesmen at 1% of their sales

Travelling salesmen's commission at 10% on their sales and expenses at 5% on their sales.

The sales during the period were estimated as follows :

Month	*Counter sales (Rs.)*	*Travelling salesmen's sales (Rs.)*
January	80,000	10,000
February	1,20,000	15,000
March	1,40,000	20,000

(*University of Delhi, B. Com.,(Hons.) April 1989*)

Solution : **Sales overhead budget**

	Jan.	*Feb.*	*March*
Estimated sales	90,000	1,35,000	1,60,000
Fixed overhead :			
Advertisement	2,500	2,500	2,500
Salaries of sales dept.	5,000	5,000	5,000
Expenses of sales dept.	1,500	1,500	1,500
Salaries of counter salesmen & their DA	6,000	6,000	6,000
	15,000	15,000	15,000
Variable overheads :			
Commission of counter salesmen—10% of counter sales	800	1,200	1,400
Commission of travelling salesmen—10% of their sales	1,000	1,500	2,000
Expenses of travelling salesmen (5% of their sales)	500	750	1,000
	2,300	3,450	4,400
Total sales overhead	17,300	18,450	19,400
Total sales	90,000	1,35,000	1,60,000
% of sales overhead to sales	19.22%	13.67%	12.13%

3. ***Advertising budget :*** In large factories, to undertake an intensive sales programme, a separate advertising department is established. It will be looked after by an advertising manager. The advertising manager will have to deal with the following while budgeting advertising cost :

(*i*) Determine the best method or methods of advertising for the business concerned.

(*ii*) Fix the total amount to be spent on advertising in the budget period. This amount is known as the advertising appropriation.

(*iii*) Co-ordinate the sales function and advertising.

(*iv*) Control the expenditure within the limits laid down and also attempt to measure the effectiveness of advertising.

The best method of advertisement to be selected depends upon reference to the product, channel of distribution, method of selling, types of consumers served. Care must be taken to see that the advertisement cost does not increase cost of production drastically. In other words, advertising cost should be incurred as long as there is an increase in sales and net profit. The matching of advertising cost and benefits derived therefrom is a vital part of advertising budget.

A specimen of advertising budget is shown below :

Advertising budget for the year ended......

Expenses	*Media of Advertisement*						
	Total (Rs.)	*News-paper*	*Magazines & journals*	*T.V.*	*Cinema*	*Catalogue*	*Samples*
Salaries							
Rent							
Travelling expenses							
Heating & lighting							
Payment to agencies							
Total							

Fig. 25.4. Specimen of advertising cost budget.

4. ***Production budget :*** This budget is prepared by production manager based upon (*a*) sales budget, (*b*) the production capacity and (*c*) the budgeted finished goods stock requirements. According to Blocker and Weltmer, a production budget deals with :

(*i*) The determination of the total estimated volume of production.

(*ii*) The division of the estimated output into different types of products.

(*iii*) The scheduling of operations by days, weeks and months.

(*iv*) The establishment of finished goods inventory requirements.

(*v*) The storage of finished products until delivery can be made in accordance with sales orders.

Advantages : The preparation of a production budget has the following advantages :

(*i*) Plans can be made to keep inventories at reasonable levels consistent with production and sales requirements.

(*ii*) The requirements of raw materials and the sources of their supply can be selected for deriving best terms of purchases along with quality.

(*iii*) By maintaining production schedule, the promised delivery dates can be maintained. This increases reputation of the business.

Procedure : According to Heckert and Wilson (*Business Budgeting and Control*) the preparation of a production budget involves the following steps :

(*i*) Determine the period of time to be used as a basis for the production budget.

(*ii*) Ascertain what physical quantities should be produced to meet the sales budget and to provide properly balanced inventories.

(*iii*) Determine when the goods should be produced.

(*iv*) Determine where the goods should be produced.

(*v*) Determine the manufacturing operations required by the production.

(*vi*) Establish standards of production performance for use in measuring production efficiency.

(*vii*) Develop a programme of materials, labour and equipment requirements.

(*viii*) Use the production budget for purpose of cost control.

(*ix*) Make necessary revisions of the production budget.

5. ***Production cost budget :*** This budget shows the cost of production taking into account the elements of costs *viz.*, direct materials cost, direct labour cost and production overheads.

Problem 5 (Production budget and production cost budget) : *X* Co. Ltd. manufactures two products *A* and *B*. Forecast of the number of units to be sold in the first seven months of the year is given below :

	Product A	*Product B*
Jan.	1,000	2,800
Feb.	1,200	2,800
Mar.	1,600	2,400
Apr.	2,000	2,000
May	2,400	1,600
June	2,400	1,600
July	2,000	1,800

It is anticipated that

(*i*) There will be no work-in-progress at the end of every month.

(*ii*) Finished units equal to half of the sales for the next month will be in stock at the end of each month (including previous December).

Budgeted production and costs for the whole year are as follows :

	Product A	Product B
Products (units)	22,000	24,000
Direct materials cost per unit	12.50	19
Direct labour cost per unit	4.50	7
Total factory overhead apportioned	66,000	96,000

Prepare for the six months period ending 30th June 1993 (*a*) production budget for each month and (*b*) summarised production cost budget.

Solution : **Production budget (in units)**

Product A	*Jan.*	*Feb.*	*Mar.*	*April*	*May*	*June*	*July*	*Total*
Sales of current month	1,000	1,200	1,600	2,000	2,400	2,400	2,000	
Add : Closing stock	600	800	1,000	1,200	1,200	1,000		
	1,600	2,000	2,600	3,200	3,600	3,400		
Less : Opening balance	500	600	800	1,000	1,200	1,200		
	1,100	1,400	1,800	2,200	2,400	2,200		11,100
Product B								
Sales of current month	2,800	2,800	2,400	2,000	1,600	1,600	1,800	
Add : Closing stock	1,400	1,200	1,000	800	800	900		
	4,200	4,000	3,400	2,800	2,400	2,500		
Less : Opening balance	1,400	1,400	1,200	1,000	800	800		
Total units to be produced	2,800	2,600	2,200	1,800	1,600	1,700		12,700

Production cost budget

	Product A	Product B
Direct material cost per unit	12.50	19.00
Direct labour cost per unit	4.50	7.00
Factory overhead	3.00	4.00
	20.00	30.00
Total budget cost	11,100 × Rs. 20 = Rs. 2,20,000	12,700 × Rs. 30 = Rs. 3,81,000

Problem 6 (Production cost budget) : The production cost of Modern Machine Co. Ltd. for the year 1992 are as under :

Direct material cost		Rs. 1,20,000
Direct wages		75,000
Overheads : Variable	70,000	
Fixed	45,000	1,15,000

The following changes are anticipated in 1993 :

(*a*) The purchase price per unit of direct materials, and of other materials included in overheads will remain unchanged.

(*b*) The average rate for direct labour will fall from Rs. 4 per hour to Rs. 3 per hour, and direct labour hours will increase by 10%.

(*c*) Production efficiency will decrease by 4%.

The overheads are absorbed on a direct wages basis. Draw up a production cost budget for 1993.

Solution : **Production cost budget for 1993**

	Original budget in 1992	*Budget for 1993*
Direct materials cost	1,20,000	1,32,000
Direct labour cost	75,000	64,350
Prime cost	1,95,000	1,96,350

Overheads	—Fixed	45,000	45,000
	—Variable	70,000	77,000
	Total cost	3,10,000	3,18,350

Notes :

1. Labour hours will increase by 10%. Therefore it is presumed that production will increase by 10% and hence 10% increase in the cost of materials.

2. Direct labour is affected by production efficiency of 4% and increase in labour hours of 10%.

$$\text{Labour hours} = \frac{\text{Rs. } 75{,}000}{\text{Rs. 4 per hour}} = 18{,}750 \text{ hrs}$$

Add : 10% increase in labour hrs. = 1,875 hrs

= 20,625 hrs

Add : 4% decrease in production efficiency

$$\frac{4}{100} \times 20{,}625 = 825 \text{ hrs}$$

= 21,450 hrs

Total labour cost = 21,450 × Rs. 3 = 64,350

3. Variable overheads are related to production, 10% rise in production will result 10% rise in variable overhead.

6. ***Plant utilisation budget :*** This budget indicates the plant capacity required to meet the production budget. While preparing this budget allowance must be made for the time lost in repairs and maintenance, setting up time, etc. For a smooth flow of production the capacity of plant must be balanced. For this purpose it is necessary to decide whether to (*a*) reduce the production volume, (*b*) purchase new machinery, (*c*) work extra shift, (*d*) use of subcontractors and so on. A specimen of plant utilisation budget is shown below :

Plant utilisation budget for the period.......

Department	*Machines*	*Number of hours available during the period (2,000)*	*Normal lost time (200)*	*Standard capacity in hrs (1,800)*	*Output per std. hr. (5)*	*Std. qty. (units) (9,000)*
A	1					
	2					
	3					
B	4					
	5					
	6					
	Total					

Fig. 25.5. Specimen showing plant utilisation budget.

7. ***Material purchase budget :*** This budget is prepared by the purchase manager for the purchase of raw materials and component parts. While preparing this budget priority must be given for the purchase of materials which are in short supply. This budget is prepared considering both quantities and value of materials. The following factors are to be considered before materials purchase budget is prepared :

(*a*) Planned increase or decrease in the stock of raw materials during the budget period.

(*b*) The date on which materials are required.
(*c*) The fluctuation in the prices of material
(*d*) The duration of credit allowed.

Problem 7 : The following are the estimated sales of a company for eight months ending 30-11-98.

Months	*Estimated sales (units)*
Apr. 1998	12,000
May 1998	13,000
June 1998	9,000
July 1998	8,000
Aug. 1998	10,000
Sept. 1998	12,000
Oct. 1998	14,000
Nov. 1998	12,000

As a matter of policy, the company maintains the closing balance of finished goods and raw materials as follows :

Stock Item	*Closing balance of a month*
Finished goods	50% of the estimated sales for the next month
Raw materials	Estimated consumption for the next month

Every unit of production requires 2 kg of raw material costing Rs. 5 per kg

Prepare production Budget (in units) and raw materials purchase budget (in units and cost) of the company for the half year ending 30th Sept. 1998. (*ICWA, Inter., June 1999*)

Solution :

Production Budget

Month	*Sales*		*Closing Balance 50% of the estimated sales for next month*		*Operating Balance*	*Production*
1998						
Apr.	12,000	+	6,500	–	6,000	12,500
May	13,000	+	4,500	–	6,500	11,000
June	9,000	+	4,000	–	4,500	8500
July	8,000	+	5,000	–	4,000	9000
Aug.	10,000	+	6,000	–	5,000	11,000
Sept.	12,000	+	7000	–	6,000	13,000
	64,000					65,000

Purchase Budget

Consumption 2 kg per unit	*Closing Balance*	*Opening Balance*	*Purchase in kg*	*Rate*	*Amt.*
25,000	22,000	25,000	22,000	5	1,10,000
22,000	17,000	22,000	17,000	5	85,000
17,000	18,000	17,000	18 000	5	90,000
18,000	22,000	18,000	22,000	5	1,10,000
22,000	26,000	22,000	26,000	5	1,30,000
26,000	26,000	26,000	26,000	5	1,30,000
1,30,000					6,55,000

Problem 8 : A company is drawing its production plan for the year 1997-98 in respect of two of its products "Gamma" and "Delta". The company's policy is not to carry any closing work-in-progress at the end of any month. However, its policy is to hold a closing stock of finished goods at 50% of the anticipated quantity of sales of the succeeding month. For the year 1997-98 the company's budgeted production is 20,000 units of "Gamma" and 25,000 units of "Delta". The following is the estimated cost data.

	Gamma	*Delta*
	Rs.	*Rs.*
Direct material per unit	50	80
Direct labour cost per unit	20	30
Other manufacturing expenses apportionable to each type of product based on production	2,00,000	3,75,000

The estimated units to be sold in the first 7 months of the year 1997-98 are as under :

	Apr.	*May*	*June*	*July*	*Aug.*	*Sept.*	*Oct.*
Gamma	900	1,100	1,400	1,800	2,200	2,200	1,800
Delta	2,900	2,900	2,500	2,100	1,700	1,700	1,900

You are required to :–

(*a*) Prepare a production budget showing month-wise number of units to be manufactured

(*b*) Present a summarised production cost budget for the half year ending 30-9-97.

(*ICWA, Inter., Dec. 1996*)

Solution : **Production budget for half year ending 30th Sept. 97**

	Apr.	*May*	*June*	*July*	*Aug.*	*Sept.*	*Total*
Product – Gama							
Budgeted sales	900	1,100	1,400	1,800	2,200	2,200	9,600
Add : Closing stock to be built up (*See note* 1)	550	700	900	1,100	1,100	900	900
	1,450	1,800	2,300	2,900	3,300	3,100	10,500
Less : Carry-over stock -opening (*See note* 2)	450	550	700	900	1,100	1,100	450
Budgeted production	1,000	1,250	1,600	2,000	2,200	2,000	10,050
Product – Delta							
Budgeted sales	2,900	2,900	2,500	2,100	1,700	1,700	13,800
Add : Closing stock to be built up	1,450	1,250	1,050	850	850	950	950
	4,350	4,150	3,550	2,950	2,550	2,650	14,750
Less : Carry-over stock -opening (*See note* 2)	1,450	1,450	1,250	1,050	850	850	1450
Budgeted production	2,900	2,700	2,300	1,900	1,700	1,800	13,300

Note-1 :

Closing stock of finished goods at the end of each month is to be ascertained as per company's policy, *i.e.*, 50% of the anticipated quantity of sales of the succeeding month. Closing stock under total column is 50% of October month, *i.e.* $\frac{50}{100} \times 1{,}800 = 900$

Note-2 :

Opening stock of each month is the closing stock of preceeding month. The opening stock under total column is 50% of Sept. closing stock, *i.e.*, $\frac{50}{100} \times 900 = 450$

Summarised production cost Budget for the half-year ending 30th Sept. 1997

	Gama		*Delta*	
Production (units)	10,050		13,300	
	Cost		Cost	
	Per unit	Amount	Per unit	Amt.
Direct Materials	50	5,02,500	80	10,64,000
Direct labour	20	2,01,000	30	3,99,000
Other manufacturing expenses	10	10,050	15	1,99,500
	80	8,04,000	125	16,62,500

Note-3 :

Other manufacturing expenses are apportioned on the following basis :

$$\frac{\text{Other Manufacturing expenses}}{\text{No. of units to be produced in 1997-98}}$$

	$\frac{2,00,000}{20,000}$	$\frac{3,75,000}{25,000}$
	= 10	15

Problem 9 (Materials purchase budget) : Draw a material procurement budget (quantitative) from the following information :

Estimated sales of a product 40,000 units. Each unit of the product requires 3 units of material *A* and 5 units of material *B*.

Estimated opening stock at the commencement of the next year :

Finished product	5,000 units
Material *A*	12,000 units
Material *B*	20,000 units
Materials on order :	
Material *A*	7,000 units
Material *B*	11,000 units

The desirable closing stock at the end of the next year :

Finished product	7,000 units
Material *A*	15,000 units
Material *B*	25,000 units
Material on order :	
Material *A*	8,000 units
Material *B*	10,000 units

Solution :

Production budget

Estimated sales	40,000 units
Add : Closing stock	7,000 units
	47,000 units
Less : Opening stock	5,000 units
Production during the year	42,000 units

Materials procurement budget

		A (units)		*B (units)*
Materials required 3 units of *A* and 5 units of *B* for 42,000 units		1,26,000		2,10,000
Add : Closing stock required	15,000		25,000	
Material on order	8,000	23,000	10,000	35,000
		1,49,000		2,45,000
Less : Opening stock	12,000		20,000	
Material on order	7,000	19,000	11,000	31,000
Unit to be procured		1,30,000		2,14,000

Problem 10 : The *XY* Company expects the following sales by month in units for the first six months of next year :

January	–	5,400	April	–	5,700
February	–	5,700	May	–	6,000
March	–	7,500	June	–	4,500

The company has a policy of maintaining an inventory equal to budgeted sales for the following two months. The beginning inventory reflects this policy. Each unit cost Rs. 10.

You are required to prepare purchase budget for as many months as you can both in units and rupees. Explain also why you had to stop where you did. *(University of Kerala, M. Com., May 1992)*

Solution :

Production budget for 3 months

	Jan.	Feb.	March
Sales	5,400	5,700	7,500
Add : Closing stock	5,700	6,000	4,500
	11,100	11,700	12,000
Less : Opening stock	7,500	5,700	6,000
Units to be produced	3,600	6,000	6,000

Purchase budget in quantity

	Jan.	Feb.	March
Units of materials required (*see note 1*)	3,600	6,000	6,000
Add : Desired stock at the end of the year	5,700	6,000	4,500
	9,300	12,000	10,500
Less : Expected stock at the beginning	7,500	5,700	6,000
Quantity of materials to be purchased	1,800	6,300	4,500

Note : In the problem the policy of opening stock is expected to be the sale units equal to the following two months. As the opening stock of every month is the closing stock of the previous month, it has been treated for every month in the same manner. The budget could be prepared only for three months because of the policy of the management in considering opening stock.

Regarding the purchase budget as separate unit of materials required for production, it is presumed that for every unit of finished goods to be produced, one unit of raw materials is required.

Purchase cost budget

Month	Qty.	Rate	Amount
Jan.	1,800	10	18,000
Feb.	6,300	10	63,000
March	4,500	10	45,000
		Total	Rs. 1,26,000

8. ***Labour cost budget :*** This budget represents the direct labour required to meet the production demand of the factory during the budget period. The labour hours required for budgeted production wiil be determined on the basis of output which must conform standard. It shows the information relating to the number of employees along with the grade required to achieve the output and the probable labour cost for budget period. The advantages of preparing a labour cost budget are as follows :

(*a*) It determines the labour force required.

(*b*) It facilitates the personnel department to plan ahead in recruitment and training of labourer.

(*c*) It helps in the preparation of production cost budget and cash budget. Aspecimen of labour cost budget is shown below :

Labour cost budget for the period......

Grade	*Number of employees*	*Hours employed*	*Rate per hour*	*Amount*
(1) Skilled (2) Semi-skilled (3) Unskilled				
			Total	

Fig. 25.6. Specimen showing labour cost budget.

Problem 11 : The sales director of a manufacturing company reports that next year he expects to sell 40,000 units of a particular product. The production department gives the following particulars :

Two kinds of raw materials *A* and *B* are required for manufacturing the product. Each product requires 3 units of material *A* and 2 units of material *B*. The estimated opening balance of the next year will be :–

Finished product	–	10,000 units
Materials *A*	–	12,000 units
Materials *B*	–	15,000 units

The desired closing balances at the end of the year are :–

Finished product	–	16,000 units
Material *A*	–	14,000 units
Material *B*	–	15,000 units

Draw up a materials purchase budget (*University of Madras, B. Com., September 1994*)

Solution :

Production Budget

Sales units	40,000
Less : Opening finished goods	10,000
	30,000
Add : Closing finished goods	16,000
Production units	46,000

Purchase Budget

	A	*B*
Raw materials consumed		
A 46,000 × 3	1,38,000	92,000
B 46,000 × 2		
Less : Opening raw materials	12,000	15,000
	1,26,000	77,000
Add : Closing raw materials	14,000	15,000
Purchase of Raw Materials required	1,40,000	92,000

Problem 12 (Labour cost budget) : The direct labour hour requirements of three of the products manufactured in a factory each involving more than one labour operation are estimated as follows :

Direct labour hours per unit (in minutes)

	Products		
	1	*2*	*3*
Operation : 1	18	42	30
2	–	12	24
3	9	6	–

The factory works 8 hours per day, 6 days in a week. The budget quarter is taken as 13 weeks and during a quarter, lost hours due to leave and holidays and other causes are estimated to be 124 hours.

The budgeted sales of the products during the quarter are :

Product 1	9,000 units
2	15,000 units
3	12,000 units

There is a opening balance of 5,000 units of product 2 and 4,000 units of product 3 and it is proposed to build up a stock at the end of the budget quarter as follows :

Product 1	1,000 units
3	2,000 units

Prepare a manpower budget for the quarter showing for each operation (*i*) Direct labour hours, (*ii*) Direct labour cost and (*iii*) The number of workers.

Solution :

Production budget

	Products		
	1 (units)	2 (units)	3 (units)
Sales	9,000	15,000	12,000
Add : Closing stock	1,000	–	2,000
	10,000	15,000	14,000
Less : Opening stock	–	5,000	4,000
	10,000	10,000	10,000

Total available hours in a quarter per man

Total hrs = 8 × 6 × 13	=	624 hrs
Less : Hours lost	=	124 hrs
Total available hours per man		500 hrs

Total time duration and manpower requirement

Products →	1		2		3		Total
Units →	10,000		10,000		10,000		hrs
Operations	Time in min.	Time in hrs	Time in min.	Time in hrs	Time in min.	Time in hrs	
1	1,80,000	3,000	4,20,000	7,000	3,00,000	5,000	15,000
2	–	–	1,20,000	2,000	2,40,000	4,000	6,000
3	90,000	1,500	60,000	1,000	–	–	2,500

Number of workers required for each operation

Operation	*Total hours*	*No. of workers requied*
1	15,000	30
2	6,000	12
3	2,500	5

Quarterly manpower budget

Opera-tion	*Hourly rate* (Rs.)	*Product1* Direct labour hours	Cost (Rs.)	*Product 2* Direct labour hours	Cost (Rs.)	*Product 3* Direct labour hours	Cost (Rs.)	*Total* Direct labour hours	Cost (Rs.)	No. of workers
1	2.00	3,000	6,000	7,000	14,000	5,000	10,000	15,000	30,000	30
2	2.50	–	–	2,000	5,000	4,000	10,000	6,000	15,000	12
3	3.00	1,500	4,500	1,000	3,000	–	–	2,500	7,500	5
		4,500	10,500	10,000	22,000	9,000	20,000	23,500	52,000	47

9. ***Factory overhead budget*** **:** This budget is prepared by production manager or persons in charge of various production departments. To facilitate control it is necessary to classify the overheads into fixed and variable and controllable and uncontrollable overhead. The budget officer may assist the production manager in supplying the past year's data to prepare this budget more comprehensively.

Problem 13 (Factory overhead budget) : The following particulars aıe extracted from the books of Jai Engineering Co. The production overhead apportionment has been prepared to show overheads for each of the production and service departments. Service departments overheads are apportioned as shown below :

Service department	*Production departments*		
	A	*B*	*C*
1	30%	20%	50%
2	25%	30%	45%

Overhead	*Basis of apportionment*	*Total*	*A*	*B*	*C*	*1*	*2*
Salaries	Actual	14,700	4,000	3,000	5,000	1,500	1,200
Indirect wages	Actual	31,600	9,000	7,000	10,000	3,000	2,600
Consumable stores	No. of employees	1,650	400	350	500	300	100
Depreciation	Value of asset	22,200	6,000	5,000	10,000	700	500
Insurance	Value of asset	2,480	750	650	900	100	80
Rent	Area occupied	3,790	1,200	1,000	1,500	50	40
Power	Meter	2,170	600	700	800	40	30
Light	Area occupied	395	100	110	140	20	25
Maintenance	Value of asset	2,525	800	700	1,000	15	10
Employee's insurance	No. of workers	3,150	900	800	1,000	250	200
Scrap	Actual	775	225	205	345	–	–
Sundries	Actual	1,105	375	235	455	25	15
	Total	86,540	24,350	19,750	31,640	6,000	4,800
Service dept. 1		–	1,800	1,200	3,000		
Service dept. 2		–	1,200	1,440	2,160		
		86,540	27,350	22,390	36,800		

Solution :

Factory overhead budget for the period

	Total	*A*	*B*	*C*
Overhead				
Variable :				
Consumable stores	1,250	400	350	500
Scrap	775	225	205	345
Fixed :				
Salaries	12,000	4,000	3,000	5,000
Depreciation	21,000	6,000	5,000	10,000
Insurance	2,300	750	650	900
Rent	3,700	1,200	1,000	1,500
Sundries	1,065	375	235	455
Service dept. 1	6,000	1,800	1,200	3,000
Service dept. 2	4,800	1,200	1,440	2,160
Semi-variable :				
Indirect wages	26,000	9,000	7,000	10,000
Power	2,100	600	700	800
Light	350	100	110	140
Maintenance	2,500	800	700	1,000
Insurance	2,700	900	800	1,000
	86,540	27,350	22,390	36,800

10. ***Administration cost budget :*** This budget is prepared by chief accountant and approved by the managing director. This budget is likely to pose some problems since most of the administration cost is fixed in nature. The main budget is divided into separate budget covering separate administrative activity such as accounting, secretarial work and so on. The factors to be considered in preparing this budget are (*a*) the existing number of staff, (*b*) their rates of pay, (*c*) change in volume of work and (*d*) legal and other administrative overheads. A specimen of administrative cost budget is shown below :

Specimen of administration cost budget

For the period________

Items of expenses	*Previous year's budget*	*Previous year's actual*	*Current budget*
Materials :			
Stationery			
Supplies			
Salaries & wages :			
Manager's salary			
Director's salary			
Clerical salary			
Expenses :			
Rent & rates			
Telephone			
Postage			
Travelling			
Insurance			
Bank charges			
Audit fee			
Subscriptions			
Total			

11. ***Research and development budget :*** The preparation of this budget is governed by the policy of the Board of Directors and head of production departments. This budget may be prepared by elements of cost or by specific project. Similarly this budget can be prepared from the point of view of short-range or long-rang activities. While long-range research programme is carried out in tune with future market trends and demands, short-range programme are carried out to achieve a satisfactory margin of profit. The research and development budget may relate to (*a*) Basic research, (*b*) New product development, (*c*) Product improvement, (*d*) Cost and capacity improvement and (*e*) Safety, health and welfare. A specimen of research and development budget is shown below :

Research and development budget for the period ....

	Projects				
	1	*2*	*3*	*4*	*Total*
Project costs :					
Materials :					
Raw materials					
Small tools					
Oil & lubricants					
Sundries					
Wages & salaries :					
Chemists					
Technicians					
Others					
Expenses :					
Professional fees					
Total					

General costs :

Supervisory salary
Laboratory cost
Technical publications
Office costs
Subscriptions

Total

12. ***Capital expenditure budget :*** This budget shows the estimated expenditure on fixed assets during the period concerned. This budget is subject to strict management control as it involves heavy amount of investment requiring the approval of top management. This budget is prepared based on the requirements of various assets for the following departments :

(*i*) Production department—For the purchase of machineries and plant either for replacing the existing machinery or new machinery for producing new products.
(*ii*) Transport department—For the purchase of new vehicles.
(*iii*) Office department—For the purchase of new office equipments.
(*iv*) Service departments—For purchasing equipments peculiar to such departments.
(*v*) Equipments to control pollution such as liquid, gaseous and noise pollution.

The capital expenditure budget offers the following advantages :

(*i*) It estimates the capital expenditure requirements and accordingly provides or arranges for it.
(i) The priority of procuring assets can be determined. Those assets which are very important and unavoidable is given first preference and others are postponed to a later period.
(*iii*) It serves as a tool of controlling capital expenditure.

13. ***Cash budget :*** This budget ir prepared to know the estimated cash balance each month along with the estimated receipts and payments during the month. It performs two important functions, viz., (*i*) to ensure sufficient availability of cash and (*ii*) to take necessary action when there is shortage of cash. If there is any surplus, which is not immediately required, the same may be invested for a short period. According to Matz-Curry-Frank, a cash budget serves the following purposes :

(*i*) It indicates the effect on the cash position of seasonal requirements, large inventories, unusual receipts and slowness in collecting bills receiveable.
(*ii*) It indicates cash requirements for a plant or equipments expansion programme.
(*iii*) It points to the need for additional funds from external sources such as bank loans, issue of securities.
(*iv*) It indicates the availability of cash for taking advantage of discounts offered.
(*v*) It helps in planning redemption of preference shares or redeemable debentures, payments of pension, etc.
(*vi*) It shows the availability of excess funds for short or long term investments.

A cash budget can be prepared under any of the following three methods.

(*i*) *The receipts and payments method :* Under this method all the cash receipts and payments expected during the budget period is considered. However care must be taken to ensure that cash adjustments and accruals are not shown in the cash budget. The cash transactions for preparing this budget is obtained from various functional budgets discussed above. For example, materials cost from material budget, labour cost from labour budget, overheads from overhead budget, sales revenue from sales budget and so on.

Problem 14 (Cash budget under receipts and payments method) : The following particulars are extracted from the books of Ajanta Co. Ltd. for the quarter ending 31.3.1993 :

Opening cash balance as on 1.1.93 Rs. 30,000

Sales budget were as follows :

	Rs.
November 1992	80,000
December 1992	90,000
January 1993	75,000
February 1993	75,000
March 1993	80,000

Analysis of records shows that debtors settle according to the following pattern :

60% within the month of sale.

25% the month following.

15% the month following.

Extracts from the purchase budget were as follows :

	Rs.
December 1992	60,000
January 1993	55,000
February 1993	45,000
March 1993	55,000

All purchase are on credit and past experience show that 90% are settled in the month of purchase and the balance settled the month after.

Wages are Rs. 15,000 per month and overheads Rs. 20,000 per month (including Rs, 5,000 depreciation) are settled monthly.

Taxation of Rs. 8,000 has to be settled in February and the company will received settlement of an insurance claim of Rs. 25,000 in March.

Prepare a cash budget for January, February and March 1993.

Solution :

Calculation of sales revenue

	January *Rs.*
November 1992 (15% of 80,000)	12,000
December 1992 (25% of 90,000)	22,500
January 1993 (60% of 75,000)	45,000
	79,500

	February Rs.
December 1992 (15% of 90,000)	13,500
January 1993 (25% of 75,000)	18,750
February 1993 (60% of 75,000)	45,000
	77,250

	March Rs.
January 1993 (15% of 75,000)	11,250
February 1993 (25% of 75,000)	18,750
March 1993 (60% of 80,000)	48,000
	78,000

Payments for purchases

	January
	Rs.
December 1992 (10% of 60,000)	6,000
January 1993 (90% of 55,000)	49,500
	55,000

	February
	Rs.
January 1993 (10% of 55,000)	5,500
February 1993 (90% of 45,000)	40,500
	46,000

	March
	Rs.
February 1993 (10% of 45,000)	4,500
March 1993 (10% of 55,000	49,500
	54,000

Cash budget for the quarter ending March 1993

	Jan.	Feb.	March
Opening balance	30,000	24,000	17,250
Receipts from sales	79,500	77,250	78,000
Insurance claim			25,000
Total cash available	1,09,500	1,01,250	1,20,250
Purchases	55,500	46,000	54,000
Wages	15,000	15,000	15,000
Overhead (less depreciation)	15,000	15,000	15,000
Taxation		8,000	
Total payment	85,500	84,000	84,000
Closing balance c/o	24,000	17,250	36,250

Problem 15 (Cash budget) : The Swadeshi Manufacturing Co. has a cash balance of Rs. 27,000 at the beginning of March 1993. you are required to prepare a cash budget for March, April and May 1993 having regard to the following information :

Creditors give 1 month credit.

Salaries are paid in the current month.

Fixed costs are paid one month in arrears and include a charge for depreciation of Rs. 5,000 per month.

Credit sales are settled as follows :

40% in month of sale, 45% in next month and 12% in the following month. The balance represents bad debts.

Month	*Cash sales (Rs.)*	*Credit sales (Rs.)*	*Purchases (Rs.)*	*Salaries (Rs.)*	*Fixed overhead (Rs.)*
Jan.	–	74,000	55,200	9,000	30,000
Feb.	–	82,000	61,200	9,000	30,000
March	20,000	80,000	60,000	9,500	30,000
April	22,000	90,000	69,000	9,500	32,000
May	25,000	1,00,000	75,000	10,000	32,000

Solution :

Statement showing receipts from debtors

	March		*April*		*May*
40% of March sales	32,000	40% of April sales	36.000	40% of May sales	40,000
45% of Feb. sales	36,900	45% of March sales	36,000	45% of April sales	40,500
12% of Jan. sales	8,880	12% of Feb. sales	9,840	12% of March sales	9,600
	77,780		81,840		90,100

Cash budget for the months of March, April & May 1993

	March	*April*	*May*
Opening balance	27,000	29,080	38,420
Receipts from debtors	77,780	81,840	90,100
Cash sales	20,000	22,000	25,000
Total cash available	1,24,780	1,32,920	1,53,520
Salaries	9,500	9,500	10,000
Fixed overheads	25,000	25,000	27,000
Purchases	61,200	60,000	69,000
Total disbursement	95,700	94,500	1,06,000
Closing balance c/o	29,080	38,420	47,520

Problem 16 (Cash budget) : From the following budgeted figures prepare a cash budget in respect of the three months to June 30, 1993 :

Month	*Sales*	*Materials*	*Wages*	*Overhead*
Jan.	30,000	20,000	5,500	3,100
Feb.	28,000	24,000	5,800	3,300
March	32,000	25,000	6,000	3,400
April	40,000	28,000	6,200	3,600
May	42,000	31,000	6,500	4,300
June	38,000	25,000	7,000	4,000

Estimated cash balance on April Ist 1993 Rs. 10,000.

Materials and overheads are paid during the month following the month of supply. Wages are paid during the month in which they are earned.

Credit items of sale are payment by the end of the month following the month of sale. It is estimated that one-half of sales are paid when due, the other half being paid during the next month.

A sales commission of 5% on sales is to be paid within the month following actual sales.

Preference share dividend of 10% on capital of Rs. 3,00,000 is to be paid on May 1, 1993.

Plant and machinery to be installed in May at a cost of Rs. 10,000 will be payable on Ist June 1993.

10% calls on equity shares capital of Rs. 2,50,000 are due on April Ist and June Ist 1993.

Solution :

Statement showing sales

	April		*May*		*June*
½ of March	16,000	½ of April	20,000	½ of May	21,000
½ of Feb.	14,000	½ of March	16,000	½ of April	20,000
	30,000		36,000		41,000

Cash budget for period ending 30th June 1993

	April	*May*	*June*
Opening balance	10,000	28,800	(5,300)
Sales	30,000	36,000	41,000
Capital	25,000	–	25,000
Total receipts	65,000	64,800	60,700

Materials	25,000	28,000	31,000
Wages	6,200	6,500	7,000
Overheads	3,400	3,600	4,300
Sales commission	1,600	2,000	2,100
Pref. share dividend	–	30,000	–
Plant & machinery	–	–	10,000
Total payment	Rs. 36,200	70,100	54,400
Balance c/o	Rs. 28,800	Rs. (5,300)	Rs. 6,300

Problem 17 : From the following data prepare a cash budget for the 3 months commercing 1st June 1996, when the bank balance was Rs. 1,00,000.

Month	*Sales* (Rs.)	*Purchases* (Rs.)	*Wages* (Rs.)	*Production expenses* (Rs.)	*Adm. expenses* (Rs.)
April	80,000	41,000	5,600	3,900	10,000
May	76,500	40,500	5,400	4,200	14,000
June	78,500	38,500	5,400	5,100	15,000
July	90,000	37,000	4,800	5,100	17,000
August	95,000	35,000	4,700	6,000	13,000

There is two month credit period allowed to customers and received from suppliers. Wages, production expenses and administration expenses are payable in the following month.

(*University of Madras, B.Com., Sept 1997*)

Solution : **Cash budget from June to August 1996**

	June	*July*	*August*
Opening balance	1,00,000	1,15,400	1,25,900
Add : Receipts :			
Collection from debtors	80,000	76,500	78,500
	1,80,000	1,91,900	204,400
Less : Payment			
paid to creditors	41,000	40,500	38,500
wages	5,400	5,400	4,800
Production expenses	4,200	5,100	5,100
Administration expenses	14,000	15,000	17,000
	64,600	66,000	65,400
Closing balance	1,15,400	1,25,900	1,39,000

Note 1 :

Delay in payment allowed to customers from suppliers is 2 montsh *i.e.*, April payment paid in June.

Note 2 :

Delay in payment allowed to wages, production expenses, administration expenses are one month *i.e.*, May payment paid in June.

Problem 18 : Infotech Ltd., commences business on 1st April 2000 and deposits Rs. 1,00,000 in the Global Trust Bank. The sum deposited would not be sufficient to finance its operations over a period of four months. As a company secretary, you are asked to prepare a cash budget from 1st April 2000 to 31st July 2000 to ascertain the monthly overhead limits to seek from the company's bankers.

Requisite data is as under :

(*i*) Sales are made to one distributor only on 30 days terms 2% discount and cheques are received on the first date of the following due date.

(*ii*) Furniture purchases for Rs. 10,000 prefferred to be made in April, 2000 (*iii*) Budget figures are :

	April	*May*	*June*	*July*
Purchases	50,000	40,000	30,000	40,000
Wages	40,000	50,000	40,000	40,000
Cash expenses	4,000	5,000	4,000	4,000
Sales	60,000	70,000	80,000	80,000

All purchases are made on net 30 days terms and cheques are posted to creditors on the last day of the month due. (*CS, Inter, June 2000*)

Solution : **Cash budget for April to July**

		Apr.	*May*	*June*	*July*
(*A*)	Cash receipts :				
	Cash receipts from distributor (Sales – 2% discount with one month time lag.)	–	58,800	68,600	78,400
(*B*)	Cash payments :				
	Payment to Creditors (one month time lag)	–	50,000	40,000	30,000
	Wages	40,000	50,000	40,000	40,000
	Cash expenses	4,000	5,000	4,000	4,000
	Furniture purchases	10,000	–	–	–
	Total cash payments	54,000	1,05,000	84,000	74,000
(*C*)	Net cash receipts/ Deficit (A – B)	(54,000)	(46,200)	(15,400)	4,400
	Balance (overdraft) at the start of the month (crummilative)	1,00,000	46,000	(200)	(15,600)
	(Overdraft) required monthwise	–	(200)	(15,400)	–

Problem 19 : Prepare a cash budget for the three months ended 30th September 1998 based on the following information :

				Rs.
Cash at bank on 1st July 1998				25,000
Monthly salaries and wages (estimated)				10,000
Interest payable in August 1998				5,000
Estimated	*June*	*July*	*August*	*September*
	Rs.	*Rs.*	*Rs.*	*Rs.*
Cash sales (actual)	1,20,000	1,40,000	1,52,000	1,21,000
Credit sales	1,00,000	80,000	1,40,000	1,20,000
Purchases	1,60,000	1,70,000	2,40,000	1,80,000
Other expenses	18,000	20,000	22,000	21,000

Credit sales are collected 50% in the month of sale and 50% in the month following. Collections from credit sales are subject to 10% discount if received in the month of sale and to 5% if received in the month following :

10% of the purchases are in cash and balance is paid in next month. (*CS, Inter, June 1999*)

Solution : **Calculation of collection from Debtors (Credit sales)**

		July	*Aug.*	*Sept.*
July	50% of 1,00,000	50,000		
	50% of 80,000	40,000		
Aug.	50% of 80,000		40,000	
	50% of 1,40,000		70,000	

Sept.	50% of 1,40,000			70,000
	50% of 1,20,000			60,000
	Total collections	90,000	1,10,000	1,30,000
Less :	Discount allowed			
(*a*)	5% on 50,000 + 10% on 40,000	6,500		
(*b*)	5% on 40,000 + 10% on 70,000		9,000	
(*c*)	5% on 70,000 + 5% on 60,000			9,500
	Net collections after discount	83,500	1,01,000	1,20,500

Calculation of payments to creditors

(*a*)	90% of 1,60,000 + 10% of 1,70,000	1,61,000		
(*b*)	90% of 1,70,000 + 10% of 2,40,000		1,77,000	
(*c*)	90% of 2,40,000 + 10% of 1,80,000			2,34,000
		1,61,000	1,77,000	2,34,000

Cash budget for three months July to Sept.

		July	*Aug.*	*Sept.*
	Opening balance	25,000	57,500	96,500
Add :	Receipts :			
	Sales cash	1,40,000	1,52,000	1,21,000
	Credit	83,500	101,000	1,20500
	Total cash	2,48,500	3,10,500	3,38,000
Payments :				
	Purchases	1,61,000	1,77,000	2,34,000
	Other expenses	20,000	22,000	21,000
	Interest	-	5,000	-
	Salaries & wages	10,000	10,000	10,000
	Total payment	1,91,000	2,14,000	2,65,000
	Closing cash balance	57,500	96,500	73,000

Problem 20 : On 30th September 1996, The balance sheet of M Ltd. (retailer) was as under :

Equity shares of		Equipment	20,000	
Rs. 10 each fully paid	20,000	*Less :* Dep.	5,000	
Reserves	10,000			15,000
Trade creditors	40,000	Stock		20,000
Proposed dividend	15,000	Trade debtors		15,000
		Bank		35,000
	85,000			85,000

The company is developing a system of forward planning and on 1st October 1996 it supplies the following information :

	Sales		Purchases
	Credit	*Cash*	*Credit*
	Rs.	*Rs.*	*Rs.*
September 1996 (actual)	15,000	14,000	40,000
October 1996 (budget)	18,000	5,000	23,000
November 1996 (budget)	20,000	6,000	27000
December 1996 (budget)	25,000	8000	26,000

All trade debtors are allowed one months credit and are expected to settle promptly. All trade creditors are paid in the month following delivery :

On 1st October 1996, all equipment were replaced at a cost of Rs. 30,000 Rs. 14,000 was allowed in exchange for the old equipment and a net payment of Rs. 16,000 was made.

The proposed dividend will be paid in December 1996.
The following expenses will be paid :
Wages Rs. 3,000 per month.
Administration Rs. 1,500 per month.
Rent Rs. 3,600 for the year upto 30th Sept. 1997 (to be paid in October 1996).
You are required to prepare a cash budget for the months of October, November and December 1996.

(CS, Inter, June 1997)

Solution : Cash budget for 3 months ending 1996

	October	*November*	*December*
Opening balance of bank/Bank overdraft	35,000	(9,100)	(12,600)
Add : Cash inflows :			
Sales : cash sales of current month	5,000	6,000	8000
Credit sales of previous month	15,000	18000	2,000
Total receipts	55,000	14,900	15,400
Less : Cash inflow :			
Credit purchases of previous month	40,000	23,000	27,000
Equipment	16,000	-	-
Wages	3,000	3,000	3,000
Administration	1,500	11,500	1,500
Rent	3,600	-	-
Dividend	-	-	15,000
Total payment	64,100	27,500	46,500
Closing balance/overdraft (A – B)	(9,100)	(12,600)	(31,100)

Problem 21 : Prepare cash budget of fashion fabrics for the months April 1999 to July 1999 (four months) from the details given below :

(*i*) Estimated sales :

	Rs.
February 1999	12,00,000
March 1999	12,00,000
April 1999	16,00,000
May 1999	20,00,000
June 1999	18,00,000
July 1999	16,00,000
August 1999	14,00,000

(*ii*) On an average 20% of sales are cash sales. The credit sales are realised in the third month (January sales in March)

(*iii*) Purchases amount to 60% of sales. Purchases made in a month are generally sold in the third month and payment for purchases is also made in the third month.

(*iv*) Variable expenses (other then sales commission) constitute 10% of sales and there is a time lag of half a month in these payment.

(*v*) Commission on sales is paid at 5% of sales value and payment is made in the third month.

(*vi*) Fixed expenses per month amount to Rs. 75,000 approximately.

(*vii*) Other items anticipated :

			Due
Interest payable on deposits	Rs.	1,60,000	(April 99)
Sales of old asserts	Rs.	1,25,000	(May 99)
Payment of Tax	Rs.	80,000	(June 99)
Purchase of fixed assets	Rs.	6,50,000	

(*viii*) Opening cash balance Rs. 1,50,000

(ICWA, Inter, December 1999)

Solution :

Cash budget for April to July 1999

	April	May	June	July
Opening balance	1,50,000	35,000	5,000	1,40,000
Add : Receipts :				
Cash sales	3,20,000	4,00,000	3,60,000	3,20,000
Collection from Debtors	9,60,000	9,60,000	12,80,000	16,00,000
Sales of old assets	–	1,25,000	–	–
Total	14,30,000	15,20,000	16,40,000	19,20,000
Payments :				
Payments for purchases	9,60,000	12,00,000	10,80,000	9,60,000
Variable expenses	1,40,000	1,80,000	1,90,000	1,70,000
Commission on sales	60,000	60,000	80,000	1,00,000
Fixed expenses	75,000	75,000	75,000	75,000
Interest on Deposits	1,60,000	–	–	–
Tax	–	–	80,000	–
Purchase of fixed asset	–	–	–	6,50,000
Total	13,95,000	15,15,000	15,05,000	19,55,000
Closing balance	35,000	5,000	1,40,000	1,05,000

Working Note :

(1) *Calculation of sales*

April

Cash sales 20% of April sales

$$\frac{20}{100} \times 16,00,000 = 3,20,000$$

Credit sales 80% of February sales

$$\frac{80}{100} \times 12,00,000 = 9,60,000$$

May

Cash sales 20% of May sales

$$\frac{20}{100} \times 20,00,000 = 4,00,000$$

Credit sales $\frac{80}{100}$ of March sales

$$\frac{80}{100} \times 12,00,000 = 9,60,000$$

June

Cash sales 20% of June sales

$$\frac{20}{100} \times 18,00,000 = 3,60,000$$

Credit sales 80% of April sales

$$\frac{80}{100} \times 16,00,000 = 12,80,000$$

July

Cash sales 20% of July sales

$\frac{20}{100} \times 16,00,000 = 3,20,000$

Credit sales 80% of May sales

$\frac{80}{100} \times 20,00,000 = 16,00,000$

(2) *Calculation of Purchases*

April $16,00,000 \times \frac{60}{100} = 9,60,000$

May $20,00,000 \times \frac{60}{100} = 12,00,000$

June $18,00,000 \times \frac{60}{100} = 10,80,000$

July $16,00,000 \times \frac{60}{100} = 9,60,000$

(3) *Calculation of variable expenses*

April

March time lag

$\frac{10}{100} \times 12,00,000 \times \frac{1}{2} = 60,000$

April sales $\frac{10}{100} \times 16,00,000 \times \frac{1}{2} = 80,000$

1,40,000

May

April sales $\frac{10}{100} \times 16,00,000 \times \frac{1}{2} = 80,000$

May sales $\frac{10}{100} \times 20,00,000 \times \frac{1}{2} = 1,00,000$

1,80,000

June

May sales $\frac{10}{100} \times 20,00,000 \times \frac{1}{2} = 1,00,000$

June sales $\frac{10}{100} \times 18,00,000 \times \frac{1}{2} = 90,000$

1,90,000

July

June sales $\frac{10}{100} \times 18,00,000 \times \frac{1}{2} = 90,000$

July sales $\frac{10}{100} \times 16,00,000 \times \frac{1}{2} = 80,000$

1,70,000

(4) *Calculation of commission on sales*

April,	Feb. sales 12,00,000 × $\frac{5}{100}$	=	60,000
May,	Mar. sales 12,00,000 × $\frac{5}{100}$	=	60,000
June,	Apr. sales 16,00,000 × $\frac{5}{100}$	=	80,000
July,	May sales 20,00,000 × $\frac{5}{100}$	=	1,00,000

(*ii*) *Adjusted profit and loss method:* This method presents the cash budget in the form of cash flow statement. When compared to receipts and payments method, this method is less detailed but more useful for long-term budgeting. In preparing a long-term budget management is concerned with overall position of cash rather than cash receipts and payments. The preparation of a cash flow statement involves the use of the following information :

(a) Cash balance in the begining.
(b) Net profit forecast for the period (before charging depreciation and other provisions)
(c) Changes in working capital.
(d) Capital expenditure and sale of plant and machinery.
(e) Capital receipts
(f) Dividents.

This method differs from the previous method in one respect, i.e., it considers particularly non-cash transactions. That is to say, this method is based on the assumption that profit = cash. In other words, if there were no credit transactions, capital transactions, accrual, provisions, or appropriation of profit, the amount of profit shown in the profit and loss account will be equal to the balance of cash shown by the cash book. But in practice such a situation rarely arises and hence requires adjustments. Hence the name adjusted profit and loss method.

(*iii*) *Balance sheet method :* This method resembles the adjusted profit and loss method explained above. In addition to a cash flow statement a budgeted balance sheet is prepared for the next period under this method. In preparing the balance sheet all assets and liabilities are taken into account except cash. The two sides of balance sheet is then balanced and the balancing figure represents cash. When the asset side is heavier than liablilities side, it denotes bank overdraft and if the liability side is heavier than asset side it denotes cash on hand or at bank.

Problem 22 (Preparation of different budgets) : Ratna Enterprises manufactures three products *A*, *B* and *C*. You are required to prepare (*a*) Sales budget, (*b*) Production budget, (*c*) Material budget for the month of January 1993.

Sales of products	*Quantity*	*Rate*
A	1,000	100
B	2,000	120
C	1,500	140

Materials used in the company's products are :

Material	M_1	M_2	M_3
Rate	Rs. 4	Rs. 6	Rs. 9

Quantities used in	*Units*	*Units*	*Units*
A	4	2	–
B	3	3	2
C	2	1	1
Finished stock as on :	*A (units)*	*B (units)*	*C (units)*
1.1.93	1,000	1,500	500
31.1.93	1,100	1,650	550
Material stocks :	M_1	M_2	M_3
1.1.93	(units) 26,000	20,000	12,000
31.1.93	(units) 31,200	24,000	14,400

Solution :

Sales budget

	A	*B*	*C*
Sales quantities	1,000	2,000	1,500
Selling price (per unit)	Rs. 100	120	140
Sales	Rs. 1,00,000	2,40,000	2,10,000

Statement showing production budget

	A	*B*	*C*
Sales units	1,000	2,000	1,500
Add : Closing stock	1,100	1,650	550
	2,100	3,650	2,050
Less : Opening stock	1,000	1,500	500
Production	1,100	2,150	1,550

Statement showing material usage budget

	M_1		M_2		M_3	
Production Budget	*Unit per product*	*Total*	*Unit per product*	*Total*	*Unit per product*	*Total*
A—1,100	4	4,400	2	2,200	–	–
B—2,150	3	6,450	3	6450	2	4,300
C—1,550	2	3,100	1	1,550	1	1,550
Material usage		13,950		10,200		5,850

Material purchase budge (Qty, and value)

		M_1	M_2	M_3
Material usage	(units)	13,950	10,200	5,850
Add : Closing stock	(units)	31,200	24,000	14,400
		45,150	34,200	20,250
Less : Opening stock		26,000	20,000	12,000
Required purchases	(units)	19,150	14,200	8,250
Unit rate		Rs. 4	6	9
Value of materials		76,600	85,200	74,250

(*b*) **Master budget :** It is a summary of all the functional budgets dicussed above. According to the ICMA terminology, "A master budet is the summary budget incorporating its component functional budgets and which is finally approved, adopted and employed. A master budget shows the operating profit of the business for the budget period and budgeted balance sheet at its close.

Problem 23 (Master budget) : A glass manufacturing company requires you to calculate and present the budget for the year from the following information :

Toughened glass	–	Rs. 3,60,000
Bent toughened glass	–	Rs. 5,40,000
Direct material cost	–	60% of sales
Direct wages of 20 workers at the rate of	–	Rs. 200 per month
Factory overheads :		
Works manager	–	Rs. 600 per month
Foreman	–	Rs. 500 per month
Stores and spares	–	2½% on sales
Depreciation on machinery	–	Rs. 12,500
Light and power	–	Rs. 5,000
Repairs and maintenance	–	Rs. 8,000
Other sundries	–	10% on direct wages
Administration, selling and distribution expenses	–	Rs. 16,000 per year.

(University of Kerala, M.Com., May 1992)

Solution : **Master budget for the period ending**

Sales budget		
Toughened glass		3,60,000
Bent toughened glass		5,40,000
		9,00,000
Less : Administration and selling and distribution overheads		16,000
	Net sales revenue	8,84,000
Prodction cost budget :		
Direct materials—60% of sales		5,30,400
Direct wages—20 × 200 × 12		48,000
	Prime cost	5,78,400
Variable factory overheads :		
Stores and spares 2½% on sales	22,500	
Light	5,000	
Repairs	5,000	37,500
Fixed factory overhead :		
Works manager's salary	7,200	
Foreman's salary	6,000	
Depreciation	12,500	
Sundries 10% of wages	4,800	30,500
	Works cost	6,46,400

Expected profit = Sales – Works cost
= 8,84,000 – 6,46,400 = 2,37,600

4. On the Basis of Capacity

On the basis of capacity operated budgets are classified into two types. They are as follows :

(*a*) **Fixed budget :** The ICMA terminology defines fixed budget as "a budget which is designed to remain unchanged irrespective of the volume of output or turnover attained. All the budgets explained above are fixed budgets, i.e., they are based on a fixed level of operation. In other words, it is assumed that the various departments of a factory work at a stated level of activity and that a specified production level is going to be achieved and that sales budget will be attained. A fixed budget does not help as a controlling tool. Hence flexible budgets are made use of.

(*b*) **Flexible budget or variable budget :** It is defined by the ICMA terminology as "a budget which by recognising the difference in behaviour between fixed and variable costs in relation to fluctuations in output, turnover or other variable factors such as number of employees, is designed to change appropriately with such fluctuation". A flexible budget is not rigid as in the case of fixed budget. Instead it adapts itself to any level of activity. The budget varies according to a change in the level of output. Hence it is also known as variable budget. It serves as a useful tool of controlling cost.

Problem 24 (Flexible budge) : Prepare a flexible budget from the following data :

Capacity	50%
Volume	10,000 units
Selling price per unit	Rs. 200
Material	Rs. 100
Labour	Rs. 30
Factory overhead	Rs. 30 (Rs. 12 fixed)
Administration overhead	Rs. 20 (Rs. 10 fixed)

At 60% working, material cost per unit increased by 2% and selling price per unit falls by 2%.

At 80% working, material cost per unit increases by 5% and selling price per unit falls by 5%. Estimate the profit at 60% and 80% working. (*Nagarjuna University, M.Com., March 1992*)

Solution :

Flexible budget

	Level of activity					
	50%		*60%*		*80%*	
	Per unit	*Amount*	*Per unit*	*Amount*	*Per unit*	*Amount*
Units	10,000		12,000		16,000	
Raw materials	100	10,00,000	102	12,24,000	105	16,80,000
Labour	30	3,00,000	30	3,60,000	30	4,80,000
Factory overhead – Fixed	12	1,20,000	10	1,20,000	7.5	1,20,000
– Variable	18	1,80,000	18	2,16,000	18.0	2,88,000
Administration overhead						
– Fixed	10	1,00,000	8.33	1,00,000	6.25	1,00,000
– Variable	10	1,00,000	10	1,20,000	10	1,60,000
Total cost	180	18,00,000	178.33	2,14,000	176.75	28,28,000
Profit	20	2,00,000	17.67	2,12,000	13.25	2,12,000
Sales	200	20,00,000	196.00	23,52,000	190	30,40,000

Problem 25 : Draw up a flexible budget for overhead expenses on the basis of the following data and determine the overhead rates at 70%, 80% and 90% plant capacity.

	Capacity level		
	70%	80%	90%
Variable overheads :			
Indirect labour	–	12,000	–
Indirect materials	–	4,000	–
Semi–variable overheads :			
Power (30% fixed)	–	20,000	–
Repairs and maintenance 60% fixed		2,000	–
Fixed overhead :			
Depreciation	–	11,000	–
Insurance	–	3,000	–
Salaries	–	10,000	–
Total overheads	–	62,000	–
Estimated direct labour hours	–	1,20,000	–

(*Madurai Kamaraj University, B.Com., April 1992*)

Solution : **Flexible budget**

	Level of activity		
	70%	80%	90%
Variable overheads			
Indirect labour	10,500	12,000	13,500
Stores	3,500	4,000	4,500
Semi-variable overhead			
Power — Fixed	6,000	6,000	6,000
— Variable	12,250	14,000	15,750
Repairs — Fixed	1,200	1,200	1,200
— Variable	700	800	900
Fixed overhead			
Depreciation	11,000	11,000	11,000
Insurance	3,000	3,000	3,000
Salaries	10,000	10,000	10,000
Total overheads	58,150	62,000	65,850
Estimated labour hours	1,08,500	1,24,000	1,39,500
Overhead rate	0.53	0.50	0.47

Problem 26 : For production of 10,000 articles the following are budgeted expenses per unit :

	Rs.
Direct materials	60.00
Direct labour	30.00
Variable overhead	20.00
Fixed overhead (Rs. 1,60,000)	16.00
Variable expenses (direct)	5,00
Selling expenses (20% fixed)	15.00
Administration expenses (Rs. 50,000 fixed for all level of production)	5.00
Distribution expenses (20% fixed)	5.00
	156.00

Prepare a flexible budget for production of 6,000, 7,000 and 8,000 units of articles, showing clearly variable cost, fixed cost and total cost. *(University of Madras, B.Com., March 1997)*

Solution : **Flexible budget**

	6,000 units		7,000 units		8,000 units		10,000 units	
	Per unit	*Amount*	*Per unit*	*Amount*	*Per unit*	*Amount*	*Per unit*	*Amount*
Material	60	3,60,000	60	4,20,000	60	4,80,000	60	6,00,000
Labour	30	1,80,000	30	2,10,000	30	2,40,000	30	3,00,000
Variable overhead	20	1,20,000	20	1,40,000	20	1,60,000	20	2,00,000
Fixed overhead	26.66	1,60,000	22.85	1,60,000	20	1,60,000	16	1,60,000
Variable expense	5	30,000	5	35,000	5	40,000	5	50,000
Selling expense :								
—Fixed	5	30,000	4.28	30,000	3.75	30,000	3	30,000
—Variable	12	72,000	12	84,000	12.00	96,000	12	1,20,000
Administration expense	8.34	50,000	7.14	50,000	6.25	50,000	5	50,000
Distribution expense								
—Fixed	1.66	10,000	1.42	10,000	1.25	10,000	1	10,000
—Variable	4.00	24,000	4.00	28,000	4.00	32,000	4	40,000
Total cost	172.66	10,36,000	166.69	11,67,000	162.25	12,98,000	156	15,60,000

Problem 27 : The following figures are available from sales and costs forecast of M/s. Asiad and Company for the year ended 31st December 1984 at 50% (5,000 units) capacity utilisation :

(*i*) Fixed expenses remain constant for all levels of production and sales.
(*ii*) Selling price between 50% and 75% capacity is Rs. 25 per unit.
(*iii*) Semi-variable expenses will remain unchanged at 50% to 65% capacity but will increase by 10% between 65% and 80% capacity and 30% between 80% and 100% capacity.
(*iv*) At 90% level, material cost increases by 5% and selling price is reduced by 5%.
(*v*) At 100% level both material and labour costs increase by 10% and selling price is reduced by 8%.
(*vi*) Semi-variable expenses are Rs. 50,000.
(*vii*) Fixed expenses are Rs. 58,000.
(*viii*) Variable expenses are, material Rs. 5 per unit, labour Rs. 2 per unit and direct expenses, Re. 1 per unit.

Prepare a profit forecast statement throught flexible budget at 60%, 75%, 90% and 100% capacity.

(*Bangalore University, M.Com., May 1989*)

Solution :

Flexible budget

	60% (6,000 units)	*75% (7,500 units)*	*90% (9,000 units)*	*100% (10,000 units)*
Materials	30,000	37,500	47,250	55,000
Labour	12,000	15,000	18,000	22,000
Expenses	6,000	7,500	9,000	10,000
Semi-variable cost	50,000	55,000	65,000	65,000
Fixed cost	58,000	58,000	58,000	58,000
Total	1,56,000	1,73,000	1,97,250	2,10,000
Profit/Loss	(6,000)	14,500	16,500	20,000
Sales	1,50,000	1,87,500	2,13,750	2,30,000

Working Note : Sales value for 9,000 units and 10,000 units

9,000 × 25 = 2,25,000		10,000 × 25 = 2,50,000	
Less : 5%	11,250	Less : 8%	20,000
	2,13,750		2,30,000

Problem 28 : The following data are available for a manufacturing company for a yearly period :

	Rs. (in lakhs)
Fixed expenses :	
Wages and salaries	9.5
Rent, rates and taxes	6.6
Depreciation	7.4
Sundry administration expenses	6.5
Semi-variable expenses (at 50% capacity)	
Maintenance and repairs	3.5
Indirect labour	7.9
Sales department salaries	3.8
Sundry administrative expenses	2,8
Variable expenses (at 50% capacity)	
Materials	21.7
Labour	20.4
Other expenses	7.9
Total cost	98.0

Assume that the fixed expenses remain constant at all levels of production, semi-variable expenses remain constant between 45% and 65% capacity increasing by 10% between 65% and 80% capacity and by 20% between 80% and 100% capacity.

Sales at various levels are :

	Rs. (in lakhs)
50% Capacity	100
60% Capacity	120
75% Capacity	150
90% Capacity	180
100% Capacity	200

Prepare a flexible budget for the year at 60% and 90% capacities and estimate the profit at these levels of buget. *(C.S., Inter, Dec. 1991)*

Solution :

Flexible budget

	Rs. (in lakhs) 60%	90%
Variable cost :		
Materials	26.04	39.06
Labour	24.48	36.72
Other expenses	9.48	14.22
Semi-variable cost :		
Maintenance	3.5	4.20
Indirect labour	7.9	9.48
Sales department salaries	3.8	4.56
Sundry administration expenses	2.8	3.36
Fixed cost :		
Wages and salaries	9.50	9.50
Rent, rates and taxes	6.60	6.60
Depreciation	7.40	7.40
Sundry administration expenses	6.50	6.50
Total cost	108	141.60
Profit	12	38.40
Sales	120	180

Problem 29 : The monthly budgets for manufacturing overhead of a concern for two levels of activity were as follows :

Capacity	*60%*	*100%*
Budgeted production (units)	600	1,000
	Rs.	*Rs.*
Wages	1,200	2,000
Consumable stores	900	1,500
Maintenance	1,100	1,500
Power and fuel	1,600	2,000
Depreciation	4,000	4,000
Insurance	1,000	1,000
	9,600	12,000

You are required to :

(*i*) Indicate which of the items are fixed, variable and semi-vairble.

(*ii*) Prepare a budget for 80% capacity and

(*iii*) Find the total cost both fixed and variable per unit of output at 60%, 80% and 100% capacity.

(C.S., Inter, December 1990)

Solution : Fixed costs are : (*i*) Depreciation

(*ii*) Insurance

Variable costs are : (*i*) Wages at Rs. 2 per unit

(*i*) Consumable stores at 1.50 p.u.

Semi-variable cost :

$$\text{Maintenance} = \left(\frac{1{,}500-1{,}100}{1{,}000-600}\right) = \frac{400}{400} = \text{Re. 1 p.u. variable}$$

Rs. 1,100 – 600 × Re. 1 = 500 fixed

$$\text{Power and fuel} = \left(\frac{2{,}000-1{,}600}{1{,}000-600}\right) = \frac{400}{400} = \text{Re. 1 p.u. variable}$$

Rs. 1,600 – 600 × Re. 1 = 1,000 fixed

Budget for 80% capacity

	Output 800 units
Wages @ Rs. 2 per unit	1,600
Consumable stores @ Rs. 1.50 per unit	1,200
Maintenance Rs. 500 + Re. 1.00 per unit	1,300
Power and fuel Rs. 1,000 + Re. 1.00 per unit	1,800
Depreciation	4,000
Insurance	1,000
Total cost	10,900

Statement showing total cost

Capacity	*60%*	*80%*	*100%*
Units	600	800	1,000
	Rs.	*Rs.*	*Rs.*
Fixed cost :			
Depreciation	4,000	4,000	4,000
Insurance	1,000	1,000	1,000
Maintenance	500	500	500
Power and fuel	1,000	1,000	1,000
Total fixed cost	6,500	6,500	6,500
Variable cost :			
Wages @ Rs. 2 per unit	1,200	1,600	2,000
Consumable stores @ Rs. 1.50 p.u.	900	1,200	1,500
Maintenance cost @ Re. 1 p.u.	600	800	1,000
Power and fuel at Re. 1 p.u.	600	800	1,000
Total variable cost	3,300	4,400	5,500
Fixed cost per unit	10.83	8.125	6.50
Variable cost per unit	5.50	5.50	5.50
Total cost per unit	16.33	13.625	12.000

ZERO BASED BUDGETING (ZBB)

Zero based budgeting is a new technique of budgeting introduced first in USA in the year 1969. This system of budgeting was developed by Peter Pyhrr of Texas Instruments of USA. This technique of budgeting is more useful in government budgeting but can also be used in factories for non-manufacturing activitites. Such as administration and selling activitites.

The ICMA terminology defines ZBB as "a method of budgeting whereby all activities are re-evaluated each time a budget is formulated. Each functional budget starts with the assumption that the function does not exist and is a zero cost. Increments of cost are compared with increments of benefits culminating in the planned maximum benefits for a given budgeted cost."

Thie technique of budgeting is considered to be an improvement over traditional method of budgeting, which is also known as 'incremental budgeting'. Under incremental budgeting every departmental manager would prepare a budget for his department based upon the previous experience and allow for a certain increase in amount in the budget for meeting contingency. However, in spite of a best forecast, sometimes the targets may not be achieved owing to inefficiency. Thus whenever previous budget is taken as a basis to prepare a current budget, the current budget involves an element of inefficiency that is carried forward from the previous year. Hence under ZBB, the budget is prepared by considering the base for the current year as zero and this eliminates the accrual of inefficiency for preparing future years budget.

The basic steps in implementing ZBB are as follows :

(*i*) Identify each function and activity of the organisation—this is referred to as a 'decision packing'.

(*ii*) Evaluate each decision package so as to ensure that is cost effective.

(*iii*) Compare each activity with possible atternatives.

(*iv*) Rank each activity—in some cases decision packages can be evaluated in terms of profitability or in any subjective terms using cost-benefit analysis.

(*v*) Allocate resources in accordance with the ranking of activitites and with resources available to the organisation.

BUDGET REPORT

The work of a budget officer does not end with the preparation and approval of budgets. The has to prepare reports on a continuous basis so as to facilitate comparison of actuals with budgets. The budgets reports are sent to various departmental managers showing favourable or adverse variance from the budget. Based on this the departmental managers will prepare a report to be submitted to the managing director pointing out the reasons for the variances. This enable remedial actions to be taken to set right unfavourable variance. The reports so furnished will also help as a guide for future planning.

According to W.W. Bigg, while preparing reports on budgets it is necessary to follow the undermentioned principles so as to make reports more effective :

1. The report should be clearly headed and the period covered shown. The unit, *viz.*, cash, tonnes, litre, etc., should be indicated.
2. Like must be compared with like and there must be no ambiguity of description. For example, it must be clear whether a sales report refers to 'deliveries made and invoiced' or to 'orders received'.
3. Information not relevant to the purpose for which the report is prepared should be omitted so that conclusions from the report can be drawn quickly and with certainty.
4. The report should not attempt to portray so much information that clarity is lost. If the information to be conveyed is complicated, more than one statement may be desirable. For example, to show actual sales compared with budet, analysed over both 'areas' and 'commodities', a separate statement for each analysis would improve clarity.
5. The information included should be limited to the sphere of the person to whom it is furnished. The data to be given to a foreman would normally be confined to that affecting his particular shop, but the factory manager would require broader information covering all departments for which he is responsible.
6. Promptness is to be prepferred to absolute accuracy, the purpose is not merely to

convey information but to convey it promptly and to the person who has the authority to take action.

7. All reports should be reviewed periodically to ensure that they are still useful and to ascertain whether they should be expanded contracted or discontinued.

QUESTIONS

I. Choose the correct answer from the following :

1. A budget that gives a summary of all the functional budgets and projected profit and loss account is known as
   (*a*) Capital budget (*c*) Master budget
   (*b*) Flexible budget (*d*) Discretionary budget [ ]
2. The fixed-variable cost classification has a speical significance in the preparation of
   (*a*) Flexible budget (*c*) Cash budget
   (*b*) Master budget (*d*) Capital budget [ ]
3. The basis difference a fixed budget and a flexible budget is that a fixed budget
   (*a*) includes only fixed costs and a flexible budget only variable cost.
   (*b*) is a budget for a single level of some measures of activity, what a flexible budget consists of several budgets based on different activity levels.
   (*c*) is concerned with future acquisition of fixed assets, while a flexible budget is concerned with expenses that vary with sales.
   (*d*) cannot be changed after a fiscal period begins, while a flexible budget can be changed after a fiscal period begins. [ ]
4. Which of the following is usually a long-term budget?
   (*a*) Sales budget (*c*) Capital expenditure budget
   (*b*) Cash budget (*d*) Fixed budget [ ]
5. Under flxeible budgeting
   (*a*) statements included in the budget report vary from period to period.
   (*b*) budget standards may be adjusted at will.
   (*c*) reporting dates vary according to the activity level reported upon.
   (*d*) planned activity level is adjusted to the actual activity level before the budget comparison report is prepared. [ ]

[***Answer :*** 1. (*c*), 2. (*a*), 3. (*b*), 4. (*c*), 5. (*d*)]

II. Mark 'T' or 'F' in the space provided

1. A budget is nothing but an estimate. *T/F*
2. Budgets are drawn up by the chief accountant. *T/F*
3. Budgets are blue prints for action. *T/F*
4. On the basis of budgets, next year's balance sheet and P & L a/c can be drawn up. *T/F*
5. Raw material supply is always the key factor. *T/F*
6. Diverse production is reduced to common basis on the basis of standard hours involved. *T/F*
7. Standing costing can operate without budgetary control. *T/F*
8. A system of budgetary control cannot be operated when standard costing system is in use. *T/F*
9. All functional budgets should be co-ordinated with sales budget which is always prepared first. *T/F*
10. A budget mannual is a summary of all the functional budget. *T/F*
11. Budgetary control system does not suit small business concern. *T/F*
12. Purchase budget and material budget is the same thing. *T/F*
13. A flexible budget is one which changes from year to year. *T/F*
14. A flexible budget system will recast quickly for changes in the volume of activity. *T/F*
15. A flexible budget carefully differentiates between fixed and variable cost. *T/F*

[***Answer :*** True—3, 4, 5, 6, 7, 14. Rest are all false]

III. Short and long answer questions

1. Define budgetary control and state its advantages. (*Kakatiya University, B.Com., Oct. 1989*)
2. Write notes on : (*a*) Limiting factor, (*b*) Budget mannual. (*Calicut University, M.Com., April 1992*)

3. What are 'budget' and 'budgetary control'? Discuss various advantages and essentials for success of budgetary control. *(Kakatiya University, M.Com., August 1991)*
4. What is budgetary control and how it is exercised? Discuss various advantages and essentials for the success of budgetary control. *(Mangalore University, B.Com., Oct. 1991)*
5. Briefly explain the steps in the installation of a system of budgetary control. *(University of Kerala, B.Com., April 1989)*
6. What is meant by 'budgetary control'? State the essentials of good budgetary control system". What are the advantages and limitations of a budgetary control system? *(Calicut University, B.Com., Oct. 1989)*
7. What is a flexible budget? How does it differ from a fixed budget? *(University of Kerala, B.Com., March 1990)*
8. What are the facts to be considered in setting up an annual sales budget? *(ICWA, Inter, Dec. 1989)*
9. What is zero base budgeting? What are the advantages of zero based approach over the traditional approach? *(ICWA, Inter, Dec. 1989)*
10. (*a*) Define the terms 'budget' and 'budgetary control'.
    (*b*) List down any five objectives of a budgetary control system. *(CA, Inter, Nov. 1990)*

EXERCISES

Exercise-1 (Sales budget) : The Royal industries has prepared its annual sales forecast expecting to achieve sales of Rs. 30,00,000 next year. The controller is uncertain about the pattern of sales to be expected by month and asks you to prepare a monthly budget of sales.

The following sales data pertain to the year, which is considered to be representative of a normal year :

Month	*Sales (Rs.)*	*Month*	*Sales (Rs.)*
Jan	1,10,000	July	2,60,000
Feb	1,15,000	Aug	3,30,000
Mar	1,00,000	Sept	3,40,000
Apr	1,40,000	Oct	3,50,000
May	1,80,000	Nov	2,00,000
June	2,25,000	Dec	1,50,000

Prepare a monthly sales budget for the coming year on the basis of the above data :

(University of Madras, B.Com., April 2000)

[**Answer :** Sales budget is to be prepared based on last years sales figures, *i.e.*, according to monthwise sales ratio.]

Jan	Rs. 1,32,000	July	Rs. 3,12,000
Feb	Rs. 1,38,000	Aug	Rs. 3,96,000
Mar	Rs. 1,20,000	Sept	Rs. 4,08,000
Apr	Rs. 1,68,000	Oct	Rs. 4,20,000
May	Rs. 2,16,000	Nov	Rs. 2,40,000
June	Rs. 2,70,000	Dec	Rs. 1,80,000
		Total	30,00,000

Exercise-2 (Sales overhead budget) : From the following estimates, prepare a sales overhead budget :

	Rs.
Advertisement	25,000
Salaries to sales department	50,000
Expenses of sales department	15,000
Counter salesman salaries	60,000

Commission to counter salesman is fixed at 10% on their sales.

Travelling salesman commission is fixed at 10% on their sales and expenses at 5% on their sales.

The sales during the period were estimated as follows :

Counter sales	Travelling salesman
Rs.	*Rs.*
8,00,000	1,00,000
12,00,000	1,50,000
14,00,000	2,00,000

(*University of Madras, B.Com., May 2000*)

[Answer : Total sales overhead budget : Rs. 1,73,000, Rs. 1,84,500, Rs. 1,94,000**]**

Exercise-3 (Materials Purchase budget)

The Sales Director of a manufacturing company reports that next year he expects to sell 50,000 units of a particular product.

Two kinds of raw materials A and B are required for manufacturing the finished product. Each unit of finished product requires 2 units of A and 3 units of B. The estimated opening balances at the commencement of next year are :

Finished goods – 10,000 units
Raw material A – 12,000 units
Raw material B – 15,000 units

The desirable closing balances at the end of next year :

Finished product – 14,000 units
A – 13,000 units, B – 16,000 units

Draw up a materials purchase budget

(*University of Madras, B.Com., April 2001*)

[Answer : (a) Production budget 54,000 units
(b) Materials consumption budget :

Material A	Material B
1,08,000 units	1,62,000 units

(c) Material purchase budget :

Material A	Material B
1,09,000 units	1,63,000 units.]

Exercise-4 (Production Cost budget)

From the following particulars, prepare production cost budget for the month of July 1999.

Particulars	*Opening stock* 1-7-1999	*Closing stock* 31-7-1999
Finished goods	12,000 units	16,000 units
Raw material-A	50,000 kgs	48,000 kgs
Raw material-B	20,000 kgs	31,000 kgs

Budgeted sales for the month-70,000 units

Raw material required to produce one unit : A - 4 kg at Rs. 8 per kg
B - 2 kg at Rs. 25 per kg.

(*University of Madras, B.Com., October 2000*)

Answer : (i) Production units budget 74,000
(ii) Raw material consumption budget for 74,000 units production
Material A - 2,96,000 kg
Material B - 1,48,00 kg
(iii) Raw materials purchase budget for 74,000 units
Material A - 2,94,000 kg
Material B - 1,59,000 kg
(iv) Purchase cost budget
Material A - Rs. 23,52,000
Material B - Rs. 39,75,000
(v) Production cost budget
Material A - Rs. 23,68,000
Material B - Rs. 37,00,000

Exercise-5 (Cash budget) : From the following information prepare a cash budget for the quarter ending 30-6-2000.

Month	*Sales*	*Purchases*	*Wages*	*Mise Expenses*
	Rs.	*Rs.*	*Rs.*	*Rs.*
Feb	1,20,000	84,000	10,000	7,000
Mar	1,30,000	1,00,000	12,000	8,000
Apr	80,000	1,04,000	8,000	6,000
May	1,16,000	1,06,000	10,000	12,000
June	88,000	80,000	8,000	6,000

Additional information :

(i) Cash on hand on 1-4-2000 Rs. 5000,

(ii) Sales – 20% realised in the month of sale, Discount allowed 2%; balance realised after two months,

(iii) Purchases are paid one month after,

(iv) Wages – 25% in arrears paid in the following month,

(v) Other expenses are paid at a lag of one month,

(vi) Income tax Rs. 25,000 due on or before 30-6-2000. *(Calcutta University, B.Com.(Hons.), 1999)*

[**Answer :** Closing cash in land
April 2000 – Rs. (–) 320
May 2000 – Rs. (+) 6916
June 2000 – Rs. (–) 63,336.]

Exercise-6 (Cash budget) : From the following data prepare a cash budget for the 3 months commencing 1st June 1996, when the bank balance was Rs. 1,00,000.

Month	*Sales*	*Purchases*	*Wages*	*Production Expenses*	*Adm. Expenses*
Apr	80,000	41,000	5,600	3,900	10,000
May	76,500	40,500	5,400	4,200	14,000
June	78,500	38,500	5,400	5,100	15,000
July	90,000	37,000	4,800	5,100	17,000
Aug	95000	35,000	4,700	6,000	13,000

There is a two month credit period allowed to customers and receipts from suppliers. Wages, production expenses and administration expenses are payable in the following month.

(Calcutta University, B.Com.(Hons.), 2000)

[**Answer :** Closing cash balance :

June	*July*	*August*
Rs. 1,15,400	1,25,900	1,39,000

Exercise-7 (Cash budget) : From the following budgeted figures a cash budget in respect of three months to June 30.

Months	*Sales*	*Materials*	*Wages*	*Overheads*
Jan	60,000	40,000	11,000	6,200
Feb	56,000	48,000	11,600	6,600
Mar	64,000	50,000	12,000	6,800
Apr	80,000	56,000	12,400	7,200
May	84,000	62,000	13,C00	8,600
June	76,000	50,000	14,000	8,000

Expected cash balance on 1st Apr – Rs. 20,000. Other information :

(a) Materials and overheads are to be paid during the month following the month of supply.

(b) Wages are to be paid during the month in which they are increased.

(c) Terms of Sales : The terms of credit sales are payment by the end of the month following the month of sales : ½ of the sales are paid when due, the other half to be paid during the next month. 5% sales commission is to be paid within the month following actual sales.

(d) Preference dividend for Rs. 30,000 is to be paid on 1st May.

(e) Share call money for Rs. 25,000 is due on 1st April and 1st June.

(f) Plant and Machinery worth Rs. 10,000 is to be installed in the month of January and the payment is to be made in the month of June. *(University of Madras, B.Com., April 1999)*

[**Answer :** Closing balance of cash

April	*May*	*June*
Rs. 32,600	(–) 5600	2,600].

Exercise-8 (Flexible budget) : The expenses for budgeted production of 10,000 units in a factory are given below :

	Per unit (Rs.)
Materials	70
Labour	25
Variable overheads	20
Fixed overhead (Rs. 1,00,000)	10
Variable expenses (Direct)	5
Selling expenses (10% fixed)	13
Distribution expenses (20% fixed)	7
Administration expenses (Rs. 50,000)	5
Total cost per unit (to make and sell)	155

Prepare a budget for production of (a) 8000 units (b) 6000 units and (c) indicate cost per unit at both the levels.

(Bangalore University, B.Com., October 2000)

[**Answer :**	*10,000 units*	*8,000 units*	*6,000 units*
Amount (Rs.)	15,50,000	12,75,400	10,00,800
Cost per unit	155	159.42	166.80.

Exercise-9 (Flexible budget) : A company incurs the following expenses to produce 1000 units of an article.

	Rs.
Direct materials	30,000
Direct Labour	15,000
Power (20% fixed)	10,000
Repairs & Maintenance (15% fixed)	8,000
Depreciation (40% variable)	6,000
Administrative expenses (100% fixed)	12,000

Prepare a flexible budget showing individual expenses of production levels at 1500 units and 2000 units *(Calcutta University, B.Com.(Hons.), 1998)*

[**Answer :**	*1000 units*	*1500 units*	*2000 units*
Amount (Rs.)	81,000	1,12,100	1,43,200
Cost per unit	81	74.73	71.60.

26

STANDARD COSTING

HISTORICAL COSTING

Historical costing is one of the techniques of ascertaining cost of production. It is based on accumulation of actual or historical cost. The National Association of Accountants has defined historical cost as "the cost which is accumulated during the process of production by the usual historical costing technique as opposed to the cost which has been determined in advance of the production process. The term 'actual' is not intended to convey any implication as to the accuracy with which costs are measured." Historical costing is not a very popular technique as it suffers from the following limitations :

(*a*) It provides cost information only after the completion of production. So cost of production cannot be ascertained until production is completed. The fixation of selling price becomes difficult under such situation.

(*b*) It is not possible to exercise control over the costs which are actually incurred.

(*c*) It becomes difficult to take decisions based on actual costs.

(*d*) Actual costs may vary from period to period and fixation of selling price on the basis of actual cost will lead to differences in selling price which may not be accepted by customers.

(*e*) It is an expensive and time consuming technique. For example, in a larger sized business, to ascertain the cost of production of say 1 lakh units involving different materials and various expenses will involve more time and clerical work.

In order to overcome the above limitations, standard costing was developed.

STANDARD COST AND STANDARD COSTING

A standard cost has been defined by Lucey (*Costing*) as "a predetermined calculation of how much costs should be under specified working conditions".

Brown and Howard in their book *Principles and Practice of Management Accountancy* define a standard cost as a predetermined cost which determines what each product or service should cost under given circumstances.

The ICMA terminology defines a standard cost as "a predetermined cost calculated in relation to a prescribed set of working conditions, correlating technical specifications and scientific measurements of materials and labour to the prices and wage rates expected to apply during the period to which the standard cost is intended to relate, with an addition of an appropriate share of budgeted overhead".

The objects of standard costs are as follows :

1. Promoting and measuring efficiencies.
2. Controlling and reducing costs.
3. Simplifying costing procedure.
4. Valuing inventories.
5. Fixing selling price.

Standard costing has been defined by Brown and Howard as "a technique of cost accounting which compares the 'standard cost' of each product or service with the actual cost to determine the efficiency of the operation, so that any remedial action may be taken immediately".

The ICMA terminology defines standard costing as "the preparation and use of standard costs, their comparison with actual cost and the analysis of variances to their causes and points of incidence".

According to the above two definitions, standard costing involves the following steps :

(*a*) Setting of standards.
(*b*) Measurement of results.
(*c*) Comparison of actuals with standards to determine the variance.
(*d*) Investigation of variance.
(*e*) Taking remedial action to set right adverse variance.

DIFFERENCES BETWEEN A BUDGET AND STANDARD

1. A standard is a unit concept, *i.e.*, the apply to a particular product, process or operation, whereas budgets are concerned with totals, *i.e.*, for the firms as a whole.
2. Standards are revised only when they are inapproporiate for current operating conditions, whereas budgets are revised on a periodic basis generally once a year.
3. Standards and the resulting variances are part of the double entry system of accounting, whereas budgets are memorandum figures and do not form part of double entry system of accounting.

DIFFERENCES BETWEEN A BUDGETARY CONTROL AND STANDARD COSTING

Budgetary control	*Standard costing*
1. It is prepared to cover various functions of a business such as purchases, sales, production. finance, etc. In other words it has a macro-approach.	1. It is prepared in respect of a cost unit. In other words it has a micro-approach.
2. It is more extensive as it covers all the operations of the business.	2. It is more intensive technique of controlling costs.
3. It is a projection of financial accounts.	3. It is a projection of cost accounts.
4. It can be implemented even in parts, *i.e.*, to cover one or more than one area of business.	4. It covers all items of expenses without leaving any item. So it cannot be operated in part.
5. It can be operated without standards.	5. It cannot exist without budget.
6. It is more management oriented.	6. It is more engineering oriented.
7. It can be implemented in all industries.	7. It is not possible in certain industries.
8. It does not involve any accounting after computing variances.	8. Variances are accounted for under standard costing.
9. Its objects are formulation of policy, co-ordination of activities, and delegation of authority.	9. Its aim is to enable management in making decisions, in price-flxing and valuation of closing stock.

STANDARD COSTING AND STANDARDISED COSTING

Standard costing should not be confused with standardised costing as both are completely different. Standard costing is a tool of cost control whereas standardised costing refers to a uniform application of costing and cost accounting principles and procedures to a firm having number of plants. The object of standardised costing is to facilitate inter-firm comparison of results.

Secondly, standard costing technique makes use of only standard cost. Whereas standardised costing can be operated with the help of historical cost also.

Thirdly standard costing is operated on the principles of exception, whereas, standardised costing in based on the principle of example.

Lastly, the objective of standard costing is to set and maintain the standard. Whereas, the objective of standardised costing is to improve upon the standard in addition to maintaining the standard.

ADVANTAGES AND LIMITATIONS OF STANDARD COSTING

The advantages of standard costing are as follows :

1. It provides a yardstick against which actuals are measured.
2. Standard costing helps in standardising the various activities of a business. Thus it enables use of standard materials and better method of production.
3. It increases the cost consciousness among all concerned by fixing targets and to achieve them.
4. This technique follow the principles of management by exception.
5. It simplifies the accounting procedure which involves less clerical work and time.
6. It helps in valuing the closing stock.
7. It pinpoints the responsibility of everybody concerned in the organisation.
8. It facilitates cost control by analysing the causes of inefficiency and by taking remedial measures. This will result in reduced cost of production.
9. It enables in periodic preparation of profit and loss account which helps management in knowing the trends of the business.
10. It helps in introducing incentives to employees and provides a basis for motivating them.
11. It helps in fixing selling price in advance of production. Thus quotations can be sent and orders secured.

The limitations of standard costing are as follows :

1. It is difficult to establish standards in practice.
2. Standards established may have to be revised owing to changing conditions. But frequent revision of standards is costly and may create problems.
3. Standards which are inaccurate, unreliable and outdated may do more harm than good.
4. If the standards set are not attained it will lead to psychological effects resulting in frustration.
5. It may not be suitable for small concerns.
6. It cannot be applied to non-standardised industries and in industries where goods are to be manufactured according to specification of customers.

PRELIMINARIES IN ESTABLISHING A SYSTEM OF STANDARD COSTING

Before establishing a system of standard costing the following preliminary factors are to be considered.

1. Establishment of Cost Centre

In order to identify the areas of efficiency or otherwise of it and to fix responsibilities for the persons who are concerned with attaining the standards, it is necessary to establish cost centre. A main cost centre can again be sub-divided into sub-cost centre for exercising better control. Having established cost centres, the next requirement is to fix up responsibility on the persons who are incharge of such cost centres.

2. Classification of Accounts

It refers to classifying the costs under a suitable accounting heading. This facilitates quick identification and collection of expenses, their analysis and in prompt reporting. As was explained under chapter 2, costs can be classified on the basis of number of characteristics. Having classified, it is desireable to give a code number for each heading of cost. For example, raw materials may be given a code number from 0 to 10, direct labour cost 11 to 20 factory overheads 21 to 30 and so on.. This results in convenience in dealing with costs and ensures secrecy.

3. Determination of Duration

This refers to the period for which standard are used. It may be a short or long duration.

4. Determine the Capacity

It refers to fixation of standard output for the sake of fixing fixed and variable overheads.

5. Types of Standard

It refers to the level of attainment accepted by management as the basis on which standard costs are determined. The following are the important types of standards.

(*a*) **Basic or fixed or static standard :** It is defined by the ICMA terminology as "a standard established for use over a long period from which a current standard can be developed. These standards remain constant for a long period of time and hence they are also termed as long-term standards. They show the trend over a period of time relating to material prices, labour rates, effects of changing methods. They serve at the most as the statistical data and is not used to evaluate current efficiency or inefficiency.

(*b*) **Ideal standard :** It is defined by the ICMA terminology as "a standard which can be attained under the most favourable conditions". Such standards are based on the best possible operating conditions. In other words the productive activity is carried out assuming that there are no breakdown in machineries, no wastage in materials, no idle time. This standard, while using is revised periodically to reflect improvement in methods, materials and technology. It is difficult to attain ideal standard in practice and hence rarely used. Therefore, such standards are used for the purpose of investigation and development but not for controlling day-to-day activities.

(*c*) **Attainable or expected or practical standard :** It is defined by the ICMA termonolgy as "a standard which can be attained if a standard unit of work is carried out efficiently, a machine properly operated or materials properly used. This is most widely used in practice. This standard is based on efficient operating condition though not a perfect condition. This standards covers allowances for normal material wastages, for fatigue, machine breakdown, etc. This standard is more realistic in nature and hence used for cost control, valuing stock and a basis for budgeting.

(*d*) **Current standard :** It is defined by the ICMA terminology as "a standard established for use over a short period of time related to current conditions". This standard is used to reflect the current condition. It can be equated to attainable standard during the period of stable prices and normal conditions.

(*e*) **Normal standard :** It is defined by the ICMA terminology as "the average standard which it is anticipated can be attained over a future period of time, preferably, long enough to cover one trade cycle". Accordingly, this standard may be prepared once in 10 years.

STANDARD HOUR

It is a measure used in standard costing by means of which products in different forms such as solid, liquid and gases are measured. The standard hour is the quantity of output or amount of work which should be produced in one hour. In other words, a standard hour is the expression of the actual output in terms of standard time instead of units. The ICMA terminology defines it as "a hypothetical unit pre-established to represent the amount of work which should be performed in one hour under standard performance". The concept of standard hour has a practical advantage in the measurement of efficiency ratio, activity ratio of an organisation.

Problem 1 : A factory produces three products *X*, *Y* and *Z*. The standard time allowed are 10 hours, 15 hours and 12 hours respectively. The actual production in January 2003 and February 2003 are as under :

		Jan. 2003 (units)	*Feb. 2003 (units)*
Product	*X*	20,000	12,000
	Y	10,000	12,000
	Z	15,000	18,000

By what percentage has production changed in February over January. If the actual hours paid for each in January and February were 6,00,000 what is the rate of labour efficiency?

Solution :

Statement showing production in Jan. & Feb.

	January		*February*	
	Units	*Std. hrs.*	*Units*	*Std. hrs.*
X	20,000	2,00,000	12,000	1,20,000
Y	10,000	1,50,000	12,000	1,80,000
Z	15,000	1,80,000	18,000	2,16,000
Total	45,000	5,30,000	42,000	5,16,000

Output in February has declined by 14,000 hrs. (5,30,000 – 5,16,000), *i.e.*, by 2.6% over January.

Labour efficiency in :

January $\frac{5,30,000}{6,00,000} \times 100 = 88.33\%$

February $\frac{5,16,000}{6,00,000} \times 100 = 86\%$

STANDARD COST CARD

A standard cost card is used for recording the standard cost. It is prepared for each product or service. It contains particulars relating to quantity and price of materials consumed, time and rate of labour required, overheads and the total cost. A specimen of standard cost card is shown below :

Standard Cost Card

Part No.______	Description______		Batch Qty.______		
Elements of cost	Standard rate	Dept. 1	Dept. 2	Dept. 3	Total
Direct material					
Direct labour					
Production overhead					
Administration overhead					
Selling and distribution					
		______	______	______	______
		______	______	______	______

Fig. 26.1. Specimen showing standard cost card.

PROCEDURE FOR INTRODUCING STANDARD COSTING

Introduction of standard costing system involves a number of steps. Setting up of standard cost for each element of cost—direct material, diect labour and overheads is a complex task. Standards must be setup carefully since a low standard which everyone can achieve does not bring out the best performance. Too high a standard on the other hand, is being impossible to achive, is treated with disdain and indifference. Setting up of standards is not merely an accounting job, it involes the cooperation of various functional departments. The following steps are to be followed while introducing a standard costing in a factory.

1. To study the technical aspects of the factory. This involves a study of the various methods of manufacture and the process involved. The input-output relationship of each process is to be worked out. For this purpose, the total production process has to be sub-divided into various sub-process of manufacture. The pattern of losses—normal and abnormal—in each sub-process over a considerable period of time should be examined. By going through the previous production records, the number of defectives and their cost of rectification should also be looked into. Previous records should be studied in order to work out the normal efficiency of labour in each production process. This study of the technical aspect of the factory is essential since a system of standard cost must be based on the actual situation in the factory.

2. The existing cost system should be reviewed with special reference to the existing records and forms. This is important since the standard costing system has to be established as an extension to the existing system of maintaining cost.

3. The organisation chart showing the various lines of authority and responsibilities should be studied so that the responsibility of supplying basic data regarding the various operations of the undertaking can be established.

4. One of the important steps involved in the implementation of standard costing is to secure the cooperation of all executive in the factory in order to fix the quality and efficient standard. The standard costing will be successful only if it receives full-fledged support from various line managers. If line managers view it merely as an imposition by the accounting department they will never cooperate with it. It is essential to classify that the system is for the benefit and would be run only if they find it useful. A standard cost committee may be formed comprising important line managers to discuss the various problems regarding standard costing system.

5. The existing cost policies specially with regard to the methods of allocation and apportionment of overheads should be studied so that what should constitutes as the standard cost can be clearly defined.

6. The budgetary control and internal control procedures should also be reviewed since the standard costing system is to be built up on the existing system of control and budgeting.

7. A detailed manual should be prepared for the guidance of the staff. This manual should briefly describe the system about to be enforced and should list benefits arising there from. It should then clearly demarcate responsibilities of generating the activity and cost data. The various definitions must be clearly defined and the following procedure of the system outlined :

(*a*) Establishment of standard cost.
(*b*) Target dates for fixing the standards.
(*c*) Target dates for fixing standard cost.
(*d*) Various reports of actual performances to be sent to accounts department for ascertaining the variances.
(*e*) Variance analysis reports to be sent by the accounts department.
(*f*) Any other relevant information.

8. The office-staff required to work the system should be properly trained. When the system goes into force, a number of alterations would be required in the scheme of making entries and in document flow.

9. To fix up the material quantity standard. The following is the procedure involved in setting material quantity standards.

(*a*) *Standardisation of products* : This involves drawing detailed specifications, blue prints, norms for normal wastage.
(*b*) *Classification of products* : This involves preparation of details lists of products to be manufactured.
(*c*) *Standardisation of materials* : This involves determination of quality, specifications, etc. to be used in the standard products.
(*d*) *Bill of materials* : This involves preparation of a bill of materials for each product showing the quantity of materials needed.
(*e*) *Test runs* : This helps in setting standards when production is to be undertaken under regulated conditions.

The material price standards are then fixed based on the following factors :
(*a*) Stock of materials on hand and its value.
(*b*) The prices at which orders for future deliveries of materials have been placed.
(*c*) Possible price fluctuations.

10. To fix up labour quantity standards by applying the following steps :
(*a*) Standardisation and classification of products.
(*b*) Training facilities required.
(*c*) Time and motion studies.
(*d*) Production planning techniques.
(*e*) Selection of right machines, deciding the method of operation.

The labour cost standard can be set up by studying data regarding the wage rates paid.

11. Determination of standard overhead rate : This involes the following steps :
(*a*) Determination of standard overhead cost.
(*b*) Estimation of the level of activity.

By dividing standard overhead for the budget period by the estimated level of activity, the standard overhead rate can be compiled.

12. Determination of standard administration cost : The purpose of setting standard administration cost is to secure maximum service at minimum cost. This objective can be achieved by a study conducted by organisation and method department. Setting up of standards also depends upon standardisation and simplification of office procedure. The standard quantity of work to be performed can be set on the following basis :

(*a*) Past performance.
(*b*) On the advise of O & M studies.
(*c*) Time and motion studies.

13. Determination of standard selling and distribution cost : Selling and distribution expenses bears a close relationship with sales volume. Hence a sales forecast is necessary before setting standard cost for selling and distribution. The classification into fixed and variable will help in setting standard cost.

VARIANCE ANALYSIS

The ICMA terminology defines a variance as "the difference between a standard cost and the comparable actual cost incurred during a given period. The purpose of knowing the variance is to enable the management to exercise control over cost. It enables to know whether the standards set is achieved or not.

Variance analysis has been defined by the terminology as "the process of computing the amount of and isolating the cause of variances between actual costs and standard cost". Thus variance analysis involves : (*a*) computation of individual variances and, (*b*) determination of the cause of each variance. The purpose of variance analysis is to enable management to improve operations, increase efficiency, utilise resources more effectively and reduce cost. To serve these purposes variance analysis must be easy to understand, they must be calculated immediately and the causes must be immediately enquired and remedial measures quickly taken.

A variance is said to be favourable when the actual results are better than the standards and an adverse or unfavourable variance when actuals are not up to the standard. Similarly, a variance is said to be controllable when it is amenable to control by an executive action and an uncontrollable variance when it is not amenable to control by executive action. An unfavourable variance is caused by external environment such as market conditions, fluctuations in demand, supply etc. In other words, no individual in the organisation can be held responsible for it.

Before calculating various cost variances it would be appropriate to know the meaning of the following concepts :

(*a*) *Actual production :* It means actual quantity produced during the actual hours worked.
(*b*) *Budgeted production :* It means the budgeted quantity to be produced during the budgeted hours to be worked.
(*c*) *Standard production :* It means the quantity which should have been produced during the actual hours worked.
(*d*) *Actual cost :* It means the actual quantity produced at the actual cost per unit.
(*e*) *Budgeted cost :* It means the budgeted quantity to be produced at the standard cost per unit.

(*f*) *Standard cost* : It means the actual quantity produced at the standard cost per unit. The various cost variances are as follows :

1. Material Variance

The various material cost variances can be shown under the following chart :

Material cost variance

- Material price variance
- Material usage variance
  - Material mix variance
  - Material yield variance

Fig. 26.2. Chart showing material cost variance.

(*a*) **Material cost variance :** It refers to the difference between the standard cost of materials specified and the actual cost of materials used. It arises owing to variation in the price of the material or in its usage. The ICMA terminology defines it as "the difference between the standard direct material cost of the actual production volume and the actual cost of direct material. The following formula is used to calculate this variance.

Material cost variance = (Standard units × Standard price) – (Actual units × Actual price)

Material cost variance is the aggregate of material price and usage variance.

(*b*) **Material price variance :** It refers to that portion of material cost variance which is due to the difference between the standard price and the actual price paid. The ICMA terminology defines it as "that portion of the direct material cost variance which is the difference between the standard price specified and the actual price paid for the direct material used". This variance arises on account of extra price paid on the units purchased. It can be calculated at the time of purchase or at the time of usage. Generally the former is preferable. The formula to calculate material price variance is as follows :

Direct material price variance = (Standard price – Actual price) × Actual quantity

The direct material price variance arises on account of the following causes :

(*a*) Higher or lower prices paid than planned.
(*b*) Discounts received or foregone depending upon quantity bought.
(*c*) Purchase of superior or inferior quality of materials than planned.
(*d*) Buying substitute materials.
(*e*) Increase in charges such as transport cost, etc.

(*c*) **Material usage variances :** It refers to that portion of material cost variance owing to the difference between the standard quantity of materials specified and the actual quantity used. The ICMA terminology defines it as "the difference between the standard quantity specified for the actual production and the actual quantity used at standard purchase price". The following formula is used to calculate this variance :

Material usage variance = (Standard quantity – Actual quantity) × Std. price

The following causes give rise to material usgage variance :

(*a*) Low or high yield from material than expected.
(*b*) Gain or loss arising out of substitue materials.
(*c*) Difference in the quality of materials than planned.
(*d*) Increased or decreased quantity of scrap than expected.
(*e*) Use of sub-standard or defective materials.

(*f*) Carelessness in the use of materials.
(*g*) Pilferage.
(*h*) Defective method of production.
(*i*) Wrong mixture of raw materials.

The material usage variance can be sub-divided into material mix and material yield variance.

(*d*) **Material mix variance :** The calculation of this variance arises in those industries where different types of raw materials are mixed to obtain required output. Examples of such industries are fertilisers, chemical, cement, food processing industries and so on. One distinct feature of such industries is, it involves losses by way of evaporation, breakage, shrinkage, etc. and are responsible for difference in the output. The ICMA terminology defines it as "the difference between total quantity in standard proportion, priced at the standard price and the actual quantity of materials used priced the standard price. In simple words it is that portion of material usage variance which is due to the difference between the standard and the actual composition of mixture.

Material mix variance may arise under the following two situations :

1. Where the ratio of standard mix differ from the ratio of actual mix, but the total quantity of both the actual mix and standard mix remaining the same.

The following formula is used in this situation.

$$\text{Material mix variance} = (\text{Revised std. qty.} - \text{Actual qty.}) \times \text{Std. price}$$

In this case the revised standard quantity is the same as the standard quantity.

2. Where both the ratio as well as total quantity differ between the standard and the actual mix.

The above formula is applicable in this situation also with a difference in calculating the revised standard quantity. The following formula is used to calculates the revised standard quantity.

$$\text{Revised std. qty.} = \frac{\text{Total weight of actual mix}}{\text{Total weight of std. mix}} \times \text{Std. qty of material in question}$$

This is because, the standard quantity of each material will be revised, when the total weight of actual mix varies from the total weight of standard mix.

(*e*) **Material yield variance :** It is the difference between the standard yield specified and the actual yield obtained. The ICMA terminology defines it as "the difference between the standard yield of the actual material input and the actual yield both valued at the standard material cost.

There are two situations under which material yield variance can arise, *viz.*, (*i*) where actual mix does not differ from standard mix. In this situation the following formula is used

$$\text{Material yield variance} = (\text{Total actual yield} - \text{Total std. yield}) \times \text{Std. yield rate}$$

$$\textit{where}, \text{ Std. yield rate} = \frac{\text{Standard cost of std. mix}}{\text{Net standard output}}$$

(*ii*) Where actual mix differ from standard mix. The following formula is used in this situation.

$$\text{Material yield variance} = (\text{Actual yield} - \text{Revised std. yield}) \times \text{Std. yield rate}$$

$$\textit{where}, \text{ Std. yield rate} = \frac{\text{Std. cost of revised std. mix}}{\text{Net std. output}}$$

Material yield variance will arise owing to the following causes :

(*a*) Use of sub-standard quality of materials.

(*b*) Losses arising out of chemical reaction.

(c) Defective method of production.

(*d*) Inadequete supervison.

Problem 2 : Bello Chemical Industries provide the following information from their records :
For making 10 kgs. of OMO, the standard material requiredment is :

Material	*Qty. (kg.)*	*Rate per kg.*
X	8	6
Y	4	4

During December 1990, 100 kgs. of OMO were produced. The actual consumption of material is as under :

Material	*Qty. (kg.)*	*Rate per kg.*
X	75	7
Y	50	5

Calculate (*i*) Material cost variance.
(*ii*) Material price variance.
(*iii*) Material usage variance. (*University of Delhi, B.Com. (Hons.), 1991*)

Solution :

For 100 kgs. of OMO

Material	*Standard*		*Actuals*	
	Qty.	*Rate*	*Qty.*	*Rate*
X	80*[1]	6	75	7
Y	40*[2]	4	50	5

(*i*) Material cost variance = (Std. units × Std. price) – (Actual units × Actual price)

X = (80 × 6) – (75 × 7)
= 480 – 525 = –45 (*A*)

Y = (40 × 4) – (50 × 5)
= 160 – 250 = – 90 (*A*)

Total (–) 135 (*A*)

(*ii*) Material price variance = (Std. price – Actual price) × Actual qty.

X = (6 – 7) × 75 = 75 (*A*)

Y = (4 – 5) × 50 = 50 (*A*)

Total 125 (*A*)

(*iii*) Material usage variance = (Std. qty. – Actual qty.) × Std. price

X = (80 – 75) × 6 = 30 *F*

Y = (40 – 50) × 4 = 40 *A*

Total 10 A

Varification :

Material cost variance = Material price variance + Material usage variance

135 (*A*) = 125 *A* + 10*A*

*[1]. For 10 kgs. → 8kg in requried

For 100 kgs. → $\frac{8}{10} \times 100 = 80$

*[2] For 10 kgs. → 4 kg. is required

For 100 kgs. → ? $\frac{4}{10} \times 100 = 40$

Problem 3 : From the given data, calculate :

(*a*) Material price variance.

(*b*) Material usage variance.
(*c*) Material cost variance.

Standard :

(1) 250 kg. of raw materials is required for producing 175 kgs. of finished products.
(2) Price of material per kgs. Rs. 4

Actuals :

(1) Production 52,500 kg.
(2) Materials consumed 70,000 kgs.
(3) Cost of materials Rs. 2,73,000

(*SV, University, B.Com., April 1999*)

Solution :

Calculation of Actual price $= \dfrac{\text{Actual Material Cost}}{\text{Actual Materials Consumed}}$

$= \dfrac{2,73,000}{70,000 \text{ kg}} = \text{Rs. } 3.90 \text{ per kg.}$

(1) Material price variance = (Std. Price – Actual Price) × Actual usage
= (4.00 – 3.90) × 70,000
= 0.10 × 70,000 = 7,000 *F*

Calculation of Standard usage

For 175 kgs. of production, 250 kgs. of raw materials
For 52,500 kgs. → ?

$\dfrac{52,500}{175} \times 250 = 75,000$ kgs.

(2) Material usage variance = Std. qty. – Actual qty.) × Std. price
= (75,000 – 70,000) × 4
= 5,000 × 4 = 20,000 *F*

(3) Material cost variance = (Std. qty. × Std. price) – (Actual qty. – Actual price)
= (75,000 × 4) – (70,000 × 3.90)
= 3,00,000 – 2,73,000
= 27,000 *F*

Varification :

Material cost variance = Material price variance + Material usage variance
27,000 *F* = 7,000 *F* + 20,000 *F*
27,000 *F* = 27,000 *F*

Problem 4 : From the given data below, calculate (*i*) the material price variance, (*ii*) Material usage variance, (*iii*) Material cost variance

Quantity of materials purchased	3,000 units
Value of materials purchased	Rs. 9,000
Standard quantity of materials required per tonne of output	30 units
Standard rate of materials	Rs. 2.50 per unit
Opening stock of materials	NIL
Closing stock of materials	500 units
Output during the period	80 tonnes

Solution :

Calculation of quantity of materials used

Qty. of opening stock of materials	Nil
Add : Qty. of materials purchased	3,000
	3,000
Less : Qty. of closing stock of materials	500
	2,500

Calculation of actual price of materials purchased

$$= \frac{\text{Value of materials purchased}}{\text{Qty. of materials purchased}}$$

$$= \frac{9,000}{3,000} = 3$$

Calculation of standard qty. of materials for actual output

= Std. qty. of materials required per tonne of output × Actual output during the year
= 30 × 80 = 2,400 units

(1) Material price variance = (Std. price – Actual price) × Actual qty.
= (2.50 – 3.00) × 2,500
= 0.50 × 2,500 = 1,250 *A*

(2) Material usage variance = (Std. qty. – Actual qty.) × Std. price
= (2,400 – 2,500) × 2.50
= 100 × 2.50 = 250

(3) Material cost variance = (Std. qty. × Std. rate) – (Actual qty. × Actual rate)
= 2,400 × 2.50) – (2,500 × 3)
= 6,000 – 7,500 = Rs. 1,500 (*A*)

Problem 4 : From the following data extracted from the books Arvind Parimal Works, calculate the material mix variance :

	Standard	*Actual*
Material *A*	70 units @ Rs. 6 per unit	60 units @ Rs. 10 per unit
Material *B*	30 units @ Rs. 4 per unit	40 units @ Rs. 2 per unit
Output	100 units	100 units

Solution : In this problem the total weight of the standard mix (70 + 30) = 100 units and the total weight of the actual mix (60 + 40) = 100 units are the same. So the revised standard quantity of each material will be the same as its standrad quantity.

Materials mix variance = (Revised Std. qty. – Actual qyt.) × Std. price
A = (70 – 60) × 6
= 10 × 6 = 60 *F*
B = (30 – 40) × 4
= 10 × 4 = 40 *A*

Total material mix variance :
Material *A* = 60 F
Material *B* = 40 A
20 F

Problem 5 : Calculate the mateial mix variance from the following data :

	Standard			*Actual*		
	Qty. *kg.*	*Rate* *Rs.*	*Amt.* *Rs.*	*Qty.* *kg.*	*Rate* *Rs.*	*Amt.* *Rs.*
Material *X*	6	1.50	9	5	2.40	12
Material *Y*	2	3.50	7	1	6.00	6
	8	2.00	16	6	3.60	18

Solution : In this problem, the total standard mix is different from the total actual mix. So, we have to calculate the revised standard quantity in respect of each materials.

$$\frac{\text{Total weight of actual mix}}{\text{Total weight of standard mix}} \times \text{Std. Qty. of the material in the mix}$$

Material A $= \frac{6}{8} \times 6 = 4.5$ kgs.

Material B $= \frac{6}{8} \times 2 = 1.5$ kgs.

Materials mix variance = (Revisred Std. Qty. – Actual Qty.) × Std. price

A = (4.5 – 5) × 1.50
= 0.5 × 1.50 = 0.75 (A)

B = (1.5 – 1) × 3.50
= 0.50 × 3.50 = 1.75 (F)

Net material mix variance :

Material A = 0.75 (A)
Material B = 1.75 (F)
1.00 (F)

Problem 6 : From the given data below, calculate the material price variance, the material usage variance, material cost variance and material mix variance.

Consumption per 100 units of product

Raw material	*Standard*	*Actual*
A	40 units @ Rs. 50 per unit	50 units @ Rs. 50 per unit
B	60 units @ Rs. 40 per unit	60 units @ Rs. 45 per unit

(*S.V. University, B.Com., October 1999*)

Solution :

Calculation of actual quantity used

A = 100 units @ 50 units per unit = 5,000 units
B = 100 units @ 60 units per unit = 6,000 units

(1) Material price variance = (Std. price – Actual price) × Actual Qty.

A = (50 – 50) × 5,000
= 0 × 5,000 = Nil

B = (40 – 45) × 6,000
= 5 – 6,000 = 30,000 A

Calculation of Standard quantity

A = 100 × 40 = 4,000 units
B = 100 × 60 = 6,000 units

(2) Materials usage variance = (Std. Qty. – Actual Qty.) × Std. price

A = (4,000 – 5,000) × 50
= 1,000 × 50 = 50,000 A

B = (6,000 – 6,000) × 40
= 0 × 40 = NIL

(3) Material cost variance = (Std. Qty. × Std. price) – (Actual Qty. × Actual price)

A = (4,000 × 50) – (5,000 × 50)
= 2,00,000 – 2,50,000 = 50,000 (A)

B = (6,000 × 40) – (6,000 × 45)
= 2,40,000 – 2,70,000 = 30,000 (A)

Verification :

	Material cost variance	=	Material price variance + Material usage variance
A	50,000 A	=	NIL + 50,000 A
B	30,000 A	=	30,000 A + NIL

(4) Calculation of Revised Std. Qty.

$$\text{Revised Std. Qty.} = \frac{\text{Total weight of Actual mix}}{\text{Total weight of Std. mix}} \times \text{Std. Qty. of material in question}$$

$$A = \frac{11,000}{10,000} \times 4,000 = 4,400$$

$$B = \frac{11,000}{10,000} \times 6,000 = 6,600$$

Material mix variance = (Revised Std. Qty. – Actual Qty.) × Std. price

A = (4,400 – 5,000) × 50
= 600 × 50 = 30,000 *A*

B = (6,600 – 6,000) × 40
= 600 × 40 = 24,000 *F*

Problem 7 : Mixers Ltd. is engaged in producing a standard mix by using 60 kgs. of Chemical *X* and 40 kgs. of Chemical *Y*. The standard loss of production is 30%. The standard price of *X* is Rs. 5 per kg. and *Y* is Rs. 10 per kgs.

The actual mix and yield were as follows :

X — 80 kgs. @ Rs. 4.5 per kg.
Y — 70 kgs. @ Rs. 8 per kg.
Actual yield is 115 kgs.
Calculate material variances. *(CS, Inter, December 1998)*

Solution :

	Standard cost			Actual cost			Standard cost for actual input qty.		
	Qty.	Rate	Amt.	Qty.	Rate	Amt.	Qty.	Rate	Amt.
$X = \frac{60}{70} \times 115$	= 98.571	5	493	80	4.50	360	80	5	400
$Y = \frac{40}{70} \times 115$	= 65.714	10	657	70	8.00	560	70	10	700
	164.3		1,150	150		920	150		1,100
Less : 30%	49.3		–	35		–			
	115		1,150	115		920			

(1) Material cost variance = (SQ × SR) – (AQ × AR)

X = (98.571 × 5) – (80 × 4.50)
= 492.86 – 360 = 132.86 *F*

Y = (65.714 × 10) – (70 × 8)
= 657.14 – 560 = 97.14 *F*

230 *F*

(2) Material usage variance = (SQ – AQ) × SP

X = (98.571 – 80) × 5 = 92.86 *F*

Y = (65.714 – 70) × 10 = 42.86 *A*

50.00 *F*

(3) Material price variance = (SP – AP) × SQ

X = (5 – 4.50) × 80 = 40 *F*

Y = (10 – 8) × 70 = 140 *F*

180 *F*

(4) *Calculation of Revised Std. Qty.*

$$\frac{\text{Total weight of Actual Mix}}{\text{Total weight of std. mix}} \times \text{Std. Qty. of material in question}$$

$$X = \frac{150}{164.3} \times 98.6 = 90$$

$Y = \frac{150}{164.3} \times 65.7 \qquad = 60$

Material mix variance = (Revised Std. Qty. – Actual Qty.) × Std. price

$X = (90 - 80) \times 5 = 50\ F$

$Y = (60 - 70) \times 10 = 100\ A$

$\qquad\qquad\qquad 50\ A$

(5) *Calculation of standard yield*

$\frac{115}{164.3} \times 150 = 105$ kgs.

Material yield variance = (Actual yield – Std. yield) × Std. price

= (115 – 105) × 10 = 100 *F*

Problem 8 : The standard cost of a certain chemical mixture was :

40% Materials *A* at Rs. 200 per ton

60% Material *B* at Rs. 300 per ton

A standard loss of 10% is expected in production. During the period the following materials were used :

90 tons. Material *A* at the cost of Rs. 180 per ton.

110 tons. Material *B* at the cost of Rs. 340 per ton.

The weight produced was 182 tons of good production.

Calculate :

(*i*) Material price variance

(*ii*) Material usage variance

(*iii*) Material mix variance

(*iv*) Material yield variance

(*CS, Inter, Dec. 1997*)

Solution : **Calculation of variances**

		Standard			*Actual*		
		Qty.	*Rate*	*Amount*	*Qty.*	*Rate*	*Amt.*
A	40%	80	200	16,000	90	180	16,200
B	60%	120	300	36,000	110	340	37,400
		200		52,000	200		53,600
Less :	Normal Loss	20			18		
		180			182		

(*i*) Material price variance = (SP – AP) × AQ

A = (200 – 180) × 90

= 20 × 90 = 1800 *F*

B = (300 – 340) × 110

= 40 × 110 = 4400 *A*

2600 *A*

(*ii*) *Material usage variance :*

Calculation of Std. Qty. for actual output

$$\frac{\text{Std. Qty.}}{\text{Std. output}} \times \text{Actual output}$$

$$A = \frac{80}{100} \times 182 = 80$$

$$B = \frac{120}{180} \times 182 = 121$$

Material usage variance = (Std. Qty. for actual output – Actual Qty.) × Std. price

A	= (80 – 90) × 200	=	2,000 A
B	= (121 – 110) × 300	=	330 F
			1,670 A

(iii) Material mix variance :

As the Std. mix (200) is equal to actual mix (200), Revised Std. Qty. for both *A* & *B* is the same as std. qty.

Material mix variance	=	(Revised Std. Qty. – Actual Qty.) × Std. price	
A	=	(80 – 90) × 200	
	=	10 × 200	= 2,000 A
B	=	(120 – 110) × 300	
	=	10 × 300	= 3,000 F
			= 1,000 F

Calculation of std. cost per unit

$$= \frac{\text{Total cost of Std. Mix}}{\text{Std. Output}}$$

$$= \frac{52,000}{180} = \text{Rs. } 288.88$$

(*iv*) Material yield variance = (Std. output for actual mix – Actual output) × Std. yield price
= (180 – 182) × 288.88
= 2 × 288.88 = 577

Problem 9 : The following information has been extracted from the records of a chemical company :

Standard price — Raw material *A* — Rs. 2 per kg.
— Raw material *B* — Rs. 10 per kg.

Standard usage — '*A*' 75% — 2,250 kgs.
— 'B' 25% — 750 kgs.

Standard yield — 90%

In a period, the actual costs, usages and output were as follows :

Used : 2,200 kgs. of '*A*' costing Rs. 4,650
800 kgs. of '*B*' costing Rs. 7,850

Output : 2,850 kgs. of products

Calculate material cost variance. (*CS, Inter, June 1994*)

Solution :

Calculation of variances

		Standard			Actual		
		Qty.	*Rate*	*Amt.*	*Qty.*	*Rate*	*Amt.*
A	75%	2,250	2	4,500	2,200	2.11	4,650
B	25%	750	10	7,500	800	9.81	7,850
		3,000			3,000		
Less :	10% loss	300			150		
		2,700			2,850		

Material cost variance	= (SQ × SP) – (AQ × AP)	
A	= (2,250 × 2) – (2,200 × 2.11)	
	= 4,500 – 4,650	= 150 *A*
B	= (750 × 10) – (800 × 9.81)	
	= 7,500 – 7,850	= 350 *A*
		500 *A*

Material price variance = (AP – SP) × AQ

A = (2.11 – 2) × 2,200

= 11 × 2,200 = 242 *A*

B = (9.81 – 10) × 800

= 0.19 × 800 = 152 *F*

90 *A*

Calculation of Std. Qty for actual output :

$$= \frac{\text{Std. Qty.}}{\text{Std. output}} \times \text{Actual output}$$

$$A = \frac{2{,}250}{2{,}700} \times 2{,}850 = 2{,}375$$

$$B = \frac{750}{2{,}700} \times 2{,}850 = 792$$

Material usage variance = (Std. Qty. for actual output – Actual Qty.) × Std. price

A = (2,375 – 2,200) × 2

= 175 × 2 = 350 *F*

B = (792 – 800) × 10

8 × 10 = 80 *A*

270 *F*

Material mix variance = (Revised Std. Qty. – Actual Qty.) × Std. price

A = (2,250 – 2,200) × 2

= 50 × 2 = 100 *F*

B = (750 – 800) × 10

= 50 × 10 = 500 *A*

400 *A*

Calculation of Std. yield price :

$$\frac{\text{Std. cost of std. mix}}{\text{Net std. output}}$$

$$= \frac{12{,}000}{2{,}700} = 4.44$$

Material yeild variance = (Total actual yield – Total Std. yield) × Std. yield price

= (2,850 – 2,700) × 4.44

= 150 × 4.44 = 666 *F*

Problem 10 : Product '*A*' is manufactured by mixing three basic raw materials *X*, *Y* and *Z* in the standard proportion of 5 : 3 : 2 and processing the mixture. Production is carried out in batches to give a standard output of 100 kg. from an input of 120 kg. per batch. The company operates standard costing system for cost control.

In the mongh of December 1998, due to non-availability of raw material, the company had to change the standard propartion. Further details regarding the standards and actual consumption during December 1998 are given below :

Materials	*Standard for 1998-99*		*Actuals for December 1998*	
	Proportion	*Price per kg. (Rs.)*	*Proportion*	*Price per kg. (Rs.)*
X	50	20	60	19
Y	30	10	20	11
Z	20	5	20	6
	100		100	

In December 1998, 50 batches were processed to produce 4,800 kg. of A.
Calculate material price usage, mix and yield variance. *(ICWA, Inter, June 1999)*

Solution :

Material	*Std. Qty of materials required per batch and standard cost*			*Actual cost incurred during December 1998*			
	Qty.	*Rate*	*Amt.*	*Qty*	*Total Qty. for 50 batches*	*Rate*	*Amt.*
X	$\frac{5}{10} \times 120 =$ 60	20	1,200	$\frac{60}{100} \times 120 =$ 72	3,600 kg.	19	68,400
Y	$\frac{3}{10} \times 120 =$ 36	10	360	$\frac{20}{100} \times 120 =$ 24	1,200 kg.	11	13,200
Z	$\frac{2}{10} \times 120 =$ 24	5	120	$\frac{20}{100} \times 120 =$ 24	1,200 kg.	6	7,200
	120		1,680	120	6,000		88,800
Less : Loss	20			20			
	100			100			

(1) Material price variance = (Std. price – Actual price) × Actual Qty.

X = (20 – 19) × 3,600 = 3,600 *F*

Y = (10 – 11) × 1,200 = 1,200 *A*

Z = (5 – 6) × 1,200 = 1,200 *A*

1,200 *A*

(2) Material usage variance = (Std. usage – Actual usage) × Std. price

X = $(4,800 \times \frac{60}{100} - 3,600) \times 20$

= (2,880 – 3600) × 20 = 14,400 *A*

Y = $(4,800 \times \frac{36}{100} - 1,200) \times 10$

= 1,728 – 1,200) × 10 = 5,280 *F*

Z = $(4,800 \times \frac{24}{100} - 1,200) \times 5$

= (1,152 – 1,200) × 5 = 240 *A*

9,360 *A*

(3) Material mix variance = (Std. mix for actual qty. of 50 batches – Actual mix of actual qty.) × Std. price

X = (50 × 60 kg. – 3,600) × 20

= (3,000 – 3,600) × 20 = 12,000 (*A*)

Y = (50 × 36 kg. – 1,200) × 10 = 6,000 (*F*)

Z = (50 – 24 kg. – 1,200) × 5 = Nil

6,000 *A*

(4) Material yield variance = (Std. yield from 50 batches – Actual yield) × Std. cost of output

= (50 × 100 kgs. – 4,800) × 16.80

= 200 × 16.80 = 3,360 *A*

Working Note :

Std. cost of output= $\frac{\text{Std. cost}}{\text{Std. output}} = \frac{1,680}{100} = 16.80$

Problem 11 : S.V. Ltd. manufactures a simple product, the standard mix of which is

Material *A* 60% at Rs. 20 per kg.

Material *B* 40% at Rs. 10 per kg.

Normal loss in production is 20% of input. Due to shortage of material *A*, the standard mix was changed. Actual result for March 1989 were :

Material *A* 105 kg. at Rs. 20 per kg.

Material *B* 95 kg. at Rs. 9 per kg.

Input	200 kg.
Loss	35 kg.
Output	165 kg.

Calculate : (*i*) Material price variance, (*ii*) Material usage variance, (*iii*) Material mix variance, (*iv*) Material yield variance. (*University of Delhi, B.Com., (Hons.) 1990*)

Solution :

Calculation of variance

	Standard			*Actual*		
	Qty.	*Rate*	*Amout*	*Qty.*	*Rate*	*Amount*
A 60%	120	20	2,400	105	20	2,100
B 40%	80	10	800	95	9	855
	200		3,200	200		2,955
Normal loss 20%	40			35		
Output	160			165		

(1) Material price variance = (Standard price – Actual price) × Actual Quantity

$A = (20 - 20) \times 105 = 0$

$B = (10 - 9) \times 95 = 95 \quad F$

Total material price variance $= 0 + 95 = 95 \quad F$

(2) Material usage variance = (Standard quantity for actul output *[1] – Actual quantity for actual output) × Std. price

$$\text{*}^{1}\text{Standard quantity for actual output} = \frac{\text{Standard quantity}}{\text{Standard output}} \times \text{Actual output}$$

$$A = \frac{120}{160} \times 165$$

$$B = \frac{80}{160} \times 165$$

$$\text{MUV for } A = \left(\frac{120}{160} \times 165 - 105\right) \times 20$$

$$= (123.75 - 105) \times 20$$

$$= \text{Rs. } 2{,}475 \quad (F)$$

$$\text{MUV for B} = \left(\frac{80}{100} \times 165 - 95\right) \times 10$$

$$= (82.5 - 95) \times 10$$

$$= \text{Rs. } 125 \ (A)$$

$$\text{Total MUV} = 2{,}475 - 125 = \text{Rs. } 2{,}350 \ (F)$$

(3) Material mix variance= (Revised standard quantity – Actual mix of actual quantity) × Std. price

$$\text{Revised standard quantity} = \frac{\text{Std. Qty. for each material}}{\text{Std. qty. total}} \times \text{Actual qty. total}$$

$$A = \frac{120}{200} \times 200 = 120$$

$$B = \frac{80}{200} \times 200 = 80$$

As Std. mix (200) = Actual mix (200

∴ Revised standard quantity for both A and B is the same as standard quantity

$$\text{MMV for } A = (120 - 105) \times 20$$
$$= 15 \times 20 = 300\ F$$
$$\text{MMB for } B = (80 - 95) \times 10$$
$$= -15 \times 10 = 150\ A$$
$$\text{Total MMV} = 300 - 150 = \text{Rs. } 150\ F$$

(4) Material yield variance= (Standard output for actual mix – Actual output) × Std. yield price

$$\text{Standard output for actual mix} = \frac{\text{Standard output}}{\text{Standard mix}} \times \text{Actual mix}$$

$$= \frac{160}{200} \times 200 = 160$$

$$\text{Standard cost per unit} = \frac{\text{Total cost of Std. mix}}{\text{Std. output}}$$

$$= \frac{3{,}200}{160} = \text{Rs. } 20 \text{ per unit}$$

$$\text{MYV} = (160 - 165) \times 20$$
$$= -5 \times 20 = 100\ (A)$$

Problem 12 : *ABC* Ltd. produces an article by blending two basic raw materials. It operates a standard costing system and the following standards have been set for raw materials.

Material	*Standard mix*	*Standard price (Rs. per kg.)*
A	40%	4
B	60%	3

The standard loss in processing is 15%. During April 1990, the company produced 1,700 kgs. of finished output.

The position of stock and purchases for the month of April 1990 are as under :

Material	*Stock on 1.4.90 (kgs.)*	*Stock on 30.4.90 (kgs.)*	*Purchased during April 1990* Cost	(Rs.)
A	35	5	800	3,400
B	40	50	1,200	3,000

Calculate the following variances :

(*i*) Material price variance.
(*ii*) Material usage variance.
(*iii*) Material yield variance.
(*iv*) Material mix variance and
(*v*) Total material cost variance. (*C.S., Inter, Dec. 1991; CA, Inter, Nov. 1991*)

Solution :

Type of material	*Standard* Qty. kg.	Rate Rs.	Amt.	*Actual* Qty. kg.	Rate Rs.	Amt.
A	800	4	3,200	35	4	140
				795	4.25	3378.75
B	1,200	3	3,600	40	3	120
				1,150	2,50	2,875
	2,000		6,800	2,020		6,513.75

(*i*) Material price variance = (Std. rate – Actual rate) × Actual qty.

Material A : Since the actual price and standard price in respect of 35 kg. of raw materials *S* are the same, there will be no price variance in respect of this quantity. Price variance will be in respect of only 795 kg. as shown below :

$$(4 - 4.25) \times 795 = \text{Rs. } 198.75\ (A)$$

Material B : In respect of material *B* also, price variance will be in respect of 1,150 kg. only as shown below :

$$(\text{Rs. } 3 - 2.50) \times 1{,}150 = \text{Rs. } 575\ (F)$$

$$\text{Total} = \text{Rs. } 198.75\ (A) + 575\ (F) = \text{Rs. } 376.25\ (F)$$

(*ii*) Material usage variance = Std. quantity for actual output – Actual qty.) × Std. rate

A	=	(800 – 830) × 4	=	120 (*A*)
B	=	(1,200 – 1,190) × 3	=	30 (*F*)
				Rs. 90 (*A*)

(*iii*) Material yield variance = (Std. output for actual mix – Actual output) × Std. cost per unit

$$= \left(\frac{1{,}700}{2{,}000} \times 2{,}020 - 1{,}700\right) \times 4$$

$$= (1{,}717 - 1{,}700) \times 4 = \text{Rs. } 68\ (A)$$

(*iv*) Material mix variance = (Revised std. quantity – Actual qty.) × Std. rate

Revised std. qty. *A* $= \dfrac{2{,}020}{2{,}000} \times 800 = 808$ kg.

Revised std. qty *B* $= \dfrac{2{,}020}{2{,}000} \times 1{,}200 = 12.12$ kg.

Material *A*	=	(808 – 830) × 4	=	88 (*A*)
Material *B*	=	(1,212 – 1,190) × 3	=	66 (*F*)
				Rs. 22 (*A*)

(*v*) Total material cost variance = Std. cost for actual output – Actual cost

6,800 – 6,513.75 = 286.25 (*F*)

Verification :

Material cost variance = Material price variance + Material usage variance
= 376.25 (*F*) + 90 (*A*) = 286.25 (F)

Material usage variance = Material mix variance + Material yield variance
= 22 (*A*) + 68 (*A*) = 90 (*A*)

Working Notes :

(1) The standard loss being 15%. It means to produce, 1,700 kg. of the article, standard quantity of material required is :

$$\frac{100}{85} \times 1{,}700 \text{ kgs.} = 2{,}000 \text{ kgs.}$$

Out of 2,000 kg. of material used 40% is of type *A* and 60% is of type *B*, *i.e.*,
Standard use for actual output

Material *A* $= 2{,}000 \times \dfrac{40}{100} = 800$ kg.

Material *B* $= 2{,}000 \times \dfrac{60}{100} = 1{,}200$ kgs.

Actaul usage of material = Opening stock + Purchases – Closing stock

A = 35 + 800 – 5 = 830 kgs.

B = 40 + 1,200 – 50 = 1,190 kgs.

(2) Standard cost per unit $= \dfrac{\text{Total standard cost}}{\text{Total standard output of std. mix}}$

$$= \frac{\text{Rs. } 6{,}800}{1{,}700} = \text{Rs. } 4 \text{ per kg.}$$

Problem 13 : One kilogram of product *K* requires two chemicals *A* and *B*. The following were the details of product *K* for the month of June 87 :

(*a*) Standard mix chemical *A* 50% and chemical *B* 50%.
(*b*) Standard price kilogram of chemical *A* Rs. 12 and chemical *B* Rs. 15.
(*c*) Actual input of chemical *B* 70 kilograms.
(*d*) Actual price per kilogram of chemical *A* Rs. 15.
(*e*) Standard normal loss 10% of total input.
(*f*) Materials cost variance total Rs. 650 adverse.
(*g*) Material yield variance total Rs. 135 adverse. (*CA, Inter, November 1987*)

Solution : In this problem actual output is not given. So let actual output be = 96 kg.

(*i*) Calculation of standard mix of input

	Qty. (Kg.)	*Price (Rs.)*	*Amount (Rs.)*
Chemical *A*	50	12	600
Chemical *B*	50	15	750
	100	13.50	1,350
Standard loss	10		
	90		1,350

(*ii*) Calculation standard rate of output

$$\frac{\text{Rs. } 1350}{90} = \text{Rs. } 15 \text{ per kg.}$$

(*iii*) Calculation of standard yield for actual output

Yield variance = (Std. yield for actual input – Actual yield) × Std. rate of output

135 (*A*) = (Std. yield for actual input – 90 kg.) × 15

Std. yield for actual input = 99 kgs.

(*iv*) Calculation of actual output

For 99 kg. of input, the output is 100 kg.

For 90 kgs. of input, output is $\frac{100}{90} \times 99 = 110$ kgs.

(*v*) Calculation of actual input of chemical A

= 110 kg. – Actual input of chemical B

= 110 kgs. – 70 kg. = 40 kg.

(*vi*) Material cost variance is given 650 (*A*). hence the actual cost of actual mix of chemical *A* and *B* will be Rs. 1,350 + 650 = 2,000

(*vii*) The actual cost of 40 kg. of chemical *A* @ Rs. 15 per kg. is Rs. 600. Thus the cost of one kg. of chemical *B* used is Rs. $\frac{2,000-600}{70}$ = Rs. 20 per kg.

(*viii*) Standard cost of actual mix

= Rs. 12 × 40 kg. + Rs. 15 × 70 kg. = Rs. 1,530

(1) Material mix variance = (per kg. std. cost of std. mix – Per kg, std. cost of actual mix) – Actual qty.

$$= \left(\frac{1,350}{100} - \frac{1,530}{110}\right) \times 110 \text{ kg.}$$

= Rs. 45 (*A*)

(2) Material usage variance = (Std. qty. – Actual qty.) × Std. price

A = (50 – 40) × 12 = 120 *F*

B = (50 – 70) × 15 = 300 *A*

180 *A*

(3) Material price variance = (Std. price – Actual price) × Actual qty.

A = (12 – 15) × 40 = 120 *A*

B = (15 – 20) × 70 = 350 *A*

470 *A*

(4) Actual loss of actual input :

Actual total input = 110 kg.

Less : Actual output = 90 kg.

Actual loss 20 kg.

(5) Actual input of chemical A = 40 kg. refer working note v.

(6) Actual price per kg. of chemical B = Rs. 20 (refer to working note vii.)

Problem 14 : *XYZ* Company manufactures a product *ABC* by mixing three raw materials. For every 100 kg. of *ABC*, 125 kg. of raw materials are used. In April 1990, there was an output of 5,600 kg. of *ABC*. The standard actual particulars of April 1990 are as follows :

Raw material	*Standard*		*Actual*	
	Mix %	*Price per kg.* Rs.	*Mix* %	*Price per kg.* Rs.
Raw material *I*	50	40	60	42
Raw material *II*	30	20	20	16
Raw material *III*	20	10	20	12

Calculate all variances (*ICWA, Inter, June 1990*)

Solution : Actual material used = $\frac{125 \text{ kg}}{100} \times 5{,}600 = 7{,}000$

(*A*) Actual cost of actual material used

I	60% of 7,000	= 4,200 kg. × 42	= 1,76,400
II	20% of 7,000	= 1,400 kg. × 16	= 22,400
III	20% of 7,000	= 1,400 kg. × 12	= 16,800
			2,15,600

(*B*) Standard cost of material used

I	4,200 × 40	= 1,68,000
II	1,400 × 20	= 28,000
III	1,400 × 10	= 14,000

(*C*) Standard cost of materials if it had been used in standard production

I	3,500 × 40	= 1,40,000
II	2,100 × 20	= 42,000
III	1,400 × 10	= 14,000
		1,96,000

(*D*) Standard cost of production (for 100 kg.)

I	62.50 kg. × 40	= 2,500
II	37.50 kg. × 20	= 750
III	25 kg. × 10	= 250

Standard cost for output of 5,600 kg. = $\frac{3{,}500}{100} \times 5{,}600$

Rs. = 1,96,000

Material price variance = *A* – *B*

= 2,15,600 – 10,000 = 5,600 (*A*)

Material mix variance = *B* – *C*

= 2,10,000 – 1,96,000 = 14,000 (*A*)

Material yield variance = *C* – *D*

= 1,96,000 – 1,96,000 = NIL

Material usage variance = $B - D$

= 2,10,000 – 1,96,000 = 14,0,000 (*A*)

Material cost variance = Material price variance + Materials usage variance

19,600 (*A*) = 5,600 (*A*) + 14,000 (*A*)

or $D - A$ = 1,96,000 – 2,15,600 = 19,600 (*A*)

2. Labour Cost Variance

The various labour cost variances can be shown under the following chart :

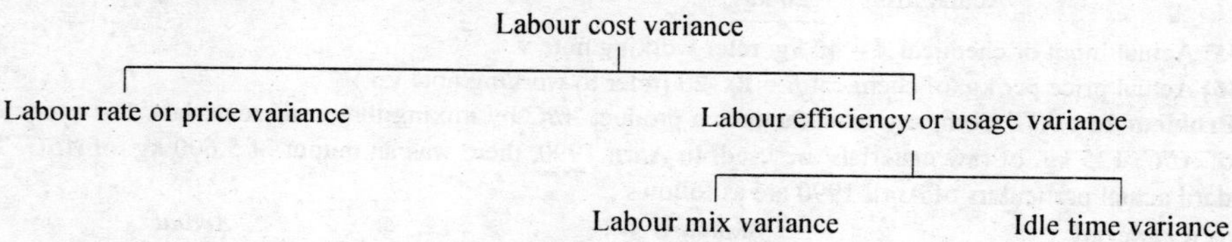

Fig. 26.3. Chart showing labour cost variance.

(A) Labour cost variance

This is also known as direct wages variance and represents the difference between standard direct wages specified for the actual production and the actual direct wages paid. The formula to calculate labour cost variance is as follows :

Labour cost variance = (Actual hours × Actual rate) – (Std. hours × Std. rate)

Labour cost variance is analysed into the following two variances.

(*a*) Labour rate or price variance : The ICMA terminology defines labour rate variance as "the difference between the standard and actual direct labour hour rate per hour for the total hours worked". In other words it is that portion of labour cost variance owing to difference between the actual rate and standard rate of pay specified. The following formula is used for calculating this variance.

Labour rate variance = (Standard rate – Actual rate) × Actual hour

The following factors are responsible for direct labour rate variance :

(*i*) Payment of high wage rate than estimated.

(*ii*) Use of more skilled or unskilled labourers than planned.

(*iii*) Payment of excess bonus than estimated.

(*iv*) Payment of more overtime premium than estimated.

(*b*) Labour Efficiency or Usage Variance : It refers to that portion of the wage variance which is due to the difference between the standard labour hours specified and the actual labour hours expended. The following formula is used to calculate this variance.

Labour efficiency variance = (Standard hours – Actual hours) × Standard rate

The following factors cause this variance :

(*a*) Use of inferior grade of labour.

(*b*) Lack of good supervision.

(*c*) Use of sub-standard quality of materials.

(*d*) Breakdown of machines during production process.

(*e*) Inadequate working conditions such as poor lighting, lack of ventilation, heating, etc.

(*f*) Lack of proper production organisation involving defective production planning, routing, scheduling, inspection, etc.

B. Idle Time Variance

Sometimes idle time may occur in spite of fixing standard carefully. Such idle time should not be included in efficiency variance but shown separately. Otherwise, employees are made responsible for inefficiency although idle time is beyond their control as for example, breakdown of machine or power supply. The following formula is used to calculate idle time variance :

Idle time variance = Idle hours × Standard rate

Idle time variance is always an adverse variance.

C. Labour Mix Variance or Gang Composition Variance

Sometimes employees of different grade may have to be used in place of specific grade because of shortage of labourers. In such a situtation a labour mix variance is calculated to show management how much of labour cost variance is due to change in labour force. It is defined as the portion of the wage variance which is due to the difference between the standard labour grades specified and the actual grades utilised. It arises under two situations.

(*a*) Where Standard composition of labour force if revised owing to shortage of a particular type of labour but the total labour time spent is equal to the total standard time. The following formula is used :

Labour mix variance = (Revised std. mix or time – Actual mix or time) × Std. wage rate per hour

Note : The revised standard mix is the same as the standard mix or time.

(*b*) Where the standard composition of labour force is revised due to shortage of a particular type of labour and total actual time of labour differs from total standard time of labour. The following formula is used :

Labour mix variance = (Revised std. mix – Actual std. mix or time) × Std. wage rate per hour

Where,

$$\text{Revised standard mix or time} = \frac{\text{Total time of actual mix of workers}}{\text{Total time of std. mix of workers}} \times \text{Std. time of the respective category of workers}$$

Problem 15 : The standard and actual figures of Ashok Metal Works are as under :

Standard time for the job	1,000 hours
Standard rate per hour	Re. 0.50
Actual time taken	900 hours
Actual wages paid	Rs. 360

Compute (*i*) Labour rate variance, (*ii*) Labour efficiency variance and (*iii*) Labour cost variance

Solution : Calculation of standard cost = 1,000 hrs. × 0.50 = 500

$$\text{Calculation of actual rate per hour} = \frac{\text{Rs. } 360}{900} = 0.40$$

(*i*) Labour rate variance = (Standard rate – Actual rate) × Actual hrs.
= (0.50 – 0.40) × 900 = Rs. 90 (*F*)

(*ii*) Labour efficiency variance = (Standard hours – Actual hrs.) × Standard rate
= (1,000 – 900) × 0.50 = Rs. 50 (*F*)

(*iii*) Labour cost variance = Standard labour cost – Actual labour cost
= (500 – 360) = 140 (*F*)

Problem 14 : From the following particulars calculate (1) Labour rate variance, (2) Labour mix variance, (3) Labour efficiency variance and (4) Labour cost variance.

	Skilled	*Semi-skilled*	*Unskilled*
No. in std. gang	16	6	3
Standard rate per hour	3	2	1
Actual number in the gang	14	9	2
Actual rate of pay	4	3	2

In a 40-hours week the gang as a whole produced 900 standard hours.

Solution : Calculation of standard hours

In a 40-hour week, the standard gang should have produced 1,000 standard hours as shown below :

Skilled	16 × 40	=	640
Semi-skilled	3 × 40	=	240
Unskilled	3 × 40	=	120
			1,000

But the actual output is 900 standard hours. Hence to find out the total labour cost variance the standard cost or cost charged to production is to be computed with reference to 900 standard hours. This is shown in the following statement.

Statement showing the standard cost actual cost and standard cost of actual gang for actual output, *i.e.*, 900 standard hours :

Gang	*Standard cost*			*Actual cost*			*Standard cost of actual gang*		
	Hrs.	*Rate*	*Amt.*	*Hrs.*	*Rate*	*Amt.*	*Hrs.*	*Rate*	*Amt.*
Skilled $\frac{640}{1,000} \times 900$	576	3	1,728	14 × 40 = 560	4	2,240	560	3	1,680
Semi-skilled $\frac{240}{1,000} \times 900$	216	2	432	9 × 40 = 360	3	1,080	360	2	720
Unskilled $\frac{120}{1,000} \times 900$	108	1	108	2 × 40 = 80	2	160	80	1	80
	900	2.52	2,268	1,000	3.84	3,480	1,000	2.48	2,480

(1) Labour rate variance = (Standard rate – Actual rate) × Actual hours
= (3 – 4) × 1,000 = 1,000 (*A*)

(2) Labour mix variance = (Std. rate of std. gang or mix – Std. rate of actual gang or mix) × Actual hours
= (2.52 – 2.48) × 1,000 = 40 (*F*)

(3) Labour efficiency variance = (Standard hours – Actual hours) × Std. rate
= (900 – 1,000) × 2.52 = 252 (*A*)

(4) Labour cost variance = (Standard labour cost – Actual labour cost)
= (2,268 – 3,480) = 1,212 (*A*)

Problem 17 : From the following particulars relating to Karnataka Toys Co. Ltd. calculate (1) Wage rate variance, (2) Labour efficiency variance, (3) Abnormal idle time variance and (4) Total labour cost variance.

Standard time per unit	2.5 hours
Actaul hours worked	2,000 hours
Standard rate of pay	Rs. 2 per hour

25% of the actual hours has been lost as abnormal idle time.

Actual output	1,000 units
Actual wages	Rs. 4,500

Solution : Calculation of standard cost charged to

Production = 1,000 units × 2.5 hrs. × Rs. 2 = Rs. 5,000

Actual wages paid = Rs. 4,500

Actual wage rate per hour = $\frac{4,500}{2,000}$ = 2.25

Standard wage rate per hour = 2.00

Ahnormal idle time = $\frac{25}{100}$ × 2,000 = 500 hrs.

(1) Wage rate variance = (Standard rate – Actual rate) × Actual hours
= (2 – 2.25) × 2,000 = 500 (*A*)

(2) Labour efficiency variance = (Standard hours – Actual hours) × Standard rate
= (2,500 – 1,500) × 2 = 2,00 (*F*)

Standard hrs. = Std. time per unit × Actual output
= (2.5 × 1,000) = hrs. 2,500

(3) Abnormal idle time variance = Idle time × Standard rate
= 500 × Rs. 2 = Rs. 1,000 (*A*)

(4) Total labour cost variance = Standard labour cost – Actual labour cost
= 5,000 – 4,500 = 500 (*F*)

Problem 18 : Quality Ice-cream factory works for 50 hours a week and employs 100 workers on production. The standard rate is Re. 1 an hour and standard output is 200 units per gang hour.

During the week, 10 employees were paid at 80 paise an hour and 5 at Re. 1.20 an hour. Rest of the employees were paid at the standard rate.

Actual number of units produced were 10,200.

Calculate (1) Labour cost variance, (2) Labour rate variance, (3) Labour efficiency variance, (4) Labour yield variance.

Solution :

Calculation of actual cost

		Rs.
85 Workers for 50 hrs. @ Re. 1 per hour	=	4,250
10 Workers for 50 hrs. @ 0.80 p per hour	=	400
5 Workers for 50 hrs @ Rs. 1.20 per hour	=	300
Total actual cost		4,950

Calculation of standard rate

$$\frac{\text{Standard cost (per gang hour)}}{\text{Standard production (per gang hour)}}$$

$$\frac{100 \text{ workers} \times 1 \text{ Re.}}{200 \text{ units}} \text{ or } \frac{\text{Rs. } 100}{200} = 0.50 \text{ per unit}$$

Calculation of standard cost

Actual production × Standard rate

10,200 units × 0.50 per unit = Rs. 5,100

(1) Labour cost variance = Standard cost – Actual cost
= 5,100 – 4,950 = Rs. 150 (*F*)

(2) Labour rate variance = (Std. rate – Actual rate) × Actual hours

As the actual wage rate has deviated from the standard in respect of only 15 workers from out of a total of 100 workers, wage rate variance would be calculated only in respect of these 15 workers. Actual hours for 10 workers for 50 hrs. will be 500 hrs. and 5 workers for 50 hrs. will be 250 hrs.

= (0.80 – Re. 1) × 500 = Rs. 100 (*F*)
= (1.20 – Re. 1) × 250 = Rs. 50 (*A*)

(3) Labour efficiency variance = (Standard hours – Actual hours) × Standard rate
= (5,100 – 5,000) × 1 = 100 (*F*)

$$\text{Standard hours} = \frac{\text{Actual production}}{\text{Std. production per hr.}} \times \text{No. of workers}$$

$$= \frac{10{,}200 \text{ units}}{200 \text{ units}} \times 100 = 5{,}100 \text{ hrs.}$$

(4) Labour yield variance = (Std. yield – Actual yield) × Std. labour cost per unit
= (10,000 – 10,200) × 0.50 = 100 (*F*)
Std. yield = 200 units × 50 hrs. = 10,000

Problem 19 : Compute labour variance from the following data of a ship building company. The particulars of labour force engaged on job on. 777, scheduled to be completed in 30 weeks are :

Category	*Standard*		*Actual*	
	Number	*Wage rate* (Rs.)	*Number*	*Wage rate* (Rs.)
Skilled	75	60	70	70
Semi-skilled	45	40	30	50
Unskilled	60	30	80	20

The actual time taken is 32 weeks. (*Nagarjuna University, M.Com., March 1992*)

Solution :

Category	*Standard*			*Actual*		
	*Weeks**	*Rate*	*Amt.*	*Weeks**	*Rate*	*Amt.*
Skilled	2,250	60	1,35,000	2,240	70	1,56,800
Semi-skilled	1,350	40	54,000	960	50	48,000
Unskilled	1,800	30	54,000	2,560	20	51,200
	5,400		2,43,000	5,760		2,56,000

*Total weeks = No. of workers × No. of weeks

(1) Labour cost variance = Standard cost – Actual cost
= 2,43,000 – 2,56,000
= Rs. 13,000 (*A*)

(2) Labour rate variance = (Standard rate – Actual rate) × Actual hours
Skilled = (60 – 70) × 2,240 = 22,400 (*A*)
Semi-skilled = (40 – 50) × 960 = 9,600 (*A*)
Unskilled = (30 – 20) × 2,560 = 25,600 (*F*)
= 6,400 (*F*)

(3) Labour efficiency variance = (Standard hours – Actual hours) × Standard rate
Skilled = (2,250 – 2,240) × 60 = 600 (*F*)
Semi-skilled = (1,350 – 960) × 40 = 15,600 (*F*)
Unskilled = (1,800 – 2,560) × 30 = 22,800 (*A*)
Total labour efficiency variance 6,600 (*A*)

Varification :

Labour cost variance = Labour rate variance + Labour efficiency variance
13,000 (*A*) = 6,400 (*A*) + 6,600a(*A*)

(4) Labour mix variance = (Revised std. time* – Actual time) × Std. rate

$$\text{Revised std. time} = \frac{\text{Actual mix}}{\text{Std. mix}} \times \text{Std. time}$$

Skilled	$= \frac{5,760}{5,400} \times 2,250$	=	2,400
Semi-skilled	$= \frac{5,760}{5,400} \times 1,350$	=	1,440
Unskilled	$= \frac{5,760}{5,400} \times 1,800$	=	1,920
Skilled	= (2,400 – 2,240) × 60	=	9,600 (*F*)
Semi-skilled	= (1,440 – 960) × 40	=	19,200 (*F*)
Unskilled	= (1,920 – 2,560) × 30	=	19,200 (*A*)
	Labour mix variance		9,600 (*F*)

Revised labour efficiency variance	=	(Std. time – Revised std. time) × Std. rate		
Skilled	=	(2,250 – 2,400) × 60	=	9,000 (*A*)
Semi-skilled	=	(1,350 – 1,440) × 40	=	3,600 (*A*)
Unskilled	=	(1,800 – 1,920) × 30	=	3,600 (A)
			=	16,200 (*A*)

Verfication :

Labour efficiency variance = (Labour mix variance + Revised labour efficiency variance)

6,600 (*A*) = (9,600 (*F*) + 16,200 (*A*)

Problem 20 : 100 skilled workmen, 40 semi-skilled workmen and 60 unskilled workmen were to work for 30 weeks to get a contract job complted. The standard weekly wages were Rs. 60, Rs. 36 and Rs. 24, respectively. The job was actually completed in 32 weeks by 80 skilled, 50 semi-skilled and 70 unskilled workmen who were paid Rs. 65, Rs. 40 and Rs. 20 respectively as weekly wages.

Find out the labour cost variance labour rate variance, labour mix variance and labour efficiency variance.

(*ICWA, Inter, June 1992*)

Solution :

Calculation of standard cost

	Rs.
100 skilled workmen @ Rs. 60 per week	6,000
40 semi-skilled workmen @ Rs. 36 per week	1,440
60 unskilled workmen @ Rs. 24 per week	1,440
	8,880

Calculation of actual cost

80 skilled workmen @ Rs. 65 per week	5,200
50 semi-skilled workmen @ Rs. 40 per week	2,000
70 unskilled workmen @ Rs. 20 per week	1,400
	8,600

	Standard wages	=	8,800 × 30	=	2,66,400	
	Actual wages	=	8,600 × 32	=	2,75,200	
1.	Labour cost variance	=	Standard wages – Actual wages			
		=	2,66,400 – 2,75,200	=	8,800	(*A*)
2.	Labour rate variance per week	=	(Std. rate – Actual rate) × Actual hrs.			
	Skilled	=	(60 – 65) × 80 × 32	=	12,800	(*A*)
	Semi-skilled	=	(36 – 40) × 50 × 32	=	6,400	(*A*)
	Unskilled	=	(24 – 20) × 70 × 32	=	8,960	(*F*)
					10,240	(*A*)

3. Labour mix variance per week

Category	*Std. mix*	*Actual mix*	*Qty. variance*	*Std. rate*	*Variance amt.*
Skilled	100	80	20 (*F*)	60	1,200 (*F*)
Semi-skilled	40	50	10 (*A*)	36	360 (*A*)
Unskilled	60	70	10 (*A*)	24	240 (*A*)
					600 (*F*)

For 32 weeks = 600 × 32 = Rs. 19,200 (*F*)

4. Labour efficiency variance =

Week lost 2

Std. weekly cost = Rs. 8,800

Labour efficiency variance = 8,800 × 2 = 17,760 (*A*)

Verification :

Labour cost variance = Labour rate variance + Labour mix variance + Labour efficiency variance

8,800 (*A*) = 10,240 (*A*) + 19,200 (*F*) + 17,760 (*A*)

Problem 21 : The standard output of product 'EXE' is 25 units per hour in manufacturing department of a company employing 100 workers. The standard wage rate per labour hour is Rs. 6.

In a 42 hour week, the department produced 1,040 units of 'EXE' despite 5% of the time paid was lost due to an abnormal reason. The hourly wage rate actually paid were Rs. 6.20, Rs. 6 and Rs. 5.70 respectively to 10, 30 and 60 of the workers.

Compute relevant variance. *(CA, Inter May 1997)*

Solution : *Working Note :*

Calculation of standard non-hours

When 100 worker work for 1 hr. — The std. output is 25 units

Std. man hour per unit $= \frac{100 \text{ hrs}}{25 \text{ units}} = 4$ hrs.

Calculation of std. man hours for actual output :

1,040 units × 4 hrs. = 4,160

Standard data			*Actual data*					
Std. man hours for actual output	*Rate per hour*	*Amount*	*No. of workers*	*Actual hours paid*	*Idle time hrs.*	*Production hours*	*Rate per hr.*	*Amt. paid*
4,160	6	24,960	10	420	21	399	6.20	2,604
			30	1,260	63	1,197	6.00	7,560
			60	2,520	126	2,394	5.70	14,364
		24,960	100	4,200	210	3,990		24,528

(1) Labour cost variance = Std. labour cost – Actual labour cost
= 24,960 – 24,528 = 432 *F*

(2) Labour rate variance = (Std. rate – Actual rate) × Actual hrs.
= (6 – 6.20) × 420 = 84 *A*
= (6 – 6) × 1,260 = NIL
= (6 – 5.70) × 2,520 = 756*F*
672 *F*

(3) Labour efficiency variance = (Std. man hours – Actual production hrs.) × Std. rate
= (4,160 – 3,990) × 6
= 170 × 6 = 1,020 (*F*)

(4) Labour Idle time variance = Idle time hrs. × Std. rate
= 210 × 6 = 1,260 (A)

Problem 22 : The following details are available from the records of *ABC* Ltd. engaged in manufacturing article *A* for the week ended 28th Feb.

The standard labour hours and rates of payment per article *A* were as follows :

	Hours	*Rate per hour*	*Total*
Skilled labour	10	3	30
Semi-skilled labour	8	1.50	12
Unskilled labour	16	1.00	16

The actual production was 1,000 articles *A* for which the actual hours worked and rates are given below :

	Hours	*Rate per hour*	*Total*
Skilled labour	9,000	4	36,000
Semi-skilled labour	8,400	1.50	12,600
Unskilled labour	20,000	0.90	18,000
			66,600

From the above set of data, you are asked to calculate :

(1) Labour cost variance.
(2) Labour rate variance.
(3) Labour efficiency variance.
(4) Labour mix variance.

(*CS, Inter, December 1994*)

Solution :

	Std. data			*Actual data*		
	Hrs.	*Rate*	*Amt.*	*Hrs.*	*Rate*	*Amt.*
Skilled	10,000	3	30,000	9,000	4	36,000
Semi-skilled	8,000	1.50	12,000	8,400	1.50	12,600
Unskilled	16,000	1.00	16,000	20,000	0.90	18,000
	34,000		58,000	37,400		66,600

(1) Labour cost variance = Std. cost – Actual cost
= 58,000 – 66,600 = 8,600 *A*

(2) Labour rate variance = (Std. rate – Actual rate) × Actual hrs.
Skilled = (3 – 4) × 9,000 = 9,000 *A*
Semi-skilled = (1.50 – 1.50) × 8,400 = NIL
Unskilled = (1 – 0.90) × 20,000 = 2,000 F
7,000 *A*

(3) Labour efficiency variance = (Std. hours – Actual hrs.) × Std. rate
Skilled = (10,000 – 9,000) × 3
= 1,000 × 3 = 3,000 *F*
Semi-skilled = (8,000 – 8,400) × 1.50
= 400 × 1.50 = 600 *A*
Unskilled = (16,000 – 20,000) × 1
= 4,000 × 1 = 4,000 *A*
1,600 *A*

Calculation of revised std. time

$$\text{Revised std. time} = \frac{\text{Actual Mix}}{\text{Std. Mix}} \times \text{Std. time}$$

$$\text{Skilled} = \frac{37,400}{34,000} \times 10,000 = 11,000$$

$$\text{Semi-skilled} = \frac{37,400}{34,000} \times 8,000 = 8,800$$

$$\text{Unskilled} = \frac{37,400}{34,000} \times 16,000 = 17,600$$

Labour mix variance	=	(Revised std. time – Actual time) × Std. rate		
Skilled	=	(11,000 – 9,000) × 3		
	=	2,000 × 3	=	6,000 *F*
Semi-skilled	=	(8,800 – 8,400) × 1.50		
	=	400 × 1.50	=	600 *F*
Unskilled	=	(17,600 – 20,000) × 1		
	=	2,400 × 1	=	2,400 *A*
				4,200 *F*

Problem 23 (Material and labour cost variance) : The following standards have been set to manufacture a product.

Direct material :

	Rs.
2 Units of *A* at Rs. 4 per unit	8
3 Units of *B* at Rs. 3 per unit	9
15 Units of *C* at Re 1 per unit	15
	32
Direct labour 3 hours @ Rs. 8 per hr.	24
Total standard prime cost	56

The company manufactured and sold 6,000 units of the product during the year. Direct material costs were as follows :

12,500 units of *A* at Rs. 4.40 per unit
18,000 units of *B* at Rs. 2.80 per unit
88,500 units of *C* at Rs. 1.20 per unit.

The company worked 17,500 direct labour hours during the year. For 2,500 of these hours the company paid at Rs. 12 per hour while for the remaining the wages were paid at the standard rate. Calculate material price and usage variance and labour rate and efficiency variances. (*University of Delhi, B.Com. (Hons.), 1988*)

Solution :

1. Material price variance	=	(Std. price – Actual price) × Actual qty.		
A	=	(4 – 4.40) × 12,500	=	5,000 (*A*)
B	=	(3 – 2.80) × 18,000	=	3,600 (*F*)
C	=	(1 – 1.20) × 88,500	=	17,700 (*A*)
Total				19,100 (*A*)
2. Material usage variance	=	(Std. qty. – Actual qty.) × Std. price		
A	=	(12,000 – 12,500) × 4	=	2,000 (*A*)
B	=	(18,000 – 18,000) × 3	=	NIL
C	=	(90,000 – 88,500) × 1	=	1,500 (*F*)
				500 (*A*)
3. Labour rate variance	=	(Std. rate – Actual rate) × Actual hours		
A	=	(8 – 12) × 2,500	=	10,000 (*A*)
B	=	(8 – 8) × 1,500	=	NIL
				10,000 (*A*)
4. Labour efficiency variance	=	(Std. hrs. – Actual hrs.) × Std. rate		
	=	(18,000 – 17,500) × 8	=	Rs. 4,000 (*F*)
	=	6,000 units × 3 hrs.	=	18,000 hrs.

Problem 24 : The following particulars are available in respect of a particular product :

Quantity of material purchased	6,000 kg.
Value of purchases	Rs. 18,000
Closing stock of materials	500 kg.

Total wage cost	Rs. 14,000
Actual hours	7,000 hrs.
Standard price of materials	Rs. 2.80 per kg.
Standard rate of wages	Rs. 2.50 per kg.
Standard time per unit	2 hrs.
Standard quantity per unit	1.50 kg.
Units produced	3,000 units
Idle time	500 hrs.

You are required to calculate :

(*a*) Total direct material cost variance analysed into price variance and wage variance.

(*b*) Total direct labour cost variance analysed to rate variance, idle time variance and efficiency variance.

Solution : 1. Standard quantity for actual production = 3,000 × 1.50 kg. = 4,500 kg.

2. Standard price = Rs. 2.80 per kg.
3. Actual quantity consumed = 6,000 kg. – 500 kg. = 5,500 kg.
4. Actual price = $\frac{\text{Rs. } 18,000}{6,000}$ = Rs. 3 per kg.
5. Standard time for actual production = 3,000 × 3 = 6,000 hrs.
6. Standard rate = Rs. 2.50 per hour
7. Time booked = 7,000 hrs. – 500 hrs. = 6,500 hrs.
8. Actual time = 7,000 hours
9. Actual rate = $\frac{14,000}{7,000}$ = Rs. 2 per hour

1. Total direct material cost variance = (Std. qty. × Std. price) – (Actual qyt. × Actual price)
   = (4,500 × 2.80) – (5,500 × 3)
   = 12,600 – 16,500 = 3,900 (*A*)
2. Material price variance = (Std. price – Actual price) × Actual qty.
   = (2.80 – 3) × 5,500 = 1,100(*A*)
3. Material usage variance = (Std. qty. – Actual qty.) × Std. price
   = (4,500 – 5,500) × 2.80 = 2,800 (*A*)
4. Labour rate variance = (Std. rate – Actual rate) × Actual hrs.
   = (2.50 – 2) × 7,000 = 3,500 (*F*)
5. Idle time variance = (Idle hours × Std. rate)
   = 500 × 2.50= 1,250 (*A*)
6. Labour efficiency variance = (Std. hrs. – Actual hrs.) × Std. rate
   = (6,000 – 7,000) × 2.50= 2,500 (*A*)

Problem 25 : From the following data prepare a unit cost statement showing the prime cost of products *A* and *B* together with anlysis of variance :

		Product A	*Product B*
Material :	Standard	600 kg @ Rs. 5	90 kg. @ Rs. 3.00
	Actual	580 kg. @ Rs. 5.50	100 kg. @ Rs. 2.80
Labour :	Standard	80 hrs. @ Rs. 2	16 hrs. @ Rs. 2.80
	Actual	92 hrs. @ Rs. 1.75	14 hrs. @ Rs. 2.60

(*ICWA, Inter, June 1998*)

Solution :

Unit cost statement

	Product A		*Product B*	
Material :	600 kgs. @ Rs. 5	3,000	90 kg. @ Rs. 3	270
Labour	80 hrs. @ Rs. 2	160	16 hrs. @ Rs. 2.80	44.80
	Std. prime cost	3,160		314.80

Material :	580 kgs. @ Rs. 5.50	3,190	100 kgs. @ Rs. 2.80	280
Labour :	92 kgs. @ Rs. 1.75	161	14 hrs. @ Rs. 2.60	36.40
	Actual prime cost	3,351		316.40
	Total cost variance	191 (*A*)		1.60 (*A*)

Material price variance	=	(5.00 – 5.50) × 580	(3 – 2.80) × 100
(SP – AP) SQ	=	290 *A*	= 20 *F*
Material usage variance	=		
(SQ – AQ) SP	=	(600 – 580) × 5	(90 – 100) × 3
	=	100 (*F*)	= 30 (*A*)
Material cost variance	=		
MPV + MUV	=	290 (*A*) – 100 (*F*)	20 (*F*) + 30 (*A*)
	=	190 (*A*)	= 10 (*A*)
Labour rate variance	=	(2 – 1.75) × 92	(2.80 – 2.60) × 14
(SR – AR) × AH	=	23 (*F*)	= 2.80 F
Labour efficiency variance	=	(80 – 92) × 2	(16 – 14) × 2.80
(SH – AH) SR		= 24 (*A*)	= 5.60 (*F*)
Labour cost variance	=	23 (*F*) + 24 (*A*)	2.80 (*F*) + 5.60 (*F*)
L.R.V. + L.E.V.	=	1 *A*	= 8.40 *F*

Problem 26 : The following information is available from the cost records of Novell & Co. for the month of March 1994

	Rs.
Materials purchased 20,000 units	88,000
Materials consumed 19,000 units	
Actual wages paid for 4,950 hrs.	24,750
Units produced 1,800 units	

Standard rates and pieces are :

Direct material rate is Rs. 4 per unit

Standard output is 10 number for one unit

Direct labour rate is Rs. 4.00 per hour

Standard requirement is 2.5 hours per unit.

You are required to compute all material and labour variances for the month. (*CA, Inter, June 1995*)

Solution :

Material variances

Material cost variance = (Std. qty for actual output × Std. price) – (Actual qty. × Actual price)

= (18,000 × 4) – (19,000 × 4.40

= 72,000 – 83,600 = 11,600 (*A*)

Note : *Calculation of std. qty. for actual output*

1,800 × 10 = 18,000 units

(2) Material price variance = (Std. price – Actual price) × Actual qty.

= (4 – 4.40) × 19,000

= 0.40 × 19,000 = 7,600 (*A*)

(3) Material usage variance = (Std. qty. – Actual qty) × Std. rate

= (18,000 – 19,000) × 4

= 1,000 × 4 = 4,000 (*A*)

Labour variances :

Labour cost variance = Std. hours for actual output × Std. rate – Actual wages

= 4,500 × 4 – 24,750

= 18,000 – 24,750 = 6,750 (*A*)

Note : *Calculation of std. hours for actual output*

1,800 × 2.5 = 4,500 hrs.

Labour rate variance = (Std. rate – Actual rate) × Actual hrs.

= (4 – 5) × 4,950 = 4,950 (*A*)

Labour efficiency variance = (Std. hrs. for actual output – Actual hrs.) × Std. rate

= (4,500 – 4,950) × 4 = 1,800 *A*

3. Overhead Variance

Overhead variances arise on account of difference between actual overhead and absorbed overheads. In order to calculate overhead variance it is necessary to know the actual and absorbed overheads. The absorbed overhead rates are also known as the standard overhead recovery rate or standard overhead absorption rate. It is calculated by applying the following steps :

(*a*) To make the estimate of probable overheads to be incurred for each department for the next year.

(*b*) This estimated overhead is to be classified into fixed and variable overheads.

(*c*) The capacity utilisation either in terms of machine hours or labour hours or production units is to be estimated.

(*d*) Apply the following formula for calculating the standard overhead absorption rate :

$$\text{Standard fixed overhead rate} = \frac{\text{Budgeted fixed overhead}}{\text{Normal volume}}$$

$$\text{Standard variable overhead rate} = \frac{\text{Budgeted variable overhead}}{\text{Normal volume}}$$

(*A*) **Variable overhead cost variance :** It is defined as the difference between the actual variable overheads incurred and the variable overheads absorbed. This variance arises on account of over or under absorption of overheads. Calculation of this variance can be based on either hours or output. The following formula is used :

Variable overhead cost variance = Standard overhead cost recovered – Actual overhead cost

Where Std. overhead cost when overhead rate is per hours

= (Std. hours for actual output × Std. overhead rate per hour)

Standard overhead cost when overhead rate is output

= (Actual output × Std. overhead rate per unit)

(*a*) ***Variable overhead expenditue variance :*** It is defined as the difference between the actual variable overheads incurred and the allowed variable overheads based on the actual hours worked. Calculation of this variance is based on hours or output. The following formula is used :

Based on rate per hour

Variable overhead expenditure variance = (Std. variable overhead absorption rate per hr. × Actual hrs. worked worked) – Actual variable overhead

Based on rate per unit

Variable overhead expenditure variance = (Std. variable overhead absorption rate per unit – Actual variable rate per unit) × Actual output

(*b*) ***Variable overhead efficiency variance :*** This is defined as the difference between the allowed variable overheads and the absorbed variable overhead. The following formula is used to calculate this variance.

Variable overhead efficiency variance = (Actual hours – Std. hours for actual output) × Standard variable overhead absorption rate

or = (Std. qty. of output – Actual qty. of output) × Std. rate per unit.

(*B*) **Fixed overhead variance :** This is defined as the difference between the standard cost of fixed overhead absorbed in the production achieved, whether completed or not, and the fixed overhead attributed and charged to that period. The formula is :

(Std. hrs. for actual output × Std. fixed overhead rate) × Actual fixed overheads

(*a*) ***Fixed overhead expenditure overhead :*** This is defined as the difference between the budget cost allowance for production for a specified control period and the actual fixed expenditure attributed and charged to that period. In other words it represents the difference between the fixed overhead as per budget and the actual fixed overhead incurred. The following formula is used to calculate this variance :

Fixed oh. expenditure variance = (budgeted qty. × Std. fixed oh. rate per unit) – Actual fixed oh.

or = (Budgeted fixed overhead – Actual fixed overhead)

(*b*) ***Fixed overhead volume variance :*** It is that portion of the fixed overhead variance which is the difference between the standard cost of the overhead absorbed in actual output and the standard allowance for that output. In this definition standard allowance means the budgeted overhead. The fixed overhead volume variance arises mainly because of the use of a pre-determined overhad recovery rate based on a normal volume of activity and of the actual level of activity being less or more than the normal volume so selected. The following formula is used to calculate this variance.

Fixed overhad volume variance = (Actual qty. – Budgeted qty.) × Standard rate

of Fixed overhead volume variance = (Std. hours for actual production – Actual hours worked) × Std. fixed overhead rate

(*c*) ***Fixed overhead efficiency variance :*** It is that portion of the volume variance which reflects the increased or reduced output arising from efficiency above or below the standard which is expected. The following formula is used to calculate this variance :

Fixed overhead efficiency variance = (Actual qty. of production – Std. qty. of production for actual capacity) × Std. fixed overhead absorption rate per unit

or = (Std. hours for actual production – Actual hours worked) × Std. fixed overhead rate

(*d*) ***Fixed overhead capacity variance :*** This is defined as that portion of the fixed overhead volume variance which is due to working at higher or lower capacity than standard capacity.

The following formula is used to calculate this variance :

Fixed overhead capacity or usage variance = (Std. qty. of production – Revised budgeted qty. of production) × Std. fixed overhead rate per unit

or = (Std. hours for actual production – Actual hours of the period) × Std. fixed overhead rate per hour

(*e*) ***Calender variance :*** It is that portion of overhead volume variance which is due to the difference between the number of working days in the period to which the budget is applied.

The following formula is used to calculate this variance.

Calender variance = (Standard units – Revised budgeted units) × Std. fixed overhead rate per unit

or = (Std. number of working days or hrs. – Possible number of working days or hours) × Std. fixed overhead rate per day or hour.

Calender variance = (Budgeted hrs. – Actual hrs.) × Std. rate

(*f*) ***Seasonal variance :*** It is that portion of the overhead volume variance which is due to the difference between the seasonally budgeted output and the average output on which standards have been calculated.

The following are the main causes for the overhead volume variance.

Causes Controllable by Management

(*i*) Employees waiting for work.
(*ii*) Avoidable machine breakdown.
(*iii*) Lack of operator.
(*iv*) Lack of tools.
(*v*) Lack of instructions.

Causes Uncontrollable by Management

(*i*) Decrease in customer demand.
(*ii*) Excess plant capacity.

Problem 27 (Overhead variance) : From the following information compute fixed overhead cost, expenditure and volume/capacity variances.

Normal capacity is 5,000 hours.

Budgeted fixed overhead rate is Rs. 10 per standard hour. Actual level of capacity utilised is 4,400 standard hours.

Actual fixed overheads Rs. 52,000. (*University of Delhi, B.Com. (Hons.), 1991*)

Solution :

(1) Fixed overhead variance = Budgeted fixed overhead – Actual fixed overhead
= 44,000 – 52,000 = 8,000 (*A*)

Budgeted fixed overhead = Std. hrs. × Budgeted fixed overhead rate
= 4,400 × Rs. 10 = 44,000

Note : Budgeted fixed overheads are taken at the actual capacity utilised.

(2) Expense variance = Budgeted total factory overhead – Actual fixed factory overhead
= 50,000 – 52,000 = 2,000 (*A*)

(3) Volume/capacity variance = (Actual capacity – Budgeted capacity) × Std. rate
= (4,400 – 5,000) × 10 = 6,000 (*A*)

Verification :

Fixed overhead variance = Expense variance + Volume variance
8,000 (*A*) = 2,000 (*A*) + 6,000 (*A*)

Problem 28 : From the following particulars calculate all variances relating to fixed overheads.

	Budgeted	*Actual*
Fixed overhead for July 1993	Rs. 10,000	Rs. 10,200
Units produced in July 1993	5,000	5,200
Standard for one unit	4 hours	
Actual hours worked		20,100 hours

Solution :

(1) Total fixed overhead variance = Absorbed fixed overhead – Actual fixed overhead
= 10,400 – 10,200 = 200 (*F*)

Absorbed fixed overhead = 5,200 × 2 = 10,400

$$= \frac{\text{Budgeted oh}}{\text{Units}} = \frac{10,000}{5,000} = 2$$

(2) Overhead expenditure variance = Actual overheads – Budgeted overheads
= 10,200 – 10,000 = 200 (*A*)

(3) Overhead volume variance = (Actual qty. – Budgeted qty.) × Std. rate
= (5,200 – 5,000) × 2 = 400 (*F*)

(4) Overhead capacity variance = (Actual hours – Budgeted hours) × Std. hourly rate
= (20,100 – 20,000) × 0.50 = 50 (*F*)

$$\text{Std. hourly rate} = \frac{\text{Rs. 2}}{\text{4 hrs.}} = 0.50$$

(5) Overhead efficiency variance = (Actual hrs. × Standard hour) × Std. rate per hr.
= (21,000 – 20,800) × 0.50 = 350 (*F*)

Standard hours produced = 5,200 × 4 = 20,800

Problem 29 : From the following data calculate the various overhead based on (1) units of production and (2) hours of production.

		Hours	Units
(*i*)	Annual budgeted production	50 weeks × 6 days × 8 hrs. = 240 hrs. or 200 hrs. per mongh	1,80,000 (or 15,000 per month)
(*ii*)	Production standard per hr.		75
(*iii*)	Annual budgeted fixed overhead		Rs. 2,70,000
	Data for June 1993	Hours	Units
(*i*)	Actual production		14,500
(*ii*)	Actual hours worked	180	
(*iii*)	Budgeted hours	4 weeks × 6 days × 8 hrs. = 192	
(*iv*)	Extra holiday	1½ days = 12 hrs.	

Solution : (A) *Calculation of overhead variance based on units of production*

Calculation of standard overhead rate = $\frac{\text{Rs. } 2,70,000}{1,80,000}$ = Rs. 1.50 per unit

(1) Volume variance = (Actual qty. – Budgeted qty.) × Std. rate
= (14,500 – 15,000) × 1.50 = 750 (*A*)

(2) Overhead capacity variance :
Change in capacity = 200 – 192 hours = 8 hrs.
Loss of output = 8 × 75 units = 600 units
∴ Capacity variance = 1.50 × 600= Rs. 900 (*A*)
or = (Standard units × Revised budgeted units for revised working hrs.) × Standard rate
(15,000 – 14,400*) × 1.50 = Rs. 900 (*A*)
*192 × 75 = 14,400

(3) Calender variance = Std. rate × Loss of output dut eo extra holiday
Rs. 1.50 × 12 × 75 = Rs. 1,350 (*A*)

(4) Overhead efficiency variance = (Actual units — Std. units) × Std. rate
(14,500 – 13,500)* = Rs. 1,500 (*F*)
Std. units = Actual hrs. worked × Std. units per hrs.
180 × 75 = 13,500

Verification :
Overhead volume variance = Capacity variance + Calender variance + Efficiency variance
75 (A) = 900 (*A*) + 1,350 (*A*) + 1,500 (*F*)

(*B*) Calculation of variance on the basis of hours of production

Calculation of standard overhead rate = $\frac{\text{Rs. } 2,70,000}{2,400}$ = 112.50 per hour

(1) Overhead volume variance = (Std. hrs. for actual production – Budgeted hrs.) × Std. rate
= (193.125* – 200) × 112.50 = 750 (*A*)

Std. hrs. for actual production = $\frac{14,500}{75}$ = 193.125

(2) Overhead efficiency variance = (Std. hrs. – Actual hrs.) × Std. rate
= (193.125 – 180) × 112.50 = Rs. 1,500 (*F*)

(3) Overhad capacity variance = (Actual hrs. – Revised budgeted hours) × Std. rate
= 8 × 112.50 = 900 (*A*)

(4) Overhead calender variance = (Revised budgeted hours – Seasonal budgeted hrs.) × Std. rate
= 12 × 112.50 = Rs. 1,350 (*A*)

Problem 30 : Assuming the expenses to be fixed, calculate from the following data (*a*) efficiency variance, (*b*) volume variance, (*c*) calender variance, (*d*) expense variance.

	Budget	*Actual*
No. of working days	20	22
Man hours per day	8,000	8,400
Output per man hour in unit	1.0	1.2
Standard overhead rate per man hour	Rs. 2	
Actual fixed expenses		Rs. 3,25,000

Solution : Actual output = 8,400 hrs. × 22 days × 1.2 units

Per hour = 2,21,760 units

Standard output per man hour = 1

Standard hours produced = 2,21,760 × 1= 2,21,760

Actual hours worked = 8,400 × 22 = 1,84,800

Overhead as per budget = 8,000 hrs. × 20 days + Rs. 2 per hour = Rs. 3,20,000

(1) Overhead efficiency overhead = (Actual hours – Std. hours) × Std. rate
= (1,84,800 – 2,21,760) × 2 = 73,920 (*F*)

(2) Capacity variance = (Actual hrs. – (budgeted hrs.) × Std. rate

Actual hrs. = 8,400 × 22 = 1,84,800

Budgeted hrs. in actual days = 8,000 × 22 = 1,76,000
= (1,84,800 – 1,76,000) × 2 = 17,600 (*F*)

(3) Calender variance = (Budgeted hrs. – Actual hrs.) × Std. rate

Budgeted hrs. = 8,000 × 20 = 1,60,000

Actual hrs. = 8,400 × 22 = 1,76,000
= (1,60,000 – 1,76,000) × 2 = 32,000 (*F*)

(4) Volume variance = (Actual qty. – Budgeted qty.) × Std. rate

Actual qty. = 8,400 × 22 × 1.2 = 2,21,760 units.

Budgeted qty. = 8,000 × 20 × 1 = 1,60,000 units
= (2,21,760 – 1,60,000) × 2 = 1,23,520 (F)

(5) Expense variance = Actual overhead cost – Budgeted overhead cost
= 3,25,000 – 3,20,000 = 5,000 (*A*)

Problem 31 : The budget for a period indicates :

	Rs.
Works overhead fixed	50,000
Works overhead variable	1,50,000
Normal activity	100%

During the period the actual activity was only 70% of the normal load for a total expenditure of Rs. 1,50,000. What are the budget and volume variance? (*ICWA, (Inter), Dec. 1990*)

Solution : Budgeted works overhead for actual qty.

		Rs.
Fixed		
Variable $\frac{1,50,000}{100} \times 70$	=	50,000
	=	1,05,000
		1,55,000
Actual works overhead for actual qty.		1,50,000
Recovered works overhead for actual qty.		
Fixed Variable $\frac{50,000}{100} \times 70$	=	35,000
	=	1,05,000
		1,40,000

(1) Overhead budget variance = Budgeted overhead – Actual overhead
= 1,55,000 – 1,50,000 = 5,000 (*F*)

(2) Overhead volume variance = Recovered overhead – Budgeted overhead
= 1,40,000 – 1,55,000 = 15,000 (*A*)

Problem 32 : Determine the budget and capacity variance from the following data :

Estimated factory overhead	Rs. 25,000
Estimated direct labour hours	5,000
Actual overhead expenses	Rs. 26,500
Applied overhead expenses	Rs. 22,500

(ICWA, Inter, June 1990)

Solution :

Overhead budget variance = Budgeted overhead – Actual overhead
= 25,000 – 26,500 = 1,500 (*A*)

Overhead capacity variance = (Std. hrs. for actual production – Actual hrs.) × Std. overhead rate per hr.
= (4,500 – 5,000) × 5 = 2,500 (*A*)

Problem 33 : The following information is available from the records of a facory

	Budgeted	*Actual*
Fixed overhead for May (Rs.)	5,000	6,000
Production in May (units)	1,000	1,050
Standard time per unit (hrs.)	10	–
Actual hours worked in May	–	11,000

Compute :

(*i*) Fixed overhead cost variance
(*ii*) Expenditure variance
(*iii*) Volume variance
(*iv*) Capacity variance
(*v*) Efficiency variance

(CS, Inter, December, 2000)

Solution :

Calculation of Std. overhead rate :

$$= \frac{\text{Budgeted Fixed overhead}}{\text{Budgeted production units}}$$

$$= \frac{5{,}000}{1{,}000} = \text{Rs. } 5$$

Calculation of hourly rate :

$$= \frac{\text{Rs. } 5}{10 \text{ hrs.}} = 0.50$$

(*i*) Fixed overhead cost variance = Overhead recovered on actual output – Actual fixed overheads
= (1,050 units × Rs. 5) – 6,000
= 5,250 – 6,000 = Rs. 750 (*A*)

(*ii*) Expenditure variance = Budgeted fixed oh. – Actual fixed oh.
= 5,000 – 6,000 = Rs. 1,000 (*A*)

(*iii*) Volume variance = (Budgeted output – Actual output) × Std. rate per unit
= (1,000 – 1,050) × 5 = 250 (*F*)

(*iv*) Capacity variance = (Budgeted hours – Actual hours) × Std. rate per hr.
= (10,000 – 11,000) × 0.50 = 500 *F*

(*v*) Efficiency variance = (Std. hours for actual output – Actual hours) × Std. rate per unit
= (10,500 – 11,000) × 0.50 = 250 (*A*)

Problem 34 : Adarsh Ltd. has furnished you the following data :

	Budgeted	*Actual for July 1998*
Number of working days	25	27
Production in units	20,000	22,000
Fixed overhead (Rs.)	30,000	31,000

Budgeted fixed overhead rate is Re. 1 per hour. In July 1998, the actual hours worked were 31,500.

Calculate the following variances :

(*i*) Efficiency variance
(*ii*) Capacity variance
(*iii*) Calender variance
(*iv*) Volume variance
(*v*) Expenditure variance
(*vi*) Total overheads variance

(*CS, Inter, June 1999*)

Solution :

Calculation of Budgeted hours

Budgeted overheads Rs. 30,000
Budgeted overhead rate per hour Re. 1

$$\text{Budgeted hours} = \frac{\text{Rs. } 30{,}000}{\text{Re. 1 per hour}} = 30{,}000 \text{ hrs.}$$

Calculation of standard time per unit of output

$$\frac{\text{Budgeted hours}}{\text{Budgeted output}} = \frac{30{,}000}{20{,}000} = 1.5 \text{ hrs.}$$

Calculation of std. hours for actual output

Actual output × Std. time per unit
22,000 × 1.5 = 33,000 hrs.

Calculation of std. rate per unit

Std. rate per unit of output = 1.5 hrs. × Re. 1 per hr.
= Rs. 1.50

(1) Efficiency variance = (Std. hrs. for actual output – Actual hrs.) × Std. rate per hr.
= (33,000 – 31,500) × 1
= 1,500 × 1 = 1,500 *F*

OR

Efficiency variance = (Std. output for actual hrs. – Actual output) × Std. rate per unit
= (21,000 units – 22,000 units) × 1.50
= 1,000 × 1.50 = 1,500 *F*

Note : Calculation of std. output for actual hours :

$$= \frac{\text{Actual Hours}}{\text{Std. time per unit of output}}$$

$$= \frac{31{,}500 \text{ hours}}{1.5 \text{ hours}} = 21{,}000 \text{ units}$$

(2) Capacity variance = (Revised budgeted hours – Actual hours) × Std. Rate per hour
= (32,400 – 31,500) × 1 = 900 *A*

Note : Calculation of revised budgeted hours :
Actual working days × Budgeted hours per day
27 × 1,200 = 32400

(3) Calender variance = (Budgeted no. of working days – Actual *No.* of working days) × Budgeted overheads/ Budgeted working days

$$= (25 - 27) \times \frac{30{,}000}{25}$$

= 2 × 1,200 = 2,400 *F*

(4) Volume variance = (Budgeted output – Actual output) × Std. rate per unit
= (20,000 – 22,000) × 1.50
= 2,000 × 1.50 = 3,000 *F*

(5) Expenditure variance = Budgeted overheads – Actual overheads
= 30,000 – 31,000 = 1,000 (*A*)

(6) Total overhead variance = (Actual output – Std. rate per unit – Actual overheads)
= (22,000 – 1.50 – 31,000)
= 33,000 – 31,000 = 2,000 (*F*)

Problem 35 : A company has a normal capacity of 120 machines, working 8 hours per day of 25 days in a month. The fixed overheads are budgeted at Rs. 1,44,000 per month. The standard time required to manufacture one unit of product is 4 hours.

In April 1998, the company worked 24 days of 840 machine hours per day and produced 5,305 units of output the actual fixed overheads were Rs. 1,42,000.

Compute :

(1) Efficiency variance
(2) Capacity variance
(3) Calender variance
(4) Expense variance
(5) Volume variance
(6) Total fixed overhead variance.

(*CA, Inter, May 1998*)

Solution :

Working Notes :

	Budget	*Actual*
(1) Fixed overhead for the month	1,44,000	1,42,000
(2) Working days per month	25	24
(3) Working hours per month =	(120 machines × 8 hrs. × 25 days) 24,000	840 machine hours × 24 days = 20,160
(4) Production units per month	$\frac{24,000 \text{ hrs.}}{4 \text{ hrs.}}$ = 6,000	5,305

(5) Standard hours for actual production
= Actual production units × Std. hours per unit
= 5,305 × 4 = 21,220 hrs.

(6) Standard fixed overhead rate per unit :

$= \frac{\text{Rs. } 1,44,000}{6000 \text{ units}}$ = Rs. 24

(7) Standard fixed overhead rate per hour :

$= \frac{\text{Rs. } 1,44,000}{24,000 \text{ hrs.}}$ = Rs. 6

(8) Standard fixed overhead per day :

$\frac{\text{Rs. } 1,44,000}{25 \text{ days}}$ = Rs. 5,760

(1) Efficiency variance = (Std. hrs. for actual production – Actual hrs.) × Std. rate per hr.
= (21,220 – 20,160) × 6 = 6,360 *F*

(2) Capacity variance = (Budgeted hours – Actual hours) × Std. rate per hour
= (24 days × 120 mach. × 8 hrs. – 20,160) × 6
= 17,280 (*A*)

(3) Calender variance = (Budgeted *No.* of days – Actual *No.* of days) × Std. rate per day
= (25 – 24) × 5,760 = 5,760 *A*

(4) Expense variance = (Budgeted fixed oh. – Actual fixed overhead)
= (1,44,000 – 1,42,000) = 2,000 *F*

(5) Volume variance = (Budgeted output – Actual output) × Std. rate per unit
= (5,305 – 6,000) × 24
= 695 × 24 = 16,680 *A*

(6) Total fixed oh. variance = (Fixed oh. for actual output – Actual fixed overheads)
= (5,305 × 24 – 1,42,000)
= 1,27,320 – 1,42,000 = 14,680 *A*

Verification :

Fixed oh. variance = Expenses variance + Volume variance
14,680 *A* = 2,000 *F* + 16,680 *A*

Volume Variance = Efficiency variance + Capacity variance + Calender variance
16,680 *A* = 6,360 *F* + 17,280 *A* + 5,760 *A*

Problem 36 (Variable overhead variances) : The following data is given :

	Budget	*Actuals*
Production (in units)	400	360
Man hours to produce above	8,000	7,000
Variable overheads (in rupees)	10,000	9,150

The standard time to produce one unit of the product is 20 hours

Calculate variable overhead variances. (*CA, Inter, November 1997*)

Solution :

Working Notes :

(1) Calculation of standard variable overhead per unit

$$= \frac{\text{Budgeted variable oh}}{\text{Budgeted production}} = \frac{10,000}{400} = \text{Rs. } 25 \text{ per unit}$$

(2) Calculation of standard variable overhead per hour :

$$= \frac{\text{Budgeted variable oh}}{\text{Budgeted man hours}} = \frac{10,000}{8,000} = 1.25 \text{ per hour}$$

(3) Calculation of Std. variable overhead for actual output

Actual output × Std. variable overhead per unit
= 360 units × Rs. 25 = Rs. 9,000

(4) Budgeted variable overhead based on actual hours worked

Actual hours worked × Std. variable overhead per hour
7,000 × 1.25 = Rs. 8,750

(5) Calculation of standard hours for actual output

Actual output × Std. hours per unit
360 units × 20 hours = 7,200 hours

(1) Variable overhead variance = Std. variable oh. – Actual variable oh.
= 9,000 – 9,150 = Rs. 150 *A*

(2) Variable overhead expenditure variable = Budgeted variable oh. – Actual variable oh.
= 8,750 – 9,150 = 400

(3) Variable overhead efficiency variable = (Std. hours for actual output – Actual hours) × Std. rate per hour
= (7,200 – 7,000) × 1.25
= 250 *F*

Verification :

Variable oh. variance = Variable expenditure variance + Variable overhead efficiency variance
150 (*A*) = 400 *A* + 250 *F*

4. Sales Variance

Sales variance is useful in controlling sales and thereby earn more profit. Sales variances can be calculated on the basis of (1) Sales margin or (2) Turnover.

(*A*) **Sales variances based on sales margin :** Before the various sales margin variances are dicussed, it is better to know the concept of standard sales margin.

Standard sales margin : This refers to the difference between the standard selling price of a product and its standard cost and it is the same as the standard profit for the product. The term 'Standard cost' used above is to indicate 'total standard cost'. It includes both fixed and variable cost. When fixed cost is excluded it becomes standard marginal cost. The difference between standard selling price and standard marginal cost is known as standard sales contribution.

The various sales margin variances are as follows :

(*a*) ***Total sales margin variance :*** This is the difference between the budgeted margin from sales and the actual margin, when the cost of sales is valued at the standard cost of production. The following formula is used to calculate this variance :

Total sales margin variance = Standard margin or profit – Actual margin or profit.

(*b*) ***Sales margin price variance :*** This is that portion of total sales margin variance which is the difference between the standard margin per unit and the actual margin per unit for the number of units sold in the period. The following formula is used to calculate this variance :

Sales margin price variance = (Std. margin per unit – Actual margin per unit) × Actual qty.

(*c*) ***Sales margin quantity variance :*** This is that portion of total sales margin variance which is the difference between the budgeted number of units sold and the actual number sold valued at standard margin per unit. The following formula is used to calculate this variance :

Standard margin qty. variance = (Standard proportion for actual sales × Budgeted qty.)
× Standard profit

When more than one product is sold, sales margin quantity variance is sub-divided into (*a*) Mix variance and (*b*) A volume variance.

(*d*) ***Sales margin mix variance :*** This is that portion of sales margin quantity variance which is the difference between the actual total number of units at the actual mix and the actual total number of units at standard mix valued at the standard margin per unit. The following formula is used to calculate this variance :

Sales margin mix variance = (Actual qty. × Std. proportion for actual sales) × Std. profit

(*e*) ***Sales margin volume variance :*** This is that portion of the sales margin quantity variance which is the difference between the actual total quantity of units sold and the budgeted total number of units at the standard mix valued at the standard margin per unit. The following formula is used to calculat this variance :

Sales margin volume variance = (Budgeted units – Actual units sold) × Std. marginal per unit

(*B*) **Sales variances based on turnover or sales value :** Sales variances based on turnover is used, by those organisations which would like to exercise control on actual sales by comparing it with budgeted sales. The following are the variances based on turnover.

(*a*) ***Sales value variance :*** This refers to the difference between the budgeted sales and the actual sales. The following formula is used to calculated this variance :

Sales value variance = Budgeted sales – Actual sales

(*b*) ***Sales price variance :*** This refers to that portion of the sales variance which is due to the difference between the standard price specified and the actual price charged. The following formula is used to calculate this variance :

Sales price variance = (Actual price – Std. price) × Actual qty.

(*c*) ***Sales volume variance :*** It refers to that portion of the sales value variance which is due to the difference between the budgeted sales and the standard value of actual mix of sales. The following formula is used to calculate this variance :

Sales volume variance = (Std. qty. of sales – Actual qty. of sales) × Std. price

(*d*) ***Sales quantity variance :*** This refers to that portion of sales volume variance which is due to the difference between standard value of actual sales at standard mix and the budgeted sales. The following formula is used to calculate this variance :

Sales quantity variance = Budgeted sales – Revised standard sales

(*e*) ***Sales mix variance :*** This refers to that portion of the sales volume variance which is due to the difference between the standard and the actual composition of the sales mix. It is the difference between the standard value of actual mix and the standard value of actual sales at standard mix. The following formula is used to calculate this variance :

$$\text{Sales mix variance} = \left(\frac{\text{Std. mix}}{\text{Revised std. mix of actual qty. sold}} - \text{Actual mix}\right) \times \text{Std. price}$$

Problem 37 (Sales variances) : Ultra Modern Cassette Ltd. had budgeted the following sales for February 1991.

Casette *A*	1,100 units @ Rs.	50 per unit
Casette *B*	950 units @ Rs.	100 per unit
Casette *C*	1,250 units @ Rs.	80 per unit

As against this, the actual sales were :

Casette *A*	1,300 units @ Rs.	55 per unit
Casette *B*	1,000 units @ Rs.	95 per unit
Casette *C*	1,200 units @ Rs.	78. per unit

The cost per unit of cassette *A*, *B* and *C* was Rs. 45, Rs. 85 and Rs. 70 respectively.

Compute the different variances to explain the difference between the budgeted and actual product.

(*C.S., Inter, June 1992*)

Solution :

	Cassette A	*Cassette B*	*Cassette C*
Standard selling price (*see assumption 1*)	50	100	80
Standard cost (*see assumption 2*)	45	85	70
Standard profit	5	15	10

Assumption 1 : Standard selling price is assumed to be equal to the budgeted selling price.

Assumption 2 : Standard cost is assumed to be equal to actual cost.

Calculation of actual profit

Actual selling price	55	95	78
Actual cost	45	85	70
Actual profit	10	10	8

Actual profit :

Cassette *A*	—	1,300 @ Rs. 10	=	13,000
Cassette *B*	—	1,000 @ Rs. 10	=	10,000
Cassette *C*	—	1,200 @ Rs. 8	=	9,600
		Total	=	32,600

Budgeted profit :

Cassette *A*	—	1,100 @ Rs. 5	=	5,500
Cassette *B*	—	950 @ Rs. 15	=	14,250
Cassette *C*	—	1,250 @ Rs. 10	=	12,500
		Total	=	32,250

(1) Total sales margin variance = (Std. profit or budgeted profit – Actual profit)
(32,250 – 32,600) = 350 (*F*)

(2) Sales margin price variance = (Std. margin per unit – Actual margin per unit) × Actual qty.

Cassette *A*	—	(50 – 55) × 1,300	=	6,500	(*F*)
Cassette *B*	—	(100 – 95) – 1,000	=	5,000	(*A*)
Cassette *C*	—	(80 – 78) × 1,200	=	2,400	(*A*)
			=	900	(*A*)

(3) Sales margin volume variance = (Budgeted sales qty. – Actual qty. sold) × Std. margin per unit

Cassette *A*	—	(1,100 – 1,300) × 5	=	1,000	(*F*)
Cassette *B*	—	(950 – 1,000) × 15	=	750	(*F*)
Cassette *C*	—	(1,250 – 1,200) × 10	=	500	(*A*)
			=	1,250	(*F*)

(4) Sales mix variance = (Actual qty. – Std. proportion for actual sales) × Std. profit

Cassette *A*	—	(1,300 – 1,67) × 5	=	665	(*F*)
Cassette *B*	—	(1,000 – 1,008) × 15	=	120	(*A*)
Cassette *C*	—	(1,200 – 1,325) 10	=	1,250	(*A*)
			=	705	(*A*)

Calculation of standard proportion for actual sales

Cassette *A* = $\frac{3,500}{3,300} \times 1,100$ = 1,167 units

Cassette *B* = $\frac{3,500}{3,300} \times 950$ = 1,008 units

Cassette *C* = $\frac{3,500}{3,300} \times 1,250$ = 1,325 units

3,500 units

(5) Sales margin qty. variance = (Std. proportion for actual sales – Budgeted qty.) × Std. profit

Cassette *A*	—	(1,167 – 1,100) × 5	=	335	(*F*)
Cassette *B*	—	(1,008 – 950) × 15	=	870	(*F*)
Cassette *C*	—	(1,325 – 1,250) × 10	=	750	(*F*)
			=	1,955	(*F*)

Volume variance = Mix variance + Quantity variance
1,250 *F* = 705 (*A*) + 1,955 (*F*)

Profit and loss statement

	Cassette *A*	*Cassette* *B*	*Cassette* *C*
Budgeted Sales	55,000	95,000	1,00,000
Less : Budgeted cost	49,500	80,750	87,500
Budgeted profit	5,500	14,250	12,500

Variances :

Price variance	6,500 (*F*)	5,000 (*A*)	2,400 (*A*)
Mix variance	665 (*F*)	120 (*A*)	1,250 (*A*)
Qty. variance	335 (*F*)	870 (*F*)	750 (*F*)
	13,000	10,000	9,600

Problem 38 : Compute the following variances from the data given below :

(1) Total sales margin variance.
(2) Sales margin volume variance.
(3) Sales margin price variance.
(4) Sales margin mix variance.
(5) Sales margin quantity (sub-volume) variance.

Product	*Budgeted quantity (Units)*	*Actual quantity (Units)*	*Budgeted sales price per unit Rs.)*	*Actual sales price per unit (Rs.)*	*Standard cost per unit (Rs.)*
X	240	400	50	45	30
Y	160	200	25	20	15

(*CA, Inter, May 1992*)

Solution : (1) Total sales margin variance = Actual profit – Budgeted profit
7,000 – 6,400 = 600 (*F*)
(*see working note 2*)

(2) Sales margin volume variance = (Actual qty. – Budgeted qty.) × Budgeted margin per unit
X = (400 – 240) × 20 = 3,200 *F*
Y = (200 – 160) × 10 = 400 *F*
3,600 *F*

(3) Sales margin price variance = (Actual margin per unit – Budgeted margin per unit × Actual Qty.
X = (15 – 20) × 400 = 2,000 (*A*)
Y = (5 – 10) × 200 = 1,000 (*A*)
3,000 (*A*)

(4) Sales margin mix variance = (Budgeted margin per unit on actual mix – Budgeted margin per unit as budgeted mix) × Total actual qty.
(*Refer working note 3*)
= (Rs. 16.666 – 16) × 600 = 400 (*F*)

(5) Sales margin qty. (sub-volume) variance = (Total actual qty. – Total budgeted qty.) × Budgeted margin per unit on budgeted mix
= (600 – 400) × 16 = 3,200 (*F*)
(*Refer working note 3*)

Verification :

Sales margin variance = Sales margin price variance + Sales margin volume variance
600 (*F*) = 3,000 (*A*) + 3,600 (*F*)
Sales margin volume variance = Sales margin mix variance + Sales margin qty. variance
3,600 (*F*) = 400 (*F*) + 3,200 (*F*)

Working Notes :

1. (*a*) Actual margin per unit = (Actual sales prices per unit – Standard cost per unit)
X = (45 – 30) = Rs. 15
Y = (20 – 15) = Rs. 5

(*b*) Budgeted margin per unit = Budgeted sales price per unit – STd. cost per unit
X = (50 – 30) = Rs. 20
Y = (25 – 15) = Rs. 10

2. (*a*) Actual profit = Actual qty. of product unit sold – Actual margin per unit

X	= 400 × 15	=	6,000
Y	= 200 × 5	=	1,000
			7,000

(*b*) Budgeted profit = Budgeted qty. of units to be sold × Budgeted margin per unit

X	= 240 × 20	=	4,800
Y	= 160 × 10	=	1,600
			6,400

3. (*a*) Budgeted margin per unit on actual mix

$$= \frac{20 \times 400 + 10 \times 200}{600}$$

$$= \frac{8{,}000 + 2{,}000}{6{,}000} = 16.666$$

(*b*) Budgeted margin per unit on budgeted mix

$$= \frac{20 \times 240 + 10 \times 160}{400}$$

$$= \frac{4{,}800 + 1{,}600}{400} = \frac{6{,}400}{400} = \text{Rs. } 16$$

Problem 39 : The following particulars are available in respect of the Sunshine Co. Ltd. for the period 1992 :

	Budgeted sales			*Actual sales*		
	Qt.	*Rate*	*Amt.*	*Qty.*	*Rate*	*Amt.*
X	1,000	2	2,000	1,800	2,50	4,500
Y	3,000	3	9,000	4,200	2,75	11,550
	4,000		11,000	6,000		16,050

You are required to calculate (*a*) Total sales variance, (*b*) Sales price variance, (*c*) Sales mix variance, (*d*) Sales qty. variance.

Solution : Sales value variance = Budgeted sales – Actual sales

X = (2,000 – 4,500) = 2,500 (*F*)

Y = (9,000 – 11,550) = 2,550 (*F*)

Alternatively total sales value variance = Total budgeted sales – Total actual sales

= 11,000 – 16,050 = 5,050 (*F*)

Sales price variance = (Budgeted selling price – Actual selling price) × Actual selling price

X = (2 – 2.50) × 1,800 = 900 (*F*)

Y = (3 – 2.75) × 4,200 = 1,050 (*F*)

150 (*F*)

Sales mix variance = (Revised std. sales mix – Actual sales mix) × Std. selling price

$$\text{Revised std. sales mix} = \frac{\text{Total actual sales mix}}{\text{Total std. sales mix}} \times \text{Std. qty. of sales}$$

$$X = \frac{6{,}000}{4{,}000} \times 1{,}000 = 1{,}500 \text{ units}$$

$$Y = \frac{6{,}000}{4{,}000} \times 3{,}000 = 4{,}500 \text{ units}$$

X	=	(1,500 – 1,800) × 2	=	6,00 (F)
Y	=	(4,500 – 4,200) – 3	=	900 (F)
				300 (A)

Sales quantity variance = (Revised std. qty. – Std. or budgeted qty.) × Std. selling price

X	=	(1,500 – 1,000) × 2	=	1,000 (F)
Y	=	(4,500 – 3,000) × 3	=	4,500 (F)
				5,500 (F)

Problem 40 : The budgeted and the actual sales for a period in respect of three products are given below :

Budgeted figures

Product	*Quantity*	*Price*	*Value*
A	1,000	5	5,000
B	750	10	7,500
C	500	15	7,500
	2,250		20,000

Actuals

A	1,200	6	7,200
B	700	9	6,300
C	600	14	8,400
	2,500		21,900

Calculate sales variances. (*CA, Inter, November 1998*)

Solution :

	Budgeted			*Actual*			*Actual qty. × Budgeted price*
Products	*Qty.*	*Rate*	*Value*	*Qty.*	*Rate*	*Value*	*Value*
A	1,000	5	5,000	1,200	6	7,200	6,000
B	750	10	7,500	700	9	6,300	7,000
C	500	15	7,500	600	14	8,400	9,000
	2,250		20,000	2,500		21,900	22,000

(1) Sales value variance = Budgeted sales – Actual sales
= 20,000 – 21,900
= 1,900 *F*

(2) Sales price variance = (Budgeted price – Actual price) × Actual qty.

A	=	(6 – 5) × 1,200	=	1,200 *F*
B	=	(10 – 9) × 700	=	700 *A*
C	=	(15 – 14) × 600	=	600 *A*
				100 *A*

(3) Sales volume variance = (Budgeted qty. – Actual qty.) × Budgeted selling price

A	=	(1,000 – 1200) × 5	
	=	1,000 *F*	1,000 *F*
B	=	(750 – 700) × 10	
	=	500 *A*	500 *A*
C	=	(500 – 600) × 15	
	=	1,500 *F*	15,000 *F*
			2,000 *F*

(4) Sales mix variance = (Budgeted price per unit of actual mix – Budgeted price per unit of budgeted – mix) × Total actual qty.

$$= \left(\frac{22,000}{2,500} - \frac{20,000}{2,250}\right) \times 2,500$$

$$= (8.80 - 8.88) \times 2,500$$

$$= 222\ (A)$$

(5) Sales qty. variance = (Total actual qty. – Total budgeted qty.) × Budgeted price per unit of budgeted mix

$$= (2,500 - 2,250) \times \frac{20,000}{2,250}$$

$$= 2,222\ (F)$$

Problem 41 : The standard cost data of three products *X*, *Y* and *Z* manufactured by a company are given below together with the budgeted sales and unit selling prices for 1995-96 :

	X	*Y*	*Z*
Budgeted sales (unit)	25,000	20,000	15,000
Selling price per unit (Rs.)	40	60	80
Cost per unit (Rs.)	28	48	64

In April 1996, the cost department of the company gathered the following details for 1995-96 :

	X	*Y*	*Z*
Actual Sales (units)	20,000	22,000	16,000
Average sales realisation per unit (Rs.)	42	56	81
Actual cost per unit (Rs.)	30	50	63

You are required to determine :

(*a*) The budgeted profit and the actual profit for 1995-96.

(*b*) The variance in profit analysed into

(*i*) Cost variance.

(*ii*) Sales price variance.

(*iii*) Sales volume variance.

(*ICWA, Inter, June 1996*)

Solution :

	Budgeted profit			Actual profit		
X	(40 – 28) × 25,000	=	3,00,000	(42 – 30) × 20,000	=	2,40,000
Y	(60 – 48) × 20,000	=	2,40,000	(56 – 50) × 22,000	=	1,32,000
Z	(80 – 64) × 15,000	=	2,40,000	(81 – 63) × 16,000	=	2,88,000
			7,80,000			6,60,000

Variance in profit = 7,80,000 – 6,60,000
= 1,20,000 *A*

(1) Cost variance = (Std. cost – Actual cost) × Actual *No.* of units sold

X	=	(28 – 30) × 20,000	=	40,000 *A*
Y	=	(48 – 50) × 22,000	=	44,000 *A*
Z	=	(64 – 63) × 16,000	=	16,000 *F*
				68,000 *A*

(2) Selling price variance= (Std. price – Actual price) × Actual *No.* of units sold

X	=	(40 – 42) × 20,000	=	40,000 *F*
Y	=	(60 – 56) × 22,000	=	88,000 *A*
Z	=	(80 – 81) × 16,000	=	16,000 *F*
				32,000 *A*

(3) Sales volume variance= (Budgeted volume – Actual volume) × Std. profit

X	=	(25,000 – 20,000) × 12	=	60,000 A
Y	=	(20,000 – 22,000) × 12	=	24,000 F
Z	=	(15,000 – 16,000) × 16	=	16,000 F
				20,000 A

CONTROL RATIOS

Ratios are often used as a control technique in addition to monetary value of variance. The following ratios are commonly used in indurstries.

Efficiency Ratio

This ratio measures the efficiency at which the factory operates. The ICMA terminology defines efficiency ratio as "the standard hours equivalent to the work produced, expressed as a percentage of the actual hours spent in producing that work. Expressed as a formula :

$$\text{Efficiency ratio} = \frac{\text{Actual production in terms of standard hrs}}{\text{Actual hours worked}} \times 100$$

Activity Ratio

This ratio measures the level of a activity at which the factory is operating. The ICMA terminology defines it as "the number of standard hours equivalent to the work produced, expressed as a percentage of the budgeted standard hours". Expressed as a formula :

$$\text{Actual ratio} = \frac{\text{Actual production in terms of std. hrs}}{\text{Budgeted production in terms of std. hrs}} \times 100$$

Capacity Ratio

The ICMA terminology defines it as "the relationship between the actual number of working hours and the budgeted number". Expressed as a formula :

$$\text{Capacity ratio} = \frac{\text{Actual hours worked}}{\text{Budgeted production in terms of standard hours}} \times 100$$

Problem 43 : In a manufacturing shop, product X required 2.5 man hours and product Y requires 6 man-hours. In a month of 25 working days of 8 hours a day 2,000 units of X and 1,000 units of Y were produced. The company employed 50 workers in the shop and the budgeted man-hours are 1,08,000 for the year. You are required to work out the capacity ratio, activity ratio, and efficiency ratio. *(ICWA, Inter, June 1990)*

Solution : Standard man-hours produced

Product X : 2,000 units @ 2.5 man-hours	=	5,000	man-hours
Product Y : 1,000 units @ 6 man-hours	=	6,000	man-hours
Total		11,000	man-hours

$$\text{Budgeted standard man-hours per month} = \frac{1,08,000}{12} = 9,000 \text{ man-hours}$$

Actual man-hours worked = 50 workers × 25 days × 8 hrs.= 10,000 man-hours

$$\text{(1) Capacity ratio} = \frac{\text{Actual man–hours worked}}{\text{Std. man–hours budgeted}} \times 100$$

$$= \frac{10,000}{9,000} \times 100 = 111.11\%$$

(2) Activity ratio $= \dfrac{\text{Standard manhours produced}}{\text{Standard manhours budgeted}} \times 100$

$= \dfrac{11{,}000}{9{,}000} \times 100 = 122.22\%$

(3) Efficiency ratio $= \text{Standard man} - \dfrac{\text{Hours produced}}{\text{Actual man}} - \text{hours worked} \times 100$

$= \dfrac{11{,}000}{10{,}000} \times 100 = 110\%$

Problem 41 : Calculate from the following figures :

(1) Efficiency ratio
(2) Activity ratio
(3) Capacity ratio

Budgeted production	**880 units**
Standard hours per unit	**10**
Actual production	**750 units**
Actual working hours	**6,000**

(CA, Inter, May 1999)

(1) Efficiency ratio $= \dfrac{\text{Std. hours for actual production}}{\text{Actual hours worked}} \times 100$

$= \dfrac{750 \text{ units} \times 10 \text{ hours}}{6{,}000} \times 100$

$= 125\%$

(2) Activity ratio $= \dfrac{\text{Std. hours for actual production}}{\text{Budgeted hours}} \times 100$

$= \dfrac{750 \times 10}{880 \text{ units} \times 10 \text{ hours}} \times 100$

$= 85.23\%$

(3) Capacity ratio $= \dfrac{\text{Actual hours worked}}{\text{Budgeted hours}} \times 100$

$= \dfrac{600}{880 \times 10}$

$= 68.18\%$

Problem 42 : If the activity ratio and capacity ratio of a company is 104% and 96% respectively find out its efficiency ratio" *(CA, Inter, May 1997)*

Solution :

Activity ratio $= \dfrac{\text{Std. hours required for actual production}}{\text{Budgeted hours}} \times 100$

Capacity ratio $= \dfrac{\text{Actual hours worked}}{\text{Budgeted hours}} \times 100$

Efficiency ratio $= \dfrac{\text{Std. hours required for actual production}}{\text{Actual hours worked}} \times 100$

From the above ratios it is clear that efficiency ratio can be obtained by dividing activity ratio by capacity ratio

So,

$$\text{Efficiencey ratio (in percentage)} = \frac{\text{Activity Ratio}}{\text{Capacity Ratio}} \times 100$$

$$= \frac{104}{96} \times 100 \quad = 108.33\%$$

INVESTIGATION OF VARIANCE AND REPORTING TO MANAGEMENT

Investigation of variance enables to take prompt control over the variance. The following benefits are derived by the process of investigating the variance :

(*a*) The person responsible for the variance is revealed.

(*b*) It reveals the accuracy of accounting system.

(*c*) Whether variance is on account of abnormal conditions and if so how to take precautionary measures in such situtation.

(*d*) To appraise the current standard and revise if need be.

Having investigated the variance, it is necessary to prepare variance analysis reports for the sake of submitting to management. In preparing and submitting such reports the following guidelines may be followed :

(*a*) The reports must be prepared and submitted promptly to the management. Otherwise its purpose is lost.

(*b*) Only those reports which are relevant to the persons jurisdiction to exercise control should be sent.

(*c*) Analysis of variance must be based on cost centre.

(*d*) Ratios, percentages, etc. can also be used while reporting in addition to monetary value of variances.

(*e*) The cost accountant should interact with variaous levels of management in addition to preparation and submission of reports.

The important reports to be sent to various levels of management are (1) Material price variance report, (2) Material usage variance report, (3) Wage rate variance report, (4) Labour efficiency variance report, (5) Sales value variance report.

Based on the reports of variance analysis, the variances are disposed off. One method of treating variance is to transfer it to costing profit and loss account. The second method advocated by some accountants is to properly distribute over closing stock and cost of sales so that both these items can be shown at actual costs in financial statement.

REVISION AND METHODS VARIANCE

Sometimes standards are revised owing to reasons such as change in wage rate, fiscal policy, etc. If such chages are incorporated in the standards, it may affect the variances and controllable factors may escape the attention of executives. Hence any changes in the factors is included in the revised budget but the standard cost is retained as a matter of policy. This process of retaining the basic standards in spite of change in the factors and analysing the variances on the basis of basic standards is known as revision variance.

A method variance refers to the difference between the standard cost of manufacture performed by normal method and the cost of manufacturing by an alternate method.

QUESTIONS

I. Fill in the blanks :

1. The system which determines what the cost 'should be' in advance of production is called ________ technique of costing.
2. For labour, the difference between actual hours at actual rate and actual hours at standard rate is called the ______ variance.
3. Gang composition variance is a sub-variance of ________ variance.
4. When the actual cost is less than the standard cost, the difference is known as ______ variance.
5. Overhead variance is the difference between the ________ cost of overhead absorbed in the output and the ________ overhead cost.
6. Material price variance = (Std. price – Actual price) × ________.

[***Answer :*** (1) standard costing, (2) labour rate, (3) labour efficiency, (4) favourable, (5) standard, actual, (6) actual quantity]

II. Choose the correct answer

1. The cost of a product as determined under standard costing is
   (*a*) fixed cost (*c*) direct cost
   (*b*) historical cost (*d*) predetermined cost [ ]
2. While evaluating deviations of actual cost from standard cost, the technique used is
   (*a*) regression analysis (*c*) trend analysis
   (*b*) variance analysis (*d*) linear progression [ ]
3. Which one of the following standards can be attained under the most favourable conditions possible?
   (*a*) theoretical standard (*c*) normal standard
   (*b*) expected standard (*d*) basic standard [ ]
4. Standard costs are useful in all of the following except
   (*a*) reducing cost (*c*) establishing records
   (*b*) speeding up preapartion of operating reports (*d*) costing inventories [ ]
5. Controllable variance are best disposed of by transferring to
   (*a*) cost of goods sold (*c*) cost of goods sold and inventories
   (*b*) inventories of work-in-progress and finished goods (*d*) costing profit and loss account

[***Answers :*** 1. (*d*), 2. (*b*), 3. (*a*), 4. (*c*), 5. (*d*)]

III. Mark true or false

1. Standard costs are fixed for each industry by the trade association concerned. *T/F*
2. Standards do not allow for any idleness and wastage and are therefore idealistic. *T/F*
3. Standards are arrived at on the basis of past performance. *T/F*
4. Standards represent achievable targets but after a purposeful effort. *T/F*
5. Standards for materials labour and overheads are inter-connected. *T/F*
6. Variance means the difference between the budget and standard costs. *T/F*
7. Favourable variances are those that increase the amounts and unfavourable ones reduce the amounts. *T/F*
8. All variances are transferred to the cost of sales account. *T/F*
9. Standard costing help management by exception by showing up the total difference between actual profit and standard profit. *T/F*
10. Price variances are calculated at actual quantity multiplied by differences in prices. *T/F*
11. Efficiency variances are concerned with quantities used and are calculated as standard quantity multiplied by difference in price. *T/F*
12. Yield variance shows the efficiency of labour. *T/F*

[***Answer :*** True—4, 5, 10, Rest are all False]

IV. Short and long answer questions

1. Explain the term 'variance' under standard costing and discuss its significance.
   (*University of Kerala, M.Com., May 1992*)
2. Discuss the utility of variance analysis in cost control. What are the major causes for efficiency, volume, capacity and calender variance? (*Calicut University, M.Com., April 1992*)

3. Distinguish between standard costing and budgetary control. Discuss the advantages and disadvantages of standard costing. *(Kakatiya University, M.Com., August 1991)*
4. Distinguish between standard costing and budgetary control. Are both these systems inter-related? *(Bangalore University, M.Com., May 1989)*
5. Define standard costing. Explain the advantages and limitations of standard costing. *(Bangalore University, M.Com., May 1990)*
6. What are the various circumstances under which material price and material usage variances are likely to arise? *(ICWA, Inter, June 1990)*

EXERCISES

Exercise-1 (Material Price Variance): From the given data calculate :

(a) Material price variance
(b) Material usage variance
(c) Material cost variance.

Standard :

(1) 250 kg of raw material is required for producing 175 kgs of finished products.
(2) Price of material per kg Rs. 4.

Actuals :

(1) Production 52,500 kgs
(2) Materials consumed 70,000 kgs
(3) Cost of materials Rs. 2,73,000.

(Sn Venkateshwara University, B.Com., April 1999)

[Answer : Material price variance Rs. 7,000 (F)
Material usage variance Rs. 20,000 (F)
Material cost variance Rs. 27,000 (F).]

Exercise-2 : The Standard Raw material costs of producing 300 units of product-A were as follows :

600 units of Raw materials @ Rs. 50 per unit Rs. 30,000

But actual Raw materials costs of producing 300 units of product-A were–1000 units of Raw materials @ Rs. 40 per unit Rs. 40,000.

Determine : (i) Raw material cost variance (ii) Raw material price variance and (iii) Raw material usage variance.

(Calcutta University, B.Com.(Hons.), 1998)

[Answer : Raw materials cost variance Rs. 10,000 (A)
Raw material price variance 10,000 (A)
Raw material usage variance 20,000 (A).]

Exercise-3 : Pragathi Company manufactures a product 'p' by mixing three raw materials. For every 100 kg of output, 125 kg of raw material input are used. In April 2002, there was an output of 5600 kg of 'p'. The standard and actual particulars of April 2002 are as follows :

	Standard		*Actual*	
Raw material	*Mix*	*Price*	*Mix*	*Price per kg*
I	50%	Rs. 40	60%	Rs. 42
II	30%	Rs. 20	20%	Rs. 16
III	20%	Rs. 10	20%	Rs. 12

Calculate all material variances. The actual quantity of material used was 7000 kg.

(Delhi University, B.Com.(Hons.), 1997)

[Answer : Material cost variance :
I = Rs. 36,400 (A)
II = Rs. 19,600 (F)
III = Rs. 2,800 (A)
19,600 (A)

Material usage variance :
I = Rs. 28,000 (A)
II = Rs. 14,000 (F)
III = Rs. Nil

14,000 (A)

Material price variance :
I = Rs. 8400 (A)
II = Rs. 5600 (F)
III = Rs. 2800 (A)

5600 (A)

Material Mix variance :
I = Rs. 28,000 (A)
II = Rs. 14,000 (F)
III = Nil

14000 (A).

Exercise-4 (Material Variances) : From the following data, calculate (a) Material cost variance (b) Price variance (c) Usage variance.

Product	*Std Qty. (in units)*	*Std Price (in Rs.)*	*Actual Qty. (in units)*	*Actual Price (in Rs.)*
A	1050	2.00	1100	2.25
B	1500	3.25	1400	3.50
C	2100	3.50	2000	3.75

(*University of Madras, B.Com., April 2001*)

[Answer : Material cost variance :
A – 375 (A)
B – 25 (A)
C – 150 (A)

550 (A)

Material price variance :
A – 275 (A)
B – 350 (A)
C – 500 (A)

1125 (A)

Material usage variance :
A – 100 (A)
B – 325 (F)
C – 350 (F)

575 (F).]

Exercise-5 (Material Cost Variance) : From the given data below, calculate the material price variance, the material usage variance, material cost variance and material mix variance. Consumption per 100 units of product.

Raw material	*Standard*	*Actual*
A	40 units @ Rs. 50 per unit	50 units @ Rs. 50 per unit
B	60 units @ Rs. 40 per unit	60 units @ Rs. 45 per unit

(*Sn Venkateshwara University, B.Com., October 1999*)

[**Answer :** Material price variance :
A – Nil
B – 30,000 (A)
Material usage variance :
A – 50,000 A
B – Nil
Material cost variance :
A – 50,000 (A)
B – 30,000 (A)
Material Mix variance – 6,000 (A).]

Exercise-6 (Labour Variance)

From the following particulars calculate

(a) Labour efficiency variance
(b) Labour rate variance
(c) Labour cost variance.

Information as per standard cost card :

Labour Rate Rs. 2 per hour
Hours 3 per unit

Actual production data :

Units produced 250
Labour Rate Rs. 2.50 per hour
Hours worked 800.

[**Answer :** (a) Labour efficiency variance – Rs. 100 (A)
(b) Labour rate variance – Rs. 400 (A)
(c) Labour cost variance – Rs. 500 (A).]

Exercise-7 (Labour Variance)

From the following information of Orient manufacturing Co. Ltd., determine (i) The Labour cost variance (ii) Labour efficiency variance (iii) Labour rate variance :

(i) Standard Labour cost per unit of production is Rs. 15
(ii) Time allowed per unit is 30 hours
(iii) During the month of March 1996, 3000 units are produced in 75000 hours
(iv) Actual payment of wages for the month is Rs. 45000 *(Calcutta University, B.Com.(Hons.) 1996)*

[**Answer :** (i) Direct Labour Cost Variance – Nil
(ii) Direct Labour Efficiency Variance – 7500 (A)
(iii) Direct Labour Rate Variance – 7500 (F).]

Exercise-8 (Material and Labour Variances)

From the following records of Appollo Bolt-nut manufacturing Company, you are required to compute material and Labour Variances :

An input of 100 kg of material yields to a standard output of 10,000 units
Standard price per kg of material – Rs. 20,
Actual quantity of materials issued and used by production department 10,000 kg,
Actual price per kg of material – Rs. 21 per kg,
Actual output – 9,00,000 units,
Number of employees – 200,
Standard wage rate per employee per day – Rs. 40,
Standard daily output per employee – 100 units,
Total number of days worked – 50 days,
(Idle time paid for and included in the above half day for cash employee.)
Actual wage rate per day – Rs. 45.

(Delhi University, B.Com.(Hons.), 1998)

[**Answer :** Material Cost Variance = Rs. 30,000 (A)
Material Price Variance = Rs. 10,000 (A)

Material Qty Variance = Rs. 20,000 (A)
Labour Cost Variance = Rs. 90,000 (A)
Labour Rate Variance = Rs. 50,000 (A)
Labour Efficiency Variance = Rs. 40,000 (A)
Idle Time Variance = Rs. 4,000 (A).]

Exercise 9 (Overhead variance) : Following information is available from the records of a factory :

	Budget	*Actual*
Fixed overhead for June	Rs. 10,000	Rs. 12,000
Production in June (units)	2,000	2,100
Standard time per unit (hrs.)	10	
Actual hours worked in June		220.00

Compute (*i*) Fixed overhead cost variance, (*ii*) Expenditure variance, (*iii*) Volume variance, (*iv*) Capacity variance, (*v*) Efficiency variance. (*CA, Inter, Nov. 1989*)

[***Answer :*** Fixed overhead expenditure variance = 2,000 (*A*)
Fixed overhead capacity variance = 1,000 (*F*)
Fixed overhead efficiency variance = 500 (*A*)
Fixed overhead volume variance = 500 (*F*)
Fixed overhead cost variance = 1,500 (*A*)]

Exercise 10 : A cost accountant of company was given the following information regarding the overhead for February 1987 :

(*a*) Overhead cost variance Rs. 1,400 adverse.
(*b*) Overhead volume variance Rs. 1,000 adverse.
(*c*) Budgeted hours for February 1987, 1,200 hrs.
(*d*) Budgeted overheads for February 1987, Rs. 6,000.
(*e*) Actual rate of recovery of overheads Rs. 8 per hour.

You are required to assist him in computing the following for Feb. 1987 : (1) overhead expenditure variance, (2) actual overhead incurred, (3) actual hours for actual production, (4) overheads capacity variance, (5) overheads efficiency variance and (6) standard hours for actual production. (*CA, Inter, May 1987*)

[***Answer :*** (1) 400 (*A*), (2) Rs. 6,400, (3) 800 hrs., (4) 2,000 (*A*), (5) 1,000 (*F*), (6) 1,000 hrs.]

Exercise 11 (Sales variance) : *X* Ltd. operates a budgetary control and standard costing system. From the following data calculate (*i*) sales variance, (*ii*) sales volume variance, (*iii*) sales price variance.

Product	*Budgeted*		*Actual*	
	Unit to be sold	*Sales value* (Rs.)	*Units sold*	*Sales value* (Rs.)
A	100	1,200	100	1,100
B	50	600	50	600
C	100	900	200	1,700
D	75	450	50	300
	325	3,150	400	3,700

(*CS, (Final), June 1987*)

[***Answer :*** Sales volume variance = Rs. 200 (*A*)
Sales price variance = Rs. 750 (*F*)
Sales variance = Rs. 550 (*F*)]

Exercise 12 : Budgeted and actual sales for the month of December 1984 of two products *A* and *B* of M/s. *XY* Ltd. were as follows :

Product	*Budgeted sales*		*Actual sales*	
	Units	*Price per unit*	*Units*	*Price per unit*
A	6,000	5	5,000	5.00
			1,500	4.75
B	10,000	2	7,500	2.00
			1,750	1.90

Budgeted cost for products *A* and *B* were Rs. 4 and Rs. 1.50 per unit respectively. Work out from the above data the following variances :

(*i*) Sales value variance.
(*ii*) Sales volume variance.
(*iii*) Sales price variance.
(*iv*) Sales mix variance.
(*v*) Sales quantity variance.

(*ICWA, (Inter), June 1985*)

[*Answer :*	Sales value price variance	=	Rs. 550	(*A*)
	Sales mix variance	=	1,781	(*F*)
	Sales qty. variance	=	781	(*A*)
	Sales volume variance	=	1,000	(*F*)]
	Sales value variance	=	450	(*F*)]

Exercise 13 (Ratios) : From the following particulars calculate :

(*a*) Capacity usage ratio, (*b*) Activity ratio and (*c*) Efficiency ratio :

	Budget	*Actual*
Direct labour hours	10,000	9,600
Number of units	5,000	5,200
Fixed overhead	Rs. 2,500	Rs. 2,600

[*Answer :*	Capacity usage ratio	=	96%
	Activity ratio	=	104%
	Efficiency ratio	=	108.5%]

SECTION F

MISCELLANEOUS TOPICS

27

UNIFORM COSTING

INTRODUCTION

Uniform costing is a system of costing which is applied to a number of plants belonging to a firm or number of firms belonging to an industry with a view to standardise accounting system under this system a uniform set of principles are allows for ascertaining cost and for fixing the selling price. Such practice of applying uniform principles of costing of facilitates comparing efficiency and as a means of controlling costs in different undertakings uniform costing is different from costing methods and techniques. The use of uniform costing system does not mean that costs in different businesses will be the same. However, it means that comparison of costs of different firms will be logical if they practice uniform costing on cost comparision it facilitates investigations into specific cost problems of the industry.

DEFINITION AND FEATURES AND APPLICATIONS OF UNIFORM COSTING

The ICMA terminology defines uniform costing as "the use by several undertakings of the same costing principles and/or practices".

The important features of uniform costing are as follows :

1. The same costing principles are applied by all member units for ascertaining costs.
2. Cost statements and reports are prepared on a uniform basis.
3. The accounting period is common for all the member units.
4. All the member units adopt the same costing methods, techniques and systems for collection, ascertainment and control of cost.

Uniform costing can be applied under the following two situations :

(*a*) Where an industry has number of firms or a firm has number of plants under same ownership and control. Where the units manufactured are identical, then cost per unit of differenct firms or plants can be compared. Where the units manufactured are dissimilar the cost comparison of similar operation process or service can be made.

(*b*) Where number of business enterprises are affiliated to a trade association in order to derive advise regarding costing problems. Under this situation the trade association undertakes to collect costing data from various member firms exchanges the ideas with them and offers valuable advise as to how to improve upon under an adverse situation. Examples of undertakings which may adopt uniform costing are printing press, hotels, sugar mill, cement mill, textile mill, plastic industries, road transport undertakings of various states and so on.

The following are the important objectives of uniform costing :

1. To facilitate cost comparison of serveral firms belonging to the same industry in order to know efficiency or otherwise of it.
2. To take suitable steps to eliminate inefficiency of firms.
3. To furnish information to the government to get subsidy and other concessions.

4. To provide cost structure to government to enable it to formulate policies relating to wage structure, pricing, import, export and so on.
5. To determine standardisation in the method of production and distribution.
6. To avoid competition among the member firms by fixing a common selling price acceptable by all.
7. To enable member firms to exchange their ideas and problems and to equip them with the current trends and technology.
8. To enable the trade association to have a general control over the member firms by way of regulating the production capacity, fixation of selling price and so on.

ADVANTAGES AND DISADVANTAGES OF UNIFORM COSTING

(*A*) Advantages to Member Units

1. It facilitates cost comparison between different firms.
2. The services of professional cost accountant and consultant can be engaged to devise a uniform costing for all firms. This would prove economical which otherwise would have become expensive if different costing methods and techniques are used.
3. It makes easier to computerise accounting system of the various firms.
4. The appointment of a full-fledged cost accountant can be dispensed with for every member unit. Instead, one competent cost accountant can be appointed at head office who can be incharge of cost accounting system of all firms.
5. It enhances efficiency and productivity.
6. It encourages standardisation of materials and labour.
7. It reveals profitable and unprofitable products or operations of all firms.

(*B*) Advantages To Workers

1. It ensures a uniform wage structure in all member units.
2. Employees will benefit in sharing bonus and other amenities because of their efficiency and productivity.

(*C*) Advantages to Trade Association

1. Trade association can exercise better control over industries in eliminating wasteful competition.
2. it regulates the output and prices of member units and improves the profitability of the organisations.
3. Trade association represents the problems of its member units to the government in terms of getting subsidy and other forms of protection.

(*D*) Advantages to the Government

1. It enables the government in formulating various policies based upon the costing information of serveral industries.
2. It enables the government to give priority to public or private sector industry, based upon their progress and prosperity.
3. It provides useful information regarding profitability of the industry. The government can formulate tax laws based on this information.

Disadvantages of Uniform Costing

1. It may not suit every firm or member unit belonging to trade association. This is particularly so when there is difference in size, structure, diversification of production, etc. in different firms.
2. It is not flexible. It can not be changed whenever the need arises.
3. In some cases the members of trade association may not furnish reliable information as they feel that confidential matters when revealed to others may lead to competitions.

PROCEDURE INVOLVED UNDER UNIFORM COSTING

The procedure that is involved in the installation of uniform costing can be outlined as follows :

1. The determination of costing technique to be adopted such as historical or marginal or standard costing, etc.
2. The determination of costing method to be adopted such as process, single or output, etc.
3. The determination of cost unit such as a kg., tonne, etc.
4. The basis for cost classification and codification.
5. The identification of production and service departments.
6. The method of pricing the material issues that is to be followed such as FIFO, LIFO, etc.
7. The method of valuing closing stock and work-in-progress.
8. The method of wage payment to be followed such as time rate, price rate, etc.
9. The method of treating O.T. and idle time wages.
10. The determination of basis of apportionment and method of absorption of overheads.
11. The method of depreciating assets and interest.
12. The method of treating notional cost.
13. The method of presentation of reports and use of standard forms.
14. Method of treating office and administration overhead and selling and distribution overheads.
15. The method of treating over and under absorption of overheads.
16. Cost accounting system to be followed such integral, non-integral accounts, etc.

UNIFORM COSTING MANUAL

It is a booklet which contains a set of guidelines relating to uniform costing system. In other words it contains details of various principles and the method of operating the system of uniform costing. It serves as a reference book for all the firms. It contains the objectives, the procedure to be followed and the rules to be followed under this system. The advantages of uniform costing manual may be outlined as under :

(*a*) It facilitates every firm to ascertain the cost of production as per the prescribed rules. Thus it simplifies the accounting procedure in all firms.
(*b*) It evokes interest with everybody concerned.
(*c*) It enables the firms to overcome problems in practising this system.
(*d*) It facilitates the preparation of reports under a definite form.

INTER-FIRM COMPARISON

It is one of the management technique which is used to control the operations of weaker firms belonging to an industry. Though it is one of the oldest technique, it is being used extensively in modern days. It is a technique by means of which the management of similar undertakings compare the relative performance with a view to know the efficiency of various firms. Uniform costing system facilitates inter-firm comparison.

Though the final accounts consisting of trading account, profit and loss account and balance sheet can be taken as a basis for inter-firm comparison, they only serve as a general basis. However, they enable to know the overall profitability and financial position of various firms. They do not help to know the efficiency, productivity and how best the firms utilise various resources available with them. Therefore different firms are compared with one another to know their performance and to take remedial steps if their performance is poor.

Objectives of Inter-firm Comparison

The objectives of inter-firm comparison may be summarised as under :

(*a*) To spot out weakness of the firms so that they can be improved upon.

(*b*) To attain and maintain overall efficiency of the firms.

(*c*) To enable the firms to standardise various functions so that wastages can be minimised.

(*d*) To enable the member-firms to know their relative position compared to other firms.

Procedure Involved Under Inter-firm Comparision

The following steps are involved under inter-firm comparision as a management technique :

(*a*) **Adoption of uniform costing :** As inter-firm comparision is based upon the uniform costing, it is essential to instal uniform costing in all the firms. To enable the system function efficiently, a uniform costing manual is also to be prepared and distributed among all firms.

(*b*) **Establishment of a central or head office :** The central office which undertakes to compare the performance of firms is to be established. It is headed by a chief cost accountant whose duty is to co-ordinate the functions of all the firms belonging to the same industry. In UK, an agency known as centre for inter-firm comparison was established in 1959. This agency undertakes to study. The data furnished by the member-firms, analyses and prepares the reports of all the firms for the sake of inter-firm comparision. The other activities performed by this agency are as follows :

(*a*) It conducts seminars on inter-firm comparision.

(*b*) It carries out research with a view to discover best method of inter-firm comparison.

(*c*) It provides opportunities for the British firms to compare their performances with similar units in other countries such as Germany, France, etc.

However, there is no specialised agency in India, though certain organisations like National Productivity Council and Trade Association facilitate inter-firm-comparison.

(*c*) **Collection of data :** The central office collects the data from member-firms by preparing and sending a questionnaire. All the member-firms will furnish the required information which will be kept in secret by the central office. The information so collected will be processed, analysed and interpreted. Usually ratios are made use of to know the solvency, profitability, efficiency, productivity and financial soundness of the firm.

(*d*) **Preparation of report :** Based on the interpretation of data, the central office will prepare comprehensive report indicating the comparative position of other firms. It also provides concrete suggestions for improving upon with reference to special problems faced by the weak firms. This enables the member firms to set right in those areas where they lack behind.

Advantages of Inter-firm Comparison

The technique of inter-firm comparison is not only useful to management of a firm in improving its activities but also to different category of people such as bankers, investors, creditors, customers, trade associations and so on. Some of the advantages derived from this technique are as follows :

(*a*) It reveals the weakness of the firm. Such weakness can be overcome by taking remedial action.
(*b*) It reveals the trend of sales, profit, costs of the firm over a period of time.
(*c*) It encourages the member firms to become more cost conscious which helps in cost reduction.
(*d*) It provides useful information to management of every firm to make proper decisions.
(*e*) It ensures standardisation of production process.
(*f*) The benefit of research is passed on to member-firms by the central office.
(*g*) External parties such as bankers, investors, creditors also benefit by the technique of inter-firm comparison.

QUESTIONS

I. Simple questions

1. Define uniform costing.
2. State the two situations under which uniform costing can be adopted.
3. State the features of uniform costing.
4. What do you mean by inter-firm comparison?
5. State any four objectives of inter-firm comparison.

II. Short answer questions

1. Outline the objectives of uniform costing.
2. State the advantages and disadvantages of uniform costing.
3. Outline the procedure involved under uniform costing.
4. Briefly explain the procedure involved under inter-firm comparison.

28

COST REDUCTION

INTRODUCTION

One of the main objectives of a business organisation is to earn maximum possible profit. Profit is the resultant of interaction of two factors, *viz.*, sales revenue and cost. Therefore it is imperative to probe into the possibilities of increasing the revenue and reducing the cost in order to achieve and desired goal. The profit may be increased through some methods such as (*a*) Increasing the selling price of the products, (*b*) Reducing the selling price to penetrate the market extensively and increase the turnover, (*c*) Increasing the demand through sales promotion and (*d*) Reducing the cost of production for a given output or increasing the production for the same cost. Though profits may be increased by one of these methods, yet the last method seems to be the best. This is because; (*a*) Increasing the selling price may other things remaining the same, result in losing the customer; (*b*) If the firm reduces the prices, competitors may also match the price cut. Thus cut-throat competition may set in, (*c*) Demand can be increased through sales promotion but other firms may also increase their sales promotion outlay.

The ICWA publication of London defines cost reduction as "cost reduction is to be understood as the achievement of real and permanent reductions in the units costs of the goods manufactured or services rendered without impassing their suitability for the use that is intended." From this definition it is clear that cost reduction must be real, permanent and should not be done sacrificing the quality of goods.

ADVANTAGES

(*A*) To the Particular Concern

(*a*) Cost reduction enables improving the profits. This leads to distributing more dividends to the shareholders, paying better remuneration and bonus to staff and permits ploughing back of profit to finance the desired growth of the firm.

(*b*) Improvement in the financial position provides the opportunities to invest the funds in research which eventually helps in providing the customers with products of improved quality.

(*c*) Cost reduction improves the competitive capabilities of the firm.

(*d*) The extent to which the costs are reduced becomes an index of efficiency attained by the organisations.

(*B*) To the Industry

Cost reduction causes benefits not only to the particular concern but to entire industry. If a particular concern is running efficiency, other concerns in the industry will have to follow and adopt the efficient practices.

(C) To the Nation

(a) If the cost reduction programme is introduced, the scarce resources can be used properly.

(b) Higher taxes will be available to the government because the firms can earn better profit through productivity.

(c) In international markets cost reduction and concomitant reduction in prices of exports help in retaining the markets and gaining new buyers.

(d) Cost reduction helps in combating inflation.

COST CONTROL AND COST REDUCTION

Cost control and cost reduction are efficient tools of management but are different concepts. The differences between these two concepts are summarised below :

(1) Cost control is the means to achieve the end, *i.e.*, cost reduction. Thus cost control is the first step to achieve end objective. Cost reduction begins where cost control ends.

(2) Cost control is exercised by fixing standards or budgets and taking remedial measures, in case actuals deviate adversely from standards. Cost reduction is achieved by improving upon standards and improving upon production methods.

(3) Cost control is management oriented whereas cost reduction is oriented towards economising all resources with a view to reduce cost of production.

(4) Cost control ends after reaching the target. But under cost reduction programme, 'products', 'process', 'procedures', 'organisation', 'methods' and 'personnel' are continuously scrutinised in order to improve efficiency and reduced cost. It is thus a process of continuous self-analysis and self-criticism.

AREAS COVERED BY COST REDUCTION

A cost reduction programme should be systematic investigation into the techniques and methods of production and other functions. It involves an analysis of every aspect of the business with the object of ascertaining the most efficient method of performing the various functions. The broad areas to be covered by a cost reduction programme are as follows :

1. Materials

In most manufacturing concerns, the materials form a substantial portion of the total cost. A small percentage of cost reduction in material cost will lead to considerable savings to the organisation. Therefore materials must be managed and controlled as carefully as the cash. The important areas on which material cost reduction can be attempted are as under :

(a) **Design :** The material cost reduction programme should always begin at the design stage. The quality and quantity of material depends upon the design of the product. Continuous research should be undertaken in selecting the design. The effect of introduction of any new design or improvement of existing design in relation to cost of production should be thoroughly investigated with the help of cost accountant.

(b) **Purchasing :** Purchasing of materials id extremely important particularly to a manufacturing concern because it has its bearing on every vital factor concerning manufacture, *i.e.*, quantity, quality, cost-efficiency, economy, prompt delivery, volume of production, etc. For efficiency buying, purchasing departments must be equipped with the list of various sources of supply and the latest prices ruling in the market for different materials. Ordering costs must be reduced as far as possible by purchasing in economic lot size quantities.

(*c*) **Storage :** After receiving the materials from the seller, they must be stored properly. The carrying cost must be reduced by keeping the inventory at optimum level. Various levels of materials, *viz.*, maximum, minimum and reordering level must be fixed properly and must be revised keeping in view the changes in production and market condition. Materials must be properly classified, coded and standardised. *A*, *B*, *C* analysis of material control is highly useful in cost reduction. Continuous check of materials must be undertaken to detect the misappropriation of or misuse of materials.

(*d*) **Transport :** External and internal transport costs must be reduced as far as possible. Costs must be reduced by eliminating or reducing empty or idle trips, the distance travelled by the vehicles and consumption of petrol and diesel.

(*e*) **Production :** Production can be improved upon by training the employees, replacing the defective machinery, ,using better quality of materials, providing adequate and proper tools, reducing the wastage scrap and defectives. Cost of production can be minimised by taking prompt action in respect of above factors.

The following are some of the techniques of materials cost reduction :

(*a*) **Value analysis :** Value analysis is one important technique of material cost reduction. This technique was first developed by Lawrence D. Miles of General Electric Company, USA. In a broad sense, it is a study of characterwise cost of an item such as quality, design, methods of manufacture, etc. with a view of reduce the ultimate cost of product. Value analysis also means the determination of the value of items proposed to be sought with a view to examine the worth of money spent on buying the materials. It is based upon the quality of materials in relation to their functional value and price. It helps in deciding what is actually required and what amount should be paid so as to derive the maximum benefit. This reduces the cost of purchase and enhances the profit of the factory. Value analysis is carried out for the following purposes :

(1) Elimination of an item altogether if possible.
(2) Examination of cheaper quality materials for their advantageous use in the factory.
(3) Examination of costlier quality in relation to its functional value and life and to give up purchase of specified cheaper quality materials.
(4) Examination of alternative source and price in relation to the money to be spent and realisation of its worth in due course.

(*b*) **Simplification and standardisation :** Simplification means elimination of superfluous varieties, size, dimension and grades of materials and component parts. It is also known as variety, reduction, as it is essentially a reduction process, a cutting down of varieties of materials. The basis principle of simplification is that a single item shall serves as many different applications as possible.

Standardisation in a production sense means the reduction of a line of product to fixed types, sizes and characteristics. It has been defined by E.C. Peck thus, "Standardisation primarily means setting up standards by which the extent, quantity, value, performance or service may be gauged or determined and is the crystallised best thought and practice of industry into definite forms for general use".

(*c*) **Linear programming :** Sometimes it is possible to reduce the cost without making any substantial change in the design of the product or price or number of items in inventory.

This is possible through the use of the linear programming. This is a quantitative technique which is used to solve problems such as inventory management, scheduling, make or buy problem transportion problem and so on.

2. Labour

According to the old theory the direct labour is a variable cost. But this does not hold good today. Once an employee is appointed it is not easy to retrench him. Therefore the selection of an employee is a very important task. Cost reduction is possible if the right worker having the right attitude is employed to do the right work. Efficiency of employees can be increased by motivating them suitable to do their best for the organisation. By increasing the productivity, the labour cost can be reduced. It is possible through introduction of incentive schemes, bonus schemes, profit sharing, accompanied by proper working conditions, welfare facilities and safety measures.

3. Overheads

Overhead can be reduced by utilising the resources to the full extent. The following are the methods which can be used by the management for reducing the overhead cost.

(*a*) **Increasing the production volume :** By undertaking the production on optimum scale the costs can be decreased as the incidence of overheads chargeable to each unit of output declines. The idle capacity can be reduced by proper planning and control.

(*b*) **Extension of market and price differentials :** Overheads can be reduced by extending the market area, increasing sales by offering discounts and charging suitable prices to attract different types of buyers.

(*c*) **Size of business units**—Expansion and contraction policies : By expanding or contracting the size of business units the overheads can be reduced. As some overheads are fixed in nature, they can be reduced by increasing the scale of production. On the contrary, costs may be more because the optimum scale of operations has been exceeded. Therefore by reducing the size, costs can be brought down.

COST REDUCTION COMMITTEE

As cost reduction plan requires co-ordination and cooperation, a high level committee must be formed. It will be entrusted with the responsibility of cost reduction programme. It is constituted by involving the heads of various functional departments. It will perform functions like agreeing on a target of cost reduction over period of time, identifying the areas to be covered for cost reduction programmes and constantly reviewing the programme from time to time.

QUESTIONS

I. Simple questions

1. Define cost reduction.
2. Distinguish between cost control and cost reduction.
3. State the advantages of reducing cost in a factory.

II. Long answer question

1. Explain the various areas covered by cost reduction programme.

29

ACTIVITY BASED COSTING

INTRODUCTION

Traditional approach to cost accounting is known by volume based cost accounting. It is a simple system of accounting whereby direct costs (*i.e.* prime cost elements) are charged to products and overheads are allocated on the basis of some arbitrary selected criteria. The various bases that are commonly used relates to MHR, LHR, percentage methods & so on. These methods have their limitations and they tend to misinterpret the apportionment of overheads to the products.

Inadequacies of Traditional Methods of overhead Absorption

The cost of product arrived in traditional cost accounting system is not so accurate owing to following reasons.

(1) The basis used in the traditional cost accounting are acceptable when valuing stock for financial reporting, but they are inappropriate when used for decision-making.

(2) The traditional basis of classification of cost into fixed and variable is often unrealistic since, as business grows they often become more complex.

(3) Traditional accounting is confined merely to furnishing information at product level. The new manufacturing technology demands feedback of performance while production is still in progress.

ABC is a recent development in cost accounting. It attempts to absorb overheads into product costs on a more realistic basis. Supporters of the technique argue that many costs are unnecessarily treated as common costs and are arbitrarily absorbed using a basis such as labour hours, machine hours etc. Many organisations have now adopted Advanced Manufacturing Technology (AMT) with the result that overheads are increasing and labour costs are becoming a small portion of total costs. Costing system which absorb overheads on a direct labour basis are therefore not relevant in an AMT environment. The basic idea of ABC is that costs are grouped according to what drives them or causes them to be incurred. The cost drivers are then used as an absorption basis.

Definition

The CIMA terminology defines ABC as a "Cost attribution to cost units on the basis of benefit received from indirect activities".

The ABC system was designed by kaplan and cooper of Harvard business school. According to them total cost should be classified into long term variable cost and short term variable cost. Traditionally, short term variable cost are known as *variable cost* and long term variable costs are known as fixed cost. Short term variable costs are volume related and change proportionately with the volume of production. Long term variable cost vary in the long term but not instantaneously. For example, production scheduling cost can be changed in the long term by changing number of runs rather than changing number of units produced.

They further claim that this approach relates overhead costs to the forces behind them. The forces behind overheads are named "cost drivers". Cost drivers can be defined as those activities or transactions that are significant determinants of costs. A cost driver is an activity which generates cost ABC system is based on the belief that activities cause costs and that a link should therefore be made between activities and products. This is done by assigning costs of activities to products based on an individual products demand for each activity.

Cost pool

A cost pool is a term used to indicate grouping of costs incurred on a particular activity which drives them. An example of cost pool is procurement of raw materials. In this transaction we see all costs associated with purchase of materials, *viz*, ordering cost, Receiving and Inspection cost, storage cost etc.

Characteristics of ABC

(1) Simple traditional distinction made between fixed and variable cost is not enough guide to provide quality of information to design a cost system.

(2) The more appropriate distinction between cost behaviour pattern are volume (scale) related, diversity (scope) related, events (decisions) related and time related.

(3) Cost drivers need to be identified. A cost driver is a structural determinant of cost related activity. The logic behind is that the cost behaviour pattern must be understood so that behaviour pattern is dictated by cost drivers.

Development of ABC system

The following steps are involved in ABC system.

(1) Identify the main activities performed in the organisation, such as manufacturing, assembly etc. as well as support activities including purchasing, packing and dispatching.

(2) Identify the factors which influence the cost of each activity-cost driver.

(3) Collect accurate data on direct materials. Direct labour and overheads.

(4) Establish the demand made by particular products on activities using the cost drivers as a measure of demand.

(5) Trace the cost of activities to products according to a products demand for each activity.

Thus ABC is the process of tracing costs first from resources to activities and then from activities to specific products. The technique of ABC lays the importance of different costs for different purposes and the identification of just those costs which are relevant to a particular decision.

IMPLEMENTATION OF ABC SYSTEM

The implementation of ABC system involves the following steps :

(*1*) Planning for ABC system

In planning stage, management's problem is identified. The questions that are to be raised here are what are the company's critical issues? What are the difficult decisions the management is faced with? What type of culture prevails in the organisation? The designer, by determining the critical decisions that management typically faces, can be able to identify the accounting information that the management would need to support decisions relating to those critical issues. Identification of the level of information (either by his analysis or interviewing the senior managers) would provide the frame work for an actual cost system using ABC concepts.

(*2*) Organising ABC Teams

Designing and implementing ABC needs support from management at every level of the organisation. A committee of Senior Managers may be constituted first to set direction & make decisions regarding the strategic use of the ABC data. The committee may appoint persons as representatives of their respective functional organisations in order to serve on the ABC work group. The work group is to assist in identifying the data to be captured and to determine the operational use of ABC data. Accordingly 3 teams are constituted as indicated below :

Level	*Teams*	*Function*
(1) Top level	Steering committee	To Monitor strategic use of cost information and determine cost objects
(2) Middle level	Project Manager & work group	To assist in identify the data to be captured and to determine the operational use of ABC data
(3) Operational	Project Teams Analyst	To identify the meaningful activities cost drivers and the sources of data.

(*3*) Management Education

The provision of better cost information does not solve the organisational problem by itself. Management needs to be educated to the multiple uses of the ABC data and must be trained to play an interactive role in the ABC process. Thus a major task in the process of implementation is to educate the managers & the employees that in turn would realise their cooperation in successful implementation.

(*4*) Designing the process

This involve :

(*a*) Defining cost objects by interviewing the top and middle level managers and perceiving their current problem such as individual product (if the problem is profitable product mix) distribution channel, customers etc.

(*b*) Analysing and defining critical activities (both production & services) with a view to establishing them as a basis for determining cost and performance.

(*c*) Calculating the activity costs by selecting appropriate first stage cost drivers and applying them to distribute the natural expenses to various activities undertaken.

(*d*) Calculating the product costs by selecting appropriate second stage cost drivers and applying them to distribute the activity costs to various products manufactured.

(*5*) Maintaining the system

Implementing ABC system is not a single time job; it needs continuous maintenance and monitoring. The cost drivers may change along with the production dynamism. Hence periodical testing of the system is necessary particularly to ensure that the cost drivers both first and second stage are working well to indicate the resource consumption. It may so happen that the cost driver chosen for a particular resource type or activity type at the time of introducing the system subsequently may fail to justify the distribution of costs. This may not only cause distrust towards the system but also create other organisational problem.

Advantages or Benefits of ABC system

ABC system besides providing more accurate basis for calculating product costs has other benefits too, *i.e.*, it serves as a mechanism for managing cost. It is in this area of cost management and resource planning ABC has the greatest potential. Its benefits may be summarised as under :

(1) Measurement of performance : This is done by identifying responsibilty or accountability for cost behaviour.

(2) Price fixation : This is done by identifying the true cost of product or services

(3) Product promotion : This is done by analysing profit contribution and impact of inter relationship of product or service.

(4) Customer profitability : It helps to know which customers yield more profit. This is done by identifying the cost or profitability of type of customer.

(5) Choosing channel of distribution : This is done by analysing the cost and performance of alternative distribution channels.

Usefulness of ABC to Management

(1) It supports management by furnishing data at operational level. Accurate product costing will help the management to compare the profits that various customers, product lines, brands or regions generate and to decide on pricing strategy, dropping unprofitable products or product lines.
(2) It helps management to redisign the products.
(3) It can be used to change technology, reduce set-up time, rationalisation of plant layout so as to reduce material handling cost, improve quality etc.
(4) It helps management in improving activities which helps in improving profits.
(5) It helps in preparing good budgets.
(6) The accurate information provided on product cost enables better decisions to be made on pricing, marketing, product design, product mix etc.

Limitations

(1) ABC is not appropriate for all companies particularly those where overheads are relatively small and which do not produce a wide range of products.
(2) This method can not be used to prepare monthly or periodical profit statement. For this, traditional cost accounting system is more suitable.
(3) ABC is more suitable to support strategic decision making, profitability analysis and control of manufacturing.

When to use ABC

ABC system is useful under the following circumstances :

(1) Products which are difficult to produce and which involve more cost of production.
(2) Where profit earned is more than the accounting system suggest.
(3) Where competitors are not able to produce more inspite of increased profit which such products yield, because of increased cost of production.

(4) In quoting tender prices.

(5) When buy or make decision is involved *i.e.*, when suppliers are able to sell at lesser price as compared to high cost of production in the organisation.

(6) Where overheads incurred are more and apportionment becomes more complex

(7) The cost of marketing and distribution of products varies considerably by distribution channel, and yet cost accounting system effectively ignores marketing cost.

Problem 1 : Sunlight company manufacturing two products *A* and *B*, using the same equipment and similar processes. An extract of the production data for these products in one period is shown below :

Particulars	*A*	*B*
Quantity produced (units)	5,000	7,000
Direct labour hours per unit	1	2
Machine hours per unit	3	1
Set ups in the period	10	40
Orders handled in the period	15	60

Overhead costs	*Rs.*
Relating to machine activity	2,20,000
Relating to production run set-ups	20,000
Relating to handling of orders	45,000
	2,85,000

You are required to calculate production overheads to be absorbed by one unit of each of the products using the following costing methods :

(1) Traditional costing approach using a direct labour hour rate to absorb overheads.

(2) An activity based costing approach using suitable cost drivers to trace overheads to products.

Solution :

(1) **Traditional costing approach** :–

Calculation of Direct labour hours :–

Product *A*	5,000 units × 1 hr	=	5,000 hrs
Product *B*	7,000 units × 2 hrs	=	14,000 hrs
		Total	19,000 hrs

$$\text{Overhead absorption Rate} = \frac{\text{Total overheads}}{\text{Total Direct labour Hours}}$$

$$= \frac{\text{Rs } 2,85,000}{19,000}$$

$$= \text{Rs. 15 per hour}$$

Overheads to be absorbed are :–

Product *A*	1 hr × Rs. 15	=	Rs. 15 per unit
Product *B*	2 hrs × Rs. 15	=	Rs. 30 per unit

(2) **ABC costing approach** :–

Calculation of machine hours :–

Product *A*	–	5,000 units × 3 hrs	=	15,000 hrs
Product *B*	–	7,000 units × 1 hr	=	7,000 hrs
				22,000 hrs

$$\text{(1) Machine – Hour driver cost} = \frac{\text{Overhead relating to machine activity}}{\text{Machine hours}}$$

$$= \frac{\text{Rs. } 2,20,000}{22,000 \text{ hrs.}} = \text{Rs. 10 per Machine Hour}$$

(2) Set up driver cost $= \dfrac{\text{Overhead relating to production setup}}{\text{No. of setups}}$

$$= \frac{20,000}{50\ (10 + 40)} = \text{Rs. 400 per set up}$$

(3) Order handling cost $= \dfrac{\text{Overhead relating to handling of orders}}{\text{No. of orders handled}}$

$$= \frac{45,000}{75\ (15 + 60)} = \text{Rs. 600 per order}$$

Overhead Cost

		Product A			*Product B*		
Machine Driver Cost	=	15,000 × 10	=	1,50,000	7000 × 10	=	70,000
Set-up cost		10 × 400	=	4,000	40 × 400	=	16,000
Order handling cost		15 × 600	=	9,000	60 × 600	=	36,000
				1,63,000			1,22,000
Overhead Rate per unit	=			$\frac{1,63,000}{5,000}$			$\frac{1,22,000}{7,000}$
	=			32.60			17.43

Problem 2 : The following particulars are extracted from the books of Mr. Colin. Calculate cost per unit under (*i*) Traditional volume based costing and (*ii*) Activity based costing

	Machine hrs per unit	*Direct labour hour per unit*	*Annual output (units)*	*Total Machine hours*	*Total direct labour hrs*	*No. of purchase order*	*No. of set ups*
Product *A*	2	4	1,000	2,000	4,000	80	40
Product *B*	2	4	10,000	20,000	40,000	160	60
				22,000	44,000	240	100

The cost of activities is as follows :–

Volume related	1,10,000
Purchasing related	1,20,000
Set-up related	2,10,000
	4,40,000

Solution :

Traditional volume based costing system

Total cost allocated to cost centre 4,40,000

Machine Hour Rate $= \dfrac{\text{Total overheads}}{\text{Total Machine hours}}$

$$= \frac{4,40,000}{22,000} = \text{Rs. } 20$$

Labour Hour Rate $= \dfrac{\text{Total overheads}}{\text{Total labour hours}}$

$$= \frac{4,40,000}{44,000} = \text{Rs. } 10$$

Cost per unit = Machine hour rate × Machine hours per unit

$= 20 \times 2 = 40$

$=$ Labour hour rate × Labour hours per unit

$= 10 \times 4 = 40$

Total cost changed to product = Annual output × Cost per unit

A = 1,000 × 40 = 40,000

B = 10,000 × 40 = 4,00,000

ABC System

Volume related cost $= \frac{1,10,000}{22,000} =$ Rs. 5 per Machine Hour

Purchase related cost $= \frac{1\ 20,000}{240} =$ Rs. 500 per order

Set-up related cost $= \frac{2,20,000}{100} =$ Rs. 2,100 per set up

Cost charged to products :–

Product *X*

Volume related cost	=	2,000 × 5	=	10,000
Purchase related cost	=	80 × 500	=	40,000
Set up related cost	=	40 × 2100	=	84,000
				1,34,000

Product *Y* :–

Volume related cost	=	20,000 × 5	=	1,00,000
Purchase related cost	=	160 × 500	=	80,000
Set up related cost	=	60 × 2,100	=	1,26,000
				3,06,000

Problem 3 : From the following particulars calculate the cost of production and profit under (*a*) Traditional method and (*b*) ABC System

Particulars	*Products*			*Total*
	A	*B*	*C*	
Selling price per unit	70	100	80	
Production & sales units	50,000	20,000	10,000	
Raw material usage (units)	5	5	12	
Direct material cost (Rs.)	20	25	10	16,00,000
Machine hours	1.0	1.5	2.5	1,05,000
Direct labour hours	1.0	2.5	1.5	1,15,000
No. of production runs	5	10	20	35
Direct labour cost (Rs.)	6	15	9	6,90,000
No. of Deliveries	5	2	20	27
No. of receipts on the basis of raw materials (units × production runs)	25	50	240	315
No. of production orders	10	5	25	40
Overhead costs :–				
Set up activities	1,00,000			
Machine activities	8,00,000			
Receiving activities	5,00,000			
Packing activities	3,00,000			
Engineering activities	6,00,000			23,00,000

Solution :

Traditional costing approach

		A per unit	B per unit	C per unit
Direct Materials		20	25	10
Direct labour		6	15	9
Overheads rate =				
$= \frac{\text{Total oh}}{\text{Total D.L.H.}}$				
$\frac{23,00,000}{1,15,000} = 20$				
A =	20 × 1 D.L.H.	20		
B =	20 × 2.5 D.L.H.		50	
C =	20 × 1.5 D.L.H.			30
	Total cost	46	90	49
	Profit	24	10	31
	Selling price	70	100	80

ABC Costing Approach

	A	B	C
Direct Material cost	20	25	10
Direct labour cost	6	15	9
Overheads :–			
(1) *Set-up cost* :–			
Cost per set up			
$= \frac{\text{Total set up cost}}{\text{Total no. of production runs}}$			
$= \frac{1,00,000}{35} = 2857.14$			
Set up cost per unit			
$= \frac{\text{Cost per set up} \times \text{No. of production run}}{\text{No. of units produced}}$			
$A = \frac{2,857.14 \times 5}{50,000}$	0.29		
$B = \frac{2,857 \times 10}{20,000}$		1.43	
$C = \frac{2,857 \times 20}{10,000}$	–	–	5.71
(2) *Machine cost* :–			
Cost per machine hour			
$= \frac{\text{Machine cost}}{\text{Machine hrs.}}$			
$= \frac{8,00,000}{1,05,000}$			
= 7.62			

	A	B	C
Machine cost per unit = Cost per machine hour × Machine hrs used per unit			
$A = 7.62 \times 1$	7.62		
$B = 7.62 \times 1.5$		11.43	
$C = 7.62 \times 2.5$			19.05
(3) *Receive cost* :–			
Cost per receiving order = $\dfrac{\text{Receiving cost}}{\text{No. of orders received}}$			
$= \dfrac{5,00,000}{315} = 1,587.30$			
Receiving cost per unit = $\dfrac{\text{Cost per receiving order} \times \text{No. of receipts}}{\text{No. of units produced}}$			
$A = \dfrac{1,587.30 \times 25}{50,000}$	0.79		
$B = \dfrac{1,587.30 \times 50}{20,000}$		3.97	
$C = \dfrac{1,587.30 \times 240}{10,000}$			38.10
(4) *Packing cost* :–			
Cost per packing = $\dfrac{\text{Packing cost}}{\text{No. of Deliveries}}$			
$= \dfrac{3,00,000}{27} = 11,111.11$			
Packing cost per unit = cost per packing order × No. of deliveries for the product/ No. of units produced			
$A = \dfrac{11,111 \times 5}{50,000}$	1.11		
$B = \dfrac{11,111 \times 2}{20,000}$		1.11	
$C = \dfrac{11,111 \times 20}{10,000}$			22.22
(5) *Engineering cost* :–			
Cost per engineering transaction $= \dfrac{\text{Engineering cost}}{\text{No. of production order}}$			
$= \dfrac{6,00,000}{40} = 15,000$			
Engineering cost per unit = $\dfrac{\text{Cost per order} \times \text{No. of production order}}{\text{No. of units produced}}$			

$A = \dfrac{15,000 \times 10}{50,000}$	3		
$B = \dfrac{15,000 \times 5}{20,000}$		3.75	
$C = \dfrac{15,000 \times 25}{10,000}$			37.50
Total production cost	38.81	61.69	141.58
Profit/Loss	31.19	38.31	– 61.52
Sales	70	100	80

PART II

MANAGEMENT ACCOUNTING

30

NATURE AND SCOPE OF MANAGEMENT ACCOUNTING

INTRODUCTION

The modern business involve several transactions. The efficiency and success of the business depend upon how management of the business deal with such transactions. The transactions which take place in a business can be measured and expressed in terms of money value. Since business is affected by such transactions, they are to be recorded, analysed and reported to management. This helps the management to evaluate the performance of the business. In fact, three branches of accounting have emerged to deal with these aspects. As a first step financial accounting system was developed and it is concerned with money. An economic resource. The American Institute of Certified Public Accountants (A I C P A) defines financial accounting as "the art of recording classifying and summarising in a significant manner and in terms of money, transactions, and events which are in part atleast of a financial character and interpreting the results thereof." "Financial accounting is concerned with preparation of two important statements, viz., income statement and position statement. Through these two statements it furnishes useful information to external parties of a business. However, financial accounting suffers from certain limitations for which reason, cost accounting system was evolved."

While financial accounting is concerned with money as an economic recource, cost accounting is concerned with money as a measure of economic performance. Cost accounting is concerned with classification, collection, recording allocation and control of costs. It consists of systems, methods and techniques which are used to measure, analyse and ascertain the cost of production. It provides useful information to management and profitability of products, departments, process etc.

Management accounting is concerned with presentation of accounting information which helps management in the formulation of policy and to facilitate management in discharging its day-to-day activities. It is the process of identification, measurement, accumulation analysis, interpretation and communication of financial information to facilitate management in planning, evaluating and controlling the activities and accountability of its resources.

NEED FOR MANAGEMENT ACCOUNTING

Modern business are complex in nature. They are large in size and their activities are wide spread. Their ownership is different from management. Instead of owners, the professional managers run and look after the business. Delegation of authority and the decentralisation of decision-making process has necessitated the use of some mechanism of performance, evaluation and responsibility accounting. The functions of planning and decision-making, control and supervision, coordination and staffing are no longer personal. A system of information is needed to help the management to analyse, measure, and check the functioning of each division and unit for their proper coordination to achieve the objectives of the business with utmost economy and efficiency. Even the development of cost accounting does not provide adequate data needed by the management. Management accounting is a system of utilising financial, costing, and other information to assist the management in the performance and evaluation of their functions. The Management Accountant basically collects, analyses, interprets and presents information regarding past activities and current and future events and helps management in decision-making. Thus, management accounting meets the need of the management.

DEFINITION AND CHARACTERISTIC FEATURES OF MANAGEMENT ACCOUNTING

The management accounting team of Anglo-American Council on Productivity defined management accounting as "The presentation of accounting information in such a way as to assist management in the creation of policy and in day-to-day operation of an undertaking."

According to J. Batty, management accounting comprises accounting methods, systems and techniques, which coupled with special knowledge and ability, assist management in its task of maximising profits or minimising losses."

The Institute of cost and Management Accountants, London, has defined management accounting as the "application of professional knowledge and skill in the preparation of accounting information in such a way as to assist management in the creation of policy and in the day-to-day operation of an undertaking".

According to Robert Anthony, "Management Accounting is concerned with accounting information which is useful to management."

Features of Management Accounting

The following are the important characteristic features of Management Accounting.

1. It is a separate branch of accounting which is devised to provide useful data to management in decision-making process.
2. It is based on anticipated events which would take place in future. In simple words it is futuristic in its approach.
3. It is not based on regular or continuous accounting system. Instead it is intemittent in nature. In other words, collection of accounting information for analysis and interpretation is made according to the requirements of the management.
4. It does not follow any prescribed accounting format for reporting. This is because information is provided according to the needs of management.
5. It is only a technique adopted by management to derive information. It cannot take part in executing the decision. In other words it cannot replace management.
6. It is subjective in nature as it is basically depends upon judgement of the person concerned rather than on measurement.
7. It is inter-disciplinary subject as it embraces within itself financial accounting. Cost accounting and financial management. According to J. Batty "management accounting is blending together into a coherent whole, financial accounting, cost accounting and all aspects of financial management."
8. It is not based on any prescribed rules and formats as in the case of financial accounts and cost accounts. It all depends upon informational needs of the management.

9. It is mainly concerned with future events. Its focus is on estimating or forecasting the future based on past results.
10. It is a service function as it provides useful information to various levels of management.

NATURE OF MANAGEMENT ACCOUNTING

The nature of management accounting can be brought out under the following headings:

1. Management Accounting is a branch of knowledge: Though management accounting is considered to be a branch of accounting, in recent time it is regarded as an important branch of knowledge, i.e. a distinct discipline by itself. It is an organised body of knowledge having its own concepts and conventions. However, the principles and rules vary from industry to industry.

2. Management Accounting is a science: Management accounting is a science as it is body of systematic knowledge relating to not only management accounting but relating to a wide variety of subjects such as financial and cost accounting. Statistics, operation research, financial management, auditing, taxation, office management and so on. It is necessary for a management accountant to have intimate knowledge of all these field of study in order to carry on his day-to-day activities. But it is to be emphasised that it is not a perfect science as in the case of natural science.

3. Management Accounting is an art: It is an art as management accountant requires the ability and skill in applying the tools and techniques of management to various management problems. By using the knowledge of management accounting, it is possible for the management accountant to present, analyse and interpret the data.

4. Management Accounting as an extension of Cost Accounting: Some authorities view management accounting as an extension of cost accounting. Management accountant employs most of the techniques of costing, such as standard costing, budgetary control, marginal costing, cost volume-profit analysis inter-firm comparision etc., to assist management in formulation of policy, preparation of plans and controlling the operations. Therefore it is also sometimes said that the management accounting is an extension of the managerial aspect of cost accounting.

5. Management Accounting is a profession: In recent years management accounting has become one of the important profession which has become more challenging. This is evident from two facts. First, the setting up of various professional bodies such as National Association of Accountants (NAA) in U.S.A, The Institute of Cost and Management Accountants, in UK, the Institute of Cost and Work Accountants, in India and similar other professional bodies both in developed and developing countries have increated the growing awareness of Management Accounting profession among people. Secondly a large number of Management Accountants are rendering the professional service to various organisations which is known as "Management Consultancy Service."

OBJECTIVES OF MANAGEMENT ACCOUNTING

The main function of management accounting is to provide useful information to management in maximising profit or minimising loss. This is undertaken by presenting various statements and reports to enable management to formulate right policies. In this regard, management accounting has set before it the following objectives:

1. Planning the activities of the business: Planning is deciding as deviding in advance what is to be done, how and when it is to be done. To undertake this task, management accountant provides information relating to past and helps in estimating future. He also furnishes data relating to alternative course of action so that management can take right decision. The information obtained from management accountant also helps the management to forecast the future. Finally management formulates the policy of the business based on facts and figures submitted by management accountant.

2. Controlling the performance of the business: Controlling is a function intended to ensure and make possible the performance of planned activities and to achieve the predetermined goals and results. For this sake, the entire organisation is divided into various segments and each segment is entrusted into the hands of a responsible person. The person in-charge of a segment is responsible for the success or failure of that segment. Further management accounting makes use of techniques such as Budgetary Control and Standard Costing, wherein actuals are compared with targets to know the favourable and adverse variances. In case of adverse variances, the causes are identified and appropriate measures are taken to set right an adverse variance.

3. Useful in organising: Organisation is the process of coordinating the physical, human and momitory resourses. It consists of conscious coordination of people towards a disired goal. It also includes delegation of authority and fixation of responsibility. Management Accounting is concerned with establishing responsibility centres, preparation of budgets, and fixing responsibilities on various persons. A good system of management accounting is helpful in creating an efficient organisational frame work in industries.

4. Motivating employees: Motivation is that function of management by which employees are stimulated to work hard by satisfying their needs, desires and wishes. Management accounting lays down the best alternative method of doing the work. It fixes the targets and on achieving the targets employees are rewarded through incentives.

5. Useful in decision making: Decision-making is concerned with choosing the best course of action from among the alternatives. In business enterprises decisions may relate to expansion or contraction, use of machinery or manual labour, make or buy the components and so on. Management accounting considers the profitability of alternative proposal and their financial implications. The information provided by management accountant helps the management to choose best alternative and to take right decisions.

6. Useful in coordination: Coordination is concerned with the unification, integration, and harmonising of the different activities of the organisation. By preparing budget of various departments, management accounting coordinates the efforts of all the departments. The Management accountant and acts as a coordinator and resolves the problems of various departments.

7. Reporting to management: One of the important objectives of management accounting is to furnish various types of reports to all levels of managements. The technique used is known as Management information system. Through this technique the management accounting appraises the performance of various departments and furnishes up to date information to management on a periodical basis.

8. Facilitates interpretation of financial information: Last but not the least the objective of management accounting is to facilitate management in understanding the financial statements. Some time managerial personnel may not understand the significance of financial statement. Management accountant by using the technique of comparative statement techniques, trend analysis ratio analysis etc., enable management to understand the contents of financial statements. Besides these techniques, statistical techniques such as graphs, charts, averages etc. can also be used to make financial statements more meaningful to management.

SCOPE OF MANAGEMENT ACCOUNTING

The scope of a subject means the areas which fall under its puriew. As for as the scope of Management Accounting is concerned it has a wide scope. The following topics fall under the scope of Management Accounting:

1. Financial accounting: Financial accounting is primarity concerned with recording of transactions in a set of books, posting them into the concerned ledger accounts, preparing trial balance and thereafter in preparing final accounts. The statements prepared under financial accounts forms the basis for analysis and interpretation which serves as a meaningful data for managerial decision making.

2. Cost Accounting: Cost accounting is primarily concerned with collection, analysis allocation apportionment and absorption of overhead with a view to ascertain the cost of production of goods or service. Cost accounting furnishes useful data to management showing areas of inefficiency and the steps to be taken to avoid losses and wastages.

3. Statistical Methods: In order to carry out the functions of management very often management relies on non-quantitative data. Such information is provided by statistical methods and they mainly include sampling techniques, diagrams, graphs, and charts, time series analysis. Index numbers, regression analysis, statistical quality control techniques etc. Thus statistical methods is an integral part of Management Accounting.

4. Operation Research: Modern business is faced with highly complicating problems in decision making process. Operation research techniques offer scientific solution to such problems. Some techniques of operation Research used to solve problems are linear programming, queing theory, waiting line models PERT, CPM, etc.

5. Organisation and Methods: O&M is the name given to any conscious attempt, scientifically applied to improve organisation, simplify and improve method and generally create and maintain an efficient administrative machine. Management accounting is also concerned with improving methods, simplifying the processes and reducing the cost. Management accounting relies on O&M with a view to achieve its objects.

6. Budgetary control: Budgetary control is concerned with fixation of budgets, comparing actuals with budgets and taking corrective measures to set right adverse deviations. In fact Management accountant acts as a coordination when budgets are prepared for various departments. Hence budgetary control is part and parcel of Management Accounting.

7. Law: Modern business functions within the legal environment. Decisions are also affected by the provisions of some of the important legistation such as companies Act, Foreign exchange Management Act, MRTP Act, and other labour legislation. Hence management accounting relies heavily on law of the country.

8. Taxation: The computation of income tax, sales tax, excise duty, import duty and filing of returns promptly is undertaken under the direct supervision of Management Accountant. So taxation is an important aspect of management accounting.

9. Internal auditing: Internal auditing is concerned with the verification of books of accounts within the organisation. Internal auditing simplifies the task of external auditing. Management Accounting arranges for internal auditing and hence it is a part of Management Accounting.

10. Management information system: Management Accountant prepares various types of reports to meet the different levels of management. The reports are prepared and submitted periodically so as to suit the needs of the management. Based on the reports, management undertakes to exercise control over the business. Hence reporting system serves as a basis for the functioning of management.

11. Capital budgeting and investment decisions: The term capital budgeting refers to long term planning for proposed capital outlay and their financing. It includes raising both long term funds and their utilisation. When current funds are invested in long term activities it results in future benefits. Capital budgeting decisions are very important as they involve large funds, risk and incertainty and they are of an irreversible nature.

FUNCTIONS OF MANAGEMENT ACCOUNTING

Management accounting is entrusted with the functions of classifying, presenting, analysing and interpreting data so as to help management in running the business efficiently and economically. The important functions performed by management accounting are as follows :

1. Recording the data: Though recording of data is originally done under financial accounting, sometimes, to make recording of transactions more meaningful to management, estimates and probabilities are taken into consideration. The management accounting classifies original recorded data into distinct groups, and sub-records are prepared. On the basis of sub-records comprehensive reports are prepared. Management accounting makes use of computers in this regard.

2. Validating the data: The efficient functioning of management depends upon the accuracy and adequacy of the financial data collected from the books of accounts. Management accounting ensures that the management is furnished with accurate and reliable information. Besides furnishing past data management accounting also provides future data based upon predetermined level of activity.

3. Interpretation of data: The recorded and validated data in its raw form may not be useful to management directly. The data requires proper analysis and classification based on their similarities and dissimilarities. This enables management to make decisions and to know its effects or expected results. Hence analysis and interpretation is considered to be an important function of management accounting.

4. Reporting the data: Having analysed and interpreted the data it is to be communicated in the form of reports to various levels of management as and when required. The reports must be promptly prepared and submitted to managers so as to facilitate them to carry out the important functions of coordination, decision-making and controlling.

5. Installation of sound Accounting System: One of the important functions of management accounting is to devise a suitable system of financial and cost accounting system and its installation in the organisation. It is also concerned with modifying and re-modifying the system depending upon the changing economic environment of the business.

6. Providing feed-back reports: The provision of feed-back report helps management in performing control function. The management accounting pin-points the deviation between actual and expected activities and by adopting the principles of selectivity helps management in following the technique of "Mangement by exception."

7. Evaluating the performance of Management: Management accounting is concerned with providing methods and techniques for evaluating the performance of the management in the hight of objectives of the business. Thus it helps in implementing the principle of "Management by objectives."

RELATIONSHIP BETWEEN MANAGEMENT ACCOUNTING AND FINANCIAL ACCOUNTING

The relationship between Management Accounting and Financial Accounting can be studied under the following heading:

Similarities between Management Accounting and Financial Accounting

Management Accounting and Financial Accounting appear to be similar in the following respects.

(*i*) They both study the impact of the business transactions and events of the enterprise.

(*ii*) They both deal with interpretation and reporting of accounting information.

(*iii*) Both the system of Accounting is concerned with providing information for internal and external use.

Dissimilarities

Management Accounting differs from Financial accounting in the following respects:

Financial Accounting	*Management Accounting*
1. It deals with the business as a whole.	1. It deals not only with the business as a whole but also each and every segment of the business.
2. Its main emphasis is external reporting. It may follow the tactics of window-dressing to project better image.	2. Its main focus is internal reporting. The reports provided reflects real situation.
3. It is historical in nature.	3. It is futuristic in its approach.
4. It is more precise being based on actual cost.	4. It may not always be precise and accurate being based on estimates.
5. The accounting information is reported once a year.	5. The reports are furnished periodically depending upon the needs of management.
6. It is governed by the generally accepted accounting principles.	6. It is not based on accounting principles. It is free to formulate its own rules pro-cedures and forms because information is meant only for internal management.
7. It is to prepared compulsorily by higher form of organisations. The preparation of accounts is laid down by the statutes concerned.	7. It is undertaken voluntorily to benefit management.
8. The statements prepared under financial accounts is expressed in monetary terms.	8. The information supplied under management accounting is both in terms of monetary as well as non-monetary such as quantities of materials, number of working hours, quantities, produced and sold etc.
9. It is objective in nature. It is based on actual measurement.	9. It is subjective in nature as it is based on judgement rather then actual measurement.
10. It is subjected to auditing.	10. It is not possible to verify and audit the transactions.
11. It is independent.	11. It is dependent on Financial accounting.

RELATIONSHIP BETWEEN COST ACCOUNTING AND MANAGEMENT ACCOUNTING

Similarities between Cost Accounting and Management Accounting:

1. Both the branches of accounting are internal to the organisation.
2. Both the branches of accounting assist management in carrying out its functions of planning, decision-making and controlling.
3. Both the branches of accounting use similar techniques such as marginal costing, budgetary control, standard costing etc.
4. There is a great deal of overlapping in their functions.

Dissimilarities:

Cost Accounting	*Management Accounting*
1. The main object of cost accounting is to ascertain and control cost.	1. The main objective of management accounting is to provide useful information to management for decision-making.
2. It is based on both present and future transactions for cost ascertainment.	2. It is concerned purely with the transactions relating to future.
3. Cost accounts has narrow scope as it covers matters relating to ascertainment and control of cost.	3. It has a wide scope in as much it covers the areas of financial accounts, cost accounts, taxation, statistics, law etc.
4. It deals only with monetary transactions, *i.e.*, it covers only quantitative aspect.	4. It deals with both monetary and non-monetary transactions *i.e.*, both quantitative and qualitative aspects.
5. Cost accounts follow a definite principle for ascertaining cost and a format for recording.	5. It does not follow a definite principle and format. Instead, the data to be presented depends upon the needs of management.
6. Cost Accountant occupies a lower position as compared to Management accountant in hierarchy of Management.	6. Management Accountant occupies a higher position in the organisational set-up.
7. Cost accounting techniques are few and includes Marginal Costing. Budgetary control and Standard Costing.	7. Management accounting techniques include apart from the costing technique, other important techniques such as fund flow, cash flow, ratio analysis etc.
8. Cost accounting is concerned with short term planning.	8. Management accounting is concerned both with short term and long term planning. Evaluating the capital investment project is the speciality of Management Accounting.
9. Cost accounting is historical in its approach and it projects the part.	9. Management accounting is futuristic in its approach. It is more predictive in nature when compared to cost accounting.
10. It is independent of Management accounting.	10. It is dependent on Cost Accounting.
11. Cost accounting is concerned merely with assisting in management functions and does not provide for the evaluation of the performance of management.	11. Management accounting is concerned with both assisting management in its functions as well as evaluation of the performence of the management as an institution.

ADVANTAGES OF MANAGEMENT ACCOUNTING

1. Management accounting assists management in the formulation of policy and in performing day-to-day activities of the business Management has to take tactical and strategic decisions to plan for the future. Decisions such as make or buy,

expand or contract, own or lease, modification and diversification of business etc. Through management accounting techniques and by providing relevant accounting data, it is possible for the management to take right decision.

2. Management accounting assists the management in performing the control function effectively. Techniques such as standard costing, budgetary control help management in controlling the operations of business.
3. Management accounting assists management in planning process and thereby attaining the targets of the business.
4. Management accounting helps management in adjusting to the changing economic environment of the business. It enables the business to overcome the seasonal and cyclical fluctuations or to prepare the business to meet such fluctuations.
5. Management accounting facilitaties coordication of activities of various departments and thus helps in attaining the objectives of the business. For this it is necessary to communicate the targets and achievements of various departments to management. Techniques such as budgeting, reporting, interpretation helps management accounting in this regard.
6. Management accounting helps management in the internal organisation of the business. The division of business into various segments, fixation of responsibility, delegation of authority etc. are integral part of management accounting.
7. It helps the management in measuring the performance of business and in evaluating the capital investments in various projects.
8. It provides employment opportunities to Management accountants.

LIMITATIONS OF MANAGEMENT ACCOUNTING``

1. Management accounting to a larger extent is based on estimates and probabilities. Hence it is not an exact science. It does not deal with actuals and thus accuracy is not ensured under management accounting.
2. Management accounting is only a tool in the hands of management. It cannot replace management.
3. Management accounting derives its information from financial accounts, cost accounts and other records. The strength and weakness of management accounting, therefore depends upon the strength and weakness of these basic records.
4. The installation of management accounting is a costly affair. Hence only big business establishments alone can think of management accounting. It is outside the purview of small scale enterprises.
5. It is very difficult to get approval of existing accounting staff for the installation of management accounting. Other managerial and lower level managerial personnel resist the installation of management accounting.
6. Management accounting is in its evolutionary stage. The tools and techniques, of management accounting requires refinement, modifications, disending, and reintroduction into the system. It takes a long time to have a full fledged management accounting system in a business.
7. Management accounting is a subject which is based upon various fields of study such as statistics, taxation, law, auditing etc. Lack of understanding or knowledge of any of these discipline will affect the management accountant in finding a solution to the problem.

MANAGEMENT ACCOUNTANT—FUNCTIONS, ROLE, DUTIES AND QUALITIES

Functions of Management Accountant

The term "Management Accountant" has many synonyms. Finance director, financial controller, financial manager, controller are some of the designations given to the person entrusted with the work of management accounting. The management accountant collects and provides accounting, cost accounting, economic and statistical information to the management to assist them in the performance of managerial functions and their evaluations. Through various techniques of recording, analysis, interpretation and presentation he makes the financial, costing and other data active and effective in the performance of management functions, *viz*. planning, decision making and control. The management accountant is forward-looking and therefore he is able to treat economic information and data to make them suitable for use by the management. His functions include the following:

1. To establish, coordinate, and administer plans to facilitate the forecasting of sales, expenses, budgets and standards that will permit profit planning, capital budgeting and financing.
2. To formulate accounting policy and procedures including submission of operating data and special reports and comparing the performance with plans and standards. Comparision of actual and expected performance helps the management in proper fixation of responsibility and in evaluation of functional and divisional heads.
3. To protect the business assets to the extent possible by external controls, internal auditing and insurance coverage.
4. To frame tax policies, and procedures and to supervise and coordinate the reports required by various authorities.
5. To be aware of economic and social forces as also the effect of Governments policies and actions on business activities.

POSITION AND ROLE OF MANAGEMENT ACCOUNTANT

The position or status of Management Accountant differs from concern to concern. It depends upon the policy and pattern of Management. In some organisations he occupies the position of an executive while in others he may be a member of Board of Directors. Generally speaking his position is that of Chief Accountant of the organisation. He works in close coordination with other departmental heads. The position of Management Accountant is exactly like the spokes in a wheel, connecting the rim of the wheel and the hub and in this process receives the information. He processes that information and then returns the processed information back to where it came from.

As regards the role and responsibility of Management Accountant, it can be said that he assists the various levels of management by furnishing useful information. More precisely, the role of Management Accountant can be discussed under the following:

1. Planning: The management accountant helps to:

(*a*) Formulate future plans by providing vital information such as what products are to be sold, condition of the market, prices to be fixed etc.

(*b*) Provides data based on past performance which guides the management for achieving the future goals.

(*c*) Plays an important role in planning the short term budget to the concern.

(*d*) Plans and prepares the master budget as a whole and presents it to the top management fcr approval.

2. Controlling: The Management Accountant:

(*a*) Controls the performance of the organisation by preparing performance reports for each responsibility centers.

(*b*) Pinpoints the areas that do not conform to plans: and quickly identify weak and troubled spots and draws the attention of the top management to take necessary steps.

3. Organising: Through responsibility accounting system, the Management Accountant represents the design and implementation of accounting system for better definition and consideration.

4. Communicating: The management accountant helps the communication function through budget and performance reports.

5. Motivating: The budgets and performance reports prepared by the management accountant motivates the personnel of the organisation. Budegts, which represent targets motivate managers in achieving the desired goals and the performance reports motivate the personnel.

DUTIES OF MANAGEMENT ACCOUNTANT

1. To serve as the chief accounting officer incharge of the organisation's accounting books, accounting records and forms.
2. To audit all pay rolls and vouchers and have them properly certified.
3. To prepare balance sheet, profit and loss account and other financial statements and reports and furnish to the Managing Director a complete report covering results of the company's operation during the past quarter and fiscal year to date.
4. To supervise the preparation, compilation, filing of all reports, statements, statistics and other data that the law requires or the Managing Director requires.
5. To receive all reports from agents and factory departments that are needed for recording the factory's general operations or for directing or supervising its accounts.
6. To maintain general control over the accounting practices of all subsidiary companies.
7. To supervise the enforcement and maintenance of the classification of accounts and any other accounting rules and regulations that any regulatory body prescribes.
8. To endorse the cheques for deposit or transfer.
9. To approve payment of all vouchers, drafts and other bills payable when required by the Managing director.
10. To prepare a budget showing the factory's future requirements as shown by its accounts and the requirements of the general manager and other officers.

QUALITIES OF MANAGEMENT ACCOUNTANT

1. Knowledge about various branches of study such as Financial Accounting, Cost Accounting, Economics, Statistics, law etc. as management accounting embraces all these field of study.

2. Knowledge of business forecast under anticipated changing environment of business.
3. Ability to appraise management from time to time regarding the current position of the business so that management can review the success or failure of the business.
4. Knowledge of various techniques of management and accounting so that he can prepare and submit reports to enable management to take prompt action to set right adverse conditions.
5. Thorough knowledge about budgeting and forecasting so as to consider alternate proposals under consideration.
6. Knowledge about sources of funds so that best source can be tapped at minimum cost of borrowing.
7. An analytical mind which can see through implications of alternate courses.
8. The ability to understand management structure so that he can submit right report to right managerial level.
9. Ability to get along with all levels of management. The reports prepared and submitted must be free from bias of any type.

INSTALLATION OF MANAGEMENT ACCOUNTING

Installation of Management accounting involves the following steps:

1. Preparation of organisation manual: An organisational manual is a comprehensive book which offers guidance to members of an organisation. It lays down the duties and responsibilities of executives in the organisational hierarchy. It facilitates delegation of authority and fixation of responsibility. Communication process is also facilitated by an organisational mannual.

2. Preparation of printed forms and returns: Management accounting to a large extent involve preparation and submission of reports to all levels of management. To avoid repetitions in preparing reports blank printed forms are made use of. The forms are appropriately filled and submitted to the concerned management.

3. Recruitment of staff: The staff and clerks who will assist management accountant must be recruited and trained.

4. Integration of cost and financial accounting: In order to enable collection and analysis of data it is desirable to classify accounts. As Management accounting uses information from both financial and cost accounting, a system of integration of there two system will help in supplying information promptly to management accounting.

5. Standard costing system: As this is one of the important techniques used by management accountant, a standard costing system is to be devised. This helps in setting up standard cost and in comparing actual costs with standard cost to locate variance. The management accountant can suggest remedial measures to eliminate such adverse variance.

6. Budgetary control system: Budgetary control system not only helps in controlling but also as a tool of coordination. The integration of departmental budgets into a master budget also helps in formulating goals of the organisation.

7. Operation research technique: With the ever charging environment of business the modern business is becoming more complex. It is faced with many challanges and opportunities. Decision making process is becoming more complicating. A system of operation research will help management accountant to solve number of problems faced by the business.

TOOLS AND TECHNIQUES OF MANAGEMENT ACCOUNTING

In order to function efficiently, management accounting makes uses of the following tools and techniques:

1. Financial accounting: Financial accounting provides accounting information to management accountant who in turn rearranages the same for reporting to management. Hence financial accounting is regarded as the backbone of management accounting.

2. Cost Accounting: Cost accounting provides information relating to cost of production. Management accounting compares actual cost with standard cost to know the efficiency of the business.

3. Financial management: Management Accounting makes use of the techniques of financial management such as the extent of trading on equity, proportion of equity, preference share and loan capital, sources of capital, evaluation of alternate investment proposals.

4. Analysis of financial statements: With a view to highlight the performance of business in simple form, management accounting uses a number of techniques of analysis and interpretation. Some such techniques are comparative financial statements, common size statements, find flow statement, cash flow statement, ratro analysis.

5. Cost control techniques: For evaluating the efficiency of business all techniques of costing such as marginal costing, differential costing, budgetary control and standard costing is increasingly used in management accounting.

6. Management information system: Management information system is concerned with furnishing information promptly to the management. This implies reporting all levels of management at appropriate time. Hence, reporting is an integral part of management accounting.

7. Statistical analysis: Of late a large member of statistical techniques are used in management accounting for making financial information more meaningful and to enable comparative study. Some such techniques used are graphs, charts, diagrams, measures of dispersion, correlation and regression analysis, time series analysis etc.

8. Inflation accounting: Thus technique is used for ensuring the maintenance of original capital during the period of rising prices.

ORGANISATION OF MANAGEMENT ACCOUNTING

Organisation of Management accounting system depends upon number of factors such as size of the business, nature of the business, policy and philosophy of management etc. In a medium sized organisation, the Management accountant may function directly under the supervision of a manager. In a large sized business, he may function in liaison with financial controller. He will work as a coordinator of various departments of an organisation. The position of Management Accountant in a large sized concern is shown below:

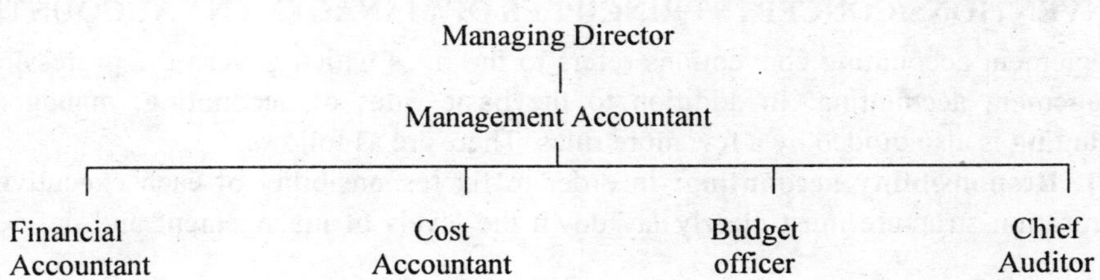

From the above chart it is clear that management accountant is directly responsible to Managing Director as for as accounting department is concerned. He can in turn delegate authority to various persons such as financial accountant (who shall be responsible for preparation of final a/cs) cost accountant (who shall be responsible for ascertaining cost). Budget officer (who shall be responsible for consolideting departmental budget) and Chief Auditor (who shall be responsible for verifying the books of accounts).

MANAGEMENT ACCOUNTING AND FINANCE FUNCTIONS

Finance is the life blood of a business. Collecting and proper utilisation of finds are the two important functions of financial management. Just as other functions of a business such as production, accounting, marketing etc., finance is regarded as a distinct function of the business. Financial management is a separate branch of management which deals with finance function of the business. Though finance function is incharge of finance manager, yet in many countries including India, this function is performaed by the accountant. In some organisations, the accounting and finance function are integrated and is looked after by chief accountant. Where a separate Finance Manager is appointed he has to work in close coordination with Management Accountant. While the Management Accountant furnishes relevant and prompt information, the finance manager based on such information will make decisions. Based on the decisions, the Management accountant has to collect new information and data.

Finance function to a large extent is determined by business environment. Generally speaking, finance is concerned with: (*a*) obtaining finds at the lowest cost and (*b*) making optimum use of these funds. The two major sources of obtaining funds are (*a*) Debt and equity and the two major uses or applications of finance are providing for: (*a*) Fixed assets and (*b*) working assets. The role of Management Accountant in raising funds are to plan for raising funds through equity shares and preference shares. He must also plan for bonus shares and right shares. Regarding loan capital, the funds may be collected through (*a*) debentures (*b*) financial institutions and (*c*) other sources. Debentures may be open or mortgage, naked or simple, redeemable or irredeemable, registered or bearer, first or second, convertible or non-convertible depending upon the financial requirement of a company. Regarding financial institutions, the long term finance is provided by the financial institutions such as IFCI, ICICI, IDBI. Insurance corporations. Miscellaneous sources include (*a*) Lease financing (*b*) Hire purchase finance (*c*) Discounting of bills (*d*) Public deposits (*e*) Trade credit (*f*) Internal source of financing (*g*) retained earnings etc.

Management accountant should ensure that the funds are obtained at the lowest cost and the same are used in the optimum manner, so as to maximise the value of the firm. The funds should be utilised for getting the maximum benefit of the firm and to ensure that there is financial discipline in the organisation.

CONVENTIONS/CONCEPTS/PRINCIPLES OF MANAGEMENT ACCOUNTING

Management accounting conventions refers to the rules which govern the profession of management accounting. In addition to the basic rules of accounting, management accounting is also guided by a few more rules. There are as follows:

1. Responsibility accounting: In order to fix responsibility of each executive the organisation structure must clearly lay down the levels of management and define the duties and responsibilities of each and every person. The process of preparing reports on the basis of level of management or according to the segments of the organisation is known as responsibility accounting. It indicates not only the results of the segment but also the person responsible for such result. Thus according to this convention for every transaction involved, some one is held responsible.

2. Management by exception: This convention is applicable at the time of reporting information to management. According to this convention normal deviation between standard and actual performance is not reported. Instead only significant variances alone are reported to management for taking corrective measures. This is to facilitate management not to be over burdened with too many information but to present only important information.

3. Principle of key areas: In every business enterprise though there are many departments found, only some departments are considered to be most important. The success or future of the entire business depends upon the efficient functioning of such key departments. According to this convention, management accountant must furnish detailed information of such key areas when desired by the management.

4. Matching cost with revenue: Matching of cost with revenue enables to know the actual profit of the business. If the matching principle is not carried out properly it leads to unrealistic profit. According to thus convention, Management Accountant should be alert in matching cost with revenue so as to avoid misleading profit.

5. Preparation of Reports in conformity with objective: According to this convention, accounting records and reports must be free from bias or prejudice. This will facilitate analysis and interpretation of reports according to the prevailing situation.

6. Flexibility: According to this convention, the accounting records, reports, statements relating to past and present must be designed to meet the needs of the business as a whole or to solve a specific problem depending upon the need.

7. Control-at-source accounting: According to this convention costs are to be controlled at the point of incurrence. Control over materials, labourers and other costs are to be exercised to establish cost consciousness in the organisation. This involves preparation of cost sheets of different segments, process, products and in designing the cost accounting system so as to facilitate effective control all over the organisation.

8. Accounting for inflation: According to this convention profit is said to be actually earned provided that capital is maintained in real terms. The convention provides that money value does not remain stable because of inflation. Hence the need for inflation accounting.

9. Use of return on capital employed: The success of business depends upon how best the capital is employed. This can be known by the technique of "Return on capital employed. Management accounting will reveal how effectively the resources are utilised for improving the business."

10. Integration: According to this convention, management information system should be integrated so as to furnish maximum information at minimum cost.

11. Recovery of overheads: According to this convention, overheads are to recovered on the most equitable basis. The overheads are to be recovered by products "on the basis of benefits received for fixed costs or responsibilities incurred for variable costs."

12. Controllable and uncontrollable cost: According to this convention, responsibility is to be fixed by classifying cost into controllable and uncontrollable by management or the department concerned.

13. Forward looking approach: According to this convention management accountant has to anticipate the problem and prevent their recurrence. This is possible through the techniques of budgetary control and standard costing.

14. Appropriate method: According to this convention management accounting must be equipped with appropriate method of collecting, classifying, and presenting information as per the requirements. Mechanisation could be followed in this regard.

15. Personal contact: According to this convention the reports and statements should not replace personal contacts. The management accountant can control cost and perform other functions such as coordination, communication, motivation etc., by means of personal contacts.

QUESTIONS

Simple Questions

1. Define Management Accounting.
2. State the similarities between management accounting and financial accounting.
3. State the similarities between management accounting and cost accounting.
4. List out any four tools and techniques of Management Accounting.
5. State the objectives of Management Accounting.
6. State the limitations of Management Accounting.
7. State any two differences between Management Accounting and financial accounting.
8. State any two differences between Management Accounting and Cost Accounting.
9. Name the concept of management accounting.

Short Answer Questions

1. Explain briefly the functions of Management Accountant. (*Bangalore University, B. Com., April 2000*)
2. Distinguish between Financial Accounting and Management Accounting. (*Bangalore University, B. Com., April 2000*)
3. "Management Accounting is bothering more than the use of financial information for management purposes." Explain this statement. (*Bangalore University, B. Com., November 1999*)
4. "Management Accounting Serves as a tool of management." Discuss. (*Bangalore University, B. Com., November 1998*)
5. Explain the scope of Management accounting. (*Bangalore University, B. Com., November 1997*)
6. "Management accounting has been evolved to meet the needs of management." Discuss. (*Bangalore University, B. Com., April 1995*)
7. "Management accounting is the adoption and analysis of accounting information and its diagnosis and explanation in such a way as to assist management." Elucidate. (*C. S. Inter, December 2000*)
8. What is the role of a management accountant in the management process? (*C. S. Inter, June 1999*)
9. Mention two major sources of finance and two major applications of finance. Explain the role of a management accountant in raising and utilising the finance. (*C. S. Iner, June 1999*)
10. Enumerate the functions of a management accountant. Show how he assists the management in exercising effective control over the business. (*C. S. Inter, December 1999*)
11. Management accounting is concerned with accounting information which is useful to management. (*C. S. Inter, December 1998*)
12. "The emphasis of" financial accounting and management accounting differ significantly." Examine it with appropriate examples. (*C. S. Inter, December 1997*)
13. "The subject of management accounting is very important and useful for optimum utilisation of resources. It is an indispensable discipline for corporate management." Elucidate this statement. (*C. S. Inter, June 1997*)
14. "There is an intimate relationship between management accounting" and "finance function." Elucidate. (*C. S. Inter, June 1996*)

15. Discuss management accounting as an effective tool of financial control. *(C. S. Inter, June 1994)*
16. What is management accounting? Discuss its usefulness for decision making and control. *(C. S. Inter, December 1992)*

Long Answer Questions

1. How does management accounting differ from financial accounting. *(S. V. University, B. Com., April 1999)*
2. Discuss in detail the functions of management accounting. Explain the nature and Scope of management accounting. *(S. V. University, B. Com., October 1999)*
3. Define Management accounting and explain clearly the need and importance of Management accounting. *(S. V. University, B. Com., April 1997)*
4. Who is Management Accountant? What are his functions and duties? *(S. V. University, B. Com., October 1997)*
5. Define management accounting. State its features and limitations. *(University of Mysore, B. Com., April 1994)*
6. Explain the meaning of Management accounting its scope, utility and limitations. In what respects it differ from financial accounting. *(University of Mysore, B. Com., October 1993)*
7. What is Management accounting? How does it differ from cost and financial accounting. *(University of Mysore, B. Com., April 1993)*
8. Explain the meaning and functions of management accounting. Also state its limitations. *(University of Mysore, B. Com., October 1991)*
9. "Management accounting is an extension of managerial aspects of financial accounting and cost accounting." Elucidate. Discuss the use of management accounting as a tool of decision making and exercising control. *(C. S. Inter, December 1991)*
10. What do you understand by Management accounting? What are its advantages? State the methods and techniques of management accounting. *(University of Mysore, B. Com., October 1994)*
11. Explain the meaning and functions of Management accounting. Also state its limitations. *(Kuvempu University, B. Com., November 1991)*
12. Explain in detail the meaning, scope and objectives of Management accounting. *(Kuvempu University, B. Com., November 1992)*
13. What is management accounting? How does it differ from cost accounting and financial accounting. *(Kuvempu University, B. Com., April 1993)*
14. "Management accounting is a coherent whole of financial accounting, cost accounting and all aspects of financial management." Examine this statement. *(Kuvempu University, B. Com., April 1994)*
15. Explain how the management accounts help in removing the limitations of financial accounting in the context of information needs of different levels of management. *(Kuvempu University, B. Com., October 1992)*
16. "Management accountancy is concerned with accounting information which is useful for management." Discuss and also distinguish between financial accounting and management accounting. *(Himachal Pradesh University, B. Com., April 1995)*
17. Define Management accounting. Discuss the main advantages and limitations of Management accounting. *(Himachal Pradesh University, B. Com., September 1994)*
18. Discuss the principal functions of Management Accountancy and show how does it help in solving management problems in key areas in business? *(Himachal Pradesh University, B. Com., September 1993)*
19. What is the usefulness of accounting information for management? State the duties and responsibilities of management accountant. *(Himachal Pradesh University, B. Com., April 1992)*
20. What is the nature of management accounting? What is the difference between financial accounting and management accounting. *(Guru Nanak Dev. University, B. Com., April 1999)*
21. Explain the meaning and objectives of Management Accounting. How does it differ from financial accounting. *(Guru Nanak Dev. University, B. Com., October 1997)*
22. Explain the various conventions of Management Accountancy.

31

FINANCIAL STATEMENTS

INTRODUCTION

The statements which are prepared from accounting information are known as financial statements. They are the end products of accounting process in an enterprise. Under accounting process, it firstly consists of recording the transactions in the books of prime entry and then posted in ledger accounts. At the end of the accounting period the balances are extracted and from these balances, final accounts are prepared. The final accounts or financial statements as they are sometimes called as, disclose the profitable and financial position of the business. A business functions with a view to attain two important objectives, *viz*., profitability and solvency. Unless a business earns sufficient profits to pay off its debts and pay a reasonable rate of return on capital employed it can not survive. The profitability position is revealed by income statement or profit and loss account. Similarly, the financial strength or solvency position is revealed by position statement or balance sheet. Based on these statements valuable decisions are taken by management and other parties interested in business.

DEFINITION OF FINANCIAL STATEMENTS

Financial statement refers to formal and original statements which are prepared to disclose financial health of the business in terms of profits, position, and prospects as on a certain data. They summarise the overall results of a business by means of grouping and classification process. They provide a systematic collection of financial data in a logical and consistent way.

In the words of John N. Myer, "The financial statements provide a summary of the accounts of a business enterprise, the balance sheet reflecting the assets, liabilities and capital as on a certain data and the income statement showing the results of operations during a certain period." According to this definition financial accounts are the end products of accounting process.

According to Robert N. Anthony, "Financial statements, essentially, are interim reports, presented annually and reflect a division of the life of an enterprise into more or less arbitrary accounting period—more frequently a year. According to this definition, financial statements are a form of reports which helps management in decision making process. Such reports are prepared periodically to enable management to carry out its day-to-day functions."

Kohler in his book Dictionary for Accountants defines financial statements as "A balance sheet, income statement, fund statement or any other supporting statement or other presentation of financial data derived from accounting records." This definition identifies the package of financial statements.

OBJECTIVES OF FINANCIAL STATEMENTS

According to A I C P A, "financial statements are prepared for the purpose of presenting a periodical review or report on the progress by the management." The main object of financial statement is to provide information for decision making for all those who are interested in the affairs of the business enterprise. The various class of people who look forward to the financial statements are the management, invistors, prospective investors, creditors etc. However it is to be emphasised that financial statements can not be tailor-made to suit all categories of persons who are interested in the business. There has to be some compromise in the preporation of financial statements. There can be preparation of only one financial statement to meet the requirements of shareholders. But it must give such significant and material information which is beneficial to the other parties as well particularly those who make decisions for the future. For example, an invertor is interested in knowing the amount of dividend his shares are going to earn and also the market value of such shares. Similarly, a supplier of goods on credit is interested to know whether the amount due to him will be paid say within a month. Such needs of various parties can be satisfied by a single set of financial statements. The precise objects of financial statements as envisaged by Accounting Principles Board (APB) of America are as follows:

1. To provide reliable financial information about economic resources and obligations, *i.e.*, inflow and outflow of cash.
2. To provide the net result, *i.e.* profit or loss of an enterprise arising from its activities.
3. To provide financial information that assist in earning capacity of the business.
4. To provide other needed information about changes in economic resources or obligations, such as change in working capital, fund flows etc.
5. To provide other information related to financial statements to others who are in need of it.

NATURE OF FINANCIAL STATEMENTS

Financial statements are prepared to portray the results and financial position of an enterprise. They reflect the totality of recorded facts, accounting principles and personal judgements. According to American Accounting Association "Every corporate statement should be based on accounting principles which are sufficiently uniform, objective and well understood to justify opinions as to the condition and progress of business enterprise. Its basic assumption is that the purpose of financial statement is to furnish information that is necessary for the formation of dependable judgements." The nature of financial statements can be explained under the following points:

1. Recorded facts: The term recorded facts means those transactions which are recorded in the books of accounts. Such transactions relate to cash in hand, bills receivable, debtors, creditors fixed assets, sales, purchases, wages, capital etc. There transactions are recorded on historical basis. Those facts which are not part of accounting books are not shown in financial statements, whatever may be its relative importance to the business.

2. Accounting conventions: These relate to accounting principles which are applied as a long standing practice. For example, the convention relating to conservatism, a provision is made for anticipated loss but not for anticipated profit. Accounting conventions are used for valuation of inventory, allocation of expenses between capital and revenue, valuation of assets etc.

3. Postulates: Postulates relate to assumptions which accountant makes while adopting conventions. One such assumption is relating to continuation of business even beyond the period which is covered by financial statements. This assumption is known as "going concern of the business." According to this assumption, assets are valued at its cost less depreciation. In the absence of this assumption, assets would have been valued at realisable value which may be negligible. Another assumption relate to stability in the value of money over a period of time and some accountants do not value assets on the basis of change in the value of money. A third assumption relates to realisation postulate. According to this assumption there has a time gap between production and sale. The revenue is earned only when sales are effected.

4. Personal judgement: The application of conventions or postulates depend upon the personal judgement of the accountant. For example, the method of Depreciating an asset, the method of valuation of stock, making provision for doubtful debts, the method of amortisation of fixed assets etc., depend upon the personal judgement of the accountant. However, the personal judgement of the Accountant is checked by the consistency principle.

5. Accounting standards and guiding notes: Accounting standards and guiding notes help to a large extent in preparing financial statements. Certain accounting standards such as disclosure of accounting policies. Revenue recognition, accounting for fixed assets etc., are compulsory in nature.

REQUISITES, ATTRIBUTES OR ESSENTIAL REQUIREMENTS OF FINANCIAL STATEMENTS

In order to serve its objectives meaningfully, financial statements must possess the following attributes.

1. Relevance: The financial statements must be relevant for the purpose for which they are meant for. Irrelevant and unwanted information should be avoided but at the same time material facts must necessarily be disclosed.

2. Accuracy: Financial accounts must disclose accurately the profitability, position and prospects of the business. Inaccurate information not only misleads the public but also attracts fines and penalties. Inaccurate information defeats the very purpose for which financial statements are prepared. There should not be any personal prejudice and window dressing of financial statements.

3. Comparability: The financial statements prepared must not only facilitate inter-firm comparision but also intra-firm comparision. Comparision of essential data over a period of time sets a trend which guides management in formulating policies and taking decisions. Inter-firm comparision facilitates the strength and weakness of the firm in the industry.

4. Promptness: In order to facilitate the functioning of the management, there should be quick preparation and prompt submission of the report to all those executives who depend on it. Any delay in presentation of information through financial statements make it difficult to take prompt action to set right adverse results of the business.

5. Generally accepted principles: Financial statements meets the requirements of wide variety of people. As such it is to be accepted and understood by everyone who is interested in it. For this reason financial statements are to be prepared according to "generally accepted accounting principles." The reliability and confidence of financial statements also depends upon the extent to which such principles are applied in preparing the financial statements.

6. Consistency: The personal judgement of accountants sometimes distort the financial statements. As far as possible unformity must be maintained while preparing financial statements. The rules and procedures should not be changed frequently unless the situation demand for a charge. Comparability of statements to a large extent depends upon consistency. For example, if different methods of labour turnover is used to measure the extent of labour turnover it will be difficult to compare as result differ from method to method.

7. Authenticity: To make financial statement reliable it should be certified by an independent and qualified person known as auditor. A statement which is authenticated by an auditor will be acceptable by all without giving room for doubt and unreliability.

8. Compliance with law: The financial statements must be prepared as per the requirements of statute. In our country section 211 of the companies Act 1956 lays down the provisions relating to preparation of financial statements. when financial statements are prepared according to the legal requirements it increases the confidence of public besides not subjected to any fines and penalties.

IMPORTANCE OF FINANCIAL STATEMENTS

Financial statements are prepared to serve the needs of wide variety of people. The beneficiaries of financial statements are as follows:

1. The management: The facts and figures provided by financial statements enable management to formulate the policies as well as to discharge their day-to-day activities of the business. A comparative study of financial statements over a period of time helps management to know the trends and modify the policies accordingly so as to avoid unfavourable situations.

2. The shareholders: Shareholders are the owners of the share capital of the company. They are interested in knowing the profitability and future prospects of the company. Financial statements serve as a guide to shareholders in this respect.

3. Creaditors and suppliers: Creaditors provide loan facilities to the companies and suppliers supply goods on credit basis. They are interested in knowing the liquidity position of the business. The ability to repay debts is revealed by financial statements.

4. Tax authorities: Tax calculations are based on income earned by the business. Both direct and indirect taxes are based on facts and figures shown by financial statements. Whereas net profit is the basis for paying income tax, sales figure constitutes the basis for paying sales tax ad valorem duty.

5. Employees and Trade Unions: The wage fixation policy, payment of bonus to employees etc., are determined on the basis of net profit as revealed by income statement of the organisation.

6. Customers: Customers are primarily interested in the price of goods and services. The cost of production, profit margin, selling price as revealed by the income statement guides the customer in selecting the suppliers.

7. Financial analyst: A financial analyst has to advise his client as to in which company, the amount can be invested. Prospective investors unable to understand financial statement may seek the advise of the financial analyst for his expert advise. Thus financial statements are more important to financial analysts.

8. Stock exchange: All those company which list their securities with the stock exchange must furnish then financial statements with stock exchanges. Based on this, the stock exchange will quote the price of shares for the benefit of shareholders and others.

9. Regulatory authority: The regulating authority of the companies such as company law board, the Registrar of joint stock companies, etc. the Lare also interested in the financial statements of companies. Based on the performance, they can amend the statute depending upon the prevailing environment of the companies.

10. Press: Economic and Commercial Journals and newspapers report the performance, position and prospects of various companies for the benefit of prospective invertors. Financial statements constitute the basis for press in such reporting.

11. Trade Associations and chamber of commerce: Trade associations and chamber of commerce collect financial statements of various companies and supply the required information to their members.

12. Government: The Government is interested in the financial statements of companies with a view to formulate policies relating to taxation, price, wage, income and national plans.

13. General public: General public is interested in the financial statements of companies so as to know the extent of social responsibility of business towards the society.

LIMITATIONS OF FINANCIAL STATEMENTS

Financial statements suffer from the following limitations:

1. Interim reports: Financial statements are essentially interim reports but not the final report of the profitable and financial position of the business. In other words they reflect the progress and position of the business at frequent intervals during its life. But the exact result and financial strength of a business can be known exactly only when the business is either sold or liquidated.

2. It reveals only quantitative information: Financial statements portrary only quantitative data which can be measured in terms of value. But there are many aspects which are qualitative and not capable of expressing in terms of money value. Such aspects may relate to harmonious relationship between employees and management reputation of management, the efficiency of employees etc., which are equally important to a business. Financial statements do not disclose all these particulars because they can not be measured in respect of money value.

3. Historical data: Financial statements are prepared on the basis of past data. They don't take into consideration the future events. So it may not be more useful for decision making.

4. It is based on accounting concepts and conventions: Financial statements are prepared on the basis of certain accounting concepts and conventions. This makes financial statements unrealistic. For example, according to going-concern concept fixed assets are shown at its cost price not at realisable value. Similarly, according to the convention of conservatism, only anticipated losses are provided for but not for anticipated profits. This distorts the profit disclosed by profit and loss account.

5. Personal judgement: The preparation of financial statements are influenced by personal judgement of accountant. Such instances relate to choice of method of depreciation, mode of amortisation of fixed assets, treatment of deferred revenue expenditure; the method of pricing material issues. The personal judgement of accountant often distorts the true picture of the business.

6. Window dressing: Financial statements may not always reveal the accurate information about the business. In order to project better image in the mind of public the management may resort to window dressing thereby revealing misleading picture of the business.

RECENT TRENDS IN PRESENTING FINANCIAL STATEMENTS

Preparation of financial statements by joint companies in India is governed by section 211 of the Companies Act. In order to make the financial statements more understandable by a layman, it is supported by other information. Such additional information include the following:

1. Summarised profit and loss a/c and balance sheet: In recent times companies are following vertical form of preparing financial statements instead of preparing them under traditional two sided P & L a/c and balance sheet.

2. Highlights: To enable readers to understand the financial report know a days important information such as sales, production, profit, capital projects, fixed assets, share capital and other landmarks are furnished at the top of the report. By going through these highlights people can make out the progress and performance of the company.

3. Cash flow statements: Preparation of cash flow statements has become compulsory in recent times. It provides the in-flow and out-flow of cash and thereby net changes in cash resulting from operations and investments in business.

4. Accounting ratios: Ratios establish relationship between various aspects of the business. This helps to understand more easily as ratios are not voluminous as in the case of other information contained in the financial statements.

5. Accounting policies: Some companies disclose the accounting policies on the basis of which accounts are prepared. This is again to enable people to understand financial statements in a better way.

6. Use of charts, graphs, diagrams: Use of charts, graphs, and diagrams are very commont in recent times while publishing financial statements. They not only attract the attention of viewers but also help them to grasp the meaning of data. They have lasting impression when compared to presenting information in the form of figures.

7. Use of schedule: In order to make the final accounts of companies more compact, the Companies Act has prescribed various schedules. The financial statements are supported by these schedules and they relate to capital, reserves and surplus, secured and unsecured loans, current liabilities, fixed assets, current assets, miscellaneous expenses etc.

8. Impact of price level changes: At prices do not remain stable, financial statements prepared on historical basis do not reflect the effect of change in price level on profitability and financial position of the business. Hence in recent time, some companies are disclosing the effect of change in price level through a supplementary statement in addition to financial statements.

9. Rounding off the figures: Following the recommondation of Sachhar Committee which has given an option for the companies to round off the figures to the nearest thousand, or hundred or ten rupees, some companies know a days portrary rounded figures to facilitate easy understanding.

BASIC FINANCIAL STATEMENTS OR PACKAGES OF FINANCIAL STATEMENTS

According to Accounting Principles Board, (APB) statement no. 4, the following are the important components or packages of financial statements.

1. Income statement
2. Position statement
3. Statement of changes in retained earnings.
4. Statement of changes in financial position.
5. Schedules and Accounting Policies.

The above statements are generally referred to as "basic financial statements. In addition to the above list we may add yet another component, *viz.*, miscellaneous statement."

1. Income Statement or Profit and Loss Account

The income statement and profit and loss account are not different but are interchangeably used. Whereas in U.S.A. income statement is a popular usage, in U.K. it is more commonly referred to as profit and loss a/c. According to AICPA terminology, income statement is defined as "a statement which shows the principal elements, the positive and negative, in the derivation of income or loss, the claims against income and the resulting net income or loss of accounting unit." In simple words, an income statement shows revenue and expenses of a business for an accounting period. It matches revenue with costs. If the revenue exceeds the cost it implies the profitability of business and of cost exceed revenue it implies the loss suffered by the business. The same view has been expressed by Haray & Guthmann when he wrote that "the statement of profit or loss is condensed and classified record of gains and losses causing changes in the owners interest in the business for a period of time." By far income statement is considered to be most important among all financial statements.

FORMAT OF PROFIT AND LOSS ACCOUNT

Though schedule VI part II of the Indian Companies Act lays down the contents and other data to be included in an income statement it is silent about the proforma according to which an income statement is to be prepared. However there are two methods which could be followed for preparing an income statement, *viz.*, (*a*) Multi-step income statement and (*b*) Single-step income statement.

1. Multi-step Income Statement: This method involves the following steps:

1. *Ascertainment of gross-profit*: From sales and other operating revenues the cost of goods sold is deducted to get gross profit (gross loss in case cost of goods sold exceeds sales).
2. *Ascertaining operating profit*: From gross profit other operating expenses such as administration. Selling and distribution expenses are deducted to get operating profit.
3. *Ascertainment of Net Profit before Tax* (*NPBT*): To the operating profit other non-operating incomes are added and therefrom other non-operating expenses are deducted. The resultant figure is known as net profit before tax.

   Non-operating incomes arise from secondary activities as for example, interest, rent, devidend received by a company whose main business is not to deal with finance, property and investment.

4. *Ascertainment of Profit after Tax* (*PAT*): The provision for tax is deducted from the net profit before tax. The result is net profit after tax.
5. *Ascertainment of Net Profit* (*NP*): Other extra ordinary gains or losses such as gain or loss on the sale of investment, loss by fire etc., are respectively added and deducted to arrive at final figure of net profit.

A proforma of Multi-stage income statement is shown below:

PROFORMA OF MULTI-STEP INCOME STATEMENT

	Net Sales			××
Less:	Cost of goods sold			××
	Gross profit			××
Less:	Office and Administration expenses:			
	Office Salaries	××		
	Office Insurance	××		
	Office Rent	××		
	Taxes	××		
			××	
Less:	Selling expenses:			
	Sales Manager's Salaries	××		
	Salesmen's Salaries	××		
	Advertisement	××		
	Travelling	××		
			××	
				××
	Operating profit			××
Add:	Other revenues:			
	Interest and Dividends	××		
	Rent Received	××		
		××		
Less:	Interest paid	××		
				××
	Net profit before tax			××
Less:	Provision for income tax			××
	Net profit after tax			××
Add:	Gains from sale of Investment			××
	Net profit			××

2. Single Step Income Statement: As multi-step income statement involves many steps it is often confusing. So many businesses use 'single-step' income statement. The following steps are involved under this method.

(*a*) To collect all items of income whether operating or non-operating at one place.

(*b*) To show all deductions from the total income as calculated in step (*a*). The difference shows net profit or net loss.

The proforma of single-step income statement is as follows:

PROFORMA OF SINGLE STEP INCOME STATEMENT

Income:			
	Sales		××
	Dividend on Investment		××
	Interest on Debentures		××
	Royalties		××
	Miscellaneous		××
			××
Less:	Expenses		
	Cost of goods sold	××	
	Selling and distribution expenses	××	
	Office and Administration expenses	××	
	Interest on Debentures	××	
	Provision for Tax	××	
	Loss on sale of Asset	××	××
		Net profit	××

Elements of Income Statement

1. Cost of goods sold: Cost of goods sold, otherwise known as cost of sales represent the cost incurred in manufacturing or purchasing the goods that have been sold to customers. The method of calculating it depends upon the nature of the business, *i.e.*, whether the business is trading or manufacturing concern. In case of trading business it is calculated as under:

Opening stock of Finished goods			××
Add:	Total purchases	××	
Add:	Carriage on purchases	××	××
			××
Less:	Purchase returns	××	
Less:	Closing stock of finished goods	××	××
	Cost of goods sold		××

In case of manufacturing business it is calculated as under:

Direct Materials Cost			××
Direct labour cost			××
Direct expenses			××
		Prime cost	××
Factory overheads			××
		Factory cost	××
Office and Administration overhead			××
		Cost of production	××
Add:	Opening stock of Finished goods		××
			××
Less:	Closing stock of Finished goods		××
		Cost of goods sold	××

However in financial accounts selling expenses are also included in the "cost of goods sold."

Cost of goods sold can also be calculated by using the following formula:

Cost of goods sold = Sales – Gross profit

Where gross profit is not given but its percentage to sales is given, cost of goods sold can be calculated by using the following formula:

$$\text{Cost of goods sold} = \text{Sales} - \frac{\text{Sales} \times \text{G.P.\%}}{100}$$

2. Operating Income: Operating income is generated from carrying on business on a day-to-day basis. Generally, sales constitutes operating income.

3. Operating expenses: Expenses which are incurred in carrying on business on a regular basis is known as operating expenses. They are also known as routine expenses and they facilitate the smooth and continuous operations of the business. Examples of operating expenses are office and administrative expenses, selling and distribution expenses, finance expenses.

4. Non-operating income and expenses: Non-operating incomes and expenses are those transactions which are not directly related to main activities of the business. Examples of such incomes and expenses are dividend, interest, rent, commission, loss or gain from sales of securities etc.

5. Net operating profit: It represents the income earned from main activities of the business. The difference between gross profit and operating expenses is known as net operating profit. Since it is the result of the main activities of the business, it is most important element of income statement for managerial planning and decision making.

Problem 1: Following is the profit and loss account of well-balanced limited for the year ended 31st March 1996. You are required to prepare vertical income statement for purpose of analysis:

To Opening stock	7,00,000	By Sales:		
To Purchases	9,00,000	Cash	5,20,000	
To Wages	1,50,000	Credit	15,00,000	
To Factory expenses	3,50,000		20,20,000	
To Office salaries	25,000	*Less:* Returns	20,000	
To Office rent	39,000			20,00,000
To Postage and telegram	5,000	By Closing stock		6,00,000
To Directors fees	6,000	By Dividend on Investment		10,000
To Salesmen's Salaries	12,000	By Profit on sale of furniture		20,000
To Advertising	18,000			
To Delivery expenses	20,000			
To Debenture Interest	20,000			
To Depreciation on:				
Office furniture	10,000			
Plant	30,000			
Delivery Van	20,000			
To Loss on sale of Van	5,000			
To Income tax	1,75,000			
To Net profit	1,45,000			
	26,30,000			26,30,000

(University of Bombay, B. Com., April 1998)

Solution:

WELL BALANCED LTD.
INCOME STATEMENT FOR THE YEAR ENDED 31ST MARCH 1996

Sales: Cash	5,20,000		
Credit		15,00,000	
		20,20,000	
Less: Returns		20,000	
			20,00,000
Less: Cost of goods sold:			
Opening stock		7,00,000	
Add: Purchases		9,00,000	
Add: Wages		1,50,000	
Add: Factory expenses		3,50,000	
Add: Depreciation on plant		30,000	
		21,30,000	
Less: Closing stock		6,00,000	
			15,30,000
Gross profit			4,70,000
Less: Operating expenses:			
(*A*) Office and administrative expenses:			
Office Salaries		25,000	
Office Rent		39,000	
Postage		5,000	
Directors fees		6,000	
Depreciation on office furniture		10,000	
		85,000	
(*B*) Selling and Distribution expenses:			
Salesman's Salaries	12,000		
Advertisement	18,000		
Delivery expenses	20,000		
Depreciation on Delivery Van	20,000		
		70,000	
(*C*) Financial expenses:			
Debenture interest		20,000	
			1,75,000
Operating profit			2,95,000
Add: Non-operating income:			
Dividend on investment		10,000	
Profit on sale of furniture		20,000	
			30,000
			3,25,000
Less: Non-operating expenses:			
Loss on sale of Van			5,000
Net profit before Tax			3,20,000
Less: Income tax			1,75,000
Net profit after tax			1,45,000

Problem 2: The following particulars are obtained from the books of Dream Flower Co. Ltd. tor the year ended 31st, March 2001. Prepare the income statement in the vertical form:

Opening stock	12,000	Sales	15,00,000
Closing stock	17,000	Purchases	10,00,000
Carriage inwards	20,000	Carriage outwards	42,000
Salaries	75,000	Debenture Interest	20,000
Interest paid	30,000	Loss on sale of machinery	30,000
Rent	20,000		
Telephone charges	12,400	Interest received on investments	25,000
Depreciation on assets	32,000	Advertisement	50,000
Dividend paid	25,000	Interest on Bank Deposits	14,000
Taxes @ 50%		Transfer to general reserve	11,000
		Wages paid	3,000

Solution: **Dream Flower Co. Ltd.**

INCOME STATEMENT FOR THE YEAR ENDED 31ST MARCH 2001

	Sales			15,00,000
Less:	Cost of goods sold:			
	Opening stock	12,000		
Add:	Purchases	10,00,000		
Add:	Carriage Inwards	20,000		
Add:	Wages	3,000		
		10,35,000		
Less:	Closing stock	17,000		
				10,18,000
	Gross profit			4,82,000
Less:	Operating expenses:			
(*A*)	Administrative expenses:			
	Salaries	75,000		
	Rent	20,000		
	Telephone charges	12,400		
	Depreciation on Assets	32,000		
			1,39,400	
(*B*)	Selling and Distribution Expenses:			
	Carriage outwards	42,000		
	Advertisement	50,000		
			92,000	
				2,31,400
				2,50,600
Add:	Operating income			Nil
	Operating profit			2,50,600
Add:	Non-operating Income:			
	Interest on Investments		25,000	
	Interest on Bank deposits		14,000	
				39,000
				2,89,600

Less:	Non-operating expenses:		
	Interest on Debentures	20,000	
	Loss on sale of Machinery	30,000	
			50,000
	Profit before Tax		2,39,600
Less:	Tax at 50%		1,19,800
	Profit after Tax		1,19,800
Less:	Appropriations:		
	Transfer to General Reserve	11,000	
	Dividends paid	25,000	
			36,000
	Profit transferred to Balance sheet		83,800

POSITION STATEMENT OR BALANCE SHEET

A Balance sheet may well be described as a statement of assets and liabilities including capital amount. It reveals the assets and liabilities and capital amount as on a period of time. It highlights the assets possessed by a business and sources of funds (from owners and creditors) used in purchasing of such assets. It discloses the financial position of the business. It records only periodic change rather than continuous one. In this sense it is static where as business is dynamic.

A Balance sheet is often discribed as a statement of equality as it equalises assets and liabilities by placing assets on right hand side and liabilities and capital on the left hand side. In the words of Howard and Upton "the balance sheet is a statement which presents property's value owned by the enterprise and the claims of creditors and owners against these properties."

Yet another new about balance sheet is to consider it as a statement of sources and uses of funds. The equality at both sides of Balance sheet can better be expressed as sources and uses or application of funds. The liability side indicates the various sources from which funds are collected and the asset side indicates the uses of funds. In this sense, the relationship of the two sides of balance sheet is rightly called as 'identity' and not 'equality'. The sources and uses of funds thus indicates the financial position of the business. For this reason a balance sheet is considered as snapshot of financial position of a business as on a given data.

FORM OR PROFORMA OF A BALANCE SHEET

Part I of schedule VI of the Companies Act 1956 lays down the proforma of balance sheet according to which all Joint Stock Companies have to prepare their balance sheets. A balance sheet can be prepared either in horizontal form or vertical form. These are shown below:

PROFORMA OF HORIZONTAL OR TRADITIONAL BALANCE SHEET

Share capital:		**Fixed Assets**	
Authorised capital	××	Goodwill	××
Issued and paid up		Land	××
capital	××	Buildings	××

Liabilities		Assets	
Reserves and Surplus		Plant and Machinery	××
Capital Reserve	××	Furniture and Fixtures	××
General Reserve	××	Patents, Trade mark,	
Share premium	××	and Designs	××
Secured loans		Vehicles	××
Debentures	××	**Investments**	
Loans and advances	××	Investment in Government	
Unsecured loans		or trust securities	××
Fixed deposit		Investment in shares	××
Loans and advances from			
Subsidiaries	××	**Current Assets Loans**	
Short-term loans and		**and Advances**	
advances	××	(*A*) **Current Assets:**	
Current Liabilities and		Interest accured on	
provisions		Investment	××
(*A*) **Current Liabilities**		Stores and spare parts	××
Sundry creditors	××	Loose Tools	××
Unclaimed dividends	××	Stock in Trade	××
Interest accrued but		Work in progress	××
not due on loan	××	Sundry Debtors	××
(*B*) **Provisions**		Cash on hand	××
Provision for Tax	××	Bank balance	××
Proposed Dividend	××	(*B*) **Loans and Advances:**	
Provident fund	××	Advances and loans	
Insurance and		to subsidiaries	××
pension for staff	××	Advances recoverable	
Other provisions		in cash or hand	
	××	(Rates, Insurance etc.)	××
		Bills of exchange	××
		Miscellaneous expenses	
		not written off	
		Preliminary expenses	××
		Expenses including	
		Commission, or brokerage	
		or underwriting of	
		shares or debentures	××
		Discount allowed on issue	
		of shares or debentures	××
	××		××

PROFORMA OF VERTICAL FORM OF BALANCE SHEET

I. Sources of Funds

(1) Shareholder's Fund	
(*a*) Capital	××
(*b*) Reserves and Surpluses	××
(2) Loan funds	
(*a*) Secured loans	××
(*b*) Unsecured loans	××
Total	××

II. Applications of Funds:		
(1) Fixed Assets		
Goss Assets	××	
Less: Depreciation	××	
Net Assets	××	××
(2) Investments		××
(3) Current assets, loans and advances:		
(*a*) Stock	××	
(*b*) Sundry Debtors	××	
(*c*) Cash and Bank balance	××	
(*d*) Other current assets	××	
(*e*) Loans and advances	××	
	××	
Less: Current liabilities and provisions	××	
Net current assets	××	××
(4) (*a*) Miscellaneous expanditure to the extent not written off		××
(*b*) Profit and loss a/c		××
Total		××

ELEMENTS OF BALANCE SHEET

1. Current assets: Assets which are readily converted into cash during a period of only year are known as current assets. Of course current assets are classified on the basis of their use and not on the basis of time. Assets which are acquired for selling in the course of business are to be treated as current assets. The following are examples of current assets:

(*a*) Cash in hand and at Bank
(*b*) Sundry Debtors
(*c*) Bills Receivables
(*d*) Stock of raw materials, work in progress and finished goods
(*e*) Marketable securities
(*f*) Prepard expenses and so on

2. Fixed assets: There are the assets, which are used for conducting the operations of the business and not for reselling to earn a profit. Examples of Fixed assets are:

(*a*) Land and Building
(*b*) Plant and Machineries
(*c*) Furniture and Fixture
(*d*) Trucks and Automobiles etc

3. Intangible assets: Assets which cannot be seen or touched are known as intangible assets. They dont exist physically in the business. Examples of such assets are:

(*a*) Patents and Trade marks
(*b*) Licence and copy right
(*c*) Good will

4. Other assets: The rest of the assets which do not fall under any of the above categories are known as other assets. Such assets are tangible in nature but are not directly used in the business. Examples of such assets are:

(*a*) Investments (excluding govt. securities and other marketable securities)
(*b*) Debenture redemption fund
(*c*) Any other fund created for redeeming a contingent liability

5. Deferred expenditure: Expenses which are not of recurring nature and which do not arise out of current operations of a business is known as deferred expenditure. Such expenses benefit the business over years. These expenses are therefore written off over a period of time and is a charge on future profit. That portion of deferred expenses which are not written off to P & C a/c is shows on the asset side of the balance sheet under the heading 'miscellaneous expenditure'.

6. Current liabilities: These are the obligations which are to be met on demand or within a period of one year. Even long term liabilities which become payable within a period of one year is also taken as current liabilities. Examples of current liabilities are as follows:

(*a*) Sundry creditors
(*b*) Bills payable
(*c*) Short term public deposits
(*d*) Bank overdraft
(*e*) Provision for tax
(*f*) Unclaimed dividends

7. Long term liabilities: There liabilities become payable over a long period of time say between 2 to 8 years. Examples of such liabilities are as follows:

(*a*) Loan on mortgage
(*b*) Debentures
(*c*) Bank loan
(*d*) Loans from specialised financial institutions.

8. Net worth: The difference between total assets and current and long term liabilities is known as net worth.

9. Other related elements:

***(a)* Liquid assets:** There are the assets which are converted into cash when desired without any loss. According to this meaning all current assets excepting stock can be converted into cash in the normal course of dealing by the business without loss. Hence :

Liquid assets = Current assets – Stock

***(b)* Working capital:** The excess of current assets over current liabilities is known as working capital. Expressed in the form of an equation:

Working Capital = Current Assets – Current liabilities

***(c)* Capital employed:** Capital employed may relate to total or gross capital or net capital employed. Gross capital employed is taken to mean the total assets of a business whereas net working capital is the difference between total assets and current liabilities. Expressed in the form of an equation:

Net Capital employed = Total assets – Current liabilities

Or

Capital employed = Fixed assets + Working Capital

Problem 3: Following is the balance sheet of Mahavir Ltd. as on 31st March 1999:

Share capital	3,00,000	Good will	40,000
Share premism	10,000	Land	1,60,000
General Reserve	1,20,000	Plant	88,000
P & C a/c	34,000	Furniture	6,000
11% Debentures	1,00,000	Trade Investment	1,60,000
Bank loan	70,000	Accounts Receivable	1,40,000
Bank overdraft	40,000	Inventories	1,20,000
Sundry creditors	1,20,000	Prepard expenses	10,000
Provision for Taxation	20,000	Cash at Bank	80,000
		Preliminary expenses	10,000
	8,14,000		8,14,000

Prepare the above balance sheet in vertical form for showing the following:

1. Fixed Assets
2. Intgible Assets.
3. Fictitions assets
4. Quick Assets.
5. Current assets
6. Net worth.
7. Long term liabilities
8. Quick liabilities.
9. Working capital.

(*University of Bombay, B. Com., October 1999*)

Solution: **Vertical Balance Sheet of Mahavir Ltd. as on 31-3-1999**

Sources of Funds:		
I. Shareholder's Funds:		
(*A*) Share capital		3,00,000
(*B*) Reserves and surplus:		
Share premium	10,000	
General Reserve	1,20,000	
P & C a/c	34,000	
	1,64,000	
Less: Fictitions assets	10,000	
		1,54,000
II. Long term liabilities:		
Secured:		
11% Debentures	1,00,000	
Bank loan	70,000	
		1,70,000
Total Fund employed		6,24,000

Application of Funds

I. Fixed Assets:			
Good will		40,000	
Land		1,60,000	
Plant		88,000	
Furniture		6,000	
			2,94,000
II. Trade Investments			1,60,000
III. Working capital:			
(*A*) Current assets:			
Accounts receivable	1,40,000		
Cash at bank	80,000		
Quick Assets	2,20,000		

Add:	Non-quick Assets			
	Inventories	1,20,000		
	Prepard expenses	10,000		
			3,50,000	
Less:	Current liabilities:			
	Sundry creditors	1,20,000		
	Provision for tax	20,000		
	Quick liabilities	1,40,000		
Add:	Non-Quick liabilities:			
	Bank overdraft	40,000		
			1,80,000	
				1,70,000
	Total fund employed			6,24,000

Problem 4: Given below is the Balance sheet of TY Ltd.

Share capital	3,75,000	Good will	62,500
Capital reserve	4,000	Land	1,14,500
General reserve	60,205	Premises	1,25,000
Debenture redemption fund	84,000	Plant	93,758
P & C a/c	37,554	Furniture	16,650
5% Debentures	1,57,500	3% G.P Notes	76,400
Sundry creditors	36,950	Stock	1,17,815
Proposed Dividend	18,750	Debtors	1,01,971
Provision for Taxation	10,000	Cash	60,140
		Advance tax	13,675
		Preliminary expenses	1,550
	7,83,959		7,83,959

Rearrange the balance sheet in vertical form and calculate the following:
1. Current assets 2. Quick assets 3. Intangible assets 4. Fictitions assets 5. Fixed assets 6. Fixed liabilities 7. Proprietors' fund 8. working capital 9. Total funds employed 10. Secured loans 11. Owned funds.

(University of Bombay, B. Com., April 1995)

Solution:

Balance Sheet as on 31- December 1994

Sources of Funds

(1)	Shareholders funds		
	(*A*) Share capital		3,75,000
	(*B*) Reserves and Surplus:		
	Capital Reserve	4,000	
	General Reserve	60,205	
	Debenture Redemption fund	84,000	
	P & C a/c	37,554	
		1,85,759	
	Less: Preliminiary expenses	1,550	
			1,84,209
(2)	Loan funds		
	5% Debentures		1,57,500
	Total sourees of funds		7,16,709

Applications of Funds

(1) *Fixed Assets:*			
Goodwill		62,500	
Land		1,14,500	
Premises		1,25,000	
Plant		93,758	
Furniture		16,650	
			4,12,408
(2) *Investments:*			
3% G. P. Notes			76,400
(3) *Working Capital:*			
Current Assets:			
Stock		1,17,815	
Debtors		1,01,971	
Cash and Bank		60,140	
Advance tax		13,675	
		(*A*) 2,93,601	
Current liabilities			
Creditors	36,950		
Proposed Divident	18,750		
Provision for Tax	10,000		
		(*B*) 65,700	
Working Capital (*A* – *B*)			2,27,901
Total fund Employed			7,16,709

(1)	Current Assets	2,93,601
(2)	Quick Assets C A = Stock – Advance Tax 2,93,601 = 1,17,815 – 13,675	1,62,111
(3)	Intangible assets	62,500
(4)	Fictitions assets	1,550
(5)	Fixed Assets	4,12,408
(6)	Fixed Liabilities	1,57,500
(7)	Proprietors funds	5,59,209
(8)	Working Capital	2,27,901
(9)	Total funds employed	7,16,709
(10)	Secured loans	1,57,500
(11)	Owned funds	5,59,209

Problem 5: The accountant of a company submits the following financial statements for 1994:

Trading and profit and loss a/c for the year ended 31st December 1994.

To opening stock	35,000	By sales	8,30,000
To purchases	7,50,000	By closing stock	80,000
To Gross profit	1,25,000		
	9,10,000		9,10,000
To Depreciation	18,000	By Gross profit	1,25,000
To other expenses	37,000	By Interest	5,000
To Tax provision	20,000		
To proposed Dividend	8,000		
To Net profit	90,000		
	1,30,000		1,30,000

Balance Sheet as at 31st December 1994

Share Capital	1,50,000	Cash	24,000
Bank overdraft	19,000	Stock	80,000
Creditors	13,000	Debtors	69,250
Depreciation provision	27,875	Land and Building	46,075
Tax provision	20,000	Machinery	64,300
Proposed Dividend	8,000	Prepard expenses	750
P & C a/c	90,000	Good will	10,000
		Preliminary expenses	3,500
		Loan	30,000
	3,27,875		3,27,875

Rearrange the above in a form suitable for analysis. *(University of Bombay, B. Com., October 1995)*

Solution:

Income Statement for the year ended 31-12-94

Sales		8,30,000
Less: Cost of sales:		
Opening stock	35,000	
Add: Purchases	7,50,000	
	78,500	
Less: Closing stock	80,000	
Gross profit		705,000
		1,25,000
Less: Operating expenses:		
Depreciation	18,000	
Other expenses	37,000	
		55,000
Operating net profit		70,000
Add: Non-operating Income		
Interest		5,000
Net profit before Tax		75,000
Less: Tax provision		20,000
Net profit after Tax		55,000
Less: Proposed Dividend		8,000
Profit transferred to balance sheet		47,000

Balance sheet as at 31-12-94

Sources of Funds			
(1) Shareholders Funds			
(*a*) Share capital		1,50,000	
(*b*) Reserves and Surplus:			
P & C a/c	90,000		
Less: Preliminary expenses	3,500		
		86,500	
Net Worth			2,36,500
(2) Loan funds			Nil
Total source of funds			2,36,500

Applications of Funds

(1) *Fixed Assets:*

Good will		10,000	
Land and Building		46,075	
Machinery		64,300	
		1,20,350	
Less: Depreciation provision		27,875	
			92,500

(2) *Working capital:*

Current assets loans and Advances

Cash		24,000	
Stock		80,000	
Debtors		69,250	
Prepared expenses		750	
Loans		30,000	
		2,04,000	
Less: Current liabilities and provisions:			
Creditors	13,000		
Bank OD	19,000		
Tax provision	20,000		
Proposed dividend	8,000		
		60,000	
			1,44,000
Total Application of funds			2,36,500

Problem 6: From the following Horizontal balance sheet extracted from the books of Moon Light Co. Ltd. as on 31st, December 2000, Redraft the same in vertical form:

Share Capital			*Fixed Assets*	
Paid-up capital			Building	150,000
60,000 Equity shares			Machinery	2,00,000
of Rs. 10 each		6,00,000	Motor Vehicles	30,000
Reserves and Surplus			Furniture	5,000
General Reserve	2,50,000			3,85,000
Additors driving the year	50,000		*Less*: Dep.	81,000
		3,00,000		3,04,000
P & C a/c		17,116		
Current Liabilities			Investment	2,88,950
Trade creditors		36,858	**Current Assets**	
Unclaimed dividend		6,526	Stock	1,48,680
Managing Directors			Book Debts	2,23,380
Remuneration		6,500	Cash on hand	72,240
Provisions			**Loans and Advances**	
Provision for taxation		60,000	Interest on Investment	2,750
Proposed dividend		24,000	Advance payment	
Staff provident fund		39,000	of Tax	50,000
		10,90,000	Accuret	10,90,000

Solution:

Vertical Form

Balance Sheet of Moon Light Co. as at 31-12-2000

I. Sources of Funds			
(1) Shareholders funds			
(*a*) Capital		6,00,000	
(*b*) Reserves and Surplus		3,17,116	9,17,116
Total			9,17,116
II. Application of Funds			
(1) Fixed Assets			
(*a*) Gross block		3,85,000	
Less: Depreciation		81,000	
			3,04,000
(2) Investments			2,88,950
(3) Current assets and loans and advances:			
(*a*) Inventories		1,48,680	
(*b*) Sundry debtors		2,23,380	
(*c*) Cash at hand		72,240	
(*d*) Loans and advances		52,750	
		4,97,050	
Less: Current Liabilities and Provisions			
(*a*) Liabilities	49,884		
(*b*) Provisions	1,23,000		
		1,72,884	
Working capital			3,24,165
			9,17,116

3. STATEMENT OF RETAINED EARNINGS

A statement of retained earnings is in fact a part of income statement or profit & loss a/c. In fact it is an extension of profit and loss a/c which reveals how the profit of the company have been utilised to meet various contingencies and the balance amount transferred to balance sheet. As this statement involves appropriating the income towards reserves and dividend it is also known as profit and loss appropriation a/c. However, on the credit side it starts with the opening balance of profit and to it is added profit earned during the current year. The term 'retained earnings' means the accumulated excess of earnings over devidends and losses.

4. STATEMENT OF CHANGES IN FINANCIAL POSITION

It is a statement which reveals the financing and investing activities of a company. It is also known as a 'statement of changes in financial position' during an accounting period. The statement discloses change in working capital. In order to know the change in financial position of a business between two period two different statements, known as fund flow statement and cash flow statement are prepared.

The fund flow statement reveals as to how working capital (*i.e.*, fund) is acquired and spent. Cash flow statement reveals a change in cash position between two accounting period. It helps to know the inflow and outflow of cash in a business.

5. SCHEDULES AND ACCOUNTING POLICES

Sometimes various schedules are prepared to supplement the information contained in profit and loss a/c and balance sheet. Such schedules relate to cost of goods sold, schedule of fixed assets, schedule of investment etc., and are attached to relevant statements.

Accounting policies followed for valuation of stock, depreciation etc., are mentioned as a foot note to the balance sheet. There help the readers to understand the financial statements in a better way.

QUESTIONS

Simple Questions

1. Define financial statement.
2. List out the objectives of financial statements.
3. Mention the various packages of financial statements.
4. What do you mean by multi-step income statement?
5. What do you mean by single-step income statement?
6. How do you ascertain cost of goods sold in case of a trading business?
7. How do you ascertain cost of goods sold in case of a manufacturing business?
8. What is "operating income"? Give an example.
9. What is operating expense? Give an example.
10. What are non-operating incomes and expenses?
11. What is net operating profit?
12. What is a current asset? Give examples.
13. What is a fixed Asset? Give examples.
14. What is an intangible asset? Give examples.
15. What is deferred expenditure? Give examples.
16. What is a current liability? Give examples.
17. What do you mean by long term liability? Give examples.
18. What is net worth?
19. What is liquid asset?
20. What is working capital?
21. What do you mean by capital employed?
22. What is statement of retained earnings?

Short Answer Questions

1. Explain the nature of financial statements.
2. Explain the attributes of financial statements.
3. Explain the importance of financial statements.
4. State the limitations of financial statements.
5. State the recent trends in presenting financial statements.

Long Answer Questions

1. Explain the packages financial statements.

Exercise 1: The following details have been obtained from the books of Mercury Co. Ltd. prepare an income statement in the vertical form for the year ended 31-12-2001.

Balance on 1-4-2000		Dividend paid	30,000
Raw materials	80,000	Sale of scrap	2,500
Work-in-progress	30,000	Purchases	89,000
Finished goods	50,000	Loss on Sale of shares	23,000
Balance on 31-3-2001			
Raw materials	90,000	Manufacturing expenses	75,000
Work-in-progress	40,000	Selling expenses	21,000
Finished goods	38,000	Office expenses	30,500
Sales	3,40,000	Interest paid	7,500

Answer: Profit 22,250.

Exercise 2: From the following particulars prepare an income statement in a vertical form:

Opening stock	1,72,058
Closing stock	1,48,680
Sales	10,83,947
Purchases	5,00,903
Manufacturing expenses	3,59,000
Interest on Investment	11,294
Establishment charges	26,814
General charges	31,078
Directors fees	1,800
Depreciation on fixed assets	10,000
Managing Directors Remuneration	6,500

Answer: Profit Rs. 7,45,268.

Exercise 3: From the following balances ascertain:
(*a*) Current assets (*b*) Fixed assets (*c*) Current liabilities and provisional (*d*) Long term debt (*e*) Shareholders funds.

Equity share capital	3,00,000	Furniture	10,000
Buildings	2,00,000	Machinery	1,50,000
Stock	50,000	Bills receivable	20,000
Debtors	1,00,000	General reserve	20,000
P & L a/c (cr.)	75,000	Bank overdraft (Permanent)	50,000
Provision for Tax	30,000	12% Debentures	1,00,000
Loan from Managing Director	90,000	Cash in hand	10,000
Cash at Bank	40,000	Unclaimed dividends	15,000
Preliminary expenses	70,000	15% Investements	90,000
Creditors	50,000	Bills payable	10,000

Answer: (*a*) Current assets Rs. 2,20,000
(*b*) Fixed Assets Rs. 3,60,000
(*c*) Current liabilities and provisions Rs. 10,5,000
(*d*) Long term debt Rs. 2,40,000
(*e*) Shareholders funds Rs. 3,95,000

Exercise 4: From the following details prepare a balance sheet in a vertical form:

36,900 equity shares of Rs. 10 each fully paid-up	3,69,000
10% cum, preference share capital	80,000
Capital reserve	71,000
Share premium a/c	10,000
P & L a/c (cr.)	24,910
Bank OD (secured by mortgage on land and buildings)	50,000
Creditors	20,000
O/s Managerial Remuneration	1,800
Provision for income-tax	26,190
Proposed dividend on pref. shares	9,600
Advance payment of income-tax	6,000
Cash at bank	5,000
Cash on hand	1,000
Debtors	47,500
Stock	40,000
Investments	1,80,000
Furniture	14,400
Buildings	68,600
Freehold land	3,00,000

Solution: Sources and Applications of funds Rs. 6,04,910.

32

ANALYSIS AND INTERPRETATION OF FINANCIAL STATEMENTS

Introduction

Financial statements prepared in an organisation conveys the financial information in absolute terms which may not be readily understood by everyone. Moreover these statements do not disclose all the relevant and required information. Further, financial statements suffer from certain inherent limitations. In order to obtain relevant and material information for knowing the strength and weakness of an organisation, analysis and interpretation of financial statements is felt necessary. Analysis and interpretation of financial statement refers to a systematic and constant effort to determine the significance and meaning of the financial statements to enable forecasting profitability, solvency, and prospects of future earning. It is designated to be the last of the four major steps of accounting which involves presentation of information that aids business managers and a large mumber of external parties such as investors, creditors, security analysts, Government and so on.

MEANING, DEFINITION AND IMPORTANCE OF ANALYSIS AND INTERPRETATION OF FINANCIAL STATEMENTS

Analysis of financial statement refers to the art of applying various tools to know the behaviour of the accounting information. It is defined by Metcalf as the "Process of evaluating the relationship between component parts of a financial statement to obtain a better understanding of a firm's position and performance." According to Kennedy and Muller, "Analysis and interpretation of financial statements are an attempt to determine the significance and meaning of the financial statements data so that the forcast may be made of the prospects for future earnings, ability to pay interest and debt maturities and profitability of a sound dividend policy." In the words of Myers, "Financial statement analysis is largely a study of relationship among various financial factors in a business as disclosed by a single set of statements and a study of the trends of these factors as shown in a series of statements." Analysis of financial statements may be compared to x-raying the financial position to diagnose the financial strength and weakness of the business.

Interpretation of financial statements refers to evaluating the performance of the business. According to F. Wood, "To interpret means to put the meaning of a statement in simple terms for the benefit of a person." It may be defined as critical examination of financial statements for a given period.

Differences between Analysis and Interpretation of financial statements

Analysis and interpretation though used synonymously, are not same. They differ in the following respects:

1. The term analysis is used in narrow sense. Whereas the term interpretation is used in a broad sense to include analysis.

2. Analysis is the first step whereas interpretation follows analysis.
3. Analysis implies classification of facts or data in a logical order. It involves splitting the complex data into various simple elements. Whereas interpretation implies explaining the meaning and significance of the facts or data so classified.

However it can be concluded that analysis and interpretation are complementary to each other. Analysis without interpretation is useless and interpretation becomes difficult without analysis.

IMPORTANCE OF ANALYSIS AND INTERPRETATION

The importance of analysis and interpretation of financial statements may be outlined under the following points:

1. Any decision taken on the basis of intution may prove to be wrong. To avoid wrong decision making it is always desireable to analyse and interpret the quantitative data. Decisions based on analysis and interpretation which is done systematically will never prove to be wrong and misleading.
2. All people may not possess knowledge and experience of understanding the financial statements in its raw-form. It can be easily understood even by layman when they are analysed and interpreted.
3. Analysis and interpretation is necessary to verify the correctness and accuracy of the decision made which must have been taken on the basis of intution.

STEPS INVOLVED IN ANALYSIS AND INTERPRETATION OF FINANCIAL STATEMENTS

Analysis and interpretation is one of the important functions of management accountant. It is not only interesting but a significant function of management accountant. In fact it may be regarded as an art as it requires good understanding and experience in this regard. The following steps are involved in the process of analysing and interpreting financial statements :

1. Analysis: Generally information presented in financial statements relate to individual accounts or group balances of many accounts. This leads to lack of homogenity and uniformity. In order to facilitate easy interpretation of information, the data is to be rearranged and reclassified. This process of methodical arrangement of presented data is known as analysis of financial statements. In this process it involves splitting of total items into various component parts. For example, if the short term solveney position of a business is to be known, it is necessary to know the current assets and current liabilities. The component of current assets can be known by analysing the asset side of the balance sheet and segregate current assets from various other components of balance sheet. Similarly, the current liabilities can be known by segregating it from other components of liability side of the balance sheet. In this way analysis includes regrouping or reclassifying of data into homogenous and comparable component parts.

2. Comparision: After division of facts into various components and sub-components, the second step involved is the comparision of figures. This step involves measuring the magnitude of the figures and knowing the extent of relationship between them. Only then it is possible to interpret the analysed data.

3. Study of trend: Having analysed and compared the magnitude of figures, the next step is to observe the data over a period of time. This study reveals the trend and the trend analysis helps in formulating a rational judgement about the performance of a business.

4. Interpretation: The process of drawing conclusions about the financial condition of a business is known as interpretation of financial statements. On the basis of findings a rational judgement is made when submitted in the form of report.

5. Criticism: Closely associated with the step of interpretation is the criticism. It may take two forms.

(*a*) **Criticism as to the form:** This goes to suggest whether the financial statements prepared is according to the law laid down by an Act. In India, the final accounts of Banking companies are to be prepared along with supportive schedules and according to the prescribed mode as required by Banking Companies Act.

(*b*) **Criticism as to reliability:** This goes to suggest that the information furnished is reliable or not. To know the reliability of accounts it is to be ensured that (*i*) Whether adequate provision is made for depreciation (*ii*) Assets are valued on a sound basis (*iii*) Deferred expenditure is gradually written off and so on.

PROCEDURE OF ANALYSIS AND INTERPRETATION

The procedure involved in the process of analysis and interpretation may be outlined as under:

1. As the technique and tools of analysis depends upon the object of analysis and interpretation, at the outset the purpose and extent of analysis is to be determined.
2. To study all data presented in financial statement for a clear understanding.
3. Collect additional information if need be for proper interpretation.
4. Divide and sub-divide the components according to their resemblences.
5. Use proper tools for analysis such as comparative statements, trend analysis etc., depending upon the purpose of interpretation.
6. Interpret the data and draw conclusions therefrom.
7. Prepare report incorporating the conclusions drawn.

Objectives of Analysis and Interpretation of Financial Statements

The objectives of financial statement analysis are as under:

1. To highlight the present and future earning capacity and the profitability of the concern.
2. To show the efficiency of the concern as a whole and department-wise.
3. To determine the solvency of the firm, both short term and long term.
4. To facilitate inter-firm and intra-firm comparisions.
5. To help in preparation of budgets.
6. To help in assessing the long term liquidity position of funds.

Types of Analysis and Interpretation of Financial Statements: Financial analysis is classified on the basis of materials used and modus operandi of the analysis. This is shown below:

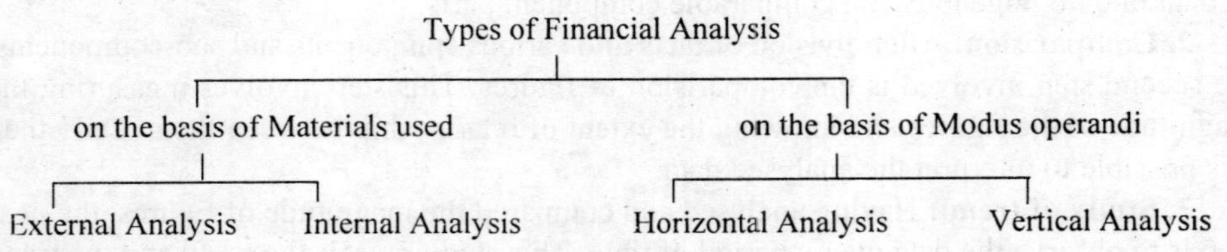

1. External analysis: Such type of analysis is made by outsiders who have no access to the books of accounts. They constitute investors, creditors, credit agencies and government agencies. As they dont have access to the books of accounts they have to depend on the published accounts for the purpose of analysis. However government regulation requiring auditing of accounts has made published accounts more reliable and dependable. As compared to internal analysis, external analysis is not done in detail and hence it serves limited purpose.

2. Internal analysis: It is done by those parties in the business who have access to books of account. Such parties can be designated as Accountant, Financial analyst. Some times it can also be done by employees to know the performance of the business. Internal analysis is done in more detail when compared to external analysis.

3. Horizontal analysis: When financial analysis is done for number of years, it is known as horizontal analysis. Such analysis sets a trend wherein the figures of various years are compared with one standard year known as base year. Based on the trend prevailing it is possible to make decision and form a rational judgement about the progress of the business. This type of analysis is also known as dynamic analysis as it measures the change of position of the business over a member of years.

4. Vertical analysis: When analysis is made for data covering one year's period it is known as vertical analysis. This type is also known as static analysis as it measures the state of affairs of the business as on given period of time. This type of analysis is useful in comparing the performance of serveral firms belonging to the same industry or various departments belonging to the same company.

Limitations of Financial Analysis

1. Because of the inflationary trend, the financial statements based on historical costs cannot be taken as an indicator for future forecasting and planning.
2. Analysis of financial statements is a tool which if used by an unskilled analyst may lead to faulty conclusions.
3. Financial statements are only interim reports and cannot be taken as final as the ultimate result of the business can be known only when the business is closed down. So analysis of these statements will not serve as conclusive evidence of the performance of the business.
4. The reliability of analysis depend upon the accuracy of the figures used in the financial statements. The analysis is distorted when the financial statements are manipulated by the accountant.
5. The results derived from analysis may be differently interpreted by different users.
6. The analysis of one year's statement will have limited use. Unless analysis is done for number of years it is not possible to compare so as to arrive at a meaningful conclusion.
7. When different firms belonging to same industry use different accounting procedures and policies the comparision will be difficult. This will not provide a reliable basis to know the performance of the industry as a whole.
8. A large number of tools are available for analysis and interpretation. Accordingly the results vary depending upon the type of tool used by the Accountant.

Tools or Techniques or Methods of Financial Analysis

For analysing the financial data and interpreting them in a systematic manner, a number of techniques or tools are available. These are as follows:

1. Comparative financial statements.
2. Common-size statement analysis.
3. Trend analysis.
4. Average analysis.
5. Ratio analysis.
6. Fund flow analysis.
7. Cash flow analysis.

1. Comparative Financial Statements: These are statements indicating the direction of movement with respect to financial position and operating results. They are very useful to the analyst because they contain not only the data appearing in a single statement but also information necessary for the study of financial and operating trends over a period of years. Comparative statements may be made to show:

(*a*) Absolute data (money values or rupee amounts).
(*b*) Increases or decreases in absolute data in terms of money values.
(*c*) Increases or decreases in absolute data in terms of percentages.
(*d*) Comparisions expressed in ratios.
(*e*) Percentage of totals.

The comparative financial statements as the name itself suggests enable comparision of financial information for two or more years placed side by side. From this it is possible to appraise, the performance, position and efficiency of business. The importance of comparative financial statement is recognised by the Indian Companies Act 1956. It makes obligatory for all companies to prepare the final accounts of companies by presenting current years as well as previous years figures.

The more common types of comparative statements are (*a*) Comparative Balance Sheet (*b*) Comparative income statement (*c*) Comparative statement of working capital and (*d*) Comparative statement of Manufacturing costs.

A comparative balance sheet is prepared to know change of Assets liabilities and capital of the business on two different dates. The changes may relate to an increase or decrease in any of the items. It contains columns for (*a*) Absolute data for the previous year (*b*) For absolute data for the current year (*c*) Changes in the items of Balance Sheet (*d*) Change in items of Balance Sheet expressed in percentages.

Similarly a comparative income statement is prepared to compare all items of profit and loss a/c and thus to know the increase or decrease in the items. By looking into the changes in expenditure and revenues it is possible to know the operating efficiency of the business.

Problem 1 (Comparative Income Statement): The following are the income statements of Swadeshi Cotton Mills for the years 2000 and 2001. Prepare comparative income statement and comment on the profitability of the company.

	2000	*2001*		*2000*	*2001*
To opening stock	85,000	2,00,000	By Sales less Returns	10,00,000	12,00,000
To purchases less returns	5,00,000	5,50,000	By closing stock	2,00,000	2,25,000
To Wages	60,000	80,000	By Income received from Investment	12,000	15,000

To Salaries	42,000	64,000	By Dividend received	5,000	7,500
To Rent, rates and insurance	35,000	40,000			
To Depreciation	40,000	60,000			
To Selling expenses	12,000	12,000			
To Discount allowed	5,000	7,000			
To Loss on sale of plant	–	8,000			
To Interest paid	12,000	14,000			
To Net profit	4,26,000	4,12,500			
	12,17,000	14,47,500		12,17,000	14,47,500

Solution:

Comparative Income Statement

		2000	*2001*	*Absolute change*	*Percentage Increase or Decrease*
Net	Sales	10,00,000	12,00,000	+ 2,00,000	+ 20%
Less:	Cost of goods sold (see working note)	4,45,000	6,05,000	+ 1,60,000	+ 35.9%
	Gross profit	5,55,000	5,95,000	+ 40,000	+ 5.41
Less:	Operating expenses:				
	Salaries	42,000	64,000	+ 22,000	+ 52.38%
	Rent, rates, insurance	35,000	40,000	+ 5,000	+ 14.29%
	Depreciation	40,000	60,000	+ 20,000	+ 50.%
	Selling expenses	12,000	12,000	–	–
	Discount allowed	5,000	7,000	+ 2,000	+ 40%
		1,34,000	1,83,000	49,000	+ 36.56%
	Operating profit	4,21,000	4,12,000	– 9,000	– 2.14%
Add:	Non-operating income:				
	Income from investment	12,000	15,000	+ 3,000	+ 25%
	Dividend received	5,000	7,500	+ 2,500	+ 50%
		17,000	22,500	+ 5,500	+ 32.35%
Less:	Non-operating expenses:				
	Loss on sale of plant	–	8,000	+ 8,000	+ 100%
	Interest paid	12,000	14,000	+ 2,000	+ 16.67%
		12,000	22,000	+ 10,000	+ 83.33%
Net	Profit	4,26,000	4,12,500	– 13,500	– 3.17%

Working Note:

Calculation of cost of goods sold:

		2000	*2001*
	Opening stock	85,000	2,00,000
Add:	Purchases	5,00,000	5,70,000
Add:	Wages	60,000	80,000
		6,45,000	8,30,000
Less:	Closing stock	2,00,000	2,25,000
Cost of goods sold		4,45,000	6,05,000

Interpretation:

1. Gross profit has shown an increase in 2001 but it is not commensurete with the increase in sales. The reason is increased cost of goods sold in 2001.
2. Among operating expenses the salary and depreciation have increased substantially. This is responsible for reduction in operating profit.
3. The total non-operating expenses is less in 2001 when compared to non-operating income in both the years.
4. Net profit decreased in 2001 when compared to 2000.

Problem 2: Following income statements of South India Metal Co. Ltd. are given for the years ending 2000 and 2001 prepare a multi-stage comparative income statement and interpret the changes.

Income statement

	2000	*2001*		*2000*	*2001*
To Cost of goods sold	9,00,000	9,50,000	By Sales	15,25,000	17,00,000
To Administration expenses	93,250	95,980	By Dividends	7,500	6,200
To Selling expenses	1,90,000	2,09,000	By profit from		
To Interest period	8,000	7,000	sale of land	6,000	8,000
To Loss on sale of machinery	2,500	800			
To Income tax	85,000	1,68,000			
To Net profit	2,59,750	2,83,420			
	15,38,500	17,14,200		15,38,500	17,14,200

Solution:

Comparative Income Statement

		2000	*2001*	*Increase or Decrease*	*Percentage change*
Sales		15,25,000	17,00,000	+ 1,75,000	+ 11.47%
Less:	Cost of sales	9,00,000	9,50,000	+ 50,000	+ 5.5%
	Gross profit	6,25,000	7,50,000	1,25,000	
Less:	Operating expenses:				
	Administration	93,250	95,980	+ 2,730	+ 2.93%
	Selling	1,90,000	2,09,000	+ 19,000	+ 10%
		2,83,250	3,04,980	+ 21,730	+ 7.67%
	Operating profit	3,41,750	4,45,020	1,03,270	
Add:	Non-operating Income:				
	Interest and Dividend	7,500	6,200	– 1,300	– 17.33%
	Profit from sale of land	6,000	8,000	+ 2,000	+ 33.33%
		13,500	14,200	+ 700	+ 5.18%
	Total Income	3,55,250	4,59,220	+ 1,03,970	
Less:	Non-operating expenses:				
	Loss on sale of Machinery	2,500	800	– 1,700	– 68%
	Income tax	85,000	1,68,000	+ 83,000	+ 92.9%
		87,500	1,68,800	81,300	+ 92.69%
	Net profit	2,67,750	2,90,420	+ 22,670	

Interpretation:

1. The increase in sales is to the extent of Rs. 1,75,000, while cost of sales increased by a sum of Rs. 50,000. The gross profit is increased by Rs. 1,25,000. This is a good indication of profitability.
2. Non-operating expenses is very high (Rs. 81,300), when compared to non-operating income (Rs. 700). This is responsible for decrease in profit.
3. Tax has gone up in 2001 by Rs. 83,000, which is also responsible for decrease in net profit.

Problem 3: From the following income statements extracted from the books of Aravind Parimal Works for the year 2000 and 2001 prepare comparative income statement and interpret the results of the business.

Income Statement (Rs. 000)

	2000	*2001*		*2000*	*2001*
To Opening stock	40.0	92.3	By sales	510.0	725.0
To Purchases	210.0	280.0	By closing stock	98.5	105.0
To Wages	25.0	32.0	By Discount	5.0	–
To Salaries	20.5	22.0	By Interest on investment	5.5	8.0
To Rent, rates and taxes	17.8	18.1	By Interest on bank deposit	5.0	7.2
To Selling expenses	5.8	6.1			
To Distribution expenses	3.2	3.9			
To Loss on sale of investment	–	10.0			
To Interest paid	7.0	7.5			
To Depreciation	35.0	40.0			
To Net profit	250.7	326.82			
	615.0	838.72		615.00	838.72

Solution:

Comparative Income Statement

		2000	*2001*	*Absolute change (Increase or Decrease)*	*Percentage change*
Net Sales		5,10,000	7,25,000	+ 2,15,000	+ 42.16%
Less:	Cost of goods sold (See working note)	1,76,500	2,99,300	+ 1,22,800	+ 69.58%
	Gross profit	3,33,500	4,25,700	+ 92,200	+ 27.65%
Less:	Operating expenses:				
	Salaries	20,500	22,000	+ 1,500	+ 7.32
	Rent, Rates, and Taxes	17,800	18,100	+ 300	+ 1.69
	Selling expenses	5,800	6,100	+ 300	+ 5.17
	Distribution expenses	3,200	3,900	+ 700	+ 21.88
	Depreciation	35,000	40,000	+ 5,000	+ 14.29
	Total operating expenses	82,300	90,100	+ 7,800	+ 9.48
		2,51,200	3,35,600	84,400	+ 18.17%
Add:	Operating Income: Discount	500	–	– 500	– 100%
	Operating profit	2,51,700	3,35,600	+ 83,900	+ 33.33%

Less:	Non-operating expenses and losses:				
	Interest paid	7,000	7,500	+ 500	+ 7.14%
	Loss on sale of Investment	–	10,000	+ 10,000	
		7,000	17,500	+ 10,500	+ 150
		2,44,700	3,18,100	+ 73,400	+ 30.0%
Add:	Non-operating Incomes:				
	Interest on Investment	5,500	8,000	+ 2,500	+ 45.45%
	Interest on Bank Deposits	500	720	+ 220	+ 44.00%
	Total Non-operating incomes	6,000	8,720	+ 2,720	+ 45.33%
	Profit before tax	2,50,700	3,26,820	+ 76,120	+ 30.36
Less:	Tax @ 50%	1,25,350	1,63,410	+ 38,060	+ 30.36
	Profit after tax	1,25,350	1,63,410	+ 38,060	+ 30.36

Working Note:

Calculation of cost of goods sold

		2000	*2001*
	Opening stock	40,000	92,300
Add:	Purchases	2,10,000	2,80,000
		2,50,000	3,72,300
Add:	Direct Wages	25,000	32,000
		2,75,000	4,04,300
Less:	Closing stock	98,500	1,05,000
	Cost of goods sold	1,76,500	2,99,300

Interpretation :

1. Though sales have increased by 42.16%. the gross profit increase is only by 27.65%. This is on account of rise in the cost of goods sold *i.e.*, 69.58%.
2. Operating expenses have increased only marginally, *i.e.*, by 9.48% which is justified with the increase in sales.
3. There is a considerable increase in non-operating income by 45.33%. This is partly responsible for increased percentage of net profit.
4. Profitability has increased in 2001 as compared to 2000 *i.e.*, by 30.36%.

Problem 4: Khaitan Fans Ltd. submitted the following particulars for the year ended 31.3.2001. Prepare a comparative income statement for the year ended 31st March 2001 for the first four quarters.

1. Sales for the first four quarters is estimated as Rs. 2,50,000, Rs. 2,10,000, Rs. 3,00,000 and Rs. 3,60,000.
2. Selling expenses are 2% and Distribution expenses are 25% of the selling expenses.
3. Cost of goods Sold-Fixed cost Rs. 40,000 fixed per quarter and variable expenses 12 1/2% of selling price.
4. Rent per quarter is Rs. 10,000 and in the last quarter an increase of 5%.
5. Administrative expenses for the first quarter is 37,250 and thereafter 5% increase of the preceding quarters expenses.
6. At the beginning of the second quarter the company borrowed a loan of Rs. 2,50,000. @ 9% and the interest is payable quarterly.
7. Rate of Tax is 25% for the first 2 quarters and 20% of the next two.

Solution:

Calculation of cost of goods sold

Working Note:

	I Qr	II Qr	III Qr	IV Qr
(1) *Fixed cost*	40,000	40,000	40,000	40,000
Add: Variable cost				
$12\frac{1}{2}$% on sales	31,250	26,250	37,500	45,000
Cost of goods sold	71,250	66,250	77,500	85,000
(2) *Rent*	10,000	10,000	10,000	10,000
Add: Increase of 5% in the last	–	–	–	500
quarter	10,000	10,000	10,000	10,500
(3) *Administrative Cost:*				
Ist quarter	37,500			
IInd quarter				
$37{,}500 + \left(37{,}500 \times \frac{10}{100}\right)$		41,250		
IIIrd quarter				
$41{,}250 + \left(41{,}250 \times \frac{10}{100}\right)$			45,375	
IVth quarter				
$45{,}375 + \left(45{,}375 \times \frac{10}{100}\right)$				49,912
(4) *Selling Cost:*				
2% on sales				
Ist quarter	5,000			
$\left(\frac{2}{100} \times 2{,}50{,}000\right)$				
IInd quarter		4,200		
$\left(\frac{2}{100} \times 2{,}10{,}000\right)$				
IIIrd quarter			6,000	
$\left(\frac{2}{100} \times 3{,}00{,}000\right)$				
IVth quarter				7,200
$\left(\frac{2}{100} \times 3{,}60{,}000\right)$				
(5) *Distribution Cost*:				
25% of Selling cost				
I Quarter	1,250			

$\left(\frac{25}{100} \times 5,000\right)$

II Quarter 1,050

$\left(\frac{25}{100} \times 4,200\right)$

III Quarter 1,500

$\left(\frac{25}{100} \times 6,000\right)$

IV Quarter 1,800

$\left(\frac{25}{100} \times 7,200\right)$

(6) Interest on loan:

II Quarter, III Quarter, IV Quarter: $2,50,000 \times \frac{9}{100} \times \frac{3}{12} = 5,625$

Comparative Income Statement

		I Qr	II Qr	III Qr	IV Qr
	Sales	2,50,000	2,10,000	3,00,000	3,60,000
Less:	Cost of goods sold	71,250	66,250	77,500	85,000
	Gross profit	1,78,750	1,43,750	2,22,500	2,75,000
Less:	Operating expenses:				
	Rent	10,000	10,000	10,000	10,500
	Administrative cost	37,500	41,250	45,375	49,912
	Selling cost	5,000	4,200	6,000	7,200
	Distribution cost	1,250	1,050	1,500	1,800
		53,750	56,500	62,875	69,412
	Operating profit	1,25,000	87,250	1,59,625	2,05,588
Less:	Non-operating expenses:				
	Interest paid	–	5,625	5,625	5,625
	Profit before Tax	1,25,000	81,625	15,4,000	1,99,963
Less:	Tax	31,250	20,406	30,800	39,993
	Profit After Tax	93,750	61,219	1,23,200	1,59,970

Problem 5 (Comparative Position Statement): Following are the Balance Sheets of a company for the years 1997 and 1998. Prepare a comparative balance sheet and explain the financial position of the concern.

Balance Sheet as on

	1997	*1998*		*1997*	*1998*
Share capital	3,00,000	4,00,000	Land and Buildings	1,85,000	1,35,000
Reserves and surplus	1,65,000	1,11,000	Plant and Machinery	2,00,000	3,00,000
Debentures	1,00,000	1,50,000	Furniture and Fixtures	10,000	12,500
Long term loan	75,000	1,00,000	Other Fixed assets	12,500	15,000
Bills payable	25,000	12,500	Cash at Bank	10,000	40,000

Creditors	50,000	60,000	Bills Receivable	75,000	46,000
Other current liabilities	2,500	5,000	Debtors	1,00,000	1,25,000
			Stock	1,25,000	1,75,000
	7,17,500	8,48,500		7,17,500	8,48,500

(*Osamania University, B. Com., October 1999*)

Solution:

Comparative Balance Sheet for the years ending 31st Dec. 1997 and 98

	1997	*1998*	*Increase/ Decrease (Rs.)*	*Increase/ Decrease (%)*
Assets:				
Fixed Assets:				
Land and Building	1,85,000	1,35,000	– 50,000	– 27.03
Plant and Machinery	2,00,000	3,00,000	+ 1,00,000	+ 50
Furniture and Fixture	10,000	12,500	+ 2,500	+ 25
Other fixed Assets	12,500	15,000	+ 2,500	+ 20
Total Fixed Assets	4,07,500	4,62,500	+ 55,000	+ 13.49
Current Assets:				
Cash of Bank	10,000	40,000	+ 30,000	+ 300
Bills Receivable	75,000	46,000	– 29,000	– 39
Debtors	1,00,000	1,25,000	+ 25,000	+ 25
Stock	1,25,000	1,75,000	+ 50,000	+ 40
Total Current Assets	3,10,000	3,86,000	+ 76,000	+ 24.52
Total assets	7,17,500	8,48,500	+ 1,31,000	+ 18.26
Liabilities:				
Equity share capital	3,00,000	4,00,000	+ 1,00,000	+ 33
Reserves and Surplus	1,65,000	1,11,000	– 54,000	– 32.73
Total	4,65,000	5,11,000	– 46,000	– 11.61
Debentures	1,00,000	1,50,000	+ 50,000	+ 50
Long term loans	75,000	1,00,000	+ 25,000	+ 33
Total				
Bills payable	25,000	22,500	– 2,500	– 10
Creditors	50,000	60,000	+ 10,000	+ 20
Other current liabilities	2,500	5,000	+ 2,500	+ 100
Total	2,52,500	3,37,500	+ 85,000	+ 33.60
Total capital and liabilities	7,17,500	8,48,500	+ 1,31,000	+ 18.26

Interpretation:

1. There is an increase in Fixed Assets in the year 1998 compared to 1997. This is as compared to long term liabilities and Share Capital which shows an increase of 75,000 (50,000 + 25,000) and Rs. 1,00,000 respectively. The company has bought fixed assets out of long term finds. The working capital is not affected.
2. Current assets show an increase of 24.52%. Whereas current liabilities show an increase of Rs. 10,000 (i.e., 12.9%). The liquidity position is therefore considered to be good.
3. Reserves and surplus has decreased by 32.73%. The company might have utilised the reserve for the issue of bouns shares or for the payment of dividend.

Problem 6: The following are the balance sheets for the year 1991 and 1992. Prepare comparative balance sheet and comment on the financial position.

Liabilities:	*1991*	*1992*
6% preference shares	30,000	30,000
Equity Share Capital	40,000	40,000
Reserves	20,000	24,500
Outstanding Tax	10,000	15,000
Sundry creditors	15,000	20,000
Bills payable	5,000	7,500
Debentures	10,000	15,000
	1,30,000	1,52,000

Assets:		
Land	10,000	10,000
Buildings	30,000	27,000
Plant	30,000	27,000
Furniture	10,000	14,000
Stock	20,000	30,000
Debtors	20,000	30,000
Cash	10,000	14,000
	1,30,000	1,52,000

(*S. V. University, B. Com., April 1999*)

Solution:

Comparative Balance Sheet

	1991	*1992*	*Absolute change*	*Percentage change*
I. *Assets*:				
(1) Current Assets:				
Stock	20,000	30,000	+ 10,000	+ 50%
Debtors	20,000	30,000	+ 10,000	+ 50%
Cash	10,000	14,000	+ 4,000	+ 40%
Total Current Assets	50,000	74,000	+ 24,000	+ 48%
(2) Fixed Assets:				
Land	10,000	10,000	–	–
Buildings	30,000	27,000	– 3,000	– 10%
Plant	30,000	27,000	– 3,000	– 10%
Furniture	10,000	14,000	+ 4,000	+ 40%
Total Fixed Assets	80,000	78,000	– 2,000	– 2.50%
Total Assets (1 + 2)	1,30,000	1,52,000	+ 22,000	+ 16.92
II. *Liabilities*:				
(1) Current liabilities:				
Creditors	15,000	20,000	+ 5,000	+ 33.33%
Bills payable	5,000	7,500	+ 2,500	+ 50
O/s Tax	10,000	15,000	+ 5,000	+ 50
Total Current liabilities	30,000	42,500	+ 12,500	+ 41.66%

(2) Long term loans:				
Debentures	10,000	15,000	+ 5,000	+ 50%
	10,000	15,000	+ 5,000	+ 50%
(3) Shareholders Funds:				
Preference Share Capital	30,000	30,000	–	–
Equity Share Capital	40,000	40,000	–	–
Reserves	20,000	24,500	+ 4,500	+ 22.5%
Total Shareholders Funds	90,000	94,500	+ 4,500	+ 5%
Total of liabilities (1 + 2 + 3)	1,30,000	1,52,000	+ 22,000	+ 16.92

Working Notes:

$$\text{Calculation of percentage change} = \frac{\text{Absolute change}}{\text{Amount of previous year}} \times 100$$

$$\text{For example : } \frac{\text{Change in Current Asset}}{\text{Total Current Asset in 1991}} \times 100$$

$$= \frac{24{,}000}{50{,}000} \times 100 = 48\%$$

Similarly other percentages are calculated.

Interpretation:

As there is slight raise in current assets over current liabilities (48% – 41.66% = 6.33%). the financial position can be stated as satisfactory. The company has not shown much change in other aspects. It is still to make effort to gain further in its financial position.

Problem 7 (Comparative Position Statement in Vertical Form): Following are the Balance Sheets as on 31 December 1997 and 1998 of M/s Gautami Ltd.

	1997	*1998*		*1997*	*1998*
Equity Share Capital	1,00,000	1,50,000	Land and Building	80,000	75,000
General Reserve	60,000	10,000	Plant and Machinery	42,000	85,000
P & L a/c	5,000	30,000	Furniture and Fittings	7,000	6,000
Bank O.D	–	65,000	Investments	6,000	12,000
Mortgage loan (Secured on plant)	–	40,000	Stock	27,500	94,500
Provision for tax	10,000	15,000	Sundry Debtors	46,500	77,250
Sundry creditors	30,000	20,000	Cash	2,000	7,250
Bills payable	10,000	30,000	Preliminary expenses	4,000	3,000
	2,15,000	3,60,000		2,15,000	3,60,000

You are required to prepare:

1. Comparative Financial statements in vertical form and to.
2. Offer your comments there on.

(*University of Bombay, B. Com., October 1999*)

Solution: **Comparative Balance Sheet**

	1997	*1998*	*Absolute change*	*Percentage change*
Sources of Fund:				
(1) Shareholders fund:				
Equity share capital	1,00,000	1,50,000	+ 50,000	+ 50%

(2) Reserves and surplus:				
General reserve	60,000	10,000	– 50,000	– 83.33%
P & L a/c	5,000	30,000	+ 25,000	+ 5%
	65,000	40,000	– 25,000	+ 38.46%
Less: Preliminary expenses	4,000	3,000	1,000	– 25%
	61,000	37,000	– 24,000	– 39.34%
(3) Long term loan:				
Mortgage loan	–	40,000	+ 40,000	–
Total funds employed (1 + 2 + 3)	1,61,000	2,27,000	66,000	41%
Application of funds:				
Fixed Assets:				
Land and Buildings	80,000	75,000	– 5,000	6.25
Plant and Machinery	42,000	85,000	+ 43,000	+ 102.39%
Furniture and Fittings	7,000	6,000	– 1,000	14.29
(*A*)	1,29,000	1,66,000	37,000	28.68
Trade Investments (*B*)	6,000	12,000	6,000	100%
Current Assets:				
Stock	27,500	94,500	67,000	243.64
Debtors	46,500	77,250	30,750	66.13
Cash	2,000	7,250	5,250	262.5
(*C*)	76,000	1,79,000	1,03,000	135.53%
Current liabilities and provisions:				
Bank overdraft	–	65,000	+ 65,000	–
Sundry creditors	30,000	20,000	– 10,000	– 33.33%
Bills payable	10,000	30,000	+ 20,000	+ 200%
Provision for tax	10,000	15,000	5,000	+ 50%
(*D*)	50,000	1,30,000	80,000	+ 16.0
Working capital	26,000	49,000	23,000	88.46
Total Funds employed	1,61,000	2,27,000	66,000	+ 41

Interpretations:

1. During the year 1998 the bouns shares of Rs. 50,000 are issued by capitalising general reserves. Also new machines were purchased which was financed through mortgaged loan.
2. Increase in current assets is partly through the plouging back of profits in business and partly by bank overdraft and bills payable.
3. Proprietors funds in proportion to total assets have been reduced as during the year mortgage loan was taken.

Problem 8: From the following data prepare comparative balance sheets in vertical form as at 31-3-1998 and 31-3-1999 of M/s APJ Ltd.

	1998	*1999*		*1998*	*1999*
Share capital	70,000	80,000	Building	55,000	80,000
P & L a/c	20,000	20,000	Machinery	43,000	50,000
Debentures	20,000	30,000	Stock	25,000	5,000
Other secured loans	10,000	20,000	Debtors	15,000	10,000
Creditors	10,000	3,000	Cash	2,000	15,000

Bank O.D	8,000	4,000		
O/s Expenses	2,000	3,000		
	1,40,000	1,60,000	1,40,000	1,60,000

Also offer your comments.

(*University of Bombay, B. Com., April 1999*)

Solution: **Comparative Balance Sheet as at 31st March 1998-99**

	1998	*1999*	*Absolute change*	*Percentage change*
Sources of Funds:				
(*A*) Shareholders fund:				
Share capital	70,000	80,000	+ 10,000	+ 14.29
P & L a/c	20,000	20,000	–	–
	90,000	1,00,000	+ 10,000	11.11%
(*B*) Loan Funds:				
Debentures	20,000	30,000	+ 10,000	+ 50%
Other secured loans	10,000	20,000	+ 10,000	+ 100%
	30,000	50,000	+ 20,000	+ 66.67%
Total Funds (*A* + *B*)	1,20,000	1,50,000	30,000	25%
Application of Funds:				
(*A*) Fixed Assets:				
Building	55,000	80,000	+ 25,000	+ 45.55%
Machinery	43,000	50,000	+ 7,000	+ 16.28
	98,000	1,30,000	+ 32,000	+ 32.65%
(*B*) Current Assets:				
Stock	25,000	5,000	– 20,000	– 80%
Debtors	15,000	10,000	– 5,000	– 33 1/3%
Cash	2,000	15,000	+ 13,000	+ 650%
	42,000	30,000	– 12,000	– 28.57%
(*C*) Current liabilities:				
Creditors	10,000	3,000	– 7,000	– 70%
Overdraft	8,000	4,000	– 4,000	– 50%
O/s expenses	2,000	3,000	1,000	+ 50%
	20,000	10,000	– 10,000	– 50%
Working capital (*B* – *C*) = *D*	22,000	20,000	– 10,000	– 50%
Total funds *A* + *D*	1,20,000	1,50,000	30,000	+ 25%

Interpretation:

1. Long term funds and building both show increase but not machinery.
2. Current liabilities and current assets show significant decline implying less commercial activity.
3. The above factors collectively indicate that the company is in process of operation.

Problem 9: The following are the balance sheets of Hindustan Ltd. for the years ending 31st March 1993 and 1994.

	1993	1994
Equity share capital	4,00,000	6,60,000
Pref. share capital	2,00,000	3,00,000
Reserves	40,000	60,000
P & L a/c	30,000	40,000
Bank O.D	1,00,000	1,00,000
Creditors	80,000	1,00,000
Provision for taxation	40,000	50,000
Proposed dividend	30,000	50,000
	9,20,000	13,60,000
Fixed assets less depreciation	4,80,000	7,00,000
Stock	80,000	1,00,000
Debtors	2,00,000	2,50,000
Bills Receivable	40,000	1,20,000
Prepaid expenses	20,000	24,000
Cash in hand	80,000	1,06,000
Cash at Bank	20,000	60,000
	9,20,000	13,60,000

Prepare the comparative Balance sheet and study its financial position.

(S. V. University, B. Com., April 1998)

Solution: **Comparative Balance Sheet as on 1993 and 1994**

	1993	1994	Absolute change	Percentage change
Assets:				
(1) Fixed assets less depreciation	4,80,000	7,00,000	+ 2,20,000	+ 45.83%
(2) Current assets:				
Stock	80,000	1,00,000	+ 20,000	+ 25%
Debtors	2,00,000	2,50,000	+ 50,000	+ 25%
Bills Receivable	40,000	1,20,000	+ 80,000	+ 200%
Prepaid expenses	20,000	24,000	+ 4,000	+ 20%
Cash in hand	80,000	1,06,000	+ 26,000	+32.5%
Cash at Bank	20,000	60,000	+ 40,000	+ 200%
	4,40,000	6,60,000	+ 2,20,000	+50%
Total Assets (1 + 2)	9,20,000	13,60,000	+ 4,40,000	+ 47.83%
Liabilities:				
(1) Shareholders funds:				
Equity share capital	4,00,000	6,60,000	+ 2,60,000	+ 65%
Pref. share capital	2,00,000	3,00,000	+ 1,00,000	+ 33 1/3%
Reserves and Surplus				
Reserve	40,000	60,000	+ 20,000	+ 50%
P & L a/c	30,000	40,000	+ 10,000	+ 33 1/3%
	6,70,000	10,60,000	+ 3,90,000	+ 58.2%
(2) Current liabilities:				
Bank O.D	1,00,000	1,00,000	–	–
Creditors	80,000	1,00,000	+ 20,000	+ 25%
	1,80,000	2,00,000	+ 20,000	+ 11.1%

(3) Provisions:				
Provision for taxation	40,000	50,000	+ 10,000	+ 25%
Proposed Dividend	30,000	50,000	+ 20,000	+ 66.67%
	70,000	1,00,000	+ 30,000	+ 42.86%
Total liabilities (1 + 2 + 3)	9,20,000	13,60,000	+ 4,40,000	+ 47.83%

Interpretation:

1. Working capital has increased by Rs. (2,20,000 – 20,000) 2,00,000.
2. The raise of shareholders fund 58.2% (Rs. 3,90,000) was utilised to raise the fixed Assets 45.83% (Rs. 2,20,000) and utilised for working capital also.
3. The dividend payable to shareholders also has increased which will increase public confidence.

Problem 10 (Comparative Income Statement and Position Statement): From the following financial statements of Vaibhav Ltd. prepare comparative financial statements in vertical form.

Revnue Statement

	31-12-95	31-12-96		31-12-95	31-12-96
Cost of goods sold	6,00,000	7,50,000	Sales	8,00,000	10,00,000
Administrative expenses	30,000	40,000			
Selling expenses	20,000	20,000			
Net profit	1,50,000	1,90,000			
	8,00,000	10,00,000		8,00,000	10,00,000

Balance Sheet

	31-12-95	31-12-96		31-12-95	31-12-96
Equity share capital	4,00,000	4,00,000	Land	2,00,000	2,40,000
9% Pref. share capital	3,00,000	3,00,000	Building	6,00,000	5,40,000
General Reserve	2,00,000	2,45,000	Stock	2,00,000	3,00,000
Tax payable	1,00,000	1,50,000	Debtors	2,00,000	3,00,000
Creditors	2,00,000	2,75,000	Cash	1,00,000	1,40,000
17% Debentures	1,00,000	1,50,000			
	13,00,000	15,20,000		13,00,000	15,20,000

Briefly comment on the difference between the stated net profit of 1996 and the increment in general reserves on 31-12-96 assuming that no amount is paid towards tax in 1996.

Also Ascertain the quantum of cash gross profit of 1996, assuming that no depreciation is provided on Land. *(University of Bombay, B. Com., October 1997)*

Solution: **Comparative Income Statement**

	31-12-95	*31-12-96*	*Absolute change*	*Percentage change*
Sales	8,00,000	10,00,000	+ 2,00,000	25%
Less: Cost of Sales	6,00,000	7,50,000	+ 1,50,000	25%
Gross profit	2,00,000	2,50,000	+ 50,000	+ 25%
Less: Operating expenses:				
Administration expenses	30,000	40,000	+ 10,000	+ 33 1/3%
Selling expenses	20,000	20,000	–	–
	50,000	60,000	+ 10,000	+ 20%
Net operating profit	1,50,000	1,90,000	+ 40,000	26.67%

Comparative Balance Sheet

	31-12-95	*31-12-96*	*Absolute change*	*Percentage change*
Sources of Funds:				
(*A*) Shareholders funds:				
Equity share capital	4,00,000	4,00,000	–	–
9% pref. share capital	3,00,000	3,00,000	–	
	7,00,000	7,00,000		
(*B*) Reserves and surplus:				
General reserve	2,00,000	2,45,000	+ 45,000	+ 22.5%
	9,00,000	9,45,000	+ 45,000	+ 5%
(*C*) Long term liabilities:				
17% Debentures	1,00,000	1,50,000	+ 50,000	+ 50%
Total funds employed	10,00,000	10,95,000	+ 95,000	+ 9.5%
Applications of Funds:				
(*A*) Fixed Assets:				
Land	2,00,000	2,40,000	+ 40,000	+ 20%
Building	6,00,000	5,40,000	– 60,000	– 10%
	8,00,000	7,80,000	– 20,000	– 2.5%
(*B*) Currents Assets:				
Stock	2,00,000	3,00,000	+ 1,00,000	50%
Debtors	2,00,000	3,00,000	+ 1,00,000	50%
Cash	1,00,000	1,40,000	+ 40,000	40%
	5,00,000	7,40,000	+ 2,40,000	+ 48%
(*C*) Current liabilities:				
Tax payable	1,00,000	1,50,000	+ 50,000	50%
Creditors	2,00,000	2,75,000	+ 75,000	+ 37.50%
	3,00,000	4,25,000	1,25,000	41.67%
Working Capital (*B* – *C*) = *D*	2,00,000	3,15,000	1,15,000	41.67%
Total funds employed (*A* + *D*)	10,00,000	10,95,000	+ 95,000	+ 9.5%

Interpretation:

1. Net profit for the year 1996 has increased by 45,000.
2. There is no change in the capital structure of the company.
3. Value of building has decreased by Rs. 60,000 indicating the loss in the value of building. Alternatively it may taken to mean depreciation on building.

Problem 11: Circle and Square are carrying on partnership business. Their position as on 31st March 1995 and 1994 is as follows:

I. The Summarised Balance Sheet

	1995	*1994*		*1995*	*1994*
Capital a/cs.	71,750	59,500	Fixed Assets	52,500	43,750
Bank loan	14,000	10,500	Investments	3,500	1,750
Sundry creditors	38,500	35,000	Stock	21,000	17,500
			Sundry debtors	31,500	26,250
			Loans and advances	14,000	14,000
			Cash and bank balance	1,750	1,750
	1,24,250	1,05,000		1,24,250	1,05,000

II. Summarised Income Statement

		1995	*1994*
Net Sales		42,000	38,500
Less:	Cost of Sales	31,500	29,750
	Gross Margin	10,500	8,750
Less:	Operating expenses	8,750	7,000
	Net profit before Tax	1,750	1,750

(*University of Bombay, B.Com., April 1995*)

Solution:

Comparative Income Statement

		1994	*1995*	*Absolute change*	*Percentage change*
Sales		38,500	42,000	+ 3,500	+ 9.09
Less:	Cost of sales	29,750	31,500	– 1,750	+ 5.88
	Gross margin	8,750	10,500	1,750	+ 20%
Less:	Operating expenses	7,000	8,750	1,750	+ 25
	Net profit	1,750	1,750	–	–

Comparative Balance Sheet

	1994	*1995*	*Absolute change*	*Percentage change*
Sources of Funds:				
Capital a/cs.	59,500	71,750	+ 12,250	+ 20.59%
Loan funds	10,500	14,000	+ 3,500	+ 33.33%
Total funds employed	70,000	85,750	+ 15,750	+ 22.50%
Application of funds:				
Fixed Assets (*A*)	43,750	52,500	+ 8,750	+ 20%
Investments (*B*)	1,750	3,500	+ 1,750	+ 100%
Current Assets:				
Stock	17,500	21,000	+ 3,500	+ 20%
Debtors	26,250	31,500	+ 5,250	+ 20%
Loans and advances	14,000	14,000	–	–
Cash and bank	1,750	1,750	–	–
	59,500	68,250	+ 8,750	+ 14.71%
Current Liabilities:				
Creditors	35,000	38,500	+ 3,500	+ 10%
Working Capital (*C*)	24,500	29,750	+ 5,250	+ 21.43%
Total funds employed (*A* + *B* + *C*)	70,000	85,750	+ 15,750	+ 22.50%

Interpretation:

1. There is an increase in partners capital as well as loans in the firm. This is utilised in financing fixed assets.
2. There is no change in profit in 1995 as compared to 1994 which means that additional capital is used in financing working capital requirements of the business.
3. Cost of sales equals operating expenses. Again both cost of sales and operating expenses equals (1,750 + 1,750 = 3,500) sales. Thus there is no absolute increase in the profit.

2. Common-Size Financial Statement Analysis: They are comparative statements that give only the percentages for financial data without giving the rupee value. They are also known as 100 per cent statements because each statement is reduced to the total of 100 and each individnal item is stated as a percentage of the total of 100. Each percentage shows the relation of the individual items to its respective total. The common size financial statements are most valuable in making comparisions between the firms in the same industry. The two common-size financial statements usually prepared are: (*a*) Common-size income statement and (*b*) Common-size balance sheet.

Computation of Common-size statements

1. In case of common-size income-statement, total net sales are stated as 100 per cent. In case of position statement either total assets or total of liabilities and capital is taken as 100.
2. The quotient of each item is found out by dividing individual money amount by the total amount in the statement. This is expressed in the form of percentage.

Illustration: If the selling expense in any particular year of a business is Rs. 60,000 and its net sales is Rs. 6,00,000 for that year, the above two steps may be illustrated as follows:

$$\frac{\text{Selling expenses}}{\text{Net Sales}} \times 100$$

$$= \frac{60,000}{6,00,000} \times 100 = 10\%$$

This denotes that selling expenses for that particular year is 10% of net sales or they amount to Rs. 10 for every Rs. 100 worth of sales.

Other items can also be incorporated in the statements in the same manner and similar conclusions can be drawn.

Problem 12 (Common-size Income Statement): Prepare common-size income statement in vertical form from the following income statement and briefly comment thereon.

P & L a/c for the year ended 31-3-99

To Cost of Sales	4,91,400	By Gross Sales	8,26,200
To Administrative expenses	81,000	Less Returns	16,200
			8,10,000
To Selling and distribution expenses	1,62,000	By Non-operating income	8,100
To Non-operating expenses	10,800		
To Tax provision	36,450		
To Proposed Dividend	7,000		
To Retained Earnings	29,450		
	8,18,100		8,18,100

(*University of Bombay, B. Com., October 1999*)

Solution:

Common-Size Income Statement

	Amount	*Percentage*
Sales	8,26,200	102
Less: Sales Returns	16,200	2
Net sales	8,10,000	100
Less: Cost of sales	4,91,400	60.67%
Gross profit	3,18,600	39.33%

Less: Operating expenses:			
Office & Adm. expenses	81,000		10%
Selling and Distribution expenses	1,62,000		20%
		2,43,000	
Net operating profit		75,600	9.33%
Add: Non-operating income		8,100	1%
		83,700	10.33%
Less: Non-operating expenses		10,800	0.133%
Net profit before Tax		72,900	9%
Less: Tax provision		36,450	4.50%
Net profit after Tax		36,450	4.50%
Less: Proposed Dividend		7,000	0.86%
Balance transferred to B/S		29,450	3.64%

Interpretation:

1. Operating expenses are high for a given cost of sales. This must be under check.
2. Non-operating expenses are high compared to non-operating income.
3. Rate of Dividend declared is very less (0.86%).

Problem 13: The following figures relate to the activities of R. R. Ltd, Mumbai for the year ending 31st march 1995.

Sales	7,50,000
Purchases	3,75,000
Opening stock	70,000
Closing stock	80,000
Administration Expenses:	
Salaries	37,000
Rent	12,000
Postage and Stationary	5,000
Provision for taxation	50,000
Selling and Distribution expenses:	
Salaries	18,000
Advertising	6,000
Commission on sales	7,500
Discount	2,000
Non-operating expenses:	
Interest	5,000
Loss on sale of assets	11,500
Non-operating income:	
Profit on sale of investments	9,500

You should study the income statement of the concern with the help of common-size statement.

(S. V. University, B. Com., October 1998)

Solution: **Common-Size Income-Statement of R. R. Ltd. for the year ended 31-3-1995**

		Amount	*Percentage*
Sales		7,50,000	100%
Less: Cost of goods sold:			
Opening stock	70,000		
Add: Purchases	3,75,000		
	4,45,000		

Less: Closing stock	80,000		
		3,65,000	48.67%
Gross profit		3,85,000	51.33%
Less: Operating expenses:			
Administration expenses:			
Salaries	37,000		
Rent	12,000		
Postage and stationary	5,000		
		54,000	7.20%
		3,31,000	44.13%
Selling and Distribution expenses:			
Salaries	18,000		
Advertising	6,000		
Commission on sales	7,500		
Discount	2,000		
		33,500	4.47
Operating profit		2,97,500	39.66%
Less: Non-operating expenses:			
Interest	5,000		0.67
Loss on sale of assets	11,500	16,500	1.53
		2,81,000	37.46%
Add: Non-operating Income:			
Profit on sale of investment		9,500	1.27%
Profit before Tax		2,90,500	38.73%
Less: Provision for Tax		50,000	6.67%
Profit after Tax		2,40,500	32.06

Interpretation:

1. Total operating expenses is 1/4th of cost of goods sold (*i.e.*, 87,500: 3,65,000). This is a satisfactory position.
2. Total Non-operating income is less than total non-operating expenses. This is not a satisfactory position.
3. Profitable percentage of 32.06% is considered to be good percentage.

Problem 14 (Common-Size Balance Sheet): Following are the Balance sheets of Vinay Ltd. for the year ended December 1996 and 1997.

Liabilities	*1996*	*1997*	*Assets*	*1996*	*1997*
Equity capital	1,00,000	1,65,000	Fixed Assets (Net)	1,20,000	1,75,000
Pref. capital	50,000	75,000			
Reserves	10,000	15,000	Stock	20,000	25,000
P & L a/c	7,500	10,000	Debtors	50,000	62,500
Bank O.D	25,000	25,000	Bills receivable	10,000	30,000
Creditors	20,000	25,000	Prepaid expense	5,000	6,000
Provision for Taxaction	10,000	12,500	Cash at Bank	20,000	26,500
Proposed dividend	7,500	12,500	Cash in hand	5,000	15,000
	2,30,000	3,40,000		2,30,000	3,40,000

Prepare a common-size balance sheet and interpret the same. (*Osmania University, B. Com., March 1999*)

Solution: **Common-size Balance Sheet of Vinay Ltd. for the year 1996 and 1997.**

	1996		1997	
	Rs.	%	Rs.	%
Assets				
Fixed Assets (Net) (*A*)	1,20,000	52.17	1,75,000	51.47
Current Assets:				
Stock	20,000	8.70	25,000	7.35
Debtors	50,000	21.74	62,500	18.38
Bills Receivable	10,000	4.34	30,000	8.82
Prepaid expenses	5,000	2.17	6,000	1.78
Cash at Bank	20,000	8.70	26,500	7.79
Cash in hand	5,000	2.18	15,000	4.41
Total (*B*)	1,10,000	47.83	1,65,000	48.53
Total Assets (*A* + *B*)	2,30,000	100.00	3,40,000	100
Liabilities:				
Capital and Reserves: (*A*)				
Equity capital	1,00,000	43.58	1,65,000	48.53
Preference capital	50,000	21.74	75,000	22.05
Reserves	10,000	4.34	15,000	4.41
P & L a/c	7,500	3.26	10,000	2.95
Total (*A*)	1,67,500	72.82	2,65,000	77.94
Current liabilities: (*B*)				
Bank overdraft	25,000	10.87	25,000	7.35
Creditors	20,000	8.70	25,000	7.35
Provision for taxation	10,000	4.35	12,500	3.68
Proposed dividend	7,500	3.26	12,500	3.68
Total (*B*)	62,500	27.18	75,000	22.06
Total liabilities (*A*) + (*B*)	2,30,000	100	3,40,000	100

Interpretation:

1. Current Assets increased from 47.83% to 48.53%. Whereas current liabilities decreased from 27.18% to 22.06%. The liquidity position is reasonably good.
2. Fixed assets increased from Rs. 1,20,000 to Rs. 1,75,000. They were purchased from the additional share capital issued.

Problem 15: Following are the Balance sheets of 'S' Ltd. for the year ending December 31, 1992 and 1993.

Liabilities	*1992*	*1993*
Equity share capital	40,000	60,000
Reserves and surplus	31,200	35,400
Debentures	5,000	10,000
Mortgage	15,000	25,500
Sundry creditor	25,500	11,700
Other current liabilities	700	1,000
	1,17,400	1,43,600
Assets:		
Land and Building	27,000	17,000
Plant and Machinery	31,000	78,600

Furniture and Fixtures	900	1,800
Other fixed assets	2,000	3,000
Long term loans	4,600	5,900
Cash in hand	11,800	1,000
Sundry Debtors	20,900	19,000
Inventory	16,000	13,000
Prepaid Expenses	300	300
Other current assets	2,500	4,000
	1,17,400	1,43,600

Analyse the financial position of the company with the help of common-size balance sheet.

(S. V. University, B. Com., October 1999)

Solution: **Comparative common-size Balance Sheets of 'S' Ltd. as on 31-12-92 and 31-12-93**

	1992		1993	
	Amount	*%*	*Amount*	*%*
Assets:				
(1) Fixed Assets:				
Land and Buildings	27,000	23%	17,000	11.84%
Plant and Machinery	31,000	26.40%	78,600	54.74%
Furniture and Fixtures	900	0.77%	1,800	1.25%
Other Fixed Assets	2,000	1.70%	3,000	2.08%
Total Fixed Assets	60,900	51.87%	1,00,400	69.91%
(2) Investments:				
Long term loans	4,600	3.92%	5,900	4.11%
(3) Current Assets:				
Cash in hand	11,800	10.05%	1,000	0.70%
Sundry Debtors	20,900	17.80%	19,000	13.23%
Inventory	16,000	13.63%	13,000	9.05%
Prepaid expenses	300	0.26%	300	0.21%
Other current assets	2,900	2.47%	4,000	2.79%
	51,900	44.21%	37,300	25.98%
Total Assets (1 + 2 + 3)	1,17,400	100%	1,43,600	100%
Liabilities:				
(1) Shareholders funds:				
Equity share capital	40,000	34.07%	60,000	41.78%
Reserves and Surplus	31,200	26.58%	35,400	24.65%
	71,200	60.65%	95,400	66.43%
(2) Long term Debts:				
Debentures	5,000	4.25%	10,000	6.96%
Mortgages	15,000	12.78%	25,500	17.76
	20,000	17.03%	35,500	24.72%
(3) Current liabilities:				
Sundry creditors	25,500	21.72%	11,700	8.15%
Other current liabilities	700	0.60%	1,000	0.70%
	26,200	22.32%	12,700	8.85%

Interpretation:

1. There is drastic fall in the working capital. In the year 1992 it was 21.89 (44.21 – 22.32) and in the year 1993 it was 17.13% (25.98 – 8.85).
2. The liquid assets also have come down which has adversely affected the business.
3. Fixed Assets have increased in 1993, the increase being 18.04% (69.91 – 51.87). This raise in fixed assets is financed partly by raising shareholder's funds and long term loans and partly by diversion from working capital, *i.e.*, 4.57%. The latter is not acceptable.
4. Reserves and Surplus have diminished in 1993, i.e., from 26.58% to 24.65%. This is not a welcome sign.

Problem 16 (Common-size Balance sheet–Vertical Method): Prepare a common-size balance sheet of M/s Ram Ltd. in vertical form from the following information and comment on it.

Balances as on 31.3.1999

	Rs.
Land and Building	6,00,000
Plant and Machinery	5,00,000
Equity capital	5,00,000
Preference capital	2,00,000
Stock	2,40,000
Debtors	2,00,000
Cash and Bank	55,000
Miscellaneous current assets	5,000
Profit and loss a/c (cr. balance)	2,00,000
General reserve	1,00,000
Sundry creditors	80,000
Bills payable	60,000
Miscellaneous current liabilities	60,000
Debentures	4,00,000

(*University of Bombay, B. Com., October 1999*)

Solution: **Common-size Balance Sheet as on 31-December 1999**

	Amount	*Percentage*
Sources of Funds:		
I. Shareholders funds:		
(*A*) Share capital–Equity	5,00,000	35.71%
–Preference	2,00,000	14.29%
(*A*)	7,00,000	50%
(*B*) Reserves and Surplus:		
P & L a/c	2,00,000	14.29%
General Reserve	1,00,000	7.14%
(*B*)	3,00,000	21.43%
II. Long term loan:		
Debentures	4,00,000	28.57
Total funds employed (*A* + *B* + *C*)	14,00,000	100%

Application of funds:		
(*A*) Fixed Assets:		
Land and Building	6,00,000	42.86%
Plant and Machinery	5,00,000	35.71%
(*A*)	11,00,000	78.57%
(*B*) Current Assets:		
Stock	2,40,000	17.14%
Debtors	2,00,000	14.29%
Cash and Bank55,000	5,500	3.93%
Miscellaneous current assets	5,000	0.36%
(*B*)	5,00,000	35.71%
(*C*) Current liabilities:		
Sundry creditors	80,000	5.71%
Bills payable	60,000	4.29%
Miscellaneous current liabilities	60,000	4.28%
(*C*)	2,00,000	14.28%
Working capital (*B* – *C*) = *D*	3,00,000	21.43%
Total funds employed *A* + *D*	14,00,000	100%

Interpretation:

1. Proprietors funds constitute 71.43% (50 + 21.43%) of total fund employed.
2. Fixed assets which constitute 78.57% are financed by proprietor's funds indicate sound financial position.
3. Currents assets are higher than current liabilities.

Problem 17 (Common-size Income and position statement): Shiv Leela Ltd. furnishes you with the following financial statement.

Balance sheet as on 31st March 1999

Liabilities		Assets		
Share capital:				
Equity	1,00,000	Building	2,00,000	
12% preference	50,000	Less Depreciation	15,000	
				1,85,000
Reserves and Surplus	35,000	Short term Investments		40,000
10% Debentures				
(Secured by Mortgage)	50,000			
Bills payable	15,000	Stock		35,000
Creditors for goods	20,000	Debtors		30,000
Outstanding expenses	10,000	Bank		10,000
Provision for taxation	10,000			
Proposed Dividend	10,000			
	3,00,000			3,00,000

Profit and Loss a/c for the year ended 31-3-1999

To Opening stock	30,000	By sales	3,00,000
To Purchases	1,80,000	By closing stock	35,000

To Expenses:		
Administration	25,000	
Selling	30,000	
Financing	5,000	
To Depreciation	150,000	
To Provision for Taxation	10,000	
To Proposed Dividend	10,000	
To Balance a/c	30,000	
	3,35,000	3,35,000

You are required to:

1. Convert the above into common-size statements in vertical form.
2. Comment on above briefly.

(University of Bombay, B. Com., April 1999)

Solution: **Common-size Income Statement for the year ended 31st March 1999**

			Amount	*Percentage*
Sales			3,00,000	100%
Less: Cost of goods sold				
Opening stock	30,000			
Add: Purchases	1,80,000			
	2,10,000			
Less: Closing stock	35,000			
			1,75,000	58.33%
Gross profit			1,25,000	41.67%
Less: Overheads:				
Administrative (25,000 + 15,000)		40,000		
Selling		30,000		
Financing		5,000		
			75,000	25.60%
Net profit before tax			50,000	16.67%
Less: Income tax			10,000	3.33%
Net profit after tax			40,000	13.34%
Less: Dividend			10,000	3.34%
Retained Earnings			30,000	10.00%

Interpretation:

1. **Gross profit is quite high as compared to overheads. This shows efficiency of business.**
2. **When compared to sales, cost of goods sold is 58.33% which indicates high profitability.**

Common-size Balance sheet for the year ended 31st March 1999

	Amount	*Percentage*
Sources of Funds:		
(1) Shareholders funds:		
Equity share capital	1,00,000	42.55%
12% preference share capital	50,000	21.28%
Reserves and Surplus	35,000	14.89%
	1,85,000	78.72%

(2) Loan funds:			
10% Debentures		50,000	21.28%
Total funds		2,35,000	100%
Application of funds:			
(1) Fixed Assets:			
Buildings	2,00,000		
Less Depreciation	15,000		
		1,85,000	78.72%
(2) Current Assets:			
Short term investments		40,000	17.02%
Stock		35,000	14.89%
Debtors		30,000	12.77%
Bank		10,000	4.26%
		1,15,000	48.94%
(3) Current liabilities:			
Creditors		20,000	8.51%
Bills payable		15,000	6.38%
Outstanding expenses		10,000	4.26%
Taxation		10,000	4.26%
Dividend		10,000	4.25%
		65,000	27.66%
Working capital (2 – 3) = 4		50,000	21.28%
Total funds (1 + 4)		2,35,000	100%

Interpretation:

1. Investment of proprietors funds is very high.
2. Fixed Assets are very high compared to current assets.
3. Current Ratio is high and it shows sound financial position.

TREND ANALYSIS OF TREND RATIOS

Trend ratios can be defined as the index numbers of the movements of the various financial items on the financial statement for a number of periods. It is a statistical device applied in the analysis of financial statements to reveal the trend of the items with the passage of time. They provide a horizontal analysis of comparative statements and reflect the behaviour of various items with passage of time. The trend ratios are the useful analytical device for management since by substitution of percentages for large amounts, the brevity and readability is achieved. It can be graphically presented for a better understanding by the management. They are very useful in predicting the behaviour of the various financial factors in future. Sometimes trends are significantly affected by external causes over which the organisation has no control. Such factors are Government policies, economic conditions, change in income and its distribution etc.

Points to be considered in calculation of trend ratios:

(*i*) The accounting principles and practices followed should be constant throughout the period for which analysis is made.

(*ii*) Trend ratios should be calculated only for items having logical relationship with one another.

(*iii*) There should be financial statement for a number of years.

(*iv*) Take one of the statements as the base with reference to which all other statements are to be studied but the selected base statements should belong to a normal year.

(*v*) Every item in the base statement should be stated as 100.

(*vi*) Trend Ratios of each item in other statement is calculated with reference to same item in the base statement by using the following formula.

$$\frac{\text{Absolute value of item in the statement under study}}{\text{Absolute value of the same item in base statement}} \times 100$$

Problem 18: From the following data, calculate trend percentage (taking 1995 as base).

	1995 Rs.	*1996* Rs.	*1997* Rs.
Sales	50,000	75,000	1,00,000
Purchases	40,000	60,000	72,000
Expenses	5,000	8,000	15,000
Profit	5,000	7,000	13,000

(*Osmania University, B. Com., March 1999*)

Solution:

Statement Showing Trend Percentages

Particulars	*1995* Rs.	*1996* Rs.	*1997* Rs.	*Trend percentages (Base 1995)*		
				1995	*1996*	*1997*
Purchases	40,000	60,000	72,000	100	150	180
Expenses	5,000	8,000	15,000	100	160	300
Profit	5,000	7,000	13,000	100	140	260
Sales	50,000	75,000	1,00,000	100	150	200

Problem 19: From the following data, calculate trend percentages (1995 as the base).

	1995 Rs.	*1996* Rs.	*1997* Rs.
Cash	200	240	160
Debtors	400	500	650
Stock	600	800	700
Other current asset	450	600	750
Land	800	1,000	1,000
Buildings	1,600	2,000	2,400
Plant	2,000	2,000	2,400

(*Osmania University, B. Com., October 1998*)

Solution: **Statement Showing Trend Percentages (Base year 1995)**

Assets	*1995*	*1996*	*1997*	*Trend percentages*		
	Rs.	*Rs.*	*Rs.*	*1995*	*1996*	*1997*
Fixed Assets:						
Land	800	1,000	1,000	100	125	125
Building	1,600	2,000	2,400	100	125	150
Plant	2,000	2,000	2,400	100	100	120
Total	4,400	5,000	5,800	100	114	132
Current Assets:						
Cash	200	240	160	100	120	80
Debtors	400	500	650	100	125	163
Stock	600	800	700	100	133	117
Other current assets	450	600	750	100	133	167
Total current assets	1,650	2,140	2,260	100	130	137

Problem 20: Calculate Trend percentages from the following information extracted from the financial statements of different entities. Give your appropriate comments on each statement.

(*a*) *Assets:*	*1992*	*1993*	*1994*	*1995*
	Rs.	*Rs.*	*Rs.*	*Rs.*
Fixed Assets	2,11,696	2,08,694	2,04,580	1,84,122
Investments	20,000	15,000	10,000	9,000
Cash in hand	41,680	30,472	20,346	18,312
Sundry Debtors	1,85,040	1,31,346	85,750	77,175
Stock	1,31,474	1,34,684	1,45,172	1,30,655
Prepaid expenses	1,690	3,236	2,440	2,196
	5,91,580	5,23,432	4,68,288	4,21,460
Liabilities:				
Sundry creditors	1,40,712	1,32,684	1,17,410	1,05,669
Liability for expenses	5,640	4,094	2,490	2,240
Share capital	4,45,228	3,86,654	3,48,388	3,13,551
	5,91,580	5,23,432	4,68,288	4,21,460

(*b*)	*1994*	*1995*	*1996*	*1997*
	Rs.	*Rs.*	*Rs.*	*Rs.*
Sales	9,880	13,640	16,400	18,040
Cost of Sales	8,810	12,490	14,970	16,460
Expenses	50	130	80	100
Indirect expenses	200	370	500	540
Tax	450	190	390	450
Profit	?	?	?	?

(*University of Bombay, B. Com., October 1999*)

Solution: **Statement Showing Trend Percentages**

Particulars	*Amount (Rs.)*				*Trend percentages*			
	1992	*1993*	*1994*	*1995*	*1992*	*1993*	*1994*	*1995*
Assets:								
Fixed Assets	2,11,696	2,08,694	2,04,580	1,84,122	100	98.58	96.64	86.97
Investments	20,000	15,000	10,000	9,000	100	75.00	50.00	45.00

Cash in hand	41,680	30,472	20,346	18,312	100	73.11	48.81	43.93
Sundry Debtors	1,85,040	1,31,346	85,750	77,175	100	70.98	46.34	41.71
Stock	1,31,474	1,34,684	1,45,172	1,30,655	100	102.44	110.42	99.38
Prepaid expenses	1,690	3,236	2,440	2,196	100	191.48	144.38	129.94
	5,91,580	5,23,432	4,68,288	4,21,460	100	88.44	79.15	71.24
Liabilities:								
Share capital	4,45,228	3,86,654	3,48,388	3,13,551	100	86.84	78.25	70.42
Sundry creditors	1,40,712	1,32,684	1,17,410	1,05,669	100	94.29	83.44	75.10
Liability for expenses	5,640	4,094	2,490	2,240	100	72,59	44.15	39.72
	5,91,580	5,23,432	4,68,288	4,21,460	100	88.48	79.15	71.24

Interpretation:

1. Share capital has reduced to 70.42% which means it includes redeemable preference shares which is redeemed in instalments.
2. During the last four years no new fixed assets were purchased.
3. Compared to the year 1992, the investments to the extant of 55% was sold to raise funds in the year 1995.
4. Cash and stock position has gone down to about 50% in 1995 compared to the year 1992.
5. It seems that company has reduced its operation. This is evident by the redemption of shares.

(*b*) **Trend Percentage**

Particulars	*Amount (in Rs.)*				*Trend percentage*			
	1994	*1995*	*1996*	*1997*	*1994*	*1995*	*1996*	*1997*
Sales	9,880	13,640	16,400	18,040	100	138.06	165.99	182.59
Less: Cost of sales	8,810	12,490	14,970	16,460	100	141.77	169.92	186.83
Gross profit (*A*)	1,070	1,150	1,430	1,580	100	107.48	133.64	147.66
Less: Expenses:								
Expenses	50	130	80	100	100	260	160	200
Interest expenses	200	370	500	540	100	185	250	270
Tax	450	190	390	450	100	42.22	86.67	100
Total (*B*)	700	690	970	1,090	100	98.57	138.57	155.71
Net profit (*A* – *B*)	370	460	460	490	100	124.32	124.32	132.43

Problem 21: Calculate the Trend percentages from the following figures of X Ltd. taking 1995 as the base and interpret them.

(*Rs. in Lakhs*)

Year	*Sales*	*Stock*	*P B T*
1995	1,881	709	321
1996	2,340	781	435
1997	2,655	816	458
1998	3,021	944	527
1999	3,768	1,154	672

(*Bangalore University, B. Com., October 2000*)

Solution: **Statement Showing Trend percentage (Base year 1995)**

Year	*Sales*		*Stock*		*Profit before Tax*	
	Amount	*Trend percentage*	*Amount*	*Trend percentage*	*Amount*	*Trend percentage*
1995	1,881	100	709	100	321	100
1996	2,340	124	781	110	435	136
1997	2,655	141	816	115	458	143
1998	3,021	161	944	133	527	164
1999	3,768	200	1,154	162	672	209

Interpretation:

1. The sales have continuously increased in all the years upto 1999. The percentage in 1999 is 2000 as compared to 100 in 1995. The increase in sales is quite satisfactory.
2. The figure of stock have also increased from 1995 to 1999. This implies the increased production capacity of the business.
3. Profit before tax has substantially increased. In the five year period it has more than doubled. The comparative increase in profit is much higher in 1998 and 1999 as compared to that in 1997.

Problem 22 (Calculation of missing information using trend percentages): On the basis of the following balances as at 31st December 1995 extracted from the books of Alpha Ltd. You are required to:

(*a*) Calculate trend statement for the year 31st December 1995, 1996 and 1997.

(*b*) Give your interpretation on the same.

Base Year

Particulars	*Balance as on 31-12-95*	*Trend as on 31-12-95*	*Balance as on 31-12-96*	*Trend as on 31-12-96*	*Balance as on 31-12-97*	*Trend as on 31-12-97*
Fixed Assets	1,60,000	100	?	150	?	200
Less: Depreciation						
Provision	60,000	100	?	150	?	250
Net Fixed Assets	1,00,000	100	?	150	?	170
Current Assets:						
Stock	3,00,000	100	?	120	?	140
Debtors	4,50,000	100	?	120	?	160
Bank Balance	1,00,000	100	?	80	?	110
Short term advance	?	?	?	?	?	?
Total current Assets	10,00,000	100	?	110	?	130
Less: Current liabilities	3,00,000	100	?	120	?	144
Working capital	?	?	?	?	?	?
Capital employed	?	?	?	?	?	?
Debentures	4,00,000	100	?	75	?	50
Net worth	?	?	?	?	?	?

(*University of Bombay, April 1998*)

Calculation of Trend statements as on December 1995, 1996, 1997

	31.12.95		*31.12.96*		*31.12.97*	
	Rs.	*Trend*	*Rs.*	*Trend*	*Rs.*	*Trend*
Fixed Assets	1,60,000	100	2,40,000	150	3,20,000	200
Less: Depreciation						
Provision	60,000	100	90,000	150	1,50,000	250
Net fixed Assets	1,00,000	100	1,50,000	150	1,70,000	170
Current Assets:						
Stock	3,00,000	100	3,60,000	120	4,20,000	140
Debtors	4,50,000	100	5,40,000	120	7,20,000	160
Bank Balance	1,00,000	100	80,000	80	1,10,000	110
Short term advance	1,50,000	100	2,20,000	146.67	1,90,000	126.67
Total current Assets	10,00,000	100	12,00,000	120	14,40,000	144
Less: Current liabilities	(–)3,00,000	100	(–)3,30,000	110	(–)3,90,000	130
Working capital	7,00,000	100	8,70,000	124.29	10,50,000	150
Capital employed	8,00,000	100	10,20,000	127.50	12,20,000	152.50
Less: Debentures	4,00,000	100	3,00,000	7,500	2,00,000	50
Net worth	4,00,000	100	7,20,000	180	10,20,000	225

QUESTIONS

Simple Questions

1. What is meant by financial analysis?
2. Distinguish between 'analysis' and 'interpretation' of financial statements.
3. What is meant by external analysis of financial statements?
4. What is meant by internal analysis of financial statements?
5. What is meant by horizontal analysis of financial statements?
6. What is meant by vertical analysis of financial statements?
7. List out the various methods of financial analysis.
8. What is meant by comparative statements?
9. What is a common-size statement?
10. What is trend analysis?

Short Answer Questions

1. "Decisions taken on the basis of financial statements may not be regarded as final and accurate"– Comment.
2. Write an analytical note on comparative income statement and state the procedure of computing them.
3. "The significance of financial statements lies not in their preparation but in their analysis and interpretation"– Comment.
4. Write an analytical note on common-size statements and state the procedure of computing it.
5. Briefly analyse the importance of "Trend percentages" as a tool of financial analysis and state the procedure of computing it.
6. Explain the procedure of financial statement analysis.
7. State the limitations of financial analysis.

Exercise 1 (Comparative Financial Statements): Balance sheet of RT Ltd, as on 31st December 1994 and 1995 is given below:

	1995	*1996*		*1995*	*1996*
Preference share capital	–	4,00,000	Fixed Assets	7,00,000	10,00,000
Equity share capital	5,00,000	5,00,000	Investments (at cost)	1,00,000	1,20,000

Reserves and surplus	1,35,000	1,71,500	Stock	1,50,000	1,80,000
12% Debentures	2,00,000	–	Debtors	2,36,000	2,44,000
Bank O.D.	50,000	80,000	Cash	24,000	2,500
Sundry creditors	1,50,000	1,25,000			
Provision for taxation	75,000	1,20,000			
Proposed dividend	1,00,000	1,50,000			
	12,10,000	15,46,000		12,10,000	15,46,000

Prepare a comparative financial statement.

(University of Bombay, B. Com., October 1996)

Exercise 2: The Balance sheets of Santhosh Ltd. is as follows:

	1993 (Rs.)	*1994 (Rs.)*
Liabilities:		
Equity share capital	2,00,000	2,50,000
10% pref. share capital	2,00,000	1,50,000
Reserve fund	80,000	1,00,000
P & L a/c	1,00,000	1,50,000
12% Debentures	2,00,000	3,00,000
Creditors	1,00,000	1,20,000
Bank O.D.	50,000	20,000
	9,30,000	10,90,000
Assets:		
Buildings	3,00,000	3,20,000
Machinery	1,50,000	1,80,000
Furniture	40,000	35,000
Investments	1,00,000	1,50,000
Stock	1,50,000	2,00,000
Debtors	1,00,000	1,20,000
Cash at Bank	90,000	85,000
	9,30,000	10,90,000

You are required to comment on the financial position of business with the help of comparative Balance sheet Technique. *(Bangalore University, B. Com., April 1996)*

Exercise 3: From the following profit and loss account and balance sheet of Radha industries, prepare a comparative income statement and a comparative balance sheet.

Profit & loss A/c (Rs. in lacs)

	1992 Rs.	*1993 Rs.*		*1992 Rs.*	*1993 Rs.*
To Cost of goods sold	500	640	By sales	700	900
To Operating expenses:					
Administrative expenses	20	20			
Selling expenses	30	40			
To Net profit	150	200			
	700	900		700	900

Balance sheet as on 31st December (Rs. in lacs)

	1992	*1993*		*1992*	*1993*
Bills payable	50	75	Cash	50	70
Tax payable	100	150	Debtors	300	450
Sundry creditors	150	200	Stock	100	200
Debentures	100	150	Land	100	120
Pref. share capital	300	300	Buildings	200	180
Equity share capital	200	200	Machinery	250	225
Reserves	200	250	Furniture	100	80
	1,100	1,325		1,100	1,325

(*University of Madras, B. Com., September 1994*)

Exercise 4 (Common-size Financial Statements): From the following particulars prepare a common-size income statement and interpret changes in 1996 as compared to 1995.

(*Amount in lakhs of Rs.*)

	1995	*1996*
Net Sales	600	800
Cost of goods sold	400	500
Gross profit	200	300
Operating expenses	40	50
Operating profit	160	250
Non-operating income	20	25
Non-operating expenses	30	40
Net profit	150	235

(*Bangalore University, B. Com., April 2001*)

Exercise 5: The profit and loss account of a company is given below:

P & L A/c

	1997	*1998*		*1997*	*1998*
To Cost of goods sold	600	750	By Net sales	800	1,000
			By Non-operating Income	50	100
To *Operating expenses:*					
Administration expenses	30	40			
Selling expenses	40	50			
To Non-operating expenses	30	40			
To Net profit	150	220			
	850	1,100		850	1,100

You are required to prepare a common-size income statement and interpret the changes.

(*Bangalore University, B. Com., April 2000*)

Exercise 6: Following are the two Balance Sheets on two different dates rearrange them in vertical form and prepare common-size statements.

	1993	*1994*		*1993*	*1994*
Equity share capital	2,25,000	2,62,500	Good will	45,000	35,250
General Reserve	15,000	22,500	Machinery	67,500	1,43,250
Capital Reserve	–	18,750	Building	75,000	56,250
P & L a/c	13,500	20,250	Long term Investment	7,500	26,250

Creditors	33,000	48,750	Stock	63,750	58,500
Provision for Tax	21,000	24,000	Debtors	45,000	67,500
Proposed Dividend	20,250	24,750	Bank	12,750	21,000
			Bills Receivable	11,250	13,500
	3,27,750	4,21,500		3,27,750	4,21,500

(University of Bombay, B. Com., October 1998)

Exercise 7: Following are the Balance sheets of Shanti & Co. and Sheela & Co. as on 31.12.1999.

Liabilities:	*Shanti & Co.* *Rs.*	*Sheela & Co.* *Rs.*
Equity share capital	3,00,000	1,50,000
Preference share capital	1,75,000	1,30,000
Reserves and Surplus	1,20,000	1,20,000
Debentures	4,55,000	2,50,000
Creditors	25,000	9,000
Bills payable	30,000	15,000
	11,05,000	6,74,000
Assets:		
Land	3,00,000	2,00,000
Building	3,00,000	1,20,000
Machinery	2,00,000	1,50,000
Investments	80,000	44,000
Debtors	1,70,000	1,40,000
Cash	55,000	20,000
	11,05,000	6,74,000

Compare the financial position of the two companies with the help of common-size Balance sheets are comment. *(Bangalore University, B. Com., April 2000)*

Exercise 8: The summarised Balance sheet of two companies are as follows:

Balance sheet as on 31.3.1998

	Top Ltd.	*Ten Ltd.*		*Top Ltd.*	*Ten Ltd.*
Equity share capital	1,20,000	3,50,000	Fixed Assets	2,45,000	4,10,000
10% Pref. shares capital	1,00,000	50,000	Current Assets	2,90,500	3,32,800
Reserves	1,40,000	56,000	Preliminary expenses	10,000	6,000
15% Debentures	50,000	50,000			
Current liabilities	1,35,500	2,42,800			
	5,45,500	7,48,800		5,45,500	7,48,800

Revenue Statement for the year 31.3.1998

	Top Ltd. *(Rs.)*	*Ten Ltd.* *(Rs.)*
Sales	10,00,000	12,00,000
Less: Cost of sales	6,00,000	8,00,000
	4,00,000	4,00,000
Less: Operating expenses (including interest)	1,40,000	2,05,000

Less:	Non-cash operating expenses (Depreciation)	10,000	20,000
		2,50,000	1,75,000
Less:	Taxes	1,00,000	70,000
Less:	Dividend	70,000	75,000
	Retained earnings	80,000	30,000

Prepare:

(*a*) Common-size balance sheet (in vertical form).

(*b*) Common-size income statement (in vertical form).

(*c*) Comment in brief.

(*University of Bombay, B. Com., April 1998*)

Exercise 9: From the following financial statements of loyal limited prepare common-size financial statements and give your comments on them.

P & L a/c for the year ended 31-3-1996

To Opening stock	4,00,000	By sales	20,00,000
To Purchases	12,00,000	By closing stock	6,00,000
To Wages	2,50,000		
To Factory overheads	2,50,000		
To G. P. cld.	5,00,000		
	26,00,000		26,00,000
To Administrative expenses	75,000	By G. P. bld.	5,00,000
To Selling and Distribution expenses	50,000	By Dividend	30,00
To Depreciation	65,000		
To Interest on Debentures	20,000		
To Net profit cld.	3,20,000		
	5,30,000		5,30,000
To Preference dividend	15,000	By Balance bld.	2,00,000
To Provision for tax (1996)	1,05,000	By Net profit bld.	3,20,000
To Surplus to Balance sheet	4,00,000		
	5,20,000		5,20,000

Balance sheet as on 31-3-1996

Equity share capital	10,00,000	Good will	5,00,000
Pref. share capital	5,00,000	Plant and Machinery	5,00,000
General Reserve	1,00,000	Land and Building	8,00,000
P & L a/c Balance	4,00,000	Furniture	1,00,000
Provision for Tax	1,05,000	Stock	5,00,000
Bills payable	1,95,000	Bills Receivable	80,000
Bank overdraft	1,00,000	Debtors	2,00,000
Creditors	5,00,000	Bank	2,20,000
	29,00,000		29,00,000

(*University of Bombay, B. Com., October 1997*)

Exercise 10 (Trend Analysis): From the following information interpret the results of operations of a manufacturing concern using Trend ratios-use 1995 as base.

(Amount in lakh of Rs.)

Particulars	*1995*	*1996*	*1997*	*1998*
Net sales	100	95	120	130
Cost of goods sold	60	58.90	69.60	72.80
Gross profit	40	36.10	50.40	57.20
Operating expenses	10	9.70	11.00	12
Net operating profit	30	26.40	39.40	45.20

(Bangalore University, B. Com., April 2001)

Exercise 11: Calculate Trend percentages.

	1994 *Rs.*	*1995* *Rs.*	*1996* *Rs.*
Sales	50,000	75,000	1,00,000
Purchases	40,000	60,000	72,000
Expenses	5,000	8,000	15,000
Profit	5,000	7,000	13,000

(Osmania University, B. Com., March 1998)

Exercise 12: Pass and Fail are partners of a firm carrying on business.

(i) **Their position as on 31st December 1992, 1993 and 1994 are as follows:**

	1994	*1993*	*1992*		*1994*	*1993*	*1992*
Partners capital a/c	4,00,000	3,40,000	3,00,000	Fixed Assets	4,00,000	3,60,000	2,80,000
General Reserve	1,00,000	1,00,000	1,00,000	Current Assets:			
Secured loans	60,000	60,000	50,000	Stock	1,60,000	1,50,000	1,35,000
Unsecured loans	1,60,000	1,80,000	1,40,000	Debtors	2,00,000	1,60,000	1,40,000
Sundry Creditors	1,60,000	90,000	45,000	Loans and advances	1,00,000	80,000	60,000
				Bank	20,000	20,000	20,000
	8,80,000	7,70,000	6,35,000		8,80,000	7,70,000	6,35,000

(ii) **Summarised Income Statement for the year ended**

	31-12-94 *Rs.*	*31-12-93* *Rs.*	*31-12-92* *Rs.*
Sales	40,00,000	36,00,000	30,00,000
Less: Cost of sales	28,00,000	24,00,000	20,00,000
Gross profit	12,00,000	12,00,000	10,00,000
Less: Expenses	8,00,000	8,00,000	7,00,000
Net profit	4,00,000	4,00,000	3,00,000

Work out trend percentages and give your interpretation on the same.

(University of Bombay, B. Com., October 1995)

33

RATIO ANALYSIS

INTRODUCTION

Ratio analysis is the process of determining and interpreting numerical relationship based on financial statements. It is the technique of interpretation of financial statements with the help of accounting ratios derived from the balance sheet and profit & loss account. It involves the comparision of existing ratios against standards established. The standards may be set by management as goals expressed in the budgets (i.e., budgetary standard) or may be historical figures showing performance of the same concern in the past (*i.e.* historical standard) or may be figures reflecting the performance of other companies (*i.e.*, industrial or market standard.)

Meaning of Accounting Ratios

A ratio is simply one number expressed in terms of another, it is an expression of relationship spelt out by dividing one figure by another. It is the quotient of two arthmetical numbers obtained from financial statements. Wixon, Kell and Bedford in their book 'Accountant's Handbook' define ratio, as "an expression of the quantitative relationship between two numbers. According to J. Batty the term accounting ratio is used to describe the significant relationship which exits between figures shown in a balance sheet and profit and loss account in a budgetary control system or any other part of accounting organisation.

Nature of Accounting Ratios

Ratios are indicators, sometimes they serve as pointers but not in themselves powerful tools of management. The ratios help to summarise the large quantities of financial data and to make qualitative judgement about the firm's financial performance.

Thorough ratios are indicators, too much reliance should not be put on the figures arrived at by the ratios. They can not be taken as the final result regarding good or bad financial position of the business. They are at best symptoms and there is always a need to investigate the facts revealed by them further. Hence ratios alone are not adequate for taking a financial decision. Infact, it must be used for what they are financial tools. Quite often ratios are looked upon as ends in themselves rather than as means to on end. The value of a ratio should not be regarded as good or bad among themselves. It may be an indication that a firm is weak or strong in a particular area but it must never be taken as a powerful tool of management.

Ratios as a matter of fact tools of quantitative analysis and it is quite possible that quantitative factors may override numerical aspects with the consequence that the conclusions from the ratio analysis may get distorted. In a way ratios are an attempt to delve in past as financial statements, (from which ratios are derived), are historical documents. But in a modern business, it is more important to have an idea of the prǫbable happening in future rather than, those in the part. These factors emphasise that ratios themselves are not powerful tools of management.

Mode of Expressing Accounting Ratios

Accounting ratios can be expressed in various ways, such as:

(*a*) Pure ratio, say ratio of current assets to current liabilities is 2: 1, or

(*b*) a rate, say current results are 2 times current liabilities

(*c*) a percentage, Say, current assets are 200% of current tiabitites.

Each method of expression has a distinct advantage over the other. The analyst will select that method which best suits his convenience and purpose. There are certain accounting ratios which can be best expressed if stated as a pure ratio, *eg.*, debt-equity ratio, current ratio etc. Some other ratios can be best expressed as a rate only, *eg.* stock turnover ratio, debtors, turnover ratio etc. While some others can most advantageously be expressed as a percentage only eg. gross profit ratio, operating ratio etc. Ratios are expressed in such a way that the first appears as the numerator and the second as the demominator.

Interpretation of Ratios

The significance of Ratio analysis lies in proper interpretation of the related items calculation by ratios as a step of ratio analysis is a simple task and it is a clerical work. Interpretation of ratios which is the ultimate step is difficult process and requires knowledge, intelligence and skill. The following are the various ways of interpreting accounting ratios.

(1) Single absolute ratio: A Ratio taken in isolation may not convey much meaning. If it is expressed in relation to another aspect it may prove to be more useful. For example if current ratio is less than one, it may reveal the insolvency position of the business, *i.e.*, current assets are not sufficient to pay current liabilitites sometimes a single ratio may fail to show the exact financial position of business.

(2) Group ratios: When group of ratios are calculated and interpreted they convey better idea about the business operation and efficiency for example, in addition to calculating current ratio, *i.e.*, current asset to current liabilities if liquid ratio, *i.e.*, liquid asset to liquid liabilities, is also used, it throws better light on the business.

(3) Historical comparision—Under this method of interpretation, the ratios of current period is companed with ratios of past year or years. Comparision of ratios over a period of time gives better indication and sets a trend which again reflects the performance and position of the business. However, care must be taken to ensure that there is no change in accounting policy and procedure during the period of comparision.

(4) Inter-firm comparision—Under this method, the ratios of one firm is compared with ratios of other firm belonging to the same industry. But this method may prove to be ineffective when different firms use different accounting policies and procedure.

(5) Projected ratios—Sometimes ratios can be calculated based on estimated financial statements. In which case they constitute standard ratios. The actual ratios are compared with standard ratios. The variance in ratios indicate the success or failure of the business.

Uses or Utility of Ratios

Ratio analysis is one of most important tools of analysing and interpreting the financial statements. It helps in understanding the financial health and trend of a business. Its past performance enables to forecast the future state of affairs of the business. It reveals the symptoms of a business as in the case of a patients temperative. Blood pressure or pulse beat which indicates the symptoms of disease in a patient. The utility of ratio analysis can be explained under the following headings:

(1) Utility to management: Management of a business uses ratio analysis in: (*a*) formulating the policies, (*b*) in making decisions, (*c*) Evaluating the performance, (*d*) in knowing the trends of the business, (*e*) in planning and forecasting the future, (*f*) communicating, (*g*) controlling.

(2) Utility to shareholders and investors: An investor would assess the financial position of a business before he invests his money in it. All investors are interested in the safety, security and profitability of their investments. Ratios enable the prospective investors to select best companies to invest their finds. The shareholders of a company uses ratios to evaluate the performance and future prospects of the company. By reviewing the operational effeciency, they are able to make out the price of their shares in the stock market.

(3) Utility to Creditors: Creditors and suppliers who supply goods on credit basis are interested in the solvency and liquidity position of the company. This can be known by looking into current ratio and acid-test ratio.

(4) Utility to employees—Employees are interested in the performance of business as their fringe benefits are related to the profits earned by the company. Profitability ratios such as gross profit ratio, net profit ratio etc. can be used by them in order to claim increased wages and other benefits.

(5) Utility to Government—The Government uses ratio analysis with a view to study the cost structure and thereby implement price control measures to protect the interest of the customers.

Limitations:

1. Usefulness of ratios depends upon the abilities and intentions of the persons who handle them. It will be affected considerably by the prejudice of such persons.
2. Ratios are worked out on the basis of money value only. They do not take into account the real values of various items involved.
3. Historical values are considered in working out the ratios. However, the effects of changes in the price levels of various items are ignored and to that extant the comparison and evaluation of proposals through ratios become unrealistic.
4. One particular ratio in isolation is not sufficient to analyse investment proposals or liquidity analysis. A group of ratios are to be considered simultaneously to arrive at the conclusion.
5. Ratio analysis is only a technique for making judgement and not a substitute for judgement.
6. Ratios are only symptoms, they may indicate what is to be investigated, only a careful investigation will bring out the correct position.
7. Liquidity ratios can mislead since current assets and liabilities can change quickly. Their utility becomes more doubtful for firms with seasonable business.
8. If there is window dressing in financial statements, ratios derived therefrom will

not serve the purpose outsiders cannot make out the window dressing of a business.

9. Financial statements buffer from inherent limitations which make ratios inaccurate. Ratios calculated on the basis of past statements need not necessarily constitute true indicator of future.

Types of Ratios—A Traditional Basis of Classification of Ratios

Accounting ratios may be classified according to the following bases:

(1) Classification on the basis of statements: This include the following:

(*a*) *Balance sheet or position ratios*: They deal with realtionship between two items or group of items which are taken from the balance sheet such as current ratio, debt-equity ratio, etc.

(*b*) *Profit and loss account or revenue ratios*: These are the Ratios which are calculated out of the figures appearing in the profit and loss account. They are also known as operating ratios. Some ratios derived from profit and loss account, are gross profit ratio, expense ratio, operating profit ratio etc.

(*c*) *Position-cum-revenue ratios*: These ratios are also known as consolidated or combined or complex ratios or inter-statement ratios. They portrary the relationship between items one of which is a part of the balance sheet and the other of the revenue statement. Examples of such ratios are, return on total resources, return on capital empolyed, turnover of debtors etc.

(2) Classification on the basis of time: On the basis of time ratios are classified into :

(*a*) Structural ratios, *i.e.*, ratios computed from data refering to the same point of time; *eg*., ratios of a particular month or year.

(*b*) Trend ratios, *i.e.*, ratios compared between the items referred to different period of time.

(3) Classification on the basis of nature: On the basis of nature of ratios, it is classified into:

(*a*) *Primary ratios*: It measures the size of profit in relation to capital employed, *e.g.*, operating profit to capital employed.

(*b*) *Secondary ratios*: Also referred to as supporting ratios, brings to light strategic facts in the profit earning structure, *e.g.* stock velocity, debtors velocity, expense ratios etc.

(4) Classfication according to functions: Ratios are grouped in accordance with certain tests which they are intended to subserve from the view point of various parties having a financial interest in on énterprise. There tests are:

(*a*) *Financial ratios*: Financial ratios include liquidity and solvency ratios. Ratios indicating the liquidity position of the firm are current ratio, quick-ratio, absolute liquidity ratio, solvency ratios include proprietory ratio, debt-equity ratio, capital gearing ratio.

(*b*) *Profitability ratios*: Profitability ratios would cover gross profit ratio, net profit ratio, return on capital employed.

(*c*) *Market Test Ratio*: Market test ratios comprise of divident yield, fixed dividend cover, price earning ratio, etc.

For the sake of clear understanding we classify ratio into the following types:

Classification of Ratios

Analysis of short term financial position or tests of liquidity	Analysis of long term financial position or tests of solvency	Activity ratios	Profitability ratios
(1) Current ratio	(1) Debt-equity ratio	(1) Stock turnover ratio	(1) Gross profit ratio
(2) Quick ratio	(2) Proprietary ratio	(2) Debtors turnover ratio	(2) Net profit ratio
(3) Absolute liquid ratio	(3) Solvency ratio	(3) Creditors Turnover ratio	(3) Operating ratio
	(4) Fixed assets to net worth ratio	(4) Working capital turnover ratio	(4) Expenses ratio
	(5) Current Assets to net worth ratio	(5) Fixed assets turnover ratio	(5) Operating profit ratio
	(6) Current liabilities to net worth ratio	(6) Current Assets Turnover ratio	(6) Return on total resource ratio
	(7) Capital gearing ratio	(7) Total Assets Turnover ratio	(7) Return on capital employed ratio
	(8) Fixed assets ratio	(8) Sales to networth ratio	(8) Return on equity share
	(9) Fixed charges cover ratio		(9) Return on equity capital ratio
	(10) Dividend cover ratio		(10) Earning per share
			(11) Dividend pay out ratio
			(12) Price earning ratio
			(13) Dividend yield ratio
			(14) Book value for share
			(15) Preference Dividend Cover

(I) ANALYSIS OF SHORT-TERM FINANCIAL POSITION OR TESTS OF LIQUIDITY

The liquidity ratios are used to test the short term solvency position or liquidity position of the business. It enables to know whether short-term liabilities can be paid out of short-term assets. This ratio also indicates whether a firm has adequate working capital to carry out routine business activity. Though commercial Banks and other short-term creditors are Primarily concerned with the analysis of short-term financial position or test of liquidity, it is a valuable aid to management in checking the efficiency with which working capital is being employed in the business. It is also of importance to shareholders and long-term creditors in determining to some extent the prospects of dividend and interest payment. The questions involved in connection with the ratio analysis of short-term financial position are :

(*a*) Will the company be able to pay its current debts promptly?
(*b*) Is the management utilising capital effectively?
(*c*) Is the current financial position improving?

The important ratios which fall under this category are as follows:

(1) Current ratio—Current ratio, also called as working capital ratio, is the most widely used of all onalytical devices based on the balance sheet. It establishes the relationship between total current assets and current liabilities. It is the barometer of general measure of liquidity and state of trading. The following formula is used to calculate current ratio:

$$\text{Current Ratio} = \frac{\text{Current Assets}}{\text{Current Liabilities}}$$

Component of Current Assets

Current assets include the following:

(*a*) Cash in level
(*b*) Cash at bank
(*c*) Bills receivable
(*d*) Sundry debtors
(*e*) Stock of raw materials, work-in-process and finished goods
(*f*) Short-term investment, *i.e.*, readily realisable investments
(*g*) Prepaid expense
(*h*) Accrued Income

Loose tools are not treated as current asset. Instead it is treated as fixed assets.

Components of current liabilities

(*a*) Sundry creditors
(*b*) Bills payable
(*c*) Bank overdraft
(*d*) Outstanding expenses
(*e*) Income received in advance
(*f*) Provision for taxation
(*g*) Short-term borrowing
(*h*) Unclaimed dividend
(*i*) Proposed dividend

Current assets are those assets which are expected to be converted into cash within a year. Current liabilities are those liabilities which are payable within one year:

Significance of current ratio

1. It indicates liquidity position of the business
2. It denotes the adequacy of working capital
3. It discloses, over or under capitalisation
4. Margin of safety for short-term creditor

Standard current ratio

A current ratio of 2: 1 is considered ideal as a rule of thumb. It means the current assets must not only be equal to current liabilities but should leave a comfortable margin of working capital after paying off the current debts. But in actual practice 1: 1 ratio is found acceptable tham 2: 1. A high ratio, *i.e.*, more than 2: 1, say, 3: 1 indicates under trading and the same also indicates one of the signs of over capitalisation. Conversely, a low ratio indicates over trading or under capitalisation of business.

Limitations of current ratio

(*a*) Current ratios differ among various industries and also between manufacturers and retailers in the same line of business.

(*b*) All current assets are treated alike but they are not equally or readily realisable in cash to meet the demand of the total current liabilities.

(*c*) The credit given to the debtors and available from the creditors in a particular business can affect the position of this ratio. If these periods are different the desirable ratio would also differ.

(2) Quick ratio or acid test ratio or liquid ratio: It is a refinement of the current ratio and a second testing device for the working capital position. It is concerned with the relationship between liquid assets and liquid liabilities. The following formula is used:

$$\text{Quick Ratio} = \frac{\text{Quick Assets}}{\text{Quick Liabilities}}$$

Components of quick assets: The assets which are converted into cash without loss within a short period of time say, 1 year is known as quick assets. Quick assets include all current assets except stock and prepaid expenses.

Components of quick liabilities: The liabilities which become payable within a short period of time, say 1 year is known as quick liabilities. It includes all current liabilities except bank overdraft and cash credit as they more or less constitute permanent arrangement and renewed periodically.

Interpretation of quick ratio: A quick ratio of 1:1 is usually considered to be ideal. This ratio is a more rigorous test of liquidity than the current ratio and when used in conjuction with it, gives a better picture of the firm's ability to meet its short-term debts out of short-term assets. However, care must be exercised in placing too much reliance on 100% acid test ratio without further investigation. This is so because the interpretation of the acid test ratio, depends on circumstances. For example, a seasonal business which seeks to stabilise production will tend to have a weak acid-test ratio during its period of slack sales, and probably a powerful one during the period of heavy selling.

(3) Absolute liquidity ratio or cash position ratio: This ratio establishes a relation between absolute liquid assets to quick liabilities. The following formula is used:

$$\text{Absolute Liquidity Ratio} = \frac{\text{Absolute Liquid Assets}}{\text{Quick Liabilities}}$$

Components of Absolute liquid assets: Absolute liquid assets include (*a*) cash in hand, (*b*) cash at bank, (*c*) Marketeable securities, (*d*) temporary investments. The following assets are not included in absolute liquid asset—(*a*) closing stock, (*b*) prepaid expenses, (*c*) outstanding income, (*d*) sundry debtors, (*e*) bills receivable.

Interpretation:

The ideal absolute liquid ratio is 1: 2. It means if the ratio is 1: 2 or more than this the concern can be taken as liquid. If the ratio is less than the standard of 1: 2, it means the concern is not liquid.

Problem 1: The following is the Balance sheet of Super Star Company Ltd. on 31st Dec., 1995. Calculate the liquidity group ratios and comment upon the same.

Equity share capital	10,00,000	Land and Building	7,00,000
Profit and loss a/c	1,50,000	Plant and Machinery	17,50,000
General reserve	3,00,000	Stock	10,00,000
Bank over draft	20,00,000	Sundry debtors	5,00,000
Sundray creditors	5,00,000	Bills receivable	50,000
Bills payable	2,50,000	Cash at Bank	2,00,000
	42,00,000		42,00,000

(Osmania University, B.Com., March 1996)

Solution: Current ratio $= \dfrac{\text{Current Assets}}{\text{Current Liabilities}}$

$$= \frac{17,50,000}{27,50,000} = 0.636$$

Current Assets:

Stock	10,00,000
Sundry Debtors	5,00,000
Bills received	50,000
Cash at Bank	2,00,000
	17,50,000

Current liabilities:

Bank overdraft	20,00,000
Sundry creditors	5,00,000
Bills payable	2,50,000
	27,50,000

Interpretation:

The current ratio is 0.636: 1. Which is much below the standard ratio if 2: 1

(2) Quick ratio $= \dfrac{\text{Quick Assets}}{\text{Quick Liabilities}}$

$$= \frac{7,50,000}{7,50,000} = 1$$

Quick Assets:

Sundry debtors	5,00,000
Bills receivable	50,000
Cash at Bank	2,00,000
	7,50,000

Quick liablities:

Sundry creditors	5,00,000
Bills payable	2,50,000
	7,50,000

Interpretation:

The quick ratio is 1:1 and the standard ratio is also 1:1. So it can meet its current obligation (except bank overdraft)

$$(3)\ \text{Absolute liquid ratio} = \frac{\text{Absolute liquid Assets}}{\text{Liquid Liabilities}}$$

$$= \frac{2,00,000}{7,50,000} = 0.26$$

Interpretation:

The absolute liquid ratio is 0.26:1 and the standard ratio is 1:2. It means the liquidity position of the company is not satisfactory.

Problem 2: The following particulars are extracted from the books of Bright star so as on 31-12-2001. Calculate absolute liquid ratio.

	(Amt. 000)
Good will	50
Plant and machinery	400
Investment	200
Marketable securities	150
Bills receivable	40
Cash in hand	45
Cash at Bank	30
Stock	75
Bank O D	70
Sundry creditors	60
Bills payable	90
O/s expenses	30

Solution: $\text{Absolute liquid ratio} = \frac{\text{Absolute liquid Assets}}{\text{Liquid liabilities}}$

$$= \frac{2,25,000}{1,80,000} = 1.25$$

Absolute liquid assets	
Marketable securities	1,50,000
Cash in hand	45,000
Cash at Bank	30,000
	2,25,000

Liquid liabilities:	
Sundry creditors	60,000
Bills payable	90,000
O/s expenses	30,000
	1,80,000

Interpretation:

The ratio of 1.25 is higher than the standard ratio of 1.2. Hence the liquidity position is satisfactory.

(II) ANALYSIS OF LONG-TERM FINANCIAL POSITION OR TESTS OF SOLVENCY

When an organisations' assets are more than its liabilitites is known as solvent organisation. Solvency indicates that position of an enterprise where it is capable of meeting long obligation. The long-term debt is contributed by debenture holders, financial institutions, other suppliers selling goods on instalment basis. All such creditors are interested in the security of loan as well as the interest due thereon. As such long term solvency ratios denote the ability of the organisation to repay the loan and interest thereon. The following ratios are used to indicate solvency position of a concern.

(1) Debt-equity ratio or external-internal equity Ratio: Debt-equity ratio expresses the relationship between debt and equity. Debt here is taken to mean long-term and short-term debt and equity means owners or shareholders funds. In other words, this ratio indicates the relaionship between external equities, *i.e.*, outsiders funds and internal equities *i.e.*, shareholders finds. The following formula is used:

$$\text{Debt-equity ratio} = \frac{\text{Debt}}{\text{Equity}}$$

OR

$$\frac{\text{External equities}}{\text{Internal equities}}$$

Components of Debt: It comprises of long term as well as short term debt.

Components of Equity: It consists of shareholders funds, reserves and accumulated profit. However, if there is any accumulated losses or fictitors assets, they are deducted from shareholders finds.

Often a question would arise as to treatment of preference share capital as a part of shareholders finds. Write some accountants are of the opinion that it must be treated as internal equity; others one of the new that it is an external equity as a fixed rate of dividend is paid on them. Further redeemable preference share may have to be pond during the life time of the company. If preference shares are redeemable it can be treated as external equity and irredeemable preperence-share is treated as internal equity. Similarly, there is a difference of opinion as to treatment of current liabilities. Some accountants are of the opinion that current liabilities are payable within a short-period of time and hence they do not constitute a long-term debt. As such no interest becomes payable on such current liabilities. But some other accountants feel that current liability is an outside debt and therefore it is a part of external equity. It is suggested that current liability is to be included in the long-term liabilities.

Interpretation:

The standard debt-equity ratio is 2: 1. It means for every 2 shares there is 1 debt. If the debt is less than 2 times the equity, it means that creditors are relatively less and the financial structure of the business is sound. If the debt as more than 2 times the equity. The state of long-term creditors are move and indicates week financial structure..

Problem 3: The comparative figures of X Ltd. and Y Ltd. are given below:

	X Ltd.	*Y Ltd.*
Total assets	2,00,000	3,00,000
Total liabilities	40,000	1,00,000
Owner's equity	1,60,000	2,00,000

Calculate Debt-equity ratio for each company and comment. (*Bangalore University, B.Com., Nov. 1995*)

Solution: Debt-equity Ratio $= \frac{\text{Debt}}{\text{Equity}}$

X Ltd. $= \frac{40,000}{1,60,000} = 0.25$

Y Ltd. $= \frac{1,00,000}{2,00,000} = 0.50$

Interpretation:

In the case of X Ltd. it is less dependent on debt (as its borrowed capital is 25%) and dependent more on equity. In the case of Y Ltd. borrowed capital as 50% and equity fund is 50%. Y Ltd. is cosidered to be more satisfactory in terms of capital structure.

(2) Proprietory ratio or net worth ratio: This ratio establishes the relationship between the proprietors fund, (equity + preference + capital reserves + free reserves + undistributed profits) and total assets. It is also called as net worth to total assets ratio. The following formula is used:

$$\text{Proprietory Ratio} = \frac{\text{Proprietor's Fund}}{\text{Total Assets}}$$

or

$$= \frac{\text{Capital employed}}{\text{Total liabilities}}$$

Interpretation:

Higher the proprietory ratio, stronger the financial position and vice-versa. A ratio of 0.5: 1 is considered ideal.

Problem 4:

Given: Total assets Rs. 8,00,000

Proprietor's equity Rs. 4,00,000

Calculate proprietory ratio *(Bangalore University, B.Com., November, 1992)*

Solution: Proprietory Ratio $= \frac{\text{Shareholders funds}}{\text{Total Assets}}$

$$= \frac{4,00,000}{8,00,000} = 0.5$$

(3) Solvency ratio: It expresses the relationship between total assets and total liabilities of a business. It is expressed as a proportion and the following formula as used:

$$\text{Solvency Ratio} = \frac{\text{Total Assets}}{\text{Total Liabilities}}$$

Interpretation:

No standard ratio is fixed in this regard. It may be compared with similar, such organisations to evaluate the solvency position. Higher the solvency ratio, the stronger is its financial position and *vice-versa.*

(4) Fixed Assets to net worth ratio: It is obtained by dividing the depreciated book value of fixed assets by the amount of proprietors funds. It is calculated by applying the following formula:

$$\text{Fixed Assets to Net Worth Ratio} = \frac{\text{Net Fixed Assets}}{\text{Net worth or proprietor's funds}}$$

This ratio shows the extent to which ownership funds are sunk into assets with relatively low turnover. When the amount of proprietor's funds exceed the value of fixed assets, a part of the net working capital is provided by the shareholders, provided there are no other non-current assets, and when proprietor's funds are less than the fixed assets, creditors obligation have been used to finance a part of fixed assets. The yordstick for this measure is 65% for industrial undertakings.

It is a sound principle that proprietors should subscribe sufficient capital to cover fixed aseets, intangible assets, investments in other companies and a reasonable figure for working capital. Some analyst deduct intangible assets from the proprietors funds, but this would depend upon the realisable value of intangibles and the purpose of analysis. Losses should also be deducted and funds payable to others should not be added:

Interpretation:

A ratio of 0.75: 1 (or 75%) is deemed to be a desirable one. A higher ratio, say, 100 per cent means that there are no outside liabilities and all the funds employed are those of shareholders. In such a case the return to shareholders would be a lower rate of dividend and this is also a sign of 'over-capitalisation'.

(5) Current assets to net worth ratio: This is obtained by dividing the value of current assets by the amount of proprietor's funds. The following formula is used:

$$\text{Current assets to net worth ratio} = \frac{\text{Current Assets}}{\text{Proprietor's fund}}$$

The purpose of this ratio is to show the percentage of proprietor's fund investment in current assets. A higher proportion of current assets to proprietor's fund, as compared with the proportion of fixed assets to proprietor's funds is advocated, as it is an indicator of the financial strength of the business. However, different industries have different standards and history of particular concern must be studied before too great a reliance is placed on this ratio. This ratio must be read alongwith the results given by the fixed assets to proprietorship funds ratio:

(6) Current liabilities to net worth ratio: This ratio is expressed as a proportion and is obtained by dividing current liabilities by proprietor's find. The following formula is used:

$$\text{Current liabilities to net worth Ratio} = \frac{\text{Current Liabilities}}{\text{Net Worth}}$$

Interpretation:

This ratio indicates the relative contribution of short-term creditors and owners to the capital of an enterprise. The standard ratio fixed is 1/3. It the ratio is high, it means it is difficult to obtom long-term funds by the business.

(7) Capital gearing ratio: It expresses the relationship between equity capital and fixed Interest bearing securities and fixed Dividend bearing shares. The following formula is used:

$$\text{Capital Gearing Ratio} = \frac{\text{Fixed Interest bearing securities} + \text{Fixed Dividend bearing Shares}}{\text{Equity Shareholders Funds}}$$

Components of fixed interest bearing securities:

1. Debentures
2. Long-term loans
3. Long-term fixed deposits

Components of Equity shareholders funds:

1. Equity share capital
2. Accumulated reserves and profits
3. Deduction of losses and fictitions assets from the total of (1) and (2)

Interpretation:

When fixed Interest-bearing securities and fixed dividend-bearing shares are higher than equity shareholders funds, the company is send to be 'highly geared'. Where the fixed Interest-bearing securities and fixed dividend bearing shares are equal to equity share capital at is said to be 'evenly geared'. Where the fixed interest-bearing securities and fixed dividend bearing shares are lower than equity share capital it is said to be 'low geared'. If capital gearing is high, further raising of long-term loans may be difficult and issue of equity shares may be attractive and *vice-versa.*

(8) Fixed Assets Ratio: It establishes the relation between fixed assets and capital employed. The following formula is used:

$$\text{Fixed Assets Ratio} = \frac{\text{Fixed Assets}}{\text{Capital employed}}$$

Components of capital employed:

1. Owners funds
2. Long-term loans
3. Long-term deposits
4. Debentures

Interpretation:

This ratio enables to know how fixed assets are financed, *i.e.*, by use of long-term funds or by short-term funds. The ideal ratio is 0.67. This ratio should not be more than 1.

(9) Fixed charges cover ratio or debt service ratio: This ratio is determined by dividing net profit by fixed interest charges. The following formula is used:

$$\text{Fixed charges cover ratio} = \frac{\text{Net profit before deduction of interest and Income tax}}{\text{Fixed Interest charges}}$$

Net profit for the purpose of this ratio means net profit before deduction of interest and Income-tax. Fixed charges include interest on long-term loans, deposits and Debentures. This ratio indicates the financial ability of the enterprise to meet interest payment out of current earning.

Interpretation:

The ideal Debt-Service cover is 6 or 7 times. If the ratio is high it means there is higher margin of safety for the long term lenders and as such it is not difficult for the business to obtain further long term funds and *vice-versa.*

(10) Dividend cover ratio: It is the ratio between disposable profit and dividend.

Disposable profit refers to profit left over after paying interest on long-term borrowing and income tax. This ratio is expressed as a rate and is calculated using the following formula.

$$\text{Dividend Cover Ratio} = \frac{\text{Net Profit after interest and Tax}}{\text{Dividend Declared}}$$

Interpretation:

This ratio indicates the ability of the business to maintain the dividend on shares in future. If this ratio is higher is indicates that there is sufficient amount of retained profit. Even if there is slight decreace in profit in the future it will not affect payment of dividend in future.

(III) ACTIVITY RATIOS OR PERFORMANCE RATIOS

Activity ratios indicate the performance of an organisation. This indicate the effective utilisation of the various assets of the organisation. Most of the ratios falling under this category is based on turnover and hence these ratios are called as turnover ratios. The various activity ratios are as follows:

(1) Stock turnover ratio: This ratio establishes the relationship between the cost of goods sold during a given period and the average stock holding during that period. It tells us as to how many times stock has turned (sold) over the period. This ratio indicates the operational and marketing efficiency of the business. It not only helps in determining the liquidity of the firm but also assets in evaluating inventory policy so as to protect the firm from any danger of over-stocking.

Normally, inventory turnover ratio is best expressed through the relationship between cost of goods sold and average inventory at cost, but ratio of sales to inventory may also be used as a substitute for the rate of cost of goods sold to average inventory, in case, cost of goods sold is not available. Besides these methods, some firms like departmental stores, customarily valuing there inventories at selling prices, compute inventory turnover ratio as the ratio between net sales and average inventory at selling prices.

The average inventory for a year is the sum of inventory at the beginning of the year and inventory at the end of the year and the total is divided by 2. The following formula is used to calculate the inventory turnover ratios:

$$\text{Inventory Turnover Ratio} = \frac{\text{Cost of goods sold}}{\text{Average stock}}$$

Interpretation:

The ideal stock turnover ratio is 8 times a year. A low inventory turnover may reflect dull business, over investment in inventory, accumulation of stock at the end of the period in anticipation of higher prices or of greater sales volume, incorrect inventory resulting from the inclusion of obsolute and unsaleable items and excessive quantitites of certain inventory items in relation to immediate requirements.

A high turnover of inventory may not be accompanied by a relatively high net income as, profits may be sacrificed in obtaining a large sale volume with the result that a higher rate of turnover is likely to prove less profitable than a lower turnover unless accompanied by a larger total gross profit. Similarly, a relatively high turnover ratio may not really be an indicator of favourable results as it may indicate serious under-investment in inventories and this may in turn result in loss of customer patronage on account of failure to make prompt deliveries. But, generally, a high stock turnover ratio means that the concern is efficient and hence it sells its goods quickly.

Problem 5: Rate of Gross profit is 25% on cost. Total sales Rs. 5,00,000. Average stock Rs. 80,000. Compute stock turnover ratio. *(Bangalore University, B.Com., November 1994)*

Solution: Gross profit ratio on cost = 25%

or Gross profit ratio on sales = 20%

$$\text{Cross profit} = \frac{20}{100} \times 5,00,000 = 1,00,000$$

$$\begin{aligned}\text{Cost of sales} &= \text{Sales} - \text{Gross profit} \\ &= 5,00,000 - 1,00,000 \\ &= 4,00,000\end{aligned}$$

$$\text{Stock Turnover Ratio} = \frac{\text{Cost of Sales}}{\text{Average stock}}$$

$$= \frac{4,00,000}{80,000} = 5 \text{ times}$$

Problem 6: Calculate the stock turnover ratio

	(Rs.)
Opening stock	45,000
Closing Stock	55,000
Sales	2,50,000
Gross profit	25% on sales

(Osmania University, B.Com., October 1997)

Solution:

Calculation of Gross Profit

$$\frac{20}{100} \times 2,50,000 = 50,000$$

Calculation of Average Stock

$$\text{Average stock} = \frac{\text{Opening stock} + \text{Closing stock}}{2}$$

$$= \frac{45,000 + 55,000}{2} = 50,000$$

$$\begin{aligned}\text{Cost of sales or cost of goods sold} &= \text{Sales} - \text{Gross profit} \\ &= 2,50,000 - 50,000 \\ &= 2,00,000\end{aligned}$$

$$\text{Stock Turnover Ratio} = \frac{\text{Cost of goods sold}}{\text{Average stock}}$$

$$= \frac{2,00,000}{50,000} = 4 \text{ times}$$

(2) Debtors turnover ratio or debtors velocity ratio: This ratio explains the relationship of net (credit) sales of a firm to its book debts indicating the rate at which cash is generated by turnover of receivables or debtors. The following formula is used:

$$\text{Debtors Turnover Ratio} = \frac{\text{Net annual credit Sales}}{\text{Average Debtors}}$$

The term debtors for the purpose of this ratio is used in a comprehansive sense and also includes the amount of bills receivable along with book debts at the end of the accounting period. Moreover debtors which do not arise from regular sales should be excluded, eg., a bill receivable from the buyer of fixed assets. Sometimes, the ratio is computed from the average of debtors at the beginning and at the end of the year. Another important point in connection with the ratio is that reserve for bad and doubtful debts is not deducted from the total amount of trade debtors.

In the absence of the break-up of sales into cash and credit, the analyst has to use total sales for computation of the ratio with the result that, to the extent cash sales are included, the ratio tends to be overstated. So far as the calculation of daily sales are concerned, the demoninator is to be the number of working days of the business during the year and while it is customary to use 360 days basis rather than 365 days exact, some writers one of the opinion that the denominator should only be 300 days owing to the remainder days being holidays, when too business is transacted.

The purpose of this ratio is to measure the liquidity of the receivable or to find out the period over which receivables remain uncollected, *i.e.*, ageing of receivables. Since debtors constitute a major element of current assets, the credit and collection policies of the business must be under continuous watch. The amount of trade debtors at the end of the accounting period should not exceed a reasonable proportion of net sales. The larger the amount of trade debtors in relation to net sales, the greater would be the expense in connection with uncontrollable accounts. An over-investment in receivables may be the result of over extension of credit, liberalisation of credit terms, ineffective credit investigation, lack of effective collection policies or the inabitity of the collection department to make collection in periods of depression.

Problem 6: Gross profit ratio 20% on sales. Total gross profit Rs. 1,00,000. Cash sales Rs. 1,20,000. Average debtors Rs. 95,000. Calculate debtors turnover ratio.

(Bangalore University, B.Com., November 1994)

Solution:

Gross profit on sales = 20%

Gross profit = Rs. 1,00,000

Total sales $= 1{,}00{,}000 \times \frac{100}{20} = 5{,}00{,}000$

Credit sales = Total sales – Cash sales
= 5,00,000 – 1,20,000
= 3,80,000

$$\text{Debtors turnover ratio} = \frac{\text{Credit Sales}}{\text{Average Debtors}}$$

$$= \frac{3{,}80{,}000}{95{,}000} = 4 \text{ times}$$

(3) Debt collection period ratio: This ratio is helpful in knowing the speed at which debts are collected. It refers to the time involved in collecting the debts by a business enterprise. The following formula is used to calculate debt collection period ratio:

$$\text{Debt Collection Period Ratio} = \frac{\text{No. of days in a year}}{\text{Debtors turnover}}$$

OR

$$= \frac{\text{Debtors}}{\text{Net annual credit Sales}} \times \text{No. of Days in a year}$$

OR

$$= \frac{\text{Net annual credit sales}}{\text{No. of Days in a year}}$$

Problem 7: Find out debtors turnover and average collection period from the following information:

	1994	*1995*
	Rs.	*Rs.*
Annual credit sales	5,00,000	6,00,000
Debtors in the beginning	80,000	90,000
Debtors at the end	1,00,000	1,10,000
No. of days for the year	360 days	360 days

(University of Madras, B.Com., March 1997)

Solution:

$$\text{Debtors Turnover Ratio} = \frac{\text{Credit Sales}}{\text{Average Debtors}}$$

$$1994 = \frac{5,00,000}{90,000} = 5.56 \text{ times}$$

$$1995 = \frac{6,00,000}{1,00,000} = 6 \text{ times}$$

Note: Calculation of Average debtors

$$\text{Average Debtors} = \text{Opening Debtors + Closing Debtors}$$

$$1994 = \frac{80,000 + 1,00,000}{2} = 90,000$$

$$1995 = \frac{90,000 + 1,10,000}{2} = 1,00,000$$

$$\text{Average Collection Period} = \frac{\text{No. of Days}}{\text{Debtors Turnover Ratio}}$$

$$1994 = \frac{360}{5.56} = 65 \text{ days}$$

$$1995 = \frac{360}{6} = 60 \text{ days}$$

(4) Crditor's turnover ratio or creditors velocity: This ratio indicates the number of times the creditors are paid in a year. The following formula is used:

$$\text{Creditors Turnover Ratio} = \frac{\text{Net annual credit purchases}}{\text{Average creditors}}$$

Components:

Credit purchases refers to credit purchase minus purchase returns. Creditors include bills payable. Average creditors is obtained by dividing opening sundry creditors and opening bills payable plus closing sundry creditors and closing bill payable divided by 2. When particulars about opening creditors and opening bills payable are not available, then closing creditors and closing bills payable is taken as denominater.

Problem 8: A company purchases goods both on cash as well as on credit terns. The following particulars are obtained from the books.

	Rs.
Total purchases	3,00,000
Cash purchases	30,000
Purchases returns	51,000
Creditors at the end	1,05,000
Bills payable at the end	60,000
Reserve for discount on creditors	8,000
Calculate average payment period	

(University of Madras, B.Com., March 1994)

Solution:

Total Purchases	3,00,000
Less cash purchases	30,000
	2,70,000
Less purchase returns	51,000
Net credit purchases	2,19,000

Accounts payable = Creditors + Bills payable

or

Total creditors = 1,05,000 + 60,000

= 1,65,000

$$\text{Creditoros Turnover Ratio} = \frac{\text{Credit purchases}}{\text{Average creditors}}$$

$$= \frac{2,19,000}{1,65,000} = 1.33$$

$$\text{Average Payment Period} = \frac{\text{No. of days}}{\text{Creditors turnover Ratio}}$$

$$= \frac{365}{1.33} = 274.44 \text{ day}$$

(4) Working capital turnover ratio: The term working capital refers to excess of current assets over current liabilities. This ratio establishes a relationship between working capital and sales. The following formula is used:

$$\text{Working Capital Turnover Ratio} = \frac{\text{Net Sales}}{\text{Working Capital}}$$

This ratio enables to know efficient utilisation of working capital of an organisation.

(5) Fixed assets turnover ratio: This ratio establishes a relationship between fixed assets and sales. The following formula is used:

$$\text{Fixed Assets Turnover Ratio} = \frac{\text{Net Sales}}{\text{Fixed Assets}}$$

Interpretation:

The standard fixed turnover ratio is 5 times. A high ratio indicates better utilisation of fixed assets. A low ratio indicates under-utilisation of fixed assets.

(6) Current assets turnover ratio: It establishes a relationship between current assets and sales. The following formula is used:

$$\text{Current Asset Turnover Ratio} = \frac{\text{Net Sales}}{\text{Current Assets}}$$

Just as fixed assets turnover ratio, this ratio indicates the contribution of current assets to sales.

(7) Total assets turnover ratio: This ratio establishes a relationship between total assets and sales. This ratio enables to know the efficient utilisation of total assets of a business. The following formula is used:

$$\text{Total Assets Turnover Ratio} = \frac{\text{Net Sales}}{\text{Total Assets}}$$

Interpretation:

A total asset turnover ratio of 2 times or more indicates that assets are utilised efficiently and a ratio below 2 indicates that the assets are under-utilised.

(8) Sales to net worth: It establishes a relationship between sales and owner's funds. This ratio enables to know the utilisation of owner's finds.

(IV) PROFITABILITY RATIOS

Profitability ratios indicate the profit earning capacity of a business. For the sake of clear understanding profitability ratios are classified into two categories, *viz.*, general profitability ratios and overall profitability ratios.

General Profitability Ratios

They include the following ratios:

1. Gross profit ratio
2. Operating ratio
3. Operating profit ratio
4. Expense ratio
5. Net profit ratio

These ratios are explained below:

(1) Gross Profit Ratio: It expresses the relationship of gross profit to net sales and is expressed in terms of percentage. Sales for this purpose means net sales, *i.e.*, sales after deducting the value of goods returned by the customers. Gross profit results from the difference between net sales and cost of goods sold without taking into account expenses generally charged to profit and loss a/c. Cost of goods sold in the case of a trading concern is the purchase of goods and all expenses directly connected with the purchases of goods, while in the case of manufacturing concern, it consists of the purchase price of raw materials and all manufacturing expenses. The following formula is used to calculate this ratio:

$$\text{Gross Profit Ratio} = \frac{\text{Gross Profit}}{\text{Net Sales}} \times 100$$

This ratio is a measure of general profitability of the business and a tool that indicates the degree to which selling price of goods per unit may decline without resulting in losses on operations for the firm. The gross profit should be adaquate to cover the operating expenses and to provide for fixed charges, dividends and buidling up of reserves.

Interpretation:

A low gross profit ratio may indicate unfavourable purchasing, the instability of management to develop sales volume thereby making it impossible to buy goods in large volume, excessive competition etc.

On the other hand an increase in the gross profit ratio may reflect an increase in the sale price of goods sold without any corresponding increase in costs; a decrease in cost without its impact on the sale price of goods, opening stock valued at a figure lower than it should have been, over valuation of closing stock of the end of accounting period etc. There is no rigid standard to this ratio. Normally 25% to 30% margin is anticipated.

(2) Operating ratio: This ratio establishes a relationship between cost of goods sold plus other operating expenses and net sales. Operating expenses consists of administrative expenses, financial expenses selling and distribution expenses. The following formula is used:

$$\text{Operating Ratio} = \frac{\text{Cost of goods sold + Operating expenses}}{\text{Net Sales}}$$

Interpretation:

This ratio is calculated mainly to ascertain the operational efficiency of the management in their business operations, as it shows the percentage of net sales that is absorbed by the cost of goods sold. Higher the operating ratio, the less favourable it is because it would leave a smaller margin to meet interest, dividend and other corporate needs. In general, for manufacturing concerns, operating retio is expected to touch a percentage of 75% to 85%. This ratio can also be used as a partial index of over-all profitability but cannot be used as a test of financial condition.

(3) Operating Profit Ratio: This ratio establishes the relationship between operating profit and net sales and is calculated as follows:

$$\text{Operating Profit Ratio} = \frac{\text{Operating profit}}{\text{Net Sales}} \times 100$$

For calculating this ratio, non-operating expenses and non-operating incomes are ignored. This ratio indicates the portion remaining out of every rupee worth of sales after all operating costs and expenses have been met.

(4) Expense Ratio: These ratios supplement the information given by the operating ratio. They are calculated by dividing each individual operating expenses (*i.e.*, administrative, selling and general expenses) by the net sales revenue.

i.e. (*a*) Material Consumed Ratio $= \frac{\text{Materials consumed}}{\text{Net Sales}} \times 100$

(*b*) Office and Administration Expenses Ratio

$$= \frac{\text{Office and Adm. expenses}}{\text{Net Sales}} \times 100$$

(*c*) Selling and Distribution Expenses Ratio

$$= \frac{\text{Selling and Distribution Expenses}}{\text{Net Sales}} \times 100$$

(*d*) Financial Expenses Ratio $= \frac{\text{Financial Expenses}}{\text{Net Sales}} \times 100$

(*e*) non-operating Expenditure Ratio

$$= \frac{\text{Non-operating expenditure Ratio}}{\text{Net Sales}} \times 100$$

These ratios which represent a summation of changes in net sales and in the expense items are valuable in comparing similar business or operating data from year to year for the same business.

(5) Net Profit Ratio: It expresses the relationship between net profit after taxes to sales. The following formula is used:

$$\text{Net Profit Ratio} = \frac{\text{Net profit after Tax}}{\text{Net Sales}} \times 100$$

This ratio is widely used as a measure of over-all profitability and is very useful to proprietors, as it gives an idea of the efficiency as well as profitability of the business to a limited extent. It different from the operating ratio in the sense it is calculated after adding non-operating income like interest or dividend on investments etc., to generating profit and deducting non-operating expenses such as loss on sale of old assets, provision for legal damages, etc., from such profit.

Tests of Overall Profitability

The ratios which test the overall profitability are concerned with measuring the overall efficiency of the business relating profit to the investment made in the business. These ratios are as follows:

1. Return on shareholders investment or net worth ratio
2. Return on equity capital
3. Return on capital employed
4. Return on total resourses
5. Dividend yield ratio
6. Preference dividend cover ratio
7. Equity dividend cover ratio
8. Price covering ratio
9. Dividend pay-out ratio
10. Earning per share

The above ratios are explained below:

(1) Return on shareholders investment or net worth ratio: Shareholders investment also called return on proprietor's finds is the ratio of net profit (after tax and interest) to proprietor's finds. It is invariably calculated by the prospective investor in the business to find out whether the investment would be worth-making in terms of return as compared to the risk involved in the business. The following formula is used:

$$\text{Return on Shareholders Investment} = \frac{\text{Net profit (After Tax and interest)}}{\text{Proprietor's fund}}$$

Shareholders investment includes all categories of share capital, capital reserves, contingency reserves, all revenue reserves, undistributed profits. Normally the average of the figures relating to shareholder's investments in the opening and closing balance sheets are considered while computing this ratio. Net profit for the purpose represents the net profit after tax and interest on long-term liabilties.

Returns on capital is one of the effective measures of the profitableness of an enterprise. The realisation of a satisfactory net income is the major objective of a business and this ratio shows the extent to which this objective has been achieved. This ratio is also used in making inter-firm comparison.

(2) Return on equity capital: Thus ratio establishes the relationship between net profit available to equity shareholders and the amount of capital invested by them. The following formula is used:

$$\text{Return on Equity Capital} = \frac{\text{Net Profit} - \text{Dividend due to preference shareholders}}{\text{Equity Share capital (paid - up)}}$$

For the purpose of calculating this return net profits are arrived at after deducting the dividend due to preference shareholders. If participating preference shares are issued, they have a right to participate further in the profits after a certain rate of dividend has been paid to equity shareholders. Such participating dividend would also have to be substracted in order to arrive at profits due to equity shareholders.

This rate of return is designed to show what percentage the earned profit of the period bears to the amount of capital invested by equity shareholders. It is used to compare the performance of company's equity capital with those of other companies, and thus help the investor in choosing a company with higher return on equity capital.

(3) Return on capital employed: This ratio is the most appropriate indicator of the earning power of the capital employed in the business. It also acts as a pointer to the management, showing the progress or deterioration in the earning capacity and efficiency of the business. The following formula is used:

$$\text{Return on Capital Employed} = \frac{\text{Net profit before Taxes and interest long-term loans, and debentures}}{\text{Capital employed}}$$

The term capital employed refers to the total long-term funds used in a business. It is calculated is shown below:

Net fixed assets	xx
Add: Trade investments, *i.e.*, investments made in associated concern to promote trade	xx
Add: Net working capital, *i.e.*, excess of current assets over current liabilitites capital employed	xx
	xx

Interpretation:

The standard return on capital employed is about 15%. If the actual ratio is equal to or above 15% it indicates higher productivity of the capital employed and *vice-versa*.

(4) Return on total resources: This ratio acts as an yordstick to assess the efficiency of the operations of the business as it indicates the extent to which assets employed in the business are utilised to result in net profit. The following formula is used:

$$\text{Return on Total Resources} = \frac{\text{Net Profit}}{\text{Total Assets}} \times 100$$

(5) Dividend yield ratio: It refers to the percentage or ratio of dividend paid per share to the market price per share. This ratio throws light on the effective rate of return on investment, which potential investors may hope to earn. The following formula is used:

$$\text{Dividend Yield Ratio} = \frac{\text{Dividend paid per equity share}}{\text{Market price per equity share}}$$

(6) Preference dividend cover: It indicates how many times the preference dividend is covered by profits after tax. This ratio measures the margin of safety for preference shareholders. Such investors normally expect their dividend to be coverd about 3 times by profits available for dividend purpose. The following formula is used:

$$\text{Preference Dividend Cover} = \frac{\text{Profit after Tax}}{\text{Annual programme dividend}}$$

(7) Equity Dividend Cover: This ratio indicates the number of times the dividend is covered by the amount of profit available for equity shareholders, *i.e.*, net profit after tax less preference dividend. The following formula is used:

$$\text{Equity Dividend Cover} = \frac{\text{Net profit (after Tax)} - \text{preference dividend}}{\text{Dividend paid on equity capital}}$$

or

$$= \frac{\text{Earnings per Equity Share}}{\text{Dividend per Equity Share}}$$

Interpretation:

An ideal equity dividend cover is 2, *i.e.*, out of every Rs. 100 profits available for dividend, Rs. 50 is distributed and Rs. 50 is retained and ploughed back in the business. Higher the dividend cover, the higher is the extent of retained earnings and higher is the degree of certainty that dividend will be repeated in future years also.

(8) Price-earning ratio: It shows how many times the annual earnings the present shareholders are willing to pay to get a share. This ratio helps investors to know the effect of earnings per share on the market price of the share. This ratio when calculated for several years can be used as trend analysis for predicting future price earning ratios and therefore, future stock prices. The following formula is used:

$$\text{Price Earning Ratio} = \frac{\text{Average Market price per share}}{\text{Earning per share}}$$

(9) Dividend pay-out ratio: This ratio indicates the proportion of earnings available which equity share-holders actually receive in the form of dividend. An investor primarily interested should invest in equity shares of a company with high pay-out ratio. A company having low-pay-out ratio need not necessarily be a bad company. A company having income may like to finance expansion out of the income earned and thus have low-pay-out ratio. An investor interested in stock-price appreciation may well invest in such a company even though the pay-out ratio is low. The following formula is used:

$$\text{Pay-out Ratio} = \frac{\text{Dividend paid per share}}{\text{Earning per share}}$$

(10) Earning per share: This ratio indicates the earnings per equity share. It establishes the relationship between net profit avaible for equity shareholders and the number of equity shares. The following formula is used:

$$\text{Earning Per Share} = \frac{\text{Net profit available for equity shareholders}}{\text{Number of equity shares}}$$

Leverage Ratios

Leverage ratios are calculated to test long-term financial position of a firm. Leverage ratios are classified into three types, *viz.*

(*a*) Financial leverage or trading on equity: Financial leverage refers to use of long-term interest bearing debt and preference share capital along with equity share capital. The following formula is used:

$$\text{Financial Leverage} = \frac{\text{Earnings before Interest and Tax}}{\text{Earnings before Interest and Tax} - \text{Interest and preference dividend}}$$

(b) Operating leverage: It is obtained by dividing 'contribution' by Earnings before interest and tax. Contribution represents the difference between the sales and variable cost. The following formula is used:

$$\text{Operating Leverage} = \frac{\text{Contribution}}{\text{Earning before interest and Tax}}$$

(c) Combined Leverage: This is a product of the above two leverages. The following formula is used:

$$\text{Combined Leverage} = \text{Financial Leverage} \times \text{Operating Leverage}$$

Problem 9: Rao Insulating Company submitted the following particulars. Calculate (*a*) financial leverage, (*b*) operating leverage under both the situations:

Sales 50,000 units @	Rs. 15
Variable cost per unit	Rs. 9
Fixed cost	Rs. 20,000
Debenture interest paid	Rs. 40,000
Tax 50%	
Increase in production	10,000 units

Solution: **Statement Showing Profit after Tax**

	50,000 *Units*	60,000 *Units*
Sales		
50,000 × 15		
60,000 × 15	7,50,000	9,00,000
Less variable cost		
50,000 × 9		
60,000 × 9	4,50,000	5,40,000
Contribution	3,00,000	3,60,000
Less Fixed expenses	2,000	20,000
	2,80,000	3,40,000
Less Interest	40,000	40,000
Profit before taxes	2,40,000	3,00,000
Less taxes	1,20,000	1,50,000
Profit after tax	1,20,000	1,50,000

$$\text{Financial Leverage} = \frac{\text{EBIT}}{\text{EBIT} - \text{Interest}}$$

$$\text{For 50,000 units level} = \frac{2,80,000}{2,80,000 - 40,000}$$

$$= \frac{2,80,000}{2,40,000} = 1.167$$

$$\text{For 60,000 units level} = \frac{3,40,000}{3,40,000 - 40,000}$$

$$= \frac{3,40,000}{3,00,000} = 1.13$$

$$\text{Operating Leverage} = \frac{\text{Contribution}}{\text{EBIT}}$$

For 50,000 units level $= \dfrac{3,00,000}{2,80,000} = 1.07$

For 60,000 units level $= \dfrac{3,60,000}{3,40,000} = 1.05$

DU-PONT CONTROL CHART

It is a chart designed by an DU-pont company of America. The chart helps management to exercise control by using ratios and their inter-relationship. The actual ratios are compared with standard ratios to judge the performance of the business. The chart is as follows:

DU-PONT CHART

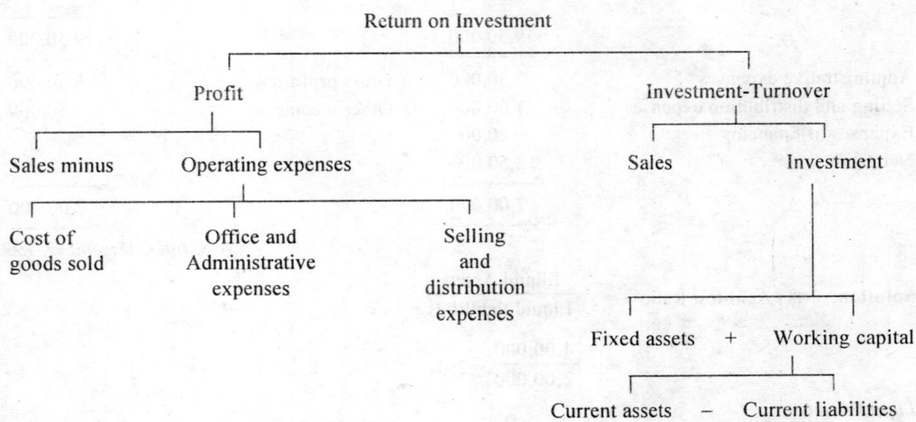

The chart is based on two aspects, *viz.* profit and investment. Profit is the difference between sales and operating expenses. When operating expenses are controlled profit margin will be increased. Earnings is the difference between sales and cost of sales. Cost of sale is the aggregate of cost of goods sold, office and administration expenses and selling and distribution expenses. Investments is the aggregate of fixed assets and working capital. Working capital is the excess of current assets over current liabilities.

The efficiency of a business depends upon the functioning of the business. The return on investment is taken as a basis to measure efficiency. The efficiency is reflected by the profit earned by the business. The efficiency can be increased by minimising costs or effective use of capital or by increasing sales. In case of inefficiency, the management can identify the areas and take remedial steps. Inter-firm comparision is used as a technique to evaluate the performance. The important ratios used in this connection are return on investment, assets turnover ratio and profitability ratios.

Problem 10: From the following final accounts of XYZ Co. Ltd. for the year ended 31st March, 1999, you are required to calculate the following:

1. Acid test ratio
2. Stock turnover ratio
3. Operating ratio
4. Debt collection period and
5. Net profit to capital employed ratio

Balance sheet as on 31st March 1999

Share capital (in shares of Rs. 10 each)	5,00,000	Land and Buildings	5,00,000
General Reserve	4,00,000	Plant and Machinery	2,00,000
Profit and loss a/c	1,50,000	Stock	1,50,000
Sundry creditors	2,00,000	Sundry debtors	2,50,000
		Cash and bank balance	1,50,000
	12,50,000		12,50,000

Profit and loss a/c for the year ended 31st March 1999

Opening stock	2,50,000	Sales	18,00,000
Purchases	10,50,000	Closing stock	1,50,000
Gross profit b/d	6,50,000		
	19,50,000		19,50,000
Administrative expenses	2,30,000	Gross profit b/d	6,50,000
Selling and distribution expenses	1,00,000	Other income	50,000
Expenses of financing	20,000		
Net profit	3,50,000		
	7,00,000		7,00,000

(*CS, Inter, December, 1999*)

Solution: (1) Acid-test Ratio $= \dfrac{\text{Liquid Assets}}{\text{Liquid liabilities}}$

$$= \frac{4,00,000}{2,00,000} = 2:1$$

Liquid Assets

Sundry debtors	=	2,50,000
Cash and Bank balance	=	1,50,000
		4,00,000

(2) Stock Turnover Ratio $= \dfrac{\text{Cost of goods sold}}{\text{Average stock}}$

$$= \frac{11,50,000}{2,00,000} = 5.75 \text{ times}$$

Cost of goods sold

Opening stock	=	2,50,000
Add: Purchases	=	10,50,000
		13,00,000
Less: Closing stock		1,50,000
		11,50,000

$$\text{Average Stock} = \frac{\text{Opening stock} + \text{closing stock}}{2}$$

$$= \frac{2,50,000 + 1,50,000}{2} = 2,00,000$$

$$\text{(3) Operating Ratio} = \frac{\text{Cost of goods sold + operating expenses}}{\text{Net Sales}} \times 100$$

$$= \frac{11,50,000 + 3,30,000}{18,00,000} \times 100$$

$$= 82.2\%$$

Operating expenses

Administrative expenses + Selling and Distribution expenses

= 2,30,000 + 1,00,000

= 3,30,000

$$\text{(4) Debt Collection Period} = \frac{\text{Total Debtors}}{\text{Sales per day}}$$

$$= \frac{2,50,000}{\frac{18,00,00}{365}}$$

$$= \frac{2,50,000 \times 365}{18,00,00} = 50.7 \text{ or } 51 \text{ days}$$

$$\text{(5) Net profit to capital employed} = \frac{\text{Net profit}}{\text{Capital employed}} \times 100$$

$$= \frac{3,50,000}{10,50,000} \times 100 = 33.33\%$$

Capital employed

Share capital	5,00,000
General reserve	4,00,000
Profit & loss a/c	1,50,000
Shareholders finds	10,50,000

Problem 11: The Balance Sheet of Punjab Auto Ltd. as on 31-12-1991 was as follows:

Liabilities		*Assets*	
Equity share capital	40,000	Plant and machinery	24,000
Capital reserve	8,000	Land and Building	40,000
8% loan on mortagage	32,000	Furniture and	
creditors	16,000	fixture	16,000
Bank overdraft	4,000	Stock	12,000
Taxation:		Debtors	12,000
—current	4,000	Investment	4,000
—Future	4,000	(short term)	
P & C a/c	12,000	Cash in hand	12,000
	1,20,000		1,20,000

From the above compute: (*a*) The Current Ratio, (*b*) Quick Ratio, (*c*) Debt-equity Ratio, (*d*) Proprietory Ratio. (*Bangalore University, B.B.M. April 2000*)

Solution: (a) $\text{Current ratio} = \frac{\text{Current Assets}}{\text{Current Liabilities}}$

$$= \frac{40,000}{28,000} = 1.42$$

Current Assets	
Stock	12,000
Debtors	12,000
Investment (Short-term)	4,000
Cash in hand	12,000
	40,000

Current liabilities	
Creditors	16,000
Bank overdraft	4,000
Taxation	8,000
	28,000

(b) Quick Ratio $= \dfrac{\text{Liquid Assets}}{\text{Liquid liabilities}}$

$= \dfrac{28,000}{24,000} = 1.16$

Liquid Assets	
Debtors	12,000
Investment (Short-term)	4,000
Cash in hand	12,000
	28,000

Liquid liabilities	
Creditors	16,000
Taxation	8,000
	24,000

(c) Debt-equity Ratio $= \dfrac{\text{External Equities}}{\text{Internal Equities}}$

$= \dfrac{52,000}{60,000} = 0.86$

External equities	
8% loan on mortgage	32,000
Creditors	16,000
Bank overdraft	4,000
	52,000

Internal equities	
Equity share capital	40,000
Capital reserve	8,000
P & C a/c	12,000
	60,000

(d) Proprietory Ratio $= \dfrac{\text{Shareholders funds}}{\text{Total Tangible assets}}$

$= \dfrac{60,000}{1,20,000} = 0.50$

Problem 12: Following is the balance sheet of Non-Such Co. Ltd. for the year ending 31st March, 1997. Calculate ratios for (*i*) testing liquidity and (*ii*) testing solvency:

Liabilitites		*Assets*	
Equity share capital	5,00,000	Goodwill	2,50,000
12% preference share capital	2,50,000	Plant and machinery	3,00,000
General reserve	50,000	Land and Building	3,50,000
Profit and loss a/c	2,00,000	Furniture	50,000
Provision for tax	88,000	Stock	3,00,000
Bills payable	62,000	Bills receivable	15,000
Bank overdraft	10,000	Sundry debtors	75,000
Sundry creditors	40,000	Bank	1,00,000
12% debentures	2,50,000	Marketable securities	10,000
	14,50,000		14,50,000

(*Sri Vanhateshwara University, B.Com., April 1999*)

Solution:

Tests of Liquidity

(a) Current ratio $= \dfrac{\text{Current Assets}}{\text{Current Liabilities}}$

$= \dfrac{5,00,000}{2,00,000} = 2.5$

Current Assets	
Stock	3,00,000
Bills receivable	15,000
Sundry debtors	75,000
Bank	1,00,000
Marketable securities	10,000
	5,00,000

Current liabilities	
Provision for tax	88,000
Bills payable	62,000
Bank OD	10,000
Sundry creditors	40,000
	2,00,000

(b) Quick or Liquid Ratio $= \dfrac{\text{Liquid Assets}}{\text{Liquid Liabilities}}$

$= \dfrac{2,00,000}{1,90,000} = 1.05$

Liquid Assets	
Bills Receivable	15,000
Sundry debtors	75,000
Bank	1,00,000
Marketable securities	10,000
	2,00,000

Liquid liabilities = Current liabilities – Bank OD
= 2,00,000 – 10,000
= 1,90,000

(c) Absolute Liquid Ratio $= \dfrac{\text{Absolute Liquid Assets}}{\text{Liquid liabilities}}$

$= \dfrac{1,10,000}{1,90,000} = 0.57$

Absolute liquid assets

Bank	1,00,000
Marketable securities	10,000
	1,10,000

(2) *Solvency Ratios*

(a) Debt-equity Ratio $= \dfrac{\text{Long term liabilities}}{\text{shareholders funds}}$

$= \dfrac{2,50,000}{10,00,000} = 0.25$

Long-term liabilities

12% Debentures = 2,50,000

Shareholders finds

Preference share capital	=	5,00,000
Equity share capital	=	2,50,000
General reserve	=	50,000
P & C a/c	=	2,00,000
		10,00,000

Note: Preference share capital is included in the shareholders funds as it is not redeemable

(b) Proprietory Ratio $= \dfrac{\text{Proprietors funds}}{\text{Total Assets}}$

$= \dfrac{10,00,000}{14,50,000} = 0.69$

(c) Capital Gearing Ratio $= \dfrac{\text{Fixed Interest bearing Securities + Fixed Dividend bearing Securities}}{\text{Equity Shareholder's funds}}$

$= \dfrac{2,50,000 + 2,50,000}{7,50,000}$

$= \dfrac{5,00,000}{7,50,000} = 0.66$

Fixed Interest Bearing Securities

12% Debentures = 2,50,000

Fixed Dividend bearing securities

12% Preference share capital = 2,50,000

Equity shareholders finds

Equity share capital	=	5,00,000
General reserve	=	50,000
P & C a/c	=	2,00,000
		7,50,000

(*d*) Fixed assets ratio $= \frac{\text{Net Fixed Assets}}{\text{proprietor's funds}}$

$= \frac{9,50,000}{10,00,000} = 0.95$

Net Fixed Assets

Goodwill	=	2,50,000
Plant and machinery	=	3,00,000
Land and building	=	3,50,000
Furniture	=	50,000
		9,50,000

Proprietors Funds

Equity share capital	=	5,00,000
General reserve	=	50,000
P & c a/c	=	2,00,000
12% pref share capital	=	2,50,000
		10,00,000

Problem 13: From the following information calculate current ratio liquid ratio, creditors turnover and average credit sales of Surya Ltd. and Chandra Ltd.

	Surya Ltd.	*Chandra Ltd.*
Credit to Debtors	*3 months*	*3 months*
	Rs.	*Rs.*
Stock	8,00,000	1,00,000
Debtors	1,70,000	1,40,000
Cash	30,000	60,000
Trade creditors	2,80,000	1,50,000
Bills payable	20,000	10,000
Bank overdraft	4,000	30,000
Creditor for expenses	60,000	10,000
Total purchases	9,30,000	6,60,000
Cash purchases	30,000	20,000

(*University of Bombay, B.Com., October 1999*)

Solution:

Current Ratio $= \frac{\text{Current Assets}}{\text{Current liabilities}}$

Surya Ltd. $= \frac{10,00,000}{4,00,000} = 2.5$ times

Current Assets

Stock		8,00,000
Debtors		1,70,000
Cash		30,000
		10,00,000

Current liabilities

Trade creditors	=	2,80,000
Bills payable	=	20,000
Bank OD	=	40,000
Creditors for expenses	=	60,000
		4,00,000

Chandra Ltd. $= \frac{3,00,000}{2,00,000} = 1.5$ times

Current Assets

Stock	=	1,00,000
Debtors	=	1,40,000
Cash	=	60,000
		3,00,000

Current liabilities

Trade creditors	=	1,50,000
Bills payable	=	10,000
Bank overdraft	=	30,000
Creditors for expenses	=	10,000
		2,00,000

(3) Liquid Ratio $= \frac{\text{Liquid Assets}}{\text{Liquid Liabilities}}$

or $= \frac{\text{Current Assets} - \text{Stock}}{\text{Current Liabilities} - \text{Bank O.D.}}$

Surya Ltd. $= \frac{2,00,000}{3,60,000} = 0.56$

Chandra Ltd. $= \frac{2,00,000}{1,70,000} = 1.18$

(3) Creditors Turnover Ratio $= \frac{\text{Credit purchases}}{\text{Creditors + Bills payable}}$

Surya Ltd. $= \frac{9,00,000}{2,80,000 + 20,000}$

$= \frac{9,00,000}{3,00,0000} = 3$ times

Chandra Ltd. $= \frac{6,40,000}{1,50,000 + 10,000}$

$= \frac{6,40,000}{1,60,000} = 4$ times

(4) *Average Credit Sales*

Surya Ltd.:-

for 3 months: Debtors are Rs. = 1,70,000

for 12 months: — ?

$\frac{1,70,000 \times 12}{3}$ = Rs. 6,80,000

Chandra Ltd.:-

for 3 months: Debtors are = 1,40,000

for 12 months: — ?

$\frac{1,40,000 \times 12}{3}$ = Rs. 5,60,000

Problem 14: From the following balance sheet of Tara Ltd. calculate: (*a*) long-term debt-equity, (*b*) proprietory ratio, (*c*) capital gearing ratio, (*d*) stock-working capital ratios.

Equity share capital	2,00,000	Land and Building	1,40,000
8% pref share capital	60,000	Plant and machinery	80,000
Reserve	30,000	Furniture and fixtures	20,000
P & C a/c	20,000	Debtors	80,000
9% Debentures	40,000	Stock	70,000
Creditors	60,000	Cash in hand	30,000
O/s expenses	5,000	Prepaid expenses	10,000
Provision for taxation	20,000	Preliminary	
Proposed dividend	15,000	expenses	20,000
	4,50,000		4,50,000

(*University of Bombay, B.Com., October 1999*)

Solution:

(1) Long-term debt equity Ratio $= \dfrac{\text{Long Term Debt}}{\text{Shareholders funds}}$

$= \dfrac{40,000}{2,90,000} = 0.138$

Long-term Debt

9% Debentures = 40,000

Shareholders finds

Equity share capital	=	2,00,000
Preference share capital	=	60,000
Reserves and surplus	=	30,000
P &C a/c	=	20,000
		3,10,000
Less fictitions assets		20,000
		2,90,000

(2) Proprietory Ratio $= \dfrac{\text{Proprietor's funds}}{\text{Total Assets}}$

$= \dfrac{2,90,000}{4,30,000} = 0.67$

Total Assets

Total of all assets			=	4,50,000
Less: Prepaid expenses	=	10,000		
Less: Preliminary expenses	=	20,000		
				30,000
				4,20,000

(3) Capital Bearing Ratio $= \dfrac{\text{Fixed Interest bearing Securities + Fixed Dividend bearing Securities}}{\text{Equity Shareholders funds}}$

$= \dfrac{40,000 + 6,00,000}{2,30,000} = 0.43$

Fixed Interest Bearing Securities

9% Debentures	=	40,000

Fixed Dividend bearing securities

8% pref shares	=	60,000

Equity shareholders finds

Equity share capital	=	2,00,000
Reserves	=	30,000
P & L a/c	=	20,000
		2,50,000
Less: Preliminary expenses		20,000
		2,30,000

(4) Stock-Working Capital Ratio $= \frac{\text{Stock}}{\text{Working Capital}}$

$$= \frac{70,000}{90,000} = 0.77$$

Working Capital

Current Assets:		
Debtors		80,000
Stock		70,000
Cash in hand		30,000
Prepaid expenses		10,000
		1,90,000
Less: Current liabilities		
Creditors	60,000	
O/s expenses	5,000	
Provision for tax	20,000	
Proposed Dividend	15,000	
	1,00,000	1,00,000
working capital		90,000

Problem 15: The following are the Trading and Profit & loss for the year ended 31st December, 1998 and the balance sheet as on that date of K Ltd.

Trading and P & L A/c

To operning stock	9,950	By Sales	85,000
To purchases	5,4525	By Closing stock	14,900
To wages	1425		
To Gross profit	34,000		
	99,900		99,900
To Administrative expenses	15,000	By Gross profit	34,000
To Selling expenses	3,000	By Interest	300
To Financial expenses	15,000	By Profit on sale of shares	600
To Loss on sale of assets	400		
To Net profit	15,000		
	34,900		34,900

Balance Sheet

Share capital	20,000	Land and Buildings	15,000
Reserves	9,000	Plant and Machinery	8,000
Current liabilities	13,000	Stock	14,900
P & L a/c	6,000	Debtors	7,100
		Cash at bank	3,000
	48,000		48,000

You are required to calculate:

(*a*) Current Ratio
(*b*) Operating Ratio
(*c*) Stock Turnover Ratio
(*d*) Net Profit Ratio
(*e*) Fixed Assets Turnover Ratio

(*Osmania University, B.Com., October 1999*)

Solution:

(*a*) Current Ratio $= \dfrac{\text{Current Assets}}{\text{Current liabilities}}$

$= \dfrac{25,000}{13,000} = 1.92$

Current Assets

Stock	14,900
Debtors	7,100
Cash at Bank	3,000
	25,000

(*b*) Operating Ratio $= \dfrac{\text{Cost of goods sold + Operating expenses}}{\text{Net Sales}}$

$= \dfrac{51,000 + 19,500}{85,000}$

$= \dfrac{70,500}{85,000} = 0.829$

Cost of Goods Sold

Opening stock	=	9,950
Purchases	=	54,525
Wages	=	1,425
		65,900
Less: Closing stock		14,900
		51,000

(*c*) Stock Turnover Ratio $= \dfrac{\text{Cost of goods sold}}{\text{Average Stock}}$

$= \dfrac{51,000}{12,425} = 4.10$ times

Average stock

$= \dfrac{\text{Opening stock + Closing stock}}{2}$

$= \dfrac{9,950 + 14,900}{2} = 12,425$

(*d*) Net Profit Ratio $= \dfrac{\text{Net profit}}{\text{Net sales}} \times 100$

$= \dfrac{15{,}000}{85{,}000} \times 100 = 17.64\%$

(*e*) Fixed Assets Turnover Ratio $= \dfrac{\text{Net Sales}}{\text{Fixed Assets}}$

$= \dfrac{85{,}000}{23{,}000} = 3.7$ times

Problem 16: The profit and loss a/c and balance sheet of XYZ Ltd. are as under:

Profit and loss A/c for the year ended 31st December, 1997

	Net sales		3,00,000
Less:	Cost of production		2,58,000
			42,000
Less:	Operating expenses		
	Selling	2,200	
	General administration	4,000	
	Rent of office	2,800	
			9,000
	Gross operating profit		33,000
Less:	Depreciation		10,000
	Net operating profit		23,000
	other income and interest on govt. securities		1,500
	Gross income (before tax)		24,500
Less:	Other expenses:		
	Interest on bank overdraft	300	
	Intrest on debentures	42,000	
			4,500
	Net income (before tax)		20,000
	Tax 50% on net income		10,000
	Net income (after tax)		10,000

Balance sheet as at 31st Dec., 1997

Equity share capital	50,000	Fixed assets	1,80,000	
7% pref share capital	10,000	*Less*: Depreciation	50,000	
Reserves and surplus	40,000			1,30,000
6% Mortgage debentures	70,000	Investment on govt. securities		15,000
Creditors	6,000	Debtors		20,000
Bills payable	10,000	Stock		30,000
O/s expenses	1,000	Cash		5,000
Provision for taxation	13,000			
	2,00,000			2,00,000

You are required to calculate the following ratios:

1. Return on investment
2. Net profit ratio
3. Current ratio
4. Net worth to capital employed
5. Cost of production to capital employed

(*CS Intermediate, June, 1999*)

Solution:

(1) Return on Investment $= \dfrac{\text{Net Profit (After Tax and Interest)}}{\text{Proprietors funds}}$

$= \dfrac{10{,}000}{1{,}00{,}000} = 0.10$

Proprietors Funds

Equity share capital	=	50,000
7% pref. share capital	=	10,000
Reserves and surplus	=	40,000
		1,00,000

(2) Net profit ratio $= \dfrac{\text{Net Profit}}{\text{Net Sales}} \times 100$

$= \dfrac{10{,}000}{3{,}00{,}000} \times 100 = 3.33\%$

(3) Current ratio $= \dfrac{\text{Current Assets}}{\text{Current Liabilities}}$

$= \dfrac{55{,}000}{30{,}000} = 1.88$

Current Assets

Debtors	20,000
Stock	30,000
Cash	5,000
	55,000

Current liabilities

Creditors	6,000
Bills payable	10,000
O/s expenses	1,000
Provision for taxation	13,000
	30,000

(4) Net worth to capital employed $= \dfrac{\text{Net Worth}}{\text{Capital employed}}$

$= \dfrac{1{,}00{,}000}{1{,}55{,}000} = 0.64$

Capital employed

Net fixed assets		1,30,000
Add: Current assets:		
Debtors	20,000	
Stock	30,000	
Cash	5,000	
		55,000
		1,85,000
Less: Current liabilities		30,000
		1,55,000

Net worth

Equity share capital	=	50,000
7% pref share capital	=	10,000
Reserves and surplus	=	40,000
		1,00,000

(5) Cost of production to capital employed $= \frac{\text{cost of production}}{\text{capital employed}} \times 100$

$= \frac{2,58,000}{1,55,000} \times 100$

$= 166.45\%$

Problem 17: The actual ratios of a company compared to the industry standard are given below. Comment on each ratio and indicate in one or two sentences the nature of action to be taken by the company:

	Ratio	*Industry standard*	*Actual for The Company*
(i)	Current ratio	2.2	2.7
(ii)	Debtors turnover ratio	6	8
(iii)	Stock turnover ratio	10	3
(iv)	Net profit ratio	5%	2.4%
(v)	Total debt to total assets	7.5%	40%

(*ICWA, Intermediate, December, 1999*)

Solution:

(1) Current Ratio: Normal value is 2. Here the company's position is above the normal value and the industry standard. This may also be due to excessive stock (Also refer to point 3 below).

(2) Debtor's Turnover Ratio· The industry standard indicates an average collection period of two months, while for the company it is only 1½ months. The companys position is better.

(3) Stock Turnover Ratio: The stock is moving very slowly obviously there is excessive stock in the company. Perhaps this has boosted up the current ratio. The sales volume has to be considerably increased and stock level brought down.

(4) Net Profit Ratio: Here the company's performance is very unsatisfactory compared to the overall position in the industry. This calls for steps to get better sales realisation and reduction of the cost of production.

(5) Total Debts to Total Assets: The percentage is disproportionately high in the company indicating a larger proportion of debt in the capital structure. Too high a debt component means too high a risk for equity shareholders.

Problem 18: The Balance Sheets of Katha Ltd., as on 31st December 1996 and 1997 were as follows:

(*Rs. in Thousand*)

Liabilities	*1996*	*1997*	*Assets*	*1996*	*1997*
Equity share capital (Rs. 10 each)	3,000	3,000	Fixed Assets	3,600	4,240
12% preference share	1,000	1,000	Sundry debtors	1,100	1,300
Reserves	1,160	1,770	Bills Receivable	860	1,050
10% Debentures	600	900	Stock	760	920
Creditors	480	640	Prepaird expenses	80	50
Bills payable	100	140	Bank Balance	120	120
Bank overdraft	200	240	Preliminary expenses	20	10
	6,540	7,690		6,540	7,690

During the year 1997, total sales were Rs. 1,80,00,000 and cash sales were 10% of total sales. Stock turnover ratio was 20 times. Net profit before payment of taxes at 40% was Rs. 22,50,000. There were no non-operating expenses and profit on sale of fixed assets Rs. 50,000. Calculate the following ratios for the year 1997.

1. Gross profit ratio
2. Operating ratio
3. Current ratio
4. Debtors turnover ratio and collection period
5. Return on capital employed
6. Earning per share

(University of Bombay, B.Com., October, 1998)

Solution: *(Fig. in Thousand)*

(1) Gross Profit Ratio $= \dfrac{\text{Gross profit}}{\text{Net Sales}} \times 100$

$= \dfrac{1,200}{18,000} \times 100 = 6.67\%$

Calculate of Gross Profit

Sales – Cost of goods sold = Gross profit

18,000 – 16,800 = 1,200

Calculation of Cost of Goods Sold

Stock Turnover Ratio $= \dfrac{\text{Cost of goods sold}}{\text{Average stock}}$

$20 = \dfrac{x}{840}$

on cross multiplying x $= 20 \times 840$

$= 16,800$

Calculation of Average Stock

$\dfrac{\text{Opening stock + Closing stock}}{2}$

$= \dfrac{760 + 920}{2} = 840$

(2) Operating Ratio $= \dfrac{\text{Operating Cost + Operating expenses}}{\text{Net Sales}}$

$= \dfrac{16,800 + 0}{18,000} = 0.93$

(3) Current Ratio $= \dfrac{\text{Current Assets}}{\text{Current Liabilities}}$

$= \dfrac{3,440}{1,020} = 3.37$

Current Assets

S. Debtors	1,300
Bills Receivable	1,050
Stock	920
Prepaid expenses	50
Bank Balance	120
	3,440

Current Liabilities

Creditors	640
Bills payable	140
Bank OD	240
	1,020

(4) Debtors Turnover Ratio $= \frac{\text{Net Credit Sales}}{\text{Average accounts recoverable}}$

$= \frac{16,200}{2,155} = 7.52$ times

Net Credit Sales

Total sales	18,000
Less: Cash sales $\frac{10}{100} \times 18,000$	1,800
	16,200

Average Accounts Receivable

$= \frac{(\text{Opening Bills Receivable} + \text{Opening Debtors}) + (\text{Closing B.R.} + \text{Closing Debtors})}{2}$

$= \frac{(860 + 1,100) + (1,050 + 1,300)}{2}$

$= \frac{4,310}{2} = 2,155$

Debtors Collection Period $= \frac{365}{\text{Debtors Turnover Ratio}}$

$= \frac{365}{7.52} = 48.53$ or 49 Days

(5) Return on Capital Employed $= \frac{\text{Net profit before Tax, Interest}}{\text{Capital employed}}$

$= \frac{2,250 + 90}{6,660}$ (Debentures Interest)

$= 0.35$

Capital Employed

Net Fixed Assets		4240	
Add: Working Capital:			
Current Assets:			
Debtors		1,300	
B.R.		1,050	
Stock		920	
Prepaid expense		50	
Bank Balance		120	
		3,440	
Less Current liabilities			
Creditors	640		
B.P.	140		
Bank OD	240	1,020	
			2,420
	Capital Employed		6,660

(6) Earning Per Share $= \frac{\text{NPAT} - \text{Preference Dividend}}{\text{No. of equity shares}}$

$= \frac{1350 - 120}{300} = 4.10$ Rs.

N.P.A.T.	
Net Profit Before Tax	2,250
Less: Tax @ 40%	900
	1,350

Problem 19: The summarised balance sheet of Good Value Traders Ltd. for the year ended 31-3-1998 is given below:

(Rs. in Lakhs)

Equity share capital	140	Fixed Assets	210	
Reserve & surplus	45	*Less:* Depreication	25	
Profit and loss a/c	20	*Current assets:*		185
Provision for taxation	10	Stock	25	
Sundry creditors	40	Debtors	30	
		Cash	15	70
	225			225

The following further particulars one also given for the year

(in Lakh of rupees)

Sales	120
Earning before Interest and Tax (EBIT)	30
Net profit after Tax (PAT)	20

Calculate the following for the company and explain the significance of each in one or two sentences:

1. Current ratio
2. Liquidity ratio
3. Profitability ratio
4. Profitability on funds employed
5. Debtors turnover
6. Stock turnover
7. Average collection period
8. Return on equity

(ICWA, Inter, June 1998)

Solution:

(Figures in Lakh of Rupees)

(1) Current Ratio $= \frac{\text{Current Assets}}{\text{Current Liabilities}}$

$= \frac{70}{40} = 1.75$

This ratio measures the liquidity of the firm and indicates its ability to meet the liabilities. Normal or ideal ratio is 2: 1.

(2) Liquidity Ratio $= \frac{\text{Liquid Assets}}{\text{Liquid liabilities}}$

$= \frac{45}{40} = 1.125$

Liquid Assets

Debtors	30
Cash	15
	45

This is more stringent than current ratio and measures the short term liquidity of the firm. Normal value is 1: 1.

(3) Profitability $= \frac{\text{EBIT}}{\text{Sales}} \times 100$

$= \frac{30}{120} \times 100 = 25\%$

This ratio indicates profit earned on sales

(4) Profitability on funds employed $= \frac{\text{EBIT}}{\text{Share Capital and Long term loans}} = \frac{30}{205}$

Share Capital and Long-term Loans

Equity share capital	140
Reserves and surplus	45
Profit and loss a/c	20
	205

This ratio measures profitability on funds employed

(5) Debtors Turnover Ratio $= \frac{\text{Sales}}{\text{Average Debtors}}$

$= \frac{120}{30} = 4$

This ratio indicates how fast debtors are converted into cash.

(6) Stock Turnover Ratio $= \frac{\text{Cost of goods sold}}{\text{Average stock}}$

$= \frac{90}{25} = 3.6 \text{ times}$

Cost of Goods Sold

Sales – EBIT

12 – 30 = 90

This ratio indicates the number of times stock is sold during the period.

(7) Average Collection Period $= \frac{\text{Debtors}}{\text{Credit Sales}} \times \text{No. of months in a year}$

$= \frac{30}{120} \times 12 = 3 \text{ months}$

This ratio indicates the normal credit allowed to customers

(8) Return on Equity $= \frac{\text{PAT}}{\text{Shareholders funds}}$

$= \frac{20}{205} = 9.76$

This ratio indicates the net return earned on shareholders funds.

Problem 20: From the following balance sheet and the sub-joined information of a company, you are required to calculate:

(*a*) Current ratio
(*b*) Quick ratio
(*c*) Inventory turnover
(*d*) Average collection period presuming 360 days in a year
(*e*) Owned finds to liabiltites ratio

Balance Sheet

Share capital	2,00,000	Goodwill	1,20,000
Reserves and surplus	58,000	Plant and machinery	1,50,000
Debentures	1,00,000	Stock	80,000

Creditors	40,000	Debtors	45,000
Bills payable	20,000	Cash	17,000
Other current liabilities	2,000	Miscellaneous current assets	8,000
	4,20,000		4,20,000

Sales (credit) for the year	Rs. 4,00,000
Gross pforit	Rs. 1,60,000

(*CS, Inter, December, 1998*)

Solution:

(1) Current Ratio $= \dfrac{\text{Current Assets}}{\text{Current Liabilities}}$

$= \dfrac{1,50,000}{62,000} = 2.4$

Current Assets	
Stock	80,000
Debtors	45,000
Cash	17,000
Miscellaneous current assets	8,000
	1,50,000

Current liabilities	
Creditors	40,000
Bills payable	20,000
Other current liabilities	2,000
	62,000

(2) Quick Ratio $= \dfrac{\text{Liquid Assets}}{\text{Liquid Liabilities}}$

$= \dfrac{70,000}{62,000} = 1.1$

(3) Inventory Turnover Ratio $= \dfrac{\text{Cost of Sales}}{\text{Average stock}}$

$= \dfrac{4,00,000 - 1,60,00}{80,000}$

$=$ 3 times

Note: In the absence of information, closing stock has been taken as the average stock.

(4) Average Collection Period $= \dfrac{\text{Debtors}}{\text{Net credit Sales per day}}$

$= \dfrac{45,000}{1.111} = 41 \text{ days}$

Credit Sales Per Day $= \dfrac{4,00,000}{360} = 1.11$

(5) Proprietor's Funds to Liabilities Ratio $= \dfrac{\text{Owners equity}}{\text{Total liabilities}}$

$= \dfrac{2,58,000}{1,62,000} = 1.6$

Problem 21: The following one the P & C a/c and The Balance Sheet of a company in summarised form

P & C a/c

To Opening stock	76,250	By Sales	5,00,000
To Purchases	3,22,250	By Closing stock	98,500
To Gross profit c/d	2,00,000		
	5,98,500		5,98,500
To Selling and Distribution expenses	22,000	By Gross profit	2,00,000
To Administrative expenses	98,000	By Dividend	9,000
To Loss on sale of assets	2,000	By Profit on sale of share	3,000
To Net profit	90,000		
	2,12,000		2,12,000

Balance Sheet

Share capital	2,60,000	Land and Buildings	1,50,000
(2600 equity)		Plant and Machinery	80,000
Shares of Rs. 100 each)		Stock	98,500
Reserves	70,000	Debtors	61,500
P & L a/c	20,000	Bills Receivable	60,000
Current liabilities	1,30,000	Bank	30,000
	4,80,000		4,80,000

Calculate

1. Gross profit ratio
2. Net profit ratio
3. Operating ratio
4. Operating profit ratio
5. Stock turnover ratio
6. Turnover of fixed assets

(Bangalore University, B.B.M., November, 1998)

Solution:

(1) Gross Profit Ratio $= \frac{\text{Gross Profit}}{\text{Net Sales}} \times 100$

$= \frac{2,00,000}{5,00,000} \times 100 = 40\%$

(2) Net Profit Ratio $= \frac{\text{Net Profit}}{\text{Sales}} \times 100$

$= \frac{90,000}{5,00,000} \times 100 = 18\%$

(3) Operating Ratio $= \frac{\text{Cost of goods sold + Operating expenses}}{\text{Net Sales}} \times 100$

$= \frac{1,01,500 + 1,20,000}{5,00,000} \times 100$

$= \frac{22,15,000}{5,00,000} \times 100 = 44.3\%$

(4) Operating Profit Ratio $= 100 - \text{Operating ratio}$

$= 100 - 44.3\% = 55.7\%$

(5) Stock Turnover Ratio $= \dfrac{\text{Cost of goods sold}}{\text{Average Inventory}}$

$= \dfrac{5,98,500 - 2,00,000}{87,375} = 4.56 \text{ times}$

Average Stock

$= \dfrac{\text{Opening stock + Closing stock}}{2}$

$= \dfrac{76,250 + 98,500}{2} = \dfrac{1,74,750}{2} = 87,375$

(6) Turnover of Fixed Assets $= \dfrac{\text{Net Sales}}{\text{Fixed Assets}}$

$= \dfrac{5,00,000}{2,30,000} = 2.17$

Problem 22: Following are the Trading Account, profit and loss a/c of Sarmer Ltd. for the year ending 31st December, 1996 and Balance Sheet on that date:

P & L A/c

To Operning Stock	1,45,000	By Sales	7,50,000
To Purchases	6,10,000	By Closing stock	1,55,000
To Gross profit c/d	1,50,000		
	9,05,000		9,05,000
To Sundry expenses	80,000	By Gross profit b/d	1,50,000
To Net profit	70,000		
	1,50,000		1,50,000

Balance Sheet

Share capital		7,00,000	Net Block	5,50,000
Reserves and surplus	5,000		Stock	2,55,000
Add: Profit for the year	70,000		Debtors	1,80,000
		1,20,000	Cash	20,000
Bank overdraft		35,000		
Creditors		1,50,000		
		10,50,000		10,50,000

You are required to calculate the following ratios:

1. Current ratio,
2. Quick ratio,
3. Gross profit to sales ratio,
4. Stock turnover ratio,
5. Debtors turnover ratio,
6. Net profit to paid up capital.

(*University of Bombay, B.Com., April, 1998*)

Solution:

(1) Current Ratio $= \dfrac{\text{Current Assets}}{\text{Current Liabilities}}$

$= \dfrac{4,55,000}{1,85,000} = 2.46$

Current Assets

Stock	2,55,000
Debtors	1,80,000
Cash	20,000
	4,55,000

Current Liabilities

Bank OD	35,000
Creditors	1,50,000
	1,85,000

(2) Quick Ratio $= \dfrac{\text{Quick Assets}}{\text{Quick Liabilities}}$

$$= \frac{2,00,000}{1,50,000} = 1.33$$

Quick Assets

Debtors	1,80,000
Cash	20,000
	2,00,000

Quick liabilities here includes only creditors

(3) Gross Profit Ratio $= \dfrac{\text{Gross profit}}{\text{Net Sales}} \times 100$

$$= \frac{1,50,000}{7,50,000} \times 100 = 20\%$$

(4) Stock Turnover Ratio $= \dfrac{\text{Cost of goods sold}}{\text{Average stock}}$

$$= \frac{6,00,000}{1,50,000} = 4 \text{ times}$$

Cost of Goods Sold

Opening stock	1,45,000
Add: Purchases	6,10,000
	7,55,000
Less: Closing stock	1,55,000
	6,00,000

Average Stock

$$= \frac{\text{Opening Stock + Closing stock}}{2}$$

$$= \frac{1,45,000 + 1,55,000}{2} = 1,50,000$$

Alternatively, Average stock may be taken as Rs. 2,00,000 $\left(i.e., \dfrac{1,45,000 + 2,55,000}{2}\right)$ and the stock turnover ratio will be 3 times *i.e.,* $\dfrac{6,00,000}{2,00,000}$

(5) Debtors Turnover Ratio $= \dfrac{\text{Debtors + Bill Receivable}}{\text{Net credit Sales}} \times 365$

$= \dfrac{1,80,000}{7,50,000} \times 365$

$=$ 88 Days App

(6) Net Profit to Paid up Share Capital $= \dfrac{\text{Net profit after Tax}}{\text{Paid up share capital}} \times 100$

$= \dfrac{70,000}{7,00,000} \times 100 = 10\%$

Problem 23: Following figures have been extracted from the books of Voodoso Ltd.

	Rs.
Land and Building	6,00,000
Plant and Machinery	5,00,000
Equity capital	5,00,000
Preference capital	2,00,000
Stock	2,40,000
Debtors	2,00,000
Cash and Bank	55,000
Miscellaneous current assets	5,000
P & L a/c	2,00,000
General reserve	1,00,000
Sundry creditors	80,000
Bills payable	60,000
Miscellaneous current liabilities	60,000
Debentures	4,00,000

You are required to:

(*a*) Rearrange above figures in the vertical form and

(*b*) Calculate

(*i*) Debt equity ratio,

(*ii*) Proprietory ratio,

(*iii*) Capital gearing ratio.

(*University of Bombay, B.Com., April 1998*)

Solution:

Voodoo Ltd.

Balance Sheet as on

Sources of Fund		
Share capital:		
Preference share capital	2,00,000	
Equity share capital	5,00,000	
		7,00,000
Reserves and surplus:		
Profit and loss a/c	2,00,000	
General Reserve	1,00,000	
		3,00,000
Loan fund:		
Debentures		4,00,000
		14,00,000

Application of Funds

Fixed Assets:			
Land and Building		6,00,000	
Plant and Machinery		5,00,000	
			11,00,000
Working Capital			
Current Assets:			
Stock		2,40,000	
Debtors		2,00,000	
Cash and Bank		55,000	
Miscellaneous current assets		5,000	
		5,00,000	
Less: Current liabilities:			
Creditors	80,000		
Bills payable	60,000		
Miscellaneous current liability	60,000		
		2,00,000	
			3,00,000
Total applications			14,00,000

(1) Debt Equity Ratio $= \dfrac{\text{Long term Debts}}{\text{Shareholders fund}}$

$= \dfrac{4,00,000}{10,00,000} = 0.4$

(2) Proprietory Ratio $= \dfrac{\text{Propritors fund}}{\text{Total Assets}}$

$= \dfrac{10,00,000}{16,00,000} = 0.62$

(3) Capital Gearing Ratio $= \dfrac{\text{Fixed Interest bearing Securities} + \text{Fixed Dividend bearing securities}}{\text{Equity Shareholders fund}}$

$= \dfrac{2,00,000 + 4,00,000}{8,00,000} = 0.75$

Equity Shareholders Funds

Equity share capital	5,00,000
Reserves and P & L a/c	3,00,000
	8,00,000

Problem 24: From the following calculate:

(*a*) Gross profit ratio
(*b*) Net profit ratio
(*c*) Operating ratio
(*d*) Current ratio
(*e*) Acid test ratio
(*f*) Stock turnover ratio
(*g*) Debtors turnover ratio
(*h*) Return on investment

Trading and Profit & Loss A/c for the year ended 31st Dec., 1996

To Opening stock	25,000	By Sales	1,80,000
To Purchases	1,05,000	By Closing stock	15,000
To Gross profit	65,000		
	1,95,000		1,95,000
To Administrative expenses	23,000	By Gross profit	65,000
To Selling and distribution expenses	10,000	By Profit on sale of fixed assets	5,000
To Financial expenses	2,000		
To Net profit	35,000		
	70,000		70,000

Balance Sheet as at 31st Dec., 1996

Share capital	50,000	Land and Buildings	50,000
General reserve	40,000	Plant and Machinery	20,000
P & L a/c	15,000	Stock	15,000
Creditors	12,000	Debtors	2,000
Bills payable	8,000	Bills receivable	5,000
		Cash at Bank	15,000
	1,25,000		1,25,000

(Osmania University, B.Com., March 1999)

Solution:

(a) Gross Profit Ratio $= \dfrac{\text{Gross profit}}{\text{Net Sales}} \times 100$

$= \dfrac{65,000}{1,80,000} \times 100 = 36.11\%$

(b) Net Profit Ratio $= \dfrac{\text{Net Profit}}{\text{Net Sales}} \times 100$

$= \dfrac{35,000}{1,80,000} \times 100 = 19.44\%$

(c) Operating Ratio $= \dfrac{\text{Cost of goods sold + Operating expenses}}{\text{Net Sales}} \times 100$

$= \dfrac{1,15,000 + 35,000}{1,80,000} \times 100$

$= \dfrac{1,50,000}{1,80,000} \times 100 = 83.33\%$

Cost of Goods Sold

Opening stock	25,000
Add: Purchases	1,05,000
	1,30,000
Less: Closing stock	15,000
	1,15,000

Operating Expenses

Administration expenses	23,000
Selling and distribution expenses	10,000
Financial expenses	2,000
	35,000

(d) Current Ratio $= \dfrac{\text{Current Assets}}{\text{Current Liabilities}}$

$= \dfrac{55,000}{20,000} = 2.75$

Current Assets

Stock	15,000
Debtors	20,000
B.R.	5,000
Cash at Bank	15,000
	55,000

Current liabilities

Creditors	12,000
B.P.	8,000
	20,000

(e) Acid Test Ratio $= \dfrac{\text{Liquid Assets}}{\text{Liquid Liabilities}}$

$= \dfrac{40,000}{20,000} = 2$

Liquid Assets = Current assets – Stock

= 55,000 – 15,000

= 40,000

(f) Stock Turnover Ratio $= \dfrac{\text{Cost of goods sold}}{\text{Average stock}}$

$= \dfrac{1,15,000}{20,000} = 5.75$ times

Average Stock $= \dfrac{\text{Opening stock} + \text{Closing stock}}{2}$

$= \dfrac{25,000 + 15,000}{2} = 20,000$

(g) Debtors Turnover Ratio $= \dfrac{\text{Net Sales}}{\text{Debtors} + \text{Bills Receivable}}$

$= \dfrac{1,80,000}{20,000 + 5,000}$

$= \dfrac{1,80,000}{25,000} = 7.2$ times

(h) Return on Investment $= \dfrac{\text{Net profit}}{\text{Capital employed}} \times 100$

$= \dfrac{35,000}{1,05,000} \times 100 = 33.33\%$

Capital Employed

= Fixed assets + Current assets – Current liabilities
= 70,000 + 55,000 – 20,000
= 105,000

Problem 25: The comparative statements of income and financial position are given below:

	1990	*1991*
	Rs.	*Rs.*
Net sales	1,00,000	1,50,000
Less: Cost of sales	70,000	1,10,000
Gross profit	30,000	40,000
Less: Operating expesnes	20,000	25,000
Net profit	10,000	15,000
Aseets		
Cash in hand	5,000	8,000
Cash at Bank	4,000	2,000
Debtors	40,000	25,000
Stock at cost	15,000	10,000
Fixed assets (Net)	56,000	65,000
	1,20,000	1,10,000
Liabilities		
Creditors	36,000	12,000
Bills payable	2,000	1,000
Mortgage loan	10,000	20,000
Equity share capital	60,000	70,000
Reserves and surplus	12,000	7,000
	1,20,000	1,10,000

You are required to calculate the following ratios for both the years:

1. Current ratio
2. Acid test ratio
3. Debtors turnover ratio
4. Average collection period
5. Stock turnover ratio
(Assume 360 days in a year)

(Sri Venkateshwara University, B.Com., April 1998)

Solution:

(1) Current Ratio $= \dfrac{\text{Current Assets}}{\text{Current Liabilities}}$

Year 1990	*Year 1991*
$= \dfrac{64,000}{38,000}$	$= \dfrac{45,000}{13,000}$
= 1.68	= 3.46

Current Assets

	1990	*1991*
Cash in hand	5,000	8,000
Cash at Bank	4,000	2,000
Debtors	40,000	25,000
Stock	15,000	10,000
	64,000	45,000

Current Liabilities

Creditors	36,000	12,000
Bills payable	2,000	1,000
	38,000	13,000

(2) Acid Test Ratio $= \dfrac{\text{Liquid Assets}}{\text{Current liabilities}}$

$$= \frac{49,000}{38,000} \qquad = \frac{35,000}{13,000}$$

$$= 1.29 \qquad = 2.69$$

Liquid Assets

	1990	*1991*
Cash in hand	5,000	8,000
Cash at Bank	4,000	2,000
Debtors	40,000	25,000
	49,000	35,000

(3) Debtors Turnover Ratio $= \dfrac{\text{Net Credit Sales}}{\text{Average Trade Debtors}}$

Year 1990   *Year 1991*

$$= \frac{1,00,000}{40,000} \qquad = \frac{1,50,000}{32,500}$$

$$= 2.5 \qquad = 4.6$$

Average Trade Debtors   1990   1991

Rs.   40,000 $\dfrac{40,000 + 25,000}{2} = 32,500$

(4) Average Colletion Period $= \dfrac{\text{Average Trade Debtors}}{\text{Net Credit Sales}} \times \text{No. of working days}$

1990 $= \dfrac{40,000}{1,00,000} \times 360 = 144$ days

1991 $= \dfrac{32,500}{1,50,000} \times 360 = 78$ days

(5) Stock Turnover Ratio $= \dfrac{\text{Cost of Sales}}{\text{Average Stock}}$

1990 $= \dfrac{70,000}{15,000} = 4.67$ times

1991 $= \dfrac{1,10,000}{12,500} = 8.8$ times

Average Stock:

1990 = Rs. 15,000

1991 $= \frac{15,000 + 10,000}{2} = 12,500$

Problem 26: From the following Balance Sheet, calculate Current ratio, Acid test ratio, Stock turnover ratio, Debtors turnover ratio and Average collection period:

Share capital	4,00,000	Goodwill	2,50,000
General Reserve	2,88,000	Buildings	4,00,000
8% Debentures	3,00,000	Machinery	3,50,000
Mortgage loan	2,50,000	Closing stock	2,00,000
Creditors	90,000	Debtors	80,000
Bills payable	35,000	Bills receivable	90,000
Bank overdraft	60,000	Cash	65,000
O/s expenses	15,000	Prepaid expenses	3,000
	14,38,000		14,38,000

Additional information opening stocks Rs. 1,50,000: Opening debtors Rs. 1,50,000 and net credit sales Rs. 6,00,000. *(University of Madras, B.Com., May 1997)*

Solution:

(1) Current Ratio $= \frac{\text{Current Assets}}{\text{Current liabilities}}$

$= \frac{4,38,000}{2,00,000} = 2.19$

Current Assets

Stock	2,00,000
Debtors	80,000
Bills receivable	90,000
Cash	65,000
Prepaid expenses	3,000
	4,38,000

Current Liabilities

Creditors	90,000
Bills payable	35,000
Bank OD	60,000
O/s expenses	15,000
	2,00,000

(2) Acid Test Ratio $= \frac{\text{Quick Assets}}{\text{Quick liabilities}}$

$= \frac{2,35,000}{1,40,000} = 1.68$

Quick Assets

= Current assets – Stock – Prepaid expenses

= 4,38,000 – 2,00,000 – 3,0000

= 2,35000

Quick Liabilities

= Current liabilities – Bank OD

= 2,00,000 – 60,000 = 1,40,000

(3) Stock Turnover Ratio $= \dfrac{\text{Cost of Sales or Sales}}{\text{Average Stock}} = \dfrac{6,00,000}{1,75,000}$ (Credit Sales)

$= 3.43$ times

Average Stock $= \dfrac{\text{Opening stock + Closing stock}}{2}$

$= \dfrac{1,50,000 + 2,00,000}{2}$

$= \dfrac{3,50,000}{2} = 1,75,000$

(4) Debtors Turnover Ratio $= \dfrac{\text{Credit Sales}}{\text{Average Accounts Receivable}}$

$= \dfrac{6,00,000}{2,05,000} = 2.93$ times

Average Accounts Receivable $= \dfrac{\text{Opening Debtor + Closing Debtor}}{2} + \text{B.R.}$

$= \dfrac{1,05,000 + 80,000}{2} + 90,000$

$= 1,15,000 + 90,000$

$= 2,05,000$

(5) Average Collection Period $= \dfrac{12}{\text{D.T.R.}}$ or $= \dfrac{365}{\text{D.T.R.}}$

$= \dfrac{12}{2.93}$ $= \dfrac{365}{2.43}$

$= 4.09$ months $= 124.57$ days

Problem 27: (*Calculate of Missing Information*)
Calculate:

(*a*) Current assets
(*b*) Inventory, from the following particulars:

Current ratio = 2.6: 1
Current liability = Rs. 40,000

(*Bangalore University. B.Com., April 2,000*)

Solution:

Current Ratio $= \dfrac{\text{Current Assets}}{\text{Current Liabilities}}$

$2.6 = \dfrac{\text{C.A.}}{40,000}$

or CA $= 2.6 \times 40,000$

CA $= 1,04,000$

Inventory is the same as current asset in the absence of liquid assets which is not given in the problem.

Problem 28: Average stock of a firm is Rs. 40,000. Its opening stock is Rs. 5,000 less than the closing stock. Find out opening stock. (*Bangalore University, B.Com., April 2,000*)

Solution:

Average stock = 40,000
Total stock = Average stock × 2
= 40,000 × 2 = 80,000

Add: Opening stock less by 5,000 = 5,000

= 85,000

Hence opening stock $\frac{85,000}{2}$ = 42,500

Problem 29: Gross profit ratio is 20% on sales. Total gross profit Rs. 1,00,000. Cash sales Rs. 1,20,000 Average debtors Rs. 95,000. Calculate debtor's turnover ratio. *(Bangalore University, B.Com., April 2,000)*

Solution:

$$\text{Gross Profit Ratio} = \frac{\text{Gross profit}}{\text{Sales}} \times 100$$

$$\frac{20}{100} = \frac{1,00,000}{\text{Sales}}$$

$$\text{or} \quad \text{Sales} = \frac{1,00,000 \times 100}{20} \text{ (on cross multiplication)}$$

$$= 5,00,000$$

Total sales = 5,00,000

Credit sales = Total sales – Cash sales

= 5,00,000 – 1,20,000

= 3,80,000

$$\text{Debtors Turnover Ratio} = \frac{\text{Credit Sales}}{\text{Average Debtors}}$$

$$= \frac{3,80,000}{95,000} = 4$$

Problem 30: Cost of sales of a firm is Rs. 2,50,000 and stock turnover ratio is 5 times. Find out the value of stock:

Solution:

$$\text{Stock Turnover Ratio} = \frac{\text{Cost of Sales}}{\text{Average Stock}}$$

Less: Average stock = x

$$5 = \frac{2,50,000}{x}$$

or $5x$ = 2,50,000

$$x = \frac{2,50,000}{5} = 50,000$$

Problem 31: Gross profit ratio of a firm is 20%. Gross profit is Rs. 30,000. Calculate the sales figure.

Solution:

$$\text{Gross Profit Ratio} = \frac{\text{Gross Profit}}{\text{Sales}} \times 100$$

$$\frac{20}{100} = \frac{30,000}{\text{Sales}}$$

20 sales = 30,000 × 100

$$\text{Sales} = \frac{30,000 \times 100}{200} = 1,50,000$$

Problem 32:
Given:
Gross profit is Rs. 3,00,000
Gross profit ratio at 25% on sales
Compute the cost of sales

Solution:

$$\text{Gross Profit Ratio} = \frac{\text{Gross profit}}{\text{Sales}}$$

$$\frac{25}{100} = \frac{3,00,000}{\text{Sales}}$$

$$\text{or} \quad 25 \text{ sales} = 3,00,000 \times 100$$

$$\text{Sales} = \frac{3,00,000 \times 100}{25}$$

$$= 12,00,000$$

$$\text{Cost of sales} = \text{Sales} - \text{Gross profit}$$

$$= 12,00,000 - 3,00,000$$

$$= 9,00,000$$

Problem 33: Turnover to fixed assets ratio is 1: 1.2 value of goods sold is Rs. 9,00,000. Compute the value of fixed assets.

Solution:

$$\text{Fixed assets to Turnover Ratio} = \frac{\text{Turnover}}{\text{Fixed Assets}}$$

$$1.2 = \frac{9,00,000}{1}$$

$$\text{or} \quad = \frac{9,00,000}{1.2} \text{ (on cross multiplication)}$$

$$= 7,50,000$$

Therefore fixed assets = Rs. 7,50,000.

Problem 34: Given long term debt to equity ratio is 2: 3. Equity amount is Rs. 50,000. Compute the value of long-term debt.

Solution:

$$\text{Long-term Debt to Equity Ratio} = \frac{\text{Long term debt}}{\text{Equity}}$$

$$\frac{2}{3} = \frac{x}{50,000}$$

$$\text{or,} \quad 3x = 2 \times 50,000 \text{ (on cross multiplication)}$$

$$x = \frac{2 \times 50,000}{3} = 33,333$$

Problem 35: Gross profit of a firm is 20% of sales. Cost of goods sold Rs. 1,60,000. Find out the sales.

Solution:

Gross profit on Sales = 20% of sales

Therefore cost of goods sold must be 80 *i.e.*, (100–20)

For cost of goods sold of 80 = 1,60,000

$$\text{For } 100 \rightarrow = \frac{1,60,000 \times 100}{80}$$

$$= 2,00,000$$

$$\text{Sales} = 2,00,000$$

Problem 36: Average stock of a firm is Rs. 40,000. Its opening stock is Rs. 5,000 less than the closing stock. Find out the opening stock.

Solution:

Average stock = 40,000

Total stock = 40,000 × 2 = 80,000

Opening stock is Rs. 5,000 less than the closing stock

= 80,000 – 5,000 = 75,000

$$= \frac{75,000}{2} = 37,500$$

Opening stock = 37,500

Closing stock = 37,500 + 5,000 = 42,500

Problem 37: Gross profit ratio is 20% on sales, stock velocity 5, average stock Rs. 1,10,000. Ascertain the sales.

Solution:

$$\text{Stock Turnover Ratio} = \frac{\text{Cost of goods sold}}{\text{Average stock}}$$

$$5 = \frac{\text{Cost of goods sold}}{1,10,000}$$

or Cost of goods sold = 1,10,000 × 5

= 5,50,000

Sales = Cost of goods sold + Profit

100 = 80 + 20

For 80; cost of goods sold is = 5,50,000

$$\text{For } 100 \rightarrow = \frac{100 \times 5,50,000}{80}$$

= 6,87,500

Problem 38: Closing stock of X Ltd. is Rs. 2,00,000. Total liquid assets are Rs. 10,00,000. Liquid ratio is 2: 1. Find out working capital.

Solution:

Closing stock = 2,00,000

Liquid assets = 10,00,000

$$\text{Liquidity Ratio} = \frac{\text{Liquid Assets}}{\text{Liquid liabilities}} = \frac{2}{1}$$

Current assets = Liquid assets + stock

= 10,00,000 + 2,00,000

= 12,00,000

Working capital = current assets – current liabilities

For liquid assets 2 : The amount is 10,00,000

For liquid asset 1 : →X→

$$= \frac{10,00,000}{2} = 5,00,000$$

Working capital = Current assets – Current liabilities

= 12,00,000 – 5,00,000

= 7,00,000

Problem 39: Total current liabilities are Rs. 80,000 current ratio is 2.5: 1. Acid test ratio 1.5: 1. Total current assets include stock, debtors and cash only. Cash is 2/3 of Debtors. Calculate debtors.

Solution:

$$\text{Current Ratio} = \frac{\text{Current Assets}}{\text{Current Liabilities}} = \frac{2.5}{1}$$

Current liabilities = $1 \times 80,000 = 80,000$

Therefore current assets = $80,000 \times 2.5$

= 2,00,000

$$\text{Acid Test Ratio} = \frac{\text{Liquid Assets}}{\text{Liquid Liabilities}} = \frac{1.5}{1}$$

1 = 80,000

Therefore liquid assets = $1.5 \times 80,000 = 1,20,000$

Stock = Current assets – Liquid assets

= 2,00,000 – 1,20,000

= 80,000

Liquid assets = Cash + Debtors

$1,20,000 = x \times \frac{2}{3} + x$ (Debtors assumed as x)

$x + \frac{2}{3}x = 1,20,000$

or $3x + 2x = 3 \times 1,20,000$

$5x = 3,60,000$

$x = 72,000$

Therefore debtors = Rs. 72,000

$$\text{Cash} = \frac{2}{3} \times 720,000 = 48,000$$

Verification = Debtors + Cash

= 72,000 + 48,000 = 1,20,000

Problem 40: Current ratio 2.5, Acid test ratio 1.75, stock Rs, 1,50,000. Calculate net working capital

Solution:

$$\text{Current Ratio} = \frac{2.5}{1}$$

$$\text{Liquidity Ratio} = \frac{1.75}{1}$$

Current Asset = 2,50

Liquid asset = 1.75

Current asset – Liquid asset = Stock

2.50 – 1.75 = 0.75

$\text{Stock} = 0.75 \text{ or } \frac{3}{4} = 1,50,000$

or $= \frac{4 \times 1,50,000}{3} = 2,00,000$

Current liability = 1 = 2,00,000

Current asset = $2,00,000 \times 2.5$

= 5,00,000

Net working capital = Current assets – Current liabilities

= 5,00,000 – 2,00,000

= 3,00,000

Problem 41: Current liabilities of a company are Rs. 3,00,000. Its current ratio is 3: 1 and quick ratio is 1: 1. Calculate the value of stock in trade.

Solution:

$$\text{Current Ratio} = \frac{\text{Current Assets}}{\text{Current Liabilities}}$$

$$\frac{3}{1} = \frac{x}{3,00,000}$$

$$x = 3 \times 3,00,000$$

$$= 9,00,000$$

$$\text{Quick Ratio} = \frac{\text{Quick Assets}}{\text{Quick Liabilities}}$$

$$\frac{1}{1} = \frac{x}{3,00,000}$$

$$x = 1 \times 3,00,000$$

$$= 3,00,000$$

Current Assets – Stock = Quick Assets

9,00,000 – x = 3,00,000

x = 6,00,000

Hence stock in Trade = Rs. 6,00,000

Problem 42: Given current ratio is 2.5, working capital is 60,000. Calculate the amount of current assets and current liabilities.

Solution:

Current Assets – Current liabilities = Working capital

2.5 – 1 = 1.5

If working capital is Rs. 1.5, then current asset is 2.5

If working capital is 1, then current asset is $\frac{2.5}{1.5}$

$$\frac{2.5}{1.5} \times 60,000 = 1,00,000$$

Current asset = 1,00,000

1,00,000 – Current liabilities = 60,000

Current liabilities = 40,000

Problem 43: Following information are available from the books of Smart Projects Ltd.

Debtors velocity	3 months
Stock velocity	6 months
Creditors velocity	2 months
Gross profit ratio	20%

Gross profit for the year ended 31st March, 1999 was Rs. 50,00,000, stock on 31st March, 1999 was more than what it was at the beginning of the year. Bills Receivable and bills payable were Rs. 60,000 and Rs. 36,667 respectively.

You are required to calculate the value of (1) Sales, (2) Sundry debtors, (3) Sundry creditors and (4) Closing stock and also prepare a note for the finance director on the overall impact of the results.

(CS, Inter, June, 2,000)

Solution: **(1) Calculation of Sales**

$$\text{Gross Profit Ratio} = \frac{\text{Gross profit}}{\text{Sales}}$$

$$\frac{20}{100} = \frac{5,00,000}{\text{Sales}}$$

$$20 \text{ sales} = 5{,}00{,}000 \times 100$$

$$\text{Sales} = \frac{5{,}00{,}000 \times 100}{20} = \text{Rs. } 25{,}00{,}000$$

(2) Calculation of Sundry Debtors

Sales	=	25,00,000
Debtor's velocity	=	3 months
Year end sales outstanding		
$25{,}00{,}000 \times \frac{3}{12}$	=	6,25,000
Less: Bills receivable	=	60,000
Sundry Debtors	=	5,65,000

(3) Calculation of Creditors

Purchases	=	Sales – Gross profit + Increase in stock
	=	25,00,000 – 5,00,000 + 20,000
Purchases	=	20,20,000
Creditor's velocity	=	2 months
Year end purchases outstanding		
$20{,}20{,}000 \times \frac{2}{12}$	=	3,36,667
Less: Bills payable	=	36,667
Sundry Creditors	=	3,00,000

(4) Calculation of Closing Stock

Cost of goods sold	=	Sales – Profit
	=	25,00,000 – 5,00,000
Cost of goods sold	=	20,00,000
Stock velocity	=	6 months
Average stock	=	$20{,}00{,}000 \times \frac{6}{12} = 10{,}00{,}000$
Let opening stock be	=	x
Closing stock	=	$x + 20{,}000$
Twice Average stock	=	$2x + 20{,}000$
20,00,000	=	$2x + 20{,}000$
$2x$	=	19,80,000
x	=	9,90,000
Thus opening stock	=	Rs. 9,90,000
Hence closing stock	=	9,90,000 + 20,000
	=	10,10,000

Overall Impact of the Results

The debtors velocity and the amount of debtors are more than what the creditors velocity and the amount of creditors. This means that the company is paying liberal credit than what it receives from the creditors. The company is having a low inventory turnover ratio which result in blocking of funds in inventory. The gross profit is merely 20% of the sales which seems to be insufficient to cover up the overheads and maintain a reasonable net profit.

Problem 44: The current ratio of a company is 2: 1 which of the following transactions would:

(*i*) Improve the ratio

(*ii*) Reduce the ratio

(*iii*) Not atter the ratio (give your reasons)

1. Pay a current liability
2. Sell machinery for cash
3. Borrow money us interest repayable at the end of 5 years
4. Purchase stock of goods for cash
5. Accept a bill of exchange drawn by a supplier
6. Issue of bouns shares.

(*University of Bombay, B.Com., October, 1998*)

Solution:

(1) Pay a Current Liability: Paying a current will decrease both in current liability and current asset by the same amount. Therefore current ratio shall improve.

(2) Sell Machinery for Cash: Selling machinery for cash will decrease the fixed assets and increases the current assets therefore current ratio shall be improved.

(3) Borrow Money at Interest Payable at The End of 5 years: This will result in increase in current asset and increase in long-term loans. Therefore current ratio shall be improved.

(4) Purchased Stock of Goods for Cash: This will result in increase in stock and decrease in cash balance. Total current assets and current liabilities remain the same and hence current ratio will not be affected.

(5) Accept a Bill of Exchange Drawn by Supplier: This will increase bills payable and reduce creditors. Total current assets and current liabilities remain the same the hence current ratio will not be affected.

(6) Issue of Bouns Shares: This will increase equity share capital and will reduce the surplus. Both effects are on non-current items, not affecting on current assets and current liabilities. Total current assets and current liabilities remain the same and hence current ratio will not be affected.

Problem 45: From the following information as certain:

(*i*) Long-term loans

(*ii*) Reserves and surplus

(*iii*) Capital employed

Capital gearing ratio	0.75
Debt equity ratio	0.40
(Long-term debts to shareholders funds)	
Equity share capital	Rs. 3,00,000
Preference share capital	Rs. 1,00,000

(*University of Bombay, B.Com., October 1998*)

Solution:

Let long-term loans $= x$

Reserves and surpluses $= y$

$$\text{Capital Gearing Ratio} = \frac{\text{Preference Share Capital + Long Term Debts}}{\text{Equity Share Capital + Reserves and Surpluses}}$$

$$0.75 = \frac{1{,}00{,}000 + x}{3{,}00{,}000 + y}$$

$$\therefore \quad 0.75\,(3{,}00{,}000 + y) = 1{,}00{,}000 + x$$

$$\therefore \quad 0.75y + 2{,}25{,}000 = 1{,}00{,}000 + x$$

$$\therefore \quad x = 0.75y + 1{,}25{,}000 \qquad \text{... (1)}$$

$$\text{Debt Equity Ratio} = \frac{\text{Long term debts}}{\text{Shareholders funds}}$$

$$0.40 = \frac{x}{\text{Equity Share capital + Reserves + Preference share capital}}$$

$$\text{or} \quad 0.40 = \frac{x}{3,00,000 + 1,00,000 + y}$$

$$x = 0.4\,(4,00,000 + y)$$

$$x = 1,60,000 + 0.4y \quad \ldots (2)$$

$$\text{or} \quad 0.75y + 1,25,000 = 1,60,000 + 0.4y$$

$$\text{or} \quad 0.75y - 0.4y = 1,60,000 - 1,25,000$$

$$\text{or} \quad 0.35y = 35,000$$

$$\text{or} \quad y = \frac{35,000}{0.35} = 1,00,000$$

Calculation of Long-term Debts, i.e., X

$$\text{Debt Equity Ratio} = \frac{\text{Long term Debt}}{\text{Eqty Shares Capital + Pref share capital + Reserves}}$$

$$0.40 = \frac{x}{3,00,000 + 1,00,000 + 1,00,000}$$

$$0.40 = \frac{x}{5,00,000}$$

$$x = 5,00,000 \times 0.40 = 20,00,000$$

Calculation of Capital Employed

Equity share capital	3,00,000
Preference share capital	1,00,000
Reserves and surplus	1,00,000
Long-term loans	2,00,000
Capital employed	7,00,000

Problem 46: From the following details find out (*a*) current assets, (*b*) current liabilities, (*c*) quick asset, (*d*) stock

Current Ratio = 2.5
Quick Ratio = 1.5
Working Capital = Rs. 60,000

(*Osmania University, B.Com., October, 1999*)

Solution:

$$\text{Current Ratio} = \frac{\text{Current Assets}}{\text{Current Liabilities}}$$

$$2.5 = \frac{\text{CA}}{\text{CL}}$$

$$\text{or} \quad \text{CA} = 2.5\ \text{CL}$$

Let current liabilities be $= x$

$\therefore$ Current assets $= 2.5\,x$

Working capital = Current assets – Current liabilities

$= 2.5\,x - x$

$= 1.5x$

But working capital = 60,000

$1.5x = 60,000$

$$x = \frac{60,000}{1.5} = 40,000$$

$$\text{Current liabilities} = 40{,}000$$

$$\therefore \quad \text{Current Assets} = 2.5 \times 40{,}000 = 1{,}00{,}000$$

$$\text{Liquidity Ratio} = \frac{\text{Quick Assets}}{\text{Quick Liabilities}}$$

$$1.5 = \frac{\text{Quick Assets}}{\text{Quick Liabilities}}$$

$$\begin{aligned} \text{Q A} &= 1.5 \times \text{Q . L} \\ &= 1.5 \times 40{,}000 \\ &= 60{,}000 \\ \text{Stock} &= \text{Current Assets} - \text{Quick Assets} \\ &= 1{,}00{,}000 - 60{,}000 \\ &= 40{,}000 \end{aligned}$$

Problem 47 (Preparation of Balance Sheet with Ratios): The gross profit of X Ltd. for the year 1998 is Rs. 80,000. This is one-fourth of the year's sales. Out of total sales, three-fourth is on credit. The stock turnover is 10 times and the average collection period is 15 days (assume 360 days). Total assets turnover is 4 times and the long-term debt to equity is 50%. Shareholder's equity is Rs. 40,000. The current ratio is 2: 1.

Find out (1) creditors, (2) long-term debt, (3) cash in hand, (4) debtors, (5) closing stock, (6) fixed assets. And also prepare Balance Sheet of 'X' Ltd. for the year 1998.

(Bangalore University, B.Com., October 2009)

Solution:

(1) Credit Sales

Gross profit = 80,000
Sales, 4 times the gross profit
i.e., 80,000 × 4 = 3,20,000

$$\text{Credit sales } \frac{3}{4} \text{ of } 3{,}20{,}000 = 2{,}40{,}000$$

(2) Inventory or Stock

$$\text{Stock Turnover Ratio} = \frac{\text{Cost of goods sold}}{\text{Average Inventory}}$$

$$10 = \frac{\text{Sales} - \text{Gross profit}}{\text{Inventory}}$$

$$10 = \frac{3{,}20{,}000 - 80{,}000}{\text{Inventory}}$$

$$\text{Inventory} = \frac{2{,}40{,}000}{10} = \text{Rs. } 24{,}000$$

(3) Debtors

$$\text{Average collection period} = 15 \text{ days}$$

$$\text{Debtors Turnover Ratio} = \frac{360}{15} = 24$$

$$24 = \frac{\text{Credit Sales}}{\text{Average Debtors}}$$

$$24 = \frac{2{,}40{,}000}{\text{Average Debtors}}$$

$$\text{Debtors} = \frac{2{,}40{,}000}{24} = 10{,}000$$

(4) Total Assets

$$\text{Assets Turnover Ratio} = \frac{\text{Sales}}{\text{Total Assets}}$$

$$4 = \frac{3,20,000}{\text{Total Assets}}$$

or, 4 total assets = 3,20,000

or $$\text{Total assets} = \frac{3,20,000}{4} = 80,000$$

(5) Long-term Debt

$$\text{Long-term Debt to Equity} = \frac{\text{Long term debt}}{\text{Equity}}$$

$$\text{50\% of 40,000 long-term debt} = \frac{50}{100} \times 40,000 = 20,000$$

(6) Cash

Current Ratio = 2: 1
Current Assets = Inventory + Debtors + Cash
4,000 = 24,000 + 10,000 + Cash
or Cash = 40,000 – 34,000 = 6,000

(7) Fixed Assets

Total assets – Current Assets
= 80,000 – 40,000 = 40,000

(8) Current Liabilities

Current Liabilities = Total Assets – Shareholders Equity – Long-term Debt
= 80,000 – 40,000 – 20,000
= 20,000

Required Information

(1) Creditors = Rs. 20,000
(2) Long-term debts = Rs. 20,000
(3) Cash in hand = 6,000
(4) Debtors = 10,000
(5) Closing Stock = 24,000
(6) Fixed Assets = 40,000

Balance Sheet

Equity share capital	40,000	Fixed Assets	40,000
Long-term liabilities	20,000	Inventory	24,000
Creditors	20,000	Debtors	10,000
		Cash	6,000
	80,000		80,000

Problem 48: From the following information, make out a statement of proprietor's funds with as many details as possible:

1. Current ratio	2.5
2. Liquid ratio	1.5
3. Proprietory ratio $\left(\frac{\text{Fixed assets}}{\text{Proprietory funds}}\right)$	0.75
4. Working capital	Rs. 60,000
5. Reserves and surplus	Rs. 40,000

6. Bank overdraft Rs. 10,000 and
7. There is no long-term loan or fictitions asset (*CS, Inter, December, 1998*)

Solution:

$$\text{Current Ratio} = \frac{\text{Current Assets}}{\text{Current Liabilities}}$$

$$2.5 = \frac{\text{Current Assets}}{\text{Current Liabilities}}$$

or $\quad CA = 2.5\ CL$

Let current liabilities $= x$

$\therefore$ Current assets $= 2.5\ x$

Working capital $=$ Current Assets – Current liabilities

$= 2.5x - x$

$= 1.5x$

(1) *Current liabilities*

But working capital is $= 60{,}000$

$\therefore \quad 1.5x = 60{,}000$

$$x = \frac{60{,}000}{1.5} = 40{,}000$$

(2) Current Assets $= 40{,}000 \times 2.5$

$= 1{,}00{,}000$

(3) Creditors = Current liabilities – Bank OD

$= 40{,}000 - 10{,}000$

$= 30{,}000$

Note: It is assumed that bank overdraft is included in current liabilities.

(4) Liquid assets $= 1.5 \times 40{,}000 =$ Rs. 60,000

(5) Stock = Current Assets – Liquid Assets

$= 1{,}00{,}000 - 60{,}000$

$= 40{,}000$

(6) Proprietary funds to fixed assets is 1: 0.75. It means 0.25 of the proprietary funds is being used as working capital.

$$\text{Hence proprietory finds} = \frac{60{,}000}{0.25}$$

$= 2{,}40{,}000$

(7) Since reserves and surplus are Rs. 40,000, paid up capital will be Rs. 2,00,000

(8) Fixed assets will be Re 0.75 of Rs. 2,40,000 = Rs. 1,80,000

Balance Sheet

Equity share capital		2,00,000	Fixed Assets	1,80,000
Reserves and surplus		40,000		
Current Liabilities			*Current Assets*	
Creditors	3,000		Stock	40,000
Bank OD	10,000		Liquid Assets	60,000
		40,000		
		2,80,000		2,80,000

Problem 49: From the following particulars prepare the balance sheet.

$$\frac{\text{Sales}}{\text{Total Assets}} = 3$$

$$\frac{\text{Sales}}{\text{Fixed Assets}} = 5$$

$\frac{\text{Sales}}{\text{Current Assets}}$ = 7.5

$\frac{\text{Sales}}{\text{Inventories}}$ = 20

$\frac{\text{Sales}}{\text{Debtors}}$ = 15

$\frac{\text{Total Assets}}{\text{Net Worth}}$ = 2.5

Current Ratio = 2

$\frac{\text{Debt}}{\text{Equity}}$ = 1

Sales = 36,00,000

(*Osmania University, B.Com., April 1998*)

Solution:

(1) $\frac{\text{Sales}}{\text{Total Assets}} = 3$

or Total Assets $= \frac{\text{Sales}}{3}$

$= \frac{36,00,000}{3} =$ Rs. 12,00,000

(2) $\frac{\text{Sales}}{\text{Fixed Assets}} = 5$

or, Fixed Assets $= \frac{\text{Sales}}{5}$

$= \frac{36,00,000}{5} =$ 7,20,000

(3) $\frac{\text{Sales}}{\text{Current Assets}} = 7.5$

Current Assets $= \frac{\text{Sales}}{7.5}$

$= \frac{36,00,000}{7.5} =$ Rs. 4,80,000

(4) $\frac{\text{Sales}}{\text{Inventories}} = 20$

Inventories $= \frac{\text{Sales}}{20}$

$= \frac{36,00,000}{20} =$ 1,80,000

(5) $\frac{\text{Sales}}{\text{Debtors}} = 15$

Debtors $= \frac{\text{Sales}}{15}$

$= \frac{36,00,000}{15} =$ 2,40,000

(6) Current Ratio = 2

or, $\frac{\text{Current assets}}{\text{Current liabilities}} = 2$

So, Current liabilities $= \frac{\text{Current assets}}{2}$

$= \frac{4,80,000}{2}$

$= 2,40,000$

(7) $\frac{\text{Total Assets}}{\text{Net worth}} = 2.5$

Net Worth $= \frac{\text{Total Assets}}{2.5}$

$= \frac{12,00,000}{2.5} = \text{Rs. } 4,80,000$

(8) $\frac{\text{Debt}}{\text{Equity}} = 1$

Debt $= \text{Equity} \times 1$

$= 4,80,000 \times 1 = \text{Rs. } 4,80,000$

(9) Liquid Assets $=$ Current Assets – (Inventories + Debtors)

$= 4,80,000 - (1,80,000 + 2,40,000)$

$=$ Rs. 60,000

Balance Sheet

Net worth	4,80,000	Fixed Assets	7,20,000
Debt	4,80,000	*Current Assets*	
Current liabilities	2,40,000	Inventories	1,80,000
		Debtors	2,40,000
		liquid assets	60,000
	12,00,000		12,00,000

Problem 50: Using the following ratios, complete the Balance Sheet given below:

$\frac{\text{Total Assets}}{\text{Net Worth}} = 3.5$

$\frac{\text{Sales}}{\text{Fixed Assets}} = 6$

$\frac{\text{Sales}}{\text{Current Assets}} = 8$

$\frac{\text{Sales}}{\text{Inventory}} = 15$

$\frac{\text{Sales}}{\text{Debtors}} = 18$

Current Ratio = 2.5

Annual sales Rs. 25 Lakhs

Balance Sheet

Net worth	....	Fixed assets	....
Long-term debt	....	Inventory	....
Current liabilities	....	Debtors	....
		Liquid assets	....
		Total current assets	....

(*Bangalore University, B.Com., April 2000*)

Solution:

(1) $\frac{\text{Sales}}{\text{Fixed Assets}} = 6$

Fixed Assets $= \frac{\text{Sales}}{6}$

$= \frac{25,00,000}{6} = 4,16,666$

(2) $\frac{\text{Sales}}{\text{Current Assets}} = 8$

Current assets $= \frac{\text{Sales}}{8}$

$= \frac{25,00,000}{8} = 3,12,500$

(3) $\frac{\text{Sales}}{\text{Inventories}} = 15$

Inventories $= \frac{\text{Sales}}{15}$

$= \frac{25,00,000}{15} = 1,66,666$

(4) $\frac{\text{Sales}}{\text{Debtors}} = 18$

Debtors $= \frac{\text{Sales}}{18}$

$= \frac{25,00,000}{18} = 1,38,888$

(5) Current Ratio $= \frac{\text{Current Assets}}{\text{Current Liabilities}} = 2.5$

Current Liabilities $= \frac{3,12,500}{25} = 1,25,000$

(6) Liquid Assets = Current assets – Inventories – Debtors

= 3,12,500 – 1,66,666 – 1,38,888

= 6946

(7) Total Assets

Fixed assets	=	4,16,666
Current Assets	=	3,12,500
Inventories	=	1,66,666
Debtors	=	1,38,888
Liquid assets	=	6946
		10,41,666

(8) $\frac{\text{Total Assets}}{\text{Net worth}} = 3.5$

Net worth $= \frac{\text{Total Assets}}{3.5}$

$= \frac{10,41,666}{3.5} = 2,97,618$

Balance Sheet

Net worth	2,97,618	Fixed Assets	4,16,666
Long-term Debt	6,19,048	Current assets	3,12,500
(Balancing figure)		Inventories	1,66,666
Current liabilities	1,25,000	Debtors	1,38,888
		Liquid assets	6,946
	10,41,666		10,41,666

Problem 51: From the following details, prepare the balance sheet of the firm concerned:

Stock velocity	6
Capital turnover ratio	2
Fixed assets turnover ratio	4
Gross profit ratio	20%
Debt collection period	2 months
Creditors payment period	73 days

The gross profit was Rs. 60,000. Closing stock was Rs. 5,000 in excess of the opening stock

(*CS, Inter, June 1998*)

Solution:

(1) Gross Profit Ratio $= \frac{\text{Gross profit}}{\text{Sales}} \times 100$

$$20 = \frac{60,000}{\text{Sales}} \times 100$$

$$20 \text{ sales} = 60,000 \times 100$$

$$\text{Sales} = \frac{60,000 \times 100}{20} = 3,00,000$$

$$\text{Cost of goods sols} = \text{Sales} - \text{Gross Profit}$$

$$= 3,00,000 - 60,000$$

$$= 2,40,000$$

(2) Stock Velocity $= \frac{\text{Cost of goods sold}}{\text{Average stock}}$

$$6 = \frac{2,40,000}{\text{Average stock}}$$

$$\text{Average stock} = \frac{2,40,000}{6} = 40,000$$

Total stock = 40,000 × 2	=	80,000
Add: Closing stock amount of Rs. 5,000 more than opening stock	=	5,000
	=	85,000
Closing Stock = $\frac{85,000}{2}$	=	42,500
Opening Stock	=	42,500 – 5,000
Rs.	=	37,500

(3) Capital Turnover Ratio $= \frac{\text{Cost of Sales}}{\text{Capital}}$

$$2 = \frac{2,40,000}{\text{Capital}}$$

$$2 \text{ capital} = 2,40,000$$

$$\text{Capital} = \frac{2,40,000}{2} = \text{Rs. } 1,20,000$$

(4) Fixed Assets Turnover Ratio $= \dfrac{\text{Cost of Sales}}{\text{Fixed Assets}}$

$$4 = \frac{2,40,000}{\text{Fixed Assets}}$$

$$4 \text{ FA} = 2,40,000$$

$$\text{FA} = \frac{2,40,000}{4} = \text{Rs. } 60,000$$

(5) Debt Colletion Period = 2 months

$$\text{Debtors Turnover Ratio} = \frac{12 \text{ months}}{\text{Debt collection period}}$$

$$= \frac{12}{2} = 6 \text{ times}$$

$$\text{Also Debtors Turnover Ratio} = \frac{\text{Credit Sales}}{\text{Average Debtors}}$$

$$6 = \frac{3,00,000}{\text{Debtors}}$$

$$\text{or Debtors} = \frac{3,00,000}{6} = 50,000$$

(6) Creditors Payment Period = 73 days

$$\text{Creditors Turnover Ratio} = \frac{365}{73} = 5 \text{ times}$$

Assuming all purchases to be credit purchases the amount of credit puchases is determined as follows:

Cost of goods sold = Opening Stock + Purchases – Closing stock

2,40,000 = 37,500 + Purchases – 42,500

Purchases = Rs. 2,45,000

$$\text{Creditors Turnover Ratio} = \frac{\text{Credit purchases}}{\text{Creditors}}$$

$$5 = \frac{2,45,000}{\text{Creditors}}$$

$$5 \text{ Creditors} = 2,45,000$$

$$\text{Creditors} = \frac{2,45,000}{5} = 49,000$$

Balance Sheet

Capital	1,20,000	Fixed Assets	60,000
Creditors	49,000	Closing stock	42,500
		Debtors	50,000
		Cash (Balancing figure)	16,500
	1,69,000		1,69,000

Problem 52:

Gross Profit	Rs. 80,000
Gross profit to cost of goods sold ratio	1/3
Stock velocity	6 times
Opening stock	Rs. 36,000
Accounts receivable velocity (year of 360 days)	72 days
Accounts payable velocity	90 days
Current assets	Rs. 1,50,000
Bills receivable	Rs. 20,000
Bills payable	Rs. 5,000
Fixed assets turnover ratio	8 times

From the above, prepare balance sheet with as many details as possible.

(University of Madras, B.Com., September, 1997)

Solution:

Gross Profit = Rs. 80,000

(1) Gross profit to cost of goods sold ratio = $\frac{1}{3}$

$$= \frac{\text{Gross profit}}{\text{Cost of goods sold}} = \frac{1}{3}$$

$$= \frac{80,000}{\text{Cost of goods sold}} = \frac{1}{3}$$

= cost of goods sold = 80,000 × 3

= 2,40,000

Sales = Cost of goods sold + Gross profit

= 2,40,000 + 80,000 = 3,20,000

(2) Stock Velocity = 6 times

$$\text{Stock Turnover Ratio} = \frac{\text{Cost of Sales}}{\text{Average stock}}$$

$$\frac{6}{1} = \frac{2,40,000}{\text{Average stock}}$$

$$\text{Average Stock} = \frac{2,40,000}{6} = 40,000$$

$$\therefore \quad \text{Average Stock} = \frac{\text{Opening stock + closing stock}}{2}$$

40,000 × 2 = 80,000

Less: Opening stock = 36,000

Closing stock = 44,000

(3) Accounts receivable velocity = 72 days

$$\text{Debtors Turnover Ratio} = \frac{360}{72} = 5 \text{ times}$$

$$\text{DTR} = \frac{\text{Sales}}{\text{Average Accounts Receivable}}$$

$$\frac{5}{1} = \frac{3,20,000}{\text{Average Accounts Receivable}}$$

$$\text{Average Accounts Receivable} = \frac{3,20,000}{5} = 64,000$$

Average Accounts Receivable = Debtors + Bills receivable

or Debtors = Average Accounts receivable – Bills receivable

Debtors = 640,000 – 20,000

= 44,000

(4) Accounts Payable Velocity = 90 days

$$\text{Creditors Turnover Ratio} = \frac{360}{90} = 4 \text{ times}$$

$$\text{Creditors Turnover Ratio} = \frac{\text{Purchases}}{\text{Average Accounts payable}}$$

Purchases = Opening stock + Cost of sales – Closing stock

= 44,000 + 2,40,000 – 36,000

= 2,48,000

$$\text{Creditor Turnover Ratio} = \frac{\text{Purchases}}{\text{Average Accounts payable}}$$

$$\frac{4}{1} = \frac{2,48,000}{\text{Average Accounts payable}}$$

$$\text{Average Accounts Payable} = \frac{2,48,000}{4} = 62,000$$

Average Account Payable = Creditors + Bills payable

Creditors = Average Accounts payable – Bills payable

= 62,000 – 5,000 = 57,000

(5) Fixed Assets Turnover Ratio = 8 times (assumed on cost of sales)

$$\frac{8}{1} = \frac{\text{Cost of Sales}}{\text{Fixed Assets}}$$

$$\text{Fixed Assets} = \frac{2,40,000}{8} = 30,000$$

Balance Sheet

Capital (Balancing figure)	1,18,000	*Current Assets*:		
Creditors	57,000	Stock	44,000	
Bills payable	5,000	Debtors	44,000	
		B.R.	20,000	
		Cash	42,000	
		(Bal figure)		1,50,000
		Fixed assets		30,000
	1,80,000			1,80,000

Problem 53: From the following details prepare a balance sheet.

Current ratio is 1.75
Liquid ratio is 1.25
Stock turnover ratio (closing stock) is 9 times
Gross profit ratio is 25%
Debt collection period is 1.5 months
Reserves to capital is 0.2
Turnover of fixed assets is 1.2
Capital gearing ratio is 0.6
Fixed assets to net worth is 1.25
Sales for the year is Rs. 12,00,000 (*CS, Inter, December 1997*)

Solution:

Sales	=	12,00,000
Less: Gross profit 25%	=	3,00,000
Cost of goods sold		9,00,000

(1) Stock Turnover Ratio $= \frac{\text{Cost of goods sold}}{\text{Closing stock}}$

$$9 = \frac{9,00,000}{\text{closing stock}}$$

$$\text{Closing Stock} = \frac{9,00,000}{9} = 1,00,000$$

(2) Debt Colletion Period = 1.5 months

$$\text{Debt Collection Ratio} = \frac{\text{Debtors}}{\text{Credit Sales}}$$

$$\frac{1.5}{12} = \frac{\text{Debtors}}{12,00,000}$$

12 Debtors = 12,00,000 × 1.5

$$\text{Debtors} = \frac{12,00,000 \times 1.5}{12} = 1,50,000$$

(3) Turnover to Fixed Assets Ratio $= \dfrac{\text{Cost of goods sold}}{\text{Fixed Assets}}$

$$1.2 = \frac{9,00,000}{\text{Fixed Assets}}$$

$$\text{F.A} = \frac{9,00,000}{1.2} = 7,50,000$$

(4) Fixed Assets to Net Worth Ratio $= \dfrac{\text{Fixed Assets}}{\text{Net worth}}$

$$1.25 = \frac{7,50,000}{\text{Net worth}}$$

$$\text{Net worth} = \frac{7,50,000}{1.25} = 6,00,000$$

Capital	=	1.0	=	5,00,000
Reserve	=	0.2	=	1,00,000
		1.2		6,00,000

(5) Capital Gearing Ratio $= \dfrac{\text{Debt}}{\text{Equity Capital}}$

$$0.6 = \frac{\text{Debt}}{5,00,000}$$

$$\text{Debt} = 0.6 \times 5,00,000 = 3,00,000$$

(6) Current Ratio $= \dfrac{\text{Current Assets}}{\text{Current Liabilities}}$

$$1.75 = \frac{\text{Current Assets}}{\text{Current Liabilities}}$$

or CA = 1.75 CL

(7) Liquid Ratio $= \dfrac{\text{Liquid Assets}}{\text{Current Liabilities}}$

$$1.25 = \frac{\text{Liquid Assets}}{\text{Current Liabilities}}$$

or LA = 1.25 CL

(8) Current Assets = L.A + Stock

1.75 CL = 1.25 CL + 1,00,000

1.75 CL – 1.25 CL = 1,00,000

0.5 CL = 1,00,000

$$\text{CL} = \frac{1,00,000}{0.5} = 2,00,000$$

CA = 1.75 × CL

= 1.75 × 2,00,000

= 3,50,000

Balance Sheet

Capital	5,00,000	Fixed Assets	7,50,000
Reserve	1,00,000	*Current Assets:*	
Debts	3,00,000	Closing stock	1,00,000
Current liabilities	2,00,000	Debtors	1,50,000
		Cash	1,00,000
	11,00,000		11,00,000

Problem 54 (Preparation of Final Accounts from Ratios): With the following ratios and further information given below, prepare a Trading account, profit and loss account and a balance sheet of Mr. Anand

1. Gross profit ratio — 25%
2. $\frac{\text{Net profit}}{\text{Sales}}$ — 20%
3. Stock Turnoveer Ratio — 10
4. $\frac{\text{Net profit}}{\text{capital}}$ — $\frac{1}{5}$
5. Capital to total liabilities — $\frac{1}{2}$
6. $\frac{\text{Fixed Assets}}{\text{Capital}}$ — $\frac{5}{4}$
7. $\frac{\text{Fixed Assets}}{\text{Total current assets}}$ — $\frac{5}{7}$
8. Fixed Assets — Rs. 10,00,000
9. Closing Stock — Rs. 1,00,000

(Bangalore University, B.B.M., November 1999)

Solution:

Trading and Profit and Loss A/c

To Opening stock	20,000	By Sales	8,00,000
To Purchases (Balancing figure)	6,80,000	By Closing stock	1,00,000
To Gross profit	2,00,000		
	9,00,000		9,00,000
To Expenses	40,000	By Gross profit	2,00,000
To Net profit	1,60,000		
	2,00,000		2,00,000

Balance Sheet

Capital			Fixed Assets	10,00,000
Opening balance	6,40,000		Closing stock	1,00,000
Add: Net profit	1,60,000		Other current assets	13,00,000
	8,00,000	8,00,000		
Liabilities		16,00,000		
		24,00,000		24,00,000

Working Note:

(1) Calculation of Capital

$$\frac{\text{Fixed Assets}}{\text{Capital}} = \frac{5}{4}$$

$$\frac{1,00,000}{\text{Capital}} = \frac{5}{4}$$

or $5 \text{ capital} = 1,00,000 \times 4$

or $\text{capital} = \frac{1,00,000 \times 4}{5} = 8,00,000$

(2) Calculation of Liabilities

Capital is $\frac{1}{2}$ of total liabilities

Liabilities = 8,00,000 × 2 = Rs. 16,00,000

(3) Calculation of Net Profit

Net profit is $\frac{1}{5}$ of capital

Net profit = $8{,}00{,}000 \times \frac{1}{5} = 1{,}60{,}000$

(4) Calculation of Sales

Net Profit is 20% of sales

Sales = $1{,}60{,}000 \times \frac{100}{20} = 8{,}00{,}000$

(5) Calculation of Gross Profit Ratio

Gross profit ratio is 25% of sales

$\frac{25}{100} \times 8{,}00{,}000 = 2{,}00{,}000$

(6) Calculation of Average Inventory

$$\text{Stock Turnover Ratio} = \frac{\text{Cost of Sales}}{\text{Average Inventory}}$$

$$10 = \frac{60{,}00{,}000}{\text{Average Inventory}}$$

$$10 \text{ Average Inventory} = 6{,}00{,}000$$

$$\text{Average Inventory} = \frac{60{,}00{,}000}{10}$$

$$= 60{,}000$$

$$\text{Cost of sales} = \text{Sales} - \text{Gross profit}$$

$$= 8{,}00{,}000 - 2{,}00{,}000$$

$$= 6{,}00{,}000$$

(7) Calculation of Opening Stock

Average Inventory = 60,000

Total Inventory = 60,000 × 2 = 1,20,000

Opening Inventory = Total Inventory – Closing Stock

= 1,20,000 – 1,00,000

= 20,000

(8) Calculation of other Current Assets

$$\frac{\text{Fixed Assets}}{\text{Total Current Assets}} = \frac{5}{7}$$

$$\frac{10{,}00{,}000}{\text{Total Current Assets}} = \frac{5}{7}$$

$$\text{or, } 5 \text{ total current assets} = 10{,}00{,}000 \times 7$$

$$\text{or, Total current assets} = \frac{10{,}00{,}000 \times 7}{5}$$

$$= 14{,}00{,}000$$

Other Current Assets = Total current assets – Closing stock

= 14,00,000 – 1,00,000

= 13,00,000

Problem 55: From the following figures and ratios, draw out balance sheet and trading and profit and loss account:

Share capital	1,80,000
Working capital	63,000
Bank overdraft	10,000

There is no fictitous asset. In current assets there is no asset other than stock, debtors and cash. Closing stock is 20% higher than the opening stock:

Current ratio	2.5
Proprietory ratio	0.7
Stock velocity	4
Net profit ratio	10% (to average capital employed)
Quick ratio	1.5
Gross profit ratio	20% to sales
Debtors velocity	36.5 days

(Sri Venkateshwara University, B.Com., October 1998)

To Opening stock	35,000	By Sales	1,92,500
To Purchases (Balancing figure)	1,61,000	By Closing stock	42,000
To Gross profit	38,500		
	2,34,500		2,34,500
To Expenses (Balancing figure)	20,500	By Gross profit b/d	38,500
To Net profit	18,000		
	38,500		38,500

Balance Sheet

Share capital	1,80,000	Fixed assets	1,47,000
Reserves and surplus		Current Assets	
Reserve	12,000	Stock	42,000
Profit and loss a/c	18,000	Debtors	19,250
Current liabilities			
Creditors	32,000	Cash	43,750
Bank OD	10,000		
	2,52,000		2,52,000

Working Notes:

(1) Calculation of Current Assets and Current Liabilities

Working capital = Current assets – Current liabilities

= 2.5 – 1.0

= 1.5

Since working capital = 63,000

$$\text{Current assets} = 63{,}000 \times \frac{2.5}{1.5} = 1{,}05{,}000$$

$$\text{Current liabilities} = 63{,}000 \times \frac{1.0}{1.5} = 42{,}000$$

(2) Calculation of Closing Stock and Opening Stock

Quick ratio = 1.5

∴ Quick assets = 1.5

$$\text{Quick assets} = 63{,}000 \times \frac{1.5}{1.5} = 63{,}000$$

Stock = Current assets – Quick assets

= 1,05,000 × 63,000 = 42,000 (closing stock)

$$\text{Opening stock} = 42{,}000 \times \frac{100}{120} = 35{,}000$$

(3) Calculation of Sales

$$\text{Average stock} = \frac{42{,}000 + 35{,}000}{2}$$

$$= \frac{7{,}70{,}000}{2} = 38{,}500$$

$$\text{Stock velocity} = \frac{\text{Cost of goods sold}}{\text{Average stock}}$$

$$4 = \frac{\text{Cost of goods sold}}{38{,}500}$$

Cost of goods sold = 38,500 × 4

= 1,54,000

Sales = Cost of goods sold + Gross profit

Cost of goods sold = 1,54,000

Gross profit $\frac{20}{100}$ × 1,54,000 = 38,500

1,92,500

(4) Calculation of Debtors

Debtors velocity = 36.5 Days

This means, sales of 36.5 days is equal to debtors

$$= 1{,}92{,}500 \times \frac{36.5}{365} = 19{,}250$$

Debtors = 19,250

(5) Calculation of Cash

Current assets – (Stock + Debtors) = Cash

1,05,000 – (42,000 + 19,250) = 43,750

(6) Calculation of Creditors

Creditors = Current liabilities – Bank OD

= 42,000 – 10,000

= 32,000

(7) Calculation of Net Profit

Net Profit to capital employed = 10%

Capital= 1,80,000

$$\text{Net Profit} = 1{,}80{,}000 \times \frac{10}{100} = 18{,}000$$

(8) Calculation of Proprietory Funds

$$\text{Proprietory ratio} = \frac{\text{Fixed Assets}}{\text{Proprietory funds}} = \frac{0.7}{1.0}$$

If proprietory Fund = x, fixed assets = 0.7 x

Proprietory Fund + Long-term loan + Current liabiliaites = Fixed assets + Current assets + Fictions assets

$$= x + 0 + 42{,}000 = 0.7x + 1{,}05{,}000 + 0$$

$$x - 0.7x = 1{,}05{,}000 - 42{,}000$$

$$0.3x = 63{,}000$$

$$x = \frac{63{,}000}{0.3} = 2{,}10{,}000$$

$$\text{Proprietory Funds} = 2{,}10{,}000$$

(9) Calculation of Fixed Assets

$$\text{Proprietory Ratio} = \frac{\text{Fixed Assets}}{\text{Proprietory funds}}$$

$$\frac{0.7}{1.0} = \frac{\text{Fixed Assets}}{2{,}10{,}000}$$

$$1 \text{ Fixed Assets} = 2{,}10{,}000 \times 0.7$$

$$\text{Fixed Assets} = \frac{2{,}10{,}000 \times 0.7}{1}$$

$$\text{Fixed Assets} = 1{,}47{,}000$$

(10) Calculation of Reserves

Reserves and surplus = 2,10,000 – 1,80,000

= 30,000

Reserve = 30,000 – 18,000, *i.e.*, Net profit

= 12,000

Problem 56: From the given ratios and other particulars, fill up the trading and profit and loss a/c and balance sheet:

Gross profit ratio	=	25%
Net profit ratio	=	20%
$\frac{\text{Sales}}{\text{Inventory ratio}}$	=	8
$\frac{\text{Fixed Assets}}{\text{Current Assets}}$	=	$\frac{3}{4}$
$\frac{\text{Fixed Assets}}{\text{Total Capital}}$	=	$\frac{3}{2}$
$\frac{\text{Capital}}{\text{Outside liabilities}}$	=	$\frac{2}{5}$
Fixed assets	=	Rs. 15,00,000
Closing stock	=	Rs. 2,00,000

Trading Profit and Loss A/c

To cost of goods sold	....	By sales	....
To gross profit	....		....
To Expenses	....	By gross profit	....
To Net profit			

Balance Sheet

Capital balance	....	Fixed assets	....
Add: Net profit	....	Current assets	....
Other liabilities	....	Stock	....
		Other current assets	....

(*Osmania University, B.Com., March 1997*)

Solution:

Trading and Profit and Loss A/c

To Cost of goods sold	12,00,000	By Sales	16,00,000
To Gross profit 25%	4,00,000		
Sales	16,00,000		16,00,000
To Expenses (Balancing figure)	80,000	By Gross profit	4,00,000
To Net profit $\left(\frac{20}{100} \times 16,00,000\right)$	3,20,000		
	4,00,000		4,00,000

Balance Sheet

Capital Balance	6,80,000		Fixed assets	15,00,000
Add: Net profit	3,20,000		*Current Assets*	
		10,00,000	Stock	2,00,000
Outside liabilities		25,00,000	Other current assets (20,00,000 – 2,00,000)	18,00,000
		35,00,000		35,00,000

Working Notes:

(1) Calculation of Sales

$$\frac{\text{Sales}}{\text{Stock}} = 8$$

$$= \frac{\text{Sales}}{2,00,000} = 8$$

Sales = 2,00,000 × 8 = 16,00,000

(2) Calculation of Gross Profit

$$\frac{25}{100} \times 16,00,000 = \text{Rs. } 4,00,000$$

(3) Calculation of Cost of Goods Sold

Sales – Gross profit = Cost of goods sold
16,00,000 – 4,00,000 = Rs. 12,00,000

(4) Calculation of Net Profit

$$\frac{20}{100} \times 16,00,000 = \text{Rs. } 3,20,000$$

(5) Calculation of Total Current Assets

$$\frac{\text{Fixed Assets}}{\text{Total current Assets}} = \frac{3}{4}$$

$$\frac{15,00,000}{\text{Total current assets}} = \frac{3}{4}$$

$$3 \text{ Total current assets} = 15,00,000 \times 4$$

$$\text{Total current assets} = 15,00,000 \times \frac{4}{3}$$

$$\text{Rs.} = 20,00,000$$

(6) Calculation of Capital

$$\frac{\text{Fixed Assets}}{\text{Capital}} = \frac{3}{2}$$

$$\frac{15,00,000}{\text{Capital}} = \frac{3}{2}$$

$$3 \text{ Capital} = 15,00,000 \times 2$$

$$\text{Capital} = \frac{15,00,000 \times 2}{3} = \text{Rs. } 10,00,000$$

(7) Calculation of Outside Liabilities

$$\frac{\text{Capital}}{\text{Outside liabilities}} = \frac{2}{5}$$

$$\frac{10,00,000}{\text{Outside liabilities}} = \frac{2}{5}$$

$$2 \text{ Outside liabilities} = 10,00,000 \times 5$$

$$\text{Outside liabilities} = \frac{10,00,000 \times 5}{2}$$

$$= \text{Rs. } 25,00,000$$

QUESTIONS

Simple Questions

1. What do you men by Accounting Ratio?
2. In what ways can ratios be expressed?
3. Define ratio analysis.
4. What are the key steps involved in ratio analysis?
5. Mention the ratios which determine the solvency of a concern.
6. What are liquidity ratios?
7. What are solvency ratios?
8. What is meant by profitability ratios?
9. What are activity ratios?
10. What do you understand by leverage ratios.
11. Explain current ratio.
12. What is 'Window dressing' in current ratio?
13. How is 'Window dressing' done?
14. What is liquid ratio? How is it calculated?
15. What is 'absolute liquidity' ratio?
16. What is a proprietory ratio?
17. What do you mean by debt-equity ratio?

18. What is gross profit ratio?
19. What is net profit ratio?
20. What is operating ratio?
21. What is operating profit ratio?
22. What is an expense ratio?
23. What is mean by 'Return on capital employed'?
24. What is stock turnover ratio?
25. What is meant by 'Debtors Turnover Ratio'?
26. What is meant by 'Creditors Turnover Ratio'?
27. What do you understand by 'Fixed assets turnover ratio'?
28. What is capital gearing?
29. What is meant by dividend coverage ratio?
30. What is interest coverage ratio?
31. How is 'Earnings per share' calculated.
32. What is price earning ratio?
33. What is dividend payout ratio?
34. What is Dupont control chart?
35. Mention any form Balance sheet ratio?
36. What is activity ratio?
37. State the significance of 'Current ratio'.
38. What is acid test ratio?
39. How do you calculate 'average collection period'?
40. What is average collection period ratio?
41. What is average payment period ratio?
42. What is price-earning ratio?
43. What is working capital turnover ratio?
44. What is return on equity capital?
45. What is capital turnover ratio?
46. What is dividend yield ratio?
47. The working capital of a firm is Rs. 80,000 and its current ratio is 5. Calculate the current assets and current liabilities. *(Osmania University, B.Com., March 1999)*

    [*Answer*: Current liabilities = Rs. 20,000
    Current assets = Rs. 1,00,000]

48. Calculation the stock turnover ratio

Opening stock	Rs. 90,000
Closing stock	Rs. 1,10,000
Sales	Rs, 5,00,000
Rate of gross profit	20%

    (Osmania University, B.Com., March 1998)
    [*Answer:* Stock turnover ratio 4 times]

49. Turnover to fixed assets ratio is 1: 1.5. Value of goods sold is Rs. 5,00,000. Compute the value of fixed assets. *(Bangalore University, B.Com., October 2,000)*

    [*Answer*: Fixed assets Rs. 3,33,333]

50. Current ratio is 2.5, liquid ratio is 1.5. Working capital is Rs. 50,000. Ascertain current assets and Inventory. *(Bangalore University, B.Com., October 2,000)*

    [*Answer*: Current assets = 83,333
    Inventory = 33,333]

51. Current ratio 2.5
    Working capital Rs. 60,000
    Calculate the amount of current assets and current liabilities
    (Sri Venkateshwara University, B.Com., October 1999)
    [*Answer*: Current assets = 1,00,000
    Current liabilities = 40,000]

52. Opening stock Rs. 29,000, Closing stock Rs. 31,000, Sales Rs. 3,20,000, Gross profit ratio 25% on sales. Calculate stock turnover ratio. *(Sri Venkateshwara University, B.Com., October 1999)*

    [*Answer:* Stock Turnover ratio 8 times]

Short Answer Questions

1. Explain the nature of Accounting ratios.
2. Explain different ways of interpreting accounting ratios.
3. Explain the uses of accounting ratios.
4. State the limitations of accounting ratios
5. Explain the various types of Balance Sheet Ratios.
6. Explain the various types of profit and loss account ratios.
7. From the following data, compute current ratio, acid-test ratio, inventory turnover ratio:
   (*a*) Assets
   Stock — Rs. 10,000, Debtors — Rs. 30,000 prepaid expenes — Rs. 2,000, cash in hand — Rs. 20,000
   (*b*) Liabilities
   Sundry Creditors — Rs. 25,000, Bank overdraft — Rs. 5,000, Bills payable — Rs. 10,000.
   (*c*) During the year sales amounted to Rs. 3,50,000 (*University of Madras, B.Com. September 19997*)
   [*Answer:* Current Ratio = 1.55; Acid test ratio = 1.43; Inventory turnover ratio = 35 times]
8. The ratios relating to a company are given below:

Gross profit ratio	15%
Stock velocity	6 months
Debtors velocity	3 months
Creditors velocity	3 months

Gross profit for the year ending 31st December, 1995 amounts to Rs. 60,000. Closing stock is equal to opening stock.
Find out (*a*) sales, (*b*) closing stock, (*c*) sundry debtors, (*d*) sundry creditors.
(*University of Madras, B.Com, September 1996*)
[*Answers:* Sales = 4,00,000; Closing Stock = 1,70,000; Sundry debtors = 1,00,000; Sundry creditors = 85,000]

9. Triveni Ltd. has the following earnings last year:

Particulars	*Rs.*
Profit before tax	26,50,000
Tax rate	40%
Proposed equity dividend	25%
Capital employed	
10% preference share capital	15,00,000
80,000 Equity shares of Rs. 50 each	40,00,000
Current market price per equity	Rs. 125

Calculate (*i*) Earning per share, (*ii*) Price earning ratio, (*iii*) Dividend payout ratio.
(*University of Bombay, B.Com., April 1997*)

Solution: Earning per share = Rs. 18; Price earning ratio = 6.94; Dividend payout ratio = 0.69

Long Answer questions

1. Explain the various types of ratios.
2. Following are the profit and loss a/c and balance sheet of a company. Calculate the following ratios:
   (*a*) Gross profit ratio (*b*) Operating ratio
   (*c*) Current ratio (*d*) Liquid ratio
   (*e*) Stock turnover ratio (*f*) Debt equity ratio

Profit and loss A/c

To Opening stock	1,50,000	By Sales	10,00,000
To Purchases	3,00,000	By Closing stock	2,50,000
To Wages	2,00,000		
To Manufacturing expenses	1,00,000		
To Gross profit	5,00,000		
	12,50,000		12,50,000

To Administration expenses	50,000	By Gross profit	5,00,000
To Selling and distribution expenses	50,000	By Profit on sale of shares	50,000
To Loss on sale of furniture	25,000		
To Interest on debentures	10,000		
To Net profit	4,15,000		
	5,50,000		5,50,000

Balance Sheet

Share capital	2,00,000	Fixed assets	2,50,000
Reserves	1,00,000	Stock	2,50,000
Debentures	2,00,000	Sundry debtors	1,00,000
Sundry debtors	1,00,000	Bank	50,000
Bills payable	50,000		
	6,50,000		6,50,000

(*Osmania University, B.Com., October 1997*)

[*Answer:* Gross profit = 50%; Operating ratio = 61%; Current ratio = 2.66; Liquid ratio = 1; Stock turnover ratio = 2.5; Debt equity ratio = 0.53

3. The balance sheets of Contractors Ltd. as on 31st December 1996 and 1997 were as follows:

	1996	*1997*		*1996*	*1997*
Equity share capital	1,500	1,700	Fixed assets	1,800	2,100
12% preference shares	500	400	Sundry debtors	550	650
Reserve	570	770	B.R.	430	525
10% Debentures	300	450	Stock	380	460
Creditors	240	320	Prepaid expenses	20	30
Bills payable	50	70	Bank	80	65
Bank OD	100	120			
	3,260	3,830		3,260	3,830

During the year 1997, total sales were Rs. 1,20,00,000 and cash sales were 20% of total sales. Stock turnover ratio was 20 times net profit before payment of taxes at 50% was Rs. 18,00,000.

There were no, non-operating expesnes and non-operating incomes. Calculate the following ratios for the year 1997:

1. Gross profit ratio
2. Operating ratio
3. Current ratio
4. Debtor turnover ratio
5. Debt collection period
6. Return on capital employed

(*University of Bombay, B.Com., April 1997*)

Solution: Gross profit ratio = 30%; Operating ratio = 85%;
Current ratio = 3.39; Debtors turnover ratio = 8.91;
Debt collection period = 40.4 days; Return on capital employed = 55.57%.

4. The following figures related to the trading activities of Z Ltd., for the year ended 31st March, 1996.

	Rs.
Sales	10,57,000
Closing stock	4,60,000
Purchases	8,35,000
Loss on sale of assets	45,000
Advertising	32,750
Rent	18,750
Profit on sale of shares	25,000

Provision for taxation	1,00,000
Salaries	35,750
Salesmen's salaries	14,250
Depreciation	36,000
Sales return	57,000
Depreciation on delivery van	8,000
Printing and stationery	17,500
Audit fees	12,000
Opening stock	2,25,000
Dividend received on shares	15,000

You are required to rearrange above income statement in vertical form and compute the following ratios:

(*a*) Gross profit ratio
(*b*) Operating ratio
(*c*) Net operating profit ratio
(*d*) Selling and distribution expenses to sales ratio

(*University of Bombay, B.Com., October 1996*)

Solution: Gross profit ratio = 40%; Operating ratio = 77.50%; Net operating profit ratio = 22.50%; Selling and distribution expenses to sales ratio = 5.50%

5. Re-arrange the following Balance Sheet and profit & loss a/c of Edens Ltd. in a form suitable for analysis and calculate the following ratios:
   1. Current ratio
   2. Stock turnover ratio
   3. Liquidity ratio
   4. Debt equity ratio
   5. Gross profit ratio
   6. Net profit ratio

Balance Sheet as at 31st March 1996

Bills payable	25,000	Fixed assets	1,25,000
Sundry creditors	50,000	Sundry debtors	50,000
Debentures	1,00,000	Bank	25,000
Reserves	50,000	Inventory	1,25,000
Equity share capital	50,000		
Preference share capital	50,000		
	3,25,000		3,25,000

P & C A/c for the year ended 31st March 1996

To Opening inventories	75,000	By Sales	5,00,000
To Purchases	1,50,000	By Closing inventories	1,25,000
To Manufacturing expenses	50,000	By Profit on sale of shares	25,000
To Direct wages	1,00,000		
To Administration expenses	25,000		
To Selling expenses	25,000		
To Loss on sale of assets	27,500		
To Interest on debentures	5,000		
To Net profit	1,92,500		
	6,50,000		6,50,000

(*University of Bombay, B.Com., April 1996*)

[*Answer:* Current ratio = 2.67; Stock turnover ratio = 2.5 times; Liquidity ratio = 1; Debt-equity ratio = 0.4; Gross profit ratio = 50%; Net profit ratio = 39%]

6. Comment on the position of Commentary Ltd., from the following:
   Profit and loss accounts and Balance Sheets after calculating stated ratios:

Balance Sheet

	31-3-95	*31-3-94*		*31-3-95*	*31-3-94*
Capital of Rs. 10 each	70,000	70,000	Fixed assets	90,000	92,000
Reserves	80,000	68,000	Current assets	1,10,000	1,12,000
Secured loans	22,000	24,000	Loans and advances	52,000	40,000

Current liabailities	26,000	30,000			
Provision	54,000	52,000			
	2,52,000	2,44,000		2,52,000	2,44,000

P & C A/c for The Year Ended

	31-3-95	*31-3-94*		*31-3-95*	*31-3-94*
To Opening stock	44,000	40,000	By Sales	2,10,000	2,00,000
To Purchases	84,000	72,000	By Closing stock	46,000	44,000
To Wages	40,000	36,000			
To Factory expenses	32,000	28,000			
To Adm. expenses	8,000	6,000			
To Selling expenses	6,000	10,000			
To Managerial remuneration	2,000	2,000			
To Transfer to reserve	2,000	2,000			
To Income-tax	22,000	24,000			
To Proposed dividend	6,000	8,000			
To Balance c/d	10,000	16,000			
	2,56,000	2,44,000		2,56,000	2,44,000

1. Current ratio, 2. Proprietory ratio, 3. Debt equity ratio, 4. Earning per share, 5. Stock working capital ratio, 6. Liquid ratio, 7. Cost of sales to sales ratio, 8. Administrative expenses to sales ratio, 9. Selling expenses to sales ratio. *(University of Bombay, B.Com., October 1995)*

Answer:

	31-3-95	31-3-96
Current ratio	2.025	1.854
Proprietory ratio	0.6	0.57
Debt equity ratio	0.15	0.17
Earning per share	2.571	3.714
Stock working capital ratio	0.56	0.62
Liquid ratio	0.80	0.82
Cost of sales to sales	73.33%	66%
Adm. expenses ratio	4.76%	4.00%
Selling expenses to sales	2.86%	5%

7. The following is the balance sheet of XYX Co. Ltd. as on 31-12-1995:

Equity share capital (Shares of Rs. 100 each)	20,00,000	Plant and equipment	12,50,000
		Land and Building	5,00,000
		Sundry Debtors	4,50,000
Returned earnings	5,00,000	Stock	7,00,000
Sundry creditors	4,00,000	B.R.	1,50,000
Bills payable	1,50,000	Prepared insurance cash	10,000
Other current liabilitites	50,000	Cash	40,000
	31,00,000		31,00,000

Statement of Profit for the year eneded 31-12-95

	Rs.
Sales	50,00,000
Less: Cost of goods sold	38,50,000
Gross profit	11,50,000
Less: Operating expenses	7,50,000
Net profit	4,00,000
Less: Tax at 40%	1,60,000
Net profit after tax	2,40,000

Sundry debtors and stock at the beginning of the year were Rs. 4,00,000 and Rs, 6,00,000 respectively.

Calculate:

1. Current ratio
2. Acid test ratio
3. Stock turnover ratio
4. Debtors turnover ratio
5. Gross profit ratio
6. Net profit ratio
7. Earning per share
8. Return on equity

(Bangalore University, B.B.M, April 1997)

Answer: Current ratio = 2.25
Acid test ratio = 1.06
Stock turnover ratio = 5.92 times
Debtors turnover ratio = 11.76
Gross profit ratio = 23%
Net profit ratio = 8%
Earning per share = 12
Return on equity = 12%

8. From the following information make out a balance sheet with as many details as possible:
   (*a*) Gross profit turnover ratio = 25%
   (*b*) Debtors velocity = 3 months
   (*c*) Creditors velocity = 2 months
   (*d*) Stock velocity = 8 times
   (*e*) Capital turnover ratio = 2.5 times
   (*f*) Fixed assets-turnover ratio = 8 times

Gross profit for the year ended 31st December, 1992 was Rs. 80,000. There was no long-term loan or overdraft, Reserves and surplus amounted to Rs. 28,000, Liquid assets were Rs. 97,333.

Closing stock of the year was Rs. 2,000 more than opening stock. Bills receivable and Bills payable were Rs. 5,000 and Rs. 2,000 respectively. *(University of Madras, B.Com., March 1996)*

[*Answer:* Total of Balance Sheet = 1,68,333]

9. From the following information, prepare a balance sheet. Show the workings:
   (*a*) Working capital = 75,000
   (*b*) Reserves and surplus = 1,00,000
   (*c*) Bank overdraft = 60,000
   (*d*) Current ratio = 1.75
   (*e*) Liquid ratio = 1.15
   (*f*) Fixed assets to proprietors funds = 0.75
   (*g*) Long-term liabilities = Nil

(University of Madras, B.Com. Correspondence Course, May 1996)

[*Answer:* Balance Sheet Total Rs. 4,00,000]

10. From the following particulars, you are required to prepare the balance sheet of a Zinc Company.

Fixed assets (after writing off 30%)	10,50,000
Fixed assets turnover ratio (on cost of sales)	2
Finished goods turnover ratio (on cost of sales)	6
G P rate on sales	25%
Net profit (before interest) to sales	8%
Fixed charges cover (debenture interest 7%)	8
Debt collection period	1.5 months
Materials consumed to sales	30%
Stock of Raw-materials (in terms of months consumption)	3
Current ratio	2.4
Quick ratio	1.0
Reserve to capital ratio	0.4

(CS, Inter, June 1997)

[*Answer:* Balance Sheet Total 20,10,000]

11. From the following details, prepare a Balance Sheet:
    Current ratio is 1.75
    Liquid ratio is 1.25
    Stock turnover ratio (closing stock) is 9 times
    Gross pforit ratio is 25%
    Debt collection period is 1.5 months
    Reserves to capital is 0.2
    Turnover of fixed assets is 1.2
    Capital gearing ratio is 0.6
    Fixed assets to net worth is 1.25
    Sales for the year is Rs. 12,00,000 (*CS, Inter, December 1997*)

    [*Answer:* Balance Sheet Total 11,00,000]

34

FUND FLOW STATEMENT

INTRODUCTION

A fund flow statement is a technical device designed to analyse, the changes in the financial condition of a business enterprise between two dates. It is also called a 'statement of sources and application of funds' as it portrays, the sources and application of working capital and highlights the basic changes in the resources and financial structure of a concern. This statement is intended to supplement and not to supplant, the balance sheet and profit and loss account in whole or in part. The fund flow statement is becoming popular with the management, because it not only helps them in analysing financial operations, providing basis for comparison with budgets, and in serving as a tool of communication, but also explains the financial consequences of such operations such as, the reason why the company is experiencing difficulty in making payments to creditors or why the bank balance is getting thinner.

CONCEPT OF 'FUND' AND 'FLOW OF FUND'

Fund

In its broadest sense, it refers to all financial resources or purchasing power or economic value possessed by a firm at a point of time. According to this concept all assets—both fixed and current would constitute fund. In a popular sense it is used to refer to working capital, *i.e.*, excess of current assets over current liabilities. In a narrow sense it is used to refer to cash and bank balance.

Concept of Flow of Fund

The flow of fund refers to the changes in the existing financial position of a business caused by in-flow and out-flow of resources owing to receipts and payments. It is generally taken to mean a change in working capital of a business. If a transaction results in an increase in fund it is known as source of fund. Where a transaction results in a decrease in the fund, it is known as application of fund. When there is no change in the fund, there is no flow of fund.

Meaning of Fund Flow Statement

It refers to a statement which incorporates working capital that brings about changes in assets, liabilities and capital of owners between two consecutive balance sheets. According to Roy A. Foulke it is a statement of sources and application of fund designed to analyse the change in the financial condition of a business enterprise between two dates.

Objective of Fund Flow Statement

Fund flow statement is a useful tool in the financial manager's analytical kit. The important objectives of this statement are:

1. to indicate the result of current financial management;
2. to lay emphasis on the most singnificant changes that have taken place, during a specific period;
3. to show how general expansion in a business has been financed or to describe the sources from which additional funds were derived;
4. to establish the relationship between profits from operations, distribution of dividend and raising of new capital or contracting of loans;
5. to give recognition to the fact that a business exists on flow of funds and is not a static organisation.

IMPORTANCE OF FUND FLOW STATEMENT

Fund Flow analysis helps in judging the efficiency of financial functions and administration of a business by providing a summary of the sources from which funds have been procured and uses to which such funds have been put to. Such on analysis is particularly useful in long range planning where projections of available liquid resources are vital and are necessarily to be made. Management can come to know about long-term debts or arrange funds for daily needs. Fund flow statement is a parametre for testing the effective use of working capital by the management during a particular period. The adequacy or inadequacy of working capital will reveal to the financial analyst about the possible steps that the management should take for effective use of working capital.

A projected fund flow statement will help the analyst in finding out as to how the management is going to allocate the scarce financial resources for meeting the productive requirements of the business. The use of funds should be phased in such an order that the available resources are put to the best use of the enterprise. Further, fund flow analysis helps in the proper postmortem of the financial policy of the business, thereby providing useful guidance to the management in the matter of debt retirement, expansion or replacement or to the payment of dividends etc. Thus the significance of funds flow statement can be summarised as follows:

(*a*) it suggests the ways of improving working capital position;
(*b*) it helps in planning for retirement of long-term debts;
(*c*) it helps in the formulation of a realistic dividerd policy;
(*d*) it helps in deciding about the mode of financing expansion or replacement of facilities;
(*e*) It evaluates the urgency of operational uses;
(*f*) it helps to explain the phenomena of high profitability with low liquidity.

Difference between Statement of Receipts and Payments and Fund Flow Statement

1. The statement of receipts and payments contains a summary of inward and outward movement of cash which is only a part of the working capital, whereas the fund flow statement contains a summary of the inward and outward movement of all items affecting the working capital of a business.
2. The statement of receipts and payments is prepared from cash book, whereas, the fund flow statement is prepared from two balance sheets and other concerned particulars.

Differences between Cash Budget and Fund Flow Statement

1. Cash budget is generally futuristic in approach whereas, fund flow statement is usually based on past data.
2. Cash budget is planning for cash before hand but fund flow is only the postmortem analysis.
3. Cash budget is prepared for a specific period and requires previous data only for the purpose of judicious forecasting whereas fund flow statement is prepared from the accounting data at two specified dates.
4. Cash budget is a tool for management for controlling cash whereas fund flow statement represents the working of the company for previous year and it is for the benefit of external parties too.

DIFFERENCE BETWEEN INCOME STATEMENT AND FUND FLOW STATEMENT

Fund Flow statement	*Profit and Loss A/c*
1. It shows sources and application of funds.	1. It shows profit or loss of the business.
2. Depreication is included in the fund from operation. So fund from operation is greater in volume compared to net profit.	2. Net profit excludes depreciation. So net profit is smaller in volume compared to fund from operation.
3. Fund flow statement explains the way the funds are generated and how it is used in making various payments such as tax, dividend, purchase of fixed assets.	3. The profit and loss account explains how profit or loss has resulted by comparing revenue with expenditure.
4. Fund flow statement does not consider outstanding and prepared expense. It does not consider the problem associated with time.	4. Profit and loss a/c takes into account out standing and prepaid expense. It takes into account problem associated with time.
5. It is meant for management for taking decisions and making policies	5. It is meant for various parties interested in business.

Superiority of fund flow statement over-income statement: Though a fund flow statement and income statement have different functions to perform a fund flow statement is a better substitute for an income statement due to the following reasons:

(*a*) The income statement discloses the operating results while a fund flow statement deals with the financial resources required for running the business. A fund flow statement translates the economic consequences of operations into their financial information as a basis for action.

(*b*) Income statement is prepared at the end of the accounting period, whereas fund flow statement is prepared as and when management wants it.

(*c*) An income statement is static in as much as it gives information on what has happened during the period covered by it. For managerial purposes funds flow statement may be prepared much before business operations and as an instrument of planning and control. It is dynamic and presents financial information in the form of a flow.

(*d*) An income statement is not very reliable as items shown in income statement can be easily maniputated by the management while a funds flow statement is more reliable.

Differences between balance sheet and a fund flow statement

Balance Sheet	*Fund Flow Statement*
1. It reveals the financial position as on a particular date.	1. It reveals the changes in the financial position between two balance sheet period.
2. It portrays all assets and liabilities.	2. It portrays a change in working capital.
3. It is an end product of an accounting system.	3. It is a by-product of balance sheet. It is under taken after the preparation of a balance sheet.
4. It is meant for external parties.	4. It is meant for the use of management.
5. Its preparation is compulsory in higher form of business organisation.	5. It is voluntarily prepared to benefit the management.

Uses and limitations of Fund Flow Analysis

Uses

1. One gets an insight into financial operations of the firm. This will help to analyse the past trends and plan future operation.
2. It is possible to know whether the firm's growth was financed from internal source or from external sources. It will also be clear whether growth was at a rapid pace and financing was strained.
3. It reveals disproportionate growth of inventories and disproportionate increase in creditors in relation to current assets affecting the credit worthiness of the firm.
4. It is possible to detect the imbalance in the use of funds. For example, one can evaluate the ratio of dividends to earnings against the background of the firm's need for funds.
5. In the case of multi-division companies, fund flow statement helps to evaluate the performance of division in the use of funds allotted to them.

Limitations

1. The fund flow statement reveals the overall change in the working capital but not the variation in individual items.
2. Fund flow statement is prepared based on historical information.
3. It is not a substitute to financial statements. Instead it is only supplementary to financial statements.
4. The management may manipulate the working capital by adopting different method of inventory valuation.
5. The concept 'fund' consists of various types of items such as cash, destors, stock, prepaid expesnes etc. Thus fund flow statement lacks homogencity.

Steps Involved in the Preparation of Fund Flow Statement

(1) Preparation of a schedule showing change in working capital: The schedule analysing changes in working capital is prepared with the help of current assets and current liabilities of the two (period) balance sheets one being the previous year, *i.e.*, opening balance sheet and the other being current year, *i.e.*, closing balance sheet. An increase in the amount of any current asset in the current year in comparision to that in the previous year results in an increase in working capital. A decrease in the amount of any current asset in the current year in comparision to that in the previous year results in a decrease in working capital. Similarly current liabilities are also compared, *i.e.*, an increase in any current liability in the current year in comparision to the previous year results in a decrease in the working capital and *vice-versa*. Finally the total increase and total decrease is compared and the difference shows the decrease or increase on the working capital. An increase of working capital is the application of funds and decrease of working capital is the source of funds.

While preparing a schedule of change in working capital, the following points must be borne in mind.

(*a*) *Provision for taxation:* Provision for tax may be treated either as a current or non-current liability. When it is treated as a current liability (*i.e.*, as a charge on profit), provision for taxation is considered while preparing statement of working capital and not used for adjusting the profit made during the year for calculating the funds from operation and also tax paid during the year is not treated as an application of fund.

As a non-current liability, the provision for tax is treated as internal appropriation of profit and it is used for adjusting the profit made during the year. In this case it will not appear in the schedule of working capital. A seperate account known as 'Provision for taxation' is prepared. It is credited with the opening balance and credited with tax paid and closing balance. The tax paid during the year is treated as an application of fund in the flow how statement. The balancing figure represents the provision made during the year and is transferred to profit and loss account.

(*b*) *Proposed Dividend:* When proposed dividend is treated as a current liability it will be shown in the schedule of working capital as an item decreasing the working capital. Any dividend paid during the current year or an earlier year is not shown as an application of funds because such payment will not change net working capital or fund, *i.e.*, it will affect two current accounts, *viz.*, cash a/c and proposed dividend.

When proposed dividend is treated as a non-current liability, it is taken as an appropriation of profit. So this item will not appear in the schedule of working capital. A separate account is opened entitled 'proposed dividend a/c" to find out proposed dividend made during the year. The adjusted profit and loss a/c is debited with this amount of proposed dividend. The payment of dividend made during the current year in response to the proposed dividend for previous year is shown as an application in the fund flow statement.

(*c*) Trade investments should be treated as long-term investments and they should not be included in statement of changes in working capital. However, if investments represent surplus fund temporarily invested in marketable securities, they are to be treated as current assets, and as such, are to be considered in determining working capital.

A proforma of a schedule of changes in working capital is shown below:

Schedule of changes in working capital

	Previous year	*Current year*	*Increase*	*Decrease*
Current Assets				
Cash in hand	xx	xx		
Cash at Bank	xx	xx		
Debtors	xx	xx		
Marketable Securities	xx	xx		
Bills receivables	xx	xx		
Stock	xx	xx		

Prepaid expenses	xx	xx
Total (A)		
Current Liabilities		
Creditors	xx	xx
Bills payable	xx	xx
O/s expenses	xx	xx
Total (B)		
Working capital (A–B)	xx	xx
Net increase/ Decrease in working capital		

(d) Preparation of Adjusted Profit and Loss a/c to calculate fund from operation: The current operations of the business is the most important single source of funds and in the long run they constitute the largest source of funds. The repayment of loans, purchase of plant, payment of dividend etc., must ultimately depend upon this source. Funds from operations which are internal in character are arrived after making adjustments in the net profit. These adjustments are necessary because the net profit has been determined after deducting non-cash expenses such as depreciation, depletion charges, amortisation of fictitions and intangible assets like amount written off by way of prelimnary expenses, goodwill, patents, discount on shares or debentures, premium on redemption of preference shares or debentures, deferred charges etc. and loss on sale of fixed assets charged to profit and loss account, which do not result in flow of funds. These transactions, in fact are book adjustments and do not involve use of resources. So the actual fund generated from operations are larger by the amount of such non-cash expenses. Similarly the non-trading or non-operating incomes like dividends and inteiest received from out side or profit on sale of fixed assets, appreciation in the value of fixed assets will have to be deducted from net profit only if they have been considered already while preparing the profit and loss account. In short, funds from operations may be arrived at by deducting all non-cash credits (incomes) and adding back non-cash debits (expenses) to the net profit. If there has been a net loss as per profit and loss account, non-cash expenses have to be deducted therefrom and non-cash income added thereto.

A proforma of adjusted profit and loss account is given below:

Adjusted Profit & Loss A/c

	Rs.		*Rs.*
To Depreciation and depletion of fictitions and intangible assets such as goodwill, patent, trade marks etc.	xx	By Opening balance of P & L a/c	xx
		By Transfer from excess provision	xx
To Appropriation of Retained earnings such as transfer to general reserve, sinking fund etc.	xx	By Appreciation in the value of fixed assets	xx
		By Dividend received	xx
		By Profit on sale of fixed assets	xx
To Loss on sale of any current or fixed asset	xx	By Funds from operation	xx
To Dividend (in cluding) interim dividend)	xx	(Balancing figure in case debt side exceeds credit side.	

To Proposed dividend (If not taken as a current liability)	xx		
To Provision for taxation (If not taken as a current liability)	xx		
To Closing balance of profit & loss a/c	xx		
To Fund lost on operation (Balancing figure in case credit side exceeds debit side)	xx		
	xx		xx

(3) Reconstruction of all non-fund accounts: The various non-fund accounts which have changed between tne two balance sheet period and in respect of which additional information is given is to be reconstructed. Such reconstruction is done by recording opening and closing balances along with additional information given. Any difference in the reconstructed account will represent either a source or application of fund. For example, a debit balance in a fixed asset account represents purchase and it relates to use of funds. If there is a credit balance, it represents sale of asset and it constitutes a source of fund. In case of non-fund liability account, if the balancing figure is on the debit side, is represents repayment and is a use of fund, while it is on the credit side, it will be a source of funds.

(4) Preparation of a statement of sources and application of funds: The final stage will involve the preparation of the statement of sources and uses of funds which portrays the avenues through which funds have been obtained and the uses to which they have been put. This statement contains the balancing figures in various non-fund accounts and the figure of fund from operation. Increase or decrease of working capital is also added as application or sources, as the case may be. The principal sources and application of funds are listed below:

Sources of Funds

1. Funds from operation
2. Issue of share capital
3. Borrowing long-term loans such as debentures, mortgage, long-term deposits, etc.
4. Sale of fixed assets such as land, building, plant, long-term investment, etc.
5. Non-trading receipts such as dividend and interest earnings, damages recovered in legal action etc.
6. Decrease in working capital (as per schedule)

Uses of Funds

1. Funds lost in operation (trading loss)
2. Redemption of preference shares
3. Repayment of long-term loans
4. Purchase of fixed assets
5. Non-trading payments, e.g., loss arising from legal action, loss of cash by embezzlement etc., and payment of taxes and dividends.
6. Increase in working capital (as per schedule)

When we prepare a fund flow statement *i.e.*, sources and application sides, would tally with each other. A specimen form of fund flow statement is shown below:

Specimen of Fund Flow Statement

Sources of Funds	
Fund from operation	xx
Issue of share capital	xx
Raising of long-term loans	xx
Receipts from partly paid shares called up	xx
Sale of fixed assets	xx
Non-trading receipts such as dividend received	xx
Sale of long-term Investments	xx
Decrease in working capital	xx
Total	xx
Application of Funds	
Fund lost in operation	xx
Redemption of preference share capital	xx
Redemption of debentures	xx
Repayment of long-term loans	xx
Purchase of fixed assets	xx
Purchase of long-term Investments	xx
Non-trading payments	xx
Payment of tax	xx
Increase in working capital	xx
Total	xx

Problem 1: (Preparation of schedule of working capital):- From the following Trail balance of 'A' Ltd. You are required to prepare a schedule of changes in working capital.

Trial Balance

	1998		*1999*	
	DR	*CR*	*DR*	*CR*
Capital	—	80,000	—	85,000
Mortage	—	—	—	5,000
Land and Buildings	50,000	—	50,000	—
Plant and Machinery	24,000	—	34,000	—
Stock	9,000	—	7,000	—
Debtors	16,500	—	19,500	—
Cash at Bank	4,000	—	9,000	—
Profit & loss a/c	—	14,500	—	24500
Creditors	—	9,000	—	5,000
	1,03,500	1,03,500	1,19,500	1,19,500

(Bangalore University, B.Com., April 2000)

Solution:

Schedule showing statement of working capital

	1998	*1999*	*Increase*	*Decrease*
Current Assets				
Stock	9,000	7,000	—	2,000
Debtors	16,500	19,500	3,000	—
Cash at Bank	4,000	9,000	5,000	—
Total (A)	29,500	35,500		

Current Liabilities				
Creditors	9,000	5,000	4,000	—
Total (B)	9,000	5,000		
Working Capital (A–B)	20,500	30,500	—	—
Net increase in working capital	10,000	—		10,000
	30,500	30,500	12,000	12,000

Problem 2: Prepare a statement showing changes in working capital:

	1990 (Rs.)	1991 (Rs.)
Assets:		
Cash	60,000	94,000
Debtors	2,40,000	2,30,000
Stock	1,60,000	1,80,000
Land	1,00,000	1,32,000
	5,60,000	6,36,000
Liabilities:		
Share capital	4,00,000	5,00,000
Creditors	1,40,000	90,000
Retained earnings	20,000	46,000
	5,60,000	6,36,000

(*Osmania University, B.Com., March 1997*)

Solution:

Schedule showing change in working capital

	1990	*1991*	*Increase*	*Decrease*
Current Assets				
CAsh	60,000	94,000	34,000	—
Debtors	2,40,000	2,30,000	—	10,000
Stock	1,60,000	1,80,000	20,000	—
Total (A)	4,60,000	5,04,000		
Current Liabilities:				
Creditors	1,40,000	90,000	50,000	—
Total (B)	1,40,000	90,000		
Working capital (A–B)	3,20,000	4,14,000		
Net increase in working capital	94,000			94,000
	4,14,000	4,14,000	10,4,000	1,04,000

Problem 3 (Problem on calculation of Fund from operation): Calculate funds from operation from the following profit and loss A/c:

P & L A/c

To Rent, salaries paid	75,000	By Gross profit	1,12,500
To Depreciation	17,500	By Grain on sale of land	15,000
To Loss on sale of machinery	1,000		
To Discount on issue of debentures	50		
To Goodwill written off	5,000		
To Net profit	28,950		
	1,27,500		1,27,500

(*Osmania University, B.Com., October 1999*)

Solution:

Adjusted Profit & Loss A/c

To Depreciation	17,500	By Gain on sale of land	15,000
To Loss on sale of machine	1,000	By Fund from operation	37,500
To Discount	50		
To Goodwill written off	5,000		
To Balance c/d	28,950		
	52,500		52,500

Problem 3 (Effect of Transactions on Working Capital): State with reasons whether the following transactions result in increase or decrease of working capital or do not affect the working capital.

(*a*) preliminary expenses written off Rs. 3,600.
(*b*) Bills receivable Rs. 4,000 was discounted for Rs. 3,850.
(*c*) Advance income tax paid Rs. 5,000.
(*d*) Rs. 50,000, 12% debentures were redeemed by purchase from open market at Rs. 95 for a debenture of Rs. 100.

Solution:

1. This is a non-current item as the amount is treated as deferred revenue expenditure. Hence this may be treated as an outflow of cash and affects the working capital.
2. This is a current liability being paid out and there is an outflow of cash and it decreases working capital.
3. There is an increase in current asset and current liability. This will not affect the working capital.
4. This is a non-current item and hence will not affect working capital.

Problem 4: State with reasons whether the following transactions result in increase or decrease in working capital or do not affect the working capital.

1. Bills accepted and issued to creditors Rs. 8,000.
2. One machine costing Rs. 30,000 (with an accumulated depreciation of Rs. 17,000) was sold for Rs. 15,000.
3. Amount paid for insurance Rs. 2,800 includes Rs. 600 prepaid insurance.
4. Dividend on investment received Rs. 800.

Solution:

1. This represents only an application of funds and it is a current liability. It decreases working capital.
2. There is a decrease in non-current assets and increase in cash. It will increase working capital.
3. There is an increase in current asset and decrease in current asset, *i.e.*, cash. It decreases working capital.
4. It is a non-current asset and does not affect working capital.

Problem 5: The balance sheets of Prasad Ltd. showed a net profit of Rs. 40,000 and Rs. 50,000 for the years 2000 and 2001 respectively. During the year 2001, proposed dividend was Rs. 30,000 and Rs. 20,000 was transferred to general Reserve Depreciation on fixed assets was Rs. 30,000. There was loss on sale of furniture to the extent of Rs. 5,000 and on plant was Rs. 10,000. Investments were sold for Rs. 40,000 and a profit of Rs. 20,000 was made. Preliminary expenses charged to the profit and loss account was Rs. 5,000. Calculate the fund from operation.

Solution:

Adjusted Profit & Loss A/c

To Proposed dividend	30,000	By Balance b/d	40,000
To Transfer to general reserve	20,000	By Profit on sale of investments	20,000
To Depreciation on fixed assets	30,000	By Fund from operation	90,000
To Loss on sale of furniture	5,000		
To Loss on sale of plant	10,000		
To Preliminary expenses	5,000		
To Balance c/d	50,000		
	1,50,000		1,50,000

Problem 6: Tanras Ltd. had the following balance sheet on 31-12-2001

Share capital	1,00,000	Buildings	40,000
Creditors	40,000	Stock	20,000
		Cash	80,000
	1,40,000		1,40,000

Following is the summary of transactions for the year

	Rs.
Purchases:	
Cash	15,000
Credit	35,000
Cash paid to creditors	5,000
Sales:	
Cash	20,000
Credit	80,000
Operating expenses (Cash paid)	20,000
Closing stock	50,000

Show the Net Change in Working Capital

Solution:

Cash A/c

To Balance b/d	80,000	By Cash purchases	15,000
To Cash sales	20,000	By Cash paid to creditors	5,000
		By Operating expenses	20,000
		By Balance c/d (Balancing figure)	60,000
	1,00,000		1,00,000

Creditors A/c

To Cash paid to creditors	5,000	By Balance b/d	40,000
To Balance c/d (Balancing figure)	70,000	By Credit purchases	35,000
	75,000		75,000

Schedule showing change working capital

	2000	*2002*	*Increase*	*Decrease*
Current Assets				
Cash	80,000	60,000		20,000
Stock	20,000	50,000	30,000	—
Total (A)	1,00,000	1,10,000		
Current Liabilities				
Creditors	40,000	70,000	—	30,000
Total (B)	40,000	70,000		
Working capital (A–B)	60,000	40,000		
Decrease in working	—	20,000	20,000	—
Capital	60,000	60,000	50,000	50,000

Problem 7: From the following particulars prepare a statement of sources and application of funds for the year ended 31.12.2000 of 'X' Co. Ltd.

(*a*) 'X' Co. Ltd. issued 1,000 shares of Rs. 100 each at a premium of Rs. 20 per share and all the shares are subscribed and fully paid up
(*b*) The company has redeemed preference shares for Rs. 1,00,000 at 10% premium
(*c*) Investments are sold for Rs. 50,000 (resulting in a profit of Rs. 20,000)
(*d*) Sale of machinery during the year Rs. 30,000 (resulting in a loss of Rs. 5,000)
(*e*) Purchase of fixed assets Rs. 1.20,000
(*f*) Dividend paid Rs. 40,000 and income tax paid Rs. 35,000
(*g*) Working capital of the company was Rs. 1,20,000 on 1-1-2000 and Rs. 1,80,000 on 31-12-2000
(*h*) Closing balance in P & L a/c was Rs. 45,000 more than opening balance as per Balance Sheets
(*i*) Depreciation provided for the year was Rs. 50,000 and preliminary expenses written off was Rs. 10,000

Solution:

Adjusted Profit & Loss A/c

To Loss on sale of machinery	5,000	By Profit on sale of investment	20,000
To Dividends	40,000	By Funds from operation	1,65,000
To Income tax	35,000		
To Depreciation	50,000		
To Preliminary expenses written off	10,000		
To Net profit	45,000		
	1,85,000		1,85,000

Fund Flow Statement

Sources		*Applications*	
Sale of machinery	30,000	Purchase of fixed assets	1,20,000
Sale of Investment	50,000	Dividend paid	40,000
Fund from operation	1,65,000	Income tax paid	35,000
Issue of shares	1,20,000	Redemption of preference shares	1,10,000
		Increase in working capital	60,000
	3,65,000		3,65,000

Problem 8: From the following particulars prepare (1) provision for depreciation A/c and (2) machinery A/c

	1.1.2001	*31.12.2001*
	Rs.	*Rs.*
Machinery a/c	1,80,000	2,50,000
Provision for depreciation a/c	50,000	60,000

The following information is also obtained:

(*a*) Machinery purchased in 2001 for Rs. 30,000 by issue of debentures
(*b*) One machine costing Rs. 40,000 on 1.1.2001 (with an accumulated depreciation of Rs. 20,000) was sold for Rs. 25,000

Solution:

Machinery A/c

To Balance b/d	1,80,000	By Sales	25,000
To Purchase of machinery by issue of debenture	30,000	By Depreciation	20,000
To Adj. P & L a/c - profit on sale of machinery	5,000	By Balance c/d	2,50,000
To Purchases of machinery for cash (Balancing figure)	80,000		
	2,95,000		2,95,000

Provision for depreciation

To Machinery a/c	20,000	By Balance b/d	50,000
To Balance c/d	60,000	By Adj. P & L a/c (Balancing figure)	30,000
	80,000		80,000

Working Note:

Calculation of profit on sale

Book value of machinery	40,000
Less: Depreciation	20,000
Depreciated value	20,000
Sales value of machinery	25,000
Profit on sale	5,000

Problem 9 (Preparation of Fund Flow Statement): Following are the summarised balance sheets of Sahana Ltd. as on 31st December, 1998 and 1999

	1998	*1999*		*1998*	*1999*
Share capital	4,50,000	4,50,000	Fixed assets	4,00,000	3,20,000
General reserve	3,00,000	3,10,000	Investments (non-current)	50,000	60,000
P & L a/c	56,000	68,000			
Creditors	1,68,000	1,34,000	Stock	2,40,000	2,10,000
Provision for taxation	75,000	10,000	Debtors	2,10,000	4,55,000
			Bank	1,49,000	1,97,000
Mortgage loan	—	2,70,000			
	10,49,000	12,42,000		10,49,000	12,42,000

Additional Information

(*a*) Investment costing Rs. 8,000 were sold during the year 1999 for Rs. 8,500

(*b*) Provision for taxation made during the year was Rs. 90,000

(*c*) During the year part of the fixed assets costing Rs. 10,000 was sold for Rs. 12,000. The profit was included in the profit and loss account.

(*d*) Dividend paid during the year amounted to Rs. 40,000

Prepare a statement showing the sources and applications of funds for the year ended 31st December 1999.

(*Bangalore University, B.Com., April 2000*)

Schedule showing changes in working capital

	1998	*1990*	*Increase*	*Decrease*
Current Assets:				
Stock	2,40,000	2,10,000		30,000
Debtors	2,10,000	4,55,000	2,45,000	—
Bank	1,49,000	1,97,000	48,000	—
Total (A)	5,99,000	8,62,000		
Current Liabilities				
Creditors	1,68,000	1,34,000	34,000	—
Total (B)	1,68,000	1,34,000		
Working capital (A–B)	4,31,000	7,28,000		
Increase in working capital	2,97,000	—	—	2,97,000
	7,28,000	7,28,000	3,27,000	3,27,000

Fixed Assets A/c

To Balance b/d	4,00,000	By Cash-sales	12,000
To P & L a/c (Profit on sale)	2,000	By Depreciation (Balancing figure)	70,000
			3,20,000
	4,02,000	Balance c/d	4,02,000

Investments

To Balance b/d	50,000	By Cash-sales	8,500
To P & L a/c - profit	500	By Balance c/d	60,000
To Cash-purchases (Balancing figure)	18,000		
	68,500		68,500

Provision for Taxation A/c

To Cash a/c (Balancing figure)	74,000	By Balance b/d	75,000
		By P & L a/c	9,000
To Balance c/d	10,000		
	84,000		84,000

Adjusted Profit & Loss A/c

To General reserve	10,000	By Balance b/d	56,000
To Dividends	40,000	By Profit on sale of investments	5,000
To Provision for taxation	9,000	By Profit on sale of fixed assets	2,000
To Depreciation on fixed assets	70,000	By Fund from operation	1,38,500
To Balance c/d	68,000		
	1,97,000		1,97,000

Statement of sources and application of funds

Sources		*Applications*	
Funf from operation	1,38,500	Dividend paid	40,000
Sale of fixed assets	12,000	Tax paid	74,000
Sale of Investments	8,500	Purchase of Investments	18,000
Mortgage loan	2,70,000	Increase in working capital	2,97,000
	4,29,000		4,29,000

Problem 10: From the following balance sheets of Joy Ltd. as on 31st December 1998 and 31st December 1999, you are required to prepare a fund flow statement for the.year 1999

Liabilities	1998	1999	*Assets*	1998	1999
Share capital	50,000	60,000	Plant and Machinery	30,000	25,000
General reserve	8,000	12,000	Land and Building	20,000	40,000
P & L a/c	6,000	10,000			
Bank loan (Long-term)	10,000	2,000	Stock	26,000	20,000
Sundry creditors	12,000	16,000	Debtors	13,000	20,000
Provision for taxation	4,000	6,000	Cash	5,000	6,000
O/s expenses	4,000	5,000			
	94,000	1,11,000		94,000	1,11,000

Additional Information

1. Interest paid on bank loan amounted to Rs. 1,000
2. Income tax paid for the year 1999 Rs. 4,400
3. Assets of another company were purchased for a consideration of Rs. 10,000 and paid in shares. Assets consisted of land and building Rs. 4,000 and stock Rs. 6,000.
4. A machinery costing Rs. 5,000 (W D V Rs. 3,000) was sold for Rs. 1,000, the loss being written off against general reserve.
5. Closing stock of 1999 was over-valued by Rs. 5,000.
6. O/s expenses paid during the year were Rs. 4,500.

(Bangalore University, B.Com., October, 2000)

Solution:

Schedule showing change in working capital

	1998	*1999*	*Increase*	*Decrease*
Current Assets				
Stock	26,000	20,000	—	6,000
Sundry debtors	13,000	20,000	7,000	—
Cash	5,000	6,000	1,000	—
Total (A)	44,000	46,000		
Current Liabilities:				
Sundry creditors	12,000	16,000	—	4,000
Total (B)	12,000	16,000		
Working capital (A–B)	32,000	30,000		
Net decrease in working capital	—	2,000	2,000	
	32,000	32,000	10,000	10,000

Outstanding expanses A/c

To Bank - O/s expenses paid	4500	By Balance b/d	4,000
		By Adj. P & L a/c	5500
To Balance c/d	5,000		
	9,500		9,500

General reserve A/c

To Loss on sale of Machinery (3,000–1,000)	2,000	By Balance b/d	8,000
To Balance c/d	12,000	By Adj. P & L a/c (Balancing figure)	6,000
	14,000		14,000

Provision for taxation

To Bank a/c –Income tax paid	4,400	By Balance b/d	4,000
To Balance c/d	6,000	By Adj. P & L a/c –provision for tax (Balancing figure)	6,400
	10,400		10,400

Machinery A/c

To Balance b/d	30,000	By Depreciation (5,000 – 3,000)	2,000
		By Loss on sale of machinery	2,000
		By Bank a/c—Sale of machinery	1,000
		By Balance c/d	25,000
	30,000		30,000

Land and buildings A/c

To Balance b/d	20,000	By Balance c/d	40,000
To Shares a/c - purchases	4,000		
To Bank a/c cash purchases (Balancing figure)	16,000		
	40,000		40,0,000

Adjusted Profit and Loss A/c

To Transfer to reserve	6,000	By Balance b/d	6,000
To Provision for tax	6400	By Over-valuation of stock	5,000
To Interest on bank loan	1,000	By Fund from operation	19,900
To Outstanding expenses	5,500		
To Depreciation on machinery	2,000		
To Balcne c/d	10,000		
	30,900		30,900

Fund flow statement

Sources		*Applications*	
Funds from operation	19,900	Loan paid	8,000
Sale of machinery	1,000	Income tax paid	4400
Issue of shares	10,000	Outstanding expenses paid	4500
Decrease in working-capital	2,000	Purchase of land & building	16,000
	32,900		32,900

Problem 11: The following is the Balance Sheets of X Ltd. on 31st December, 1992 and 1993

	1992 *(Rs.)*	*1993* *(Rs.)*
Liabilities:		
Equity capital	3,00,000	4,00,000
Cum preference shares	1,50,000	1,00,000
General Reserve	40,000	70,000
P & L a/c	30,000	48,000
Proposed Dividend	42,000	50,000
Sundry creditors	55,000	83,000
Bills payable	20,000	16,000
Provision for taxation	40,000	50,000
	6,77,000	8,17,000

Assets:		
Goodwill	1,15,000	90,000
Buildings	2,00,000	1,70,000
Machinery	8,000	2,00,000
Sundry Debtors	1,60,000	2,00,000
Stock	77,000	1,09,000
Bills receivable	20,000	30,000
Cash in hand and at Bank	25,000	18,000
	6,77,000	8,17,000

Additional Information

(*i*) Depreciation written off on machinery and building in 1993 were Rs. 10,000 and 20,000 respectively.
(*ii*) During the year 1993, dividends of Rs. 20,000 were paid.
(*iii*) The income tax paid during the year was Rs. 35,000.
Prepare Fund Flow Statement. (*Sri Venkateshwara University, B.Com., October 1999*)

Solution: **Schedule of changes in working capital**

	1992	*1993*	*Increase*	*Decrease*
Current Assets				
Sundry debtors	1,60,000	2,00,000	40,000	—
Stock	77,000	1,09,000	32,000	—
Bills receivable	20,000	30,000	10,000	—
Cash and Bank	25,000	18,000	—	7,000
Total (A)	2,82,000	3,57,000		
Current Liabilities				
Sundry creditors	55,000	83,000	—	28,000
Bills payable	20,000	16,000	4,000	—
Total (B)	75,000	99,000		
Working capital (A–B)	2,07,000	2,58,000		
Increase in working capital	51,000	—	—	51,000
	2,58,000	2,58,000	86,000	86,000

Equity Share capital

To Balance c/d	4,00,000	By Balance b/d	3,00,000
		By Bank (Balancing figure)	1,00,000
	4,00,000		4,00,000

Cum pref. share capital A/c

To Bank (Balance figure)	50,000	By Balance b/d	1,50,000
To Balance c/d	1,00,000		
	1,50,000		1,50,000

General reserve

To Balance c/d	70,000	By Balance b/d	40,000
		By P & L a/c (Balancing figure)	30,000
	70,000		70,000

Proposed dividend A/c

To Bank A/c	20,000	By Balance b/d	42,000
To Balance c/d	50,000	By P & L a/c (Balancing figure)	28,000
	70,000		70,000

Provision for taxation A/c

To Bank	35,000	By Balance b/d	40,000
To Balance c/d	50,000	By P & L a/c (Balancing figure)	45,000
	85,000		85,000

Goodwill A/c

To Balance b/d	1,15,000	By P & L a/c (Balancing figure)	25,000
		By Balance c/d	90,000
	1,15,000		1,15,000

Buildings A/c

To Balance b/d	2,00,000	By Depreciation	20,000
		By Bank-sales (Balancing figure)	10,000
		By Balance c/d	1,70,000
	2,00,000		2,00,000

Machinery A/c

To Balance b/d	80,000	By Depreciation	10,000
To Bank-purchases (Balancing figure)	1,30,000	By Balance c/d	2,00,000
	2,10,000		2,10,000

Adjusted Profit & Loss A/c

To General reserve	30,000	By Balance b/d	30,000
To Proposed dividend	28,000	By Fund from operation	1,76,000
To Provision for taxation	45,000		
To Goodwill written off	25,000		
To Depreciation on:			
Building	20,000		
Machinery	10,000		
To Balance c/d	48,000		
	2,06,000		2,06,000

Fund flow statement

Sources		*Applications*	
Fund from operation	1,76,000	Redemption of cum pref shares	50,000
Issue of equity shares	1,00,000	Dividend paid	20,000
Sale of building	10,000	Income-tax paid	35,000
		Purchase of machinery	1,30,000
		Increase in working capital	51,000
	2,86,000		2,86,000

Problem 12: From the following balance sheet of X Ltd., as on 31st December, 1997 and 31st December 1998, you are required to prepare fund flow statement:

Liabilities	*1997*	*1998*	*Assets*	*1997*	*1998*
Share capital	4,00,000	5,00,000	Land & building	4,00,000	4,80,000
General reserve	80,000	1,40,000			
P & L a/c	64,000	78,000	Machinery	3,60,000	2,60,000
Bank loan	3,20,000	80,000	Stock	2,00,000	2,52,000
(long-term)			Debtors	1,60,000	1,28,000
Creditors	3,00,000	2,60,000	Cash at Bank	1,04,000	18,000
Provision for Taxation	60,000	80,000			
	12,24,000	11,38,000		12,24,000	11,38,000

Additional Information

1. During the year ended 31st December, 1998, dividend of Rs. 84,000 was paid.
2. Assets of another company were purchased for a consideration of Rs. 1,00,000, payable by the issue of shares. The assets included land and building of Rs. 50,000 and stock of Rs. 50,000.
3. Depreciation written off an machinery is Rs. 24,000 and on land & building is Rs. 45,000
4. Income tax paid during the year was Rs. 70,000.
5. Addition to buildings were Rs. 75,000.

(*Osmania University, B.Com., October 1999*)

Solution:

Schedule showing changes in working capital

	1997	*1998*	*Increase*	*Decrease*
Current Assets:				
Cash at Bank	1,04,000	18,000	—	86,000
Debtors	1,60,000	1,28,000	—	32,000
Stock	2,00,000	2,52,000	52,000	—
Total (A)	4,64,000	3,98,000		
Current liabilities				
Creditors	3,00,000	2,60,000	40,000	—
Total (B)	3,00,000	2,60,000		
Working capital (A–B)	1,64,000	1,38,000		
Decrease in working capital	—	26,000		
	1,64,000	1,64,000	1,08,000	1,08,000

Provision for taxation A/c

To Cash	70,000	By Balance b/d	60,000
To Balance c/d	80,000	By Adj. P & L a/c	90,000
	1,50,000		1,50,000

Machinery A/c

To Balance b/d	3,60,000	By Adj. P & L a/c depreciation	24,000
		By Sale of machinery	76,000
		By Balance c/d	2,60,000
	3,60,000		3,60,000

Land & buildings A/c

To Balance b/d	4,00,000	By Adj. P & L a/c —Depreciation	45,000
To Share capital	50,000	By Balance c/d	4,80,000
To Cash	75,000		
	5,25,000		5,25,000

General reserve A/c

To Balance c/d	1,40,000	By Balance b/d	80,000
		By Adj P & L a/c	60,000
	1,40,000		1,40,000

Adjusted Profit & Loss A/c

To Machinery a/c	24,000	By Balance b/d	64,000
To Land & Buildings	45,000	By Fund from operation	3,17,000
To Provision for tax	90,000		
To General reserve	60,000		
To Dividend paid	84,000		
To Balance c/d	78,000		
	3,81,000		3,81,000

Fund Flow Statement

Sources		*Application*	
Issue of shares	50,000	Purchase of land & building	75,000
Sale of machinery	76,000	Bank loan paid	2,40,000
Fund from operation	3,17,000	Dividend paid	84,000
Decrease in working capital	26,000	Income tax paid	70,000
	4,69,000		4,69,000

Problem 13: Following are the Balance Sheets of fertilizers India Limited as at 31st December, 1997 and 1998 respectively.

	31.12.97 *Rs.*	*31.12.98* *Rs.*
Liabilities		
Share capital of Rs. 100 each	20,00,000	25,00,000
Reserve and surplus	8,00,000	8,70,000
8% convertible debentures	10,00,000	8,00,000
Public deposits	3,00,000	2,50,000
Current liabilities & provisions	6,20,000	7,10,000
Proposed dividend	2,00,000	2,50,000
	49,20,000	53,80,000

Assets		
Fixed assets at cost	25,00,000	30,00,000
Less: Depreciation till date	6,80,000	8,20,000
	18,20,000	21,80,000
Trade investments	12,50,000	13,50,000
Marketable Investments	60,000	30,000
Inventories	4,10,000	5,20,000
Book Debts	5,30,000	5,05,000
Cash and Bank	1,20,000	1,40,000
Preliminary expenses	1,00,000	50,000
Capital work-in-progress	6,30,000	6,05,000
	49,20,000	53,80,000

You are informed that during 1998:

1. **Debentures of Rs. 2,00,000 were converted into shares at par.**
2. **Shares of Rs. 2,00,000 were issued as fully paid bouns shares out of reserves.**
3. **Shares worth Rs. 1,00,000 at par were issued to a vendor in part payment of a machine costing Rs. 1,.20,000 supplied by him.**
4. **A machine costing Rs. 50,000 (Book value Rs. 30,000 as on 31st December 1997) was disposed off for Rs. 20,000.**
5. **Trade Investments costing Rs. 30,000 were disposed off for Rs. 36,000.**

Prepare fund flow statement along with detailed schedule of changes in working capital for the year 1998.

(University of Bombay, B.Com., October 1999)

Solution:

Schedule showing change in working capital

	1997	*1998*	*Increase*	*Decrease*
Current Assets				
Inventories	4,10,000	5,20,000	1,10,000	—
Book debts	5,30,000	5,05,000	—	25,000
Cash & Bank	1,20,000	1,40,000	20,000	—
Capital work-in-progress	6,30,000	6,05,000	—	25,000
Marketable Investment	60,000	30,000	—	30,000
Total (A)	17,50,000	18,00,000		
Current Liabilities				
Current liabilties & provisions	6,20,000	7,10,000	—	90,000
Total (B)	6,20,000	7,10,000		
Net Working capital	11,30,000	10,90,000	—	—
Decrease in Working capital		40,000	40,000	—
	11,30,000	11,30,000	1,70,000	1,70,000

Proposed dividend A/c

To Bank	2,00,000	By Balance b/d	2,00,000
To Balance c/d	2,50,000	By P & L a/c	2,50,000
	4,50,000		4,50,000

Fixed Assets A/c

To Balance b/d	25,00,000	By Machine sold	50,000
To Equity share capital	1,00,000	By Balance c/d	30,00,000
To Cash a/c	20,000		
To Cash-purchases (Balancing figure)	4,30,000		
	30,50,000		30,50,000

Provision for Depreciation A/c

To Depreciation on machine sold	20,000	By Balance b/d	6,80,000
To Balance c/d	8,20,000	By Depreciation a/c	1,60,000
	8,40,000		8,40,000

Trade Investment

To Balance b/d	12,50,000	By Bank a/c	36,000
To Reserves	6,000	By Balance c/d	13,50,000
To Bank a/c	1,30,000		
	13,86,000		13,86,000

Calculation of Loss on Sale of Machine

Cost price	50,000
Less: Depreciation	20,000
Written down value	30,000
Sold	20,000
Loss on sale	10,000

Adjusted Profit & Loss A/c

To Preliminary expenses	50,000	By Balance b/d	8,00,000
To Equity share capital (Bonus)	2,00,000	By Profit on sale	6,000
To Proposed Dividend	2,50,000	By Fund from operation	7,34,000
To Loss on sale of machine	10,000		
To Depreciation	1,60,000		
To Balance c/d	8,70,000		
	15,40,000		15,40,000

Fund Flow Statement

Sources		*Application*	
Sale of machine	20,000	Dividend for last year paid	2,00,000
Sale of investment	36,000	Public deposit repaid	50,000
Decrease in working capital	40,000	Purchase of machine	4,50,000
Fund from operation on	7,34,000	Purchase of trade investment	1,30,000
	8,30,000		8,30,000

Problem 14: Prepare (*i*) statement of changes in working capital and (*ii*) fund flow statement for the year ended 31st December, 1998 from the following balance sheets of Shivani Ltd.

Liabilities	*1997*	*1998*	*Assets*	*1997*	*1998*
Equity share capital (Shares of Rs. 10 each Rs. 8 paid up)	1,20,000		Fixed assets	2,10,000	2,30,000
			Investments	40,000	52,000
			Stock	1,10,000	1,36,000
Equity share capital (shares of Rs. 10 each fully paid)		1,80,000	Debtors	90,000	88,000
			Cash & Bank	14,000	33,000
12% Preference share capital	1,00,000	70,000	Preliminary expenses	2,000	1,000
Share premium	5,000	3,500			
General reserve	80,000	40,000			
Profit & loss A/c	26,600	45,000			
15% Debentures	20,000	60,000			
Creditors	80,000	95,000			
Proposed equity dividend	14,400	22,500			
Provision for taxation	20,000	24,000			
	4,66,000	5,40,000		4,66,000	5,40,000

Additional information is as follows:

1. During the year (*i.e.*, 1998) the company has paid a bouns of Rs. 2 per share to make the partly paid shares fully paid up and for this purpose general reserve was utilised.
2. During the year, the company then issued equity shares as rights, shares in the ratio of one for every fire held.
3. Prepference shares were redeemed at 5% premium on 31st December, 1998.
4. During the year, a machine costing Rs. 12,000 on which depreciation written off to data was Rs. 3,000 was sold for Rs. 9,500 and current years depreciation provided on fixed assets was Rs. 15,000
5. Paid proposed equity dividend of last year and also paid in term dividend of Rs. 9,000.
6. The preference share dividend was paid on 31st December each year.
7. Income-tax of Rs. 24,000 was paid during the year. *(University of Bombay, B.Com., April 1999)*

Solution:

Schedule showing change in working capital

	1997	*1998*	*Increase*	*Decrease*
Current Assets				
Stock	1,10,000	1,36,000	26,000	—
Debtors	90,000	88,000	—	20,000
Cash & Bank	14,000	33,000	19,000	—
Total (A)	2,14,000	2,57,000		
Current Liabilities				
Sundry creditors	80,000	95,000		
Total (B)	80,000	95,000		
Working capital (A–B)	1,34,000	1,62,000		
Increase in working capital	28,000	—	—	—
	1,62,000	1,62,000	45,000	45,000

Working Notes:

(1) Calculation of amount utilised from general reserve for issue of bouns

No. of shares $\frac{1,20,000}{8}$ = 15,000 shares

15,000 shares @ Rs. 2 per share = 30,000

(2) Issue of right shares

No. of shares already issued = 15,000
For 5 shares 1 New shares

For 15,000 shares = $\frac{15,000 \times 1}{5}$ = 3,000 shares

3,000 shares of Rs. 10 each = 30,000
Total share capital on 31.12.1998
15,000 + 3,000 = 18,000 shares of Rs. 10 each, *i.e.*, 1,80,000

Fixed Assets A/c

To Balance b/d	2,10,000	By Bank-sale	9,500
To P & L a/c profit sale	500	By Depreciation	15,000
To Cash-purchases (Balancing figure)	44,000	By Balance c/d	2,30,000
	2,54,500		2,54,500

Calculation of Profit on sale of Machine

Cost price	12,000
Less: Depreciation	3,000
Written down value	9,000
Sold for	9500
Profit on sale	500

Equity Share Capital A/c

To Balance c/d	1,80,000	By Balance b/d	1,20,000
		By General Reserve	30,000
		By Cash (Balancing figure)	30,000
	1,80,000		1,80,000

General Reserve A/c

To Equity capital	30,000	By Balance b/d	80,000
To P & C a/c	10,000		
To Balance c/d	40,000		
	80,000		80,000

Proposed Equity Dividend A/c

To Bank	14,400	By Balance b/d	14,400
To Balance c/d	22,500	By P & L a/c	22,500
	36,900		36,900

Provision for taxation

To Cash	24,000	By Balance b/d	20,000
To Balance c/d	24,000	By P & L a/c	28,000
	48,000		48,000

Adjusted Profit & Loss A/c

To Preliminary expenses	1,000	By Balance b/d	26,600
To Depreciation	15,000	By Profit on sale of machinery	500
To Interim Dividend	9,000	To Transfer from general reserve	10,000
To Pref dividend	12,000		
To Provision for tax	28,000	By Fund from operation	95,400
To Proposed dividend	22,500		
To Balance c/d	45,000		
	1,32,500		1,32,500

Fund Flow Statement

Sources		*Application*		
Issue of Debentures	40,000	Investment purchased		12,000
Issue of Right shares	30,000	Redemption of pref shares	30,000	
Sale of machinery	9,500	*Add:* Premium	1500	
Fund from operation	95,400			31,500
		Increase in working capital		28,000
		Equity dividend paid		14,400
		Interim dividend paid		9,000
		Preference dividend		12,000
		Income tax paid		24,000
		Fixed assets purchased		44,000
	1,74,900			1,74,900

Problem 15: From the following Balance Sheets of ABC Ltd. on 31st December, 1996 and 1997, you are required to prepare (*i*) A schedule of changes in working capital, (*ii*) A fund flow statement:

	1996	*1997*		*1996*	*1997*
Share capital	2,00,000	2,00,000	Goodwill	24,000	24,000
Gen. reserve	28,000	36,000	Building	80,000	72,000
P & L a/c	32,000	26,000	Plant	74,000	72,000
Creditors	16,000	10,800	Investments	20,000	22,000
Bills payable	2,400	1,600	stock	60,000	46,800
Provision for taxation	32,000	36,000	B.R.	4,000	6,400
Provision for doubtful debts	800	1200	Debtors	36,000	38,000
			Cash	13,200	30,400
	3,11,200	2,11,600		3,11,200	3,11,600

Additional Information

(*a*) Depreciation provided on plant was Rs. 8,000 and on Buildings Rs. 8,000.

(*b*) Provision for taxation made during the year Rs. 38,000.

(*c*) Interim dividend paid during the year Rs. 16,000 (*Osmania University, B.Com., March 1999*)

Solution:

Schedule showing change in working capital

	1996	*1997*	*Increase*	*Decrease*
Current Assets				
Cash	13,200	30,400	17,200	—
Debtors	36,000	38,000	2,000	—
B.R.	4,000	6,400	2400	—
Stock	60,000	46,800	—	13,200
Total (A)	1,13,200	1,21,600		

Current Liabilities				
Provision for doubtful debts	800	1,200	—	400
Bills payable	2,400	1,600	800	—
Creditors	16,000	10,800	—	—
Total (B)	19,200	13,600		
Working capital (A–B)	94,000	1,08,000		
Increase in working capital	14,000	—	—	14,000
	1,08,000	1,08,000	27,600	27,600

Provision for taxation A/c

To Bank-tax paid	34,000	By Balance b/d	32,000
To Balance c/d	36,000	By P & L a/c	38,000
	70,000		70,000

Plant A/c

To Balance b/d	74,000	By Depreciation	8,000
To Bank-purchase	6,000	By Balance c/d	72,000
	80,000		80,000

Buildings A/c

To Balance b/d	80,000	By Depreciation	8,000
		By Balance c/d	72,000
	80,000		80,000

Investment A/c

To Balance b/d	20,000	By Balance c/d	22,000
To Bank-purchases	2,000		
	22,000		22,000

Adjusted Profit & Loss A/c

To Transfer to general reserve	8,000	By Balance b/d	32,000
To Provision for tax	38,000	By Fund from operation	72,000
To Depreciation on:			
–plant	8,000		
–Building	8,000		
To Interim dividend	16,000		
To Balance c/d	26,000		
	1,04,000		1,04,000

General Reserve A/c

To Balance c/d	36,000	By Balance b/d	28,000
		By P & L A/c	8,000
	36,000		36,000

Fund Flow Statement

Sources		*Applications*	
Funds from operation	72,000	Purchase of plant	6,000
		Tax paid	34,000
		Purchase of investment	2,000
		Interim dividend paid	16,000
		Increase in working capital	14,000
	72,000		72,000

Problem 16: Following are the summarised balance sheets of the Gamges Ltd. as on 31st December, 1996 and 1997

	1996	*1997* (*Rs. '000*)		*1996*	*1997* (*Rs. '000*)
Share capital	200	250	Land & building	200	190
General Reserve	50	60	Plant & machinery	150	169
P & C a/c	30.5	30.6	Stock	100	74
Bank loan	70	—	Sundry debtors	80	64.2
Sundry creditors	150	135.2	Cash balance	0.5	0.6
Provision for taxation	30	35	Bank balance	—	8
			Goodwill	—	5
	530.5	510.8		530.5	510.8

The following additional information is available:

(*a*) During the year ended 31st December, 1997:
 (*i*) Dividend of Rs. 23,000 was paid
 (*ii*) Assets of another company were purchased for Rs. 50,000 payable in shares, assets purchased were: stock Rs. 20,000 and machinery Rs. 25,000
 (*iii*) Machinery of Rs. 8,000 was purchased in addition to that of (*ii*) above.

(*b*) Depreciation written off during the year 1997:
Building Rs. 10,000 and machinery Rs. 14,000.

(*c*) The net profit for the year 1997 was Rs. 66,100.

(*d*) Income-tax paid during the year 1997 was Rs. 28,000 and provision of Rs. 33,000 was made to profit & loss a/c.

Preare a statement of sources and applications of funds for the year ended 31st December, 1997 and a schedule setting out the changes in working capital. (*CS, Inter, December 1998*)

Solution: **Schedule showing change in working capital**

	1996	*1997*	*Increase*	*Decrease*
Current Assets				
Stock	1,00,000	74,000	—	26,000
Sundry Debtors	80,000	64,200	—	15,800
Cash	500	600	100	—
Bank	—	8,000	8,000	—
Total (A)	1,80,500	1,46,800		
Current Liabilities				
Sundry creditors	1,50,000	1,35,200	14,800	—
Total (B)	1,50,000	1,35,200		
Working capital	30,500	11,600		
Decrease in working capital	—	18,900	18,900	—
	30,500	30,500	41,800	41,800

Machinery A/c

To Balance b/d	1,50,000	By Depreiciation	14,000
To Vendor	25,000	By Balance c/d	1,69,000
To Cash-purchases	8,000		
	1,83,000		1,83,000

Provision for income tax

To Cash	28,000	By Balance b/d	30,000
To Balance c/d	35,000	By P & L A/c	33,000
	63,000		63,000

Share Capital A/c

To Balance c/d	2,50,000	By Balance b/d	2,00,000
		By Vendor's A/c	50,000
	2,50,000		2,50,000

Goodwill A/c

To Vendor	5,000	By Balance c/d	5,000

Adjusted Profit & Loss A/c

To Dividend	23,000	By Balance b/d	30,500
To Depreciation (10,000+14,000)	24,000	By Fund from operation	90,100
To Provision for taxation	33,000		
To General reserve	10,000		
To Balance c/d	30,600		
	1,20,600		1,20,600

Fund Flow Statement

Sources		*Applications*	
Issue of shares (for stock)	20,000	Dividend paid machinery	23,000
Fund from operation	90,100	Purchased	8,000
Decrease in working capital	18,900	Income tax paid	28,000
		Bank loan paid	70,000
	1,29,000		1,29,000

Problem 17: From the following information of XYZ Ltd. prepare a statement showing changes in working capital position along with funds flow statement:

	31st December Previous year Rs.	*31st December current year* Rs.
Current assets	1,35,000	1,27,200
Investments	15,000	21,400
Land	9,000	9,000
Plant and machinery	81,100	1,05,000
(Accumulated depreciation)	(24,000)	(26,000)
Patents	16,200	12,600
Total assets	2,32,200	2,32,200
Current liabilities	24,600	34,800
12% debentures	43,400	—
14% debentures	—	39,000

Equity share capital	90,000	1,00,000
Reserve for future losses on investments	6,000	36,000
Retained earnings	68,200	71,800
Total liabilities and capital	2,32,200	2,32,200

Additional Information

(*i*) a reconciliation of the balances in retained earnings is as follows:

	Rs.
Beginning balance	68,200
Net income for current year	3,000
Award received from settlement of patent, infringement case	15,600
Dividends	(15,000)
Ending Balance	71,800

(*ii*) Net income of the current year includes a loss of Rs. 48,000 on the sale of a part of plant. The plant was for Rs. 19,000 at the beginning of the year, accumulated depreciation being Rs. 6,000.

(*iii*) Investments of Rs. 15,000 were sold during the year at a loss. The loss was charged to the reserve for future losses on investments and did not appear on the income statement.

(*iv*) During the current year the 12% debentures were called for redemption. Most of them were refunded through the issuanee of new 14% debentures, and the rest were retired for cash.

(v) The equity shares were issued in exchange of machinery. The rest of the plant and machinery were purchased for cash. (*CS, Intermediate, June, 1998*)

Solution:

Schedule showing change in Working Capital

	Previous year	*Current year*	*Increase*	*Decrease*
Current assets	1,35,000	1,27,200	—	78,00
Less: Current liabilities	24,600	34,800	—	10,200
Working capital	1,10,400	92,400		
Decrease in working capital	—	18,000	18,000	—
	1,10,400	1,10,400	18,000	18,000

Accumulated Depreciation

To Plant & machinery A/c	6,000	By Balance b/d	24,000
To Balance c/d	26,000	By P & L a/c - (Balancing figure)	8,000
	32,000		32,000

Calculation fo sale of machinery

Book value	19,000
Less: Depreciation	6,000
Written down value	13,000
Less; Loss on sale	4,800
Sale of machinery	8,200

Plant & Machinery A/c

To Balance b/d	81,000	By Cash-sales	8,200
To Share capital (1,00,000–90,000)	10,000	By Accumulated depreciation a/c	6,000
To Bank-purchases (Balancing figure)	33,000	By Loss on sale machinery	4,800
		By Balance c/d	1,05,000
	1,24,000		1,24,000

Calculation of sale of Investments

Book value	15,000
Less: Loss (6,000–3600)	2400
	12,600
Sale of investments	12,600

Investments A/c

To Balance b/d	15,000	By Cash-sales	12,600
To Bank-purchases (Balancing figure)	21,400	By Reserve for future loss	2,400
		By Balance c/d	21,400
	36,400		36,400

Adjusted Profit & Loss A/c

To Patent written off	3600	By Balance b/d	68,200
To Depreciation on plant & machinery	8,000	By Award received	15,600
To Loss on sale of plant	4,800	By Fund from operation	19,400
To Dividend	15,000		
To Balance c/d	71,800		
	1,03,200		1,03,200

Fund Flow Statement

Sources		*Applications*	
Issue of 14% debentures	39,000	Purchase of plant	33,000
Sale of Investments	12,600	Redemption of 12% debentures	43,400
Award received	15,600	Purchase of investments	21,400
Sale of plant	8,200	Dividend paid	15,000
Fund from operation	19,400		
Decrease in working capital	18,000		
	1,12,800		1,12,800

Problem 18: Timbaktu Limited furnishes the following details with the direction to prepare fund flow statement for the year 1997:

Balance Sheet

	1997	*1996*		*1997*	*1996*
Share capital	90,000	80,000	Working capital:		
Profit & loss a/c	46,000	30,000	Current assets	1,20,000	96,000
			Less: current liabilities	42,000	30,000
				78,000	66,000
			Fixed assets	56,000	40,000
			Share Issue expenses	2,000	4,000
	1,30,000	1,10,000		1,36,000	1,10,000

Other Information

1. An old machine costing Rs. 8,000 (W D V Rs. 6,000) was sold during the year for Rs. 7,000.
2. Depreciation for the year was Rs. 2,000.
3. Interim devidend of Rs. 4,000 was paid during the year. Final dividend was not declared.
4. The company made the bonus issue of shares during the year at one equity share for 8 equity shares held by the existing shareholders by utilising the profits.

(University of Bombay, B.Com., October 1998)

Solution:

Statement showing change in Working Capital

	1996	1997	Increase	Decrease
Current assets	96,000	1,20,000	24,000	—
Less: Current liabilities	30,000	42,000	—	12,000
Working capital	66,000	78,000		
Increase in working capital	12,000		—	12,000
	78,000	78,000	24,000	24,000

Working Notes:

(1) Calculation of profit on sale of machinery

Machinery at cost	8,000
Less: Accumulated depreciation	2,000
Written down value	6,000
Sold for	700
Profit on sale	1,000

(2) Calculation of Bonus issue of shares

For 8 equity shares → 1 Bonus share

For 80,000 → $\frac{80,000 \times 1}{8}$ = Rs. 10,000

Fixed Assets A/c

To Balance b/d	40,000	By Sale of machine	7,000
To Profit on sale	1,000	By Depreciation	2,000
To Bank-purchases (Balancing figure)	24,000	By Balance c/d	56,000
	65,000		65,000

Adjusted Profit & Loss A/c

To Depreciation on fixed assets	2,000	By Balance b/d	30,000
To Interim dividend	4,000	By Profit on sale of machinery	1,000
To Bonus to share-holders	10,000	By Fund from operation	33,000
To Share issue expenses	2,000		
To Balance c/d	46,000		
	64,000		64,000

Fund Flow Statement

Sources		*Applications*	
Sale of machinery	7,000	Purchase of fixed assets	24,000
Fund from operation	33,000	Interim dividend paid	4,000
		Increase in working capital	12,000
	40,000		40.000

Problem 19: From the following Balance Sheets of X, Y and Z Ltd. as on 31.12.1996 and 31.12.1997 you are required to prepare:

(*a*) Schedule of changes in working capital.

(*b*) Fund flow statement.

	1996	1997		1996	1997
Share capital	1,00,000	1,00,000	Goodwill	12,000	12,000
General reserve	14,000	18,000	Building	40,000	36,000
P & L a/c	16,000	13,000	Plant	37,000	36,000
Sundry creditors	8,000	5,400	Investment	10,000	11,000
Bills payable	1,200	800	Stock	30,000	23,400
Provision for taxation	16,000	18,000	B.R.	2,000	3,200
Provision for doubtful debts	400	600	Debtors	18,000	19,000
			Bank	6,600	15,200
	1,55,600	1,55,800		1,55,600	1,55,800

Further Information

1. Depreciation charged on plant was Rs. 4,000 and on building Rs. 4,000.
2. Provision for taxation Rs. 19,000 was made during the year 1997.
3. Interim dividend of Rs. 8,000 was paid during 1997.

(Bangalore University, B.B.M., November 1998)

Solution:

Schedule of changes in Working Capital

	1996	1997	Increase	Decrease
Current Assets				
Cash at Bank	6,600	15,200	8,600	—
Debtors	18,000	19,000	1,000	—
B.R.	2,000	3,200	1,200	
Stock	30,000	23,400	—	6,600
Total (A)	56,600	60,800		
Current Liabilities				
Provision for doubtful debts	400	600	—	200
Bills payable	1,200	800	400	—
Sundry	8,000	5,400	2,600	—
Total (B)	9,600	6,800		
Working capital (A–B)	47,000	54,000		
Increase in working capital	7,000	—	—	7,000
	54,000	54,000	13,800	13,800

Plant A/c

To Balance b/d	37,000	By Depreication	4,000
To Bank-purchases (Balancing figure)	3,000	By Balance c/d	36,000
	40,000		40,000

Provision for Tax A/c

To Bank-tax paid (Balancing figure)	17,000	By Balance b/d	16,000
		By P & L a/c	19,000
To Balance c/d	18,000		
	35,000		35,000

Adjusted Profit & Loss A/c

To Transfer to general reserve	4,000	By Balance b/d	16,000
To Provision for tax	19,000	By Fund from operation	36,000
To Depreciation on plant	4,000		
To Depreciation on building	4,000		
To Interim dividend paid	8,000		
To Balance c/d	13,000		
	52,000		52,000

Fund Flow Statement

Sources		*Applications*	
Fund from operation	36,000	Purchase of plant	3,000
		Tax paid	17,000
		Investments purchased	1,000
		Interim dividend paid	8,000
		Increase in working capital	7,000
	36,000		36,000

Problem 20: Following are the summarised balance sheets of 'X' Ltd. as 31st December, 1996 and 1997. You are required to prepare a funds flow statement for the year ended 31st December, 1997:

	1996	*1997*		*1996*	*1997*
Share capital	1,00,000	1,25,000	Goodwill	—	2,500
General reserve	25,000	30,000	Buildings	1,00,000	95,000
P & L A/c	15,250	15,300	Plant	75,000	84,500
Bank loan	35,000	67,600	Stock	50,000	37,000
(long-term)			Debtors	40,000	32,100
Creditors	75,000	—	Bank	—	4,000
Provision for tax	15,000	17,500	Cash	250	300
	2,65,250	2,55,400		2,65,250	2,55,400

Additional Information

1. Dividend of Rs. 11,500 was paid.
2. Depreciation written off on plant Rs. 7,000 and on building Rs. 5,000.
3. Provision for tax was made during the year Rs. 16,500.*(Osmania University, B.Com., October 1998)*

Solution:

Schedule of changes in working capital

	1996	*1997*	*Increase*	*Decrease*
Current Assets				
Cash	250	300	50	—
Bank	—	4,000	4,000	
Debtors	40,000	32,100	—	7900
Stock	50,000	37,000	—	13,000
Total (A)	90,250	73,400		
Current Liabilities				
Creditors	75,000	—	75,000	—
Total (B)	75,000	—		
Working capital (A–B)	15,250	73,400		
Increase in working capital	58,150	—	—	58,150
	73,400	73,400	79,050	79,050

Share Capital A/c

To Balance c/d	1,25,000	By Balance b/d	1,00,000
		By Bank a/c	25,000
	1,25,000		1,25,000

General Reserve A/c

To Balance c/d	30,000	By Balance b/d	25,000
		By P & L a/c	5,000
	30,000		30,000

Provision for Taxation A/c

To Bank A/c	14,000	By Balance b/d	15,000
To Balance c/d	17,500	By P & L A/c	16,500
	31,500		31,500

Bank Loan A/c

To Balance c/d	67,600	By Balance b/d	35,000
		By Bank a/c	32,600
	67,600		67,600

Land & Building A/c

To Balance b/d	1,00,000	By Depreciation a/c	5,000
		By (P & L a/c)	
		By Balance c/d	95,000
	1,00,000		1,00,000

Plant A/c

To Balance b/d	75,000	By Depreciation	7,000
To Bank a/c	16,500	(P & L a/c)	
		By Balance c/d	84,500
	91,500		91,500

Goodwill A/c

To Bank a/c	2,500	By Balance c/d	2,500

Adjusted Profit & Loss A/c

To General reserve a/c	5,000	By Balance b/d	15,250
To Provision for tax a/c	16,500	By Fund from operation	45,050
To Dividend paid	11,500		
To Depreciation on:			
—Building	5,000		
—Plant	7,000		
To Balance c/d	15,300		
	60,300		60,300

Fund Flow Statement

Sources		*Applications*	
Fund from operation	45,050	Purchase of plant	16,500
Issue of shares	25,000	Income tax paid	14,000
Bank loan	32,600	Dividend paid	11,500
		Goodwill paid	2,500
		Net increase in working capital	58,150
	1,02,650		1,02,650

Problem 21: The Balance Sheets of XYZ Co. Ltd. as on 31st December 1992 and 1993 are given below:

Liabilities & Capital	*1992*	*1993*
Share capital	1,00,000	1,50,000
Share premium	—	5,000
General reserve	50,000	60,000
Profit & loss a/c	10,000	17,000
6% Debentures	70,000	50,000
Provision for depreciation:		
on plant	50,000	56,000
on furniture	5,000	6,000
Provision for taxation	20,000	30,000
Sundry creditors	86,000	95,000
	3,91,000	4,69,000
Assets		
Freehold land	1,00,000	1,00,000
Plant at cost	1,04,000	1,00,000
Furniture at cost	7,000	9,000
Investment at cost	60,000	80,000
Debtors	30,000	70,000
Stock	60,000	65,000
Cash	30,000	45,000
	3,91,000	4,69,000

A plant purchased for Rs. 4,000 (Depreciation Rs. 2,000) was sold for cash Rs. 800 on 30th September 1993. On 30th June 1993 an item of furniture was purchased for Rs. 2,000. These were the only transactions concerning fixed assets during 1993.

Depreciation was provided on plant at 8% on cost (the sold out item is not taken into consideration) and on furniture at 12½% on average cost. A dividend of 22½% on original shares are paid.

(*Sri Venkateshwara University, B.Com., October 1998*)

Solution:

Schedule showing changes in Working Capital

	1992	*1993*	*Increase*	*Decrease*
Current Assets				
Debtors	30,000	70,000	40,000	—
Stock	60,000	65,000	5,000	—
Cash	30,000	45,000	15,000	—
Total (A)	1,20,000	180,000		
Current Liabilities				
Creditors	86,000	95,000	—	9,000
Total (B)	86,000	95,000		

Working capital (A–B)	34,000	85,000		
Increase in working capital	51,000	—	—	51,000
	85,000	85,000	60,000	60,000

Plant & Machinery A/c

To Balance b/d	1,04,000	By Cash a/c	800
		By Provision for depreciation	2,000
		By P & L a/c – loss on sale (Balancing figure)	1,200
		By Balance c/d	1,00,000
	1,04,000		1,04,000

Provision for Depreciation on Plant A/c

To Plant & machinery A/c	2,000	By Balance b/d	50,000
To Balance c/d	56,000	By P & L a/c $\left(\frac{8}{100} \times 1,00,000\right)$	8,000
	58,000		58,000

Furniture A/c

To Balance b/d	7,000	By Balance c/d	9,000
To Cash-purchases	2,000		
	9,000		9,000

Provision for Depreciation on Furniture A/c

To Balance c/d	6,000	By Balance b/d	5,000
		By P & L a/c $\left(\frac{12.5}{100} \times 8,000\right)$	1,000
	6,000		6,000

Investment A/c

To Balance b/d	60,000	By Balance c/d	80,000
To Cash-purchases	20,000		
	80,000		80,000

Share Capital A/c

To Balance c/d	1,50,000	By Balance b/d	1,00,000
		By Cash-Issue	50,000
	1,50,000		1,50,000

Share Premium A/c

To Balance c/d	5,000	By Cash	5,000

General Reserve

To Balance c/d	60,000	By Balance b/d	50,000
		By P & L a/c (Balancing figure)	10,000
	60,000		60,000

6% Debentures A/c

To Cash (Balancing figure)	20,000	By Balance b/d	70,000
To Balance c/d	50,000		
	70,000		70,000

Provision for Taxation a/c

To Balance c/d	30,000	By Balance b/d	20,000
		By P & L a/c (Balancing figure)	10,000
	30,000		30,000

Adjusted Profit & Loss A/c

To Loss on sale of plant	1,200	By Balance b/d	10,000
To Depreciation on plant & machinery	800	By Fund from operation	59,700
To Depreciation on furniture	1,000		
To General reserve	10,000		
To Dividend $\left(\frac{22.5}{100} \times 1{,}00{,}000\right)$	22,500		
To Provision for taxation	10,000		
To Balance c/d	17,000		
	69,700		69,700

Fund Flow Statement

Sources		*Applications*	
Fund from operation	59,700	Increase in working capital	51,000
Sale of plant	800	Purchase of Furniture	2,000
Issue of shares	50,000	Purchase of investment	20,000
Share premium	5,000	Redemption of debentures	20,000
		Payment of dividend	22,500
	1,15,000		1,15,000

Problem 22: The balance sheets of Parasman Ltd. are given below:

	31.12.96	*31.12.97*		*31.12.96.*	*31.12.97*
Share capital	3,00,000	4,00,000	Fixed assets	5,70,000	6,60,000
Capital reserve	—	10,000	Trade investment	1,00,000	80,000
General reserve	1,70,000	2,00,000	Current assets	2,80,000	3,30,000
Profit & loss A/c	60,000	75,000	Preliminary expenses	20,000	10,000
Debentures (of Rs. 100)	2,00,000	1,40,000			
Current liabilities	1,20,000	1,30,000			
Provision on tax	90,000	85,000			
Proposed dividend	30,000	36,000			
Unpaid dividend	—	4,000			
	9,70,000	10,80,000		9,70,000	10,80,000

For 1997 the following information is given:

1. Sold one machine for Rs. 25,000, the cost of which was Rs. 50,000 and the depreciation provided on it was Rs. 21,000.
2. The provision for depreciation (accumulated) was Rs. 2,90,000 on 31-12-97 which was Rs. 60,000 more than that on 31.12.96.
3. Some debentures were redeemed @ Rs. 103.
4. Fixed assets costing Rs. 14,000 which were fully depreciation were written off.
5. Some trade investments were sold at some profit which was adjusted in capital reserve.
6. Decided to value stock at cost on 31.12.97 whereas previously it was valued at cost less 10% on 31.12.96 which was Rs. 54,000.

You are required to prepare statement of sources and application of funds during 1997, showing the detailed changes in working capital and provision for taxation, proposed dividend account.

(University of Bombay, B.Com., April 1998)

Solution:

Schedule of changes in Working Capital

	31.12.96	*31.12.97*	*Increase*	*Decrease*
Current assets	2,80,000	3,30,000		
Add: Increase in stock value	6,000			
Total (A)	2,86,000	3,30,000	44,000	—
Current Liabilities	1,20,000	1,30,000	—	10,000
Total (B)	1,20,000	1,30,000		
Working capital (A–B)	1,66,000	2,00,000		
Increase in working capital	34,000	—	—	34,000
	2,00,000	2,00,000	44,000	44,000

Working Notes:

(1) Calculation of Loss on sale of Machine

Cost	50,000
Less: Accumulated depreciation	21,000
	29,000
Sold for	25,000
Loss on sale	4,000

(2) Calculation of Premium on Debenture Redemption

Face value of 100 Redeemed at Rs. 103

For face value of 60,000 → ?

$$\frac{103 \times 60,000}{100} = 61,800$$

So premium on Redemption = 61,800 – 60,000 = 1,800.

This is shown as a loss on the debit side of adjusted profit & loss account and also shown as application of fund.

(3) Fixed assets fully depreciated means accumulated depreciation is equal to cost of fixed assets. The accumulated depreciation is debited to provision for depreciation a/c and credited to fixed assets account.

(4) Calculation of undervalued opening stock

For 90 → 54,000
For 10 → ?

$$54{,}000 \times \frac{10}{90} = \text{Rs. } 6{,}000$$

Proposed Divident A/c

To Cash	26,000	By Balance b/d	30,000
To Unpaid dividend a/c	4,000	By P & L a/c	36,000
To Balance c/d	36,000	(Balancing figure)	
	66,000		66,000

Provision for Taxation

To Cash	90,000	By Balance b/d	90,000
To Balance c/d	85,000	By P & L a/c	85,000
	1,75,000		1,75,000

Fixed Assets A/c

To Balance b/d	8,00,000	By Cash	
To Profit on sale of machine	25,000	Sale of machine	25,000
To Cash purchases	2,14,000	By Provision for	
(Balancing figure)		depreciation a/c	14,000
		By balance	9,50,000
	10,14,000		10,14,000

Note:

1. Opening Balance of fixed assets	5,70,000
Add: Provision for depreciation on fixed assets (2,90,000 – 60,000)	2,30,000
	8,00,000
2. Closing Balance of fixed assets	6,60,000
Add: Provision for depreciation on fixed assets	2,90,000
	9,50,000

Provision for Depreciation A/c

To Depreciation on machinery sold	21,000	By Balance b/d (2,90,000 – 60,000)	2,30,000
To Machinery written off	14,000	By P & L a/c	95,000
To Balance c/d	2,90,000	(Balancing figure)	
	3,25,000		3,25,000

Trade Investment A/c

To Balance b/d	1,00,000	By Cash-sales	30,000
To Capital Reserve	10,000	(Balancing figure)	
–profit on sale		By Balance c/d	80,000
	1,10,000		1,10,000

Adjusted P & L a/c

To Loss on sale of machinery	4,000	By Balance b/d	60,000
To Proposed dividend	36,000	By Opening stock	6,000
To Provision for taxation	85,000	By Fund from operation	2,70,800
To Premium on redemption of debentures	1,800		
To Transfer to general reserve	30,000		
To Preliminary expenses written off	10,000		
To Provision for depreciation on fixed assets	95,000		
To Balance c/d	75,000		
	3,36,800		3,36,800

Fund Flow Statement

Sources		*Applications*	
Issue of share capital	1,00,000	Proposed dividend of 1996 paid	26,000
Sale of machinery	25,000	Income tax paid	90,000
Sale of Investment	30,000	Debentures redeemed	61,800
Fund from operation	2,70,800	Purchase of fixed assets	2,14,000
		Increase in working capital	34,000
	4,25,800		4,25,800

Problem 23: Following are the summaries of balance sheets of a Limited Company as on 31st December 1997 and 1998

	1997 *Rs.*	*1998* *Rs.*
Paid up share capital	1,00,000	1,00,000
General reserve	21,400	26,000
Profit & loss a/c	17,000	16,000
Creditors	9,750	6,380
Provision for taxation (non-current)	19,000	21,000
Provision for doubtful debts	1,000	1200
	1,68,150	1,70,580
Buildings	46,800	45,000
Machinery	38,280	42,030
Goodwill	13,000	13,000
Investments	10,000	11,250
Stock	30,000	28,000
Debtors	22,000	22,000
Prepaid expenses	70	300
Cash balance	8,000	9,000
	1,68,150	1,70,580

Additional Information

1. The profit for the year 1998 was Rs. 8,600 which has been arrived at after charging Rs. 3,050 by way of depreciation and increase in provision for doubtful debts Rs. 200.
2. An interim dividend of Rs. 5,000 was paid in October 1998.
3. Additional machinery was purchased in May 1998 for Rs. 5,000.
4. Investments (cost Rs. 5,000) were sold in November 1998 for Rs. 4,800 and on 1st December, 1998 another investment was made for Rs. 6,250.
5. Income tax Rs. 18,000 was paid during the year and charged against the provision.

(*Sri Venkateshwara University, B.Com., April 1998*)

Solution: **Schedule of changes in Working Capital**

	1997	*1998*	*Increase*	*Decrease*
Current Assets				
Stock	30,000	28,000	—	2,000
Debtors	22,000	22,000		
Prepaid expenses	70	300	230	
Cash	8,000	9,000	1,000	
Total (A)	60,070	59,300		
Current Liabilities				
Creditors	9,750	6,380	3,370	—
Provision for doubtful debts	1,000	1,200	—	200
Total (B)	10,750	7,580		
Working Capital (A–B)	49,320	51,720		
Increase in working capital	2,400	—		2,400
	51,720	51,720	4,600	4,600

General Reserve A/c

To Balance c/d	26,000	By Balance b/d	21,400
		By P & L a/c	4,600
	26,000		26,000

Provision for Taxation

To Income tax paid	18,000	By Balance b/d	19,000
To Balance c/d	21,000	By P & L a/c (Balancing figure)	20,000
	39,000		39,000

Buildings A/c

To Balance b/d	46,800	By P & L a/c (Balancing figure)	1800
		By Balance c/d	45,000
	46,800		46,800

Machinery A/c

To Balance b/d	38,280	By P & L a/c (Balancing figure)	1,250
To Cash	5,000	By Balance c/d 2	42,030
	43,280		43,280

Investments A/c

To Balance b/d	10,000	By Cash-sale of investment	4,800
To Cash	6,250	By Loss on sale of investment	200
		By Balance c/d	11,250
	16,250		16,250

Adjusted Profit & Loss A/c

To Depreciation on:		By Balance b/d	17,000
Building	1,800	By Fund from operation	31,850
Machinery	1,250		
To Interim dividend	5,000		
To Loss on sale of investment	200		
To Provision for taxation	20,000		
To Transferred to general reserve	4,600		
To Balance c/d	16,000		
	48,850		48,850

Fund Flow Statement

Sources		*Applications*	
Fund from operation	31,850	Increase in working capital	2,400
Sale of investment	4,800	Machinery purchased	5,000
		Investment purchased	6,250
		Interim dividend paid	5,000
		Income tax paid	18,000
	36,650		36,650

Problem 24: From the following balance sheets of Bharat Ltd. prepare (*a*) statement of changes in working capital and (*b*) funds flow statement.

Balance Sheet as on

	1995	*1996*		*1995*	*1996*
Equity share capital	30,000	40,000	Goodwill	10,000	8,000
8% Redeemable preference shares	15,000	10,000	Land & Building	20,000	17,000
Capital Reserve	—	2,000	Plant	8,000	2,000
General reserve	4,000	5,000	Investment	2,000	3,000
P & L a/c	3,000	48,000	Debtors	14,000	17,000
Proposed dividend	4,200	5,000	Stock	7,700	10,900
Sundry Creditors	2,500	4,700	Bills receivable	2,000	3,000
Bills payable	2,000	1,600	Cash in hand	1,500	1,000
Liability for expenses	3,000	3,600	Cash at Bank	1,000	800
Provision for taxation	4,000	5,000	Preliminary expenses	1,500	1,000
	67,700	81,700		67,700	81,700

Additonal Information

1. A piece of land has been sold out in 1996 and the profit on sale has been credited to capital reserve.
2. A machine has been sold for Rs. 1,000. The written down value of the machine was Rs. 1200. Depreciation of Rs. 1,000 is charged on plant account in 1996.
3. The investments are trade investment. Rs. 300 by way of dividend is received including Rs. 100 from pre-acquisition profit which has been credited to investment account.
4. An interim dividend of Rs. 2,000 has been paid on 1996.

(Sri Sathya Sai University, B.Com., March 1997)

Solution: **Schedule of change in Working Capital**

	1995	1996	Increase	Decrease
Current Assets:				
Sundry debtors	14,000	17,000	3,000	—
Stock	7,700	10,900	3,200	—
Bills receivable	2,000	3,000	1,000	—
Cash in hand	1,500	1,000	—	500
Cash at Bank	1,000	800	—	200
Total (A)	26,200	32,700		
Current Liabilities				
Sundry creditors	2,500	4,700	—	2,200
Bills payable	2,000	1,600	400	—
Liability for expenses	3,000	3,600	—	600
Provision for taxation	4,000	5,000	—	1,000
Total (B)	11,500	14,900		
Working capital (A–B)	14,700	17,800		
Increase in working capital	3,100	—	—	3,100
	17,800	17,800	7,600	7,600

Land A/c

To Balance b/d	20,000	By Cash - sale	5,000
To Profit on sale-capital reserve	2,000	(Balancing figure)	
		By Balance c/d	17,000
	22,000		22,000

Adjusted Profit & Loss A/c

To Depreciation	1,000	By Balance b/d	3,000
To General reserve	1,000	By Dividend received out	
To Proposed dividend	5,000	of post acquisition	
To Interim dividend	2,000	profit (300–100)	200
To Good will written off	2,000	By Fund from operation	13,300
To Loss on sale of machinery (1,200–1,000)	200		
To Preliminary expenses written off	500		
To Balance c/d	4,800		
	16,500		16,500

Fund Flow Statement

Sources		*Applications*	
Issue of share capital	10,000	Redemption of preference shares	5,000
Sale of land	5,000		
Sale of machinery	10,000	Purchase of plant	14,200
Dividend received	300	Purchase of investment (1,000+100)	1,100
Fund from operation	13,300		

		Dividend paid:	
		Interim	2,000
		for 1995	4,200
			6,200
		Increase in working capital	3,100
	29,600		29,600

Problem 25: Prepare fund flow statement from the following data:

	31-12-96	*31-12-97*
Assets:		
Cash	2,000	2,500
Accounts receivable	2,400	2,700
Inventories	3,100	3,200
Other assets	800	700
Fixed assets	5,000	5,800
	13,300	14,900
Liabilities		
Accumulated depreciation	2,100	2,500
Accounts payable	2,000	2,100
Long-term debt	1,400	1,300
Equity capital	5,000	5,300
Retained earnings	2,800	3,700
	13,300	14,900

Note:

1. Fixed assets costing Rs. 1,200 were purchased for cash.
2. Fixed assets (original cost Rs. 400, accumulated depreciation Rs. 150) were sold for Rs. 200.
3. Depreciation for the year 1997 amounted to Rs. 550 and duly debited to profit & loss account.
4. Dividend paid amounted to Rs. 300 in 1997.
5. Reported income for 1997 was Rs. 1,200. *(Bangalore University, B.B.M., April 1998)*

Solution:

Schedule of changes in working capital

	1996	*1997*	*Increase*	*Decrease*
Current Assets:				
Cash	2,000	2,500	500	—
Accounts receivable	2,400	2,700	300	—
Inventories	3,100	3,200	100	—
Other assets	800	700	—	100
Total (A)	8,300	9,100		
Current Liabilities				
Accounts payable	2,000	2,100	—	100
Total (B)	2,000	2,100		
Working capital (A–B)	6,300	7,000		
Increase in working capital	700	—	—	700
	7,000	7,000	900	900

Fixed Assets A/c

To Balance b/d	5,000	By Bank a/c	200
To Bank-purchases	1,200	By Loss on sale	50
		By Accumulated depreciation	150
		By Balance c/d	5,800
	6,200		6,200

Accumulated Depreciation A/c

To Fixed assets	150	By Balance b/d	2,100
To Balance c/d	2,500	By P & L a/c	550
	2,650		2,650

Adjusted P & L A/c

To Accumulated depreciation a/c	550	By Balance b/d	2,800
To Loss on sale	50	By Income	1,200
To Dividend paid	300	By Fund from operation	600
To Balance c/d	3,700		
	4,600		4,600

Fund Flow Statement

Sources		*Applications*	
Fund from operation	600	Payment of long-term debt	100
Issue of equity capital	300	Dividend paid	300
Sale of fixed assets	200	Fixed assets purchased	1,200
Income received	1,200	Increase in working capital	700
	2,300		2,300

Problem 26: The comparative balance sheets of star Ltd. are given below:

	1995	*1996*		*1995*	*1996*
12% preference share capital	2,00,000	1,00,000	Goodwill	85,000	80,000
Equity share capital	6,00,000	8,00,000	Land & Building	2,02,000	2,16,000
Share premium	10,000	30,000	Investments	1,00,000	75,000
Reserves	52,000	70,000	Patents	30,000	24,000
Profit & loss a/c	1,75,000	1,50,000	Plant	4,20,000	5,10,000
6% debentures	1,25,000	1,00,000	Stock	2,85,000	3,37,000
Sundry creditors	1,02,000	1,33,000	Sundry debtors	1,30,800	1,46,400
Interim dividend payable	—	2,000	Prepaid expenses	3,200	4,600
Provision fo taxation	38,000	48,000	Advance income tax	40,000	35,000
			Discount on issue of debentures	6,000	5,000
	13,02,000	14,33,000		13,02,000	14,33,000

Additional Information

1. Preference share redemption was carried out on 31st December, 1996.
2. Dividend 12% p.a was paid on preference shares and Interim dividend on equity shares Rs. 43,000 was paid in the year 1996.
3. Depreciation of Rs. 26,000 and Rs. 79,000 has been provided on land and buidlings and plant respectively in the year 1996.

4. Plant costing Rs. 60,000 purchased on 1st Januarey, 1994, depreciated by 20% (on W.D.V.) was sold on 1st January 1996 for Rs. 30,000.
5. Investment having book value Rs. 57,000 sold for Rs. 49,000.
6. Income tax assessment for the year ended 31st December, 1995 was completed on 1st April, 1996 for a gross demand of Rs. 45,000. The Balance amount of demand after adjusting advance-tax (1995) was paid on 10th April, 1996.

You are required to prepare:

1. Statement of funds flow during the year 1996.
2. Schedule of changes in working capital showing individual item wise figures therein.
3. Provision for taxation account and advance tax account.

(University of Bombay, B.Com., October 1997)

Solution:

Schedule of changes in Working Capital

	1995	*1996*	*Increase*	*Decrease*
Current Assets:				
Stock	2,85,000	3,37,000	52,000	—
Sundry debtors	1,30,800	1,46,400	15,600	—
Prepaid expenses	3,200	4,600	1,400	—
	4,19,000	4,88,000		
Current Liabilities				
Sundry creditors	1,02,000	1,33,000	—	31,000
Working capital	3,17,000	3,55,000		
Increase in working capital	38,000	—	—	38,000
	3,55,000	3,55,000	69,000	69,000

Working Notes

(1) Calculation of loss on sale of plant

Cost	60,000
20% Depreciation for 1994	12,000
	48,000
20% Depreciation for 1995	9600
W.D.V.	38,400
Sold for	30,000
Loss on sale	8,400

(2) Loss on sale of Investment

Cost	57,000
Sold at	49,000
Loss on sale	8,000

Plant A/c

To Balance b/d	4,20,000	By Depreciation	79,000
To Bank-plant purchased (Balancing figure)	2,07,400	By Plant sold -Bank	38,400
		By Balance c/d	5,10,000
	6,27,400		6,27,400

Land & Building

To Balance b/d	2,02,000	By Depreciation	26,000
To Bank-land purchased	40,000	By Balance c/d	2,16,000
	2,42,000		2,42,000

Investment A/c

To Balance b/d	1,00,000	By Bank-sale of investment	57,000
To Bank-Investment purchased	32,000	By Balance c/d	75,000
	1,32,000		1,32,000

Provision for Tax A/c

To Advance tax a/c	45,000	By Balance b/d	38,000
To Balance c/d	48,000	By P & L a/c (Balancing figure)	55,000
	93,000		93,000

Advance Tax A/c

To Balance b/d	40,000	By Provision for tax	45,000
To Bank a/c	5,000		
To Bank a/c	35,000	By Balance c/d	35,000
	80,000		80,000

Interim Dividend Payable A/c

To Bank a/c	43,000	By Balance b/d	—
To Balance c/d	2,000	By P & L a/c (Balancing fig.)	45,000
	45,000		45,000

Adjusted Profit & Loss A/c

To Depreciation on:		By Balance b/d	1,75,000
Land & building	26,000	By Fund from operation	2,50,400
Plant	79,000		
To Loss on sale of:			
Plant	8,400		
Investment	800		
To Provision for tax	55,000		
To Dividend on preference shares	24,000		
To Interim dividend	45,000		
To Transfer to reserve	18,000		
To Goodwill written off	5,000		
To Patent written off	6,000		
To Discount on debentures	1,000		
To Balance c/d	1,50,000		
	4,25,400		4,25,000

Fund Flow Statement

Sources		*Applications*	
Plant sold	30,000	Increase in working capital	38,000
Investment sold	49,000	Plant purchased	2,07,400
Issue of shares	2,00,000	Land & Building purchased	40,000
Share premium	20,000	Investment purchased	32,000
Fund from operation	2,50,400	Tax paid (35,000+5,000)	40,000
		Redemption of pref. shares	1,00,000
		Dividend on pref. shares	24,000
		Interim dividend paid	43,000
		Redemption of debentures	25,000
	5,49,400		5,49,400

QUESTIONS

Simple Questions

1. What is a fund?
2. What is meant by flow of funds?
3. Define a funds flow statement.
4. State the need for fund flow statement?
5. State two uses of funds flow statement to management.
6. Mention any two limitations of fund flow statement analysis.
7. What are the major sources of funds for a business?
8. State two points of differences between funds flow statement and an income statement.
9. State two points of differences between funds flow statement and position statement.
10. State the common 'inflows' to working capital.
11. State the common 'outflows' from working capital.
12. What is 'positive' and 'negative' changes in working capital?
13. Mention the important steps involved in the preparation of funds flow statement.
14. Give the meaning of working capital.
15. How do you treat provision for taxation while preparing a funds flow statement.
16. State the rules to ascertain which transaction give rise to a source or use of working capital.
17. What is 'Fund from operation'?
18. State the significance of preparing a funds flow statement.
19. How do you treat 'proposed dividend'? While preparing a funds flow statement?

Short Answer Questions

1. Analyse the managerial uses of funds flow analysis.
2. A fund flow statement is a better substitute for an income statement comment.
3. State the reasons whether the following transactions result in increase or decrease of working capital or do not effect the working capital.
   (*a*) A company issued 10,000 shares of Rs. 10 each at par fully paid up.
   (*b*) Debentures for Rs. 1,00,000 are commented into equity shares.
   (*c*) Investments were sold for Rs. 50,000
   (*d*) Building was purchased for Rs. 1,50,000
   (*e*) Bills payable accepted and issued to creditors Rs. 40,000
   (*f*) Bills receivable Rs. 10,000 discounted for 9,500.
   (*g*) Fixed assets purchased by issue of shares for Rs. 1,00,000
   (*h*) Cash paid to creditors Rs. 30,000
   (*i*) Preliminary expenses written off Rs. 5,000.
   (*j*) Advance income tax paid Rs. 50,000. (*Bangalore University, B.Com., April 1994*)

Exercise 1: From the following information, calculate fund from operation:

Profit & Loss A/c

To Expenses:		By Gross profit		2,00,000
Operation	1,00,000	By Gain on sale of building		20,000
Depreciation	40,000			
To Loss on sale of machinery	10,000	By Other incomes		2,000
To Advertisement suspense a/c	5,000			
To Discount on debtors	500			
To Discount on issue of shares	500			
To Goodwill	12,000			
To Preliminary expenses	2,000			
To Net profit	52,000			
	2,22,000			2,22,000

(*University of Madras, B.Com., May 1997*)
[*Answer:* Rs. 1,01,500]

Exercise 2: Calculate fund from operation from the following profit & loss a/c.

Profit & Loss A/c

To Rent	10,000	By Gross profit	9,86,000
To Salary	25,000		
To Depreciation on furniture	3,000		
To Discount on issue of shares	10,000		
To Goodwill written off	5,000		
To Preliminary expenses	6,000		
To New profit	9,27,000		
	9,86,000		9,86,000

(*University of Madras, B.Com., March, 1996*)
[*Answer:* Rs.9,51,000]

Exercise 3: Prepare an adjusted profit & loss account to determine the funds from operations from the following information extracted from Crown Ltd. for the year 2000:

Profit & loss a/c balance on 1.1.2000	Rs. 2,00,000
Profit & loss a/c balance on 31.12.2000	Rs. 6,40,000
Profit earned during the year was	Rs. 6,40,000

After the following adjustments were made:

Depreciation on assets	2,80,000
Preliminary expenses written off	20,000
Patents written off	30,000
Provision for tax	3,20,000
Proposed dividend	1,20,000
Provision for doubtful debts	40,000
Profit on sale of fixed assets	10,000
Loss on sale of investments	5,000

In addition the profit was overstated by Rs. 20,000 due to change in the method of revaluation of closing stock. There was also a transfer of Rs. 2,00,000 to reserves (out of Rs. 6,40,000)

Prepare a profit & loss (adjusted) account for arriving at your answer. [*Answer:* Rs. 12,85,000]

Exercise 4: Following information is extracted from the books of Omega Ltd. for the year 2000:

Opening balance of P & L a/c	25,000
Closing balance of P & L a/c	60,000
Salaries paid	5,000
Rent paid	3,000
Refund of tax paid	3,000
Profit on sale of building	5,000
Depreciation on plant	5,000

Provision for tax	4,000
Loss on sale of plant	2,000
Discount on issue of debentures	2,000
Provision for bad debts	1,000
Transfer to general reserve	1,000
Preliminary expenses written off	3,000
Goodwill written off	2,000
Proposed dividend	6,000
Dividend received	5,000

Prepare a statement showing funds from operations through an adjusted profit & loss account.

[*Answer:* Rs. 48,000]

Exercise 5: Prepare a statment showing changes in working capital from the following balance sheets of excel for the years 1999-2000

	1990	*2000*		*1999*	*2000*
Equity share capital	15,00,000	6,00,000	Fixed assets	10,00,000	11,20,000
			Less: Dep.	3,70,000	4,60,000
Reserves	1,50,000	1,80,000		6,30,000	6,60,000
P & L a/c	40,000	65,000	Stock	2,40,000	3,70,000
7% Debentures	3,00,000	2,50,000	A/c Receivable	2,50,000	2,30,000
A/c payable	1,70,000	1,60,000	Cash at bank	80,000	60,000
Provision for income tax	60,000	80,000	Preliminary expenses	20,000	15,000
	12,20,000	13,35,000		12,20,000	13,35,000

[*Answer:* Increase in working capital Rs. 10,00,000]

Exercise 6: From the following information prepare a funds flow statement including a schedule of changes in working capital for the year ended 31.12.96:

Balance Sheet

	31.12.95	*31.12.96*		*31.12.95*	*31.12.96*
Share capital	1,40,000	1,48,000	Cash	18,000	15,600
Debentures	24,000	12,000	Debtors	29,800	35,400
Reserve for doubtful debts	14,000	1,600	Stock	98,400	85,400
Creditors	20,720	23,680	Land	40,000	60,000
P & L a/c	20,080	21,120	Goodwill	20,000	10,000
	2,06,200	2,06,400		2,06,200	2,06,400

Additional Information

(*a*) Dividends paid Rs. 7,000

(*b*) During the year 1996 land purchased for Rs. 20,000. (*Osmania University, B.Com., March 1998*)

[*Answer*: Total of fund flow statement Rs. 39,000

Exercise 7: From the following Balance sheets of Nav Bharat Ltd. as on 31st December, 1995 and 1996 you are required to prepare a fund flow statement.

	1995	*1996*		*1995*	*1996*
Share capital	2,00,000	2,50,000	Land & building	2,00,000	1,90,000
General reserve	50,000	60,000	Plant	1,50,000	1,69,000
P & L a/c	30,500	30,600	Stock	90,000	74,000
Bank loan (short-term)	70,000	—	Debtors	80,000	64,200
Creditors	1,50,000	1,35,200	Cash	2,500	8,600
Provision for tax	30,000	35,000	Goodwill	8,000	5,000
	5,30,500	5,10,800		5,30,500	5,10,800

Additional Information

1. Dividends paid during the year 1996 Rs. 23,000.
2. Depreciation written off on plant Rs. 14,000 and on building Rs. 10,000.
3. Income tax provision made during the year 1996 Rs. 33,000.

(Osmania University, B.Com., October 1997)

[*Answer*: Total by Fund Flow Statement Rs. 1,43,100]

Exercise 8: The comparative balance-sheets of Star Ltd, are given below:

Liabilities	*1995*	*1996*
12% pref share capital	2,00,000	1,00,000
Equity share capital	6,00,000	8,00,000
Share premium	10,000	30,000
Reserves	52,000	70,000
P & L a/c	1,75,000	1,50,000
6% Debentures	1,25,000	1,00,000
Sundry creditors	1,02,000	1,33,000
Interim dividend payablae	—	2,000
Provision for taxation	38,000	48,000
	13,02,000	14,33,000
Assets		
Goodwill	85,000	80,000
Land & Building	2,02,000	2,16,000
Investments	1,00,000	75,000
Patents	30,000	24,000
Plant	4,20,000	5,10,000
Stock	2,85,000	3,37,000
Sundry debtors	1,30,800	1,46,400
Prepaid expenses	3,200	4,600
Advance income tax	40,000	35,000
Discount on issue of debentures	6,000	5,000
	13,02,000	14,33,000

Additional Information

1. Preference share redemption was carried out on 31st December, 1996.
2. Dividend 12% p.a was paid on preference share and interim dividend on equity shares Rs. 43,000 was paid in the year 1996.
3. Depreciation of Rs. 26,000 and Rs. 79,000 has been provided on land and buidling and plant respectively in the year 1996.
4. Plant costing Rs. 60,000 purchased on 1st January 1994, depreciated by 20% (on WDV) was sold on 1st January 1996 for Rs. 30,000
5. Investments having book value Rs. 57,000 sold for Rs. 49,000.
6. Income tax assessment for the year ended 31st December 1995 was completed on 1st April 1996 for a gross demand of Rs. 45,000. The balance amount of demend often adjusting advance-tax (1995) was paid on 10th April, 1996.

You are required to prepare

1. Statement of funds flow during the year 1996.
2. Schedule of changes in working capital showing separate item wise figures therein.
3. Provision for taxation a/c and advance-tax a/c. *(University of Bombay, B.Com., October 1997)*

[*Answer:* Fund from operation Rs. 2,50,400
Total of fund flow statement Rs. 5,49,400]

Exercist 9: From the following balance sheets of Ananth Co. Ltd., prepare a statement of changes in the working capital and the fund flow statement for the year ended 31st March 1996.

	1995	1996		1995	1996
Share capital	3,00,000	3,50,000	Goodwill	1,00,000	80,000
Debentures	1,50,000	2,50,000	Machinery	4,10,000	5,40,000
P & L a/c	60,000	70,000	Investments	30,000	80,000
General reserve	1,00,000	1,50,000	Discount on issue of debentures	5,000	—
Provision for Depreciation on Machinery	90,000	1,30,000	Cash at Bank	1,20,000	1,30,000
Sundry creditors	75,000	1,10,000	Sundry debtors	80,000	1,90,000
Bills payable	10,000	15,000	Stock in trade	40,000	55,000
	7,85,000	10,75,000		7,85,000	10,75,000

During the year investments costing Rs. 30,000 were sold for Rs. 28,000. A new machine was purchased for Rs. 45,000 and payment was made in fully paid shares. *(Bangalore University, B.B.M., November 1997)*

[*Answer:* Total of FFS Rs. 3,50,000]

Exercise 10: From the following balance sheets of XYZ Co. Ltd., prepare funds flow statement:

	(Rs. 000) 1995	1996		*(Rs. 000)* 1995	1996
Equity share capital	600	800	Goodwill	230	180
Preference share capital	300	200	Land & buildings	400	340
General reserve	80	140	Plant & machinery	160	400
P & L a/c	60	96	Debtors	320	400
Proposed dividend	84	100	Stock	154	218
Creditors	110	166	Bills receivable	40	60
Bills payable	40	32	CAsh	30	20
Tax provision	80	100	Bank	20	16
	1,354	1,634		1,354	1,634

Additional Information

1. Proposed dividend made during 1995 has been paid during 1996.
2. Depreciation: (*a*) Rs. 20,000 on plant & machinery
   (*b*) Rs. 4,000 on land & buildings.
3. Interim dividend has been paid Rs. 40,000 in 1996.
4. Income-tax Rs. 70,000 has been paid during 1996. *(CS, Inter, December 1997)*

[*Answer:* Fund from operation Rs. 4,36,000
Total of fund flow statement Rs. 6,56,000]

Exercise 11: Prepare a funds flow statement and a statement of changes in working capital from the following particulars furnished by X Company Ltd.

(Rs. in Lakhs)

Owner's Equity & Liabilities	*End of 1995*	*End of 1996*
Share capital	50	50
Reserves & surpluses	60	70
Long-term debt	95	80
Short-term bank borrowings	70	80
Trade creditors	50	60
Provisions	20	15
	345	355
Assets:		
Fixed assets (net)	180	190
Inventories	70	60
Debtors	60	70
Cash	20	15
Other assets	15	20
	345	355

The income statement of X Company Ltd. for the year 1996 is given below:

	(Rs. in Lakhs)		(Rs. in Lakhs)
To Cost of goods sold	520	By Sales	800
To Operational expenses	150		
To Non-operational expenses	50		
To Interest	30		
To Tax	20		
To Dividend	20		
To Balance c/d	10		
	800		800

(*CS, Inter, June 1997*)
[*Answer:* Fund from operation Rs. 35 (lakhs)
Total of fund flow statement Rs. 95 (in lakhs)]

Exercise 12: From the following balance sheets of X Ltd. prepare a schedule of changes in working capital and fund flow statement:

	31.12.90	*31.12.91*		*31.12.90*	*31.12.91*
Share capital	6,00,000	8,00,000	Machinery (cost)	4,00,000	6,45,000
Debentures	2,00,000	3,00,000	Buildings (cost)	3,00,000	4,00,000
P & L a/c	1,25,000	2,50,000	Stock	20,000	40,000
Creditors	1,15,000	90,000	Preliminary expenses	7,000	6,000
Provision for bad debts	6,000	3,000	Debtors	69,000	61,000
Provision for depreciation:					
on building	20,000	24,000			
on machinery	30,000	35,000			
	10,96,000	15,02,000		10,96,000	15,02,000

Additional Information

(*a*) During the year a part of the machinery costing Rs. 70,000 (accumulated depreciation thereon Rs. 2,000) was sold for Rs. 6,000.

(*b*) Dividend of Rs. 50,000 were paid during the year 1991.(*University of Madras, B.Com., September 1997*)

[*Answer*: Fund from operation Rs. 2,49,000
Total of fund flow statement Rs. 5,55,000.]

Exercise 13: The following are the summarised balance sheets of Archana Polygraph Limited as on 31st March, 1995 and 1996.

	31.12.95	*31.12.96*		*31.12.95*	*31.12.96*
Share capital	4,60,000	4,60,000	Land & building	3,00,000	3,00,000
P & L A/c	32,000	46,000	Machinery	1,04,000	1,40,000
Reserve for contingency	1,20,000	1,20,000	Investments	2,20,000	1,48,000
8% Debentures	1,80,000	1,40,000	Stock	1,64,000	2,12,000
Depreciation fund	80,000	88,000	Debtors	1,34,000	86,000
Creditors	2,06,000	1,92,000	Cash	1,80,000	1,80,000
O/s liability for expenses	26,000	24,000	Prepaid expenses	2,000	4,000
	11,04,000	10,70,000		11,04,000	10,70,000

Additional Informations

1. 10% Dividend was paid during the year 1996.
2. Machinery for Rs. 6,000 was purchased and old machinery costing Rs. 24,000 (accumulated depreciation Rs. 12,000) was sold for Rs. 8,000.
3. Rs. 40,000, 8% debentures were redeemed by purchase from open market at Rs. 96 for a debenture of Rs. 100.
4. Investments worth Rs. 72,000 were sold at book value.

You are required to prepare a schedule of changes in working capital and a statement showing sources and application of funds.

(University of Bombay, B.Com., April 1997)

[*Answer:* Fund from operation Rs. 28,400
Total of fund flow statement Rs. 1,08,400]

Exercise 14: From the following balance sheets of 'A' Ltd. for the year ending 31st December, 1994 and 1995 draw out a fund flow statement and a statement of changes in working capital:

	1994	*1995*		*1994*	*1995*
Equity share capital	3,00,000	4,00,000	Goodwill	60,000	55,000
9% Redeemable	80,000	50,000	Land & building	1,25,000	85,000
pref share capital			Plant & machinery	1,20,000	2,25,000
Capital revenue	—	20,000	Furniture	15,000	12,000
General reserve	30,000	40,000	Investment	12,000	48,000
P & L A/c	26,000	35,000	Sundry debtors	65,000	1,05,000
Sundry creditors	30,000	58,000	Stock	90,000	84,000
Bills payable	12,000	8,000	Bills receivable	16,000	30,000
O/s expenses	6,000	5,000	Cash in hand	13,000	20,000
Proposed dividend	30,000	42,000	Cash at bank	15,000	20,000
Provision for Taxation	32,000	36,000	Preliminary expenses	15,000	10,000
	5,46,000	6,94,000		5,46,000	6,94,000

Additional Information

(*a*) A piece of land has been sold out in 1995 and the balance has been revalued. Profits on sale and revaluation being transferred to capital reserve a/c.

(*b*) Depreciation on plant & machinery has been written off Rs. 24,000 in 1995 and no depreciation has been charged on land and buildings.

(*c*) A machinery was sold for Rs. 16,000 (written down value being Rs. 20,000) and no furniture has been sold during the year.

(*d*) An interim dividend of Rs. 20,000 has been paid in 1995.

(*e*) Rs. 3,000 has been received as dividend on investment.

(Sri Sathya Sai University, B.Com. (Hons), March 1996)

[*Answer:* Fund from operation Rs. 77,000
Total of fund flow statement Rs. 2,56,000]

Exercise 15: Balance sheet of Govind as on 31.12.1989.

Capital	50,000	Machinery	60,000
P & L A/c	20,000	Furniture	5,000
Long-term loan	30,000	Investments	25,000
Creditors	40,000	Debtors	25,000
General reserve	10,000	Cash	5,000
		Stock	30,000
	1,50,000		1,50,000

The following transactions took place in the year 1990:

1. Machinery (Book value Rs. 20,000 on 1.1.1990) was sold on 1.4.1990 for Rs. 18,000.
2. Investments were sold for Rs. 30,000.
3. Depreciation was provided at 10% p.a on machinery and 20% p.a on furniture.
4. New machinery was purchased on 1.7.1990.
5. Total depreciation provided on machinery was Rs. 6,500 for the year 1990.
6. Drowings of Mr. Govind was Rs. 15,000 in the year 1990 and additional capital was Rs. 25,000.
7. Loan Rs. 10,000 was paid.
8. Transfer to general reserve was Rs. 10,000.
9. On 31.12.1990 it was found that there was increase in creditors by Rs. 20,000, stock by Rs. 20,000; debtors by Rs. 35,000 and total increase in working capital was Rs. 52,000.

(Bangalore University, B.Com., April 1996)

[*Answer:* Closing balance of P & L a/c on preparing a balance sheet is Rs. 50,000.
Fund from operation Rs. 49,000
Total of fund flow statement Rs. 1,17,000]

Exercise 16: From the figures given below, prepare a statement showing the application and sources of funds during the year 1995:

Assets	*31.3.1994*	*31.12.1995*
Fixed assets (net)	5,10,000	6,20,000
Investments	30,000	80,000
Current assets	2,40,000	3,75,000
Discount on debentures	10,000	5,000
	7,90,000	10,80,000
Liabilities:		
Share capital (equity)	3,00,000	3,50,000
Share capital (preference)	2,00,000	1,00,000
Debentures	1,00,000	2,00,000
Reserves	1,10,000	2,70,000
Provision for doubtful debts	10,000	15,000
Current liabilities	70,000	1,45,000
	7,90,000	10,80,000

You are informed that during the year:

(*i*) A machine costing Rs. 70,000 (book value Rs. 40,000) was disposed off for Rs. 25,000.

(*ii*) Preference share redemption was carried out at a premium of 5%.

(*iii*) Divdend at 15% was paid on equity shares for the year 1994.

Further:

(*a*) The provision for depreciation stood at Rs. 1,50,000 on 31.3.1994 and at Rs. 1,90,000 on 31.3.1995.

(*b*) Stock which was valued at Rs. 90,000 as on 31.3.1994 was written up to its cost Rs. 1,00,000 for preparing the profit and loss account for 1995. (*CS, Inter, June 1996*)

[*Answer:* Fund from operation Rs. 2,90,000;
Total of fund flow statement Rs. 4,65,000]

35

CASH FLOW STATEMENT

INTRODUCTION

Cash flow statement is one of the analytical tool used by the management Accountant to interpret the financial soundness of the business. It shows the changes in the cash position between two dates of balance sheet. This change in cash position is known by considering the inflow and outflow of cash. This statement indicates the sources from where cash is obtained and the uses to which cash is utilised. The term 'cash' used in 'cash flow' includes cash as well as bank balance. Cash flow refers to the movement of cash in and out of business. Sometimes the inflow of cash is referred to as positive flow and the outflow as negative flow. The difference between them is net cash flow. Inflow of cash takes place when a transaction increases the cash position. Examples of transactions which increases cash position are sale of assets, issue of shares and debentures etc., outflow of cash takes place when a transaction decreases the cash position. Examples of transactions which decreases cash position are purchase of assets, redemption of debentures.

Cash flow are of two types, *viz.*, (*a*) actual cash flow and (*b*) notional cash flow. Actual cash flow implies direct flow of cash into or out of the business. For example, when shares are issued, there is direct inflow of cash. Notional cash flow refers to indirect flow of cash into or out of business. This takes place when there is increase or decrease in current assets such as bills receivable, debtors, stock etc.

Cash Flow Statement

It is a statement designed to high light upon the causes which brings changes in cash position between two balance sheet dates. This statement depicts the various sources of cash and the uses to which it is put. Cash flow results on account of three activities, viz., (*a*) operating, (*b*) investing and (*c*) financing activities.

(*a*) Cash flow from operating activities : These are the transactions which determine the net profit or loss of the business. The business operations result in cash receipts and cash payments. Cash receipts arise from sale of goods. Operating expenses and cost of goods sold result in cash payment. Cash receipts arising from operating activities are listed below :

(*i*) Cash receipts from sale of goods.
(*ii*) Cash receipts from royalities, commission.
(*iii*) Collection from sundry debtors.
(*iv*) Dividend and interest received on investment.
(*v*) Cash sale of fixed assets and current investment.
(*vi*) Refund of tax.

Cash payments arising from operating activities are listed below :

(*i*) Cash payment to suppliers for having suplied raw-materials.
(*ii*) Cash payment to employees.
(*iii*) Cash payment to creditors and bills payable.
(*iv*) Cash payment of interest and dividend.

(*v*) Cash payment as fines and penalty.
(*vi*) Cash payment of Income-tax.

(*b*) Cash flow from investing activities : Investing activities are those activities relating to acquisition and disposal of fixed assets and long-term investment. Cash receipts arising from investing activities are listed below :

(*i*) Cash receipt from sale of fixed and intangible assets.
(*ii*) Cash receipt from the disposal of shares, warrants or debt instrument of other companies.

The cash payment arising from investing activities are listed below :

(*i*) Cash payment to acquire fixed assets.
(*ii*) Cash payment to acquire shares, warrants or debt instrument of other enterprises.
(*iii*) Cash advances and loans made to third parties.

(*c*) Cash flow from financing activities : Whenever there is change in capital (both equity and preference) and borrowings by a business, it is referred to as financing activities. The cash receipts arising from financing activities are listed below :

(*i*) Cash received on issue of shares.
(*ii*) Cash received on issue of debentures.

The cash payments arising from financing activities are listed below :

(*i*) Redemption of redeemable preference shares.
(*ii*) Redemption of debentures.
(*iii*) Payment of dividend.

Importance or Utility of Cash Flow Statement

A cash flow statement is an important tool in the hands of management to evaluate financial policies and current cash position. A business needs sufficient cash to meet its various obligations in near future. Cash flow statement helps the management to know the sources and applications of cash and in turn enables the management to plan for investment of cash. The utility of cash flow can be stated as under :

(1) Helps in efficient management of cash : No business operation can be carried out without cash. It is therefore necessary to know the requirements of cash, the internal and external sources of cash, and proper use of cash. The projected cash flow statement enables the management to plan and coordinate the financial operations properly. It helps in evaluating financial policies and current cash position. The management knows how much finds are needed, how much can be generated internally, and how much should be obtained externally.

(2) It helps in internal financial management : Cash flow statement reveals the cash from trading operations, *i.e.*, internal source of cash. The replacement of assets, repayment of long term debts, dividend policies and such other programme can be chalked out on this basis.

(3) Discloses movement of Cash: It throws light on the factors causing low cash balance when the operating profit are high or for heavy cash balance when the operating profits are low. Inflows of cash and outflows of cash indicate the movement of cash, which otherwise would not have been known.

(4) Discloses success or failure of cash planning : Comparision of projected cash flow statement with the actual cash flow statement reveals the variation in actual cash flow statement. This interim throws light on financial planning and enables the management to take remedial measures.

(5) Helps to control cash expenditure : Cash budget can be prepared with the help of cash flow statement. A comparision of the cash flow statement and the budgeted forecast of cash is helpful in comparing and controlling cash expenditure.

(6) It provides a better measure for inter-period and inter-firm comparision.

Limitation of Cash Flow Statement

1. It reveals only the movement of cash but fails to show liquidity position of the business.
2. It shows cash income of the business, but to determine the income of the business, non-cash income should also be considered.
3. In cash flow statement, the term 'fund' is used in a narrow sense, *i.e.*, cash only. This will not therefore give a complete picture of financial position of the business.
4. It connot replace income statement and find flow statement as they have specific purpose of there own.

Types of Cash Flow Statement

Cash Flow Statement may relate to past or future. In the former case it is referred to as historical cash flow statement and projected cash flow or cash budget in the case of latter. Historical cash flow statement is prepared at the end of accounting year to know sources and uses of cash. In fact the cash flow statement which is normally prepared relates to historical cash flow statement.

Difference between Cash Flow Statement and Cash Budget

Cash budget is different from cash flow statement. Cash budget reveals the probable cash position as a result of planned operation and thus the excess or shortage of cash is known. This helps in arranging short-term borrowings in advance to meet the situations of shortage of cash or making investment in times of cash in excess. Cash can be coordinated in relation to total working capital, sales, investment and debt. On the other hand, a statement of cash flow provides detailed information about how particular assets, liabilities and owners equity elements changed as a result of cash receipts and cash payment from business's operating, investing and financiang activities.

Differences between cash flow statement and fund flow statement

Fund flow statement	*Cash flow statement*
1. It is based on the concept of working capital.	1. It is based on the concept of cash.
2. It reveals changes in working capital position between two balance sheet dates.	2. It reveals change in cash position between two balance sheet dates.
3. It is of primary importance.	3. It is of secondary importance.
4. Classification of assets and liabilities into current and non-current category is essential.	4. No such classification is necessary.
5. This statement match sources and application of fund.	5. It commences with opening cash balance and ends with closing cash balance.
6. An improvement in cash position results. in improvement in working capital.	6. An increase in cash on hand does not result in increase in working capital.
7. It is long-term tool of financial analysis.	7. It is a short-term tool of financial analysis.

Procedure Involved in Preparing Cash Flow Statement

The following steps are involved in the preparetion of cash flow statement :

(1) Calculation of cash flow from operation : Ascertainment of cash flow from operation involves the following two steps :

(*a*) *Ascertainment of operating profit or operating cash profit* : Operating profit is to be ascertained because net profit shownn in the income statement contain non-cash and non-operating expenses and non-operating incomes. Hence specifically operating cash profit has to be calculated. The operating cash profit can be ascertained by preparing an adjusted profit and loss account which resembles to the one prepared under fund flow statement. A proforma of adjusted profit and loss account is shown below :

Adjusted Profit & Loss A/c

To Non-cash and non-operating expesnes :			By Balance b/d	xx
– Depreciation on fixed assets	xx		By Non-operating and non-cash incomes :	
– Preliminary expenses	xx		– Interest received	xx
– Discount on issue of shares & debentures	xx		– Dividend received	xx
– Underwriting commission wirtten off			– Compensation received	xx
– Reserve for bad debts	xx		– Donation received	xx
– Reserve for discount on debtors	xx		– Profit on sale of investment	xx
– Provision for taxtaion	xx		– Profit on sale of fixed assets	xx
– Donation given	xx		By Operating cash profit (Balancing figure)	xx
– Compensation paid	xx			
– Fines & penalties	xx			
		xx		
To Appropriation of profit :				
– Transfer to reserve		xx		
– Dividend declared		xx		
To Balance c/d		xx		
		xx		xx

Problem 1 (Ascertainment of cash from operation) : From the following profit & loss account, you are required to compute cash from operation :

Profit & Loss A/c for the year ended 31.12.98

To Salaries	5,000	By Gross profit	25,000
To Rent	1,000	By Profit on sale of land	5,000
To Depreciation	2,000	By Income on investment	3,000
To Loss on sale of plant	1,000		
To Goodwill written off	4,000		
To Proposed dividend	5,000		
To Provision for taxation	5,000		
To Net profit	10,000		
	33,000		33,000

(*Bangalore University, B.B.M., April 2002*), (*CS, Inter December, 1997*)

Solution :

Adjusted Profit & Loss A/c

To Depreciation	2,000	By Balance b/d	Nil
To Loss on sale of plant	1,000	By Profit on sale of land	5,000
To Goodwill written off	4,000	By Income on investment	3,000
To Proposed dividend	5,000	By Opering cash	8,000
To Provision for taxation	5,000	By Profit (Balancing figure)	19,000
To Balance c/d	10,000		
	27,000		27,000

(b) Ascertainment of Cash Flow from Operation : Cash flow from operation consists of both operating cash profit and changes in current assets and changes in current liabilities. The total cash flow from operation can be shown under the following proforma :

Proforma showing the Cash Flow from the Operation

Operating cash profit (as ascertained by preparing adjusted P & L a/c)		xx
Add : Decrease in current assets	xx	
Add : Increase in current liabilities	xx	
		xx
		xx
Less : Increase in current assets	xx	
Less : Decrease in current liabilities	xx	
		xx
Cash Flow from Operation		xx

Problem 2 (Ascertainment of Cash flow from operation) : From the following information, you are required to ascertain cash flow from operation :

	31-12-96 (*Rs.*)	*31-12-97* (*Rs.*)
Net profit	–	70,000
Debtors	42,000	40,000
Bills receivable	8,000	13,000
Creditors	47,000	50,000
Bills payable	15,000	10,000
Stock	58,000	65,000

(*Osmania University, B.Com., March 1999*)

Solution :

Calculation of Cash from Operation

Profit made during the year		70,000
Add : Decrease in debtors	2,000	
Add : Increase in creditors	3,000	5,000
		75,000
Less : Increase in bills receivable	5,000	
Less : Increase in stock	7,000	
Less : Decrease in bills payable	5,000	
		17,000
Cash from Operation		58,000

Problem 3 : From the following balances you are required to calculate cash from operation :

	31.12.1989	*31.12.1990*
Debtors	50,000	47,000
Bills receivable	10,000	12,500
Creditors	20,000	25,000
Bills payable	8,000	6,000
O/s expenses	1,000	1,200
Prepaid expenses	800	700
Accrued income	600	750
Income received from advance	300	250
Profit made during the year	–	1,30,000

(*Bangalore University, B.B.M., November 1999*)

Solution :

Cash from Operation

Profit made during the year		1,30,000
Add : Decrease in debtors	3,000	
Decrease in prepaid expenses	100	
Increase in creditors	5,000	
Increase in O/s expenses	200	
		8,300
		1,38,300
Less : Increase in Bills receivable	2,500	
Increase in Accrued Income	150	
Decrease in Bills payable	2,000	
Decrease in Income received in advance	50	
		4,700
Cash from operation		1,33,600

Problem 4 : From the following information, calculation cash from operation :

	1996 *Rs.*	*1997* *Rs.*
P & L a/c (Credit)	40,000	50,000
Debtors	20,000	26,000
Bills receivable	20,000	12,000
Prepaid rent	2,000	3,000
Prepaid insurance	1,000	800
Goodwill	20,000	14,000
Depreciation	32,000	40,000
Creditors	20,000	30,000

(*Osmania University, B.Com., October 1999*)

Solution :

Adjusted P & L A/c

To Goodwill written off	6,000	By Balance b/d	40,000
To Depreciation	8,000	By Operating cash profit	24,000
To Balance c/d	50,000		
	64,000		64,000

Cash from Operation

Operating cash profit			24,000
Add :	Decrease in bills receivable	8,000	
	Decrease in prepaid insurance	200	
	Increase in creditors	10,000	
			18,200
			42,200
Less :	Increase in debtors	6,000	
	Increase in prepaid rent	1,000	
			7,000
	Cash from operation		35,200

Problem 5 (Preparation of cash flow statement):
Balance sheets of A and B on 1.1.1990 and 31.12.1990 were as follows :

	1.1.1990 *Rs.*	*31.12.1990* *Rs.*		*1.1.90* *Rs.*	*31.12.90* *Rs.*
Creditors	40,000	44,000	Cash	10,000	7,000
Mrs A's loan	25,000	-	Debtors	30,000	50,000
Loan from bank	40,000	50,000	Stock	35,000	25,000
Capital	1,25,000	1,53,000	Machinery	80,000	55,000
			Land	40,000	50,000
			Building	35,000	60,000
	2,30,000	2,47,000		2,30,000	2,47,000

During the year, a machine costing Rs. 10,000 (accumulated depreciation Rs. 3,000) was sold for Rs. 5,000. The provisions for depreciation against machinery as on 1.1.1990 was Rs. 25,000 and on 31.12.1990 Rs. 40,000. Net profit for the year 1990 amounted to Rs. 45,000. You are required to prepare a cash flow statement. *(Bangalore University, B.B.M., April 1999)*

Solution :

Adjusted P & L A/c

To Depreciation on machinery	18,000	By Balance b/d	Nil
To Loss on sale of machinery	2,000	By Operating profit	65,000
To Balance c/d	45,000		
	65,000		65,000

Statement showing Cash from Operation

Operating profit			65,000
Add :	Decrease in stock	10,000	
	Increase in creditors	4,000	14,000
			79,000
Less :	Increase in debtors		20,000
	Cash from operation		59,000

Machinery A/c

To Balance b/d	1,05,000	By Bank	5,000
		By Loss on sale of machinery	2,000
		By Provision for depreciation	3,000
		By Balance c/d	95,000
	1,05,000		1,05,000

Provision for Depreciation

To Machinery a/c	3,000	By Balance b/d	25,000
To Balance c/d	40,000	By P & L a/c (Balancing figure)	18,000
	43,000		43,000

Cash Flow Statement

Sources		*Uses*	
Cash balance (1.1.1990)	10,000	Purchase of land	10,000
Cash from operation	59,000	Purchase of building	25,000
Loan from bank	10,000	Mrs A's loan paid	25,000
Sale of machinery	5,000	Drawings	17,000
		Cash balance (31-12-1990)	7,000
	84,000		84,000

Problem 6 : Balance sheets of Aneeta Ltd. as on 31.12.1997 and 31.12.1998

	1997	*1998*		*1997*	*1998*
Share capital	2,00,000	3,00,000	Plant & machinery	2,00,000	3,00,000
Share premium	–	10,000	Land & buildings	50,000	1,10,000
8% Debentures	1,00,000	50,000	Investments	10,000	50,000
General reserve	50,000	80,000	Stock	80,000	60,000
P & L a/c	50,000	70,000	Debtors	90,000	80,000
Provision for taxation	30,000	40,000	Cash and bank	70,000	50,000
Proposed dividend	20,000	30,000			
Sundry creditors	50,000	70,000			
	5,00,000	6,50,000		5,00,000	6,50,000

Additional Information

1. Investment costing Rs. 8,000 was sold for Rs. 15,000, the profit being credited to P & L a/c.
2. An interim dividend of Rs. 20,000 was paid during the year.
3. Accumulated depreciation on :

	1997 Rs.	*1998* Rs.
Land & building	30,000	40,000
Plant & machinery	40,000	60,000

4. Depreciation charged during the year :

Land & building	10,000
Plant & machinery	20,000

5. Debentures were redeemed at par
6. Profit and loss a/c (balance) 1997

Profit and loss a/c (balance) 1997	Rs. 50,000
Add : Profit for 1998	40,000
	90,000
Less : Interim dividend	20,000
	70,000

Prepare a cash flow statement. *(Bangalore University, B.Com., October 2000)*

Solution :

Plant & Machinery A/c

To Balance b/d	2,00,000	By Balance c/d	3,00,000
To Accumulated depreciation	40,000	By Accumulated depreciation	60,000
	2,40,000		

To Bank-purchases (Balancing figure)	1,20,000		
	3,60,000		3,60,000

Provision for Depreciation in Plant

To Balance c/d	60,000	By Balance b/d	40,000
		By P & L a/c - Dep. on machinery (Balancing figure)	20,000
	60,000		60,000

Land & Building A/c

To Balance b/d	50,000	By Balance c/d	1,10,000
To Accumulated depreciation	30,000	By Accumulated depreciation	40,000
To Bank-purchases (Balancing figure)	70,000		
	1,50,000		1,50,000

Provision for Depreciation on Land & Building

To Balance c/d	40,000	By Balance b/d	30,000
		By P & L a/c - depreciation	10,000
	40,000		40,000

Investment A/c

To Balance b/d	10,000	By Bank-sale	15,000
To P & L a/c - profit	7,000	By Balance c/d	50,000
To Bank-purchases (Balancing figure)	48,000		
	65,000		65,000

Adjusted P & L A/c

To Provision for depreciation on plant & machinery	20,000	By Balance b/d	50,000
To Provision for depreciation on land & building	10,000	By Profit on sale of investment	7,000
To Interim dividend	20,000	By Operating profit	93,000
To General reserve	30,000		
To Balance c/d	70,000		
	1,50,000		1,50,000

Cash from Operation

Operating Profit		93,000
Add: Decrease in debtors	10,000	
Decrease in stock	20,000	
Increase in creditors	20,000	
Increase in proposed dividend	10,000	
Increase in provision for tax	10,000	
		70,000
Cash from operation		1,63,000

Cash Flow Statement

Cash Balance (1.1.97)	70,000	Purchase of plant & machinery	1,20,000
Cash from operation	1,63,000	Purchase of land & building	70,000
Sale of investment	15,000	Purchase of investment	48,000
Issue of share with premium	1,10,000	Payment of interim dividend	20,000
		Redemption of debentures	50,000
		Closing cash balance	50,000
	3,58,000		3,58,000

Problem 7 : From the following Balance Sheets of Mr. 'X' prepare a cash flow statement for the year 1999 indicating therein separately the cash from operations :

Balance Sheet

	1999	*1998*		*1999*	*1998*
Capital	4,00,000	3,00,000	Fixed assets	4,90,000	5,44,000
Loans	1,20,000	2,60,000	Stock	44,000	30,000
Creditors	30,800	51,200	Debtors	90,000	60,000
Provision for taxation	8,000	20,000	Cash	11,200	15,000
			Bank	40,000	30,000
Bills payable	1,17,200	57,400	Deferred-Revenue expenses	2,800	9,600
Unpaid income tax	2,000	—			
	6,78,000	6,88,600		6,78,000	6,88,600

Other Particulars

1. An item of fixed assets having book value of Rs. 5,000 was sold for Rs. 6,000 during the year 1999.
2. Capital st the end of 1999 was arrived after making adjustment of the newly introduced capital of Rs. 20,000 and drawings of Rs. 50,000.
3. Income-tax assessment for the year 1998 was completed resulting in a gross demand of Rs. 22,000 out of which Rs. 20,000 being undisputed demand was paid.(*University of Mumbai, B.Com., October 1999*)

Solution :

X's Capital A/c

To Drawings	50,000	By Balance b/d	3,00,000
To Balance c/d	4,00,000	By Cash	20,000
		By P & L a/c -profit for the year (Balancing figure)	1,30,000
	4,50,000		4,50,000

Fixed Assets a/c

To Balance b/d	5,44,000	By Depreciation -P & L a/c	49,000
		By Bank-sale of fixed assets	5,000
		By Balance c/d	4,90,000
	5,44,000		5,44,000

Provision for Tax

To Cash	20,000	By Balance b/d	20,000
To Unpaid income tax	2,000	By P & L a/c (Balancing figure)	10,000
To Balance c/d	8,000		
	30,000		30,000

Adjusted P & L A/c

To Provision for tax	10,000	By Profit on sale of fixed assets	1,000
To Deferred revenue expenses written off	6,800	By Operating profit	1,94,800
To Depreciation on fixed assets	49,000		
To Net profit transfered to capital a/c	1,30,000		
	1,95,800		1,95,800

Statement of Cash from Operation

Operating profit		1,94,800
Add : Increase in Bills payable		59,800
		2,54,600
Less : Increase in stock	14,000	
Increase in debtors	30,000	
Decrease in creditors	29,400	
		64,400
Cash from operation		1,90,200

Cash Flow Statement

Opening balance of			Loans repaid		1,40,000
Cash	15,000		Tax amount of 1998 paid		20,000
Bank	30,000				
		45,000	X's Drawings		50,000
Capital Introduced		20,000	Closing balance		
Sale of fixed assets		6,000	Cash	11,200	
Cash from operation		1,90,200	Bank	40,000	
					51,200
		2,61,200			2,61,200

Problem 8 : Balance sheets of MN Rao as on 1-1-1993 and 31-12-1993 was as follows ;

	1-1-1993 *(Rs.)*	*31-12-1993* *(Rs.)*
Liabilities		
Capital	1,25,000	1,53,000
Creditors	1,40,000	1,44,000
Bank loan	65,000	50,000
Bills payable	20,000	30,000
	3,50,000	3,77,000
Assets		
Cash	20,000	17,000
Debtors	30,000	80,000
Stock	45,000	35,000
Machinery	80,000	65,000
Land	90,000	80,000
Buildings	65,000	70,000
Goodwill	20,000	30,000
	3,50,000	3,77,000

During the year, a machine costing Rs. 12,000 (accumulated depreciation Rs. 4,000) was sold for Rs. 7,000. Balance of provision for depreciation against machinery as on 1.1.93 was Rs. 35,000 and on 31.12.93 Rs. 50,000.

Prepare cash flow statement. Net profit for the year 1993 Rs. 55,000.

(*Sri Venkateshwara University, B.Com., October 1999*)

Solution :

Capital A/c

	Rs.		Rs.
To Drawings (Balancing figure)	27,000	By Balance b/d	1,25,000
To Balance c/d	1,53,000	By P & L a/c –Net profit	55,000
	1,80,000		1,80,000

Bank Loan

	Rs.		Rs.
To Bank (Balancing figure)	15,000	By Balance b/d	65,000
To Balance c/d	50,000		
	65,000		65,000

Machinery A/c

	Rs.		Rs.
To Balance b/d (80,000+35,000)	1,15,000	By Provision for depreciation	4,000
To Bank (Balancing figure)	12,000	By Bank-sale	7,000
		By P & L a/c - loss on sale	1,000
		By Balance c/d (65,000+50,000)	1,15,000
	1,27,000		1,27,000

Provision for Depreciation on Machinery A/c

	Rs.		Rs.
To Machinery a/c	4,000	By Balance b/d	35,000
To Balance c/d	50,000	By P & L A/c (Balancing figure)	19,000
	54,000		54,000

Land A/c

	Rs.		Rs.
To Balance b/d	90,000	By Bank (Balancing figure)	10,000
		By Balance c/d	80,000
	90,000		90,000

Buildings A/c

	Rs.		Rs.
To Balance b/d	65,000	By Balance c/d	70,000
To Bank (Balancing figure)	5,000		
	70,000		70,000

Goodwill A/c

	Rs.		Rs.
To Balance b/d	20,000	By Balance c/d	30,000
To P & L a/c (Balancing figure)	10,000		
	30,000		30,000

Adj. P & L A/c

To Loss on sale of machinery	1,000	By Balance b/d	Nil
To Depreciation on machinery	19,000	By Appreciation in goodwill	10,000
To Balance c/d	55,000	By Operating profit	65,000
	75,000		75,000

Statement showing Cash from Operation

Operating profit		65,000
Add : Increase in creditors	4,000	
Increase in bills payable	10,000	
Decrease in stock	1,000	
		24,000
		89,000
Less : Increase in debtors		50,000
Cash from operation		39,000

Cash flow Statement

Balance of cash on 1.1.93	20,000	Drawings	27,000
Sale of land	10,000	Bank loan repaid	15,000
Sale of machinery	7,000	Building purchased	5,000
Cash from operation	39,000	Machinery purchased	12,000
		Balance of cash on 31.3.93	17,000
	76,000		76,000

Problem 9 : Umesh Ltd. has provided the following Balance sheets and requests you to prepare cash flow statement :

	1997	*1998*
Liabilities :		
Share capital	3,00,000	3,75,000
Reserve fund	75,000	90,000
Profit & loss a/c	45,000	46,000
Mortgage loan	1,00,000	–
Creditors	2,25,000	2,10,000
Provision for taxation	45,000	52,500
	7,90,000	7,73,500
Assets		
Land and building	3,00,000	2,85,000
Plant & machinery	2,25,000	2,53,500
Stock	1,50,000	1,20,000
Debtors	1,14,000	96,000
Cash	1,000	1,500
Bank	–	10,000
Goodwill	–	7,500
	7,90,000	7,73,500

Additional Information

1. Dividend paid Rs. 32,000.
2. Assets of another company were purchased for a consideration of Rs. 75,000 payable in shares. The following assets were purchased, stock, Rs. 30,000, machinery Rs. 37,500.

3. Machinery was further purchased for Rs. 12,000.
4. Loss on sale of machinery Rs. 300 was written off to reserve fund.
5. Income tax provided during the year Rs. 50,000. (*Bangalore University, B.Com., April 2001*)

Solution :

Machinery A/c

To Balance b/d	2,25,000	By General reserve	300
To Share capital	37,500	By Bank-sales (Balancing figure)	20,700
To Bank-purchases	12,000	By Balance c/d	2,53,500
	2,74,500		2,74,500

General Reserve

To Machinery	300	By Balance b/d	75,000
To Balance c/d	90,000	By P & L a/c - transfer	15,300
	90,300		90,300

Provision for Tax

To Bank-Tax paid (Balancing figure)	42,500	By Balance b/d	45,000
To Balance c/d	52,500	By P & L a/c	50,000
	95,000		95,000

Share Capital A/c

To Balance c/d	3,75,000	To Balance b/d	3,00,000
		To Machinery –Shares issued	37,500
		By Stock –shares issued	30,000
		By Goodwill	7,500
	3,75,000		3,75,000

Adj. P & L A/c

To Dividend	32,000	By Balance b/d	45,000
To Depreciation on building	15,000	By Operating profit	1,13,300
To Provision for tax	50,000		
To General reserve Transfer	15,300		
To Balance c/d	46,000		
	1,58,300		1,58,300

Statement showing Cash from Operation

Operating profit	1,13,300
Add : Decrease in stock (1,50,000+30,000–1,20,000)	60,000
Add : Decrease in debtors	18,000
	1.91,300
Less : Decrease in creditors	15,000
Cash from operation	1,76,300

Cash Flow Statement

Opening balance of cash	1,000	Payment of mortgage loan		1,00,000
Sale of machinery	20,700	Purchase of machinery		12,000
Cash from operation	1,76,300			
		Payment of tax		42,500
		Payment of dividend		32,000
		Closing Balance :		
		Cash	1500	
		Bank	10,000	
				11,500
	1,98,000			1,98,000

Problem 10 : The financial position of Anu and Parmanu as on 1st July, 1997 and 30th June, 1998 was as follows :

	1.7.1997	*30.6.1998*
Assets :		
Cash	4,000	3,600
Debtors	35,000	38,400
Stock	25,000	22,000
Land	20,000	30,000
Building	50,000	55,000
Machinery	80,000	86,000
	2,14,000	2,35,000
Liabilities		
Mrs Anu's loan	–	20,000
Bank loan	30,000	25,000
Current liabilities	36,000	41,000
Capital accounts	1,48,000	1,49,000
	2,14,000	2,35,000

Other Information

1. Drawings during the year Rs. 26,000.
2. Provision for depreciation :

	1.7.1997	*30.6.1998*
Machinery	27,000	36,000
Building	8,000	10,000

Prepare cash flow statement showing cash from operations separately for the year ended 30th June, 1998.

(University of Mumbai, B.Com., April 1999)

Solution :

Machinery A/c (At Cost)

To Balance b/d (80,000+27,000)	1,07,000	By Balance c/d (86,000+36,000)	1,22,000
To Cash (Balancing figure)	15,000		
	1,22,000		1,22,000

Building A/c (At Cost)

To Balance b/d (50,000+8,000)	58,000	By Balance c/d (55,000+10,000)	65,000
To Cash (Balancing figure)	7,000		
	65,000		65,000

Provision for Taxation

To Drawings	26,000	By Balance b/d	1,48,000
To Balance c/d	1,49,000	By P & L a/c (Balancing figure)	27,000
	1,75,000		1,75,000

Capital A/c

To Drawings	26,000	By Balance b/d	1,48,000
To Balance c/d	1,49,000	By P & L a/c (Balancing figure)	27,000
	1,75,000		1,75,000

Adj. P & L A/c

To Depreciation :- Machinary	9,000	By Balance b/d	Nil
Building	2,000	By Operating profit	38,000
To Balance c/d	27,000		
	38,000		38,000

Statement showing Cash from Operation

Operating profit		38,000
Add : Increase in current liability	5,000	
Decrease in stock	3,000	
		8,000
Less : Increase in debtors		46,000
		3,400
Cash from operation		42,600

Cash Flow Statement

Opening Balance of cash	4,000	Repayment of bank loan	5,000
Loan from Mrs. Anu	20,000	Purchase of land	10,000
Cash from operation	42,600	Purchase of building	7,000
		Purchase of machinery	15,000
		Drawings	26,000
		Closing balance of cash	3,600
	66,600		66,600

Problem 11 : B Ltd., supplies you the following balance sheets as on December:

	1988	*1989*
Liabilities		
Share capital	70,000	74,000
Bonds	12,000	6,000
Sundry creditors	10,360	11,840
Provision for doubtful debts	700	800
Reserves and surplus	10,040	10,560
	1,03,100	1,03,200

Assets :		
Bank balance	9,000	7,800
Debtors	14,900	17,700
Inventories	49,200	42,700
Land	20,000	30,000
Goodwill	10,000	5,000
	1,03,100	1,03,200

Following additional information is also supplied to you :

(*a*) Dividend amounted to Rs. 3,500 were paid during the year.

(*b*) Land was purchased for Rs. 10,000.

(*c*) Rs. 5,000 were written off on goodwill during the year.

(*d*) Bonds of Rs. 6,000 were paid during the course of the year.

You are required to prepare a cash flow statement. (*Sri Venkateshwara University, B.Com., April 1999*)

Solution :

Land A/c

To Balance b/d	20,000	By Balance c/d	30,000
To Cash	10,000		
	30,000		30,000

Goodwill A/c

To Balance b/d	10,000	By P & L A/c	5,000
		By Balance c/d	5,000
	10,000		10,000

Share Capital A/c

To Balance c/d	74,000	By Balance b/d	70,000
		By Cash	4,000
	74,000		74,000

Bonds A/c

To Cash	6,000	By Balance b/d	12,000
To Balance c/d	6,000		
	12,000		12,000

Adjusted P & L A/c

To Dividend	3,500	By Reserve & surplus —Opening Balance	10,040
To Goodwill written off	5,000	By Operating profit	9,120
To Provision for D.D.	100		
To Reserves & surplus —Closing balance	10,560		
	19,160		19,160

Statement of Cash from Operation

Operating profit		9,120
Add : Decrease in stock	6,500	
Increase in creditors	1,480	7,980
		17,100
Less : Increase in debtors		2,800
Cash from operation		14,300

Cash Flow Statement

Opening Bank balance	9,000	Purchase of land	10,000
Issue of shares	4,000	Payment of Bonds	6,000
Cash from operation	14,300	Dividend paid	3,500
		Closing bank balance	7,800
	27,300		27,300

Problem 12 : From the following Balance Sheet of 'X' Company Ltd. for the year ending 31st December 1997 and 31st December, 1998, prepare cash flow statment for 1998.

	1997	*1998*		*1997*	*1998*
Equity share capital	2,00,000	2,50,000	Goodwill	50,000	45,000
9% Preference share capital	60,000	40,000	Land & building	80,000	55,000
			Plant & machinery	90,000	1,60,000
Capital reserve	–	10,000	Furniture	12,000	10,000
General reserve	15,000	20,000	Trade Investment	10,000	45,000
P & L a/c	25,000	40,000	Sundry debtors	32,000	25,000
Sundry creditors	28,000	52,000	Stock	64,000	45,000
Bills payable	8,000	10,000	Bills Receivable	10,000	35,000
O/s expenses	4,000	3,000	Cash in hand	10,000	25,000
Proposed dividend	18,000	25,000	Cash at Bank	15,000	26,000
Provision for taxation	20,000	24,000	Preliminary expenses	5,000	3,000
	3,78,000	4,74,000		3,78,000	4,74,000

Additional Information

1. An interim dividend of Rs. 10,000 has been paid in 1998.
2. Rs. 2,000 has been received as dividend on trade investment.
3. A piece of land has been sold out in 1998 and the remaining has been revalued. Profit on sale and revaluation being transferred to capital reserve.
4. Depreciation on plant and machinery has been written off Rs. 15,000 in 1998 and no depreciation has been charged on land and building.
5. A machinery was sold for Rs. 18,000 (W.D.V. being Rs. 20,000) and no furniture has been sold during the year. *(Bangalore University, B.Com., April 2000)*

Solution :

Land & Building A/c

To Balance b/d	80,000	By Bank-sales (Balancing figure)	35,000
To Capital reserve (profit on sale)	10,000	By Balance c/d	55,000
	90,000		90,000

Plant A/c

To Balance b/d	90,000	By P & L a/c —Depreciation	15,000
To Bank-purchases (Balancing figure)	1,05,00	By P & L a/c —Loss on sale	2,000
		By Bank a/c sales	18,000
		By Balance c/d	1,60,000
	1,95,000		1,95,000

Investments

To Balance b/d	10,000	By Balance c/d	47,000
To Dividend	2,000		
To Bank-purchases (Balancing figure)	35,000		
	47,000		47,000

Adjusted P & L A/c

To Plant-Depreciation	15,000	By Balance b/d	25,000
To General reserve (20,000–15,000)	5,000	By Dividend received	2,000
To Goodwill written off	5,000	By Operating	86,000
To Preliminary expenses written off	2,000		
To Interim dividend	10,000		
To Provision for tax	4,000		
To O/s expenses	3,000		
To Depreciation on furniture	2,000		
To Loss on sale of plant	2,000		
To Proposed dividend	25,000		
To Balance c/d	40,000		
	1,13,000		1,13,000

Statement of Cash from Operation

Operating profit		86,000
Add : Decrease in debtors	7,000	
Decrease in stock	19,000	
Increase in creditors	24,000	
Increase in B.P	2,000	
		52,000
		1,38,000
Less : Increase in B.R		25,000
Cash from operation		1,13,000

Cash Flow Statement

Opening cash and Bank Balance (10,000+15,000)	25,000	Purchase of plant	1,05,000
Issue of shares	50,000	Purchase of Investment	35,000
Sale of land	35,000	Redemption of pref shares	20,000
Sale of Plant	18,000	Interim dividend	10,000
Dividend received	2,000	Proposed dividend	18,000
Cash from operation	1,13,000	Payment of liability for expenses	4,000
		Closing cash and bank balance (25,000+26,000)	51,000
	2,43,000		2,43,000

Problem 13 : Following are the balance sheets of Young India Ltd.:

	1998	*1997*		*1998*	*1997*
Share capital	7,00,000	6,00,000	Fixed assets	6,50,000	4,00,000
General reserve	2,00,000	1,50,000	Debtors	3,50,000	2,00,000

P & L A/c	2,00,000	1,00,000	Stock	2,50,000	1,50,000
14% Debentures issued for purchase of fixed assets	2,00,000	Nil	Cash	1,30,000	1,00,000
Proposed dividend	80,000	70,000	Underwriting Commission	Nil	70,000
	13,80,000	9,20,000		13,80,000	9,20,000

Assuming the depreciation for the year to be Rs. 50,000 and interim dividend paid during the year to be 5% on opening capital. Prepare cash flow statement indicating therein separately cash from operations.

(*University of Mumbai, B.Com., October 1998*)

Solution :

Fixed Assets A/c

To Balance b/d	4,00,000	By Depreciation	50,000
To 14% Debentures	2,00,000	By Balance c/d	6,50,000
To Cash (Balancing figure)	1,00,000		
	7,00,000		7,00,000

Adjusted P & L A/c

To Interim dividend	30,000	By Balance b/d	1,00,000
To Proposed dividend	80,000	By Operating profit	3,80,000
To Depreciation on fixed assets	50,000		
To Transfer to general reserve	50,000		
To Underwriting commission	70,000		
To Balance c/d	2,00,000		
	4,80,000		4,80,000

Statement of Cash from Operation

Operating profit		3,80,000
Less : Increase in debtors	1,50,000	
Increase in stock	1,00,000	
		2,50,000
Cash from operation		1,30,000

Cash Flow Statement

Opening cash balance	1,00,000	Interim dividend	30,000
Issue of equity shares	1,00,000	Dividend paid	70,000
Cash from operation	1,30,000	Fixed assets purchased	1,00,000
		Closing cash Balance	1,30,000
	3,30,000		3,30,000

Problem 14 : Ayodhya Limited has provided the following balance sheets as on 31.3.95 and 31.3.96:

	1995	*1996*		*1995*	*1996*
Share capital	17,00,000	18,35,000	Building	8,00,000	10,00,000
Reserves	40,000	83,700	Furniture	5,000	6,000
P & L a/c	1,00,000	1,30,000	Machinery	2,50,000	3,70,000
Creditors	1,00,000	95,000	Book debts	1,00,000	45,000
Provision for dividend	70,000	50,000	B.R.	8,000	9,000
Bank OD	8,000	18,000	Inventories	4,00,000	3,43,700
Bills payable	14,000	13,000	Investments	1,64,000	1,70,000

Long-term loan	10,000	70,000	Patents	3,00,000	3,43,700
			Cash	2,000	2,200
			Preliminary expenses	10,000	2,000
			Prepaid insurance	3,000	3,100
	20,42,000	22,94,700		20,42,000	22,94,700

Additional Information

(*a*) Depreciation charged on building at 3% of cost of 9,00,000; on machinery 8% of cost of Rs. 4,00,000; on furniture at 5% of cost of Rs. 8,000.

(*b*) Investments were purchased and interest of Rs. 3,000 was received which was used in writing down the book value of investments.

(*c*) The declared dividend for 1995 was paid and interim dividend for Rs. 20,000 paid out of P & L A/c.

(Bangalore University, B.Com., April 1999)

Solution :

(1) Calculation of Depreciation

(*a*) on Buildings $= 9{,}00{,}000 \times \frac{3}{100} = 27{,}000$

(*b*) on Machinery $= 4{,}00{,}000 \times \frac{8}{100} = 32{,}000$

(*c*) on Furniture $= 8{,}000 \times \frac{5}{100} = 400$

(2) Share Capital A/c

To Closing balance	18,35,000	By Balance b/d	17,00,000
		By Bank-issue of shares	1,35,000
	18,35,000		18,35,000

(3) Reserve A/c

To Balance c/d	83,700	By Balance b/d	40,000
		By P & L a/c transfer	43,700
	83,700		83,700

(4) Provision for dividends

(*a*) Balance of 1995 : It is paid in 1996, so it is an item of cash outflow.

(*b*) Balance of 1996 : Opening balance is completely utilised to pay dividend. So the closing balance of Rs. 50,000 is an item of appropriation.

(*c*) Interim dividend paid for 1996 :- It is an item of appropriation and also cash flow.

Loan A/c

To Balance c/d	70,000	By Balance b/d	10,000
		By Bank-loan raised	60,000
	70,000		70,000

Building A/c

To Balance b/d	8,00,000	By Depreciation	27,000
To Bank-purchases (Balancing figure)	2,27,000	By Balance c/d	10,00,000
	10,27,000		10,27,000

Machinery A/c

To Balance b/d	2,50,000	By Depreciation		32,000
To Bank-purchases	1,52,000	By Balance c/d		3,70,000
	4,02,000			4,02,000

Furniture A/c

To Balance b/d	5,000	By Depreciation	400
To Bank-purchases	1,400	By Balance c/d	6,000
	6,400		6,400

Investment A/c

To Balance b/d	1,64,000	By Bank-Interest received credited	3,000
To Bank-purchases	9,000	By Balance c/d	1,70,000
	1,73,000		1,73,000

Patents A/c

To Balance b/d	3,00,000	By Balance c/d	3,43,700
To Bank-purchases	43,700		
	3,43,700		3,43,700

Preliminary Expenses

To Balance b/d	10,000	By P & L a/c wirtten off	8,000
		By Balance c/d	2,000
	10,000		10,000

Adjusted P & L A/c

To Depreciation on building	27,000	By Balance b/d	1,00,000
To Depreciation on machinery	32,000	By Operating profit	2,14,100
To Depreciation on fixtures	400		
To Preliminary expenses written off	8,000		
To Transfer to reserve	43,700		
To Provision for dividends	50,000		
To Interim dividend	20,000		
To Prepaid expenses at the beginning of the year	3,000		
To Balance c/d	1,30,000		
	3,14,100		3,14,100

Statement of cash from Operation

Operating profit		2,14,100
Add : Decrease in debtors	55,000	
Decrease in stock	56,300	
		1,11,300
		3,25,400

Less : Increase in bills receivables	1,000	
Decrease in creditors	5,000	
Decrease in bills payable	1,000	
		7,000
Cash from operation		3,18,400

Cash Flow Statement

Opening balance :		Dividend paid for 1995	70,000
Cash	2,000	Interim dividend paid	20,000
Bank overdraft	(–) 8,000	Purchase of buildings	2,27,000
Issue of shares	1,35,000	Purchase of machinery	1,52,000
Long-term loan	60,000	Puchase of furniture	1,400
Cash from operation	3,18,400	Purchase of investment	9,000
Interest on Investment	3,000	Purchase of patent	43,700
		Prepaid expenses (Paid in the current year)	3,100
		Closing Balance:	
		Cash	2,200
		Bank overdraft (–)	18,000
	5,10,400		5,10,400

Problem 15 : The following are the summarised balance sheets of a company as on 31st December, 1997 and 1998

Liabilities	*1997*	*1998*
Share capital	2,00,000	2,50,000
General reserve	50,000	60,000
Profit & loss A/c	30,500	30,600
Bank loan (long-term)	70,000	–
Sundry creditors	1,50,000	1,35,200
Provision for taxation	30,000	35,000
	5,30,500	5,10,800
Assets :		
Land and Buildings	2,00,000	1,90,000
Machinery	1,50,000	1,69,000
Stock	1,00,000	74,000
Sundry debtors	80,000	64,200
Cash	500	600
Bank	–	8,000
Goodwill	–	5,000
	5,30,500	5,10,800

Additional Information

1. During the year ended 31st December, 1998 dividend of Rs. 23,000 was paid.
2. Assets of another company were purchased for a consideration of Rs. 50,000 payable in shares. The following assets were purchased stock Rs. 20,000, machinery Rs. 25,000.
3. Machinery was further purchased for Rs. 8,000.
4. Depreciation written off on machinery Rs. 12,000.
5. Income tax provided during the year Rs. 33,000.
6. Loss on sale of machinery Rs. 200 was written off to general reserve.

You are required to prepare cash flow statement. *(Sri Venkateshwara University, B.Com., April 1998)*

Solution :

Machinery A/c

To Balance b/d	1,50,000	By Depreciation	12,000
To Cash	8,000	By Sale of machinery	
To Vendor company	25,000	–Cash	1,800
		(Balancing figure)	
		By Loss on sale of machinery	200
		By Balance c/d	1,69,000
	1,83,000		1,83,000

Provision for Taxation

To Cash	28,000	By Balance b/d	30,000
(Balancing figure)		By P & L a/c	33,000
To Balance c/d	35,000		
	63,000		63,000

Purchase of Assets from another company

Purchase consideration payable in shares		50,000
Less : Assets purchased		
Stock	20,000	
Machinery	25,000	
		45,000
Goodwill (Balancing figure)		5,000

Adjusted P & L A/c

To Transfer to general reserve	10,000	By Balance b/d	30,500
To Provision for taxation	33,000	By Operating profit	88,300
To Dividend	23,000		
To Depreciation on machinery	12,000		
To Depreciation on land & building	10,000		
To Loss on sale of machinery	200		
To Balance c/d	30,600		
	1,18,800		1,18,800

Cash from Operation

Operating profit		88,300
Add : Decrease in debtors	15,800	
Decrease in stock	46,000	
		61,800
		1,05,100
Less : Decrease in creditors	14,800	14,800
Cash from operation		1,35,300

Cash Flow Statement

Balance on 1.1.98	500	Bank loan paid	70,000
Cash	.	Income tax paid	28,000
Cash from operation	1,35,300	Dividend paid	23,000
Sale of machinery	1,800	Machinery purchased	8,000
		closing balance on 31.12.98	
		Cash	600
		Bank	8,000
	1,37,600		1,37,600

Problem 16 : Following are the comparative Balance Sheet of Company of two different dates :

Balance Sheet

	1995	*1996*		*1995*	*1996*
Share capital	30,000	40,000	Plant & machinery	40,000	45,000
Share premium	–	1,000	*Less* : Depreciation	14,000	15,000
P & L a/c	10,000	10,000	Net	26,000	30,000
Profit for the year	–	20,000	Property	20,000	25,000
Debentures	15,000	10,000	Shares in subsidiary co.	–	1,500
Profit on Redemption of debentures	–	200	Stock	14,000	15,000
			Debtors	10,000	15,000
Creditors	14,000	11,000	Bank balance	3,500	15,700
Provision for taxation	5,000	10,000			
Proposed dividend	1,500	2,000			
	75,500	1,04,200		75,500	1,04,200

Additional Information

1. Plant costing Rs. 5,000, accumulated depreciation thereon being Rs. 3,000 was sold for Rs. 1,000. The loss on sale has been charged to P & L a/c.
2. Taxation paid for the year amounts to Rs. 6,000.
3. An interim dividend of Rs. 1,000 has been paid during the year 1996. You are required to prepare a cash flow statement from the above information. Also ascertain cash from operation.

(*University of Mumbai, B.Com., April 1998*)

Solution :

Plant & Machinery A/c

To Balance b/d	40,000	By Plant sold	5,000
To Cash	10,000	–Cash	
		By Balance c/d	45,000
	50,000		50,000

Provision for depreciation A/c

To P & L a/c	3,000	By Balance b/d	14,000
To Balance c/d	15,000	By P & L a/c	4,000
	18,000		18,000

Provision for Tax A/c

To Cash	6,000	By Balance b/d	5,000
To Balance c/d	10,000	By P & L a/c	11,000
	16,000		16,000

Proposed Dividend A/c

To Cash	1,500	By Balance b/d	1,500
To Balance c/d	2,000	By P & L a/c	2,000
	3,500		3,500

Adjusted P & L A/c

To Loss on sale of plant & machinery		1,000	By Balance b/d	10,000
To Depreciation on		4,000	By Operating profit	39,000
To Proposed dividend		2,000		
To Provision for tax		11,000		
To Interim dividend paid		1,000		
To Profit for the year	20,000			
To Balance c/d	10,000			
		30,000		
		49,000		49,000

Statement of Cash from Operation

Operating profit		30,000
Less : Increase in loan to subsidiary Company	1,500	
Increase in stock	1,000	
Increase in debtors	5,000	
Decrease in creditors	3,000	
		10,500
Cash from operation		28,500

Cash Flow Statement

Opening Balance of cash	3,500	Purchase of property	5,000
Cash from operation	28,500	Tax paid for 1995	6,000
Sale of plant & machinery	1,000	Interim dividend paid	1,000
Issue of shares at premium	11,000	Plant & machinery purchased	10,000
		Proposed dividend paid	1,500
		Debentures redeemed	4,800
		Closing Balance of bank	15,700
	44,000		44,000

Problem 17 : From the following balance sheets of Exe. Ltd. make out the statement of sources and uses of cash :

Liabilities	*1996*	*1997*
Equity share capital	3,00,000	4,00,000
8% Redeemable preference Share capital	1,50,000	1,00,000
General reserve	40,000	70,000
Profit & loss a/c	30,000	48,000
Proposed dividend	42,000	50,000
Creditors	55,000	83,000
Bills payable	20,000	16,000
Provision for taxation	40,000	50,000
	6,77,000	8,17,000

Assets		
Goodwill	1,15,000	90,000
Land & buildings	2,00,000	1,70,000
Plant	80,000	2,00,000
Debtors	1,60,000	2,00,000
Stock	77,000	1,09,000
Bills receivable	20,000	30,000
Cash at Bank	10,000	8,000
Cash in hand	15,000	10,000
	6,77,000	8,17,000

Additional Information

(*a*) Depreciation of Rs. 10,000 and Rs. 20,000 have been charged on plant and land and buildings respectively in 1997.

(*b*) An interim dividend of Rs. 20,000 has been paid in 1997.

(*c*) Rs. 35,000 Income-tax was paid during the year 1997.

(*Sri Venkateshwara University, B.Com., October 1998*)

Solution :

Equity Share Capital A/

	Rs.		Rs.
To Balance c/d	4,00,000	By Balance b/d	3,00,000
		By Cash (Balancing figure)	1,00,000
	4,00,000		4,00,000

8% Redeemable Pref Share Capital

	Rs.		Rs.
To Cash (Balancing figure)	50,000	By Balance b/d	1,50,000
To Balance c/d	1,00,000		
	1,50,000		1,50,000

General Reserve A/c

	Rs.		Rs.
To Balance c/d	70,000	By Balance b/d	40,000
		By P & L a/c (Balancing figure)	30,000
	70,000		70,000

Provision for Taxation A/c

	Rs.		Rs.
To Cash	35,000	By Balance b/d	40,000
To Balance c/d	50,000	By P & L a/c (Balancing figure)	45,000
	85,000		85,000

Goodwill A/c

	Rs.		Rs.
To Balance b/d	1,15,000	By P & L a/c (Balancing figure)	25,000
		By Balance c/d	90,000
	1,15,000		1,15,000

Land & Building A/c

To Balance b/d	2,00,000	By P & L a/c –Depreciation	20,000
		By Cash-sales (Balancing figure)	10,000
		By Balance c/d	1,70,000
	2,00,000		2,00,000

Plant & Machinery A/c

To Balance b/d	80,000	By P & L a/c –Depreciation	10,000
To Cash (Balancing figure)	1,30,000	By Balance c/d	2,00,000
	2,10,000		2,10,000

Adjusted P & L A/c

To General reserve	30,000	By Balance b/d	30,000
To Proposed dividend	50,000	By Operating profit	2,18,000
To Interim dividend	20,000		
To Provision for tax	45,000		
To Depreciation on plant & building	30,000		
To Goodwill written off	25,000		
To Balance c/d	48,000		
	2,48,000		2,48,000

Statement of Cash from Operation

Operating profit			2,18,000
Add:	Increase in creditors		28,000
			2,46,000
Less:	Increase in debtors	40,000	
	Increase in stock	32,000	
	Increase in B.R.	10,000	
	Decrease in B.P	4,000	
	Cash from operation		86,000
			1,60,000

Cash Flow Statement

Cash & Bank balance (31.12.96)	25,000	Redemption of 8% pref shares	50,000
Issue of equity shares	1,00,000	Proposed dividend of 1986 paid	42,000
Sale of building	10,000	Income tax paid	35,000
Cash from operation	1,60,000	Plant purchased	1,30,000
		Interim dividend paid	20,000
		Closing cash & bank balance	18,000
	2,95,000		2,95,000

Problem 18 : Following are balance sheets of X Co. for 1996 and 1997 :

Liabilities	*1996*	*1997*
Shareholders fund	60,000	70,000
Long-term loan	–	15,000
Outstanding salaries	2,000	2,000
Provision for tax	3,000	5,000
Creditors	5,000	8,000
Bills payable	20,000	–
	90,000	1,00,000
Assets		
Buildings	50,000	55,000
Other fixed assets	8,000	5,000
Investments	5,000	7,000
Stock	12,000	15,000
Debtors	10,000	15,000
Cash	5,000	3,000
	90,000	1,00,000

Profit & loss a/c for the year ending 31.12.97		
Net Sales		50,000
Expenses :		
Cost of goods sold	25,000	
Administration and selling expenses	5,000	
Depreciation on building	5,000	
Interest	1,000	
		36,000
		14,000
Provision for tax (50%)		7,000
		7,000
Profit & loss a/c on 1.1.97		40,000
		47,000
Dividend paid		3,000
Profit & loss a/c on 31.12.97		44,000

Prepare Cash Flow Statement (*Bangalore University, B.Com., April 1998*)

Solution :

Buildings A/c

To Balance b/d	50,000	By P & L a/c depreciation	5,000
To Cash-purchases	10,000	By Balance c/d	55,000
	60,000		60,000

Provision for tax

To Cash-tax paid	5,000	By Balance b/d	3,000
To Balance c/d	5,000	By P & L a/c	7,000
	10,000		10,000

Adjusted P & L A/c

To Depreciation on building	5,000	By Balance b/d	40,000
To Provision for tax	7,000	By Operating profit	18,000
To O/s expenses	2,000		
To Balance c/d	44,000		
	58,000		58,000

Cash from Operation

Operating profit		18,000
Add : Increase in creditors		3,000
		21,000
Less : Increase in Debtors	5,000	
Increase in stock	3,000	
Decrease in B.P	20,000	
		28,000
Cash lost in operation		7,000

Cash Flow Statement

Opening cash balance	5,000	Tax paid	5,000
Issue of share capital	10,000	Purchase of building	10,000
Long-term loan	15,000	Interest paid	1,000
Sale of fixed assets	3,000	Dividend paid	3,000
		O/s expenses paid	2,000
		Purchase of investment	2,000
		Cash lost in operation	7,000
		Closing cash balance	3,000
	33,000		33,000

AS-3* (REVISED) CASH FLOW STATEMENTS

The following is the text of the revised Accounting Standard (AS 3), Cash Flow Statements, issued by the Council of the Institute of Chartered Accountants of India. This Standard supersedes Accounting Standard (AS 3), Changes In Financial Position, issued in June, 1981.

In the initial years, this Accounting Standard (AS) will be recommendatory in character. During this period, this standard is recommended for use by companies listed on a recognised stock exchange and other commercial, industrial and business enterprises in the public and private sectors.

Objective

Information about the cash flows of an enterprise is useful in providing users of financial statements with a basis to assess the ability of the enterprise to generate cash and cash equivalents and the needs of the enterprise to utilise those cash flows. The economic decisions that are taken by users require an evaluation of the ability of an enterprise to generate cash and cash equivalents and the timing and certainty of their generation.

* Revised in March, 1999

The Statement deals with the provision of information about the historical changes in cash and cash equivalents of an enterprise by means of a cash flow statement which classifies cash flows during the period from operating, investing and financing activities.

Scope

1. ***An enterprise should prepare a cash flow statement and should present it for each period for which financial statements are presented.***
2. Users of an enterprise's financial statements are interested in how the enterprise generates and uses cash and cash equivalents. This is the case regardless of the nature of the enterprise's activities and irrespective of whether cash can be viewed as the product of the enterprise, as may be the case with financial enterprise. Enterprises need cash for essentially the same reasons, however different their principal revenue-producing activities might be. They need cash to conduct their operations, to pay their obligations, and to provide returns to their investors.

Benefits of Cash Flow Information

3. A cash flow statement, when used in conjunction with the other financial statements, provides information that enables users to evaluate the changes in net assets of an enterprise, its financial structure (including its liquidity and solvency), and its ability to affect the amounts and timing of cash flows in order to adapt to changing circumstances and opportunities. Cash flow information is useful in assessing the ability of the enterprise to generate cash and cash equivalents and enables users to develop models to assess and compare the present value of the future cash flows of different enterprises. It also enhances the comparability of the reporting of operating performance by different enterprises because it eliminates the effects of using different accounting treatments for the same transactions and events.
4. Historical cash flow information is often used as an indicator of the amount, timing and certainty of future cash flows. It is also useful in checking the accuracy of past assessments of future cash flows and in examining the relationship between profitability and net cash flow and the impact of changing prices.

Definitions

5. The following terms are used in this Statement with the meanings specified :

   Cash comprises cash on hand and demand deposits with banks.

   Cash equivalents are short-term, highly liquid investments that are readily convertible into known amounts of cash and which are subject to an insignificant risk of changes in value.

   Cash flows are inflows and outflows of cash and cash equivalents.

   Operating activities are the principal revenue-producing activities of the enterprise an other activities that are not investing or financing activities.

   Investing activities are the acquisition and disposal of long-term assets and other investments not included in cash equivalents.

   Financing activities are activities that result in changes in the size and composition of the owners' capital (including preference share capital in the case of a company) and borrowings of the enterprise.)

Cash and Cash Equivalents

6. Cash equivalents are held for the purpose of meeting short-term cash commitments rather than for investment or other purposes. For an investment to qualify as a cash equivalent, it must be readily convertible to a known amount of cash and be subject to an insignificant risk of changes in value. Therefore, an investment normally qualifies as a cash equivalent only when it has a short maturity of, say, three months or less from the date of acquisition. Investments in shares are excluded from cash equivalents unless they are, in substance, cash equivalents; for example, preference shares of a company acquired shortly before their specified redemption date (provided there is only an insignificant risk of failure of the company to repay the amount at maturity).
7. Cash flows exclude movements between items that constitute cash or cash equivalents because these components are part of the cash management of an enterprise rather than part of its operating, investing and financing activities. Cash management includes the investment of excess cash in cash equivalents.

Presentation of a Cash Flow Statement

8. ***The cash flow statement should report cash flows during the period classified by operating, investing and financing activities.***
9. An enterprise presents its cash flows from operating, investing and financing activities in a manner which is most appropriate to its business. Classification by activity provides information that allows users to assess the impact of those activities on the financial position of the enterprise and the amount of its cash and cash equivalents. This information may also be used to evaluate the relationships among those activities.
10. A single transaction may include cash flows that are classified differently. For example, when the instalment paid in respect of a fixed asset acquired on deferred payment basis includes both interest and loan, the interest element is classified under financing activities and the loan element is classified under investing activities.

Operating Activities

11. The amount of cash flows arising from operating activities is a key indicator of the extent to which the operations of the enterprise have generated sufficient cash flows to maintain the operating capability of the enterprise, pay dividends, repay loans, and make new investments without recourse to external sources of financing. Information about the specific components of historical operating cash flows is useful, in conjunction with other information, in forecasting future operating cash flows.
12. Cash flows operating activities are primarily derived from the principal revenue-producing activities of the enterprise. Therefore, they generally result from the transactions and other events that enter into the determination of net profit or loss. Examples of cash flows from operating activities are :

(*a*) cash receipts from the sale of goods and the rendering of services;

(*b*) cash receipts from royalties, fees, commissions, and other revenue;
(*c*) cash payments to suppliers for goods and services;
(*d*) cash payments to and on behalf of employees;
(*e*) cash receipts and cash payments of an insurance enterprise for premiums and claims, annuities and other policy benefits;
(*f*) cash payments or refunds of income taxes unless they can be specifically identified with financing and investing activities; and
(*g*) cash receipts and payments relating to futures contracts, forward contracts, option contracts, and swap contracts when the contracts are held for dealing or trading purposes.

13. Some transactions, such as the sale of an item of plant, may give rise to a gain or loss which is included in the determination of net profit or loss. However, the cash flows relating to such transactions are cash flows from investing activities.
14. An enterprise may hold securities and loans for dealing or trading purposes, in which case they are similar to inventory acquired specifically for resale. Therefore, cash flows arising from the purchase and sale of dealing or trading securities are classified as operating activities. Similarly, cash advances and loans made by financial enterprises are usually classified as operating activities since they relate to the main revenue-producing activity of that enterprise.

Investing Activities

15. The separate disclosure of cash flows arising from investing activities is important because the cash flows represent the extent to which expenditures have been made for resources intended to generate future income and cash flows. Examples of cash flows arising from investing activities are :
(a) cash payments to acquire fixed assets (including intangibles). These payments include those relating to capitablised research and development costs and self-constructed fixed assets;
(b) cash receipts from disposal of fixed assets (including intangibles);
(c) cash payments to acquire shares, warrants, or debt instruments of other enterprises and interests in joint ventures (other than payments for those instruments considered to be cash equivalents and those held for dealing or trading purposes);
(d) cash receipts from disposal of shares, warrants, or debt instruments of other enterprises and interests in joint ventures (other than receipts from those instruments considered to be cash equivalents and those held for dealing or trading purposes);
(e) cash advances and loans made to third parties (other than advances and loans made by a financial enterprise);
(f) cash receipts from the repayment of advances and loans made to third parties (other than advances and loans of a financial enterprise);
(g) cash payments for futures contracts, forward contracts, option contracts, and swap contracts except when the contracts are held for dealing or trading purposes, or the payments are classified as financing activities; and
(h) cash receipts from futures contracts, forward contracts, option contracts, and swap contracts except when the contract are held for dealing or trading purposes, or the receipt are classified as financing activities.

16. When a contract is accounted for as a hedge of an identifiable position, the cash flows of the contract are classified in the same manner as the cash flows of the position being hedged.

Financing Activities

17. The separate disclosure of cash flows arising from financing activities is important because it is useful in predicting claims on future cash flows by providers of funds (both capital and borrowings) to the enterprise. Examples of cash flows arising from financing activities are :
   (a) cash proceeds from issuing shares or other similar instruments;
   (b) cash proceeds from issuing debentures, loans, notes, bonds and other short or long-term borrowings; and
   (c) cash repayments of amounts borrowed.

Reporting Cash Flows from Operating Activities

18. ***An enterprise should report cash flows from operating activities using either :***
   (a) the direct method, whereby major classes of gross cash receipts and gross cash payments are disclosed; or
   (b) the indirect method, whereby net profit or loss is adjusted for the effects of transactions of a non-cash nature, any deferrals or accruals of past or future operating cash receipts or payments, and items of income or expense associated with investing or financing cash flows.

19. The direct method provides information which may be useful in estimating future cash flows and which is not available under the indirect method and is, therefore, considered more appropriate than the indirect method. Under the direct method, information about major classes of gross cash receipts and gross cash payments may be obtained either :
   (a) from the accounting records of the enterprise; or
   (b) by adjusting sales, cost of sales (interest and similar income and interest expense and similar charges for a financial enterprise) and other items in the statement of profit and loss for :
      (i) changes during the period in inventories and operating receivables and payables;
      (ii) other non-cash items; and
      (iii) other items for which the cash effects are investing or financing cash flows.

20. Under the indirect method, the net cash flow from operating activities is determined by adjusting net profit or loss for the effects of :
   (a) changes during the period in inventories and operating receivables and payables;
   (b) non-cash items such as depreciation, provisions, deferred taxes, and unrealised foreign exchange gains and losses; and
   (c) all other items for which the cash effects are investing or financing cash flows.

Alternatively, the net cash flow from operating activities may be presented under the indirect method by showing the operating revenues and expenses, excluding non-cash items disclosed in the statement of profit and loss and the changes during the period in inventories and operating receivables and payables.

Reporting Cash Flows from Investing and Financing Activities

21. ***An enterprise should report separately major classes of gross cash receipts and gross cash payments arising from investing and financing activities, except to the extent that cash flows described in Paragraphs 22 and 24 are reported on a net basis.***

Reporting Cash Flows on a Net Basis

22. ***Cash flows arising from the following operating, investing or financing activities may be reported on a net basis :***
    - ***(a) cash receipts and payments on behalf of customers when the cash flows reflect the activities of the customer rather than those of the enterprise; and***
    - ***(b) cash receipts and payments for items in which the turnover is quick, the amounts are large, and the maturities are short.***
23. Examples of cash receipts and payments referred to in Paragraph 22(a) are :
    - (a) the acceptance and repayment of demand deposits by a bank;
    - (b) funds held for customers by an investment enterprise; and
    - (c) rents collected on behalf of, and paid over to, the owners of properties.

    Examples of cash receipts and payments referred to in Paragraph 22(b) are advances made for, and the repayments of :
    - (a) principal amounts relating to credit card customers;
    - (b) the purchase and sale of investments; and
    - (c) other short-term borrowings, for example, those which have a maturity period of three months or less.
24. ***Cash flows arising from each of the following activities of a financial enterprise may be reported on a net basis :***
    - ***(a) cash receipts and payments for the acceptance and repayment of deposits with a fixed maturity date;***
    - ***(b) the placement of deposits with and withdrawal of deposits from other financial enterprises; and***
    - ***(c) cash advances and loans made to customers and the repayment of those advances and loans.***

Foreign Currency Cash Flows

25. ***Cash flows arising from transactions in a foreign currency should be recorded in an enterprise's reporting currency by applying to the foreign currency amount the exchange rate between the reporting currency and the foreign currency at the date of the cash flow. A rate that approximates the actual rate may be used if the result is substancially the same as would arise if the rates at the dates of the cash flows were used. The effect of changes in exchange rates on cash and cash equivalents held in a foreign currency should be reported as a separate part of the reconciliation of the changes in cash and cash equivalents during the period.***
26. Cash flows denominated in foreign currency are reported in a manner consistent with Accounting Standard (AS) 11, Accounting for the Effects of Changes in

Foreign Exchange Rates. This permits the use of an exchange rate that approximates the actual rate. For example, a weighted average exchange rate for a period may be used for recording foreign currency transactions.

27. Unrealised gains and losses arising from changes in foreign exchange rates are not cash flows. However, the effect of exchange rate changes on cash and cash equivalents held or due in foreign currency is reported in the cash flow statement in order to reconcile cash and cash equivalents at the beginning and the end of the period. This amount is presented separately from cash flows from operating, investing and financing activities and includes the differences, if any had those cash flows been reported at the end-of-period exchange rates.

Extraordinary Items

28. ***The cash flows associated with extraordinary items should be classified as arising from operating, investing or financing activities as appropriate and separately disclosed.***
29. The cash flows associated with extraordinary items are disclosed separately as arising from operating, investing or financing activities in the cash flow statement, to enable users to understand their nature and effect on the present and future cash flows of the enterprise. These disclosures are in addition to the separate disclosures of the nature and amount of extraordinary items required by Accounting Standard (AS) 5, Net Profit or loss for the Period, Prior Period Items, and Changes in Accounting Policies.

Interest and Dividends

30. ***Cash flows from interest and dividends received and paid should each be disclosed separately. Cash flows arising from interest paid and interest and dividends received in the case of a financial enterprise should be classified as cash flows arising from operating activities. In the case of other enterprises, cash flows arising from interest paid should be classified as cash flows from financing activities while interest and dividends received should be classified as cash flows from investing activities. Dividends paid should be classified as cash flows from financing activities.***
31. The total amount of interest paid during the period is disclosed in the cash flow statement whether it has been recognised as an expense in the statement of profit and loss or capitalised in accordance with Accounting Standard (AS) 10, Accounting for Fixed Assets.
32. Interest paid and interest and dividends received are usually classified as operating cash flows for a financial enterprise. However, there is no consensus on the classification of these cash flows for other enterprises. Some argue that interest paid and interest and dividends received may be classified as operating cash flows because they enter into the determination of net profit or loss. However, it is more appropriate that interest paid and interest and dividends received are classified as financing cash flows and investing cash flows respectively, because they are cost of obtaining financial resources or returns on investments.
33. Some argue that dividends paid may be classified as a component of cash flows from operating activities in order to assist users to determine the ability of an enterprise to pay dividends out of operating cash flows. However, it is considered

more appropriate that dividends paid should be classified as cash flows from financing activities because they are cost of obtaining financial resources.

Taxes on Income

34. ***Cash flows arising from taxes on income should be separately disclosed and should be classified as cash flows from operating activities unless they can be specifically identified with financing and investing activities.***

35. Taxes on income arise on transactions that give rise to cash flows that are classified as operating, investing or financing activities in a cash flow statement. While tax expense may be readily identifiable with investing or financing activities, the related tax cash flows are often impracticable to identify and may arise in a different period from the cash flows of the underlying transactions. Therefore, taxes paid are usually classified as cash flows from operating activities. However, when it is practicable to identify the tax cash flow with an individual transaction that gives rise to cash flows that are classified as investing or financing activities, the tax cash flow is classified as an investing or financing activity as appropriate. When tax cash flows are allocated over more than one class of activity, the total amount of taxes paid is disclosed.

Investments in Subsidiaries, Associates, and Joint Ventures

36. ***When accounting for an investment in an associate or a subsidiary or a joint venture, an investor restricts its reporting in the cash flow statement to the cash flows between itself and the investee/joint venture, for example, cash flows relating to dividends and advances.***

Acquisitions and Disposals of Subsidiaries and Other Business Units

37. ***The aggregate cash flows arising from acquisitions and from disposals of subsidiaries or other business units should be presented separately and classified as investing activities.***

38. ***An enterprise should disclose, in aggregate, in respect of both acquisition and disposal of subsidiaries or other business units during the period each of the following :***

    (a) the total purchase or disposal consideration; and

    (b) the portion of the purchase or disposal consideration discharged by means of cash and cash equivalents.

39. The separate presentation of the cash flow effects of acquisitions and disposals of subsidiaries and other business units as single line items helps to distinguish those cash flows from other cash flows. The cash flow effects of disposals are not deducted from those of acquisitions.

Non-Cash Transactions

40. ***Investing and financing transactions that do not require the use of cash or cash equivalents should be excluded from a cash flow statement. Such transactions should be disclosed elsewhere in the financial statements in a way that provides all the relevant information about these investing and financing activities.***

41. Many investing and financing activities do not have a direct impact on current cash flows although they do affect the capital and asset structure of an enterprise.

The exclusion of non-cash transactions from the cash flow statement is consistent with the objective of a cash flow statement as these items do not involve cash flows in the current period. Examples of non-cash transactions are :

(a) the acquisition of assets by assuming directly related liabilities;
(b) the acquisition of an enterprise by means of issue of shares; and
(c) the conversion of debt to equity.

Components of Cash and Cash Equivalents

42. ***An enterprise should disclose the components of cash and cash equivalents and should present a reconciliation of the amounts in its cash flow statement with the equivalent items reported in the balance sheet.***

43. In view of the variety of cash management practices, an enterprise discloses the policy which it adopts in determining the composition of cash and cash equivalents.

44. The effect of any change in the policy for determining components of cash and cash equivalents is reported in accordance with Accounting Standard (AS) 5, Net Profit or Loss for the Period, Prior Period Items, and Changes in Accounting Policies.

Other Disclosures

45. ***An enterprise should disclose, together with a commentary management, the amount of significant cash and cash equivalent balances held by the enterprise that are not available for use by it.***

46. There are various circumstances in which cash and cash equivalent balances held by an enterprise are not available for use by it. Examples include cash and cash equivalent balances held by a branch of the enterprise that operates in a country where exchange controls or other legal restrictions apply as a result of which the balances are not available for use by the enterprise.

47. Additional information may be relevant to users in understanding the financial position and liquidity of an enterprise. Disclosure of this information, together with a commentary by management, is encouraged and may include :

(a) the amount of undrawn borrowing facilities that may be available for future operating activities and to settle capital commitments, indicating any restrictions on the use of these facilities; and
(b) the aggregate amount of cash flows that represent increases in operating capacity separately from those cash flows that are required to maintain operating capacity.

48. The separate disclosure of cash flows that represent increases in operating capacity and cash flows that are required to maintain operating capacity is useful in enabling the user to determine whether the enterprise is investing adequately in the maintenance of its operating capacity. An enterprise that does not invest adequately in the maintenance of its operating capacity may be prejudicing future profitability for the sake of current liquidity and distributions to owners.

Format of Cash Flow Statement

Though Accounting Standard 3 (Revised) has not provided any format for the preparation of cash flow statement the following proforma is suggested.

CASH FLOW STATEMENT (DIRECT METHOD)

(A) Cash flows from operating activities :

Cash receipts from customers
Cash paid to suppliers and employees
Cash generated from operations
Income tax paid.
Cash flow before extraordinary item
Proceeds from earthquake disaster settlement
NET cash from operating activities.

(B) Cash flows from investing activities :

Purchase of fixed assets
Proceeds from sale of equipment
Interest received
Dividend received
NET cash from investing activities

(C) Cash flows from financing activities :

Proceeds from issuance of share capital
Proceeds from long-term borrowings
Less : Repayment of long term borrowings
Less : Interest paid
Less : Dividend paid
NET cash from financing activities
NET Increase (Decrease) in cash and
Cash equivalents (A + B + C)
Cash and Cash Equivalents at Beginning of period
Cash and Cash Equivalent at the end of period

CASH FLOW STATEMENT (INDIRECT METHOD)

(A) Cash Flows from Operating Activities :

Net profit before tax and extraordinary items
Adjustment for :
Depreciation
Foreign Exchange
Investments
Gain or loss on sale of fixed assets
Interest/Dividend
Operating profit before working capital changes
Adjustments for :
Trade and other receivables
Inventories
Trade payables
Cash generation from operations
Interest paid
Direct taxes
Cash before extraordinary items
Deferred revenue
NET cash from operating activities

(B) Cash Flow from Investing activities :
Purchase of Fixed Assets
Sale of fixed assets
Sale of Investment
Purchase of investments
Interest received
Dividend received
Loans to Subsidiaries
NET cash from investing activities

(C) Cash Flow from financing activities :
Proceeds from issue of share capital
Proceeds from long term borrowings
Repayment to finance/lease liabilities
Dividend paid
NET cash from financing activities
Net increase (Decrease) in cash and
Cash equivalents (A + B + C)
Cash and Cash Equivalents at the
beginning of the period
Cash and cash equivalents at the
end of the period

Problem-19 : From the following information as contained in income statement and Balance Sheet of Ril Ltd, you are required to prepare a cash flow statement using (i) direct method and (ii) indirect method.

Income Statement for the year ended 31st March, 2002

			Rs. in Crores
Net Sales			20,301
Less :	Cost of Sales	15,984	
	Depreciation	2534	
	Salaries & Wages	375	
	Operating expenses	891	
	Provision for tax	57	
			19,841
	Net operating profit		460
Add :	Other income	645	
	Profit on sale of asset	42	
			687
	Profit for the year		1147
Add :	Balance of profit & loss a/c brought forward		11183
			12,330
Less :	Dividend declared	420	
	Tax on dividend	46	466
			11,864
Add :	Share premium a/c		772
	profit & loss a/c on 31st March 2000		12,636

Comparative Balance Sheet

		As on 31-3-2000 (Rs. in crores)		As on 31-3-1999 (Rs. in crores)
Assets :				
Fixed Assets :				
Land		1029		901
Building & equipment		23634		21,187
Gross block		24,663		22,088
Less : Accumulated depreciation		9214		6692
Net block		15,449		15,396
Investments		6067		4295
Current Assets :				
Cash	1082		4898	
Debtors	842		457	
Stock	1823		1409	
Advances	4059		1676	
Other current assets	48	7854	25	8465
		29,370		28,156

Liabilities	As on 31-3-2000 (Rs. in crores)	As on 31-3-1999 (Rs. in crores)
Equity capital	1053	933
Preference capital	293	253
Reserves & Surplus	12636	11,183
Loans	11,520	11,650
Sundary Creditors	2959	3345
Provision for tax	266	544
Other liabilities	643	248
	29,370	28156

Cost of equipment sold was Rs. 40 crore

(*C.S. Intermediate December 2000*)

Solution :

Direct Method

Cash flow statement for the year ended 31-3-2000

Rs. in crores

Cash flow from operating activities :		
Cash receipts from customers	19,916	
Less : Cash paid to suppliers and employees	20061	
Cash generated from operations	(–) 145	
Less : Income tax paid	(–) 335	
	(–) 480	
Other income	645	
		165
Cash flow from investing activities :		
Purchase of land	(–) 128	
Purchase of building and equipment	(–) 2487	
Purchase of Investments	(–) 1772	
	(–) 4387	

Sale of equipment		70	
Net cash used in investing activities			(–) 4317
Cash from financing activities :			
Issue of equity shares		120	
Issue of preference shares		40	
Share premium		772	
		932	
Less : Loan repaid	130		
Dividend	420		
Tax on dividend	46		
		596	
			336
Net increase in cash and cash equivalents			– 3816
Cash and cash equivalents at the beginning			4898
Cash and cash equivalents at the end			1082

Working Notes :

(i) Cash receipts from customers :

Sales		20301
Add : Debtors at the beginning		457
		20,758
Less : Debtors at the end		842
		19,916

(ii) Cash paid to suppliers & employees :

Cost of goods sold		15,984
Add : Operating expenses		891
Salaries and Wages		375
		17,250
Add : Other liabilities at the beginning	248	
Creditors at the beginning	3345	
Stock at the end	1823	
Advances at the end	4059	
Other current assets at the end	48	
		9523
		26,773
Less : Creditors at the end	2959	
Other liabilities at the end	643	
Stock at the beginning	1409	
Advances at the beginning	1676	
Other current assets at the beginning	25	6712
		20061

(iii) Income tax paid :

Income Tax payable at the beginning	544
Add : Provision for taxation	57
	601

Less : Tax payable at the end	266
Tax paid during the year	335

(iv) Accumulated depreciation written off on equipment sold :

Accumulated depreciation at the beginning	6692
Add : Depreciation for the year	2534
	9226
Less : Accumulated depreciation at the end	9214
	12

(v) Sale price of equipment :

Cost of equipment	40
Less : Accumulated depreciation	12
	28
Add : Profit on sale	42
	70

(vi) Purchase of Building and equipment :

Balance at the end	23,634
Add : Cost of equipment sold	40
	23,674
Less : Balance at the beginning	21,187
	2487

Indirect Method

Cash Flow Statement for the year ended 30-3-2000

Cash flow from Operating Activities :		
Net profit before taxation and extra ordinary item (1147 + 57 – 42)		1162
Adjustments for Depreciation		2534
Operating profit before working capital changes :		3696
Less : Increase in Debtors	385	
Increase in stock	414	
Increase in advances	2383	
Increase in other current assets	23	
Decrease in Creditors	386	
Income tax paid	335	
		3926
		– 230
Add : Increase in other liabilities		395
Net cash from operating activities		165
Cash flow from investing activities		(–) 4317
Cash flow from financing activities		336
Net increase in cash and cash equipments		(–) 3816
Cash and cash equivalents at the beginning		4898
Cash and equivalents at the end		1082

Note : Since tax on dividend (corporate dividend tax) is paid on declaration on/payment of dividend, it is treated as a cash out flow from financing activities.

Problem-20 : From the following information as contained in the income statement and the balance sheet of Strong Ltd. you are required to prepare a cash flow statement using (i) Direct method and (ii) Indirect method.

Income Statement and Reconciliation of Earnings for the year ended 31st March 1998

Net sales		40,32,000
Less : Cash of sales	31,68,000	
Depreciation	96,000	
Salaries & Wages	3,84,000	
Operating expenses	1,28,000	
Provision for taxation	1,40,000	
		39,16,800
Net operating profit		1,15,200
Non-recurring income :		
Profit on sale of equipment		19,200
Profit for the year		1,34,000
Retained earnings (balance of profit & loss a/c brought forward)		2,42,880
		3,77,280
Dividend declared and paid during the year		1,15,200
Profit & loss account balance as on 31st March 1998		2,62,080

Comparative Balance Sheets

	As on 31-3-1997 Rs.	As on 31-3-1998 Rs.
Fixed Assets :		
Land	76800	1,53,600
Building and equipment	5,76,000	9,21,600
Current assets :		
Cash	96,000	1,15,200
Debtors	2,68,800	2,97,600
Stock	4,22,400	1,53,600
Advances	12,480	14,400
Total	14,52,480	16,56,000
Capital	5,76,000	7,10,400
Surplus in P & C a/c	2,42,880	2,62,080
Sundry creditors	3,84,000	3,74,400
Outstanding expenses	38,400	76,800
Income-tax payable	19,200	21,120
Accumulated depreciation on building & equipment	1,92,000	2,11,200
Total	14,52,480	16,56,000

Cost of equipment sold was Rs. 1,15,200

(*C S, Inter, December 1999*)

Solution : **Direct Method**

Cash Flow Statement for the year ended 31-3-1998

Cash flows from operating activities :	
Cash receipts from customers	40,03,200
Less : Cash paid to suppliers & employees	33,84,320

Cash generated from operations	6,18,880	
Less : Income tax paid	1,38,880	
Net cash from operating activities		4,80,000
Cash flows from Investing activities :		
Purchase of land	(–) 76800	
Purchase of building & equipment	(–) 4,60,800	
Sale of equipment	+ 57600	
Net cash used in investing activities		(–) 4,80,000
Cash flows from financing activities :		
Issue of share capital	1,34,400	
Dividend paid	(–) 1,15,200	
Net cash from financing activities		19,200
Net increase in cash and cash equivalents		19,200
Cash and cash equivalents at the beginning		96000
Cash and cash equivalents at the end		1,15,200

Working Notes :

(i) *Cash receipts from customers :*

Sales	40,32,000
Add : Debtors at the beginning	2,68,800
	43,00,800
Less : Debtors at the end	2,97,600
	40,03,200

(ii) Cash paid to suppliers and Employees :

Cost of goods sold		31,68,000
Add : Operating expenses		1,28,000
Add : Salaries & Wages		3,84,000
		36,80,000
Add : Creditors at the beginning	3,84000	
O/s expenses at the beginning	38,400	
Stock at the end	1,53,600	
Advances at the end	14,400	
		5,90,400
		42,70,400
Less : Creditors at the end	3,74,400	
O/s expenses at the end	76,800	
Stock at the beginning	4,22,400	
Advances at the beginning	12,480	
		8,86,080
		33,84,320

(iii) *Income-tax paid :*

Income tax payable at the beginning	19,200
Add : Provision for taxation	1,40,800
	1,60,000
Less : Tax payable at the end	21,120
	1,38,880

(iv) *Accumulated Depreciation Written off on equipment sold :*

Accumulated Depreciation at the beginning	1,92,000
Add : Depreciation for the year	96,000
	2,88,000
Less : Accumulated Depreciation at the end	2,11,200
	76,800

(v) *Sale price of equipment :*

Cost price	1,15,200
Less : Accumulated depreciation	76,800
	38,400
Add : Profit on sale	19,200
	57,600

(vi) Purchase of building and equipment :

Balance at the beginning	5,76,000
Less : Cost of equipment sold	1,15,200
	4,60,800
Balance at the end	9,21,600
	4,60,800

Indirect Method

Cash Flow Statement for the year ended 31-3-1998

Cash Flow from Operating Activities :		
Net profit before taxation and extraordinary items		2,56,000
Add : Adjustment for Depreciation		96,000
Operating profit before working capital changes		3,52,000
Add : Decrease in stock	2,68,800	
Increase in o/s expenses	38,400	
		3,07,200
		6,59,200
Less : Increase in Debtors	28,800	
Increase in advances	1,920	
Decrease in creditors	9,600	
		40,320
Cash generated from operations		6,18,880
Less : Income tax paid		1,38,880
Net cash from operating activities		4,80,000
Cash Flow from Investing Activities :		
Purchase of land	(–) 76,800	
Purchase of building & equipment	(–) 4,60,800	
Sale of equipment	(+) 57,600	
Net cash used in investing activities		(–) 4,80,000

Cash flows from financing activities :		
Issue of share capital	1,34,400	
Dividend paid	(–) 1,15,200	
Net cash from financing activities		19,200
Net increase in cash and cash equivalents		19,200
Cash and cash equivalents at the beginning		96,000
Cash and cash equivalents at the end		1,15,200

QUESTIONS

Simple questions

1. What is cash flow?
2. Distinguish between 'Fund' and 'Cash'.
3. State the objectives of cash flow analysis.
4. State limitations of cash flow analysis.
5. How are cash flows classified?
6. What are cash flows from operating activities?
7. What are cash flows from investing activities?
8. What are the cash flows from financing activities?
9. What is meant by historical cash flow statement?
10. What is meant by projected cash flow statement?
11. What do you mean by actual cash flow.
12. What is meant by notional cash flow?
13. What is cash flow statement?

Short Answer Question

1. Explain the utility of cash flos statement.
2. Distinguish between fund flow statement and cash flow statement.
3. State the various sources and uses of cash flow.

Exercise 1 (Cash from Operation) : From the following information, you are required to calculate cash from operations :

	31.12 96	*31.12.97*
Net profit for the year	—	35,000
Debtors	21,000	20,000
Bills receivable	4,000	6,500
Creditors	23,500	25,000
Bills payable	7,500	5,000
Stock	29,000	32,500

(Osmania University, B.Com., October 1998)

(*Answer* : Cash from operation Rs. 29,000)

Exercise 2 : Following information is available from the books of Standard Company Ltd. :

	1994-95	*1993-94*
Profit made during the year	2,50,000	—
Income received in advance	500	600
Prepaid expenses	1,600	1,400
Debtors	80,000	95,000
Bills receivable	25,000	20,000
Creditors	45,000	40,000
Bills payable	13,000	15,000
Outstanding expenses	2,500	2,000
Accrued income	1,500	1,200

Calculate cash flow from operation

(CS, Inter, December 1996)

[*Answer* : Cash from operation Rs. 2.62,900]

Exercise 3 : The current assets and current liabilities of the business for the years ending 31st December 1992 and 1993 are as follows :

Compute cash from operation, given profit for the year 1993 is Rs. 10,000 after providing depreciation of Rs. 2,000.

	31.12.92	*31.12.93*
Sundry debtors	10,000	12,000
Provision for bad debts	1,000	1,200
Bills receivable	4,000	30,000
Bills payable	5,000	6,000
Sundry creditors	8,000	9,000
Inventories	5,000	8,000
Short-term investments	10,000	12,000
O/s expenses	1,000	1,500
Prepaid expenses	2,000	1,000
Accrued income	3,000	4,000
Income received in advance	2,000	1,000

(*University of Madras, B.Com., September 1994*)

[*Answer* : Cash from operation Rs. 7,700]

Exercise 4 (Cash Flow Statement): The following are the Balance Sheets of X Ltd. on 1.1.1996 and 31.12.1996:

	1.1.96	*31.12.96*		*1.1.96*	*31.12.96*
Capital	1,25,000	1,53,000	Cash	10,000	47,000
Bank loan	40,000	50,000	Sundry debtors	30,000	50,000
Loan from Financial Co.	25,000	—	Stock	35,000	25,000
			Machinery	80,000	55,000
Sundry creditors	40,000	44,000	Land	40,000	50,000
P & L a/c	1,00,000	1,20,000	Buildings	35,000	60,000
			Goodwill	1,00,000	80,000
	3,30,000	3,67,000		3,30,000	3,67,000

Additional Information

1. Dividend paid during the year amounted to Rs. 15,000.
2. Rs. 20,000 worth of machinery was sold prepare the cash flow statement from the above particulars.

(*Osmania University, B.Com., March 1997*)

[*Asnwer* : Total of cash flow statement Rs. 1,42,000]

Exercise 5 : The following are the balance sheets of Mrs. Sridhar:

	1.1.96	*31.12.96*		*1.1.96*	*31.12.96*
Capital	2,96,000	3,08,000	Cash	8,000	7,200
Hire-purchase Vendor	—	40,000	Debtors	70,000	75,800
			Stock	50,000	44,000
Loan from bank	60,000	50,000	Land	40,000	60,000
Current liabilities	72,000	82,000	Buildings	1,00,000	1,10,000
Mrs. Sridhar's loan	—	40,000	Machinery less dep.	1,60,000	1,72,000
			Delivery van	—	50,000
	4,28,000	5,20,000		4,28,000	5,20,000

The delivery van was purchased on hire-purchase basis in December 1996, a payment of Rs. 10,000 was made at the time of agreement and the balance amount is to be paid in 20 monthly instalments of Rs. 2,000 each together with interest @ 12% p.a. During the year the proprietor with draw Rs. 52,000 for household expenses. The provision for depreciation on machinery as on 1.1.96 was Rs. 54,000 and on 31.12.96 was Rs. 72,000. You are required to prepare a cash flow statement.

(*Sri Sathya Sai University, B.Com. (Hons) March 1997*)

[*Answer* : Total of Cash Flow Statement Rs. 1,39,200]

Exercise 6 : Following are the summarised balance sheets of Mayur Industries Private Ltd. as on 31st March 1995 and 31st March, 1996.

Balance Sheet

	1996	1995
Assets		
Premises	4,75,000	5,00,000
Machinery	4,22,500	3,75,000
Equipments	40,500	45,000
Stock	74,000	1,00,000
Sundry debtors	1,60,000	2,00,000
Cash	7,000	3,000
Bank	10,000	—
Goodwill	—	12,500
	11,89,000	12,35,500
Liabilities		
Share capital	5,00,000	5,00,000
General reserve	1,50,000	1,25,000
Profit & loss a/c	76,500	76,250
Term loan from ICICI	1,55,000	1,75,000
Sundry creditors	2,31,250	2,75,000
Provision for taxation	76,250	84,250
	11,89,000	12,35,000

Other Information

(*i*) Interim dividend of Rs. 25,000 was paid during the year.
(*ii*) Depreciation on Premises is provided at 5%
(*iii*) Machinery of Rs. 75,000 was a acquired during the year.
(*iv*) Income tax provision for the year was Rs. 75,000.

Prepare (*a*) cash flow statement, (*b*) statement showing cash from operation.

(*University of Mumbai, B.Com., October 1997*)

[*Answer* : Total of cash flow statement Rs. 2.20,000; Cash from operation Rs. 2,17,000]

Exercise 7 : The balance sheet of Yash Ltd. as on 31st December, 1995, 1996 are as under :

(*Figures in thousand*)

	31.12.95	31.12.96		31.12.95	31.12.96
Equity share capital	350	400	Fixed assets	210	320
General reserve	20	—	Stock	90	140
P & L a/c	40	—	Sundry debtors	60	55
Secured loan	—	180	Bills receivable	50	75
Sundry creditors	30	45	Investments	70	40
Bills payable	50	25	Cash	30	20
O/s expenses	10	30	P & L a/c	—	30
Unpaid dividend	10	—			
	510	680		510	680

Accumulated Depreciation was Rs. 60,000 on 31st December, 1995 and on 31st December, 1996. It was Rs. 57,000. Machinery having written down value Rs. 90,000 was sold for Rs. 15,000 on 1.7.1996, plant costing Rs. 2,30,000 purchased on 1st July, 1996, prepare :

(*i*) Statement showing cash from operation.
(*ii*) Statement of cash flow for the year ended 31st December, 1996.

(*University of Mumbai, B.Com., April 1997*)

[*Answer* : (1) Total of cash flow statement Rs. 305 (000)
(2) Cash lost in operation (–) 45 (000)]

Exercise 8 : The financial position of M/s A and B on 1st July, 1994 and 30th June, 1995 was as follows :

	1.7.1994	*30.6.1995*
Cash	4,000	3,600
Debtors	35,000	38,400
Stock	25,000	22,000
Land	20,000	30,000
Buildings	50,000	55,000
Machinery	80,000	86,000
	2,14,000	2,35,000
Current liabilities	36,000	41,000
Mrs A's loan	—	20,000
Loan from bank	30,000	25,000
Capital	1,48,000	1,49,000
	2,14,000	2,35,000

During the year, the partners withdraw Rs. 26,000 for domestic expenditure. The provision for depreciation against machinery as on 1.7.1994 was Rs. 27,000 and on 30.6.1995 was Rs. 36,000.

You are required to prepare a cash flow statement. (*Sri Sathya Sai University, B.Com. (Hons), March 1996*)

[*Answer* : Total of cash flow statement Rs. 68,000]

Exercise 9 : From the following particulars prepare a cash flow statement of AB Traders :

	1.1.95	*31.12.95*
Cash	7,500	6,000
Debtors	60,000	67,500
Stock	45,000	37,500
Land	45,000	60,000
Building	75,000	82,500
Machinery	1,05,000	1,20,000
	3,37,500	3,73,500
Current liability	52,500	60,000
Loan from Mr. K	—	37,500
Bank loan	60,000	45,000
Capital	2,25,000	2,31,000
	3,27,500	3,73,500

During the year the firm brought in additional capital of Rs. 15,000 and the drawings during the year was Rs. 46,500.

Provision for depreciation on machinery; opening balance Rs. 45,000, closing balance Rs. 60,000. No depreciation need be provided on other assets. (*Bangalore University, B.B.M., November 1996*)

[*Answer* : Total of cash flow statement Rs. 1.20,000]

Exercise 10 : The following details are available from a Company:

	31.12.85	*31.12.86*		*31.12.85*	*31.12.86*
Share capital	70,000	74,000	Cash	9,000	7,800
Debentures	12,000	6,000	Debtors	14,900	17,700
Reserve for D.D	700	800	Stock	49,200	42,700
Trade creditors	10,360	11,840	Land	20,000	30,000
P & L a/c	10,040	10,560	Goodwill	10,000	5,000
	1,03,100	1,03,200		1,03,100	1,03,200

(a) Dividend paid Rs. 3,500.
(b) Land was purchased for Rs. 10,000.
(c) Amount provided for amortisation of goodwill Rs. 5,000.
(d) Debentures paid off Rs. 6,000.

Prepare cash flow statement.

(*University of Madras, B.Com., September 1996*)
[*Answer* : Cash flow from operation Rs. 14,300
Total of cash flow statement Rs. 27,300]

Exercise 11 : The following are the Summarised balance sheets of M/s Rahul Brothers Private Limited as on March 31, 1992 and 1993 :

	1992	*1993*		*1992*	*1993*
7% Redeemable preferecen shares	—	1,000	Fixed assets	4,100	4,000
Equity shares	4,000	4,000	*Less* : Depreciation	1,100	1,500
				3,000	2,500
General reserve	200	200			
P & L a/c	100	120	Debtors	2,000	2,400
Debentures	600	700	Stock	3,000	3,500
Creditors	1,200	1,100	Prepaid expenses	30	50
Provision for taxation	300	420	Cash	120	350
Proposed dividend	500	580			
Bank overdraft	1,250	680			
	8,150	8,800		8,150	8,800

(*University of Madras, B.Com., May 1996*)
[*Answer* : Cash from operation 400
Total of cash flow statement Rs. 470]

Exercise-12 (AS-3) : The Balance Sheet and Statement of profit & loss account of ...... Co. Ltd. for the period 31-12-2002 is given below prepare cash flow statement (a) under Direct method (b) Indirect method Balance Sheet as at 31-12-2002.

(Rs. 000)

			2002		*2001*
Assets :					
Cash on land and balances with banks			200		25
Short term investments			670		135
Sundry Debtors			1700		1200
Interest receivable			100		–
Inventories			900		1950
Long term Investments			2500		2500
Fixed cost at cost	2180	1910			
Less : Accumulated depreciation	1450	1060			
Fixed Assets (net)			730		850
Total Assets			6800		6660
Liabilities :					
Sundry creditors			150		1890
Interest payable			230		100
Income tax payable			400		1000
Long term debt			1110		1040
Share Capital			1500		1250
Reserves			3410		1380
Total Assets			6800		6660

Statement of profit & loss for the period ended 31-12-2002

			(Rs. 000)
Sales			30,650
Less : Cost of sales			26000
		Gross profit	4650
Less : Depreciation	450		
Adm. & Selling expenses	910		
Indirect expense	400		
Foreign exchange loss	40		
			1800
			2850
Add : Interest income	300		
Dividend income	200		
			500
Net profit before taxation & extraordinary item			3350
Extraordinary item-Insurance proceeds from earthquake disaster settlement			180
Net profit after extraordinary item			3530
Less : Income tax			300
		Net profit	3230

Additional information :

(a) An amount of 250 was raised from the issue of share capital and a further 250 was raised from long-term borrowing.

(b) Interest expense was 400 of which 170 was paid during the period Rs. 100 relating to interest expense of the prior period was also paid during the period.

(c) Dividend paid was Rs. 1200.

(d) Tax deducted at source on dividend received (included in the Tax expense of 300 for the year) amounted to 40.

(e) During the period, the enterprize acquired fixed assets for 350. The payment was made in cash.

(f) Plant with original cost of 80 and accumulated depreciation of 60 was sold for 20.

(g) Foreign exchange loss of 40 represents the reduction in the carrying amount of a short term investment in foreign currency designated bonds arising out of a change in exchange rate between the date of acquisition of the investment and the balance sheet date.

(h) Sundry debtors and Sundry creditors include amounts relating to credit sales and credit purchase only.

[*Answer : Cash equivalent at the end of the period Rs. 910*]

Exercise-13 : From the information as contained in the income statement and the balance sheet of Ashok Ltd., you are required to prepare a cash flow statement using (i) Direct method and (ii) Indirect method.

Income Statement and Reconciliation of Earnings for the year ended 31-3-2003

Net Sales		25,20,000
Less : Cost of sales	19,80,000	
Depreciation	60,000	
Salaries & Wages	2,40,000	
Operating expenses	80000	
Provision for taxation	88000	
		24,48,000
Net operating profit		72000
Non-recurring income :		
Profit on sale of equipment		12000
		84,000

Retained earnings (balance in profit & loss a/c brought forward)	1,51,800
	2,35,800
Dividend declared and paid during the year	72000
P & C a/c balance as on 31-3-2003	1,63,800

Comparative Balance Sheet

	As at 31-3-2002 Rs.	*As at 31-3-2003 Rs.*
Fixed Assets :		
Land	48000	96000
Building & equipment	3,60,000	5,76,000
Current Assets		
Cash	60000	72000
Debtors	1,68,000	1,86,000
Stock	2,64,000	96,000
Advances	7800	9000
	9,07,800	10,35,000
Capital	3,60,000	4,44,000
Surplus in P & C a/c	1,51,800	1,63,800
Sundry Creditors	2,40,000	2,34,000
o/s expenses	24000	48,000
Income tax payable	12000	13,200
Accumulated depreciation on building & equipments	1,20,000	1,32,000
	9,07,800	10,35,000

Cost of equipment sold was Rs. 72000

[*Answer : Cash and cash equivalents at the end Rs. 72000*]

36

INFLATION ACCOUNTING (ACCOUNTING FOR PRICE LEVEL CHANGES)

INTRODUCTION

Inflation is a state in which purchasing power of money goes down or conversely, there is more money in circulation than is justified by goods and services. The effect of inflation is that the prices of assets go up and the accounts prepared on the basis of conventional accounting system present very distorted figures to the users of accounts.

Inflation Accounting is a method derised to show the effect of changing cost and prices on affairs of a company during course of relative accounting period. It is not a panacea for difficulties confronted by a company during period of inflation but it provides a leeway to see in right perspective the inpact of inflation on the company's operation during the course of relative accounting period.

Accounting for price level changes (popularly known as inflation accounting) has recently been seriously engaging the attention of accountants. So far accountants have been measuring business transactions in terms of monetary units, *i.e.*, rupees. etc. but this standard of measurment is highly unstable and keeps on changing in value particularly on the high side due to inflation almost all over the world.

Features of Inflation Account

(*a*) It is assumed that the unit of measurement is not stable

(*b*) The procedure of recording is automatic

(*c*) All elements of the financial statements are taken into account

(*d*) Realisation principles are not followed strictly, e.g. fixed assets and long term loans are recorded at their current values.

Objectives of Inflation Accounting

1. It portrays the real profit or loss for the period under consideration as against the profit or loss on the basis of historical cost. Inflation accounting shows the true picture of profitablility of the business. In cases when prices have substantially risen, the profit and loss account prepared on the basis of historical cost does not show the proper appraisal of the performance of the organisation. This is because of the fact that though sales revenue is recorded in terms of current rupees, some of important charges (say depreciation) against the revenue are in terms of historical cost.
2. It sets out the real financial position in present day terms rather then conventional position on historical cost basis and indicates the real capital employed. As a result of inflation the value of various assets and liabilities may vary, the same can be represented only by inflation accounting.
3. It ensures that sufficient funds will be available to replace the various assets when the replacement becomes due. At the time of replacement of assets huge

funds are required on account of inflationary condition and if historical method of a ccounting is followed the concern will be experiencing scarcity of funds to replace the assets. If assets are not replaced in time it willl adversely affect the operational efficiency of the organisation.

4. It indicates the profits in constant rupees, *i.e.*, having regard to the general movement in prices for the reference of shareholders as well as the management. The price level adjusted accounts provide the basis for rational appraisal of managerial effectiveness in terms of preservation of the current rupee equivalent of capital invested in the business. The management would greatly benefit by such accounts for the determination of management policies with respect to pricing, credit, dividend, expansion, etc.

A number of studies established that many companies had been taking unsound financial policy decisions because of their sole reliance on accounting statements based on historical costs. The growth rate in real terms was lower than shown and the profit increase in real terms was much less than what is was supposed to be earlier.

A committee under the chairmanship of F.E.P. Sandilands was set up in U.K. in January, 1974 to study the effects of inflation on accounts and suggest remedial measures. The committee presented its report to the British Parliament in September, 1975 which spot lighted certain concepts very dominantly. Among the many recommendations of Sandilands Committee, the following are the important ones.

(1) Definitions

A company's gains (or losses) may be classified into a number of categories.

(*a*) Holding gains: A holding gain is the difference between the measured value to a company of an asset at any point of time and the original cost incurred by the company in purchasing that asset. Such gains may be either realised or unrealised. This value to the business of an asset on a particular point of time will be arrived at in the light of guidelines set by management after due deliberations.

(*b*) Operating gain: An operating gain is the difference between the amount realised for a company's output (its earnings from goods or services provided) and the 'value to the business' of the inputs used by the company in generating those amounts. A company's profit should be equated with its operating gains.

(*c*) Extraordinary gains: An extraordinary gain is the difference between the amounts realised for items which do not form part of a company's normal output and their value to the company at the time of disposal. The distinction between operative and extraordinary gains is essential for their adjustment and operation at the time of presentation.

(*d*) Realised gains: Total gain may be either realised or unrealised during the year. A realised gain is a gain arising from sale or disposal by the company of any kind of goods, services, assets or liabilities.

(*e*) Unrealised gains: 'Unrealised gain' arise, when measured value of any asset held by company increase during the life time of the company and the asset is still retained by the company.

(2) Limitations of Historical Costing

Historical costing is more useful where it is desired to measure a company's performance in terms of cost incurred and when prices are stable. But its utility is reduced during a period of inflation. This is because of its limitations which are as follows :

(*a*) Historical cost accounts in their basic form do not recognise unrealised holding gains. Assets are shown in the accounts at cost less depreciation and as such the unrealised holding gains arising from the increase in monetary value of assets due to inflation are not shown. This deprives the shareholders, employees, creditors, etc. from getting useful information on a type of gain which is increasingly important during the time of inflation.

(*b*) Under the historical cost accounting realised holding gains are usually included together with operations gains as profit for the year. When due to inflation, holding gains are large, this factor reduce the usefulness of historical cost accounts since they do not give the correct information required by the users of accounts. This results in exaggerated profit being shown by historical accounting method due to the valuation of the same quantities of closing stocks at higher level in successive years of inflation. If for example, a company maintains a consistent stock which was valued at Rs. 1 lakh at the end of one of the past years and which due to progressive inflation during last several years now stands valued at Rs. 8 lakhs, this will have an important and major impact. This progressive valuation of closing stock at higher amounts will result in acute shortage of funds, and profit shown will not be there in real terms.

(*c*) The aim of calculating and charging depreciation under historical cost accounting is to spread the cost of an asset over its useful life. The depreciation so charged is inadequate because it does not take into account the changes in the replacement value of the fixed assets under inflationary conditions. The depreciation provided for at a reduced rate may be totally inadequate to purchase a new machine the cost of which would have appreciably gone up. It follows that the profits shown by the company during this period were over-stated and that they did not truly reflect the surpluses from the business activities after maintaining the capital assets in tact.

TECHNIQUES OF INFLATION ACCOUNTING

The two techniques used for presenting correct accounts during inflation are as follows :

(1) Current Purchasing Power Method

This method is also known as general purchasing power method. It seeks to show the affairs of an enterprise in terms of a unit of measurement of constant value where costs and prices are changing. According to this method all items in the financial statements are to be restated for changes in the general price level for this purpose any approved price index is used to convert the various items of the balance sheet and the profit and loss account. This method eliminates the effects on account of changes in the value of money. It should be noted that under this method only the changes in general purchasing power of money is taken into account. It does not consider the changes in the value of individuals assets. Since the conversion of each figure in terms of index number of the date of transactions is practically very difficult, it is assumed that all operating trnasactions take place evenly throughout the year. Moreover in respect of monetary terms purchasing power gain or loss is computed.

The system of adjustment underlying the current purchasing power method may be presented under the following three heads.

(a) Common Features

(*i*) All items in the balance sheet and the income statement are adjusted in terms of current rupees.

(*ii*) Items appearing in historical cost accounts are classified into monetary and non-monetary groups. Monetary items are simply related in current rupees; they do not require adjustment. Non-monetary items on the other hand are adjusted in accordance with changes in the purchasing power of money.

(*iii*) Transactions, both capital and revenue are assumed to have taken place evenly throughout the year at the average price level of the year.

(b) Adjustment of Profit and Loss Account

(*i*) Items such as sales, purchases, expenses, taxes, dividends etc. are adjusted in terms of the year and rupee by applying the average index for the year.

(*ii*) Opening and closing stock are adjusted by the price index of the average date of their acquisition.

(*iii*) For computing adjusted depreciation, the fixed assets are first aged and grouped according to the date of their acquisition and then their cost, in current rupees is obtained. The depreciation charges are computed with reference to such adjusted cost either by applying regular rates of depreciation or on a proportionate basis.

(c) Adjustment of Balance Sheet

(*i*) Fixed assets are adjusted in accordance with the index numbers of the dates of their acquisition or if deemed satisfactory, with reference to the index number of the average date of their acquisition.

(*ii*) The method of conversion of inventory is the same as stated above in 2 (*ii*)

(*iii*) The remaining current assets and all liabilities (*i.e.*, monetary assets and liabilities) need no adjustment as they are already stated in current rupees.

(*iv*) The index number at the date of issue or if deemed satisfactory, the average index of the year; is used to adjust equity capital. The preference capital is treated as a monetary item and is simply restated.

Limitations of Current Purchasing Powers

(*a*) In the long run, the CPP method does not remedy the deficiencies of historic cost accounting and so it does not provide the best long term solution to the problem of accounting for inflation.

(*b*) The retail price index is an index of prices of wide range of goods and services purchased by domestic consumers. In many cases, such an index will give a misleading indication of the effects of inflation on individual companies.

(*c*) The method introduces a new set of problems by expressing company accounts in a new unit of measurement, viz. units of current purchasing power, instead of monetary units. The unit of current purchasing power is likely to be conceptually difficult for most users of accounts to understand.

(*d*) The recommendation that CPP statements should be supplementary to the basic accounts weakens their impact.

(2) Current Cost Accounting Method

Current cost accounting is a system of inflation accounting in which each item of financial statements is restated in terms of current value of that item. This method recognises the changes in the prices of individual assets irrespective of the quantum and direction of changes in the general price level. It takes into account the price changes relevant to particular firm or industry rather than the economy as a whole. This method seeks to ensure that adequate provisions or adjustments are made for the maintenance and replacement of the operating assets of the company. Assets are shown in terms of what such assets whould currently cost. Similarly, profits are computed on the basis of what the cost would currently cost. Similarly, profits are computed on the basis of what the cost would have been at the date of sale rather then the actual amount paid. In other words, it seeks to arrive at a profit which can be safely distributed as dividend without impairing the operational capacity of the firm. In addition to adjustment for depreciation and cost of sales, it deals with the working capital and also loan raised.

Features of Current Cost Accounting Technique

(*a*) The accounts will continue as at present to be drawn-up in terms of monetary units.

(*b*) The accounts should show the value to the business of the company's assets at the balance sheet date.

(*c*) It measures the income after matching current costs with current revenues. It is based on the concept of operational capability. This method seeks to achieve this by substituting the current cost of assets consumed in place of corresponding historical cost.

(*d*) Depreciation for the year is to be calculated on the current value of the relevant fixed assets.

(*e*) The cost of stock consumed during the year is to be calculated on the value of the stock of business at the date of consumption and not at the date of purchase.

(*f*) The effects of loss or gain from loans will be computed and set-off against interest.

(*g*) The current cost operating profit is arrived at by making three adjustments to trading profits before interest is calculated on historical cost basis, *i.e.*, depreciation adjustment, cost of sales adjustment and monetary working capital adjustment. The current cost attributable to shareholders is obtained by making gearing adjustment.

(*h*) Profit for the year should consists of the company's operating gains, and should exclude all holding gains.

(*i*) The current cost balance sheet includes a new reserve 'current cost reserve', which is created to take the credits relating to the revaluation of fixed assets and stock as also those relating to the depreciation adjustment, cost of sales adjustment, the working capital adjustment and the gearing adjustment.

Advantages

(*a*) The principle of showing assets and liabilities at their 'value to the business' will enable the comparative returns on capital employed of different companies to be assessed in a more useful way during a time of inflation that is possible with existing accounting convention.

(*b*) The clear separation in the accounts of holding, operating and extraordinary gains will lead to clear distinction being made between gains which due to a company's productive efforts and gains due to luck or skill in the timing of purchases of assets during a period of inflation. Such accounting presentation will enable the performance of companies to be assessed and compared in a more useful way than with existing methods which do not make such distinction. It is also particularly important for internal management purposes during a period of inflation to have information which clearly distinguishes between operating and holding gain.

(*c*) The principle of current cost accounting are developments of accounting techniques already in use by number of companies. For example, the revaluation of properly assets in company accounts is already widespread and the principle underlying the 'cost of sales adjustment' forms the basis of the 'base stock' method of accounting for stock. Current cost accounting is an evolutionary rather than a revolutionary system of accounting.

QUESTIONS

Simple Questions

1. What do you mean by inflation accounting?
2. State the features of inflation accounting.
3. State the objectives of inflation accounting.
4. What do you mean by holding gain?
5. What do you mean by operating gain?
6. What do you mean by extraordinary gain?
7. State the limitations of historical costing.

Short Answer Questions

1. Explain current purchasing power as a technique of inflation accounting.
2. Explain the current cost accounting as a technique of inflation accounting.

37

RESPONSIBILITY ACCOUNTING

INTRODUCTION

Responsibility accounting is one of the technique of Management Accounting which is used for managerial control. Whole other techniques are used to control the organisation as a whole, responsibility accounting is used to appraise the performance of various segments of an organisation. These segments are called by responsibility centres. This technique is also known as profitability accounting.

Definition

"Responsibility accounting is concerned with collecting and reporting planned and actual accounting information about the inputs and outputs of responsibility centres."

An analysis of the above definition reveals the following features of responsibility accounting.

(*a*) Input and output: Input and output constitutes the basis for responsibility accounting. The input used in an organisation is in the form of physical resources and it takes the form of raw-materials consumed, hours of labour expended and so on. These resources are expressed in monetary terms and is referred to as cost. Similarly, the output when expressed in monetary term is known as revenue. Responsibility accounting is based on cost and revenue data which is also known as financial information.

(*b*) Planned and actual data: In order to facilitate managerial control, financial information is needed both in respect of planned and actual. Actual data is compared with planned or budgeted data and in case of adverse variations the management can focus its attention on the causes responsible for such variation.

(*c*) Fixation of responsibility: Responsibility accounting centres around the organisation structure of an enterprise. If involves fixation of responsibilities among the superiors and subordinates. Though authrority can be delegated, responsibility can never be delegated. However authority must be coupled with responsibility as without responsibility a person cannot discharge his duties satisfactorily. For the successful functioning of responsibility accounting a clear cut authority and responsibility is to be laid down. The performance of an individual can be evaluated based on the authority and responsibility assigned.

(*d*) Responsibility centres: The establishment of responsibility centre is the nucleus of responsibility accounting. The entire organisation is divided into various segments in such a way that the person who is in-charge of that segment is responsible for the success or failure of that segment. Responsibility centres are classified into three types based on control exercised, *viz*.

(*i*) ***Cost centre***: Under this type the person in-charge is responsible for cost incurred in that centre. In other words, he is responsible only for the cost incurred for input but not for output. The record maintained in the cost centre records only the cost incurred but excludes the revenue earned (*i.e.*, output value). Thus it is clear that a cost centre is a segment whose financial performance is measured in terms of cost. The performance of managers is evaluated by comparing the cost incurred and the estimated cost. The focus of the management is only to exercise control over cost.

(*ii*) ***Profit centre***: Under this type the manager is responsibile for cost (input), revenue (output) and the profit (*i.e.*, excess of revenue over cost). Where cost exceed revenue it results in a loss. Though, according to generally accepted accounting principle, revenue is recognised only when goods are sold to external parties, for evaluating profit centre, revenue represents a monetary measure of output, irrespective of whether the revenue is realised or not. The underlying principle is that a department has output representing goods and services which are capable of monetary measurement. Profit for the sake of evaluation of profit centre is taken as pre-tax profit. The Manager's performance is decided by the profit earned by that profit centre.

(*iii*) ***Investment centre***: Under this type the manager is responsible for cost, revenue, and investments made on assets of a responsibility centre. The basis for evaluating the performance of a manager is not by the profit earned by that centre, but on the return on investment. One of the popular tool for reporting performance of an investment centre is the rate of return on investment in assets. Symbollically

$$\text{RoI} = \frac{\text{Net Income}}{\text{Total Assets}}$$

□□□